Good Hot Stuff

The Life and Times of Queer Film Pioneer Jack Deveau

A MARCO SIEDELMANN JOINT

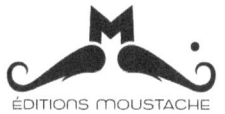
ÉDITIONS MOUSTACHE

"It is going to be like literature. It will be around forever as long as we can keep it alive, as long as we can keep it from being destroyed, it will be here. And we will be able to have a whole vision of what it was like being alive in this period of the time."

Robert Alvarez

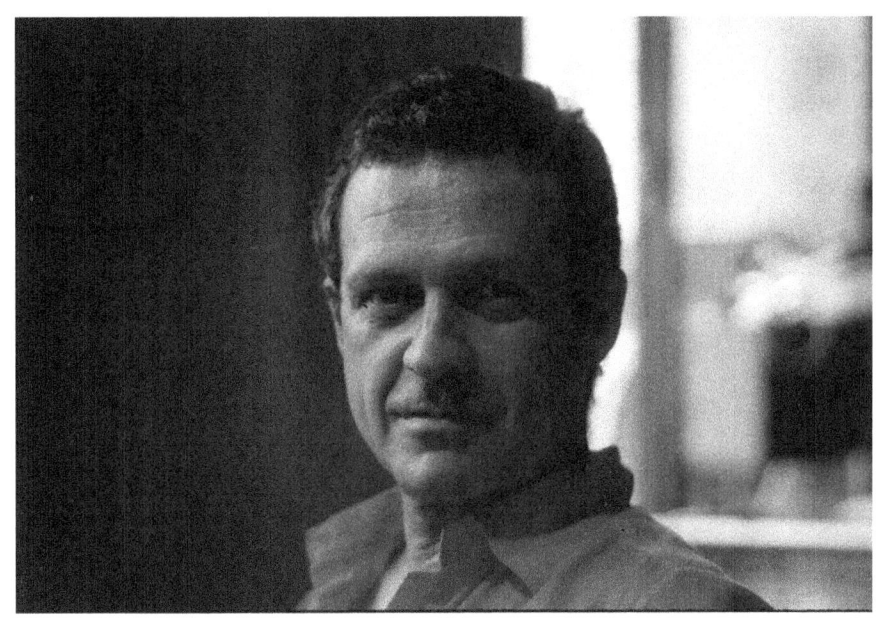

This book is dedicated to the memory of Jack Deveau (1935-1982)

PLEASE CREDIT PHOTO TO HAND MADE FILMS, INC.

to be used only in connection with the
promotion of Hand Made Films, Inc.
or its productions.

TABLE OF CONTENTS

PROMISCUITY AND EVERYDAY LIFE: JACK DEVEAU'S PORN CINEMA // INTRODUCTION by Jeffrey Escoffier **7**

JACK DEVEAU: GAY FILM PIONEER by Tom Udo **16**

FRANK ROSS: UNDER THE TUTELAGE OF JACK DEVEAU by Marco Siedelmann **24**

WHAT MAKES A PORNSTAR MOST? ARCH BROWN'S LATEST DISCOVERIES by Arch Brown **38**

MEMORIES ARE MADE OF THIS by David Earnest **40**

PRESS REVIEWS 1: Left-Handed, The Night Before, The Back Row, Casey!, Jack, Drive **45**

PLAYGUY IN AMERICA - MARK WOODWARD by Clarke Taylor **92**

ENTER CHRISTOPHER RAGE by Christopher Rage **98**

HENK VAN DIJK: BALLET DOWN THE TIMES SQUARE by Marco Siedelmann **102**

LORENZO MANS: THE RELUCTANT GAY PORN WRITER by Marco Siedelmann **111**

PRESS REVIEWS 2: Ballet Down The Highway, Rough Trades **123**

TOM DESIMONE - HOLLYWOOD'S MODERN MOVIE MOGUL by Barnaby Shackleford **154**

PRESS REVIEWS 3: Good Hot Stuff, Catching Up, The Idol, Station To Station, Everything Goes **158**

TOM DESIMONE: MAKING 'THE IDOL' by Jerry Douglas **182**

KEVIN REDDING: YESTERDAY, TODAY, AND TOMORROW **188**

TOM DESIMONE: BEHIND THE CAMERA by Jerry Douglas **196**

ROBERT ALVAREZ: HAND IN HAND - A LOVE STORY by Marco Siedelmannn **220**

PETER DE ROME AND HIS EROTIC MOVIES by Peter Argus **246**

GENESIS OF THE DESTROYING ANGEL by Peter De Rome **248**

PRESS REVIEWS 4: The Erotic Films of Peter De Rome, Adam and Yves, The Destroying Angel **252**

PETER DE ROME: GRANDFATHER OF GAY PORN by Grigoris Daskalogrogorakis **268**

WORLD REPORTS: PARIS - WALLACE POTTS PORTRAIT by Peter Adams **278**

JEAN ÉTIENNE SIRY: THE FRENCH CONNECTION by Gary Vanisian **281**

FRANÇOIS ABOUT: FRENCH PORN'S FIRST CINEMATOGRAPHER by Gary Vanisian **296**

A STAR IS PORN by Bill Hunter **314**

PRESS REVIEWS 5: Hot House, A Night At The Adonis, Boy Napped **322**

JIM DELEGATTI: SOME MOMENTS IN TIME by Marco Siedelmann **368**

KEN SCHNETZER: A DECADE AT THE ADONIS by Marco Siedelmann **376**

ROLF PARDULA: COMING OUT WITH HAND IN HAND by Marco Siedelmann **382**

MOOSE 100: IMITATION OF LIFE - THE SCREENWRITER OF HAND IN HAND by Marco Siedelmann **388**

SHADOW: A BRIEF ENCOUNTER WITH HAND IN HAND by Marco Siedelmann **396**

PRESS REVIEWS 6: Wanted - Billy The Kid, Sex Magic, Dune Buddies, Fire Island Fever **402**

ROBERT W. RICHARDS: THE WAY WE WERE - REMEMBERING JACK DEVEAU by Marco Siedelmann **474**

JACK DEVEAU - A BLUEMOVIEMAKER'S PRIVATE THOUGHTS by Robert W. Richards **480**

PRESS REVIEWS 7: The Boys from Riverside Drive, Private Collection, Centurians Of Rome, Times Square Strip, Hand In Hand Preview Tape, In Heat **492**

ROBERT ALVAREZ AND KEES CHAPMAN: THE LEGACY OF JACK DEVEAU by Jerry Douglas **568**

JACK DEVEAU OBITUARY by Arthur Bell **579**

HAND IN HAND LIBRARY: Film Credits **581**

INTRODUCTION

PROMISCUITY AND EVERYDAY LIFE: JACK DEVEAU'S PORN CINEMA

by Jeffrey Escoffier

"Sex is a pleasurable experience repeated many, many times during our lives that, if experienced with the same person each time, is considered responsible, adult, mature; if experienced with a different person each time, is considered promiscuous."

Andrew Holleran, Notes on Promiscuity

"The willingness to have sex immediately, promiscuously, with people about whom one knows nothing and from whom one demands only physical contact, can be seen as a sort of Whitmanesque democracy, a desire to know and trust other men in a type of brotherhood far removed from the male bonding of rank, hierarchy, and competition that characterizes much of the outside world. It is equally true, however, that age and beauty set up their hierarchies and barriers."

Dennis Altman, The Homosexualization of America

Pornography became an integral part of American popular culture during the sexual revolution of the 1960s and 70s. Hardcore gay pornographic films, however, only became widely available after the Stonewall riots in June 1969—coincidently, the same month that the first straight hardcore pornographic movies were shown in theaters in San Francisco. Initially, most of the gay hardcore movies shown in theaters were either cheaply made 16mm shorts originally produced for private distribution or soft-core features with extraneous sex scenes interjectet.

Pornography, however, has long played a particularly important role in the life of gay men in the last fifty or sixty years—not only because homosexuality has been a stigmatized form of behavior, but also because historically there have been so few homoerotic representations of any kind . Up until very recently, most gay men become sexually active adults without any socialization in the social or sexual codes of the gay male subculture. In its absence, pornography has provided an education—limited in some ways, to be sure—in homosexual desire. Pornography was, as John Preston wrote "how we learned the parameters of our sexual life...[it] was how we developed our fantasies, both sexual and emotional."

By the end of 1972, five feature-length gay hardcore movies had been released in theaters in Los Angeles, San Francisco and New York. Wakefield Poole's BOYS IN THE SAND opened first (late in December 1971), and was an immediate critical and financial success. BOYS IN THE SAND was followed by J. Brian's SEVEN IN A BARN (1971), which had been made in the Bay Area. In the following year, Fred Halsted's gritty sadomasochistic feature, LA PLAYS ITSELF (1972) opened; then Jack Deveau's LEFT-HANDED (1972), a tale of sex and betrayal set in New York City, and lastly Jerry Douglas' THE BACK ROW (1972), a documentary-like portrait of New York's raunchy post-gay-liberation sexual scene. Casey Donovan, who starred in two of these movies – BOYS IN THE SAND and THE BACK ROW – went on to become the first nationally recognized gay porn star. These five films launched the new wave of post-liberation gay hardcore pornographic cinema.

LEFT-HANDED and THE BACK ROW were both made in New York. Jack Deveau and his lover Robert Alvarez began making LEFT-HANDED even before Poole's film had premiered. Encouraged by actor Sal Mineo, the actor who had played James Dean and Natalie Wood's friend in the REBEL WITHOUT A CAUSE, Deveau and Alvarez were actively involved in both the City's avant-garde cultural scene and in the new gay sexual scene that had emerged in the sixties. Deveau was an industrial designer and Alvarez had worked for a number of years as a film editor on documentaries for National Educational Television (NET) as well as a few 'underground' films.

Jack Deveau was born in 1935 and grew up in Manhattan. He attended Cornell University for one semester before moving back to Manhattan where he became a partner in an architectural and design firm. Once he had begun making pornographic films, he thought of it as a business. He and Alvarez, set up Hand In Hand Films to produce and distribute gay erotic films. They had decided that they would not lease the films but only sell final prints —thus avoiding the problem of distributors and exhibitors making copies of the leased films to avoid paying the leasing fees. As soon as LEFT-HANDED was done, they traveled across the country and visited theater owners in all the major cities.

"We're in the movie business," Deveau and Alvarez told exhibitors, "and we're going to be making a lot movies. ... We will have product. You'll get better prints. You'll get better services from us." They sought out films made by others filmmakers to distribute. One of the first projects after LEFT-HANDED was releasing a collection of Peter DeRome's 8mm. shorts in a 16mm format. In 1972, Deveau and Alvarez also acquired the Lincoln Art Theatre on West 57th Street as a showcase for the films they made and distributed through Hand In Hand. However, before they even started showing gay porn, they booked THE DEVIL IN MISS JONES, the acclaimed straight adult film of 1972 that Alvarez considered, as many others did, one of "the best pornographic films" ever made. But it ran for years and by the time it closed the need for a local theater to showcase their own films had become superfluous; in fact, Hand In Hand had become a national distributor. Deveau died on December 2, 1982, his pioneering film career cut short, after a long bout with cancer.

Stonewall, Promiscuity and Pornography

Before the 1970s in the United States, pornographic materials, whether print or visual, were difficult to obtain in the United States, as well as ex-pensive and even dangerous to possess. It was illegal to send sexually explicit images through the mails. Homoerotic images—that is, photographs of nude men or drawings of erotic scenes—were available only through private networks or to 'select mail-order customers.' Starting out as an underground phenomenon during the 1950s, smallmagazines with photographs of almost nude men were sold on newsstands in larger cities – New York, Chicago and Los Angeles. These 'physique magazines' and the mail order businesses based upon them became central to the development of a gay erotic imagination. These magazines were not merely one aspect of a wider gay male culture, but as Valentine Hooven argues in his history of beefcake magazines, "they virtually *were* gay culture."
Without a long history of sexually explicit imagery, early gay films focused on sexual content such as soft-core beefcake movies or were" experimental avant-garde artistic works like those of Kenneth Anger, Andy Warhol and Jack Smith. With the breakthrough to hardcore production, new genres of pornographic movies began to emerge. The shift to hardcore was extremely important for gay men. The primary focus

of beefcake publications had been on men as *objects of desire*, not as *agents of desire*. While there was a select and furtive underground business in sexually explicit drawings of men having sex with one another, the beefcake magazines were never able to publically show men having sex. In images that were often coy and suggestive, the illustrations that were published in the magazines did imply (especially in the drawings and illustrations) that the men portrayed might have some potentially 'erotic' interest in one another. Hardcore films, however, offered images, roles and sexual scenarios that could serve as models and to legitimate active sex in place of the 'worship' of ideal bodies sponsored by beefcake publications. The advent of gay hardcore movies that showed publically in theaters thus enabled gay audiences to see gay men as active *agents of homosexual desire*.

Since making feature-length porn movies for theatrical viewing was a relatively new activity after 1969, there were no well-established formulas for making a hard-core film. Some kind of plot, however, was required. After the US Supreme Court decision in *Miller v. California*, pornographic films needed to have a plot or tell a story to satisfy the Court's requirement that works with sexually explicit imagery must exhibit "serious" literary, artistic, political or scientific value or be deemed as obscene and "utterly without redeeming social worth," and thus be banned.

In everyday life, we maintain a sharp distinction between social reality and fantasy, but due to the film medium's basic 'photographic realism,' the line between reality and fantasy is often blurred in porn movies. Porn films portray a seemingly 'real world' where the improbable and the desired take place—when, for instance, straight men drop their clothes without hesitation and have sex with other men in the locker room.

Thus a number of different 'genres' or types of porn films emerged. Many of the early gay porn movies portrayed sexual activity in idyllic or fantasy settings, primarily as a way of creating an imaginary world in which sex between men was free from the social, legal and cultural obstacles that traditionally limited homosexual activity. During early seventies, the everyday reality of casual sex anywhere anytime exceeded the fantasies that many pre-Stonewall gay erotic films showed. Among the new wave of gay porn films in 1971 and 1972, Wakefield Poole's BOYS IN THE SAND and BIJOU were both fantasy features. Poole's BOYS IN THE SAND was set, for example, on Fire Island, an idyllic vacation resort outside New York City, where a gay man sees a beautiful man arise from the sea or throw a magic pill into a backyard pool to produce a sexy man. Poole's second feature, BIJOU, was also a fantasy film. Though set in a New York bathhouse, the sexual action was initiated by or set in fantasy contexts—that is one removed from the course of everyday life. For example, J. Brian's SEVEN IN A BARN portrayed an orgy set in a barn in the California countryside. In these films, real sex was set in the context created by a fantasy scenario.

Many other early hardcore features adopted melodramatic or comic plots organized around the sexual action. Instead of attempting to make Hollywood-style melodramas or comedy skits like many other porn directors, Deveau created a unique genre of hardcore pornography that stands apart from the work of almost every other hardcore filmmaker from the period. And while Deveau did make a number of porn films with fantasy scenarios, he created porn films—melodramas and comedies—that explored the tensions and complications that arose between a new sense of sexual freedom that allowed for an increase in casual and impersonal sex and gay men's desire for intimacy and domestic relationships. In fact, it even extended to the conflict between sexual availability and other aspects of a gay man's everyday life—career, friendship and neighborliness.

Deveau adopted the *cinema verite* style to record the underground sexual lifestyle that had emerged in the years just before and immediately after the Stonewall riots of 1969, using 'naturalistic' techniques that originated in documentary filmmaking to capture the rough and gritty feel of New York City. Pioneered by documentary photographers during the 1960s, it allowed Deveau to capture the uninhibited and adventurous sexual activity occurring throughout New York City during that period. His films thus joined together documentary-style photography and psycho-political themes of sexual liberation.

Deveau's porn movies were examples of what film critic Leo Braudy called 'open films.' In a closed film, the film's action is completely determined by the actors and events portrayed within the film. Nothing outside the setting affects the action of the film's action. Most contemporary porn films (or scenes, for that matter) represent closed forms: the sexual action is completely determined by the film's performers or the premise of the setup. Nothing outside enters to shape the sexual action. But the early gay documentary-style hardcore films were open films. The world outside the camera's frame entered the story and affected its action—working in an area where "the accidental prevails over the providential, and happenings in the nature of unexpected incidents are all but the rule." They were often shot on the streets, in cruising sites, bars, theaters, restrooms, and subway stations.

Other porn filmmakers adopted the same style. This group, who I have called, "homo-realists," included Peter de Rome, Arch Brown, Avery Willard (as Bruce King), and Ian McGraw, all of whom shot porn films that portrayed the gay male subculture in bathhouses, porn theaters and on the piers. These movies were thus both 'pornographic movies' and 'documentaries' of the gay male sexual subculture of the seventies. These films reveled in the sexual subculture that had Stonewall, amidst the seedy, rundown and unused industrial spaces that supplied so many opportunities for uninterrupted sexual activity with multiple and unknown partners. They all made a point to show the streets and the landmarks of the city's sexual landscape. But Deveau's movies also did something more. They explored the conflicts that gay men experienced during the 1970s between the vast field of sexual possibilities available and attempts to establish and maintain some sort of domestic life and other everyday activities.

Promiscuity and everyday Life

In the introduction to a catalogue for a show of paintings and photographs portraying the everyday lives of lesbians and gay men at New York's Lesley Lohman Museum of Gay and Lesbian Art, the show's curator, James Saslow, recounted an anecdote from his own life:

> Before coming out to my father, I tested the waters by casually remarking that I'd met a gay couple who'd lived together for twenty years and had a nice relationship. "People like that don't have relationships," he sneered, "they just have sex." Before and after which, implicitly, they vanished intobnsome limbo of suspended animation with no "real life."

Both Saslow and his father were partially correct—gay men did have long-term relationships that were meaningful, but many gay men, even ones in relationships, did have a lot of casual sex. The tension between the sexually exciting possibilities and the desire to create stable domestic relationships was explored by psychologist Charles Silverstein in his book, *Man to Man: Gay Couples in America* (1981) written and published just before the advent of AIDS. One of the gay men interviewed by Silverstein summed up the situation that many gay men experienced during the 1970s:

> I have a lover, but we don't put any stress on fidelity. That's not the driving force in our life, but we don't lie to the other.

> Marriage is wonderful and warm and affectionate and all kinds of terrific things. One of things it isn't is exciting, and I guess I just don't want to let go of that excitement. I've never articulated this before, but— I love the hunt. I love going out finding sex. I love cruising. I love going to the baths, cruising, prowling. ...I'm not the most physically attractive man in the world; I'm not big and muscular. I'm twenty-five years older than most of the people, and I really like seducing and getting people to come home with me or doing it with me in the baths. I love sex itself, and I love to suck cock. I love to turn other men on because it turns me on, too. .

Silverstein found that the tension between the excitement of easy sex and desire to create a satisfactory domestic life with a long-term partner was a frequent source of conflict between gay male couples during that period.

Starting with his first film, LEFT-HANDED (1972) and then in BALLET DOWN THE HIGHWAY (1975), WANTED; BILLY THE KID, (1976), HOT HOUSE (1977), DUNE BUDDIES (1978), A NIGHT AT THE ADONIS (1978), FIRE ISLAND FEVER (1979), and up until one of his last films THE BOYS FROM RIVERSIDE DRIVE (1981), Deveau's movies explored the everyday life of gay men in post-Stonewall New York. Stonewall had legitimated, as writer Michael Bronski noted, "the promise of sex: free sex, better sex, lots of sex, sex without guilt, sex without repression, sex without harassment, sex at home and sex in the streets." Though Deveau's films are porn films and full of wonderful and exciting sex, they also seriously explored the chaotic impact of the rampant sexual availability and above all the difficulties of forging a new sexual subculture that also made roo m for enduring romantic or domestic relationships and intimacy. Deveau's movies contain the DNA of their times.

LEFT-HANDED, Deveau's first film, showed a cross-section of gay male life in Manhattan in the early seventies. A romantic melodrama, it focuses on an affair between a gay man (who happens to be a hustler) and a straight man (who happens to be a drug dealer)—an almost iconic story of the 1960s and the early seventies. Ray, the gay man, is challenged by a friend to seduce Bob, the straight man. Soon Ray and Bob embark on an affair, but as Bob becomes more emotionally involved and breaks up with his girlfriend, Ray loses interest in the sexually curious 'straight' man. He de-clares that he is bored and wants something new. Thus LEFT-HANDED introduces the theme that runs through much of Deveau's work- the challenges to establishing an intimate relationship in a period when sex had become easily available and less guilt-ridden.

LEFT-HANDED also reflects the fluid boundary that existed between gay and sexual liberation in the early seventies. In the years immediately after Stonewall, the gay movement did not at first focus on the question of a gay identity, or even strictly on civil rights but on *sexual liberation*. Gay liberation, as Dennis Altman, one of its early theorists, noted, was "not only for those of us who are homosexuals, who are finding the courage and self-assurance to come out in public, but indeed . . . for everyone else." The early movement also emphasized "polymorphous perversity," the undifferentiated ability to take pleasure from all parts of the body. Thus homosexual sex represented an expression of pleasure and love free from the social requirements of heterosexuality. LEFT-HANDED acknowledges the sexual atmosphere of the period and includes a hardcore sex scene between Bob and his girlfriend, along with sex scenes in a tearoom, an antiques shop, several scenes between the gay man and his straight lover, and an orgy.

Many of Deveau's films addressed the theme of the tensions generated between promiscuous sex and other aspects of everyday life. BALLET DOWN THE HIGHWAY (1975) is about a ballet dancer who has an affair with a straight truck driver. The affair interrupts his developing relationship with a fellow dancer, though they engage happily in a threesome with the truck driver. The film culminates in a dramatic scene in the dancer's apartment in which the straight man's straight friends discover the affair and go to the dancer's apartment to confront him, but all quite drunk, and instead of a confrontation, they all participate in an orgy. For the dancer, that is the end of the affair, and his new boyfriend, a fellow dancer, moves in. WANTED: BILLY THE KID (1976) focused again on a hustler, basically a struggling actor, who both earns his living and pays for essential needs such as his rent through prostitution. While sex seems to be freely available, most of the sex that Billy engages with is part of an economic exchange, and not as part of a personal relationship.

In HOT HOUSE (1977), all the neighbors end up having sex with one another, despite various misunderstandings and minor abuses of hospitality. Thus, while most of the movies illustrate the conflict, they also show an acceptance of the situation.

Fire Island came to symbolize the wild promiscuity of the 1970s. Andrew Holleran's *Dancer from the Dance* and Larry Kramer's *Faggots* represent two opposed views on the centrality of the Fire Island experience Holleran portrayed Fire Island as a sort of Paradise, though one with dark overtones, while Kramer ranted against what he saw as its devastating superficiality. Deveau uses Fire Island to test his characters ability to resist the disruptions of sexual freedom. DUNE BUDDIES (1978), unlike most of Deveau's other films, shows how one gay man refuses to accept the disruptions that promiscuous sex has had on his life. Set on Fire Island, it tells the story of a college professor who wants to get away from the sex that dominates his life in New York City on his summer vacation. "Career considerations aside," he explains, "I came to New York for the sex and that's exactly what I got. All the sex I wanted and more—in fact, too much! I got picked up on the way to work, on the way home from work and at work. It happened at the supermarket, the laundry, … . It got so crazy, in fact, that I stopped enjoying it." When someone offers him a cheap rental for a month on Fire Island, he accepts hoping that he will have some peace and quiet. However within his first twenty-four hours he has had so many uninvited sexual encounters— he cannot turn any of them down—that he decides to go back to the city and find another way to escape from the sex. He calls Fire Island paradise, but it's not what he needed. Deveau made another movie set on Fire Island to test another possibility. In FIRE ISLAND FEVER (1979) a pair of lovers go to vacation on the Island and decide to experiment by opening up their relationship. But they experience drug mishaps and fits of jealousy and thus decide to return to their previous status.

Deveau's most ambitious film to explore the ramifications of promiscuous sex was A NIGHT AT THE ADONIS (1977) set in the theatre where most of his films were shown in New York and which was renowned for its untrammeled public sex. One former patron called it "a fuck palace." The film was a tribute in part to the great role that porn theaters played in creating a sexual environment for gay men during the seventies and, in part, to Jerry Douglas' 1972 film THE BACK ROW. A NIGHT AT THE ADONIS is considered to be one Deveau's best movies. Each of the film's characters ends up at the Adonis because some sexual or emotional disappointment leads him there as a distraction - for example, Jack Wrangler, who goes to the Adonis when he fails to have sex with his boss, or like the 'kept man' whose lover isn't spending enough time him. A NIGHT AT THE ADONIS (1978) is the most elaborate exploration of the tension between promiscuity and gay men's everyday lives.

Sex takes place throughout the Adonis, in the seats (in the balcony and the back rows), the passageways, in the offices, behind the counters, and in the men's room, the site of a grand orgy. Some of the men at the Adonis are friends, others are regulars, but everyone is there to have sex. People keep propositioning a young 'management trainee' who turns everyone down because he has chosen to act professionally and is serious about learning the business, but the juice bar manager dismisses the trainee's reserve and admonishes him to acknowledge the sexual scene that exists at the Adonis: "The only way to learn this business," he explains, "If you're not willing to play yourself, you shouldn't be running a playground." Yet everyone ends up connected to the person with whom they started out wanting to have sex. In the world of the Adonis there are no boundaries that separate casual sex from everyday life.

THE BOYS FROM RIVERSIDE DRIVE (1981), one of Deveau's last films, focuses on a couple celebrating their anniversary. They get into a fight before they start their dinner and both go off and end up having sex with various people—the doorman, the super's son, etc. When they both return home, they find a messenger who was supposed to deliver an anniversary greeting having sex with the super's son. They make up and have sex.

Fantasy Worlds

Deveau made other kinds of movies as well. The second movie he made was DRIVE (1974) an extravagant and flamboyant satirical film about the evil drag queen, Arachne who sought to eliminate the male sex drive, who almost seems to prefigure the HIV-inspired critics' rants against the promiscuity of the 1970s. With a script by Christopher Rage (later to become famous on his own as a director) who also played the role of the villainess Arachne in drag, it had a cast of more than 50 people. The movie singles out the male sex drive that so often generated the conflict in so many of Deveau's other movies. In 1975, he made GOOD HOT STUFF, a behind the scenes account of pornographic filmmaking at Hand In Hand Productions. GOOD HOT STUFF was the first gay porn movie to be shown in France, where it encouraged a wave of pornographic filmmaking that brought French filmmaker Jacques Scandelari to New York to shoot the first French gay porn films—NEW YORK CITY INFERNO, NEW YORK AFTER MIDNIGHT, and ERIC À NEW YORK, all of which adopted Deveau's homorealist style.

But Deveau made a couple of fantasy films as well. They show worlds that depart from the rules of everyday reality. In STRICTLY FORBIDDEN (1974) which was made in Paris, the beautiful erotic male statues in an art museum come to life and in JUST BLONDS (1980), he enacts the fantasies of a young man on LSD, who leaves home to camp out in the woods and explore his erotic desires. He encounters numerous extremely attractive young men as well as the demons who haunted him. ROUGH TRADES (1977) is a heavily plotted film that does not focus on the everyday life of gay men, but demonstrates, once more, the sexual openness of the 1970s among a group of construction workers. SEX MAGIC (1977) is an extravagant erotic fantasy about a hunky window washer in Manhattan, played by super-star Jack Wrangler, who finds a magic ring, which connects him back to ancient Egypt, but immediately lets him have sex without anyone in his presence. After he loses the ring, the men who find it have hot sexual encounters with whomever comes into contact with them.

The sex in Jack Deveau's movies all takes place in context—the sex scenes do not focus exclusively on straight-on sexual action, but are framed naturalistically by the physical context (bed room, forest, bathroom, truck), the lighting (day or night), and full of interruptions that reveal character, circumstance (a quickie, a break-up) or narrative significance – in other words, it is like real everyday sex. And because of that, it often has a kind of excitement that a lot of porn doesn't often have.

It is difficult to look back at the promiscuity of the 1970s, or for that matter at the casual and unprotected sex so visibly portrayed in the early porn films without reflecting on its relation to the AIDS epidemic. Deveau treated the promiscuity and casual sex of the era as a problem that posed complications for the everyday life of gay men. He noted the conflict between the pleasures and joys of casual sex and the emotional limitations—he portrayed it, in part, as a comic problem. Neither he nor anyone had any idea that HIV existed or that it was circulating among gay men at the time. With the new forms of treatment, and the new ease of hooking up with smart phone apps and over the Internet, we may need to approach our own sex lives with some of the attentiveness and sympathy that Jack Deveau did.

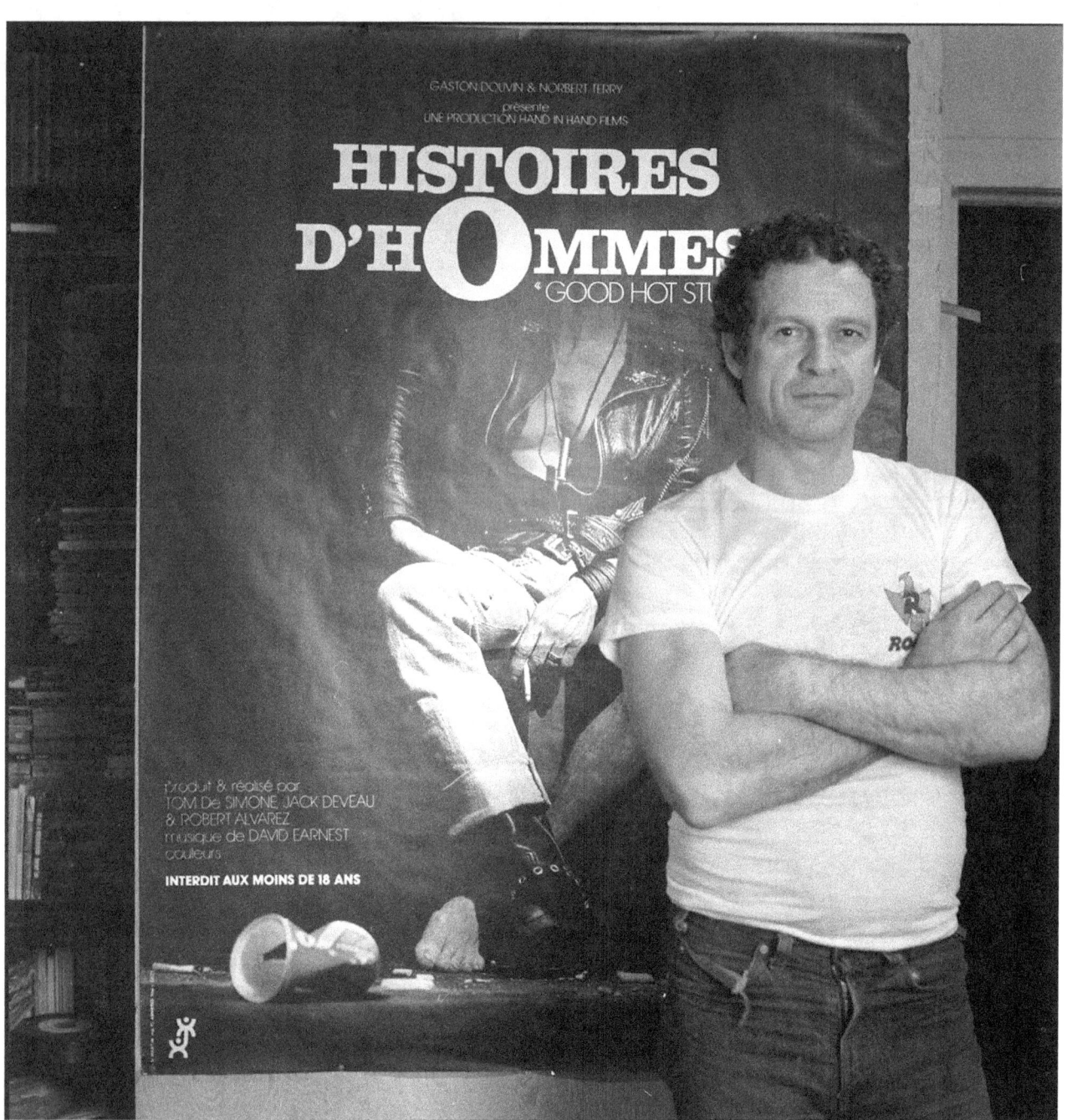

"In relation to Hollywood films, gay films have reached 1940" **JACK DEVEAU**, 1975

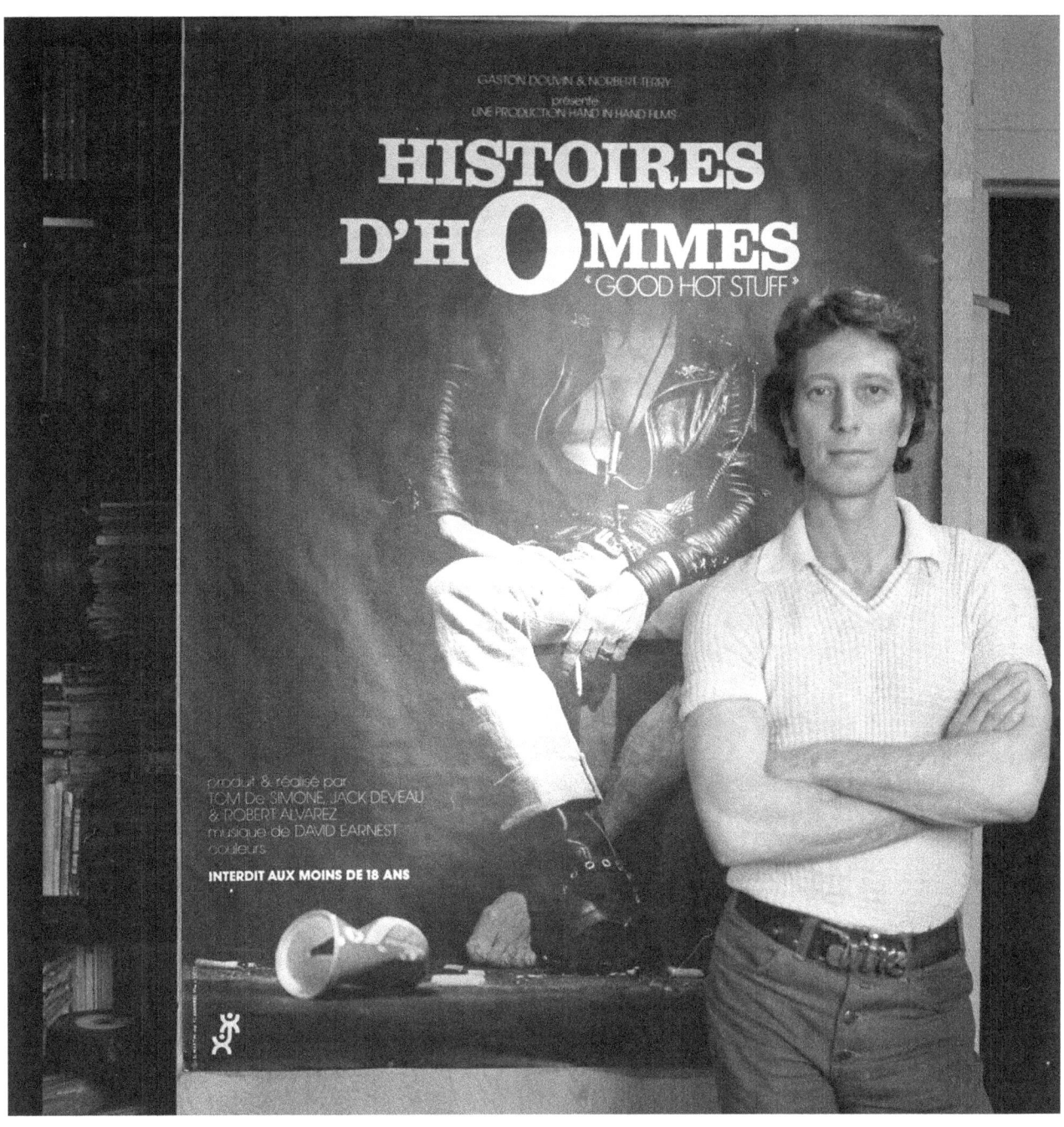

"We were very different than other filmmakers of that genre and had different goals and hopes for the future. Sometimes we were brilliant and sometimes not, but we were trying to raise the bar and challenge ourselves as well, all the while having a great time doing it." **ROBERT ALVAREZ**

JACK DEVEAU
Gay Film Pioneer

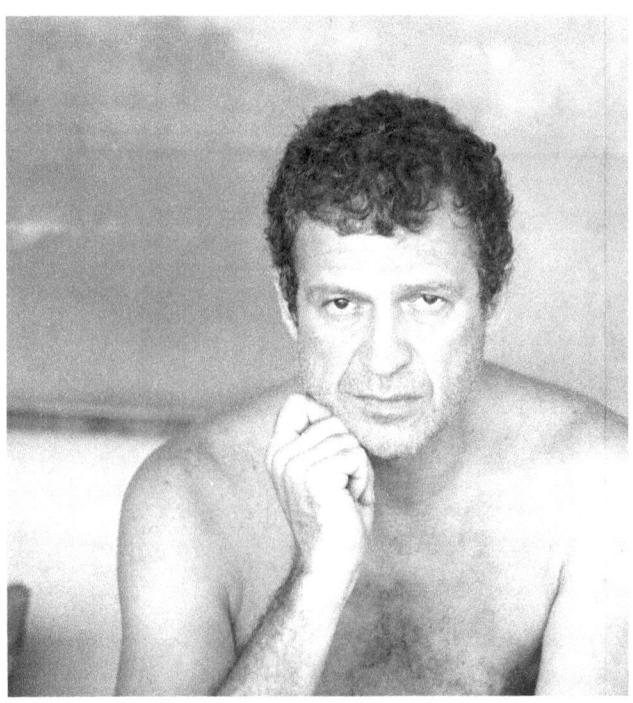

Despite rumors of a new ice age being spread by the more freaked and frozen natives of Manhattan Island, there are still some warm, inviting places to visit that provide welcome relief from the urban tundra. The sun-filled Westside penthouse of Jack Deveau, acknowledged Zuzu Mamu of gay porn films, is one of them. Amidst the muted ringing of phones, the seductive purring of Vera (the most proudass of the four resident Siamese cats) and the aroma of freshly-brewed coffee, it's actually possible to ignore the zero-degree weather. The living room is spacious and comfortable, and holds enough sound equipment for a disco. Deveau is president of Hand In Hand Films, arguably the most highly regarded producer of "all-male-cast" pies. Among his directorial credits are LEFT-HANDED ('72), DRIVE ('74), GOOD HOT STUFF, BALLET DOWN THE HIGHWAY ('75) and WANTED: BILLY THE KID ('75). Coming up this year are LE MUSEE (retitled DREAMBOY in U.S.), ROUGH TRADES and MONDO HOMO. Laid-back and easy to be around, Deveau is earnestly involved in expanding his horizons as a filmmaker, and still giving his public hot films for the cold spell.

Tom Udo: How do you interview a potential actor for a part in a Hand In Hand film?
Jack Deveau: The first thing I'd have him do is fill out a questionnaire. When we first started, it was a checklist of will do's, won't do's ... very specific, almost clinical. Well, it tended to make people uptight. Since people tend to lie on questionnaires of this kind anyway, we decided to tone the questions down to a more general category and go by our instincts. When you're looking for men who can suck and fuck for the screen in front of a crew of technicians, there's a poise and confidence that emanates from those who can. You can feel it just sitting and talking to someone. We also ask why the applicant wants to appear in a pornographic movie. If money is the only answer, I'm rarely interested in going any further. The work of being in a porn film, the physical and mental demands, just can't be bought with money alone. You have to have some interest in being in front of a camera, whether through sheer narcissism or attempting to ply your craft as an actor. And corny as it sounds, there is such a thing as star quality, a sense of himself a man can have that sets him apart.
Udo: Since porn, like all movies, operates on schedules and budgets, what happens if you have, say, a certain location in which a sex scene must be shot in two hours, and your actors aren't turning on to each other?
Deveau: In order to accommodate a situation where we wouldn't get anyone else or reschedule the scene, we'd have to change the character of the scene. For example, the original leads in ADAM & YVES had to be recast after shooting a thousand feet of film on them. But usually that doesn't happen. There's enough time between casting and filming to spend some time with the cast and crew socially, get everybody used to each other. That often means people are propositioning each other and going home together. Ideally, by the first day of shooting, you have an idea of what to expect. This has to be done, of course, as unobtrusively as possible. We found that, like an interview or questionnaire that's overly specific, it's a

a turn-off, like picking up someone in a bar and asking, "What do you do?"

Udo: Didn't you spend some of the last year in France?

Deveau: Well, I usually go over for the Cannes Festival, but last year, when the French censorship system was temporarily relaxed, we opened the first gay hardcore film ever to play in a Paris movie house – GOOD HOT STUFF, our Hand In Hand anthology film. It was retitled HISTOIRE D'HOMMES ("Stories of Men"), and it was a great success for us. Not only did we get lots of interesting press and critical attention, most of it quite favorable, but the film outgrossed NASHVILLE our opening week. The most satisfying part of the whole experience, though, was to be treated as a serious filmmaker.

Udo: Did you remain in Paris and shoot LE MUSEE?

Deveau: No, we flew back to New York, cast the film and gathered a small, essential crew to take back to Paris with us. I had acquired the script not long before. It was perfect for us. An American student traveling in France finds himself one day in a Paris art museum. Wandering around, he comes upon an unlocked door to a private collection. A guard shoos him away, but his curiosity has gotten the best of him. He returns to the museum, managing to sequester himself there overnight. What he finds in the room is a collection of erotic male statues, which come to life and guide the boy from one sexual act into another. In the end, the boy becomes one of them, a statue. The film is seen from the boy's point of view, and takes on the feeling of one sexual act, an initiation into homosexuality.

Udo: As an American hardcore production, filming in a foreign country, did you have any difficulty with the authorities?

Deveau: Not at all. Having French co-producers made things simpler for us, but LE MUSEE was registered with the French government, same as any other film. We were permitted to shoot much of the film at the Musee Rodin – The Thinker, The Kiss – and we also used Musee Gravin, a wax museum. All the special effects work, the transformations from statues into men and back, was done at a studio.

Udo: What was your impression of Paris gay life?

Deveau: Although Paris is an outrageous city, it's several years behind New York for most middle class gays. If you're an artist, it's fine, but you couldn't be a bureaucrat and a known homosexual. You'd probably lose your job.

Udo: You returned to the States right in the middle of the Harry Reems case. What did you think about it?

Deveau: When it comes to the First Amendment, like my lawyer says, make sure that someday one of your films doesn't show in some Neanderthal part of the country. It gives them the right to pick the ground on which to fight you.

Udo: Before we started today, you showed me some promotional material for ROUGH TRADES. What's the story behind it?

Deveau: Gay people nowadays really respond to the image of the workman, which were among the first male images used in stag films: plumbers, telephone men, window washers. So we decided to put a young man in a New York apartment and surround him with half a dozen of these uniformed men.

Udo: Audiences have come to expect more story elements in your films than most others. Is this true for ROUGH TRADES?

Deveau: No. Some of our films have been criticized for having too much plot and not enough sex, so ROUGH TRADES was conceived as what might be called a "classical" sex movie – take a very simple plot, fill it with handsome men with the biggest cocks, nicest round buns and most impressive pecs and biceps I could find, and shoot them in focus, interestingly dressed and well-lit, fucking and sucking. It's a sort of comic strip tribute to the roots of the porno film.

Udo: How did you wind up producing films?

Deveau: Sal Mineo and Bob Alvarez, my lover, talked me into it. I was in the business of architectural and graphic design at the time. Though I was always intrigued by the thought of producing films, and Bob was editing commercial films and video (WOODSTOCK, AN AMERICAN FAMILY), I couldn't take the idea too seriously. Then Sal asked me if I'd go with him to a production meeting for an upcoming film of his. I didn't really know what he had in mind, but I went, and sat quietly in a corner while a room full of film executives said some of the dumbest things I'd ever heard. I thought, I could do better than that, so with a little more encouragement, I became a film producer.

Udo: Do you think that porn films and commercial films are influencing one another?

Deveau: Porn has clearly influenced commercial films, with LAST TANGO the obvious example. But it hasn't worked the other way around, with rare exceptions. Porno could be a proving ground for com mercial movies, but the level of

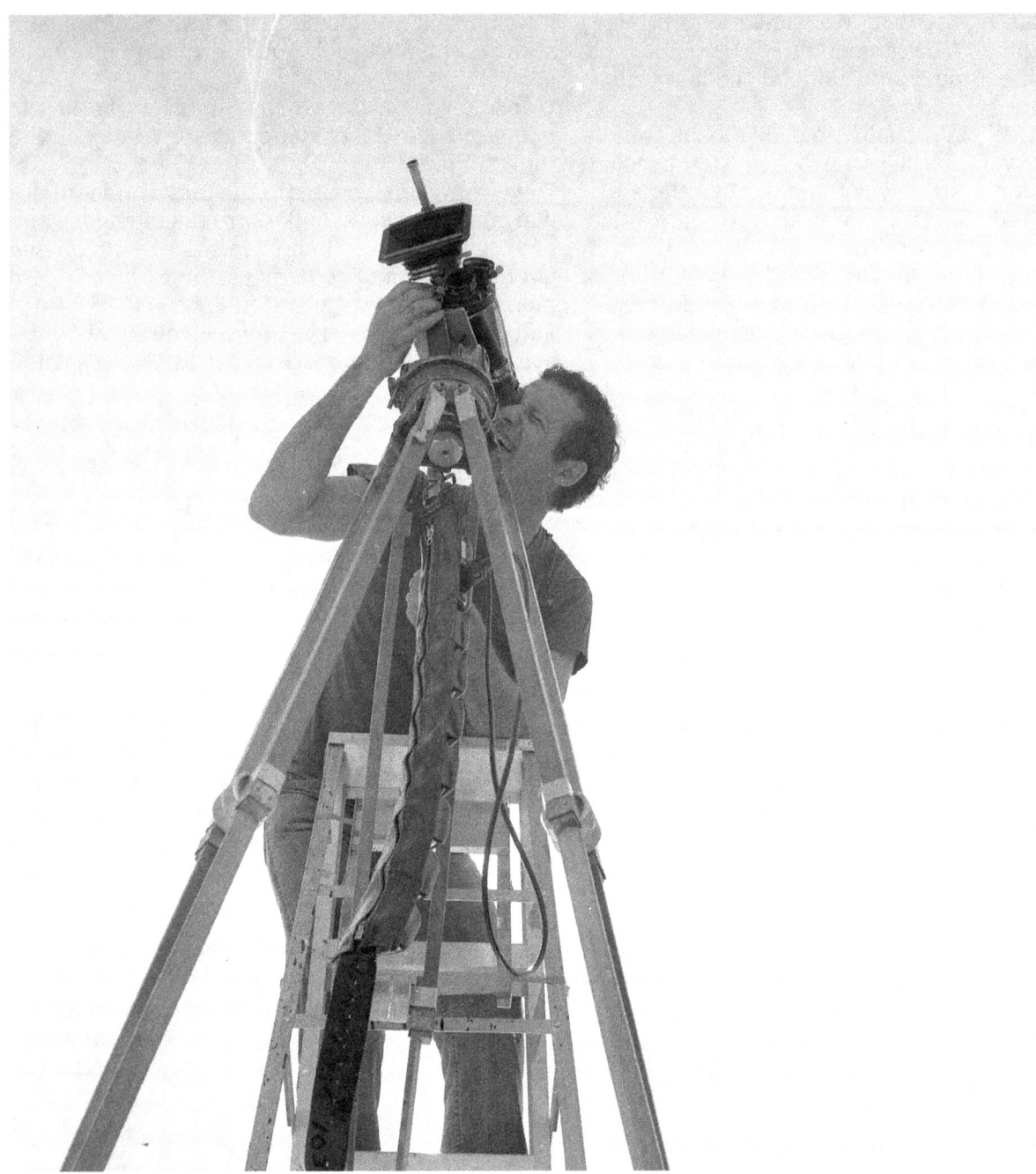
Jack Deveau during the shooting of *Fire Island Fever*

structure, writing and acting hasn't much improved. To some extent this can be attributed to economics. Porn budgets are so miniscule that there are a world of things you *cannot* do and very few things you can. Also, in terms of distribution, there are only 15 cities in this country that will book a gay porno film, which makes the profit margin low.

Udo: What do you project for yourself and Hand In Hand in the next few years?

Deveau: We intend to continue producing a range of gay porn, and we're developing some projects with writers which don't depend on their sexual content and can reach a larger audience. There are many stories to be told, as people finally listen to and begin to understand the experiences of gay men and woman. I think there'll soon be a larger audience for movies about the way gay people feel about themselves and how they interact with the rest of society. And from a purely commercial standpoint, gay people have been supporting the film industry for years. It's about time they started getting some feedback.

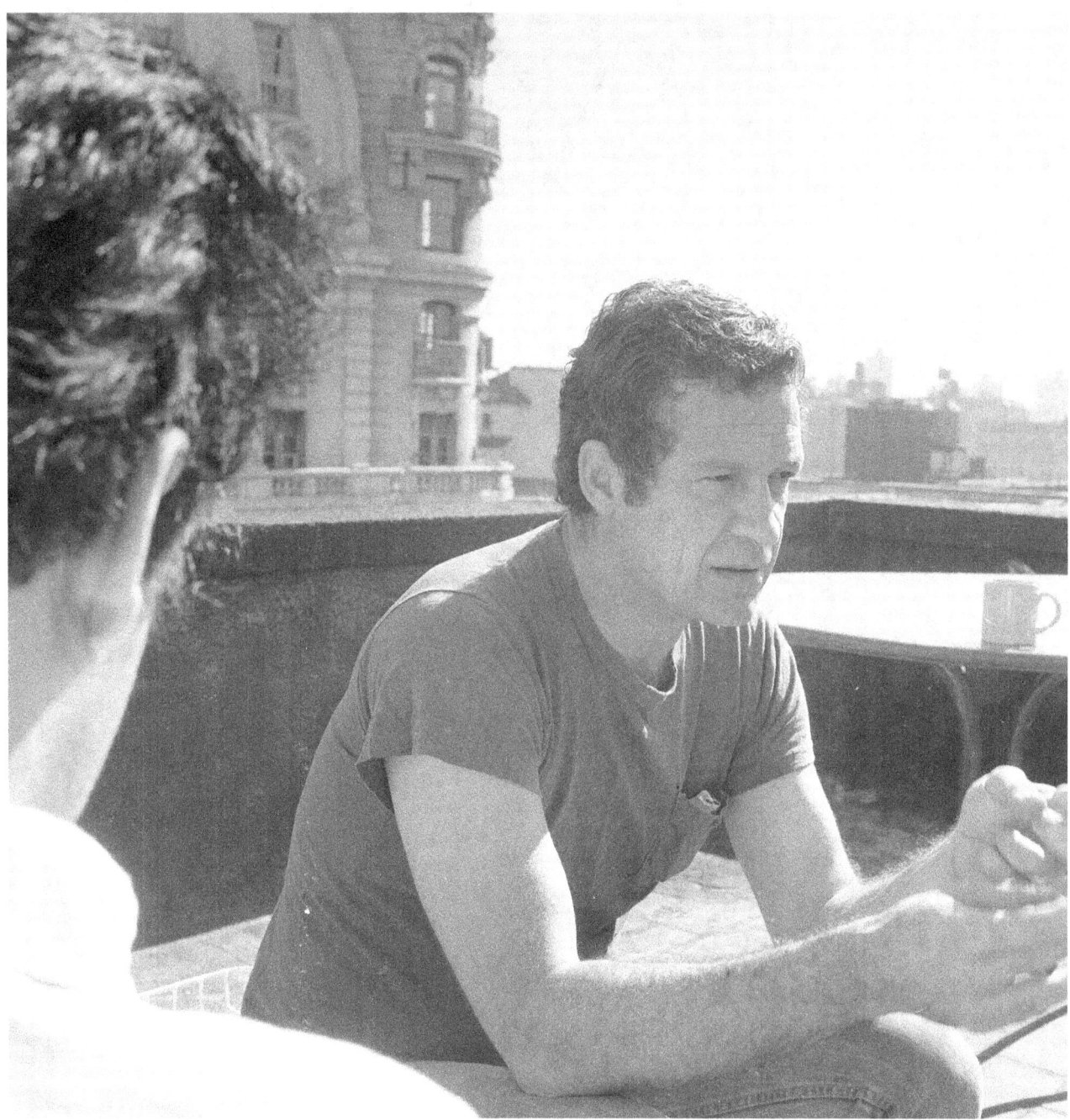
Jack Deveau in front of the Ansonia Building

Interview: JACK DEVEAU

By TOM UDO

Dan Donovan as a statue in *Dream Boy*

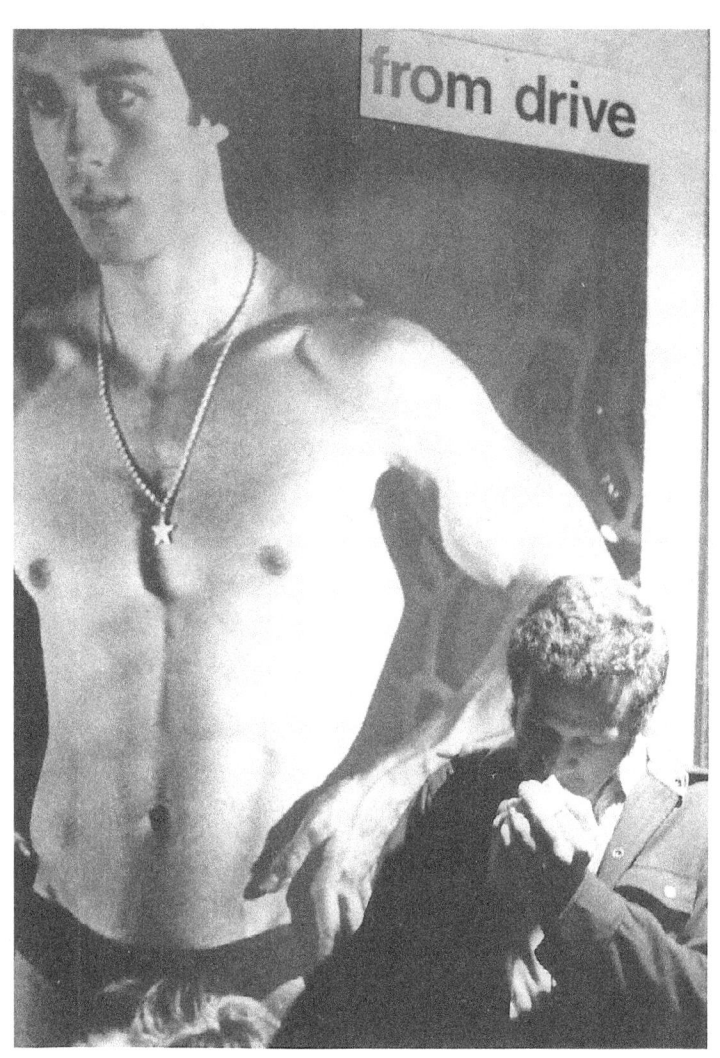

Jack Deveau in front of a cinema, on poster Brian Destazio

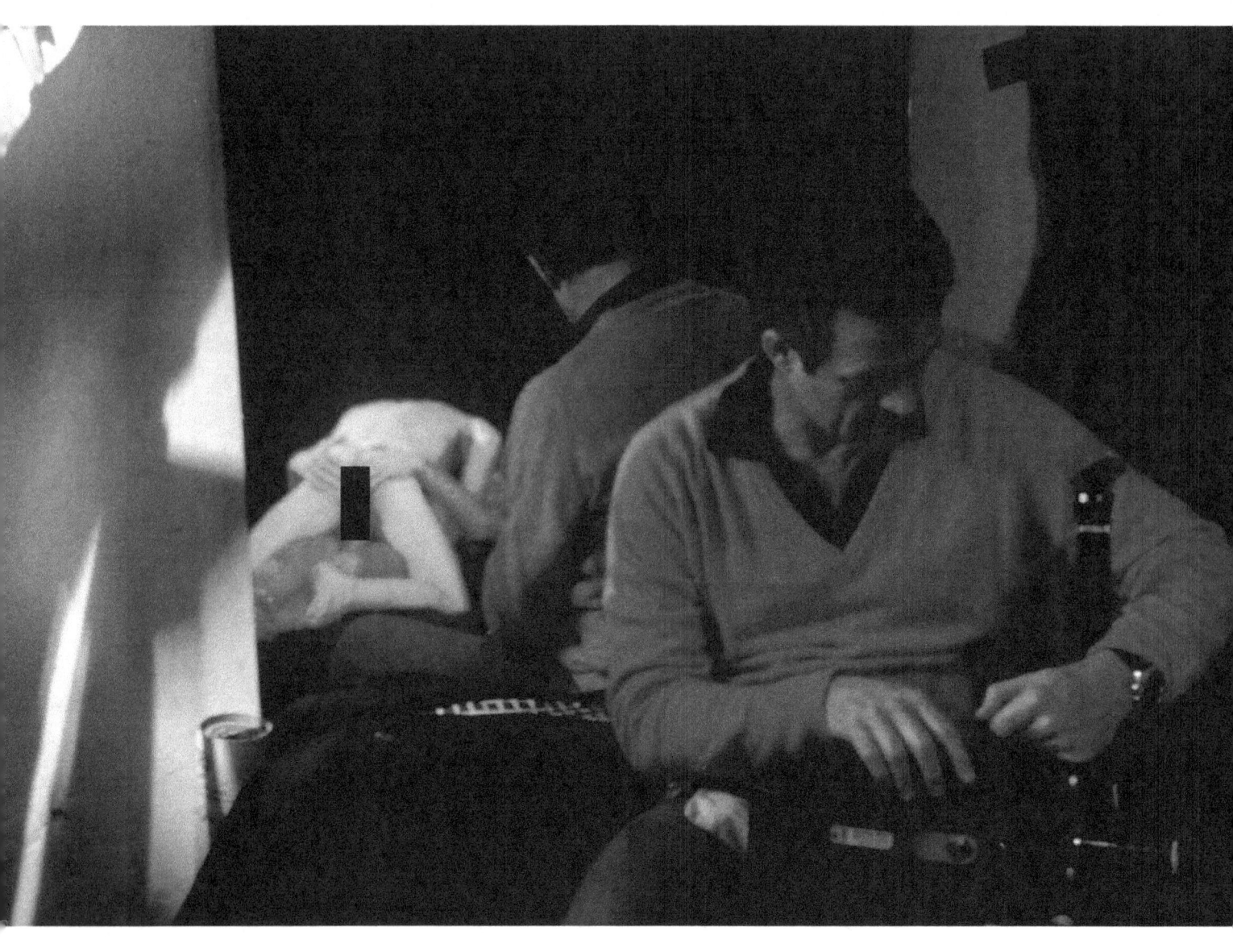

Jack Deveau behind the scenes of *Times Square Strip*

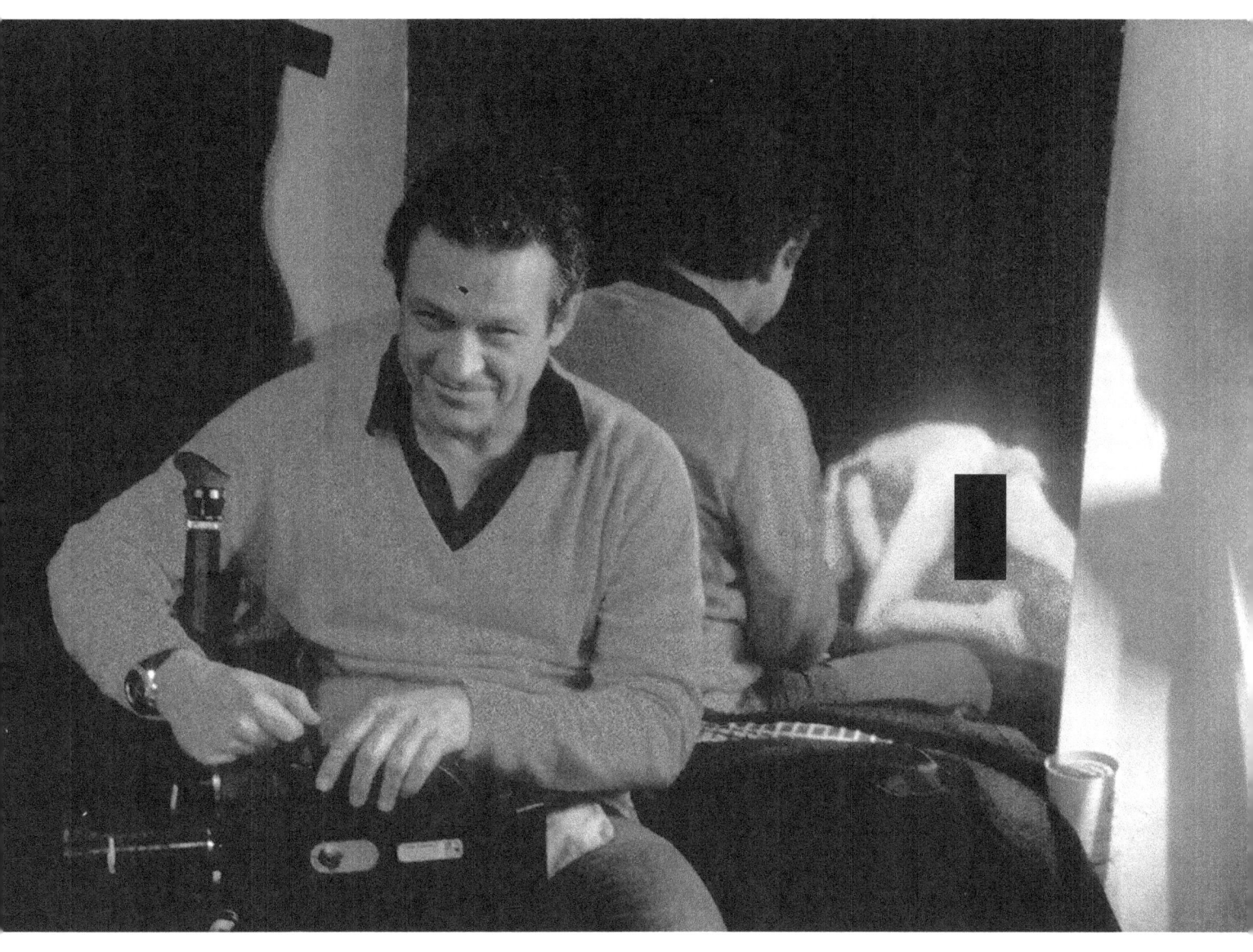

FRANK ROSS

Under the Tutelage of Jack Deveau

Marco Siedelmann: Mr. Ross, you are looking back on a career in gay porn business that's almost lasting four decades. You have contributed in many ways to the porn legacy, earning credits as director, producer, editor and more. The first chapter takes us back to the early days of Jack Deveau and his film studio Hand In Hand Films. Let's start with the usual: When did you see your first all-male porn, and how did you join the scene?

Frank Ross: Keep in mind that in the period you're talking about, 1970 and before, everything was shot on 8 mm, mostly without sound and there weren't any theatrical venues in those days since it was still considered illegal. That is, until Wakefield Poole released BOYS IN THE SAND and previewed it, I believe, but not sure, at the Park Miller Theater in Manhattan. This followed the first straight porn movie to open theatrically, DEEP THROAT, which shocked the world, and Poole was inspired to do the same with BOYS IN THE SAND, and put gay porn on the map. I also believe it was the first gay porn shot on 16 mm with synchronized sound. Until that time, gay porn was mostly shot on hand-held, manual winding Bolex cameras that did not have synch sound and were quite noisy when they ran. But they were very light and easy to use and allowed one to experiment with various camera angles. The early 8 mm films could only be seen at the grungy peep shows that existed, mostly underground, around the country. One could also buy 8 mm loops from the producers and some peep shows, if you had an 8 mm projector at home. But generally, it was hard to find, and the porn magazine business at that time was in its heyday. I believe the first gay porn I ever saw was a loop by a very talented and often forgotten pioneer in gay porn, Avery Willard. I was introduced to Hand In Hand in 1973 when my roommate at the time began an affair with Jack Deveau. Jack was producing a new film directed by Arch Brown, and my roommate told me they were looking for performers. So I met with Arch Brown and was hired on the spot. I co-starred in the movie which was titled THE NIGHT BEFORE. I had not chosen a professional name yet, since this was my first time, so I don't remember how I was billed. I was also a photographer at the time and was more interested in the other side of the camera, so I began doing still photography for Hand In Hand and generally all around production assistant, learning everything I knew about film from Jack and Bob Alvarez. Jack was a willing teacher if he thought you had a passion for filmmaking, and it was under his tutelage that I learned so much about the craft of filmmaking. Nobody on the crew had any one specific job. We all wore many hats, from general assistants to lighting, propping, set decoration, sound recording, and slating scenes. I even learned how to load fresh film into the 16 mm film magazines, which involved placing the double magazine in a light-proof black bag. There were two openings for both hands to insert, and then you had to do all the threading and loading, all by feel alone without seeing what you were doing. It was very intricate, and you needed patience and total concentration. It was an excellent school for learning filmmaking from the ground up.

Siedelmann: Were you good friends with David Earnest, Robert Alvarez or Deveau himself? The rare background footage draws the picture of a company built of friends and lovers; almost like a family. Is this too simple and naive?

Ross: David Earnest and I have been friends for over 40 years - long before Hand In Hand. We are still best friends today. I introduced David to Jack Deveau because Jack wanted to use original music only, and David was a talented young composer, and he and Jack hit it off right away. Yes, at the time we were like one big family. We all hung out at Jack and Bob's famous penthouse apartment on West 73rd St. That was headquarters, a sometimes location and generally, when not filming, hanging out, drinking and doing cocaine a lot. But yes, we were all very close and friends. It had to be that way. If you didn't fit in to the crowd, you were not brought into the group. So you had to have a sort of intelligence and passion. This Jack always demanded from everyone who worked for him. There were always intrigues and affairs, especially between the performers and the crew members. We were quite sexually liberated by this time so anything went when it came to sexual behavior. But play never interfered with our work. We were very proud of the work we did. It was an honor and a privilege to have Jack Deveau as a mentor. He was an extraordinary man and way ahead of his time whose life was cut short at an early age.

Siedelmann: Sounds magical and like a "Golden Age" in many ways - you must have had the time of your life. But cocaine parties were already very expensive in the seventies. The members of the Hand In Hand family obviously were making a good living at this time?

Ross: Please don't misunderstand. None of us were drug addicts or had a "problem" with drugs. Most people of that era smoked pot and did cocaine as we did earlier, experimenting with LSD; casual use, for fun only. Drugs were never allowed on the set, and we were very professional in that way. Any "partying" we did was when we were not filming a movie, and it was occasional, maybe in the case of a premiere party or something like that. And I must point out that the crew made very little money in those days. We really did it for love more than money; both for the excitement of filmmaking and because we all loved Jack so much.

Siedelmann: Pioneer Wakefield Poole had to struggle with drug addiction and lost a huge part of his capability, he had to sell most of his art collection as well. Did it happen at some point (to you or someone else) who was a close friend at Hand In Hand?

Ross: As I mentioned in the previous question, none of us were drug addicts. We used drugs just for casual entertainment. No one that I know of in the Hand In Hand group had, nor as far as I know, ever had such a problem, during and after our time with the studio.

Siedelmann: Jack Deveau is clearly one of the key directors within the gay golden age legacy: What do you think about his skills as a filmmaker? Do you still sometimes take a look at the Hand In Hand stuff?

Ross: Jack was a genius, period! His skills as a filmmaker, porn or not, were unrivaled. He was rather Hitchcockian in his approach to directing. He was always interested in the performer's private life and always drew on their experiences, fears, perversions, addictions, to bring out the character he wanted. He was a master at psychoanalyzing these performers without them realizing what he was doing. He always built his characters around the individual performer, because these were not trained actors, and it was difficult to make a narrative movie with untrained actors. Jack was very talented at getting from them what they would do best and not sticking to any script or idea of just an imaginary character. The performer became the character. By the way, he did the same thing with his crew. Always probing, questioning, and observing who they really were. I haven't seen a Hand In Hand film in many years. It's kind of what I do with my own movies. Once shot and edited, I never look at them again.

Siedelmann: The later films lost quality and got more conventional. Were you into strictly narrative porn films as LEFT-HANDED at all, or did you prefer the more sex-orientated stuff as loops and compilations from Old Reliable, Falcon or Magnum Griffin?

Ross: Personally, I was never very interested in narrative porn, nor as a director. But learning my craft by working on narrative films allowed me to hone my skills in what we might call "traditional filmmaking"; in other words, Hollywood-type films. Jack was all Hollywood and taught us how to make a proper film from scratch. I preferred in those early days Old Reliable as my source of erotic pleasure. The boys were hot; the sex was hot in a natural way. Not acting. They were sexual beings just performing in front of a camera.

Siedelmann: Did the work of Hand In Hand have some political and social dimension?

Ross: I wouldn't say there was an obvious political edge to porn in those days. Everyone who made movies just did it for the sheer love of it. Of course, at the time, we were all going through an amazing liberation; politically, socially and sexually. It was a time of radical changes in our society as a whole. So I think making porn, in itself, was a statement of freedom and equality, but it was not overtly political.

Siedelmann: You are best friends with David Earnest, who takes credit as composer for some of the greatest classics in gay porn, such as THE NIGHT BEFORE or DRIVE. Don't you think his music is very underrated? Do you think film historians have ever noticed his work just because it was done for gay porn?

Ross: On the contrary: David Earnest has had a long and thriving career as a composer and teacher. He was young and unknown in the music world of the time and loved having the opportunity to write some good music for Jack's movies. But he did not do that for very long. He went on to do many other works using his professional name, John David Earnest. He is quite an accomplished composer.

Siedelmann: As far as I know your uncredited on-screen-time in THE NIGHT BEFORE, directed by the legendary Arch Brown, is counted as your one and only job in front of the camera. Do you remember the shooting; were you close to Mr. Brown? How long was the working period on films like this, from the very first idea until holding the copies in hands?

Ross: Arch Brown and I were friends for many years. THE NIGHT BEFORE was my only appearance in front of the camera and my introduction to the fascinating world of porn. Arch liked to shoot lots of outdoor, non-hard core stuff to add to his propensity for the narrative. So we often all got on the subway and did walk-by shots on various city streets, accidental meetings, things like that. Arch worked rather quickly, and I think that movie was done in less than a week. We shot some sex scenes at his house and some at other private locations in the city. Actually, the post-production usually took longer that the shoot. This was mainly because Jack Deveau was a perfectionist, and narrative films involved a lot of work, especially films shot on 16 mm with synchronized sound and music. Starting with a work print, editing picture and sound, adding music, mixing, negative cutting, and then the final 1st print; this could take sometimes several months to complete. Keep in mind, at the time there weren't any post-production houses that generally would work on gay porn, and there weren't any gay post-production people who were experts. But we found negative cutters, sound mixing studios, and film labs that created work prints and the final release print. They were all straight and most did it quietly. The labs would run our prints at night when no one was around. The point is, in those days, we had all professional post-production facilities that at the same time were also working on mainstream Hollywood and TV productions. So we had the best! This was very sophisticated for gay porn at the time. Now people shoot a video, edit it on a computer and it's out to the market. Getting my education in the pre-video period made it so much easier for me to transfer into video production when it first appeared. Even the modern editing programs are based on the traditional way we edited film, except it is digital and much faster. We sat at flatbed or upright Moviolas and edited picture and sound by hand. Every splice was done by hand, one by one, taped manually and these cuts had to match to the audio track, which was on a separate reel and ran in synch with the picture; well, hopefully. If one lost synch, it was sometimes a nightmare to re-synch the two. It helped if you were a good sound editor too, because sometimes you had to re-synch the picture by matching exactly the movement of a performers lips to the sound track. Sometimes it would involve matching a sound, like a bang or a moan, and it had to be exactly line-up or the rest of the picture would never be in synch. Imagine! But it was wonderful, and I still miss the process. With video editing now, it's almost impossible to lose synch in that way.

Siedelmann: Can you give estimation about the number of fabricated copies? How many were made for common productions of Hand In Hand, compared with Steve Scott's WANTED, or both Toby Ross films you contributed on? And how long could they be seen in theatres, a few months or even years?

Ross: In the early days of 16 mm theatrical releases, there was a very small network of distributors and theater owners. As I remember, there were only about six major gay theaters in the country: New York, Boston, Philadelphia, Chicago, San Francisco, and Los Angeles. When I went to work for Mustang Studios, I handled theatrical distribution. Usually, there weren't many release prints made. When a new film was released there might have been maybe a few prints made, and they were sent to the major theaters around the country. Those same prints were then recycled over and over again, so much so that eventually when they reached secondary markets the quality of the film had degraded from overuse. Remember, this was before video and people could only see these movies at theaters. As is the case today, for a studio to make any money, they had to keep in constant production with new releases every few months to feed the theaters with new product. The new releases usually would reach the theaters within a month after completion, and the turnaround was feverish.

Siedelmann: Are there many other friendships left from the very early years? Do you remember bad vibrations between some studios or filmmakers or was there something like a bond between those who contributed to gay adult films? Rumors say there was no need for conflicts in the first decade because the need of new film material had more or less some space for everybody's films?

Ross: Except for Toby Ross and Wakefield Poole, there were not many friendships that endured. Since most directors at the time were independent, they worked for numerous studios who wanted their films, and there was a lot of interaction between us. That is how I met Arch Brown, Toby Ross, Wakefield Poole, Steve Scott, Peter de Rome, Joe Gage and others at the time. Of course there was some competition among the directors but as you say, there was room enough for everyone. But each director wanted to be recognized as the best, so yes; healthy competition existed, which was only natural for these artists and auteurs. The real issues were not among the directors but the studios/distributors. A key issue to remember here is that most studios were run by straight porn people who went into the gay market when theatrical gay films began to appear. They appeared on the gay porn scene like the Huns descending on Rome. They were truly barbarians at the gate, and the gay porn community had no choice but to submit to their occupation. Here is where the real conflicts began because truthfully, the straight owners almost always exploited the gay directors. They were often never paid for their work completely, and gay directors were at their mercy because at the time no gay-owned studios really existed. There were many infamous straight studio owners, who I will not mention by name, who were particularly nothing but common thieves, and they knew that gay directors had no way to fight back, especially not legally. Wakefield Poole is a prime example of this practice. He often had to beg for his money from these scoundrels. William Higgins is another example, when he released his first movie, BOYS OF VENICE. And, these straight studios often literally stole prints from other studios, making deals with the labs that made the prints and then releasing them without any rights to the films. This was common practice at the time, and law suits were out of the question, and everyone knew that. An example of this practice happened in New York, while I was managing the 55th St. Playhouse. William Higgins had just released his famous, classic movie about the boys of Southern California, BOYS OF VENICE. It had its New York premiere at the 55th St. Playhouse. Higgins came to New York with his film after he had made a deal with Mustang. Since he had no place to stay and obviously no money for a hotel, and Mustang wouldn't pay for one, they made him sleep in an upper lobby chair at the theater. It must have been so humiliating for Higgins, and I was personally embarrassed and sympathetic from both a general distaste for his treatment but also aware of the obvious mistreatment of gay directors by straight studios. He was literally imprisoned in the theater at night when the theater was closed and locked up. Higgins, who had just made one of the classic movies of the period, was treated no better than a homeless person and he was very unhappy. But, there were obviously money problems between Higgins and Mustang. Again, with no written contract as far as I know, Higgins was not getting paid as promised. One day, while I was in the projection room screening THE BOYS OF VENICE, I had just switched to the 2nd reel of the movie and had the 1st reel on the re-wind table, when suddenly Higgins burst into the door and ripped the 1st reel off the table and ran out with it. He disappeared out of the theater and was never seen again. Now since I didn't have reel 1 of the movie, we were in big trouble because the movie was very popular, and we had large crowds every day coming to see it. While we had to temporarily start screening another movie, Mustang was able, within two days, to get a copy of reel 1 from someone in California, probably the film lab in California. Since most "Master" reels were kept at the labs, a lot of labs were unscrupulous and sold unauthorized prints. It was obviously a pirated copy, but we continued to do the movie, and Higgins got nothing and could not do anything about it. But in the end, it was Mustang's loss, as Higgins went on to become one of the most successful directors in California and would never do business with Mustang again. In New York at least, Hand In Hand Films was the first gay-owned studio, and that's when gay directors started to be treated fairly.

Siedelmann: The films directed by Christopher Rage are very notorious examples of gay adult filmmaking. He was a crew member at Hand In Hand, for example THE NIGHT BEFORE and HOT HOUSE by Jack Deveau. Was he a part of the inner circle?

Ross: Christopher Rage was a very integral part of Hand In Hand. Like me, he changed his professional name when he began his own company. The name he sometimes used back then was Tray Christopher, so you might find credits for him under that name. He was the production manager for Hand In Hand when we shot THE NIGHT BEFORE, and that's how we met and became lifelong friends until his death. I think he might have appeared in some films under that name. At the time, this is pre-video, he was the advertising director for an advertising company that was called, I believe, Sampson/Craynor. They designed and placed ads in the local newspapers for new films coming out in the theaters. This company almost exclusively handled all advertising in NY for all the gay theaters, and the straight ones too.

Siedelmann: How many films did you accompany at Hand In Hand as a still photographer? Do you still own this early work of yours? And have you continued photography until now?

Ross: I really don't remember the titles of all the films I worked on for Hand In Hand. I know the only one I didn't work on was LEFT-HANDED. I arrived on the scene after this was made. I worked with Jack until he became ill and stopped producing movies. I did not own the stills. They were owned by the studio. Yes, I continued to do still photography throughout my career and still do.

Siedelmann: Still photography was mostly done for advertising purposes - every studio needed them for selling the films better in theatres. How much attention and interest had the studio owner for these work?

Ross: It's true that stills were primarily used for advertising purposes in the local newspapers when a new film was released to a theater, but also, the magazines were always starved for content, so most studios used to give stills from a film to the magazines in exchange for some publicity. Sometimes studios even got free advertising from the magazines in exchange for stills. In the earlier days, slide sets were also reproduced and sold to consumers. It was another way to make money on the movies. Even today in the world of Pay Per View, stills are considered very valuable to the studios and secondary producers. If you don't have quality stills, it's difficult to get your movie on a PPV site.

Siedelmann: Indeed, Deveau was one of the few great directors of the era, maybe the most important and best when it comes to narrative structures in gay porn. I think he should be named next to Bob Rafelson, John Schlesinger or even Robert Altman.

Ross: I agree!

Siedelmann: Deveau's first feature LEFT-HANDED already showed this remarkable talent. His wildly moving camera sets the bar high for the whole era, the acting is far away from the often clumsy-looking standards, and scripts are well-written. Did most of the group keep up their friendship until the tragic passing of Deveau? If I'm free to ask this, when was the last time you saw him?

Ross: Yes, I worked with Jack Deveau from the time I starred in THE NIGHT BEFORE until the last film he made, which I cannot remember the title of. The last time I saw Jack was at his home, and he was already ill. After a while, he really didn't want to see too many people. He knew he was dying. Unfortunately, this was also around the time that the AIDS epidemic had started, and during those years I lost many friends and associates to this disease. So many of them, sadly; they are long gone.

Siedelmann: Please describe a film example you worked on for Hand In Hand. Did you have instructions all by Deveau?

Ross: One I remember very well was BALLET DOWN THE HIGHWAY. Although he was not always the director of some films, he was always the consumate producer. He conceived and ran every aspect of a shoot, and yes, we all took direction directly from him. BALLET was shot at various locations. One scene was shot in the country, and it was a lot of work, and we had a large crew, traveling like a Bedouin caravan. But the scene that was the longest scene I ever worked on was the ballet scene which we shot at the very famous Adonis Theater on 8th Ave. in New York. It was once a legitimate movie theater, so it was huge, with a stage and large screen, balconies and lots of dark corners one could play. The Adonis premiered lots of new films, including Jack's, and in fact, THE NIGHT BEFORE was premiered there. Jack had hired a limo for me and my co-star, Coke Henessey, and as we got out there were scores of gay paparazzi. Believe me; it was like a Hollywood premiere and quite glamorous. Jack had the theater for the entire evening, and we started shooting in the morning and didn't leave the shoot until the next morning. That's correct. 24 hours of non-stop shooting one scene. It was exhausting, but the kind of thing that happened in those days, and for Jack, it was always about perfection. This kind of attention to detail is unheard of now. For your information, I was on screen as the stage manager. Back in the early days I did not have a professional name so I used my real name. This is the name you might find on other credits from Hand In Hand, including crew credits. I prefer to keep this name confidential if you don't mind as I haven't used it in over 30 years, and I've always been known professionally as Frank Ross.

Siedelmann: At some point you decided working with other studios. It's not easy following your career steps by looking in databases and random sources. Tell me about your main stations after Hand In Hand. Among others you joined the Mustang Studios and worked with Al Parker and Steve Scott in WANTED.

Ross: Well, while working for Hand In Hand, I became good friends with Tray Christopher, who was primarily their advertising liaison. He would later go on to start his own studio, Live Video, and changed his professional name to Christopher Rage. We remained very close friends until his death. He also did publicity for Mustang Studios and these two straight Israeli brothers owned several theaters in New York. The major theater was called the 55th St. Playhouse, and it often premiered new gay films. When Jack Deveau premiered one of his movies there, I believe it was JUST BLONDS, I was asked to be the house counter. In other words, Jack knew these guys might not be honest, and I was responsible for counting heads, so to speak, so Jack would be able to compare my count with the count the theater owner gave to him since they were paying Jack by a percentage of the house. This was not very common at the time as prints were usually rented at a flat rate. The latter was an example of Jack Deveau's clever business acumen. It was then that I became acquainted with the two Israelis, the Mamane Brothers. Danny Mamane was the chief honcho at the time and head of Mustang Studios. He was the Louis B. Mayer of gay porn in every sense. I remember a funny incident while Toby Ross and I were in his office as we watched Danny brood over what his next move should be. As he sat behind his desk, twirling his giant moustache, as he tended to do when he was try to strategize, like a general on the frontline of battle. He then sat up and, banging his fist on the desk, shouted to us: "Get me Gordon Grant, he's a *star*!!" Gordon Grant, the legendary Colt model and mega-star in porn in the 70's was long gone from the scene and had literally disappeared. Toby and I just looked at each other with amazement. That's how they were. Greedy, and wanting something that other studios had, and his perception was that they were making money that he wasn't. It made people like Danny totally crazy. Danny eventually went to Los Angeles and became a multi-millionaire as a distributor by buying product at very low prices in large quantity and underselling all the other distributors. I must say, I don't judge Danny, he was a product of the times, and he was always good to me, and we had a very close relationship. When they opened new straight porn theaters on 54th St. Tray Christopher was made manager. When he wanted to leave to start working on plans to start his own studio, he asked me to take over management of the theater, which I did; thus started a very long and difficult climb up the porn ladder with Mustang. I later moved to San Francisco temporarily to manage a theater there that the Mamane's had just purchased; it was called The Screening Room. I remember another interesting experience when I first arrived there. San Francisco had a very strong projectionist union, and the projectionist who was working there when we took over was a straight union man and could not be fired. Since we needed a second projectionist to work the second shift, Danny came to San Francisco, and we met with the union president at his office, who happened to be Jewish. The purpose of the meeting was because the union would only allow a non-union 2nd projectionist if he was the owner/operator. So Danny had to negotiate with him so that I could be considered a legal representative of the owner and be allowed to operate the projectors in his absence. The Union president did not agree and kept refusing Danny's insistence that I should be allowed to be 2nd projectionist. Of course, since I had no idea how to operate a very complicated projector - they were carbon arc projectors which required a trained operator - I just sat there wondering how all this would turn out. Finally, in desperation, Danny turned to the union president and said, "Listen, I'm a Jew, you're a Jew". I was startled and very uncomfortable, especially since I was the only Gentile in the room. Within minutes, the union president agreed, and I was now the second projectionist and had no idea how to operate a carbon arc projector. The union allowed our union projectionist to teach me, and soon I was an expert at operating these very complicated projectors. Another amusing incident I had with Danny while he was in San Francisco was one evening he asked me to take him to a straight bar because he was dying to get laid. So I did, and he eventually picked up two chicks at the bar and he asked me to drive them all back to hotel. While in the car he suggested that I join them for a 4-way; well, he knew I was gay but that didn't seem to matter to him. I thought that my loyalty to Danny had a breaking point and sleeping with him and these two shiksas [Yiddish word for a Gentile woman] was that point. I told him I would drop them off because I had to go and close the theater. He suggested I return after I closed the theater. Well, of course I didn't, and not another word was ever spoken about it again. I don't know if Danny wanted to experiment with a gay man or if he might have thought he could turn me straight. This is how little understood gay men were understood by these straight guys. They dealt with them when it came to making money off them, but they probably thought we were all freaks. It was during this period that I was made producer to oversee productions that were being done in California. This is how I first met Steve Scott and Toby Ross, as producer for Mustang. I eventually moved back to New York and directed my very first movie for Mustang titled ONE NIGHT STAND; around 1983 or so.

Siedelmann: So, after years shooting stills on so many sets, you finally came to directing films on your own. First entry in most databases is the cult favorite HUNK (1981). Is this a compilation and were you directing short films before?

Ross: The first film I ever directed was in 1983 for Mustang Studio titled, ONE NIGHT STAND, although I had been working for Mustang since 1979 and did a variety of things during that period. I managed The Screening Room in 1980 and also learned my film editing skills from a great editor. I truly don't remember editing HUNK, but it's quite possible. I looked at the production credits and knew most of the people in the cast who were working in NY at the time. Also, studios over the years have taken to changing titles of movies, especially films they bought but did not produce. Bijou is well known for this practice.

Siedelmann: I assume this was the major league, the gay porn mainstream?

Ross: Indeed this was so. Really the golden age of porn where gay premieres were held at major theaters, big glitzy openings with gay paparazzi, limos for the stars, huge, lavish parties after the screenings, reviews in the major gay magazines. This is when the real gay stars first began to emerge, through this kind of mass media exposure. It was really the beginning of where porn is at now. I remember while I was working with Steve Scott on WANTED, which starred the iconic Al Parker and the then well known star Jack Wrangler. We were shooting a scene somewhere outside L.A., on some ranch that was miles away from the nearest town. In those days we didn't have food or refreshments on the set, especially when it was location. During a break, Jack asked Steve Scott for coffee. Well the nearest coffee to be found was miles away, but Steve asked me to please fetch some coffee for Jack. So I drove about 20 miles to get the coffee for him, just to keep him happy. This is a good example of how the real stars were treated. I personally wanted to strangle Jack Wrangler, but I kept my mouth shut and learned a good lesson about how to treat valuable performers.

Siedelmann: You are also still in lively contact with Toby Ross. How did both of you get together? In the early 80s you were the producer for two of his very last films, shot on celluloid: THE DIARY and THE LAST SURFER. There was no further work together and both films are the latest produced by Hornbill, the label of Toby Ross. Was there a financial disaster?

Ross: As I mention, I met Toby while managing the Screening Room Theater for the Mamane Brothers. They had hired Toby to do a film for them, THE DIARY, and since I was already in California, it was convenient to make me the producer, basically the "money man" for them. Not to mention I didn't get paid for that role, ever. We first met in L.A., and we immediately bonded and that bond lasted over many years. I also was the producer with Toby when we shot THE LAST SURFER in L.A. Although that may be the only two that were credited, Toby and I worked on many other movies together, both mine and his, usually uncredited, and we also did a lot of post-production work together. We were very, very close friends and are still in contact to this day. This was also how I met Steve Scott in L.A., producing his first film for Mustang, WANTED. We also became good friends for a while and worked on a subsequent film for Mustang, I believe it was titled CALIFORNIA BOYS, until we had a falling out over the film lab that Mustang instructed me to use in L.A. - we had one more scene to shoot to finish the movie, and apparently Steve Scott had some issues with them and threatened to walk out on the film if I continued using them. When Mustang refused, I finished the last scene of the movie with Toby Ross directing. Steve Scott and I never spoke again. The film was eventually bought by Bijou Studios in

Chicago, and the title was changed to L.A. BOYS.

Siedelmann: THE LAST SURFER is a rare film of its kind: not only elusive, nostalgic and melancholic, also a period piece, located in the early sixties. More specific: The longboard-era and the origins of surf sport as we know it until today. Which topics come to your mind when you think of the sixties?

Ross: The gay liberation movement started in New York while California kept "dreamin' on", and something of that 60's culture held on in California and still does in some ways. Now, Toby always had a fascination for things American, especially young American men, and that is where he decided to settle. In a rather classic Greek way, Toby idolized the essence of American youth, which he saw at its best in California. He was transfixed by the innocent, naive natural beauty of American youth, or as he often referred to them as, "corn-fed". This very American expression arose as a way of describing healthy, young, handsome, naturally innocent boys from the mid-west, which is where all our corn is grown. Such boys would charm the pants off of Toby, and it was in California that many of these "corn-fed" boys flocked to in the 70's. You say elusive, nostalgic and melancholic? Yes, exactly, that was the sense one got from his movies, especially THE LAST SURFER. It was his version of THE LAST PICTURE SHOW. He was nostalgic for the period of innocence that existed in the US before all the social upheavals of the late sixties. Since he never got to see that, he used his movies to invoke that period and idealize American youth.

Siedelmann: What about the sport - were you ever a surfer?

Ross: Sorry, but I had to laugh at your question. I am born and bred in New York, actually the Bronx, and the nearest wave big enough to surf on was 3,000 miles away. In the sixties, there were two different cultures going on between the East and West Coast. As an example, while West Coasters were listening to music such as the Beach Boys, we in New York were listening to doo-wop and Motown which came from Detroit. We were very different in the way we dressed, spoke and danced.

Siedelmann: THE LAST SURFER was shot by cinematographer Tom Howard. To me and many other enthusiasts, his work for the films of Steve Scott [celluloid and video] brought out some of the finest images in vintage porn. Did you meet him while shooting WANTED in 1980? Was it hard to get him convinced for smaller projects?

Ross: Tom Howard was by far the best cinematographer in the industry, not to mention the nicest guy you would ever hope to meet. He was cool, always confident, and one found a certain security in his ability to do things correctly and beautifully. He added a lot to the quality of films being made then. He was formally trained in the great Hollywood tradition, as was Steve Scott. In fact, Tom's father was a very famous cinematographer in Hollywood who worked on many well know mainstream films. I met him when we filmed WANTED, through Steve Scott and subsequently worked on many films with him. You say "smaller" projects? In those days everything was smaller, at least budget-wise, and nobody made a lot of money. As I may have mentioned earlier, we were able to get highly skilled, professional people to work on our films. I don't think they did it so much for the money but just for the love of their craft and the opportunity to work. I think I was the one to introduce Tom to Jack Deveau. Tom was strictly an L.A. person. Lived and worked there, but eventually Jack was able to get him to come to NY for some film projects. Unfortunately, I'm not able to recall what those films were.

Siedelmann: You were producing many different films and were therefore, in most cases, the owner, right? After the sunset of the golden age of porn there was much discord in the industry: most filmmakers were literally robbed of their remaining copies, films were sold without permission or simply used because they were orphaned. Without dropping names, did you have some of these bitter experiences as well?

Ross: I didn't own a single film until I started 3rd World Video in 1995. I didn't have such bad experiences, because I wasn't directing movies at the time, but I often was witness to such out and out exploitation and robbery. Don't misunderstand what "producer" meant in those days. These films were all financed by straight studios and distributors. As I mentioned earlier, it was these guys who did the stealing. Most gay directors of the time had no studio of their own and independently made movies for them for a fee only. They never owned the movies. Except for Wakefield Poole, who was robbed blind by these greedy worms! I was basically the money man, and was the gay representative for these straight producers. My job was to pay everyone, make sure the production didn't go over budget and handle the executive end of the production.

Siedelmann: It seems to me, the use of unlicensed music [often huge hits] reinforced this legal situation and the distribution problems worldwide. Most golden age gay porn films are sadly not able to appear on an official and fully legal DVD. Were you using such music without rights, and were you regretful about this sometime?

Ross: I have never used unlicensed music in any of my movies. I always used original music performed and recorded by hired musicians. In my later productions, I actually started to eliminate music completely, favoring all live, synchronized sound instead. In the old days, music was necessary because very little of the film, if any, used live sound. Everything was shot MOS (an abbreviation for Mid out sound.) Legend has it, according to *The Screenwriter's Bible*, David Trottier credits the term to Austrian director Erich von Stroheim, who allegedly would tell his crew: "Ve'll shoot dis mid out sound." - Which remained an industry standard. This was the reason most filmmakers of the day had to add some kind of music to their movies, often infringing on copyrights, but since they were so limited to a select audience and not public, filmmakers could have never foreseen the future of porn and its worldwide exposure. I remember the very favorite choice of film makers in those days was Indian raga music. It was hard to trace and not easily identified. Yes, it is sad that so many of the early movies cannot be legally released now because of copyright infringements.

Siedelmann: Have you ever worked with David Hurles, the man behind Old Reliable, one of the most influencing porn filmmakers of all time?

Ross: I never met David but was very familiar with his films. In fact, he was a strong influence on my later movies when I started 3rd World Video.

Siedelmann: For Satellite, you directed a bunch of porn films focusing on black guys. Have you ever experienced any kind of racism or derogatory attitude within the industry? All in all there were plenty actors in a few films but long time nothing as genuine black porn existed. These films were commissioned work? Or have you always had a thing for black guys?

Ross: Personally, I have always been attracted to African-American men. I had a very good relationship with Eddie Mishkin, who was the owner of Satellite Video. He was an old-timer in the porn business and quite a character. I really liked him a lot, even though he was a scoundrel. At the time, he was not really a studio. Their main business was video sales and rentals to subscribers. And he also made a lot of money during the heyday of the old peep shows. It's no secret that these types of companies would buy one VHS copy of a movie from various producers and then illegally copy the tape over and over again. This was common practice, and the producers never saw another penny from these movies except the sale of that one copy. This re-copying of VHS tapes eventually degraded the quality of the original, and sadly they continued to sell and rent them regardless of the bad quality. The sad story is that this is one example, as I mentioned a few times earlier, that gay people were exploited, both producers, directors and eventually, the consumers. It was a business of greed. Anyway, there was a total lack of black performers in gay porn, not to mention an all-black cast. I began a series of all-black movies for Satellite, I think maybe 8 or 9. The first and most popular was titled MADE IN THE SHADE, which starred the soon-to-become famous first black porn star, Joe Simmons, who was the most wonderful person and performer. I adored him and made several movies with him until he was picked up by some studios in California where he found his fame. Without a doubt, there was a considerable amount of racism, not only in porn but in the general gay culture. It just mirrored the racism that was rampant in our society as a whole then and in some way still is. By the way, speaking of Toby Ross and our uncredited collaborations over the years, he was very involved in helping me produce these Satellite movies, and I couldn't have done it without his valuable help and advice. I was interested in why there was such a lack of "ethnic types" in gay porn, and sometime after the Satellite movies, I started a new, short-lived studio called True Blue Video. I produced and directed two movies with Asian and Caucasian performers. I don't believe there were any American porn films that featured Asian performers. Those movies were titled SECRET ASIAN MAN and PACIFIC FEVER. SECRET ASIAN MAN was a huge hit with both Asians and the Caucasian men that were attracted to them. Again, Toby Ross took a major, uncredited role in helping me produce these movies, which were both shot in San Francisco. They are still available on PPV sites such as AEBN.

Siedelmann: Talking about Afro-American men in gay porn: Was there an equality

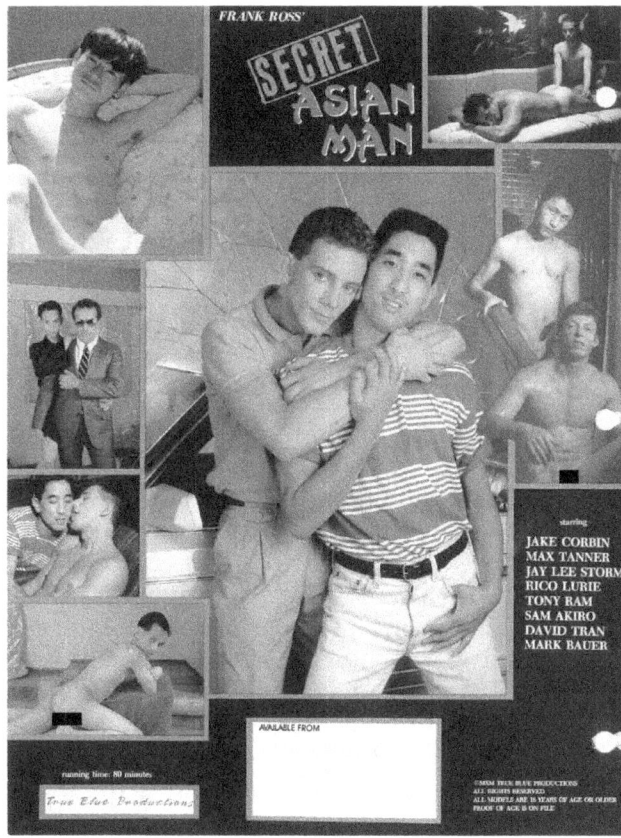
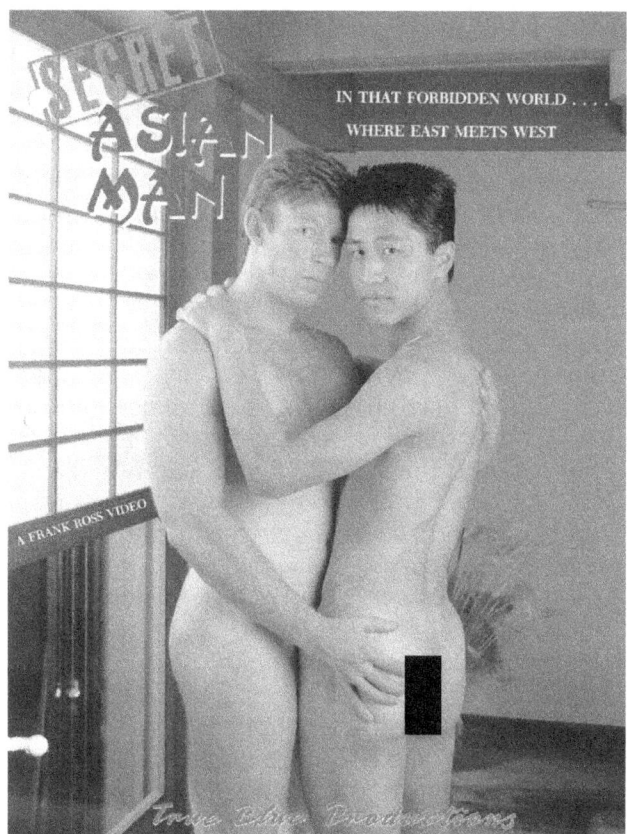

of opportunities for black guys within the the Golden Age? In the clubs, theatres and parties, were many black men taking part of the seventies gay community?

Ross: During the seventies, both in and out of the porn industry, there were few opportunities for black men. Socially, there was still a division to some extent between white and black men. Culturally they were slow in coming out of the closet, because in the straight black community there was a big stigma attached to being gay. Although gay people were ostensibly more liberal, there remained a cultural gap that was mirrored by the general racial attitudes of the times. To an extent, that gap remains to this day in some ways. Black men were rarely used in early porn, except Black Forest in L.A. Socially, they hardly mixed with whites, even having their own gay bars to go to. When I made my first all-black movie, MADE IN THE SHADE, it starred a wonderful black performer named Joe Simmons. He was handsome, sexy, great body, big dick and very open-minded sexually. He was a dream to work with, and eventually he became a big star in L.A., making inter-racial porn. The inter-racial gay scene, at least in New York, still remains a sub-culture, although racism has changed dramatically in this country.

Siedelmann: Among the first directors who established an authentic Afro-American style and view in gay porn is the nearly forgotten Dwight Anthony, founder of Black Forest. Have you ever met him or at least seen his films?

Ross: I never had the pleasure of meeting Dwight as he was L.A.-based, and I was in NY. In those days, the West Coast and East Coast porn industry were very set apart, and we did not have the opportunity to exchange ideas. Black Forest was the only studio making all-black movies back then, and they catered generally to an all-black market. Very few white men ever knew of these movies. I was introduced to his movies when I joined Satellite Video, and it was from my exposure to those movies that I was inspired to make all those black movies for them. It helped a lot that I was personally attracted to black men and had many sexual experiences, which at the time was not so common for white men.

Siedelmann: Among many other magazines with focus on black men, Black Forest has been publisher of *BFP Tribune* - great articles and interviews were reflecting the situation of black men in gay porn. Any idea what happened to Black Forest during the 90s?

Ross: I was not familiar with this magazine and

don't know what happened to Black Forest. Back then, East was East and West was West. The scene on the East Coast was very different from the West Coast. Camaraderie was more local then.

Siedelmann: BLACK SHAFTS, BLACK BOOK, BLACK & BI - mostly All-Black-Films are branded blatantly obvious by the studio or distributor. Have you ever been criticized by a black audience?

Ross: When I was asked by Satellite Video to create some movies for them with all black casts, they insisted that the titles be blatantly obvious that these were black movies for a black audience and those that liked black men. At the time, I was a bit reluctant to do this, but the studio insisted. I was never criticized for this, because the movies were well made and I was very respectful with all my performers. They sensed this, we got along well, and they worked hard to get these movies done. I never exploited them for their race and never portrayed them in any sort of racial stereotyping.

Siedelmann: Next to many other contributors to the history of gay adult films, you were interviewed for the well-known magazine *Manshots* (Vol 5, No. 3 - Feb. 1993). Your interview-partner, David Babbitt, was at that point already a director himself. Have you seen his films and do you like them?

Ross: At the time I met David Babbitt, he was writing film reviews for *Manshots*. He was not yet a director. He contacted me one day and told me he had shot a movie, his first. I believe it was titled BEAT COP, which starred Donnie Russo. By this time everyone was shooting on video, so it was easy for anyone to shoot a movie; they needed no formal training or experience as we did when shooting 16mm. Babbitt really had no idea what he was doing, as he didn't understand the need for shooting a movie with editing in mind. So he brought me this movie and asked me to edit it, which I did. During these sessions I think I taught David a lot in terms of shooting a cohesive movie that was editable. His was not, and it was a grueling experience to put it together. We were friends for a while but I never did see any of his later movies. During this time, anyone who wanted to pick up a video camera and shoot a movie did so. Everyone wanted to be a famous director, and to be honest, most of us who were making movies on 16mm did not take these interlopers very seriously. Those of us who came from a film background before video considered ourselves somewhat superior, I think. The era of video had arrived, and movies would never be the same again. To this day, I still prefer 16mm to video and would, if I could afford it, continue to shoot on film.

Siedelmann: About the conversation with Babbitt: Was it an honor speaking as a representing veteran a filmmaker to a younger generation, who seriously is aware of gay porn tradition?

Ross: David was a very intelligent interviewer and had a great sense of humor, so I liked him. But we all wanted publicity, so doing an interview was a great opportunity for me to express my views on the gay porn scene of the time. In that interview, I believed I expressed my dismay over all the new people coming into the industry without any training and much talent. So yes, I was very nostalgic about the old days of 16mm because it was a whole process that required many hands to put them together. With video, one person could shoot, direct and edit, so it didn't take much talent, and there wasn't the atmosphere we enjoyed, working with a group of like-minded people who each contributed to the final film. We were a family. In a way, it echoed the name of our studio, Hand In Hand.

Siedelmann: Magazines from *Beefcake* to *Unzipped* had been an important part within gay culture, early porn film and the leather scene. Have you been a magazine reader as well? Which did you prefer?

Ross: Personally, I was never much interested in the magazine scene. Not so much interested in getting off on the photos as much as keeping up with the news about performers, directors and new movies. For this the magazines were highly valuable.

Siedelmann: Very low information about a studio/distributor that worked with Joe Gage, Steve Scott, Matt Sterling, Wakefield Poole and more legendary directors: Can you tell any details about the studio TMX?

Ross: TMX was a secondary studio run by the same people who ran Mustang. It was active during the early period of video, before they started making the large video boxes that became the standard for years. During this time we used small, slip-in boxes that were cheap to make and easy to ship. The large boxes that would come to dominate the porn industry and straight too, were very expensive and involved a lot of work with designers, printer, etc., and also most printers demanded a minimum quantity to print them. I do believe the minimum was 2,500 boxes, and most studios couldn't afford that nor had that kind of distribution to sell all of them. For some reason unknown to me, Mustang discontinued TMX when they started doing the larger standard boxes. It was not uncommon for studios to create sub-studios, especially if the content was specific, like a fetish line, or twink line.

Siedelmann: BORN TO RAISE HELL - directed by Roger Earl and produced by Terry Le Grand - is counted as the awakening of the leather film. Were you part of the audience at the theatrical release?

Ross: Of course, BORN TO RAISE HELL is a classic film, and Roger Earl was a very talented director. I first saw the movie well after its premiere. Again, I lived in NY and the movie was premiered in L.A. We were not bicoastal people, so we waited for the movies to come to us.

Siedelmann: Avery Willard has been founder of the gay porn studio, PM Productions. Are you familiar with the PM films, partly directed by cult directors as Joe Gage, Kennith Holloway, Jason Sato or Francis Ellie?

Ross: I wasn't aware that Avery Willard founded PM Productions. As far as I remember, it was run by Bill Perry, who owned a famous movie theater/bath house in Times Square. I knew him very well, and although I never directed a movie for him, I did edit many of them over the years. He eventually was indicted in Florida for distribution of offensive material and spent several years in prison. This experience was very difficult for him, and he never worked in the industry again. This was the kind of oppression the U.S. government used to run people in porn out of business, and often they succeeded. Although I never worked with Joe Gage nor Francis Ellie, I knew them very well and respected them enormously for their talents and visions.

Siedelmann: Absolutely true, SECRET ASIAN MAN mostly is mentioned as a pioneer film when it comes to Asians in American gay porn. I assumed it must have been a success - how much budget was needed and did the film first flop? If not, why were these two True Blue Productions not followed by more of their kind?

Ross: The budgets were very high when I made SECRET ASIAN MAN. I believe that cost $10,000.00, as did PACIFIC FEVER. I rented houseboats, schooners, studios that all cost money. I think the high production value made these movies very successful, especially in light of the fact that they were considered "ethnic". One associated such ethnic movies with cheap, amateur, low-budget productions. I was living in San Francisco at the time and not only had all these locations available to me but also the Asian performers. It wasn't easy considering that, at the time, Asians were very much in the closet. Eventually I moved back to NY and started doing other things, so True Blue was a short-lived company. Finding Asians in New York willing to perform in front of a camera was near impossible, but SECRET ASIAN MAN was, and still is, one of the best movies I ever made and it is still available on PPV sites.

Siedelmann: You are directing and producing gay porn until today for your very own company 3rd World Kink. What was the main idea when you founded the company in 1995?

Ross: As you know, Christopher Rage and I were very close friends, and I often worked on some of his productions with LIVE Video. It was my introduction both personally and professionally to "kink". Eventually, he became very ill due to AIDS and was no longer able to shoot movies, so he asked me to direct one for him. I did, and the movie was titled Lovers. It was a commercial success and received rave reviews. I was astonished and very pleased that my first attempt at kink was such a success. I shot a second movie for him, and while on the set, received a phone call that he had died. The last time I saw him, he knew he was dying and told me if he did, to just continue making the movie. So, I hung up the phone and continued shooting while grieving for my good friend who I had just lost. After his death, a woman who was his bookkeeper somehow got control of the company and asked me to work for them. I did, and eventually became vice president of the company. Unfortunately, we clashed a lot, and I finally decided to leave and start my own "kink" company.

Siedelmann: A research through the known databases isn't very credible, so what can you say about the company? How many people are involved, how many films have been made until today?

Ross: 3rd World Video has produced over 65 movies since our start. The crews are small and local and only get together when we are shooting. I tried to continue the legacy of Christopher Rage, who always attempted to break barriers sexually and bring to the screen the reality and popularity of extreme fetishes, which no one else would consider or produce, especially the studios on the West Coast. I happily became a porn pariah and enjoyed shocking the world in any way I could, while keeping the erotic nature of fetish sex foremost. Many scenes that I shot were considered borderline illegal, and I loved the danger of it all. I loved shocking people who knew nothing about sex except the boring, mainstream porn that was coming out of California. You know the standard formula, first I suck you, then you suck me, then we kiss, then I fuck you. My movies generally have no storylines and very little non-sexual dialog, preferring live sound and no music.

Siedelmann: The reason, fetish and leather films developed that much after the sundown of the golden age era? Was it easy to get eyes on SM films during the 70s or has it been more difficult compared to the "mainstream" gay porn?

Ross: The SM scene in New York in the 70's was very underground. They had their own bars and didn't mix much with other gays who were more mainstream sexually. I don't recall seeing many truly SM movies back then. After all, this was the 70's. Even mainstream porn was borderline illegal, and SM sex was considered by the authorities to be obscene, in the same class as sex with animals, so it remained a secret society and not the kind of behavior one would chance putting on film. I think leather/SM films became more acceptable in the 80's, when video arrived and when the government loosened restrictions on the kind of sex you could portray. Christopher Rage was a true pioneer in bringing this kind of movie to the general public.

Siedelmann: The most popular regular actor at 3rd World is Donnie Russo, who has worked for studios as Palm Drive, Fox, Catalina, Falcon and many more. In addition, he made some films for your company behind the camera. Are you friends with him?

Ross: Donnie and I were friends for many years. I met him after I edited BEAT COP for David Babbitt, and Donnie was the star of the movie. He was a beautiful young man, with a killer body and just oozing with sexuality. He had made his mark doing films for L.A. studios as you mentioned, but he lived in NY. He appeared in many of my movies for 3rd World Video. Donnie had worked a lot for many studios and at some point wanted to try his hand at producing and directing his own movies. So he enlisted me to join in a partnership called R&R Productions. He was the consummate performer, and you always could rely on him to give you a very hot scene; a real professional. It was easy to get other performers because everyone wanted to have sex with Donnie. He was a true narcissist, and sometimes it was difficult for me to work with him because of that. He performed in the movies, I shot and edited them, and then I marketed them. I had a lot of connections with distributors in L.A., and we made money selling these movies wholesale even though the cost of packaging had become astronomical. Eventually, when the distribution venue started to dry up, I sold them to my mail order customers of 3rd World Video. Eventually Donnie and I had a falling out over profits, and we never spoke again.

Siedelmann: Were you a regular visitor to the legendary Mineshaft or the fetish-club-scene in general?

Ross: Ah, the Mineshaft. I was indeed a regular visitor to the Mineshaft. It was a one-of-a-kind place. A sex club, open to all, where one could have any kind of sex they wanted. But it was also a great place for voyeurs. There was no checking your clothes at the door as most other sex clubs required, and one could just get a drink at the bar, fully clothed and just walk around watching the various sex acts. They had this long wall with glory holes and cocksuckers would just kneel at the holes and wait for anonymous cocks to come through. It was part theater, part circus. There were bathtubs for naked guys to just sit and wait for guys to piss on them; the areas were all like small tableaus really. There were other areas that had all sorts of SM equipment for those into bondage, mummification, whippings. You name it, no matter what your fetish was, you could get it at the Mineshaft. When it finally closed, we all mourned the loss of such an amazing sex theater.

Siedelmann: Do you have some kind of favorite films list?

Ross: I was never much interested in awards and "best of" contests. In fact, I think it was the start of these "gay Academy Awards" that ruined what gay porn had been about. It became glamorized, and was a product of the Hollywood crowd, not the New York industry so much. All of a sudden we had stars, famous directors, top studios, best films, etc. This really had nothing to do with porn of the 70's. It became silly and vain and most of those awards were mostly "fixed" by the major L.A. studios who were connected to such award ceremonies and always managed to garner all the awards anyway. To me, the "best movies" were those that were never nominated or recognized. The only category I will address is the fetish/leather/sm. The

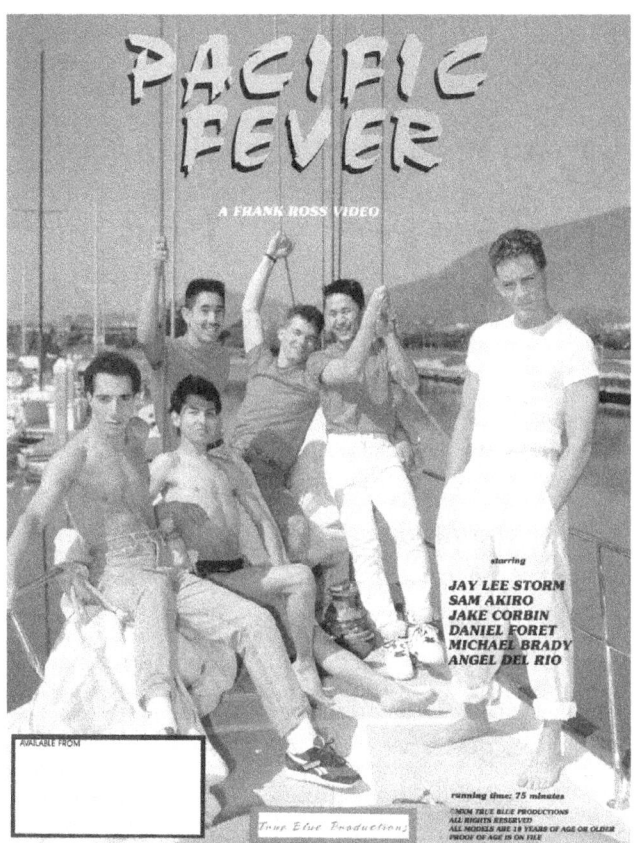 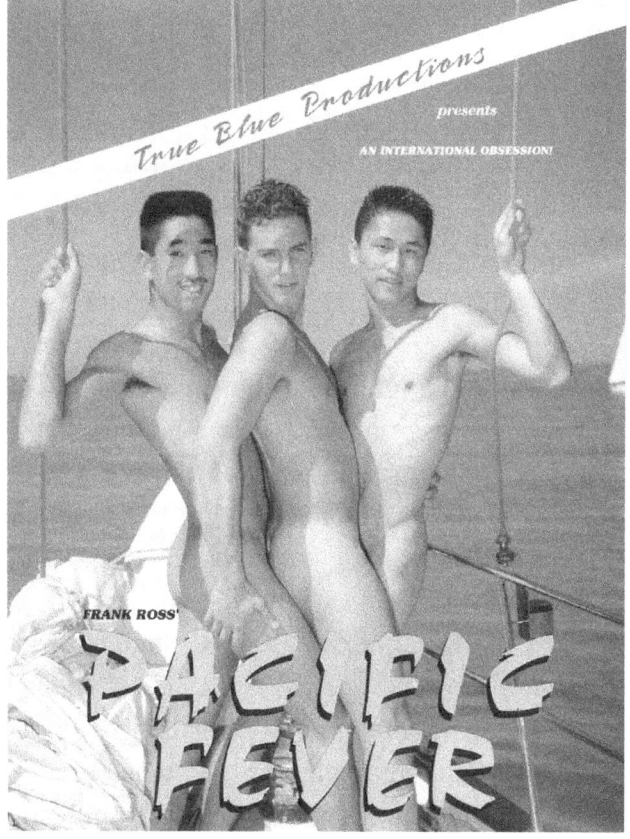

greatest and most talented filmmaker in this genre was Christopher Rage, and his Live Video studio. He was NY based, made amazing, graphic and mostly banned movies that Hollywood ignored. They were actually horrified by the content. Some of the things he featured was bareback fucking, fisting and watersports. At the time, the L.A. scene was very political and, I think, hypocrites in denouncing such content. It's ironic that when such movies began to sell in the past decade, the Hollywood crowd jumped on the bandwagon, and now most studios make their living making such movies. Rage was truly a pioneer and overcame all criticism in order to do what he liked and shocked a nation of prudes. This to me is great porn.

What makes a porn Arch Brown's latest

by Arch Brown

The talents needed to be a porn star are obvious. You need to get it up and keep it up. You must know how and when to get your co-star worked up, and in the gay marketplace, you have to be able to be top and bottom. I can't recall a guy who's made it to the top being just a fucker, or just a cocksucker, no matter how deep his throat is. This is very different from straight porn where roles are so easily defined. What makes a man hot, apparently for most of the all-male audience, is a stud who does it all – on both sides of the fence. But not only do you have to know your business, you have to know the business that you're in. And this can be difficult and tricky. When you are fucking, your concentration is on pleasure and technique. Your mind is focused on what you're doing, and this concentration keeps the action and the hard-on going. But good porn stars also manage to keep some of their concentration on the filmmaking. Wrangler, Scorpio and Locke *always* know exactly where the camera is. They never get in the way of the light or the lens. Sounds easy. But try it. And try keeping everything else going too! It's not easy. In fact, it's damned hard. And even harder to keep it hard! This special talent comes in part from what I call the Ego-Drive category. The one statement that comes through in almost every porn star's talk is that they are hot, sexy, and proud of it. They're showing it to you 'cause they wanna show it to you and it's this push that allows them the split concentration ... "I'm a good assfucker ... see!" This is a fairly unique Ego type, and is nearly necessary in the business. Most of us think of sex as a private thing. We want to show off to our bed-partners. But these men want to show off to everybody, and in almost every case, this self-knowledge is apparent to them and everyone around them. This may make them all sound like egotistical showoffs, obnoxious as hell maybe. Wrong! I find it charming and yet disarming. To admire yourself and your sexuality so much that you want to share it is not necessarily a bad quality. In fact, if the rest of the world were a little less uptight about their dicks, this just might be a hell of a lot better place to live!

These guys also have business drive. They *want* to be in films and magazines. For the most part, they find us, the producers and the photographers. They *want* to work in this business. For years I have heard, "You're using these people. They are being exploited." Bullshit! No one is ever coerced into anything. They do it 'cause they want to. And they love it. Occasionally I have asked a friend, a fuck-buddy or a stranger to be in a film and

STAR MOST? DISCOVERIES

"WRANGLER, SCORPIO AND LOCKE ALWAYS KNOW EXACTLY WHERE THE CAMERA IS."

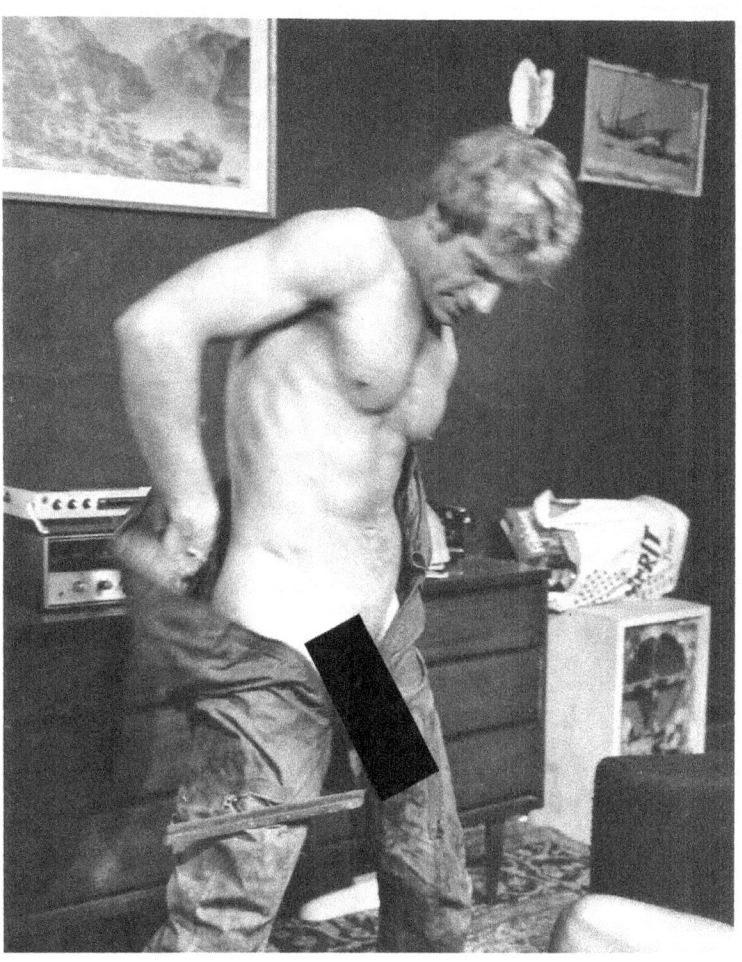

Jack Wrangler in *Sex Magic*

they do it for the lark. Most get off on it, but it's a one or two time thing. They have other careers to get on with. But the stars, the ones with the names above the titles, work hard at it. It's no accident that these men are where they are. They go after it. Most are beautiful, sexy, built, hung, handsome, and have that special charismatic magic. This is a very unique necessity, this complete all-over perfection. Redford could have a teeny weeny and Streisand could have pimples on her ass, but Halsted and Donovan have to have good faces, bodies, muscles, asses, and cocks (and they have to *work* at it). All of this and an audience willing to pay to see them, and the ability to keep it hot and heavy is what it's all about.

These guys work. Sure they enjoy it; indeed get off on it. But remember, nothing worthwhile ever comes easy! Take it from one who knows.

Memories are Made of

by David Earnest

I should alert you that although my memory of the early 1970s in New York is still somewhat vivid, the intervening 40-plus years have eroded many details. But I'll do my best...

Born in 1940 in Texas, I attended the University of Texas at Austin from 1960-67, earning my bachelor and master's degrees in music composition. As anyone who matured during the turbulent 60s knows, tremendous cultural changes were taking place during that decade. Coming out as a young gay man was my own personal realization of those changes. After finishing graduate school in 1967, I moved to Philadelphia for a brief period, and then to New York in January 1968. I got an apartment on the Upper West Side, and I worked as a music copyist (in those days , music for concert, ballet, and Broadway was all copied by hand - there were no computers). But I was always writing my own music as well, mostly songs, chamber music, and one very spare score for a student film based on Tennessee Williams' short story, Desire and the Black Masseur, around 1972. Gradually I became acquainted with an ever-widening circle of composers and performers, some of whom became life-long friends and colleagues. At the same time, as a gay man in my early thirties in New York City, I took eager advantage of all the endless sexual adventures that were available to all of us during the extraordinary post-Stonewall decade of the 1970s. But you don't need my testimony to tell you about that period - that history is already amply documented by many other contemporaries of the time. Life was a rich experience for a young gay man living in New York, and I had many terrific adventures during my early years in the city: a lot of music, a lot of work, a lot of sex, several boyfriends, and I loved every minute of it!

In 1969, I met Frank Ross. He was introduced to me by a Texas friend who had just moved to New York. Frank, a native New Yorker, and I became good friends, a friendship that is still as vital and wonderful as the day we met 45 years ago. Frank and I discovered that we shared many common interests: in music, art, film, and history. Since he was a photographer, and I was a composer, we both were interested in working in film production, and we both had the good fortune to be guided in that direction. Around 1972, Frank and a friend, Tom Hinckley, had just started doing some technical and crew work for Jack Deveau's new gay-porno studio, Hand In Hand Films. So Frank wanted me to meet Jack and Bob Alvarez, Jack's business and life-partner, knowing that both Jack and Bob wanted to have original music for their new films. I was terrifically excited by the possibility of writing film scores!

Even through the memory-haze of over 40 years, I still remember my first meeting with Jack Deveau and Bob Alvarez. They lived in a penthouse on top of a hotel on the upper West Side, and when I called Jack to introduce myself, he invited me to meet with him and Bob at their penthouse. When I arrived, Jack and Bob were there, but there was

THIS

also a fourth person there - Tray Christopher, a talented writer who had been recruited by Jack to join the Hand In Hand team. Over the next 30 years, Tray became a major influence in my life, both as a dear friend and as an artistic collaborator. Frank was also very close to Tray and we all shared many wonderful times together until Tray's passing in 1991. During the course of the evening, I played a reel-to-reel tape of some of my music, most of it written in graduate school. Jack and Bob liked what they heard, and recognized that I was serious about my composing, so they asked me to be a part of Hand In Hand. It was a great moment for me. That evening in the penthouse was my first experience of observing Jack Deveau's extraordinary personality and skills - he was fluently articulate about his vision for his new studio, and conveyed his enthusiasms with such energy and dedication that I felt completely caught up in the excitement of the new venture he and Bob were creating. Jack's genius as an innovative producer became more apparent after I began working for Hand In Hand: he had an unerring sense of how to find talented people, how to energize them, and how to encourage them to generate their best work.

My first project for Hand In Hand was to compose music for Jack's production of a new film by Arch Brown titled THE NIGHT BEFORE Arch Brown, though still early in his career, already had achieved some notoriety as a gay filmmaker, so I was pleased to be working with someone who had clear ideas about what he wanted for his film score. Since the film had a generally playful attitude, Arch wanted the music to reflect that sensibility. So I wrote quite a lot of music for a chamber ensemble of flute, clarinet, keyboard, and percussion, some of it in a bright tempo with jauntily tuneful melodies and snappy rhythms, and some of it in a languorously sensual mood. I recently watched THE NIGHT BEFORE having not seen it in 40 years, and was surprised and delighted with the movie and its quality of playful innocence, supported by my music. THE NIGHT BEFORE was a great success for Hand In Hand, for Arch Brown, for Jack and Bob, and for me. Jack Deveau then moved toward more ambitious projects: the next two films I worked on were ADAM & YVES written and directed by Peter de Rome, and DRIVE co-written by Tray Christopher and Jack Deveau, and directed by Jack Deveau. Both films were made during 1974-75.

It was a delightful pleasure to work with Peter de Rome - he had very a clear concept of the atmosphere he wanted the music to create for his emotionally intricate scenario of two men, an American and a Parisian, sharing the pleasures of each other's bodies and of Paris. I wrote the score for ADAM & YVES for a large chamber ensemble of flute, clarinet, saxophone, horn, trumpet, string quartet, keyboard, percussion, guitar and bass. Since Peter wanted each segment of his film to be an homage to a specific famous film he admired, he asked me to write music in a variety of different styles, among them: a lively, bright, fast Parisian traffic cue; a sexy tango; a lushly romantic string quartet; a mysterious, moody cue for flutes; and a funky rhythm and blues number for an orgy scene called *Honey Man*. It was a welcome challenge and involved many recording sessions, and I was especially proud of the music I created for the film. Peter's film was another great success for Hand In Hand and for all of us who worked on it. DRIVE was probably Jack's most ambitious project in the Hand In Hand catalog. The screenplay was co-written by Jack and Tray Christopher [aka Christopher Rage]. An elaborate thriller-mystery-psychopath-action scenario, the music I wrote for the production required a studio orchestra of woodwinds, brass, percussion, keyboard, and strings. It was a huge piece of work for the studio and for me, and was a great creative success. Once again, the music I wrote had to reflect several different styles and attitudes, each one appropriate to the narrative quality of a specific scene. I continued to work for Hand In Hand during 1975-76, mostly as a music director and music supervisor for a number of other films, GOOD HOT STUFF, BALLET DOWN THE HIGHWAY and WANTED: BILLY THE KID among them. I also continued to work with Arch Brown on several of his independently produced films. We had a long and productive friendship and collaboration on other non-film projects until his passing in 2012.

Gradually, my career as a composer began to move productively in other directions, writing chamber music, choral music, and vocal music. By 1977, I was busy with composing my concert music and getting performances, and was no longer working with Hand In Hand. But my experience during those 4 years of working with the studio was one of the most professionally and personally satisfying experiences of my life, and I still remember that period, even after 47 years in New York, with great fondness and pride. The music I wrote during that period was an important early predictor of certain stylistic traits that have been part of my creative life ever since. The lessons I learned about musical economy, thematic development, orchestration, and recording technique were invaluable assets to my future as a composer - those lessons have served me well for many decades. Of those years with Hand In Hand, I especially remember Jack Deveau and Bob Alvarez. Their generosity to me, and their recognition of my commitment to writing music, were remarkable gifts for me as a young, inexperienced composer. Jack was a larger-than-life personality who really opened up to me the experience of living creatively. His extraordinary intelligence and perception helped shape my maturity during those years. He was exactly the mentor I needed at that formative time in my life, and I shall always be grateful that he was in my life. Bob will always have my admiration and gratitude for the guidance, tutelage, counseling, and support I received from him during our many long hours of working together at his editing table. His soft-spoken thoughtfulness and gentle patience were a welcome anodyne to the constant pressures of filmmaking for us all.

New York, January 2015

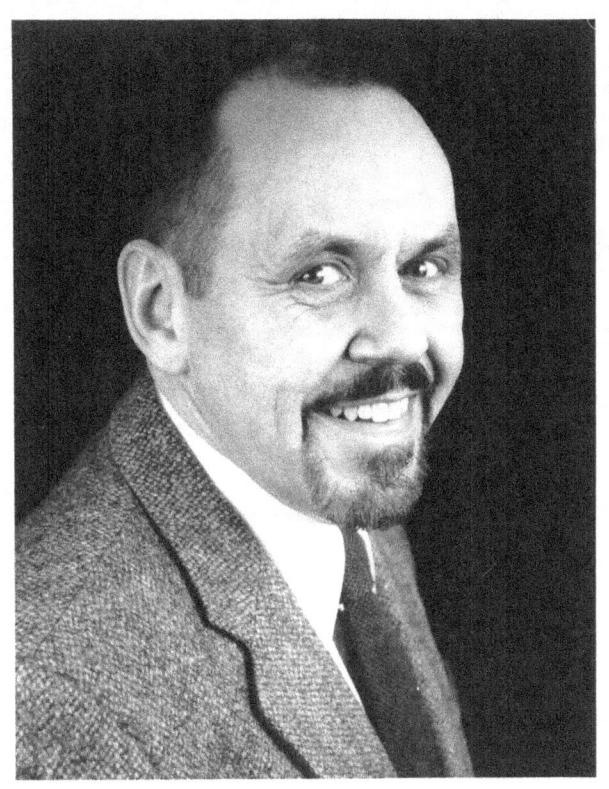

David Earnest

The ADVOCATE
Newspaper of America's Homophile Community

'Left-Handed' is classy but erotic and trippy

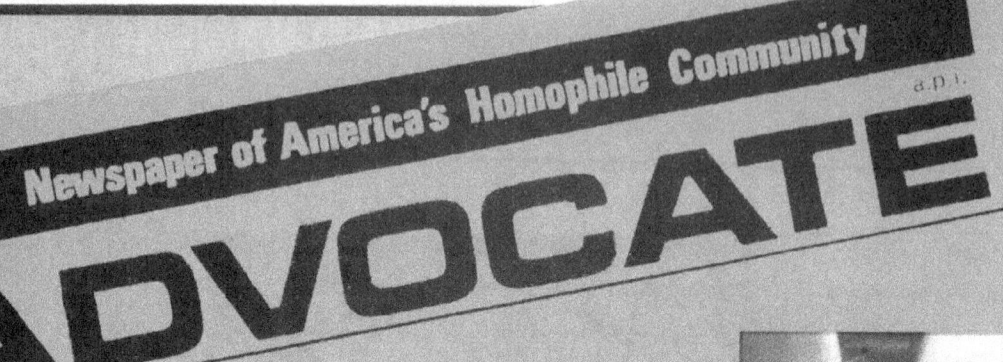

On the occasion of *Left-Handed's* Los Angeles opening, we'd like to amplify on some of the comments this excellent film received in the initial review (ADVOCATE, Issue 84) when it premiered in New York.

Left-Handed is a fine example of class porno filmmaking, boasting a polished production and technical values equal to major studio product. It was shot on locations in Manhattan and Woodstock, N.Y., and has an original background music score including five songs written especially for the picture (the best of which is the title tune). The sound is sharp and clear, having been mixed from eight-track at a recording studio, and the visual effects are very sophisticated, among them a fantasy sequence with desaturated color.

But technical excellence aside, *Left-Handed* is a film filled with very sensual and erotic imagery, a story that is presented in abstract terms, creating a mood that is—for want of a better word—trippy. As long as *Fantasia* isn't playing anywhere this week, heads would be well-advised to spend their time on *Left-Handed*.

But this is not to say that the film's appeal is confined exclusively to them. There is something for everyone, sexually speaking. It has a boy-girl scene, a tearoom encounter, an orgy, a fantastic show-exotic tastes, pedestrian tastes, and everything in-between.

Ray Frank stars as a footloose, uncommitted Gay, wandering from one trick to the next until he picks up on Robert Rikas, who has come down to the city from Woodstock to deliver some grass. Frank makes several trips north to visit Rikas but, true to form, tires of the affair and leaves him, returning to his former sexual meanderings. The last scene of the film shows the audience just what emotional damage this has inflicted on Rikas.

Los Angeles audiences will probably appreciate the refreshing change of locales from those usually found in locally produced films. New York City still looks as grim as ever, but it's photogenic.

— Harold Fairbanks

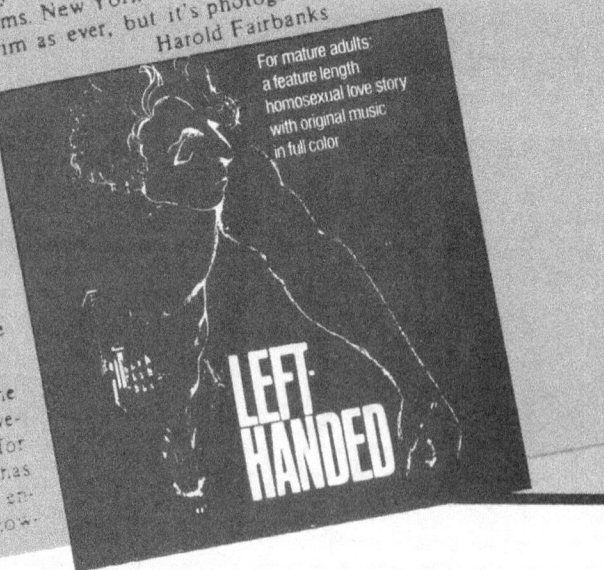

For mature adults: a feature length homosexual love story with original music in full color

LEFT-HANDED

PRESS REVIEWS 1

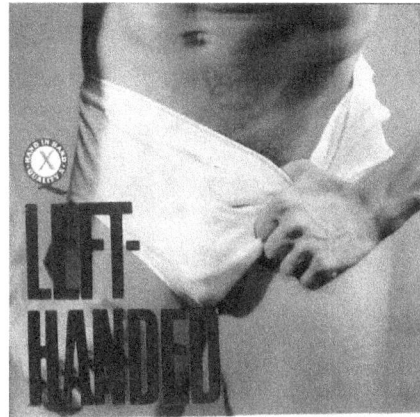

In Color • Running time: 88 minutes
The first film to come from HAND IN HAND is now a classic. It's a beautiful and passionate story of all male lust and love, featuring the incredibly handsome Ray Frank. It ends with the orgy scene that people are still talking about. MX-017
All Male Cast • Rated XXX

On the occasion of LEFT-HANDED's Los Angeles opening, we'd like to amplify on some of the comments this excellent film received in the initial review (*Advocate*, Issue 89) when it premiered in New York. LEFT-HANDED is a fine example of class porno filmmaking, boasting a polished production and technical values equal to major studio product. It was shot on locations in Manhattan and Woodstock, N.Y., and has an original background music score including five songs written especially for the picture (the best of which is the title tune). The sound is sharp and clear, having been mixed from eight-track at a recording studio, and the visual effects are very sophisticated, among them a fantasy sequence with desaturated color. But technical excellence aside, LEFT-HANDED is a film filled with very sensual and erotic imagery, a story that is presented in abstract terms, creating a mood that is – for want of a better word – trippy. As long as FANTASIA isn't playing anywhere this week, heads would be well-advised to spend their time on LEFT-HANDED. But this is not to say that the film's appeal is confined exclusively to them. There is something for everyone, sexually speaking. It has a boy-girl scene, a tearoom encounter, an orgy, a fantastic show, exotic tastes, pedestrian tastes, and everything in-between. Ray Frank stars as a footloose, uncommitted Gay, wandering from one trick to the next until he picks up on Robert Rikas, who has come down to the city from Woodstock to deliver some grass. Frank makes several trips north to visit Rikas but, true to form, tires of the affair and leaves him, returning to his former sexual meanderings. The last scene of the film shows the audience just what emotional damage this has inflicted on Rikas. Los Angeles audiences will probably appreciate the refreshing change of locales from those usually found in locally produced films. New York City still looks as grim as ever, but it's photogenic.

*Harold Fairbanks, *The Advocate*

HAND IN HAND VIDEO

A DIVISION OF
Quality X Video Cassette Company
356 WEST 44TH STREET
NEW YORK, NEW YORK 10036
(212) 541-7860 Outside N.Y. (800) 223-7981

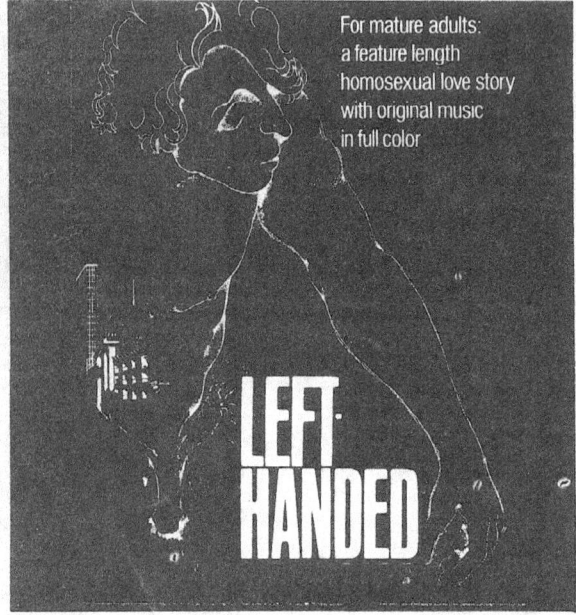

For mature adults: a feature length homosexual love story with original music in full color

LEFT-HANDED

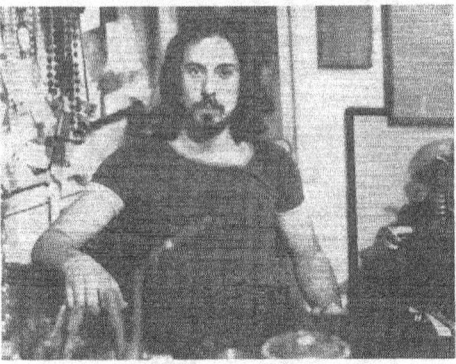

Larry Burns plays the dope dealer that everybody wants to meet

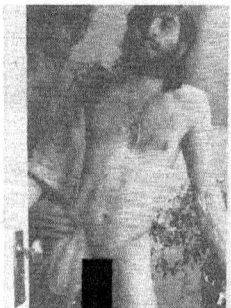

Robert Rikas and Ray Frank are the lovers in this scorching romance.

Ray Frank and Robert Rikas bathe after having a hot, hot sex scene.

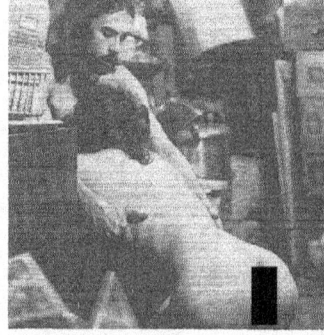

Larry Burns and Ray Frank get it on in the back of an antique shop in the fantasy sequence from the film.

When LEFT-HANDED first opened, **Gay Scene** raved: "Eureka! It's here at last. A gay sex film of inherent quality, delicate beauty and imposing scope....Genet and Cocteau, move over—Jack Deveau has arrived to take his place beside you as a filmmaker of consummate skill and artistry."

Since its first showing, LEFT-HANDED HAS BEEN EXCITING AUDIENCES AROUND THE WORLD, WITH SCREENINGS FROM Los Angeles to Paris. Never in the history of the gay film has any single effort so captured the minds and libidos of the public and the press. **The Advocate** called LEFT-HANDED a "fuck-fest" the first time it was reviewed, and in its unprecedented *second* review raved that the film was "sensual and erotic...A fine example of class porno filmmaking." **Variety** hailid the "eroticism of LEFT-HANDED", while the **Chicago READER** was amazed by the accurate presentation of SEX BETWEEN MEN in New York.

The incredibly handsome RAY FRANK and the horny, versatile porno star ROBERT RIKAS are the central figures in this moving story of sex and love which takes place in New York and Woodstock. The two leads go after each other with unbridled passion, lusting and loving with an authenticity and excitement that has never been equalled.

LEFT-HANDED director Jack Deveau's first feature, presents a cast of beautiful men in explicit, beautifully photographed scenes that will please everyone "from those with exotic tastes to those with pedestrian tastes, and everyone in between." **(The Advocate)**

And saving the best for last, the orgy sequence which concludes the film will become an instant favorite of yours (if it isn't already.) The men are spectacular. What they do to each other is very HOT, and they keep on doing it to each other until everyone, themselves and you, is satisfied.

StudioSound is a special process that guarantees a high fidelity like you've never heard. Instead of the usual optical transfer of sound from film to tape, which limits the reproduction of sound to a narrow range of frequencies, StudioSound is a magnetic transfer of the ORIGINAL MAGNETIC STUDIO sound tracks for the feature, transferred directly to the magnetic tape in your video cassette. This process actually gives you BETTER QUALITY than can be achieved in a cinema. For further enhancement, you can patch your video system into your stereo system and surround yourself with the excitement of these sensual sounds.

Cast: Ray Frank, Robert Rikas, Larry Burns, Teri Reardon, Al Mineo, Alex Marks, Bob Williams, Warren Mans

Produced and directed by Jack Deveau • Edited by Robert Alvarez
Music by Stan Freeman

| LEFT-HANDED | 88 MINUTES | COLOR | ALL-MALE CAST | **StudioSound** |

LEFT-HANDED

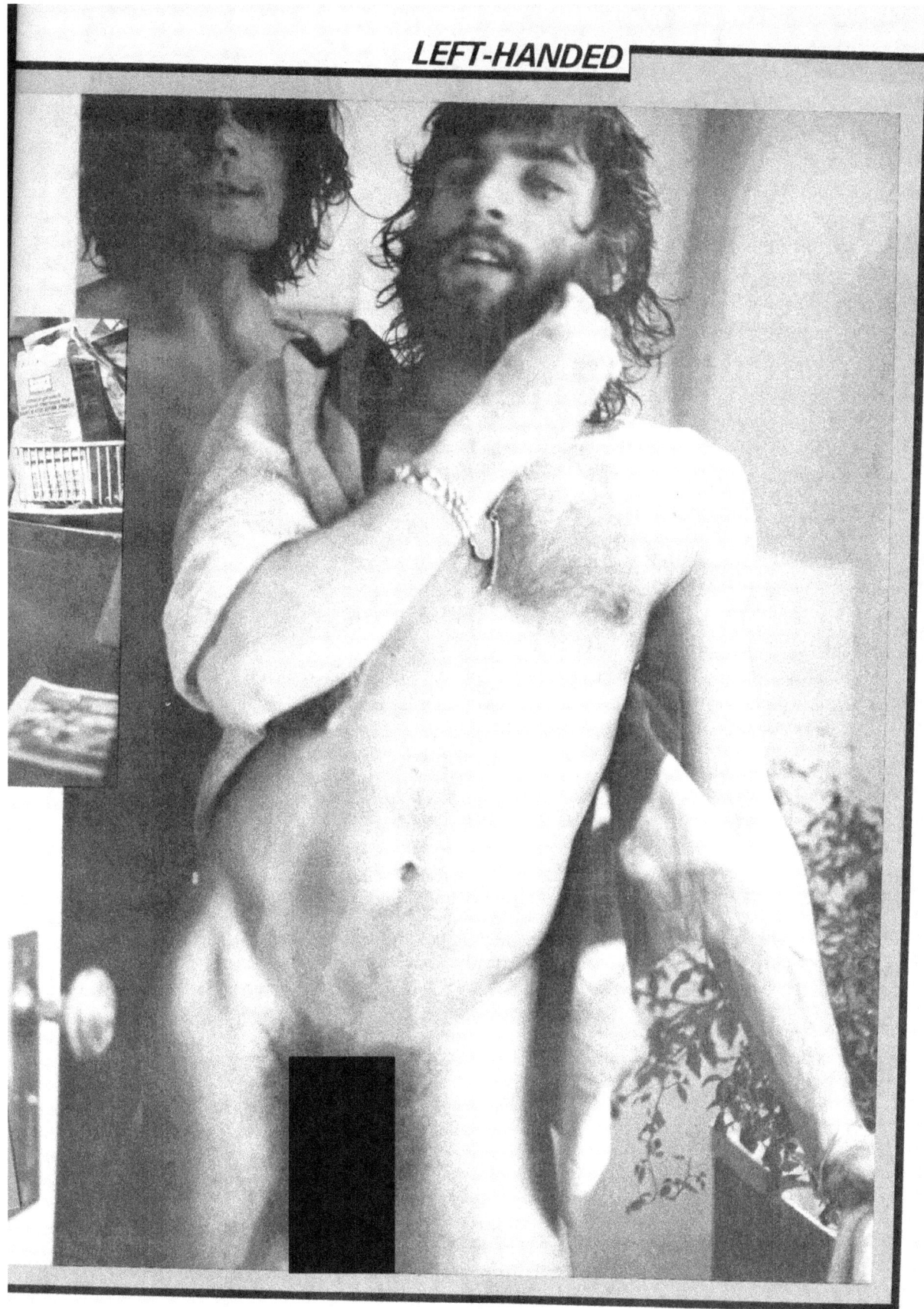

One of the earliest gay films to achieve widespread commercial and critical success, LEFT-HANDED was the first effort of legendary filmmaker Jack Deveau, and today it remains both engrossing and arousing, not merely an historical curio. The tale of a brief romance between a hedonistic hustler (Ray Frank) and a bisexual drug dealer (Robert Rikas), this landmark film has a European feel to it, and seems most particularly influenced by the *cinema verite* of the French.

Its men are human animals (not suntanned Adonises), its story is biting and uncompromising, its cinematography is gritty and harsh, and its editing provides a relentlessly pulsating momentum – all of which enhance its bald sexuality.

The action of the film alternates between the seamier side of New York's Greenwich Village and the barren wintry landscape of Woodstock, not so long after the summer of The Festival. The long-haired hustler is first seen whipping through a quick blowjob in a public john, then hurrying off to the antique store of a friend (Larry Burns), where he meets the dealer: Burns, obviously harboring a non-reciprocal lust for Frank, tells him that the guy has a girlfriend; this does not deter Frank, however, who vows to have him the next time they meet.

In neat juxtaposition, the next scene shows Rikas and his lady (Teri Reardon) balling at their upstate farm. The device of a heterosexual coupling explicitly serves to enhance the fascinating desirability of the seemingly unattainable dealer. By the time the two men have met again, then, the viewer has firsthand knowledge of the dealer's heterosexual performance, which heightens the suspense and tension of the prolonged, very believable homosexual seduction which follows. Joints rolled in American flag papers, butterfly appliques sewn on bell-bottom jeans, and period song hits place this scene smack in the pansexual heart of the sixties sexual revolution.

In subsequent vignettes, the two men's affair escalates and consumes both in the most romantic moments of the film, including an acid trip shot entirely through a red filter (which unfortunately does not transfer well to video). In time, however, Frank decides he needs a change, shaves off his beard, and leaves his idyll to head back to the city and one of Burns' orgies – a sequence in which no orifice is left unfilled, including some striking handball footage. In this basically silent film, the plot unfolds through a series of voice-overs, most particularly a final telephone conversation in which the dealer learns his newfound lover has moved on, leaving him in stony, silent tears. The script, acting, direction, and visual imagery are all first quality; the transfer from film to video is not, often turning the atmosphere from moody to muddy. Still, even in its video incarnation, LEFT-HANDED's impact remains potent.

*Jerry Douglas, *Manshots*

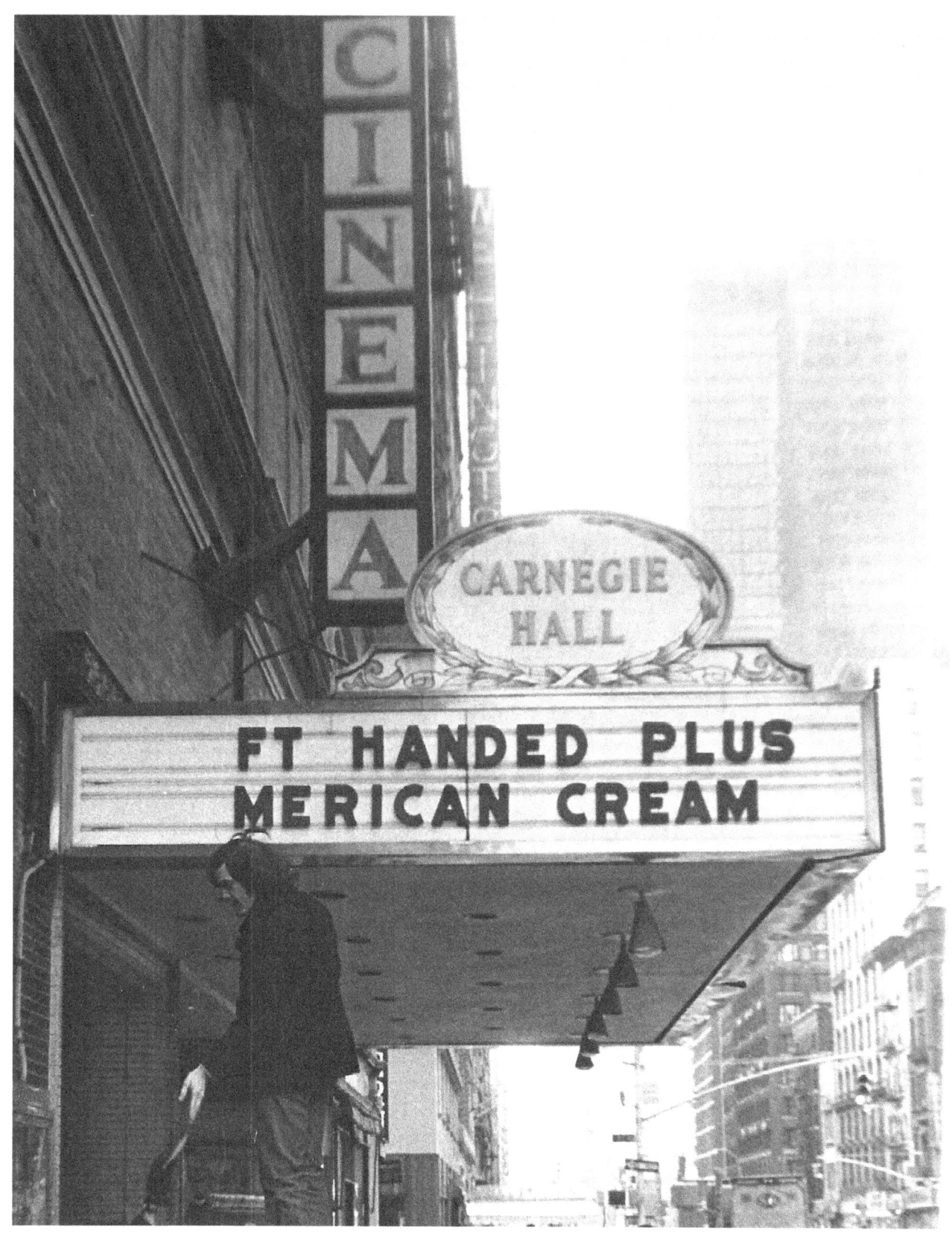

Carnegie Hall Cinema: Two Hand In Hand films are advertised in the marquee
Jack Deveau's *Left-Handed* and *American Cream*, which was distributed by Hand In Hand

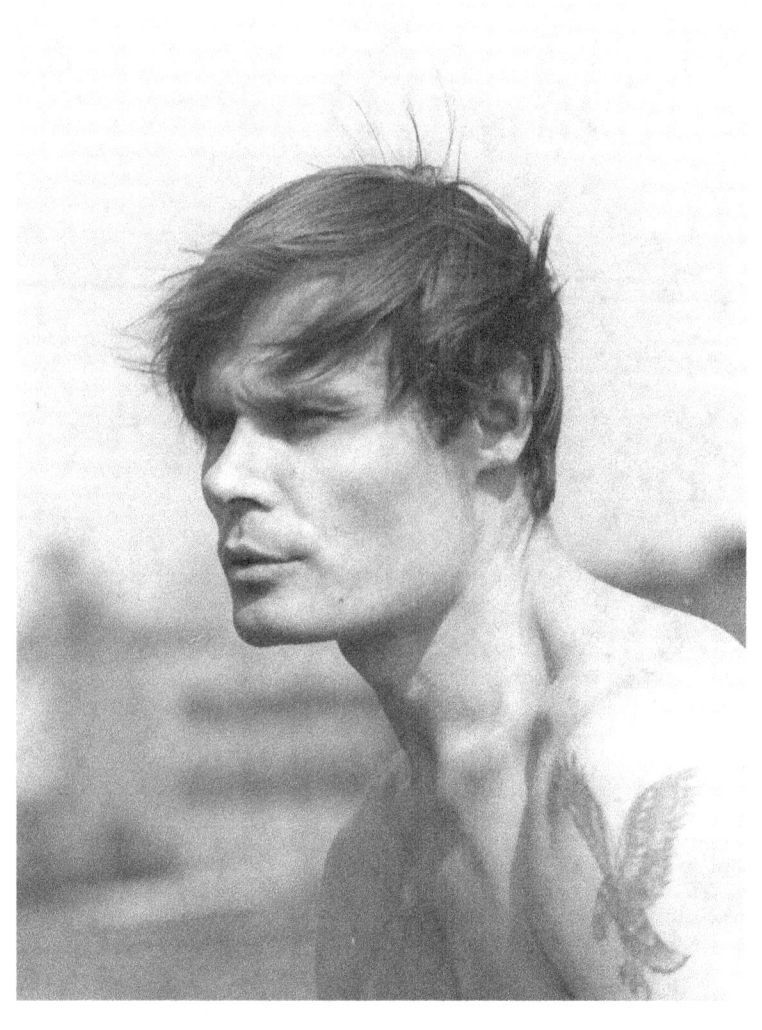

Robert Rikas in *Left-Handed*

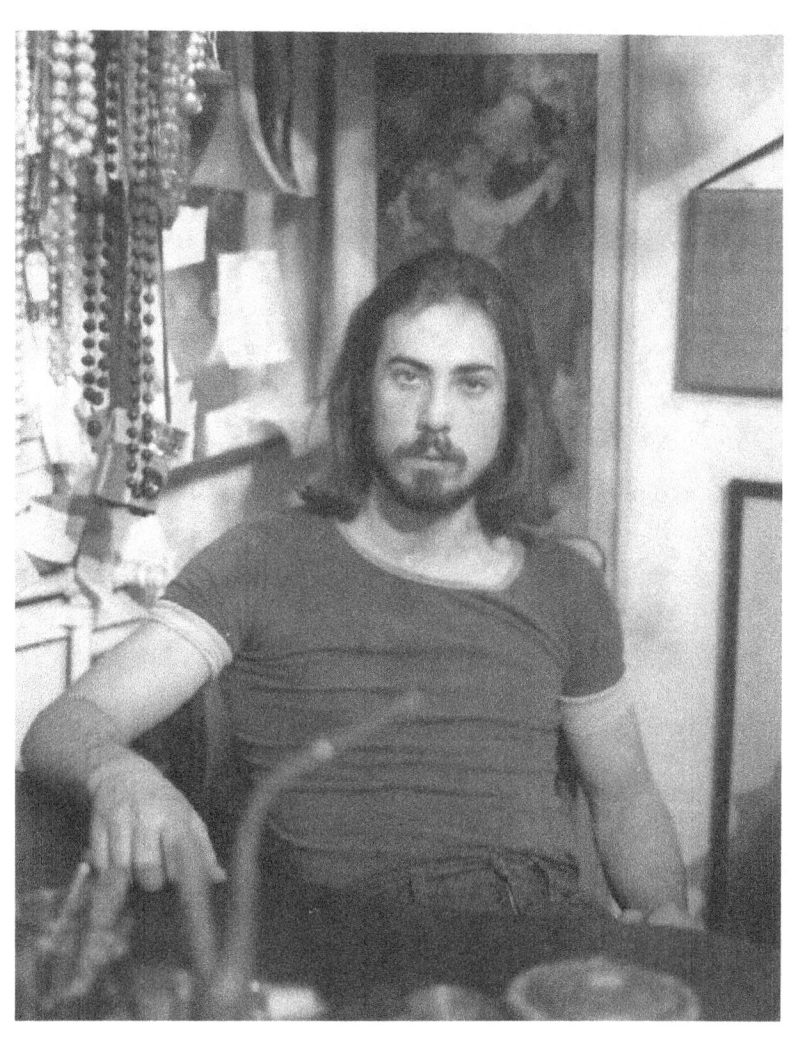

Left-Handed: Larry Burns plays the dope dealer that everybody wants to meet

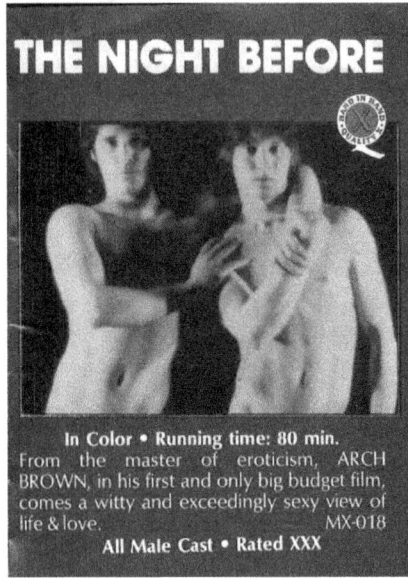

To explain the full significance of this magnificent descent into the labyrinth of fear and guilt would require a volume unto itself, for THE NIGHT BEFORE is the most complex, the most richly symbolic, the most stylistically sophisticated gay film yet made. And it can hold its own in comparison with any mainstream title from even the most renowned director. Perhaps the most underrated director of them all, Arch Brown equaled this achievement in none of his other films, although HOT FLASHES (1976) and FIVE EASY PIECES (1977), come tantalizingly close. The menacing mood is established during the credits; a voiceover recitation of numbers (4-5-6-2-1-7-3-9-8) accompanied by the loud ticking of a clock reminds us that time is running out in a random countdown with no fixed goal in view. The first visual image is a curtain with black and white stripes and a series of stenciled numbers, much like a prison uniform. Suddenly we see that Hank (Coke Hennesy) is sewing the curtain as he stares out his bedroom window into the apartments of his neighbors: Paul (Michael Kade) shaves in his bathroom; a young woman (Mimmi Garth) prepares morning coffee, then (with a kiss) awakens her boyfriend, Pete (Bill Yort), who lies nude in bed. As Hank brushes his teeth, dresses, and gathers in his laundry, Paul telephones the young woman, arranging a photography shoot and telling her to bring Pete along. The minor characters are also introduced through Hank's eyes. On the street Hank bumps into a delivery man (Jamal Jones), knocks several packages out of his hand, and helps him pick them up. After he happens upon Paul in Central Park and helps him with the photography shoot, Hank passes a young man (Alexis Knight) working on his bicycle and again offers his assistance. When the young man replies, "No, thanks," Hank continues on his way and meets Paul at the corner. The photographer invites Hank home to watch him develop the film, and on the way waves at Tim (Nick Kastroff), a former "roommate" with whom he "split up two months ago." In Paul's apartment Hank becomes fascinated with a black and white photograph of two nude men (Tim Clarke and Jeffrey Etting) as Paul talks on the phone with Bill (Bob Plummer) about adopting a kitten.

When Hank accompanies Paul to Bill's apartment, we meet the final member of the cast. Brown's elaborate but completely realistic method of introducing his cast underscores two important traits in Hank's character: his obvious sexual interest in other men and his inability to act directly and aggressively upon his own desires. The commonplace methods of introduction also emphasize Hank's immersion in a commonplace world, his alienation from any openly gay environment. Only after he is convinced of Paul's interest in him does he make a sexual move: to Paul's suggestive question, "What are you doing the rest of the day?," Hank replies, "Just hoping to ball with you." His boldness, compounded by the series of frustrating encounters that he was afraid to follow up and tempered by his macho posturing even with Paul, leads to a sexual experience in which he chooses the receptive role, as if to place the main burden on his partner. As the two men talk in bed afterward, Hank insists that this is his first time since he "tried it at twelve" with "a couple of neighbor boys" near the farm where he grew up. "I'm straight," Hank asserts, ignoring Paul's response, "You could've fooled me." Having painted his portrait of a gay man imprisoned by his own fear and guilt, Brown now launches a dream sequence that explores Hank's unconscious with surrealistic images and sounds, so rapidly changing, so enigmatic, and so complexly interrelated that it is virtually impossible to disentangle the separate threads. The climactic sequence occurs when Hank follows an unwinding ball of string into an underground club where he participates in a bizarre orgy with Paul, Tim, the bicyclist, and the delivery man. The sequence ends when Paul awakens Hank with the ironic question, "Sleep well?" When Paul tells Hank that after breakfast, "I have to kick you out," Hank is stunned: he equates the reality of the morning after with the dream of the night before, a prophecy of where his relationship with Paul will lead. As the camera focuses on Hank's face, we again heard the ticking of a clock and the random countdowns that accompanied the opening credits. What does it all mean? Only everything – about being gay, male, and human.

*S.W., *Manshots*

Hand In Hand Films has gathered its most recent NYC successes into a package with its latest releases and brought them to Southern California for a film festival that promises to raise the standard of pornography in filmland. The promise is well kept with Arch Brown's THE NIGHT BEFORE. By no means a classic, it does manage to have the grace that made THE BACK ROW the enjoyable milestone it now has become recognized to be. The script for THE NIGHT BEFORE (written by Arch and Bruce Brown) can easily be said to be pretentious but Arch Brown's fluid direction plays down all the absurdist-abstract intellectual fun and emphasizes the realistic sensual fun with a style that is fitting to the flesh film. The story, of course, is not ignored and certainly represents a pound of artful social redeeming value.

More interesting than the cute plot or the sensual style is the extremely human development of characters. Everything in the film is good but the handling of the characters is one of the more hopeful signs in pornography today and hopefully a sign of the standard that the Hand In Hand Festival will be setting. Coke Hennesy as Hank, the film's hero, is a surprise in a pornographic film, especially a gay one. You could have fooled me. He walks through the film as if it were an odyssey of gay life, to which he has as yet to become at ease with, but no, he has been sucking for quite some time. It is hard to tell from his mono-level role what kind of an actor he is but it is easy to suspect he could be another Michael Moriarity, underplaying everything story and saving up for anything glimpsing of human contact. The film is after all merely a low-budget pornographic venture and it is hard to tell where he would go with a full role.

Michael Cade as Paul may not have the professional restraint that Coke Hennesy seemed to be operating within but he is vital. His performance never stops being a turn on. It didn't matter if he was acting or not. It was a joy to watch him move, to listen to him talk his lines, and to watch thoughts cross his mind at varying speeds of personality. Michael Cade should only become the hottest attraction in any kind of film he appears. Put his name up on the marquee and you'll have my money on the counter and my ass looking for the closest seat to the screen. The ballet fantasy sequence danced by Tim Clark and Jeffrey Etting was tasteful and approached the exquisite. Tray Christopher knows something about how to get us with his choreography. The film is full of talent and the direction and editing allows the more talented sequences to shine forth without destroying the author's intentions. Not a great film, THE NIGHT BEFORE is an enjoyable success, full of beauty, humor, and a playful flirtation with the magic that accompanies falling in love.

*David Minton, *In Touch*

HAND IN HAND VIDEO

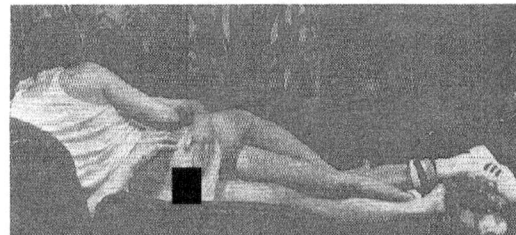

A DIVISION OF
Quality X Video Cassette Company
356 WEST 44TH STREET
NEW YORK, NEW YORK 10036
(212) 541-7860 Outside N.Y. (800) 223-7981

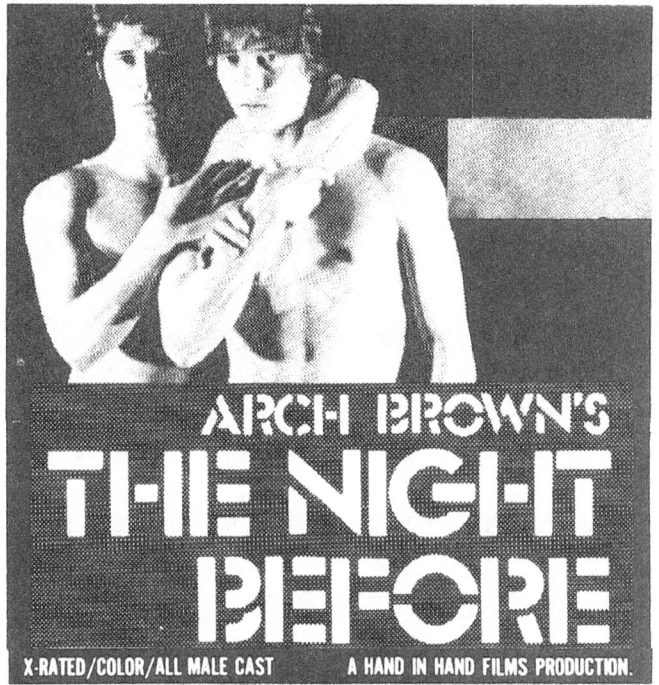

ARCH BROWN'S THE NIGHT BEFORE
X-RATED/COLOR/ALL MALE CAST — A HAND IN HAND FILMS PRODUCTION.

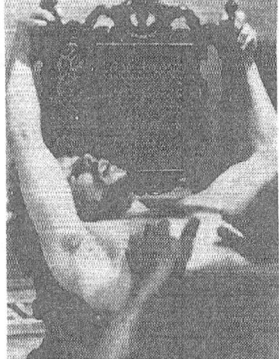

A tangle of bodies from the incredible orgy that ends the film.

Caught at the moment of orgasm in the Orgy

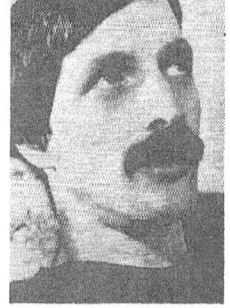

Michael Cade, the beauty that plays one of the lovers in the film.

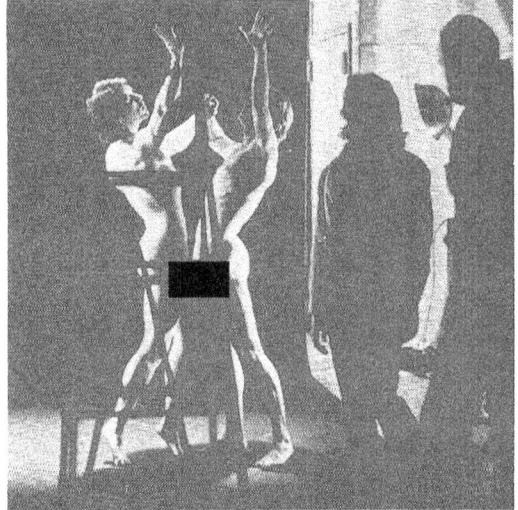

The erotic ballet from THE NIGHT BEFORE.

While filmmakers come and go, there is one man who has created more popular pieces of hard-core excitement than almost anyone else in the business: ARCH BROWN. And the film he made for HAND IN HAND has been as extravagantly praised as any ever shown. It is also one of the highest grossing and most popular gay films ever made. **The Advocate** called THE NIGHT BEFORE "Clever, erotic, romantic and a work of art." "It charges out like THUNDER," claimed **Gay Scene** and **Screw Magazine** said simply it is "one of the best gay films ever made...with plenty of hard-core sex and all attractive men."

The "Dream Orgy in New York" (**Gay Magazine**) features dozens of the most attractive men ever filmed and includes fantastic scenes that have yet to be equalled for inventiveness and horniness.

Hank (Coke Hennessy) meets Paul (Michael Cade) and what should have been just another day in his sexy life turns into a fantasy sequence with sexual encounter piled on sexual encounter. Erect cocks come and go from the most unexpected places and lead us into chases and adventures that only Arch Brown could conceive.

There is an amazing nude ballet (featuring professional dancers, Tim Clarke and Jeffrey Etting) which is as erotic as it is handsome. And there are surprise sequences that will have you gasping in astonishment.

Arch Brown, one of the first and always one of the most successful gay filmmakers, presents the viewer with a touching, funny and most of all sexually arousing descent into the world of all-male sex.

STUDIOSOUND is a special process that guarantees a high fidelity like you've never heard. Instead of the usual optical transfer of sound from film to tape, which limits the reproduction of sound to a narrow range of frequencies, StudioSound is a magnetic transfer of the ORIGINAL MAGNETIC STUDIO sound tracks for the feature, transferred directly to the magnetic tape in your video cassette. This process actually gives you BETTER QUALITY than can be achieved in a cinema. For further enhancement, you can patch your video system into your stereo system and surround yourself with the excitement of these sensual sounds.

Cast: Coke Hennessy, Michael Cade, Jamal Jones, Nick Kastroff, Alexis Knight, Bob Plummer and Bill Yort.
Featuring Tim Clark and Jeffrey Etting as The Dancers.

Directed by Arch Brown • Produced by Jack Deveau
Edited by Robert Alvarez • Music by David Earnest

| THE NIGHT BEFORE | 80 MINUTES | COLOR | ALL-MALE CAST | STUDIOSOUND |

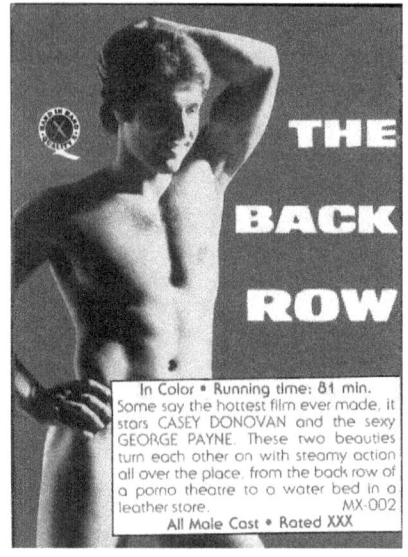

THE BACK ROW was Casey Donovan's first film after his acclaimed discovery in BOYS IN THE SAND, and solidified his legitimacy as a superstar in a day when stars were few and far between. Here, his character takes on a new dimension as he moves from the idyllic days of summer sun and surf on Fire Island (in BOYS IN THE SAND) to the bleaker, colder winter of New York City (THE BACK ROW). Though likeable, Donovan's character is not always the nicest as he moves around the city engaging in back row and tearoom sex. More of the sympathy goes to George Payne, in his screen debut, as the kid from Montana discovering the ambience of big city gay life. Donovan's character is attracted to Payne's, but his eye never stops roving, something Payne's naïve character can't understand. As the two central figures, they are perfect foils for each other, providing interesting conflict. The film, covering one afternoon in the art of cruising and contact sex, is a first effort by Doug Richards. He has combined the elements of fantasy and harsh reality into a slice of life that instructs the uninitiated into all aspects and ramifications of impersonal, no-commitment sex. Donovan serves as the instructor, while Payne is the initiate. Before the titles, the audience is barraged by a jumble of Forty-Second Street marquees. This motif of signs, reminiscent of Berthold Brecht, is carried throughout the film, underscoring and/or signaling the action. The recurring one is the pedestrian "Walk/Don't Walk" sign which underscores the ever-shifting status of the Donovan/Payne relationship. Richards incorporates a vivid scene in the Pleasure Chest sex boutique as Donovan inspects various leather goods and toys. Payne fantasizes Donovan using the items in quick staccato flashes. Later, in a tearoom, Donovan uses some of them to full advantage in a three-way scene with Warren Carlton and Chris Villette. In this film of contrasts, Richards' most profound use comes in a movie-within-the-movie entitled, WANTED - ROOMMATE. (The title is another Brechtian sign.) Payne fantasizes that he and Donovan are doing what they see being done on the screen. In a series of cross-cuts, we see the cinema of a student and his roommate making love, and the fantasy of Payne mimicking it with Donovan. Both pairs enact the same sequence on the same set - the roommates in normal lighting, Payne and Donovan in the soft focus of candlelight. The entire film is an allegory of reality (Donovan) vs. fantasy (Payne). Richards has woven these factors together seamlessly. And like Brecht, Richards doesn't give us all the answers. Life is real, but not much without fantasy, and vice-versa. Although there is no dialogue, the film is still timely. If you are historically interested in the development of gay feature porn films, as well as the sex contained therein, then THE BACK ROW should not be missed.

*Christopher Parrish, *Stallion*

HAND IN HAND VIDEO

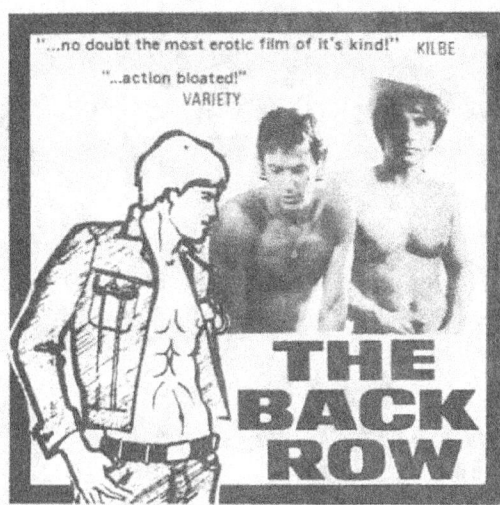

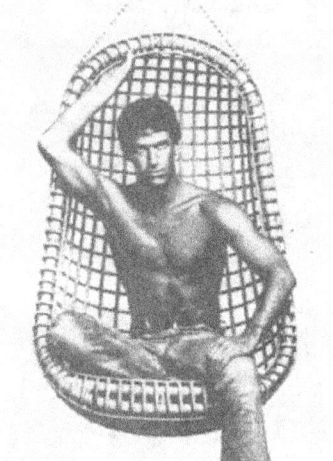

Superstar Casey Donovan certainly deserves his fame and he's never looked better than in THE BACK ROW.

What goes on in THE BACK ROW? A better question would be what doesn't? You've heard of hot combinations before, but try this one. The biggest of the all-male stars, CASEY DONOVAN, and the most popular new-comer in years, Colt and Target model, GEORGE PAYNE. The director (Doug Richard) is the man who brought you SCORE, TUBSTRIP and BOTH WAYS, and THE BACK ROW is certainly one of his most successfully erotic efforts. The perfect fusion of fantasy and lust.

Casey Donovan, the blond that nobody gets enough of, is riding the subway when George gives him "the look". The two of them end up in a Village leather shop called THE PLEASURE CHEST for a scene you'll re-run in your mind as often as you do on your television. With every piece of leather, every dildo, chain and toy in the place, they make waves on the water bed. What a fantasy!

But it's just the begining. George follows Casey to the movies and he shyly observes Casey begin his adventures with the horny man who sells him a ticket (Warren Carlton from LEFT-HANDED) — more of him later in the orgy in the bathroom. Casey wanders into the theatre and finds all kinds of steamy action in progress. He finds a sailor in the seats and even imagines himself involved in the action on the screen (in a very sexy fantasy.) But the best, the hottest, the sexiest of all is George's shy observance of Casey. It's George Payne (in his film debut) and he's got to have Casey. Through all the rest of his adventures in the theatre, George keeps trying to get his hands on Casey, but Casey's a busy young man.

What's your fantasy? You'll find it in THE BACK ROW. The orgy in the men's room is all-male and all-action. Sombody's brought all the equipment and by the time it's over, leather and toys are everywhere, and the group of men are all over each other and into every conceivable position. You'll be as hot as all the other guys by the time you get through this scene.

The ending will surprise and please you, as will all of THE BACK ROW. Over and over.

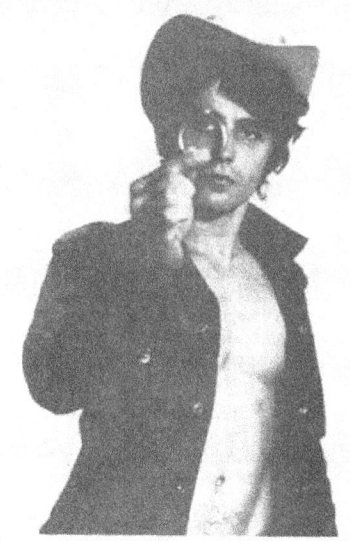

George Payne was introduced to audiences in THE BACK ROW as the "Midnight Cowboy" busting after Casey Donovan.

Cast: Casey Donovan, George Payne, Robin Anderson, Warren Carlton, David Knox, Chris Villette, Arthur Gramah, Robert Tristan.

Produced and directed by Doug Richards

| THE BACK ROW | 81 MINUTES | COLOR | ALL-MALE CAST |

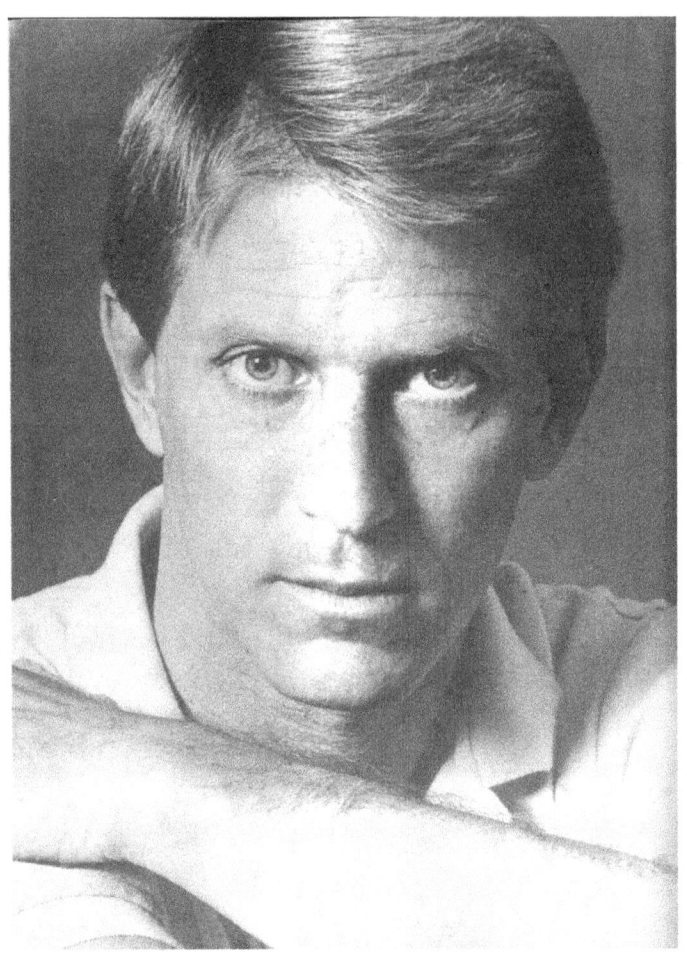

"I can honestly say that in any job I have ever had, I have never fucked for a job. In every film I have always had written agreements. In the first one I got $20 a day which always pissed me off because the girls were getting $50. In *Casey* I got $125 a day and it took four days to shoot it. For *Boys in the Sand* I never signed a contract until after we started making it. I never discussed salary with Wakefield. I got $125 a day for four days of shooting. After it opened in January and was such a huge success, he gave each of us a $500 bonus. So altogether I made $900 on *Boys*. On *Back Row* I got $150. I think we shot for ten days and with retakes maybe 13. I also had 3% of the profits. But to this day I have never seen a penny of them. The producer skipped off to Canada. That film has been a rip-off. It never did very well in New York. It did its best business right here in L.A."

CASEY DONOVAN

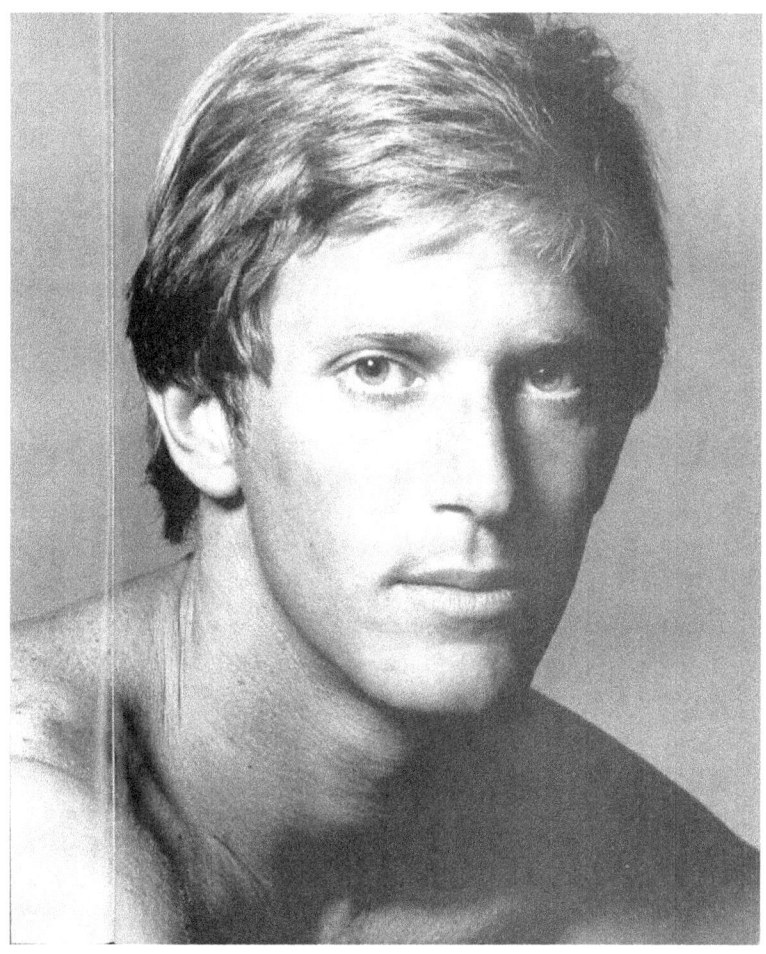

"Most of the directors have left the sex scenes up to me— with some guidance. I always think back of *Casey* my really first hard-core porno. Everyone was straight and I really had to work hard at making myself hard and everyone else too. When I did *Boys* and *Back Row* I got along very well with my directors. I knew what they wanted and they knew what they wanted. When I am doing a film, I am always adding to the script. I think that I have pretty good film sense, and I can feel in front of the camera what I think is right. And I have been in different types of movies too. *Casey* actually was a talkie with a message. *Boys in the Sand* was just an erotic fantasy. One reviewer complained about all the walking in it. Wakefield said that it is a statement on all thé walking that is part of a gay's life— the pursuing, the cruising, the walking on the streets, the walking at the baths, the walking up and down the theatre aisles. *Boys* had a loose structure. *Back Row* had a complete script, shot by shot."

CASEY DONOVAN (Iconic porn actor,
star of *Casey!* and *The Back Row*)

CASEY!

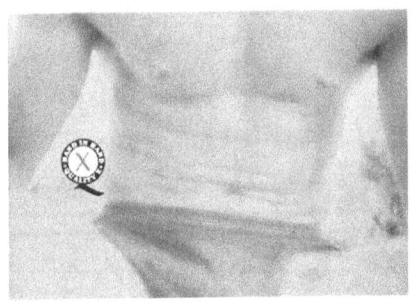

In Color • Running time: 88 min.
This is the film that gave superstar CASEY DONOVAN his name. The scene with the delivery boy is one of the hottest sequences around, with the two of them all over the floor, romping and rolling to a huge climax. MX-006
All Male Cast • Rated XXX

CASEY is the film that gave sex superstar Casey Donovan (BOYS IN THE SAND, THE BACK ROW) his name, and you'll only need a few minutes of this fabulous fantasy to see why. Follow Casey on his erotic romp and find out how this blond manages to have more fun. And more fun. Casey is a sensitive (and beautiful and *hot*) young man who is trying to find himself. Along the way he finds adventure in the form of several stunning studs, much to his (and *your*) satisfaction. First there's fun with the fairy godmother (also played by Casey) followed by a quick romp with Steven, and handsome hump who happens by. But you haven't seen anything till you watch Casey and the delivery boy. And boy does this boy deliver. He and the incredible Casey start in the kitchen and suddenly find themselves in the middle of the groceries. They're all over the floor, surrounded by everything from potatoes to beer cans. But nothing stops these two young bucks from getting into, in on and over each other. They can't seem to get enough of each other's hot bodies and you won't have trouble figuring out why. The contrast of the two perfect forms, one the swimmer's body of the blond bombshell Casey, and the musky sensuality of the dark delivery boy are the ideal combination for action the way you like it. If you enjoyed Casey in BOYS IN THE SAND and THE BACK ROW, you'll want to be sure to invite him into your home as *Casey*, the first (and the *greatest*) sex star. This is the man who can do it all, and in his first film he does. For many nights to come you'll enjoy all that this most famous of all the SuperStuds has to offer.

*Hand In Hand Promo

HAND IN HAND VIDEO

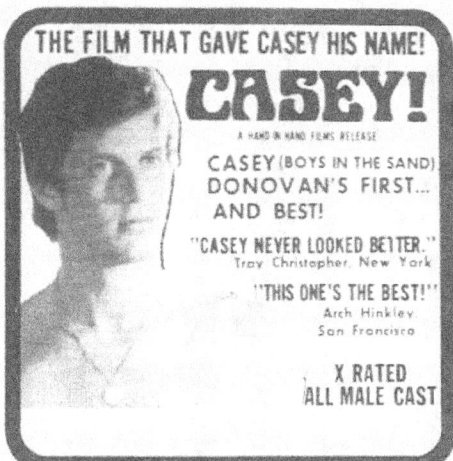

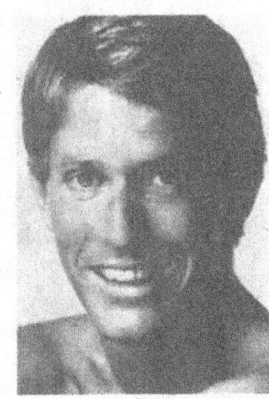

Casey Donovan as he looked in his film debut, the film that gave him his name

CASEY IS THE FILM THAT GAVE SEX Superstar Casey (BOYS IN THE SAND, THE BACK ROW) Donovan his name, and you'll only need a few minutes of this fabulous fantasy to see why. Follow Casey on his erotic romp and find out how this blond manages to have more fun. And more fun.

Casey is a sensitive (and beautiful and HOT) young man who is trying to find himself. Along the way he finds adventure in the form of several stunning studs, much to his (and your) satisfaction.

First there's fun with the fairy godmother (also played by Casey) followed by a quick romp with Steven, and handsome hump who happens by. But you haven't seen anything till you watch Casey and the delivery boy. And boy does this boy deliver. He and the incredible Casey start in the kitchen and suddenly find themselves in the middle of the groceries. They're all over the floor, surrounded by everything from potatoes to beer cans. But nothing stops these two young bucks from getting into, in on and over each other. They can't seem to get enough of each other's hot bodies and you won't have trouble figuring out why. The contrast of the two perfect forms, one the swimmer's body of the blond bombshell Casey, and the musky sensuality of the dark delivery boy are the ideal combination for action the way you like it.

If you enjoyed Casey in BOYS IN THE SAND and THE BACK ROW, you'll want to be sure to invite him into your home as CASEY, the first (and the greatest) sex star. This is the man who can do it all, and in his first film he does. For many nights to come you'll enjoy all that this most famous of all the SuperStuds has to offer.

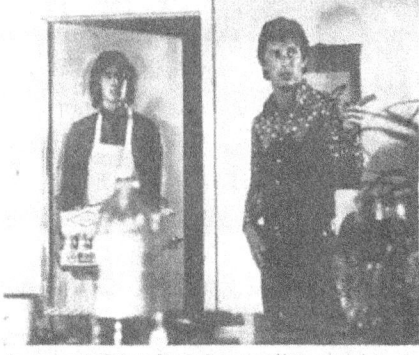

Casey gives the Delivery Boy the first series of instructions that ends up with a super hot duo on the kitchen floor.

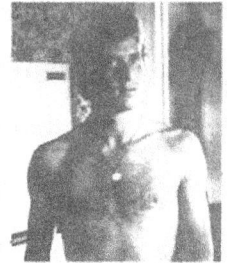

The boyish Casey is the engaging young man you'll meet in this Hand in Hand hot video release.

Cast: CASEY DONOVAN, Nat Grey, Angelo Warne Sparrow Goano

Directed by Donald Crane • Edited by Frank Tondo
Produced by Carl Fromuius

| CASEY | 88 MINUTES | COLOR | ALL-MALE CAST |

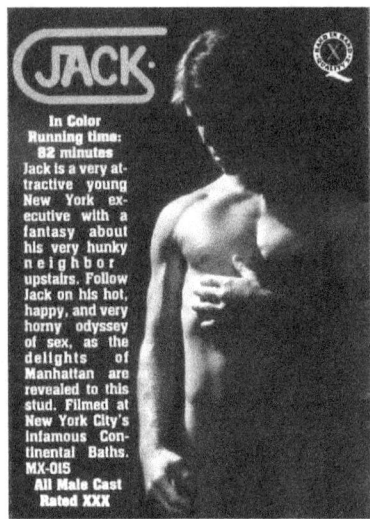

"The men are spectacularly attractive and the sex is top notch," is what New York's *Gay Magazine* said about JACK. The *Village Voice* loved Jack's enthusiastic foreplay and handsome humpings, and found the film "refreshing." You'll say it's *hot* and here's why: Jack, our title character, is a Manhattan executive who has this fantasy – he wants to make it with the hunky man who lives in the apartment upstairs. (Once you see the neighbor, you'll share the fantasy.) The trouble is that the neighbor has a wife and a kid and doesn't seem to be at all available. Jack decides to try and replace his fantasy with some real, warm flesh, and sets out to find another man. As you surely know, in New York, another man is never very far away. Just look around the next corner or under the next bush and that's exactly what our man Jack does. He's successful in finding other men, of course. Men as good looking as Jack always are successful in the search for sex. He finds a shoeshine boy who's hot for more than a big tip. Jack is all too happy to oblige. Next Jack heads for a bathhouse for the kinds of adventures that most of us only dream about. But this isn't just any bathhouse. This is the famous (infamous?) Continental Baths, the legendary home of Bette Midler and the most beautiful men in the world. The place is full of sexy males, all of whom are as eager to please and be pleased as Jack is. There is a wonderfully erotic and entertaining scene with Jack and the two lovers who pick him up. The torrid footage is enough to make you re-think three ways as these humpers go at it all ways. And how about an underwater jerk-off? It's wild and wet and very good. Throughout the film, however, Jack can't get his mind off the beauty who lives upstairs. (Don't we all have someone like this in our lives?) This story has a very happy ending, though. Happy and horny. And it's one you'll love each and every time you put on this sexy and exciting film.

*Hand In Hand Promo

HAND IN HAND VIDEO

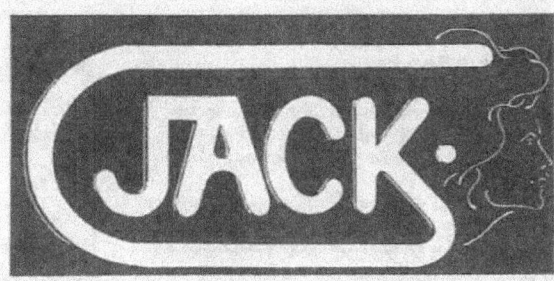

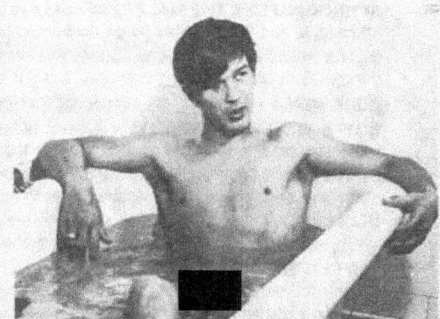
Our man underwater, getting ready for something wet and wild.

"The men are spectacularly attractive and the sex is top notch," is what New York's **Gay Magazine** said about JACK. The **Village Voice** loved Jack's "enthusiastic foreplay and handsome humpings," and found the film "refreshing." You'll say it's "HOT!" and here's why.

Jack, our title character, is a Manhattan executive who has this fantasy—he wants to make it with the hunky man who lives in the apartment upstairs. (Once you see the neighbor, you'll share the fantasy.) The trouble is that the neighbor has a wife and a kid and doesn't seem to be at all available.

Jack decides to try and replace his fantasy with some real, warm flesh, and sets out to find another man. As you surely know, in New York, another man is never very far away. Just look around the next corner or under the next bush and that's exactly what our man Jack does. He's successful in finding other men, of course. Men as good looking as Jack always are successful in the search for sex. He finds a shoeshine boy who's hot for more than a big tip. Jack is all too happy to oblige.

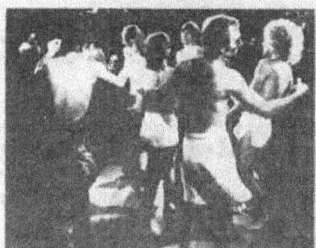
These are the men you heard about at the famous Continental Baths.

Next Jack heads for a bathhouse for the kinds of adventures that most of us only dream about. But this isn't just any bathhouse. This is the famous (infamous?) Continental Baths, the legendary home of Bette Midler and the most beautiful men in the world. The place is full of sexy males, all of whom are as eager to please and be pleased as Jack is.

There is a wonderfully erotic and entertaining scene with Jack and the two lovers who pick him up. The torrid footage is enough to make you re-think three ways as these humpers go at it all ways. And how about an underwater jerk-off? It's wild and wet and very good.

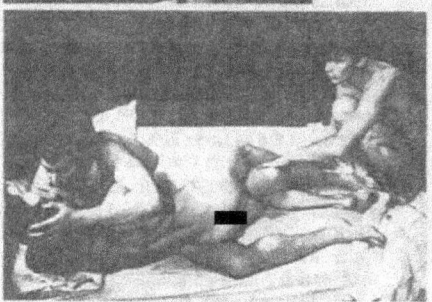
Jack gets it on with two very hunger lovers.

Throughout the film, however, Jack can't get his mind off the beauty who lives upstairs. (Don't we all have someone like this in our lives?) This story has a very happy ending, though. Happy and horny. And it's one you'll love each and every time you put on this sexy and exciting film.

Starring:
DANO MARTIN as JACK
with
Leo Link, Robert Lamb, Bob Jones,
Phil D'Angelo, Bob Benelli
Produced by: John Stephens and Geoffrey Knower
Written and Directed by: John Stephens
First Camera: Dom Mori • Second Camera: Chris Larkin
Editor: Terry Charles • Music: The Beautiful People (Original Score)

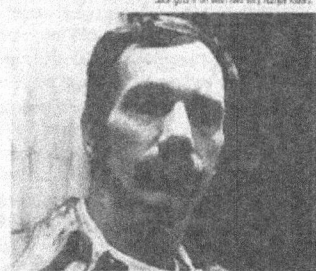
This is the object of Jack's affection. Can you blame him?

| JACK | 82 MINUTES | COLOR | ALL-MALE CAST |

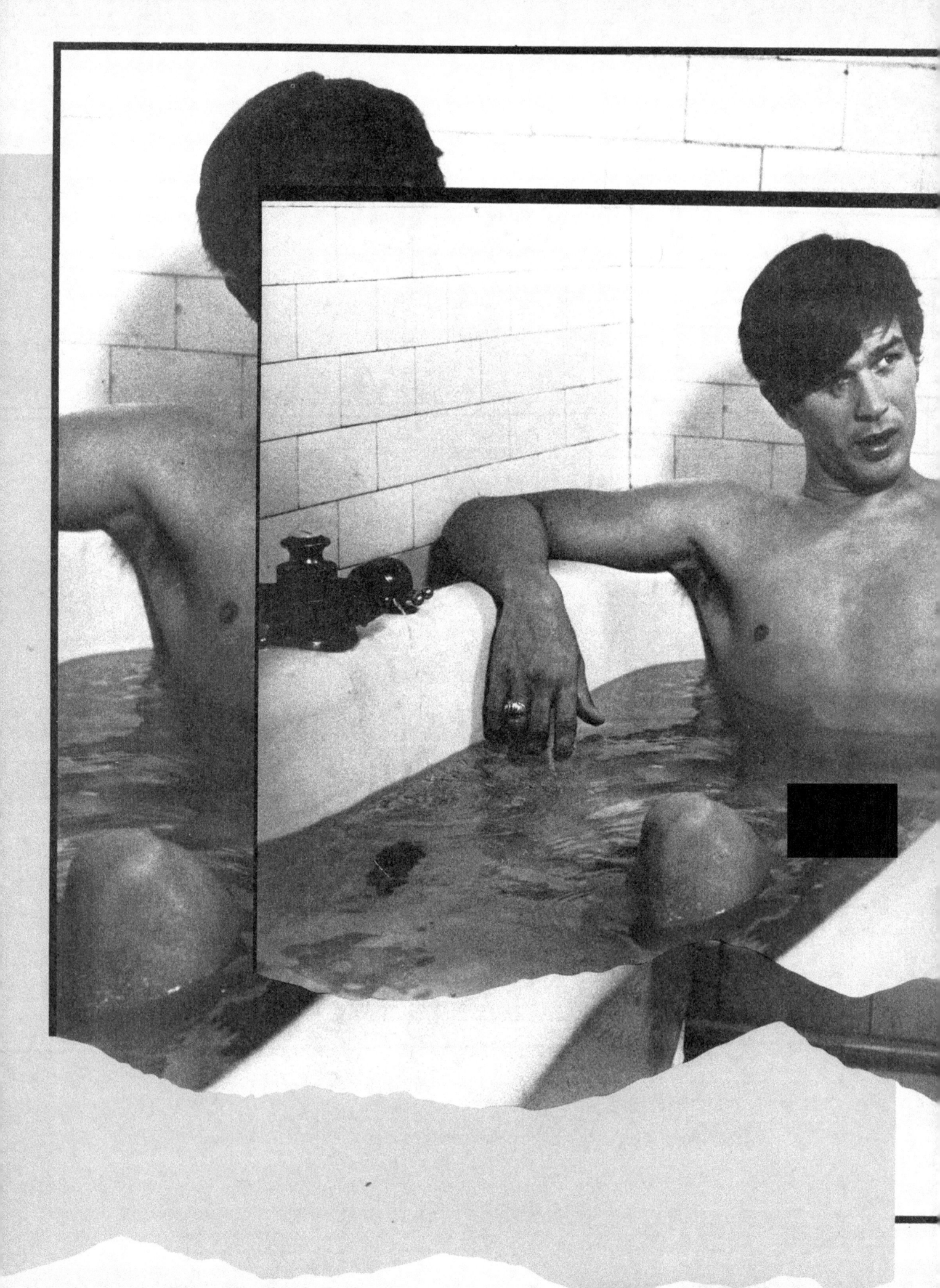

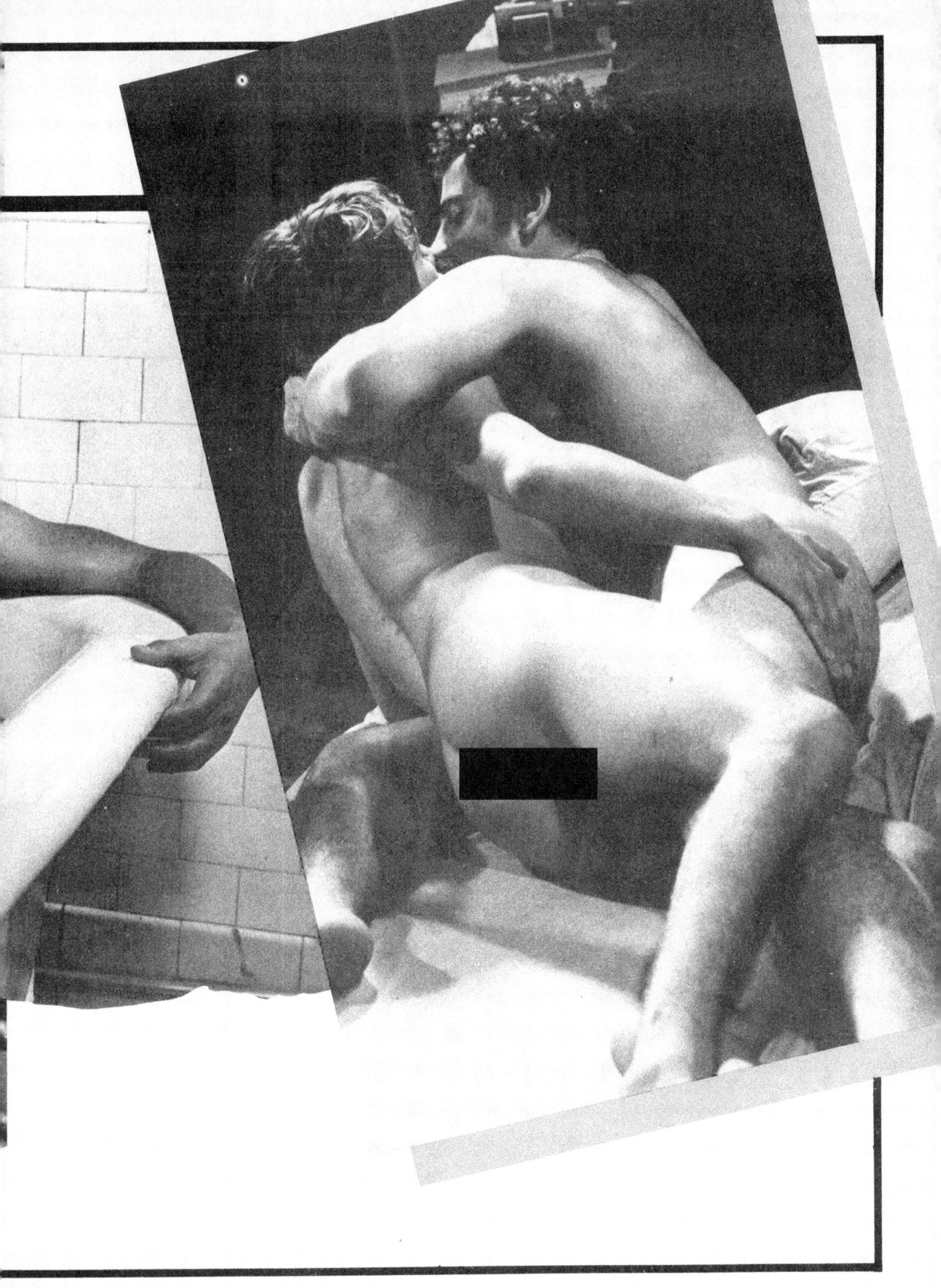

JACK

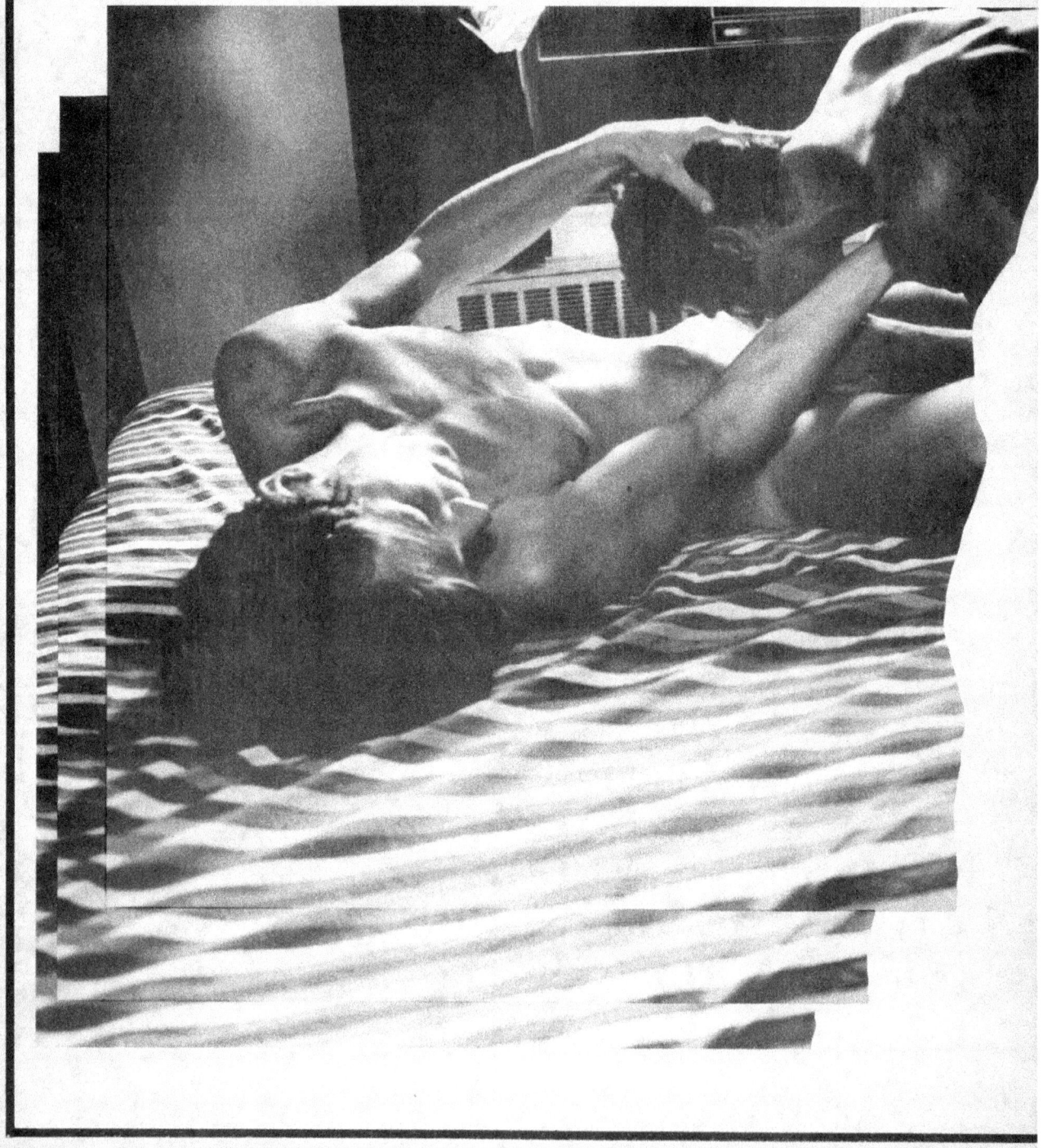

JACK is a young Manhattan executive. His habits and life style resemble those of thousands of others living and working in the city, right down to his fantasies: He wants to make it with the guy next door (or rather, upstairs). The only trouble is that the object of his affection already seems to be involved with a wife and child, and it doesn't look like he's ever going to be available for JACK. So Jack tries to find someone, something else. He looks in Central Park's famed Rambles, picks up a shoeshine boy, checks into the tubs, makes it with two lovers.

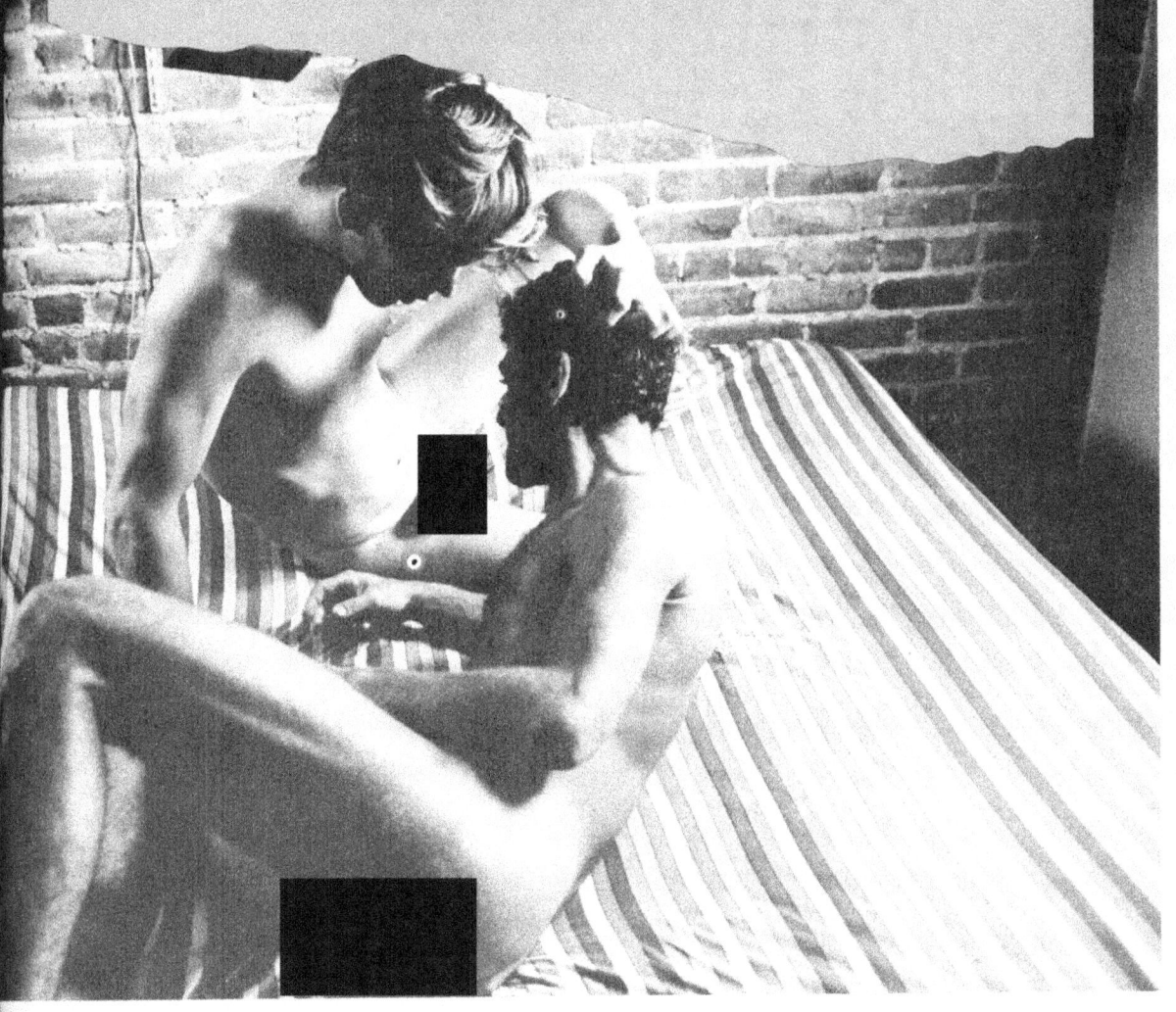

49

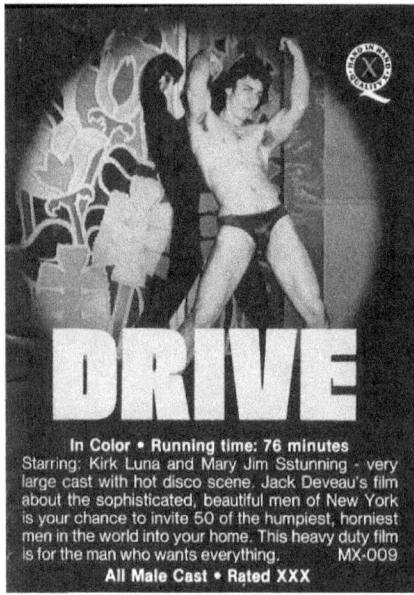

Never let it be said that Jack Deveau lacked chutzpah. In DRIVE he manipulates the formula of a James Bond film to attack the anti-sex fervor of a society driven to madness by its own obsessions with such diverse forces as feminism, religion, and technology. Mary Jim Stunning (actor-director Christopher Rage, in full drag) gives a remarkable performance as the mad Arachne, a transvestite who wishes to rid the world of sexuality by chemical castration of all males. Peter De Rome plays the head of a secret agency who assigns operator Kirk Luna to break through Arachne's web of deceit and insanity. As the name itself suggests, Arachne is the quintessential black widow spider, luring men to their doom with her perversity. Luna succeeds only after a near brush with castration himself: his salvation is an erection that refuses to fall even under duress. The mere sight sends Arachne into a fit of despair, from which she can arouse herself only by composing her memoirs to tell the world her side of the story. Arachne's polemics against male sexuality – its promiscuity, its instability, its emotional and psychological havoc – sound very much like the sermons of a right-wing evangelist, while her attempt at chemical castration recalls both the rhetoric of extreme feminists (who advocate the same punishment for rapists) and the technologic conspiracies of a repressive government against its own populace. In the current age of AIDS and censorship, it is difficult to dismiss this distrust of the government as simple paranoia. In fact, the film may well contain an ironic element of prophecy. In pointing out the meeting ground between fundamentalism, feminism, and fascism – the three "F'"s that constitute the target of his satire – Deveau reveals how seemingly disparate forces converge to create an anti-sex campaign capable of infiltrating every level of society. The current crusade against "pornography," let us remember, consists of just such a triple alliance. We are in no position to play doubting Thomases.

As a sub-theme of his film, Deveau examines the nature of gay male sexuality with the experienced eye of one who has done as well as seen it all. Luna is presumably involved in a committed relationship – at least he has a live-in lover (Fersen) who cooks his breakfast. On the other hand, the relationship is not monogamous, and he has no scruples about exercising his sexual prowess in a variety of situations throughout the film, some directed at achieving necessary information to fulfill his assignment, some just for fun.

The contradiction may strike some viewers as perverse, but to Deveau it reflects the reality of gay life in the New York City of his time. Commitment and love are indeed desirable to give one a home base and a degree of security, he seems to be saying, but a little extramarital activity and a willingness to experiment never hurt anyone. The very qualities that Arachne detests are to Deveau the true landmarks of male sexuality, which receive their "purest" and most extreme expression in the lifestyles of gay men, which are uncomplicated by legal obligations and children. The double standard, furthermore, is not operative: Luna extends to his temporarily abandoned lover the same freedom that he claims for himself. The sexual morality of the film stands solely on the basis of mutual consent between informed adults.

Because of its large cast, its complicated plot, its fondness for chase scenes, and its frequent forays into explicit sex that include virtually every act two men can perform together, DRIVE may well be the most ambitious gay adult film yet made. Deveau involved nearly everyone in the adult business (New York branch) in the project, both in front of and behind the camera.

The film's main failure is not in its production values and special effects, but in the superficial characters that populate the script. Only the mad Arachne compels our attention. But even this factor works to the film's advantage if we accept it on its own terms as primarily a political satire in the tradition of James Bond. After all, no one has ever accused Ian Fleming – much less Sean Connery or Roger Moore – of depth. Ironically, the potentially offensive element in DRIVE lies less in its attack on Dworkinesque feminism – which deserves whatever punches it receives – than in its perhaps accidental suggestion that transvestism involves a total rejection of maleness. Although Deveau avoids explicit generalization on this matter, the implication remains. And Stunning's brilliantly perverse performance as Arachne lends the implication dramatic as well as psychological support. As an element alien to his overall vision, transvestism does not fare well at Deveau's hand; but in spite of this problem, DRIVE deserves to be remembered as a powerful weapon against the three "F'"s that still threaten the freedom of our society.

*M.L., *Manshots*

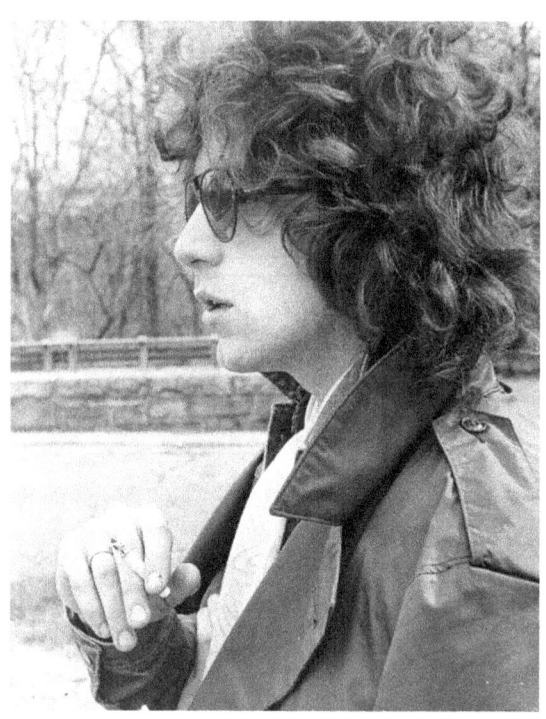

Shaun Roberts

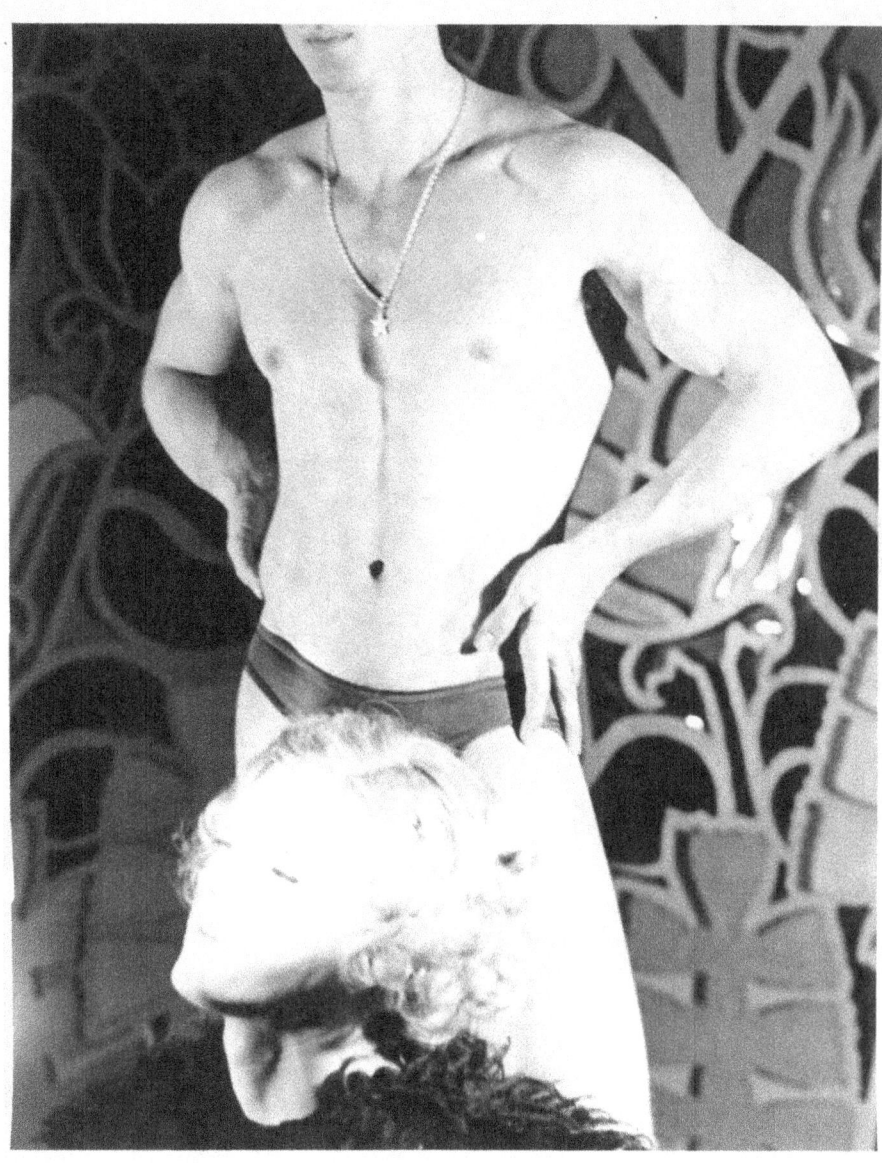

Arachne is a transvestite who has been driven mad by an unrequited love. Scorned, she makes it her mission to kill the sex drives of all men, her crude methodology being the castration of gay men who come to her disco (we see Arachne holding a blade to an anonymous man's cock.) In this first scene at the disco, numerous sexy men are seen dancning, some shirtless, some drinking and indulging in coke. A hot muscular dancer (Brian Destazio) strips down to his underwear and takes the stage go-go dancer style, then Arachne arrives in a gorilla costume, a la Marlene Dietrich in Hot Vodoo. She picks up Destazio's discarded clothes from the dancefloor and Destazio helps her remove the gorilla mask, as she welcomes the unsuspecting men to her club.

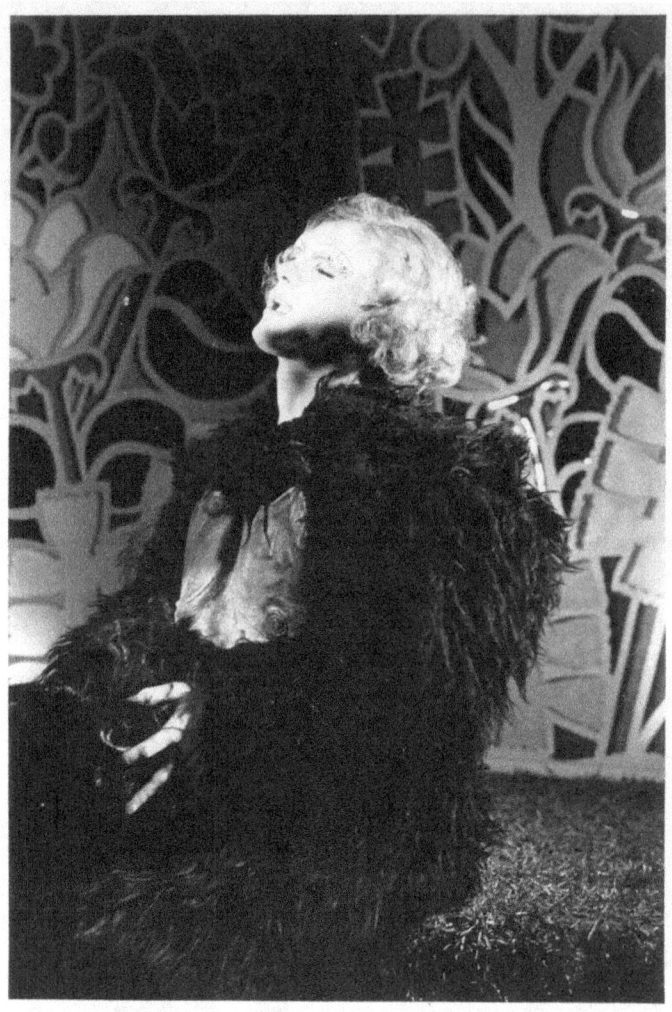

Drive: Christopher Rage aka Mary Jean Stunning as Arachne

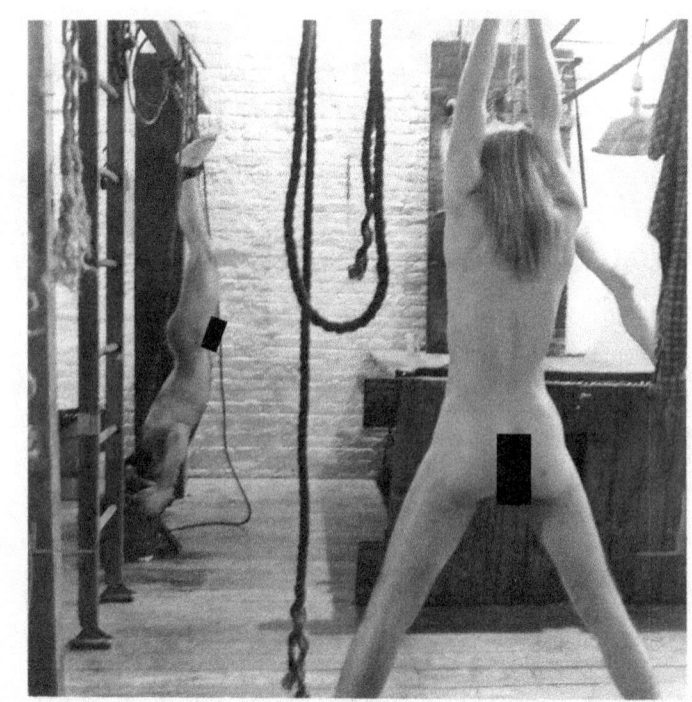

Mark Woodward (right) hanging handcuffed in the dungeon scene in *Drive*

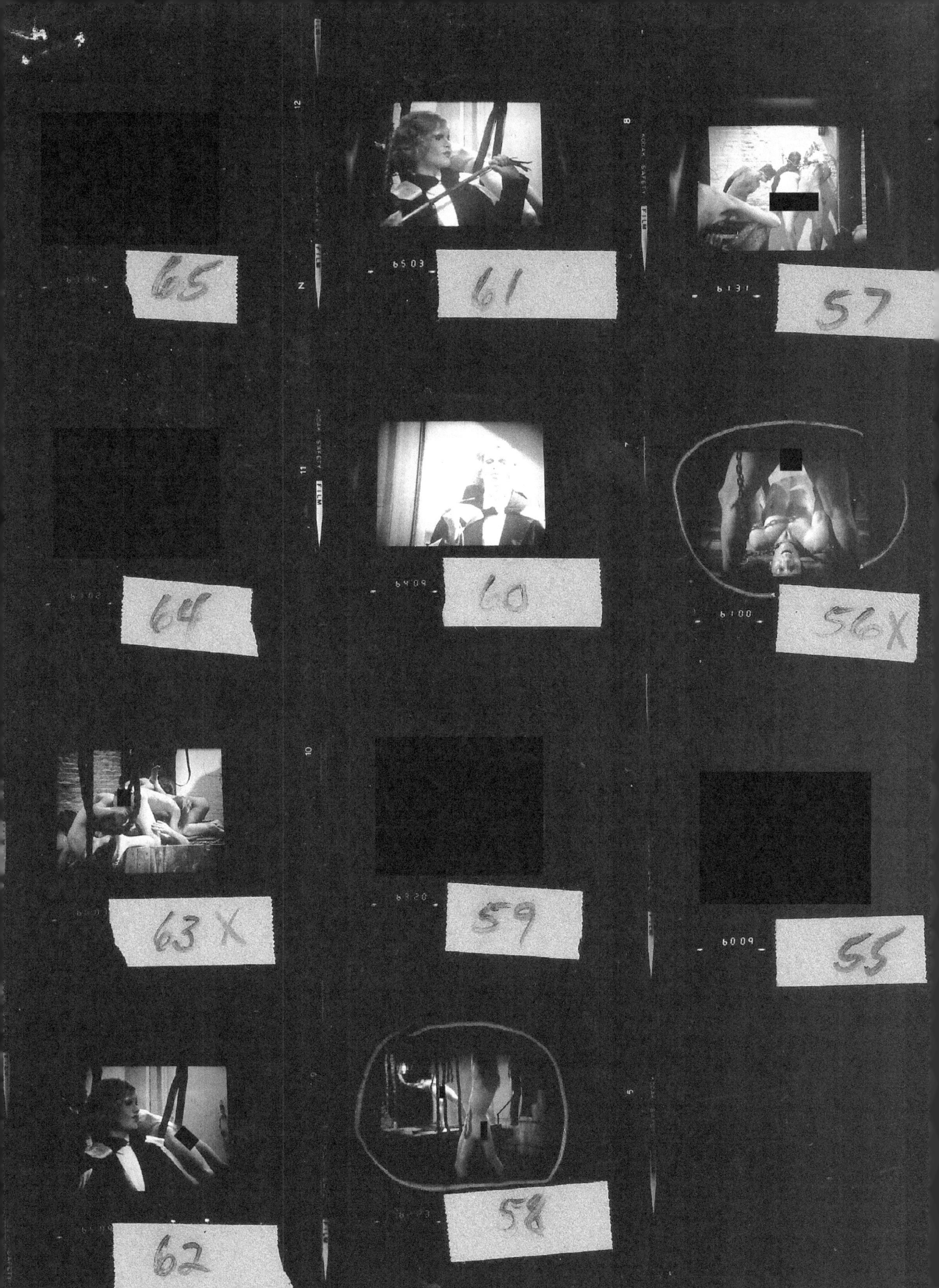

DRIVE

JACK DEVEAU'S

DRIVE

...ABOUT FIFTY VERY COMPULSIVE MEN.

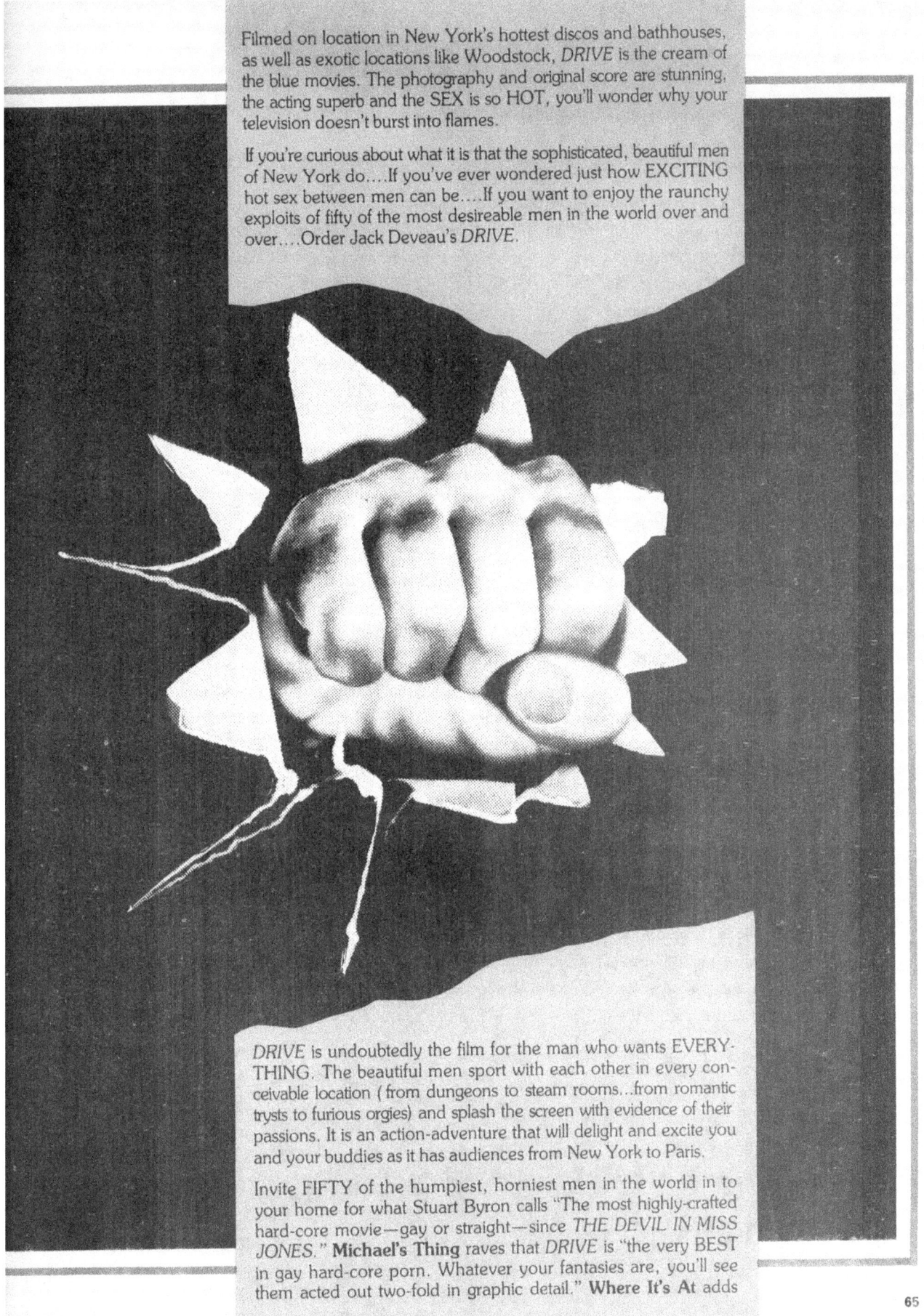

Filmed on location in New York's hottest discos and bathhouses, as well as exotic locations like Woodstock, *DRIVE* is the cream of the blue movies. The photography and original score are stunning, the acting superb and the SEX is so HOT, you'll wonder why your television doesn't burst into flames.

If you're curious about what it is that the sophisticated, beautiful men of New York do....If you've ever wondered just how EXCITING hot sex between men can be.....If you want to enjoy the raunchy exploits of fifty of the most desireable men in the world over and over....Order Jack Deveau's *DRIVE*.

DRIVE is undoubtedly the film for the man who wants EVERYTHING. The beautiful men sport with each other in every conceivable location (from dungeons to steam rooms...from romantic trysts to furious orgies) and splash the screen with evidence of their passions. It is an action-adventure that will delight and excite you and your buddies as it has audiences from New York to Paris.

Invite FIFTY of the humpiest, horniest men in the world in to your home for what Stuart Byron calls "The most highly-crafted hard-core movie—gay or straight—since *THE DEVIL IN MISS JONES.*" **Michael's Thing** raves that *DRIVE* is "the very BEST in gay hard-core porn. Whatever your fantasies are, you'll see them acted out two-fold in graphic detail." **Where It's At** adds

Arachne's tale of a secret drug to eradicate sexual desires, to eliminate sexual DRIVE. A tale perhaps too funny to be told without being told exceptionally well, DRIVE is not a telling of Arachne's tale exceptionally well. It is more, perhaps, too much more. DRIVE is not only the telling of Arachne's undoing but also an overly ambitious display of super-spy pyrotechnics that depletes the film's humor with spectacle. Director of Cinematography Jack Deveau has no spread his talents so thin that he neglected to deliver a beautiful looking film with plenty of intelligent movement. DRIVE is a production achievement in most respects except direction. Perhaps the greatest reason for this is the casting. Although the cast includes a few professional actors, not all the performers in DRIVE earn their living in front of the camera. Their current occupations include fashion photographer, jewelry designer, student, playwright, waiter, manager of a dance company, policeman, bartender, magazine editor, filmmaker, business manager, art director, adult fiction writer, manager of a nightclub, hustler, film editor, dancer and a bank teller. DRIVE ... about fifty very compulsive men, is certainly that.

Sex drive pushes the film over the brink and into the sink, a raunchy, nasty, dirty, bloody sink of exploitable scenes, that are nonetheless brought to life artistically with all the luridness of trash comics. Generally the sex in the film is slow in getting off but get off it does. Undoubtedly the first penetration shot is the best this reviewer has ever seen. It was graceful but hot. The film is narrated by Arachne with a flip delivery from Mary Jim Stunning of lines that are too tacky to be funny for too long. She begins her seedy tale at the typewriter, making a plea to her "public" that her side of the story not be lost: Under the direction of the government, a brilliant young scientist named Hardison has developed a secret drug reported to eradicate sexual desire. Arachne, having heard about the drug through her massive spy network, realizes that it is the final solution to fulfilling a dream of ending sex in the world. Arachne sends her henchmen to capture fellatiatingly silly scientist Dr. Hardison, hoping to force him to make the drug so that she might pollute the water supplies of the world. (Certainly a faster and neater procedure than her current practice of castration).

The kidnapping is bungled and the silly scientist escapes. The government wants to find Dr. Hardison before the evil Arachne. So, enter the hero. Clark, played excitingly by Kirk Luna, is the beautiful young super-agent stud. All his scenes blow the trumpets before he enters but instead of jumping out of his civvies into his cape he ambles in front of the camera. The character is enmeshed in the manipulations of everyone around him and in his own aimlessness; always moving, always alert; almost as if he were "everyman" whose facelessness as a real person is allegorized by his wordlessness. When a film is stringing several sex scenes of diverse nature and proportions into one production it is very convenient to have the central character wander about from one scene to another. But Clark is not supposed to be the central character. As evil as Arachne could be seen to be, it is her story and she insists that she is the protagonist out to save man from his misery. Clar, the antagonist, finally jumps into his leathers and drives off on

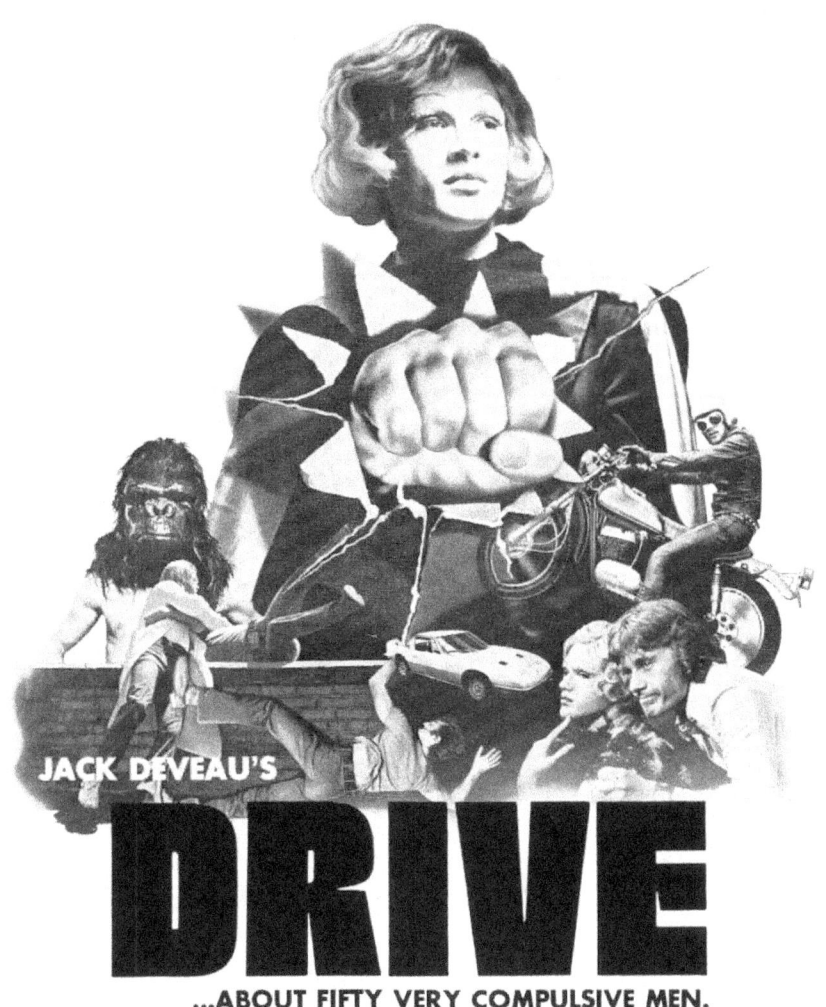

his bike up to Woodstock to rendezvous with Dr. Hardison. Their wuick but beautiful affair is interrupted by Arachne's henchmen, who abduct the two young stud-lovelies and carry them off to Arachne's dungeon, where she has decided that if the good scientist won't give her the secret formula she is quite willing to return to her old-style crusade. And, if he does not cough up, it will be super-spy stud Clark who will be *cut off* from the pleasures first. Clark's self-control prevails in what could have been one of the funniest gags in porno history but unlike Clark's tool's performance the scene goes limp. And that is indicative of the film's basic problem. The script is hilarious and the direction is somber. As a whole it fails to meet its own intent but as a collection of entertainment it can hardly be topped.

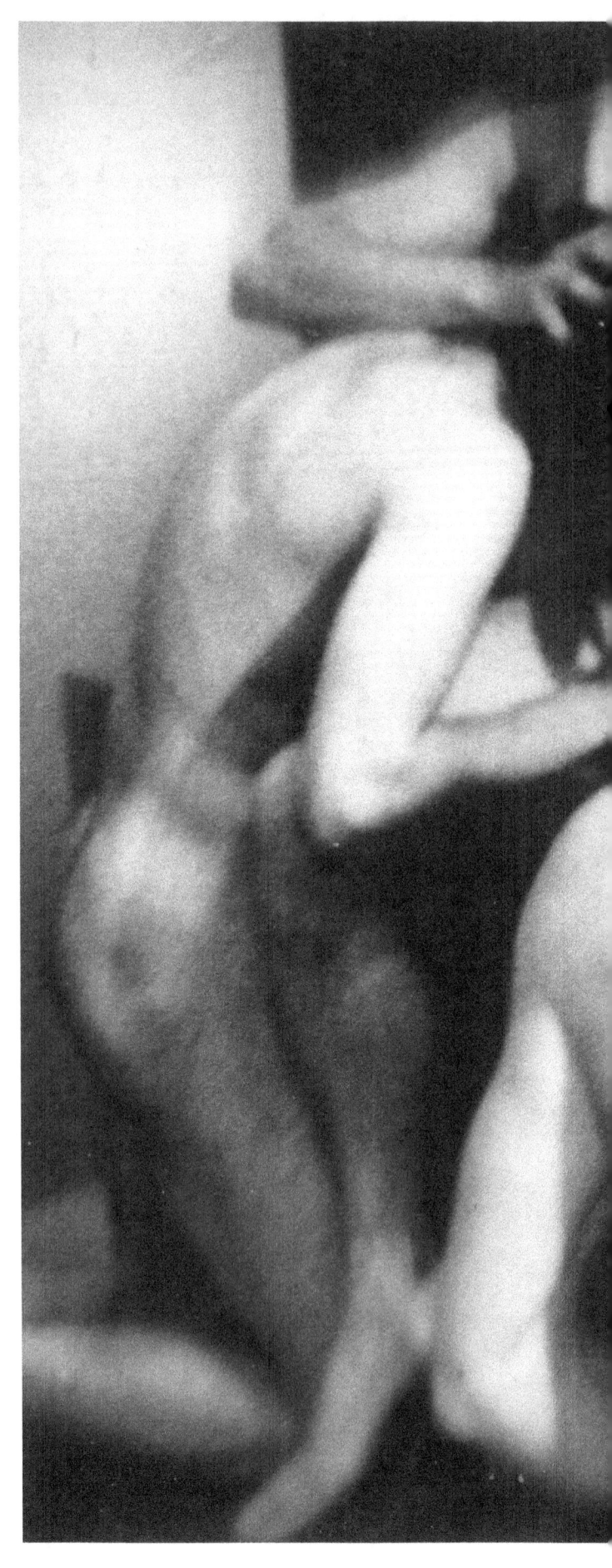
The orgy scene in *Drive*

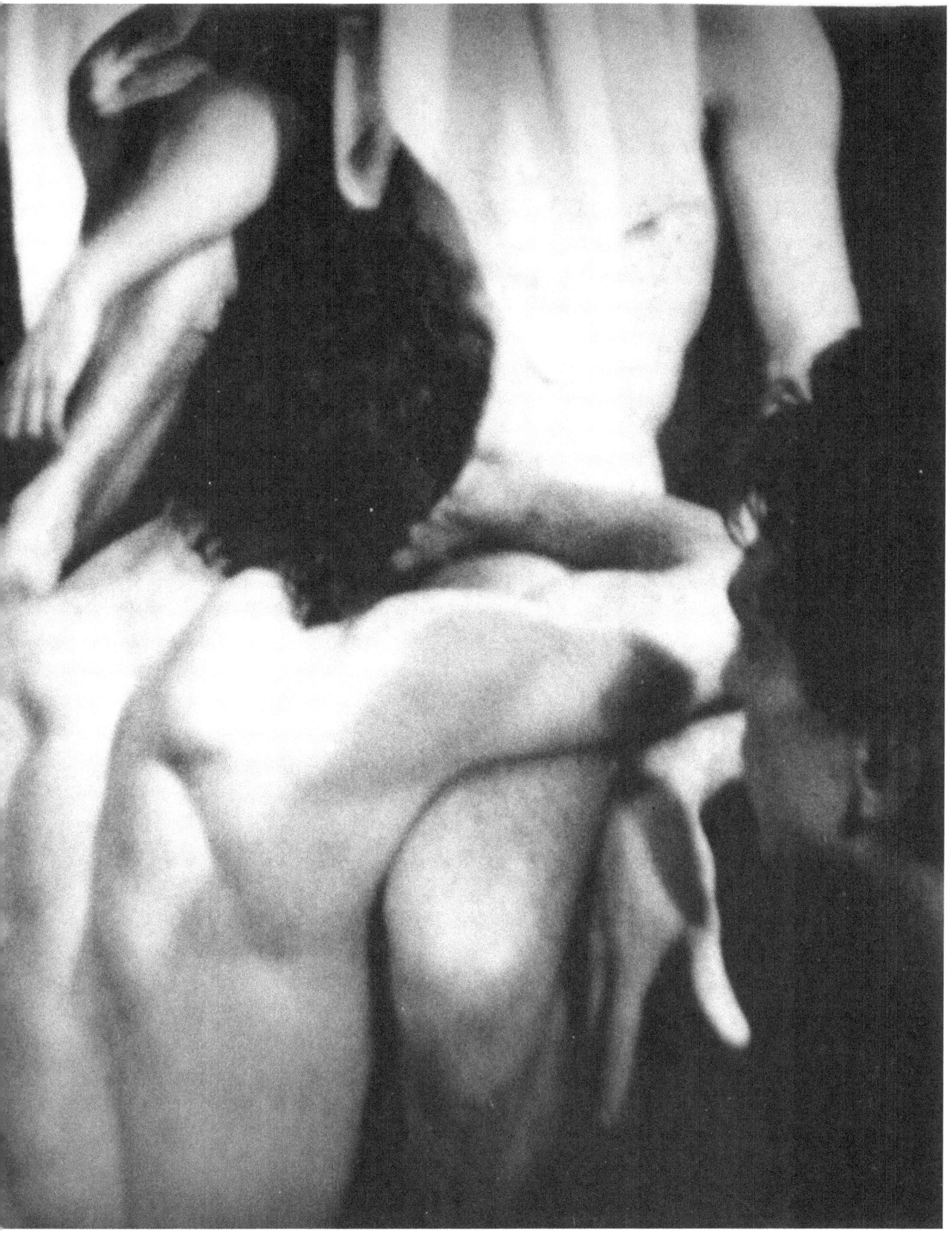

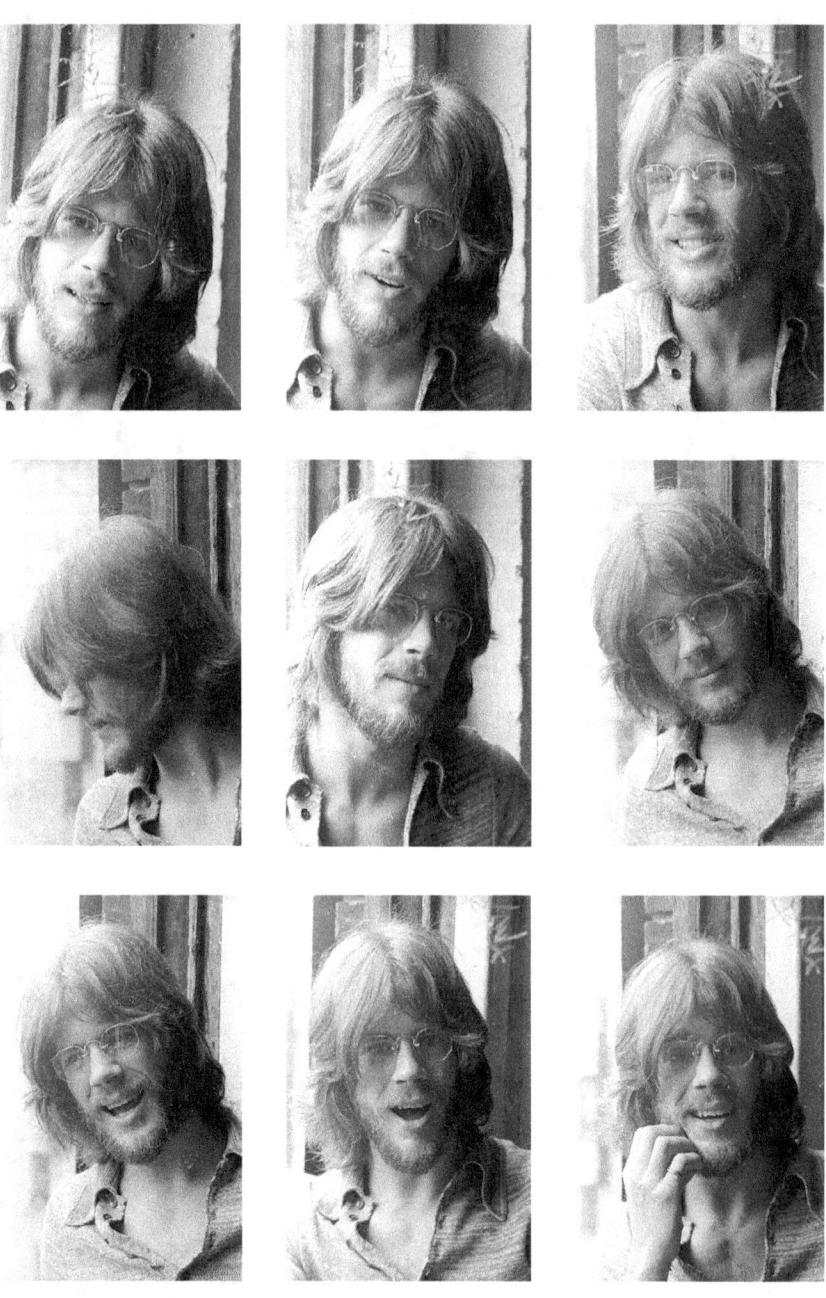

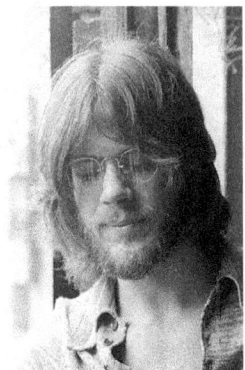

"Kirk Luna came to us out of curiosity. He was good looking, and just the right type for the role. He was masculine, but more in the way of traditional movie leading men type. He had a nice body and a nice dick. He filled all the requirements."

ROBERT ALVAREZ

Kirk Luna: Photo session for the casting of *Drive*

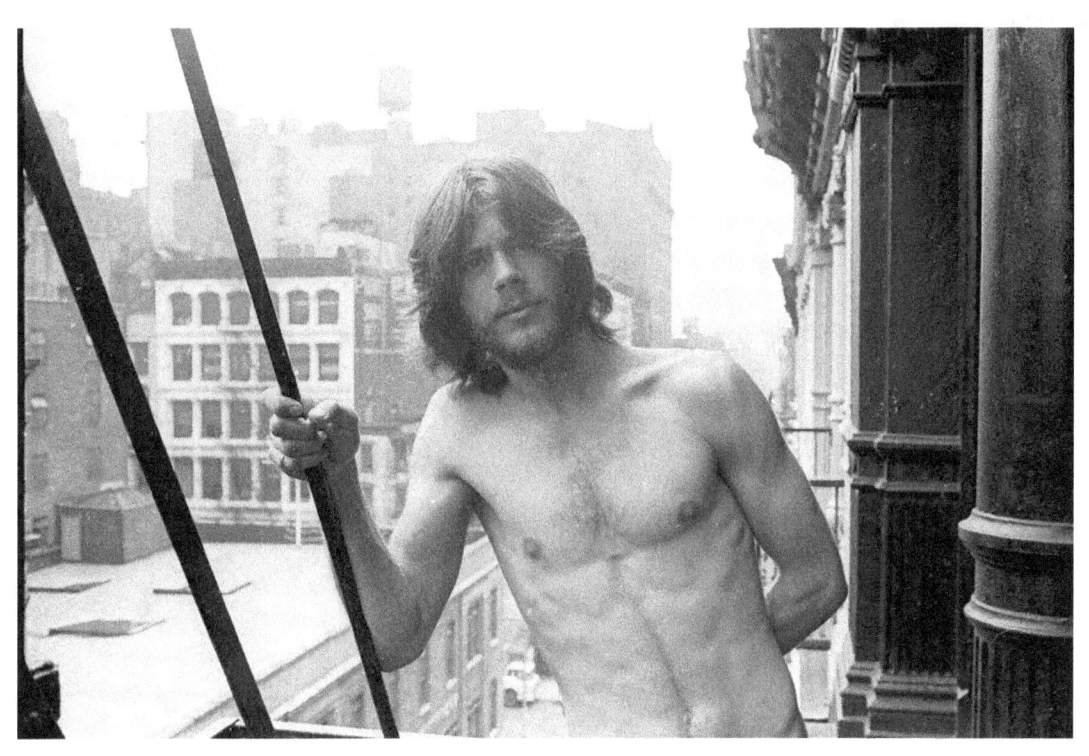
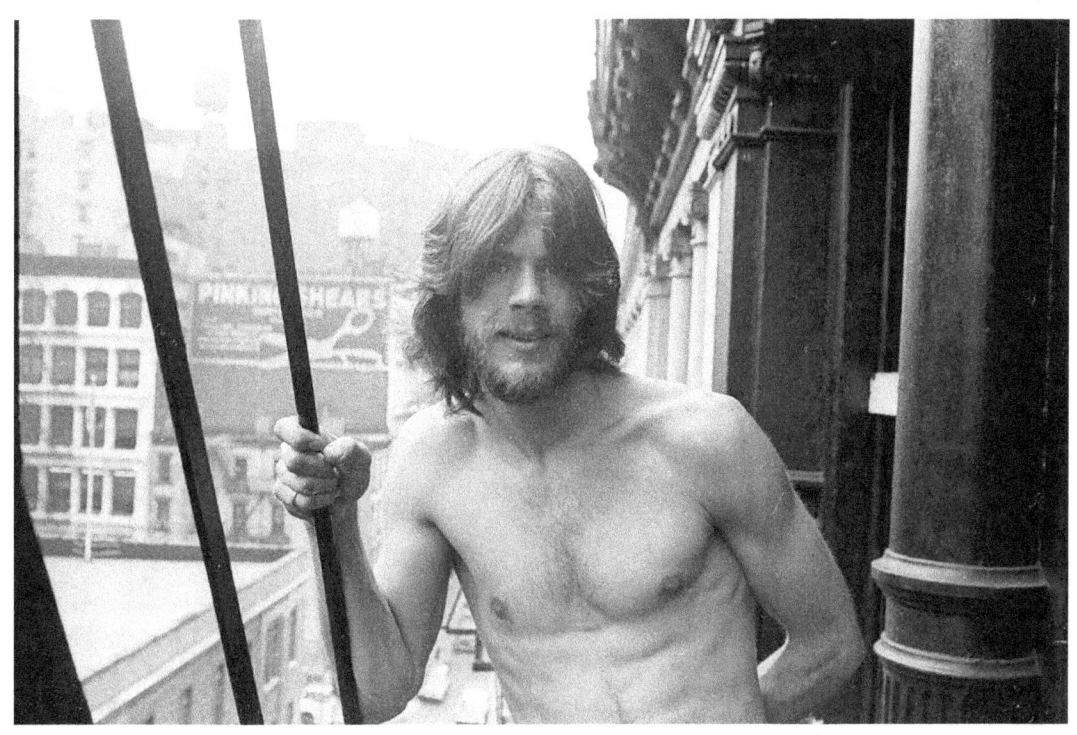

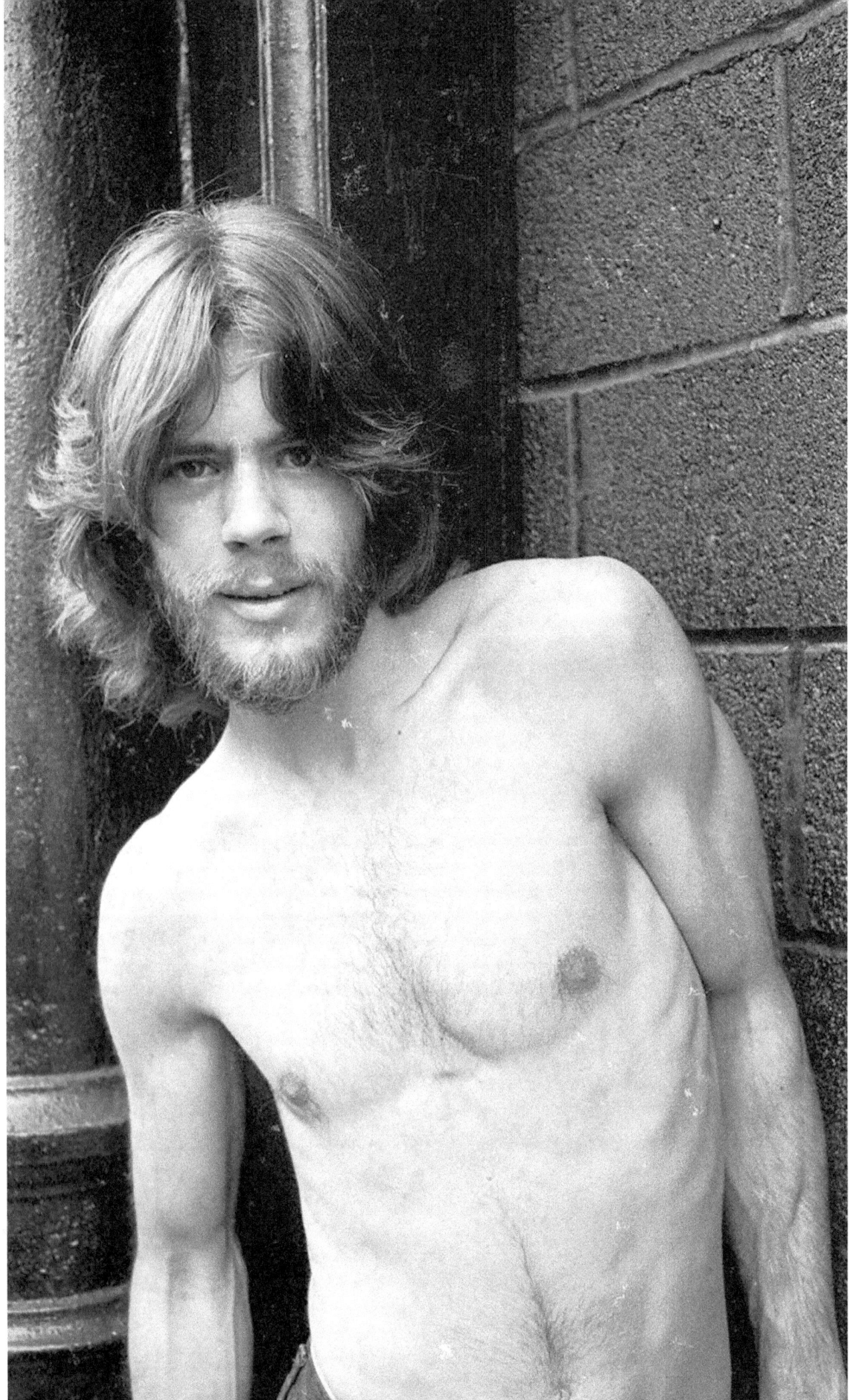

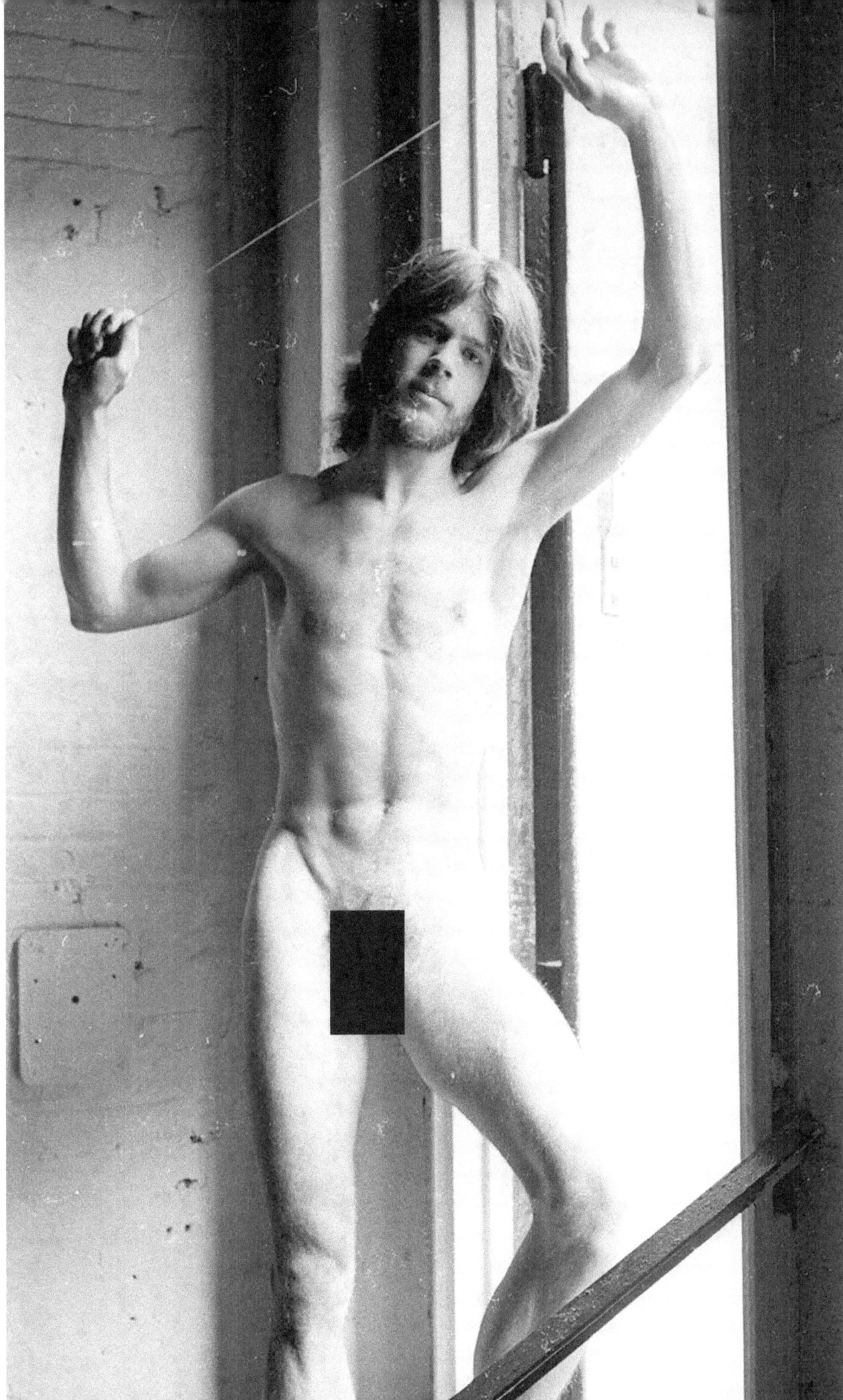

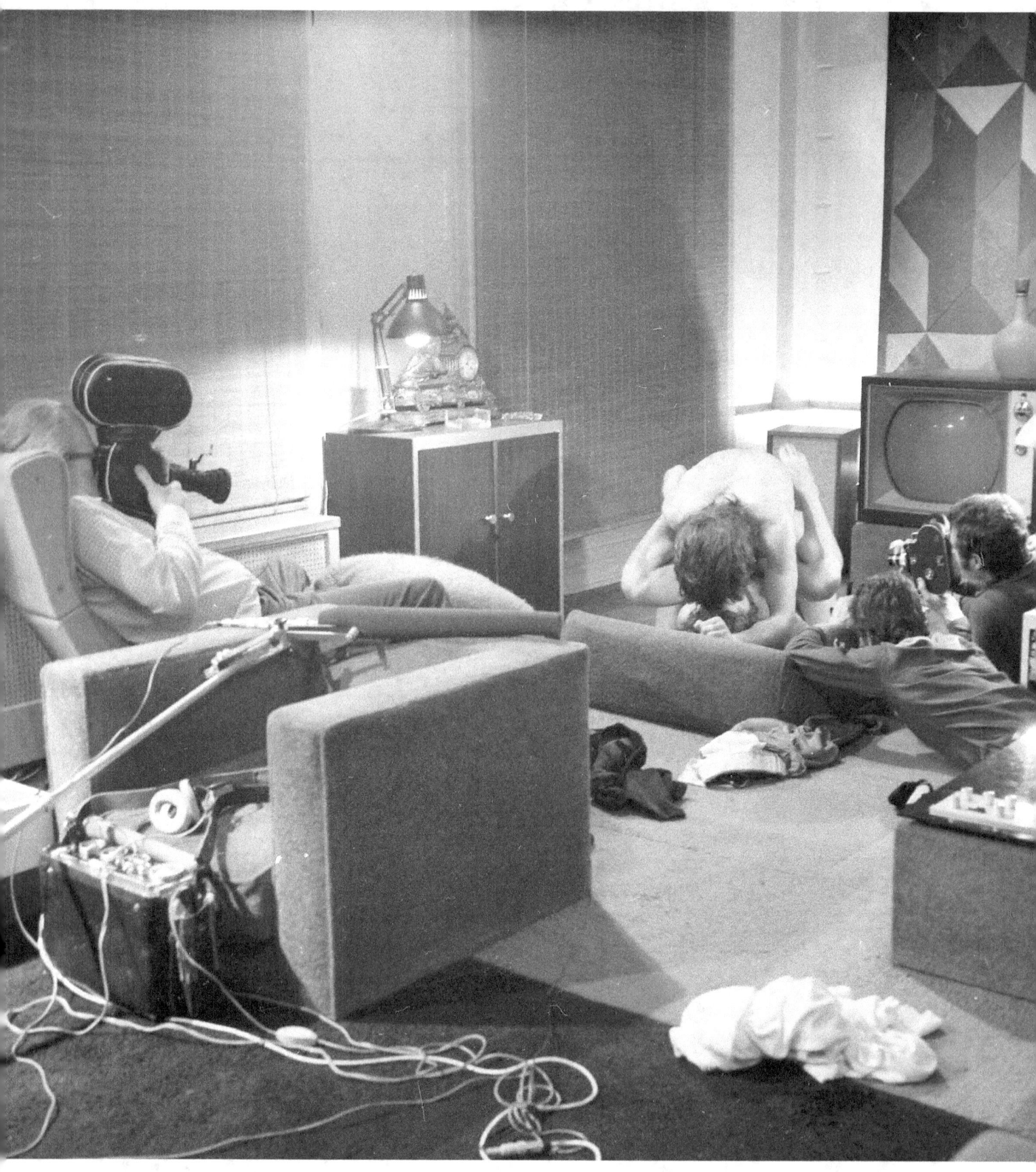

Behind the scenes of *Drive*

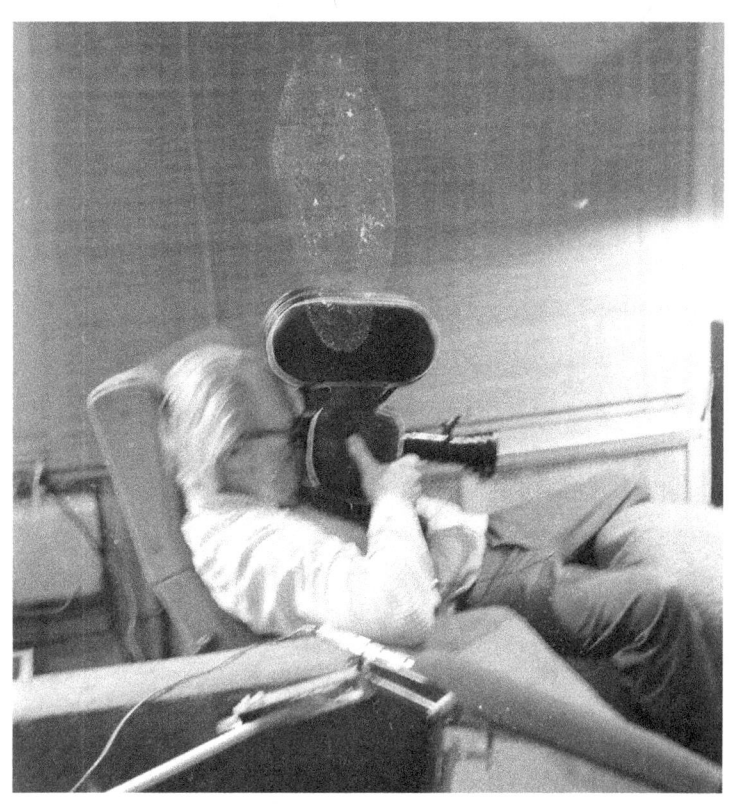

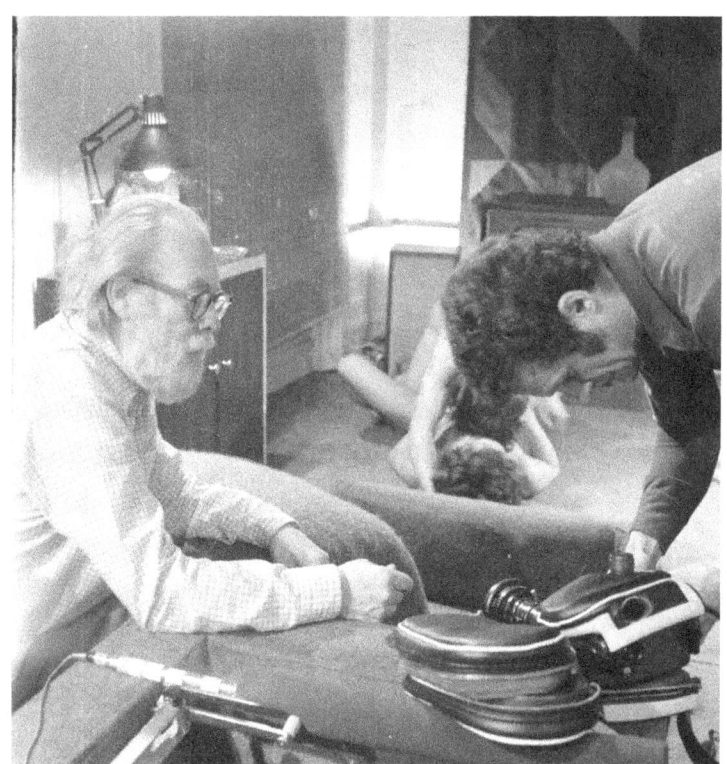

Jaap Penraat (left) and Jack Deveau

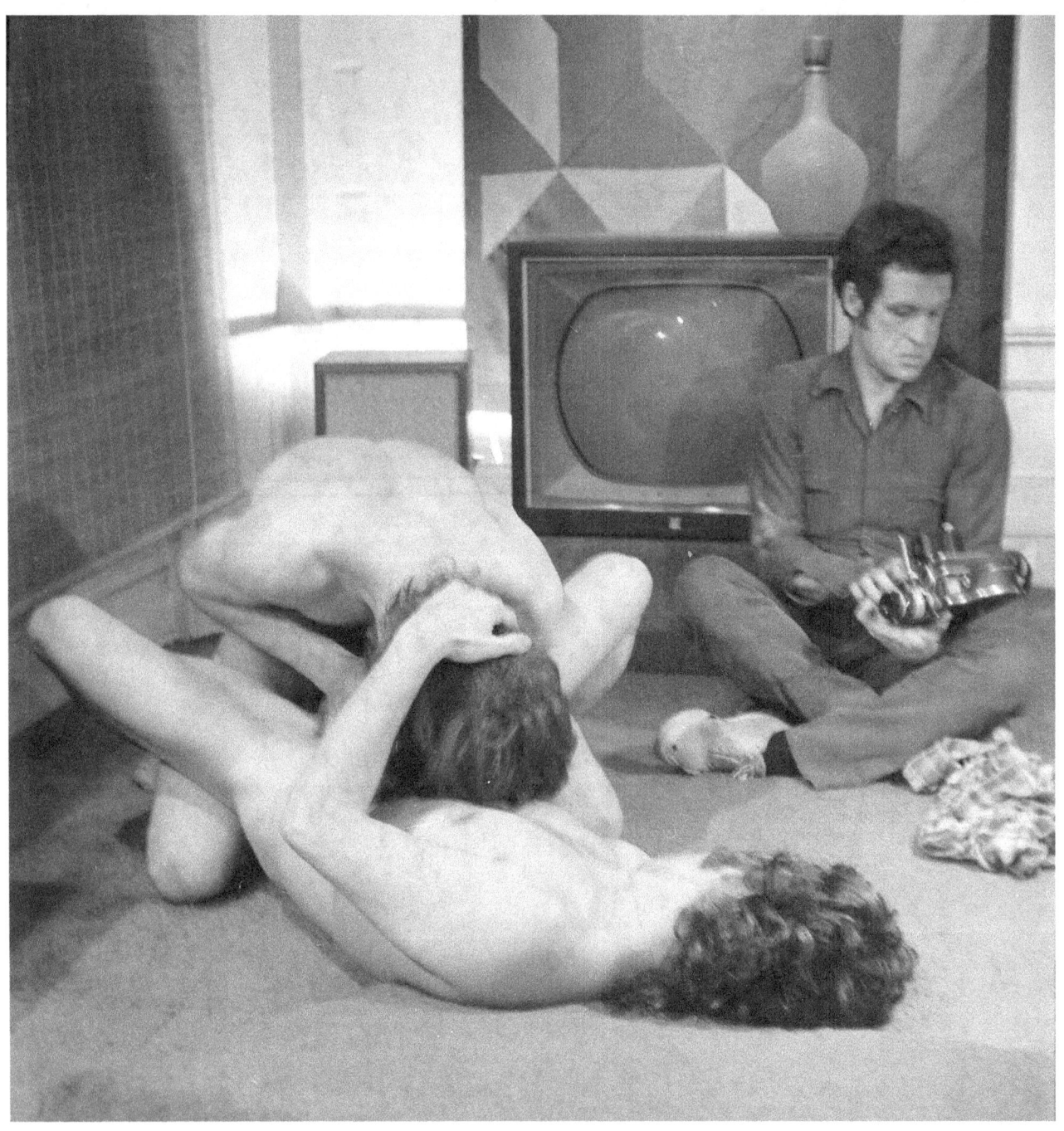

Intercut with the disco scene is a domestic sex scene with special agent Clark (Kirk Luna) and his needy lover Robby (Shaun Roberts). Robby whines a lot, but manages to goad Clark into having sex on their living room floor. Clark sucks Robby at first, they 69, then Clark fucks Robby.

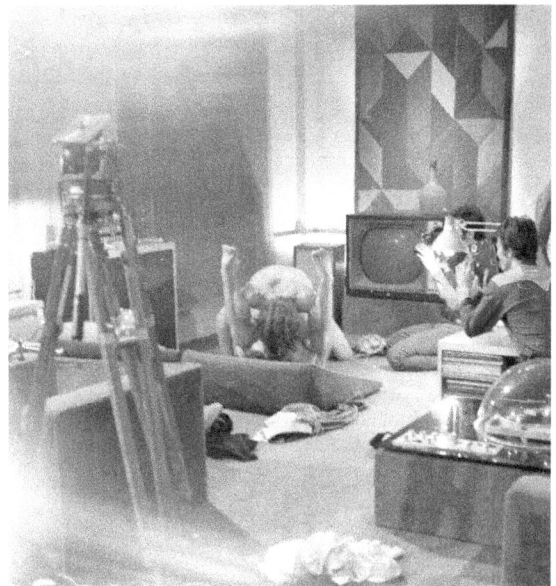
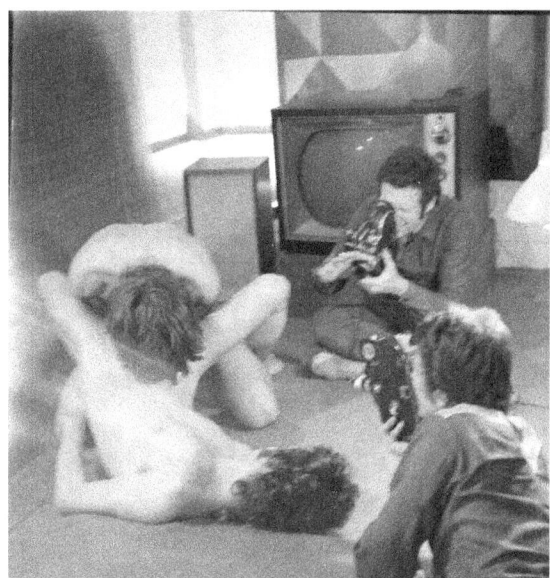
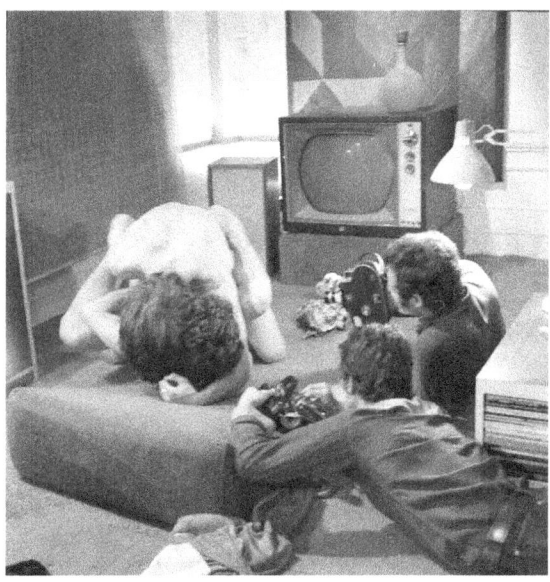

Robert Alvarez and Jack Deveau shooting *Drive*

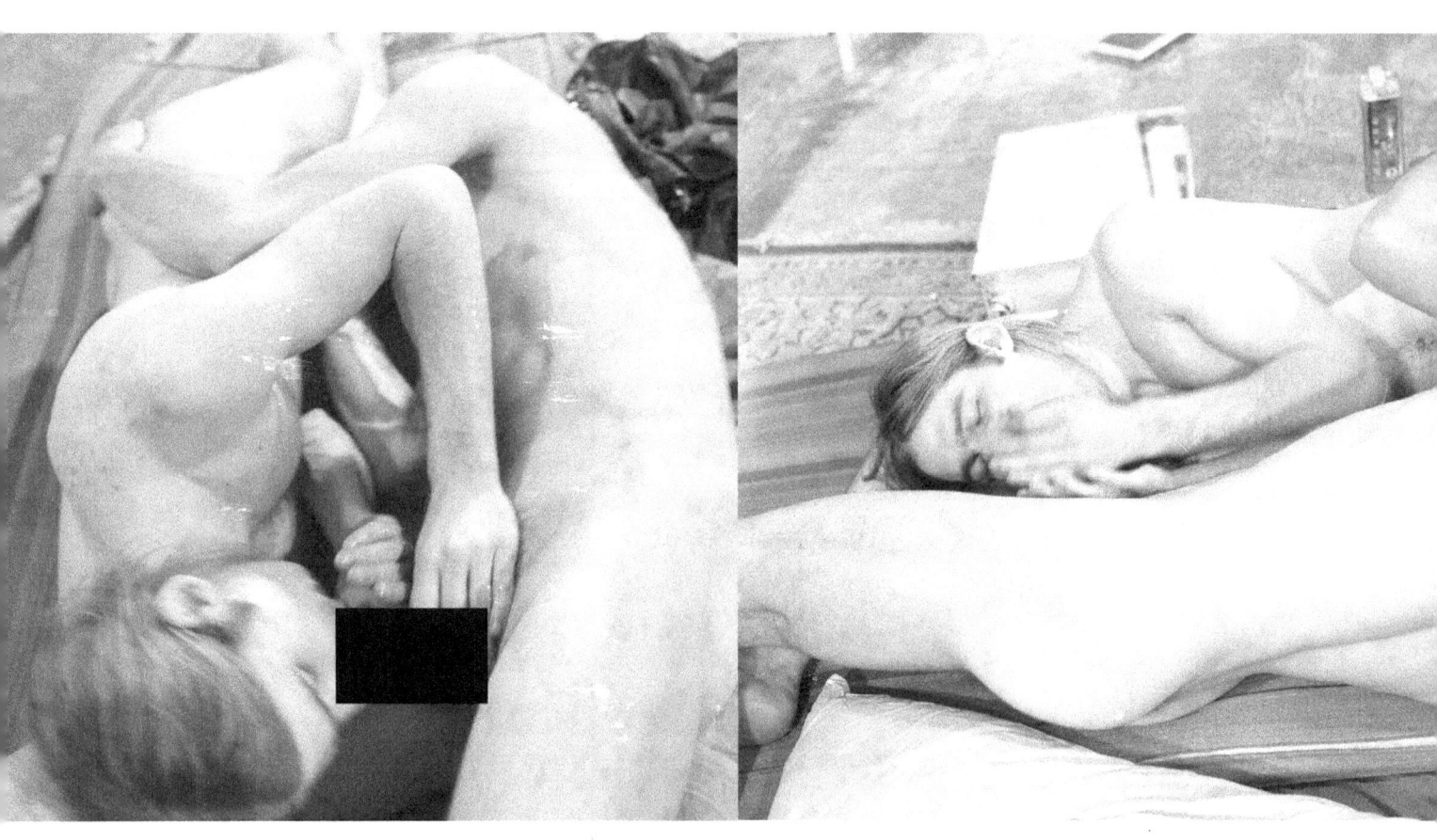

The doctor sucks Clark's cock, they 69 on the floor and finally Hardison rides Clark's cock. This scene is very hard to see because Deveau has superimposed footage of aerialists and lion tamers from a circus on top of the sex in a double exposure.

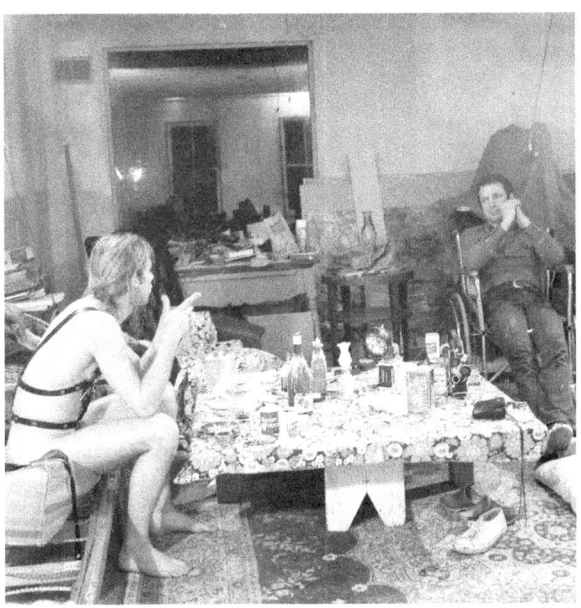
Mark Woodward and Jack Deveau

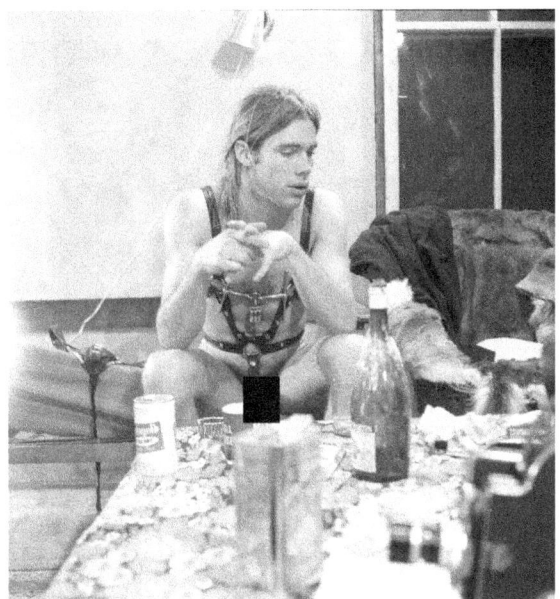
Mark Woodward

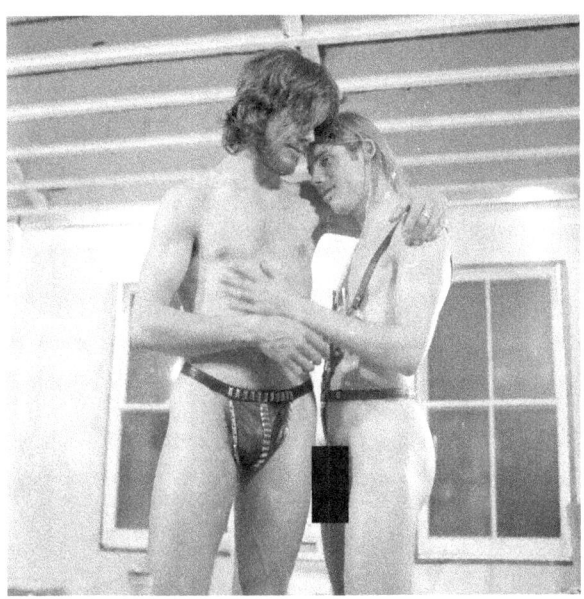
Kirk Luna (left) and Mark Woodward

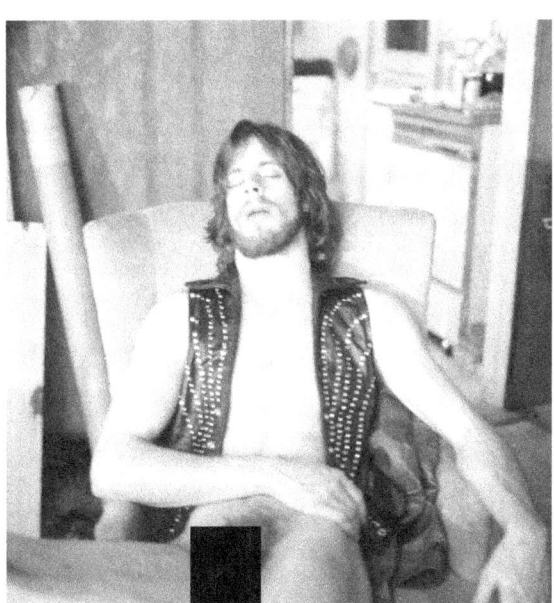
A tired Kirk Luna after a hard day of shooting

HAND IN HAND VIDEO

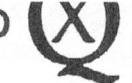

Quality X Video Cassette Company
356 WEST 44TH STREET
NEW YORK, NEW YORK 10036
(212) 541 7860 Outside N.Y. (800) 223-7981

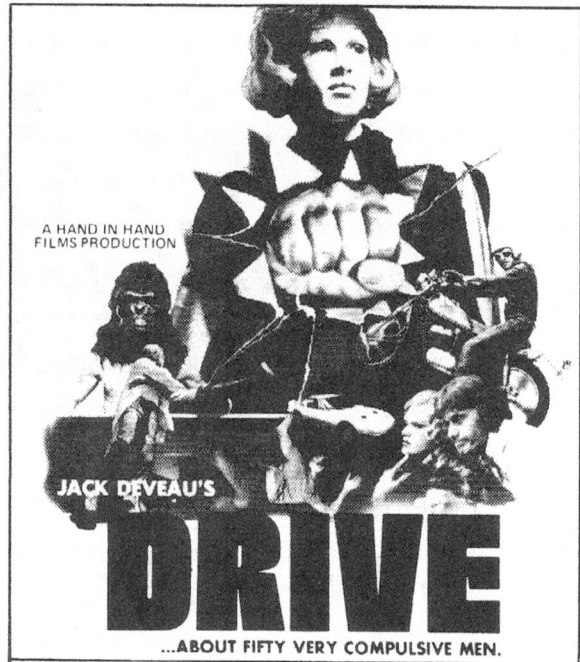

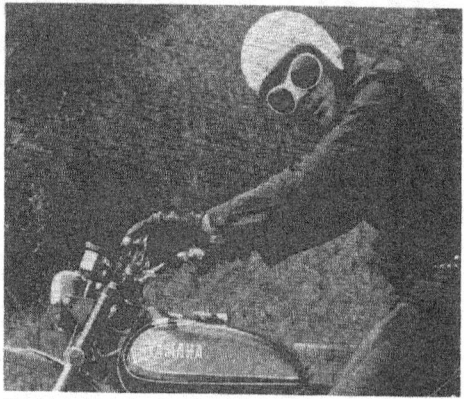

The incredible hero of DRIVE, Kirk Luna, decked out for action.

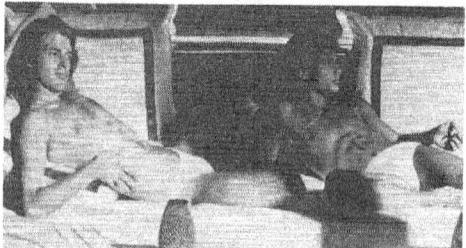

Two of the FIFTY beauties in a hot scene from a New York disco.

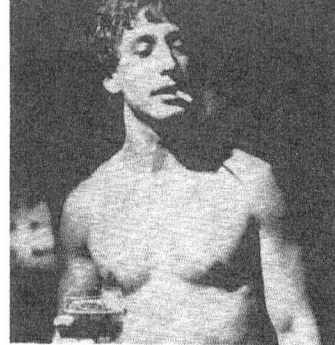

A humpy henchman, ready to serve you.

Invite FIFTY of the humpiest, horniest men in the world in to your home for what Stuart Byron calls "The most highly-crafted hard-core movie—gay or straight—since *THE DEVIL IN MISS JONES*." **Michael's Thing** raves that *DRIVE* is "the very BEST in gay hard-core porn. Whatever your fantasies are, you'll see them acted out two-fold in graphic detail." **Where It's At** adds that "for members of the FFA there is a scene to tingle their elbows." **In Touch** says "As a collection of entertainment it can hardly be topped."

DRIVE is undoubtedly the film for the man who wants EVERYTHING. The beautiful men sport with each other in every conceivable location (from dungeons to steam rooms...from romantic trysts to furious orgies) and splash the screen with evidence of their passions. It is an action-adventure that will delight and excite you and your buddies as it has audiences from New York to Paris.

Filmed on location in New York's hottest discos and bathhouses, as well as exotic locations like Woodstock, *DRIVE* is the cream of the blue movies. The photography and original score are stunning, the acting superb and the SEX is so HOT, you'll wonder why your television doesn't burst into flames.

If you're curious about what it is that the sophisticated, beautiful men of New York do....If you've ever wondered just how EXCITING hot sex between men can be....If you want to enjoy the raunchy exploits of fifty of the most desireable men in the world over and over....Order Jack Deveau's *DRIVE*.

STUDIOSOUND is a special process that guarantees a high fidelity like you've never heard. Instead of the usual optical transfer of sound from film to tape, which limits the reproduction of sound to a narrow range of frequencies, StudioSound is a magnetic transfer of the ORIGINAL MAGNETIC STUDIO sound tracks for the feature, transferred directly to the magnetic tape in your video cassette. This process actually gives you BETTER QUALITY than can be achieved in a cinema. For further enhancement, you can patch your video system into your stereo system and surround yourself with the excitement of these sensual sounds.

Cast: Mary Jim Sstunning, Kirk Luna, Mark Woodward, Brian Destazio, Peter Fersen, Jack Brusca, Shawn Roberts and FIFTY VERY COMPULSIVE MEN.

Produced and directed by Jack Deveau • Edited by Robert Alvarez
Music by Stan Freeman and David Earnest

| JACK DEVEAU'S **DRIVE** | 76 MINUTES | COLOR | ALL-MALE CAST | **STUDIOSOUND** |

© Quality X Video Cassette Company, 1979

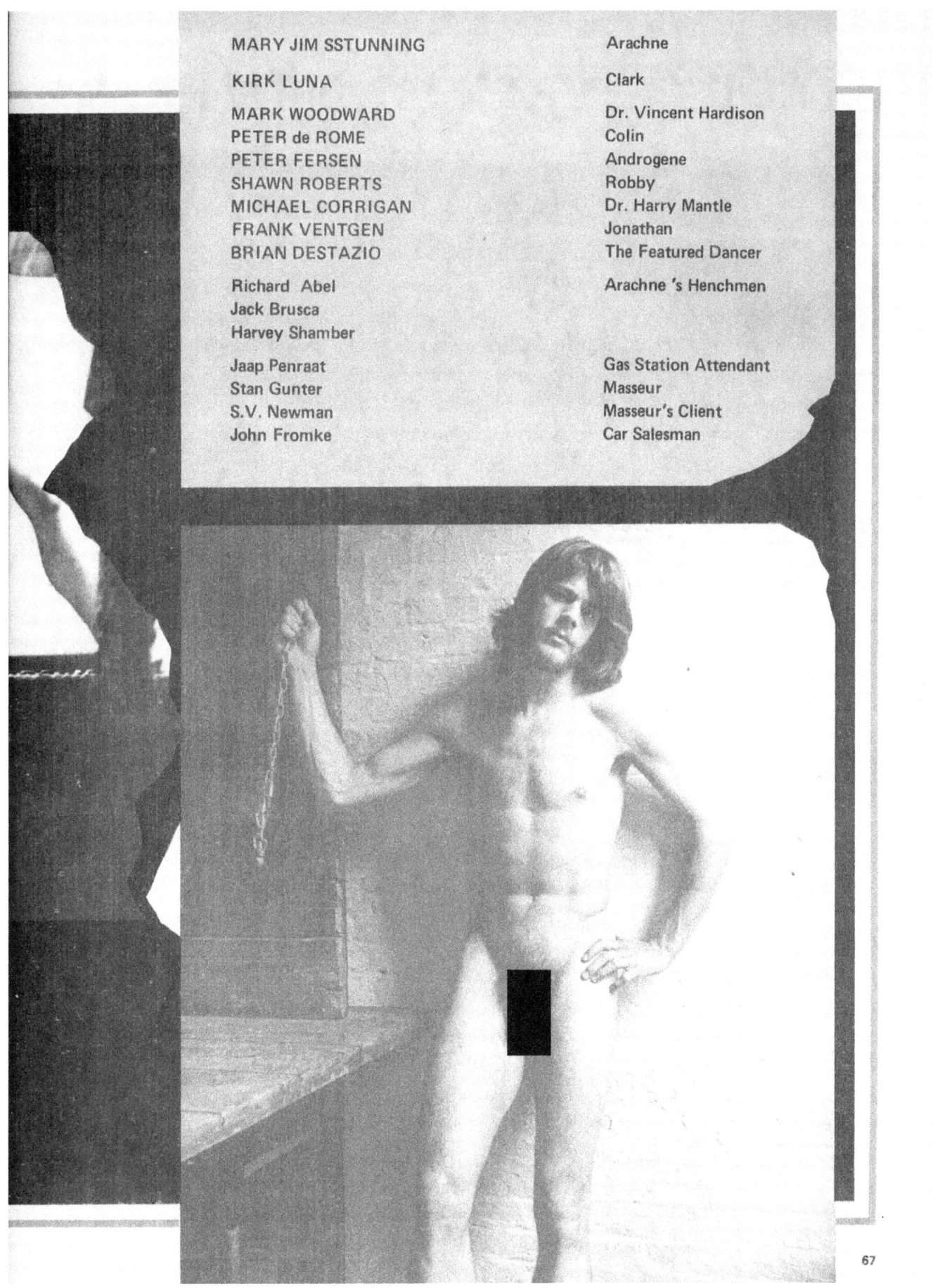

MARY JIM SSTUNNING	Arachne
KIRK LUNA	Clark
MARK WOODWARD	Dr. Vincent Hardison
PETER de ROME	Colin
PETER FERSEN	Androgene
SHAWN ROBERTS	Robby
MICHAEL CORRIGAN	Dr. Harry Mantle
FRANK VENTGEN	Jonathan
BRIAN DESTAZIO	The Featured Dancer
Richard Abel	Arachne's Henchmen
Jack Brusca	
Harvey Shamber	
Jaap Penraat	Gas Station Attendant
Stan Gunter	Masseur
S.V. Newman	Masseur's Client
John Fromke	Car Salesman

PLAYGUY IN AMERICA

by Clarke Taylor

Mark Woodward is interested in power politics. Strange, for a young man of twenty-six who manages the office of America's leading male pornographic film company. And yet, not so strange. As a student of political science at New Jersey's Farleigh-Dickinson University, Mark soon learned that he was interested in "subversive power" rather than "power up front." It was largely out of this realization that he began looking for alternatives to the "bullshit of school" during his sophomore year. One such alternative passed his way one night while haunting one of New York's gay bars, the Ninth Circle. Strangers often pass in the night here, but not so many who offer a change of lifestyle to bored young men. Mark (a pseudonym because his father is a prestigious attorney, not because he is concerned with his own position) is attractive. Blond, with a slim, muscular build, he would be sought out by many a stranger. This particular bar stranger asked him if he'd like to make a porno film, and with apparently little hesitation, he accepted the notion. It was while riding the elevator to the film producer's apartment for an audition that Mark met Case. The two became lovers after three days and remain so "for the rest of our lives." Case didn't get a part in the film, Mark did. The film was called DRIVE, now a classic in the catalogue of Hand In Hand Films. It was 1972. Mark's return to school *must* have seemed out of step to him. DRIVE introduced him to sex, drugs, parties, and an understanding of what there is about him – his mind and body – that will serve him best: where his power lies. The second film offer came by way of GOOD HOT STUFF, a compilation of film episodes intended to show how a porno film is made. Mark was asked to be in the now-classic Bagdad scene from that film. As a concubine to this fictitious Sultan, Mark's function was to perform an erotic dance which would entice the Sultan into a giant pool for a mass orgy. Above the pool, two huge, jade legs spread to form a hefty arched entrance. Between them, a giant cock pouring wine into the pool. Real panache. Determined for more eroticism and less academe, Mark spent the subsequent summer in Provincetown, Massachusetts, Mecca for gay Sultans, with encouragement from Case to go his own way for a while. Returning to New York Mark looked to Hand In Hand once more, this time for a more "subversive" role. It was 1974. He was made Production Coordinator, at fifty cents an hour, and was soon promoted to "Librarian," the guy who repairs the legions of film distributed by this company. He also started working with Peter De Rome on his latest film THE DESTROYING ANGEL. As of June 1, 1975 he has been Business Manager for the company, which amounts to organizing bookings, planning publicity, and, of course, keeping the till. He has, simply, been involved in every aspect of porno filmmaking but for wielding the camera, and this may not be far off. "I don't have time now to make films, but if Case and I wanted to make one, Hand In Hand would help us." The same self-confidence demonstrated here runs throughout Mark's dialogue. He is

MARK WOODWARD

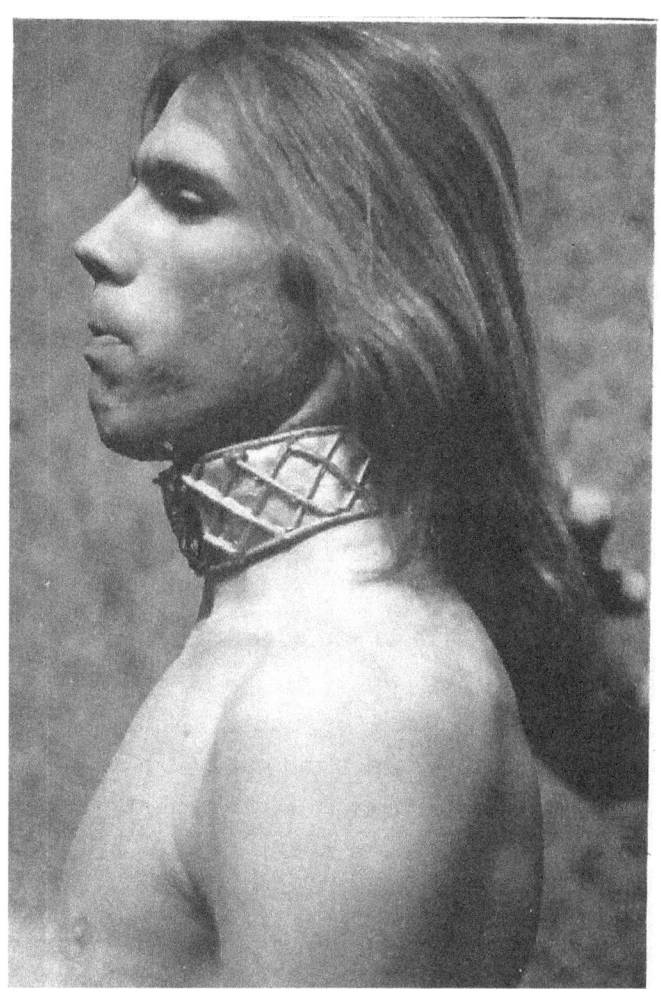

Mark Woodward in *Good Hot Stuff*

determined to do as he pleases, when he pleases. And while this may involve certain amounts of self-centredness, there is a certain freedom as well. So long as there is an understanding, Case and a bit of good fortune. "I have to be able to do whatever I want all the time. The first film gave me a lot of confidence. I had only come out nine months previous and I was very vulnerable. I needed attention; I was insecure. I feel a little less towards myself for having made a porno film, it's true, and I don't particularly want to be seen in one. It's not going to be *my* claim to fame. But I wanted to see myself on screen. I'm the vainest person I know. I want people to like me the way I am, but seeing myself on screen put me in an objective position; I wanted to see what people were seeing. And I see kids in Englewood (Mark's suburban New Jersey hometown) who are so narrow, they've not had experience. Anything is valuable if you can turn it into a good thing. I look very good in GOOD HOT STUFF. I may never look as good again. People tell me there's something about my style, the way I move, that I find interesting. I get off more on people's vibrations." Mark claims to have as much insight into why others make – and watch – films as he does into his own participation. "A lot of guys are interested in being in a movie. For one thing, they're introduced to a group of people who deal in sex. And it's difficult to find a good looking person who has his shit together. It's even more difficult to find one who'll make a film. People want to see a lot of fucking and sucking. And you don't need nice looking people for this; only two guys who can get off balling together. I've never really got off on the people I've had sex with in the films." It's difficult to judge who Mark *does* "get off on," except for Case, or whether he even wants to. "I like to stand in a bar's darkest corner and just watch other people doing their thing. I'm not usually there for the sex. The other night a guy was bothering me, so I put a cigarette out in his hand as he drew it near to me." Power politics. "As for long-range goals, well, I'd like to get into straight movie-making. I've always wanted to have enough money to do just what I want to do. But I'll stick with Hand In Hand as long as I get something out of it. I'm pretty much running the show now, the day-to-day part of it; the amount of work I do is inexhaustible. It's true that my chances of running for public office are not very good now that I've been involved in this business. But I wouldn't want to hold office representing people who are down on gay porno films – or on someone who has been in them – anyway, I don't want the office, because that's power up front. I'd rather be David Rockefeller (brother of the Vice-President, and real magnate of the family fortune) than Nelson."

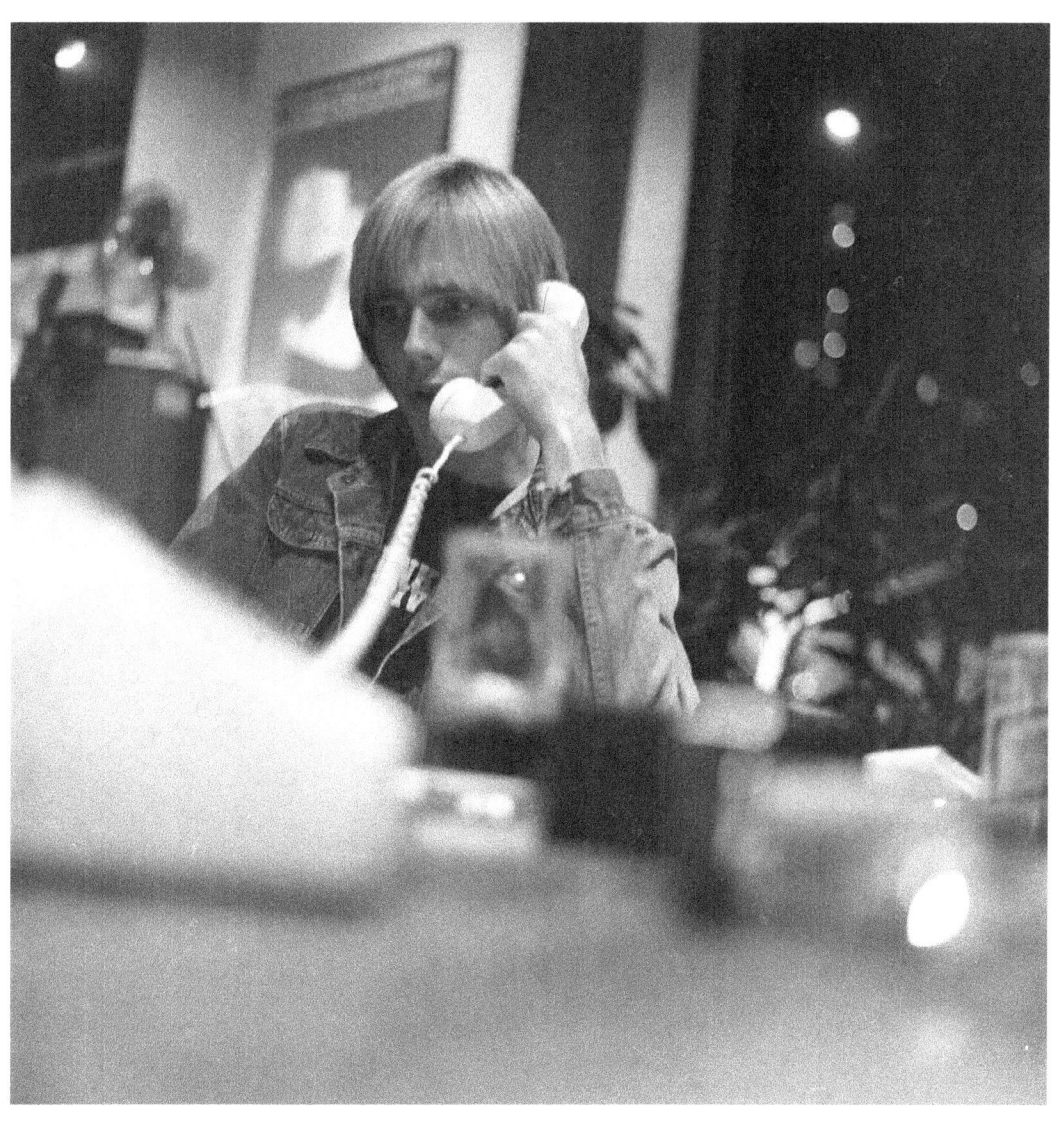

Mark Woodward doin´ work - behind the scenes of *A Night At The Adonis*.

to see myself on screen. I'm the vainest person I know. I want people to like me the way I am, but seeing myself on screen put me in an objective position; I wanted to see what people were seeing. And I see kids in Englewood (Mark's suburban New Jersey hometown) who are so narrow, they've not had experience. Anything is valuable if you can turn it into a good thing.

'I look very good in *Good Hot Stuff.* I may never look as good again. People tell me there's something about my style, the way I move, that I find interesting. *I* get off more on people's vibrations.'

Mark claims to have as much insight into why others make —and watch—films as he does into his own participation. 'A lot of guys are interested in being in a movie. For one thing, they're introduced to a group of people who deal in sex. And it's difficult to find a good looking person who has his shit together. It's even more difficult to find one who'll make a film. People want to see a lot of fucking and sucking. And you don't need nice looking people for this; only two guys who can get off balling together. I've never really got off on the people I've had sex with in the films.

It's difficult to judge who Mark *does* 'get off on', except for Case, or whether he even wants to.

'I like to stand in a bar's darkest corner and just watch other people do their thing. I'm not usually there for the sex. The other night a guy was bothering me, so I put a cigarette out in his hand as he drew it near to me.'

Power politics.

'As for long-range goals, well, I'd like to get into straight movie-making. I've always wanted to have enough money to do just what I want to do. But I'll stick with Hand 'n Hand as long as I get something out of it. I'm pretty much running the show now, the day-to-day part of it; the amount of work I do is inexhaustible.

'It's true that my chances of running for public office are not very good now that I've been involved in this business. But I wouldn't want to hold office representing people who are down on gay porno films—or on someone who has been in them—anyway. I don't want the office, because that's power up front. I'd rather be David Rockefeller (brother of the Vice-President, and real magnate of the family fortune) than Nelson.'

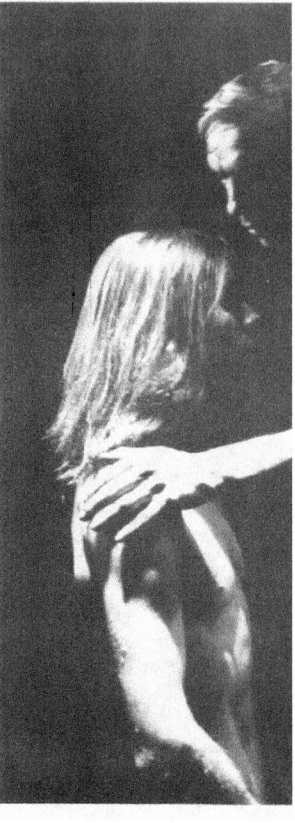

Woodward and James Bidgood

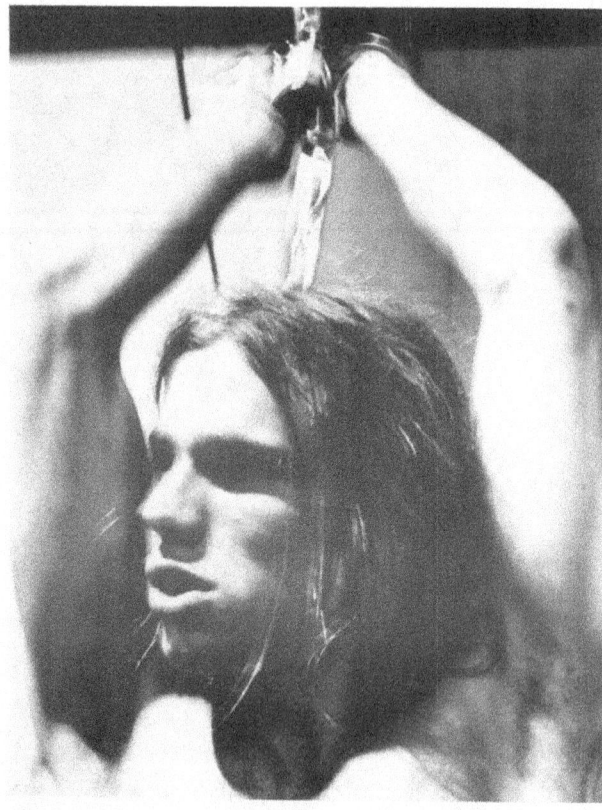

Woodward in *Drive*

Playguy in America.

Mark Woodward.

By Clarke Taylor—

Mark Woodward is interested in power politics. Strange, for a young man of twenty-six who manages the office of America's leading male pornographic film company. And yet, not so strange.

As a student of political science at New Jersey's Fairleigh-Dickinson University, Mark soon learned that he was interested in 'subversive power' rather than 'power up front'. It was largely out of this realisation that he began looking for alternatives to the "bullshit of school" during his sophomore year.

One such alternative passed his way one night while haunting one of New York's gay bars, the Ninth Circle. Strangers often pass in the night here, but not so many who offer a change of lifestyle to bored young men.

Mark (a pseudonym because his father is a prestigious attorney, not because he is concerned with his own position) is attractive. Blond, with a slim, muscular build, he would be sought out by many a stranger. This particular but stranger asked him if he'd like to make a porno film, and with apparently little hesitation, he accepted the notion.

It was while riding the elevator to the film producer's apartment for an audition that Mark met Case. The two became lovers after three days and remain so "for the rest of our lives". Case didn't get a part in the film. Mark did.

The film was called *Drive*, now a classic in the catalogue of Hand 'n Hand films. It was 1972.

Mark's return to school must have seemed out of step to him. *Drive* introduced him to sex, drugs, parties, and an understanding of what there is about him—his mind and body—that will serve him best: where his power lies.

The second film offer came by way of *Hot Stuff*, a compilation of film episodes intended to show how a porno film is made. Mark was asked to be the now-classic Bagdad scene from that film. As a concubine to this fictitious Sultan, Mark's function was to perform an erotic dance which would entice the Sultan into a giant pool for a mass orgy. Above the pool, two huge, jade legs spread to form a hefty arched entrance. Between them, a giant cock pouring wine into the pool. Real panache.

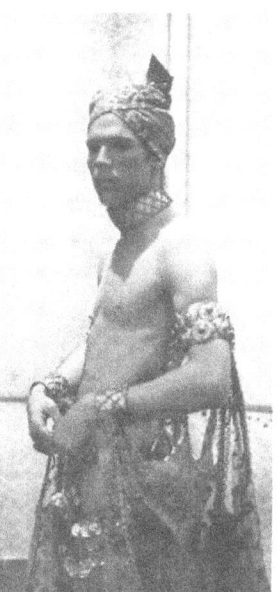

Mark Woodward waits for the cameras to roll in the Bagdad scene from 'Hot Stuff'. *Pictures courtesy of HAND IN HAND FILMS.*

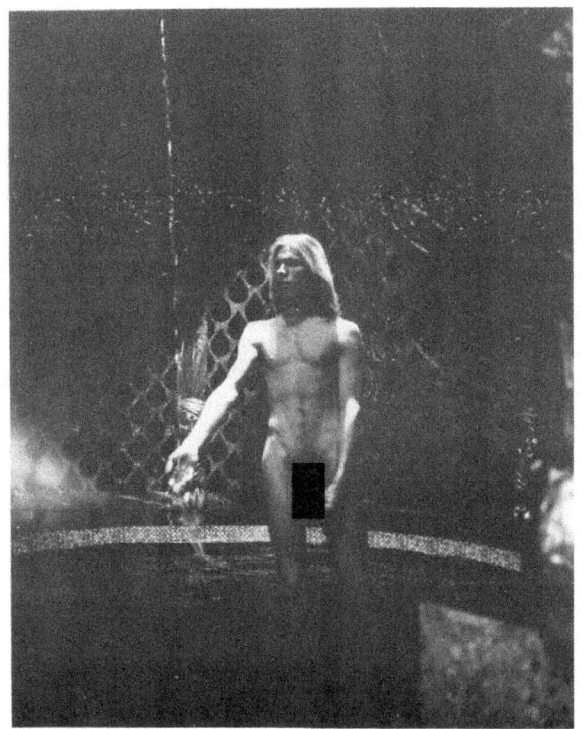

Waiting for the Sultan to arrive in 'Good Hot Stuff'.

Mark Woodward waits for the cameras to roll in the Bagdad scene from *Good Hot Stuff*.

Enter Christopher Rage

by Christopher Rage

Today I received in the mail a request from the editor of this magazine to contribute a few words about myself and my work for his thoughtfully sleazy magazine. He wrote that he was quite willing to accept any drivel I cared to pen, in any format that suited me. He suggested, "probably easier for you and a lot more honest for the magazine would be a brief piece in first person." Now I have to admit that in my ten or more years in and around pornography (excluding the years prior when I was only a masturbating consumer) this is the first and only time someone has brought up the topic of "honesty" at all. I was so shocked by the very idea that (in spite of my trepidations about such self-serving efforts) I could hardly refuse. Therefore, with the assurance that the reader understands I am only out for self-aggrandizement, I will proceed. Speaking of the truth, I have always felt that I came by my career in pornography honestly. The very first thing I ever remember writing for myself (outside of class assignments) was a one-page, one-paragraph description of a man standing at a urinal stroking his cock. I must have been about twelve when I wrote this and was no doubt describing an early sexual encounter. I don't remember much about it except that it got me so aroused that I went immediately to the bathroom and masturbated, after which I tore the paper into tiny pieces that I flushed. My mother could be trusted to discover any wandering from the proper path to salvation and I didn't dare save the thing, however erotic I thought it was.

It was ten or so years before I attempted any more graphic sexual writing. I had just moved to New York and was making a feeble attempt to support myself by hustling at the infamous intersection of 53rd Street and Third Avenue. My chief problems as a hustler were two-fold; I hated having sex with men I didn't find attractive; I was only good for one trick a night. Since this meant that I made forty dollars on a good night and nothing on an average night, I was forced to try and find some way to supplement my income. As is true of many would-be performers, I resisted the idea of taking a regular job since it would interfere with opportunities to audition. In reading the *Village Voice* I came across an ad soliciting pornographic manuscripts. I decided this was work I could do without having it get in the way of my acting or my prostitution and I immediately set to writing the first of twenty-six dirty books. Twenty of the books were "straight" and the remainder were gay. The longest it took me to write a book was three months (the first one) and the shortest was eighteen hours (the last). Practice may not make perfect in the case, but it did make speedy. At about the same time, I was strolling through Central Park one summer afternoon when I happened across a beautiful young man who was tripping. I took him home and later he invited me to a private screening of a porno film he had just performed in. At the screening, I met the director of the film, Arch Brown, who eventually asked if I would like to do a film for him. Although by then I didn't desperately need the money, it did sound like fun and I agreed immediately. A few months later when Arch asked if I'd like to do another one for him,

I *did* need the money and again agreed. It was during the filming of the second movie that Arch introduced me to Jack Deveau who was just setting up his own film production company, Hand In Hand Films. Jack first asked me to write and then appear in his second feature, DRIVE. The script I wrote with Jack called for an evil drag queen (the part was originally written for Lyn Carter) who was out to eliminate sex from the world. Carter was interested but unavailable. Jack and his partner Bob Alvarez decided I would be perfect for the part, although I'd never appeared in drag before, on or off screen. I guess they say potential. DRIVE was some eighteen months from conception to completion and during the time I worked on several of Jack's other films. For the first time I found out what it was like to be on the other side of the camera; casting, writing, promoting, advertising, and partying. Jack Deveau is without a doubt the *best* party-person I have ever met. He could easily be the basis for an "Uncle Mame" book. During succeeding years I worked primarily in advertising and spent some time managing several of New York's premiere and not-so-premiere all-male theatres. About six months ago, several of the people with whom I had worked approached me with the idea of putting together a video tape production on my own. Since I had done quite a bit of still photography for Arch Brown and others, and since I had managed several live sex shows in Manhattan, I had the contact with performers to get a cast of good-looking men together for the tapes. They had the money. Now we have the tapes. What was originally going to be one tape starring Richard Locke quickly turned into a three-tape project. The stars we rounded up included George Payne (very image conscious, always with a hard-on during taping, somewhat difficult, always The Star); Scorpio (one of the sweetest and most attractive men alive today); Lee Marlin (looks tough, acts likeable, one of the better actors in hardcore films); Richard Locke (handsome, articulate, perfectionist and a royal pain in the ass); Casey Donovan (who gets my vote as the most cooperative and sexiest man I've ever had in front of my camera); and many "newcomers" who were for the most part sexy and easy to work with. The question I'm asked second most (the first is "What is ___ really like?") is do I fuck with all the people I take pictures of. The answer is, of course, no. No more than I fuck with everyone I meet in bars. The trouble with most of the performers (trouble isn't really the right word) is that they are very into their own lifestyles, which frequently involve hustling and almost always involve "performing" which is to say being on stage. Those of you who've had (or tried to have) affairs with actors, models, hustlers or bartenders must know what I mean: These are very difficult people to become involved with, mostly because they tend to be very self-involved. I don't hold it against them. On the contrary, it's what makes them who they are. I just would rather be on the opposite side of the camera. And behind the camera is where you'll probably find me in the immediate future. If the public goes for these tapes as I think they will, then we'll be making more of them. And I'll continue looking for the hottest men around … not just for me, but for you too.

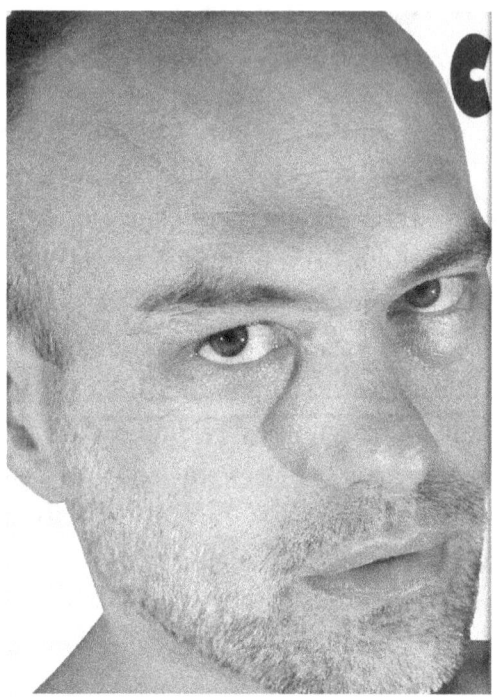

The late Christopher Rage

"I was a very horny kid. I was caught playing doctor with the little neighbor girls when I was three or four and I got into trouble for that. I didn't like getting into trouble so from then on, I avoided the little girls and started playing around with the little boys. And I liked that even better! Later, I discovered Athletic Model Guild. I'll never get over those gorgeous oiled bodies and those bulging posing straps. That was it! The beginning of Christopher Rage."

CHRISTOPHER RAGE

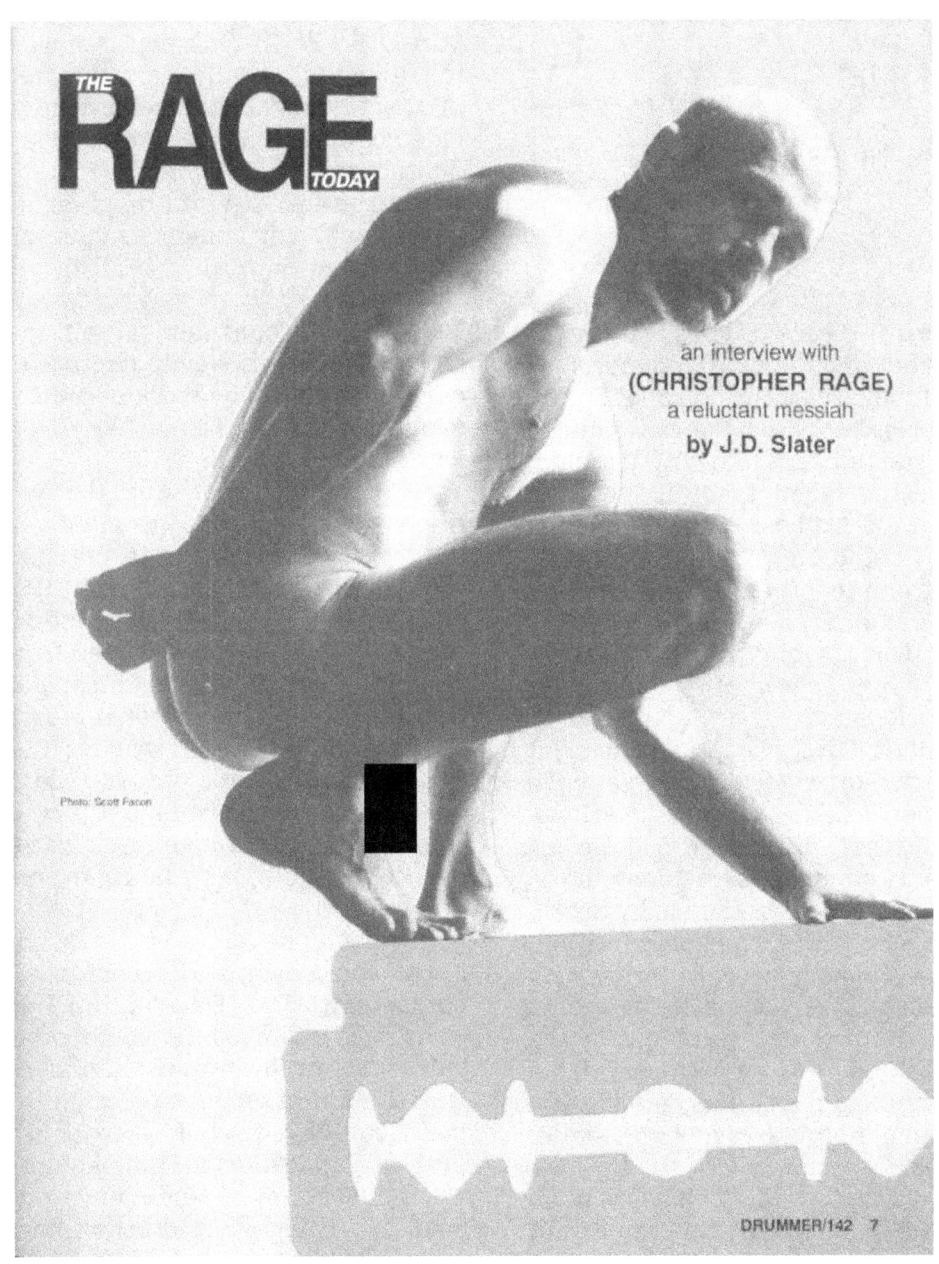

"I have no higher ambitions, I'm not compromising, and it's still physically sexy for me to make movies. Not while I'm actually filming, because obviously I have other things to consider during that time. But the idea of capturing the sexual act on film excites me and, of course, seeing the footage during the editing process gets me off."

CHRISTOPHER RAGE

HENK VAN DIJK
Ballet Down The Times Square

Marco Siedelmann: Please tell me about your relationship to ballet and dancing in general.
Henk Van Dijk: I took a class at National Ballet; I just joined the class for about ten years until I was thirty-one. I started very late with dancing, and I didn't have the talent to do it on a top level. Jack Deveau did his best to make me look as a top dancer. I could only do one pirouette. They put four of them together, so it looked like four pirouettes. *(Laughter)*
Siedelmann: So what's your profession, what do you do for a living, and what's your career all about?
Van Dijk: Actually I have two professions. At first I'm a cameraman, since 1974 I've been recording the performers for the National Ballet, and I still do that. Other than that, I work for several different companies, fashion shows, operas. I made documentaries, especially for my partner Hans van Manen. He's a choreographer. The other career is the body work. I started with massages, and then I became a professional Rolfing therapist. Both things came out of the dance for me. Both come from capturing from a distance, and knowing the bodies very close. I know what's happening to a body when I see it. I see the emotions.
Siedelmann: You didn't want to have a huge career in it, but the dancing was very important for you?
Van Dijk: I enjoyed doing it, and I got involved in the dance world. I already knew my partner back then, almost 45 years now. He was filming his own ballets, which wasn't usual at the time. He used the first semi-industrial video cameras for that. He bought one right away when it came to the market. I got interested in the equipment, and after a few years, he asked me if I would like to try it. I never thought about it before in a serious way, but I tried it, and sort of copied his formula to capture the choreography. You follow the dancers in a dynamic way, you know? Basically I stretched his formula throughout the years and made it more filmic.
Siedelmann: Have you always been fascinated by the camera eye, were you a movie lover or into still photography earlier in your life?
Van Dijk: Yes, I took pictures when I was a teenager, but I really started to gain interest in the technical side of it when I started video work. But I always liked film and photography. I still do.
Siedelmann: Are you more of a technical person when it comes to your profession? Do you film with an eye of an architect or an artist?
Van Dijk: I consider myself more of an artist. My art is a way to capture dance. You can see some of my work in public.
Siedelmann: BALLET DOWN THE HIGHWAY was made in 1975...
Van Dijk: No, that was the year of the release, it was shot in 1974. They were filming another movie at the same time, I think it was WANTED: BILLY THE KID. The editing and the post-production process took a long time. It was filmed from October to December 1974, and the release was in September the year after. I was 22 during the time we did BALLET DOWN THE HIGHWAY.
Siedelmann: How did you come to the project? When did you meet Jack Deveau?
Van Dijk: I had a love affair with a dancer – Ernest - who was American, and he was going back to the United States to dance with a company in New York. He wanted me to come over, and he actually made the contact with Jack Deveau, but I don't know if he was involved in some other project with him, or just knew him personally. It was the idea that he was going to play the main part, my part. I was going to do the part of Jeff Sullivan, the younger dancer. Then Ernest got an engagement and wasn't available anymore to do the filming, so the main role shifted to me. I had to send some pictures of myself. My partner, Hans, also had a photography career, so we did a series of stills of me. The next thing that happened was that Jack Deveau sent me the tickets for a flight; he invited me to come over. I was supposed to be there for six weeks, but some scenes had to be re-done, so it turned out to be more than two and a half months.
Siedelmann: So you were really confident about your sexuality at the time, did you have an early coming out?
Van Dijk: Hmm... rather around seventeen

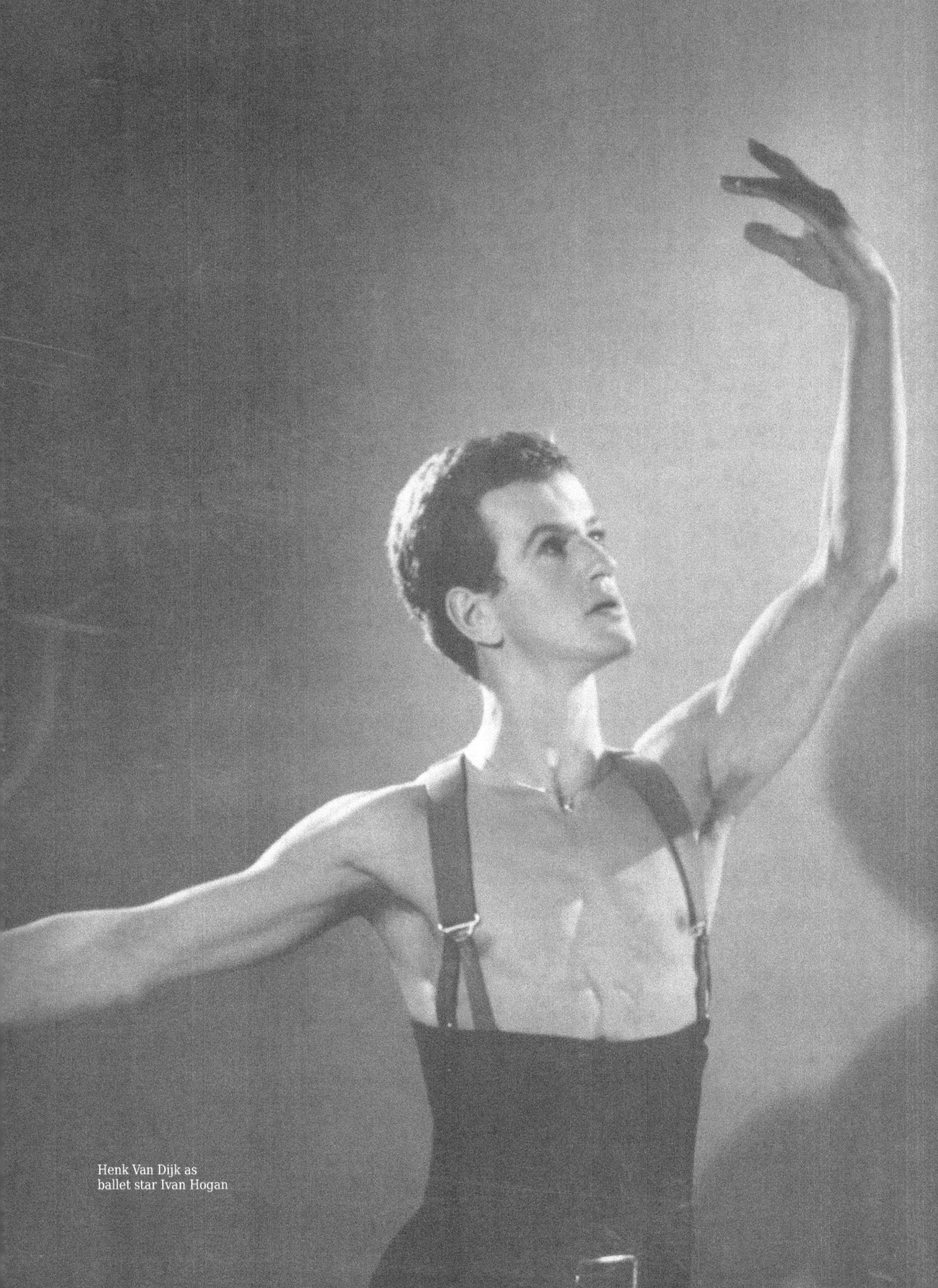

Henk Van Dijk as ballet star Ivan Hogan

or eighteen, yeah. I was still in high school.
Siedelmann: Of course it's always a difficult process, but was it very hard for you? Did you grow up in a liberal environment?
Van Dijk: There were some issues, but for me it wasn't very difficult. The nice thing was that I always was playing with boys and men from a very early age on. At the time I discovered gay life, I realized there was something like a gay culture. There was a possibility not only to have gay sex, but to be in love, to be exclusive with a man in a relationship. That was new for me at the time. Of course there were social issues in school, and at home. It just happened. And time was on my side. In the sixties things would become more liberal in general, so I was comfortable about myself. I never suffered from it. I didn't have a religious background; I quit going to church when I was twelve.
Siedelmann: Did you experience the Netherlands as a very liberal country as well? Was it very open?
Van Dijk: Indeed, it was very progressive at the time.
Siedelmann: And how did you experience New York at the time?
Van Dijk: I was born and raised in Amsterdam, so for me the next big city to go to would be New York. I was always fascinated, especially with music from the United States. Then my partner started to work in America. He did some ballet dance in Pennsylvania, and at the weekends he would go to New York, so when he came back he told me we should go there. I was completely overwhelmed when we did that, and with the love affair on top, it was heaven. Then of course I went there to do the movie a few months after. It was very nice to have such an experience at that age. It was very self-sufficient, and I got to know that big city really fast: when people asked me about directions in the streets they used to think I was a native New Yorker. *(laughing)* New York always was a special place for me. I also did my Rolfing studies there, and I spent a lot of holidays in New York and Fire Island when it was very popular and lively. But looking back, I'm kind of glad I never moved there. I still love to live in Amsterdam. But putting all the times together I went there I almost spent two years of my life in New York. I know the city quite well.
Siedelmann: Did you go to the gay clubs with Jack Deveau and the people from the Hand In Hand circle? Or was that separated?
Van Dijk: Yes, it was more or less separated. Hand In Hand was the work part. Of course, we got private a little, but we never engaged real friendship with all the people. But I remember some of them very well, for example Tom De Simone.
Siedelmann: Tom De Simone suffered from the work schedules and the production process by Hand In Hand films; did that show?
Van Dijk: I can imagine that, he was involved both in BALLET DOWN THE HIGHWAY and WANTED: BILLY THE KID, so he probably had a very busy schedule. But I remember him as a very kind person, very talented, respectful, and professional. The whole atmosphere was nice, and I also enjoyed that some parts of BALLET DOWN THE HIGHWAY were shot in Jack and Bob's apartment.
Siedelmann: Was working with Jack Deveau like working with a "pornographer"? Do you consider the Hand In Hand films as more than all-male adult movies?
Van Dijk: No, of course not. Jack Deveau made feature films with sex in them; they always tried to put the sex into a regular narrative film at the time. Hand In Hand always had the special feeling in their films, as it was normal to show hardcore in a feature.
Siedelmann: What also makes a difference: BALLET DOWN THE HIGHWAY is not only a light feature film, it's also very sad in many ways...
Van Dijk: You think so?
Siedelmann: Yes, don't you agree on that?
Van Dijk: No. I think it's just a love story about me and the younger dancer, and the truck driver affair.
Siedelmann: I think the Garry Hunt character is very tragic.
Van Dijk: Tragic... – why?
Siedelmann: Because of his sexual desires he doesn't really belong to the heterosexual community and his working class friends, but he also doesn't fit into the sophisticated people of Manhattan.
Van Dijk: Well, that's true. It's never nice to be rejected in such a situation, but the romantic part of the love story is really between the two dancers. The truck driver storyline is the rough part. Don't forget that he's making it all worse again and again during the movie. I wouldn't feel too sorry about him.
Siedelmann: How do you remember Garry Hunt, who played the part of the truck driver?
Van Dijk: He was a nice person for sure. I must say he was the best actor in the film.
Siedelmann: In other films he shows lots

of humorous talent, so I agree that he was a remarkable actor. Was he serious about the acting, or was he more of a relaxed person during the shooting?
Van Dijk: I think everybody was very laid back. We had a good working relationship, and he was fun to be around with. So yes, I also think he had sense for humor.
Siedelmann: Have you ever questioned yourself before having sex on camera?
Van Dijk: No, this just came my way. I had no objections about it; I was eager to get into that experience. It was one thing when I accepted the role, I thought to myself: "I can never be the prime minister of Holland." But that was really the only thing in terms of career chances, and so forth. *(laughing)* – All of my friends were very open for that, and it was very exciting to talk about it. A few years later – I think it was 1978, or something – the movie was shown here in Holland at the Gay and Lesbian Film Festival. Of course I went to see it, and afterwards when I was standing at the exit the people came out of the theatre. Some of them recognized me, some of them looked at me with a lot of aspiration, and others of them looked at me with disgust. *(laughing)* – Well, I didn't want my parents to know about it, of course. My brothers and sisters knew a little bit, but we never told my parents.
Siedelmann: Before BALLET DOWN THE HIGHWAY was shown at the festival, was there any chance to see it or buy it in the Netherlands anyway?
Van Dijk: No. I got my own copy years after when the VHS or Betamax. Actually I bought it myself in New York. Of course there were gay movies here in Amsterdam, but all regular ones, none of the Hand In Hand films, or other feature films from the Golden Age era. That was a very different genre, and totally unknown here. They were never really widespread, basically Hand In Hand was only known in the United States. Also in America, BALLET DOWN THE HIGHWAY was shown in porn theaters, but only in a few cities – New York, Chicago, and Los Angeles – and as a very limited release.
Siedelmann: What kind of gay pornography was available in the Netherlands in those days?
Van Dijk: Hmm, there was nothing on TV of course. There were porn theaters, but they didn't show feature films. Later there were videos, and also there were a few magazines. The industry here wasn't that big.

Siedelmann: And how about New York, did you go to an X-rated cinema there? Have you ever been to the legendary Adonis?
Van Dijk: Yes!
Siedelmann: Was it an exciting experience?
Van Dijk: Well, everything new was exciting at the time, but you get used to it very fast. The setting and the atmosphere was very important. Have you ever heard about the gay live shows in small theaters around Times Square? They were very popular at the time. I mean boys doing striptease; masturbation and real sex was forbidden there. But we had a huge gay scene here in Amsterdam, a lot of parties in clubs and warehouses, also a very big leather and fetish scene.
Siedelmann: Hand In Hand films also were very popular for using more raunchy stuff like fisting scenes or urination.
Van Dijk: Yes, they used pretty much all the clichés from that time, and all kind of types. The construction worker, the cowboy, whatever…
Siedelmann: How did you experience Jack Deveau as a director during the shooting of BALLET DOWN THE HIGHWAY? Did he give you a lot of advice?
Van Dijk: No, very limited. He trusted me a lot, and he let it happen in a very free and open way. I rehearsed a lot with Lorenzo Mans, the guy who wrote the script. Getting to know the text was usually ok, and I felt very confident about the fact that I had never acted before. I must say that Jack Deveau gave me a lot of freedom. The way I did it, he usually agreed with. But I think the sex part of the film is not the strongest part. I wish I could have performed better. I think in terms of the sex it wasn't so easy, because I was all covered with body make-up which gets into your mouth when you kiss or suck someone, and then the soundman comes, asking to do it another time. That can be very distracting, you know? – Fun fact: Jim Delegatti, who assisted the make-up artist Gene Kelton, did one cumshot for me. I just couldn't do in time, and he helped out. *(Laughs)* – Jim was a very sexy guy! By the way, I'm very glad to hear that so many guys of the Hand In Hand circle are still around; I thought that nearly all of them died during the AIDS era. At least that happened to Jeff Sullivan, my acting partner in BALLET DOWN THE HIGHWAY. He was dancing with a ballet company as well, and he came to Holland in 1977, that was the last time I saw him.
Siedelmann: Was it romantic between the both of you during the shooting of BALLET?
Van Dijk: Not really. No, but sex was easy at that age and in that time. It was just normal,

part of our life. We were all very much uncomplicated about it. BALLET DOWN THE HIGHWAY shows a very natural image of gay life during that era.

Siedelmann: Yes, more or less the films of Jack Deveau are pretty much the beginning of queer cinema.

Van Dijk: Probably, yes. The movie tells you about the issues, but not really in a problematic way. It's not like it is specifically socially engaged to something. But it tells a lot how it was back then, about the atmosphere of that time, that's true. It's about being free, enjoying your body and the sex with several partners, but also about the search for a fulfilling love. That always goes together. Afterwards it all had a different weight, and it was less free than in the 70s.

Siedelmann: BALLET DOWN THE HIGHWAY is one of the very rare examples that created a symbiotic dualism between porno and regular feature film.

Van Dijk: That's true, in a way it was quite progressive. It was forward for its time.

Siedelmann: You did not see the film at the premier in New York, right?

Van Dijk: No, I didn't. But my lover was there, and he told me about it afterwards. I couldn't go at the time. Maybe it was because of money, or because of another engagement – I don't know.

Siedelmann: Did you ever meet Jack Deveau again?

Van Dijk: No, I don't think so. I met Bob Alvarez again when he came here one time to show some Hand In Hand films – including BALLET DOWN THE HIGHWAY – at a gay film festival. And that was it, other than that I never met someone of Hand In Hand again. Many of them died early, though – in the Netherlands the AIDS epidemic wasn't as extreme as in the United States. But of course I lost many friends, too. It was definitely happening, but not on the same scale as in New York or San Francisco.

Siedelmann: Has that changed your view on sexuality? Many people gave up on sex, at least for a while, because it was so depressing and frightening at the same time.

Van Dijk: Yes, that was definitely the case for a few years. Of course in the beginning the rules weren't clear, you know? There was so little known about it. There was some unsafe behavior. And I did that too. Looking back I have the feeling that I passed through the eye of a needle, I easily could have been infected as well. For example I gave a blow-job to a well-known dancer here, and shortly afterwards it got into the public that he was positive as well. Especially at that time I was quite worried. The tests were very complex at the time, you had to wait three months, and another three months to be absolutely sure. There were lots of insecurities around.

Siedelmann: It really ended the party of a whole era.

Van Dijk: That's true, because the sixties were the first time in history people could have sex open and unprotected. There was basically only syphilis to worry about, but that was curable. AIDS was the death sentence, so it was the end of the so-called Golden Age.

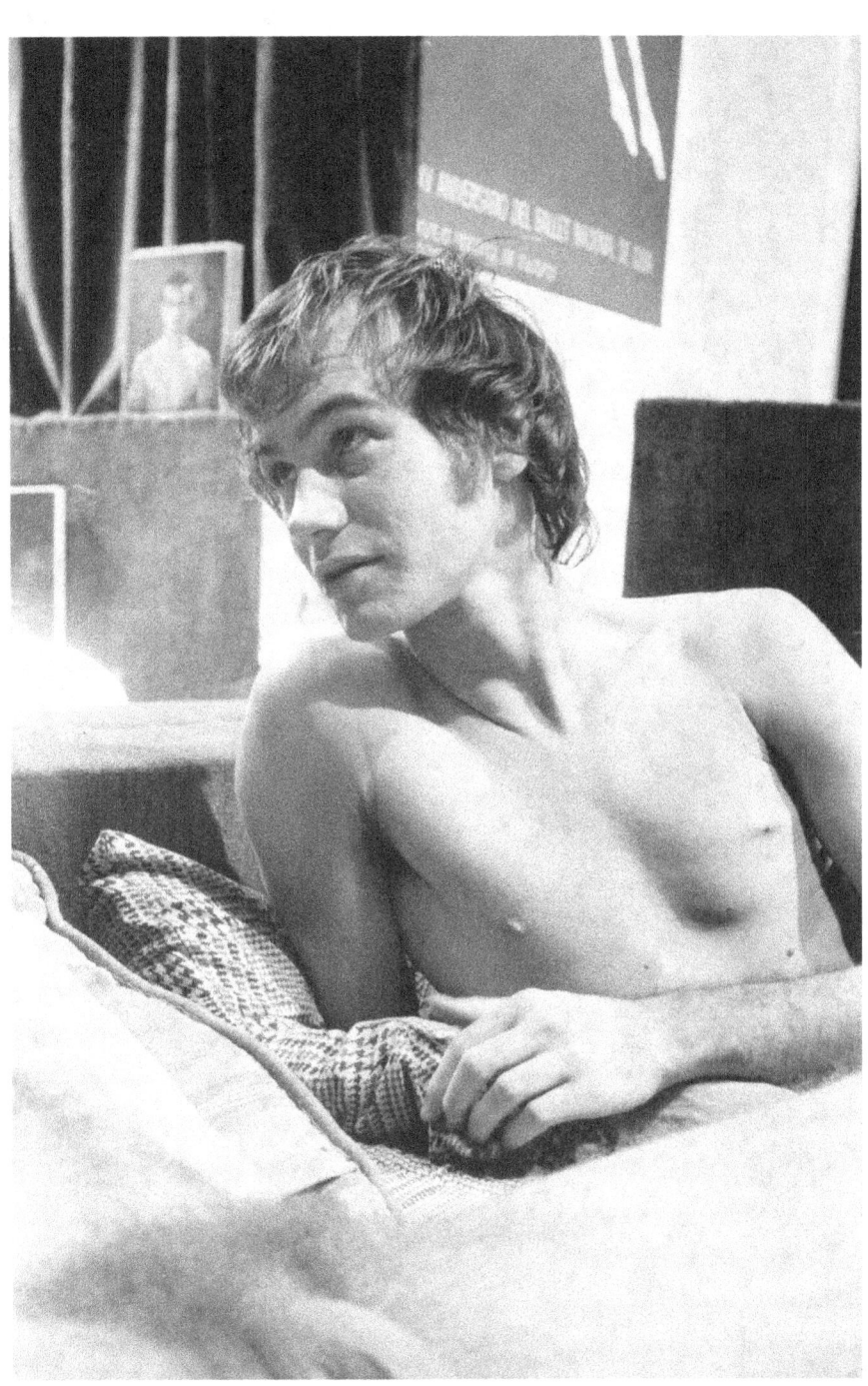
Jeff Sullivan in *Ballet Down The Highway*

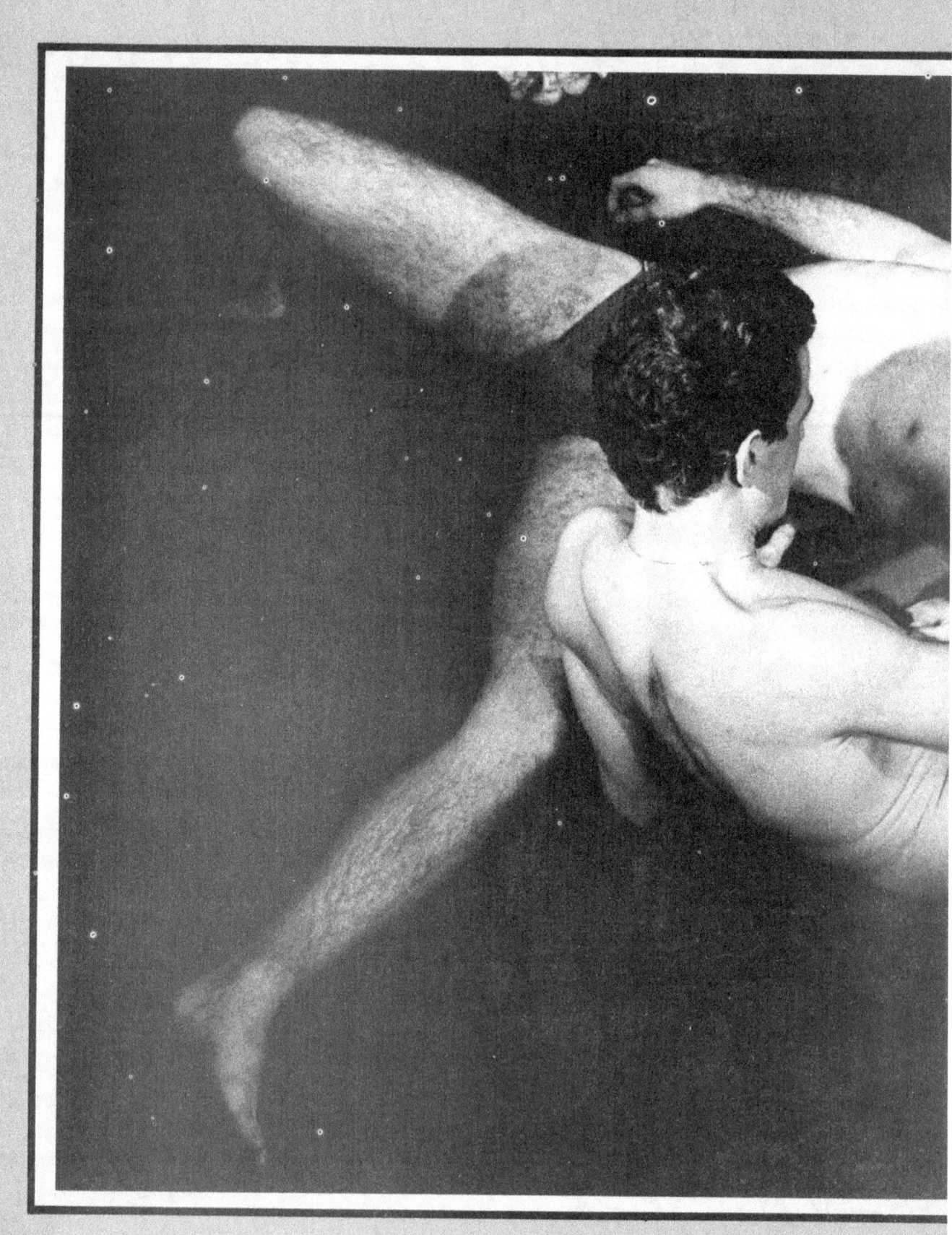

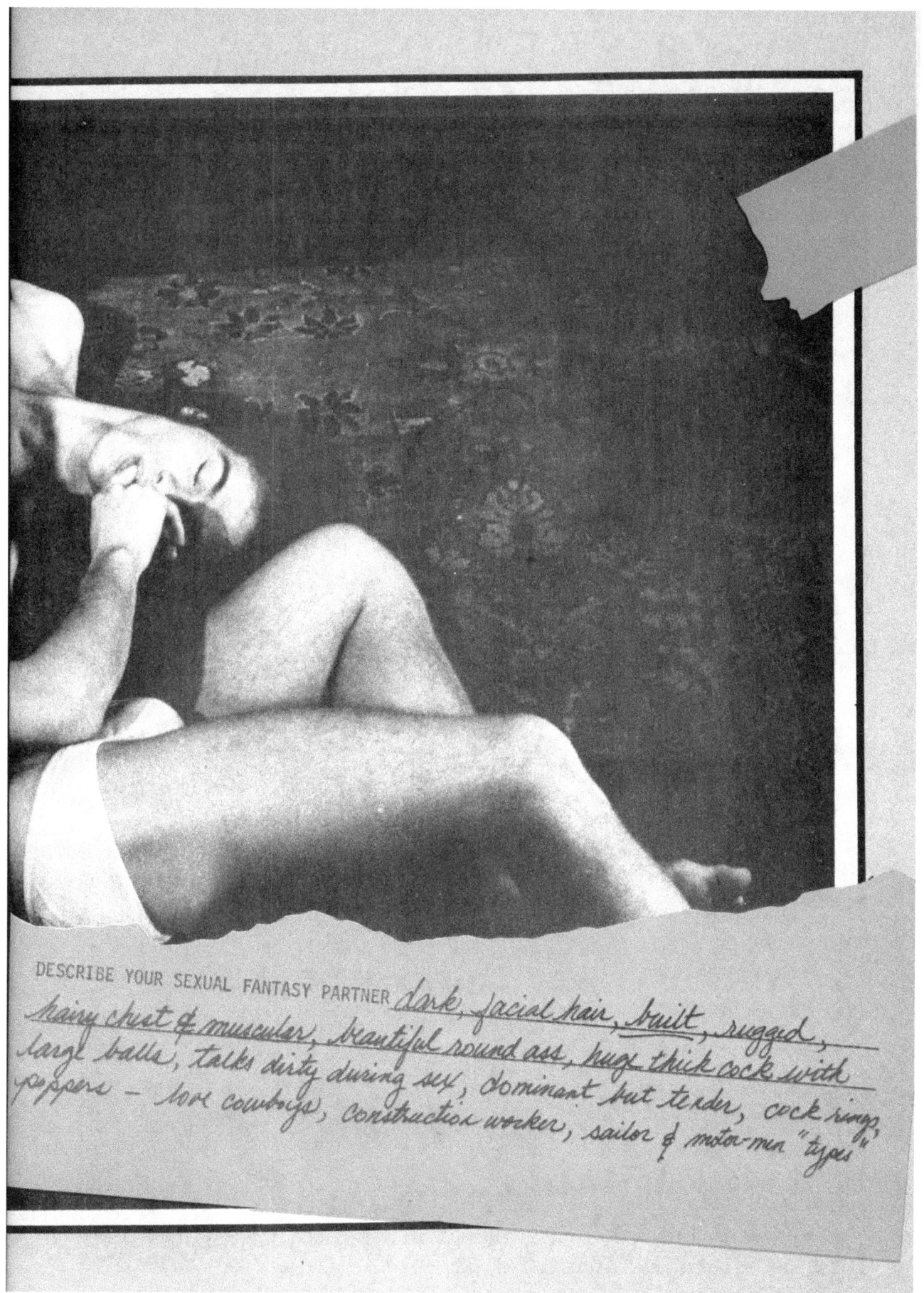

DESCRIBE YOUR SEXUAL FANTASY PARTNER dark, facial hair, built, rugged, hairy chest & muscular, beautiful round ass, huge thick cock with large balls, talks dirty during sex, dominant but tender, cock rings, poppers — love cowboys, construction worker, sailor & motor-men "types"

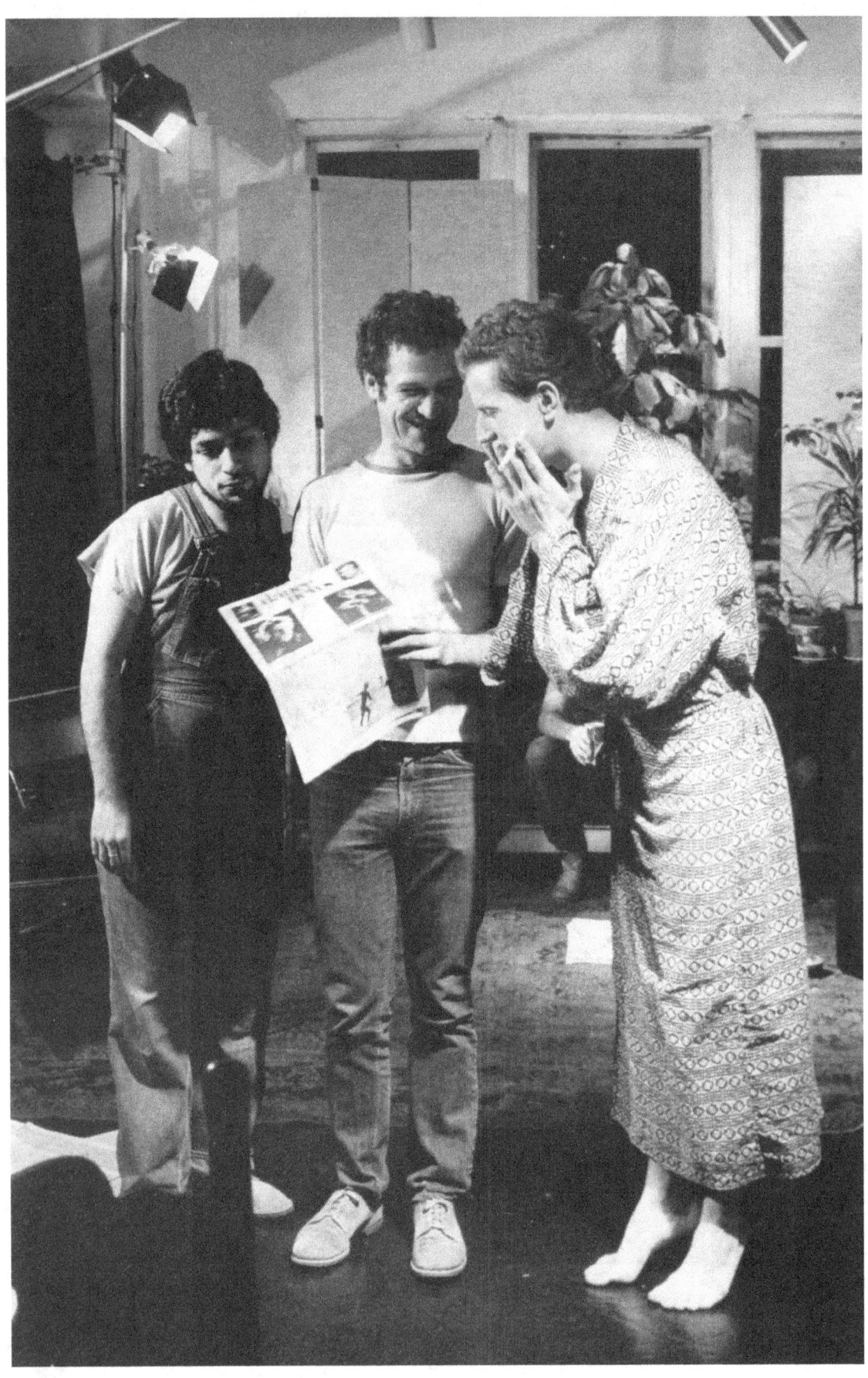

Fun at work: Lorenzo Mans, Jack Deveau, and Henk Van Dijk during the shooting of *Ballet Down the Highway*

LORENZO MANS
The Reluctant Gay Porn Writer

Marco Siedelmann: What do you remember mostly about Jack Deveau?
Lorenzo Mans: Well, I don't know if you know that about him, but he was a very good cook. Before he delved into film – whatever sort – he was very into this passion. I'm very vague about it, but it wasn't cooking books, I don't remember what form or shape, but he learned it totally on his own. He didn't take classes; he didn't go to school, or any of that. He had a little business, I don't recall what it was, but his first enterprise was involved in trying to teach cooking. Maybe there were cassettes, but I'm not really sure what form they took.
Siedelmann: You were a professional writer already at the time, is this correct?
Mans: Yeah. I have written screenplays. Some of which have been produced. Then I have written plays. Some of which have been produced. And I have had other professions in film, like I was a production designer. Oh, and I also acted in a couple of films as a very young person. So I did all kinds of things. But about Jack Deveau, what really comes back to me – and that is pretty much the only honest memory, I'm disturbed by anything else – was that he and Bob Alvarez lived in a beautiful penthouse. I'm not sure; I think Bob Alvarez kept it.
Siedelmann: Yes, that's true; he still lives in the same apartment. I can hook you guys up if you like to meet him again.
Mans: No, I would much rather not. It's not that I don't still like him, but I really just feel that I don't have any nostalgia or desires to keep up with memories that have faded. I like to keep 'em that way, but I can tell you that during the first years when I was friends with Jack, I was invited over lots of times to eat. It wasn't Nouvelle Cuisine, but still kind of French Cuisine. It was very traditional French, and those were really meals that I remember liking. Of course I don't remember exactly what we ate, but I certainly remember what a wonderful host he was for all of his friends. The conversations were ... light.
Siedelmann: You were around in some independent film and avant-garde film circles.
Mans: Yes. *(laughing)* You can look me up at imdb if you want.
Siedelmann: I did. You also were involved with the legendary INTAR Theater.
Mans: Right. That was a company for which I worked, I would say as a dramaturge and a manager. I was working with them for a long time.
Siedelmann: It specialized in Latino topics?
Mans: Well; it specialized in Latino plays in English language. For example, we worked with Mario Vargas Llosa and Manuel Puig, the author of *Kiss of the Spider Woman*. So they were involved with lots of acclaimed writers. They supported Latino playwrights who wrote in English or even hardly knew Spanish, and we produced some American playwrights as well. We got pretty good reviews for a while, and then the whole thing just died out, technically. *(Laughter)*
Siedelmann: You worked under an alias with Hand In Hand, which was P.P. Mans.
Mans: That was Jack's idea. See, I was a member of the Writer's Guild, and a couple of other things, and I have to admit: I was a little shy using my real name. Somehow Jack came up with giving me a synonym. But I think I only used it one time on something called BALLET DOWN THE HIGHWAY. That's it. But I was around sometimes. Basically not as a writer, but somehow when they needed a little dialogue I would give it to them. Eventually Jack thought that my kind of style was too humorous for that kind of porn that sold better.
Siedelmann: At least you are credited for some dialogue and continuity in another movie called ROUGH TRADES.
Mans: ...and quite a few others. Basically I hung around as something they normally call script girl. You know, some work here and there. There was a British person who made films for them; I cannot recall his name...
Siedelmann: Peter De Rome?
Mans: Oh yes, thank you. I remember him being a wonderful person. He was really charming. Before he made films for Jack Deveau just by himself, he made little films, somewhere between home movies and underground art. They were quite nice. I remember a guerilla film of him where two men kind of have sex – not totally hardcore – in a subway.
Siedelmann: That's UNDERGROUND.
Mans: Yes, exactly.
Siedelmann: Were you at the shooting?

Mans: Yeah, I was there. I was kinda like scouting to see if there was any danger. I was looking for cops! That was my role with Peter De Rome when he went underground and for a few other ventures. *(laughing)* I pretended not to be there, I wasn't exactly in the same car. I was always ready to show up and prevent any arrest.
Siedelmann: Was there any incident with the cops?
Mans: No!
Siedelmann: So you did a good job.
Mans: Probably, yes. There were also some shootings in busses. You know, now everybody's taking pictures and little videos on whatever, but at that time it was very strange to see somebody taking pictures of strangers without asking for permission.
Siedelmann: So were you introduced to Peter De Rome by Jack Deveau, or did you know him before?
Mans: Actually, I knew everybody because Bob Alvarez very early on was an assistant film editor for some movies directed by Jim McBride. Sometimes Bob worked for him as an assistant editor, but other times he was a little more than that for Jim McBride. That's how I met Alvarez, and then one thing led to another, and at some point he invited me for dinner. That's the way I became a friend of Jack Deveau.
Siedelmann: That was probably when Jim McBride started out as a filmmaker?
Mans: Right!
Siedelmann: With DAVID HOLZMAN'S DIARY...
Mans: ... which I acted in, yes. Well, that's basically how my connection with Hand In Hand started. I was friends with a lot of people around Michael Wadleigh, who was the cinematographer on DAVID HOLZMAN'S DIARY. He was kind of like the main person on WOODSTOCK, and he worked together on that film with Bob Alvarez. Even Martin Scorsese was an editor back then. I got to know everybody, because there was this revival at a movie house called Bleecker Street Cinema which was run by Lionel Rogsin. That was my first real job: house manager for the Bleecker Street Cinema.
Siedelmann: How old were you at the time?
Mans: A teenager. *(laughing)*
Siedelmann: Originally you are Cuban?
Mans: Well, yes, I was born in Cuba. My family comes from the Pyrenees, they are originally Huguenot, and so they were sort of rebellious Protestants. My last name has to do with that my family a long, long time ago came from Le Mans. At some point they had to leave because they were Huguenot, and they went to the Dutch part of Belgium I believe. Somehow there were old people always in my family who talked about the persecution of the Huguenots. I guess centuries afterwards. *(laughing)* – Just like the Jewish people will talk about the Holocaust for centuries. I kinda inherited that, and even when I was a young boy in Cuba, it seemed to me that my family lived more in centuries past than in the present.
Siedelmann: So you were an eye witness of the Cuban revolution, is this possible?
Mans: No. *(laughing)* – Well, I was there as a young person during the very beginning of the revolution, but *(whispering)* my family pretended it wasn't happening. *(laughing)* Also, somehow they pretended we weren't living there at all. You know, my family migrated so many times during the centuries, and we ended up in the Pyrenees where a lot of people came to, running away from whatever. We went to Cuba mostly because my father got a job teaching math. That's what he did. And because he taught math he lived kind of in a very abstract world. My mother was a classical musician, so she also lived in an abstract world. At some point, when I first came to the United States people kept asking me questions about the Cuban (pre-)revolution, and I actually was embarrassed. Just because I grew up pretending it wasn't happening. I never ended up thinking of myself as Cuban, and once when I came to New York it was very easy to be a New Yorker; simple as that.
Siedelmann: Was it the first city you came to in the United States?
Mans: Yes.
Siedelmann: Did you stay there for your whole career, or did you move around in the USA?
Mans: Not really. I made a film with Jim McBride in California and then got hired to write a script that never got made into a film. You know, it was the usual story: We sold it, started shooting, but for some reason it didn't evolve. Jim stayed in California, but I was always very anxious to go back to New York City. From all the places I could have been, I always preferred to be not only in New York City, but in Manhattan.
Siedelmann: Jim McBride and Michael Wadleigh; were they also friends with Jack Deveau?
Mans: No, they never met him.
Siedelmann: But you are still friends with Jim McBride?
Mans: Yes, actually we exchange long emails almost daily.

Siedelmann: I also did extended interviews with another filmmaker you once worked with: Joseph Zito.
Mans: Oh, my God.
Siedelmann: *(laughing)* So you remember Joe Zito?
Mans: Oh, do I ever. *(laughing)* – Yes. See, throughout my life I always tried to figure out what I am going to do in terms of having a career. At least I wanted to make a little bit of money. For some crazy circumstances I ended up meeting somebody called Louis Jackson who made a film about a man who believed that he's the real Santa Claus. It's called CHRISTMAS EVIL. I ended up being the production designer for that film, because I had inherited an enormous amount of Christmas decor.
Siedelmann: Oh, of course. Another title is YOU BETTER WATCH OUT.
Mans: Correct! That was the original title, but for the commercial release it was titled CHRISTMAS EVIL. Anyhow, don't ask me why I inherited this entire Christmas decor, but my collection included some plastic Santas with light in them, all kinds of stuff – you just name it. That's why I got the job; I could furnish all these props for YOU BETTER WATCH OUT. Joe Zito saw it, loved it, and asked me to be the production designer of THE PROWLER. Anyhow, I enjoyed working for that one, especially working with the famous Tom Savini, who did the special effects for it. I was treated by everybody as I was the artist during the production. I didn't create it as a typical slasher movie; I wanted it to be very classy. We shot it in Cape May, which is this gingerbread weird town in the most southern part of New Jersey. I also knew some old people who owned houses there, and they rented them to us. So I provided kinda real places, and then we hired a guy who rented us a huge warehouse where we did the ... bloody parts. *(laughing)* We reproduced a corner of the real places there, and Savini let the blood flow.
Siedelmann: It was a really bloody movie indeed.
Mans: Yes, that's for sure. But somehow afterwards I didn't want to pursue this career; I didn't want to do more slasher movies at all.
Siedelmann: But you didn't have some difficulties with Joe Zito and the crew?
Mans: No, not at all. Actually the shooting of YOU BETTER WATCH OUT was very difficult. We were creating fake snow, but sometimes getting real snow, and stuff like that. It was just physically exhausting. The Zito movie was all fun! I just moved on.
Siedelmann: So THE PROWLER had bigger production values than YOU BETTER WATCH OUT, correct?
Mans: It really had to do with the difference between the two directors. It had to do with crazy Zito being a professional, and Savini being even more than that, a genius. I am very grateful for that, it was a very nice experience. – You know, as a very young person I had gone swimming a lot at Cape May. And let's say the old ladies I knew there that had rented us their houses weren't very happy when they found out what kind of a movie we were shooting there. *(laughing)* So I was no longer welcome as a summer guest there.
Siedelmann: And Louis Jackson stopped filmmaking after YOU BETTER WATCH OUT...
Mans: Not because he wanted, but he never got any other film together. But YOU BETTER WATCH OUT – or whatever title it has – ended up having a lot of screenings. Every Christmas, Jackson got an opportunity to show the film somewhere else. Let's call it a cult movie! – The thing is, even now that I'm pretty old, for the first time I'm writing a novel. I always tried out different fields.
Siedelmann: Is it an autobiographical topic?
Mans: Kind of, yes. Did you know that BALLET DOWN THE HIGHWAY at some point was shown to the Museum of Modern Art in New York? It never happened that the film went into their collection, but they did give us a cine-probe. That basically happened because I was friends with the people from the film department of MoMA, which had to do with those old Bleecker Street Cinema contacts, as I said it was sort of where I met everybody – including crazy Nicholas Ray. Oh, was that a crazy man.
Siedelmann: A brilliant filmmaker!
Mans: Brilliant filmmaker, crazy man. I always thought there was something mad about him. I met him in the mid-60s, when he came back from shooting 55 DAYS AT PEKING, and he showed up for a screening deal at the cinema. He sneaked into my office and made a lot of long-distance phone calls, and ran up a bill – as you know, in those days long-distance was very expensive. When the bill arrived, we couldn't figure out at first who actually made these phone calls. *(laughing)*
Siedelmann: Were you fascinated by ballet and dance at the time you wrote BALLET DOWN THE HIGHWAY?
Mans: No, I never liked ballet at all. It all had

to do with the fact that Jack Deveau found this Dutch, not-so-good ballet dancer who agreed to star in the film. You have to know I don't feel any guilt or shame; it's just that those memories have faded away. And actually I'm ok with that.
Siedelmann: Can you remember when the film was finished, did you like it.
Mans: No, not at all. The thing is that the films that I have always liked are kinda like highbrow, intellectual. Jean-Luc Godard and filmmakers like that.
Siedelmann: Did you have some kind of conflict with Jack Deveau because of the way the movie turned out?
Mans: No, absolutely not. But as I told you, the kind of humor that I contributed to it wasn't very welcome if you wanted to make successful porno movies. Before he worked on pornos, the first film script we worked on together was totally different. Jack found something like a low-grade paperback called THE WATERGATE GIRLS, and it was all about the scandal at Watergate, he bought the rights, and I wrote a silly script. *(whispering)* I mean a really silly script. It's funny, I always liked the more pretentious films, but everything I've ever written is kind of on the silly side. One of the things Jack Deveau was receptive about me was that all of my friends were kinda pretentious, but I wasn't. That's what he thought. His goal was to actually raise money to make a film based on THE WATERGATE GIRLS. It took him a while, and by that time he could have done it nobody cared about the Watergate scandal anymore. So the jokes became outdated, and we realized that we had to make it incidentally, or not at all.
Siedelmann: Yeah, it's always about the timing.
Mans: Yes. Of course the real big Hollywood films may take a long time, but if you make low-budget movies you've got to be quick.
Siedelmann: Were you around at the parties Jack Deveau gave in his apartment?
Mans: Parties? I don't think I was ever invited. *(laughing)* Like I said, in the beginning of our friendship, when he was involved in cooking he invited me a couple of times. Not too many, just a few dinners. Then we got involved in THE WATERGATE GIRLS, which I think I wrote in a week or so. *(laughing)* We actually made a table reading for it, that's how far we got. Actually, I never met many people from that business at all, and I never watched any of those films by Hand In Hand, or whatever company. I wasn't prude, but I've never been interested in pornography. And I remember another thing that actually might be not part of my resume anywhere, is that Andy Warhol made a film that he called FOUR STARS, and it lasted 24 hours. And somehow Andy was told that the one person who might actually want to watch all of it and write a review was me. And I did. *(laughing)*
Siedelmann: Wow, you sat through the whole 24 hours?
Mans: Well, I took breaks. I had to drink water and go to the bathroom, and whatever. And I didn't take drugs of any kind. That was kinda like part of what the people Andy surrounded himself with did. I don't remember clearly, but I proposed to write a review for the *Village Voice*, and they said, "Sure! Who else?!?"
Siedelmann: Did you write regularly for the *Village Voice*?
Mans: Only once. One review for them: FOUR STARS. It was after CHELSEA GIRLS and all of those. I don't remember what year it was, but it was much later. It was about shooting in color, and having people who couldn't stop talking, and especially there was somebody who was reading that Christian book *The Imitation of Christ*. I don't remember who the characters were, but I sort of knew all those people and didn't want to be near them at all. Definitely didn't want to be part of that druggy world.
Siedelmann: ... oh, that's the reason you weren't invited to the Hand In Hand parties... *(laughing)*
Mans: ... or any parties. *(laughing)* – But I thought watching all of these crazy people on film wasn't as bad filmed as some of the earlier Warhol movies. I could have walked out on it, but it made me think of a film by Jacques Rivette called OUT 1, which I actually sat through, and my friend Jonathan Rosenbaum had the commission to write a review about it, and I sat with it. Sometimes one of us went to the bathroom, and we kinda said to each other what we have missed. Jonathan and I still have long phone conversations. He travels a lot, but I hate it. I even hate leaving Manhattan. I'm a Manhattan person. Once in a while, whenever he returns from a trip, he calls me on the phone and tells me about movies and persons he cared for, and the events and meals he went to. Other than that I don't have any friends. Well, I do have friends, but not really old friends.

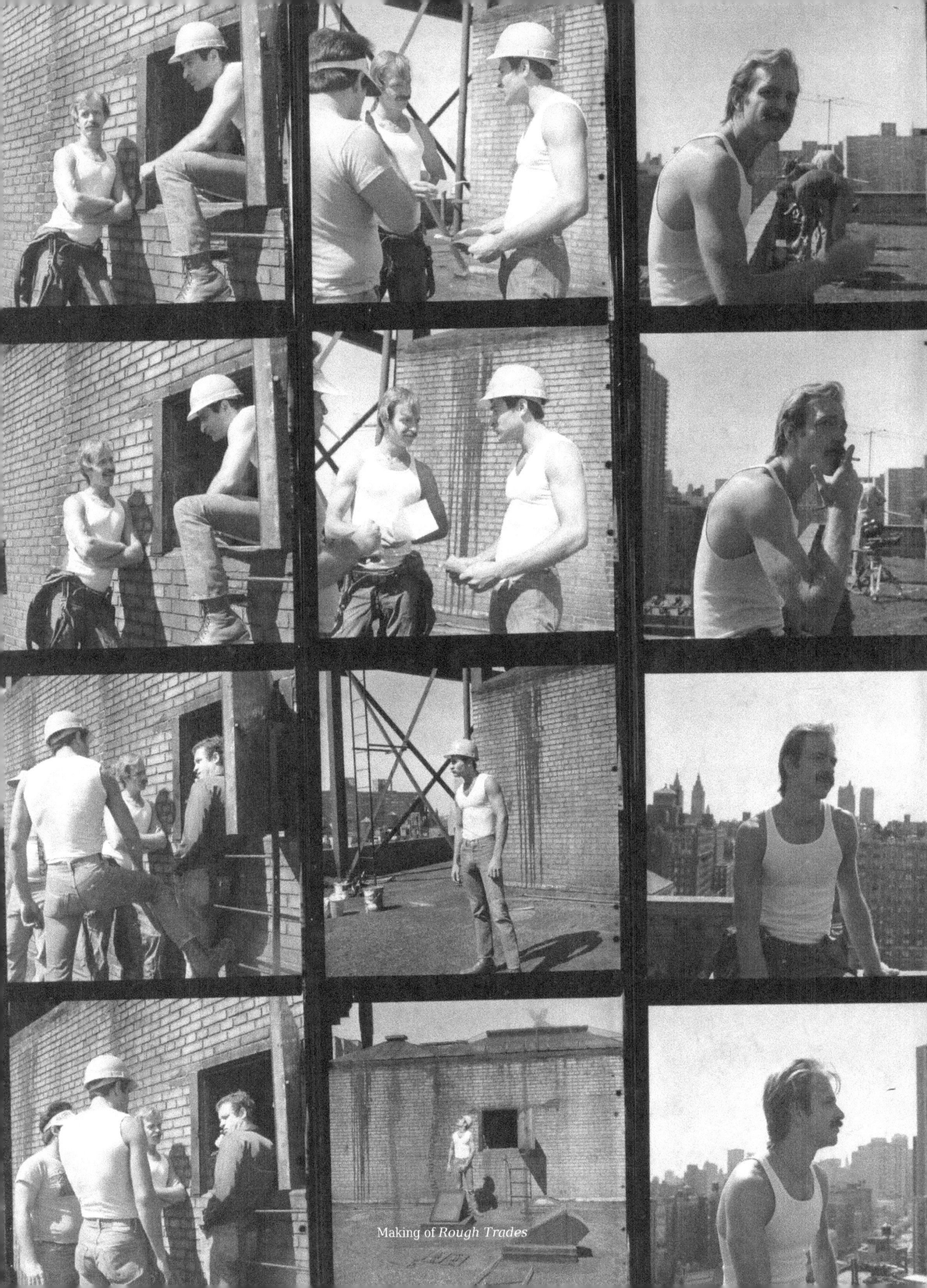
Making of *Rough Trades*

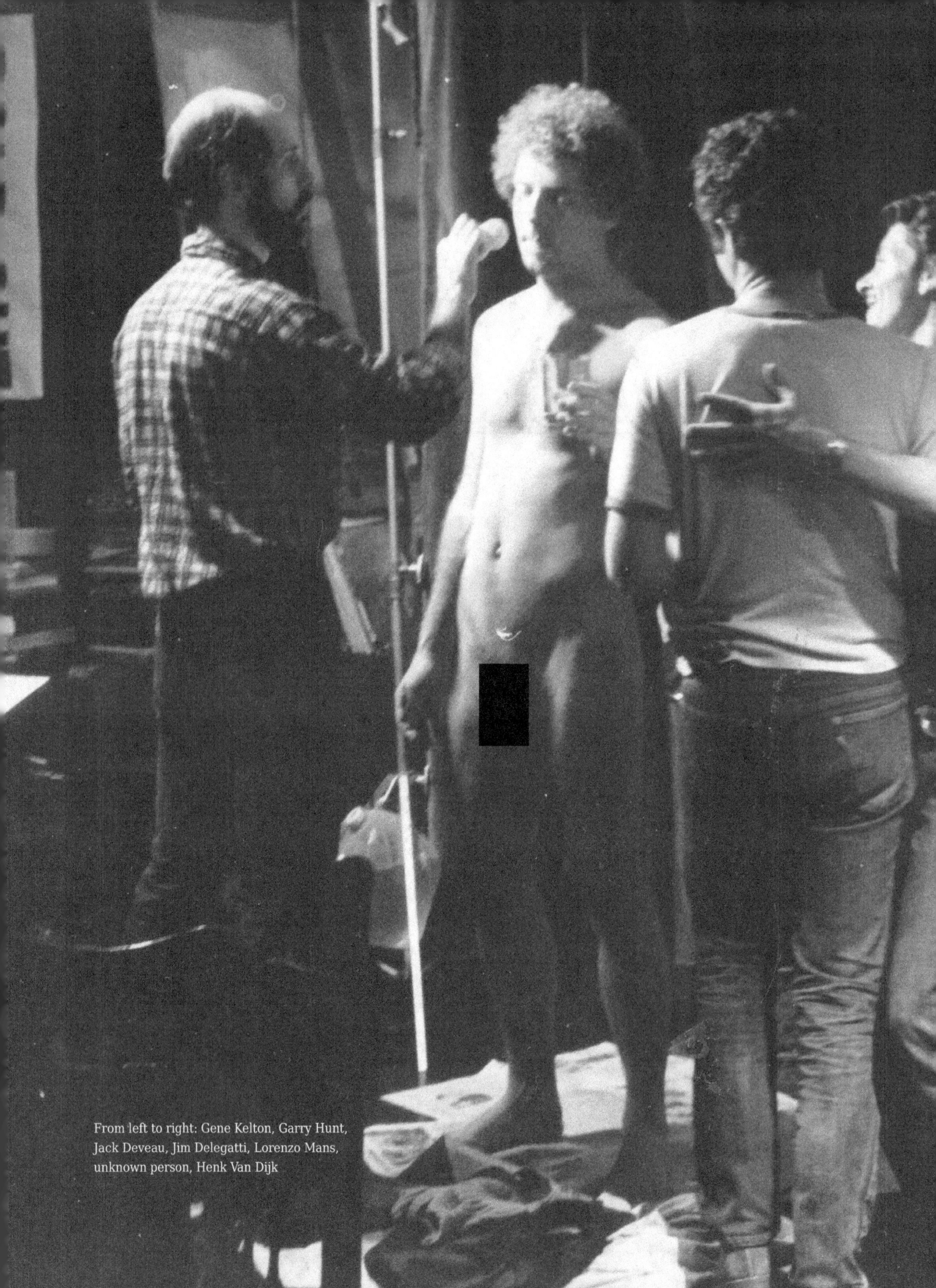

From left to right: Gene Kelton, Garry Hunt, Jack Deveau, Jim Delegatti, Lorenzo Mans, unknown person, Henk Van Dijk

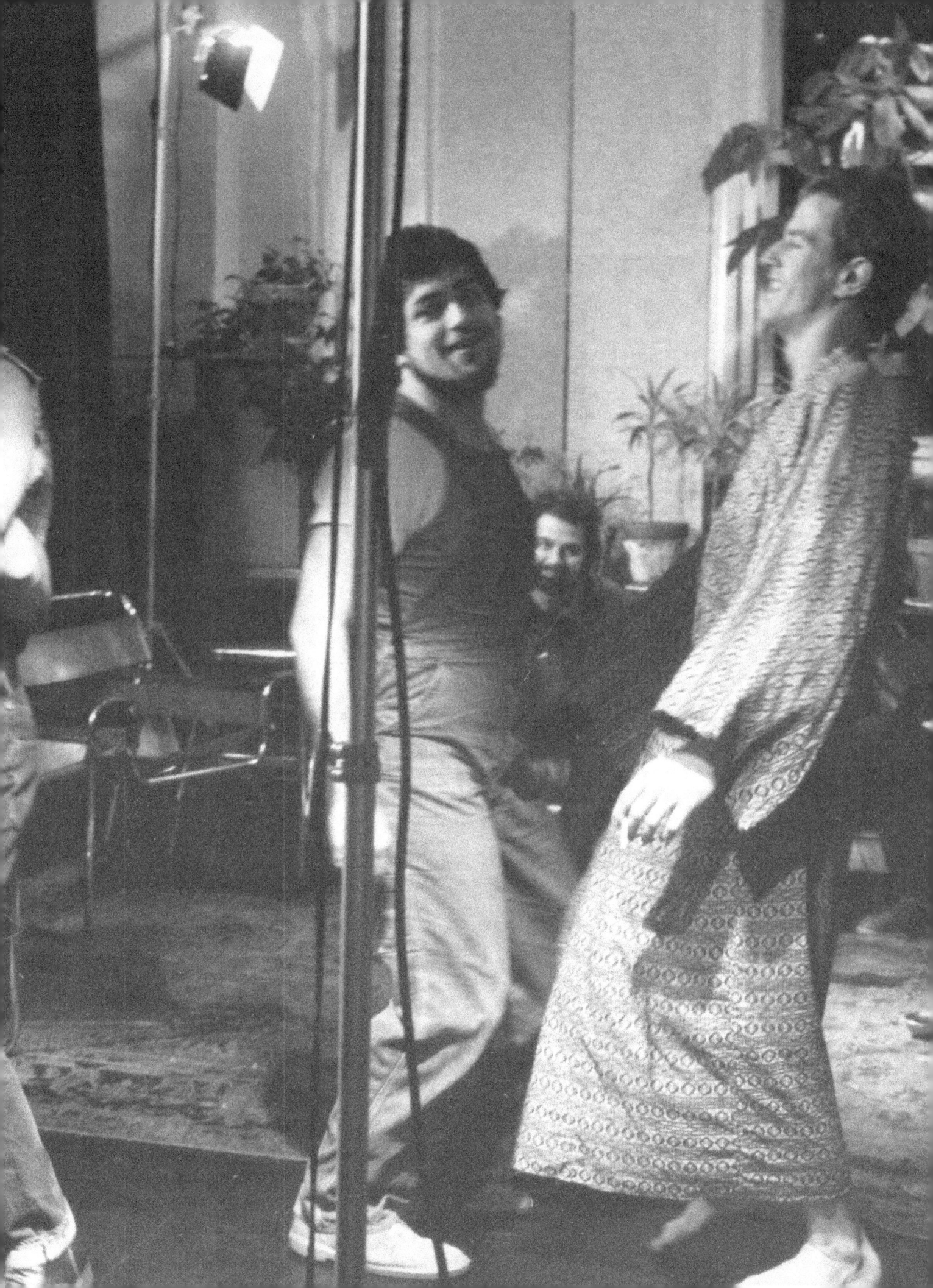

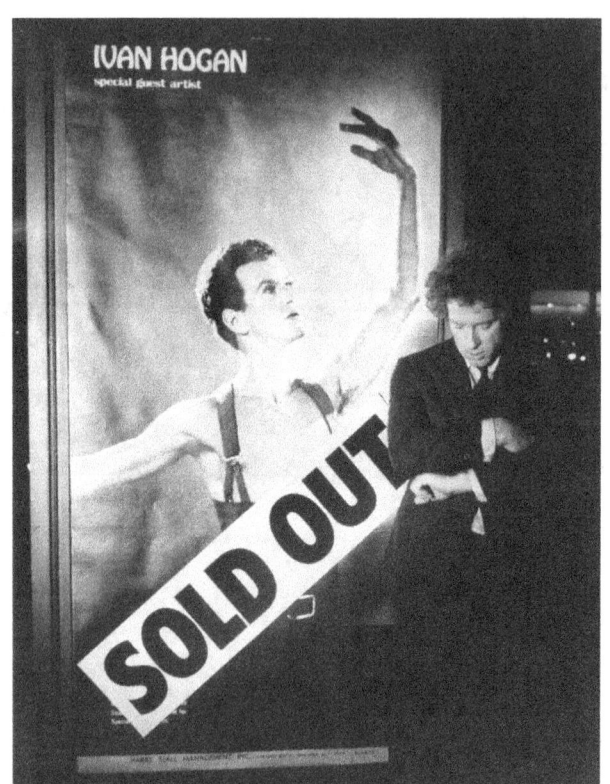

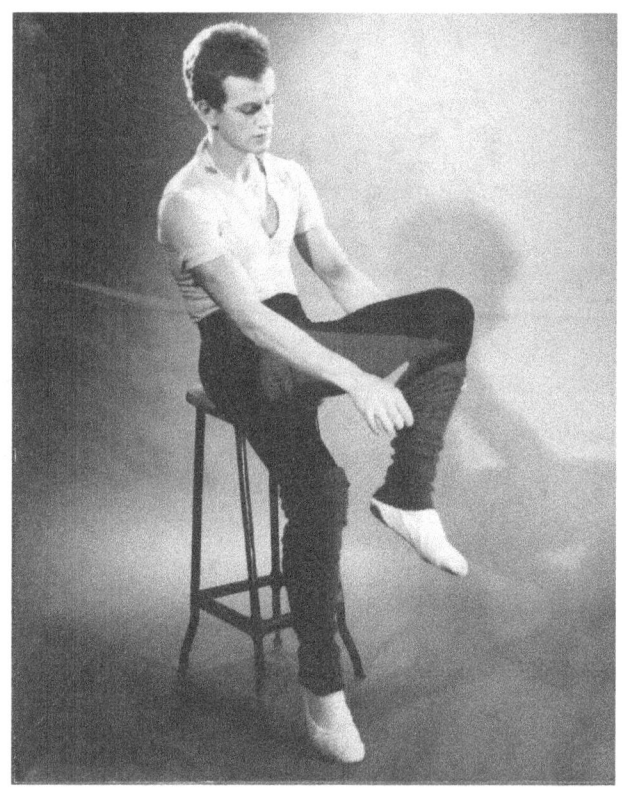

Waiting for the man - Garry Hunt in *Ballet Down the Highway*

Henk Van Dijk in *Ballet Down the Highway* - "A fabulous classic gay porn movie directed by Hand In Hand Films founder Jack Deveau. This film delivers a compelling story, raunchy gay porn action, along with wonderful ballet footage. This is a fascinating vintage gay porn movie -- the realism makes the gay sex so much more interesting; it´s like you´re watching real people having sex and not stiff mechanical sex." (Bijou World promotional material)

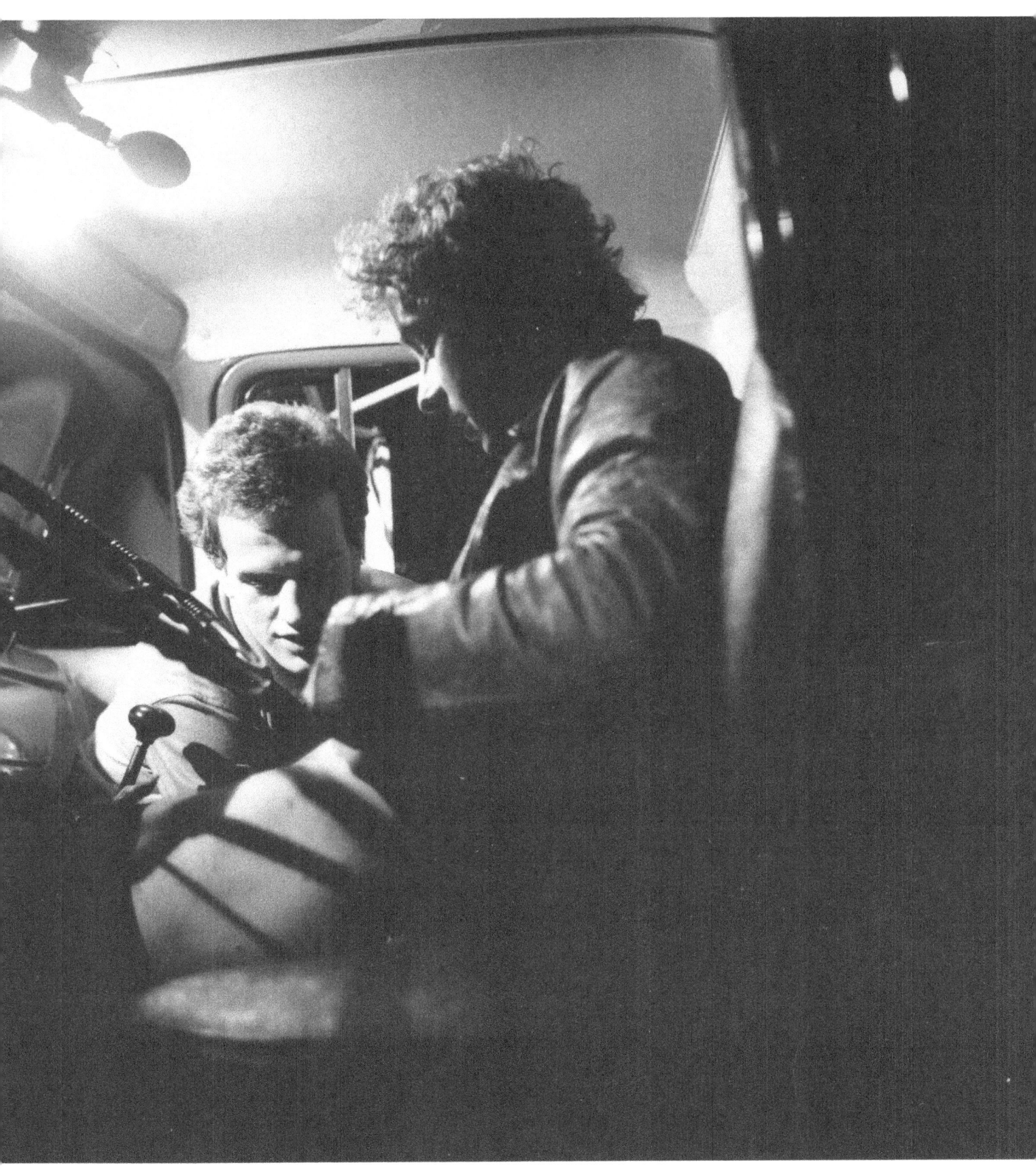

Truck suck: Henk Van Dijk (left) gives Garry Hunt a blowjob

HAND IN HAND VIDEO

A DIVISION OF Quality X Video Cassette Company
358 WEST 44TH STREET
NEW YORK, NEW YORK 10036
(212) 541-7860 Outside N.Y. (800) 223-7981

Ballet down the HIGHWAY

Produced & Directed by JACK DEVEAU
A Hand in Hand Films Production

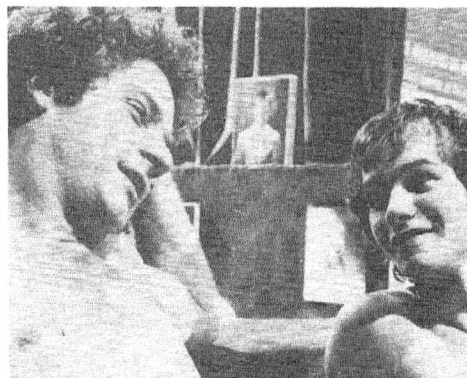

Garry Hunt and Jeff Sullivan relax after a sexual encounter of the best kind.

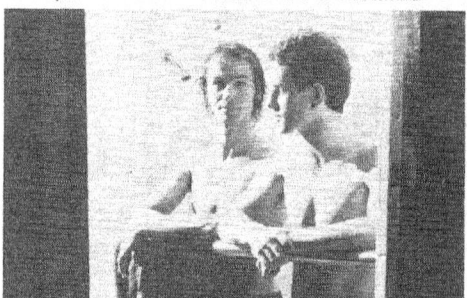

Jeff Sullivan and Henk van Dijk share a shower in one of the many erotic scenes between the dancer/lovers.

What do truckers and ballet dancers have in common? Not very much on the surface, but in BALLET DOWN THE HIGHWAY, master filmmaker Jack Deveau delves beneath the surface into the world of eroticism, where what you do for a living isn't as important as what you do in bed.

BALLET DOWN THE HIGHWAY (honored in a film festival in Holland for its craftsmanship and eroticism) was named one of the year's best films by the **Soho Weekly News** and called "The Big One for 1975" by **Michael's Thing**. It is a sensual fantasy that combines the rugged world of trucking with the lyricism of ballet. A chance encounter between the trucker Joe (Garry Hunt) and Ivan Hogan (Henk van Dijk), a principal dancer with a major ballet company, leads to seemingly endless sexual encounters of a variety that was highly recommended (three "V's") by Arthur Bell in the **Village Voice**.

Who hasn't watched the perfectly muscled bodies of dancers and yearned to see them in another kind of action.... Who hasn't fantasized about the tough masculinity of truck drivers? BALLET DOWN THE HIGHWAY brings all of these fantasies to life with a perfect synthesis of Hot Sex and poetic motion. And the GANG RAPE of Joe the trucker by three of his trucker buddies is the kind of horny banging that puts the "X" into X-rated films.

A moving and provocative score enhances both the beauty and the raw sexuality of this lusty tale. You'll be as excited as the gorgeous hunks on the screen by the time you see the romantic conclusion: An all-night love-feast that continues even as a spectacular dawn bathes the sky and the lovers in lush shades of violet.

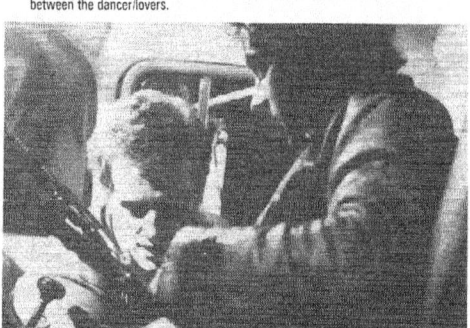

Henk van Dijk and Garry Hunt get it on in the cab of a truck.

STUDIOSOUND is a special process that guarantees a high fidelity like you've never heard. Instead of the usual optical transfer of sound from film to tape, which limits the reproduction of sound to a narrow range of frequencies, StudioSound is a magnetic transfer of the ORIGINAL MAGNETIC STUDIO sound tracks for the feature, transferred directly to the magnetic tape in your video cassette. This process actually gives you BETTER QUALITY than can be achieved in a cinema. For further enhancement, you can patch your video system into your stereo system and surround yourself with the excitement of these sensual sounds.

Cast: Garry Hunt, Henk van Dijk, Jeff Sullivan, Tom DeMastri, and Tony Duva, Charles Drucker and Joe Major as the Truckers, along with a large supporting cast of rugged, hot men.

Produced and directed by Jack Deveau
Edited by Robert Alvarez • Music by Stan Freeman and Ian Herman

BALLET DOWN THE HIGHWAY   93 MINUTES   COLOR   ALL-MALE CAST   **StudioSound**

© Quality X Video Cassette Company 1979

Mark Woodward aka Sydney Soons
(Behind the scenes of *Ballet Down the Highway*)

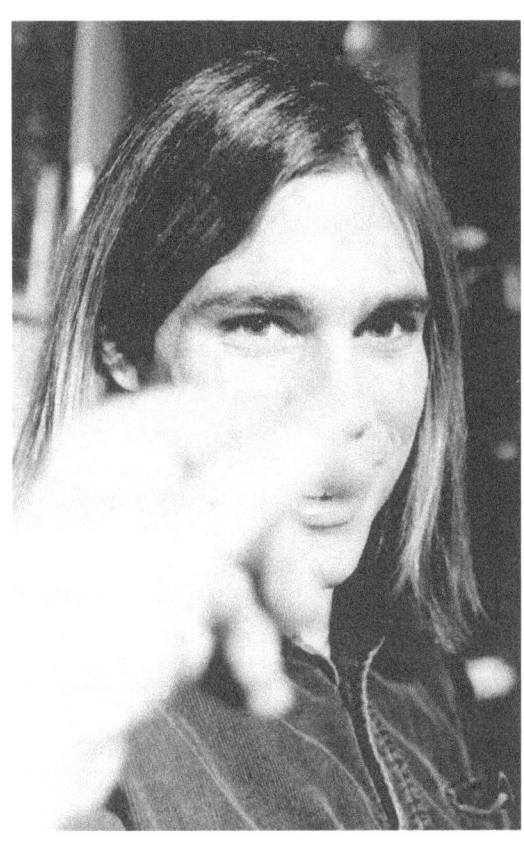

Ballet Down the Highway - Opening Party with Asst. Directors Tom De Simone (left) and Jaap Penraat in Background: Jack Deveau (left), Bob Alvarez (middle) and Sydney Soons

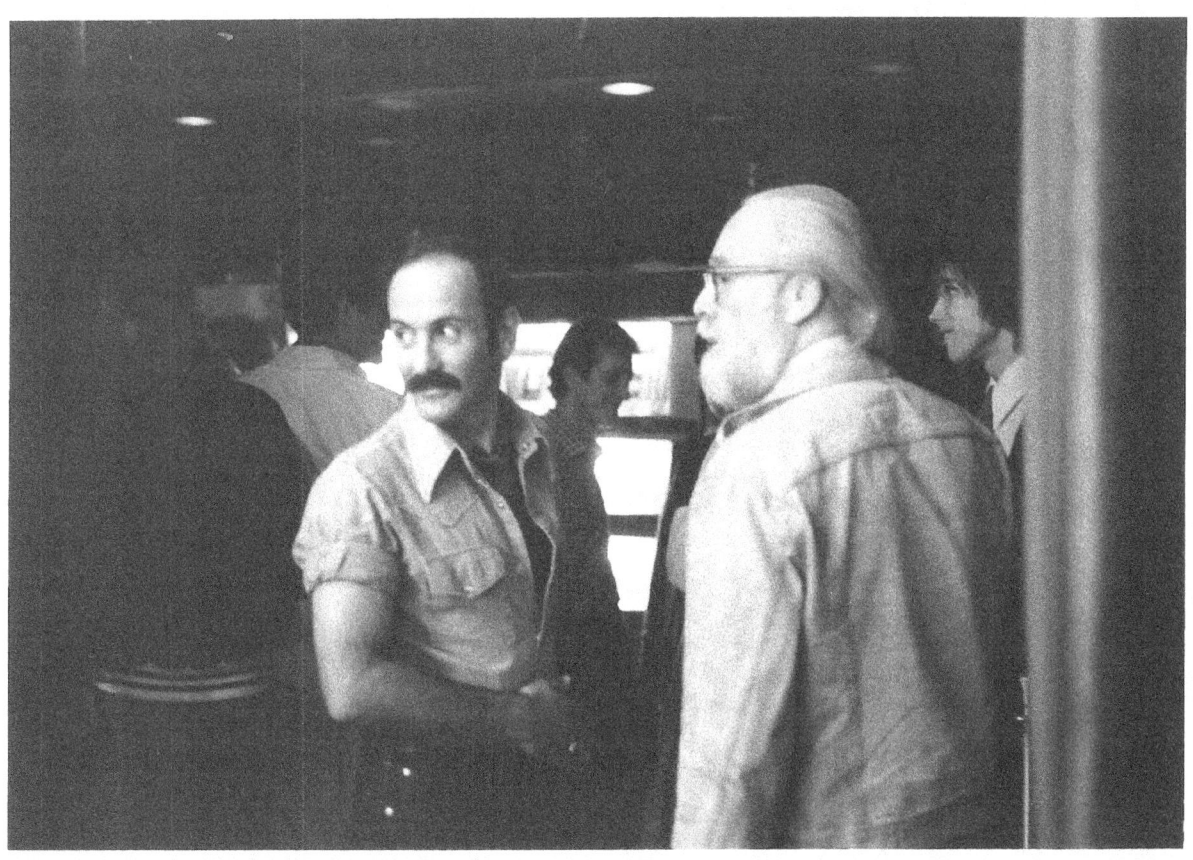

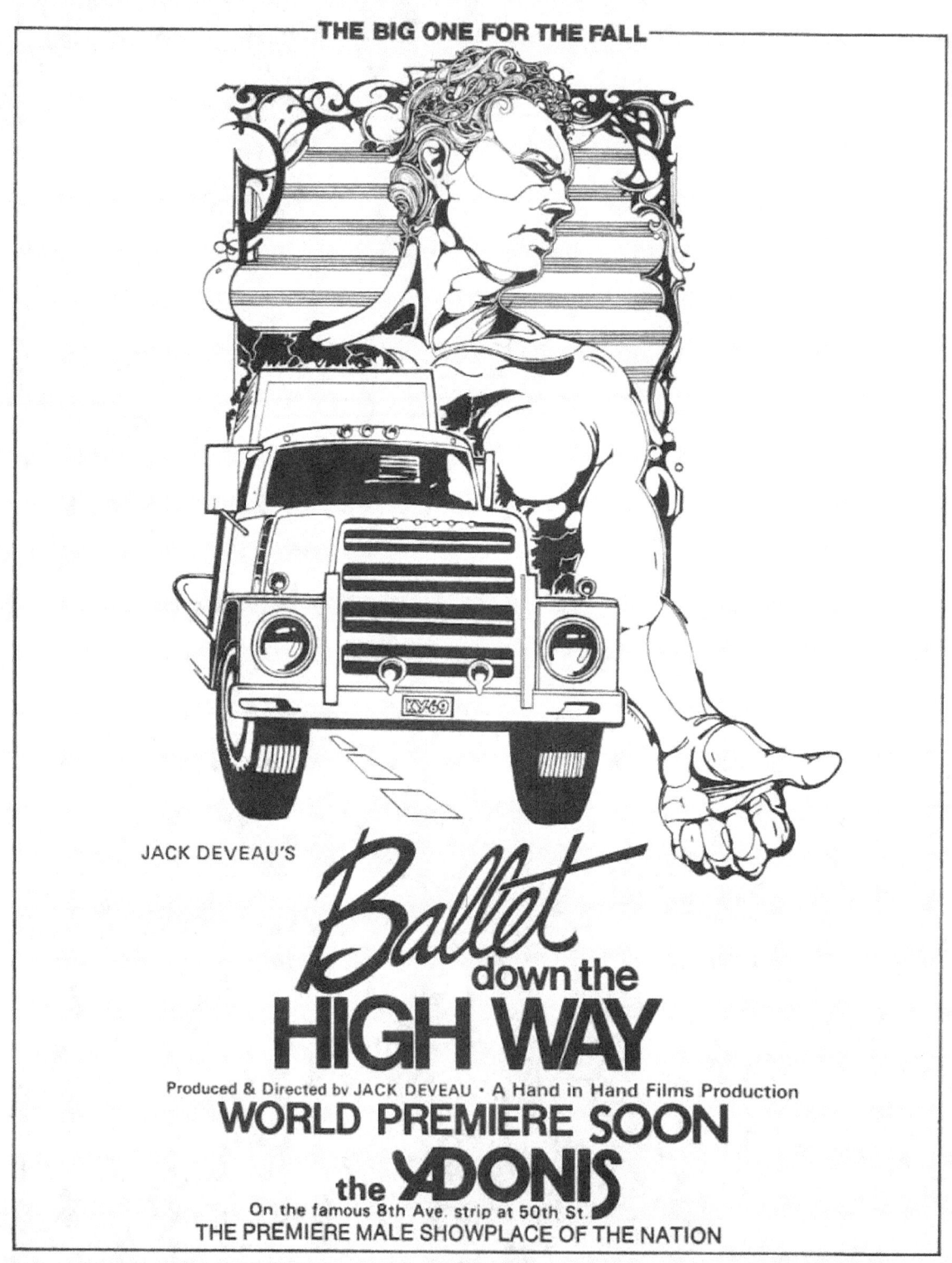

Original poster artwork - "Noted for creative use of graphic art in their film promotion, Hand In Hand's beautifully stylized logo for *Ballet Down the Highway* is by artist Chris Santoro, a master of suggestive line." Freeman Gunter

PRESS REVIEWS 2

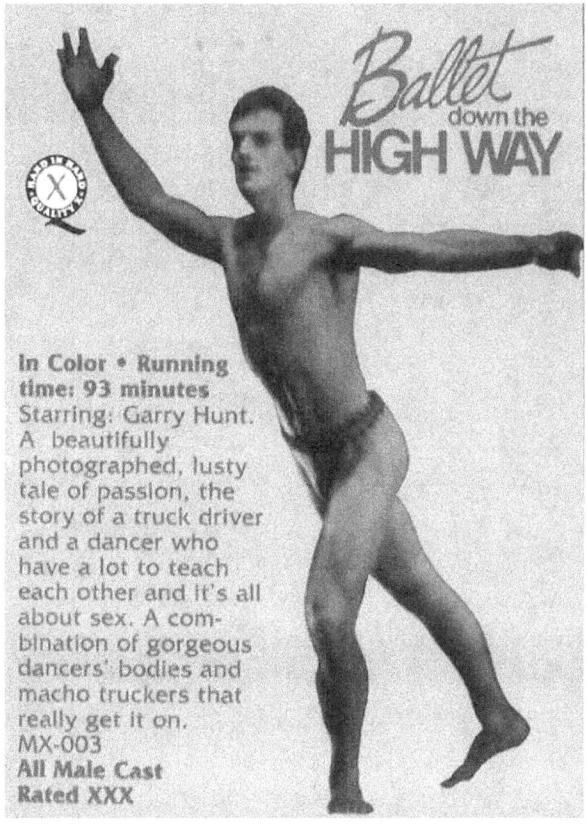

In Color • Running time: 93 minutes
Starring: Garry Hunt.
A beautifully photographed, lusty tale of passion, the story of a truck driver and a dancer who have a lot to teach each other and it's all about sex. A combination of gorgeous dancers' bodies and macho truckers that really get it on.
MX-003
All Male Cast
Rated XXX

"In relation to Hollywood films, gay films have reached 1940," says Jack Deveau, pioneer maker of male action flicks and guiding hand of Hand In Hand Films, a company that at least one reviewer has dubbed "the MGM of gay hardcore." "The problem, of course, is money," Deveau continues. "The economics of gay films are crazy. One of our films costs about one percent of what it costs to make the cheapest Hollywood feature. One percent! The advertising bill from the New York Times for BALLET DOWN THE HIGHWAY, our latest film, is larger than the film's entire budget." In spite of this, and maybe in part because of it, Deveau has managed to turn out films which are literate, artistically ambitious and, of course, sexually hot. "Well," Jack Deveau said with a laugh and a shrug, "necessity *is* the mother..."

BALLET DOWN THE HIGHWAY is Deveau's most ambitious film to date and it is also his most successful; it is the first of the male porno films that is not just a skin flick. BALLET's success stems from the fact that it is a full-fledged *movie*. It was shot, completely in sync, from an uncommonly subtle and adult screenplay by P.P. Mans. The film is full of genuine humor, not mere gags, which develops from the characterizations and clearly demonstrates that sex can be at once funny and hot. "For this film," Deveau explains, "we have hired talented, experienced actors and dancers, not just studs off the street. These men have given me the kind of controlled performances that have made it possible for us to attempt some effects, some subtleties which have not been possible before in a gay hardcore movie. Without sacrificing the spontaneity that's needed for good, hot sex on the screen," he hastens to add.

BALLET DOWN THE HIGHWAY is a sexual comedy of manners which plays some games with the sexual stereotypes which gay men themselves are often all too willing to accept. Each of the protagonists in BALLET embodies the flexible and three-dimensional masculinity that exists in actual experience but seldom, if ever, is portrayed in a film of this type. The plot concerns a famous ballet star, Ivan Hogan (Henk Van Dijk) whose narcissistic and self-confident life-style is briefly but dramatically upset by a truck driver named Joe (Garry Hunt), a macho closet type who soon becomes hooked on the dancer's sinewy, defined and versatile body. To further complicate matters and to provide a third side for the eternal triangle there is a young student dancer named John (Jeff Sullivan) who manages to get Ivan Hogan in the end, so to speak. The telling of their story demonstrates some facts and fallacies about two opposing gay lifestyles, that of a dancer in an occupation many would regard as feminine and of a truck driver in an occupation which many would consider to be the epitome of masculinity. But it ain't necessarily so. "I can identify with this material," Deveau says, "Hard-working New Yorkers have no time for anarchic men. They may talk a lot about spontaneity, but it drives them crazy when someone like Joe, the trucker, shows up." Attention must be called to the film's fine musical score. It is the joint work of two accomplished professionals, and its quality further demonstrates the coming of age of the pornographic film genre. Stan Freeman is a distinguished Broadway composer (*I Had A Ball*) who has done musical direction for many of the major stars in the country, most recently for Marlene Dietrich. Ian Herman, the other composer, is a young rock musician and this, his first film score, is an impressive achievement which could stand on its own quite well on an LP record. As we said at the beginning, Jack Deveau's BALLET DOWN THE HIGHWAY is more than just another skin flick. It is a real, honest-to-God motion picture, one which deserves to be seen.

*Freeman Gunter, *Mandate*

Ballet down the HIGH WAY

By Freeman Gunter

MANDATE
THE NATIONAL MAGAZINE
OF ENTERTAINMENT & E[ROTICA]
DECEMBER 1975
$1.25

"In relation to Hollywood films, gay films have reached 1940," says Jack Deveau, pioneer maker of male action flicks and guiding hand of Hand-in-Hand Films, a company that at least one reviewer has dubbed "the M-G-M of gay hardcore." The problem, of course, is money," Deveau continues. "The economics of gay films are crazy. One of our films costs about one percent of what it costs to make the cheapest Hollywood feature. One percent! The advertising bill from the New York Times for Ballet Down the Highway, our latest film, is larger than the film's entire budget."

In spite of this, and maybe in part because of it, Deveau has managed to turn out films which are literate, artistically ambitious and, of course, sexually hot. "Well," Jack Deveau said with a laugh and a shrug, "necessity is the mother . . ."

Ballet Down the High Way is Deveau's most ambitious film to date and it is also his most successful; it is the first of the male porno films that is not just a skin flick. Ballet's success stems from the fact that it is a full-fledged movie. It was shot, compl-etely in sync, from an [un]subtle and adult screenp[lay by Moe] Mans. The film is full [of] humor, not mere gags, w[hich] ops from the characteriza[tions and] clearly demonstrates that s[ex can be] at once funny and hot.

"For this film," Deveau [said,] "we have hired talented, exp[erienced] actors and dancers, not just s[tuds off] the street. These men have giv[en us] the kind of controlled perform[ances] that have made it possible for [us to] attempt some effects, some subt[leties] which have not been possible b[efore]."

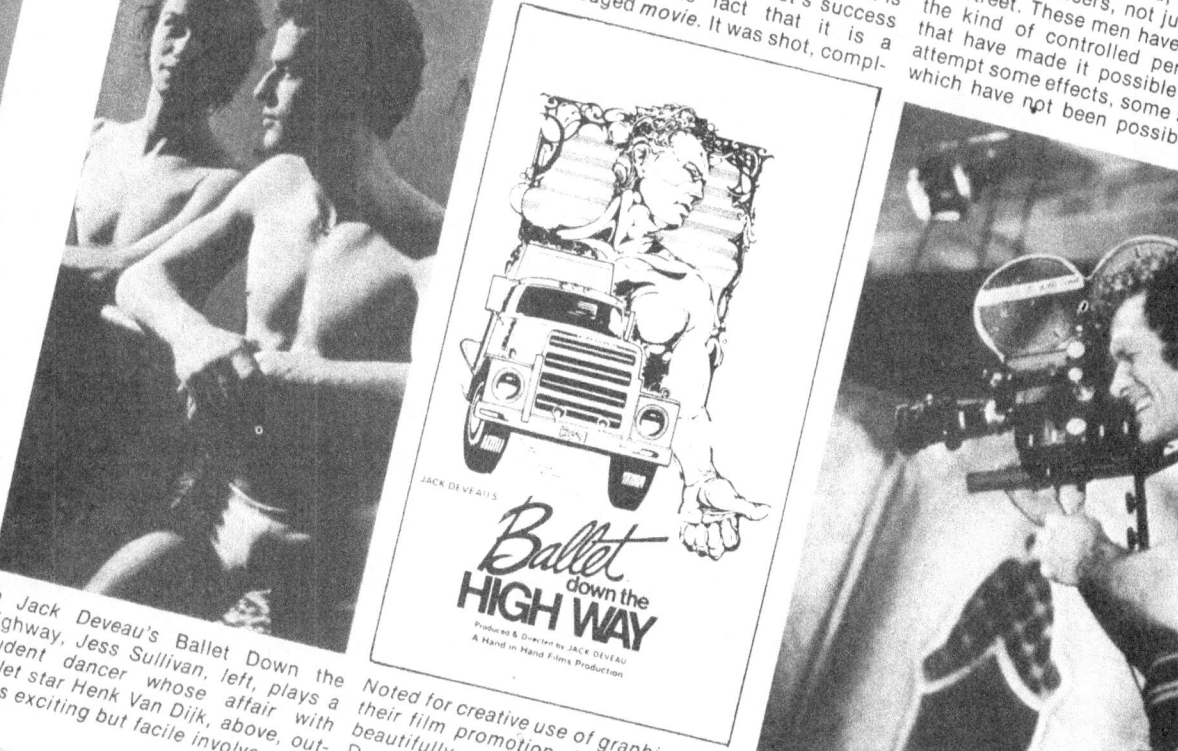

In Jack Deveau's Ballet Down the Highway, Jess Sullivan, left, plays a student dancer whose affair with ballet star Henk Van Dijk, above, outlasts exciting but facile involvements.

Noted for creative use of graphic art in their film promotion, Hand-in-Hand's beautifully stylized logo for Ballet Down the Highway is by artist [S.] Santoro, a master of...

If Hand-in-Hand is [the MGM of] porno, the...

During the credits of BALLET DOWN THE HIGHWAY, director Jack Deveau uses an almost kaleidoscope technique to interweave the three major threads of his thematic tapestry: the self-deceiving machismo of highway cowboys, the self-centered refinement of the ballet studio, and the all-accepting, all-inclusive cityscape of New York. His film celebrates the diversity of an urban life that, for gay men in the 1970s, offered almost total freedom. The story: Ivan Hogan (Henk Van Dijk), an internationally famous ballet dancer, returns to the city where his career began for a series of master classes at his former school. His first sexual encounter involves a student named John (Jeff Sullivan), whose dancing slippers he borrows to demonstrate a pas de deux. As he bends over to put on the slippers, he stares directly into John's crotch. "Are we the same size?" the student asks with a slight smile. "We'll find out." Responds Ivan – and, of course, they do. The sexual encounter, which takes place in front of a long mirror at the head of Ivan's bed, suggests an almost narcissistic fantasy, in which each dancer makes love primarily to himself. When Ivan has a Dutch music box delivered to his country home, he meets Joe (Garry Hunt), a truck driver who hides his homosexuality behind a macho pose. Immediately infatuated with the dancer's sleek body, Joe guiltily masturbates into a pair of dirty shorts as he watches Ivan perform stretching exercises in the nude. Their second meeting occurs by accident. When Ivan's sports car breaks down, he walks to O'Neill's, a nearby truck stop, to catch a bus into the city. Joe, a regular at O'Neill's, immediately approaches Ivan and offers him a ride. Ivan gives Joe a blowjob in the truck and then invites him home for a full-fledged fuck – with Joe, of course, on top. Joe agrees to attend one of Ivan's performances, but feels so out of place at the theatre that he makes a run for it – breaking his after-performance commitment with Ivan and seeking safety in booze at O'Neill's. Ivan settles for his student, John, and the two are in bed when Joe shows up, totally drunk, and is easily coaxed into a three-way, sucking cock for the first time. Joe's fellow truck drivers (Tony Duva, Charles Drucker, Joe Mayor) suspect that Joe is having an affair with the dancer and dare him to introduce them to his "girlfriend." When they discover the truth, they gangbang Joe in Ivan's apartment, as Ivan listens to classical music through his headphones. The final scene is masterfully ironic. John moves into Ivan's apartment, and even before he is unpacked, the two men fall to the floor for a sixty-nine. Afterward they dance nude on the roof of Ivan's building, silhouetted against the city lights. But their relationship is not one of love and commitment; it is a game in which each is using the other for his own purpose. The real hero of the film is New York City, the magic land of light and fantasy that makes possible the lifestyles of the various characters. Its choices are unlimited, Deveau implies, except by the perceptions of the gay men who call it home.

*M.L., *Manshots*

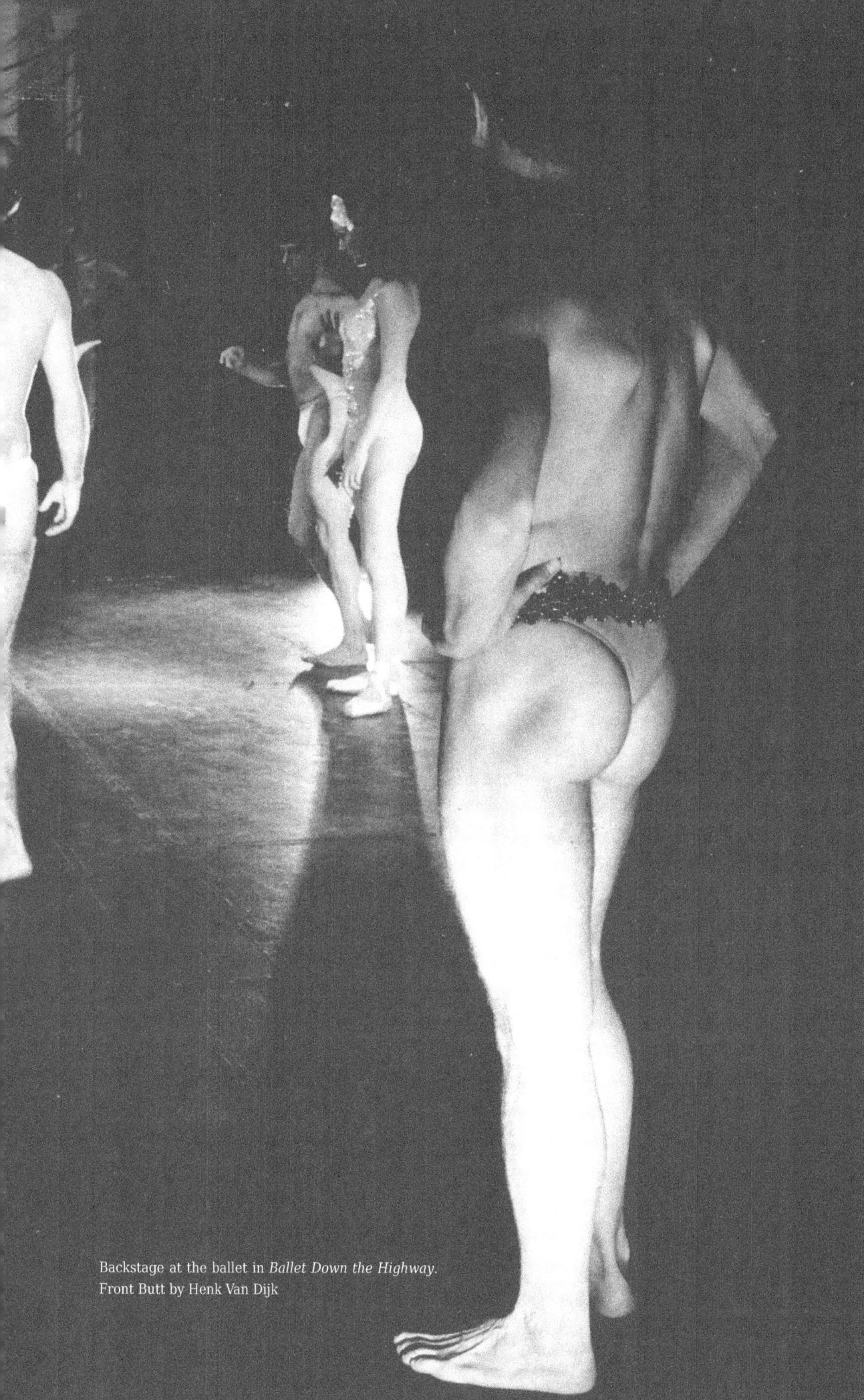

Backstage at the ballet in *Ballet Down the Highway*.
Front Butt by Henk Van Dijk

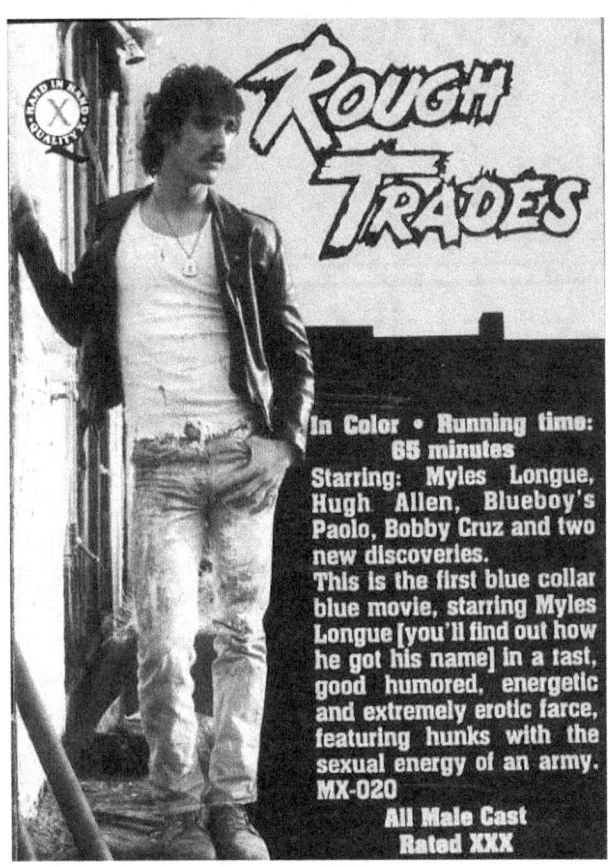

If you're looking for sizzling sex with hot studs in some unusual places, ROUGH TRADES is for you. The somewhat unbelievable plot (an apartment building overrun by cock-hungry fix-it en all on the same day) makes for some great encounters on the roof, in the elevator, and everywhere in between. Jack Deveau seems to never miss when the cameras begin to roll; he's always on target. And once again he's proven he's one of the few who really know how to make a fuck film. Your loins will ache, you'll grab your balls and soon find yourself working over your growing cock, excelling to explosion. It's a guaranteed turn-on. Shot in the late 70's, ROUGH TRADES is just as potent as it was back then – and that's unusual. But, as I said, when director Deveau is at the helm, you're guaranteed nothing but the best.

*John Mensior, *Torso*

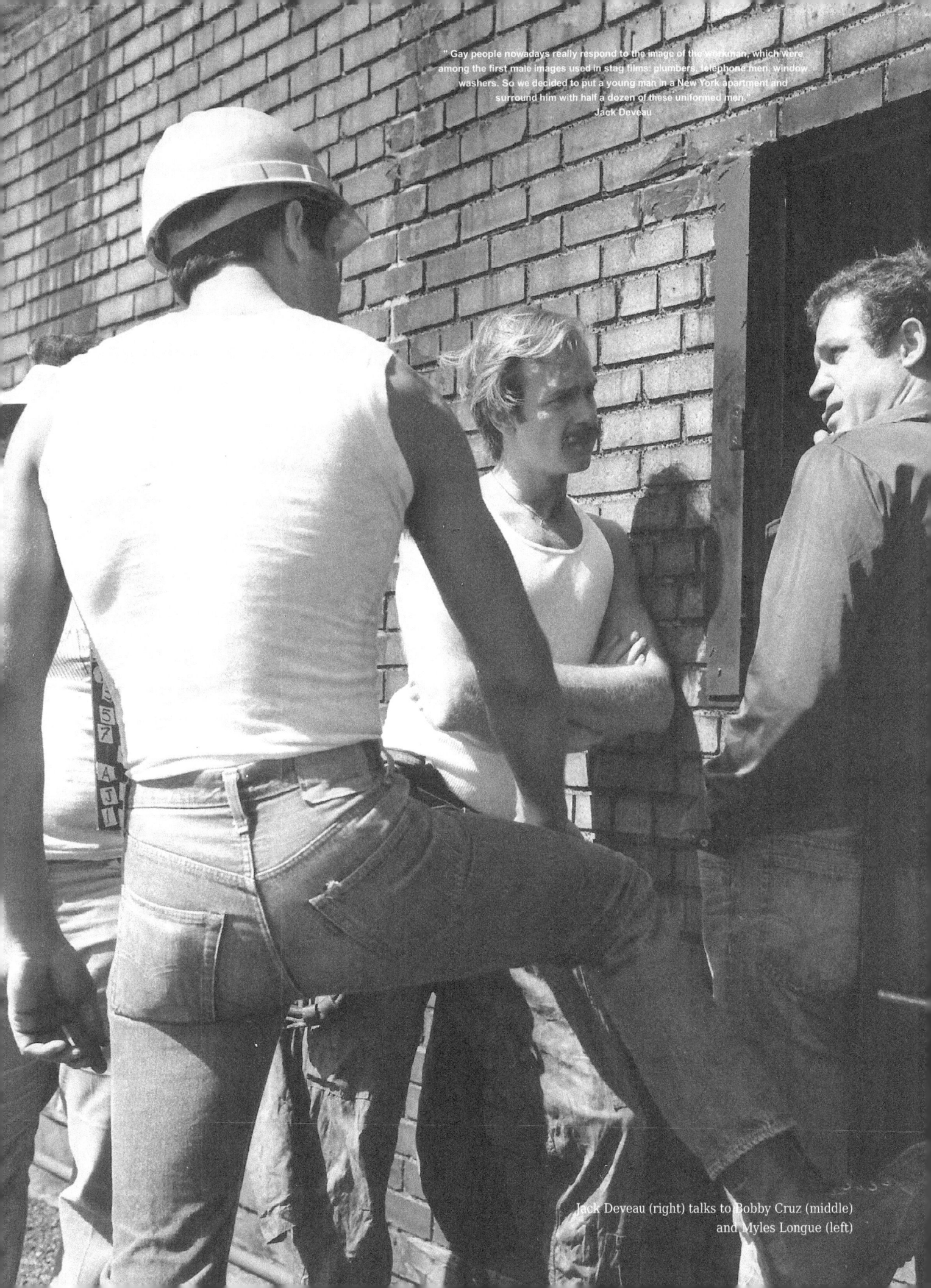

" Gay people nowadays really respond to the image of the workman, which were among the first male images used in stag films: plumbers, telephone men, window washers. So we decided to put a young man in a New York apartment and surround him with half a dozen of these uniformed men.
Jack Deveau

Jack Deveau (right) talks to Bobby Cruz (middle) and Myles Longue (left)

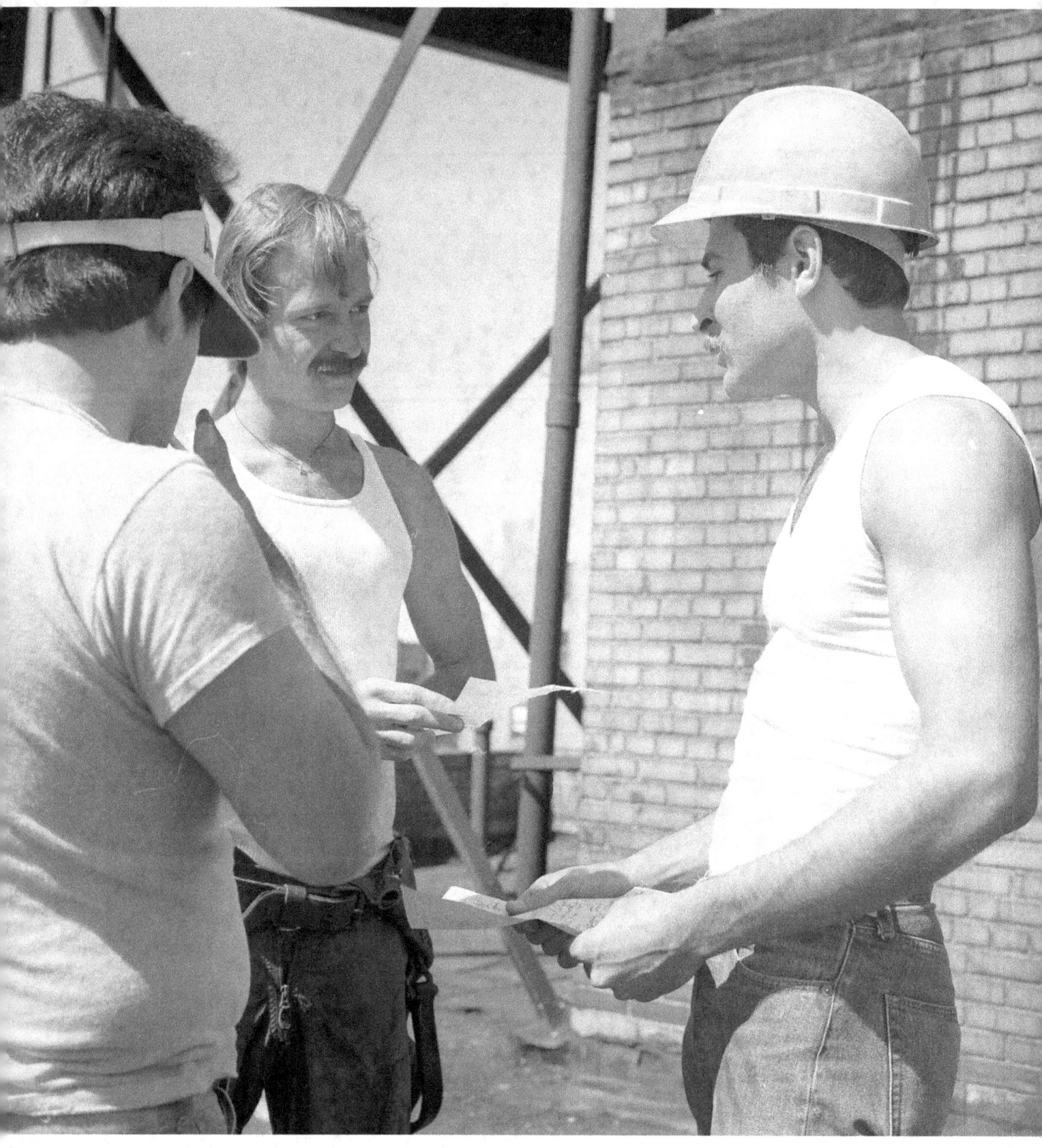

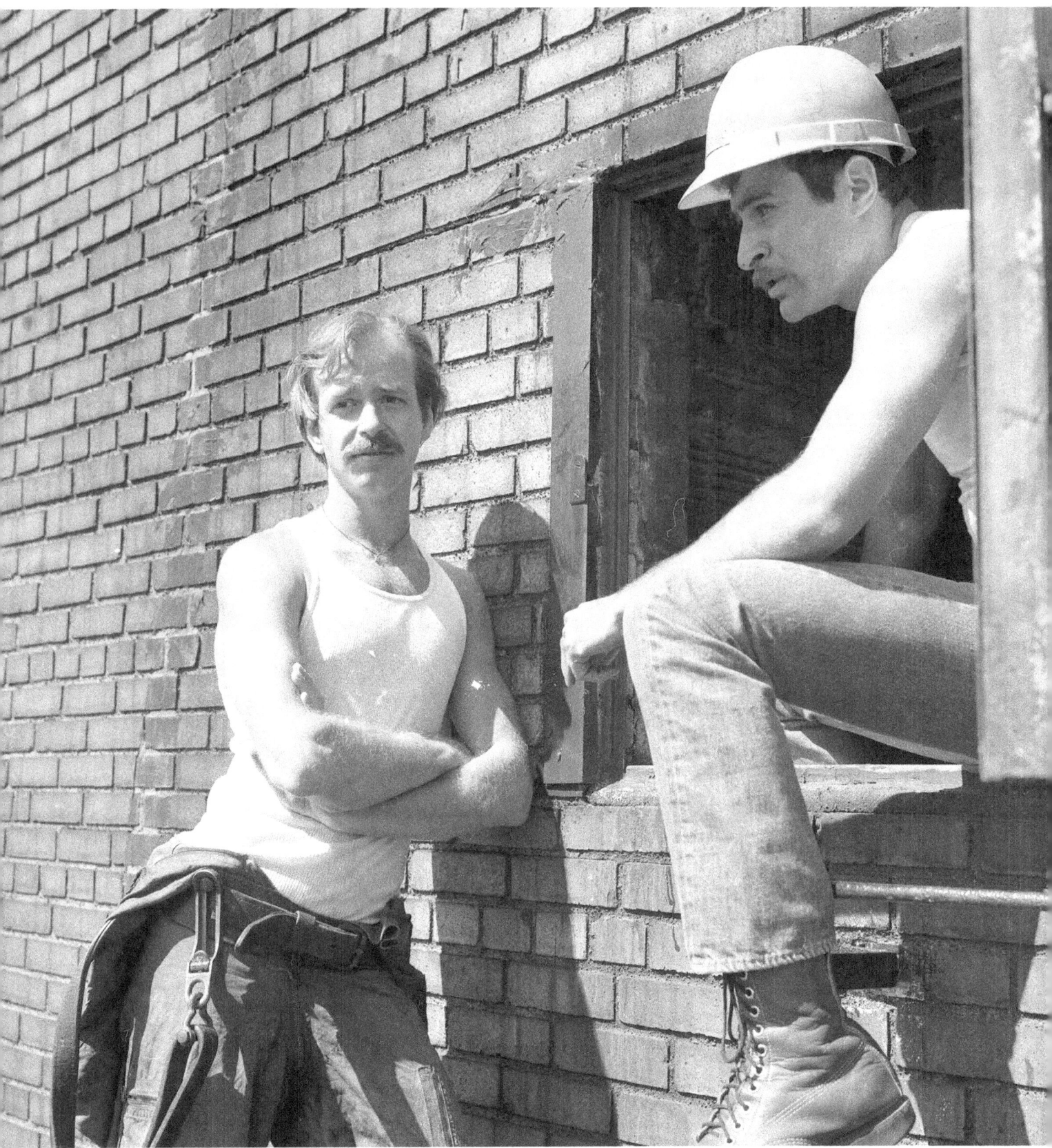

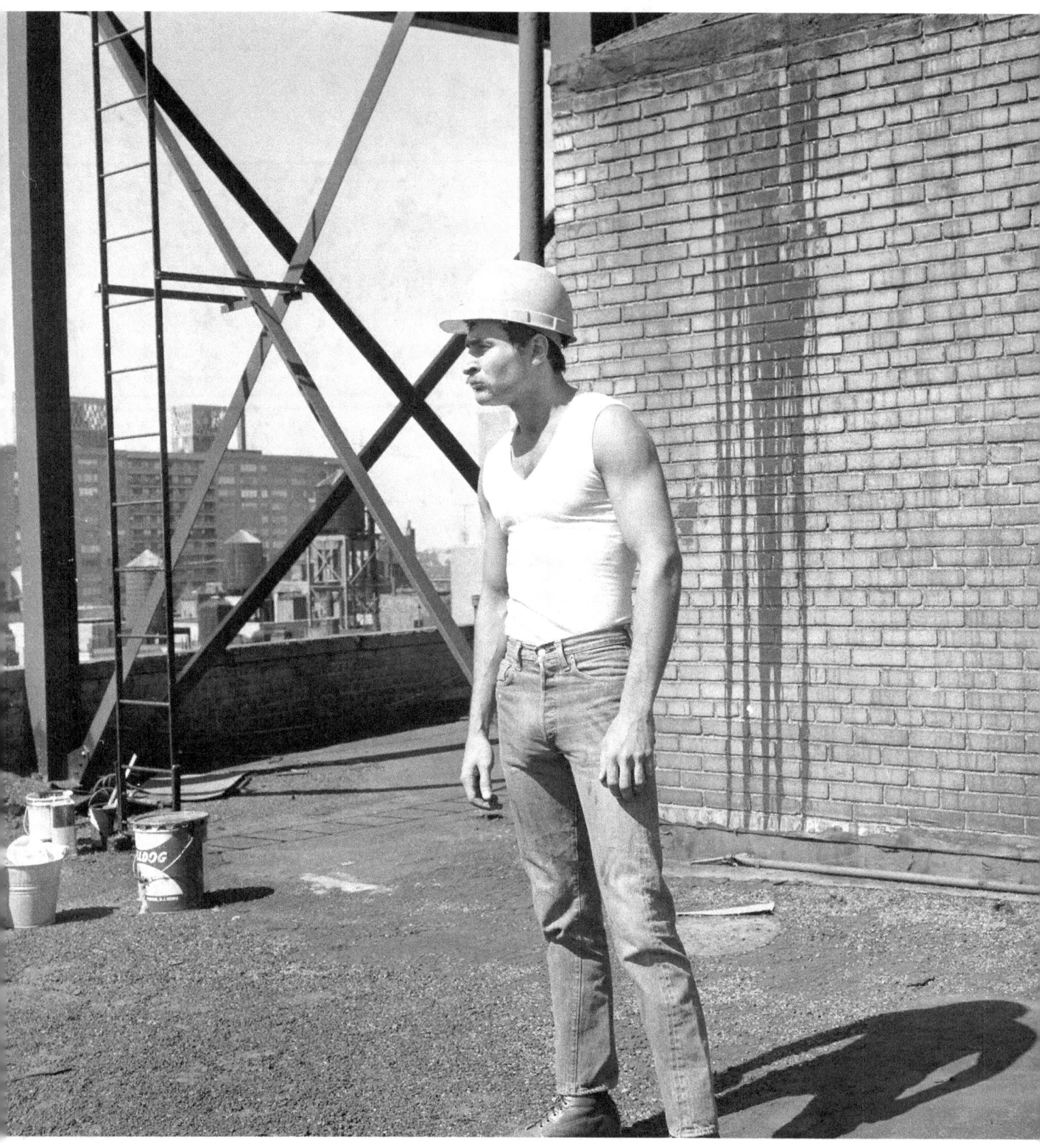

Myles Longue

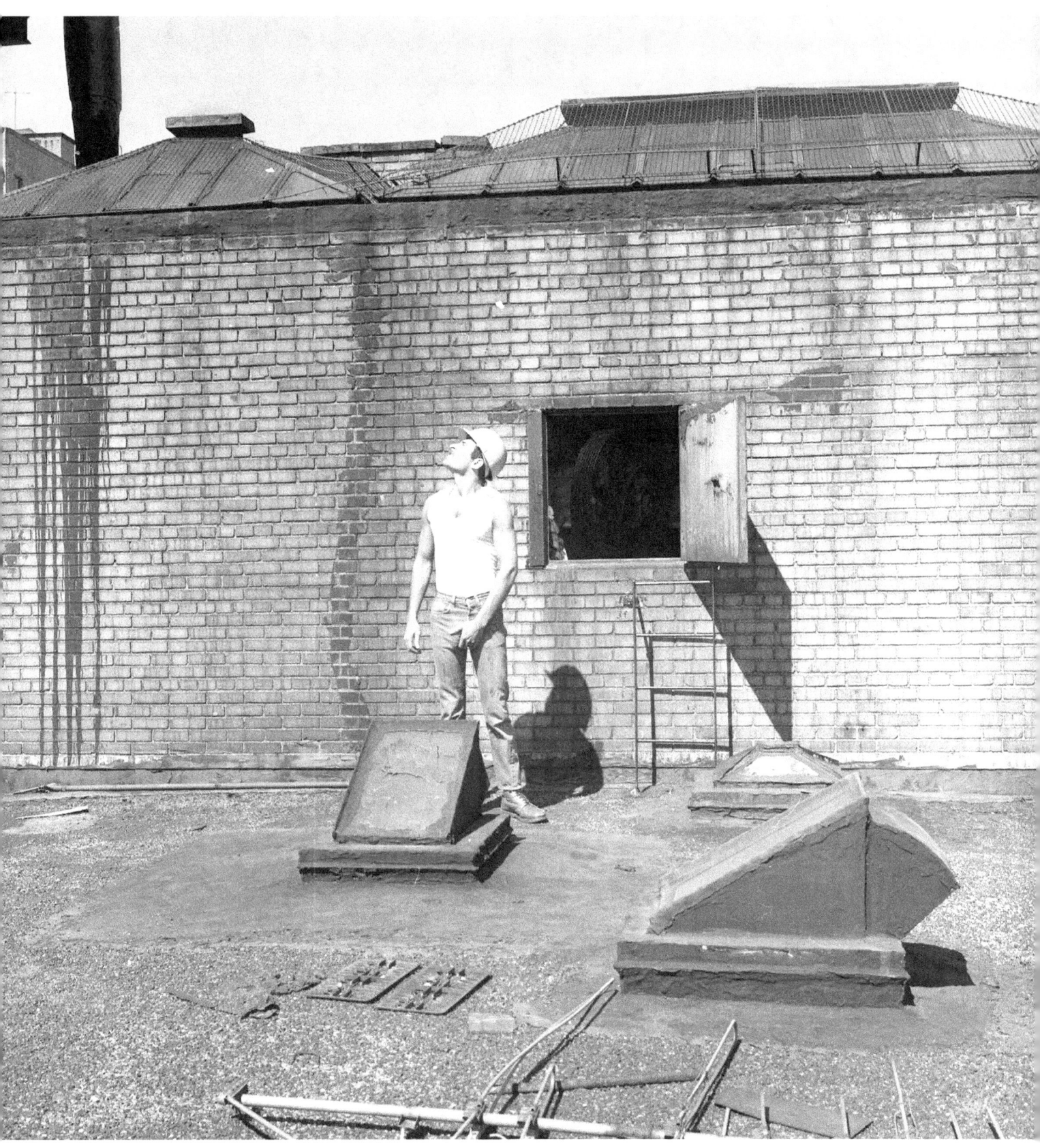

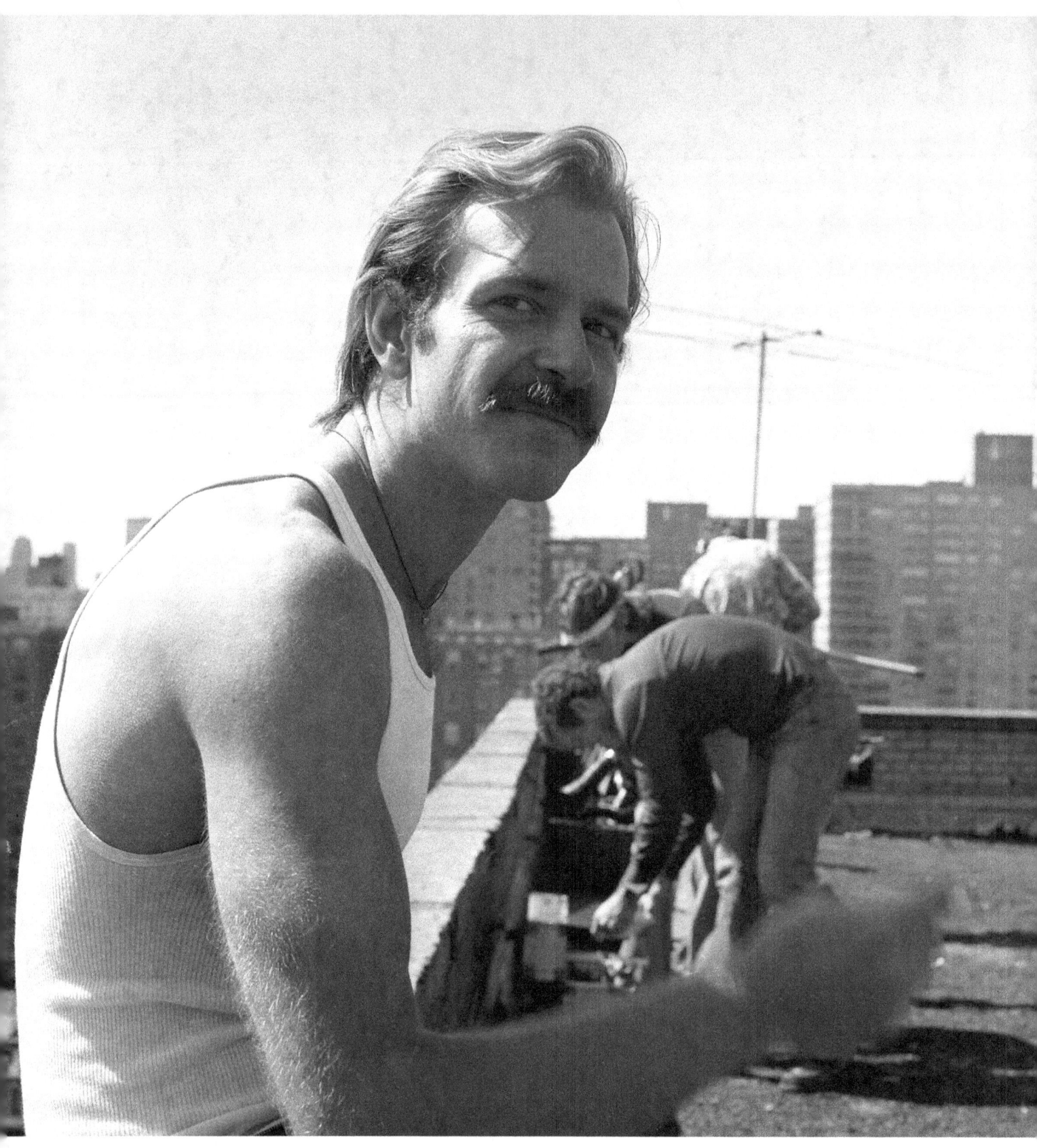

Bobby Cruz

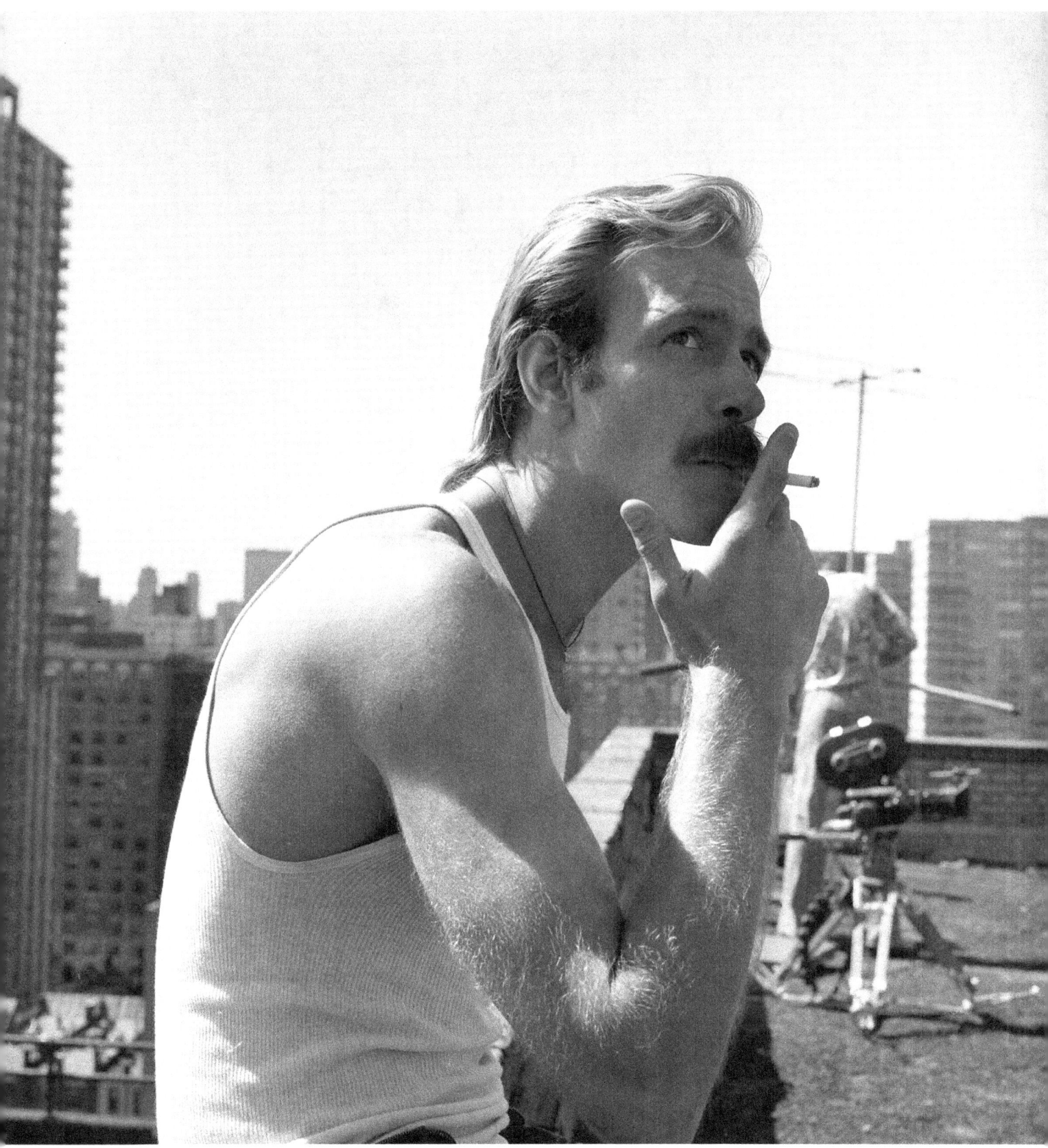

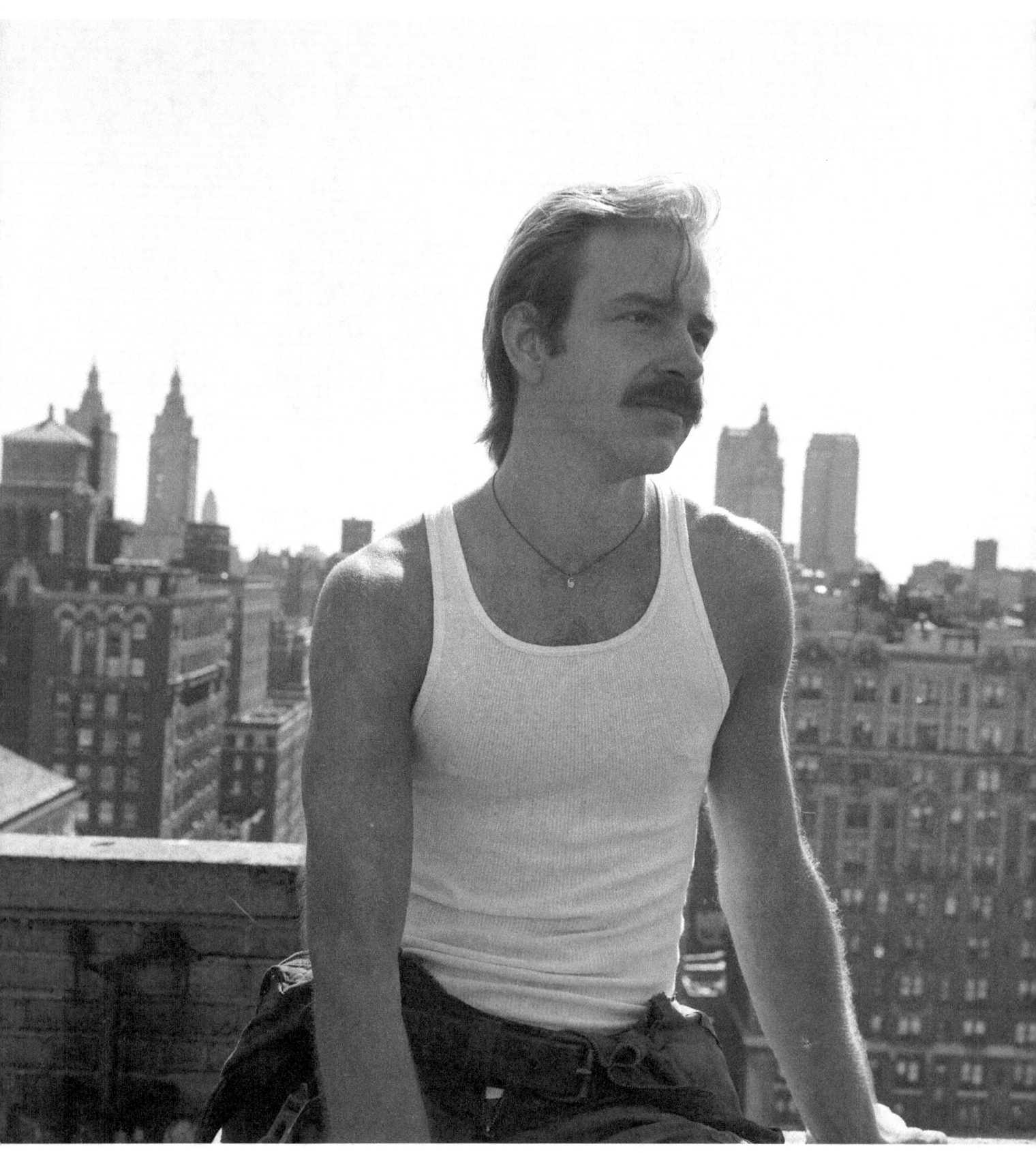

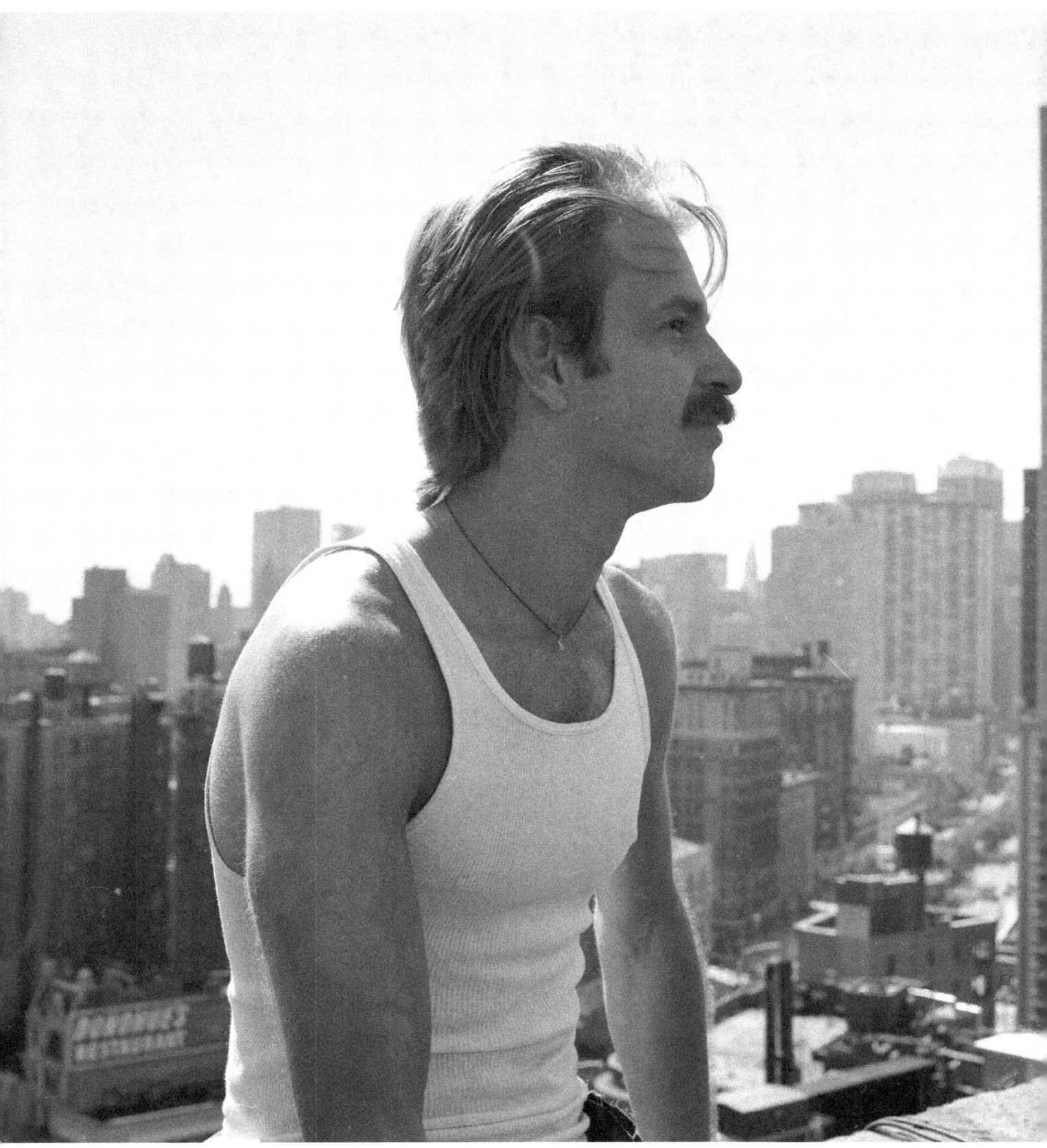

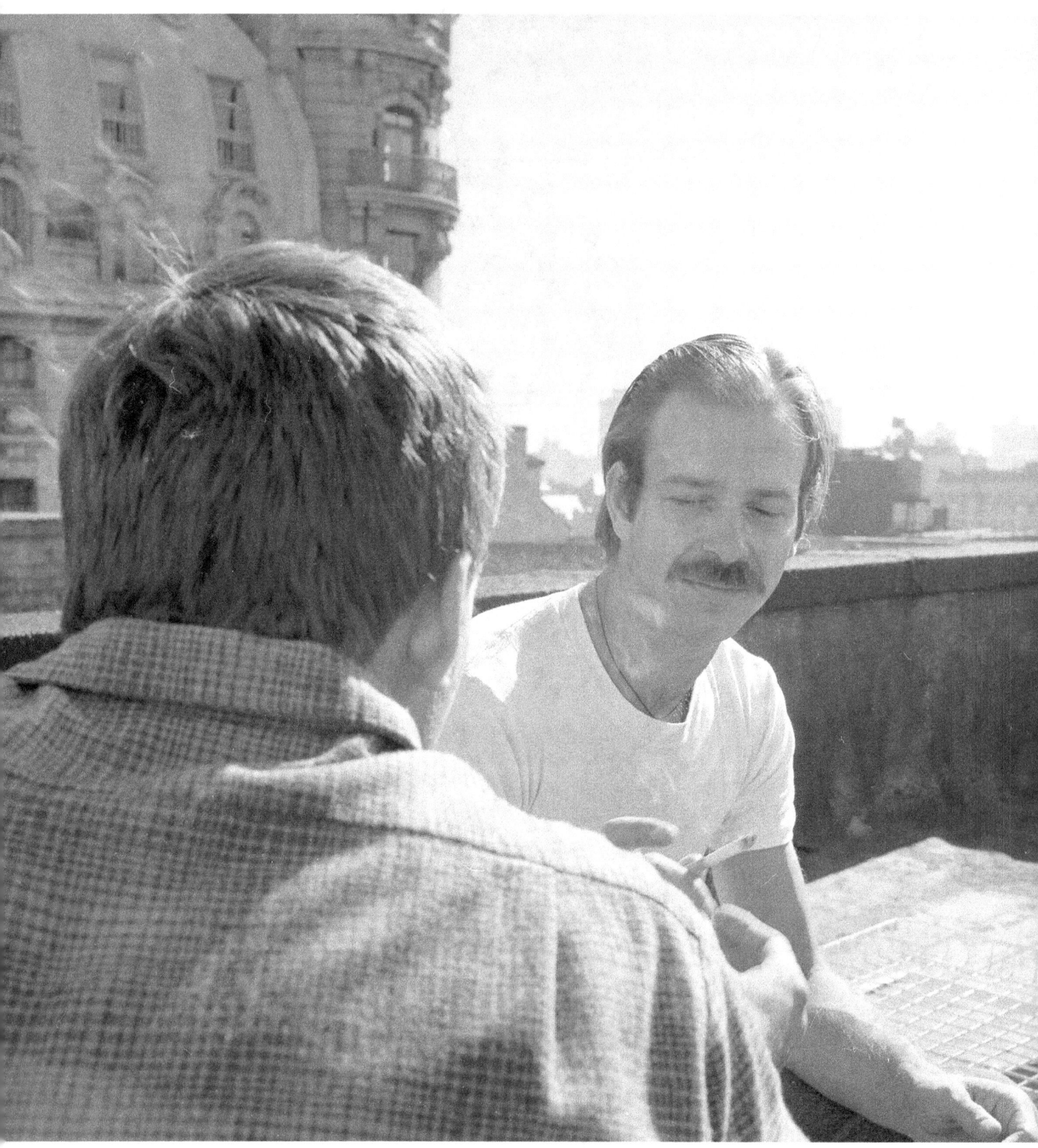

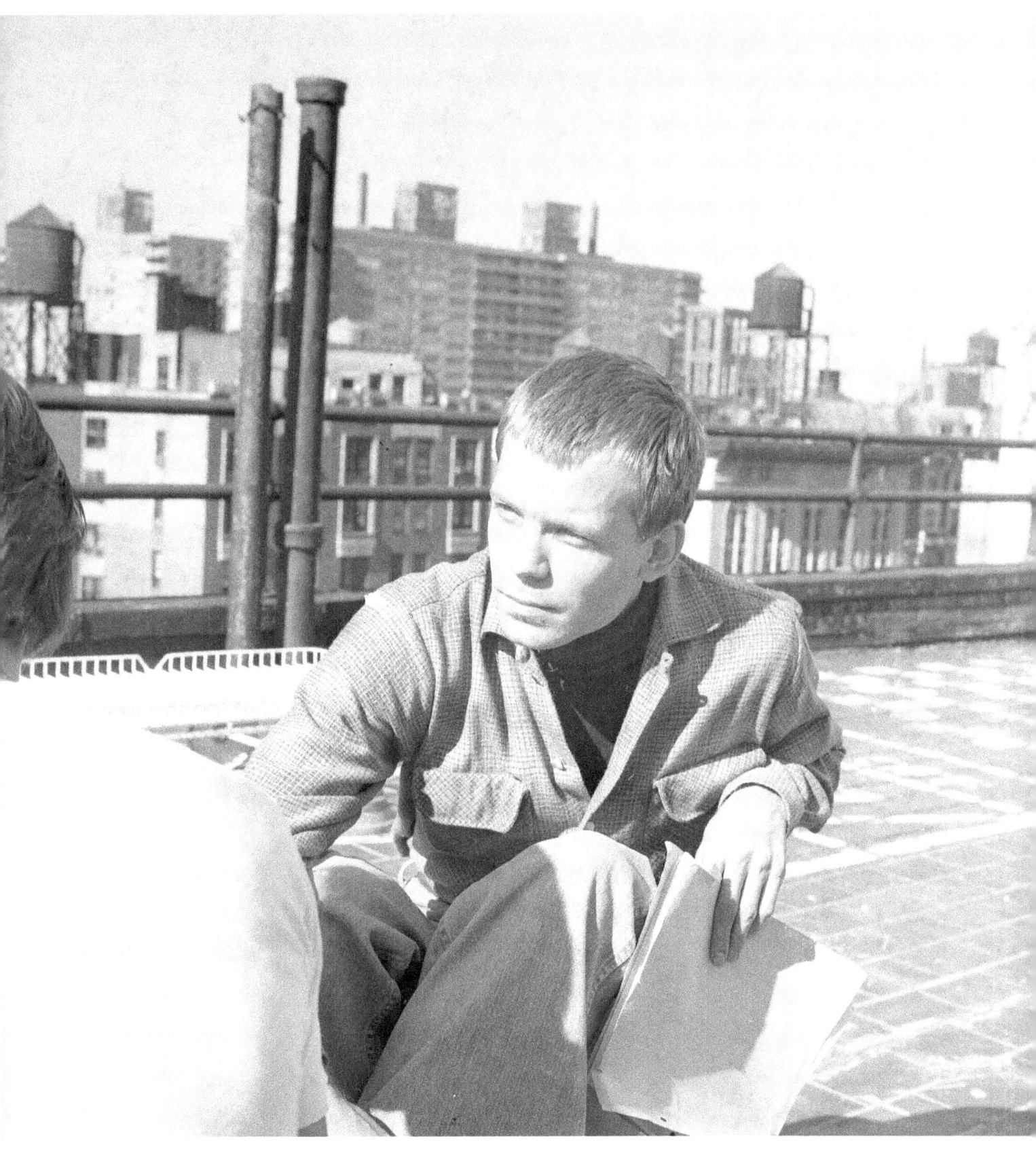

Hugh Allen

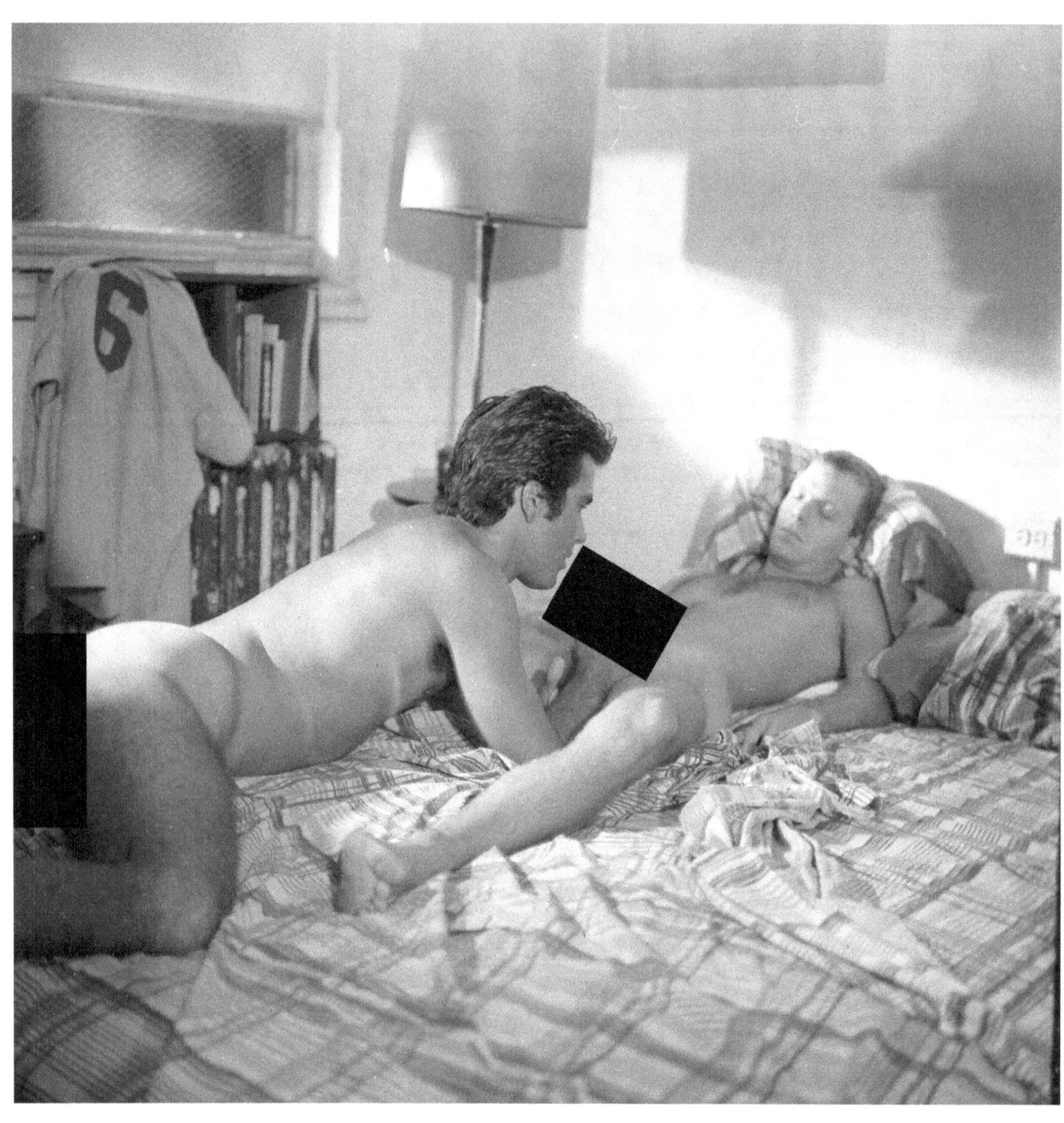

Rit Young and Hugh Allen

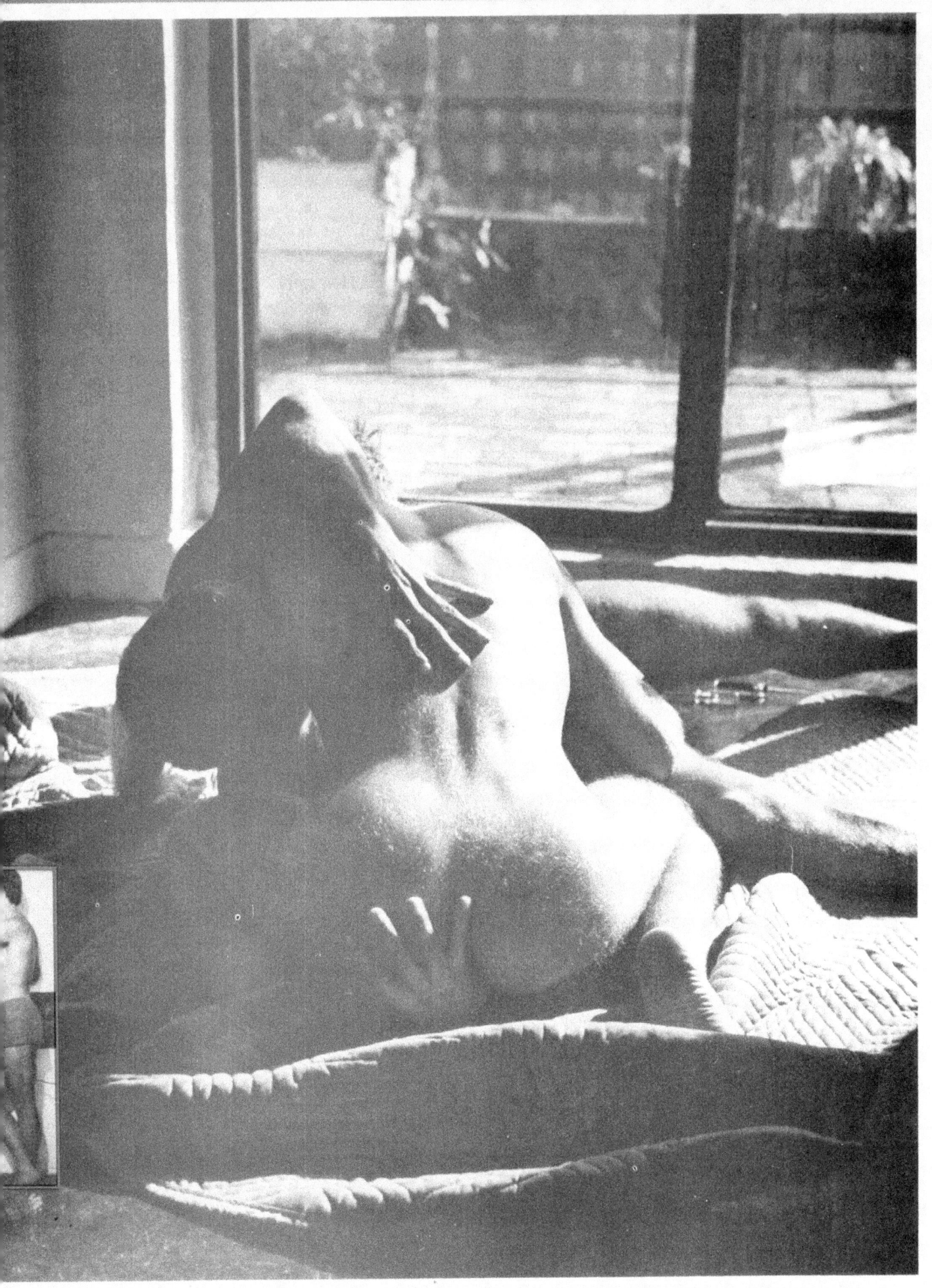

A decade after its initial theatrical release, Jack Deveau's ROUGH TRADES remains a compact little fuckfest featuring half a dozen blue collar fantasy prototypes: a taxi driver, a telephone installer, a handyman, an elevator repairman, a delivery boy – and the host through whose New York apartment they pass. The years have been kind to the film; the fashions of the tradesmen have not dated – do faded Levi's ever go out of style? – and once out of their work-clothes, the six men together constitute, without exception, a Size Queen's Smorgasbord. Nothing much beyond the strictly sexual happens in ROUGH TRADES. Hugh Allen is first-billed in the role of an upwardly mobile yuppy (in the days before the word was coined, when the clone look was still "in"). One day, he leaves his job as an engineer in a recording studio, agrees to a quickie with a friendly cabby (Rit Young), but cuts it short to hurry home to his penthouse apartment, so that he "won't miss the phone man." The phone man (Paolo) arrives, and in time so do the building handyman (Bobby Cruz), an elevator repairman (Myles Longue), and a delivery boy (Steve Cory). The action moves from the terrace to the apartment, from the water tower on top of the building to the elevator shaft to the elevator itself, and the inventive cinematography and editing constantly open up the confines within which the low budget project was made. There are no specific sequences per se, for the constantly changing combinations are constantly cross-cut from one to another in kaleidoscopic fragments of pre-epidemic excess. Rimming, drugs, fisting, and other high risk practices are the order of the day. Among the more memorable images: the telephone man, his tool belt dangling invitingly, casually announcing "I give good head," and then proceeding to prove that that is only one of his talents; the blond handyman and the dark moustachiod repairman – equally hung, equally hard – balling their brains out on top of the elevator shaft; the delivery boy, stalled between floors in the elevator with the telephone man, dildoing the guy's accommodating ass with celery, cucumber, eggplant, bologna, corn on the cob, and finally his own fist; and the climactic three-way in which the top man host finally gets topped. Originally shot on film and transferred to video, ROUGH TRADES has lost color and crispness in the transfer, but none of its nearly non-stop heat.

*Jerry Douglas, *Stallion*

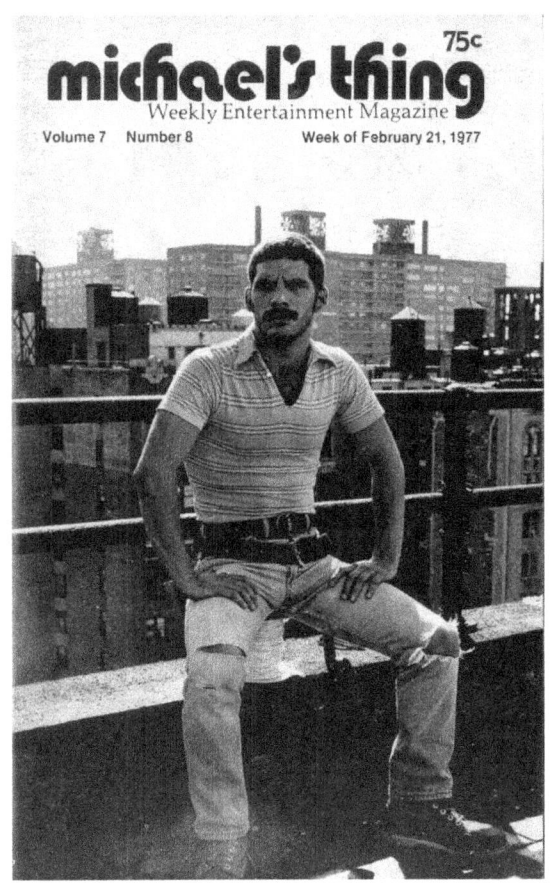

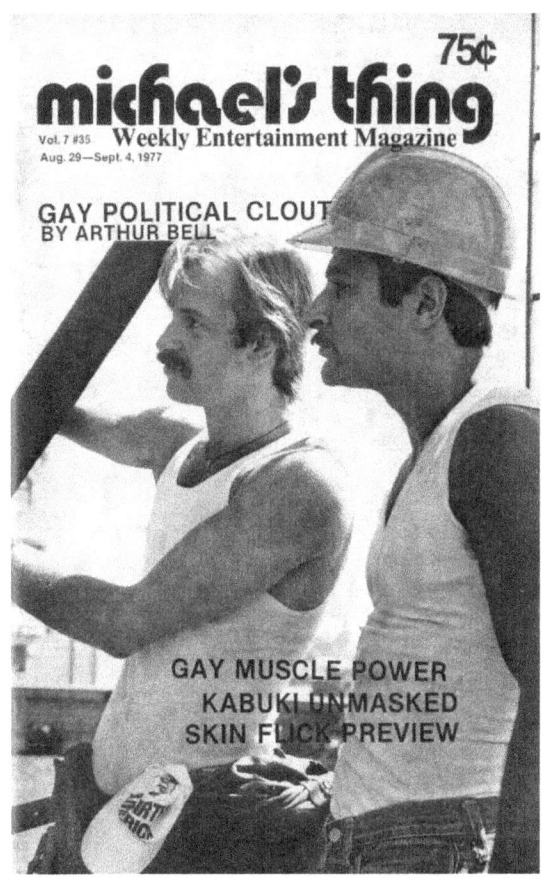

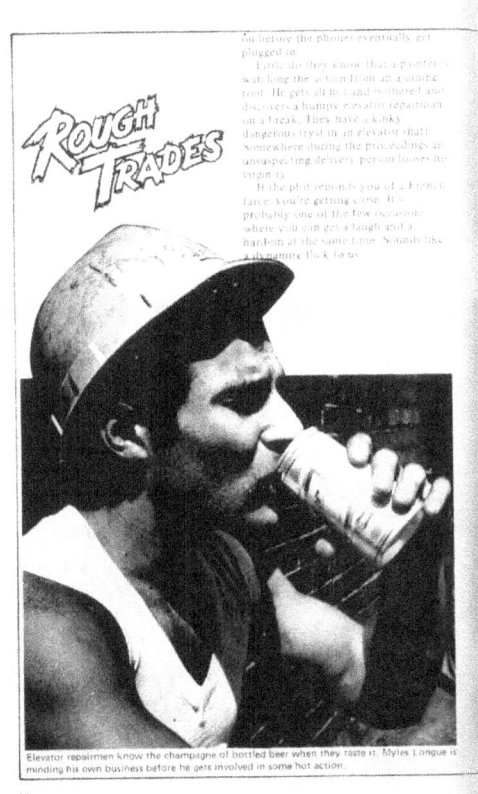

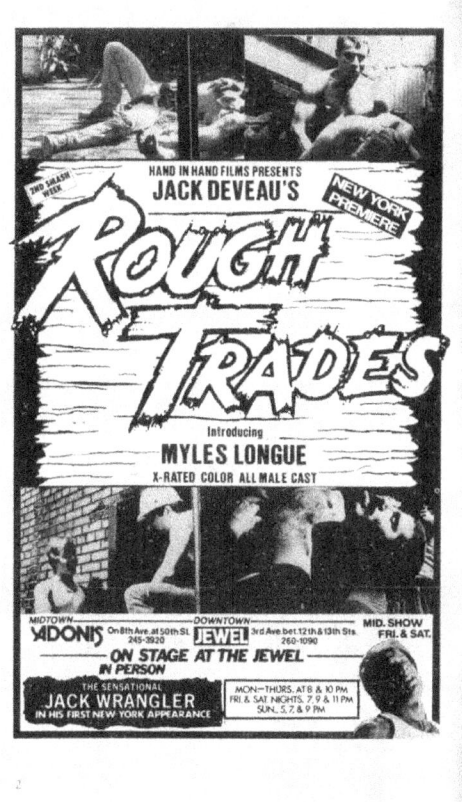

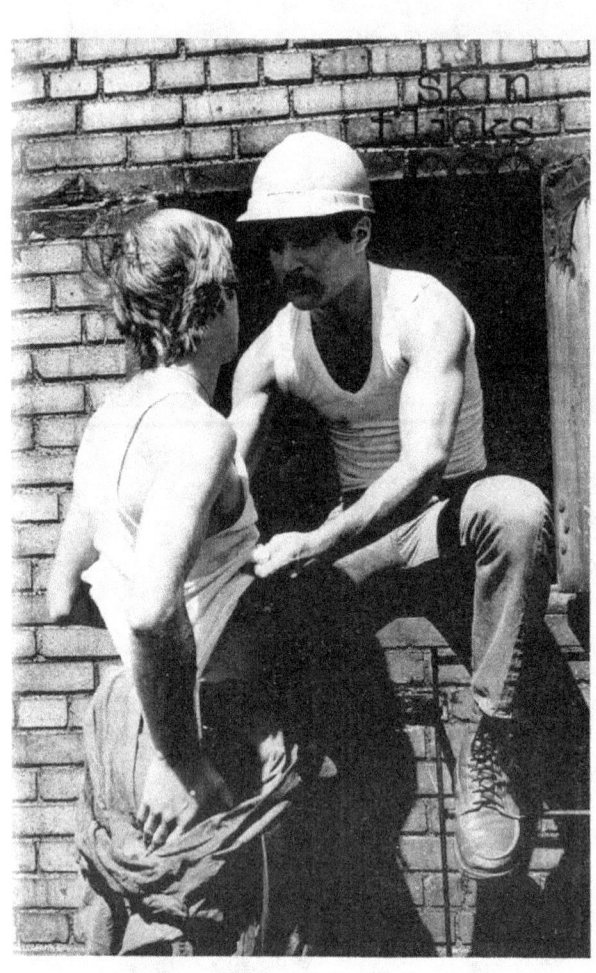

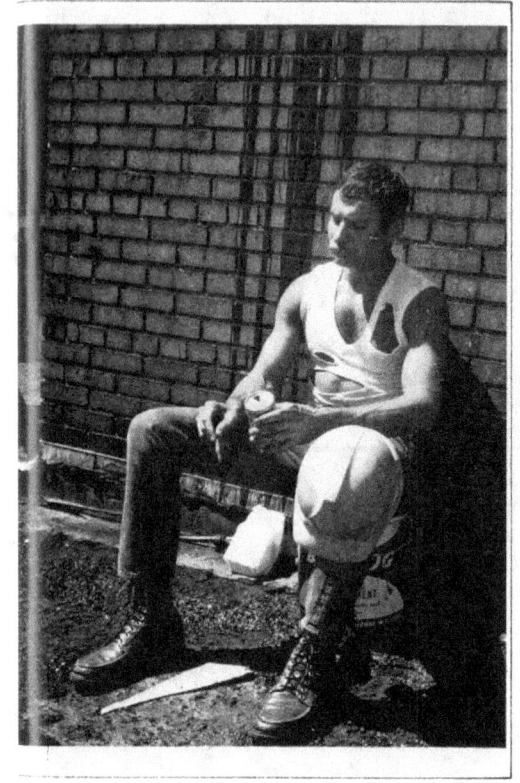

The situation comedy, known in the trade as sit-com, has gone the hard-core porn route in a gay way. The good people at Hand In Hand Films – they always do everything right – will unleash their latest erotic entry, ROUGH TRADES, at the Adonis and Jewel Theatres next week. It'll be a back-to-back engagement, if you know what we mean. The plot (for those who need one) concerns a rock promoter who's just rented a penthouse. When the telephone man comes to install the phones the rock promoter finds him irresistible. You will too. A lot of hot hanky-pank goes on before the phones eventually get plugged in. Little do they know that a painter is watching the action from an ajoining roof. He gets all hot and bothered and discovers a humpy elevator repairman on a break. They have a kinky, dangerous tryst in an elevator shaft. Somewhere during the proceedings an unsuspecting delivery person looses his virginity. If the plot reminds you of a French farce, you're getting close. It's probably one of the few occasions where you can get a laugh and a hard-on at the same time. Sounds like a dynamite flick to us.

*Rough Trades preview, Michael's Thing

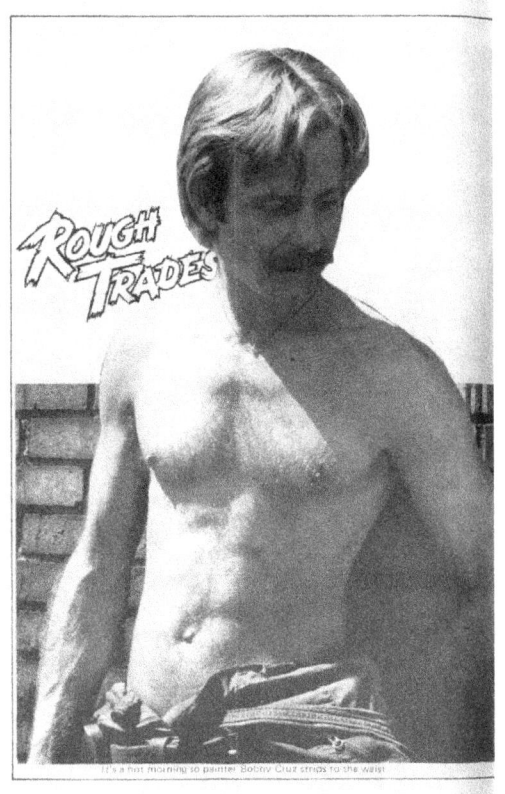

It's a hot morning so painter Bobby Cruz strips to the waist.

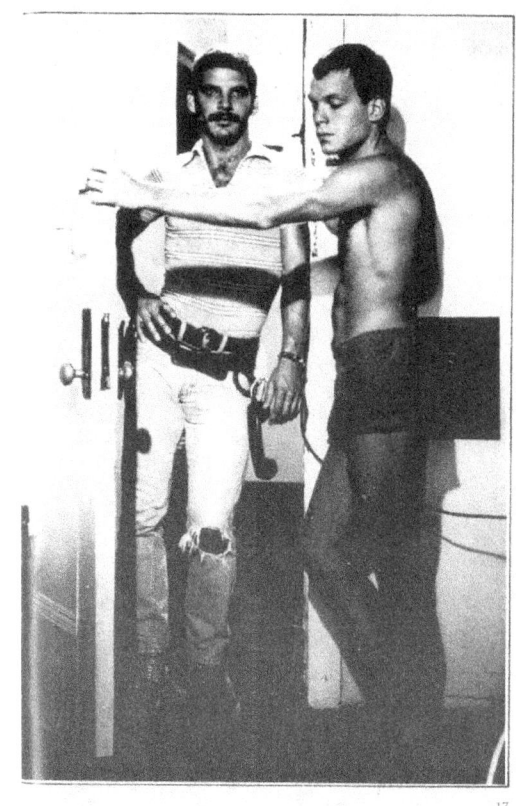

skin flicks ⬥⬥⬥ PREVIEW

Rough Trades

The situation comedy, known in the trade as sit-com, has gone the hard-core porn route in a gay way. The good people at Hand-in-Hand Films—they always do everything right—will unleash their latest erotic entry, *Rough Trades* at the Adonis and Jewel Theatres next week. It'll be a back-to-back engagement, if you know what we mean. The plot (for those who need one) concerns a rock promoter who's just rented a penthouse. When the telephone man comes to install the phones the rock promoter finds him irresistible. You will too. A lot of hot hanky-pank goes

David Gorsky arrives to install the phone. Hugh Allen, a rock producer, knows a hot number when he sees one →

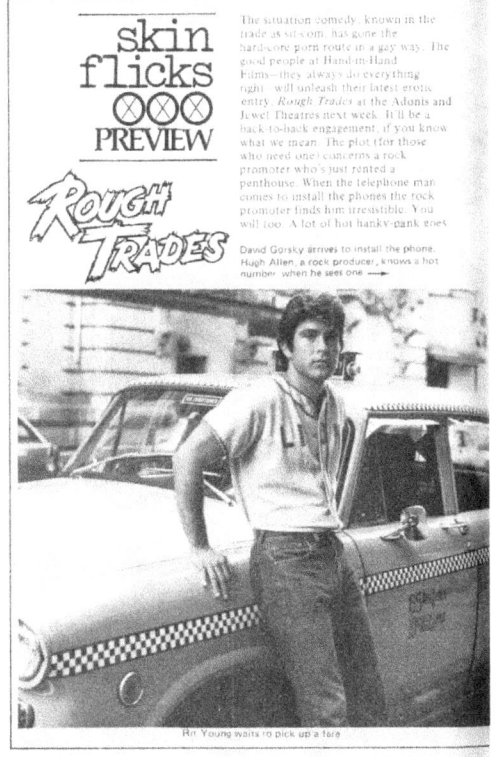

Bo Young waits to pick up a fare.

Steve Dory is a delivery person with more in his bag than sandwiches

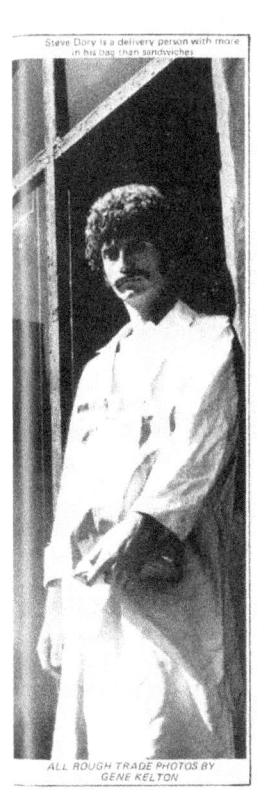

ALL ROUGH TRADE PHOTOS BY GENE KELTON

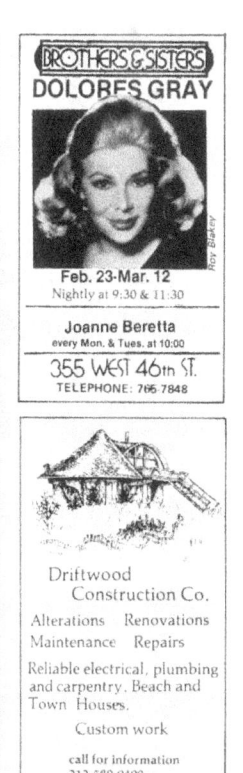

BROTHERS & SISTERS
DOLORES GRAY

Feb. 23–Mar. 12
Nightly at 9:30 & 11:30

Joanne Beretta
every Mon. & Tues. at 10:00

355 WEST 46th ST.
TELEPHONE: 765-7848

Driftwood
Construction Co.

Alterations Renovations
Maintenance Repairs

Reliable electrical, plumbing and carpentry. Beach and Town Houses.

Custom work

call for information
212-580-0490

"Most of the sex in the Hand In Hand movies is almost like documentary filming. You cannot really direct people to be sexually hot, you know? They have to have that in them. And they had to be caught up with it. That's how we built the scenes."

ROBERT ALVAREZ

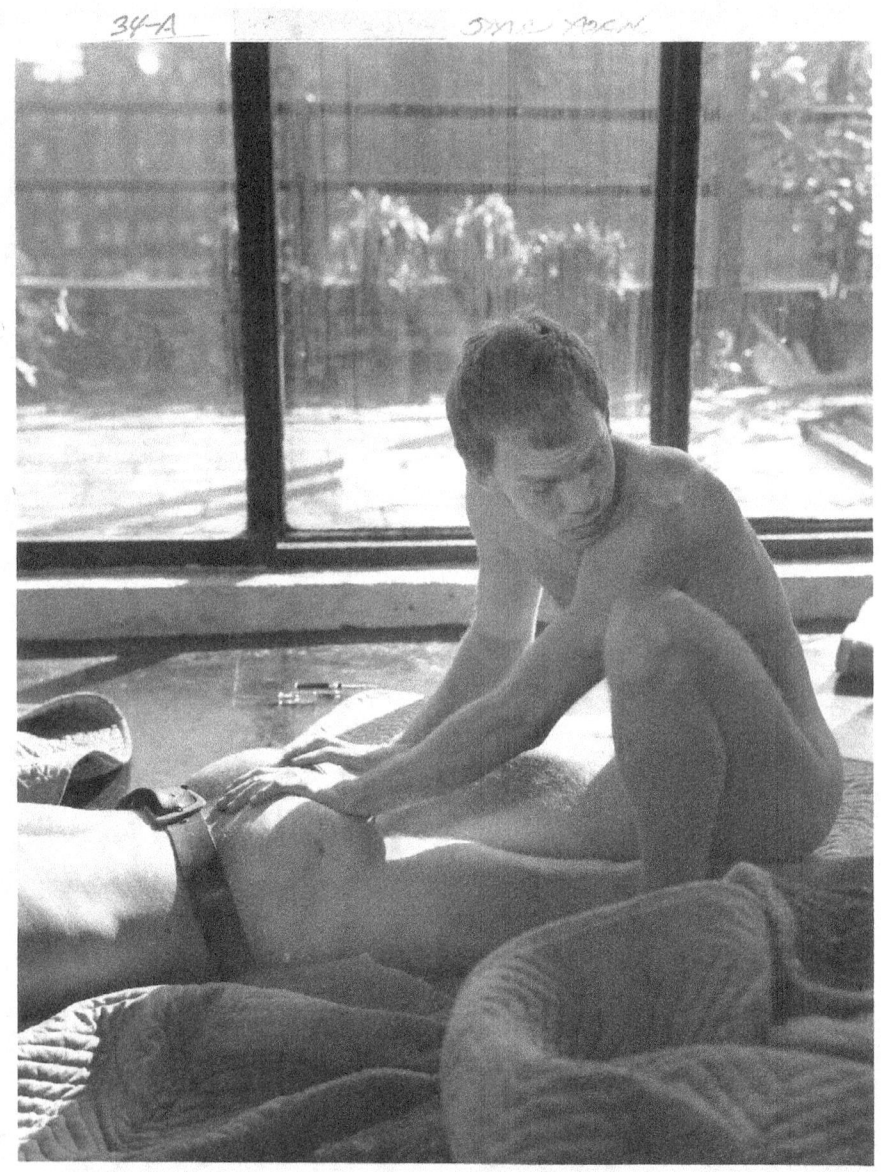

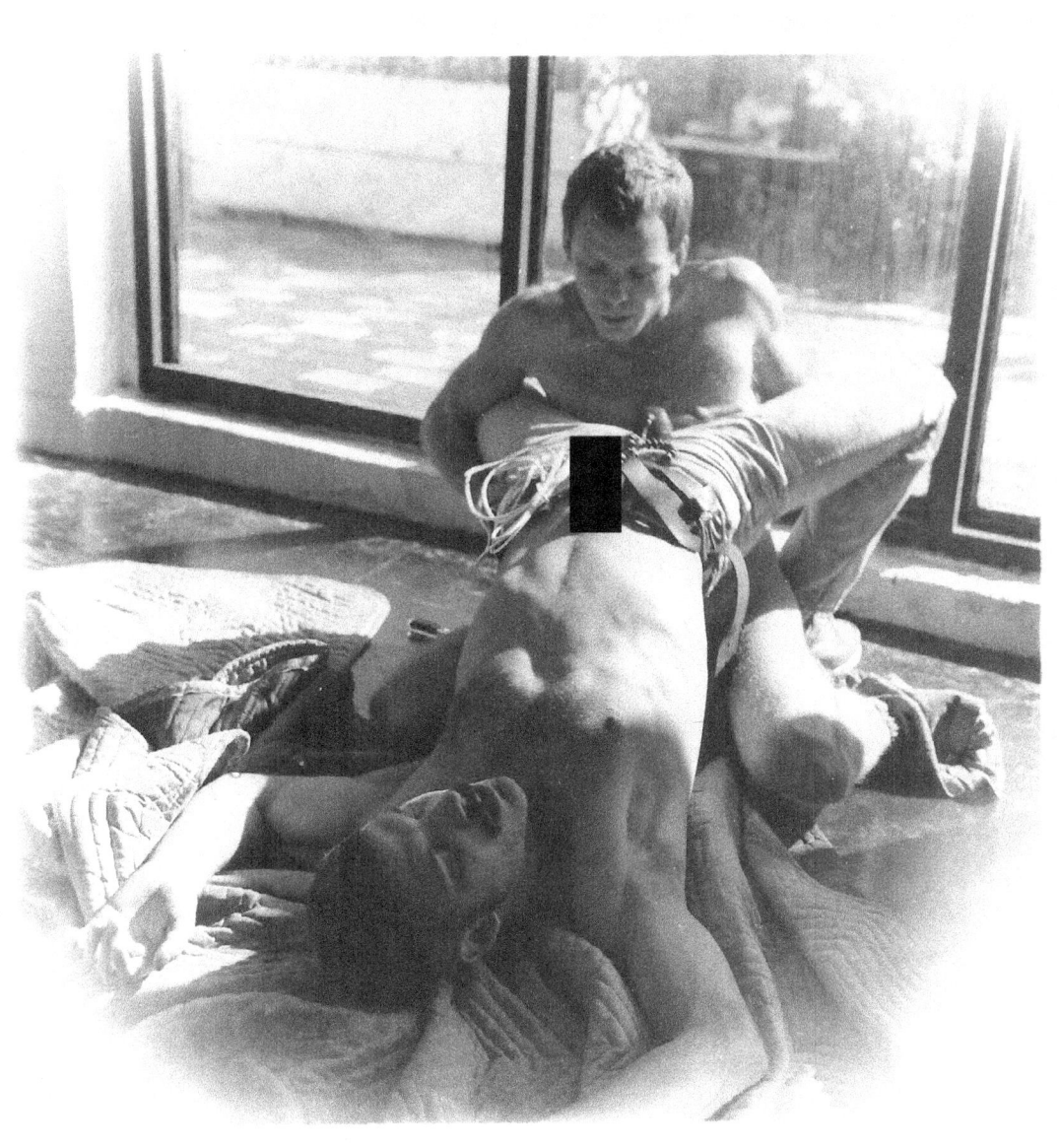

David "Paolo" Gorsky (down) and Hugh Allen in *Rough Trades*

"I like being versatile. I like being more of a top, but it depends on the person."

MYLES LONGUE

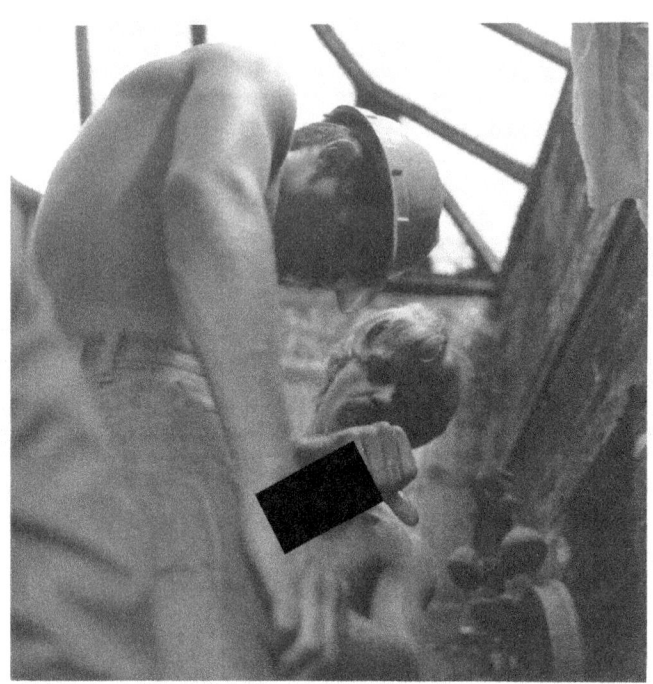

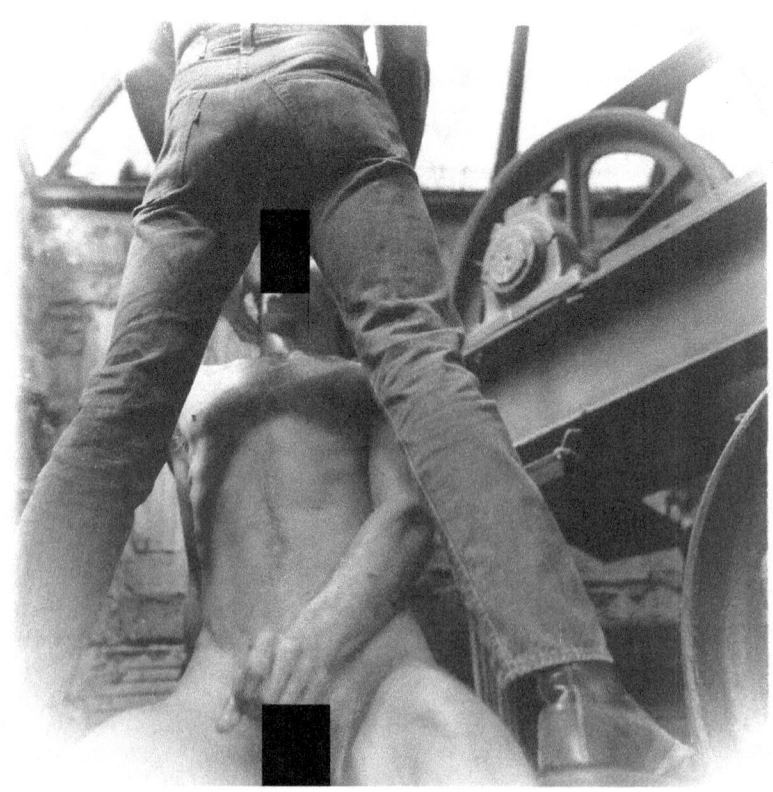

Myles Longue gives it to Bobby Cruz

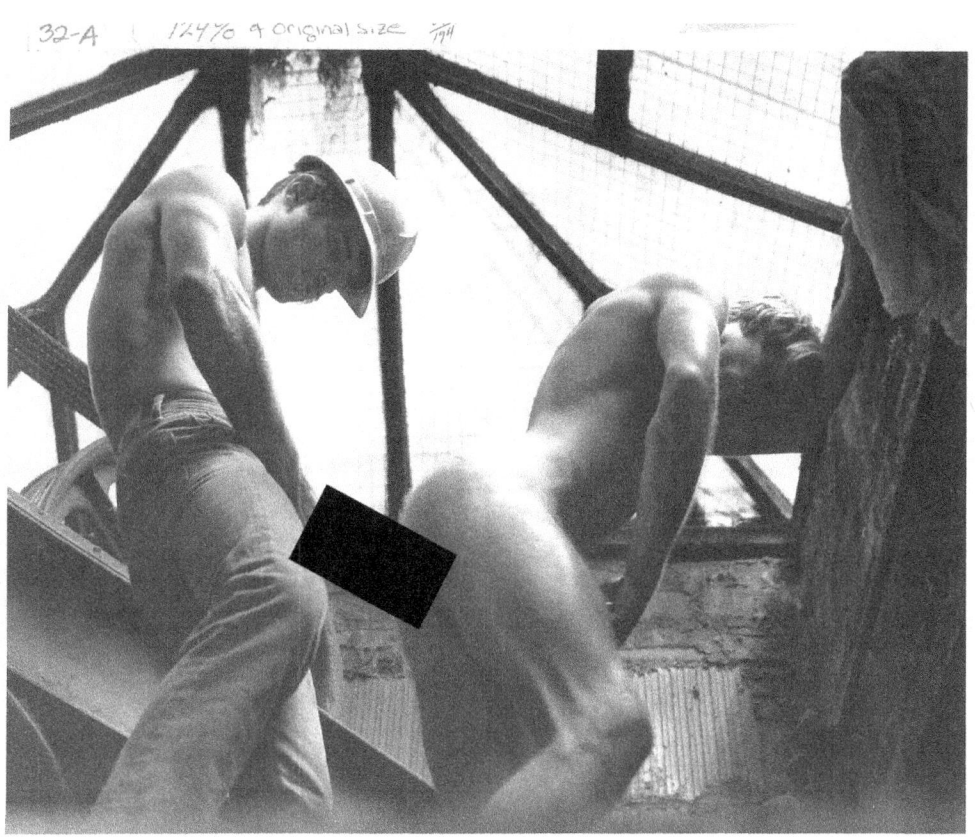

"How did you get the name Myles Longue?" "I'm not sure. I remember on a film set, someone said, 'Your dick is a mile long.' And that's all I heard. The next thing I knew I saw it on paper – Myles Longue. What a name! I didn't want to deal with Myles Longue."
Manshots interview by Tony Hartman

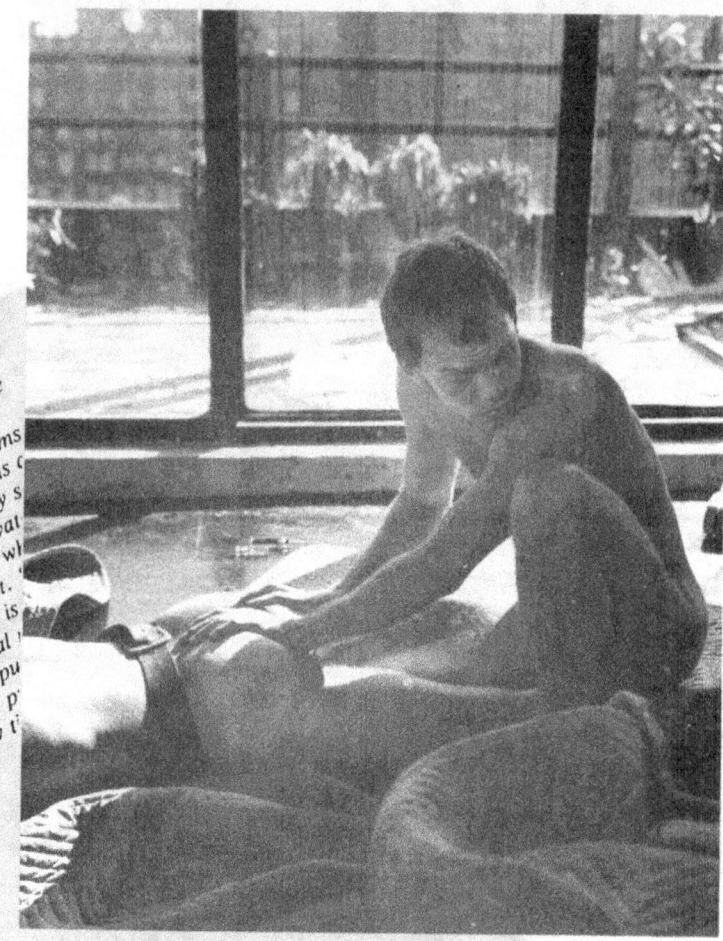

A Festival of Hand in Hand Films continues on its erotic way this week at the Jewel, 3rd Ave. bet. 12th and 13th Sts., with **Rough Trades** and "The Erotic Films of Peter de Rome." "Rough Trades" is a working man's film just full of sweaty s... and hot action. The scene in the eleva... shaft is positively riviting. You see w... happening but you don't believe it. ... Erotic Films of Peter de Rome" is ... of intimate studies on the sexual ... men on the prowl. It kind of pu... back into fuck films without t... off. Call 260-1090 for show t...

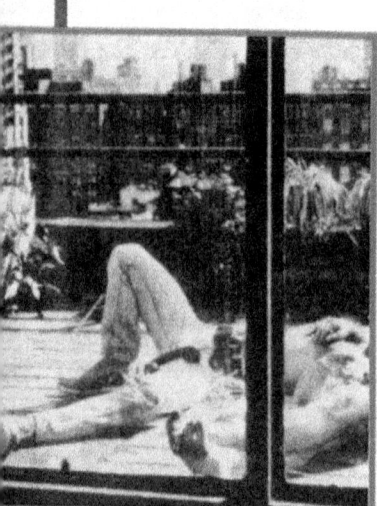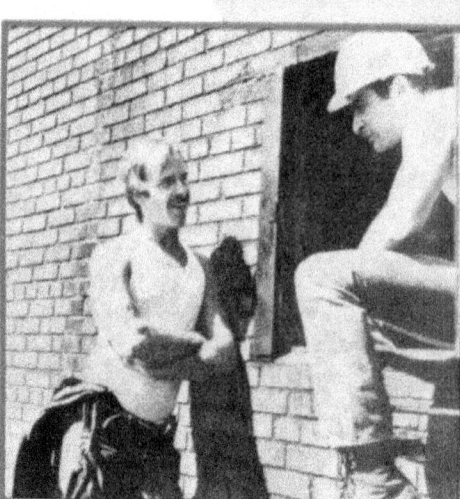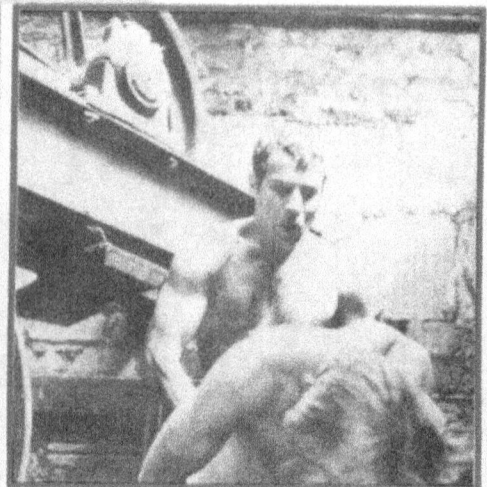

don't get

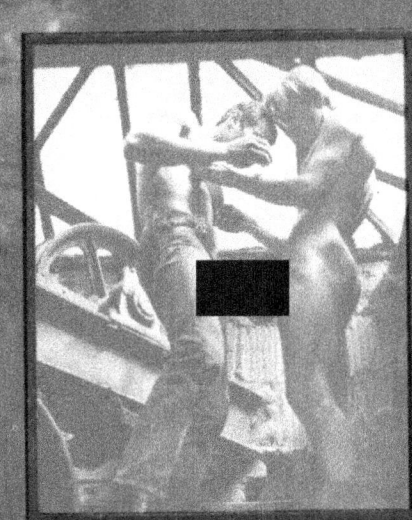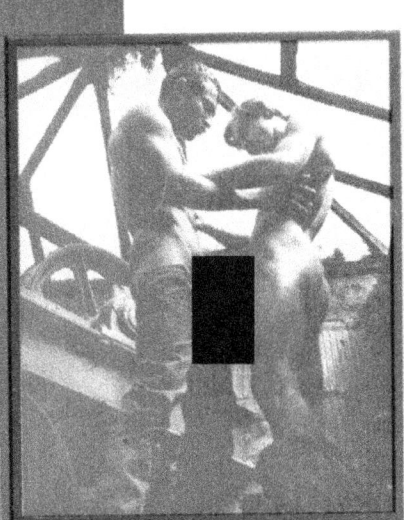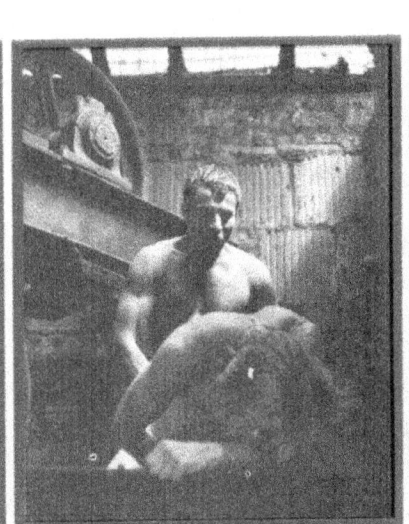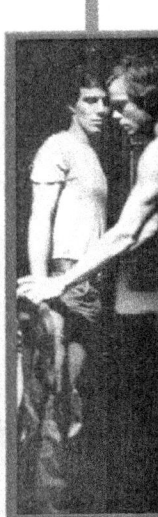

NEW FROM HAND IN HAND

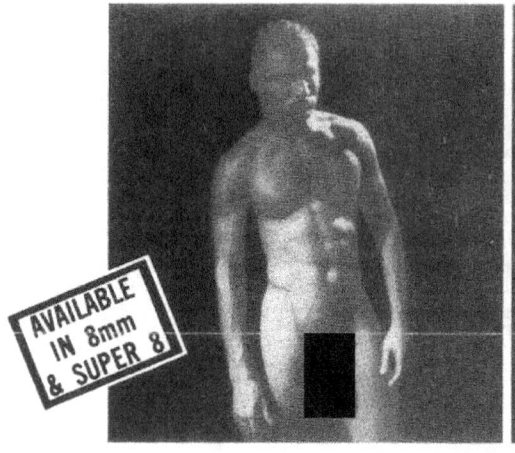
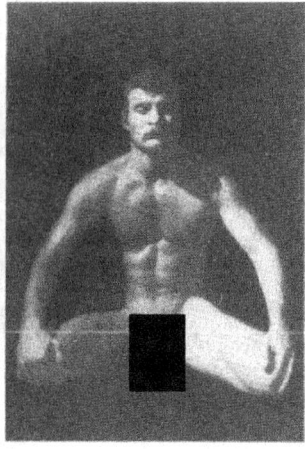

AVAILABLE IN 8mm & SUPER 8

MYLES LONGUE in
NARCISSUS II

Hand in Hand's newest discovery, the star of the forthcoming "Rough Trades", Myles Longue appears in this extra hot, extra special film. Myles, who's equipment has to be seen in action to be believed, meets his own hard image and the exchange of looks, sweat, and strokes will set fire to your projector. Filmed with a special camera process, Myles meets Myles, and in a double long narcissistic fantasy. The film sizzles with pecks, abdominals, biceps and 10 plus hard cocks. Their meeting and appreciation of each others own muscular bodies produces two of the longest and hottest orgasms ever. Each of them drip with cum as one after the other gets off in two big ball busting orgasms. When he tastes his own cum, you'll want to taste it too. This is truly an amazing film, starring an amazing man. Narcissus II is 200 feet of hard action color film. It's the hot stuff your dreams are made of. If you like Bill Young, you'll cream over Myles Longue.

ORDER FORM

PAUL SONNEBERG ● 9 PATCHIN PLACE #9, NEW YORK, N.Y. 10011

MAKE CHECKS PAYABLE TO ABOVE

IMPORTANT NOTICE: We have secured the services of a new lab. All prints are of superb quality, clarity, focus and color.

Enclosed is $_____ by ☐ Check ☐ Money Order ☐ Bank Check

	8mm COLOR $28.00	SUPER 8 COLOR $28.00	TOTAL
NARCISSUS from Peter de Rome's Adam & Yves			
NARCISSUS II with Myles Longue			
THE BLACK ORGY from Peter de Rome's Adam & Yves			
TOTAL			
HANDLING			
PLUS AIRMAIL			
PLUS REGISTERED MAIL			
TOTAL			

Name _____
Address _____
City _____
State _____
Zip _____
Print clearly, ZIP Code must be included.

A. AIRMAIL: U.S., Canada, and Mexico please include 50c extra for each film ordered. Overseas: Please include $4.00 extra for each film.

B. REGISTERED MAIL: (U.S.Only) If you wish, we will send your order via Registered Mail, which insures delivery to you personally. Please include $2.00 Registration Fee for this purpose.

C. FOREIGN ORDERS: Please make payment by cash, International Bank, or Postal Money Order, made out in American Dollars only.

SHIPMENT: All packages are sent in safe shipping bags. Orders by Money Order, Bank Check, or Personal Check from established clientele take about a week for shipment. Personal checks from new clients must await minimum clearance time, averaging 2 weeks.

YOU MUST COMPLETE REVERSE SIDE OF ORDER FORM

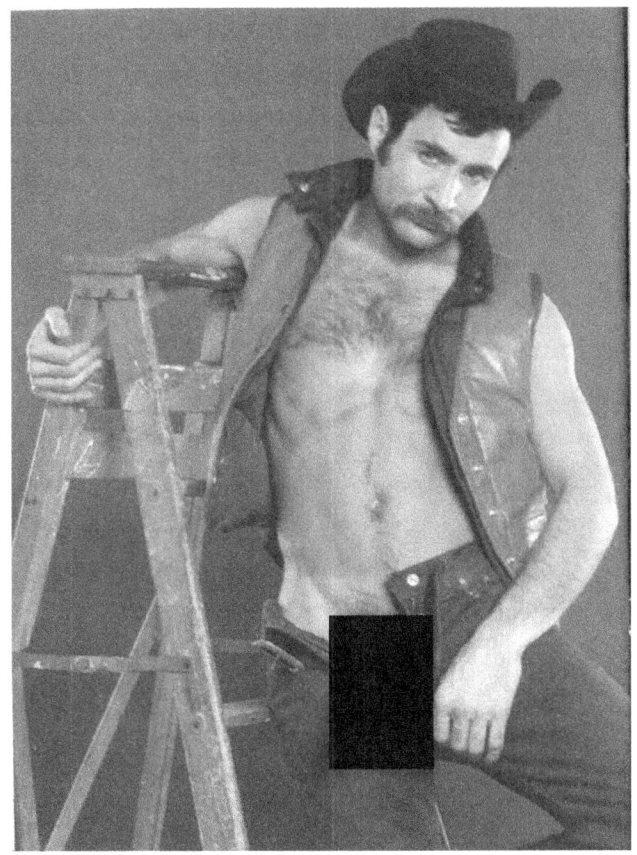 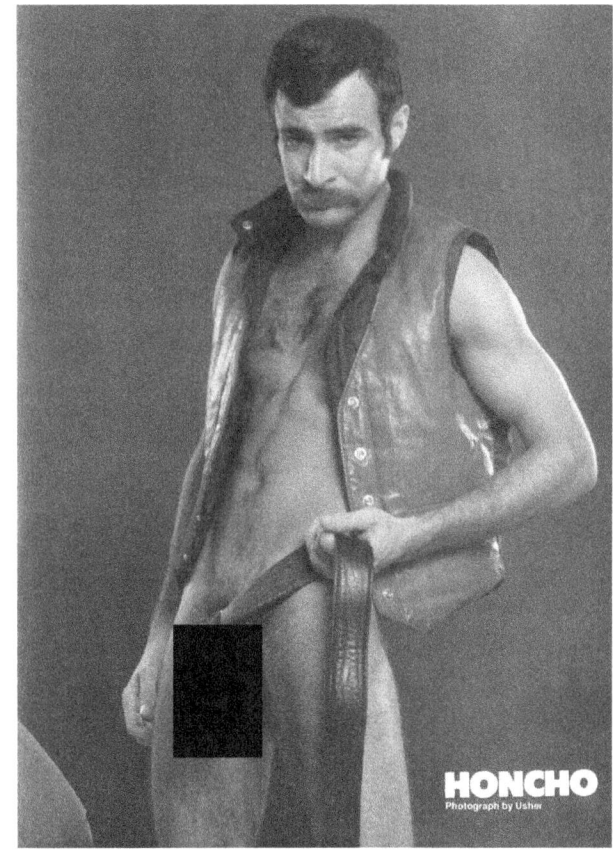

"Actually, farming is very sexual, because you see animals constantly having sex. It was a trip watching my horse jack off… where they beat their dicks against their stomachs and they do it long enough until they shoot. That was how a horse jacked off. I used to get really excited watching that shit."

MYLES LONGUE AKA ED WILEY

"My dad and my brother and my cousins are very well endowed, too. My father was German and thick. Once, when my brother and I were young, we were watching my father take a shower and we could see in the side window, and my brother turned to me and said, "I hope we grow up like that!" And I said, "Well, I hope so, too!"

Tom DeSimone - Hollywood's

by Barnaby Shackleford

"Hollywood is not the glitter of false tinsel. When you peel away the false tinsel, there is real tinsel underneath." – Fred Allen

Filmmaker Tom DeSimone settled comfortably into a chair in his Hollywood office. The room is decorated to accommodate a modern movie mogul which, in every sense, Tom DeSimone is. The office looks much the way Sam Goldwyn's must have looked, or Darryl Zanuck's - except, of course, it's smaller; and the pictures which line the walls aren't of willowy starlets, but of hunky, handsome young men in various states of undress and excitement. Although he looked tanned, fit and successful as he settled in, DeSimone was a man with a complaint; several, in fact. "People expect porno filmmakers to be fat, bald, old men with big cigars," he said, smiling the faintly, rueful smile of the frequently misunderstood. "They're always mildly shocked when I turn out to be normal." Normally, of course, is relative. The producer of DUST UNTO DUST, CONFESSIONS OF A MALE GROUPIE, and EROTIKUS is unlikely to be elected Man of the Year by the Hollywood Chamber of Commerce. On the other hand, it isn't difficult to see the personable DeSimone as he sees himself as a professional filmmaker who only coincidentally makes male films featuring explicit sex. Even *Daily Variety*, Hollywood's prestigious trade paper, concedes that CATCHING UP – DeSimone's most recent release – demonstrates "assured, professional competence." Actually, that's not surprising. DeSimone holds an M.A. from UCLA and has produced more than 50 films – everything from the most dingy, 400 foot, backroom "loop" to semi-sociological features like ONE, a study of teenage masturbation. And in his most recent film, DeSimone handles writing and directing chores as well. He is as close to being an "auteur" as it's possible to get without being Bergman or Jerry Lewis.

DeSimone's trademark is fully developed characterization. He likes to take the time to create people you can care about; so, when the time comes to hop into bed, you give a damn what happens to them. "In most pornos they start sucking right away," he says, "You don't know who the people are and you don't care. I think that's cheating. I like to provide something more." In CATCHING UP the extra ingredient is humor – satire mingles with the sex. The laughs, however, don't diminish the film's erotic appeal. DeSimone concedes the porno business isn't famous for respecting the audience. He quite candidly says there are only three theatres in the country (the Adonis in New York, the Vista in L.A., and the Nob Hill in San Francisco) that care about what they are doing or about who they are doing it to. "The others

MODERN   MOVIE   MOGUL

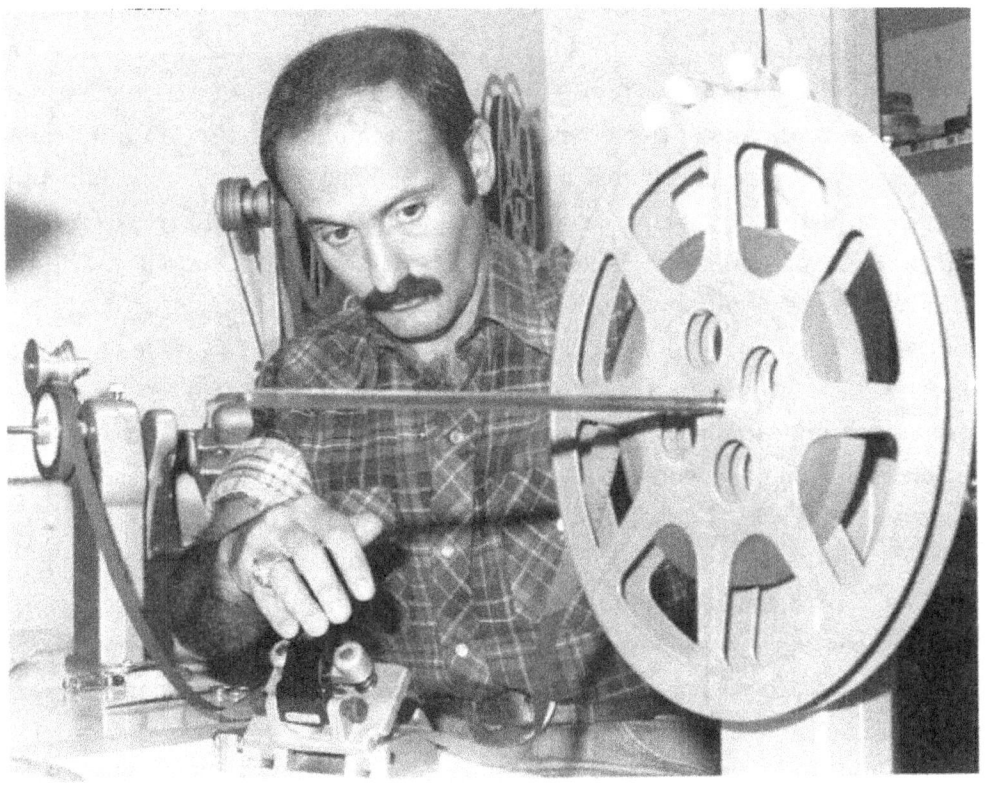

TOM DeSIMONE
hollywood's modern movie mogul

By BARNABY SHACKLEFORD

"Hollywood is not the glitter of false tinsel. When you peel away the false tinsel, there is real tinsel underneath."
— Fred Allen

Filmmaker Tom DeSimone settled comfortably into a chair in his Hollywood office. The room is decorated to accommodate a modern movie mogul which, in every sense, Tom DeSimone is. The office looks much the way Sam Goldwyn's must have looked, or Darryl Zanuck's — except, of course, it's smaller; and the pictures which line the walls aren't of willowy startlets, but of hunky, handsome young men in various states of undress and excitement.

Although he looked tanned, fit and successful as he settled in, DeSimone was a man with a complaint, several, in fact.

"People expect porno filmmakers to be fat, bald, old men with big cigars," he said, smiling the faintly rueful smile of the frequently misunderstood.

"They're always mildly shocked when I turn out to be normal."

Normalcy, of course, is relative. The producer of "*Dust to Dust*," "*Confessions of a Male Groupie*," and "*Erotikus*" is unlikely to be elected Man of the Year by the Hollywood Chamber of Commerce.

On the other hand, it isn't difficult to see the personable DeSimone as he sees himself, as a professional filmmaker who only coincidentally makes male films featuring explicit sex.

Even *Daily Variety*, Hollywood's prestigious trade paper, concedes that "*Catching Up*" — DeSimone's most recent release — demonstrates "assured, professional competence."

Actually, that's not surprising. DeSimone holds an M.A. from UCLA and has produced more than 50 films — everything from the most dingy, 400 foot, backroom "loop" to semi-sociological features like "*One*," a study of teenage masturbation.

And in his most recent film, DeSimone handles writing and directing chores as well. He is as close to being an "auteur" as it's possible to get without being Bergman or Jerry Lewis.

don't give a damn," he says, "Their attitude is, 'Aw, hell, they're just beating off in there anyway.' The audience picks up on it, of course, and sort of slinks in – eyes cast down, collar turned up – as though they were doing something wrong." DeSimone reacts strongly to this self-perpetuating cycle of sleaze because he is one of those who brought the male hard action film from a position just above white slavery to one just below respectability. "There is incredible acceptance now," he says, "largely due, I suppose, to the success of DEEP THROAT and BEHIND THE GREEN DOOR. But when I started in this business in the late '60s, everybody was paranoid all the time. Actors were never told where the location was beforehand. And when they were finally taken there, they weren't allowed to make telephone calls. It was kind of creepy. But it was necessary. People got busted all the time. My first film – an S&M feature called THE COLLECTION – was busted twice while it was running at the old Avon Theater on Hollywood Boulevard. That was one of our biggest problems. Managers were always calling and complaining they had nothing to show because the Vice had confiscated the film."

Lately, however the porno film has become a cult phenomenon. The intellectuals have taken them up. They are discussed on late night talk shows. Ann Landers is preparing a position paper. Ironically, success has created problems of a different kind. Pornos are so chic these days that there is some dispute about who made the classics. Since most of the early films were made anonymously, credit is easy to claim. Porno pioneers often selected names at random. "We called ourselves anything that popped into our heads. I made some films as 'I.M. Horney' and others as 'Lancer Brooks.' I finally settled on 'Lancer Brooks' because the distributor said it was easier to sell a film if he could point to something else the guy had done. The irritating thing is that 'Lancer' did some of my best work," DeSimone says. "Even though 'Lancer Brooks' is a ridiculous name," he says, "at least it's better than 'I.M. Horney'." DeSimone, who seems to specialize in demolishing preconceptions, is also irritated by people who believe porno filmmakers live incredibly decadent lives, surrounded by beautiful, naked boys. He flatly denies it. But the graphic photographs which adorn the walls seem to contradict him. Smiling slightly, DeSimone, when pressed, admits his work does require him *occasionally* to be surrounded by a *few* naked boys. And *some* of them are beautiful. And one or two are as sexy as hell. "Actually, the sex scenes are the most difficult part of the film. They're hard (no pun intended) because so many things can go wrong. One thing I've learned," he says, "is to keep the actors apart until the scene is ready to go. I had two actors once who couldn't keep away from each other. While I was directing a complicated dramatic scene they were in the bedroom doing everything to one another. When I was finally ready for them they were exhausted. They had cock ring on up to *there* and still nothing. I should have had the camera in the bedroom. Sex isn't very filmic," DeSimone has

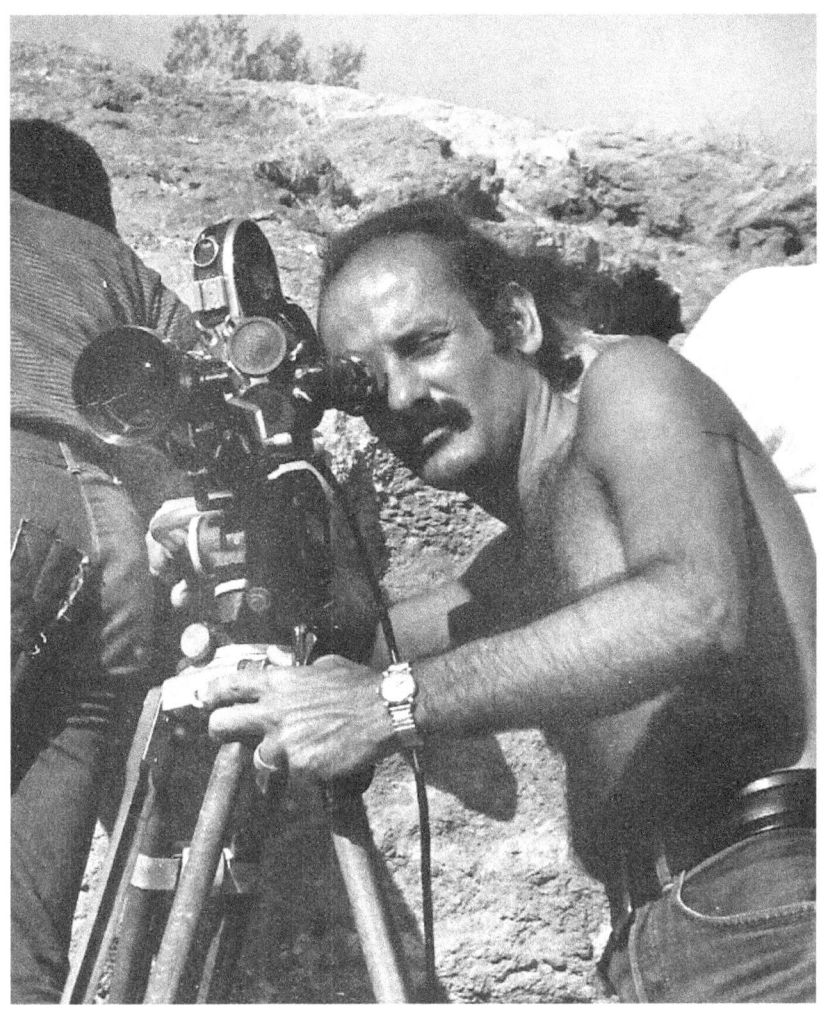

has discovered. "Something may feel good, but not be very attractive or interesting to look at. Much of the time, it's like open heart surgery." However much DeSimone would like to see himself as just another businessman – and, obviously, there are parallels; there are, just as obviously, vast dissimilarities. For instance, where does he find the actors for his numerous projects. Surely he doesn't run an ad in the *Los Angeles Times*. "Well," he says, "for one thing we don't use many real actors. Actors worry about their 'image.' Particularly in a gay film. If you are up there on the screen sucking some guy's cock you are doing something more than acting." Plenty of people, though, are eager to appear in DeSimone's minor epics. "I go through the ads in *The Advocate* and call up the models. I ask them if they want to be in a film. Many of them say no. Others come in and fill out an application. The application, to put it mildly, is frank, i.e. *circle your choice* - A.) Sexually I am: Aggressive. Passive. Either. B.) The type of sex I like is: Romantic. Rough. Dirty. S&M. Other. C.) I dig: Butch. Fems. Thin. Heavy. Hairy. Younger. Older. Blondes. Dark. Negro. Caucasian. Makes no difference.

yes or no – Are you into: Bondage. Being Tied. Slapping. Being Slapped. Whipping. Being Whipped. Other.
Yes, yes, yes, yes, yes, yes, yes, yes. Everything.

"In fact," DeSimone says, suddenly all business, "you can fill one of these out if you like." Ah, how sweet," I said, blushing becomingly. So, as the sun sets slowly over pornoland, we leave Tom DeSimone as he rummages through stacks of pictures and applications, mumbling gently that no one understands what a serious business he's in.

PRESS REVIEWS 3

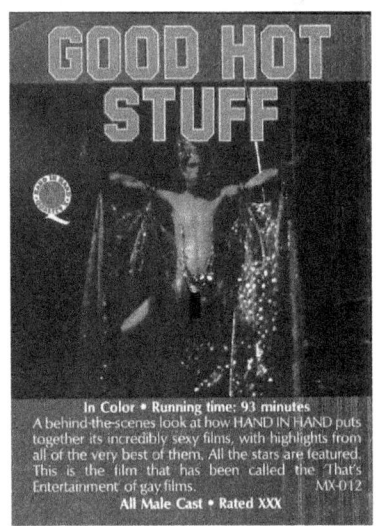

A behind-the-scenes look at porno filmmaking during the Seventies, as well as an hour and a half commercial for Hand In Hand films, GOOD HOT STUFF is a compendium of the best moments from that studio's films, each good hot sequence being used to illustrate one aspect of the craft. (It is not to be confused with the Buckshot Video of the same title.) Narrated by actor Mark Woodward, this anthology begins with three different scenes from the landmark LEFT-HANDED, the company's first (and enormously successful) effort. One of the most intriguing inclusions is the short piece, UNDERGROUND, from THE EROTIC FILMS OF PETER DE ROME. Shot entirely (and illegally) in the New York subway, the film actually manages to record a blow job, a stand-up fuck, and the obligatory cum shot, with passengers and even, at one point, a policeman nearby. Talk about danger scenes! As Woodward points out, "Shooting porn requires not only ingenuity, but balls of brass." After discussing scripts and shooting, GOOD HOT STUFF next provides an insight into the editing process, using Bill Eld's onanistic solo, NARCISSUS, from ADAM & YVES. Next, between the sizzling orgy scene from THE NIGHT BEFORE and the handballing episode from DRIVE, there is a quick selection of "outtakes, bloopers, and fuck-ups" which provides a delightful change of pace in the rhythms of the film. Vignettes from BALLET DOWN THE HIGHWAY (a blow job in the cab of a trailertruck) and WANTED: BILLY THE KID (a bisexual three-way) round out the piece, but the most unusual is saved for last. Footage from an uncompleted film, BEYOND THESE DOORS, brings GOOD HOT STUFF to its close. A lavish epic of ancient Baghdad, what film was actually shot reminds one more than a little of those old Maria Montez tits-and-sand epics. In this instance, however, the men (including Woodward himself) are the most striking in the film, and if the chiffon walls and crotchless satin pantaloons seem a bit silly, the action does not. As Woodward points out, pornography documents our sexual attitudes and acts as no sociological tract can. He adds, in conclusion, that in the future "the good hot stuff will even get hotter." – and all one has to do is look through the pages of this magazine to know he was absolutely right.

*Jerry Douglas, *Stallion*

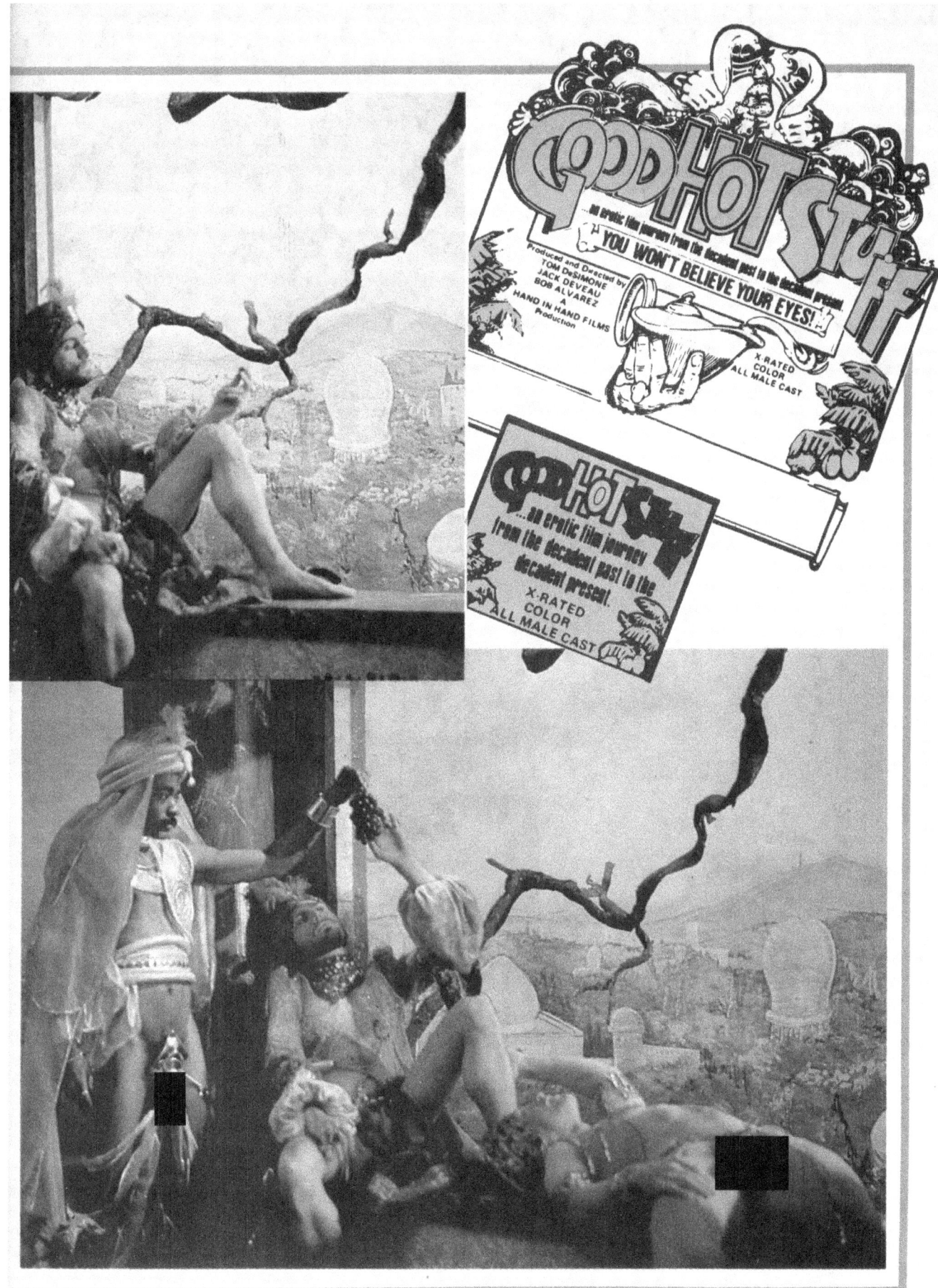

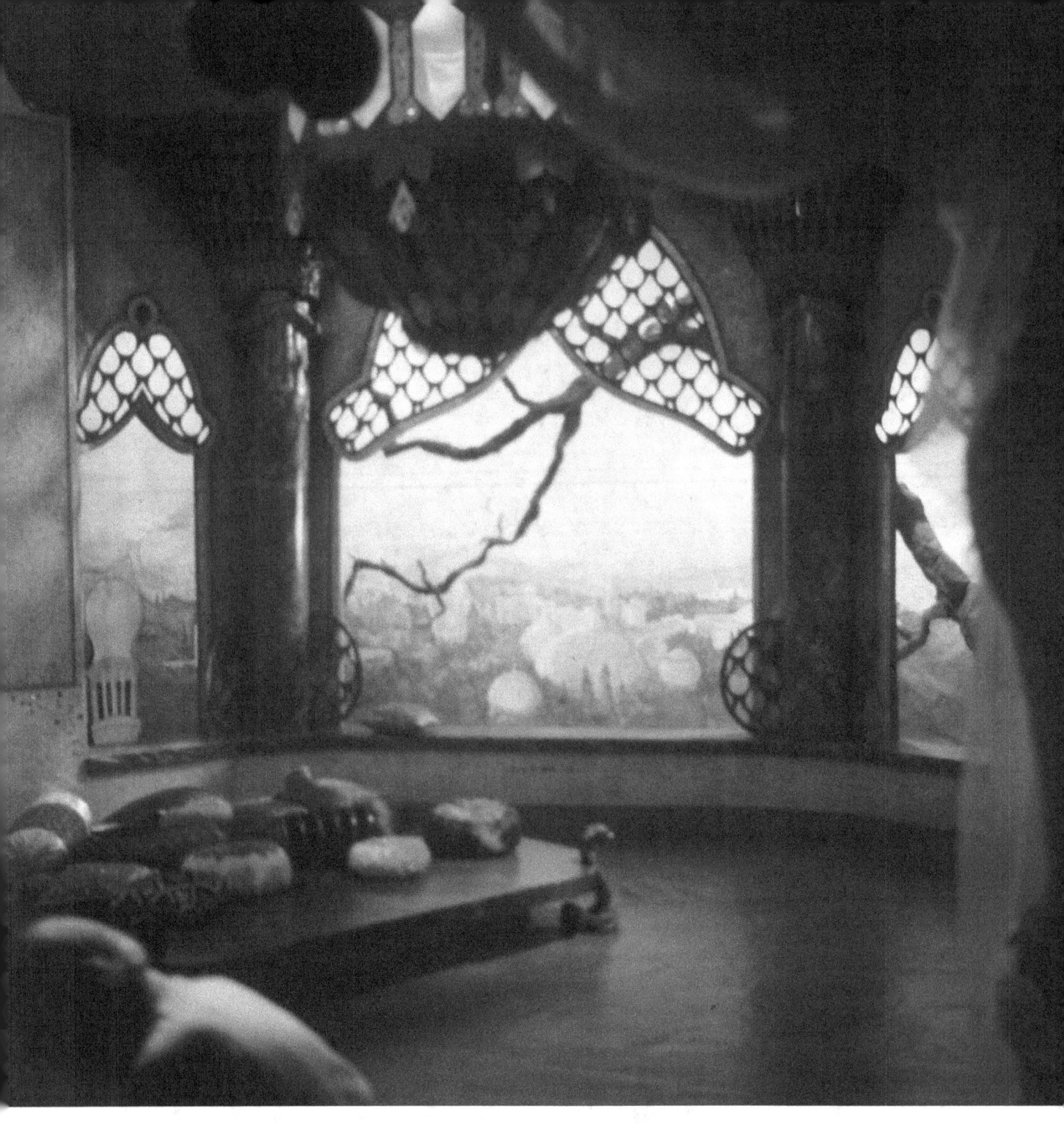

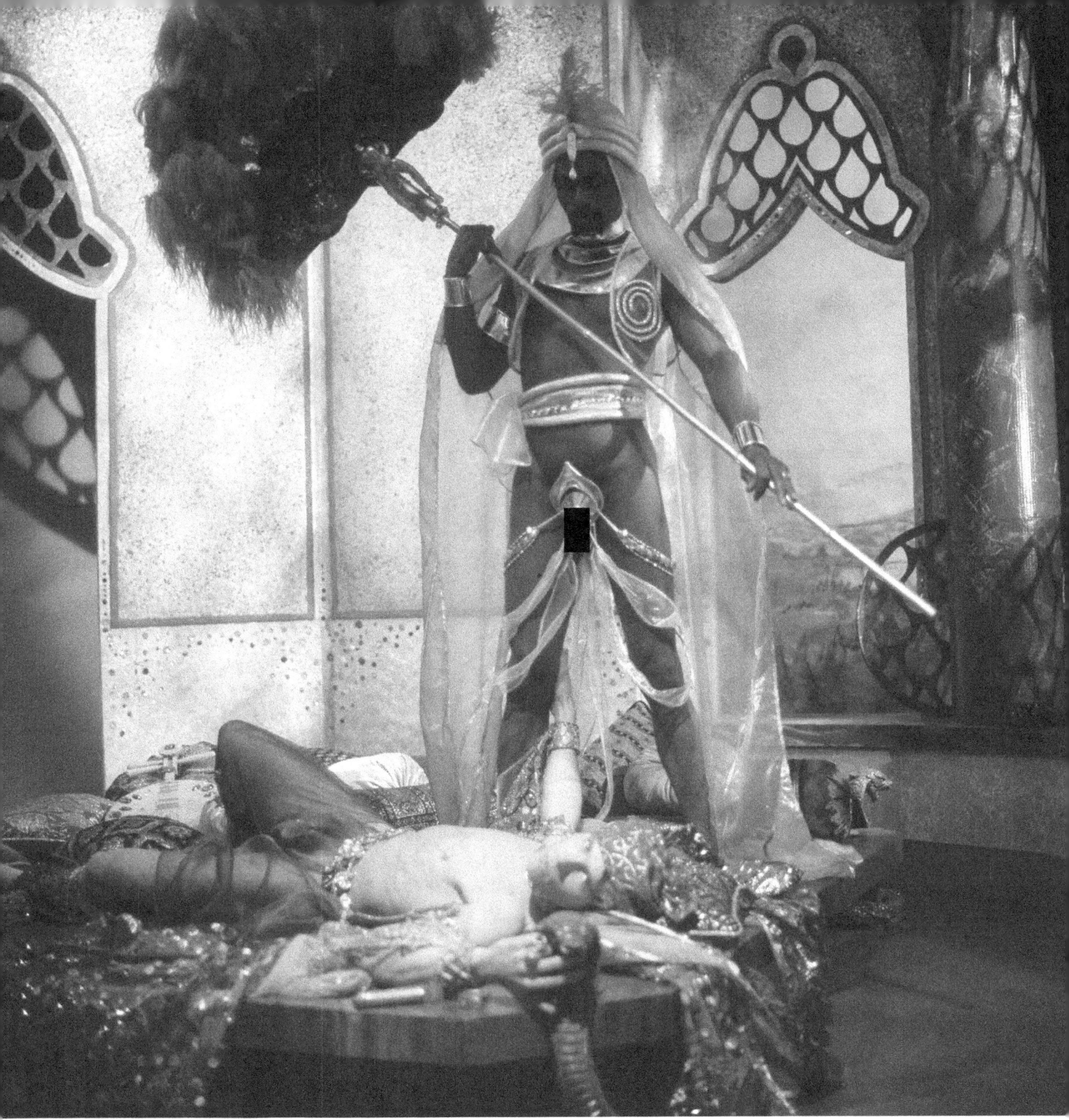

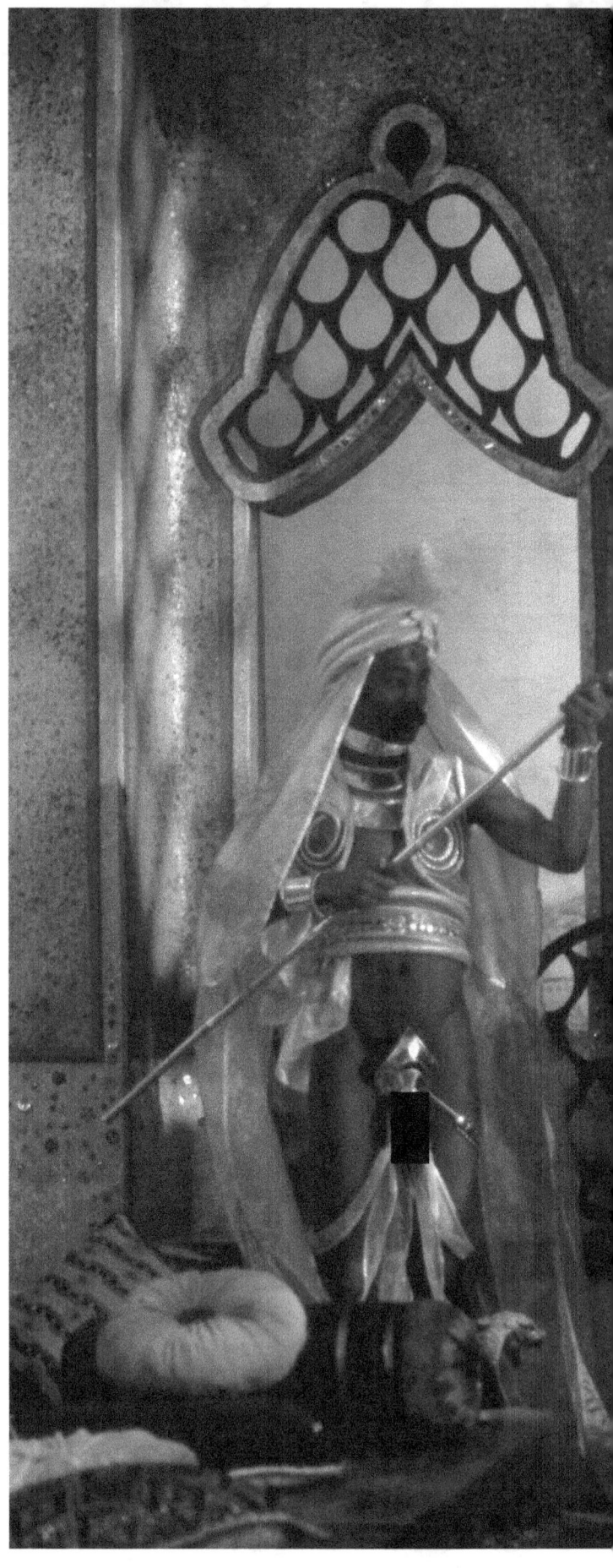

"Promo for Hand in Hand's back catalogue features extracts from the films the company made or distributed up until 1975. The clips (mostly far too long) are introduced by actor Mark Woodward (one of several participants not listed on IMDb) and interspersed with mostly feeble inserts (out takes and non-analytical interviews). The chief interest is that it includes "making of" footage and presumably much of what was shot of James Bidgood's abandoned follow-up to *Pink Narcissus*. It's absolutely untrue that the footage at the end of *Good Hot Stuff* is *Pink Narcissus* itself. It is in fact all we'll ever see of *Bagdad* starring Woodward. Throughout, *Good Hot Stuff* transfers are extremely variable. Some clips are sharp; others look as though they've been telerecorded (kinescoped in US). Hand In Hand boss Jack Deveau is interviewed, once with director Peter de Rome while they're allegedly editing the trailer for de Rome's *Adam & Yves*. This is of interest. However the *Bagdad* footage is of major importance. It's impossible to know for sure but it appears as though this film could have been a worthy follow-up to Bidgood's cult hit. It's certainly in his inimitable style (and, unlike *Pink Narcissus*, hardcore). It's been given an appropriate Middle Eastern score by Hand In Hand regular David Earnest. An excerpt runs under the end credits. Worth seeking out."

DAVID MCGILLIVRAY, *imdb*

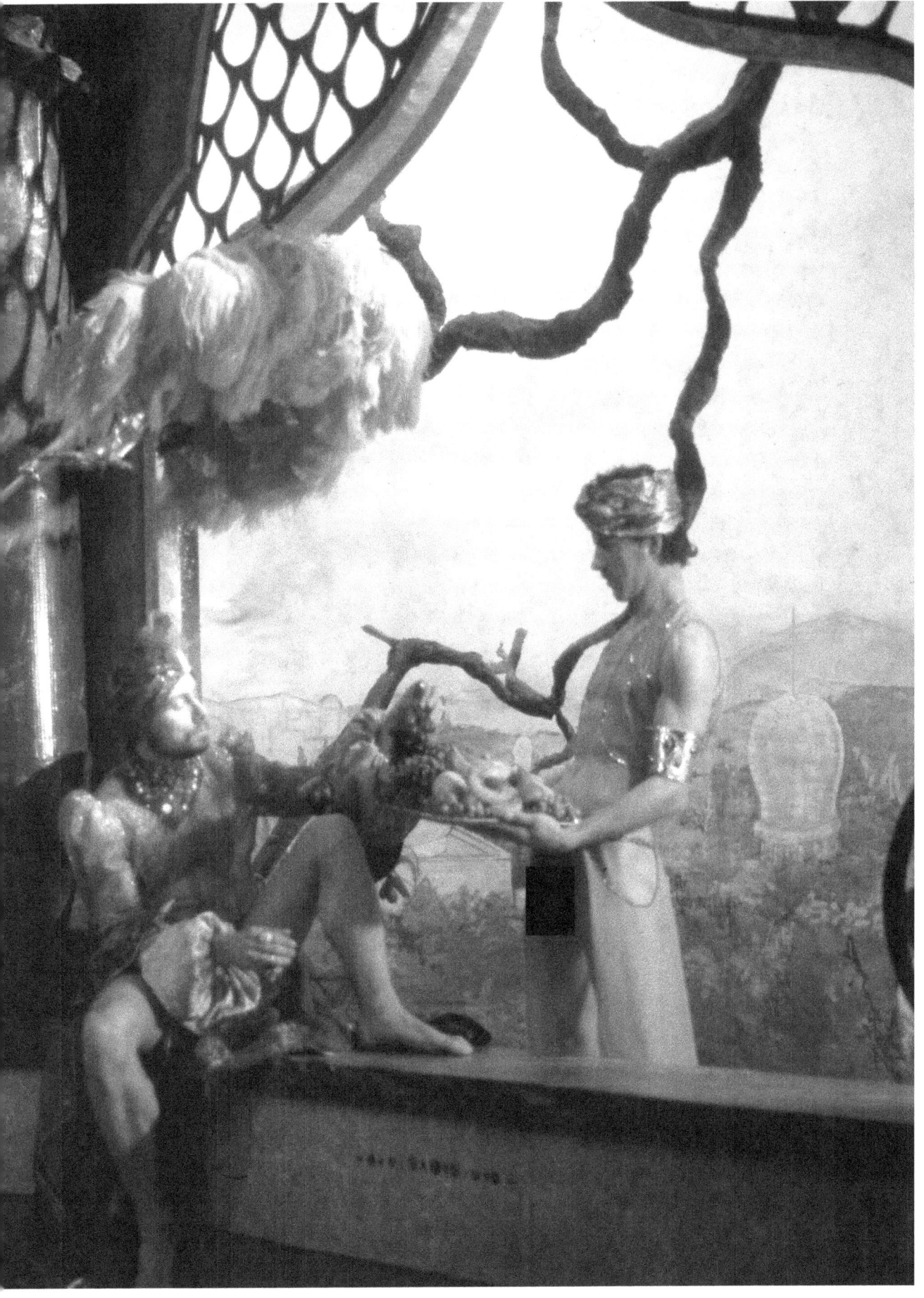

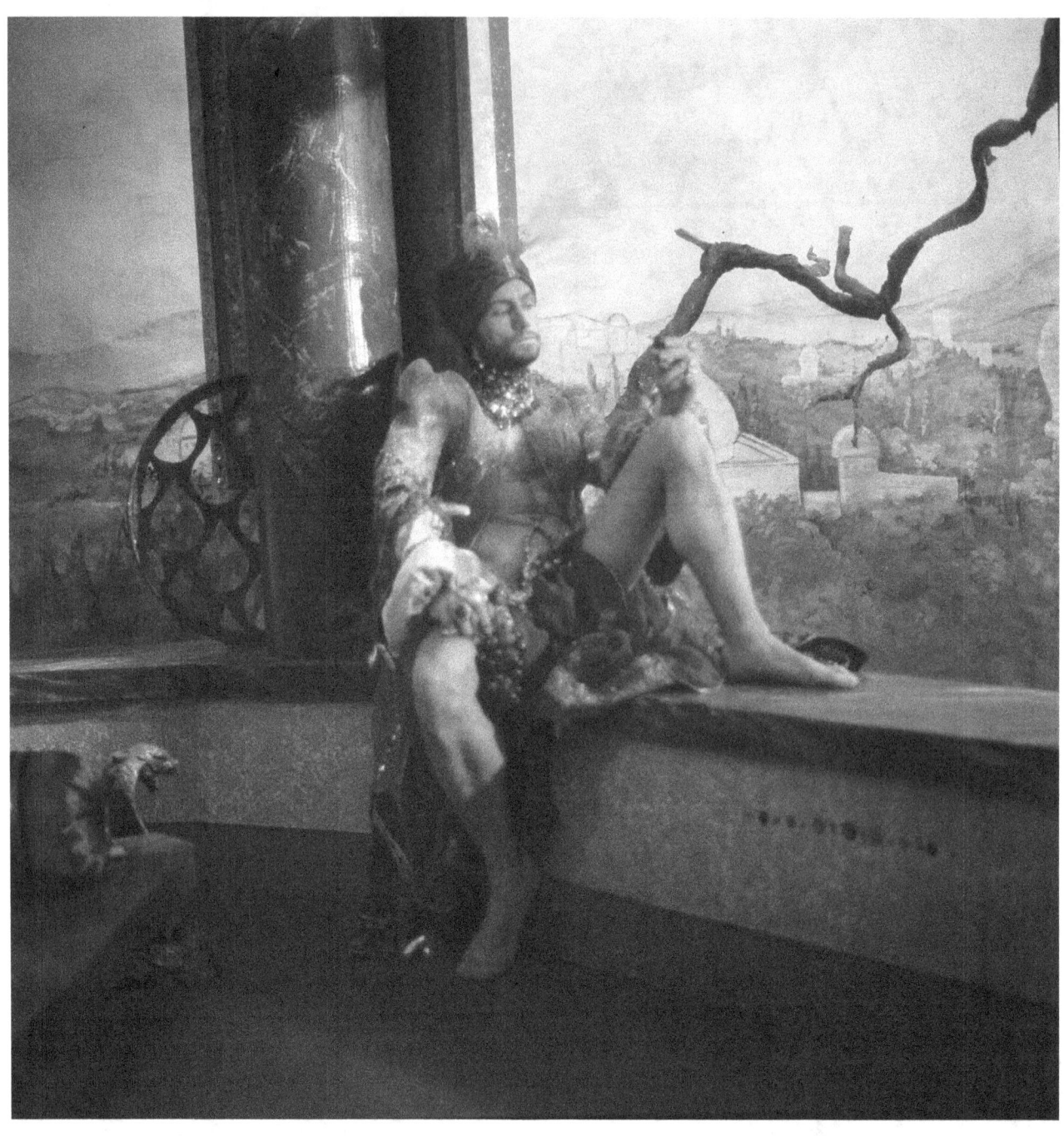

"In 1975, James Bidgood contracted with Jack Deveau of Hand In Hand Films to make a porno film partly inspired by Genet's *The Balcony*. His agreement was to develop the lush aesthetic of *Pink Narcissus* on a more permissive scale, with triple-X-rated action. He'd designed a jade-screen genie whose spread legs framed an arch over a huge swimming pool and whose crotch spewed red wine surrounded by golden penises that pumped incense. The project was a disaster. After working day and night building the set, Bidgood found himself having to begin filming without his customary storyboard. To his surprise, other cameramen had been installed to film simultaneously with him. According to him, Hand In Hand had little interest in his rigorous standards and his tradition of minutely controlling the angles and lighting for each scene. There were explosive arguments. Bidgood got so paranoid he began to think that he'd been handed a camera without film. In a short time, he was banished from the set, and the film was never finished. Eventually, scenes from it under the title *Bagdad* were released on a compilation of Hand In Hand excerpts called *Good Hot Stuff*. Touches of Bidgood remain in these scenes, but they lack the exquisite detailing and oneiric imagery of his other work."

BRUCE BENDERSON, *Bidgood*

HAND IN HAND VIDEO

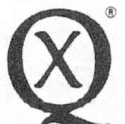

A DIVISION OF
Quality X Video Cassette Company
356 WEST 44TH STREET
NEW YORK, NEW YORK 10036
(212) 541-7860 Outside N.Y. (800) 223-7981

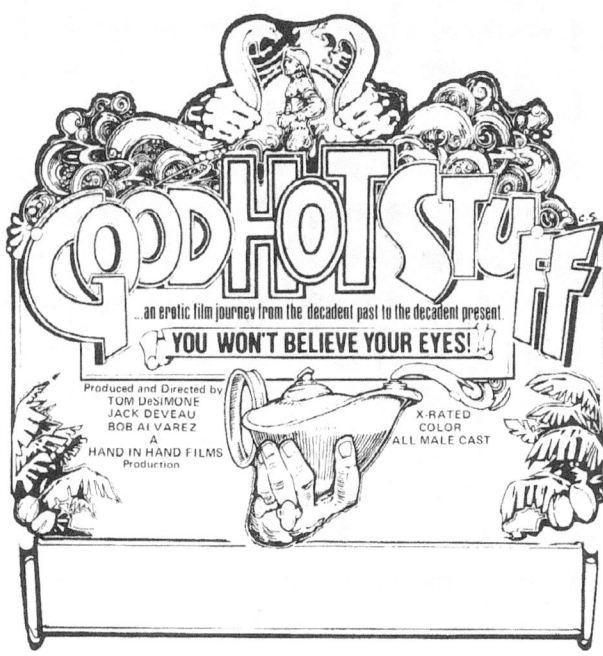

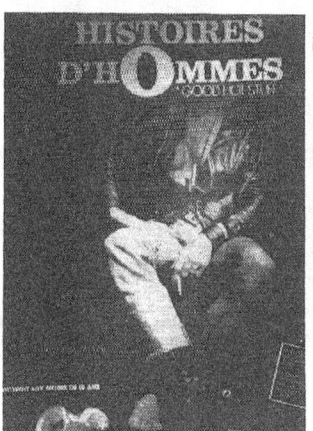

The French poster for the film, used in its highly successful Paris run.

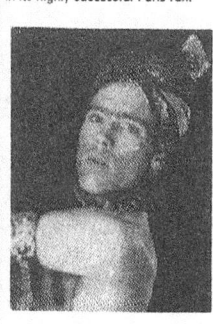

Mark Woodward, the sultan's favorite dancer, in the BAGDAD section of GOOD HOT STUFF.

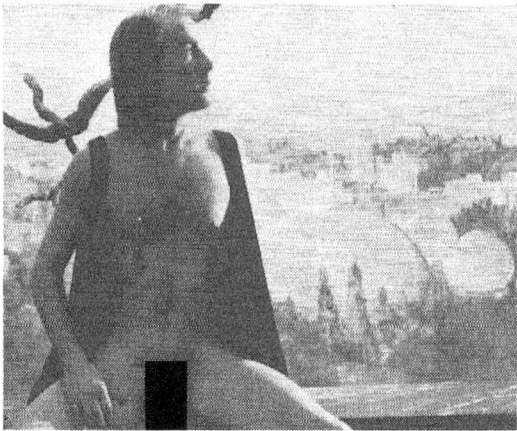

A harem slave boy awaits his master in the BAGDAD sequence.

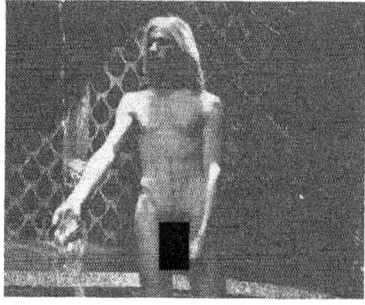

Mark Woodward bathes in the Sultan's fantastic pool in BAGDAD.

GOOD HOT STUFF is first and foremost exactly what it says. It is GOOD. And it is very, very HOT. How could it not be? It features the best...the Very Best from the company that brings you the very best, HAND IN HAND.

GOOD HOT STUFF has a story. It is the story of how these hot films come into being. You are taken through the entire process of putting a gay hard-core film together by Producer/Director extraordinaire, Jack Deveau. Let him be your guide behind the cameras for the making of LEFT-HANDED, THE NIGHT BEFORE, THE EROTIC FILMS OF PETER de ROME, ADAM & YVES, DRIVE, BALLET DOWN THE HIGHWAY, WANTED: BILLY THE KID, and the amazing BAGDAD.

You will see the most exciting sequences from all of the above films, as well as footage that has never been shown before in a genuine masterpiece of eroticism. GOOD HOT STUFF was honored by being the first explicitly gay film ever shown in France (under a visa from the Minister of Culture.) And if its pedigree doesn't impress you, its MEN certainly will.

In your own home you will enjoy all of the men that made HAND IN HAND famous around the world for presenting the finest specimens of male perfection available captured in every conceivable type of sexual encounter. Orgy scenes like you've never seen; pairs and trios, romantic and frantic; with an original score that would be terrific entertainment all by itself.

Invite everyone over to see the famous SUBWAY SEX SCENE (**Underground**) from THE EROTIC FILMS OF PETER de ROME; share the extraordinary BAGDAD episode that was never released (a mind and sense boggling trip into the world of sultans and harem boys) see the "fantasy and exceptionally handsome men of LEFT-HANDED" (**Michael's Thing**) as well as the erotic, fantastic and priceless excerpts from all the other HAND IN HAND hits.

You will own a collector's item in this film, one that will entertain and excite you for years to come.

STUDIOSOUND is a special process that guarantees a high fidelity like you've never heard. Instead of the usual optical transfer of sound from film to tape, which limits the reproduction of sound to a narrow range of frequencies, StudioSound is a magnetic transfer of the ORIGINAL MAGNETIC STUDIO sound tracks for the feature, transferred directly to the magnetic tape in your video cassette. This process actually gives you BETTER QUALITY than can be achieved in a cinema. For further enhancement, you can patch your video system into your stereo system and surround yourself with the excitement of these sensual sounds.

Cast: Kirk Luna, Al Mineo, Dennis Walsh, Shawn Roberts, Henk van Dyjk, BIG BILL Eld Young, Robert Rikas, David Savage, Brian Destazio, Peter de Rome, Jack Deveau, Garry Hunt, Rene, Mark Woodward, Jamal Jones, Mary Jim Sstunning, the Fifty Very Compulsive Men of DRIVE, AND DOZENS OF THE MOST BEAUTIFUL MEN IN THE WORLD.

Produced and directed by Jack Deveau
Edited by Robert Alvarez and Thomas De Simone
Music by David Earnest

| **GOOD HOT STUFF** | 93 MINUTES | COLOR | ALL-MALE-CAST | **StudioSound** |

© Quality X Video Cassette Company, 1979

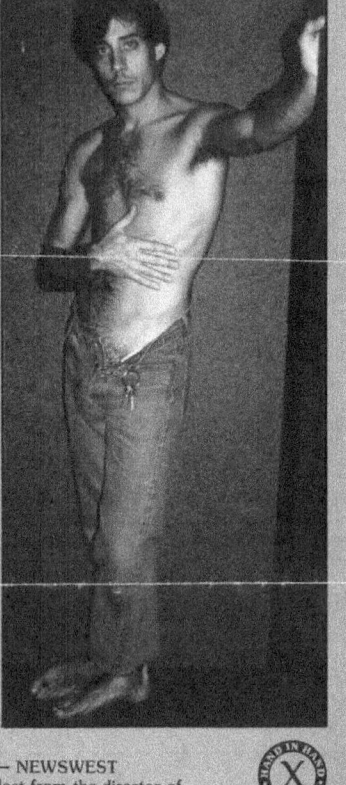

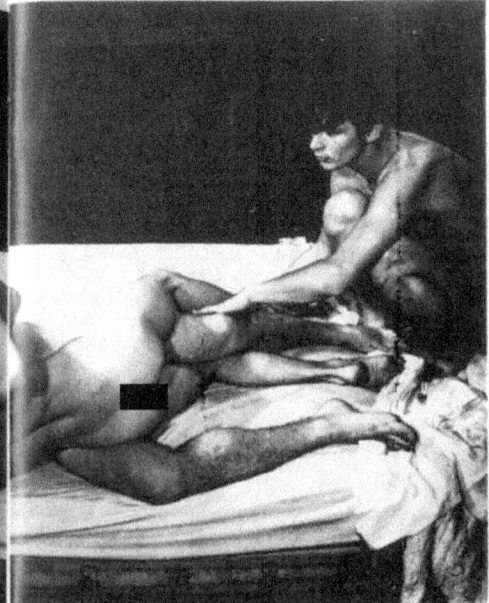

the 1939 *Three Comrades*, an 8mm short job that is a milestone in the history of the homoerotic film, being the first hardcore one.

It was a silent and had titles in the silent screen manner. Snappy ones like "These guys are hung big from being blowed off so much." Earthy comedy too, such as a closeup of a grinning comrade plucking hairs from his teeth. It was unique not only in being gay but that its cast actually had orgasms. American straight porn was long distinguished by its heroes rarely having climaxes.

You could get away with murder more easily than making a sexually explicit film in those days. The dating of the 1939 production is underscored by the fact that it was 25 years before another gay hardcore film appeared.

Filmmakers Co-Op screened *Le Chant d'Amour* on W. 23rd Street in 1963. A short film by Jean Genet made in Europe in the early 1950's was soft core but enormously erotic, or so it seemed then. It was candid about something all those "up the river" Hollywood flicks never hinted at: that men have homosexual liasons in prison. They also masturbate. *Le Chant D'Amour* is still around, and you should see it, but in '63 it was busted quicker than you can say First Amendment.

Those first innocuous loops of nude males wrestling, doing push-ups, running in place and lifting weights (mostly lifting weights!) appeared in the 42nd Street bookstores in 1964. Only to disappear, re-appear, then vanish again.

These *physical fitness* numbers were about as shocking as a locker room at the N.Y. Athletic Club. No actor touched himself or his co-star, there wasn't a tremor of tumescence, it was all long-shots, and everything played straight, so to speak. But they shocked the gendarmes, these films, and I remember a bookstore clerk at one point telling me, and so self-righteously, "You will never see another movie with naked men on sale in New York City."

Talk about a clouded crystal ball. Just a few months later an 8mm *hardcore* gay loop was offered to me for a mere $35—from under the counter in a 6th Avenue store. This untitled divertissement, featuring three Hispanics stoned out of their heads, was short on plot but long on endowments.

The underground classics that followed in the late 60's were few and far between: *Boys Will Be Boys*, *Gay Judo*, *Sailor and the Marine*, the made-in-France *Lucky Pierre* and the first chicken delight, *Over The Barrel*.

Although domino-masked men were the rule in early straight porn, the only homoerotic film with masked revelers was a '67 item introducing a young man who went on to stardom in major features.

In 1970, a loft theatre on W. 14th Street started showing male movies on

From "Catching Up" — A Hand in Hand film classic

In the years after CATCHING UP was first released in 1975, adult filmmakers, with few exceptions, moved further and further away from the narrative form, contenting themselves with feature films that were often no more than a series of loops, sometimes tied together with a common theme, milieu, or star, more often than not simply lumped together under a catchy title. While this approach gained more screen time for explicit sex play, it also suffered the loss of dramatic values that can so often heighten sexual heat. It has been only in recent years that the story film has gained popularity once again. CATCHING UP, created by that pioneer master Tom DeSimone (THE IDOL, SKIN DEEP, BI-COASTAL), reminds us once again that quantity per se is not necessarily as arousing as quality. The problem of course is to balance the narrative and erotic ingredients so that they enhance, rather than impugn each other. Under the sure hand of DeSimone, CATCHING UP remains a banquet for both the brains and the balls. Its action begins in a restaurant when older lover Frank (John Farrel) tells younger lover Dennis (Keith Anthoni in his shimmering film debut) that after three months in their relationship, he feels "trapped," needs some "freedom." Wounded, the young neophyte sets out to get even, to discover other facets of gay life – in short, to "catch up." The first trick with whom he connects is a waiter (Jayson McBride) who believes "that love stuff is a bunch of crap anyway," but quickly proves that lust is quite another matter. A macho munchkin, McBride proves a perfect match for the lanky, doe-eyed Anthoni, who next explores public sex in the balcony of a skinflick house, experiencing his first three-way with Scott Heith and Tim Christy. This sleazy action is cross-cut with a black and white film-within-the-film, in which a model (Paul Strand) and a masseur (Bob Perry) make idealized romantic love to a satiric voice-over soundtrack of every cliché in the fuck-book canon. Moving right along, Anthoni next answers the underground ad of a kink freak (Dave Daniels) who plays games with a double-headed dildo, cuts off his guest's undershorts with a menacing pair of shears, and turns out to be a pussycat bottom. The film concludes with an unexpected twist, as Anthoni returns home, a new and different man determined to change the dynamics of the original relationship. CATCHING UP provides knowing insights into a gay relationship, views the human condition with compassionate humor, and never fails to generate sexual heat. The acting – in particular Anthoni's and McBride's – is eminently professional, and the camera work is slick and inobtrusive. One small complaint: the transfer from film to video is uneven, the color often flat and dark. In spite of these problems, however, the film's humanity shines through.

*Jerry Douglas, *Manshots*

"Suddenly, I was out of work, and someone, I don't remember who, asked me to do a porn film, and I found myself in Tom DeSimone's *Catching Up* with Jayson MacBride. I've forgotten a great deal about that part of my life – it all happened too fast – too much excitement – too many drugs." **KEITH ANTHONI**

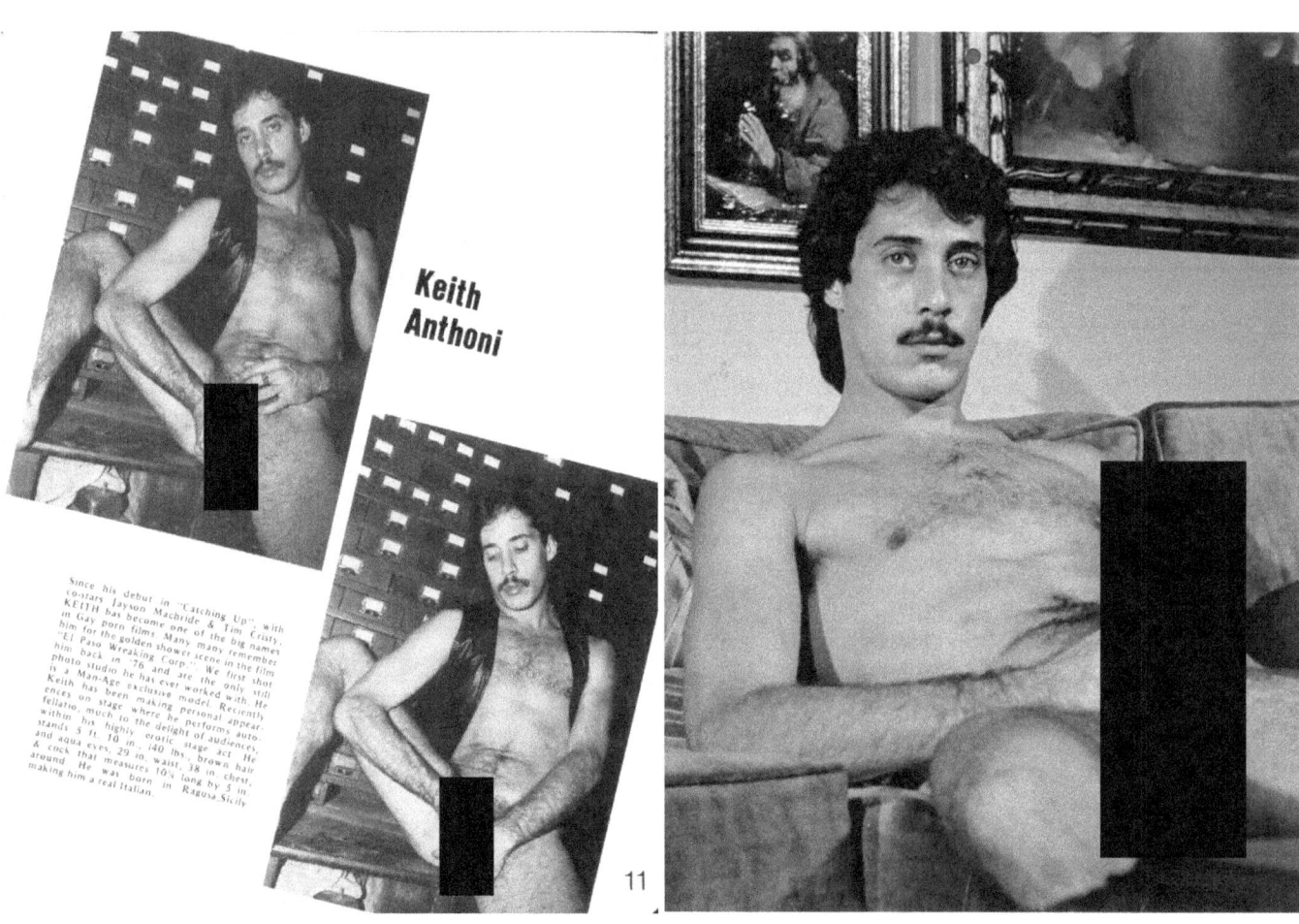

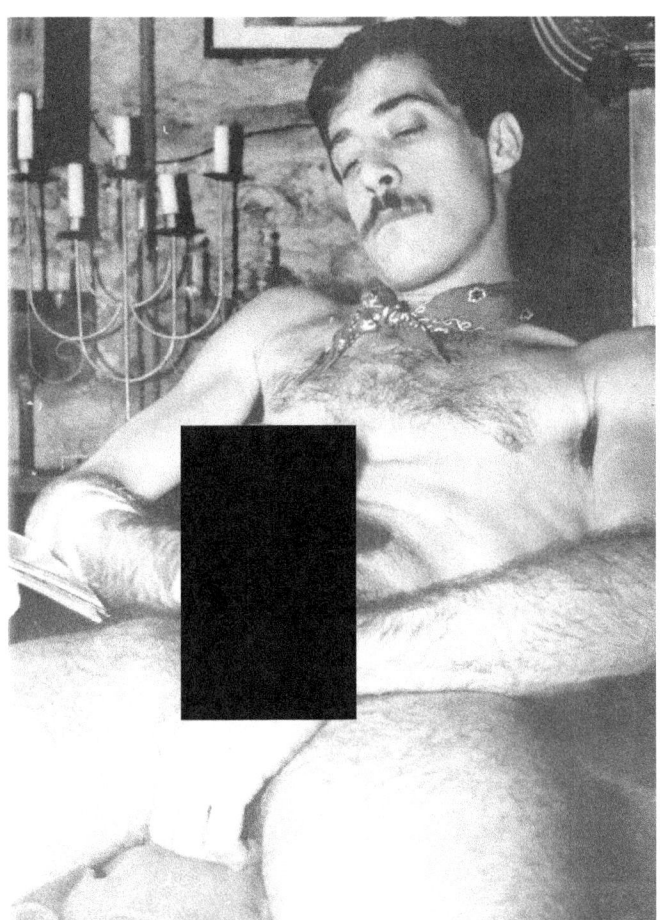 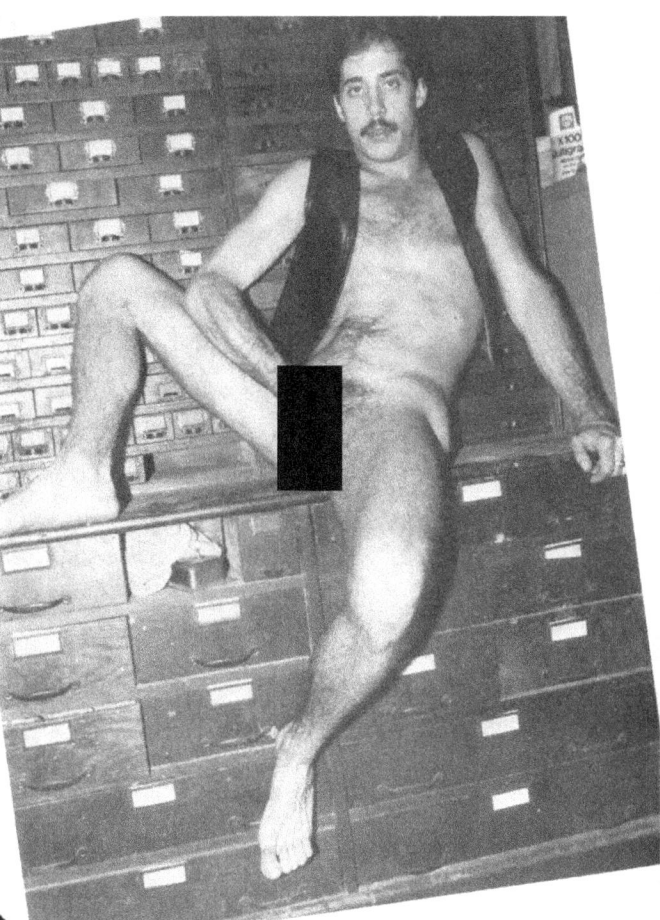

"I must tell you, and you can print this, that I am totally oral sexually. I go crazy when someone's working on my cock - I love the feeling, and the visual, and I love having a dick down my throat. I was on Fire Island once, and I met this pair of lovers on the beach who wanted to fist me. I'd probably not been fucked even ten times in my life at that point, and I'd only liked it twice - maybe that's why I've become an excellent cocksucker. I've never found one I couldn't take all the way down, but I've never been crazy about getting fucked. Anyway, I protested, told them I hardly ever got screwed, let alone fisted - then one of them stuck his dick down my throat, and before I knew it the other one had his hand up my ass halfway to the elbow. I can't believe how far I'll go when I'm sucking cock! When the man I was doing pulled out of my mouth, I suddenly couldn't handle the scene. I panicked when I realized what was going on. I was terrified of being hurt. I just go into another world when someone's fucking my face. Maybe that's why I'm good in front of the camera - I get carried away."

KEITH ANTHONI

"*Catching Up* was pretty good. I could probably look at it today and not throw up. [...] I think Deveau's *Hot House* was the biggest box-office hit I was in, though. And *Night at the Adonis* was a big success. What a busy movie that was! [...] We shot everything backwards - sex first and dialogue after. I like to get the speaking and acting out of the way as fast as possible. Once that's in the can - you feel less responsible. They can always substitute a dick."

JAYSON MACBRIDE

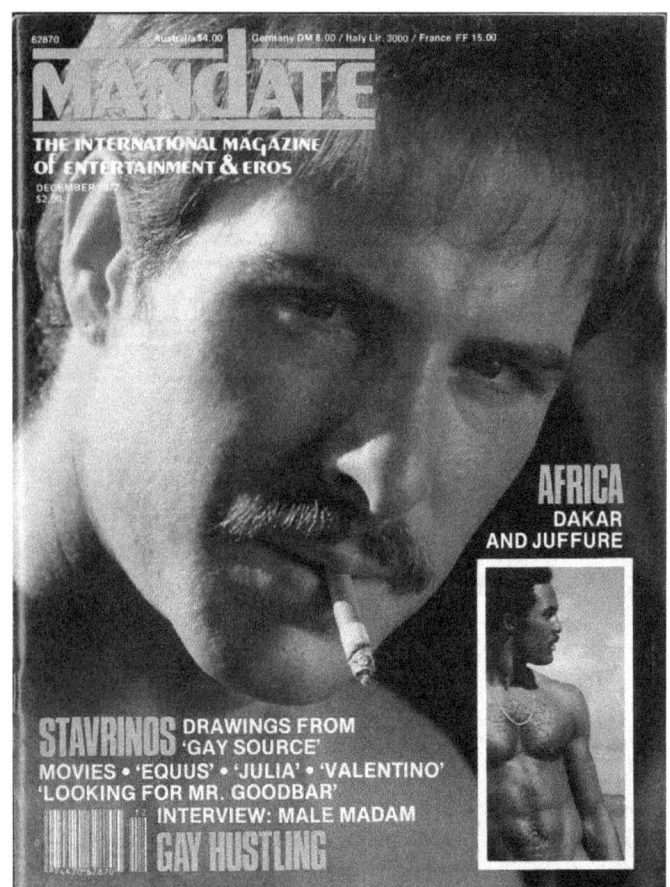
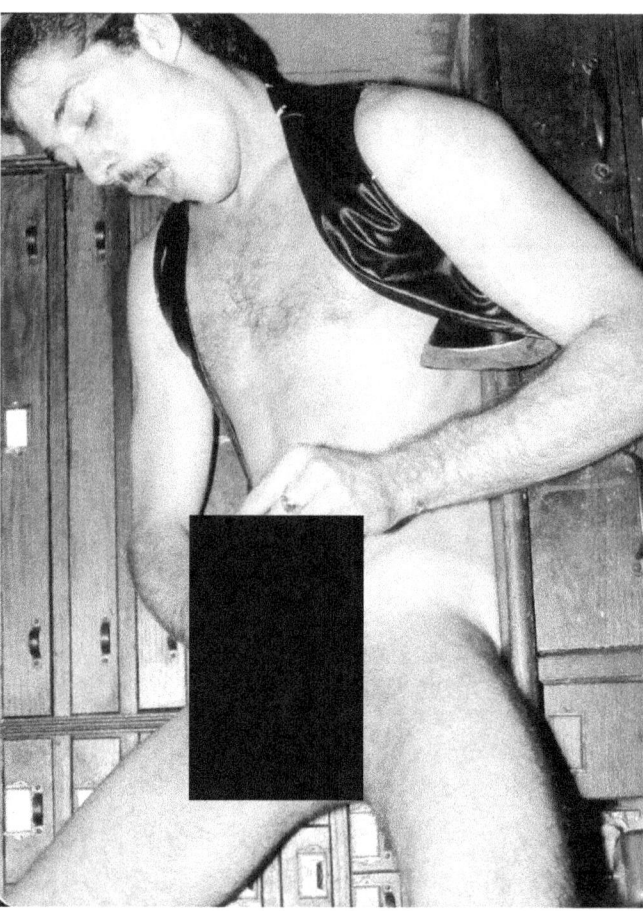

Hand In Hand star Jayson MacBride - Started acting at the age of eight. Discovered by *Champion* in the late 60s. Did a softcore magazine for them with Douglas Campbell. Moved to New York in 1967. MacBride did some work in conventional performance including *Sweet Charity* on Broadway and toured with several George M. productions. Other roles were in *Fidler on the Roof, Gypsy, West Side Story, Enter Laught, The Happy Time* and *Anniversary Waltz*. He enjoyed his porn work, did some hustling but didn't like stripping because it didn't pay well and "wasn't a big fan" of watching porn. His "9 to 5" job was a successful career in market research. MacBride had let it be known that he was interested in doing some porn work and Tom deSimone heard about that and called him up. When describing the films he liked, he singled out the scripts as the deciding factors. When filming *Red Ball Express*, Jayson invited his boy friend "Mikey" to be in the film and bottom for Jayson. "Mikey" was too shy for that but he was the fluffer for the entire cast and when the closing orgy was being filmed, he went wild and "worked that room!" He quit doing porn for a period of time but started up again when he found producers had reused his scenes, presumably in compilations. In about 1974 he lost all his possessions, music, costumes, pictures, memorabilia and a host of plants in a home fire.

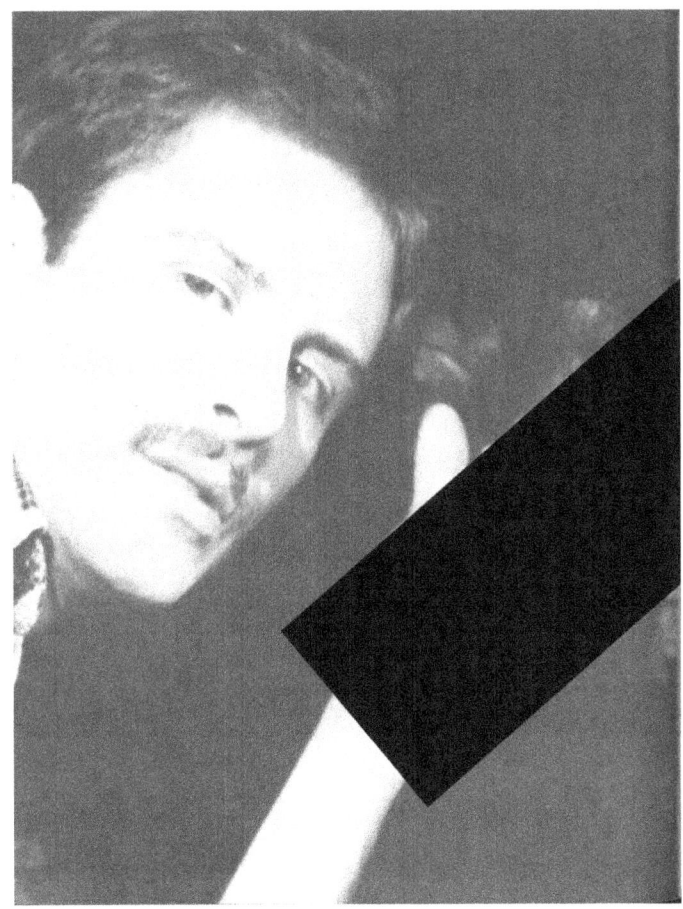
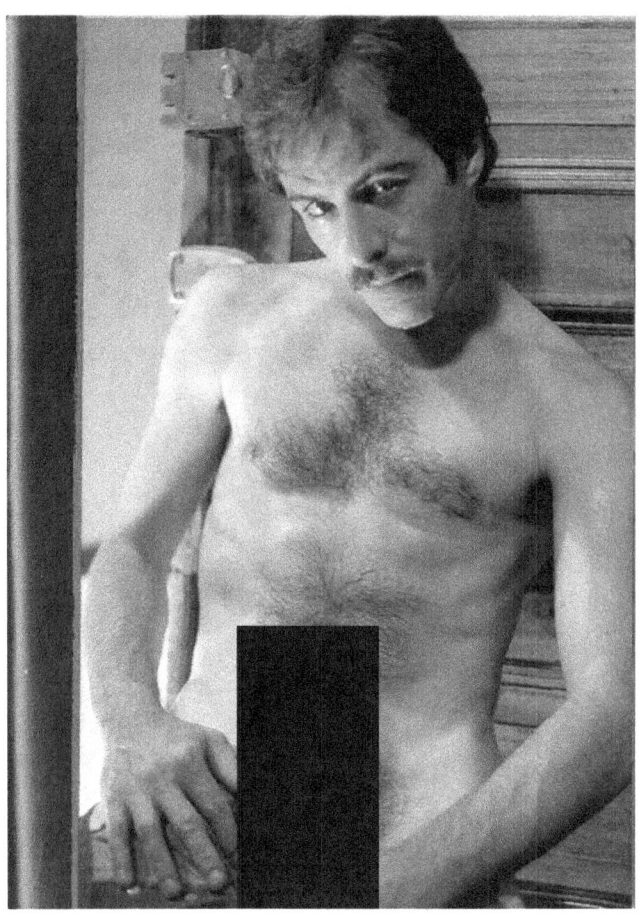

"Jack Deveau is wonderful to work with – he treats actors so well. On any set of any movie we've made together there was always everything you wanted or needed. A lot of people want you to pick up lights and cameras. Jack has a great crew – they've been a unit for a long time, and they work together so well. For them, I wouldn't hesitate to move a cable or push furniture around because they don't expect it of you. They realize you're not doing the easiest thing in the world to begin with – it's not like being a hooker. You don't lie back and let it happen." **JAYSON MACBRIDE**

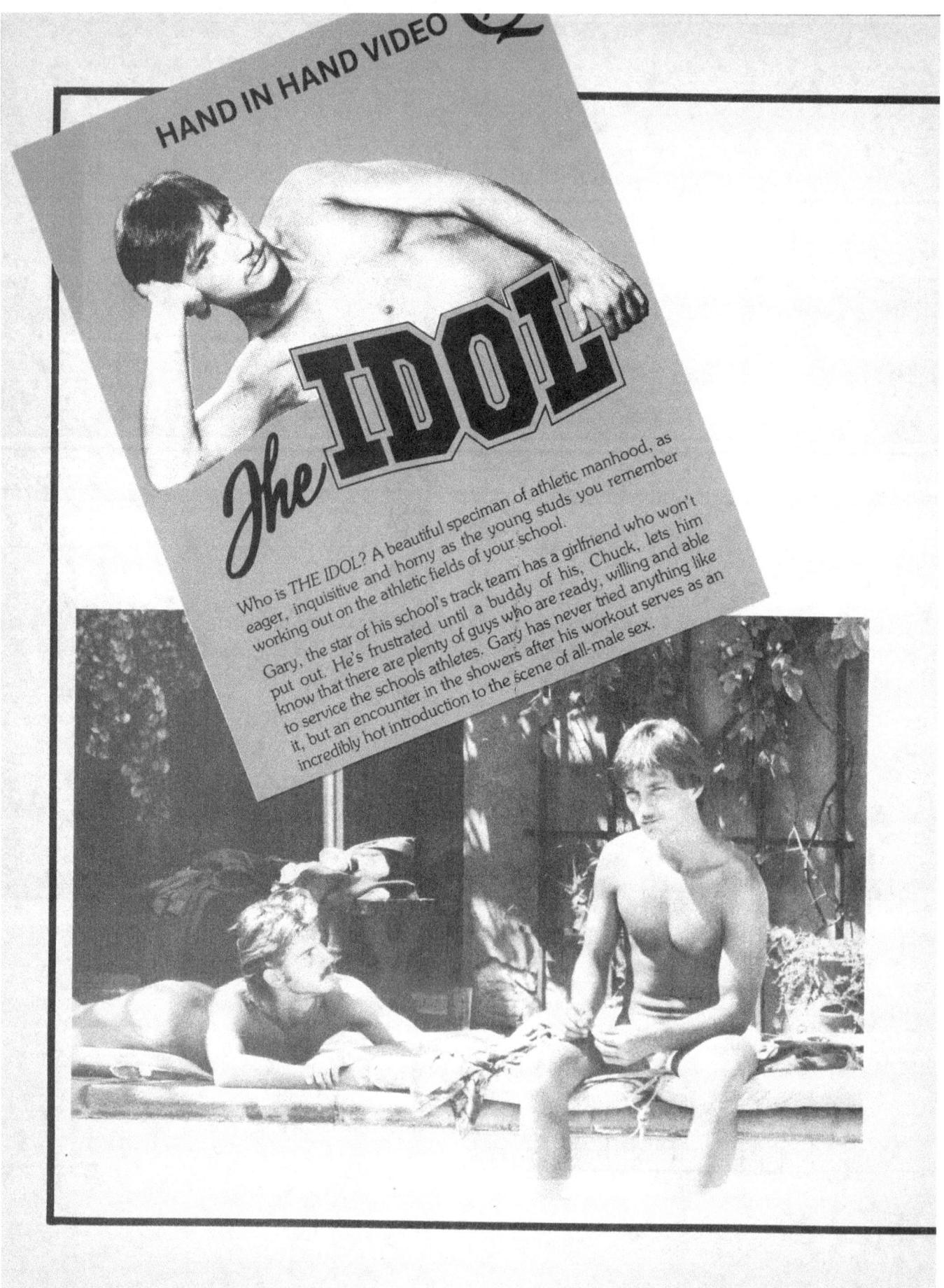

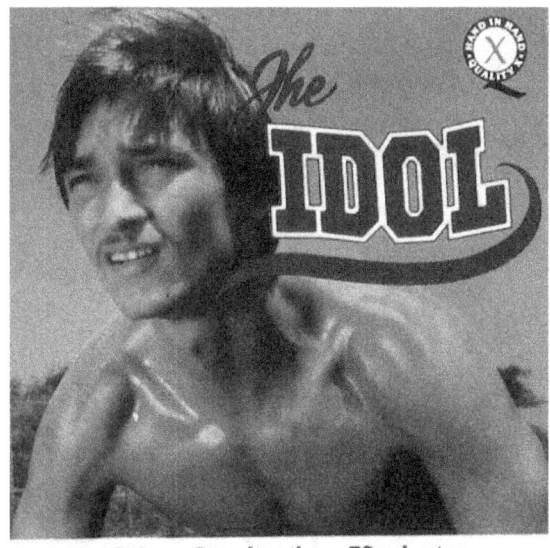

In Color • Running time: 73 minutes

This is a story of a beautiful young athlete's entrance into the world of sex and love, a tender and extremely arousing saga of a boy finding himself. An erotic tale not to be missed. Produced, written, and directed by Tom DeSimone. Starring: Kevin Redding, Nick Rogers, Greg Dale and Jim Bataglia. MX-014

All Male Cast • Rated XXX

Today, nearly a decade after its theatrical release, Tom DeSimone's THE IDOL remains as fresh and sensuous as ever, arguably the best piece of gay erotica ever filmed. The classic Coming Out story, the picture begins with a black and white image of a vibrant all-American adolescent. Gradually, the camera pans back to reveal that it is a news photo under the headline "College Athlete Dies in Auto Aaccident." A blond bicyclist picks up the newspaper from the dusty road and begins to reminisce about the loss. There are many reasons for THE IDOL's enduring popularity. First of all, it is so honestly written and directed that virtually any gay male can relate to it. Second, because of its honesty and the remarkable presence of its star, the sexual encounters it records are infinitely more erotic than most of the impersonal couplings in all too many of today's videos. Finally, such care has been lavished on the casting, the cinematography, the editing, and the production values that THE IDOL emerges as something to touch the mind and the heart without in any way ignoring the gonads. Shamelessly romantic, the film is seen basically through the eyes of Terry, the boy on the bike (nicely played in low-key style by Mark Bitler), who proves to be a consummate voyeur in the hero worship of his idol, Gary (portrayed by Kevin Redding in his only film appearance ever, and what a pity that is, for he is facially, physically, and genitally breathtaking). The film begins at this funeral, and is neatly divided into five flashbacks, each of which realistically represents a step in his coming out: a solo masturbation sequence on the front seat of his car when his girlfriend leaves him hot-rocked in a lovers' lane; tentative experimentation in the school shower with three of his buddies, in which he remains strictly trade; a massage session with his coach, in which he kisses a man for the first time; a poolside encounter with his cousin, in which he cautiously experiments with oral sex (after smoking a joint), progresses to active anal sex, and eventually throws his legs in the air to whisper "Let me see what it feels like"; and finally, the culminating interlude with Terry, in which he reveals the ardor, commitment, and versatility of sexual maturity. THE IDOL is a must for any gay video library. There is not a false moment in the entire work, either dramatically or erotically, and if the final fadeout reminds you a bit of the ending of *Maytime*, who says you can't cry and come at the same time?

*Jerry Douglas, *Manshots*

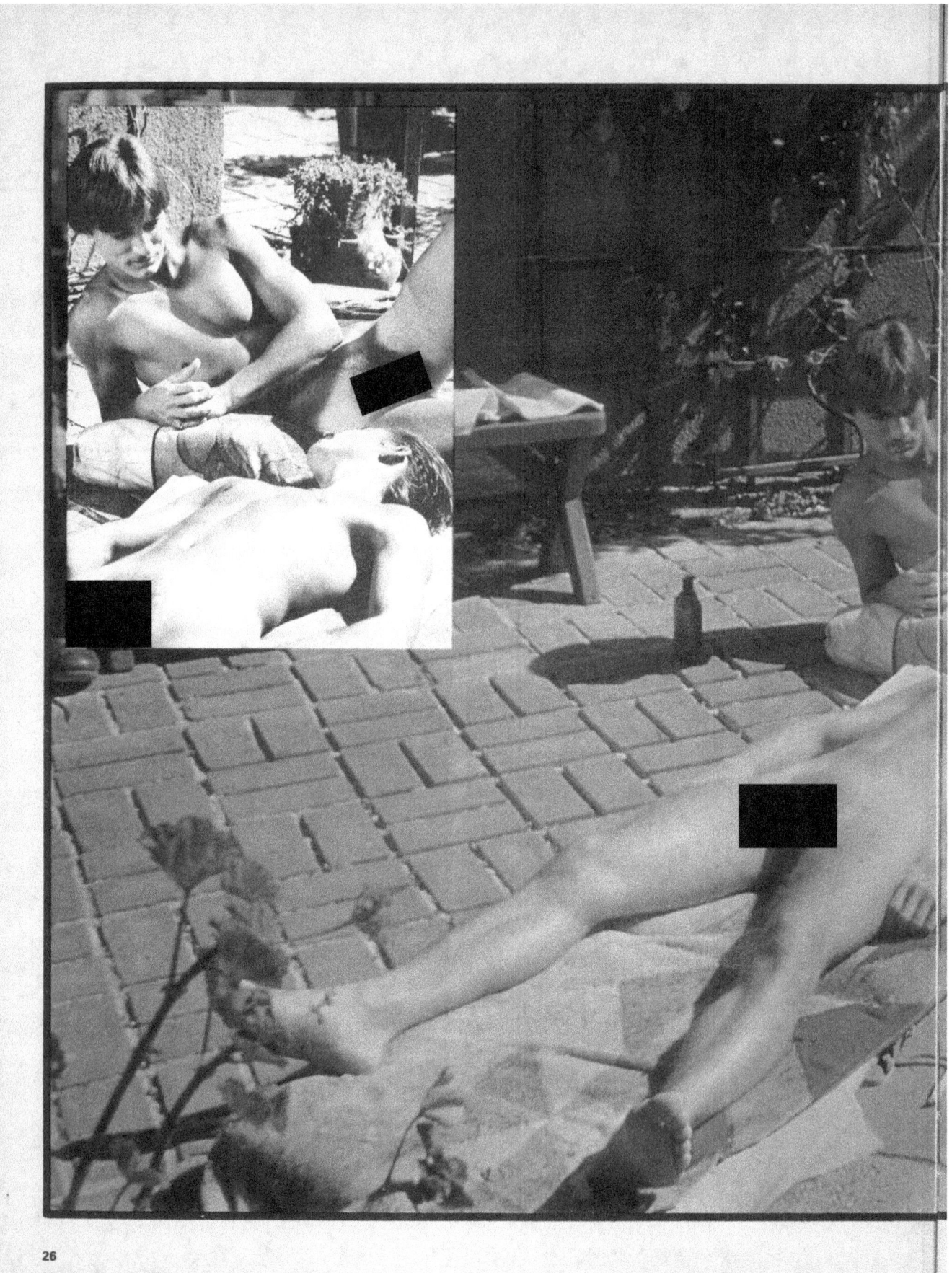

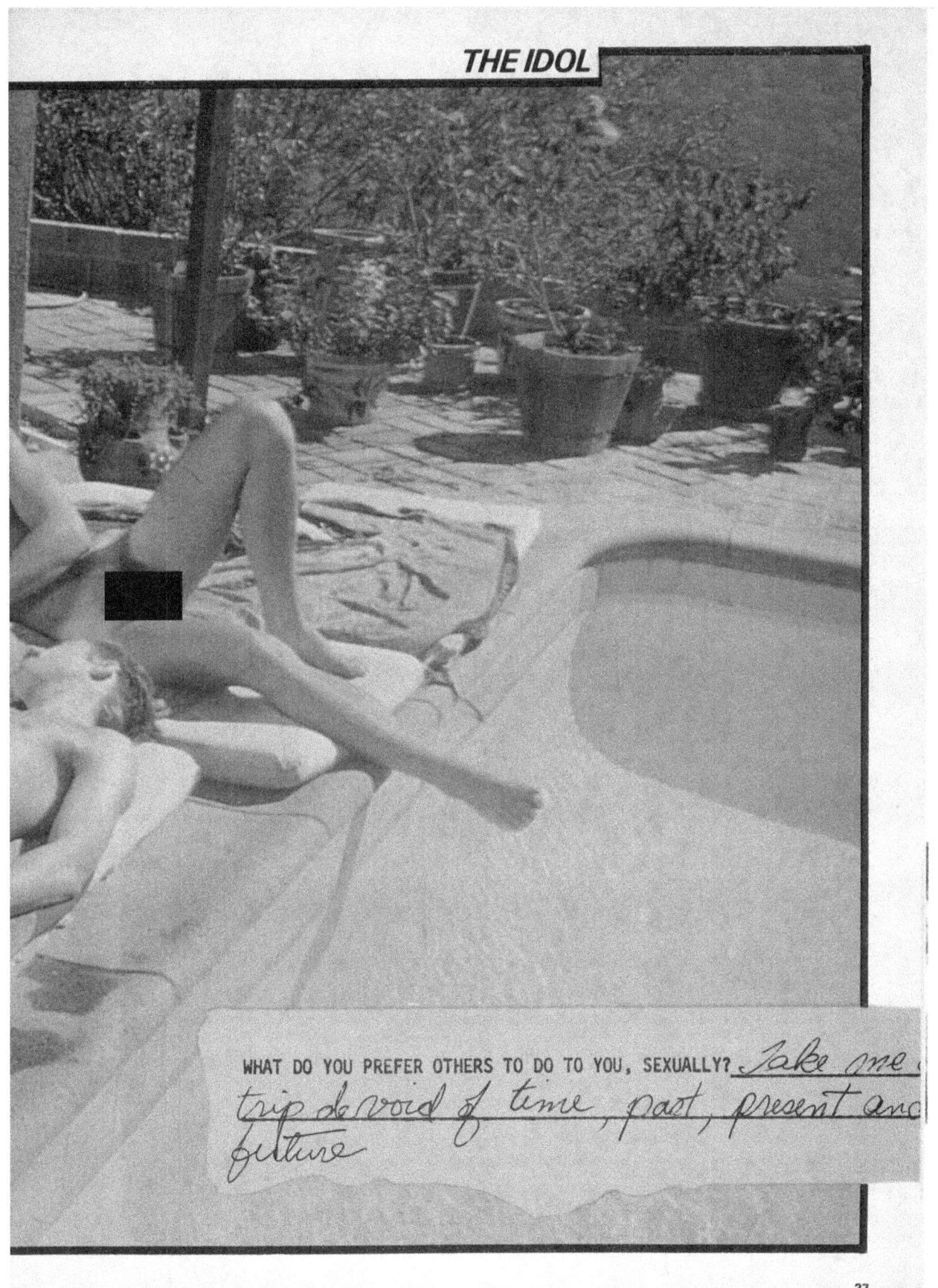

THE IDOL

WHAT DO YOU PREFER OTHERS TO DO TO YOU, SEXUALLY? _Take me a trip devoid of time, past, present and future_

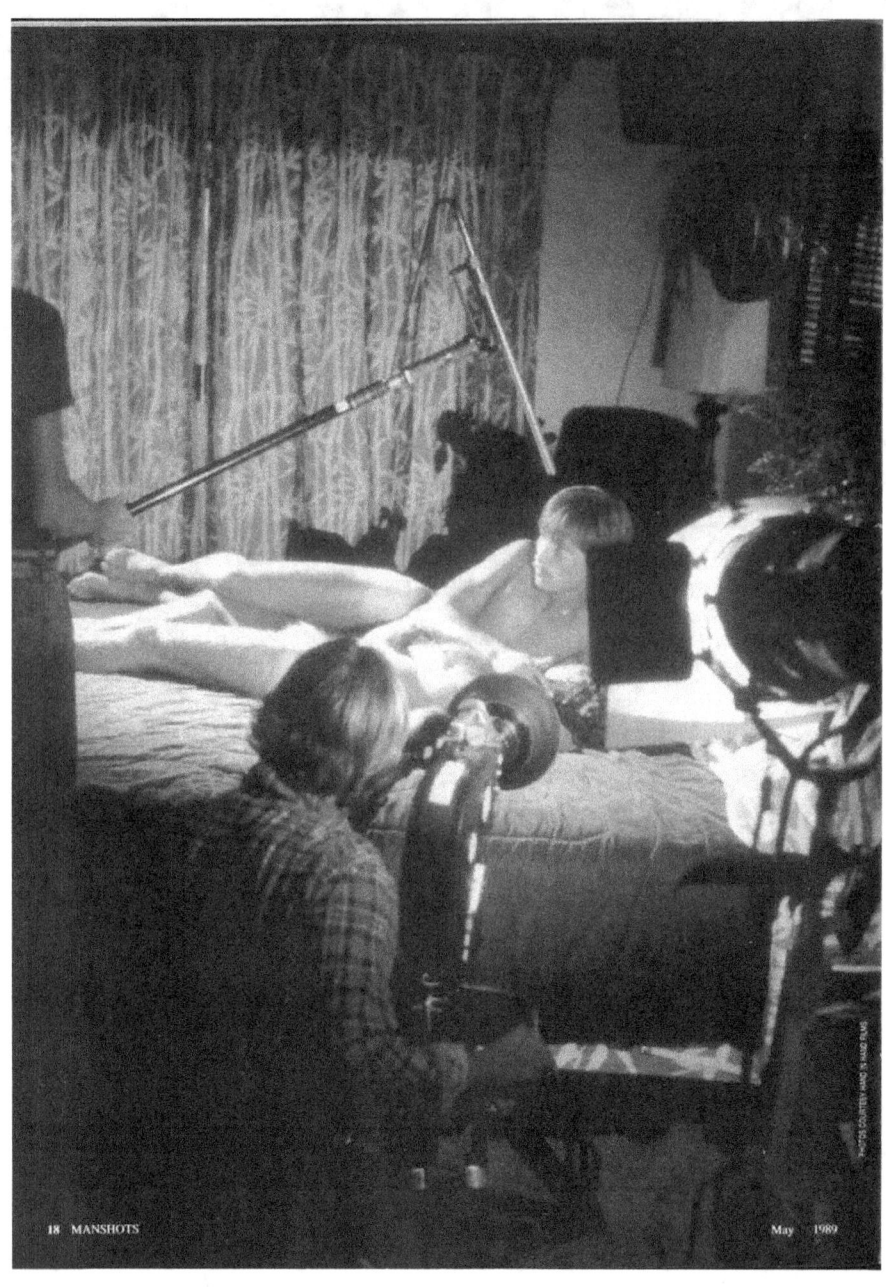

"I did the picture, and in all honesty, I'm very proud of it. It was a real movie, and I was very pleased with that. Up until I saw the film for the first time, I went through a lot of emotional stress about it, because I really felt guilty about doing it. I mean, hey - I was raised a Southern Baptist - what can I tell you? My anatomy, for a couple of months, broke down. Broke down. But then I saw it, and I was just proud. I'm really a funny person. It's like, you know, I do something because I want to know what it's like."

KEVIN REDDING

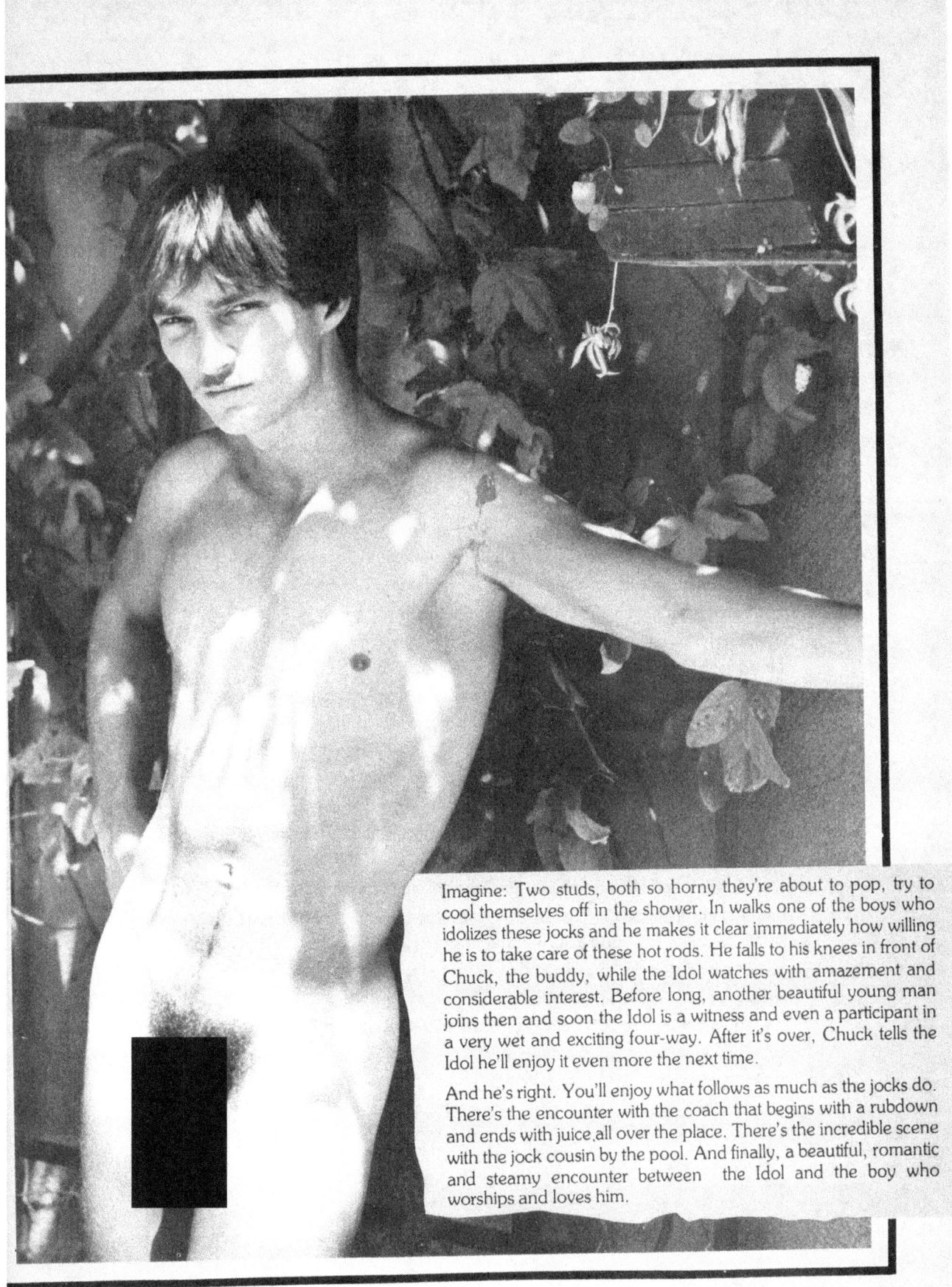

Imagine: Two studs, both so horny they're about to pop, try to cool themselves off in the shower. In walks one of the boys who idolizes these jocks and he makes it clear immediately how willing he is to take care of these hot rods. He falls to his knees in front of Chuck, the buddy, while the Idol watches with amazement and considerable interest. Before long, another beautiful young man joins then and soon the Idol is a witness and even a participant in a very wet and exciting four-way. After it's over, Chuck tells the Idol he'll enjoy it even more the next time.

And he's right. You'll enjoy what follows as much as the jocks do. There's the encounter with the coach that begins with a rubdown and ends with juice all over the place. There's the incredible scene with the jock cousin by the pool. And finally, a beautiful, romantic and steamy encounter between the Idol and the boy who worships and loves him.

Like his 1979 classic THE IDOL, Tom DeSimone's 1974 STATION TO STATION details the steps in a young man's coming out, though it is little more than a blueprint for the masterpiece that was to follow. Obviously, DeSimone was preoccupied with this aspect of the gay experience, for many of the same ideas, attitudes, and situations appear in both films. In STATION TO STATION, the central figure is played by Tim Christy (without his twin brother anywhere in sight). Under the titles, he is discovered in a lush, leafy grove, getting a blow job from an anonymous trick. The scene seems out of context, for in it he is already no innocent. The story proper begins with a phone call to his parents saying that their son has been arrested on a morals charge. (Perhaps that is what the opening scene is about, although there is no suggestion that the idyll in the bushes ends with anything but a post orgasmic glow). After much angst on the part of the parents, and a series of flashbacks revealing the youth's relationship to his distant father (Ron Fischer) and manipulative mother (Liz Wolfe), sex finally rears its head again when he goes to a photographic studio to meet his girlfriend (Linda Hartley) and observes instead a porn photo shoot. The romantic sexplay between the two models (Tom Payne and Steve Fox) obviously mesmerizes him. The second and most effective sex scene occurs that evening. He flops on his bed, and begins to play with himself as he fantasizes himself into the action he has just observed. The episode is a triumph of ingenious editing, especially in the cross-cutting between Christy jacking off on the bed and Christy jacking off at the studio - almost as if he were twins. The final action sequence finds him returning to the studio to actually make it with the photographer Tony (Carl Ford). They smoke a joint, split a beer, and explore each other manually and orally before Tony gradually loosens him up, then enters him in an excruciatingly slow penetration shot. We can almost believe we are witness to an actual deflowering. Although the rhythm of the film suggests that we are about to move toward a hot finale, there is none - only a brief dialogue scene where his father brings him home from the police station, and they agree to "talk it over tomorrow morning." A blackout brings the proceedings to a rather abrupt and unsatisfying end. STATION TO STATION was originally shot on film, and the transfer to tape is not ideal. The color has faded some, and the sound is often muddy. Its greatest fascination, aside from its place in the oeuvre of DeSimone's work, is the presence of Tim Christy, the perfect all-American boy archetype, since he is not quite perfect and therefore an attainable rather than a fantasy figure. And for those of you who love THE IDOL, STATION TO STATION makes an interesting, if pale, companion piece.

*Jerry Douglas, *Stallion*

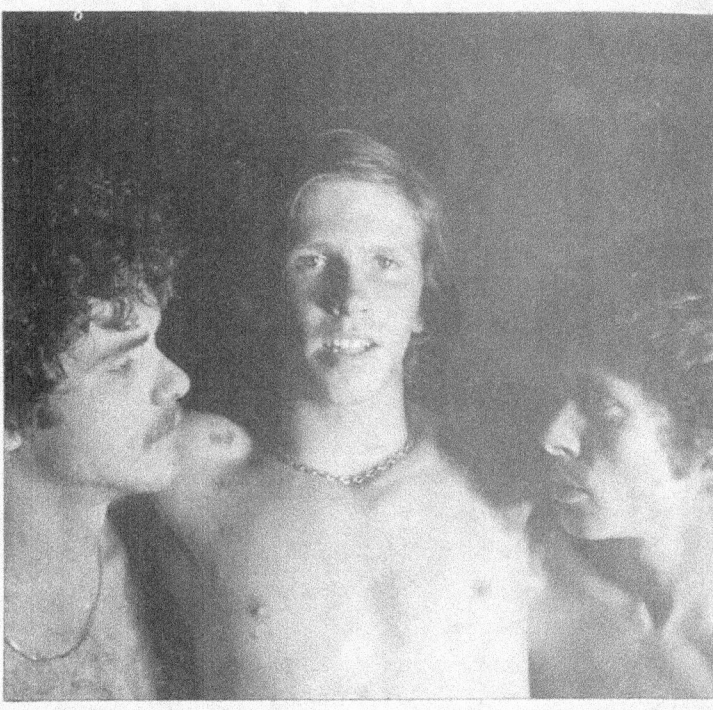

Tom Payne, Tim Christy, & Steve Fox in "Station to Station."

STATION TO STATION

STATION TO STATION (1974); Video Pix; Hand in Hand Films; Times Productions; Directed by L. Brooks (Tom DeSimone); Produced by Max Blue; Sound by Mark Holt; Camera, Noel Kent. Cast: Ron Fischer; Tim Christy; Linda Hartley; Liz Wolfe; Carl Ford; Tom Payne; Steve Fox. Running time: 66 minutes.

Like his 1979 classic *The Idol*, Tom DeSimone's 1974 *Station to Station* details the steps in a young man's coming out, though it is little more than a blueprint for the masterpiece that was to follow. Obviously, DeSimone was preoccupied with this aspect of the gay experience, for many of the same ideas, attitudes, and situations appear in both films.

In *Station to Station*, the central figure is played by Tim Christy (without his twin brother anywhere in sight). Under the titles, he is discovered in a lush, leafy grove, getting a blow job from an anonymous trick. The scene seems out of context, for in it he is already no innocent.

The story proper begins with a phone call to his parents saying that their son has been arrested on a morals charge. (Perhaps that is what the opening scene is about, although there is no suggestion that the idyll in the bushes ends with anything but a post orgasmic glow.) After much angst on the part of the parents, and a series of flashbacks revealing the youth's relationship to his distant father (Ron Fischer) and manipulative mother (Liz Wolfe), sex finally rears its head again when he goes to a photographic studio to meet his girlfriend (Linda Hartley) and observes instead a porn photo shoot. The romantic sexplay between the two models (Tom Payne and Steve Fox) obviously mesmerizes him.

The second and most effective sex scene occurs that evening. He flops on his bed, and begins to play with himself as he fantasizes himself into the action he has just observed. The episode is a triumph of ingenious editing, especially in the cross-cutting between Christy jacking off on the bed and Christy jacking off at the studio — almost as if he were twins.

The final action sequence finds him returning to the studio to actually make it with the photographer Tony (Carl Ford). They smoke a joint, split a beer, and explore each other manually and orally before Tony gradually loosens him up, then enters him in an excruciatingly slow penetration shot. We can almost believe we are witness to an actual deflowering.

Although the rhythm of the film suggests that we are about to move toward a hot finale, there is none — only a brief dialogue scene where his father brings him home from the police station, and they agree to "talk it over tomorrow morning." A blackout brings the proceedings to a rather abrupt and unsatisfying end.

Station to Station was originally shot on film, and the transfer to tape is not ideal. The color has faded some, and the sound is often muddy. Its greatest fascination, aside from its place in the oeuvre of DeSimone's work, is the presence of Tim Christy, the perfect All American boy archetype, since he is not quite perfect and therefore an attainable rather than a fantasy figure. And for those of you who love *The Idol*, *Station to Station* makes an interesting, if pale, companion piece.

STATION TO STATION is available from Hand In Hand Films, 240 West 73 St., Suite 1701S, New York, N.Y. 10023 for $49.95 plus $3.00 shipping and handling. Mastercard or Visa accepted. Specify VHS or Beta.

FULL GROWN, FULL BLOWN

FULL GROWN, FULL BLOWN (1987); Catalina Video; A John Summers Production; Produced, Directed, and Edited by B. Savage; Director of Lighting, Earnest Robles; Production Design, Mel Garrett; Sound, James Smitty. Cast: Vladimir Correa; Jean-Jacques LeBon; John Davenport; Matt Hawks; Chris Thompson; Ricky Rhodes; Bobbie Davis; Matt Forrest; Tony Franco; Cole Taylor. Running time: 80 minutes.

Full Grown, Full Blown, an uneven series of loops, is webbed together by the presence of a beefy bodybuilder named Vladimir Correa, reportedly a big name in straight porn circles down in Brazil. Starting out in white shorts and tank top, he fantasizes the various loops, as he gradually strips, fondles himself, and fucks the bedspread in a flurry of frottage, but has some trouble maintaining his erection throughout. Perhaps that is because the badly recorded voiceover — supposedly his thoughts — is so riddled with stroke book cliches as to be almost a parody of the genre. Most viewers these days have become sophisticated enough not to be aroused by lines like "... my horniness has grown out of control... when will I have what I so desperately

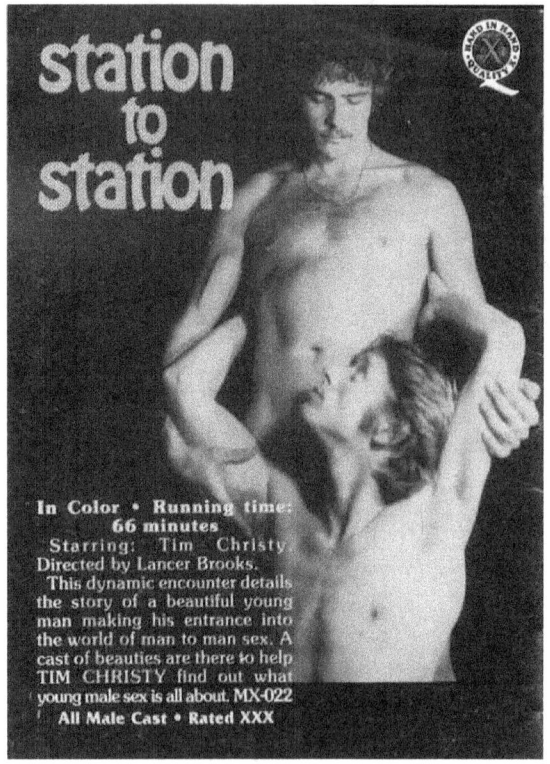

An early attempt with the camera by famed director Lancer Brooks. Most pieces of erotic entertainment that are worth watching have passed through this man's hands. His talent is unnerving; he rarely misses. And STATION TO STATION is no exception. It is the story of young Ron who is arrested for soliciting a plainclothes cop in a bar. Through a series of flashbacks we see what led up to this predicament. Ron was a mama's boy; she kept him away from his father, away from athletics, and when the time came, even found a girlfriend, Linda, for Ron to date. Linda, a fashion model, introduces Ron to her photographer, Tony. One day in his studio, Tony puts the make on Ron. It's only casual sex, but Ron mistakes it as commitment, and when he wants to get together again with Tony, the answer is, "Sorry kid, no seconds." Ron takes to the bar, and is unknowingly trapped and jailed. An emotional ending surfaces with his parents as Ron faces them with a decision and a promise to help them understand. Typical of Lancer Brooks, STATION TO STATION is filled with emotion, sexual turmoil, story, and above all, erotic action that few directors have been able to bring to the video screen.

*John Mensior, *Torso*

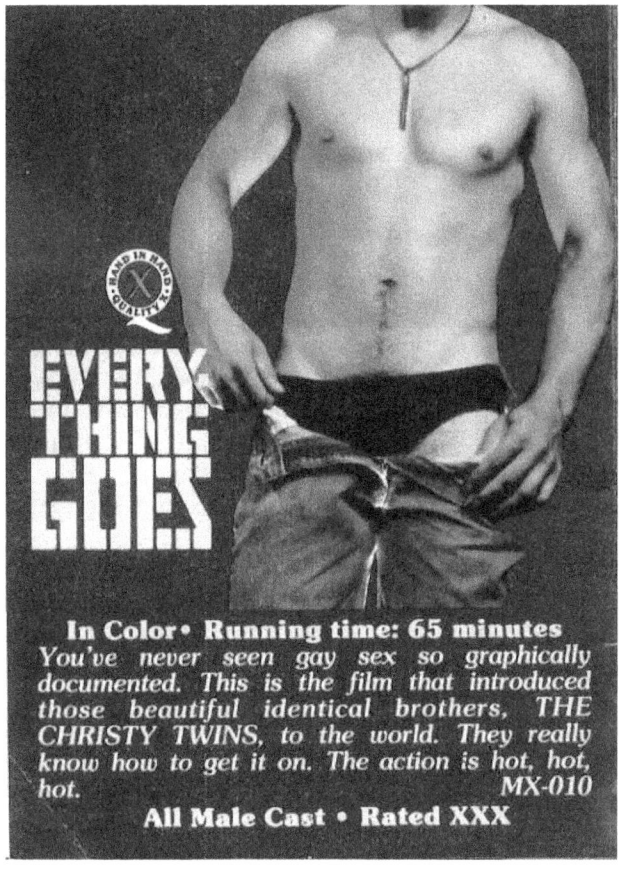

A fascinating curio from the early days of hard-core is this pseudo-documentary entitled EVERYTHING GOES. (The original title on the print itself remains ANYTHING GOES, but perhaps the Cole Porter estate did not approve. At any rate, today the film is generally known by the EVERYTHING title.) Don't be misled by the term "documentary," for the dramatic device of a psychiatrist presenting patients from his "aberration file" provides nothing more than brief webbing between meaty segments, each of which is a most unusual look at The Sexual Self. The most notable sequence is the third one, in which the identical Christy twins make love to - not just have sex with - each other. Today, a decade and a half later, the sequence fairly crackles with sexual electricity in its exploration of The Twin as an extension of The Self. Early on, one of these vibrant blond twins (who knows which?) says, "I could feel my own cock getting worked on when I touched him down there," and thus begins the melding that encompasses oral, anal, and manual give-and-take, and leads the viewer through a rhythmically harmonious sixty-nine to perfectly synchronized orgasms that seem as one. This scene begs for replays, as one contemplates its many provocative implications andovertones. The first and third segments - the auto-fellationist (Marc Taylor) and the sex toy devotee (Shannon Paul) - are almost as unusual, and both provide solo scenes that are far from ordinary in their revelations of two men who make love to themselves. The second one, which features the notorious AcuJac machine, is especially arousing. The final S&M sequence, a public danger scene in a park shed, features two footloose California beach types (Bill Travis and Bob Burke) in a lengthy handballing exercise that is absolutely riveting. Fisting is an activity that is rarely filmed these days, and as such, this footage remains something of an historical rarity. Although the sound leaves a lot to be desired, the color has hardly faded at all, and the subject matter is photographed exceptionally well. EVERYTHING GOES is an offbeat treasure for the connoisseur of the unusual.

*Jerry Douglas, *Manshots*

TOM DeSIMONE

Making 'The Idol'

Although Tom DeSimone has in recent years devoted himself exclusively to such mainstream films as HELL NIGHT with Linda Blair, CONCRETE JUNGLE with Jill St. John, REFORM SCHOOL GIRLS, and his most recent release, ANGEL 3 with Maude Adams and Richard Roundtree, his work in gay erotica during the seventies and early eighties includes such classics as SKIN DEEP, CATCHING UP, STATION TO STATION, HOT TRUCKIN', BI-COASTAL, and of course THE IDOL, a film widely regarded as the best gay porno film ever made. DeSimone, who says he has no plans at the present time to make another gay porn flick, however, is quick to add "but that is not to say I won't."

Jerry Douglas: Let's go back as far as we can. Where did the idea for THE IDOL come from?
Tom DeSimone: I can tell you exactly where the idea came from. Jack Deveau, the head of Hand in Hand films in New York, had a treatment - a three-page outline of a story about a high school jock who has a love affair with one of the kids at school, but it was not fleshed out, it was just an idea. It was actually written by a guy who was Sal Mineo's lover at the time. Anyway, Jack sent it to me and said, "Do you think there's anything we can do with this?" I read it over and said I'd like to write the screenplay.
Douglas: How did you go about casting it?
DeSimone: It was very hard casting in those days. Very often, you had to get people almost off the street, or you'd go to bars and proposition people. I rarely knew what their backgrounds were or where they came from, and many times they were hustlers who just needed some money. I would always treat them with respect and I always treated them well. I was paying them for a job, and they were doing a job. But I always wanted the relationship to end right after that. Nowadays it's a legitimate industry - there are models and model agencies, and these actors have followings and fan clubs, but I've been in the business since 1969, and in those days you were very underground about what you were doing.
Douglas: Yes, for a long time you were Lancer Brooks.
DeSimone: *(Laughs)* Still am.
Douglas: How did you find your star, Kevin Redding?
DeSimone: I knew Nick Rogers - I'd done HOT TRUCKIN' with him - and I figured he'd be good for the role of the coach. Kevin - his real name is Don - was Nick's lover at the time. He'd never done a picture before, and he wasn't sure he wanted to do it. I shouldn't say they were lovers, they were having an affair at the time. So Nick brought him by, and I talked to him, and I guess he felt secure. Interestingly enough, he's never done another film since.
Douglas: That's one of the legends surrounding THE IDOL.
DeSimone: Well, many people approached him after the film's release, including myself. I continued to call him pretty regularly. I wanted him for another picture, because THE IDOL was so popular. But he just said flat out that he never wanted to do another picture - not that he had any bad feelings about it. In fact, he was thrilled by it. But he was afraid that if he did others, he would become "just another porn star," and this way, he could always remain THE IDOL. In so doing, he created a mystique around himself, and the film.
Douglas: What were your first impressions of him? Do you remember the day you first met him?
DeSimone: Yes. In fact, I still have his photo, model release, and questionnaire. I always have models fill out a questionnaire, and I take a Polaroid.
Douglas: What sort of questionnaire?
DeSimone: Well, that came about because so many times in the early days, I'd be making a picture, shooting a scene, and I'd want somebody to do something, and he'd say, "Oh, I don't do that." We'd be stuck. So, to avoid this problem, I had two questionnaires made up. One was just the general information - name, age, how do I reach you, etc. - and the second one was a sexual questionnaire, and there was no name on it.
Douglas: Can you remember any of Kevin Redding's answers?
DeSimone: Well, I have it right here. Would you like me to go get it?

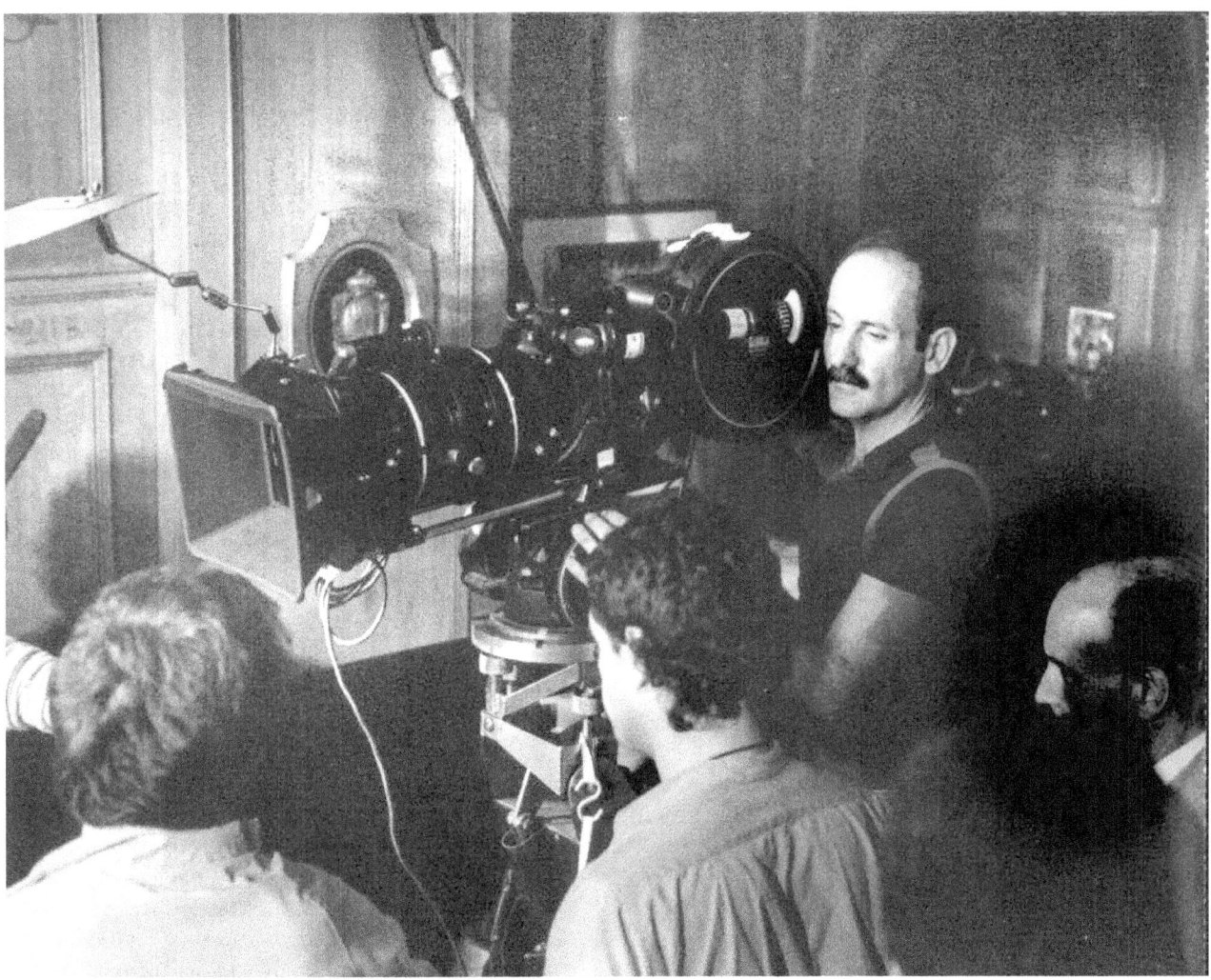

Douglas: Go get it.
(In no time, DeSimone has produced the model releases and Polaroids for the entire cast of THE IDOL, and graciously agreed to let us reprint them in this article.)
DeSimone: The model releases were signed in July, 1978, so that must be when I shot the film. And this is the Polaroid of Kevin – standing by the window here because I needed some sunlight. I remember he was very nervous. As soon as he got undressed, he got an erection – which was a good sign.
Douglas: That he was an exhibitionist?
DeSimone: Yes. And he was a little bit turned on to the whole idea, so I felt he would probably be good.
Douglas: Your films have always demanded a certain acting ability.
DeSimone: I didn't make loop pictures, where it's just one fuck scene after another, and the only dialogue is, "Hi, Delivery Man, come on in and, gee, why don't you get undressed!" There's nothing wrong with those pictures, but just because a film was a sex film, I didn't want to cheat the audience or myself.
Douglas: What was Kevin Redding's background?
DeSimone: He was a waiter.
Douglas: How tall was he?
DeSimone: Five-eight, five-nine, I guess – an inch or two taller than I am.
Douglas: How old was he when he made THE IDOL?
DeSimone: You know, I can't really say, but he must have been in his early twenties. I never stayed in touch with him socially. After we did THE IDOL, we only talked a few times.
Douglas: The camera certainly loved him.
DeSimone: It did, it really did. And Nick Elliot, who has been my cameraman on most of my pictures, did a beautiful job.
Douglas: Before we talk about the shooting, can we talk a bit more about casting? Where did you find Mark Bitler to play the boy on the bicycle who idolizes the idol?

DeSimone: I don't remember where he came from, and I don't think he made another film.
Douglas: What about the boy who played the cousin? He was billed as Jerry Foxe.
DeSimone: He flew in from Phoenix, and this was the only picture he ever did. There were a lot of "only" people in this picture.
Douglas: After you decided to use Kevin Redding as the idol, how did your pre-production work proceed?
DeSimone: Well, I gave him a copy of the script and we discussed the schedule as to which scenes would be shot when. You always have to work out a schedule, because these kids always have other jobs, you know. We always shot on weekends, because we had to rent the equipment. We'd pick it up on Friday afternoon – always after four – try to shoot a scene Friday night, shoot all day Saturday and all day Sunday, and then return the equipment Monday morning. Basically, you were paying for Saturday and getting an extra day and a half free shooting out of it. So I gave Kevin the script, and he wanted to know who he'd be working with. The scene with the coach was no problem, since Nick was his boyfriend. I showed him stills of the cousin, and that was fine. In the shower, he doesn't really have sex, just watches. So the only one he wasn't thrilled about was Mark Bitler, but we were stuck. He was the only one I had for the role. None of the other boys seemed right to me.
Douglas: Did you allow for any rehearsal time?
DeSimone: We didn't rehearse. As we shot, we worked on it, scene by scene. Kevin was good about having his lines down – very good about that. I don't shoot long masters in porno films. I shoot in steps. I cut exactly where I know I'm going to do a close-up, because it's difficult to ask these actors to memorize a whole scene. These are not professional actors who can carry a scene. They can invariably get three or four lines out, and then they go up on their lines.
Douglas: One of the most impressive things about THE IDOL is its structure, the way it traces the archetypal steps in coming out: the masturbation scene in the car after his girl friend leaves, the voyeurism in the shower scene, the passive participation and first kiss in the scene with the coach, the experimentation with the cousin at the pool, and finally the total commitment of the final scene.
DeSimone: Well, the thing I wanted to do was gradually bring this boy out. The problem I have with a lot of porno films is these actors pretending to be straight – you always see this scene where to guys are sitting there looking at a Playboy and they're getting hard, and instantly – *(He snaps his finger.)* – they're into gay sex of every conceivable combination.
Douglas: Were you able to shoot any of the film in order?
DeSimone: No. The very first stuff we shot was the footage of Kevin out on the playing field, early in the morning, with the coach, and the boy watching. We just went up here to a local high school and stole the shots. When I say the word "stole," I mean we just grabbed what we could. You know, you're not supposed to shoot in these places without permits, and you don't get a permit to do a porno film.
Douglas: This was a Saturday morning?
DeSimone: I think so, it must have been.
Douglas: What came next?
DeSimone: We went from there to a building downtown – sort of a warehouse that a friend of mine has – lots of space, and one of the rooms worked for the massage room in the film, with the coach and Kevin. The first sex scene to be shot. It was mid-afternoon by this time. I remember we had a little trouble with Nick. Kevin was very turned on and hard through the whole scene, and everything worked very well. We got the dialog out of the way first and then we had to get into the sex, but Nick had a problem staying hard. Nick always had that problem. As many times as I worked with him, that was always a problem. I had thought I wanted the coach to fuck the boy on the massage table, but Nick just couldn't get it hard enough to fuck him. I just couldn't get a cum shot out of him. We were there forever, and everybody was taking a turn trying to get him off, and finally he realized he just couldn't do it. He felt real bad about it and promised that he would come back another afternoon with just me and the camera, and I said, "Okay." So the week after we wrapped, I rented this massage table again and we went out to my garage. I just got under the table and he jacked off under the table and I was able to film it – a pick-up scene we inserted later.
Douglas: Well, whether it was by design or by accident, the film works much better without the coach fucking him.
DeSimone: Yes, it's true. It worked out fine that the coach just sort of introduces him to man-to-man sexuality. Originally, I was just thinking in terms of turning the audience on early in the film by showing them a good hot fuck scene with Nick, who also had a big dick, but it actually worked much better for the film this way. I'm glad now the coach

didn't fuck him.
Douglas: Which scene did you shoot next?
DeSimone: I think we did the beach stuff on Saturday, too. Yeah. We went to a deserted beach – not too deserted, but away from the public. Again, we had to "steal" everything. You know, in this particular instance, I think we shot more than a weekend. I can't actually remember now, for sure – it's been so long. But thinking back to what we covered, I don't think we could have done it in a weekend. I know we shot the cemetery stuff on Sunday morning. Again, we had to "steal" everything – which isn't easy to do when you've got extras and flowers and a grave site, and you're setting up lights and sound and everything. That took longer than we thought, and we had to get to a health club in Hollywood that was going to let us use their place for the shower scene. By the time we got there, we only had an hour to do it. So we were frantically trying to get everything ready. And of course we were dealing with water and cable and lights. The fact that I even got that scene was a miracle. It was late, and the guy was in a hurry to get out of there. I remember, though, as we were shooting it, I was watching Kevin, and I thought this was going to be very effective because he had exactly what I was going for in the scene.
Douglas: And then?
DeSimone: I guess the scene with the cousin was next. That had to be the next day, I think. We had a little trouble getting that scene, but it plays real well. The scene with the cousin was certainly the one in which Kevin was the most turned on.
Douglas: When you sense that kind of sexual electricity on the set, how do you make sure it's maintained?
DeSimone: It's never very easy. Basically, what I do beforehand is sit down with the actors – after the dialogue is out of the way – and I clear the set of everyone that isn't really necessary, although I always shoot with a very small crew anyway: a cameraman, myself, the sound man, and an assistant who helped out.
Douglas: Did you shoot with one camera?
DeSimone: Always. Anyway, I would sit with the actors, discuss briefly what I thought was the tone of the scene. The scene with the cousin I wanted to be very romantic – it was the first time the idol had ever sucked cock, fucked, or gotten fucked. Everything leading up to the sex – the questioning – had to be gradual, not start off like gangbusters. So I talked to them about that, reminded them that they were playing guys who were doing these things for the first time.
Douglas: And then you just let nature take its course?
DeSimone: I tell them I will probably talk to them while they're having sex. I'll say, "Don't respond and don't look at me. Just listen to what I have to say. If you can do what I say, continue doing what you're doing and gradually do what I've requested." Generally, I stand next to the cameraman, and I may tap his arm and signal him to move this way or that, or to get this. Obviously, it's easy to shatter the mood. And when you shatter the mood, you shatter everything, and then you're waiting around for them to get their hard-ons back.
Douglas: Give us an example of what you might say to the actors.
DeSimone: Very quietly, I might say something like, "Keep kissing, but when I tell you to, I want Kevin to go down and suck on Jerry's nipples a little bit ... and then down on his stomach ... and when I tell you to, go down on him ..."
Douglas: In a sex scene, such as the one with the cousin, do you lay out a sexual "road map" of what each is to do?
DeSimone: We always discuss that first. Naturally, you have to know who's going to do what to whom, and you don't want any surprises. I tell them in very technical terms, "First, I'm going to shoot four hundred feet – which is ten minutes of screen time. The first four hundred feet is to be devoted to foreplay, kissing, and sucking. Then we stop to reload, and the second hour hundred feet is going to be the penetration, the fucking, and the cum shot." That way I have twenty minutes of footage on each sex scene. In the editing room I trim that twenty minutes down to eight or ten. While we load the second four hundred feet, whoever was going to be the receiver would douche and clean up.
Douglas: There were no surprises, then, in shooting the scene with the cousin?
DeSimone: I think probably the only mistake I made in that scene was I didn't shoot the sex first, I shot the dialog first. What happened is what often happens – two people meet and they know they're going to fuck, and initially there's this chemistry. The actors show up, they look each other over, they're turned on, they want to do it. Then, if they have to spend a lot of time waiting or doing technical things, very often that can kill everything. By talking and interrelating socially, you begin to see this person not as the sexual fantasy you thought he was, but as the

person he really is, and he may not appeal to you anymore. The chemistry is dissipated or gone. And I think a little of that happened in this scene. They showed up, they were very turned on to each other. There was a lot of kidding and ass-grabbing. Then we did all the dialog and broke for lunch, and by midafternoon when we were ready to do the sex scene, they were kind of burned out on each other. So I had to somehow get them re-stimulated. Talking about what they were going to do kind of turned them on again. It's not the easiest thing in the world to do a sex scene, and certainly not the easiest thing to shoot. It was always my least favorite part of filmmaking, believe it or not.

Douglas: Whatever problems you had, I personally think it is the hottest scene in the film.

DeSimone: About midway through the shooting – after the first four hundred foot roll – we took a break, and I remember we were down for about an hour, which was very unnerving. But Kevin needed a break. He couldn't keep it up, and he was uncomfortable about something. So we took a break, and they smoked a joint and relaxed, and they got back into it. So it was a two-part scene as shot.

Douglas: The seam doesn't show. Did you ever find out why Kevin was uncomfortable about something?

DeSimone: Halfway through the shooting, I think he lost interest.

Douglas: The game was over.

DeSimone: Exactly.

Douglas: And it became work.

DeSimone: That was exactly the problem. It wasn't anything I hadn't dealt with before. I've actually had actors not finish a picture. At least, he finished – he stayed and fulfilled his commitment, but the bloom was off the rose. A lot of these kids don't realize that making a porno film is hard work. They think all you have to do is show up, drop your pants, have hot sex, be paid some money, and go home.

Douglas: That only leaves the first and last sex scenes of the picture: the masturbation scene in the car and the sex scene with the kid who idolizes him.

DeSimone: Well, Mark was very turned on to Kevin, but Kevin didn't really want to do the scene. He was really turned off to the idea of finishing the picture. So it was like pulling teeth to get that scene out of him. But that last day he was tired, because he had an awful lot to do that day. He had three sex scenes to do in one day. I don't usually ask an actor to do more than one sex scene a day. Maybe I'm remembering wrong. I can't believe I asked him to do three sex scenes in one day – maybe two, but not three.

Douglas: That explains why the last scene doesn't quite top the scene with the cousin. Now, you've talked about every scene in the film except the masturbation scene in the car.

DeSimone: That was done at night – the very last thing we shot, and it was done in my garage here. We shot the long shots in a park up here – where she gets out of the car and the kid on the bicycle is watching. We quickly got that shot where the car door is open and his legs are sticking out. We "stole" it in a hurry and got out of there. Then we came back to the garage, put some branches outside the windows of the car, and finished the masturbation sequence.

Douglas: How long did it take you to edit the film?

DeSimone: Usually it takes me six to eight weeks, because I do everything myself. I cut the picture and then cut in the music and sound effects. I've always edited my own pictures. Because the budgets were so low and we shot them so quickly, I always did a lot of cutting in the camera, so when I got to the cutting room, there weren't miles of footage to go through. In a mainstream movie, everything is catalogued, and labeled, and slated, but shooting a porno film, there's no time. The shooting of the sex scenes is a little different. You shoot it just like a documentary – as if you were at a sporting event over which you had no control You cover it from as many angles as you can, and it's really creative editing.

Douglas: Did the film change at all in the editing room? Did you shoot any scene that wasn't used?

DeSimone: Oh, no, no. Everything is in it that I intended to use. This picture was very well thought out in my head – a picture I really and truly wanted to make. It was a very personal film. Porno films are almost never about love, they're always just about sex. And I'm a firm believer in love. I'd wanted to do a love story for homosexuals. I wanted people to go sit in a theatre and not just get hard-ons, but something in their hearts as well.

Douglas: Do you remember the first time you showed a rough cut of THE IDOL to anyone?

DeSimone: I never show a rough cut. As soon as I finish, though, I have a screening here in my home, and I always have the cast and the crew and invited guests. Generally, when I had these screenings, there would be eight or ten people, but this night, so many people showed up that I had to remove all the furniture. Kevin, you remember, had not been too thrilled about finishing the picture, but when he saw it that night he was absolutely amazed. And when the film opened, Kevin went over and over again and took as many people as he could. He took his whole family to see the picture when it played over here at the Vista Theatre. He took his mother, aunts and uncles, relatives. I knew the manager of the theatre at that time, and he called me, quite surprised. He said, "You know, that kid who's in the picture – he's here every day. And every time he comes in, he introduces his family to us. I'm just amazed." I just said, "More power to him. I wish we could all be so open about our sexuality."

Douglas: What do you suppose prompted him to bring his family?

DeSimone: I never talked to him about it, but I suppose he was suddenly seeing himself in what many people considered to be an actual movie, and I guess he was proud of it. Maybe he wanted his family to see him in a different light, maybe he wanted them to be exposed to his sexuality, maybe he thought it was a way for them to understand what homosexuality is all about. I don't know.

Douglas: Did you ever have any sense of his having a goal in life?

DeSimone: Interestingly enough, after the picture, he did start to take acting lessons. Don't forget, this was a kid who'd never been on a movie set before, a kid just out of school who was a waiter in a gay bar, and suddenly had this thrust upon him. I remember, a long time after that, I was doing a regular Hollywood feature and needed several young boys for a locker room scene, and I thought of giving him a call, but at the time, I had no idea of how to find him anymore.

Douglas: So he just vanished?

DeSimone: Well, just this past Thanksgiving I was in Palm Springs, at the CC Construction Company – it's one of the big discos there where the beautiful people go – somehow, they let me in. Anyway, I was standing there. It was very crowded, and I looked across the dance floor, and there he was, just dancing his little tush off. He looked spectacular. He really did. He had a tank top on. And not much older than I remember him in the film – just more pumped up, and more ... butch, if that's the word. He's been going to the gym and pumping up. He's got a huge chest and massive arms. It's not unattractive, but he looks different. So I saw him and he saw me, and I went over, and we hugged. I guess we were both just so happy to see each other alive and still looking good. These days, when you run into someone you haven't seen in years, you say "Whew!" I said, "I'm just so happy to see you well and happy."

Douglas: What's he doing these days?

DeSimone: He's still a waiter.

Douglas: Did you speak of Nick's death? *(Editor's note: Nick Rogers died January 10, 1987 of AIDS complications in Houston, Texas.)*

DeSimone: No, we didn't talk about Nick. It was just one of those dance floor hugs. You know, "Happy Holidays!" and all that. And he danced away, and I danced away, and that was it.

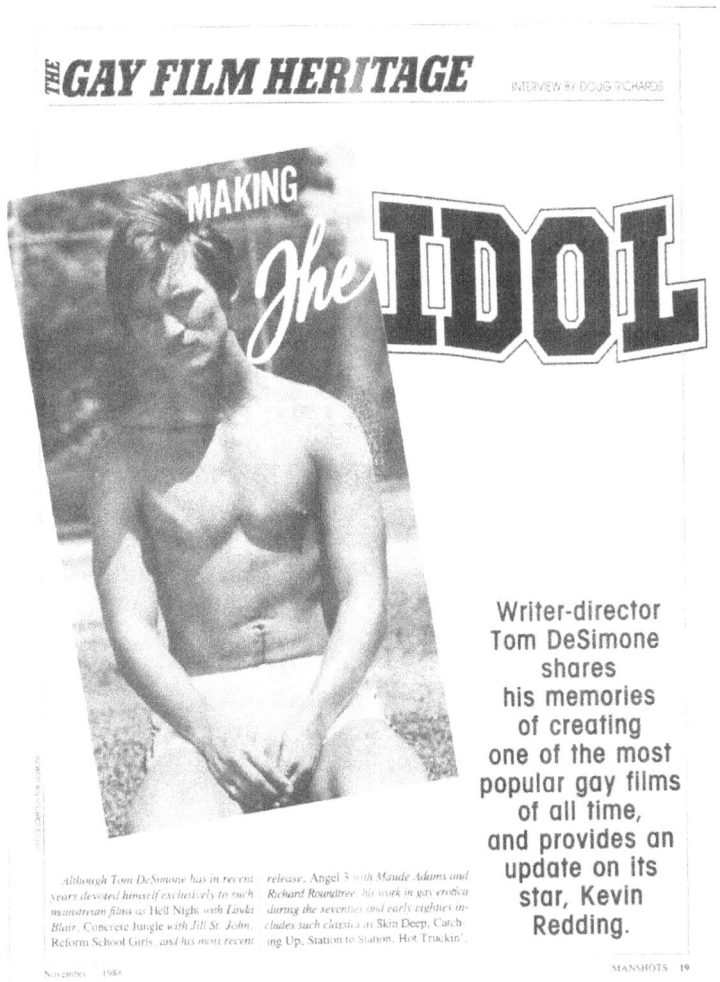

Writer-director Tom DeSimone shares his memories of creating one of the most popular gay films of all time, and provides an update on its star, Kevin Redding.

KEVIN REDDING

Yesterday, Today, and Tomorrow

Shortly after an article entitled "Making THE IDOL" appeared in last November's issue of Manshots, *a friend of Kevin Redding's told this interviewer that Redding, the star of THE IDOL, had read the piece and was willing to share his memories about the shooting of that erotic classic, and to discuss what has happened to him since that film was made, including those factors that contributed to his decision never to make another film. An interview was instantly arranged. Redding arrives at the West Hollywood apartment where the New York-based interviewer is visiting. He is wearing snug black jeans and Polo shirt, a bright red webbed belt, and Reeboks. He is as lean and handsome as ever, his moustache a bit fuller, his face only days older than he was a decade ago when he became an instant legend. He clutches a pack of cigarettes and a lighter in one hand, and almost the first thing he says is: "Oh, good, you smoke. I was afraid I'd have to get through this without..." He laughs and doesn't complete the line. It is a speech habit he repeats throughout the interview. This is not the last sentence he will leave unfinished. We chat idly for a few moments about the weather, mutual friends, and restaurants in Los Angeles, and then the tape recorder is activated.*

Kevin Redding: Well, I don't understand why anybody would want to interview me, anyway. I just don't understand that. I don't look at myself as ... I did the picture, and in all honesty, I'm very proud of it. It was a real movie, and I was very pleased with that. Up until I saw the film for the first time, I went through a lot of emotional stress about it, because I really felt guilty about doing it. I mean, hey - I was raised a Southern Baptist - what can I tell you? *(He laughs)* My anatomy, for a couple of months, broke down. Broke down. But then I saw it, and I was just proud. I'm really a funny person. It's like, you know, I do something because I want to know what it's like.
Jerry Douglas: "Try anything once"?
Redding: Sure, why not. *(A pause)* I'm not quite that way anymore. Not quite as adventuresome as I used to be.
Douglas: Let's go back a bit. Where was your head at, when you were approached to do the film?
Redding: Christ, I don't even remember. I know I didn't hear about this film through Nick. *(Editor's note: Nick Rogers, who played the coach in the film.)* No. No, I will tell you exactly what happened. I was going with Nick's roommate - not Nick - at the time. And we had gone to this party, and I was introduced to these two guys. One of them said, "I really think you'd be nice for this film that this guy I know is doing." He said it was a porn film, and I said, "No." Well, about two months later I called Tom. *(Editor's note: Tom DeSimone, the director of THE IDOL, who was interviewed for the first article.)* I said, "Yeah, I'd be interested in doing it."
Douglas: What happened in those two months to make you change your mind?
Redding: I was going back and forth about it.
Douglas: Were you flattered that you'd been asked?
Redding: Sure. Are you kidding? Of course. Who wouldn't be?
Douglas: Had you seen much porn at that time?
Redding: A little bit, yah. I don't watch it that much now, either. I do READ. But I don't watch it. *(Laughs)* I'd rather do it. But I just said, "What the hell - why not?" And I did need the money at the time. A thousand bucks back then was a great deal of money. Still a lot of money now. So I did it. I called Tom. I'm not sure if I called Tom or Nick, because Nick and I did have a little thing going ... But he did have a lover at the time - and that rubs me the wrong way. And now, I wouldn't do it. Just won't. Because I've been hurt, other people have been hurt. So, what's the point? I mean, just to suck on somebody's dick? Big deal. It's just not worth it to me. So, anyway, I had somehow gotten through to Tom, whether I called him directly - I did have a card to call - or arranged it through Nick...
Douglas: Perhaps that is why Tom assumed you were having a thing with Nick?
Redding: Could be. You know, I think Nick and I went to bed a total of twice. The first time he got it up, and I was really - *Whoa!* You know? And the second time, he couldn't.
Douglas: Tom mentioned he had that problem from time to time.
Redding: Yeah, well, you know. I guess he had to be really ... He just didn't find anybody

that excited him that much ... I guess.
Douglas: Back to the audition with Tom.
Redding: At any rate, I went, and I was very nervous. Jesus, I was scared to death. Oh, yeah.
Douglas: What did you think was going to happen?
Redding: I don't know. Basically, my fears were: Would I like the people that would be in the movie with me? What if I couldn't get it up? That was a biggie with me.
Douglas: Do you remember that first interview at all?
Redding: I remember being really attracted to Tom. *(Laughs)* Very much, as a matter of fact. I remember him getting the Polaroid shots, and I remember filling out the questionnaire.
Douglas: Tom told me, "As soon as he got undressed, he got an erection – which was a good sign."
Redding: When I read that, I laughed. I mean, I laughed! And I probably still would get an erection in a situation like that.
Douglas: A new sexual sensation?
Redding: Sure. A very exciting thing.
Douglas: How soon did you start filming?
Redding: Right away, a week or two.
Douglas: Tom talked a lot about your concern over the men you'd be working with.
Redding: As I said, that was one of my fears when I went into the interview. I mean, who wants to ... I was worried I would be with someone I wasn't attracted to. So Tom showed me pictures of a few of them, and I thought they were okay. It wasn't like: "I have to have this type of approval."
Douglas: You'd had sex with Nick already.
Redding: And I think that was a major influence in me deciding to go ahead and do the film – because I still had the hots for him. But a lot of people, said to me, "Don't do it." I discussed it with this friend of mine, sort of a mentor, father figure. *(Editor's note: This friend will be called Ray, although that is not his real name.)* Ray tried to talk me out of it, but he could see already that I was going to do it anyway.
Douglas: At that point, did you envision a long career, or did you know from the start that you would make only one film?
Redding: I envisioned a quick thousand bucks and leaving. I don't know – that's being very honest. I didn't do it because I wanted to be some sort of a star. I did it because I was curious. The idea of it was very hot to me at the time.
Douglas: Were you concerned about your parents finding out?
Redding: Very much so. God, that was one of my biggest fears – my mother. She was living in Santa Barbara at the time. I do have a gay brother. I'm sure he knows, although I don't think I've ever discussed it with him. He's younger, lives in Santa Barbara, twenty-two. Good kid.
Douglas: Is your father alive?
Redding: Yes, but he lives in Florida. So he might know. But my mother, that was the biggest thing with me. God, I was afraid – and still am.
Douglas: But Tom was under the impression that you took your entire family to the premiere of the film.
Redding: Yes, and I want to correct that. I would never have taken my mother to that film. Never. I took a lot of friends to see it, but not my family. Never. I just could do nothing to hurt my mother intentionally.
Douglas: Does she know you're gay? Have you come out to her?
Redding: Oh, God, when I was seventeen. SHE asked me. Because I was living with my first lover.
Douglas: And nowadays she deals with the matter well?
Redding: Oh, yah, very much so. It's no problem; this would be.
Douglas: Well, let's talk about the first day of shooting. What did you do the night before?
Redding: I was scared shitless. I used to go out all the time, but I stayed home the night before the shooting, so I could rest up, which is what Tom had told me to do for a week, but I didn't do it. I said, "Okay, fine." And just went on my merry way. I did what I wanted to do, which is part of my problem – I never listen to people.
Douglas: What sign are you?
Redding: Sagittarius – what can I tell you? *(Laughs)* I can't remember how early I got up. But it was early. We went to the school and shot the opening scene. Then I remember going to this warehouse in downtown L.A. While we were shooting, God, I was scared to death the cops would break in the door in. I was lying on this table and I can remember thinking, "God, somebody's going to come through here and say, 'Okay, freeze.'" I was very naïve.
Douglas: Where were you born?
Redding: Florida. Born in Miami, moved to L.A. when I was seven, lived there till I was thirteen, moved to Santa Barbara, moved back to L.A. when I was twenty-one.
Douglas: Okay, let's talk about the scene with

the coach.

Redding: We're in the set for the coach's office, and I'm on the table, I'm really excited about the prospect of doing the sex scene. I really am. And then, at the same time, I was scared to death that we were going to be raided. The whole time we were filming, that was the big thing with me – that we were going to get caught.

Douglas: That tension shows in the film. Okay, let's talk about the moment of truth: when it was time to produce an erection.

Redding: I think I was hard as soon as we parked. *(Laughs)* Oh, yeah. There was no problem. It was just like: a-l-l-r-i-g-h-t! I remember lying on that table. I remember Nick not being able to get a hard-on. I remember being extremely disappointed.

Douglas: I believe the shower scene was shot next.

Redding: No, the coach scene was the last scene of the day. It was night time when we shot that scene. The following day we went to the gym on Santa Monica Boulevard for the shower scene. I remember I was hot for the blond guy, the curly haired one – Jim.

Douglas: Bartolotta, also known as Jim Battaglia.

Redding: He was the only one in the whole scene I was attracted to. And I remember the real gym instructor watching, and *that* made me nervous. I was just really nervous about outsiders watching.

Douglas: Well, it worked. There's so much tension in that scene.

Redding: *(Wrily)* Well, I kind of like to think maybe it might have been my acting, too. *(Laughs)* But I doubt it.

Douglas: Okay, let's talk about the scene with the **cousin**, played by the actor named Jerry Foxe.

Redding: The best. My favorite. Beautiful. It was in the afternoon of the second day. We were high on a hill in Coldwater Canyon.

Douglas: Had you ever met the actor before?

Redding: Never met him, and boy, let me tell you something, when I first laid eyes on him, I just thought he was so cute. And that was, and still is ... I don't think there's ever been a sex scene in a pornographic film like that. Ever. I was very much attracted to him, and he was to me.

Douglas: You arrived at the house, and he was there?

Redding: You know, when you walk into a room, and your eyes ... Christ, I think we would have gotten it on right then and there, had there been nobody around. Now, I think Tom said something about my losing interest midway through the scene. I don't think that was quite the case. I was just tired. I wasn't used to working from eight in the morning till nine at night, you know? But I was excited about doing that scene with Jerry. I always thought he was so hot, and we promised to keep in touch with each other, and I never saw him again.

Douglas: Maybe, if he reads this, he'll try to contact you through the magazine.

Redding: I do remember watching the movie for the first time at Tom's house. I liked the quality right away, but I think when I saw that scene – that was when I fell in love with the movie. I guess that's when my pride came out – when I saw that, and the scene with Mark Bitler. *(Editor's note: The boy on the bicycle who worships the character played by Redding.)*

Douglas: Is Tom accurate in his memory of your being disinterested in that actor?

Redding: Tom's memory is *extremely accurate*. *(Quickly)* Now, I liked him as a friend. I'd seen him out at the bars and we'd danced together – I used to go to Oil Can Harry's all the time – and he was always interested in me. And he'd come up and say, "Let's go home." I just liked him as a person, but I was not interested in him sexually.

Douglas: Do you know anything about him?

Redding: Nothing whatsoever. Except his brother was a pretty well-known female impersonator. Anyway, Tom is very accurate. I wasn't turned on to Mark, and I remember his saying to me – like it was yesterday – "Now I've got you." And I looked at him and said, "No, you don't." How can you have somebody unless he wants you to? And that's why I had such a problem with the erection in that scene. Tom's memory serves him well. Now, he'll know. Let me tell you something: Because of what that kid said to me, I hated every moment of that scene. Looking back, I'm very proud of the way it came out.

Douglas: How old were you when you made THE IDOL?

Redding: Twenty-two.

Douglas: Is Tom's memory accurate that you lost interest during the course of shooting the film?

Redding: It was the fact of: "God, when is this going to end?" It was like: "Now we've got to go over here and do this. Now we've got to go over here and do that. You've got to get it up now." It was a lot of pressure.

Douglas: How many days did you shoot?

Redding: I think we shot two or three days, and then a week's time lapsed, and we began shooting again. I'd gone out and partied a lot, which I shouldn't have done. So that contributed to my fatigue.
Douglas: The last scene shot was the solo, right?
Redding: Yes, yes. I remember saying, "What should I wear?" and Tom saying, "Wear your own clothes." So I wore my favorite shirt in that scene. I remember I had a little problem getting an erection. Then I got my erection and we shot the scene, and that was it. I remember the girl was there for that scene. Yeah, we'd just shot her scene. The scene with the girl – I didn't even want to do, because she tried to talk Tom into writing in a sex scene with me. I said, "No way." Period.
Douglas: Do you remember going home that last night?
Redding: Yah. I was very tired, and really glad it was over – not because of any guilt feelings – that didn't start for a few days.
Douglas: When did the guilt set in and how did it manifest itself?
Redding: I started thinking: "What if my mother finds out?" "What if this happens? What if that happens?" "People aren't going to like me anymore." What if, what if, what if. Then Ray and his lover – with whom I lived – were moving to Palm Springs at the time, picking up the only stable home that I'd ever lived in, and I didn't want to go. At the time, I felt like a prostitute, and I'm not that way. All of a sudden, my attitude just went downhill. I couldn't go to the john for a week – I finally had to have a catheter put in me – at the Eisenhower in Palm Springs. Figure it out. I can't. It was just all psychological.
Douglas: You had recovered by the time of the screening?
Redding: *(Nodding)* And that really changed my feelings.
Douglas: What did you think the first time you saw yourself nude, with an erection, on film?
Redding: *(Long pause)* I didn't – and I still don't – see the attraction. I'm flattered other people do, but ... You know.
Douglas: So the guilt was gone.
Redding: I got in my mind that if I did it, thank God, *that's* what I did. Because I don't know how I would have reacted, if I'd seen a piece of shit. But I was very proud. And then I sort of thought for a while I'd like to do THE FRONT RUNNER. *(Laughs)*

Douglas: Tell us about the premiere.
Redding: All my friends at Oil Can Harry's knew about it. I remember everybody going. I sat in the back row. I was very embarrassed. I remember two lovers who were friends of mine, sitting in the row in front of me. I remember wanting, just wanting to get both of them in the sack at the same time, and I remember one looking at the other and saying, "Jesus, how would you like to sit on that?" I just smiled. *(A pause)* What else? And then just kind of looking here, looking there, and seeing the people's reactions. And when it was over, I went into the lobby, and I was right there in the center, and it was like, *Whoosh!* And I was scared to death and thinking, "Get me out of here." I remember this one guy who relieved the whole tension for me. He came up to me and said, "Jeez, I thought you were taller."
Douglas: How tall are you?
Redding: Five-nine. Tom was right.
Douglas: Do you remember the first time someone asked you for your autograph?
Redding: Yes, I was bowled over. It was like: "C'mon, you've got to be kidding."
Douglas: Had you ever written the words "Kevin Redding" before?
Redding: No. But I remember who it was and everything. As a matter of fact, just last year I was asked for an autograph. It was just bizarre, because I don't look at myself that way at all, you understand? I really don't. Christ, if I was Robert Redford or Barbra Streisand, I could understand all of this, but I don't, because I'm not. I'm me. I did this thing. And that was it.
Douglas: When did you decide not to make another film?
Redding: That last night. Yeah.
Douglas: Why?
Redding: Because I didn't want to be ... I didn't want people to have the wrong impression of me, I guess. I didn't want people to think I was some piece of meat. I'm a human being, you know. I have feelings and ... People think you have no intelligence. And that you'll do it for any amount of money, and I guess ... *(Snorts)* Hell, we all have our price. I found that out, but I don't want that stigma associated with me. *(Quickly)* I like to think I'm above judging somebody because of what he does for a living. But it's not for me, it's not something I want to do or that I want to be known for.
Douglas: How did you deal with subsequent film offers?
Redding: I can't remember people calling and asking me, to tell the truth. I think maybe once or twice. But I think it was out that I just

wasn't interested. Tom asked me if I wanted to do another one, during the filming, and I said no, but I wasn't sure then. I do know he called me a couple of other times and asked me if I'd changed my mind, and I said I had not.

Douglas: Did you ever have a sense that you were a celebrity?

Redding: *(Roars with laughter)* I never bought a pair of dark sunglasses.

Douglas: Did you do much press for the film? I've never read an interview with you.

Redding: There hasn't been one.

Douglas: This is your first interview?

Redding: Yah. It's really bizarre. Ten years later.

Douglas: If you had it to do over, would you make this film?

Redding: *(Instantly)* Yah.

Douglas: But you've never considered making another one?

Redding: There's no price tag high enough. *(Pause)* Well, hey, what can I tell you? Everybody's a whore. "Name your price, honey."

Douglas: If you could get the money, say, that Elizabeth Taylor commands.

Redding: Well, I doubt anyone would offer me Elizabeth Taylor's money. *(Pause)* I really resent the fact that ... I'd like to know just exactly how much money this movie's made. *(Sighs)* A thousand dollars flat. It kind of bothers me at times. I went through a period of my life – through my own fault...

Douglas: Want to talk about it?

Redding: Sure. It doesn't bother me. I was a coke addict. I went through some heavy drug addiction for a long time, I'll tell you.

Douglas: When did you first do coke?

Redding: Oh ... when did I first do coke? I remember exactly where I was when I did it, and I remember who gave it to me. *(Pause)* From '80 up to '85. Oh, it just had me by the balls and wouldn't let go. It just wouldn't. And for two, three years, people would say to me, "Do you know you're a drug addict?" *(Soft)* And I'd say, "No, I'm not..." And I didn't believe it ... and I was.

Douglas: How did you get out of it?

Redding: *(Chuckles)* Well, it's a funny thing. Everybody has his bottom, and he has to hit it. And I guess I hit mine. I had a landscaping business up in Fresno, when the drugs just took over. Well, I needed money real quick, so I got back into waiting tables, and then I worked for a restaurant chain and they put me into their assistant manager program. I was with them for two years, and moved to Palm Springs. I had written $300-$400 worth of checks to the restaurant, and when I couldn't cover them, I had to go to my regional manager, and tell him. I could go without the stuff for days at a time – I could go without the stuff for two, three weeks at a time. I didn't realize I was an addict till then. My lights were turned off three times. I was being evicted from my apartment. Just things that a responsible, clean human being wouldn't go through, you know? Anyway, I didn't get fired. I was too good to fire, and they knew that, but they insisted that it should never happen again, and asked if I wanted to go get treatment. I went to two or three AA meetings, and those were depressing. So I just quit on my own. My lover and I had broken up, and I got a call from Palm Springs that Ray had AIDS, so I quit the restaurant anyway and moved there. Not before I had another job – I'm not that stupid. *I do* stupid things, but I'm not totally stupid. And I didn't do any of it for another year, and then last November I went on a binge for like, two weeks, and I could see I was heading for the same thing again. And ... *I will never do it again*.

Douglas: What are you doing for a living now?

Redding: I have my own business, and it's doing very well – landscaping and design. *(Pause)* We are what we choose to be.

Douglas: What do you see for the rest of your life?

Redding: I see ... myself having a ranch up in the high desert. A lot of land surrounding me. I see myself owing a chain of nurseries. I love plants, and I have a very green thumb.

Douglas: I thought your answer would be more romantic. You didn't mention another person.

Redding: I do see myself with someone in the future. I'm very much a romantic person. Very much so. I've had two lovers – one for four years and one for seven years, and there are times when I'm very lonely. But when it happens, *it will be the last time*. I will not go through the breakup and shit again. I just won't. *(Sighs)* I'm not as free with myself as I used to be. I don't go out and meet somebody and take him home with me, regardless of whether I think he's hot or not. There has to be a process. You have to get to know somebody. I mean, do you really want to give yourself to somebody for one night and then, all of a sudden, you never see him again? I've felt that emptiness so many times in my life. I don't want to feel that anymore. You know what I mean...?

THE GAY FILM HERITAGE

INTERVIEW BY DOUG RICHARDS

KEVIN REDDING
Yesterday, Today, and Tomorrow

Shortly after an article entitled "Making The Idol" appeared in last November's issue of Manshots, *a friend of Kevin Redding's told this interviewer that Redding, the star of* The Idol, *had read the piece and was willing to share his memories about the shooting of that erotic classic, and to discuss what has happened to him since that film was made, including those factors that contributed to his decision never to make another film. An interview was instantly arranged.*

Redding arrives at the West Hollywood apartment where the New York-based interviewer is visiting. He is wearing snug black jeans and Polo shirt, a bright red webbed belt, and Reeboks. He is as lean and handsome as ever, his moustache a bit fuller, his face only days older than he was a decade ago when he became an instant legend. He clutches a pack of cigarettes and a lighter in one hand, and almost the first thing he says is: "Oh, good, you smoke. I was afraid I'd have to get through this without..." He laughs and doesn't complete the line. It is a speech habit he repeats throughout the interview. This is not the last sentence he will leave unfinished.

We chat idly for a few moments about the weather, mutual friends, and restaurants in Los Angeles, and then the tape recorder is activated.

Redding: Well, I don't understand why anybody would want to interview me, anyway. I just don't understand that. I don't look at myself as... I did the picture, and in all honesty, I'm very proud of it. It was a real movie, and I was very pleased with that. Up until I saw the film for the first time, I went through a lot of emotional stress about it, because I really felt guilty about doing it. I mean, hey — I was raised a Southern Baptist — what can I tell you? (*He laughs*) My anatomy, for a couple of months, broke down. Broke down. But then I saw it, and I was just proud. I'm really a funny person. It's like, you know, I do something because I want to know what it's like.
Manshots: "Try anything once"?
Redding: Sure, why not. (*A pause*) I'm not quite that way anymore. Not quite as

---

Ten years after the release of "The Idol," its star surfaces to sit for his first interview ever!

---

adventuresome as I used to be.
Manshots: Let's go back a bit. Where was your head at, when you were approached to do the film?
Redding: Christ, I don't even remember. I know I didn't hear about this film through Nick. (*Editor's note: Nick Rogers, who played the coach in the film.*) No. No, I will tell you exactly what happened. I was going with Nick's roommate — not Nick — at the time. And we had gone to this party, and I was introduced to these two guys. One of them said, "I really think you'd be nice for this film that this guy I know is doing." He said it was a porn film, and I said, "No." Well, about two months later I called Tom. (*Editor's note: Tom DeSimone, the director of* The Idol, *who was interviewed for the first article.*) I said, "Yeah, I'd be interested in doing it."
Manshots: What happened in those two months to make you change your mind?
Redding: I was going back and forth about it.
Manshots: Were you flattered that you'd been asked?
Redding: Sure. Are you kidding? Of course. Who wouldn't be?
Manshots: Had you seen much porn at that time?
Redding: A little bit, yah. I don't watch it that much now, either. I do *read*. But I don't watch it. (*Laughs*) I'd rather do it. But I just said, "What the hell — why not?" And I did need the money at the time. A thousand bucks back then was a great deal of money. Still a lot of money now. So I did it. I called Tom. I'm not sure if I called Tom or Nick, because Nick and I did have a little thing going... But he did have a lover at the time — and that rubs me the wrong way. Going to bed with somebody else's lover just rubs me the wrong way. And now, I wouldn't do it. Just won't. Because I've been hurt, other people have been hurt. So, what's the point? I mean, just to suck on somebody's dick? Big deal. It's just not worth it to me. So, anyway, I had somehow gotten through to Tom, whether I called him directly — I did have a card to call — or arranged it through Nick...

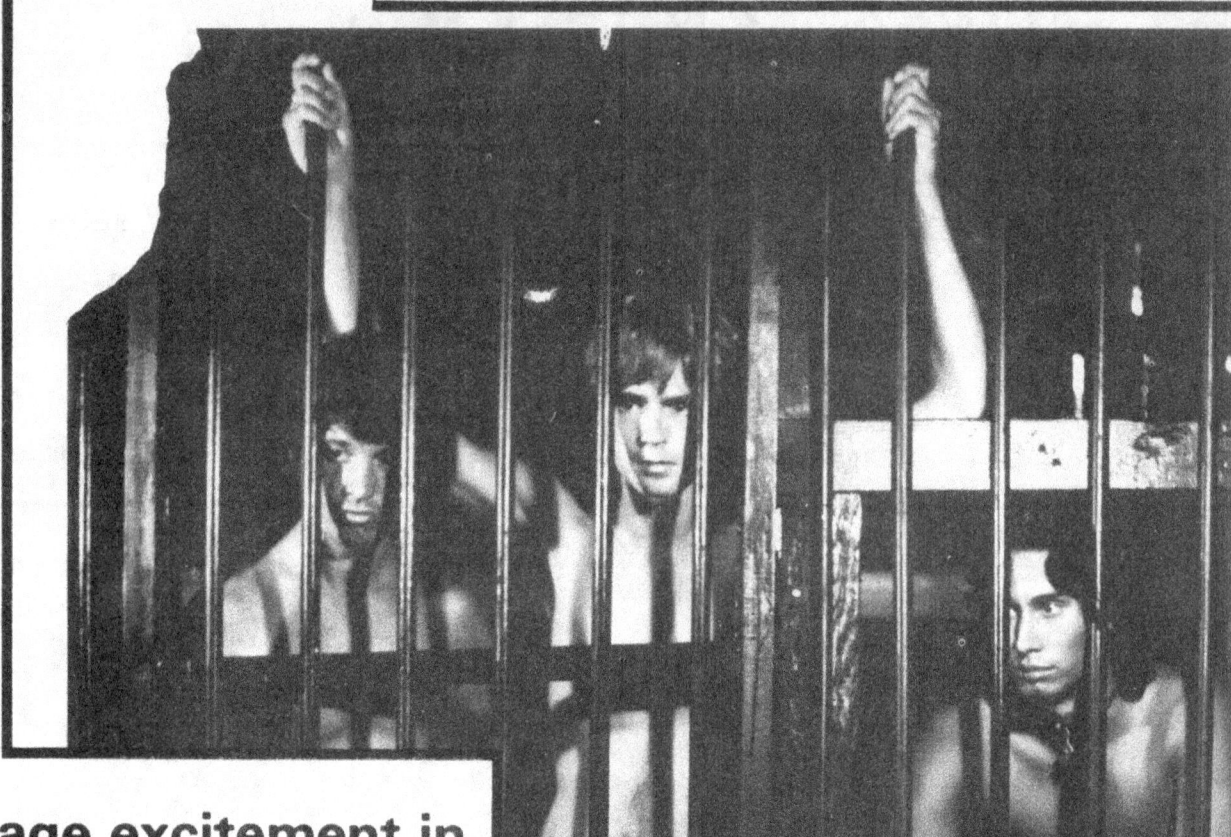

THE COLLECTION

Savage excitement in a classic all-male film.

The Collection

X-RATED/COLOR/ALL MALE CAST
A HAND-IN-HAND FILMS RELEASE

Terry is locked in a strawfilled cage already occupied by another beautiful boy (Jim). Both boys are naked. In an effort to befriend Terry, Jim seduces him - not realizing that the seduction is being carefully watched by the kidnapper through a knothole in the wall. After their love-making they reason that now there are two of them to one kidnapper (although he is admittedly a very pwerful foe) and they decide to be on the watch for an escape.

68

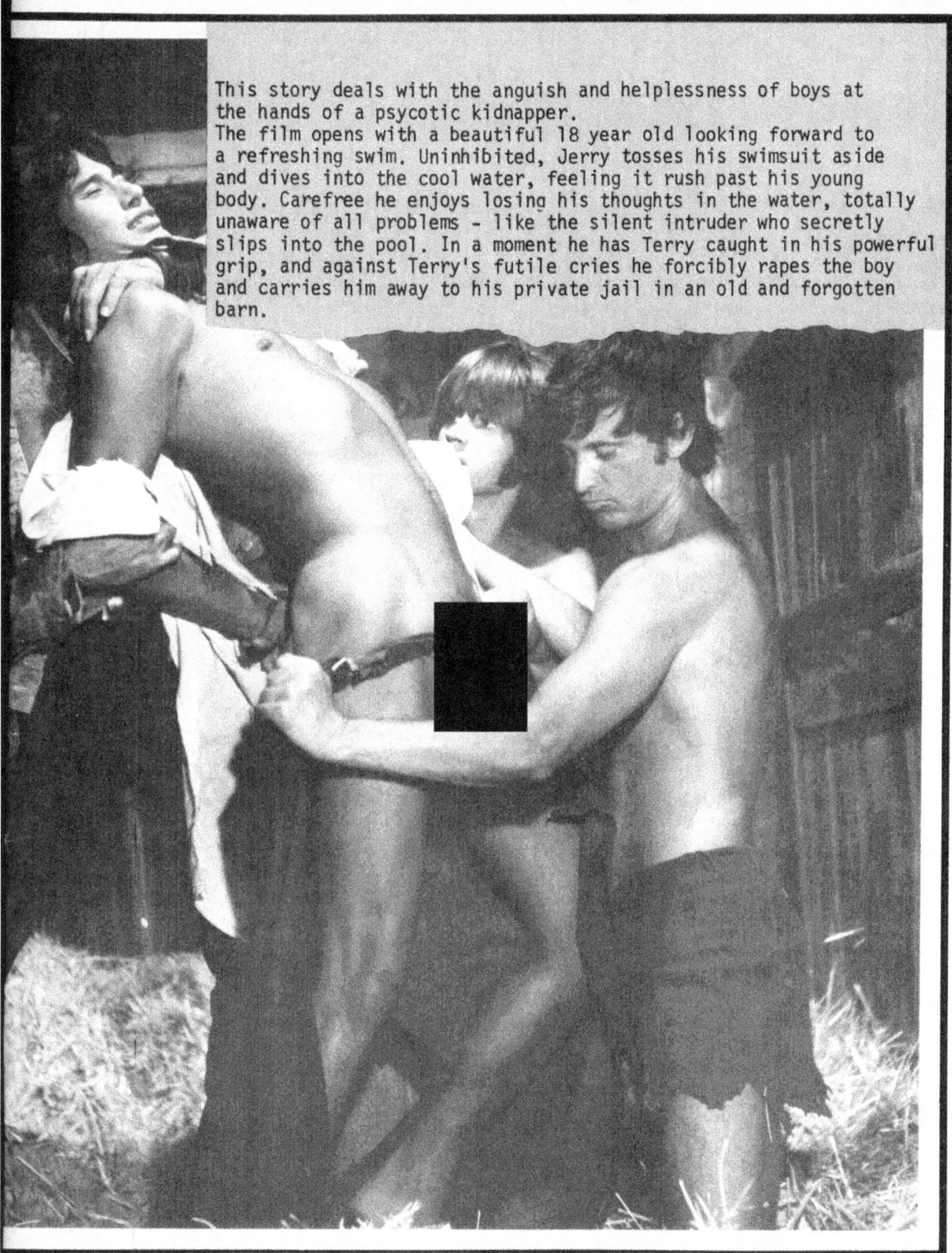

This story deals with the anguish and helplessness of boys at the hands of a psycotic kidnapper.
The film opens with a beautiful 18 year old looking forward to a refreshing swim. Uninhibited, Jerry tosses his swimsuit aside and dives into the cool water, feeling it rush past his young body. Carefree he enjoys losing his thoughts in the water, totally unaware of all problems - like the silent intruder who secretly slips into the pool. In a moment he has Terry caught in his powerful grip, and against Terry's futile cries he forcibly rapes the boy and carries him away to his private jail in an old and forgotten barn.

TOM DeSIMONE

Behind the Camera

I.
Tom DeSimone, one of the pioneers in the field of gay erotica, is now working in mainstream television, but continues to live in the comfortable home in North Hollywood where he has lived for many years. He is as gracious and articulate as ever, and this interview is conducted around the same oversized coffeetable where he shared tales on the making of his most famous film, THE IDOL, for one of the earliest issues of Manshots. Today, we talk not about one film but his entire career.

Jerry Douglas: The way I usually start these interviews is to ask how you got into this business in the first place.
Tom DeSimone: Well, I was working as an editor for a company that made children's films, educational films. I was right out of film school.
Douglas: You did go to film school?
DeSimone: Yes, I have a master's in motion picture production from UCLA, and a BA in theatre, in directing, from Emerson College in Boston.
Douglas: Are you from Boston originally?
DeSimone: New England.
Douglas: Had you gone to film school with the idea of being an editor?
DeSimone: Hopefully, of being a director. That's all I ever wanted to do. In fact, when I was a kid, I had an eight-millimeter camera and my own editing equipment. I had rheumatic fever when I was ten, and I had to stay in bed for about three months, so my dad asked if there was anything I wanted. And I said I wanted a movie projector, 'cause I loved movies. So, he bought me a little eight-millimeter projector and a bunch of films, cartoons, Abbott and Costello, and westerns. I would just lie in bed all day and run these movies over and over and over, and drive them crazy. Finally, then, I decided I wanted to make pictures, so he bought me a camera. Suddenly, I became the one in the family who recorded all of the events, weddings, parties, birthdays, and so, with each birthday and each Christmas, my parents would buy me something like a splicer, some take-up reels, a screen, and through the years, I just collected more and (got) more sophisticated in what I could do. All through high school, I shot films.
Douglas: What did you find film school to be like?
DeSimone: Well, I was fascinated to be working in the medium, and I felt that I knew a little more than most of the kids, especially in classes like editing, because I had been doing it for so many years. I developed, through the years, a feel for it. And, actually, working in the porno business helped me a lot in the work I do now, because when I was making porno films, the budgets were so low and there was a limit on it and you had to learn to shoot quickly and how to edit in the camera and how to break down a script so you're not wasting a lot of time and footage. And that has helped me immensely now, because now I work in television, and I work continually because all the producers in town know that I'm the one that can bring it in on time and on budget. A few people know my background. *(Laughs)*
Douglas: Let's talk about that.
DeSimone: When I got out of school, it was the late sixties, when porno was beginning to happen – not even porno, just "nudies," Pat Rocco stuff, kids on pogo sticks, that kind of stuff. Very barely suggested homosexuality. I mean, there would be male nudes, but you would see them in a long shot walking hand in hand, their silhouette against the sunset, and you'd have to imagine that this was going to lead to something else. Or else, there would be lots of the wrestling films like those that Bob Mizer did. For awhile there, before I got into film, I actually had a studio that did still photography, called Thomas Studio – male nudes – but I never achieved any great fame. So, someone said, "If you make an X-rated movie, you could probably make some money." I didn't know anything about the business, so I started doing some research. First I called the Park Theatre, which was the only theatre in town at the time showing male nudes, and I went down to see what they were showing, and that was the Pat Rocco stuff. Then I called the theatre and asked where they got their stuff, who distributed their pictures, 'cause I figured I should go to the source. They gave me the name of a company called Signature. So, I made an appointment with Signature, and talked to the man there – that was Mr.

Shan Sayles. I showed him a couple of my student films, and he was impressed, but he said, "You know, what we do is very different. A lot of people come in this office and think they can make these pictures and they can't." He suggested that I go out and shoot something and bring it back. So, I went out on the weekend with a sixteen-millimeter camera and two friends. What I shot was all simulated and very artsy. I cut it together, put some classical music on it, and brought it to him. And that was the picture, a little short called YES. Part of it appears in EROTIKUS. So, I showed that to him as my audition, and he said, "Sure, make pictures for me, I'll distribute anything," so I made THE COLLECTION.

Douglas: Tell us about THE COLLECTION. It's a film that, to the best of my recollection, I've never seen.

DeSimone: Well, it was the first real gay feature film. It had a plot, it had acting, it had editing, it had titles, music. Up to that point, they were just loops, and the loops were not even simulated sex. THE COLLECTION was just a takeoff on a picture that was popular then called THE COLLECTOR.

Douglas: Oh, yes, based on the John Fowles novel.

DeSimone: In my version, of course, the man was gay, and he collected young boys and would keep them in cages. It was an S & M picture. And it just went through the roof when it opened.

Douglas: Where did it open?

DeSimone: It opened at the Park Theatre. 1969, I believe. The problem is, the film started to get busted, because of the subject matter. There was no hard core in it - in fact, even no erections. There was a lot of simulated sex - and they hadn't seen that yet. And there was a lot of hard core simulated S & M stuff, like branding. The police got really uptight about it. And then in '72, Nixon did this report on pornography in America, and THE COLLECTION was cited as an example of the kind of stuff we shouldn't be watching. That was my entrée into the business. And then Mr. Sayles said, "Come work for me and I'll give you anything you want."

Douglas: In spite of all the busts?

DeSimone: Oh, sure. There's no substitute for money. In those days, everything got busted. And anybody in this business was used to being hauled in or at least fingerprinted and questioned. And you always had to have a lawyer on retainer.

Douglas: Were you ever busted?

DeSimone: No, I always managed to avoid all that. It was distributors and theatre owners, because they were the ones who were in the forefront, they were the ones easy to get, you know. And each time a bust came - and because of civil rights and the First Amendment, the police would lose - that meant you could go further and further. And it was finally, I think, in the early seventies that everything started to go hard-core.

Douglas: What was the first hard-core film you made?

DeSimone: Well, the first one that actually had hard-ons and ejaculations was that documentary called ONE. It was on teenage masturbation.

Douglas: How did you move from soft core to hard core?

DeSimone: Well, I had made a bunch of films for Signature. These were all soft core. Then we had this big meeting at the company, and it was decided that the competition in New York and San Francisco was starting to show hard core.

Douglas: And the defining characteristic of hard core, then as now, was "insertion."

DeSimone: Yeah, in soft core we showed erections, we showed people giving head and getting fucked, but you didn't see penetration - that's what constituted hard core. In fact, you could put your face close to an erect penis, and you could lick it. Each film began to test the limits and see how far they could go. So there was a lot of licking of the stomach, guys dry humping or humping each other without showing the penetration. It was much easier to make those pictures, because a) you could get models to do anything, and b) you could fake it. You didn't have to wait for the erection, didn't have to wait for the cum shot. When the decision came that we should switch to hard core, it was like: stay with it or get out. And, of course, we all knew that we'd have to go even further underground, because everything was getting busted. So I just kept a very low profile, never used my name, was careful who I hired. And then, after DEEP THROAT, and pictures like that, started to become mainstream - in '72, I think - theatres were opening up in every city, and porno was suddenly chic and not underground at all. So there wasn't as much hiding and there wasn't as much trouble from the police. The city began to look the other way and that's when everything flourished.

Douglas: Do you remember the first day you shot penetration, and had to get it and get it right?

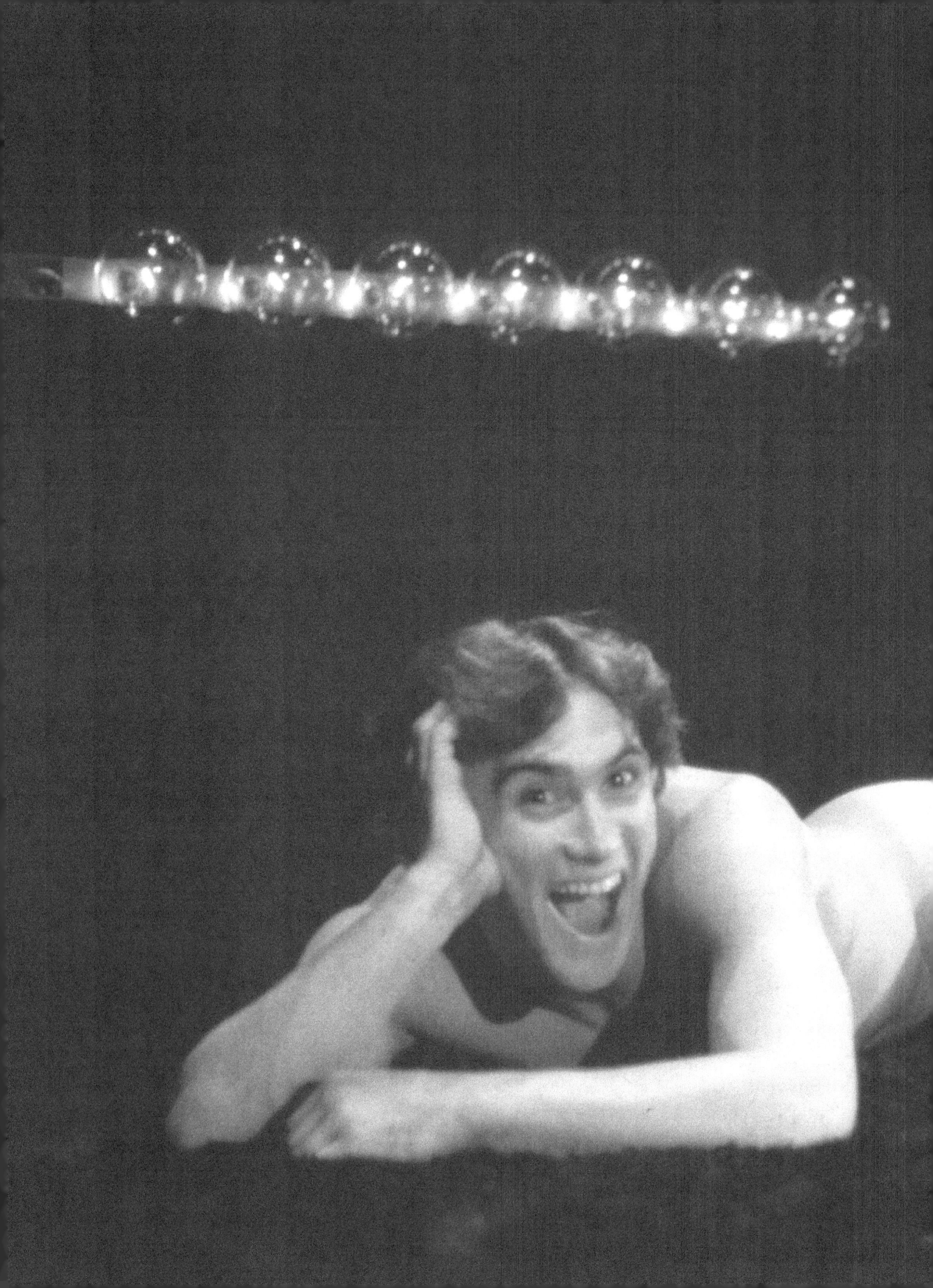

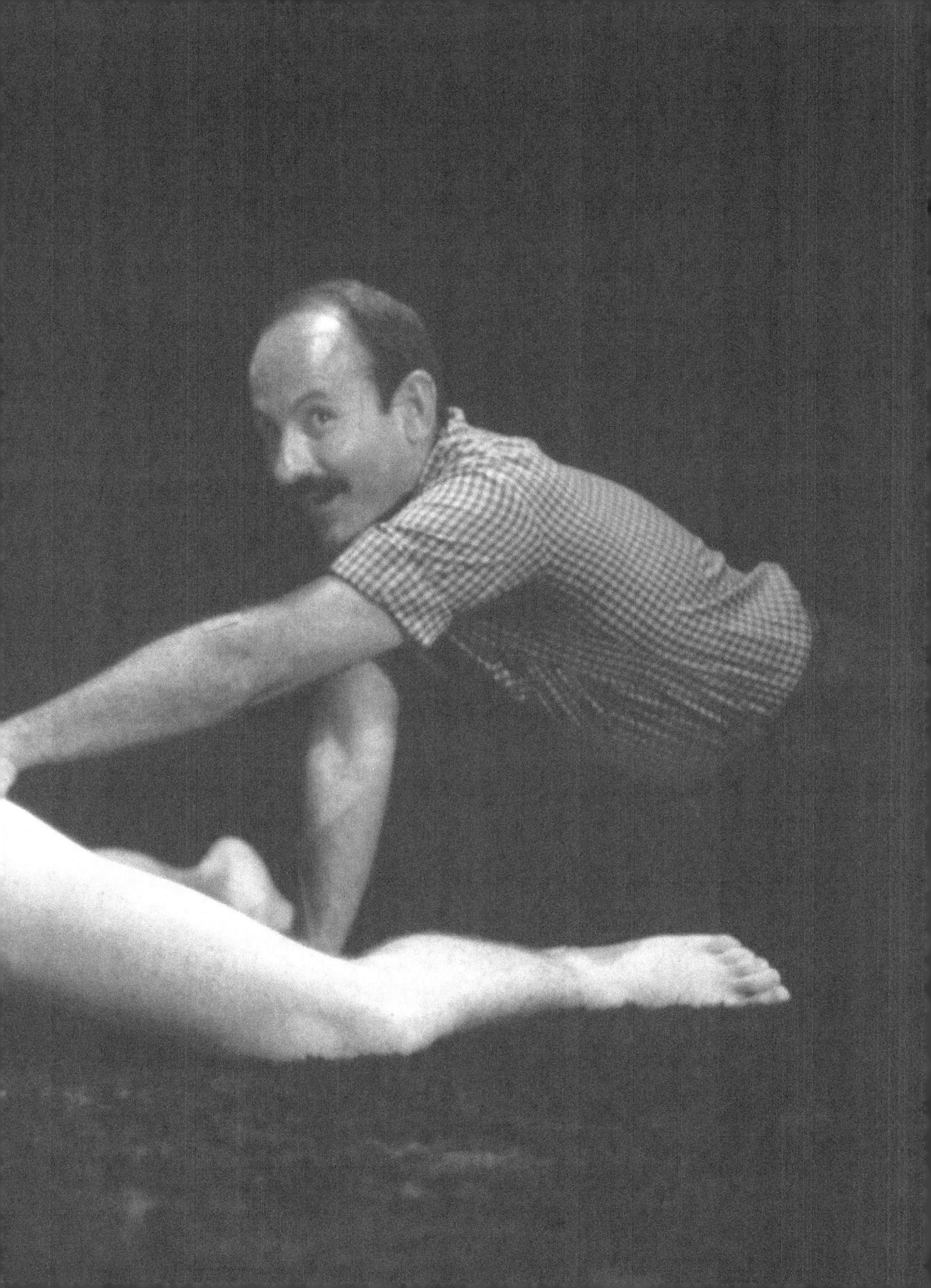

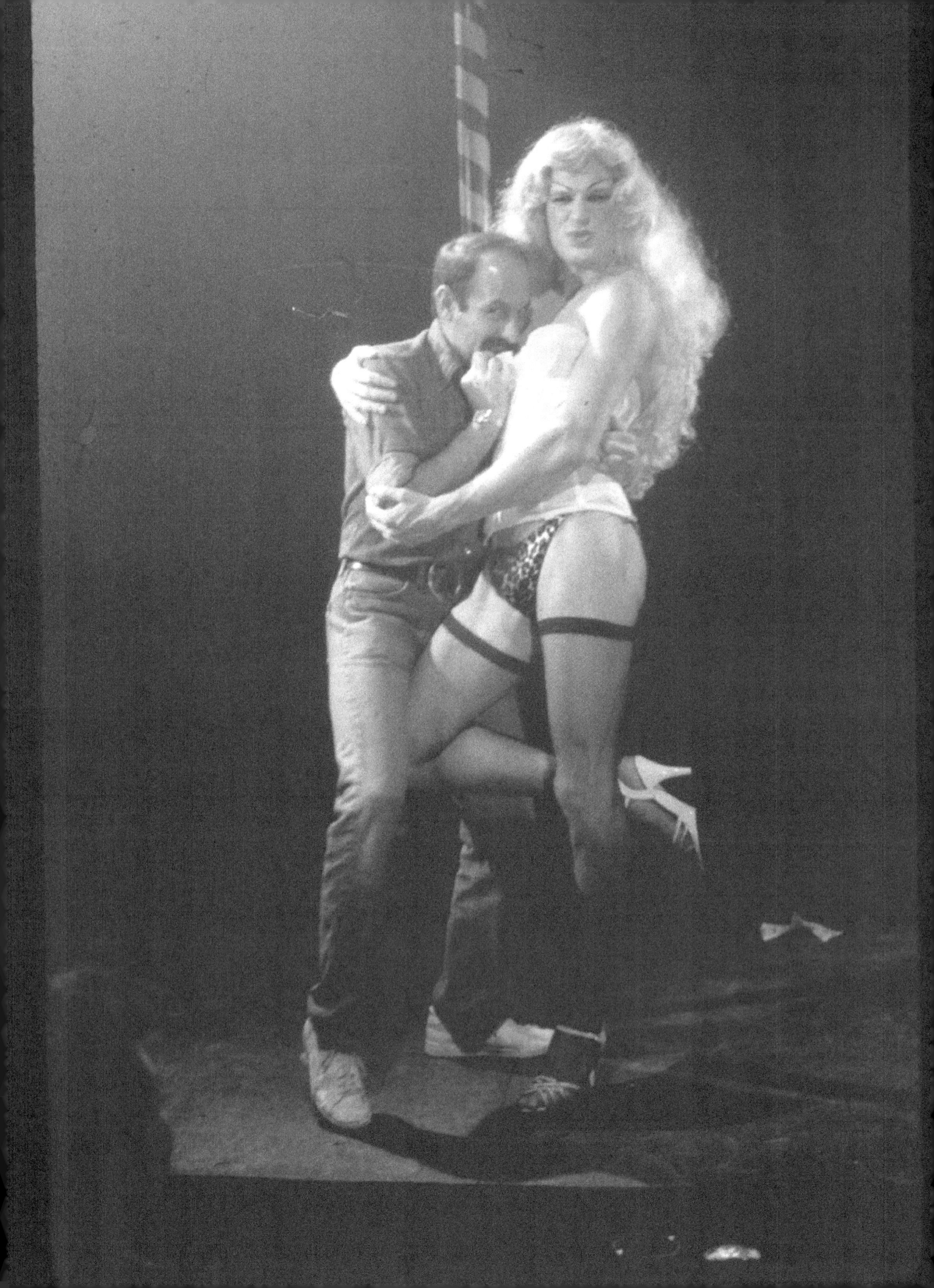

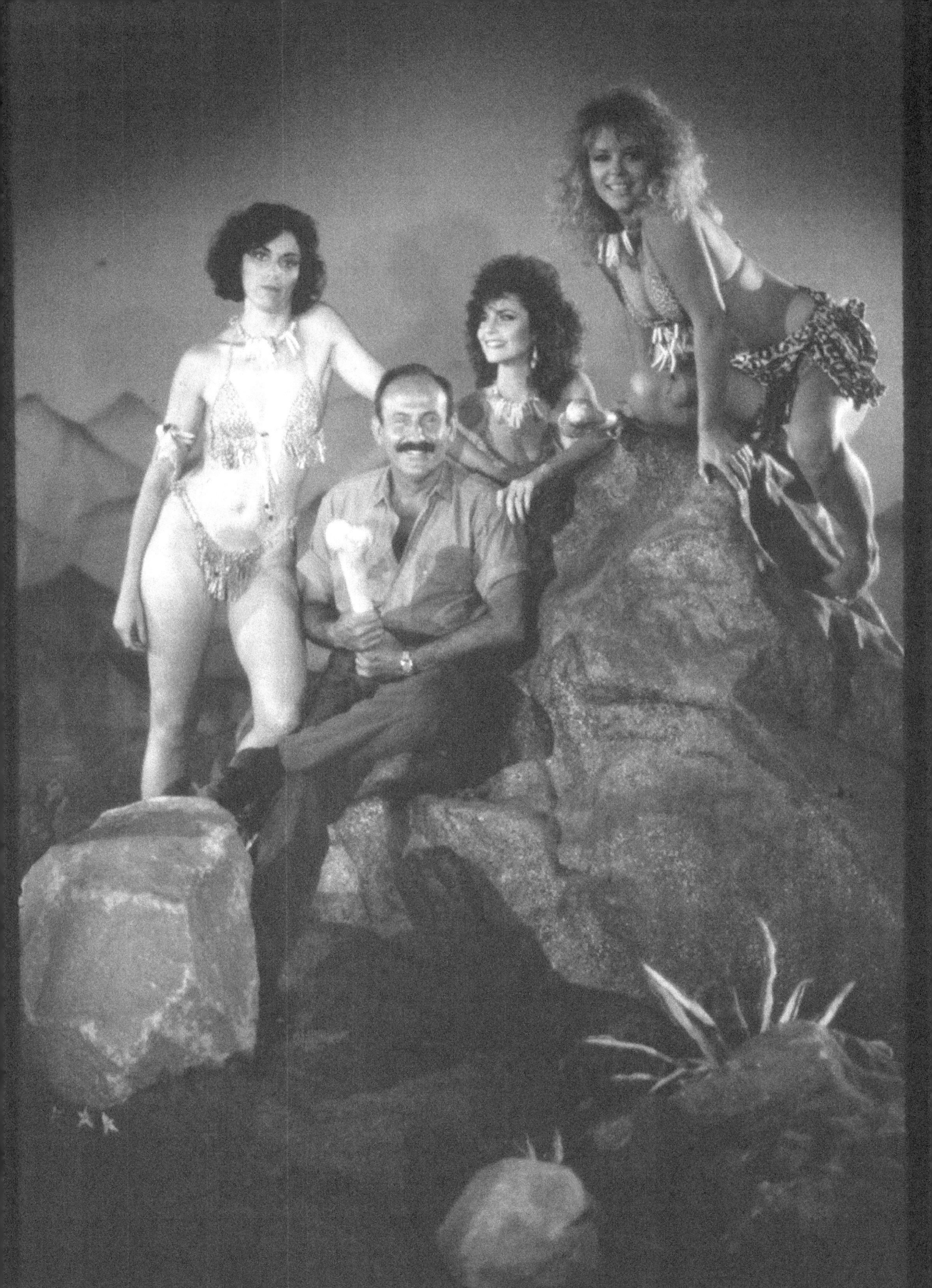

DeSimone: I think it was a film called MALE EROTIC FESTIVAL. Yeah, this was a series of hard-core loops, because we were in a hurry to get a hard-core picture out, you know, with some penetration. And these were a bunch of models I had used before in the simulated stuff, and they agreed to do harder stuff. I remember it was three or four short stories. One of them was set in sort of an Arabian harem, because we knew someone who had this set, and lots of big pillows, draped fabric, and all that stuff. We just called it MALE EROTIC FESTIVAL. It wasn't much different doing the hard core, because, actually, when I was doing the simulated stuff, lots of times there would be penetration. We just had to hide it from the camera. You get two gay guys together, and they're turned on, and they're nude, and they're pretending to have sex – they have sex. There would often be sucking, and I found that if you let them actually do the sucking, it looked more real, even though it was hidden from the camera. The movement of the head, and the reaction of the man getting head, was much more real than if they faked it. So, it wasn't a big leap for me, doing the hard core.

Douglas: Do copies of these early films still exist?

DeSimone: No. No, because we didn't save anything in those days. I mean, who knew that this would be something that anybody would be interested in years later?

Douglas: Or an art form.

DeSimone: Or an art form ... true. I found out from Mr. Sayles that his entire library of all the films he made when he had Signature Films, he donated to the Kinsey Institute. They weren't just films I made for him, but many films he had bought from other producers, and acquired by running those theatres. He had a warehouse full of films. (He asked me) if there was anything in there that I wanted before he donated them, and I said, "No. I have no use for any of those."

Douglas: Let's talk about finding actors and finding locations in those days.

DeSimone: Well, locations were easy in those days, because we always knew somebody who had a house. Casting was the most difficult, because there was the fear of being busted.

Douglas: During the shooting?

DeSimone: Well, yes, because what happened was the vice squad used to send people out there posing as models. Very sexy guys. So you had to be very careful when you interviewed these people what you said, because you were hiring them to perform sex for money and that was pandering. And that was how they used to get you. They were trying everything possible to get at us, and we had to keep one step ahead. Lawyers kept saying, "Now don't say this and don't do that." It was still very underground and very few people doing it, so you really had to rely on friends, someone you had tricked with who maybe needed a hundred-and-fifty dollars, and you'd pay them to appear. You just got whatever you could.

Douglas: It was all the grapevine, then.

DeSimone: Absolutely. And often, we'd be putting wigs on men or changing their appearance, because they didn't want to be recognized. And then, when they were hired, they had to meet a designated spot, and we'd pick them up and drive them to the location. Nobody knew ahead of time where the location was, so that nobody could find us or they could tell anyone. And no phone calls were allowed to be made from the set either. There was always that fear when you were starting to do a scene, because stories were that these people would pose as models and just as you were about to do the sex, you'd get busted. So, there was always that moment or two before they actually got into the action. Once they started kissing and fondling and got erect, you pretty much knew that they were into the scene. I never got busted, so I don't know how it would happen. But I can't imagine, if a guy was a vice squad posing as a model, that he would go beyond getting undressed. I think all they needed was to find out where you were and to have proof that that's what you were doing. They would wait till you got something on film that was incriminating, because then that became evidence. So there was a practice among many filmmakers and cameramen that if ever there was a bust or anything that looked like a bust, you immediately opened the camera to expose the film to light, because then it just became their word against yours as to what actually was happening. Even if you had shot for a whole day, even if you wasted that day's work, it was still cheaper than having to fight it in court.

Douglas: Who was the first "star" that you ever worked with?

DeSimone: I guess that would be Jack Wrangler, and he was kind of self-made. He was the first of the porno stars who was actually what you would call buffed. Gyms weren't popular then. That look – that clone look – of being buffed and muscular was not the look yet. He was one of the first to adopt

that look and promote it. Up till then, guys were still looking like hippies. We had a lot of tall, thin, lanky guys with moustaches and beards and love beads.
Douglas: What was the first film that you did with Jack Wrangler?
DeSimone: He was the first one to become a star, but I didn't work with him until I did a 3-D movie, I think.
Douglas: HEAVY EQUIPMENT?
DeSimone: HEAVY EQUIPMENT. I think that was the first film – the only film – I worked with Jack on. I knew him personally, and he was working for other people.
Douglas: In earlier interviews, you have said that you put a different name credit on each film for a long time, and as it happened, Lancer Brooks was the one they decided they wanted to keep.
DeSimone: We always used different names, for obvious reasons.
Douglas: Was this part of the running and the hiding?
DeSimone: Yeah, well, first of all, who wanted his name on the stuff? At the time, it was only considered sleazy and underground and just a means to make money. I mean, nobody was considering it an art form yet.
Douglas: Except people like you, subconsciously, mabe.
DeSimone: Yes, I was working to make them good, but at the same time, I was always fearful that it would come back to haunt me or that I'd get in trouble with the law, and I didn't want to. I think on THE COLLECTION, I used my real name. And I regretted it for many years. So, we would just make up names – all silly ones, like R.U. Horny. And the actors would do the same thing – like Myles Longue. Ruffin Tumble was an actor friend of mine. Just silliness, because we weren't taking it that seriously. And then ... I think the first picture I used Lancer Brooks on was APHRODISIACS AND THE MALE ANIMAL. We were just joking around, and I was stoned, and we were up at my friend's house, and we were shooting the titles, and we were trying to come up with names. I don't know how Lancer Brooks came out, but it did, and so I used it on that film. At this time, I was making films for myself, and we had a distributor. When I was doing the next picture, he said, "Use the same name that you used on the last film, because the theatre owners like your stuff. And when I give them your stuff, I can ask for more money." So I was stuck with Lancer Brooks.

Douglas: When did you leave Signature Films and form your own company?
DeSimone: CONFESSIONS OF A MALE GROUPIE was the last for Signature and PETER THE PEEKER was my first independent.
Douglas: Tell us about the man who came to be known as Max Blue, your producer.
DeSimone: He was a friend of mine from film school, and we chummed around together. We're still very good friends, as a matter of fact. When I went to work for Signature, I hired him as my casting director, because he was more outgoing than me, and he knew people in town, and he was out and about. So his job was to find me guys so that we could use them in films. He was my partner on THE COLLECTION. In fact, he ended up acting in it, much against his will, but we had lost the lead actor, the day we were shooting. We had rented equipment that weekend, and we had to shoot. I said, "Max, guess who's going to be the Collector?" It always bothered him.
Douglas: He is the Collector?
DeSimone: He is the actual Collector.
Douglas: What kind of working relationship did you have? Was it a traditional producer/director relationship?
DeSimone: I did all of the production work, and he sort of went around and made the deals and found the distributors and handled the money and that kind of stuff. He also helped with the casting.
Douglas: He was business, you were creative.
DeSimone: Exactly, exactly. It was called Times Productions. I did all the editing, I did the shooting, I did the writing, I did the music. When the picture was finished, he would take it under his arm and he would make the deals. The most he got involved in a creative sense was in the casting. 'Cause, in those days, it was fun to cast, 'cause you always tried people out first.
Douglas: How many films did the two of you make independently?
DeSimone: Let's see – SONS OF SATAN, CHAINED, SWAP MEAT, DIRTY BOOKS, DAFFY'S TAVERN, DUST UNTO DUST, GAMES WITHOUT RULES, GYPSY'S BALL, CLASSIFIED CAPERS. EROTIKUS was our last picture together. Then he went to New York to try to sell that, and he met Jack Deveau, Hand in Hand Films, while he was trying to sell EROTIKUS.
Douglas: And had you met Jack before?
DeSimone: No, he met him first. Jack saw the film and was very impressed and wanted to know who the director was.
Douglas: And that moved you into your Hand in Hand period.
DeSimone: What happened was: Jack Deveau

offered us money to make some pictures, and we made STATION TO STATION and EVERYTHING GOES for Hand In Hand, and then Max and I ended our relationship. After our partnership ended, I began working independently for Hand in Hand. I was working on my own.

Douglas: Of your films made during your partnership with Max Blue, which would you say was your best?

DeSimone: Oh, DUST UNTO DUST.

Douglas: Okay, let's talk about that.

DeSimone: Well, that was one of those pictures that just happened. I mean, we had the money to make a picture – we had to make a picture. We would get something like three thousand dollars from the distributor, and he wanted a picture in three weeks, something like that. I had no script, we had no cast, but we had a couple of friends who lived out in the desert. One fella, whose name was Creed, was very sexy, very handsome, big, part Polish/part American Indian. He was living in the desert and he needed money, so we went out to the desert, and he was living there with his lover, whose name was Nilo, and another friend of ours, Poco, who was also Spanish and Indian. Well, I had these three guys, and they all had long hair and stuff, so I decided to do this Indian picture. We got there on a Friday night, went to dinner with them, saw where they were living, and then I went back to the motel and I just sat at the typewriter. I began to write, and it just sort of came to me, because I was limited in that I only had three people, and had Saturday and Sunday – a day and a half. I don't know how it happened, but I finished it in a matter of hours.

Douglas: Tell us what it's about.

DeSimone: It's a story about ... about a family who come to the West to find gold and they don't find it. This is all prologue, in voice-over, and you see this old homesteader's cabin in the dust and abandoned, and it talks about how they did and left behind a young child. This is a very interesting story, because when we went to the desert, my friend, Nicholas, - his son at the time was just a little five or six year-old kid. We took him with us, and Nilo had a dog who had just had pups. I got this great shot where we had the boy walking naked in the desert, sort of going behind some trees, and as he walked, we panned with him, and he had a little puppy following him. As he went through the trees, we dissolved, and then it was the full grown man walking nude with the full grown dog. It was a beautiful transition. Well, we sent the dailies in to the lab and they just went crazy; they wouldn't release our film or anything because it had a child in it. They called me and said, "We've just developed your film, and you've got a child in here, and you know, we can't have child pornography." There was a lengthy discussion, and I couldn't convince them that this was an artistic thing, and the child wasn't involved in any of the sex, but their position was that they knew they were processing what they considered pornographic film, and this child was in the film; therefore, they would either destroy everything or just that scene. I had to give them written permission to destroy that piece of film. It doesn't exist anymore, and it was a beautiful moment. I had to go back to the desert and shoot it with just the dog ... Anyway, the film is about this man who grows up alone in the desert, having never seen anyone other than his parents. Then we cut to two Indians who are outcasts from their tribe, because they're homosexual. And you see these two Indian brothers wandering the desert – and they come across the white man. And they've never seen a white man, so there's this lovely scene where they circle around, sizing each other up. Anyway, the older of the two brothers teaches the white man about love. We see them having sex – and the white man, of course, being naïve, - the language of the film is much more lyrical than the way I'm presenting it – he wants to experience this same magic, for he considers it magic that the Indians have brought him this feeling of love. He wants to experience that with the other brother, as well. And he does, but he doesn't realize that he's now set up a situation of jealousy between the two brothers. So the two brothers become enemies over the love of this white man. They begin hunting each other down, and the white man becomes hunted as well, because he's now caused this. They all come together, finally, in this wooded glen. The two Indians have guns, and the white man doesn't, and they both come to him, and one of them kisses him, and the other brother begins kissing, and the three of them are kissing all together, and the guns go off and they die. They've killed each other. The last shot is the three of them, running naked in slow motion through the sand of the desert, and the narration goes that they've liberated themselves from the earthly bonds and are free to express their love forever. Years from now, when all these other pictures are just dust themselves, this picture will hold up.

Douglas: Where is it today?

DeSimone: I have a print of it.

Douglas: But, is it available commercially?
DeSimone: It's never been put on video and I wish it were.
Douglas: Who owns it?
DeSimone: I don't even know who owns it, to tell you the truth. It's been passed around through hands, and I have a print that's kind of faded. There are some scenes from it, a lengthy section of it, in the film EROTIKUS, which is on video, and most people who know about DUST UNTO DUST know it from EROTIKUS. I was always very proud of the film and very happy, and I wish today that I did own it or that today I had a good print of it or a tape. But, a lot of these things fell by the wayside.
Douglas: Let's talk a little bit about CHAINED, because it is obviously the link between THE DEFIANT ONES and Steve Scott's WANTED, which is almost a shot-by-shot remake of CHAINED. Have you ever seen WANTED?
DeSimone: No, no. I didn't even know that is was the same as CHAINED. But, something happened to CHAINED. When it went to video, they lost part of the last reel or something. I don't remember what. I just remember something happened, and the lab ruined the last reel or part of the last reel, and then they were going to go to tape, and then they just said fuck it. In those days, we didn't strike many prints. We'd make one or two prints and send it to one theatre for two weeks and then it would go to the next theatre for two weeks. That was the way you saved money. But, when I went into business for myself, I struck a print for each city and I sold it to them – they owned it. Because, the problem was, when you used to show films at these theatres, trying to collect your money afterward, you were always chasing your money. Finally, when I was making the pictures strictly for myself, I said, "No, no more of this rental shit." I would go to the Adonis – that was the biggest theatre in New York – they had the most money. And I would go to the Nob Hill in San Francisco, or I would go to the Century in L.A. The deal was: you could buy a print and own it for all time, and show it whenever you wanted to, but you'd have to pay dearly for it. It took me years to get that smart; I don't know what took me that long. The thing is: I never made a dime on all of the pictures I made. I made a living, and that was all. It was always hand-to-mouth. You know, people thought for years that I was filthy rich from the porno, and I wasn't.
Douglas: Where did the idea for CHAINED come from? Was it clearly from THE DEFIANT ONES?
DeSimone: Oh, sure, yeah. When I was making these pictures, there was no video market. People would come into movie theatres to sit down and watch a movie. They wanted to see "a movie" – but with sex in it. So, where do you get your ideas for movies, but from the movies? People were familiar with those plots, and oftentimes, the plots that we would lift were popular, and people would have liked to have seen some sex in those plots. In other words, everyone who went to see Sidney Poitier and Tony Curtis would have loved to have seen them naked, rolling around together. So, we just did that. We gave them that pleasure of watching the same story, but with sex implied or heavily implied.
Douglas: Since the very beginning of adult films, there have always been two schools of thought: That people who wanted to watch the old in-out and not much else. There are other people, like you and like me, who believe that viewers would rather see two people they have gotten to know fuck than two impersonal robots.
DeSimone: Than two pieces of meat. Well, that was what made my pictures different or unique, and why people always liked them. Once the picture started, there would always be that section of the film early on where you got to know the characters, and so viewers would get sucked into the story. You can't not, if you're watching. By the time the sex scenes came, they were more erotic, because it wasn't like disembodied cocks. You were watching people you knew having sex, and so it became more real and more erotic. I can't sit and watch loops, unless the people are drop-dead gorgeous, and even that doesn't matter to me as much as if the sex seems real to me. And what makes the sex real is if I sense that I know those people.
Douglas: You say you are turned-on when two people are actually sexually hot for each other. How did you make that happen?
DeSimone: I would always meet the models first. I would interview them and they would fill out the famous questionnaire that everyone has talked about, listing their likes and dislikes, what they would do, what they wouldn't do on film. Then I would pair people up, but I always cast for the story, for type. I didn't want to cast just anybody in any role, because to me it was very important that these people look the part and could act the part. So it was difficult for me, because not only was I looking for someone who could play this particular role, but then they

would also have to be a top if the role required that, or a bottom if the role required it. Most of the time when producers would cast this type of film, they would just get two guys - one that wanted to get fucked and one to do the fucking - and just film it. But mine - if the guy had to be the top in the film, he had to look like the right character, he had to be able to play the lines, and be believable in the role, and vice-versa, the bottom. Casting was always the most difficult for me. If I had one guy lined up for the part and if I had a picture of him, I would show the picture to the other guy, we'd discuss it. And then I would just hope and pray that when they got together the chemistry would be there.
Douglas: And how often was it and how often wasn't it?
DeSimone: I would say about seventy per cent of the time it wasn't there and thirty per cent of the time it was.
Douglas: And, when it wasn't, how did you deal with it?
DeSimone: Then I had to ... I had to then make it happen in the camera. Lots of times they'd get hard to a certain point and they would lose it. When it was real and it was happening, then it was very easy for me, because I had any choice of angles I could get. But, often, I'd have to talk them through the whole sex scene.
Douglas: Choreograph it?
DeSimone: Yes, I would tell them, "We'll start out with some kissing," and I would say to them, "While we're shooting, I will talk to you. Don't look at me or respond. Just do what I say. Stay in what you're doing until I tell you to do something else." And then I would roll and I would say, "All right, start kissing." So, that would get some footage on that, and then I would say, "Slowly move down and lick his neck and then go down to his nipple, and suck on his nipple." Later on, Nick Elliot used to shoot all my stuff. I would be standing right next to him, and I would whisper in his ear, "Go down, go down, move" - stuff like that, so as not to distract them. Or he would listen to me as I directed the actors, and he anticipated, knew where to be with the lens. If I said, "Now, run your tongue down his stomach, lick his navel," he knew where the actor was going and he would pan. If it wasn't really happening, I would then have to choreograph it and I would try to get angles that I knew would look hotter than it really was. The opposite problem was: sometimes you couldn't keep 'em off each other, and they would be burned out before the cameras even rolled.
Douglas: During any of these early periods, did you ever use more than one camera on a shoot?
DeSimone: I've never used more than one camera. I never could do it with two, because my point of view on a particular scene is one point of view, and that's what I see, and that's what the camera's filming. Anything else, to me, would be extraneous. *(Pause)* I shouldn't say never ever. When I was making the pictures for Bill Higgins, NIGHTCRAWLER and BI-COASTAL, I used his crew, his equipment, and they always used two or three cameras. So I would have those extra cameras around just for the cum shots. When the models were getting ready, we'd set up position for this one and that one. One would be slow motion, but, I never used two cameras during the sex scenes, except just to get the wet shots. Now, it's funny, because today in television, we use two or three cameras, and I'm very used to it, and I'm always setting up the shot for the A camera and the B camera, and then the C camera would be here if we need it. But that's just something that came out of the business I'm in now, and I got used to doing it. No, I shot everything just like the old Hollywood days, where you had a camera and that was it.

II.

In Part I of this article, published in the last issue of Manshots, *Tom DeSimone discussed the early days of the gay adult film industry. Here, he continues the story of his career with such legendary films as CATCHING UP, HEAVY EQUIPMENT, WET SHORTS, and SKIN DEEP, and also reveals little known facts about his crossover into mainstream television.*

Jerry Douglas: Before we talk about the third section of your career, your relationship with Hand in Hand Films, would you say something to us about Fred Halsted, with whom you made EROTIKUS?
Tom DeSimone: Well, I didn't make it with him, I used him in the film. It was a very unpleasant relationship, and I always hate to say bad things about people who have died, but I didn't have the best relationship with him. What happened was: When I decided to make EROTIKUS, I went to my partner with the idea, and it then became his job and mine to contact as many people as we could within the industry and ask them for clips. And everybody volunteered their stuff. I

mean, everybody was thrilled. Fred was not. Fred wanted five thousand dollars to use the clip. So I said to him, "Well, why don't you appear in the film, and we'll pay you to appear?" And then he made some sort of deal with my partner that there would be a percentage of the profits. We gave him some money up front, and then I guess there was to be some money which would come out of the profits of the film. But he was the only one that charged, and he wanted a lot of money. In the early Seventies, five thousand dollars was a lot of money. It was more than the whole picture was gonna cost me. So we made the picture, and of course, he was very difficult shooting that narrative stuff. It was all to be done in one day. He was just going to come in and do the narration, and then he was supposed to masturbate at the end. Well, he couldn't even stay hard. So we stopped the filming, and he called his boyfriend to come up and help him.

Douglas: This was Joey Yale?

DeSimone: No, it wasn't Joey at the time. It was someone else that he was just sort of with at the time. The boyfriend came up, and they did all kinds of sucking and carrying on, and he just never ... I never could get the shot I needed. So, then, I used my lover – that's actually my lover at the end of the film, that masturbation, that big close-up and the slow motion cum shot at the end of EROTIKUS. That's not Fred Halsted. Now, I'm sure people know it's not Fred, because the dick is much bigger and the body is much different. Fred always had this sort of thing – he felt that we owed him money, that we'd gypped him out of something. Years later, he approached me and asked if he could release it in eight-millimeter through his company, and I said, "Sure." I gave him the print, so that he could make eight-millimeter reductions. He duped it and began selling it around the country. Joey started going around – I found out through sources, that they were selling prints of EROTIKUS for like five hundred dollars – and then, of course, I never got a penny from the eight-millimeter, either. I contacted him about it, and he gave me some bullshit about how I had screwed him years ago when I made EROTIKUS, so he was getting even. Anyway, it was all very unpleasant. Then, years later, when I was working in legit films, he began coming to me, begging for work in the industry. It's funny how people forget.

Douglas: Okay, now let's talk about Jack Deveau and Hand in Hand Films.

DeSimone: He met my partner in New York, and he booked EROTIKUS at the Fifty-Fifth Street Playhouse, which he was operating at the time, and then he began talking to me about making pictures for him. So we made those two pictures for him, STATION TO STATION and EVERYTHING GOES. My partner and I were sorta ... it was the end of our relationship, anyway. There was no point in being partners anymore, I felt. The business wasn't going anywhere, we weren't getting any richer, and if I was doing all the production work, I could easily do it on my own. I didn't need a partner to share the money with. So, that was the end of the relationship. And then Jack made me a very handsome offer to come to New York for awhile and shoot some pictures for him. That's when I did BALLET DOWN THE HIGHWAY.

Douglas: Okay, but before that, let's talk about STATION TO STATION and EVERYTHING GOES – and most particularly, about the Christy Twins.

DeSimone: I met the Christy Twins through a man who was a camera operator, and he used to shoot a lot of these pictures for me. And the Christy Twins, they were living with him. He had met them on the beach – he was sort of their Svengali. They were surfers, and he was older, and he sort of took them under his wing and they ended up living with him. They lived in Venice in a shack – in a house that was so filthy, you couldn't breathe in there.

Douglas: Where were the parents?

DeSimone: I never quite knew the story, except that the cameraman, he sort of met them, and I guess they just moved in with him. He offered to let them, and the parents didn't care, or he went to the parents and said, "I'll take care of them." It was very strange, and there was always this thing that they weren't really gay. I always suspected that they were gay not by choice, but by manipulation, through this person. I found out years later that one of them got in trouble with drugs and alcohol. I can't remember their names, because those were made-up names. The one who appeared in many of my films is now married and has children, and isn't with this cameraman anymore.

Douglas: I find that amazing, because I've seen almost everything that the Christy Twins have done on film, and the sexplay seems so enthusiastically real.

DeSimone: Yeah, well, they did it and they were enjoying it when they were doing it. But I don't think they were gay by choice. I was convinced of it. See, I was there on the set, and I remember how they were told to do what they were doing.

It was an order from him. And they never were comfortable doing it with anyone else, except each other. You know, they rarely wanted to do it with anyone else. Tim was always my sound man, and the other one, Chris, was always off. Tim was the one that stayed. Even after Chris went off and disappeared, Tim stayed with this guy, and they lived together for a long time. They shared another business together. They kept trying to find other ways to make money after the porno thing ended. I heard through the grapevine that Tim finally left him, finally broke away and got married and has a family and all that kind of stuff.

Douglas: And the other one just vanished, as far as you know?

DeSimone: Yeah, into drugs and alcohol. I guess he had been arrested several times, and they kept trying to rescue him, and he kept trying to get away from them.

Douglas: You have no idea where either of them is today?

DeSimone: No, and I don't know where that cameraman is.

Douglas: Then, you began to make such films as GOOD HOT STUFF and HOT TRUCKIN' for Jack. And CATCHING UP, POOL PARTY, THE IDOL, HEAVY EQUIPMENT.

DeSimone: No. POOL PARTY wasn't theirs. The only films I made for Hand in Hand were GOOD HOT STUFF, HOT TRUCKIN', CATCHING UP, THE IDOL, and THE COLLECTION I contributed to. And all the rest were just done on my own, independently. THE FALL was another one done independently. And then WET SHORTS and FLESH AND FANTASY were two films that someone approached me and he owned a mail order company and he wanted some loops. I said, "Well, I don't do loops." He said, "Look, just shoot me some loops and you can keep them afterwards." So he was willing to pay for them, and all he wanted was the eight-millimeter rights, so then I put them together and strung them together with some theme. The first one became WET SHORTS and the second became FLESH AND FANTASY. I owned those film rights – sixteen-millimeter and video. Then I sold video rights to Bill Higgins, and after that, he wanted me to do some more – SKIN DEEP and THE DIRTY PICTURE SHOW – and then, of course, BI-BI LOVE and BI-COASTAL. Those all became pictures for Higgins, and NIGHTCRAWLER.

Douglas: You said something about BALLET DOWN THE HIGHWAY.

DeSimone: Yeah, I shot that for Jack. I was the camera operator for that and also for BILLY THE KID. We shot those both simultaneously. It was two or three weeks' work. I went to New York and I stayed at Jack's place. We went out and shot every day, and it was very frustrating to me, because he worked very differently than I did. His stuff was all sort of improvised, and there was a lot of partying. They never took anything seriously, and money was just being wasted. It was driving me crazy, and I remember after the fourth for fifth day, we had this big blowup, and I said, to him, "Look, you gotta sit down – this is how it's done." His scripts were very loose and not coherent. You'd spend hours and hours on one scene – trying to figure it out and make it work. Jack and I became friends, but I didn't want to stay in New York. I said, "No, I live in L.A., and I want to work in L.A., so we set up a little office here and he would funnel money to me, and that's when I did THE IDOL, which we've already talked about.

Douglas: Let's talk about CATCHING UP and Keith Anthoni. How did you find him?

DeSimone: Just had an ad in – I dunno, I think it was The Advocate, advertising for models, and I had one day set up where I would interview these people. And he walked in.

Douglas: What was it about him that made him interesting?

DeSimone: The size of his dick, frankly, and he seemed right for the part for the lover who goes out and has all these adventures. He read a few lines, and we talked.

Douglas: Did you meet Jayson McBride in much the same way?

DeSimone: Uh, no. Jayson was the lover of someone I knew here on the West Coast. He was working as a waiter and living with someone I knew who had mentioned to me that this guy had a big dick and might want to do a film. So, I went and talked to him. He was never quite turned on to people who were his own age. He was more into older, macho men than someone like Keith, but the scene was okay.

Douglas: Why do you think CATCHING UP works so well, and stands up today so well?

DeSimone: Well, it's a story, I think, that's easy to relate to. The characters and the situation that they're in is quite real – we've all been there. Or many of us have. And I think the fact that the lead character – Keith – experiments with sex is something that a lot of us have done. You know, to the porno theatres, classified ads. It's a story that anyone can relate to, and also, it looks very good. I think it's well acted and well put together. It got raves everywhere that it got reviewed. It's still one of my favorites. You know, I've never seen it on tape. I don't watch my own stuff. I got a brochure in the mail from some company selling a whole bunch of stuff very cheaply, like nineteen-ninety-five, and in there were six of my titles. And, I actually sent away for them, just to have tapes of my work.

Douglas: Let's back up a little. Let's talk a little about HOT TRUCKIN' and Gordon Grant.

DeSimone: Just a loop picture.

Douglas: How did you find Gordon Grant?

DeSimone: Through someone who knew him. He was very boring to work with.

Douglas: In what way?

DeSimone: He never said two words. He would just show up and do what he had to do. He was totally inexpressive during the sex scenes and even off camera. He was just like a robot.

Douglas: But he could get it up.

DeSimone: He could get it up. But if you watch him in sex scenes, he's so totally uninvolved, it's unbelievable. If he's fucking – from his navel to his knees is the part of him that works. Those hips would go in the same motion, the same thing, and his expression never changed. He never broke a bead or opened his eyes. He literally was a piston with a body attached. And that was it. He never really cared to suck dick, and if somebody sucked him, he would just lie there. They could suck him for three hours, and he wouldn't move or change his expression. It was very bizarre. It was strange working with him. He was very unisexual.

Douglas: Did you have any sense of what prompted this façade?

DeSimone: No, except that he lived with someone at the time who was a transsexual – very domineering, bossy, kind of, and they had a very strange relationship. From what I understood from people who knew him, she really had him by the balls and ran him around her finger. When we were finished, he would leave and go immediately home, because she wanted him there.

Douglas: Did he speak of himself as a straight man or a gay man, or did you have any sense of that?

DeSimone: I never got a clue as to what he thought of himself.

Douglas: Did you ever have more than three words to say to each other?

DeSimone: No, strictly professional. I'd tell him what to do and stuff and he'd just nod. He never offered an opinion, asked a question, or made a suggestion. He said the lines that were handed to him and never discussed anything. He just was not there mentally. He was strictly a body with a big dick attached. It seemed to me and everybody on the picture how uncommitted he was to what he was doing.

Douglas: What about getting fucked?

DeSimone: No. He said that just wasn't his thing.

Douglas: But, he gets fucked in several movies.

DeSimone: Yeah, later he did, but at this time he was strictly topping. He wasn't much even for giving head. Sort of like Roger – the things Roger wouldn't do on film: he wouldn't kiss and he wouldn't suck dick. Of course, Roger was straight. I knew him and his wife.

Douglas: Let's talk about HEAVY EQUIPMENT. That was the first 3-D skin flick. How did it come about?

DeSimone: A friend called me and he said, "Why don't we make a picture together?" He was running the Paris Theatre on La Cienega at the time, but he wanted a gimmick. He said, "We gotta do something that'll make a lot of money." I said, "How about a 3-D movie? I've always wanted to do a 3-D movie." I found this guy – it was the same cameraman that I'd met the Christy Twins through – an optical crazy guy, anyway, who devised a system whereby we could shoot in 3-D. It was very limiting, because we could only use a twenty-five-millimeter lens, and it was a prism that was put right in front of the lens that split the image like that, so you couldn't really pan – you could barely move the camera. To me, in that picture, the sex is all very vanilla. If you look at it, it's so boring. And I didn't want to call it HEAVY EQUIPMENT. I had the story of the kid with the magic potion and all that, and my friend said, "I want you to call this picture HEAVY EQUIPMENT. That's a title that'll do business." I said, "Why, it's got nothing to do with ..." He said, "I don't care – just have a scene in there with construction workers or a bulldozer or something." I said, "Oh, God ..." So for that last scene, with Al Parker, we drove out to this field where there was a parked skip-loader, and I did the sex scene there. HEAVY EQUIPMENT was something I shot over a period of time, and it was very difficult to shoot the 3-D, because the set had to be flooded with light, and everybody was wringing wet. And, then, of course, the prism didn't allow you to do much, and every time you moved the camera, you had to then readjust everything. So, when you cut, you were down for sometimes half an hour, forty minutes, and of course the models were totally turned off by that. I never liked it, although it did business.

Douglas: What parts of PRIVATE COLLECTION did you do?

DeSimone: Two parts. There's the scene in the hot tub. It's a guy and a girl sitting in a hot tub, drinking wine. You assume that they're lovers, but when she goes in to answer the phone, he looks over the fence, and there's a guy raking leaves. Typical loop story – the guy comes over and they have quick sex, and then he leaves, and then she comes back and sits in the hot tub. And then the last scene is a threeway rape scene. Very hot, I remember. A big black guy, and a kid who was my boyfriend at the time, and a night watchman, something like that. I did two of them and Peter de Rome did one.

Douglas: Let's talk about THE HARDER THEY FALL.

DeSimone: I just did that independently with some money that someone gave me. And then it went through a lot of hands and the title was changed. I've heard three different titles. I made it as THE HARDER THEY FALL, and then I've also seen it advertised as HOT something, like HOT EXPECTATIONS, and now Bijou has re-released it as THE FRENCHMAN AND THE LOVER. I wonder why they slapped that title on it.

Douglas: These two films, WET SHORTS and FLESH AND FANTASY. They're very much alike.

DeSimone: 'Cause I shot them all at once. There are lots of interesting actors. By this time, of course, we were having stars.

Douglas: Did you prefer working with newcomers or with stars?

DeSimone: See, I never approached those people because I couldn't afford to pay that kind of money or didn't want to. When I did HEAVY EQUIPMENT, I wasn't footing the bill, so I approached Jack Wrangler, Roger, Al Parker. But when I made pictures for myself, I was more interested in making the picture I wanted to make and not featuring some star, who was going to bring something to the picture other than what I wanted. If I had used Al Parker in THE IDOL, it would have been a different movie.

Douglas: J.W. King was in both WET SHORTS and FLESH AND FANTASY.

DeSimone: Uh huh. WET SHORTS was his first gay picture. The fellow who was with him – he used to use the name R.J. Reynolds – he brought J.W. to me. R.J. had done a picture for me once before – he was in BAD, BAD BOYS. And that was his first gay picture. And then when I approached him to do WET SHORTS, he said, "I have a buddy." At the time, they had been doing hetero films because, even though they were gay, they didn't want to do gay pictures. But like everybody else in those days, they needed money. So he brought J.W. to me. In fact, I met him the day we were going to shoot. J.W. was gorgeous. I used him again for FLESH AND FANTASY. We sorta chummed around – not a lot, but we'd go to parties and things, he and R.J. and myself. There were certain ones that I stayed friends with, because we sort of had the same head. And there were others I wanted nothing to do with – as soon as I said "cut," that was it.

Douglas: Can you talk a little about working with King?

DeSimone: Well, he was a lot of fun. I liked him and that's why I used him again. He and R.J. were buddies; they used to go fuck together. They would throw sex parties at their house. I those days, when I was getting high, and he was getting high, we used to joke around and kid around. I always enjoyed working with him, because he was easy to work with, he loved doing what he was doing, and he always had fun in the sex scenes. I remember when we did WET SHORTS, that young blond kid that he does the carpenter scene with –

Douglas: Eric Clement.

DeSimone: He's the same one that's the Frenchman in THE HARDER THEY FALL. He and J.W. had a little affair for a long time – not a long time. In those days, anything over a month was a long time.

Douglas: This is the first time, in any of my discussions about J.W. King, that I've ever heard anything about heterosexual movies.

DeSimone: He did quite a few of them. In fact, I filmed some of them, right here in this house.

Douglas: Did he think of himself as bisexual? You said earlier that they were gay, but –

DeSimone: I don't think that he thought of himself as bisexual.

Douglas: To my knowledge, there's no film record of him ever bottoming. Was that ever an issue that was made clear?

DeSimone: Yeah, he wouldn't be a bottom.

Douglas: Onscreen.

DeSimone: Onscreen.

Douglas: I would say, probably, after THE IDOL, your finest hour is widely considered to be SKIN DEEP. Let's talk about that.

DeSimone: Yeah, how did that happen? I needed money. I remember, I needed money and I wasn't working and I did that after I'd already done a couple of legit pictures, I'd already done HELL NIGHT with Linda Blair.

Douglas: Well, do you want to talk about how you moved away from the industry and how you came back for SKIN DEEP? Let's fill that gap.

DeSimone: Well, how I moved away: It was never my plan to be a pornographer. It was just one of those things I got into assbackwards, and I got caught up in the fun of it. I just woke up one day and I was forty years old, and I thought, "Jesus Christ, is this going to be my life?" I always had bigger plans. I started seriously pursuing the other, but at the same time, making films to stay alive – you know, making the porno. I had a picture that I wrote a synopsis of, called LIPS, and my partner and I were going to do this right after DEEP THROAT became a big hit. We thought maybe we should do a hetero picture, because there's more entrée to those pictures than with gay. So, I wrote this story called LIPS, about a girl with a talking vagina. I had a friend in town who had written several hit movies and TV shows and stuff, and he was having a New Year's party. I was invited, and there were many Hollywood people there. And he introduced me to a producer, who was at the party who was also gay. He arranged a screening up at his home, and there were several very closeted Hollywood people there, and we had a dinner and I ran a couple of my films. And he was very impressed. He wanted to make an X-rated movie, but soft X. He wanted something like EMANUELLE. I said, "Well, I have this script called LIPS." He read it and liked it, so we got a writer to work on it, and that became the picture known as CHATTERBOX, which was my first crossover film. It was my entrée into the legit world. And then I got the Linda Blair after that and CONCRETE JUNGLE with Jill St. John.

Douglas: And how you came back?

DeSimone: There was a dry spell, and I wasn't working, so I called Bill Higgins and I said, "I'm gonna do a picture," and he said, "Yeah, okay." I just sat down and wrote SKIN DEEP.

Douglas: Do you know where the idea for it came from?

DeSimone: Well, I usually get my ideas, believe it or not, either from music or from one scene that I want to do, and then the rest of it happens. The ones that turn out to be my best ones are the ones that aren't lifted from something else, but just come out of me.

Douglas: And they're the easiest to write.

DeSimone: Yeah, yeah. In my file over there, I've got several other scripts, one of them that I would love to do, called HARD MUSCLE. I wrote it for Roger, and then, of course, he got out of the business, and I never did it. In SKIN DEEP, the one scene where he picks up the hustler in the car and that little exchange of dialogue is something that I had in my file, because I was going to use it in one of these WET SHORTS analogies, and I never did it. So I thought, "Oh, I'll use that music for the opening, and then I'll take that scene where he picks up the hustler and I'll go from there ..."

Douglas: And then it wrote itself.

DeSimone: Yeah, suddenly he was a writer and the models of his characters came to life.

Douglas: How did you like working with Bill Higgins?

DeSimone: Oh, Bill was always very generous. Bill was a fan of mine. When I was in the business and really grinding them out, he came to me. He was new in town, he called me up, introduced himself. He had spent something like ten thousand dollars to twelve thousand dollars on this picture called A MARRIED MAN – and he had all this footage, and it wasn't finished, and he ran out of money. Would I look at it, would I be interested in finishing it? He came here and he screened his stuff for me, and I just thought it was god-awful. I'll never forget the advice I gave him. I said, "You really want my advice? Get out of this business before you waste any more money." But we always remained friends and he contacted me often: "Do you wanna make a picture, do you wanna make a picture?" And I always said no. And then when I wanted to make a picture, I'd call him and he'd say, "Sure." So, I'd make the picture and just sell it to him.

Douglas: And that's how SKIN DEEP came about?

DeSimone: Well, I made the picture for myself, because I needed money and I had about seventy-five hundred dollars to my name and I put it all into the film. I shot it at a friend's loft here in L.A. And Nick Elliot was the cameraman and we shot it in two days – two afternoons.

Douglas: What prompted you to cast Johnny Daws and Michael Christopher in the leads?

DeSimone: Higgins suggested Michael Christopher. He wasn't what I had in mind, per se, but I went to meet him and I thought, "Well, he'll be good for the hustler." And, Johnny I knew, and I thought, "Well, he'll be okay for the writer." First I hired Christopher – and he wanted a lot of money – he wanted more than I

was going to pay, but I thought, "He'll be worth it." Also, there was the fact that Bill wanted him in the picture; I knew Bill could promote him. But I remember Michael was really surprised about the fact that he had to do dialogue and memorize lines. But he did quite well, I thought.
Douglas: He was unhappy or pleased?
DeSimone: Unhappy, that he had to "work" for his money. Also, he couldn't believe that I wanted to start at like eight-thirty, nine o'clock in the morning. And I told him, "Please don't go out and party the night before," because I knew that he was a party guy, and also he'd told me that he was doing this because he needed the money. I said, "Okay, but I'll pay you after the picture." That was my only leverage, I thought, "If I give him the money now, he'll go off and blow it, and I won't see him."
Douglas: Where did the idea for the gangbang at the end come from?
DeSimone: Well, that was always part of the script. So, we all knew we had to do it. That was the last scene we shot on the first day. And everybody was hanging around. That was one of those days when I had trouble with the models, because Beau Matthews and Giorgio Canali were picked up early and brought there to do the scene in the hot tub, but I was still upstairs filming the first scene. They were downstairs, and I couldn't keep them apart. And I kept saying, "Guys …" What happened was they got into it with each other, and they fucked, and they both came, and I was pissed off. And then we went downstairs to do the scene, and the scene with them was very difficult to get, because neither one of them could stay hard. And by then, they were "finished" with each other. The bloom was off the rose. And I really had to work to get the scene. And then, of course, it took forever to get the cum shots, because they couldn't stay hard, and then Canali started getting pissed off because he had an appointment. He wanted to get out of there. I said, "I can't let you go till I get …" It was not pleasant.
Douglas: Let's talk about the bisexual films.
DeSimone: What happened on BI-COASTAL – a friend approached me with some money; he wanted me to tape a video of nude aerobics. I set up an appointment with Bill Higgins. Bill was sort of only mildly interested and he said, "If you really want to get back in the porno business" – he was talking to me – "and you want to make a picture that would really make money, I'll tell you what the new wave is gonna be. The future," he said, "is bisexual … Everybody's bored with what's out there. There's a million gay films, there's a million straight films. They're looking for something new. The only thing left, other than animals or children, is bisexual." So, that's where BI-COASTAL came from. I wrote the script and we did it, and then he wanted me to do another, so I did BI-BI LOVE. And the very last film I did was NIGHTCRAWLER.
Douglas: By then, you were well into your so-called "legit" career.
DeSimone: Yeah, but there were periods of time when I wasn't working. See, I wasn't doing television then, I was doing features. You know, you do a feature and then, suddenly, you don't work for six or eight months. Suddenly, Bill called me. He said, "I need a picture – I need a dark picture, something like the Gage Brothers do. I don't know how to make those kind of pictures, I can't do that. I want you to make one of those pictures for me." And I said, "Well, all right. Let me think of an idea." And I had this idea about this place. You know, it bothers me that in the film it's perceived to be a bathhouse, but it never was supposed to be. It is supposed to be this strange sex club. I had far more bizarre things that were going to be going on in this place, and I sent the script over to Bill. He liked it, but he said, "Listen, we gotta take out a lot of this stuff. You know with AIDS and everything." I mean, when the character went into each of these different rooms – it was going to be far more bizarre than it is. There were these strange devices with tubes going into guys, and funnels, and men masturbating into them. It was going to be like fantasex. Bill liked it, but he said, "I don't think we should do this." It wasn't a picture that I was longing to make, although once I started making it, I was very happy with it. And then, right after I finished shooting it, my deal came through on REFORM SCHOOL GIRLS. Then I was in a pickle, because I said, "I can't edit this." I was very unhappy, because I like to edit my own work. I hate to have anyone else touch it.
Douglas: Absolutely.
DeSimone: And I wanted to wait. And Bill said, "I can't wait. I gotta get it out. I gotta release it." So, he said, "We'll edit it. You can look at the cut and you can approve it." I said, "Okay." And when I was off doing REFORM SCHOOL GIRLS, his people cut it. I was very happy with the cut, and I particularly like the score. Costello Presley did a particularly good job on the score. So I liked the way that picture turned out.
Douglas: Was the cast handed to you by

Bill?
DeSimone: Pretty much. See, he had access to all these people.
Douglas: So, casting has never been real important to you, in one sense, and in another way, totally important.
DeSimone: Yeah, yeah. See, I always conceived a picture first. I never go after somebody and say, "I want you to do a picture."
Douglas: You've never written a film for anyone?
DeSimone: Never, never. Always, it's the story I want to tell first. And then I find people to fit the story.
Douglas: When you finished NIGHTCRAWLER, did you know that that would be your last adult film?
DeSimone: Pretty much, yeah. Because I knew when I did REFORM SCHOOL GIRLS that ...
Douglas: That it would open the door?
DeSimone: Yeah. I haven't stopped working since then.
Douglas: How many people in the "legit" industry know about your past, and how do they deal with it?
DeSimone: Only a handful know. Most of the people I work with now, on the series, know my background as porno, but they don't know that it's gay. I don't volunteer any information. No one has ever said anything negative about it. I don't make that information known. I don't flaunt it or hide it.
Douglas: That's the best way.
DeSimone: And it's the same with my gay lifestyle. If they know it, fine. I don't flaunt it, nor do I hide it. My only fear is that some day this may come back to haunt me, because my name is on some of these things.
Douglas: One last question: Over the last two years, I've heard on three separate occasions, rumors that you were in the process of being wooed back to make one more gay film. Is that totally unfounded?
DeSimone: Totally. I mean, no one has even approached me. Nor would I consider it.
Douglas: You cannot imagine any circumstances under which you would make another X-rated film?
DeSimone: Uhm. No, not really. Not now, with the way things are going with my career. It would be too risky. I mean, it wouldn't serve any purpose. I certainly don't need the money anymore, and I don't need the fame or the notoriety, because I'm working toward the other direction. So, it would really be detrimental. My agent would have a stroke, for one thing, because he's tried desperately to get me away from pictures even like REFORM SCHOOL GIRLS. He's trying to groom me toward loftier things, like Movie of the Week, and primetime television, and you know I've done pictures like REFORM SCHOOL GIRLS and CHATTERBOX and CONCRETE JUNGLE and HELL NIGHT, which are, in part, exploitation. They're not porno – they're not even X-rated – but they were drive-in movies, and he's trying to erase that sort of thing. And, God forbid I should ever do an X-rated movie! I'd probably be dropped from the agency. No, it's too risky now for me. And the interest isn't even there any more. I mean, I did it. It was part of my life. I enjoyed it when I did it, I'm proud of several of the things I've done. But it's a chapter that's really closed.

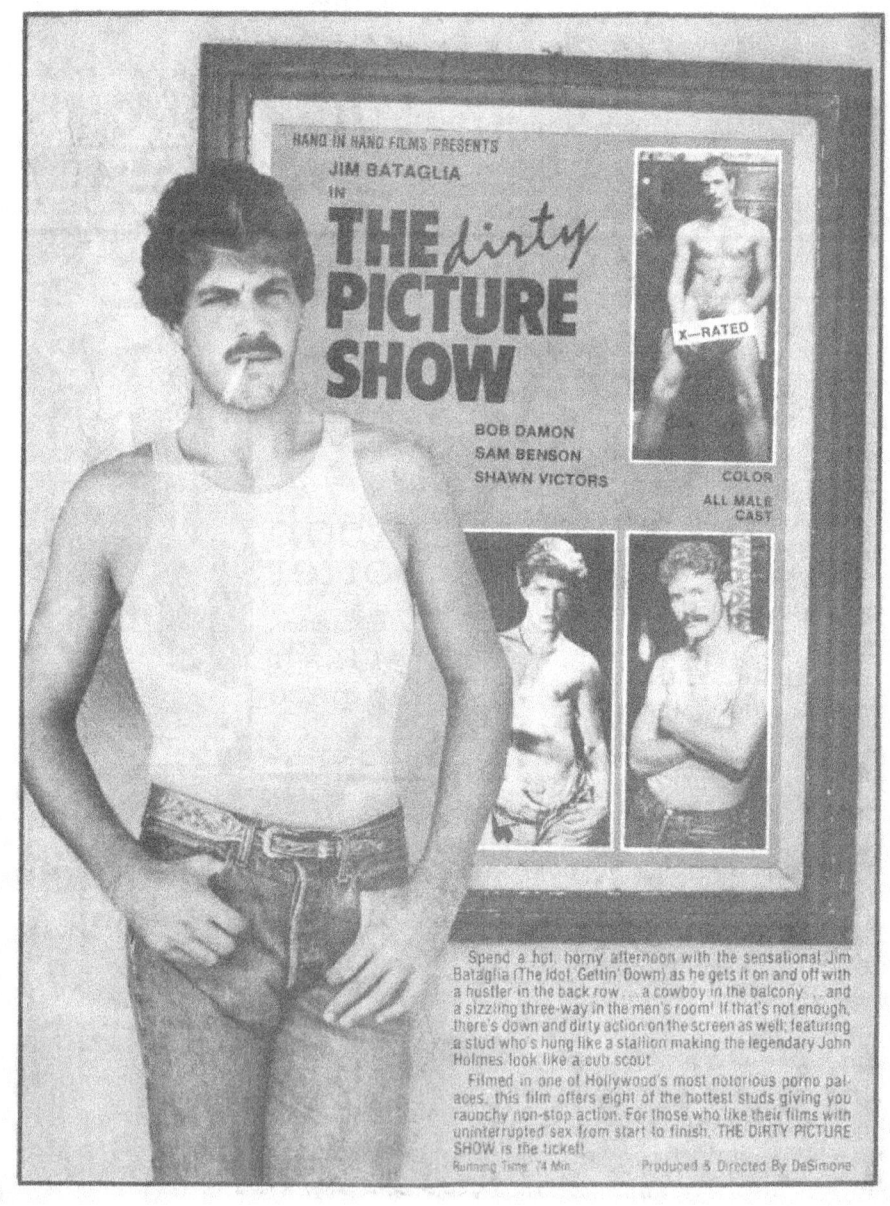

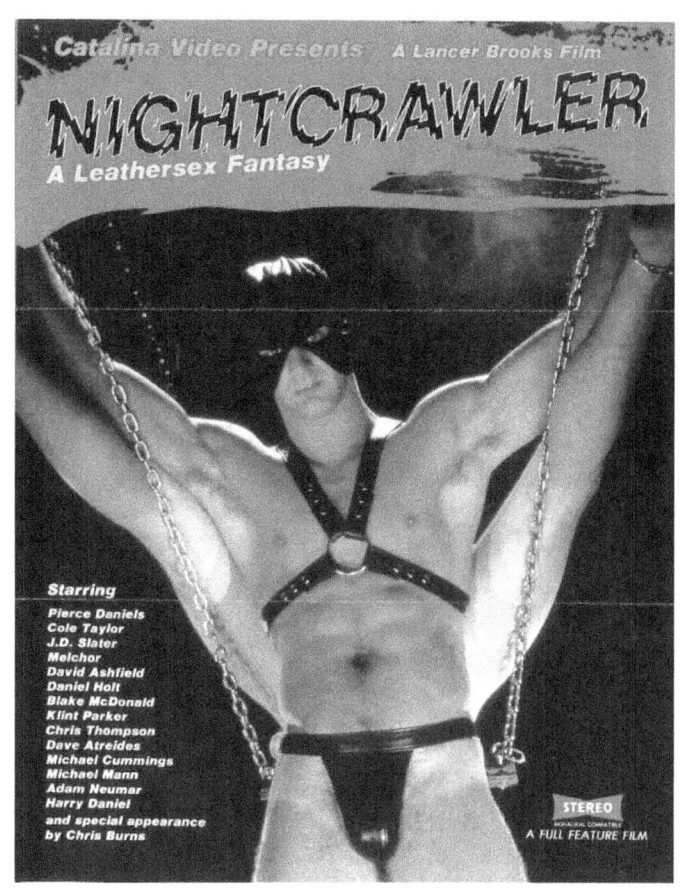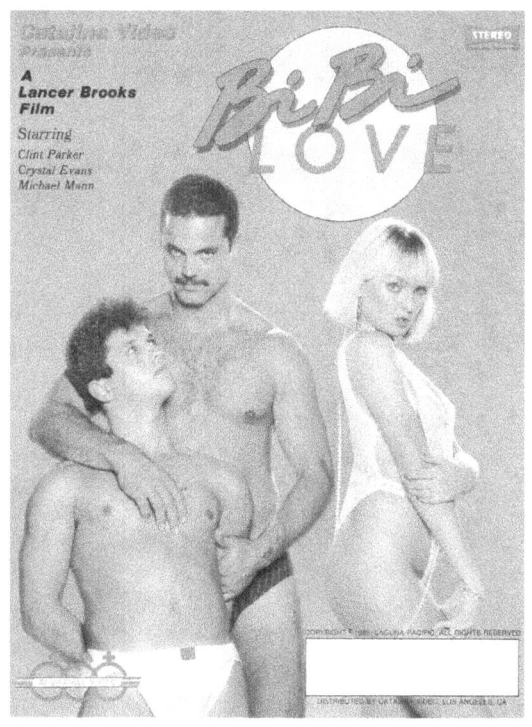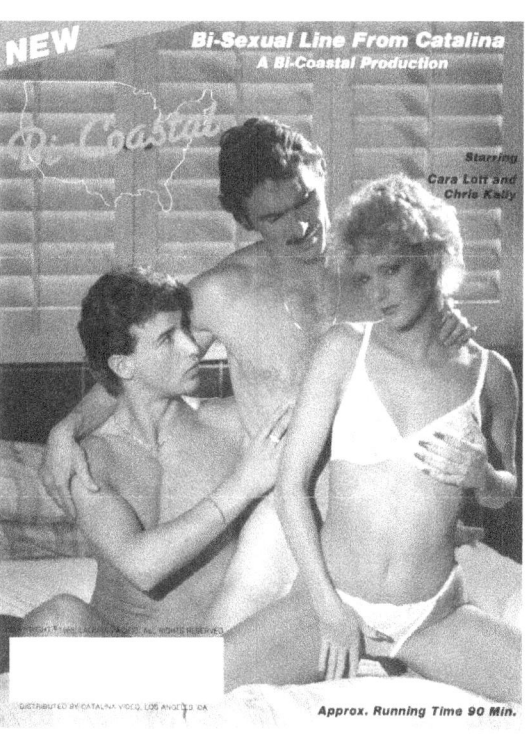

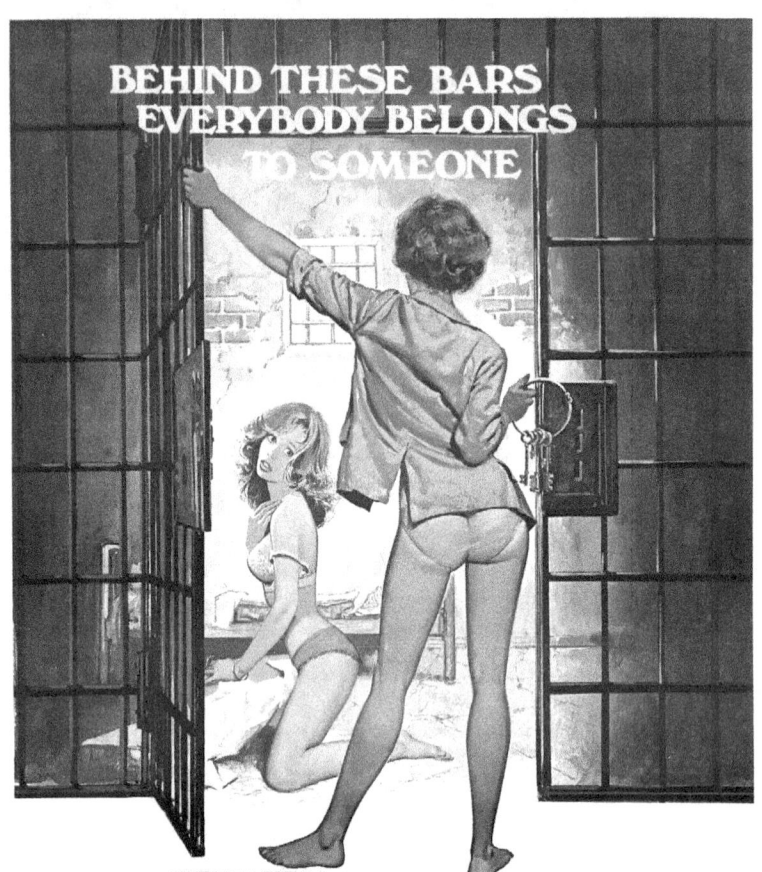

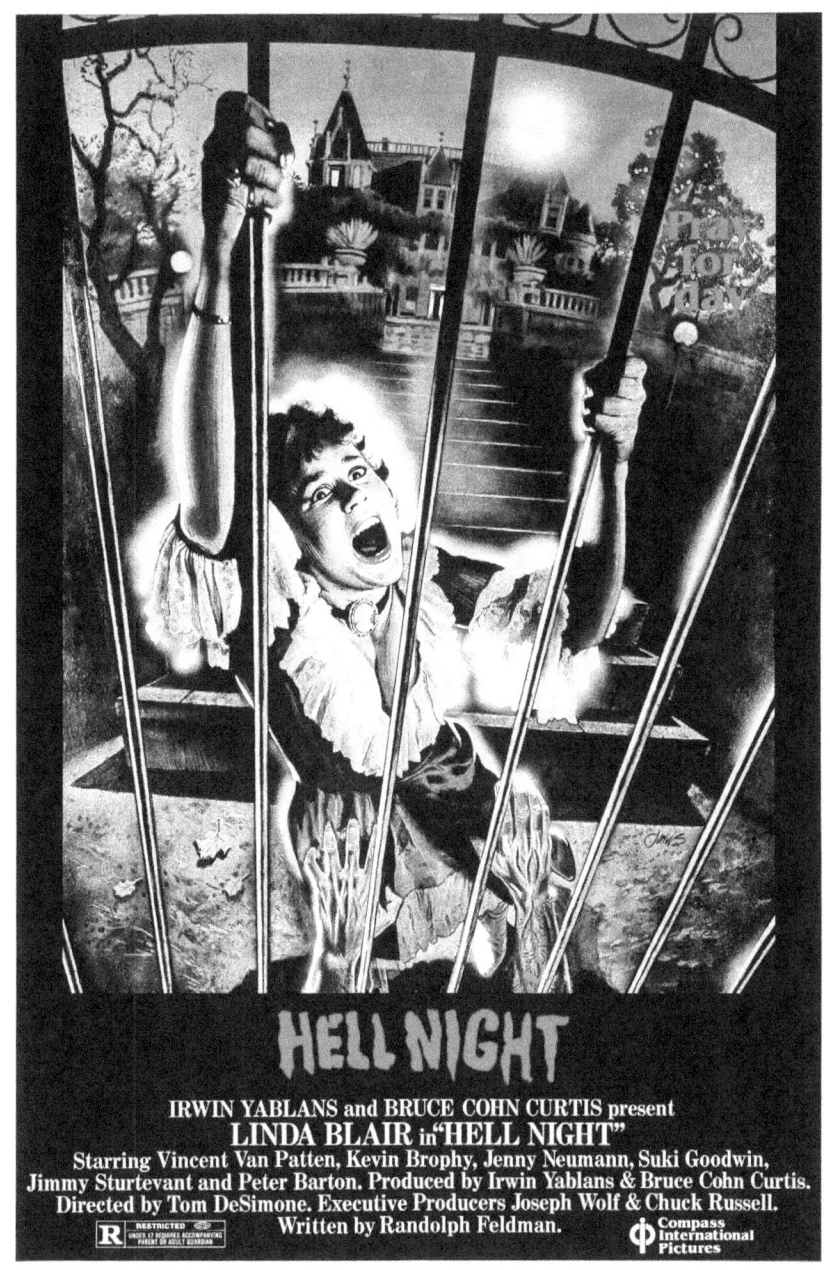

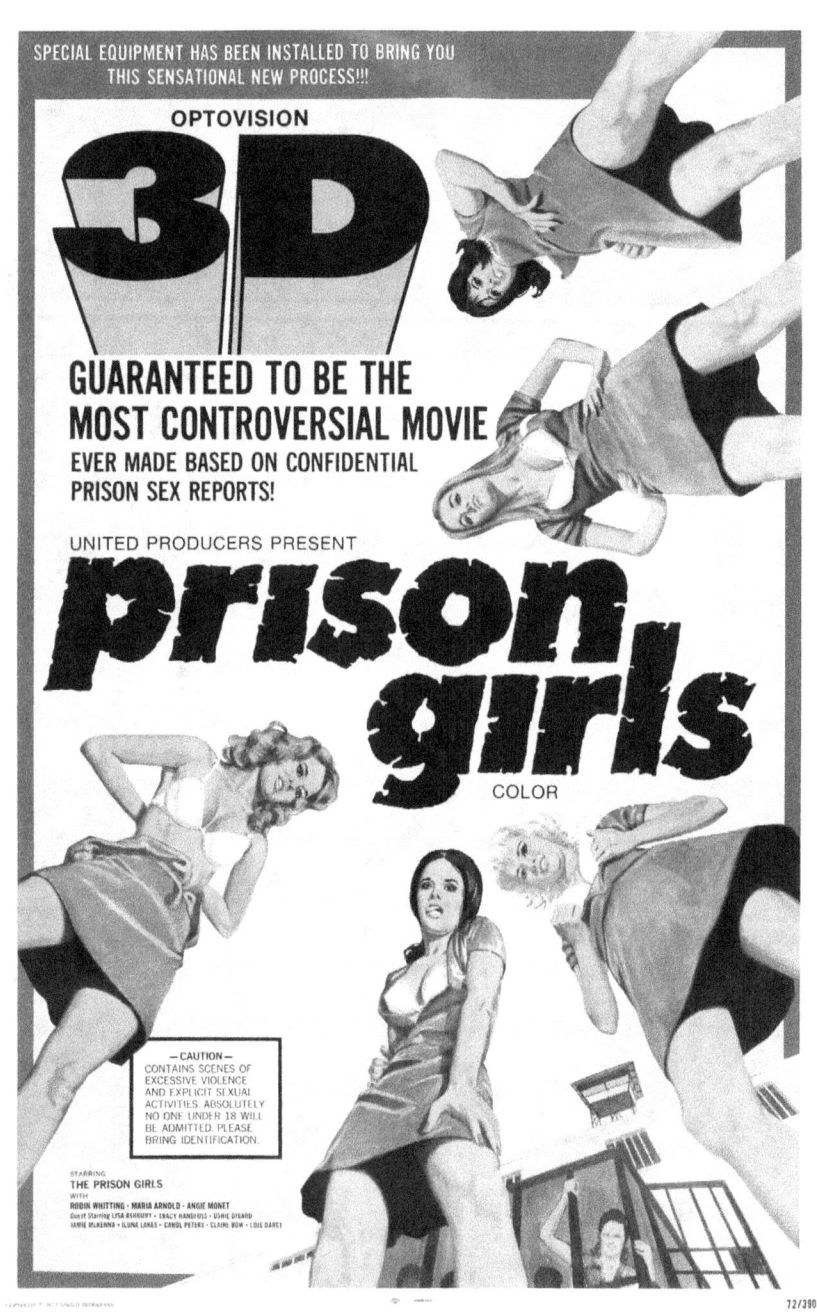

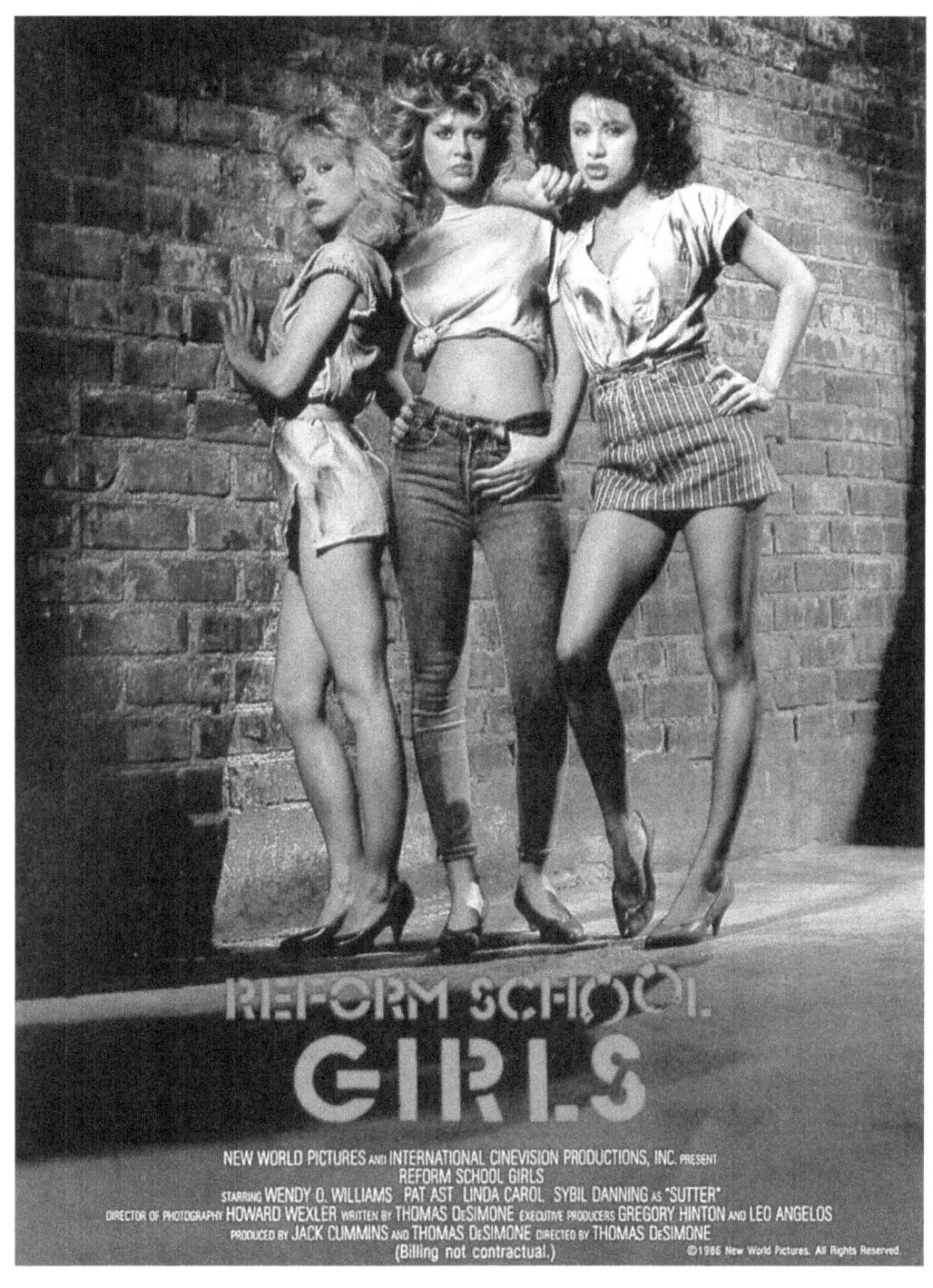

ROBERT ALVAREZ

Hand In Hand - A Love Story

Marco Siedelmann: Before we start talking about Jack Deveau, please tell me about Kees Chapman. He became an important artistic collaborator at some point.
Robert Alvarez: He came to us actually as the partner of Sydney Soons. Sydney came to our office, and you would might say he worked as a production assistant. He also was in DRIVE of course. But he was way more interested in the jobs behind the camera, and so he ended up working for us in production. Kees then was working as a waiter downtown. He came in, hung out, and next thing you know he also was doing work for us. He helped making the movies behind the scenes. At a later point in the game, Kees and Sydney split up. Sydney went to live in Florida, and Kees more or less took over the job that Sydney had. Kees became another partner, because he was very valuable to us. He was a huge help in the later years of Hand In Hand Films existence. He organized a lot, and he also got into camera work. He actually shot some of the stuff in the later films with Jack. He had no specific artistic background; I guess it just came out while working with us. He was very ambitious to learn the different aspects of filmmaking. He was able to work with actors very well, especially after Jack died. More or less he took over the directing of the actors. We always worked well together.
Siedelmann: He also died very early.
Alvarez: Yes, and I was very shocked about that. He wasn't like most of us. He was pretty conventional, not much of a risk-taker - I was very surprised when he came out with AIDS. Honestly, I'm surprised that I am still alive. Jack and I had a rather open relationship that way. We always had a lot of sex with each other, and with other people. I escaped somehow.
Siedelmann: You always need luck in life, no matter what. Sydney Soons also died. If I'm not wrong, was he 35 years old, and he passed away in 1984?
Alvarez: Yes. He also died of AIDS. He moved down to Key West, and once I went there on a little vacation, and I saw him. We always were friends; we had a good time together. He was working as a waiter. I don't think I knew about his illness at that point, at least he had no symptoms. It was the beginning height of the epidemic about 1984, until the mid-90s.
Siedelmann: Wakefield Poole gave up sex completely at the point all those people around him left this world. Did you also give up on sex for a while?
Alvarez: Yes. And I also gave up on lots of other things. Alcohol, drugs, even cigarettes. I never gave up sex completely, there were always exceptional encounters. But I was very careful, doing safe sex at the time. Although I hated it, I always used a condom.
Siedelmann: I think safe sex certainly is better than no sex at all.
Alvarez: Yeah, that's what I thought. You just have to adapt to the situation, just like you have to adapt to a lot of things in life. Kees lived a while in the apartment next to ours. There are two apartments on this floor. We had the other one for an office, my editing room, and things like that. It became a guest room as well. It wasn't as big as the apartment we lived in, but big enough for a small bedroom. We had many people staying there for a while. Sal Mineo, Peter Berlin, Sydney Soons, Kees Chapman, Tom De Simone - all these people. *(laughing)*
Siedelmann: Oh, if these walls could talk. *(both laughing)*
Alvarez: Yeah. - Finally I ended up renting it to a friend, but unfortunately the landlord found out about it. He took it away from me, because it's not allowed to have more than one apartment when it's ruled by rent stabilization. It's like rent control. Both apartments are right across from each other, and they would have made a great, huge apartment together. But they were never interested in such a solution.
Siedelmann: So you still live in the same apartment where the whole Hand In Hand story took place?
Alvarez: Yeah, I'm living here for way more than 40 years now. I think we moved in here in '68.
Siedelmann: Had Jack already lived there, and you moved in?
Alvarez: No. We moved in together.
Siedelmann: Ok. And where did you live before?
Alvarez: We lived in some kind of studio apartment actually, Mid-town. As you might

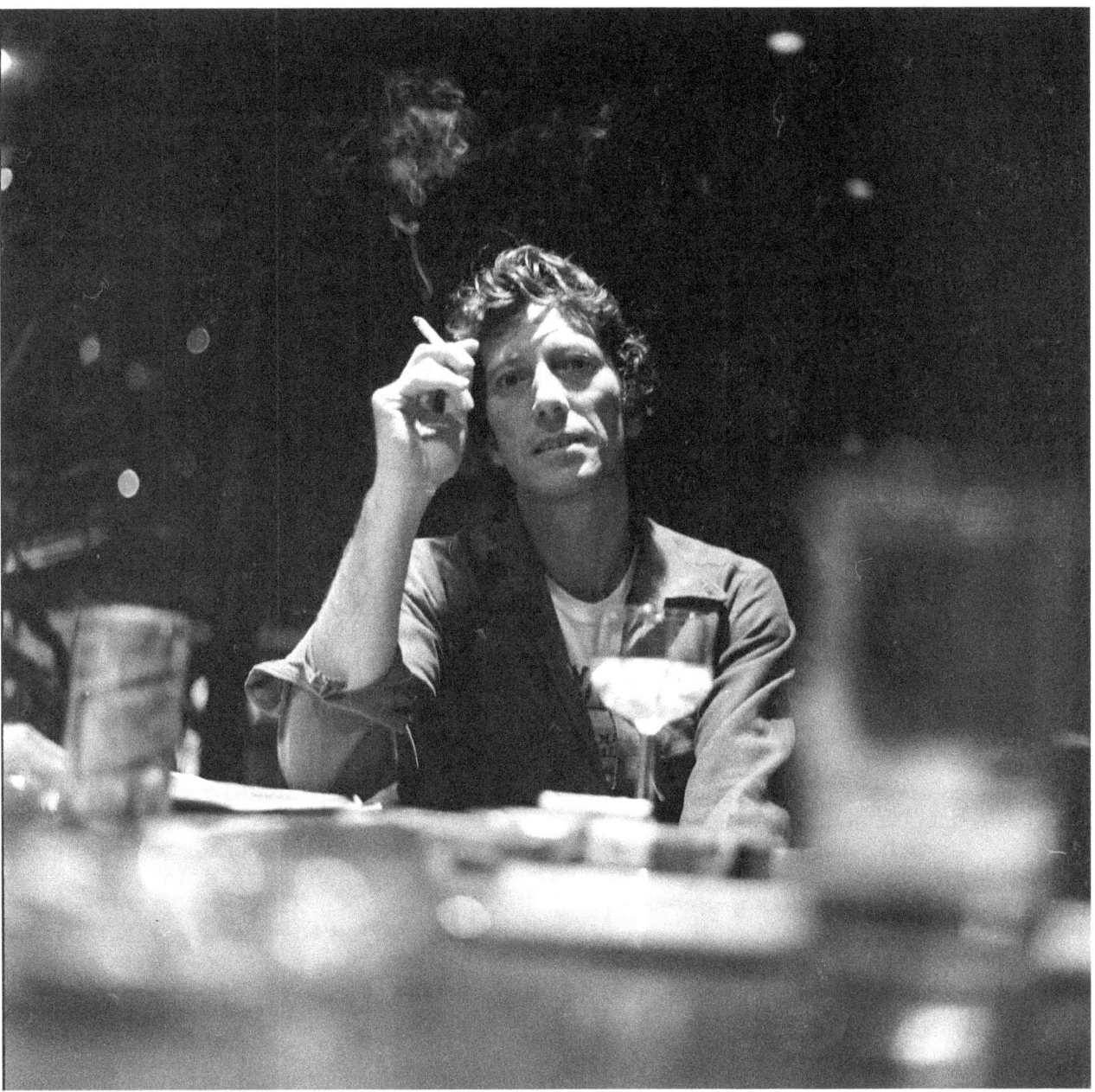

Robert Alvarez at the editing table

know Jack liked the coke a lot.
Siedelmann: So he was already into cocaine at this point?
Alvarez: Yes.
Siedelmann: And that was the time even before the studio apartment. At the beginning of your relationship, did you move in an apartment he lived in, or otherwise did he move into an apartment you already rented before?
Alvarez: Let's see. When I met Jack he was living in a very nice first-class hotel that his father used to manage. His father was working in a good position for the Sheraton chain. Naturally, he always had a nice apartment, and so Jack did have a studio apartment also in there. When I met him, I used to live downtown in the Village with a room-mate, but the more we settled and the more we were committed to our relationship, we thought about living together. Then he had to move because his father had been transferred to another city. Jack didn't want to go this time. So we had to find an apartment, and that was the studio apartment.
Siedelmann: So actually this was Jack's first external apartment ever?
Alvarez: Yes. He was treated like a royalty most of his life. *(laughing)*
Siedelmann: But he had found a home in New York and wanted to stay there with you; for good.

Alvarez: Yes.
Siedelmann: How old was he at that point?
Alvarez: He was 24 or 25.
Siedelmann: What about Jack's parents? I guess they were very liberal?
Alvarez: Yes, they were ... in a sense; his mother especially. She was a very devout Catholic, but she also was a musician, and so she knew about this bohemian world as well. For the matter of fact: She was a classical viola player, and she worked with several companies in New York. She used to have string quartet meetings and things like that. She was very into the arts. Jack's father was not, he was a businessman - period. He was somehow distant; he wasn't someone who could express his emotions. The manner I got from him is he was actually running away from being a husband, and the whole fatherhood role. He was very involved in his business, in making money. I never got to know him very well; we had not much in common. He was accepting the situation, but he wasn't necessarily happy with it.
Siedelmann: But he was never hateful against your relationship?
Alvarez: No.
Siedelmann: Was Jack a single child?
Alvarez: No, he had an older brother, but only a few years difference between them. They were very close in childhood, but at some point their lives drifted apart. He was straight, and very uptight. He was much more like his father, and Jack was more like his mother. His name was Tom Deveau.
Siedelmann: Tom was his brother?
Alvarez: It was the name of his father, and also the name of his brother.
Siedelmann: Did they know about your hedonistic lifestyle? Did they ever try to swing by for a coffee, and you had an orgy going on at that moment?
Alvarez: His mother certainly knew more than she would admit. *(laughing)* I give you an example: The first night that I met Jack - It was at an opera downtown. It was *The Saint of Bleecker Street* by Gian Carlo Menotti. Jack's mother was playing the viola in the orchestra. It was almost impossible that I was there, because I'm not an opera fan at all, but I do like that particular opera. I went there with one of my Village friends, and during the intermission Jack came up and started talking to me. He obviously was looking to pick me up. I was thinking: He's not my type, but there's something about him. *(laughing)* We talked some more, and at one point he said: "Tell me your name, because here comes my mother, and I need to introduce you."

- She was a wonderful sparky woman with a great personality. She was very, very nice. To make a long story short: We ended up going home together. His studio apartment was right next to the apartment that his parents had in the hotel. And in the morning I heard someone knocking at the door. *(laughing)* And she walks right in. She said: "Oh, hello. How are you?", and to Jack: "You must get up now." - She was very motherly in an average way during the situation. She was not shocked, or upset; at least not in appearance. She knew he was gay, there's absolutely no question there. She was religious, but not one of the persons who think there's only one way of living.
Siedelmann: So Jack really came from big wealth?
Alvarez: There was some money on his father's side of the family, but I don't know where it came from. Of course he was making a lot of money while doing the hotel management thing, and also they had the opportunity of living in these big hotels.
Siedelmann: So his parents financed his lifestyle? Was he ever under pressure because of the situation?
Alvarez: Jack worked in a design company, and he was into public relations and that kind of stuff. They did industrial design, and his boss was one of his friends. They formed a well working company in a very short time, and when I met him, he was working there. That ended at one point, because the owner decided to go off somewhere. He made his fortune, and just decided to retire in a very early age. Jack was left without a job, but soon he met Jaap Penraat, who was a very well-known designer from Holland at the time. He knew a lot of people who were survivors of WWII.
Siedelmann: He was a victim of the Nazis himself, correct? He helped smuggling people, I guess, to save their lives.
Alvarez: Yes, he somehow got caught and was put in a concentration camp where he was tortured. Somehow he managed to get out. I don't know about his story in detail.
Siedelmann: Were you the jealous type sometimes? For example, were you upset when Jack and Peter flew to Paris?
Alvarez: Not so much. My relationship with Jack was a whole other story. Like I said, it was open, but I had a broad mind approach to most things. There were no set rules between our relationships with each other and other people. Sometimes it was hard.

Siedelmann: Besides the sex there's always the chance you fell hard in love with some of your affairs.
Alvarez: Yeah, and he did. There were a couple of people during our times together he couldn't just say goodbye to. He had a very long affair with one person, but it finally died out on its own. I was psychologically threatened to whether I should stay or leave. I decided that I would stay. I believed in our relationship. I think it was different, and much deeper than most people experience it. I don't think many people can handle such a relationship. Many people are so much self-involved that they really can't give anything to anyone. They're very often afraid, angry, and competitive.
Siedelmann: So I assume there were many people who envied you.
Alvarez: Yes, I think some utterly wanted what I had. Gay people today have become way more sophisticated about being in relationships. More like ordinary straight couple. Back then, being gay was much more about finding that one person. More fairy tale. Bigger expectations. If you did not have someone who was dying to make love to you every minute of the day you were too insecure to feel like a whole person. I think I represented a special thing for many people. This was what I wanted; a long lasting, not threatening relationship. Even when Jack had an affair, it was easier for me to accept it, so it did not become threatening. It worked itself out. I had my life too, and it was important not to get hysterical about it.
Siedelmann: Was it easier for you to cut off affairs?
Alvarez: I liked a lot of variety. *(laughing)* Maybe I was attracted to someone, and it happened to connect. When I was in bed with somebody, I did not necessarily want to do it again; at least not right away with the same person. Of course a few weren't like that. For some of them I had stronger feelings. But looking back now, I know it wasn't any more real than a fantasy. I made the right decision stay close to Jack, and went not too far.
Siedelmann: I guess many people became more confident and optimistic because of your relationship as well; real love, a successful and exciting life. You lived and worked together...
Alvarez: Yes, that was an important aspect. We did something together, we created something. We had similar hobbies, we both just happened to like the same things. That wasn't made up artificially. Also Jack's intelligence kept us together. I knew that of all the people I met, I never experienced some sort of connection. It was worth all the imperfections, just to have that in my life. I figured that out with a little psychiatry. *(laughing)* As Jack got older, he became more dissatisfied, just in general. There were certain things that haunted him about his life. But nothing he could do anything about, so he became more and more un-enchanted.
Siedelmann: Was he very into his looks? Was it hard for him to get older? I mean, we all hate it, of course...
Alvarez: Jack was handsome and good-looking. A lot of people found him very attractive - including me. He wasn't that gorgeous gay model type. So I think he never felt he was looking good enough. He also abused alcohol and cigarettes. He was an incredible smoker; always Camel, without filters. He did many self-destructive things. I don't know exactly what kind of demons haunted him. Maybe something about his family, I really don't know. He became less funny. He got more introspective when he got older. And of course when he got sick, he was completely somewhere else. I don't know where his mind was. He was making sense and everything, but he knew he had a fatal disease. How do you handle that? I don't know.
Siedelmann: I think there's nothing special needed for someone to be haunted and unhappy. It's just the way life works: You get older every day. At the end, you can take nothing with you. I think a lot of sensitive people suffer from that because it's hard to imagine that at some point everything and everyone around us will be gone.
Alvarez: That's true.
Siedelmann: How long did he know about that there would no chance to get through the disease?
Alvarez: He died about six months after he got the diagnosis. He took it very well, I mean he did not impose his grief and all the bitter feelings he had on the rest of the people around him. He was still the same personality. He just was no more energetic. He faded out. They were very honest with him about the type of lung cancer he had. It was a tumor that grows very quickly and spreads everywhere. The idea was to shrink the tumor, which we did. But it was more about giving him a few more days to live. There was no chance for him to survive. He had seen no alternative so he went with it.
Siedelmann: Did he want to clarify some things with family members or old friends before his

passing?

Alvarez: Not anything I was aware of. I think his mother found some strength in her Catholic beliefs, but she also became ill critically. She died relatively quick after he was gone. I think that's not unusual. She was in her seventies, I don't know exactly.

Siedelmann: So did you see the family members ever again?

Alvarez: The father maybe died before Jack, I'm not sure. I went to visit his mother once after Jack died. It was very sad. She looked so different. I think Jack had his joie de vivre from his mother, who once had such a lively personality. She got less and less communicative. I guess she just wanted to die at that point.

Siedelmann: The 70s had passed, and a new era was about to begin. At the time he became the diagnosis - was there still the hard party lifestyle ongoing, or had it become a little quieter anyway?

Alvarez: I remember it that he quit smoking, and a day later he was diagnosed. Of course it wasn't that way, but it just felt that way. It was maybe three or four months after he stopped smoking. He did start to clean up. He cut down alcohol. There wasn't as much cocaine around. *(laughing)* - But finally it didn't help him.

Siedelmann: Yes. Life is often cruel with timing.

Alvarez: Oh yes. It surely is.

Siedelmann: Were there some of the people from the inner Hand In Hand circle who made their living with the films, like full-time employees?

Alvarez: No, i didn't think anybody was in that kind of way supported by our films. We got together for a short period of time, and they did get a fee for what they had been doing. Afterwards they went on with their lives, and we went on with ours. So we would come together again for parties, premier events, and other things like this.

Siedelmann: But there were some regular "jobs" like in any other office, correct? Someone had to do the books, the distribution of the films, the selling of Super 8 copies...

Alvarez: About the 8mm copies: This wasn't a great success. Jaap Penraat was going to be in charge for that. I don't know; something happened there. I think it wasn't too legal. I guess he was pulling some of the money up for himself, and that caused a huge rift between Jack and him. Their friendship split up, and it was never restored again. Jaap went on with his industrial design work. He still had a lot attention from the Netherlands, so he always had some income by that.

Siedelmann: So Jaap Penraat wasn't much into filmmaking in general?

Alvarez: I think he never made films again in any way. I guess he was more into other things. As you know, his daughter Noelle went on with filmmaking, but in a whole other field compared to production and direction. She started her career as a negative matcher at Hand In Hand.

Siedelmann: I wanted to ask about that point. Noelle Penraat almost was a teenager back then, correct?

Alvarez: Yeah, she was very young; also very smart and talented.

Siedelmann: Well - she must have been, because the negative matching is so very important. You can do serious damage with making mistakes there, right?

Alvarez: Yes. But she was great, and she learned very fast. Noelle was trained before by a well-known and very respected negative cutter for several years. That's how she learned the trade. At some point, she wanted to do it on her own. At the time we made BALLET DOWN THE HIGHWAY she knew enough of the business to be able to make it professionally. She did it. She wasn't someone who made a lot of mistakes - in anything, I guess. Her mentor let her do it, because it was an important step for her. And it was from his perspective the perfect training film: He would not do it anyway because it was an adult film. Also he was way above such small independent features. I don't remember his name, but he was responsible for the negative matching of huge motion pictures.

Siedelmann: Moose 100 was the man who was called out for the screwball comedies?

Alvarez: Yes, he was one out of two writers who used to work with us who were very much into this Hollywood type of storytelling. The writing style of Moose 100 was kind of light and comedic. So he was scripting movies like FIRE ISLAND FEVER, DUNE BUDDIES, HOT HOUSE...

Siedelmann: ...but not BALLET DOWN THE HIGHWAY, correct?

Alvarez: No, that one was written by P.P. Mans. He was a - I would not say: avant-garde writer - but he was around a lot of people who were shooting non-pornography independent movies at the time. He was a friend of ours. But yeah, the light ones were definitely more Moose 100. Because they were comedies, they naturally had a whole different flavor. They often kept inside jokes

only certain people would react to. Then were the darker ones, like THE DESTROYING ANGEL or LEFT-HANDED. Some might would say LEFT-HANDED is a romantic film, but...
Siedelmann: ...it's kind of heartbreakingly sad. Definitely not light!
Alvarez: *(both laughing)* Exactly. - Those are the different categories of the Hand In Hand work.
Siedelmann: So I assume Moose 100 was a professional writer in his real life as well?
Alvarez: Yes. As a playwright, he has done several things; mostly Off-Broadway. I don't think he had done any film scripts prior to that. So yeah, he always was a professional writer in his separate real life persona.
Siedelmann: The dialogue in films like THE BOYS FROM RIVERSIDE DRIVE isn't easy to handle for inexperienced actors. Was most of it improvised on set?
Alvarez: It was mostly scripted. I mean - there was improvisation, but it was taken from the scripted situations. At least it was suggested by the script, but the actors may not remember the text exactly, and used different words. Everything was very well written in films like RIVERSIDE DRIVE, FIRE ISLAND FEVER, DUNE BUDDIES, etc.
Siedelmann: So RIVERSIDE DRIVE was very much conceived in its remarkable mockumen-tary style?
Alvarez: Yes. It was presented as a kind of classroom style study about gay people in New York, and their significant habits. Just like ethnological documentaries about certain African countries. The professor was played by a professional actor who met through one of our friends - who was another actor and Hand In Hand regular, Garry Hunt. He did that segment, and also the voiceover. A touch of Old Hollywood short film presentations, but kind of shown realistically.
Siedelmann: We can see a few pop cultural references in RIVERSIDE DRIVE; for example the FLESH GORDON poster artwork in Raul's room. Are some of these details just random, or was Jack very into the smallest details?
Alvarez: He was definitely aware of it. I remember that poster. We owned it, but I cannot recall what happened to it. It's from the soft-core porn remake.
Siedelmann: Also the pieces of pop art we can see?
Alvarez: Again - you can be sure that none of the material was on accident in the movies. We owned the stuff, or we just had another connection to it.
Siedelmann: Do you remember the apartment?
Alvarez: Yeah, for a matter of fact, one of our partners - Kees Chapman - lived in the building we made the film in. Most parts of the film were shot there - so the dining room scene, or the one in the elevator. I have a feeling the basement scene was shot in another house, maybe the house Jack and I lived in. I remember we made the room look like a boiler room.
Siedelmann: Would you agree that comedy - compared to more experimental or avant-garde movies - is much harder to handle under this low budget circumstances? Because we know how painful a bad comedy can be!
Alvarez: Jack was very good at these things. He just knew how to direct. He knew when something sounded right. He would work on it until it came out right.
Siedelmann: Do you recognize the company Brentwood?
Alvarez: Oh, yes. Sure.
Siedelmann: Were their films around a lot, very popular?
Alvarez: Yes, they were. Jerry Douglas would know better about that because the gay magazines at the time were packed with advertisements for Super 8 porno movies. Most of them came from the West Coast, California; for example Brentwood. So did Falcon. They also had been distributed in theaters, but the main focus was to make super 8 copies for mail order business, so people could collect the films. They sold 8mm and Super-8, mostly Super-8.
Siedelmann: Brentwood produced, as one of the very first companies, narrative short films.
Alvarez: Oh, did they?
Siedelmann: Kind of, yah. *(laughing)*
Alvarez: I know they had stories, but they were very basic, and really not very interesting. I'm not being critical here, it's just a fact. They were almost childish. Maybe naive is the word.
Siedelmann: So have you ever been connected to Joe Dallessandro at some point?
Alvarez: No, not at all; this was a small movie he made when he was just a teenager I guess. He was Andy Warhol's superstar, you know. He made some underground adult short films.
Siedelmann: How did you get the footage?
Alvarez: I don't remember exactly how I found him, but I knew about that collector, and tracked him down. When I bought it I wasn't intending to use it anywhere. I just thought it would be an interesting film to have. And it is, it's quite hot actually. When we did HOT HOUSE, there happened to be the sequence where all were looking at a porn film. So I got the perfect one

for that situation. *(laughing)*
Siedelmann: Weren't you afraid to get in trouble because he was such a popular iconic actor at the time?
Alvarez: It was shot at a time when, especially on porno, there was not really such a thing as copyright. It was one of the things nobody could ever sue you for something like that. So that was impossible, and the only risk left was he might be able to get mad about it. Also we never published the fact that it was Joe Dallessandro. So we skipped the name of a superstar while advertising the film. We never pointed out who he was. It remained an inside joke. From time to time someone in the audience recognized it. You know, Joe did that before he went on becoming a popular actor.
Siedelmann: There was an animated short film distributed by Hand In Hand. Do you remember DEMI-GODS, directed by Wallace Potts?
Alvarez: It was kind of a collage film that Wallace had made completely on his own, and it appeared as an animated film. I don't know what's happened to it. He owned the rights the whole time. It was his film. We just distributed it, but it actually was quite interesting. It was a cut-out animation technique. That's an example for a very off-beat kind of films we also sometimes promoted. We did it a few times with the films by other directors. An interesting film about Wallace Potts: He was from the South, and he lived in New York. Actually he was the lover of Rudolf Nureyev for a while, but Wallace had his own career. He also was kind of a social person. He circulated around and met new people. He got to know a very famous Hollywood cinematographer. Unfortunately he is dead now; I think he died of AIDS. Wallace went to Paris for a while, and he directed LE BEAU MAC there, which became a classic adult movie.
Siedelmann: I guess Peter De Rome never went on doing a film with another company.
Alvarez: That's because we knew about his strangeness, and his weaknesses. He liked Jack a lot, and he always came to him when he had an idea. He once had an idea about a take-off of GRAND HOTEL. It was a very Peter De Romisch idea. *(laughing)* - Instead of the Hollywood-Cast with Greta Garbo and others, he wanted to cast porn stars like Casey Donovan, some stars from Falcon and Colt. He wanted to write all these little plots, and they should be connected to each other. He never got around with it, which is a shame. It was a really great idea. Jack really was the co-director on most of the films Peter De Rome made. THE DESTROYING ANGEL is definitely directed by Peter De Rome and Jack Deveau, although it's not credited that way. That's the truth of the matter. And ADAM & YVES, oh my goodness! Jack shot lots of the footage.
Siedelmann: So how did that happen? Was it re-made by Steve Toushin?
Alvarez: No, actually that was done before Steve bought the Hand In Hand library. When we decided to go venture on video sale especially the straight porn industry did very well in that field. So we found a company in NY that was interested in our stuff. We had copyrighted music on a number of films, for example HOT HOUSE. Music we hadn't paid anybody for, or at least had no clearance about. We took the chance, and it was never a problem showing the films in theaters. It was a very calculated risk. We never got in trouble. I think Peter de Rome once was caught by James Brown's company, and was taught not to show the film with that soundtrack any longer. That was HOT PANTS, and for a matter of fact we won a prize for it in Amsterdam. It's part of THE EROTIC FILMS OF PETER DE ROME. Anyway, we decided for some of our films that we couldn't afford original music any longer. I picked up music I thought would work in the films, and we just used it. Only two or three movies we made had popular music in it. HOT HOUSE was one of them, DUNE BUDDIES was another. For certain films we had to decide changing the music to avoid all risks. We did several things. I paid for so-called stock music which is very generic sounding. It has the flavor of different kinds and tempos, but it's really not that exciting. We had to go with those soundtracks. So I had to do remixing with lot of the music. That's how we released these videos. A lot of times I had to think: What a shame! I spend so much time on choosing the right music, and now we had to go on with second rate soundtracks. Same thing happened with Tom De Simone's THE IDOL. But we had to do it. That wasn't any longer such a limited market like the theatrical releases, or the super 8 market. It was a much bigger industry. And it was everywhere available. We also used popular music on THE DESTROYING ANGEL. We used *Dark Side of The Moon* by Pink Floyd. We hired a guy to re-do the music for the video release, and it was ok. You know, it wasn't terrible; if you don't know about the difference. It works beautifully with the original music; some of it classical, some of it modern. Also the

music used in the short film UNDERGROUND was copyrighted. But it sounds so dissonant, almost like sound effects.

Siedelmann: Jack's personality was very much affecting the way he worked as a director?

Alvarez: Absolutely; it's everything. If Jack had not had the kind of magnetism he had, he would never been able to convince people to perform in the way they did in a gay film. During that time a lot of people were still frightened of being exposed. They maybe had a secret longing to do it, but Jack had a very persuasive kind of personality without being threatening the same time. He was a wizard.

Siedelmann: I have the feeling he was like Fred Halsted without being angry and hateful.

Alvarez: Totally, yeah!

Siedelmann: You were not so much involved in ADAM & YVES as in the regular Hand In Hand films. So what did you do?

Alvarez: I definitely worked with David on it. With everything he did for us, I was involved and worked pretty close to him. We talked in great extent about the details - what kind of music should it be for a particular scene, what kind of move, etc; the whole flavor of it. I would give him ideas. Then he worked on that, and he came back with something we both would agree on.

Siedelmann: You told me that you like two scenes in the movie very much. Which segments are those?

Alvarez: The fantasy sequences. From a sexual perspective, I like the *Narcissus* section very much. It's a very beautiful erotic film on its own. It's in black and white, starring Bill Eld solo. The other one would be *A day for a Lay*, in which he is recounting an experience he had with a man in Paris. It's with Kirk Luna who was in DRIVE also. Peter was very clever in using a poem that is signed Anonymous, but it is well known among people who are knowledgeable about that period of poetry that it's written by W. H. Auden. I don't know if he acknowledged that it was his at the time. But it was, definitely. It's another piece of beautiful and very romantic - kinda steamy - way of sex. Very laid back, you could feel the summertime in it. It's set in the summer, and if you ever have been in Paris during the summertime, it almost put you there; very moody. It made you feel, oh yes! I would enjoy a day like that! Nothing to do, and just sex on your mind; coming across to somebody new. No one you ever had known before; just an interlude of great sex. - So I think that's a very good sequence also.

Siedelmann: The *Narcissus* segment was also a hit as a single short movie, distributed on Super 8 - correct?

Alvarez: Yes. Partially because Bill Eld already was popular at the time; he was in many photo shoots for magazines prior to working with us. And I'm pretty sure he had been in movies before. There were rumors of him being straight, but I think it was more of a bisexual thing. He definitely seemed attracted to certain men.

Siedelmann: Was he really a narcissus? A little bit of Peter Berlin there?

Alvarez: Not in personality. They were very different. Peter was much more directed toward being some sort of superstar. I'm not sure. But he enjoyed being a celebrity. Bill Eld had not the inclination, or the drive to focus on a particular path for him. He had this incredible body. I think he worked very hard on keeping it that way. He would make money hustling. You know, selling his body. That's how he existed, I guess. I was never a real part of his personal life, but I think he had many upper class clients. He had a huge penis, an exceptional body, and he had a popular face. So I think he did very well at the time, he certainly knew how to negotiate this.

Siedelmann: He probably was with an agency about this?

Alvarez: As far as I know, yes. I would not be surprised if it was more than just one agency. It's hard to imagine that it did not happen at a certain point. I mean, anybody who was a madam at the time would definitely look for someone like him to represent. Like a trophy. But again, I cannot guarantee such things. Jack might would have known better. He had a special and confidential way to get into these people. So he mostly had information about the people no one else had.

Siedelmann: A lot of your actors were from the West Coast, right?

Alvarez: Certainly initially when we were starting out we got our casts. The people from New York came to us; because of ads they had seen somewhere. This was at the very beginning of course. So we got known very quickly to people who were interested in being in our movies. We made a few casting calls, and many men reacted on that. We would interview them, they filled out a form. I still have these forms, they are actually pretty funny. Later, when we started a new movie, we placed ads in some of the well-known magazines. We described the types we were looking for, things like this. This actually led to the fact that more and more actors and models from the West Coast recognized our company. Peter Berlin got to know us this way, and he was certainly part of the first wave of artists who saw gay porn as worthy products. All in all, the people came from everywhere. We established ourselves as real legitimate gay filmmakers. We constantly had people calling us after a while to interview for the next film, whatever it might be. There was a lot of interest from the people just coming by into the office and being interviewed. We had various questions about their sexuality in our forms. They were very important for the production process, and rather humorous because of the things people came up with sometimes. Those interview sheets were one of the very best things.

Siedelmann: ADAM & YVES shows a very romantic image of Paris. You have been to the city before, right? What kind of feeling did you get?

Alvarez: I'm seeing it way more as Peter De Rome's vision of Paris than mine would be. I think some of the points he touches in the movie are definitely related to him and not for many other people. Anyway, I think it's a very beautiful film, but almost in your imagination still. The truth of the manner is: The exteriors were all shot in Paris, but any of the interiors - so all the sex scenes as well - were shot in New York. The scene with Greta Garbo and all that is taken from Peter's apartment, I believe. Also the sequence based on the poet was done in New York. So the truth is, I can't look at it and be reminded of Paris completely. When they are moving around, I recognize some places, actually you can't get away from that. Particular landmarks will always evoke memories of the places you've been. Paris has lots of unique places you could find nowhere else.

Siedelmann: So were you in love with Paris?

Alvarez: I loved Paris, I loved being there. I love France, period. We drove around to South France, in the Provence. I'm not a big traveller, but Paris has always been one of my most favorite cities. I always thought I do well when I have only been in the US and in Europe; and maybe some Caribbean Island. *(laughing)* Very important: Fire Island as a place on its very own. All those locations have magical qualities for me. I somehow feel more alive in those places.

Siedelmann: How do you remember your holiday trips with Jack?

Alvarez: Some of the museums, places where you can spend days and days, even weeks and weeks - without seeing everything in them. The Rodin Museum was a wonderful place. As you know we shot some footage there for LA MUSEE. The city itself has so many different colors and qualities. It's just incredible and beautiful. The artwork is all around you. You don't even have to go to a museum! All those wonderful sculptures and monuments; it's a knockout, just gorgeous. At night, with all the lights up, it's pure magic. I would have been very sad if I had not seen the city. Places like this are essential for my life. They helped me appreciate things, and they brought me experience. Maybe that sounds soapy, but I really feel very strongly about it.

Siedelmann: ADAM & YVES clearly was influenced by the French New Wave; and the films by young European directors of the time in general.

Alvarez: Yes. Especially it's influenced by THE LAST TANGO IN PARIS. The storyline follows a similar pattern, and also the first sex scene is referencing on the legendary erotic sequence in LAST TANGO.

Siedelmann: I like the scene, actually it kinda moved me. It's great how both of them sort of fall out after they are done.

Alvarez: Exactly!

Siedelmann: It had been the first unsimulated sex filmed by Peter De Rome. Before that he only shot soft-core.

Alvarez: I wasn't very close to the actual shooting. I'm kind of foggy about my role in it. Something technical, and certainly I worked with the sound and music.

Siedelmann: How many years did you spend with Jack Deveau?

Alvarez: Well, let's see, we were together for about 21 years. Jack died in 1982. Before we met I wasn't into film yet, I was still pursuing dancing at that point. I tried getting into the theater. I came to New York when I was nineteen. I spent a lot of time going to auditions, but not much happened. I got a job for performing in a musical called Irma La Douce. I was in that phase when I met Jack Deveau. You know, we hit it off and got together. Before that there isn't much to tell, because I hadn't been in New York that long.

Siedelmann: Maybe we add some basic information, in which year were you born?

Alvarez: I was born in 1938, August 30, in Tampa, Florida. I was raised there, and like I said I stayed there until I was about nineteen. I came to study in Massachusetts one summer, and after that I moved to New

York. I knew that it was what I wanted to do. I didn't go to College or anything like that. I put all my energy in trying to be a dancer. Before I met Jack, I did a little performing, but not a lot. We met in 1961.

Siedelmann: Did you have your coming out before you came to New York? Did you know about your sexuality back then?

Alvarez: Oh yeah. I did in my last year at high school, actually. *(laughing)* - More or less I was out of the closet. And I had to pay for it, because in Tampa, Florida, it wasn't cool to be gay. I had a lot of problems with some of the other students there. They didn't see it as being ... okay. So I had kind of hard last two years there. I guess it's one of the reasons why I decided to go away. Mostly because of the dancing, and I knew New York was the only place to come for this. I made this decision quite a long time before I left. I just felt it was the right thing to do for me. Then I got this opportunity to be a scholarship student at a place called Jacob's Pillow in Massachusetts, which is very well-known here in the East. They put on a summer festival, and they had different performers every week, all summer long. And they teach, they had students as well. I went there, and in exchange for the classes and so forth I did some jobs there. It's a really beautiful place, almost like a big farm; very rustic. I was one of the students that helped take care of the place. I had certain duties to perform. Anyway, after the summer that's what led me to New York, I didn't want to return to Florida. And I didn't, much tothe sadness of my parents, especially of my mother who never wanted me to be a dancer in the first place. When she found out that I wanted to go to New York she was even more upset, but I was determined to come here. So I did it anyway. Of course I didn't have any brothers or sisters, so I'm sure it was hard for them. I'm sorry for that, but I'm not sorry that I left. My life really began after I came to New York.

Siedelmann: I can understand that, you have to follow your heart.

Alvarez: True. And I had no future in Florida anyway, especially without a College education. I don't know what would have happened, but I wouldn't be a happy person if I stayed.

Siedelmann: Did you got along with your parents later on?

Alvarez: Yes, I did. My mother loved me a lot. More or less she swallowed her pride and accepted me. We never talked much about the gay business. They knew I was gay, but they didn't discuss it at all. The whole relationship was very tenuous. They kinda made it hard on me when they found out about it. We got past that, but I never really got over it.

Siedelmann: How did they find out? Did you have a coming out moment?

Alvarez: Not exactly. My mother got suspicious, because I had some friends that were gay, and I guess I wasn't smart enough to realize that she was thinking about it. There was a guy that I was seeing. He was in the Air Force, and he became a friend. He wasn't feminine at all, but we had something going on, and he stayed over some nights. We fooled around and had sex. He wrote me letters, and I, of course, saved them. One day my mother was snooping around, trying to find something – and she did. She confronted me with the letters when I got home from work one day. She made it really tough for me. She did everything you would expect a non-tolerant parent would do. She just made me feel horrible. I never really forgave her for that. Hell, she kept on going like everything was ok afterwards, so I always had the feeling that she betrayed me in a way. She never mentioned it again, she just assumed that I was going through a phase, or something – and that I would come out of it. I don't know if she really believed that, but that was her attitude.

Siedelmann: That was what she wanted to believe.

Alvarez: Yes. My father too, but actually he was much more understanding than she was.

Siedelmann: What did they do for a living, what kind of jobs did they have?

Alvarez: They had very ordinary jobs. My mother was a nurse, and my father was a workman in a factory. He was about twenty years older than her. I think maybe he had a little bit more experience because of his age. He was less upset by things life threw at him. You know, we did get along the best we could after that, but it was never the same again.

Siedelmann: How did it happen that you become an editor, which is a very technical job?

Alvarez: It's different, but I tried to find a relationship between dancing and film editing. Both deal with movement, rhythm, and putting pieces together. This is what choreography is, too. I kind of related it to that. I always loved movies, and after I reached the age of twenty-five I saw that I wasn't getting very far with the dancing. I've done a few things, but I hated auditioning though. At one point I discussed it with Jack, and he said that he didn't think I had the temperament for performing. He didn't say I was bad, and I wasn't. Actually I was pretty good, but he thought it wasn't the best choice for my personality. I decided that I would stop, and go into something else. I was still young enough to make a switch over, and I appreciate the years that I had as a dancer, which I never regret. I kinda floated around for a while, not knowing which way to go. Then I got involved with some underground filmmakers, or as they were called in those days: experimental filmmakers. I appeared in a couple of films directed by Gregory J. Markopoulos. More or less I drifted into production of films. I worked for a while with an animator and assisted him, which was very interesting for me. Then I went on with trying to get a job, which I did. I worked for the NBC network here, also as an assistant editor. I stayed with that for several years, and I tried to become an assistant for the chief editor there. After that I got my first full-flesh editing job for a company that did movie trailers. That wasn't a very good experience, so I just stayed for a short time there. After that I became a freelancer and went from job to job as they came up. Finally, after working for a guy who did commercials, I got all fired up with the fact that WOODSTOCK was going to be done as a film documentary, and they were editing it in New York. So I went for an interview, and I got it! So I worked as an assistant editor on that, next to the very young Martin Scorsese. And that was the beginning; this is where it all started. When I finished working on WOODSTOCK, I worked for numerous television stations here, on several documentaries. Again, always as an assistant, I had to learn the craft. During that time I became interested in maybe doing some X-rated stuff, because Wakefield Poole had just come around at that time. I recognized that he did very well with BOYS IN THE SAND, and I was very excited about it. I knew Wakefield from years ago, because he used to be a dancer as well.

Siedelmann: ... and he also lived in Florida before, right?

Alvarez: Yes, that's where I met him. I already studied dance in Florida for a while. I met him at some kind of convention. We didn't know each other well, but we remembered each other – and I followed his career when he was working here in New York on Broadway. At some point I got to know him a little bit better. Of course when he decided to do BOYS IN THE SAND, I was around, and I was editing by that time. He needed some help with laying down the soundtrack, the music track for the movie, so I helped out – in fact he mentions it in his book, *Dirty Poole*. Because of that I got together with Jack, we talked about it, and at time Sal Mineo was a friend of ours as well. He encouraged Jack to go ahead and try it. We decided to give it a shot. That's where Hand In Hand started. We opened LEFT-HANDED, and it received a good reception, so it gave us a pretty positive feeling. From that point on, we decided to keep going and make more. We were in business, and we decided from the very beginning that we would distribute our own films, because we didn't want to get screwed by other distributors who always seemed to be very dishonest. That decision helped us to keep our business going as well throughout the years. Instead of selling our films like most gay adult film makers, we took ownership to ours. For others, they only became available as rental products, not as things they could purchase in their library. That seemed to work out very well, too. At least better than it would have to turn it the other way round. At that point we got to know people like Shan Sayles, the big producers of these films in California. We took a trip across the country, and went to all of the gay cinemas. We told them about our stuff and what we were doing. That's how we picked up our clients, more or less during this trip. That all kinda clicked into place.

Siedelmann: Yeah, that was a wise decision.

Alvarez: And that helped us getting to know other gay filmmakers, and they were all disappointed about the way they were treated, almost all of them had the feeling of being cheated because of money. We tried our very best not to have that happen to us. And for the most part we succeeded. Of course later on we got to know Nick Justin, the owner of the Adonis. We made a deal with him to show our first release with him, so he would more or less finance the films. We used the first run to pay our debt to him, which also worked out quite well.

Siedelmann: Did you hear about Shan Sayles? He passed away a couple of weeks ago...

Alvarez: Oh no, I didn't. I know he wasn't well. Tom De Simone told me about it; Shan - more or less - only existed in the last chapter of his life.

Siedelmann: Did you have a good relationship to Shan Sayles?

Alvarez: Well, I would say good, but also very cautious. He also was an operator, you know? He would take advantage of you if he could – financially, or any other way. But he was an interesting guy, very much a product of the old Hollywood style and system. He did it on a different scale. He had "his" filmmakers like Tom De Simone, he had "his" actors. His way of making movies was usually fast and cheap, he had his own theatres. So he knew what he was doing, and he made himself a lot of money. I respect that, but I wouldn't trust him as far as I could throw him – and he was a big man, so that wouldn't be very far. Actually we became friends, and he was around when Jack died. He saw him before he passed away, and after that we ended up one night going out together, doing something that Jack would have loved. We went to see performers Jack liked to see very much when he was alive. I had a wonderful time, and it really helped me in that difficult situation. Shan Sayles was a very complicated person though, and he was an interesting person all the way. I know he took advantage of Tom De Simone, but they remained friends as well until his death. Shan wasn't just one thing.

Siedelmann: Are you still a movie lover, or isn't cinema a passion of yours any longer?

Alvarez: I still like movies, although I haven't got the enthusiasm I used to have, but yeah; I keep up with them, I go to see the ones that I think I'll enjoy. I haven't done so much experimenting as far as choices, you know? I used to be much more adventurous in terms of the range of movies I would go to see. I'm a little more conventional now. There's not enough time to do everything. Now that I'm retired I will certainly go to see some more movies, but they have gotten expensive over here. You just can't follow everything up. And there's so much, just an incredible amount. I just read an article about the Cannes Film Festival; we used to show our movies there as well. That was an interesting adventure. And I always was interested in foreign films, so at least I try to read about what's happening over there. Same with Broadway, it's also very expensive, so it's hard to see as much as I would like to.

Siedelmann: When you were a dancer, was it more ballet dancing or Broadway?

Alvarez: Mostly Broadway, yeah.

Siedelmann: It's sad when you think of it: people like Wakefield Poole told me the same thing about the prices for the shows. So he worked for many years on Broadway and now he cannot afford the tickets.

Alvarez: Yes, it is sad, because it has become very elite. You have to make a great deal of money in order to afford to go to Broadway shows.

Siedelmann: I think your first film LEFT-HANDED still holds up as one of the most important Hand In Hand productions. Let's start with the cinematography. There isn't a cameraman credited. Was it shot by Jack Deveau himself, just like most of his films?

Alvarez: Yes, he was primarily the photographer on that, although I did some work on it, too. I'm not sure if Jaap Penraat also did some or not, but I don't think he did. So it was me and Jack, yeah.

Siedelmann: Was it for Jack clear from the beginning that he would be his own photographer?

Alvarez: He already was into it, because he did some still photography as a hobby. He knew stuff about how a camera works, and so forth. He took on the role of a cinematographer as well. Most of LEFT- HANDED was shot by him.

Siedelmann: It was shot on 16mm, correct?

Alvarez: That's right.

Siedelmann: Do you remember the pre-production? I guess the intention was to make something more serious than BOYS IN THE SAND, because that's more of a fantasy.

Alvarez: Yes, it was more about the characters. There's more of suggestion of personality. You know the type of persons that were caught up in this brief, but intense relationship. We tried to do something close to a real commercial film. Not that we thought it would be commercial, but we wanted to go along the lines of a traditional film as much as possible. We wanted to tell a story.

Siedelmann: There's a lot of human drama in it, and it has a very interesting anti-hero as a main character.

Alvarez: Yeah, exactly. He is a somewhat immoral person; he always gets what he wants. Then once he has it, he doesn't want it any longer. Then there's the other character, the man who runs the antique shop, and he has secret desires for this person as well. Then there's the young man who was a marijuana dealer, actually. To that point he had been for all practical purposes straight. He gets charmed by the hero, and it's much to his disappointment. In other words he gets shafted in the end. So definitely there are three different types of people in it. We tried to show their differences within the story.

Siedelmann: Robert Rikas worked with Peter de Rome before.

Alvarez: Yes, he was in one or two shorts that

Peter produced and directed. He hadn't done many films before; I think Peter was the one who more or less discovered him. He liked him, and we liked him as well: The way he looked like, he was very handsome and he had personality. We thought he would be perfect for LEFT-HANDED, and what can I say? He was perfect for the role.

Siedelmann: I think it's interesting that his character not only has a girl-friend in the story, there's also a longish hardcore sex scene between him and her.

Alvarez: We did that because we wanted to show this aspect of his life as well. Therefore we had to show him with a woman, so we found a woman who did straight porno and we hired her to have a scene with him. Which I really think is quite beautiful.

Siedelmann: Do you remember how the gay audience reacted on that?

Alvarez: I think it gave the film a little more weight to have that scene in it. People accepted it, and I tried to make it as artistic as possible while I was editing it. I worked with a lot of dissolves and things like that to give it some lyrical quality. I wanted to show that they are really into each other at the beginning – before he met the guy who seduced him. I hope it came across that way.

Siedelmann: Another beautiful sequence is the next one; Ray Frank is masturbating and fantasizing.

Alvarez: There again, I wanted to show his own desires and his fantasies, you know? I gave him this scene where he has sex with the hero. Again, I think it went really well, but he's a devious person, which comes out later when he more or less sets it up that the new lover will find him in the middle of an orgy. Scenes like that tell you about his nature.

Siedelmann: Was it your idea to separate the fantasy from the reality using the black and white material?

Alvarez: Jack and I both came to that conclusion. We knew we should do something to set it apart, and I think we thought about THE WIZARD OF OZ. Reality is in black and white, and the fantasy is in color, so we reversed it. We made the fantasy black and white, and the rest of the film was in color.

Siedelmann: Also very obvious on LEFT-HANDED is that it's a New York film all the way; many authentic locations, outdoor shootings, etc.

Alvarez: We wanted to make that clear that it was New York City the story takes place in. We showed buildings and subways, places where gay people cruise or have sex. Like in the beginning when he goes to the trucks. This used to be a place where trucks would park, and at night they would turn into cruising locations as well, they used to be open in the back. We showed these things to make clear what New York was like during that time. We wanted to illustrate what was going on socially and sexually. Indeed, LEFT-HANDED was very much emphasized with New York, and places outside of New York. There is country and city included, and the country was definitely another location that was important to the story. We shot that in Jaap Penraats weekend house out there near Woodstock. It kinda gave it a flavor away from the city, the two characters were isolated from New York, and their relationship could evolve without the patterns of the city.

Siedelmann: Jaap Penraat was heavily involved in the movie; he also shares the directing credit with Jack Deveau.

Alvarez: When we started out, Jaap was an important part of the group. Jaap and Jack worked together before Hand In Hand started out; Jaap had his industrial design firm. So they decided to do this together as well. Jaap wasn't gay or anything, but he was very excited about the idea of doing something like this. He was part of the original circle. Basically we were a trio.

Siedelmann: Did they also join you in the editing room?

Alvarez: That was pretty much my thing, my job. I was the element that they didn't have any knowledge about. I already worked as an editor for a while, and of course I also was very excited about the project. I took over all the editing.

Siedelmann: But you were around during the shootings as well?

Alvarez: Yes, all the time. As I said before, I did some of the photography on LEFT-HANDED, especially during the sex scenes; I was controlling the extra camera. My shots were always the ones that were in strange places. *(laughing)* – Like the overhead shots when they first meet and have sex for the first time. Those were shot by me, and in the orgy I shot a lot of stuff as well. Also various snippets throughout the movie, but I didn't do much more shooting after LEFT-HANDED. I did a little bit more on DRIVE, and then I stopped shooting and stuck to editing.

Siedelmann: So all the sex scenes were shot with two cameras?

Alvarez: Yes, right.

Siedelmann: Do you remember about the production process itself? How long did you take from the script to the finished movie?
Alvarez: I don't remember exactly, but we did it all pretty efficiently. Definitely we shot one scene at least every time we used to meet. It probably took us about, I would say, a month, or let's say six weeks. To do the whole thing.
Siedelmann: Including the editing? That's pretty fast.
Alvarez: Right, that was one of our more efficient ones. *(laughing)* It was our first film, and we knew we had to get it together in order not to lose the momentum of it, so it was important that we would work on it intensely.
Siedelmann: The world premier was on June 1, 1972 – that means the film has its 45th anniversary in the next days.
Alvarez: Oh, wow. I hadn't realized that. That's amazing.
Siedelmann: Did you throw a big party event for the premier?
Alvarez: No, I know we had some advertising in the newspaper. In those days, you could advertise in the mainstream papers. We had ads in the New York Times, Daily News, and so forth. It was mostly promoted that way, and we showed a movie trailer in the theater, prior to our opening. We opened at the Carnegie Hall Cinema. It was strictly advertising, as far as I remember we didn't have any party at that point. We didn't have the money to spend on parties and premiers and that sort of thing at the beginning. We tried to have it built through word of mouth. After BOYS IN THE SAND sort of became a thing in New York to go to, we got this Carnegie Hall Cinema, and actually rented the theater without them realizing that they were going to be showing an X-Rated feature. It was actually used as an art-house, to show foreign films and classic films. Unfortunately, when they found out they stopped the cooperation. We had a run there, I don't remember how many weeks, but it took a while for them to realize what LEFT-HANDED was. So we had all kinds of audiences coming to see it, not knowing what it was. Then I guess somebody complaint, or whatever; the owner of that theater made us stop using it, but by that time another theater became available. It was the same theater where BOYS IN THE SAND premiered, and so we moved over there. We wanted it originally to open there, but they were already booked with some other gay film. So we couldn't play there and find another one, and we were kind of lucky with the Carnegie Hall Cinema. That's how it all started.
Siedelmann: That theater was the 55th Playhouse?
Alvarez: That's correct, yes.
Siedelmann: Sal Mineo was one of the people who encouraged Jack Deveau to start into filmmaking. Was he in any way involved in LEFT-HANDED?
Alvarez: No, he wasn't involved in our movies directly, but he was at the time working on an Off-Broadway show. He was directing it. He had several meetings with backers, producers, etc. – so he indeed was encouraging Jack to do that, he went to lots of production meetings with him so Jack would know what goes on when you are producing something. So in that sense he was very helpful. I think he wasn't around when LEFT-HANDED was produced.
Siedelmann: There's an actor in the movie credited as Al Mineo.
Alvarez: Yeah, that was a made-up name. We wanted to give him some sort of tribute. *(laughing)*
Siedelmann: I think LEFT-HANDED is structured very well. First we have a diversity of scenes, we have the scene with the girl, the masturbating and the fantasy, the scenes with Ray Ross and Robert Rikas. Then it's climaxing in an orgy scene. Was it part of the conception to give it something like a big bang for the end?
Alvarez: Absolutely, yeah! We wanted to build on the intensity of the sex in it. So we finished with an orgy, and also it made a good accomplishment to the dramatic action in the film. Robert Rikas stumbles into the orgy, and actually he didn't intend to go there for an orgy, to his surprise he finds out that his boyfriend is there, too; that kinds of puts an accent on the sadness of that moment.
Siedelmann: Yes, it's very unusual until today that a porno film ends with a heartbroken main character. It's one thing I appreciate very much, that the movie doesn't only focus on the positive sides of sexuality.
Alvarez: Right. I think that's what we set out to do in the beginning. Jack used to say about LEFT-HANDED that it is the story of a city-mouse and a country-mouse; and the fact that they are very different people. We wanted to illustrate that they were very incompatible.
Siedelmann: I think it's an important thing for most of the Hand In Hand movies: Even if a character isn't the nicest guy on earth, the films never judge about the characters.

Alvarez: It was very much in the style of... say a foreign film. It wasn't our intention to make judgments; we just wanted to have a conflict situation as it is. The characters are what they are. One of my favorite scenes in LEFT-HANDED is when Ray decides to re-invent himself, so to speak. He just conquered his person of interest and gotten his way with him, and then he more or less goes through a change; without dialogue or anything. That's the scene where he shaves his beard that he was wearing most of the time in the movie. This symbolizes that he's going through a change. I always liked that because without any words it tells you that something is different now.

Siedelmann: Even more than the later movies, LEFT-HANDED isn't for everybody – I don't mean it's narrative only, but also the type of guys that appear in front of the camera.

Alvarez: True, they are not sex symbols necessarily, but more – real. More typical of what the majority of people looked like. But I mean they were definitely not unattractive, there weren't many people into bodybuilding and that sort of thing back in those days anyway, that came later. The actors in LEFT-HANDED were not chosen because of their physical exception, they were nice looking people that you would find in situations like that.

Siedelmann: Was the movie shot silent and dubbed afterwards?

Alvarez: Absolutely, and that's why it's very crude in that sense. All the dialogue scenes were done separately, and dubbed afterwards. You can tell that it's not actual sync sound. But I think it works anyway. It is what it is, you know: our first attempt in making a film, telling a story. We didn't have cameras that could record sound and take the pictures at the same time. We had to do it separately.

Siedelmann: But as you said, the movie does a nice job in telling the story with very little dialogue. It shares this quality with THE BACK ROW by Jerry Douglas.

Alvarez: Yes.

Siedelmann: Did the people dubb their own dialogue, or did you find other people to speak?

Alvarez: We did both. I think Jack used his voice for the lead. For other scenes we used some of the actual people. I don't think Robert Rikas had a voice in the film at all...

Siedelmann: It's interesting, I didn't know about the fact that Jack Deveau's voice can be heard in the film.

Alvarez: We wanted to downplay the fact that it wasn't synced sound. So it's not a well-known detail. *(laughing)*

Siedelmann: In many books and articles, LEFT-HANDED is mentioned as the first X-rated gay film ever produced with an original score.

Alvarez: I don't know if that's actually true or not, but I would say it certainly seems like it to me. I'm pretty sure that this is true, because all the other ones I remember had music that was either well-known, or they used classical music sometimes, anything they could come up with. *(laughing)* We had an original score for it. I used some stock music for it, but mostly it was originally composed for the movie by Stan Freeman, a fairly well known pianist and composer here in New York. He had done a Broadway show, and he had a nightclub act, and composed a lot of material himself. That was kind of an unusual thing in itself.

Siedelmann: And that was important for you and Jack?

Alvarez: Very much so, we didn't just want to lift music that didn't have anything to do with the meaning of what was going on. We did the same thing with DRIVE. One of the songs in LEFT-HANDED was composed by Stan Freeman already, and we used it because it seemed to be fitting for the sequence. Also I had a guy who was a sound mixer who had a band of his own, and he composed music for us for the first draft of LEFT-HANDED, you can still hear it in the shower scene, and many other small parts of the movie. For the most part it was original music.

Siedelmann: As an editor, you also did the sound editing.

Alvarez: Yes, in fact I enjoy that part of the editing as much as cutting the picture. I always liked how music plays a part in films, and so I had fun with using the music properly for whatever was happening on screen.

Siedelmann: Right after LEFT-HANDED Hand In Hand released THE NIGHT BEFORE, directed by Arch Brown.

Alvarez: Yes, I think that was the second one. We didn't really make that, we were working with the director. He came to us because he had shot this film. It wasn't quite finished, but it was close; and he wanted to do something with it as far as distribution. He had heard about our company. THE NIGHT BEFORE was the first one that we took on as a part of our library. But it wasn't made by Hand In Hand. We picked it up

and received a percentage on it wherever we showed it. That's how that worked.
Siedelmann: But you also edited the film, right?
Alvarez: I did some editing on it, yes, but it wasn't the same as with Jack's films. I think Arch Brown had a rough cut of it when we saw it, and I just did some more things with it. I edited that scene with the two dancers – not a sex scene, it's a naked dance piece. Both men involved are nude, it's very erotic. They do a lot of lifts, it's very balletic.
Siedelmann: That scene was used in GOOD HOT STUFF, right?
Alvarez: Yes.
Siedelmann: It's a good example for your editing style, I guess. You are using a lot of cross-fades; you like to overlay a lot of images.
Alvarez: Yes, that was something I learned when I was involved with underground filmmakers. The person that I was helping – I appeared in a couple of his films – was very into doing long dissolves, overlays, and things like that. That's where I picked up this part of the style and made it my own. It creates a very lyrical atmosphere.
Siedelmann: In DRIVE, it's mostly the editing technique that allows the film to tell a rather complex story.
Alvarez: It suggests that the work the agent is doing highly involves sexual activity: To be sexually available all the time, even though he was essentially married with another guy. The other guy is somewhat disturbed by that fact. It shows when he had tickets for the circus, and the agent couldn't make it, so he had to go alone. Or the scene when the agent has sex with the doctor in a cabin, it is contrasted with the scenes of the boyfriend/husband or whatever who is looking for him in the audience and he doesn't show up. To make it clear, I used long dissolves and superimpositions, the circus is kind of a contrast to the actual sex that is going on in the cabin. That kinda makes a comment on their relationship.
Siedelmann: Can you remember which parts you photographed in DRIVE? Was it the disco scene?
Alvarez: Yes, definitely parts of the dancing scene in the club. And I shot parts of the scene which it is intercut with. The agent and his boyfriend are having sex in the living room. I added some special angle shots that I used in the editing. That were the scenes that I had to do with as far as a cameraman. Most of the filming in DRIVE was done by Jack Deveau himself.
Siedelmann: In GOOD HOT STUFF, we can see that Jack Deveau really believed in a collaborative process, and I would say DRIVE is a perfect example for that.
Alvarez: Yes, very true.
Siedelmann: There is an unusual double fisting scene in DRIVE. Was that in the script?
Alvarez: It wasn't necessarily scripted, but we found some actors that were willing to do that. We had a scene in a steam room and it was supposed to represent a special room, one that was cut off from the rest of the steam bath. This particular kind of sex went on there; we cast it with people that were into that kind of thing. One of them was a policeman by the way. *(laughing)* Jack more or less directed the movements for them, but once they start going he couldn't say, do this or turn this way, without destroying the hotness of the moment. He would tell them basically what to do, or the positions they would get into, and they would take it from there. Most of the sex in the Hand In Hand movies is almost like documentary filming. You cannot really direct people to be sexually hot, you know? They have to have that in them. And they had to be caught up with it. That's how we built the scenes. Of course any dialogue scenes and things like that were rehearsed and very definitely scripted.
Siedelmann: So the choreography comes from the editing, not from advising the actors what to do?
Alvarez: Yes, basically. You hope that you would have enough material that you'll be able to cut into something.
Siedelmann: The anti-hero in DRIVE is one of the most fascinating characters in the Hand In Hand universe: The drag queen Arachne. Was the character a creation by Christopher Rage himself?
Alvarez: He was. We always intended a drag queen to play the part, and we tried to get a well-known drag queen from New York at the time, but he couldn't do it. So Trey Christopher who worked for us – he took on the part and he created the character. I still think to this day that he did a terrific job on that. Because he wasn't a feminine person at all, he didn't particular look feminine. Whatever feminine was there all came from the make-up and his acting ability.
Siedelmann: Was he a performer in any way?
Alvarez: He had been an actor. Later on he became a manager for two or three singers. Then he also worked with our company, doing publicity. He created the ads, he used to work

with the agency that would use it for different newspapers and magazines. So he originally was an actor, and I think he always was interested in that aspect. He also liked the idea of being behind the scenes. He was a good publicity man; he knew what he was doing.

Siedelmann: In both films – DRIVE and THE NIGHT BEFORE – the score by David Earnest is really important. Do you agree that DRIVE is even more complicated in terms of sound editing and mixing?

Alvarez: It is. David came in during the making of THE NIGHT BEFORE. Of course I laid in all the music once he composed it, and he also did ADAM & YVES, and the music for DRIVE. He seemed to enjoy it very much, being surrounded by that milieu of people, and he was very close with Jack. His music is very important to the actual film itself. But remember that the DRIVE theme song that we can hear at the end of the movie was written by Stan Freeman, who also did some of the music of THE NIGHT BEFORE and LEFT-HANDED. So first they worked both on our films before David Earnest took over.

Siedelmann: Did you conceive DRIVE as a spoof about the James Bond films?

Alvarez: Oh, absolutely, it wasn't meant to be taken seriously. *(laughing)* - In no way we could ever be tempted to do that. It was a satire type of film, and its uniqueness was the fact that the sex was real; and all-male of course. Of course you'll find some sex in the James Bond films, but never to that extent. *(laughing)*

Siedelmann: DRIVE is very overwhelming. There's despair in the movie, pain, and humor. It's sometimes experimental, sometimes very light, even funny – but still not a comedy.

Alvarez: Totally, yes. The whole idea was to make a dark sex film that had lots of different layers to it: different people, different types of characters, and to be somewhat comic at the same time. So it's really a little complex, yeah. It was way too elaborate for most people who would sit in the audience. But it was our intention from the beginning. Our mutual agreement was trying to make these films reflect something that had to do with real life. Use them as a model for maybe later on getting into making a film that would reach a mass market, rather than a specialized market like pornography, or gay-themed films. Our goal was to make real movies eventually. Unfortunately that never happened, because of various reasons. Making X-rated films gave us a lot of freedom as long we delivered a required number of sex scenes. It was a good place to start filmmaking, because within a small scale, any kind of story was possible. And some critics of ours kind of were upset that we wanted more than the traditional sex film. They just wanted to see boys getting together and doing it. It was like: What's that storytelling all about? *(laughing)* – Other people loved it, and in the long run it's a good reason why the films have lasted, because there's more to them than just raw sex. There certainly is an attempt to say something, or at least do something else; something artistic without sticking it to your face. Hand In Hand wanted to produce films that were a little more intelligent, I think.

Siedelmann: Do you have a particular anecdote regarding Kirk Luna, who played the lead character in DRIVE?

Alvarez: Not really. He never had done a film before, and I think we interviewed him based on an ad we created to search people for DRIVE. We needed even more men for this movie. We used several magazines that were floating around as well as liberal mainstream newspapers like *The Village Voice*. Immediately we had people coming to us constantly, submitting photos, and we had a resume for them to fill out; based on that, we would do the interview. Kirk Luna came to us out of curiosity. He was good looking, and just the right type for the role. He was masculine, but more in the way of traditional movie leading man type. He had a nice body and a nice dick. He filled all the requirements. *(laughing)* – He was just perfect for the part, which is not true for some of the other people in DRIVE. But I think we managed around that. Some of the voiceovers, at least one person in particular who did some of the voiceovers. He wasn't right for it, but luckily we hadn't much. Plus a couple of the actors I would have preferred to have different types. But for the most part it worked out quite fine. In my opinion especially the group sex scenes work very well. All the casting in those was good. It's still a convincing movie, I would say.

Siedelmann: Was a group sex – or orgy – scene a bigger challenge to put together?

Alvarez: Absolutely, the steam room sequence was the hardest, mainly because it was all constructed here in our living room. We had to make it look like that it was much bigger as the space actually was. So we had to build these flats, thanks to Jaap Penraat who did a terrific job in designing the sets. We could move these panels around, so it looks like a different configuration, as if there could be another room. That's more or less how we did it. We didn't actually use steam, so I had to superimpose it afterwards in the printing. That was rather complicated, technically. A lot of the actors were doubling up as other characters that made it look like more people were involved. That really was a creative challenge, making sure that the same persons surely would look like different characters. Another complicated scene is the one in the night club that Arachne owns. There's a whole dance sequence that she does, including a gorilla costume. I think this was very well choreographed. It was filmed in an actual club, I don't remember if we were allowed to film there or if we had to rent it, but we had to do the shootings in the off hours. Fortunately it was perfectly well decorated; it totally looked like as what it supposed to be. It was very dark, so we had problems with the light. Other than that, it was just the thing we needed for that key scene.

Siedelmann: There's a dungeon sequence; was that also a real location or a built set?

Alvarez: No, neither. That was an actual room somewhere in New York. We found it after a while, and it absolutely looked like a dark dungeon.

Siedelmann: Sounds as if DRIVE needed lots of location scouting.

Alvarez: True, it did. Actually, DRIVE was the movie that took us the longest to make, we had to start and stop constantly. We need to dig up the cast, and then have 'em wait maybe a week or so before we could shoot again. We were heavily involved with preparing the sets for the next scenes, sometimes it was quite a mess.

Siedelmann: DRIVE had some extended press at the time; many magazines printed advertisements for the movie. It's often the case that you need the same amount of money for the marketing as for the film making itself, right?

Alvarez: Yes, but not in this case. A lot of the magazines depended on that kind of revenue, so we did have a certain amount of ads, but they weren't extraordinarily expensive at the time. The most expensive ones were those for the regular newspapers we were able to get into. But the film itself was a pricy proposition. It cost more money than probably any other of our movies to make. The major expense went directly on the screen, I can say that.

Siedelmann: Even by Hand In Hand standards, it's a really unusual porn film. Was it accepted by the audience or was it less successful than LEFT-HANDED?

Alvarez: I think it was our least successful film. People saw it and didn't know how to take it. At least here in New York, people didn't understand it. We did get an audience, but we had to cut our run short, because at that time we were involved with another producer in Boston. He made distribution deals of all kind, and he took over a regular legit movie theater here in New York. It was right on 57th street which was a popular area, and we opened with DRIVE. It ran for a while, but compared to the other ones a short time. It was doing all right, and it looked like we could stay there for some time, but what happened was that this other producer had picked up the rights for another straight porno film called THE DEVIL IN MISS JONES. It became a huge hit, and we wanted to put it in that theater – which he did. So DRIVE ended up at the 55th Playhouse when we left the 57th Street Theater. Then we began to play it in other cities, so it had a good first run. We did make money on it, but we hoped that it would be more of a new groundbreaking kind of gay film; which it kind of became later on. I'm very satisfied with DRIVE. The only thing I have to say about it: It's essential to have a very good print, because a lot of scenes are pretty dark, and if you don't have a nice print many details will fade out. I think it's important to present the film as pristine as possible. That's why the best is always a 16mm print. But I have to say the last version I've seen from Bijou DVD is quite good. Steve Toushin cared for the quality; he lightened up some of the scenes that have been too dark before. It was almost as good as a film print.

Siedelmann: Someday the early films of Hand In Hand will end up in the collection of the Museum of Modern Art, I'm pretty sure about that.

Alvarez: We came close with BALLET DOWN THE HIGHWAY with that, but they didn't like the fact that there was so much sex in it and not enough plot development. It's maybe our most heavily plotted movie. I don't know, the person who reviewed it liked it very much, but felt that there's too much sex in it. And I agree, if I could have it my way now I would take out some of the minor sex scenes, or shorten them anyway. I think the movie should be more concentrated on telling a story. At least some of the films of our collection definitely are going to last for a long time, if not forever. There are many archives that will be interested in taking them, but for better or worse Steve Toushin kept the films alive. He made a real attempt to give the best quality that he's able to. They are still around, and that's good.

Siedelmann: There are a lot of art pieces in the beginning of DRIVE, in the exhibition sequence. What can you say about the artist?

Alvarez: First, I think it's a very good opening for the film, to introduce the characters in a rather sophisticated way. The person who did the paintings that you mentioned was a friend of ours. He had several shows already, and at the time we were shooting he was just preparing for a new exhibition. We asked him if we could film in the gallery – he checked with the owners and they thought it was fine. That's how that happened, so it's a very authentic contemporary exhibition you can see there. The name of the artist was Jack Brusca. He had somewhat of a name, especially in New York during that era he was very popular. In fact I still have one of his paintings that he did for us on a special consignment. Besides from the fact that he was a friend – he also passed away – I think his work is really good.

Siedelmann: He's also credited for that, as well as one of the many actors in the movie.

Alvarez: He was one of the bad guys.

Siedelmann: Was CENTURIANS OF ROME a Hand In Hand production?

Alvarez: No, we just picked it up for distribution. At one point the director, who actually wound up with the film ... it's a long and kinda complicated story. He died, and we inherited it. We kept it in distribution, and treated it like our own movie, but it wasn't.

Siedelmann: What's your opinion about the movie? Did you like it very much and picked it up because of its quality?

Alvarez: Yes, I liked it, because it was almost done like a spoof about the old gladiator films that were so popular in the 60s and the 70s. It had a great cast, people like Steve Reeves – the bodybuilder – as a lead character like Hercules. It was in that mood, it had a lot of details. It was supposed to take place in ancient Rome; it had a cruel emperor who was somewhat modeled after Caligula. It had sex that took place in Roman baths. CENTURIANS OF ROME was pretty much a throwback to that genre. We liked it. And it was rather elaborate also, for a gay sex film. So we took it on.

Siedelmann: There are rumors and legends about this movie. Do you have any information about its background? Is it true that the money came from a robbery?

Alvarez: Yes, it did. The person who produced the film was someone who had gotten away with a robbery. He worked in a big company, and he was somehow able to steal a lot of money from them. He kinda disappeared and created a whole new personality and everything. No one knew who he was or where his money came from. But he seemed to be very wealthy, so he travelled in exclusive gay circles, and he did a lot of drugs with the money. *(laughing)* And he had a lot of sex with hustlers. One of the other things he did, he became an investor; the principal investor in this movie, actually. He was eventually caught, and put in jail. The guy who became the director of the film more or less took it over. He finished it and got it into distribution. Then the guy who was in jail died – I think he died of AIDS also – and the director was left alone with the movie. He had never tried to distribute any film, so he came to us and asked if we were interested in taking it on. So we did. More or less, that's the short version of what happened.

Siedelmann: If you have another anecdote about this particular movie, go ahead.

Alvarez: Well, I feel a little strange talking about it; we didn't have a direct relationship to it. We made some money out of it, and just by some circumstances the film ended up in our library. We never had anything to do with it production-wise. And the fact that the money that was used for the film was stolen makes it also scary. In fact, when Kees Chapman was alive, he had to go to a court room. There wasn't a trial or anything, but he had to give them an accounting on what he knew about the film. The company people who had been robbed were looking for if any money was available, but at that point it was all gone. He used it up with drugs and sex. Just pissed it away, you know?

Siedelmann: So there were no legal problems Hand In Hand had with CENTURIANS OF ROME?

Alvarez: Right, at that point there was no money to be had, no money to get back to the original owner. We also didn't make any real money out of it, so there wasn't a reason for them to come after us. We didn't have any either.

Siedelmann: Quite an interesting story for sure! It's always fascinating if someone comes from outside the film business and simply has the money and the ability to produce a film. These are often very interesting projects.

Alvarez: Yeah, and if you see the films you really can see that the investor had great illusions about the film. He was up to create an ancient Rome spectacle. He put a lot of money on the screen.

Siedelmann: The film was released at the time Jack Deveau already was ill. So it was the last chapter in the distribution history of Hand In Hand. There wasn't an unfinished feature film Jack Deveau was working on?

Alvarez: We used some unfinished material for the compilation film IN HEAT; I directed two short parts for it as well. We also started to shoot a feature film after Jack died, but we couldn't use the material because it was too dark. That was Kees and me. We kept it going until he got sick, and when he died I didn't care to go on. I wasn't a business person, not really a producer. I was the editor. Also I had enough of the business by that time. It had changed a lot, and video became more and more the medium for which it was used. I decided that I would sell the business afterwards; which I did.

Siedelmann: Tell me the story about the stolen print of STRICTLY FORBIDDEN. I'm curious about that. *(laughing)*

Alvarez: Ok, let me see where to begin. We had been in Paris a few times, and we connected with a distributor, who just started coming out with regular heterosexual porn and some gay stuff too, I think. He was the owner of a theater, I think it was called The Hollywood Theater. It was right in the middle of Paris, and we had... actually I should say *they* had a big success with two of our films. One of them was GOOD HOT STUFF, which, they re-named; they called it HISTOIRES D HOMME. And I think we showed our first movie there, LEFT-HANDED. Anyway, these people that owned the theater were also involved in producing. They had worked with people like Jean-Paul Belmondo, and some other famous actors. So they were professional, and it looked like they had their fingers in a lot of different pots. Just one of them was in producing porn. I think they were triggered by our success in their theater, so they talked to Jack, and he talked them into maybe doing a film in Paris, which would turned out to be LE MUSEE. They went with it, and everything was very amicable in the beginning. You probably know this information, but we had a professional cinematographer, guidance, assistance; also we brought a few people with us from the United States. One of them was make-up artist Gene Kelton. And we brought some actors, like Bill Eld, and the boy who played the lead. Of course we worked with Jean-Etienne Siry on it. He was an intermediary; he spoke the language so he worked very well with the French people involved. I don't know whether he had any connection with the actual producers of it, but I think he might have sat in on some meetings with Jack and them. Anyway, we got along fine for a while. We shot the film in a very quick time; I don't think it took us more than a week. We had created a set which was supposed to be the museum in where this boy kind of gets lost, and discovers different things happen, like the statues coming to life, they start having sex, and of course they are all men. It was actually quite interesting because some of the effects in it were interesting too. Especially the scenes when the statues transform into real people. So there was a lot of attempt to make it special, and visually interesting. Everything was going fine until we got to a point where I think – I'm not sure exactly – Jack went to them for some more money. The producers apparently had not told us, but they were not happy with how the spending of the money was going. We stayed in a nice hotel in Paris, and so did the actors. There was money flowing freely for a while, but then they started to try not to pay for certain bills. I guess for lodging and things like that. I don't know if Jack had some of his own money in it. It seemed to me that we must have had some monetary connection as well, because our deal with the producers was that we would do the film, but usually when we produced a film it got help from either an exhibitor, someone who owned the theater or something like that. Then they would have exclusive rights to open the film and let it play for a certain amount of time. I'm pretty sure that our French arrangement was something like that; more or less all the deals were the same. Somehow at one point they got the feeling they would be cheated. By this time I had assembled a work print. When we assembled the work print – the film was shot in color, of course – so it was basically printed off the original negative. From there on you can cut it and edit, which is what I did. So such a working print was my tool. Some of the material for this work print we didn't print in color. We did it in black & white in order to save money. Supposedly when it was finished – which it practically was – I assembled a rough cut of the movie. So all the scenes were in their place, and we had an assemblance of the finished film. We even already worked with the composer, Didier Vasseur. We had the dialogue, we had the music, and this all went into the work print. It was basically the movie, just partly black & white. Obviously this was not meant to be used as a release print or anything like that. Then the producers got suspicious and refused to give us some more money, and then they refused to give us the original negative, which was in the laboratory that we used in Paris. So we were stuck with that work print and with no money, and that was it. *(laughing)* – They came after us; in fact they came to our hotel, although we saw them through a window. They were out on the streets, and it looked like something from a French gangster movie. There were a lot of guys, circled around a limousine; standing, waiting for us to come out. They didn't want to hold back the original negative only; they also wanted to get the work print, which we had with us in the hotel. What we did was, we appealed to the concierge who knew us very well by this time. We said, "Look, we have to do something here! We have got to get away from these people because we don't know what they are supposed to do."

Siedelmann: And they helped you in this critical situation?

Alvarez: Yes, they gave us a room to hide in, in the basement. We took the film, boxed it, and put it in the basement. We sneaked out of the back door, but anyway – they never got the work print, and we escaped more or less from those guys. *(laughing)* – That was the end of that, and we were never been able to reconcile with the producers, for a continuation of the deal. They just sort of pulled out completely. No more money, no more prints, no original negative. Nothing! They took over, and what happened was that they hired another post-production team; some of them were working for us during the shooting of the film! They were young kids, not even real film editors. But supposedly they put together a release print from the original negative and that's what got released in Paris as LE MUSEE. We still had the half-colored work print, and… it looked interesting, but it didn't represent at all what we had intended. But this material that was sitting in the basement of the hotel in Paris finally got – and I'm not clear on this at all – but somehow it wound up in the possession of some man in Amsterdam. He owned a laboratory, a film lab. We were able to track it down, this was several years after this all happened. Anyway, one day we were able to go to Amsterdam and get the material from this person. He died, or he wasn't any longer in business; something had changed. Sorry that I'm not clear on this, but I really wasn't that close to it at this point. The end result is that we got the work print back. A partner of ours flew to the Netherlands and brought it back to us. At that point, I started re-working on it, re-cutting parts of the film. I was curious about what I could do with it. At the end it only was a ghost of what we intended to do, because without the color material it seems very strange. Why would we have black & white switching to color without any particular reason? Nevertheless, we were kind of stuck, and we felt that we had to come out with something. In the end we were able to use the modified work print as our own release print. I mean I used the work print just as I would use the original negative material. We finally released it as STRICTLY FORBIDDEN. It played around, but I always hated it, because I know what it should have been. I don't know if it would ever been a great movie, but there was the version in Paris. I have no idea what that version looks like, or anything – but it certainly couldn't be nearly what we planned to do with it. I don't think we lost money on it, but I can say we didn't make any great money, because it was a strange film, and people didn't understand how to take it anyway. There's no real reason for some of the material in it. But it still has some scenes: It looks like a hybrid, experimental film almost.

Siedelmann: That's true.

Alvarez: Anyway, it wasn't a big hit. We just heard from here that their version was released, probably at the theater that they owned.

Siedelmann: So STRICTLY FORBIDDEN aka LE MUSEE was shot in 1974 and released in 1976?

Alvarez: That sounds correct, although I'm not sure about the release year. It may have been even later, but probably it's accurate. It just seems like something that went on forever in my life, you know? *(laughing)* I was already on something else; when we came back from Paris we started to work on the next films. We always thought if we would get it back some day we would release it as a new film in our library. In fact it had been shot years ago before it could be seen in New York.

Siedelmann: That's a shame, because it was such an ambitious project for Hand In Hand.

Alvarez: Yes, it really was. Some of the special effects that we used were kind of remarkable, initially for such a small-budget film. Like I said, I'm still pleased with the statues that come to life. We projected marble slides on to their bodies which were made up with white make-up. When the projections hit their bodies it looks like their bodies were made out of marble, too. When they slowly come to life we used some tricks with the lighting and dissolves. So we created the illusion of a full-marbleized figure to a real life person; maybe a little white skin, but nevertheless alive. *(laughing)* It wasn't all special effects, but the things we did in the movie were unusual, at least not seen in any other film that I've ever seen. For me it felt more of a Cocteau film.

Siedelmann: Was Francois About very much involved in the look of the film?

Alvarez: He certainly was; he was involved in all of the shooting. But he wasn't involved anymore after the backers refused to go on any further. He originally was hired by them, and I assume he was paid for the work that he did, but after we were out of the picture, he didn't go on as well. But I could be wrong about that, maybe they hired him again, but it would seem almost redundant, because he would have been finished completely with the shooting of the film. So I doubt that they used him again after they took over the film.

Siedelmann: He continued to work with Jean-Etienne Siry. Siry also worked with Hand In Hand distribution afterwards, so this story didn't destroy your friendship with him?

Alvarez: No, although I think Jean-Etienne was a little detached from it. He didn't like how things went out between the producers and us, and I don't think he cared for the film any longer, neither when the producers came up with their version, nor when we later on released it as STRICTLY FORBIDDEN. I can understand his reaction, because either way what he saw was an unfinished product. He didn't see the whole thing. As far as his relationship with Jack, it was fine. They didn't have a problem. Personally, I am completely detached as well from what happened afterwards. It's possible that some of the people who were involved with us might have also helped them finish the film. I don't know what the creative result was. In any case, I heard it was terrible! *(laughing)* I don't know whatever happened to it after the first release, but I still would love to see it. Maybe it flopped miserably at the time, and they would just take what they got from the one showing run of it.

Siedelmann: Rene Chateau was involved in this?

Alvarez: Oh yes, of course. Rene Chateau was the big boss, I think. I could offer him a deal so I could finally re-edit it. *(laughing)* But I don't think that will happen. I'm sure it would be better than what they made with it.

Siedelmann: In some circles of adult filmmaking in New York, there also were members of the mafia and other gangsters involved in the financing, right?

Alvarez: I guess, but that I don't know for sure. Luckily we were able to produce and distribute our films completely independently. There's always a lot of speculation about Rene Chateau, and his connections with the mob. This is just what I heard; I never knew any details about it. In France, I got the feeling that at least people were involved that were not so clean; underground people. They may have gotten parts of their money illegally, but I don't know for sure. I remember that he mentioned a connection to Jean-Paul Belmondo. Well, it wasn't BREATHLESS, that's for sure. *(laughing)* – But he had supposedly some good connection to the film industry. From what I understand is that he was rather wealthy.

Siedelmann: And how do you remember him as a person?

Alvarez: I don't remember him very well, because Jack did most of the business connections with him. I was pretty much outside of that part of Hand In Hand. I would just cut my film, and that was it.

Siedelmann: Jack Deveau once said in an interview that STRICTLY FORBIDDEN is kind of a metaphor for the awakening of homosexual desires.

Alvarez: I assume that would be true. It's a little bit simple, but yeah, there is an awakening of a homosexual side that the protagonist didn't know about. The things that happen in the museum help to bring him out of the closet, so to speak.

Siedelmann: How did you experience the work with French actors and American actors?

Alvarez: *(laughing)* It was kind of crazy. The French actors were fine, and Jack spoke enough French to be able to communicate with them, so there wasn't a great barrier there. Most of the main actors were American. We brought Hugh Allen, Big Bill Eld, Thomas Jeffries, one of the actors was a steward from an airline, and he was talked into the project by Jack Deveau. There wasn't a big problem; the only conflict by that respect might have been with Francois About, because they had to communicate much more. Actually it wasn't hard to communicate with the actors: "Now you can fuck." *(laughing)* With About, Jack had to relate much more specifically

what he wanted. About had an assistant, and luckily he spoke some English; between the two of them they were able to work pretty easily with Jack on this.
Siedelmann: It's interesting, because STRICTLY FORBIDDEN was the first film directed by Jack with another cinematographer in charge.
Alvarez: Jack worked a little bit on the photography of this one. He may have been the second cameraman on some of the shots There were some shots that were not specifically related to the plot, but were little abstract pieces. I remember they were kind of surreal looking. I'm pretty sure he shot some of that stuff. About shot anything with motion, all the tracking shots, the transitional shots of statues becoming human beings. Of course that was combined with the lighting in an essential way. I don't remember, was Gene Kelton in the crew?
Siedelmann: Yes, he even was on camera, he's the museum guard.
Alvarez: Oh right, I've forgotten that. Now I remember, Gene Kelton did the make-up and the lighting. Actually it was his most outstanding job in one of our films.
Siedelmann: Did you distribute the first film directed by Jean-Etienne Siry?
Alvarez: I can't say, but I don't think we did. We were not that much interested in distributing short films unless we could make them part of a collection.
Siedelmann: Did you like POING DE FORCE; have you seen it?
Alvarez: Yeah, I did like it! It's very gruesome. The guy in it looks like someone who has been through a fire. I found it a little hard to look at sometimes... *(laughing)*, but I'm not so squeamish anymore. I can look at things much easier. But I liked it, and I still think Jean-Etienne is very creative. He's very intelligent and has a wonderful offbeat-mind. I am not a huge fan of the average porn short film, but actually I think POING DE FORCE should be shown. There's a definite twist to it, and it has a very kinky point of view. I would be interested in what happened to the film. Did you ever see his feature film UN ESCARGOT DANS LA TÊTE?
Siedelmann: No, actually I didn't have the chance, but ET... DIEU CRÉA LES HOMMES is a masterpiece!
Alvarez: I heard a lot of this film, but I've never seen it.
Siedelmann: So the end of that story is that your fruitful business connection to France stopped?
Alvarez: Well, yes. But it's an interesting story, right? It certainly has some thriller elements in it. *(laughing)* Thank god it never got violent, or too dangerous.
Siedelmann: Did you go to Paris afterwards?
Alvarez: Oh yeah, every time I have the chance I go to Paris. I love it there! To me it's the most beautiful city I've ever seen; perhaps because I went there for the first time with Jack. In many ways it was a wonderful life experience. I love Rome, I love Berlin, but Paris has this special thing in my heart, and I guess it will always be there. I know it's changing a lot, politically it's a mess, and I really feel bad about it but I just don't remember that part. So...
Siedelmann: So Jack Deveau was also very much into cooking. For you that were a great win I guess. *(laughing)*
Alvarez: Oh, you bet! I was well fed. *(laughing)*
Siedelmann: French cuisine?
Alvarez: Yes, in fact that was one of the reasons why we liked Paris so much. We always loved to eat there in several restaurants. Jack was very intrigued by the whole process of cooking. And yes, especially French cuisine! He was a big fan of Julia Child, do you know about her?
Siedelmann: Yes, because there was a movie starring Meryl Streep about Julia Child.
Alvarez: She was extremely popular here back in the day. She turned America in a new place and discovered the kitchen for the people. Because of her, Americans learned a lot about enjoying food, and the art of cooking. She was very funny as well, quite a character. That's what we liked about her.
Siedelmann: What kind of hobby did you have?
Alvarez: Well, I also like to cook, but I didn't do it when Jack was around. It was one of these things: He was so good and opinioned about it. So it was his domain, more or less. He did it all so well. And I was lazy too, I suppose. I always loved sex; I loved the theater and the cinema. I wouldn't call it a hobby, but it was really important to me: To have a relationship. The fact that I did wind up with someone like Jack is still a bit surprising for me. He just had a certain type of personality that could easily turn me off when I met him, but it didn't. It worked the other way. I decided very early on that this is what I wanted. Like many people – and like many gay people especially – I had certain fantasies what I would like as a partner and a lover. Jack wasn't those

things at all, and yet he's the one that had the strongest effect on me. Talking about hobbies and stuff like this – I would say that everything we did together was a hobby. *(laughing)* One day we built a tape recorder together, that was also one of our passions.

Siedelmann: After this episode, Moose 100 came into the company, right?

Alvarez: I guess that's correct. That's where we downsized a little bit to what we became later on. Those last few films were done much faster and in smaller scale. There's a funny thing on those films – I mean, I like them, and I certainly think Moose contributed to them to make 'em work. I just wish we had been able to continue our original plan, which was to make the industry more compatible with the regular marketed films, and so on. It became less and less interesting, less and less artistic, more and more ... I don't know, cut-throat I guess. That's the way it goes, that's the way it is. – Here's a thought I had, it has nothing to do directly with our interview: Incidentally I've been watching a TV show called FLESH AND BONE, it is aired on STARZ, one of those subscription channels. They show some interesting stuff, and I was watching this one recently. I think it's amazing! It's sexy, and it's real. It's about a girl who joins this ballet company, and the series shows kind of her coming out, in a way. It has all sorts of things that are very unusual for something on television. Except that things are changing a lot now, they have become more and more open and sexual. Almost to a point where you need just one little step more and it would be hardcore. It is very well produced anyway, and it got me trapped. *(laughing)* I've never seen something about ballet that's so gritty. It has a lot of reality in it. You believe it, this could be a real company and real situations. – As I said, the series doesn't have to do with our work, but still it illustrates where we wanted to go with Hand In Hand.

Siedelmann: One of the lesser plotted films of Hand In Hand is ROUGH TRADES, another one with Hugh Allen. What was the main idea on that one? Was it about fetishizing these hardhats?

Alvarez: Um, yeah, I think among the homosexual community there tends to be a certain share of that romanticizing and making anything like that to a very masculine fetish. All kinds of situations with plumbers, construction workers, telephone repairmen – there's a lot of eroticism in that fetish; lots of tension for homosexual characters. Certain fantasies are pretty much part of the scene. Most of the gay people have the mentality and the emotional intelligence to know that this isn't the real world. It's still a fantasy. They love to pretend. When it comes to me, I would love to take a ballet dancer anytime. *(laughing)* – There's also just certain hotness in a guy who's riding a motorcycle, you know?

Siedelmann: Yes, and all kinds of hyper-masculinity are reflected in many gay porn movies from the golden age of porn, think of Joe Gage or Christopher Rage.

Alvarez: Yes, especially Chris Rage.

Siedelmann: So when he left Hand In Hand?

Alvarez: He had a lot of things going on as a singer, actor and as an agent. He was very intrigued by show business. He was also very horny all the time. *(laughing)* It just seemed like a natural thing for him to go on his own. He took enormous chances; a lot of his subjects were heavy duty for most people. But there also was a group of people that appreciated his work very much. I think he always was a true artist. Tom De Simone, for instance, once said that Christopher Rage was the closest one of us to being an artist. I think his movies are fascinating, but I also find them hard to look at. There always comes a point in my head where the eroticism of his films turns off. The grossness of it becomes too much for me to see it as a real experience. I mean if someone shits in another guy's mouth, that doesn't turn me on.

Siedelmann: Wow, this kind of stuff also happens in his movies?

Alvarez: Well, it's not the real thing, but the assimilated version of it. It's enough to make me think it's real.

Siedelmann: Were you surprised to see how heavy these films are?

Alvarez: Not really surprised, no. I mean, I'm always waiting for the next step; the next daring move, so to speak. The films of Chris Rage certainly fit in that category. But I also think sometimes it maybe is creative, but also could be exploitative. Not unethical, but too sensational for its own sake. I think sometimes there are no real connections with anything, sometimes it's just sensationalism. How can I shock them most? Sometimes I feel that, and I feel that's not art to me. But it could be my own limitation, too. I mean, I don't necessarily want to go into that, because I'm afraid, or perhaps it simply turns off what I think is sexual and sensual. I think I'm somewhat of a romantic. I like ballet, I like dancers. I also like rough looking guys, but they have to have some sensitive side to them as

well. I'm not trying to be critical, I'm just saying what he was - Christopher Rage was always like: Fuck romance! - The more shocking, the better.
Siedelmann: At least his last film was titled FUCKED UP.
Alvarez: I've seen that one. There is a reality to FUCKED UP, that's why it's really hard to take. The man in the movie is Casey Donovan, the lead man from BOYS IN THE SAND. And if you look deeply in his eyes, you can see it. I mean, he was always very sexual, a beautiful man. He was the whole thing. He was always ready to go, very open to everything. That's one of the things I really liked about him, but as the years went by it went darker. Later on his enjoyment was more into taking more risks. Down and dirty sex, kind of the same philosophy that Chris Rage had about all this: as shocking as possible. Casey became like that, and during that time he became HIV-positive. At the same time he went deeper into drugs, and deeper in being abused sexually. His real life certainly wasn't everybody's real life. It's a very sad movie, because Casey looks fucked up indeed. There's nothing sexy about him anymore. He's given in to life's mess and tragedy. Casey probably knew he was going to die. This was his way of striking back, I think.
Siedelmann: Wakefield Poole called the movie "The Burning of an Icon."
Alvarez: Yes, that's very true.
Siedelmann: But was that always the personality of Christopher Rage, was he a dark character?
Alvarez: Not in the beginning. At first he was typically Broadway-hopeful. He was very involved in that, and very close to Ellen Greene; he became her manager for a while. At some point he realized that he himself was interested in performing and developing a career out of that. In fact, he knew some real talented people, many directors in the business. For some reason he took another road. He chose the dark side.
Siedelmann: Did you stay in touch with him?
Alvarez: I saw him periodically. I remember one day I went to his apartment, when he already was dying from AIDS. He showed me his films; he gave me the whole library. Actually I never became a close friend of his. I mean, during Hand In Hand, he was a different kind of person. I always admired him in that era. He was very lively and aggressive. Not in a bad way, more like: Hey, let's go, we'll get this done! – A very energetic young man. When he went on to do his thing I didn't dislike him for that. That was part what I liked about him: He took chances, he wasn't like anybody else. Just his personal choices, sexually and privately, were not my cup of tea.
Siedelmann: At one point you started to shoot the Hand In Hand films back to back, so two movies in a row.
Alvarez: I think it was closely after the French episode that we realized we had to change our method of producing these films. We needed to change the way they were made, so we did our best to cut down. We did them faster, more simply. That was the time we got hooked up with the owner of the Adonis. His name was Nick Justin. He was another closeted film fanatic. He even worked for Mike Todd – who was married to Liz Taylor - earlier in his life. Todd died in a plane crash, but he produced some much admired work in Hollywood. I guess that's when Nick Justin got the knowledge about running a theater. He also was fascinated by Jack and his personality. He made a deal with Jack to put up a certain amount of money to make a film as long as he would get the release rights on it. He was guaranteed to make the first amount of profit. It was a business deal. Nick Justin used to laugh at us because we took so much time and paying with films like DRIVE. We spent more money than we should have, because we desperately wanted to make real movies. *(laughing)* At one point the industry got bigger and bigger, and it became a necessity to make two films instead of one in the same amount of time. That's when we started with films like ROUGH TRADES and SEX MAGIC. Well, A NIGHT AT THE ADONIS kind of stands on its own. JUST BLONDS, DUNE BUDDIES, FIRE ISLAND FEVER and all those films don't have the same meaning to me as our early ambitious ones. Those films were our way to stay in business, same with the short pieces like IN HEAT or PRIVATE COLLECTION. We still didn't make a huge amount of money on these films. The saving grace of them is that they all lasted, because the audiences that we got were a little bit more sophisticated than the usual. Throughout the years they understood better what we were trying to do. For that reason there's also the fact that we held on to the original films for a very long time, until I decided to sell to Steve Toushin of Bijou. So our material is always available, which is important for me.
Siedelmann: At the time the movies were shown theatrically, Nick Justin was your most important business partner, correct?

Alvarez: Jack and Justin were working very close businesswise; I would almost call it a friendship. We all think he was gay, but he was definitely closeted. He was a Greek man, I don't know if he had to be in the closet because of his family. Or maybe he was because he worked in the film business, and had to be seen as a heterosexual man. Nevertheless he liked Jack a lot, and had a lot in common with him. They would go out to dinner occasionally, and do things. Actually he was more than just a business contact. He was more enthusiastic than other theater owners. I mean, he also was always interested in making money, that's for sure. But he would pretty much do what we wanted to do as long as it came in under certain requirements.

Siedelmann: Did he organize events for the movies?

Alvarez: Yes, he did. We had some great openings in the Adonis, because at the time it was kind of a show palace for gay films. It was a big theater, it had a long history. It was once owned by one of the big Broadway producers in the past. Nick Justin had kind of taken it when it was for sale. More or less he fixed it up, did some repairs, and turned it into a gay movie palace. He liked the whole glitter of the film business, so he tried as much as possible to repeat that glamour in the gay world. That's why he liked the fact that Jack Deveau was more ambitious than most of the people from the adult film business. He never took credit for being a producer of one of our films, but he did put money into the films. There was a good deal between him and Hand In Hand where he would be guaranteed a certain amount of money from the first run of the movie. Wewould get our percentage collected when the movie would start making a profit. Then from any future showings of it, plus we made money through renting the films to other venues. That combination seemed to work for us the best. But of course the owners of the theaters were the ones that made the real money out of the films. Nick Justin in New York, Steve Toushin in Chicago. Shan Sayles in Los Angeles and San Francisco; he was the one who started the whole thing. He was the first theater owner who decided to make his own films for the upcoming adult film industry. It's an interesting point by itself: people like Shan Sayles, and especially producers from the film and show business: That's their whole world. Once that leaves, they are left without any resources to do something else. They are so used to the whole mentality and lifestyle of the business, because all the years everything went on along making movies. I think that's Shan: He truly did love movies. Not just gay films, he always invited people to his house over the weekend, and he would rent 16mm versions of popular and classical movies that were made in the 40s and 50s. He just liked to show them to people. *(laughing)* So he was very tied into the whole business. He started out very young. He worked in several positions in Hollywood; he was hired for small jobs by the huge studios. But he knew what he wanted, and he went for it. I guess Shan Sayles thinks of himself as the CITIZEN KANE character, because it's pretty much like that. He made his money; he was on the top of the heap in his specialty. He bought himself fancy homes, and now at the end of his life he was pretty much alone. He wasn't like Jack Deveau.

Peter DeRome and his Erotic

by Peter Argus

Peter De Rome is an expatriate Englishman who chose New York City as his base some years ago and began making movies. One of his best known works is undoubtedly ADAM & YVES, made in Paris and for a long time very popular at New York gay movie houses. But Peter's first success was with a series of eight short movies entitled THE EROTIC FILMS OF PETER DE ROME, blown up from 8mm to 16 for release in commercial theatres. ADAM & YVES was a fully produced feature and it's just been joined by a second which will be on view in New York this autumn – THE DESTROYING ANGEL. Believe it or not, it's about a mushroom...

Filming began for Peter when he purchased an 8mm camera "just for fun, having seen an ad in a movie magazine." He began experimenting, almost at once, making little story movies rather than "baby in the garden type of thing" and found himself really enjoying it. Before long he was working at getting little bits of nudity through the film developers. "I'd shoot a bit of skin – say myself stark naked in front of a mirror – and send it off to Kodak, waiting tremulously until it got back!" He smiles at those early days. "Touch wood it always came back. Over a period of ten years I only lost two or three sequences because they could only spot-check film." Do they still do it? "No, I think they've finally given up. Since the US Supreme Court declared that it was not illegal to have pornographic films at home, they quickly decided not to bother." How does he describe his movies? Does he call them pornographic himself? "I don't mind what they're called. Basically they're gay sex movies – but then you see you get into all that boring categorization of whether it's soft-core or hard-core. Now of course all the films we make in the US have to be hard-core because people won't accept anything else. Hard-core literally means hard cock and action. Now of course it's getting into pretty advanced forms of sex – S&M, fist-fucking and so on. I'm *not* really intrigued with all that – my feeling is for eroticism. And that for me is 'leading up to the sex.' Once you're at the sex stage it can quickly get terribly boring. For me, again, a lot of the arousal is in the mind and the imagination. That is what really turns me on. Most of my ideas, therefore, are concerned with how we get there."

So for him movies must be titillating and exciting? "Absolutely," he agrees, "Movies that start off with sex in the first minute are, to me, a failure. That was brought home to me at the 1971 Wet Dream Festival in Amsterdam, to which I sent some films. Most of the films presented there were straight and all sex. You know, they put me to sleep in five minutes most of them. Because, let's face it, straightforward sex is pretty limited. It's either anal, or

MOVIES

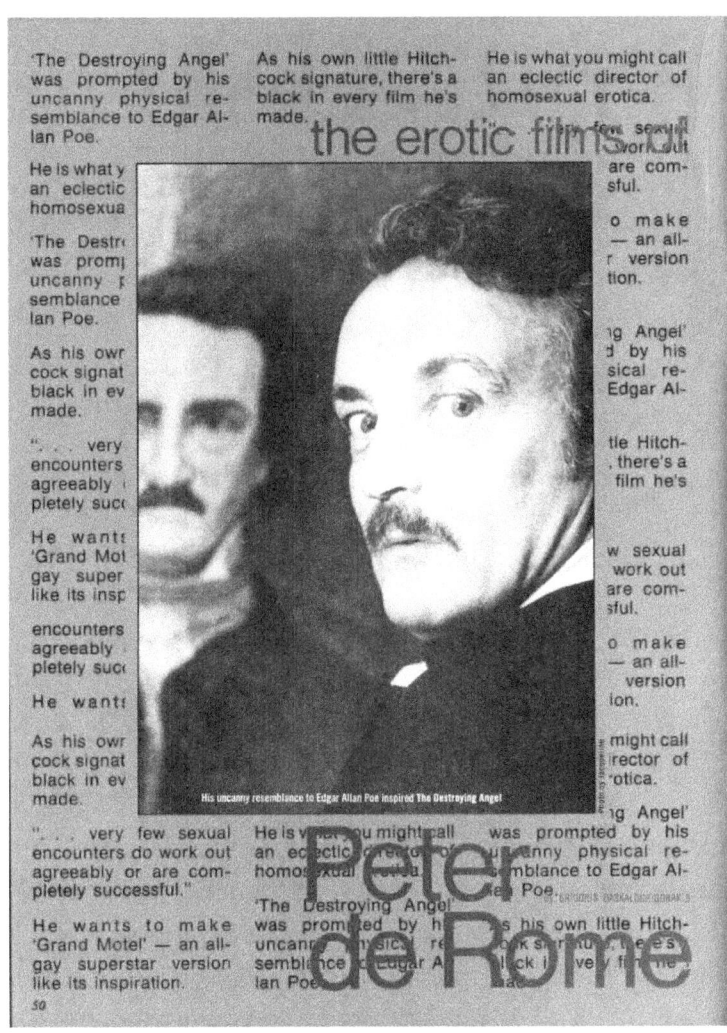

oral, or sado-masochistic. For me shooting sex scenes is getting more and more difficult, and I find it a great challenge to make it exciting, *really* exciting. You get much more demanding of yourself. Of course, as one gets more professional and you have a crew with you, that tends to make the atmosphere chilly. So you strive for a controlled but vital spontaneity. You hope that the actors will get carried away – but that in itself poses problems when you have to get in really close. What about the challenges of the new movie? "Well, THE DESTROYING ANGEL is actually the name of a poisonous mushroom, with hallucinogenic properties. The story concerns a boy who has an alter ego and at one time he has sex with his alter ego. No, it's not mirror sex, it's a double with a very similar body cut to look as though it is himself. It's a complicated story – a sex film with a strong storyline to do with the supernatural, loosely based on a story by Edgar Allan Poe. There's about eight people in the cast and it's color and synch-sound with original music. It's about the most advanced film the company – it's called Hand In Hand – has made so far. We distribute about thirty gay features. Public show in the States is restricted to about twenty-five cities, but straight porn shows absolutely *everywhere* in America – college campuses, everywhere. It's really high time they changed the law in England – it's getting beyond a joke. And I don't know why they still try such cases by jury – it's avoiding the question."

Does he usually do the camera work too? "Not all the time. As a matter of fact I was so busy directing the last one my producer, Jack Deveau, did the camera. But usually I do – and I also cut them as well as writing them. No one in Hollywood has that freedom of doing everything with the right of final cut too, so they're very much personal movies. Which is a great joy.

GENESIS OF THE DESTROY

by Peter De Rome

It started with the thought that gay films had been made in various forms, but that they hadn't yet tackled the horror genre. Almost at the same time came the idea to write a story about twins – one that had been lurking in the back of my mind for a long time. Then, by chance, I happened to read John Allegro's fascinating study, *The Sacred Mushroom and the Cross*, that seeks to equate Jesus Christ with a mushroom, the Amanita Muscaria. This, in turn, led me to R.G. Wasson's *Soma: Divine Mushroom of Immortality*, which traces the same mushroom to the Soma plant in the ancient Rig Veda of India. The whole incredible story seemed to me to be a natural for erotic treatment. But how to blend the two ideas together?

    I sat down at the typewriter and looked up at the painting hanging on the wall before me. It could have been a portrait of myself, except for the way he was clothed and the caption underneath: Edgar Allan Poe. Was this a sign? Maybe, but inspiration eluded me. So I went back to his stories and, sure enough, there was the answer. William Wilson provided just the sort of structure I was looking for with one important change: the twins became one troubled young man and his alter ego. A few scenes in the film are direct parallels to the story, but mostly only the structure is retained. And then, because of the religious aspect of the mushroom story, it seemed logical to make the principle character a young priest, sorely tempted beyond his means to resist. The urination scene derives from the hypothesis that the sacred plant called the Soma in the Vedic culture was, in fact, a hallucinogenic mushroom, a plant with miraculous inebriating virtue, enjoyed both by the peoples of the Valley of the Indus and the cattle they tended. The juice of the Soma had a similar intoxicating effect on the animals, and is excreted still in its purest form in the urine, only to be ingested once more by the peasants. This way they could stay high for days! Small wonder that the sun became a compelling metaphor for the gleaming red-topped mushroom, and the urine its golden rays.

ing Angel

Pass on me the flowing Soma
Divine Inebriant – Holy Water
Urinate your juices on me
Fruit of my esoteric dreams
Hari Krishna – Flaming Fungus
Spill yourself onto the belly of Indra
Penetrate my entrails, enter into my heart
O Soma juice, light of the sun.

Peter De Rome

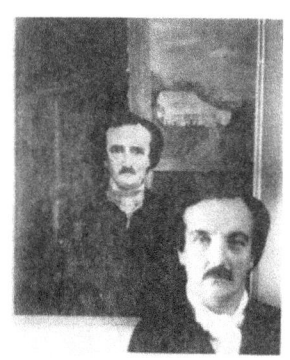

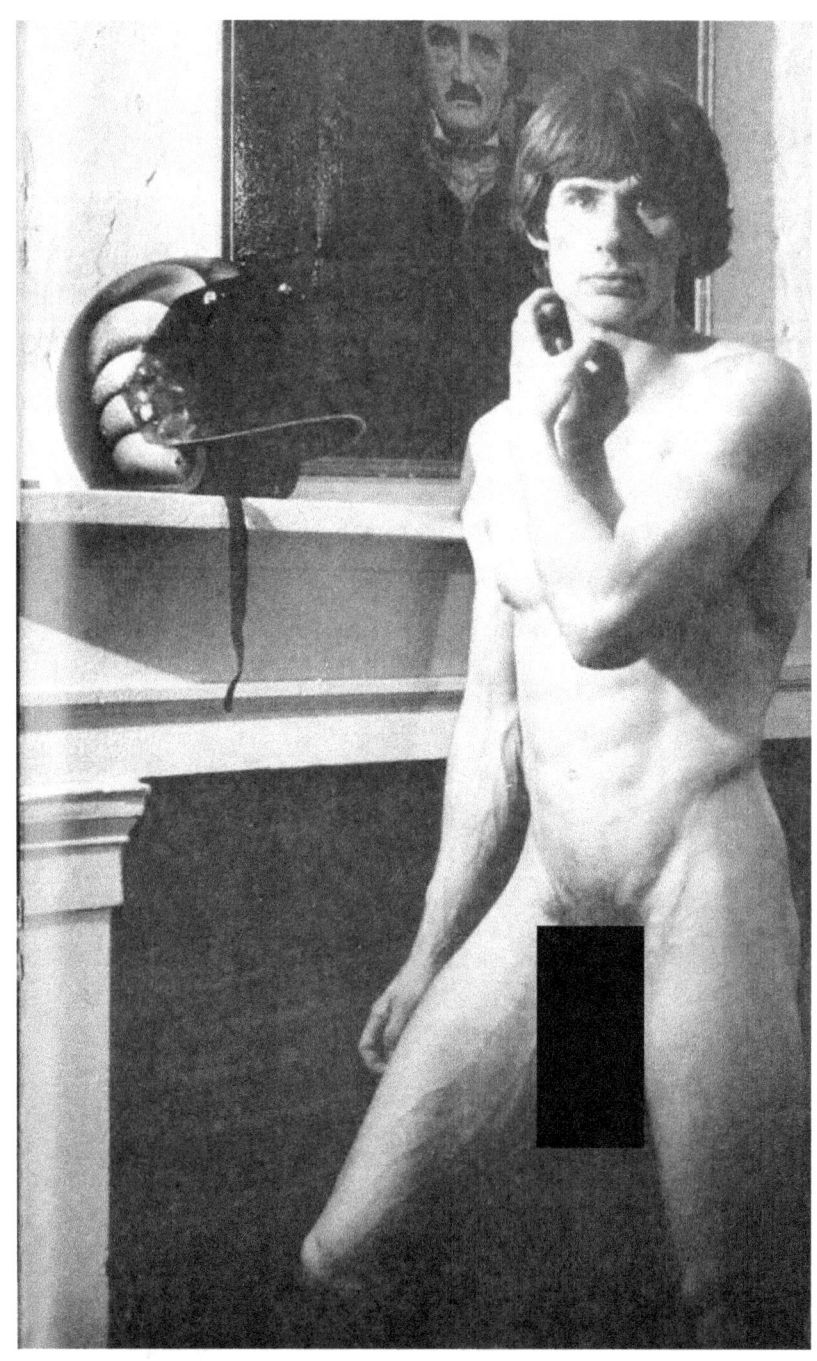

"Jack Deveau was one of the true and few artists in this business. He was a great man ... a good friend."

BIG BILL ELD (Still from *The Destroying Angel*)

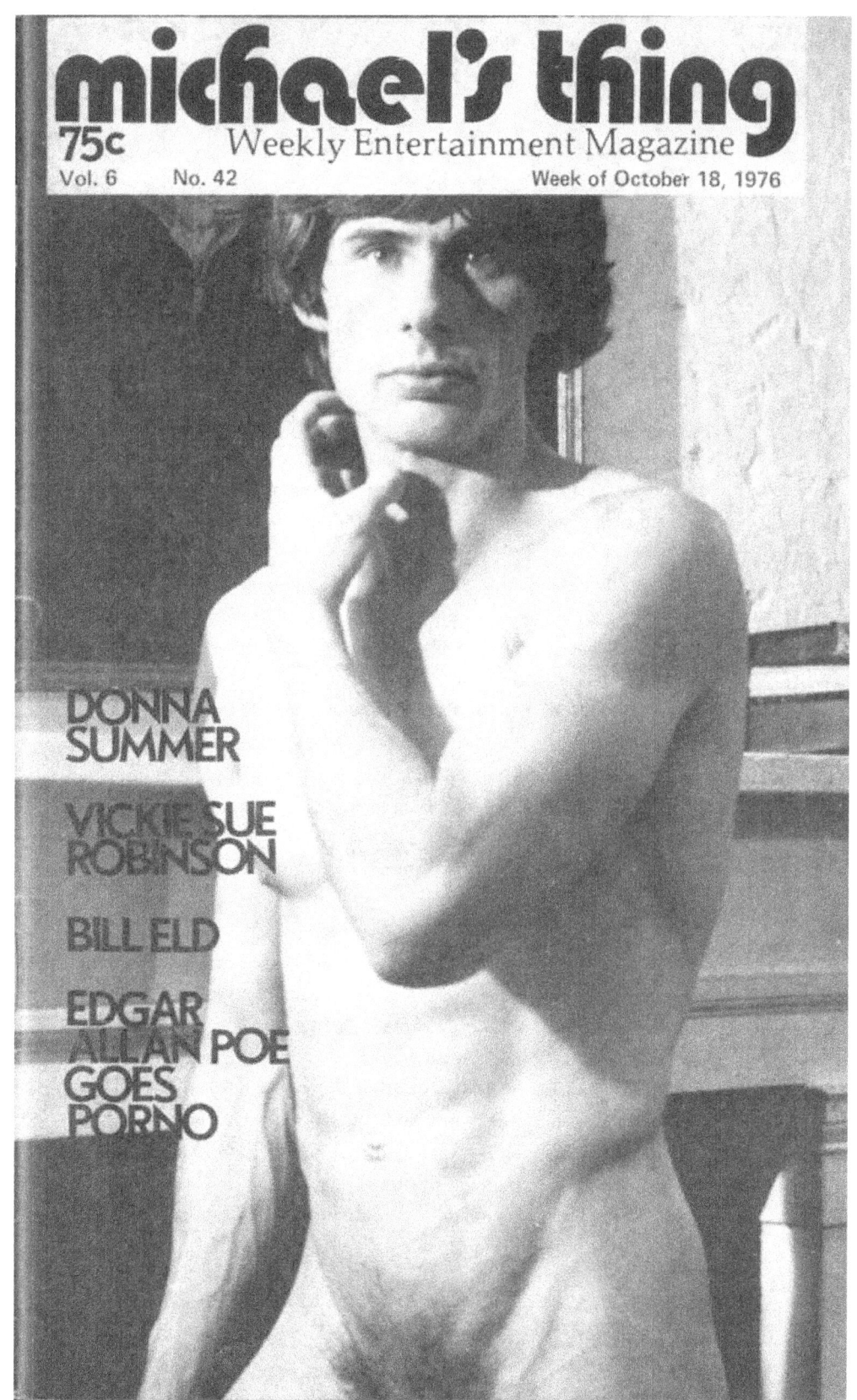

PRESS REVIEWS 4

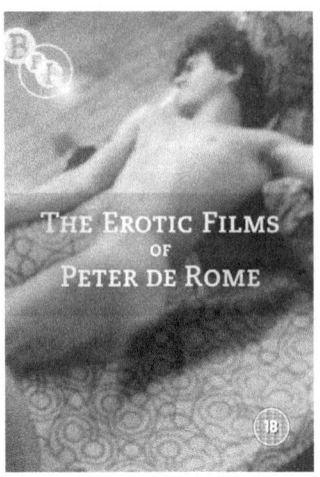

The eight films that make up THE EROTIC FILMS OF PETER DE ROME were filmed in Paris, London, Malaga, Marbella, and New York by an artist with a fine discriminating eye for the magic of place. The interweaving images of magical places give warmth to chasings and cruising filled with psychological excitement of symbolic threat and just plain realistic horniness. From a sacrificial crucifixion in Spain that turns into an orgasm to a blow job on the subway, the art of Peter De Rome is sensational and yet sensitive. The first short film, DOUBLE EXPOSURE, is a spiraling structured glimpse at the other side of reality. Its delicate, graceful balance is an almost perfect underscoring of a strange moment in the twilight zone. The camera work is itself a ballet and the editing is a musical tune of an unknown eerie time. What spirals in to a lovely little idea slowly crawls up your spine and unwinds again leaving you with an unexplained tingle. The second film, HOT PANTS, was shot with the kind of simplicity that demands much skill and precision. THE SECOND COMING is filled with beautiful compositions of Spanish alleys. DAYDREAMS FROM A CROSSTOWN BUS has a prize-winning student film look. MUMBO JUMBO also has a student film look but is hilariously weird. GREEN THOUGHTS returns you for a few moments to Eden.

UNDERGROUND is one of those sensational ideas that filmmakers only talk about and never do. UNDERGROUND is more than just the realization of the sensational fantasy on film, however. It works not only as gimmick but also in terms of great character and story development. A blow job on the subway is hard enough to pull off but Peter De Rome has captured the entire encounter as it would actually happen between two real human beings with real nervousness, horniness, and sensitivity pent up inside of them. It is great theatre and worth the entire show. The last film, PROMETHEUS, I must admit is beyond my grasp but it felt right. Perhaps it was the modern camera style that doesn't fit with the classic story as told by De Rome, I don't know. Something didn't fit and maybe it was me. Robert Rikas makes a wonderful masochistic Prometheus and seemed to understand the role as De Rome plotted it. You may like watching what is done to him.

*David Minton, *In Touch*

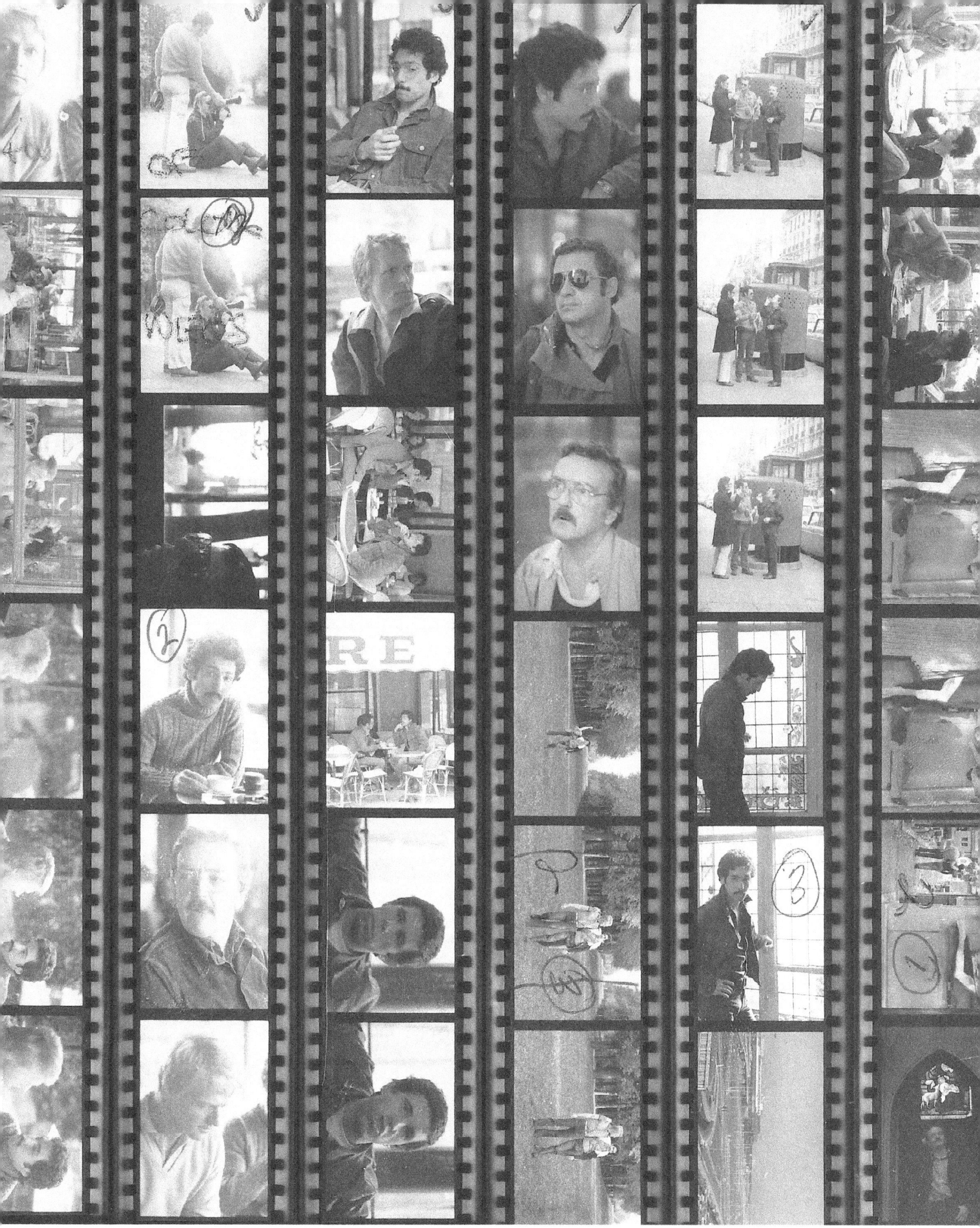

The Making Of *Adam & Yves* (Negatives lost)

To a generation of viewers raised on William Higgins, Matt Sterling, and the endless list of their imitators, the work of Peter De Rome often seems lacking in sexual fireworks: penetration always subservient to thematic and stylistic priorities. THE EROTIC FILMS OF PETER DE ROME, a collection of eight short films, which ranged in date of execution from 1969 to 1984, offers the best introduction to the world of this director – and hopefully it will inspire a generation of youthful viewers to rediscover the value of sex in a rich and multilayered context. Intended only for private circulation, the first two entries – DOUBLE EXPOSURE and HOT PANTS – are by today's standards soft-core. The first contains only nudity, with no sex at all, while the second incorporates masturbation with the usual money shot. Their purpose is less to offer fodder for the J.O. crowd than to tease the libido into achieving satisfaction elsewhere – and, of course, to serve as records of the sexual sensibility of the late Sixties and early Seventies. THE SECOND COMING, which ranges in locale from London and Paris to Malaga in Spain, centers on the quest for a statue of the crucified Christ that has the miraculous ability to get an erection and ejaculate. More than an irreverent satire, its purpose is to redeem traditional Christianity from its absurdly anti-sexual stance.

DAYDREAMS, which focuses on the sexual fantasies of a young man as he rides a cross-town Manhattan bus, includes the usual menu of sexual activity, oral and anal, but in such fragmented and nontraditional frames that most viewers will be hard put to find a focus for fantasies of their own. But the stream-of-consciousness style reveals the arbitrary and obsessive nature of sexual fantasizing with more imagination and psychological truth than any later exploration of the same theme by more explicit directors. MUMBO JUMBO satirizes the slogan-crazed world of advertising, with intercuts of male nudity amid the many references to contemporary ad campaigns. Though it provokes more laughter than lust, its revelation of the homosexual subtext to Madison Avenue's ostensibly "middle American" view of reality rings compellingly true. GREEN THOUGHTS includes masturbation in its satire of the "back-to-nature" and "save the environment" movements among young people of the Seventies. Since neither movement has yet run its course, the satire remains as striking today as when the film was first made. Undoubtedly the most daring and risk-taking of the collection is UNDERGROUND, which was actually filmed on the New York City subway system at late hours when the trains were near empty. Two unidentified actors cruise each other and then actually fuck as the train winds its way through the underground of New York. The title refers, of course, not only to the subway, but to an entire way of life buried beneath the city's veneer of civilization. The spotty, often wavering camerawork adds to the overall effect of this classic achievement – guerrilla filmmaking at its most daring and dangerous.

UNDERGROUND may well be the ultimate tribute to the sexual revolution in general and to gay liberation in specific. If you haven't seen this film, you know next to nothing about the gay adult industry. As for the eighth entry, it is perhaps the most

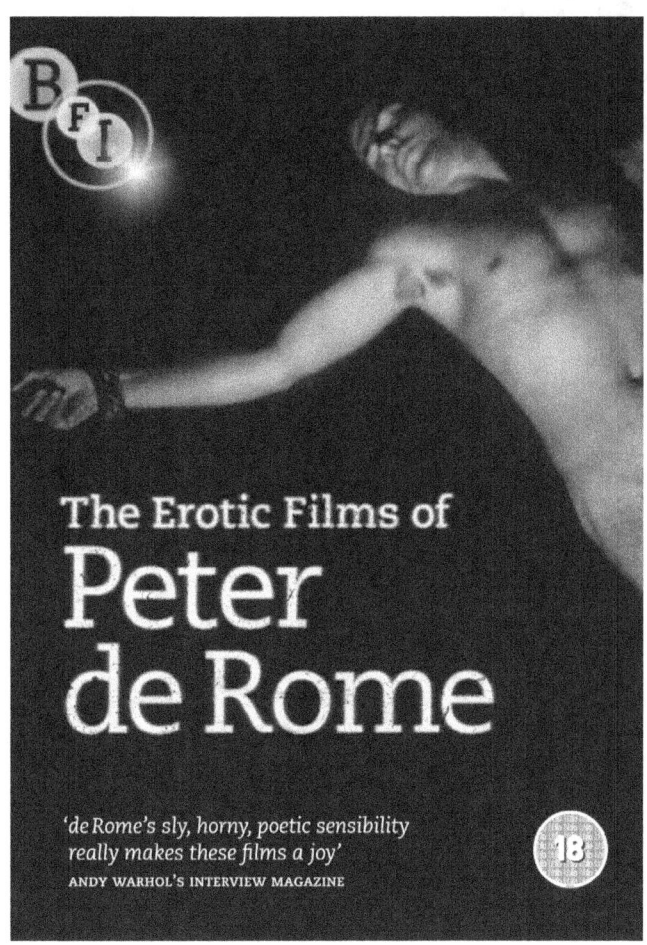

compelling exploration of bondage on film. Entitled PROMETHEUS, it combines classical mythology with contemporary sexual practices, revealing the archetypal timelessness of both. The Greek story of the hero chained to a rock as punishment for giving fire to humankind becomes an allegory of gay bondage when Prometheus is rescued by Hercules with all the elements of ritual involved in gay bondage. The gift of "fire" becomes the gift of sexual freedom and the "punishment" becomes the reward of sexual fulfillment with another man. Although the eight films were made at different periods of De Rome's evolution as a director, they are clearly unified by his overriding vision of gay sexuality as a positive expression of human nature. More than an artistic vision, De Rome's work constitutes a political manifesto of revolutionary proportions, more eloquent in style and more persuasive in argument than the rhetoric of any activist organization. Here is one of our greatest poets, Walt Whitman released from his closet, a true prophet of our age.

*S.W., *Manshots*

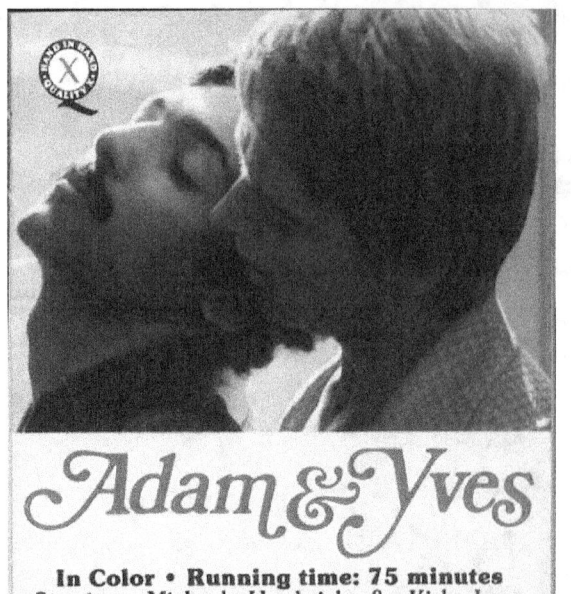

Adam & Yves

In Color • Running time: 75 minutes
Starring: Michael Hardwick & Kirk Luna
Peter de Rome's tale of of an American in Paris contains two of the hottest sequences ever requested: The Black Orgy with eight of New York's hottest black men going to it, and the Narcissus scene, which shows off all of 'Big' Bill Eld's perfect manhood. MX-001
All Male Cast • Rated XXX

There's a mystique attached to the name Peter De Rome, which may or may not be deserved. It's based simply on the viewer's particular taste or proclivities, and how well De Rome chooses to satisfy them – or not satisfy them. Be warned: ADAM & YVES is most often found playing in big city art film houses, not porn emporiums, and that is good news or bad, depending on one's point of view.

The photography and production values cannot be faulted. The camera frequently and lovingly caresses balls and buttocks, as well as Paris landmarks, but the work is trying to be Cocteau with cock, and if a hot night's J.O. session with the help of the home VCR is what you're after, this may not be the cup of tea – or glass of Pernod – for you. Both Michael Hardwick as Adam, the American tourist, and Marcus Giovanni, as the Parisian Yves, who will never tell his name (for reasons which remain forever unclear), are beautiful to look at. They also manage to remain convincingly and impressively erect through some beautifully photographed fuck episodes – including one tribute to LAST TANGO IN PARIS, which reminds us that butter is more than just the seventy-cent spread.

Other sequences move into memory and fantasy – most notably Bill Eld's classic Narcissus turn – with a variety of musical underscorings and somewhat rudimentary live sound. The chief distraction would seem to be De Rome's insistence that we follow him through endless montage shots of everything from tourist views of Notre Dame to theatre posters. There is, as well, a certain obviousness in the images chosen. For example, anyone who missed the significance of the stick of butter as lube will have his memory refreshed by several loving pans across Marlon Brando's form on the original LAST TANGO movie poster. If a person is viewing this film one quarter at a time in an arcade peep show machine, bankruptcy might well occur before orgasm.

But when orgasms come, as it were, they are copius, generous, romantic, and/or poetic, depending on the mood chosen for the particular sequence. One remembered fantasy is accompanied by a rhymed voice-over, which makes Jeff Stryker's oft-repeated "Lick them balls" pale by comparison. Another, a tearoom sequence provides several yards of black cock in full and imaginative action, while the sound track pumps out funky soul.

The actual dialogue between Adam and Yves remains obscure right up to the final farewell at the airport – the sound quality varies greatly – and the film ends with yet another montage of French countryside before the rolling of the final credits. The transfer to tape is respectable. Peter De Rome has created an art film with low-hanging balls, if the viewer has the patience to just sit back and wait for them to swing.

*J.E.,Manshots

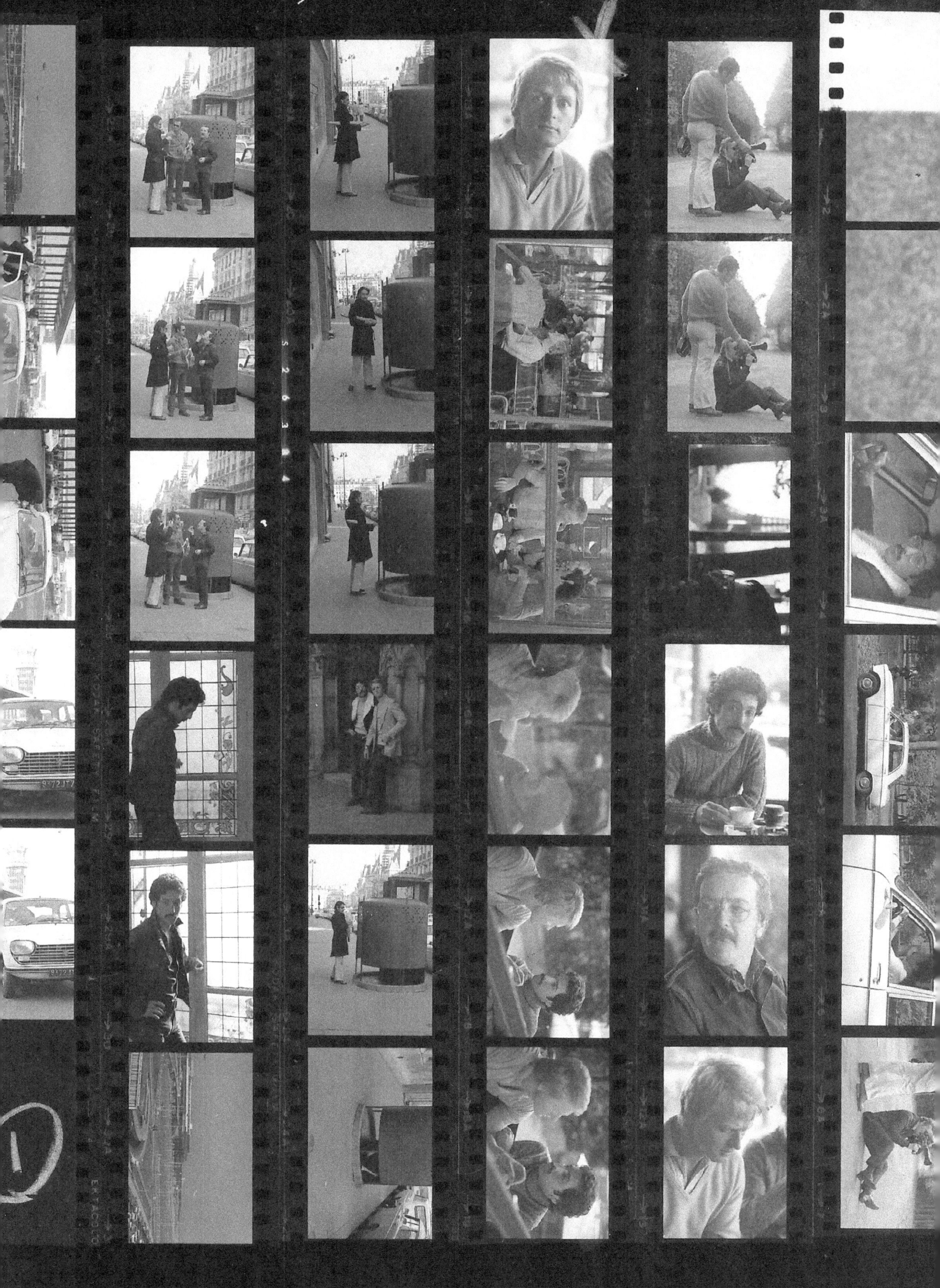

ADAM AND YVES

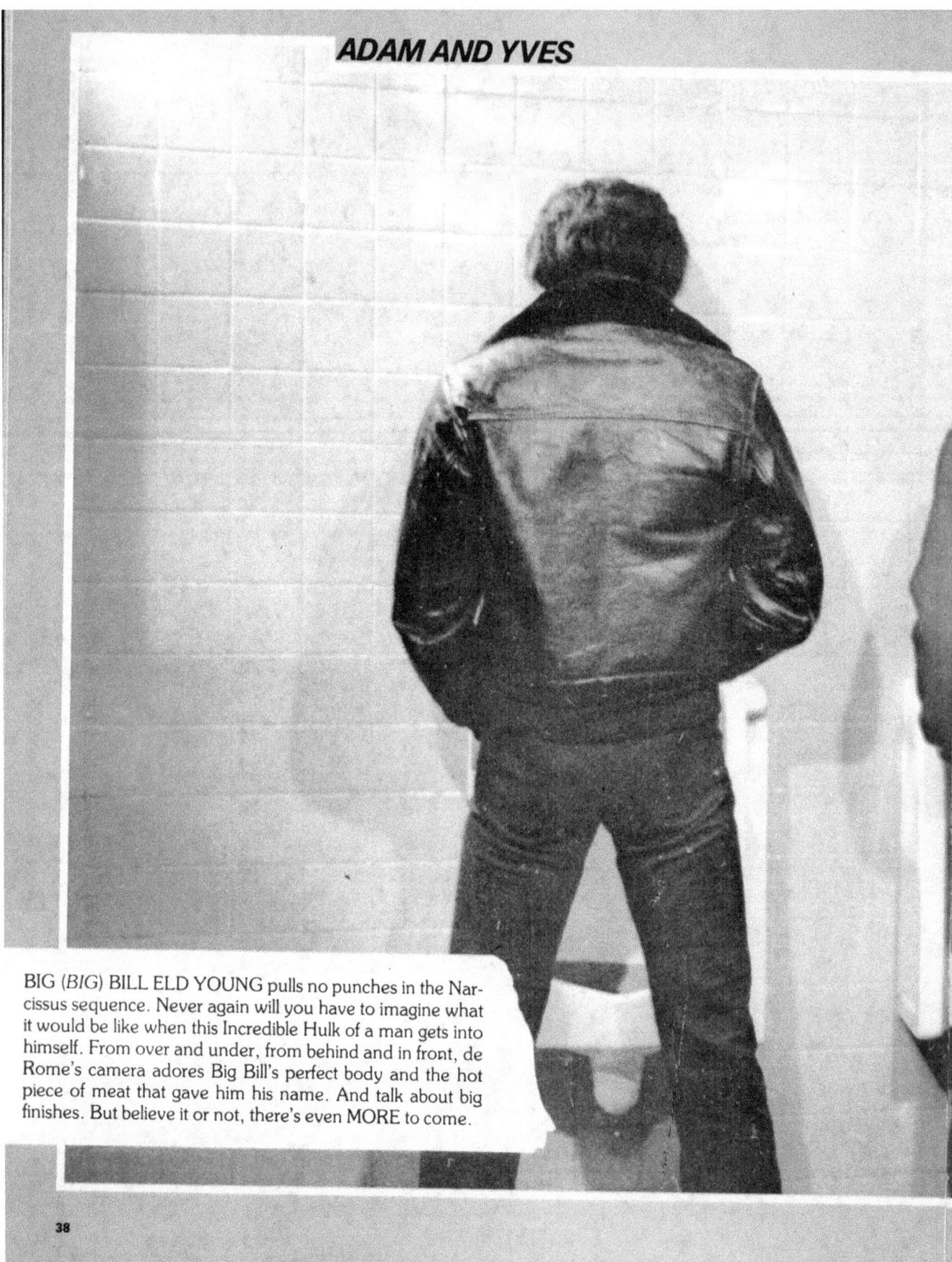

BIG (*BIG*) BILL ELD YOUNG pulls no punches in the Narcissus sequence. Never again will you have to imagine what it would be like when this Incredible Hulk of a man gets into himself. From over and under, from behind and in front, de Rome's camera adores Big Bill's perfect body and the hot piece of meat that gave him his name. And talk about big finishes. But believe it or not, there's even MORE to come.

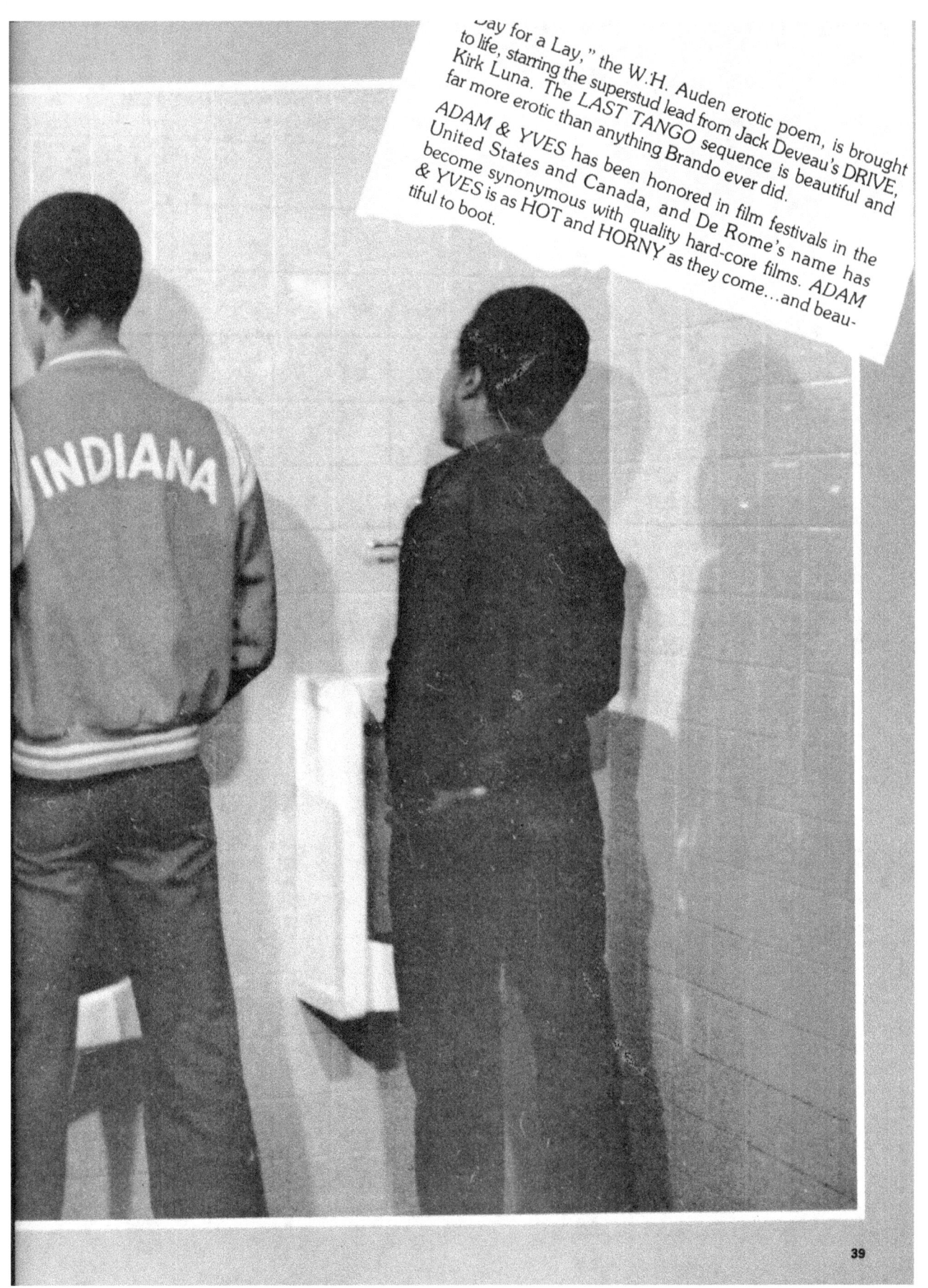

...ay for a Lay," the W.H. Auden erotic poem, is brought to life, starring the superstud lead from Jack Deveau's DRIVE, Kirk Luna. The LAST TANGO sequence is beautiful and far more erotic than anything Brando ever did. ADAM & YVES has been honored in film festivals in the United States and Canada, and De Rome's name has become synonymous with quality hard-core films. ADAM & YVES is as HOT and HORNY as they come...and beautiful to boot.

Adam & Yves

PETER DE ROME, whose first full-length feature *Adam and Yves* opens in New York shortly, entered film production in an unusual way. For ten years he had been making short erotic films in 8mm, and showing them to friends. Word of their unusual content and quality spread until invitations to a showing of Peter de Rome's films in Paris, London or New York became the hottest underground ticket in town, with international celebrities vieing with each other for a screening.

When de Rome showed just one 8-minute short at the Amsterdam Wet Dream Film Festival in 1972 he walked away with the first prize. This triggered distributor interest, and in 1973 a programme of eight shorts under the title *The Erotic Films of Peter de Rome* opened in New York to glowing notices, and has since played all over the USA.

Now *Adam and Yves*, a tale of an American in Paris, is almost ready. Described as an erotic film game in five sequences, the story concerns two young men, an American and a Frenchman, who meet in an unfurnished apartment in circumstances strangely similar to another famous recent movie made in Paris.

From then on, each of their adventures has its film counterpart, and it becomes a guessing game to discover which film they are 'playing', from a novel and startling view of Greta Garbo to the erotic extreme in black exploitation movies.

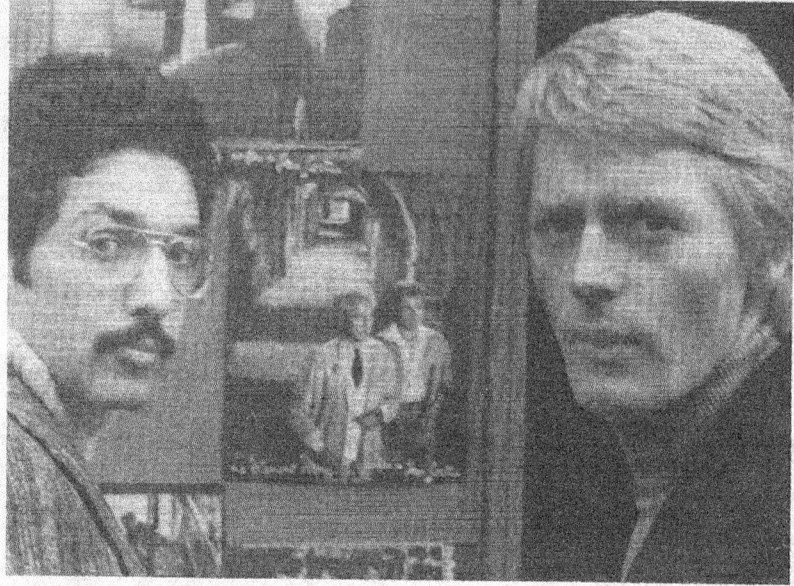

Yves (Marcus Giovanni) and Adam (Michael Hardwick) visit a cinema showing a festival of Cocteau movies

In a flashback, Adam reminisces about a certain day in New York, telling the story of his meeting with Bud (Kirk Luna) in poetry

Kirk Luna and Michael Hardwick, in the sequence entitled 'A Day for a Lay' after the poem by W H Auden

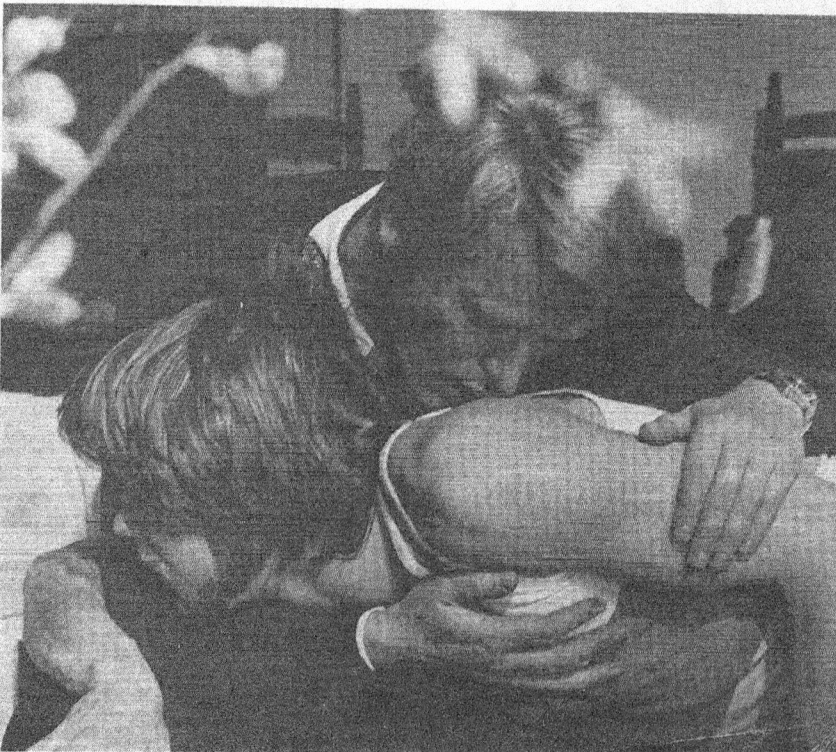

HAND IN HAND VIDEO

A DIVISION OF
Quality X Video Cassette Company
356 WEST 44TH STREET
NEW YORK, NEW YORK 10036
(212) 541-7860 Outside N.Y. (800) 223-7981

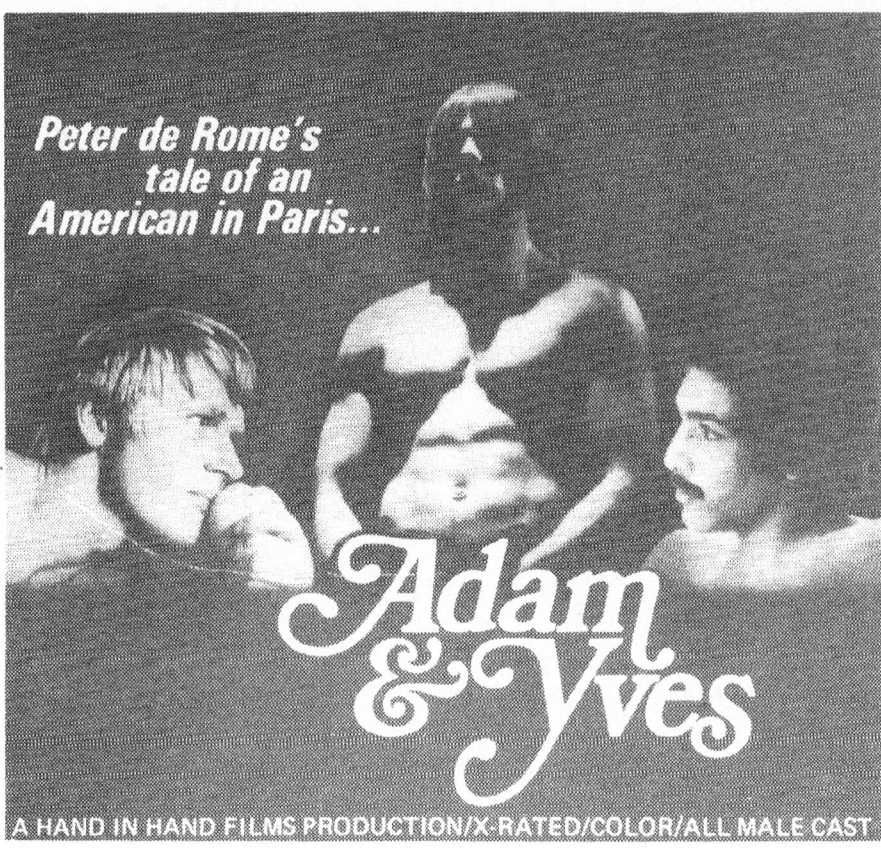

Peter de Rome's tale of an American in Paris...

Adam & Yves

A HAND IN HAND FILMS PRODUCTION/X-RATED/COLOR/ALL MALE CAST

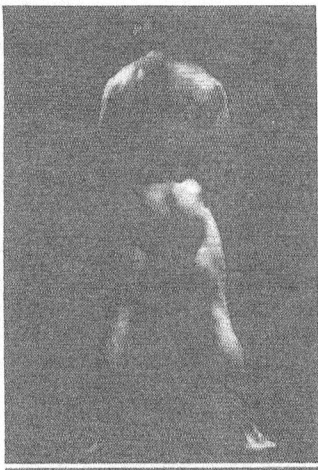

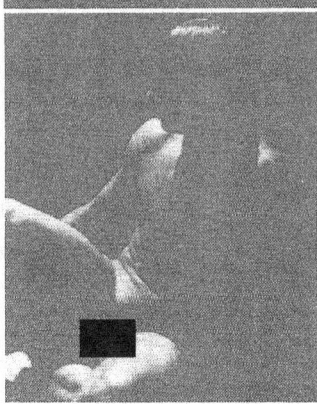

BIG BILL ELD YOUNG...There was never a better package of prime meat, and he's captures at his best.

BIG (*BIG*) BILL ELD YOUNG pulls no punches in the Narcissus sequence. Never again will you have to imagine what it would be like when this Incredible Hulk of a man gets into himself. From over and under, from behind and in front, de Rome's camera adores Big Bill's perfect body and the hot piece of meat that gave him his name. And talk about big finishes. But believe it or not, there's even MORE to come.

"Day for a Lay," the W.H. Auden erotic poem, is brought to life, starring the superstud lead from Jack Deveau's DRIVE, Kirk Luna. The *LAST TANGO* sequence is beautiful and far more erotic than anything Brando ever did.

ADAM & YVES has been honored in film festivals in the United States and Canada, and De Rome's name has become synonymous with quality hard-core films. *ADAM & YVES* is as HOT and HORNY as they come...and beautiful to boot.

Cast: Michael Hardwick, Marcus Giovanni, Kirk Luna, Bill Young, Jack Deveau, Charles Pooney, Eric Crawford, Bob Jones, Luther LeVale, Tony Skinner, Mark Connors, John Davis. Featuring GERALDO

Directed by Peter de Rome • Produced by Jack Deveau
Edited By Robert Alvarez • Music by David Earnest

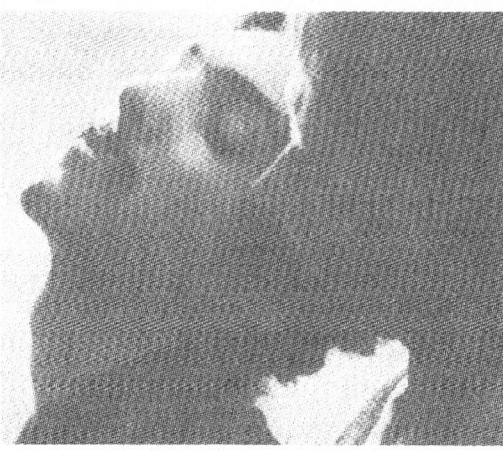

ADAM and YVES...The lovers around which the film revolves...in the LAST TANGO sequence.

StudioSound is a special process that guarantees a high fidelity like you've never heard. Instead of the usual optical transfer of sound from film to tape, which limits the reproduction of sound to a narrow range of frequencies, StudioSound is a magnetic transfer of the ORIGINAL MAGNETIC STUDIO sound tracks for the feature, transferred directly to the magnetic tape in your video cassette. This process actually gives you BETTER QUALITY than can be achieved in a cinema. For further enhancement, you can patch your video system into your stereo system and surround yourself with the excitement of these sensual sounds.

| ADAM & YVES | 75 MINUTES | COLOR | ALL-MALE CAST | StudioSound |

Sex and Drugs and Death
Peter De Rome's Destroying Angel

The second feature by artsy gay pornographer Peter De Rome is a crazed, visionary piece loosely based on an unnamed short story by Edgar Allan Poe (the story is probably William Wilson). A conflicted young seminarian called Caswell Campbell takes a three month sabbatical from his studies to explore his less Judeo-Christian impulses: casual gay sex and drugs. He picks up a callous trick at a bar and takes the man home, where Caswell gets brutally fucked. Afterwards, the man makes no bones about expressing his disappointment, and when he leaves Caswell ingests one of the red-headed mushrooms he has in his hall. There follows a vision of himself sucking built men and being pissed on.

Caswell then goes to a party, and seems to be haunted by a voice saying his name. At the party he gets off with a handsome young man, and they retire back to Caswell's for another session of intense sex and hallucinogenic mushrooms. Things are beginning to turn very strange for our protagonist, as at one point he finds himself in bed with his pick-up and a double of himself. After this, he retreats to the beach where he goes searching for some more mushrooms - directed by his double, who now seems to be his companion.

Caswell picks some 'shrooms, some red-headed and some white. He then picks up a man on the dunes and takes him home. Caswell takes one of the white 'shrooms and there follows an intense session of somewhat brutal and physically challenging sex, with the man cramming a baseball bat handle, a courgette and a banana inside Caswell. The next day, Caswell isn't looking too good, and when he consults his book of mushroom lore, he finds out why: he has ingested a deadly Amanita mushroom, also known as the Destroying Angel because of its extreme and lethal toxicity. Caswell leans that he is dying, and is sent into the grave by the laughing voice of his double. There's a final short scene, with Caswell in black priest's garb masturbating on his own newly filled-in grave.

As you can see, THE DESTROYING ANGEL isn't your usual porno. It's hallucinatory montages and fractured narrative make it a kind of avant-garde nightmare, at times reminiscent of the more Black Magic orientated works of Kenneth Anger. Gay life is depicted as driven, compulsive and brutal - anyone who thinks Cruising is a negative image better stay away from this. The film very successfully suggests a riven consciousness, torn between Christian conformism and the need to experience more intense pleasures. Consciousness is divided, with a trickster Higher Self providing kicks and death. Most of the acting is pretty amateurish, except for Tim Kent as Caswell, who manages to suggest the protagonist's inner torment both in and out of the bed.

It's only available on DVD from gay porn dealers, which is kind of a shame as it's an underground film with explicit sex rather than a porno. It's probably one of the best films out there about the altered states hallucinogenic drugs can provide. It also, in a strangely prophetic way, prefigures the AIDS epidemic, as the sick and drawn Caswell languishes and sweats in his room, dying from a mistake in his lifestyle.

*jaibo, *imdb*

Dixie Review (83-1) ✱✱✱

HAND IN HAND VIDEO

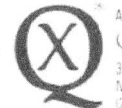

A DIVISION OF
Quality X Video Cassette Company
356 WEST 44TH STREET
NEW YORK, NEW YORK 10036
(212) 941-7860 Outside N.Y. (800) 223-7961

Peter de Rome's The Destroying Angel

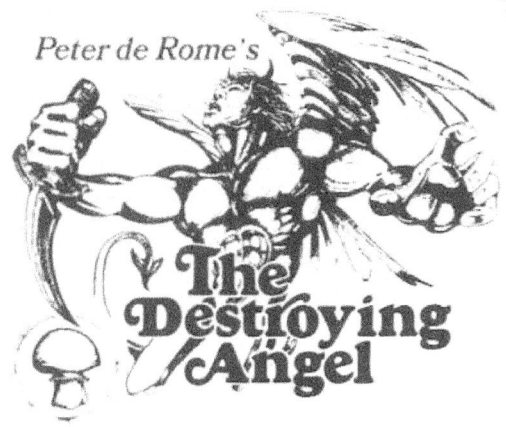

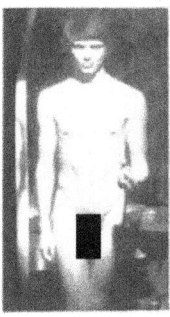
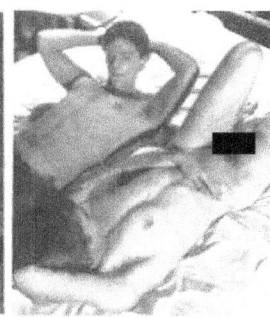

Rick Scott is the mysterious hitchhiker vision that starts Caswell Campbell on the road to the erotic and bizarre.

Tim Kent (eighth) isn't prepared for the sexual suggestions Philip Darden makes in the Gothic tale of THE DESTROYING ANGEL.

Peter de Rome works his magic again in the hauntingly beautiful story of all male sex. Caswell Campbell is a haunted young man. He is torn between the call of the cloth and the lure of the flesh. On a three month sabbatical from the seminary, his sex life has its decided problems until he is offered a mysterious mushroom. After the first bite, he is witness to a view of sex he has never known before and his whole world takes on intimate new possibilities.

Bedeviled by repeated glimpses of his alter ego, he is drawn into a nightmare world of hallucinogenic drugs and supernatural sex.

But the supply of mushrooms dries up. His craving leads to a desperate search for the Soma, magic mushroom of Vedic folklore, but when he finally finds it there is a foreign fungus among them. And in his greed and haste, Caswell is not at all prepared for the hideous fate that awaits him.

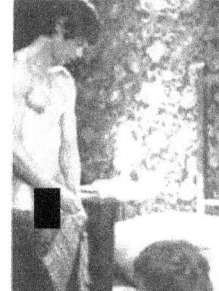
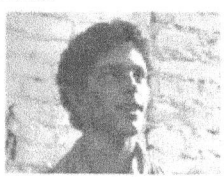

Handsome Philip Darden makes his movie debut in Peter de Rome's haunting story based upon a short story by Edgar Allan Poe.

de Rome has always been known for his unique view of sex and life and in DESTROYING ANGEL he brings together all of his remarkable abilities to present a tale that is as disturbing as it is erotic. Featuring the talents of BIG BILL ELD, DESTROYING ANGEL is de Rome's finest effort. You will thrill to the delights of the flesh that de Rome presents with his humpy cast, and will definitely be intrigued by the magic spell that de Rome casts around them. In addition to the gorgeous body and huge meat of ELD, you'll enjoy de Rome's incredible discoveries: TIM KENT, PHILIP DARDEN, PAUL EDEN, EVAN DE BRAYE, ALAIN MONCEAU, and THOM AARON.

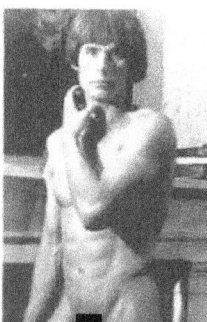

"Big" Bill Eld introduces Tim Kent to the role of sexual penitent in Tim's first of many encounters with sex and the supernatural.

THE DESTROYING ANGEL is Bill Eld's finest film. You will be amazed at the acting ability he has, nothing of his physical perfection.

The story is a moving one, but since DESTROYING ANGEL comes from HAND IN HAND, you know that sex plays a very important part in it. The sex scenes are as explicit and arousing as any you've ever seen and you will no doubt enjoy them over and over as the weird mysterious tale of the DESTROYING ANGEL unfolds before you.

Cast: Tim Kent, Bill Eld, Philip Darden, Paul Eden, Evan De Braye, Alain Monceau, Thom Aaron and Glenn Middleton, Gian Paolo Corto, Billy White, Rick Scott. Written and Directed by Peter de Rome. Based on a story by Edgar Allan Poe. Produced by Jack Deveau, Director of Photography Jack Deveau. Editor Robert Alvarez. Original Electronic Music Composed and Performed by Joe Mann.

STUDIOSOUND is a special process that guarantees a high fidelity like you've never heard. Instead of the usual optical transfer of sound from film to tape, which limits the reproduction of sound to a narrow range of frequencies, StudioSound is a magnetic transfer of the ORIGINAL MAGNETIC STUDIO sound tracks for the feature, transferred directly to the magnetic tape in your video cassette. This process actually gives you BETTER QUALITY than can be achieved in a cinema. For further enhancement, you can patch your video system into your stereo system and surround yourself with the excitement of these sensual sounds.

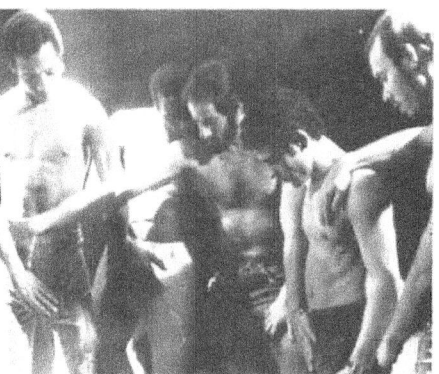

The orgy sequence in THE DESTROYING ANGEL is a "golden" opportunity for connoisseurs of the unusual.

| THE DESTROYING ANGEL | 70 MINUTES | COLOR | ALL-MALE CAST | STUDIOSOUND |

Quality X Video Cassette Company, 1982

The Devil In Mr. Campell
Peter De Rome's Destroying Angel

In the envelope-pushing "Me Decade", pornography very nearly went mainstream after DEEP THROAT played to packed houses across the country and a good many porno chic films from this "Golden Age" had decent budgets, actual plot lines, and attractive stars. One such film was THE DEVIL IN MISS JONES (1973), which was considered "thinking man's porn" due to the intelligent, *No Exit*-esque narrative wherein a virginal suicide makes a pact with the devil to come back for a few days and earn her consignment to hell ("If you have to go to hell go for a reason", the tag line urged). Peter De Rome's all-male XXX THE DESTROYING ANGEL is a gay version that re-"tool"s the Edgar Allan Poe yarn "William Wilson" into the story of Caswell Campbell, a conflicted seminary student who's given a three-month sabbatical to find himself and come back to God a stronger man. He straight-away gives in to lust and magic mushrooms which, of course, is just another way of saying "If you have to go to hell go for a reason."

Caswell literally "finds himself" being haunted by his dark side, a doppelganger he even has a threesome with in a cleverly staged scene. Despite the low budget and amateur acting, this is an expertly executed vision of a homosexual hell and it's dark theme is brought home through shadowy, seemingly candlelit mis-en-scène inter-cut with religious iconography. The last scene is a black attack on organized religion's denial of natural desires. The oil painting of Poe and his raven over the mantle in Caswell's apartment was also a nice touch.

The sex -and there's lots of it- is on the masochistic side and includes watersports, sex toys, and a cucumber. De Rome's wetdream-cum-nightmare is obviously very personal, the creation of a man with some interesting issues -which begs the question, who was this film intended for? Like Jonas Middleton's XXX THROUGH THE LOOKING GLASS (made the same year), the disturbing imagery of a phantasmagorical universe would be a guaranteed "wood-killer" for the trenchcoat crowd. It's interesting to note that all three films (MISS JONES, ANGEL, LOOKING GLASS) hypnotically chant the same mantra: heaven and hell are one and the same. Life also imitated art at the time with the LOOKING FOR MR. GOODBAR crime.

These are excellent films made pornographically and the 1970s actually might have been on to something but, alas, AIDS and the '80s killed that party -literally- and porn went back to being smut kept behind closed doors thanks to the VHS home-video boom. THE DESTROYING ANGEL deserves to be much better-known ...and not just in jerk circles.

*melvelvit-16, *imdb*

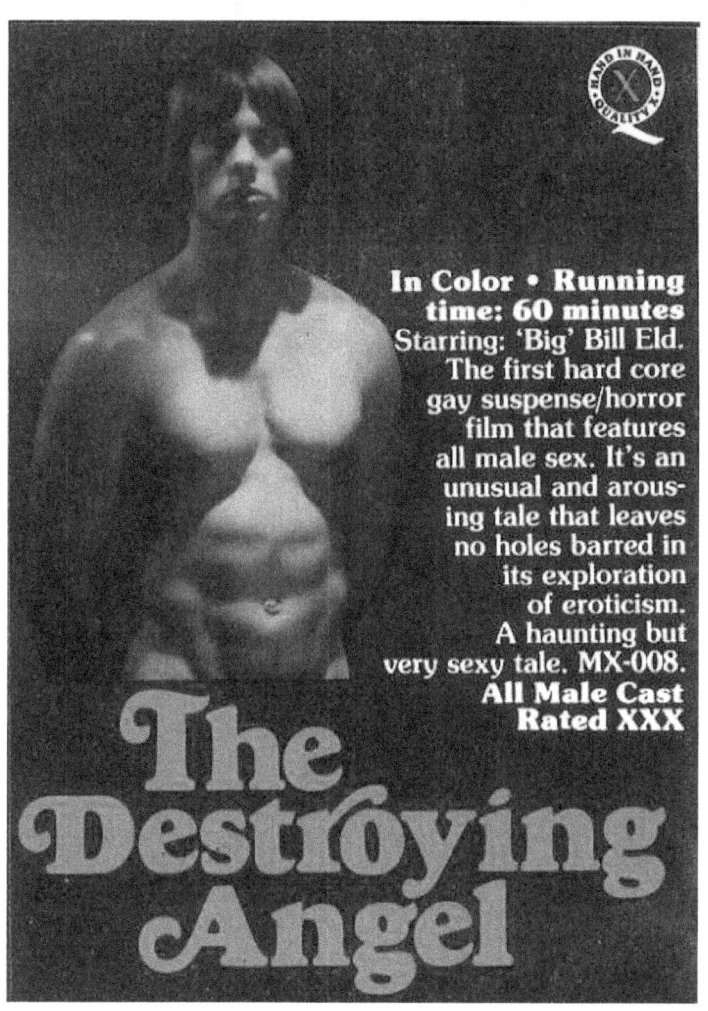

Peter De Rome brings a balanced measure of storyline, emotion, and steamy sex to the video screen in DESTROYING ANGEL, a film he completed in 1976. The story focuses on Caswell Campbell, a haunted young man torn between the call of the cloth and his own unnatural feelings pent up inside. Campbell takes a three-month sabbatical from the seminary, and plunges himself into a world of man-sex. After a bite of a mysterious mushroom, he becomes witness to a view of sex he has never known before and his whole world takes on infinite new possibilities. Bedeviled by repeated glimpses of his alter ego, Campbell finds himself drawn into a nightmare world of hallucinogenic drugs and supernatural sex. Campbell's hideous fate is a sad, albeit appropriate ending. The intensity that De Rome creates with his combination of bizarre story and spectacular sex culminates in a nerve-shattering climax of frenzied emotion. Once again Peter De Rome has managed to successfully bring together the right ingredients to produce an appealing erotic video. Though slightly dated, DESTROYING ANGEL is a spectacular feature that should really be seen even today.

*John Mensior, *Torso*

Hand In Hand Film's long-awaited release of Peter De Rome's THE DESTROYING ANGEL offers several striking surprises. The foremost being that it is probably the first hard-core porno flick, gay or straight, where the sex scenes are an integral part of the action and necessary to clarify the plot. The plot, of course, is based on "William Wilson," an Edgar Allan Poe story that De Rome has adapted to suit his purposes. It was a bold attempt on De Rome's part, but he has pulled it off. THE DESTROYING ANGEL has a compact script and is dizzyingly complex. As Caswell Campbell (Tim Kent), the haunted hero, hallucinates the screen vibrates with erotic images of earlier, as well as present and future occurrences. Reality and fantasy intermix to produce a supernatural continuance. One moment the mirror faithfully reflects an image, and the next moment it offers Campbell a glimpse of his psyche. There are several sexually explosive sequences that De Rome fulfills to perfection. One if the "golden shower" scene. He turns what is basically a touchy subject into an almost balletic statement. It's almost over before you realize what is happening. De Rome believes in easing the viewer into a situation, but once he has them there he pulls out all visual stops. In another scene he shows a ménage a tois where two of the three participants are the same person. Great grandpa Freud would be smiling up at the screen were he still with us. As with people who are haunted and live by inner visions, out protagonist is eventually done in by mistaken identity. If you don't know what you want, you never know what you'll end up with. In the case of THE DESTROYING ANGEL, the end is bizarre destruction and death. Technically the film is superior to De Rome's other works (THE EROTIC FILMS OF PETER DE ROME and ADAM & YVES). His interest in erotica goes beyond voyeurism, and his perceptions into man's sensual nature are those of an artist. The cast is virile and handsome, and the film is one of the best acted pornos in a long time. De Rome uses Tim Kent, Philip Darden and Bill (Eld) Young to their full advantage. Their roles are not necessarily easy because of the constant play with actuality and invention. If you're looking for a good film THE DESTROYING ANGEL is highly recommended. The fact that it's hot and heavy at times should only serve to heighten your enjoyment and involvement with it. After all, anything "X" rated and all-male deserves whatever attention you can give it.

*Frank Schmitt, *Michael's Thing*

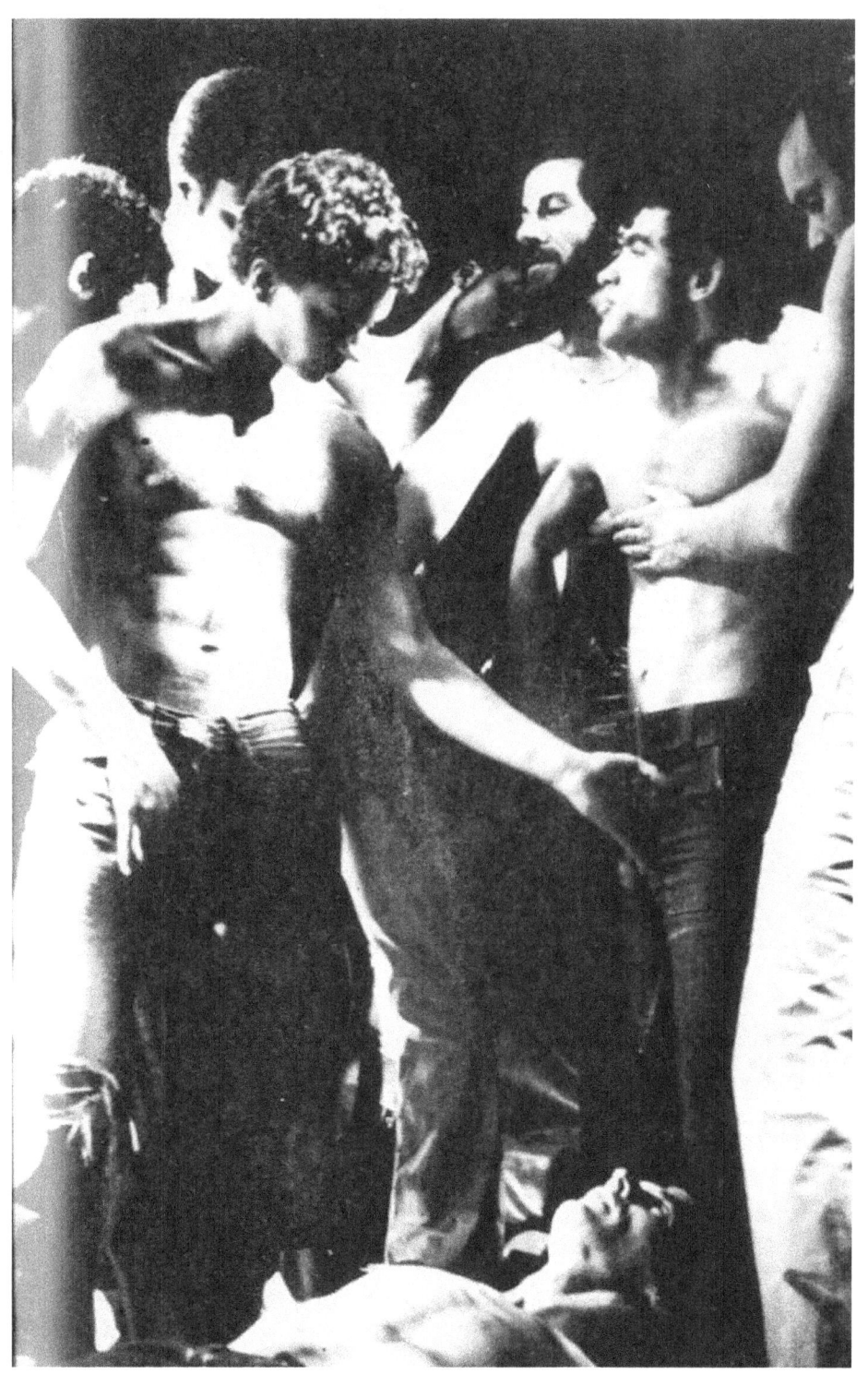

The controversial golden shower / orgasm scene in *The Destroying Angel*

PETER DE ROME
Grandfather of Gay Porn

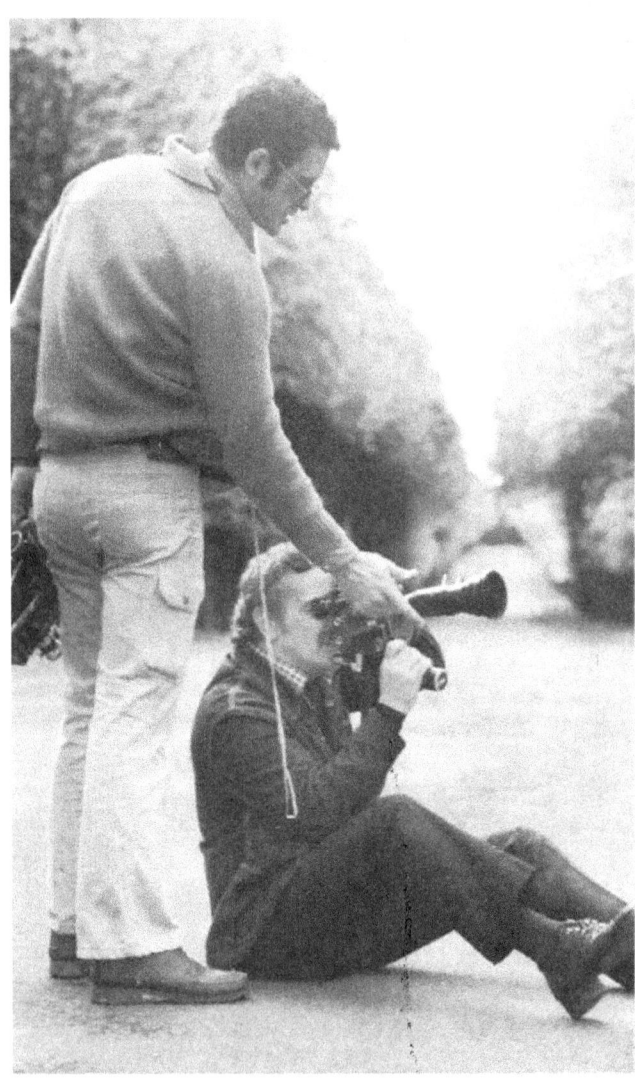

Peter De Rome is an auteur among gay porn filmmakers. Many of the original EROTIC FILMS OF PETER DE ROME are little sexual conundrums painstakingly crafted and originally made for the amusement of friends who urged him to have them blown up and made commercially available. He is what you might call an aclectic director of homosexual erotica. His 30-odd-short films are in fact an amalgamation of bits and pieces of his life and the tangents he's gone off on. In one of them he has captured a vivid picture of the Garden District of New Orleans in the early '60s, which almost teems with repressed eroticism. Of these small gems, some consider UNDERGROUND his masterpiece. The film takes off from one of those fantasies that everyone must have had sometime in New York, in which you actually consummate a sex act on a subway train.

In his cozy apartment near Sutton Place, where he's lived for 20 years, he is firmly ensconced in one of New York's poshest neighborhoods – thanks to rent control – and lives just around the corner from Greta Garbo. Garbo even makes a brief appearance in ADAM & YVES when Adam, in a mutual sharing of personal experiences, tells Yves, a new French playmate he's found in Paris, about how he once saw Greta Garbo in the street. By incorporating things from his own life in this way, Peter De Rome addsa a sense of self to his films that's unique. ADAM & YVES is full of affectionate hommages to Bertolucci (LAST TANGO IN PARIS), W.H. Auden (A DAY FOR A LAY) and Cocteau (BLOOD OF A POET). In his film THE DESTROYING ANGEL, he plumbed the complex duplicities of a sexual Doppelganger, a lapsed priest who is haunted by his debauched alter ego in an almost reversed Dorian Gray.

Sitting with him in his quaint (unheated) pad, he is a short man with large, vigilant eyes and a high forehead. He's only a year or so older than Paul Newman or Marlon Brando, he tells me; Peter De Rome (his real name) was born in the South of France (Juan-les-Pins) and raised in the South of England (Kent). He worked in the movies in England and Europe for 10 years as a film publicist – with J. Arthur Rank, Alexander Korda, David O. Selznick – and came to the U.S. to work for Selznick, "but he died." He spent 2 years in the South working in the Civil Rights movement, and was once arrested with an actress friend – Madeleine Sherwood – at a demonstration in Alabama. Subsequently he worked with the Free Southern Theatre in New Orleans – a city he came to love and where he experienced "many bizarre sexual encounters straight out of Tennessee Williams."

He started making sex pics in '65 when he bought his first 8mm camera. At first "I would shoot myself with a hard-on in front of a mirror, and would bury the shot in the middle of otherwise innocent footage and then wait breathlessly to see if Kodak would send it back. They usually did." Then he got bolder and bolder, ending up sending 50-foot sex scenes thru at a time. He has made about 30 private films in this way. He showed just one – HOT PANTS – at the

Wet Dream Film Festival in Amsterdam in '71, and won 1st prize. Producer Jack Deveau saw his films and decided to blow 8 of them up to 16mm for commercial release as THE EROTIC FILMS OF PETER DE ROME.

Grigoris Daskalogrigorakis: Do you think there is any difference between pornography and eroticism?
Peter De Rome: Yes, I most certainly do. And, in fact, I've got a few aphorisms on that subject. It's very important to me, and I'd try to sum it up in this way: Pornography is to eroticism as vulgarity is to humor. And then to back that up I have three more: Eroticism is to arousal as pornography is to performance. Arousal is to promise as performance is to completion. Promise is to infinity as completion is to limitation. I did a lot of thinking about that *(Laughs)*, but it does sum up what I think is the difference.
Daskalogrigorakis: How do you conceive of your highly plotted and complex plots?
De Rome: They come to me in various inexplicable ways. I really can't tell you how I conceive of them. It might be a picture (such as the one that demonstrated my uncanny physical resemblance to Edgar Allan Poe, and which prompted THE DESTROYING ANGEL), or a phrase from a tune, a tiny incident ... for instance, I can tell you about one idea, the origin of it. I've longed for many years to do a little film called I LOVE A PARADE. And it's about a guy who goes out on parade days and cruises some of the onlookers, feeling their buns and groping them and getting close like a lot of people do in parades and gradually getting so carried away that he actually goes down on one of the onlookers while they're all there watching the parade go by. And that actually did take place with a friend of mine years and years ago on Coronation Day in England. There was this mass of people outside Buckingham Palace all waving like mad at the royal family and I looked around to say something to my friend and there he was down on his knees blowing a soldier in the crowd. And I'd just love to make a little movie based on that idea – maybe *this* year, as it's the Silver Jubilee!
Daskalogrigorakis: You are one of the only persons who has explored black eroticism in sex films. How did you come about this?
De Rome: Mainly because I happen to like black people very much. I have a great affinity with and for black people and I try to get somebody black or several black people into

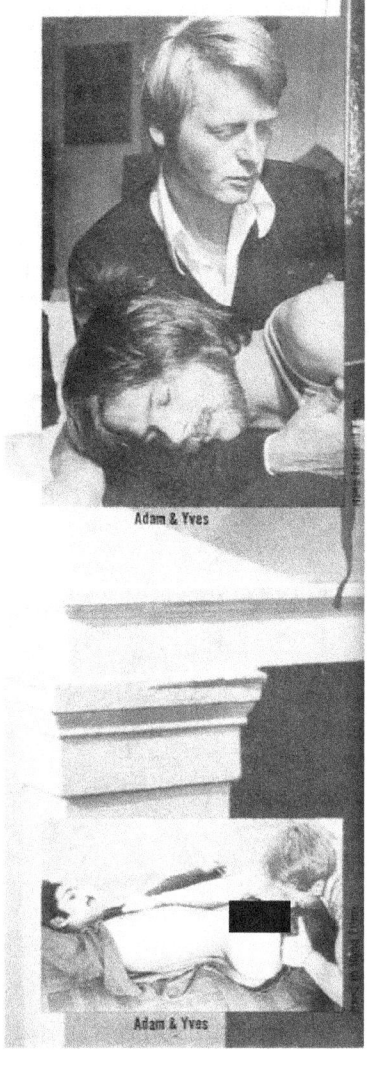

every film I make. In fact, it's become a sort of signature with me, my little personal Hitchcock signature, so that if you look very closely you'll see somebody black in every film I've made, even if it's only a picture of somebody black. And in ADAM & YVES in particular, I wanted to do an important scene with black people and I conceived of that black orgy. I like working with black people and I find them extremely erotic.
Daskalogrigorakis: Do you still yearn to wade into the murky waters of legitimate film?
De Rome: Well, that's a very thorny question. What I would like very much is if some wealthy patron came along and I told them an idea I had and they said here, here's the money, we don't care if it's not commercial, go ahead and do it. I'd love that. I suppose it's just castles in the air. But who knows? If like Cocteau, I could find a Vicomtesse de Noailles, who put up the money for BLOOD OF A POET, I'd like that to happen. But I just don't think anyone's ever going to ask me, that's all. Although I do have some *great* ideas!
Daskalogrigorakis: What constitutes to you the ideal homoerotic film?
De Rome: Well, I must say the field is wide open. I think so far to me the model erotic film is UN CHANT D'AMOUR, the Jean Genet thing. Even though *that* was made over 20 years ago, to me it still has much more going for it than

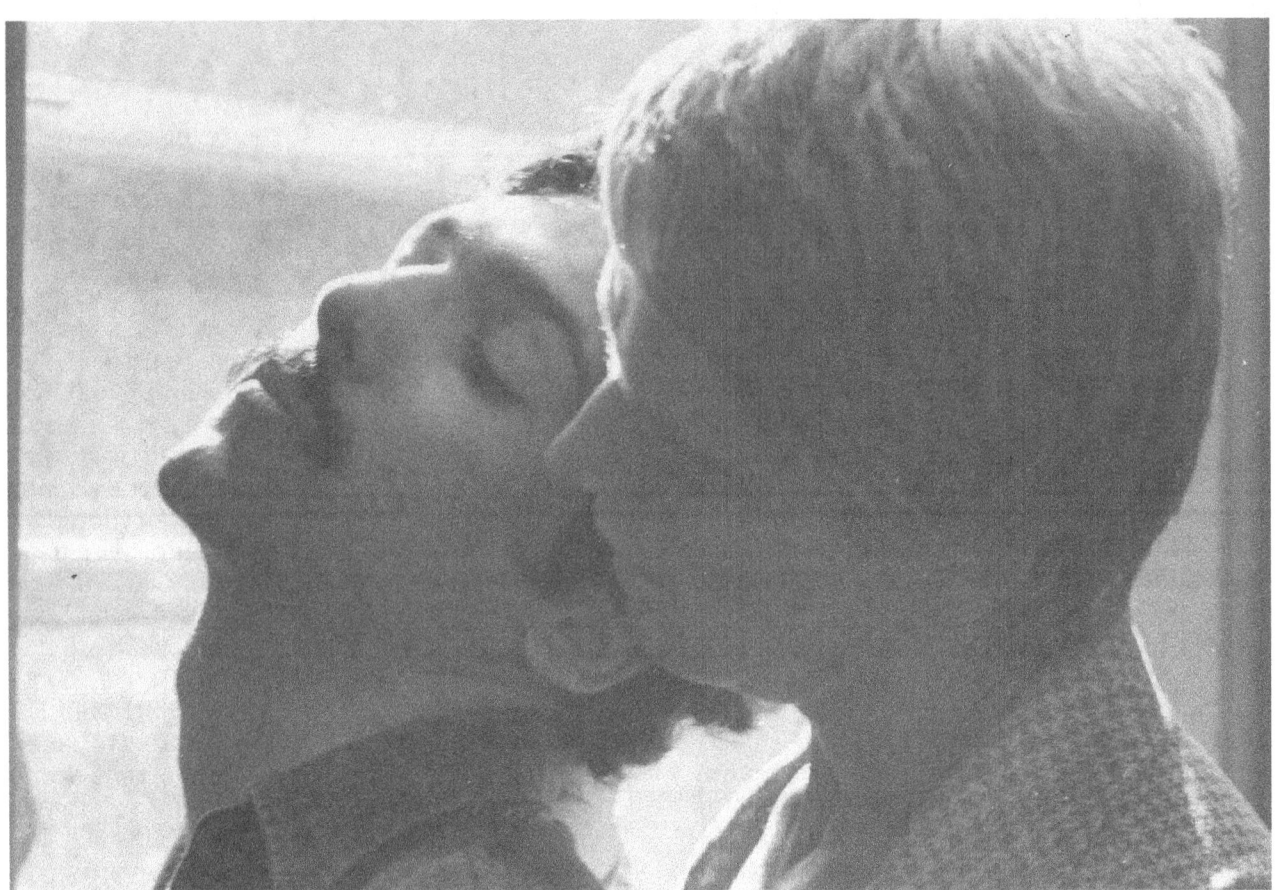
Adam (Michael Hardwick) and Yves (Marcus Giovanni) ...the lovers around which the film revolves...in the *Last Tango* sequence.

much that has taken place since. I think that we've barely scratched the surface of pornography in filmmaking, and that it has become a sort of mandatory thing in sex films to show a positive view of sex and all of sex is supposed to be the ultimate, the pinnacle of excitement and life simply isn't like that. It seems to me that sometime we've got to get honest about sex and admit to ourselves that very few sexual encounters do work out agreeably or are completely successful. And that's one of the reasons that I did the first scene in DESTROYING ANGEL as a "down": it was meant to be an unsuccessful sex trip. And apparently it was as it turned a lot of people off, and they don't want to be reminded. But why not for God's sake? I think we can learn from our failures as from our successes. I have a very simple if not simplistic attitude toward sex films, and that is that sex is just as much a part of life as living - eating - breathing - sleeping, it's just another function of life and I don't see why it can't be depicted dramatically just as those other functions are and as honestly, too. And I think we have to show every aspect of sex in films before we can really say we are making sex films. At the moment it seems that we are titillating a certain section, a certain segment of the audience who are mostly repeaters, who go back again and again mostly to cruise the theatre, and that's okay, but that's not really why I am interested in sex films, and they're not really the people I'm making my sex films for. And even though I agree with a lot of what J. Brian said in his article in *In Touch*, I cannot myself approach sex films in the same way he does.

Daskalogrigorakis: What are your plans for a gay GRAND HOTEL called GRAND MOTEL?

De Rome: Well, I hope very much I can do it if we find the financing. I want it to be an all-gay superstar version like the original, and it does seem to work terribly well as a gay story - with Garbo and Crawford being played by two of our leading gay porno men!

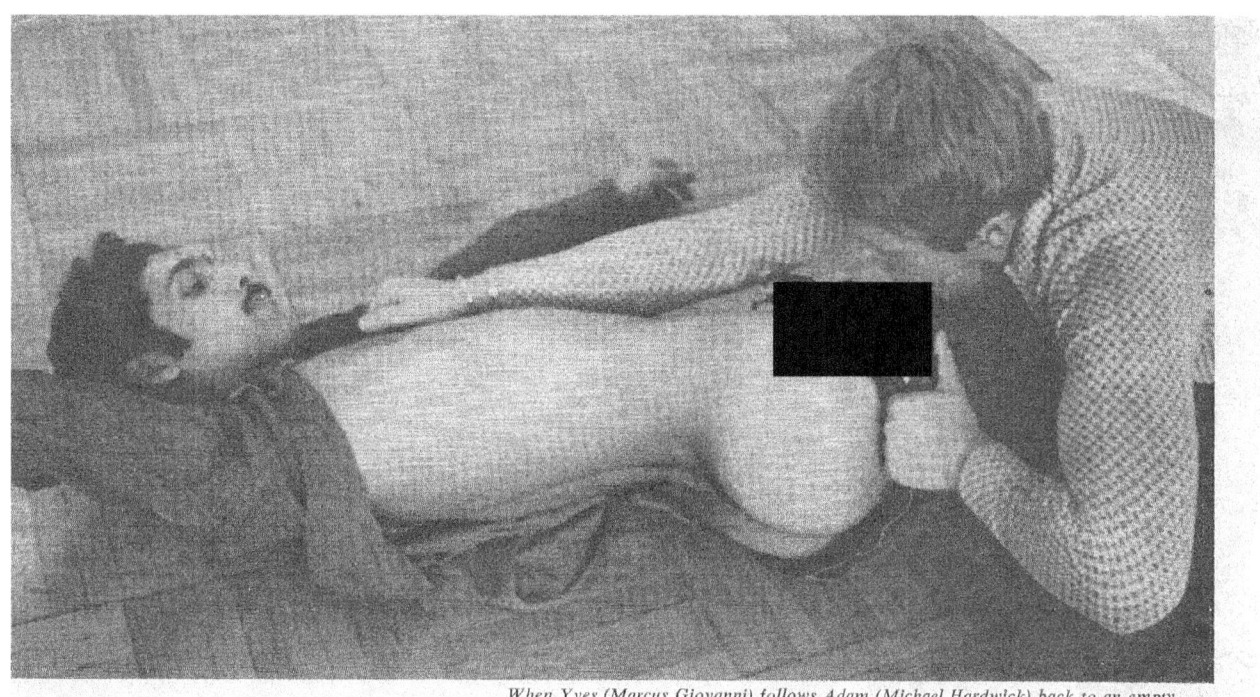

ADAM & YVES

When Yves (Marcus Giovanni) follows Adam (Michael Hardwick) back to an empty apartment in Paris, it is a prelude to a scene strangely similar to that in another recent film made in Paris

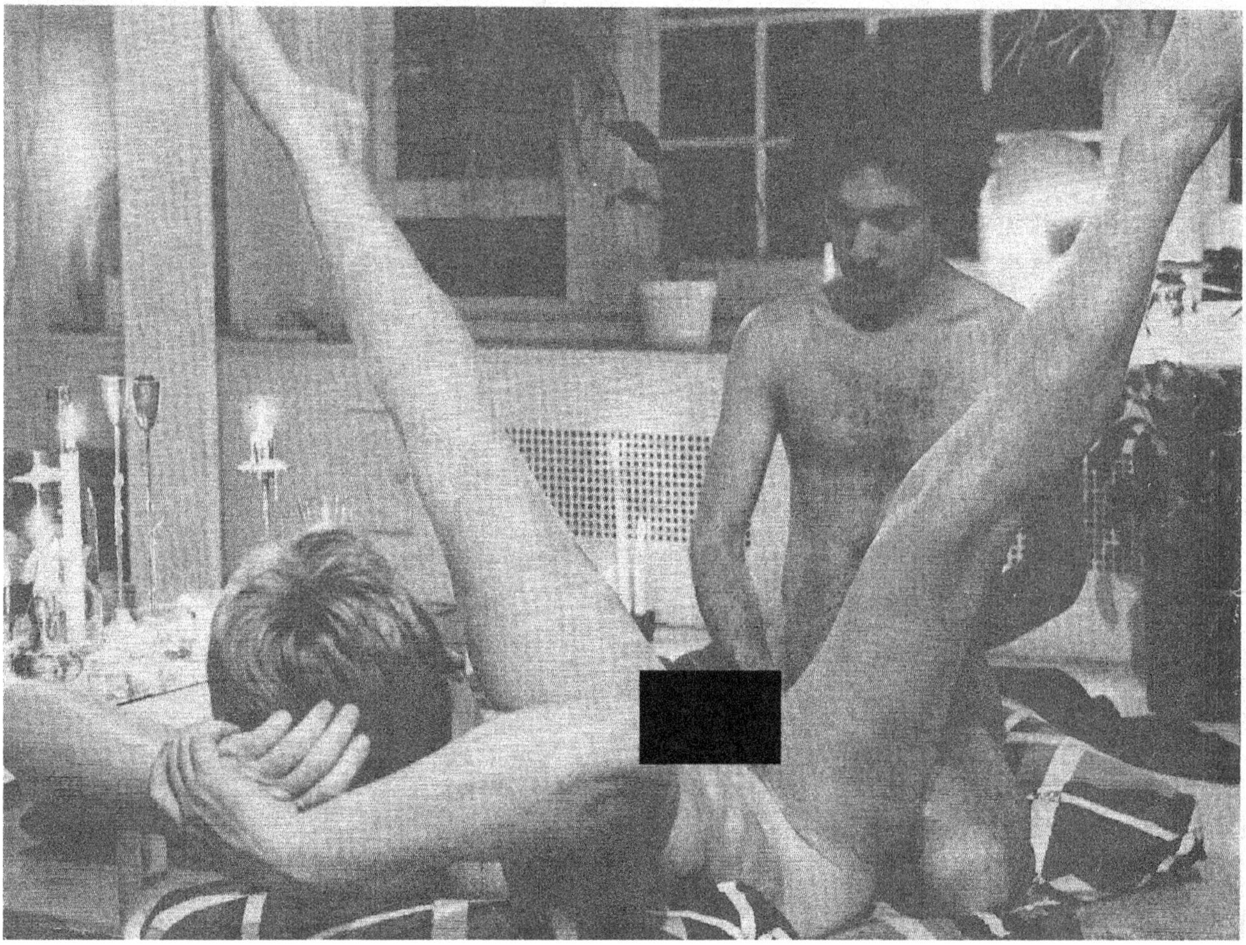

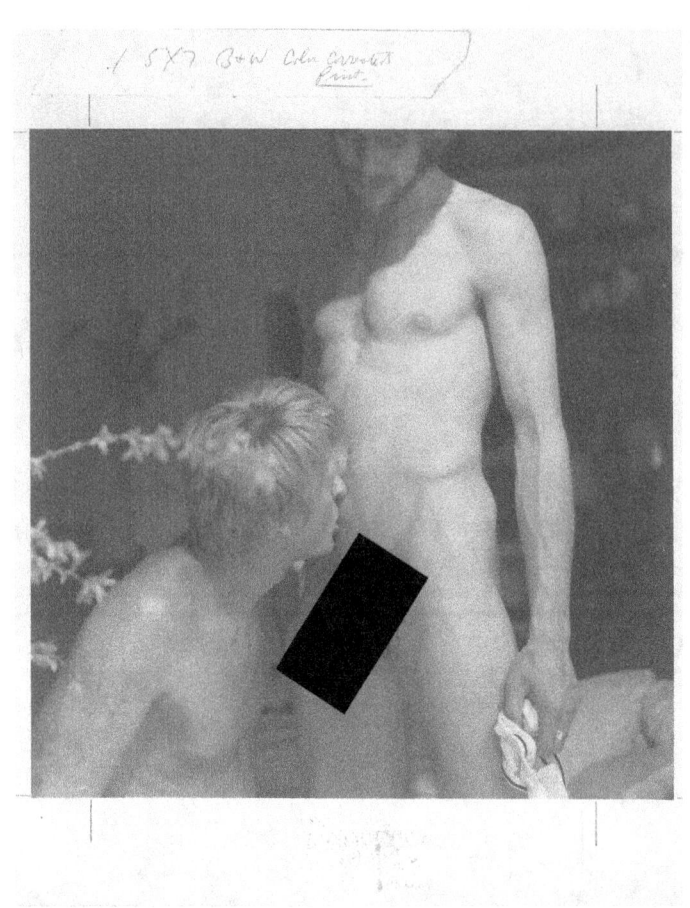

Adam (Michael Hardwick, left) and Bud (Kirk Luna) in *Adam & Yves*

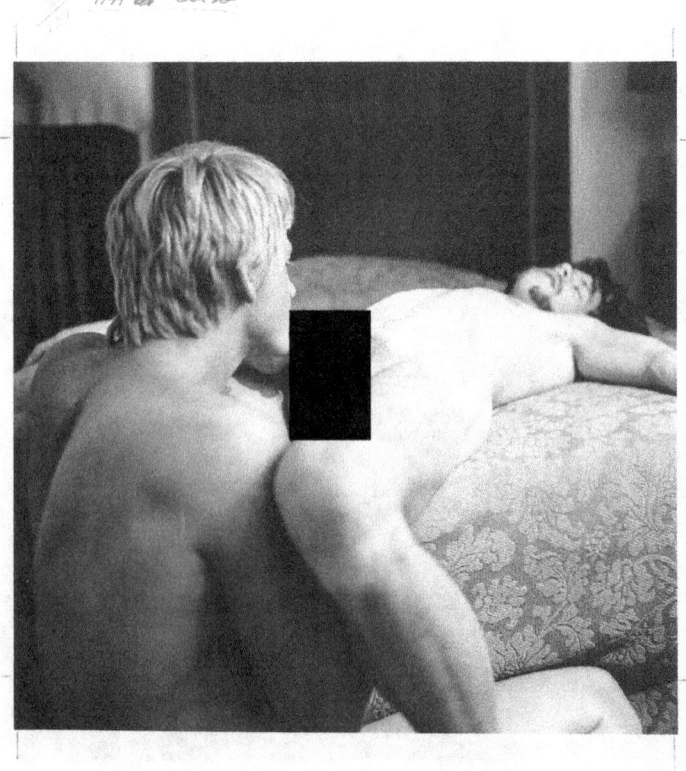

...TO YOU, SEXUALLY? MISTRESSES, AMAZON TYPES
... & TO SUCK ME OFF

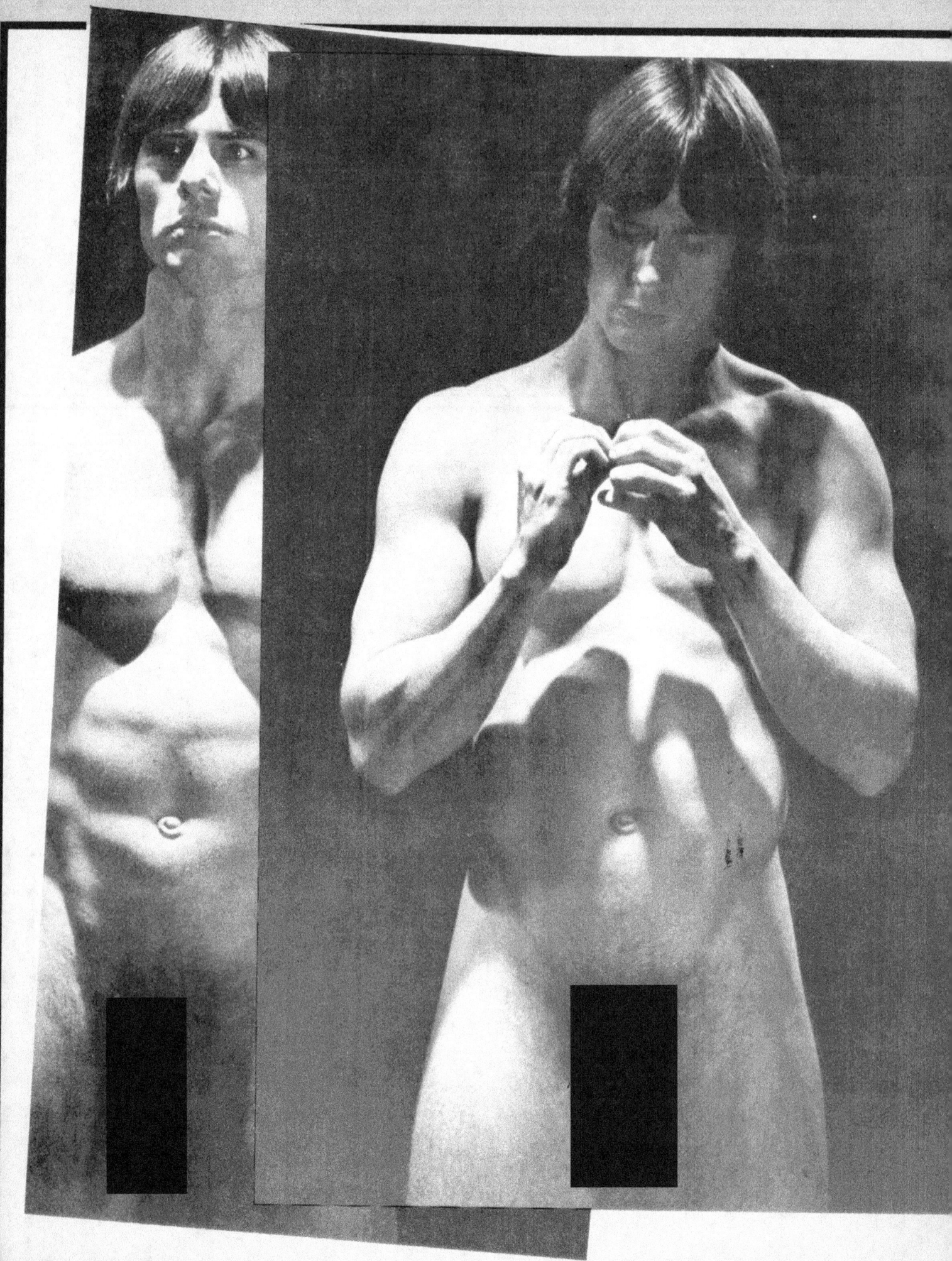

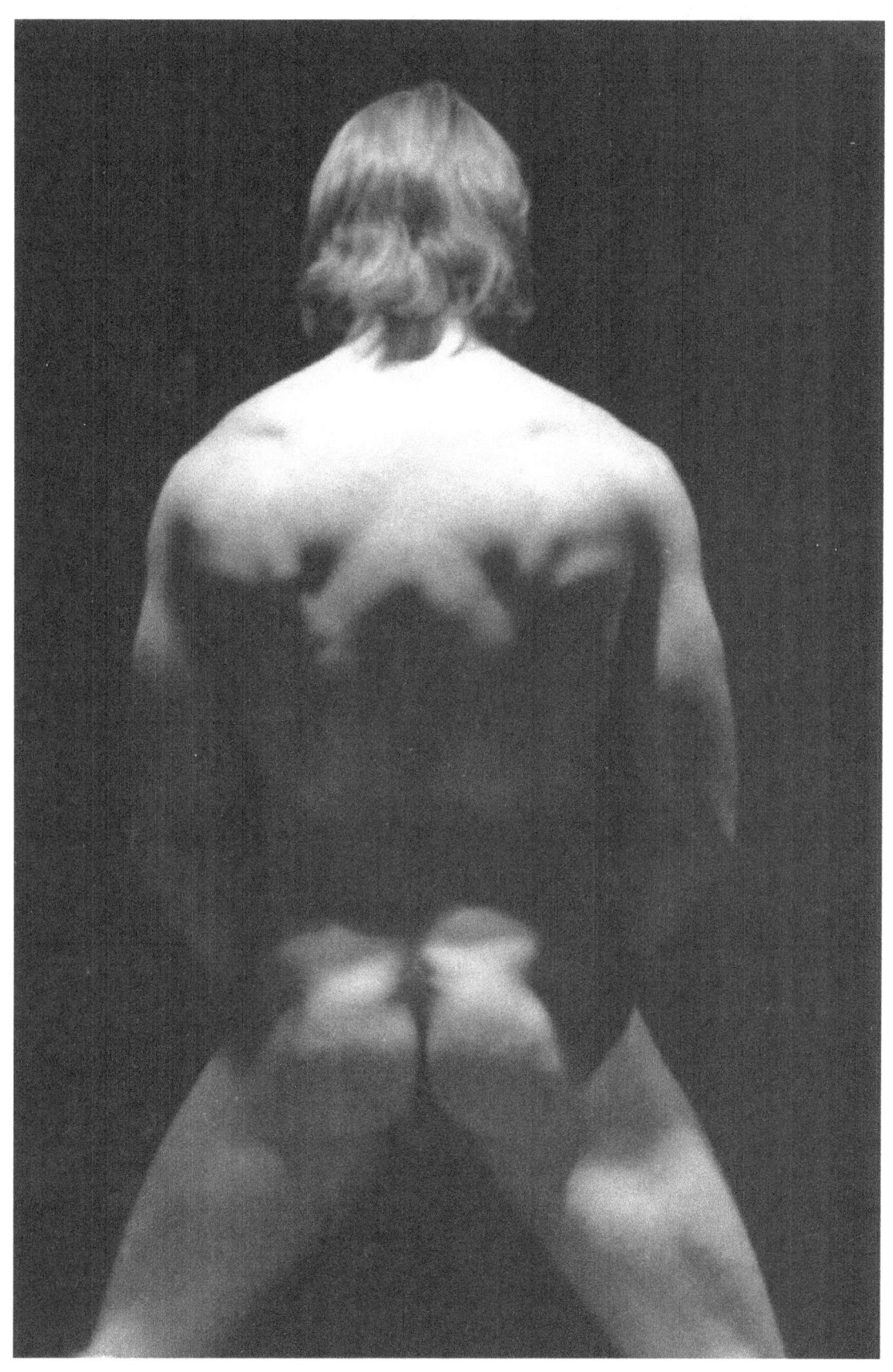

Big Bill Eld in his famous solo sequence Narcissus in *Adam & Yves*

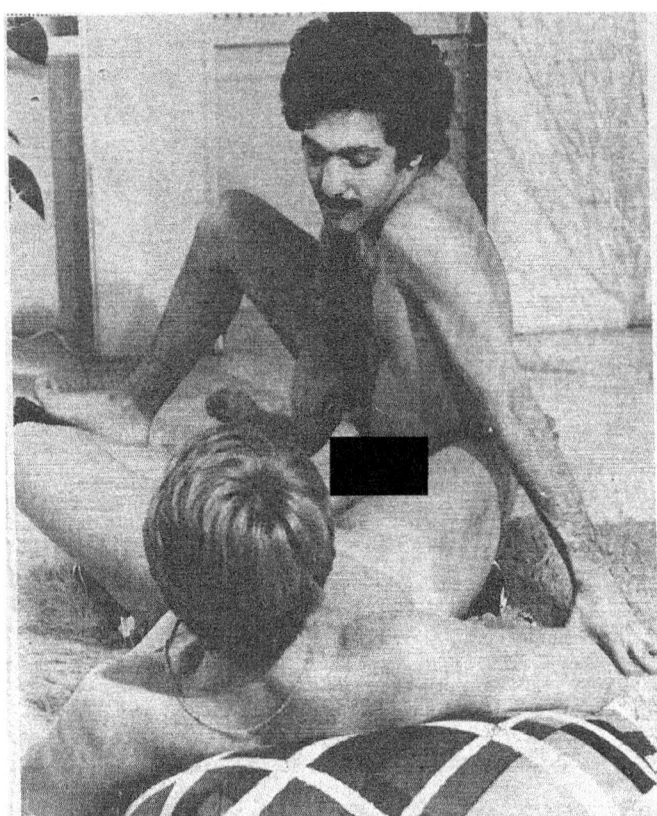

It's all part of a guessing game...

...to discover which film they are 'playing'

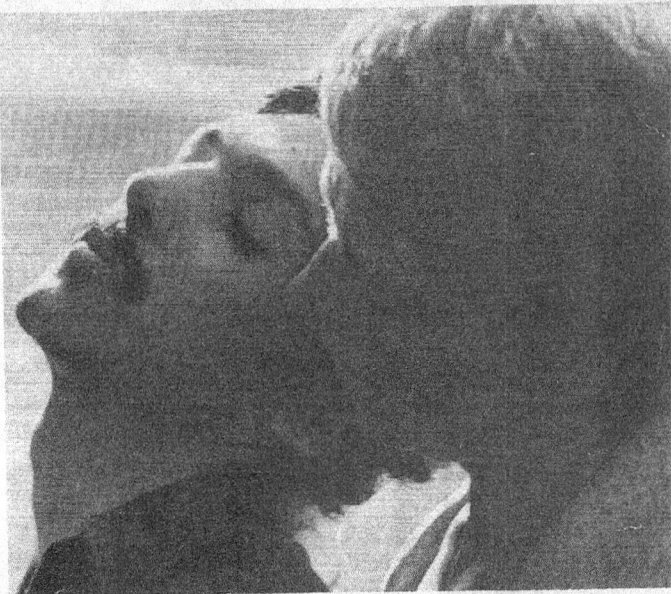

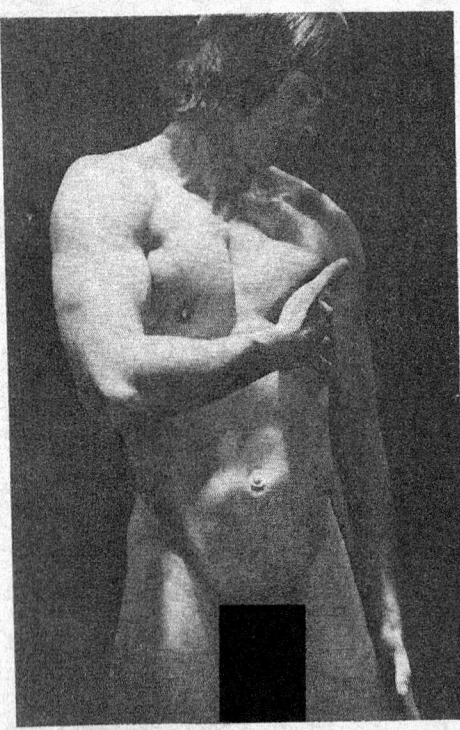

Bill Young as Narcissus

Adam and Yves continue their film guessing game, and they are just about to start on Queen Christina

Charles Pooney, Jack Deveau (producer) and Peter de Rome (writer and director) during location filming in Paris

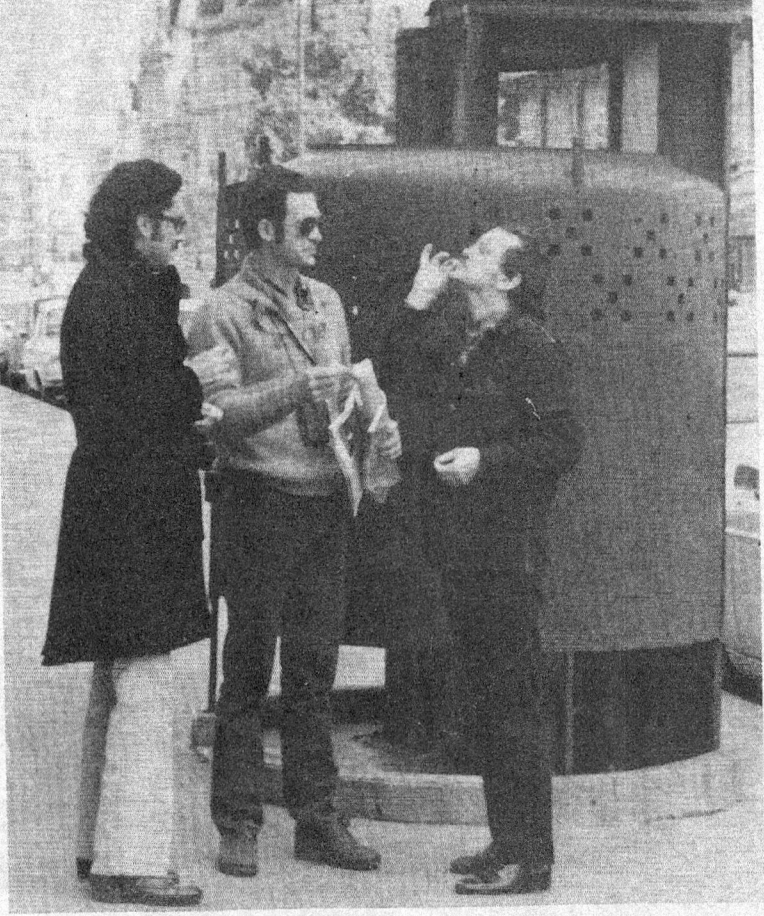

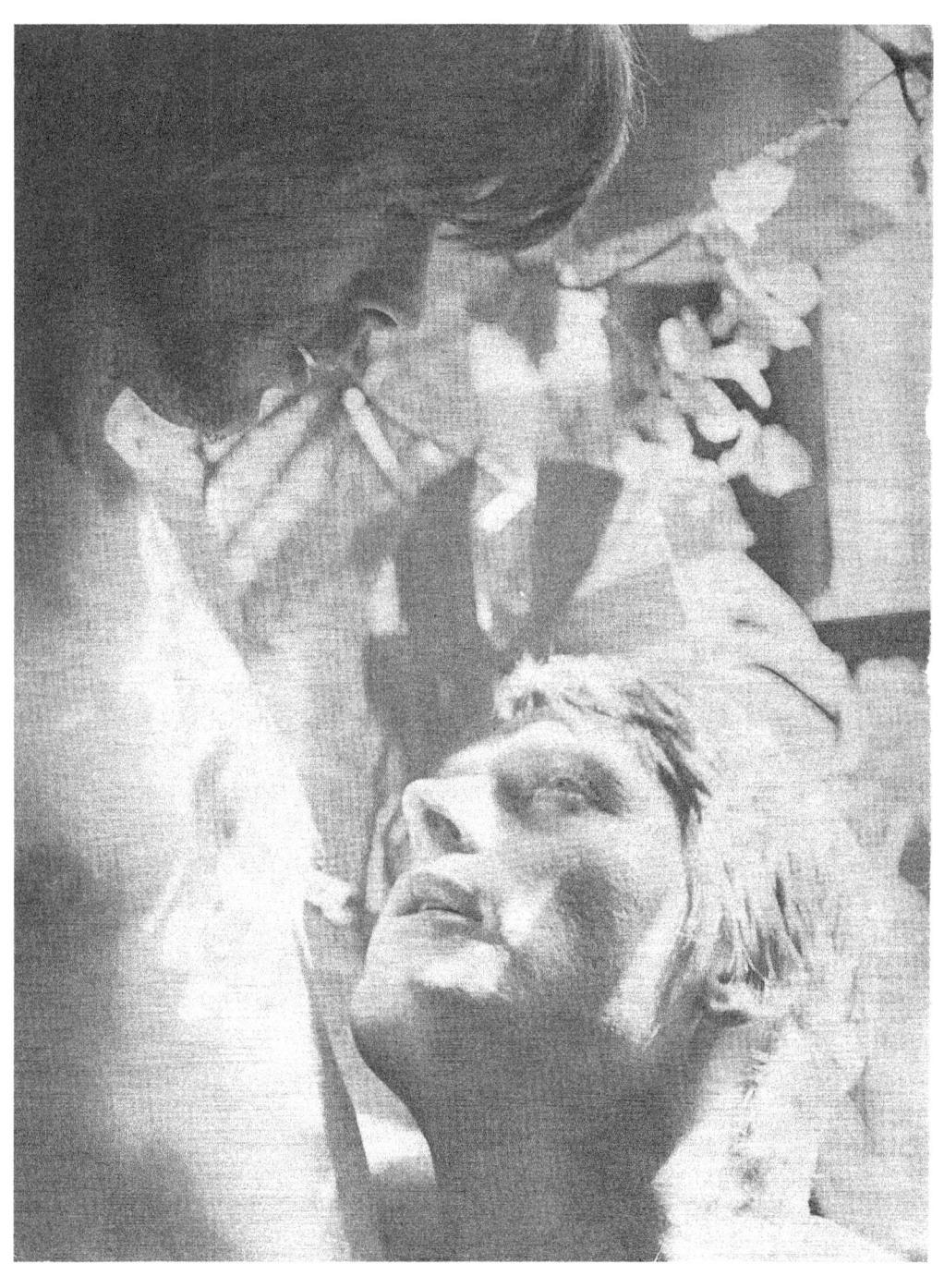

Kirk Luna and Michael Hardwick in *Adam & Yves*

WORLD REPORTS: PARIS - WALLACE POTTS PORTRAIT

Who is Wallace Potts and what's he doing in Paris? Well, he came to France last year to attend the Cannes Film Festival with hopes of selling his newest porno film, MORE, MORE, MORE which he wrote and directed. He did manage to sell it; and although, to his knowledge, it hasn't opened in the States, it did have a run here in Paris.

Wallace, who is thirty, hails from Alabama. He attended a film school in New York and also spent some time at U.S.C. in California. His film credits include a three minute experimental film, an eight minute film on Einstein's "Theory of Relativity" with dancers from the Royal Ballet, and a thirty minute porno cartoon entitled DEMIGODS, a collage of sorts with characters with musclemen bodies and the faces of Hollywood actors Marlon Brando, Paul Newman and Burt Lancaster superimposed. DEMIGODS can be seen today at porno theatres throughout the United States. He also worked with Pasolini in London on CANTERBURY TALES.

MORE, MORE, MORE cost $30,000 to make; and although Wallace described the "story" to me, it didn't make me want to rush out and see it. But Wallace is the first to agree that male porno films have little or no story – which he feels is a problem, but he also feels that finding actors who can act a bigger problem. "To be in a porno film," he says, "you really need to be part exhibitionist and get your kicks by having sex with somebody watching – in this case, the camera."

We spoke briefly of Jack Deveau's LE MUSEE (DREAMBOY in the States – see *In Touch* '29), which opened in paris in June and which starred Hugh Allen and Dan Donovan. Wallace was not particularly impressed. "It started out with a story," he said, "but the story was abandoned halfway through the film in favor of sucking and fucking." And this, of course, ruined the film.

Wallace is presently working on re-writing a science-fiction porno film which, if it gets off the ground, will star French porno star Jean-Paul Doux, who starred in LE BEAU MEC (A BEAUTIFUL GUY). Wallace's next project, for which he wrote the script, will be DISCO QUEEN – not be a porno film but rather a story on homosexual life in Los Angeles. He has written a part for Peter Berlin, but it will not be the lead.

Changing the subject rather abruptly, Wallace asked: "How do you like French cocks as opposed to American cocks?" I told him I really didn't find any difference. "But they're (French cocks) not circumcised," he persisted in a surprising tone of voice. Whether this is a criticism or not (I didn't ask) Wallace likes Paris and apparently the French, although he admits the "gay life in Paris is not the same" (as in the States). "Gay life is very easy. I mean you can go through it quite quickly here. You know, I feel like I've fucked Paris."

*Peter Adams, *In Touch*

WORLD REPORTS

Paris

Who is Wallace Potts and what's he doing in Paris? Well, he came to France last year to attend the Cannes Film Festival with hopes of selling his newest porno film, *More, More, More* which he wrote and directed. He did manage to sell it; and although, to his knowledge, it hasn't opened in the States, it did have a run here in Paris.

Wallace, who is thirty, hails from Alabama. He attended a film school in New York and also spent some time at U.S.C. in California. His film credits include a three minute experimental film, an eight minute film on Einstein's "Theory of Relativity" with dancers from the Royal Ballet, and a thirty minute porno cartoon entitled *Demigods*, a collage of sorts with characters with musclemen bodies and the faces of Hollywood actors Marlon Brando, Paul Newman and Burt Lancaster superimposed. *Demigods* can be seen today at porno theatres throughout the United States. He also worked with Pasolini in London on *Canterbury Tales*.

More, More, More cost $30,000 to make; and although Wallace described the "story" to me, it didn't make me want to rush out and see it. But Wallace is the first to agree that male porno films have little or no story—which he feels is a problem, but he also feels that finding actors who can act a bigger problem. "To be in a porno film," he says, "you really need to be part exhibitionist and get your kicks by having sex with somebody watching — in this case, the camera."

We spoke briefly of Jack Deveau's *Le Musee* (*Dreamboy* in the States—see IN TOUCH #29), which opened in Paris in June and which starred Hugh Allen and Dan Donovan. Wallace was not particularly impressd. "It started out with a story," he said, "but the story was abandoned halfway through the film in favor of sucking and fucking." And this, of course, ruined the film.

Wallace is presently working on re-writing a science-fiction porno film which, if it gets off the ground, will star French porno star Jean Paul Doux, who starred in *Le Beau Mec* ("A Beautiful Guy"). Wallace's next project, for which he wrote the script, will be *Disco Queen* — not be a porno film but rather a story on homosexual life in Los Angeles. He has written a part for Peter Berlin, but it will not be the lead.

Changing the subject rather abruptly, Wallace asked: "How do you like French cocks as opposed to American cocks?" I told him I really didn't find any difference. "But they're (French cocks) not

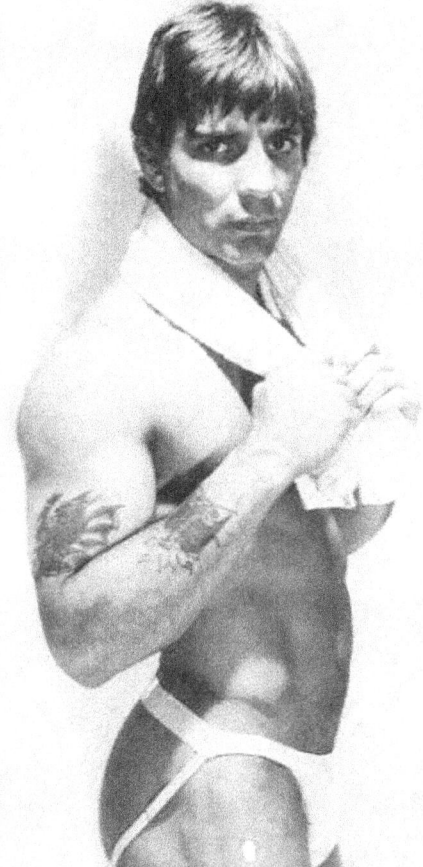
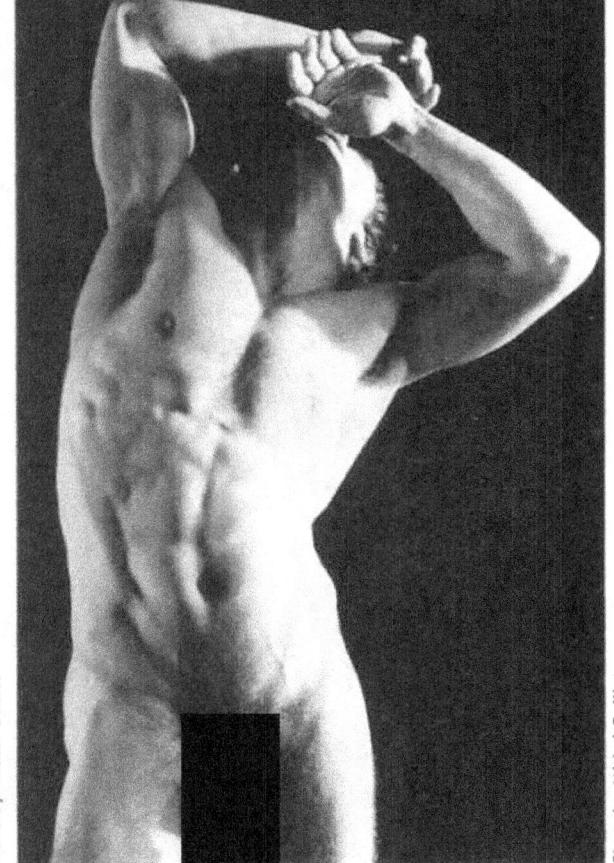

Photo by Michel Guillot

Hunky French porno star Jean Paul Doux is slated to lead the cast of Wallace Potts' new, as yet untitled, erotic sci-fi film.

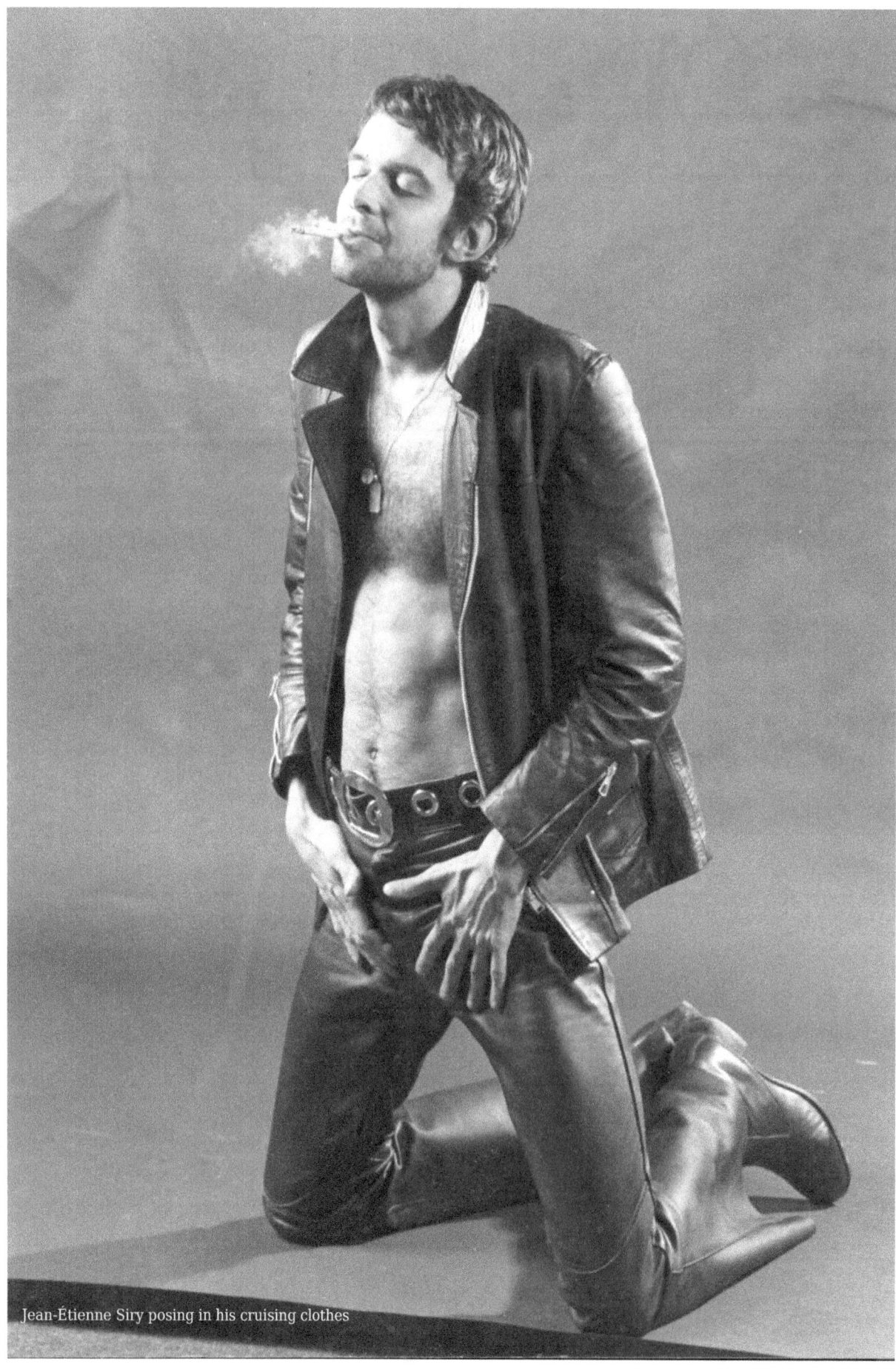
Jean-Étienne Siry posing in his cruising clothes

JEAN ÉTIENNE SIRY
The French Connection

Jean-Etienne Siry: I have to say that the people were completely enthusiastic about POING DE FORCE. This astonished me, this astonished me! That the film could have been a phantasm for homosexuals. That people, young people, would masturbate while watching it even 40 years later – but why not? This was something delirious. The fetishes I could have had, how sordid it was. For me it was really horrible, what I had made. Yet, I shot it in a relaxed atmosphere. We made it laughing, giggling and without knowing it would have such an impact on the spectator. We saw the answer print, and I thought: that's too strong, that's too strong, I went too far. Compared to it, ET... DIEU CRÉA LES HOMMES was gentle. It was a commissioned film, more or less. I had to learn the profession. Thus it is far from being a masterpiece, but I put all my abilities into it. However, for me, my real film, the film I am most proud of, is UN ESCARGOT DANS LA TÊTE, a film about the difficulty of communicating, namely between women and man, about alcoholism, a bit also about dementia, and about incommunicability. Not being able to communicate with somebody. Everything on which I drew upon back then. The film had all together good reviews, but, unfortunately, due to a conflict between the producers and the distribution company, Gaumont, the release of the film was scuttled. They released the film absolutely indifferently, without caring at all about it. The film was removed after only 15 days in the cinemas. And so the people interested in the film, thanks to the press reviews, had only 15 days to make it to the cinemas to see it – mouth-to-mouth-propaganda still functioned well then. There were still posters in the subway and bus stations, but the film had already disappeared from the movie theaters. For me it was a shock. I was shocked, and I dropped it, which I now regret because I still keep receiving messages from people who watch it on YouTube and who tell me: It was a film ahead of its time; we are impressed by it. Despite my 76 years and health problems, I feel very young. Despite my age and my physics, I feel as if I were 30 years old. For instance, I could talk with you about Beyoncé, Kim Kardashian, the lot of these assholes, I am keeping up with all this. Regarding my comic book *Félice*: It had an enormous success but it was banned by the French censorship committee, in 1970. I was 30 years old when I made this book and had been doing comical drawings at the same time. My "little girl" just entered my mind one day. In the beginning, she was nice and didn't say dirty things. It was the editor of the book who told me during a meeting: "Sir, if you want me to publish your book, your little girl has to be much more brazen, debauched." Therefore there are two parts in the book: In the first one, she is nice and behaves well, whereas in the end she liberates herself completely. The book sold itself very, very well, until the day the censorship banned it because it said things which were too bawdy: A girl doing orgies and talking about love, it was shocking at that time. Now, everybody laughs about it.

Gary Vanisian: Did you have any other artists in your family?

Siry: My great-grandfather was a dress-maker, the first one in France. He was the dressmaker of the Empress Eugénie, the wife of Napoléon III. His name was Charles Frederick Worth; he was from England, and very famous. He was the only artist in the family, except a cousin of mine, Jean-Claude Pascal, a well-known, "playboy"-type actor from the 1950s. All the girls were in love with him.

Vanisian: At what age did you start to work as an artist?

Siry: But you can look this up on Wikipedia! There you will find everything about me. *(laughing)* Initially, I had started as a movie poster designer. The most successful poster I ever did was for LES TONTONS FLINGEURS. I designed it when I was 23 years old, and until today I receive royalties for it, because the film has become a cult film and the poster likewise. I had entered an art school, after finishing high school; I was around 18 years old. Then a sordid thing happened: The director of the school, a very well-known poster designer, took one of my posters, erased my signature and put his own onto it. I sued the agency to which he had sent it, and simultaneously I went knocking at the door of the advertising department of the Societè Pathé, since I was a fanatic cinema lover. When Pathé published my first poster, I was 18 years old. That's how it all started! And I made cinema posters until the age of 30. I worked for Americans, English, a whole pile of distribution companies, and I worked "freelance". Afterwards, I got the opportunity to become the artistic director of a publicity agency. After working there for a few years, the agency went more or less bankrupt, and I resigned. I received a compensation fee and then for the next three years was able to pursue my cinema education.

Vanisian: As for Wikipedia - there e.g. one can read that Roger Vadim explicitly asked to work with you on a poster for one of his films.

Siry: Yes, the poster for ET SATAN CONDUIT LE BAL.

Vanisian: How exactly did a collaboration such as this begin? Did Vadim contact you personally?

Siry: No. I was the regular model maker of a press agent who worked for all the celebrities of that time. It was him who created the GENDARME DE SAINT-TROPEZ series, Richard Balducci. He introduced me to a lot of people; I knew all the contemporary yet-set, Johnny Halliday, Vadim, Catherine Deneuve and Brigitte Bardot, at the age of 18. It was an insane era.

Vanisian: How did you conceive a movie poster? Did you see the movie before starting, or did you speak with the director about it, about what he imagined?

Siry: No, I didn't watch the movies. For example, I didn't watch LES TONTONS FLINGEURS before designing the poster. Later, I saw this film on television and found it incredibly stupid; I have no idea why it was so successful. No, I didn't like to see the films before starting to work on the posters; it put me on the wrong trail. I preferred not to see them, but instead to get an idea of them through the film stills or the screenplay. In contrast, I talked with the directors, yes. They told me what they wanted. For example Roger Vadim told me: Look, give me something "oléolé", and I gave him this "oléolé", just like he asked. *(laughs)*

Vanisian: And then you also designed the poster for Jack Deveau's GOOD HOT STUFF.

Siry: Yes, it is here somewhere. A rare piece, because at that time posters for pornographic films were forbidden. And this was the last poster made for a pornographic film. It was quite striking for me because it symbolizes for me everything that homosexuality was, at the time of the Village People and all that.

Vanisian: I suppose it was an evident thing for you to design the poster for Jack since at that time you were his friend, and he approached you directly to do it.

Siry: Not at all. It was Norbert Thierry who asked me, the producer of ET... DIEU CRÉA LES HOMMES, he was - to tell you a nasty thing - a real bandit. A genuine bandit. Him I got to know because he was a friend of the mother of Georges Lautner, the author of LES TONTONS FLINGEURS, and she presented me to him. He was a very boastful guy, and one day he said to me he wanted to do hardcore cinema, homosexual cinema, and I thought about it and said to myself: "Why not?" Though I have to be precise that it was not my cup of tea. I did it because I was keen on learning the profession. I made a sketch which was terrific, namely POING DE FORCE, it was shot at in a place close to the Bastille. It was a short film, but it was very tough. Without realizing it, I made very violent things because otherwise I am good and generous. Meaning that I would give everything to one who is in need, but once somebody does malice to me, does me harm, then it's over. Well, after POING DE FORCE was made, it was entirely banned by the censorship. Only many years later I retrieved it, and together with a young man called Jean Daniel Cadinot, a gay photographer who also made gay films, I commercialized POING DE FORCE on VHS. The incredible thing about this film, I'm repeating, is that it was really shot rigorously. It was done in a small attic room, in one day. It was lent to us for free, and before we could start shooting in there - it was a construction site, the owner used it as a storeroom - we had to remove everything. Inside, there was a bidet, dating back to the beginning of the century, on feet. And we used it to a maximum extent. Everybody was sweating, we were in an incredible condition, and we laughed, we laughed while we were doing it, without realizing the impact that the film was about to have. When Jack Deveau saw it, he said to me: "But Jean-Étienne, how did you come up with all these ideas?" "Jack," I replied, "it was all spontaneous." Stemming from the taste of the youth of that time. It was the first and only film I produced myself, the others were financed by Norbert Thierry. And it's the only film where I was not cheated. POING DE FORCE was done in 1976, ET... DIEU CRÉA LES HOMMES was made in 1977, 1978. In 1979 then, together with producers who had nothing to do with hardcore movies, I made ESCARGOT DANS LA TÊTE, which, however, was done thanks to the impact of the porn films.

Vanisian: There is such a dark side of sexuality in your films, the interior, the small "storyline", and especially the haunting image when the rapist shows his burned face. Was this your main idea in conceiving and shooting POING DE FORCE?

Siry: Yes. Yes, I admit it. Objectively, I wanted it to be dirty. I wanted it to be dirty because it matched certain individuals of that time. If you asked me to do it again today, I would be incapable. I couldn't show anything as sordid today. This burned face you mention - it was in the script already, completely preconceived. And my staging was a mixture between natural development on the set and precise instructions.

Vanisian: How did you find the actors for this movie? Were they part of your community, your friends?

Siry: They were friends, yes. Furthermore, there was a cameraman, François About, and one other person in a small room, plus the 16mm-camera, the lighting, a deadly heat. It was shot among friends.

Vanisian: POING DE FORCE was distributed in the US by Jack Deveau and Hand In Hand, is this correct? Do you remember any business aspects you experienced with the movie?

Siry: Honestly, I didn't know that Hand In Hand Films distributed it there, and this surprises me. I didn't think that Bob Alvarez would do something like this to me. If it is true, it disappoints me.

Vanisian: Do you remember when you first met Jack Deveau? How did that happen, and what was your impression of him? Both as an artist and in a personal way, did you connect right away?

Siry: Yes, it took place in Paris. Through an intermediate, the named Norbert Thierry. There was a kind of seduction, Jack seduced me, and later I seduced him. There was a kind of complicity, friendship created between us. I am not talking of sexual friendship! Because he was not my lover. He was simply a friend. To be frank: I have always been bisexual, be it towards men or women, I never had a particular preference. And Jack, well, it was very spontaneous, a special friendship because he felt in me the artist who I am and always have been. He knew how to make use of it.

Vanisian: Why did Jack come to Paris? Because he loved the city.

Siry: He enjoyed it as many other Americans did. He also had some French origin. So he loved to go to Paris, and when he was here, he needed somebody to help him around, I was his representative, delegate, if you will. To show him places, shooting locations and all that. I was in charge of this. And I did this gladly, because I had a lot of sympathy for him. I can't recall how he spent his time in Paris otherwise, but when we were together, we were mostly surrounded by his shooting team or having lunch or dinner, actually we went hardly at all to gay places. That didn't interest us too much. What interested him above all was the work we were about to do.

Vanisian: How do you remember the atmosphere in the 70s in Paris – I believe there were certain gay areas in Paris at that time, such as the Rue Sainte-Anne close to Opéra?

Siry: Oh no, no. With Jack at least it was not this area. I knew the owner of a nightclub at Saint-German-des-Près, it was called "The Go-Go-Boy". I stayed there for a little while, since it didn't accord much to my nature to stay out at night until seven in the morning, to listen to the stupidities of the one or the other. But at the time when Jack was here we went to this nightclub together. The film LE MUSÉE/STRICTY FORBIDDEN was shot in a nightclub at Rue de la Villette, I think, and that was something unbelievable. How on earth we could shoot there, I don't know.

Vanisian: And how was the situation regarding the porn cinemas in Paris? Do you have any particular anecdotes about the films, the theaters and the audience at the time? Have adult movies been an important part for the cultural life of a gay man back then?

Siry: There was a cinema called "Hollywood Boulevard" on the Grands Boulevards, also one at Saint-German where these kinds of films would be shown. LEFT-HANDED also was released in the Hollywood Boulevard before the distribution of gay hardcore films ended due to a new law. But until then, there was advertisement, posters and so on. Afterwards, the films were shown in cinemas specialized on gay cinema, the cinemas of Norbert Thierry, "Le Vivienne", and another cinema at Saint-Germain-des-Près, I forget the name, but that's where ET... DIEU CRÉA LES HOMMES was screened and quite successfully. The man who released these films was also the press agent of Jean-Paul Belmondo, Réné Chateau. There were big conflicts with him, though Jack was also not completely honest with him.

Vanisian: Was there a lot of cruising in the cinemas?

Siry: Indeed. When I was, for example, attending a screening of ET... DIEU CRÉA LES HOMMES at this cinema in Saint-Germain, the main actor was there, but instead of watching the film, he stood at the entrance of the toilet. I found this lamentable. What interested me was to see how many people bought tickets and entered the cinema. I never made a fortune with these films, however.

Vanisian: Tell me about the creative process of scripting STRICTLY FORBIDDEN. Did you show Jack Deveau the completed script, or did you develop parts of it together?

Siry: I am the author of the script. Jack shot the film in France. It could have been very good, he had made good films before, but unfortunately here he made a real shit; a shit that cost Jack a fortune. He returned to the US, took with him the rushes of the film and left Réné Chateau with some other thousand meters of film. Chateau then made another editing with it, the version titled LE MUSÉE, which didn't go well, because it was shitty. In the US, Jack had made a different editing with the material he had brought back to the US. STRICTLY FORBIDDEN is the US-title, right? It's a good title. In fact, there is an American actor who took directly inspiration from Jack Deveau's film, stole the script, Ben Stiller with his NIGHT AT THE MUSEUM. I was actually paid for writing the script, I had a contract with Réné Chateau who was obliged to pay me even despite the difficulties he had with Jack.

Vanisian: How did the idea for this script come, and did you write it together with Jack Deveau, at least to some extent?

Siry: I wrote it alone. And the idea just came one day. You know, I have quite some ideas. And here was the idea to write a kind of fantastic cinema. Jack immediately approved it. It could have been wonderful, even with the little means we had, because the idea was charming, interesting. But it turned out a total shit, in both versions.

Vanisian: Could you explain what makes you consider it such a failure?

Siry: Because it is badly edited, the script was not respected at all, it was done very negligently. Whereas the script had a little suspense in it: A young man, who arrives at the museum, has himself locked up there and violated by all the sculptures there. The special effects, however, are not bad; the projections of the marble on the bodies are well done.

Vanisian: Were you present at the shooting?

Siry: Oh yes. The exteriors were shot at the Musée Rodin, all the interior scenes at a place called "La Villette" at Pigalle, a gay nightclub, on the first floor. We set up the decoration there, shot during daytime and at 6pm each day we had to take everything down to let the evening guests enter the room to have a "fiesta" there.

Vanisian: What was the key aspect for you, in terms of storytelling and symbolism? Jack Deveau once said in an interview that the movie reflects different steps of someone who is about to discover the nature of his own sexuality, a metaphor about coming out as a gay man. Can you agree on that?

Siry: Oh well, some blabla... Puh.

Vanisian: Another future regular collaborator of yours, apart from François About, on this film was composer Didier Vasseur. After STRICTLY FORBIDDEN he made the sounds and original music for POING DE FORCE and also for ET... DIEU CRÉA LES HOMMES. Describe your working relationship a little bit, how did his creative process work?

Siry: Aahh, yes, Didier Vasseur! He was a friend of mine! I didn't know that he did the sound effects for Jack, but he wrote the music for my film ESCARGOT. He died in pitiful circumstances, very young, from diabetes. He was a genius, an extraordinary guy.

Vanisian: Did you ever visit Jack and Bob in New York? You remained friends after STRICTLY FORBIDDEN, correct? How do you remember the end of the shooting of STRICTLY FORBIDDEN? The print was sneaked out, the movie remained unfinished.

Siry: Yes, I went there. Once with my best friend, who appeared as a model on the poster for ET... DIEU CRÉA LES HOMMES. We went there, and I stayed in a sordid hotel with bugs. Oh, a nightmare this was, the stay with Jack and Bob. I keep very good memories of our time together in Paris, but

New York was dreadful.

Vanisian: As far as I can judge it ET... DIEU CRÉA LES HOMMES (1978) can be called your best movie, do you agree on that? Was it recognized outside the adult movie niche? (I think it's a masterpiece in many ways and sadly not remembered enough – and in cinematic terms I always compare it to the No Wave filmmakers of the time, Amos Poe, Jim Jarmusch) Also it seems to me a very personal film, driven by your own experiences and thoughts. Did you think at the time adult movies and regular movies would get more and more interactions?

Siry: No, but those people wouldn't go to see such a film. There were good reviews indeed, but solely in the gay circles. Now it's a film which makes the people laugh because there is a scene with a telephone. I often hear people talking about it: "The telephone scene, the telephone scene!" It was a nice one, but compared to what I did in POING DE FORCE, it's nothing, that one is much harder, stronger.

Vanisian: It seems to me that dialogue isn't too much important for you; the language of your films is way more cinematic and created by editing, sounds, impressionistic images and camera movements. Was that your preferred style, or was it partly conceived because adult movie actors were not always able to "act" and "speak" in a classical sense?

Siry: In POING DE FORCE there are no dialogues. In ET... DIEU CRÉA LES HOMMES there are. It was, if I remember well, about the search, through different experiences, of love by somebody who was loved and who died. It is a sensitive film, its hero is searching for love. Love is not an evident thing, right? I am now 76 years old, I had quite a few experiences in my life, with men and women alike, and now I am all alone. That's how it is. I have somebody who is calling me up, I got connected with him by chance through Twitter. He fell in love with me 42 years ago. Now he lives together with somebody who is 68 years old and calls me each day. We talked via Skype, and I don't recognize him, which shames me a bit, I wonder how it is possible that I don't recognize him, whilst he keeps on reminding me of memories that I am supposed to have lived through with him. I have no memory! And still I am very sensitive.

Vanisian: Were there have any directors which inspired you for your own films? Did Jack's films have any influence on your own hardcore films?

Siry: No, not at all. I will tell you one thing: On the day when I showed to Jack POING DE FORCE, I thought: I am stronger than you. And when he saw ESCARGOT – it was very shortly before his death – he was very surprised, because he loved me as a friend, considered me a companion in work, but he was surprised that I had gone so far.

Vanisian: The lead actor in ET... DIEU CRÉA LES HOMMES – Yvon Sauders – wasn't a professional adult film model, is this correct?

Siry: He was not a professional actor and was brought to me one day. I chose him because he was banal, though beautiful; an ordinary-looking man. But this fit the role very well. What was very strange: He shot the film, and when he later watched it, he said: I can't show this to my parents.

Vanisian: Whereas ESCARGOT is shot entirely with professional actors.

Siry: Yes, there were all professionals. But I'll tell you: Be it with professional or non-professionals, I was always very polite. I respected extras just as much as the actors. It was the same with the pornographic films; I treated them just like normal persons. I gave orders such as: Calm down, don't get nervous!

Vanisian: How was it with Jack in this regard?

Siry: Well... For instance one day there was a problem while shooting a scene where a male actor was supposed to have an erection and he didn't manage to, and Jack said: "Oh well, if he can't do it, we won't force him to." Definitely he was not a despot, but rather relaxed; except once, oh yes, once it happened that he treated me really like a dog. I couldn't bear this, because I had always been helpful and attentive with him, and he really treated me like a piece of shit, during a shooting, at the "La Villette", the nightclub. So I left the set, in front of everybody, the technicians and actors. I have never seen anything like this: He ran, took the stairs in a flight and then, for the first time in my life, I saw him crying. He said to me: "Jean-Étienne, I implore you, please don't go, stay here." And I stayed. I would have left in any other circumstance, but it was accidental from his side, and seeing his tears and his behavior, I thought that he was in need of me. So I stayed.

"THIS WAS THE LAST POSTER MADE FOR A PORNOGRAPHIC FILM. IT WAS QUITE STRIKING FOR ME BECAUSE IT SYMBOLIZES FOR ME EVERYTHING THAT HOMOSEXUALITY WAS, AT THE TIME OF THE VILLAGE PEOPLE AND ALL THAT."

JEAN-ÉTIENNE SIRY

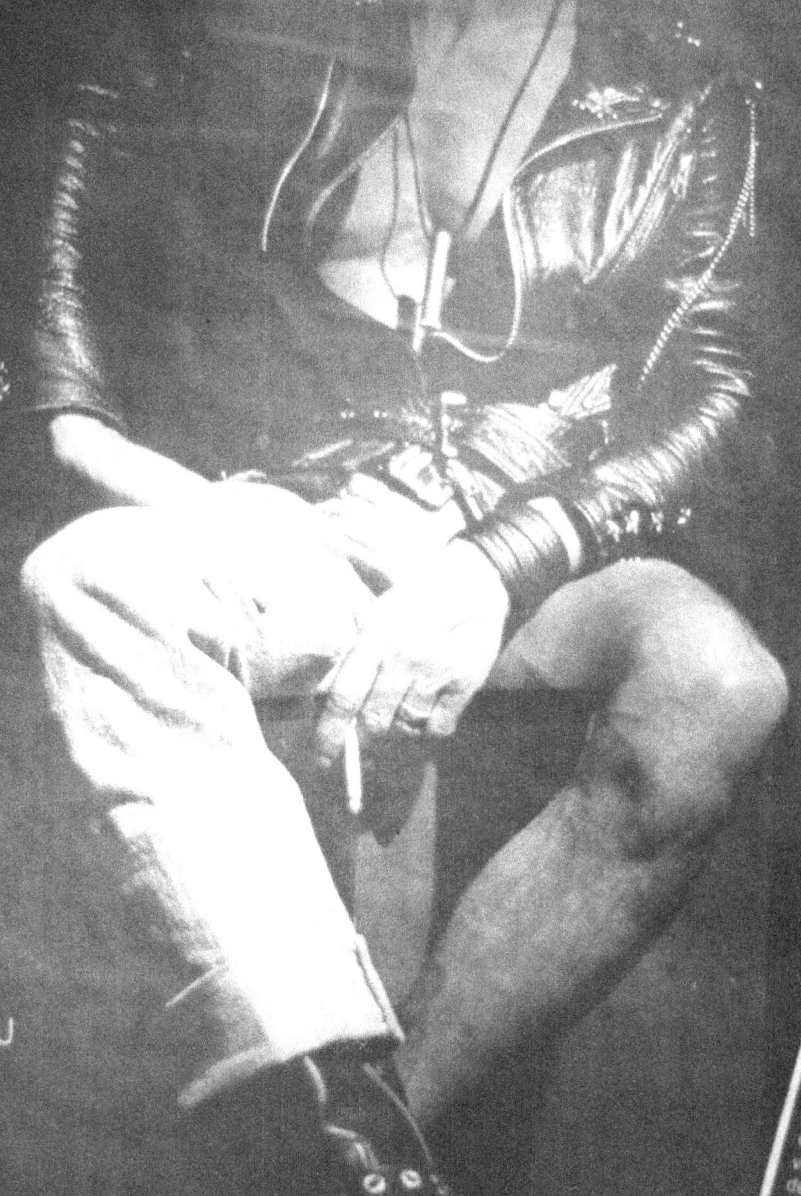

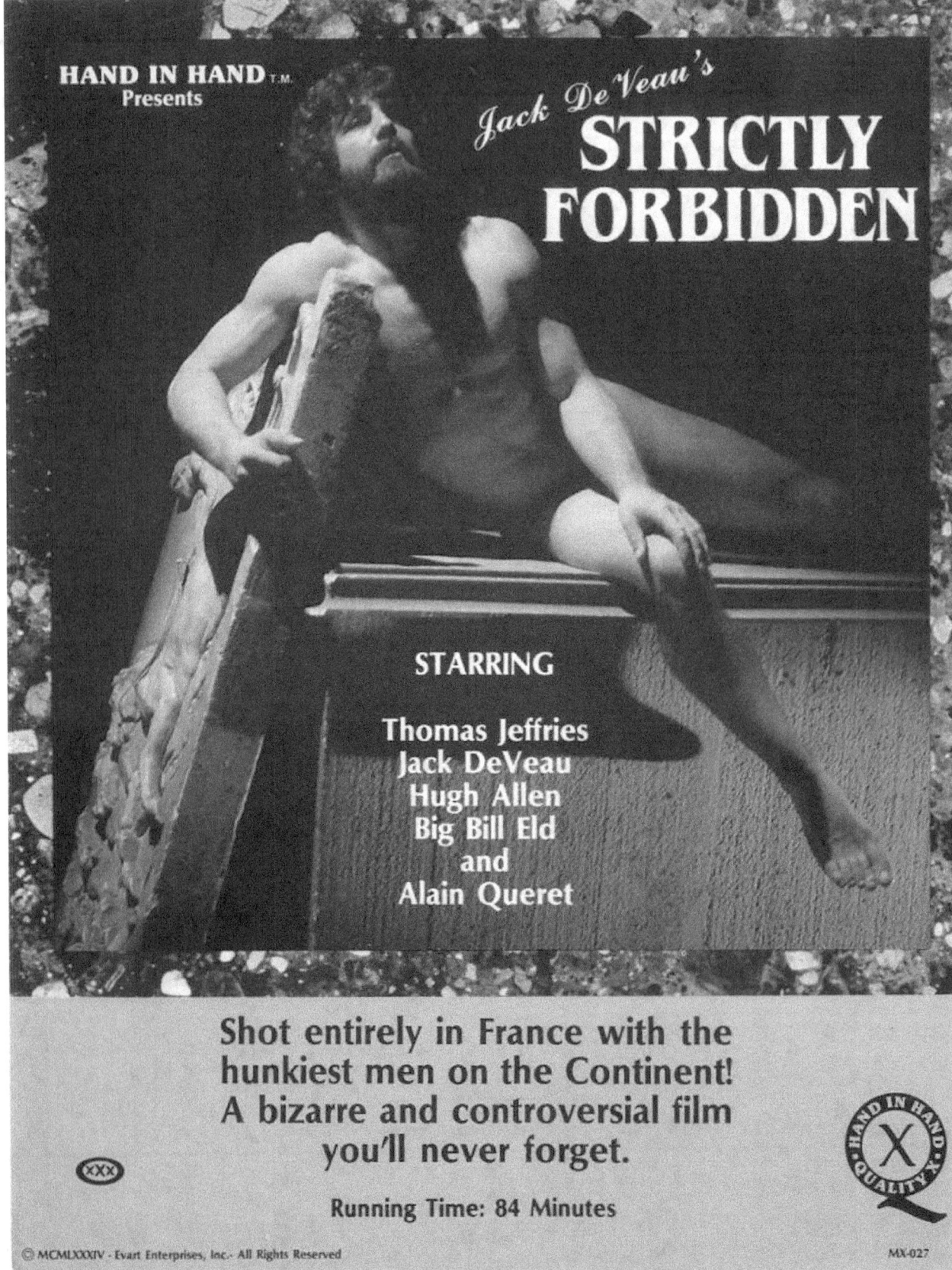

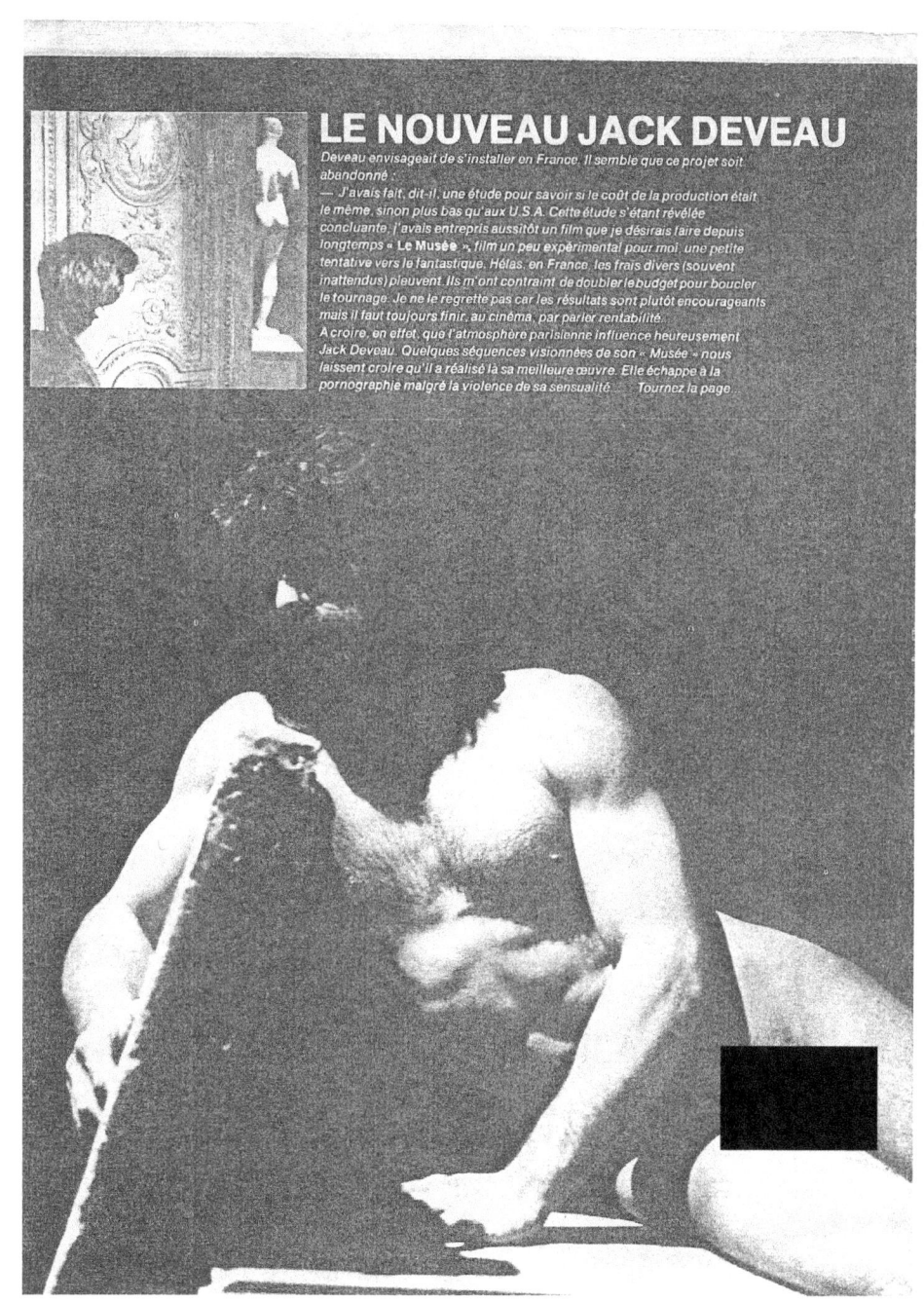

LE NOUVEAU JACK DEVEAU

Deveau envisageait de s'installer en France. Il semble que ce projet soit abandonné :
— J'avais fait, dit-il, une étude pour savoir si le coût de la production était le même, sinon plus bas qu'aux U.S.A. Cette étude s'étant révélée concluante, j'avais entrepris aussitôt un film que je désirais faire depuis longtemps « Le Musée », film un peu expérimental pour moi, une petite tentative vers le fantastique. Hélas, en France, les frais divers (souvent inattendus) pleuvent. Ils m'ont contraint de doubler le budget pour boucler le tournage. Je ne le regrette pas car les résultats sont plutôt encourageants mais il faut toujours finir, au cinéma, par parler rentabilité.
A croire, en effet, que l'atmosphère parisienne influence heureusement Jack Deveau. Quelques séquences visionnées de son « Musée » nous laissent croire qu'il a réalisé là sa meilleure œuvre. Elle échappe à la pornographie malgré la violence de sa sensualité.   Tournez la page

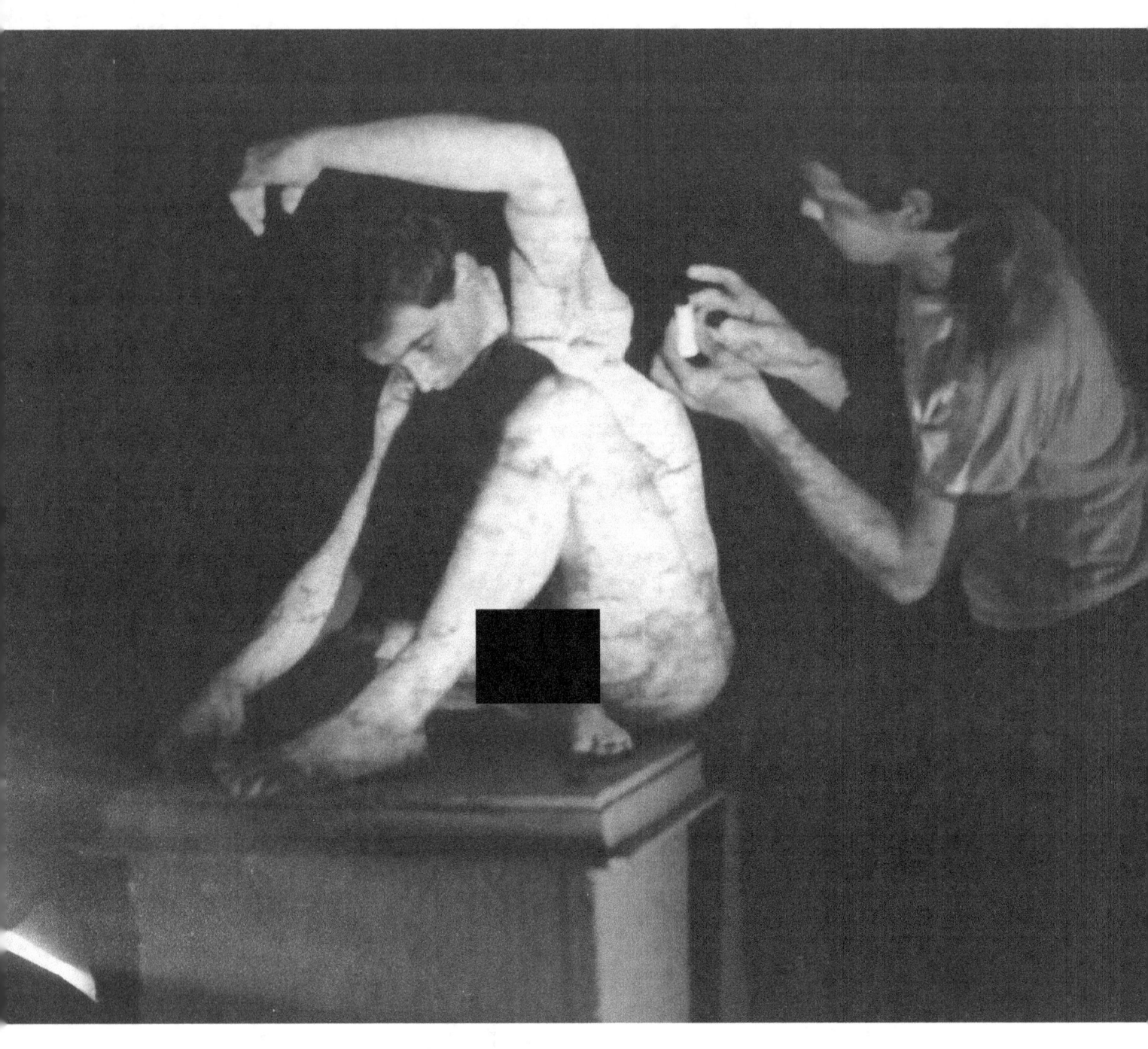

Thomas Jeffries being made up as a statue by a local make up man for the final sequence in *La Musee*.

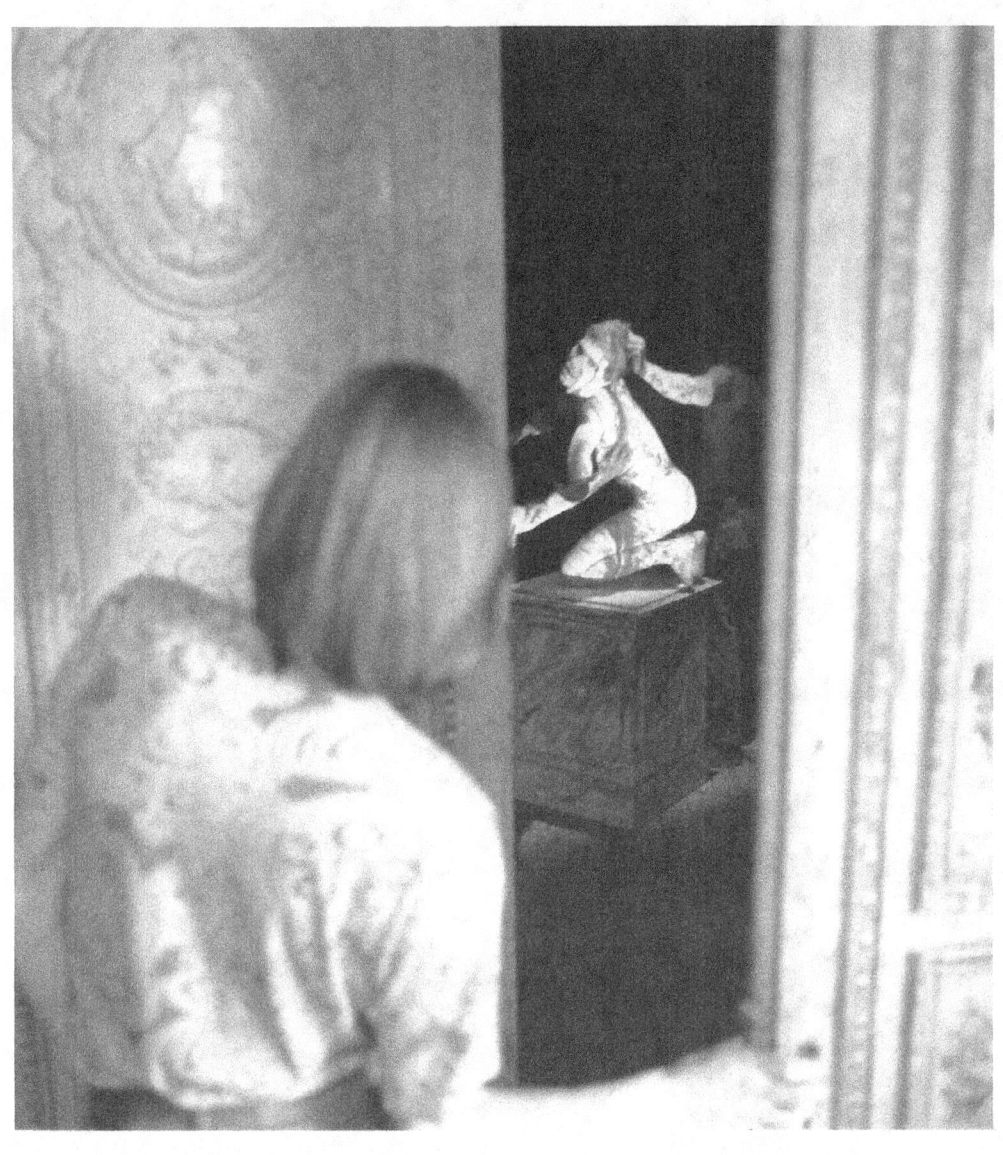

The next day (no one could ever explain it), yet another marble statue hab appeared in the gallery.
Daniel Mesplet looking into the museum.

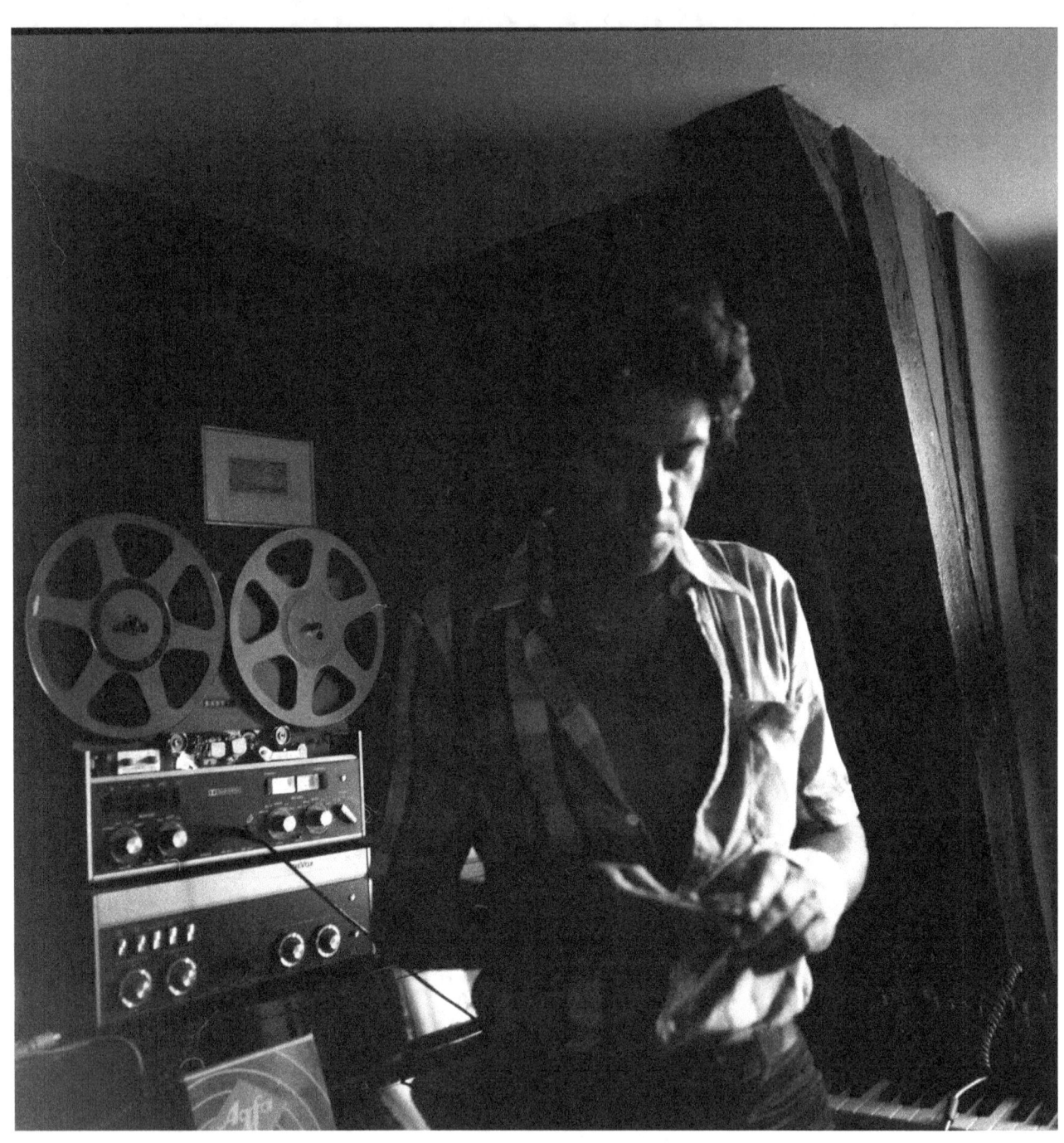

Didier Vasseur, the composer of the music for *La Musee* in his recording studio.

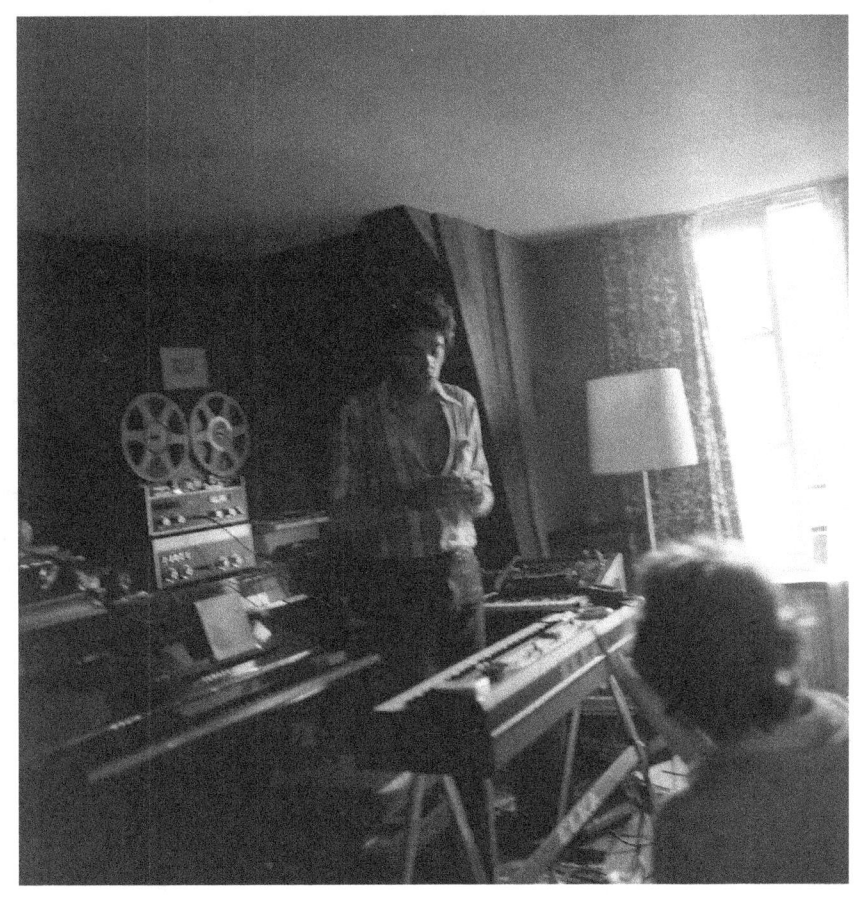

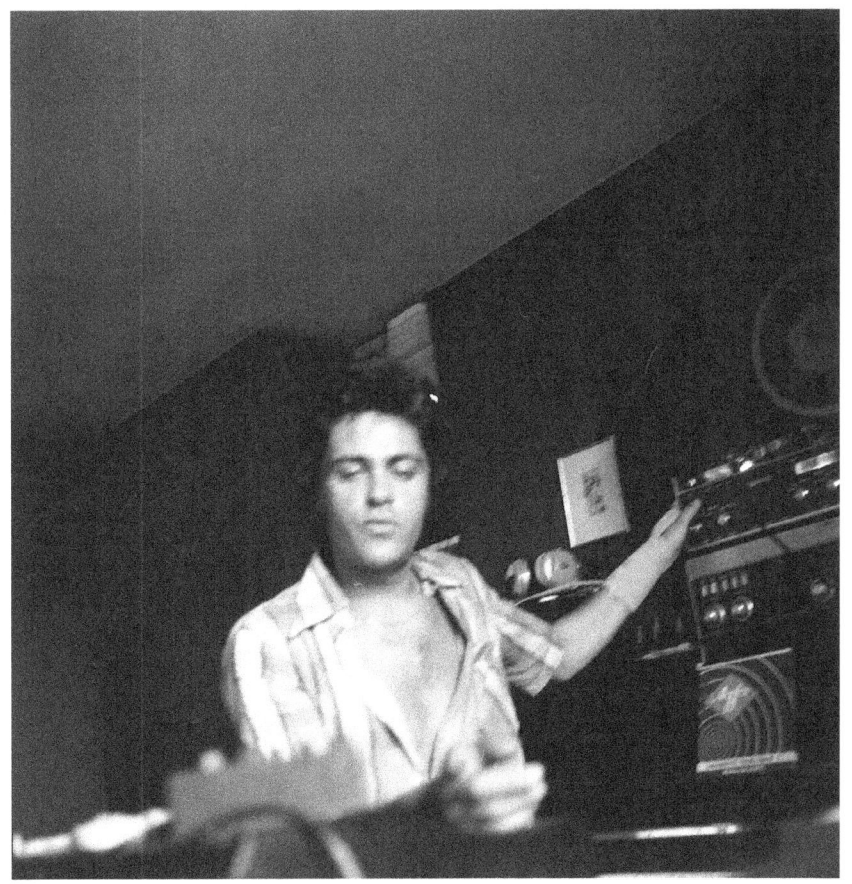

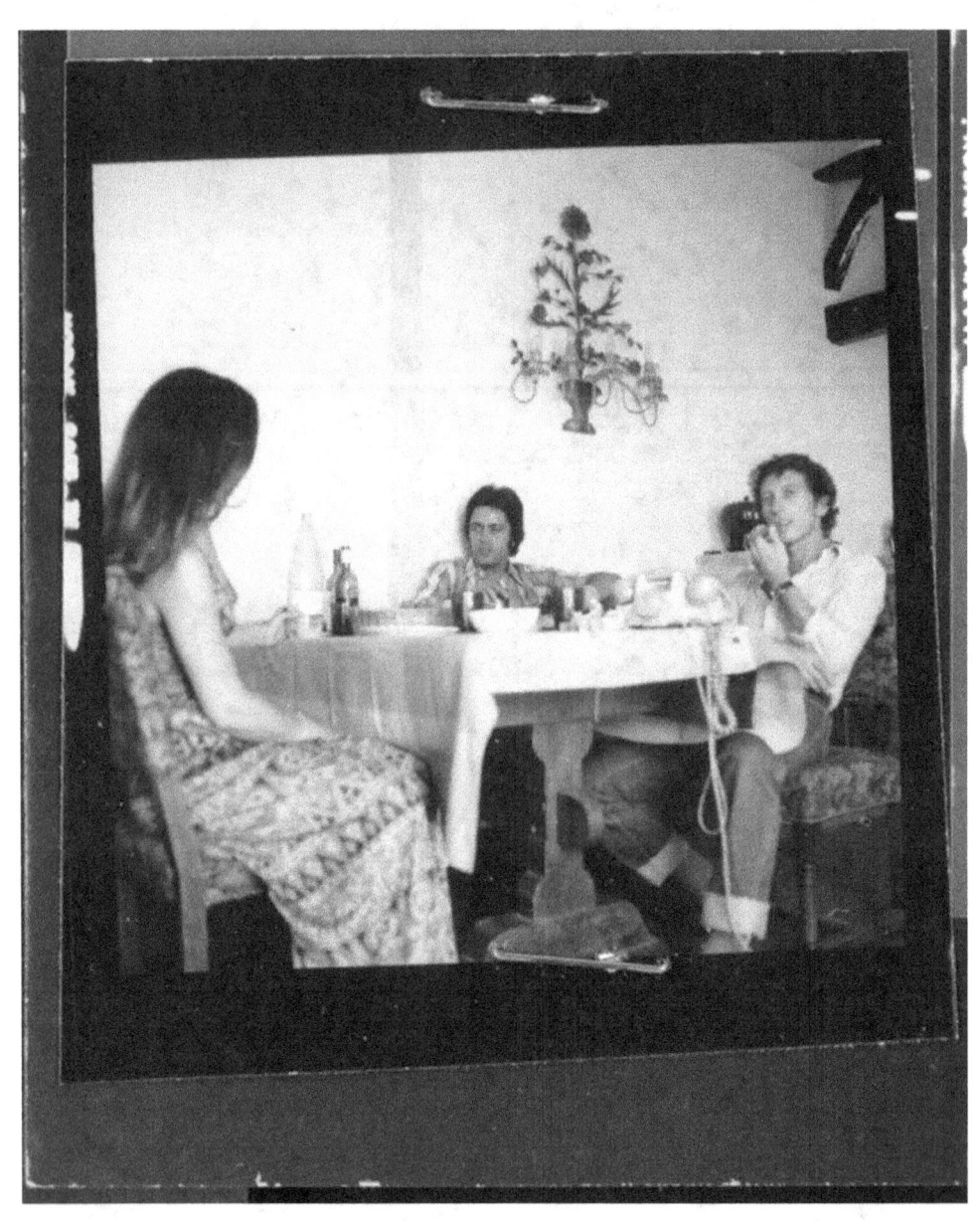

"Prior to *La Musee*, the session we had to go over the music. Didier Vasseur (middle), his wife (left) and me." **ROBERT ALVAREZ**

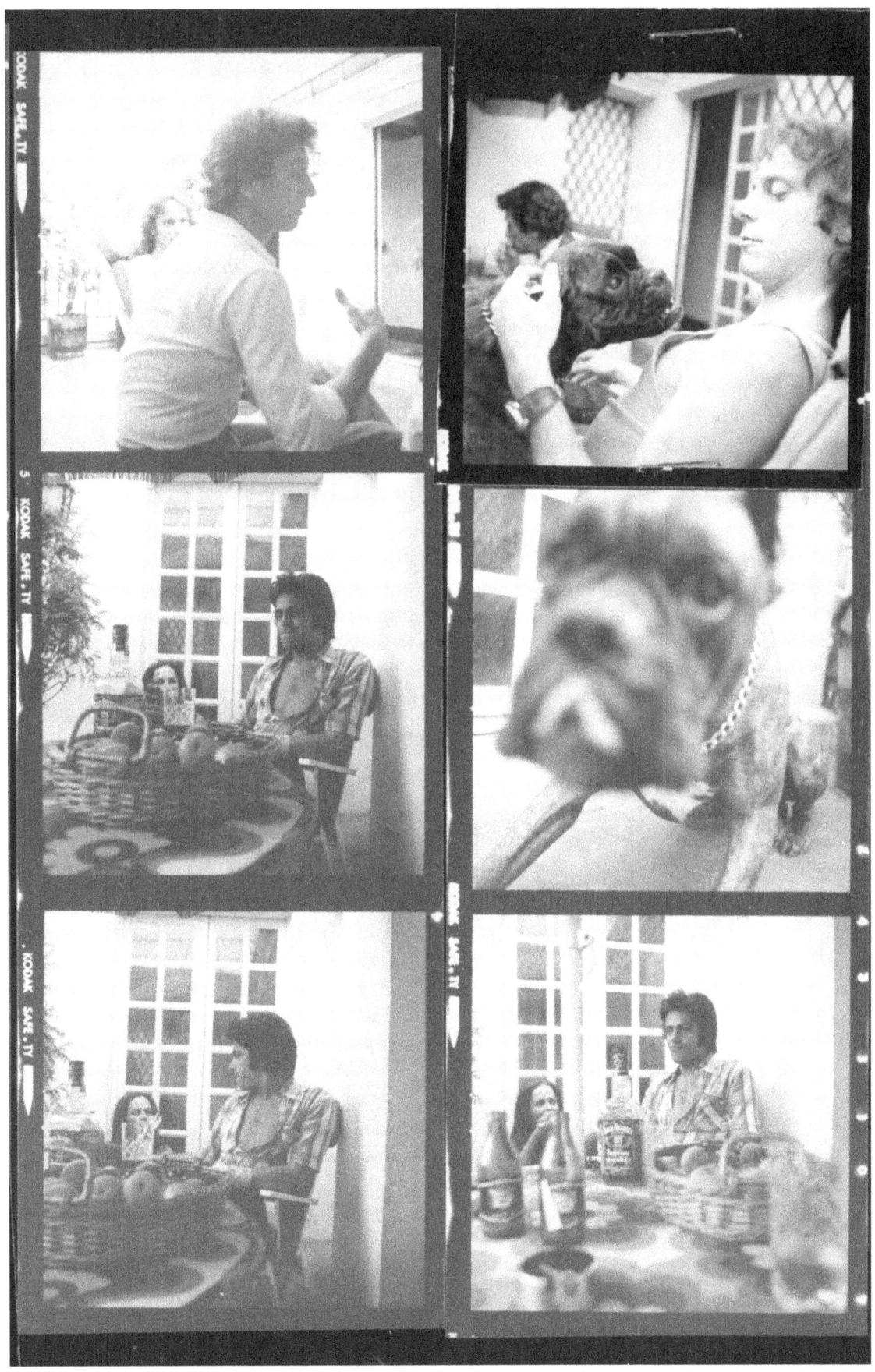

FRANÇOIS ABOUT

French Porn's First Cinematographer

The conversation with François About, on a lovely sunny afternoon in the Paris suburb Argenteuil, famous for the paintings Claude Monet made on the banks of the river, starts by talking about the most important thing: love.

François About: Philippe Vallois, the director with whom I made three, four films, said to me: François, if you haven't infected yourself with AIDS it's because you always fall in love with hetero boys. And this is my problem! *(laughs)*
Gary Vanisian: I think it would be correct to call you the first cinematographer in the history of French adult gay movies. Please tell me about your background.
About: Before moving to Paris to study at the École Louis Lumière, a film school formerly situated in Paris and now close to Paris, I wanted to please my parents who stayed behind in Morocco, where my father worked as a functionary. I had finished the "bac C" [an old high school diploma], and afterwards wanted to make a science degree. In Morocco this wouldn't have been easy, so I went to Marseille all alone and enrolled myself in the local university. I took quite difficult scientific courses. I did my best! *(laughs)* We students were also offered to work in a factory. During that time, I fell in love with a boy called Nano Cecchini.
Vanisian: You also signed some of your films as Nano Cecchini.
About: Well, Nano Cecchini was my first love.
Vanisian: He was Italian, I suppose?
About: Yes, he had Italian origins, and he lived in Nice at that time, so I visited Nice many times. At other times, he would stay at my place, and we tried to study natural sciences. *(laughs)* And one day I couldn't restrain myself any longer and start biting his ear and kissing him like a madman, whereupon he ran away. He wasn't homosexual. And anytime later when I wanted to make love to him, he ran away. While continuing my studies in Marseille, having courses such as Chemistry 1, Chemistry 2, General Chemistry etc., I was hopelessly in love with this boy who rejected me. So, I apply for the qualifying examination at the École Louis Lumière –bam, I made it and moved to Paris! Thus I quit my life in Marseille and my science studies because of a boy with whom I fell in love and who rejected me.
Vanisian: Why did you choose to apply at the École Louis Lumière at all? Were you interested in photography and film before?
About: Well, what did I do while I was studying in Marseille? It was I who took care of the local ciné-club. I was projecting the films. Before each film, I held an introduction. I realized then that I was very interested in cinema and not made to become an engineer in a factory. Therefore I left everything and moved to Paris and became a "cinéaste." At the film school, there were courses in which I could use my knowledge of chemistry, but what interested me most was to make films. All of the school's cameras were more or less broken, so I also started mending them. There were directors who would visit the school, for example Philippe de Broca, together with the famous DoP Pierre L'homme who took me for his assistant. The assistant-cameraman of Pierre L'homme died this year, and do you know how I found out about it? I watched the César award ceremony. At one point, all the people are remembered who left us this year. And I heard almost exclusively names of people whom I had known, technicians, editors, cameramen, sound engineers and so on. At the École Louis Lumière, I had learned to charge almost any kind of camera, be it an Éclair or an Arri or whatsoever. Nowadays, one has forgotten all about it, you just use memory cards. *(laughs)* Which explains why DoPs are not important anymore. Just look at the camera magazines, even the specialized ones, they don't mention the name of the DoP anymore. In the 1970s, everyone knew the name of the DoP for any film one saw. At that time you also had to be registered by your name in order to execute your part in the crew. The production had to forward the name of each member of the technical crew and the crew member's professional number. However, for certain films, I would indicate another name than my own. I took the name of a lover of mine who had died, Serge de Beaurivage. Certain films which

I shot are credited to Serge de Beaurivage. That's me! *(laughs)*

Vanisian: You worked with acclaimed directors of French cinema as a camera operator and assistant cinematographer, so you learned the craft from the tops of the business. How did it come that you came to adult movies in the early 70s?

About: Well, so I studied at the École Louis Lumière. Upon leaving it after two years of studies and completing my promotion, I myself was a patron of promotions. Through this I got to know a young cinematographer who learned I was homosexual – I didn't hide it – and who told me: "François, there is a director who is asking me to make a film with him with a gay screenplay, and I can't do it." So he presented me to Philippe Vallois, and I accepted to photograph the first homosexual feature film in Paris in the 1970s, moreover, using my flat as a set. A film that was called Johan. Because Philippe Vallois had fallen in love with a boy of that name, Johan, – who, unfortunately, is still in prison as of now, he had killed somebody – and wanted to shoot a movie with him. The problem was that the boy got locked up in jail shortly before we could start. I said to Philippe: "Let's do the film with an actor who has all the characteristics of this Johan." So Philippe Vallois is responsible for my having started working in homosexual cinema. It would be worthwhile that his filmography be studied properly, especially since he is still making films; he even wanted to have me for one of his last films which I had to decline for health reasons. After JOHAN I made another film with him, NOUS ÉTIONS UN SEUL HOMME, with Serge Avedikian, who is not homosexual, and another guy. Vallois was very doubtful, while I, taking the camera on my shoulders, filming him, told to Vallois: "It will work!" The story takes place during the German occupation of France: the young actor, Piotr Stanislas, falls in love with a German soldier. It was complex and about the fact that a young French man falls in love with a Nazi. That's the story of the film.

Vanisian: In many countries the sexual revolution opened a huge market for erotic movies and unsimulated sex on the screen. How was it with gay pornography, was that accepted as part of the sexual revolution and the new industry? Was it more closeted than straight porn first?

About: Well, the atmosphere of this era, it was 1975, was like this: in Paris homosexuality was still a crime, according to the law. Thus it's true that since there were only a few homosexual clubs labeled as "gay", close to the Opéra, nowhere else, because the police wouldn't allow them elsewhere. They were surveilling the area around Opéra, in the Rue Sainte-Anne, this was the center.

Vanisian: Which nowadays is the "Japanese street" with many Japanese restaurants and shops?

About: That's true, now the Japanese are there.

Vanisian: Why was this particular area the center for homosexual bars and clubs?

About: I couldn't tell how it developed but there was even a café, a brasserie, where one would meet each other. This was where I met all the young directors who were about to start their career. It was in the Avenue de l'Opéra, I forgot the name of the place. But suddenly, in this area around the opera, all the homosexual clubs opened up in the 1970s. What would happen occasionally was that – at that time I was young and hanging around a lot in these places *(laughs)* – suddenly the police would enter the club and ask all people inside for their documents, having them stand against the wall and spreading their legs. And so at that time a major duty of the French police was to make lists of the queers. Thus I had to pay a high price for this film Johan for which I let Philippe Vallois shoot at my place. The neighbors complained. I was renting the place, had a contract for six years with a society that was loaning the apartments, very beautiful artists' studios, which is why, obviously, Philippe Vallois wanted to shoot there. Another director had actually shot before at my place, Guy Gilles, who died very young, he made LE JARDIN QUI BASCULE at my place. So, the neighbors filed a complaint because two homosexual films where shot at my place.

Vanisian: How did the neighbors notice it at all?

About: Because they saw the actors passing by, they asked them questions. When Guy Gilles shot at my place, I was not there because I was working on another film and couldn't be his DoP. And once a guy who was at my promotion in Vaugirard at the École Louis Lumière brought some spotlights up to my apartment and immediately the neighbors realized that a film was being shot there. When I asked for my rental agreement to be renewed, I was told: "Normally it wouldn't be a problem since you always paid your rent on time, but your neighbors don't accept anymore that a homosexual lives in this apartment." Here you have the atmosphere of the 1970s. The socialists had to come to power, Mitterrand, to change something. Mitterrand was elected in 1982 and decriminalized homosexuality, he abolished the law. Nowadays, one doesn't talk much about this anymore, more often the Simone-Weill-law is mentioned, but one rarely speaks about the fact that Mitterrand was responsible for homosexuals not being persecuted anymore. Because what had happened before all around me? There was the Jardin de Sacre Coeur, and the police would regularly come with buses and gathered all the boys there. It was a horror. And thus to make a homosexual film – for me it turned out a catastrophe. Suddenly my name was branded as "homosexual." All the people with whom I had worked, Philippe Garrel, Maurice Pialat, great filmmakers, started avoiding me. With Garrel I had worked on LA CICATRICE INTÉRIEURE, which starred Nico. I got along very well with Nico because I spoke German and she didn't speak very well French. Philippe Garrel even got mad at me, he was very young at that time: "You are speaking to Nico?!" And I: "Yes, because I can speak German with her." She liked me a lot. But I can tell you that there was another actor with whom I was very much in love during this film: Pierre Clémenti. He was a provocative person, and I adored this. Once we passed a border, and we were controlled by the border police. I saw Clémenti taking out a piece of shit and asking: "Are you looking for this?" These are fond memories. We shot LA CICATRICE INTÉRIEURE in 1969. After that I also made a film for a Hungarian filmmaker who had left Hungary for political reasons. The DoP was Jean Badal, who died just recently, and his assistant was Peter Kassovitz, whose son is Mathieu Kassovitz. I held Mathieu in my hands when he was small. When Peter Kassovitz later found out that I was homosexual, he didn't ask for my services anymore. And thus I realized that certain persons didn't hire me anymore because they had learned that I am homosexual. I was locked up in the homosexual cinema.

Vanisian: But did you feel that those colleagues were avoiding you because they really had a problem with homosexuality or was it rather for opportunistic reasons?

About: It's a complex issue. Often it could have to do with the producers. Actually, I received confirmation of this sentiment by a true champion, who later became a great DoP, a good friend at that time whom I saw once a week: Nestor Almendros. When I was finishing the École Louis Lumière, it was in 1965, I was hired for a job by the school television. At the shooting I saw a Cuban, Almendros, he wasn't known at all at that time. And why did he leave Cuba for France? Because in Cuba he had been in jail. I told him that I was openly homosexual, and he said: "François, you are lost. I, too, am homosexual, but I am hiding it, I never tell this to anyone." And so he became the DoP of Truffaut and many other great filmmakers, but he was hiding his homosexuality. His lover at that time was an American with whom I, too, have worked later. He even invited me to come to San Francisco and shoot a gay film with him but it didn't work out, however, I worked with him on another film. I also once went to New York and worked as a set photographer. With Jacques Scandelari I worked together in this function on a film whose screenplay went as follows: A French woman falls in love with a young American, they are going to marry in New York, but once they arrive there she realizes that her husband is homosexual! *(laughs)* This was Scandelari's screenplay, who didn't sign this film by the name Scandelari, but took a pseudonym instead. He told me: "François, I am doing films for French television – if they found out I am homosexual, they won't hire me anymore." Once again I am relating you the atmosphere of the 1970s. And during this time there was only one person who was calling me, who had seen the homosexual films I had done before – it was Marc Dorcel. He was a specialist of hardcore films, but with straight sex. He called me up: "You have been doing homosexual films, would you accept to work on hetero films?" "Of course, why not?" He had seen my way of photographing and understood that I was not working like most of the others. Because I wasn't interested in all the genital close-ups. What interested me foremost was the look on the actors' faces. Thus I became the first DoP to shoot the great Italian X-actor, Rocco Siffredi. He did his first film with me being DoP, in France, the director was Michel Ricault, who died under mysterious circumstances. Why did I film Siffredi nicely? He was a good looking boy, he knew I am homosexual, and when he saw me getting behind the camera, he tried his best to look as good as possible, he knew I was somebody who would appreciate it. *(laughs)* I became good friend with Siffredi, he was a good actor and subsequently also cast in "normal" films, by Catherine Breillat, for instance.

Vanisian: Jack Deveau and the people of

Hand In Hand had a thing for Paris, they loved to visit, made friends there, shot ADAM & YVES in the city. Were you familiar with Deveau's work, or did you know him in person? Can you remember when you met him first?

About: So, one day Jack Deveau made some inquiries and finally wanted to meet me. Deveau stayed in a big hotel in the 5th arrondissement during his time in Paris. We got in touch and immediately understood each other perfectly. He said to me: "I will shoot a film with you but you have to help me because this film will be titled LE MUSEE [The Museum]. It's about a young American who visits a museum and has himself locked up inside. Later at night, all the statues become alive and violate him." So I took my 16mm Éclair camera on my shoulders and together with Jack Deveau and the young American, we present ourselves at the entrance of the Musée Rodin, in the center of Paris, not far from the Invalides. Looking back, I find this incredible! Nowadays I wouldn't be able to do this. Yet, back then I started talking to the person at the entrance of the museum and told him I was accompanying an American tourist who had to return to the US very soon and didn't have enough time to ask for permission to shoot inside. The friendly lady at the entrance allowed us to go in. Thus, my loaded camera on my shoulders, like a tourist, and together with Jack Deveau and the young American, we enter the museum. All the shots in the film where you see the young man looking at the Rodin sculptures, we made them there. Afterwards, we shot all the hardcore scenes in a nightclub in Paris, a location of no great interest. But what was surprising was that Jack Deveau thought that all the French were lousy, and he brought everybody with him, even equipment, e.g. the flag, the thing you put in front of a spotlight to let through the light, a kind of black plate, he even brought this kind of stuff with him to Paris – and then he realized I had this kind of equipment myself, and we didn't need this at all. All the actors came over from New York, they were quite tired when they arrived here and weren't in good shape. This caused some problems, the scenes in the nightclub weren't very exciting, the guys didn't do so well, so Jack became annoyed… By the way, he spoke very well French, extremely well. What I liked about him: he was a true filmmaker.

Vanisian: How do you remember Jack Deveau as a person and how long did you stay in contact afterwards?

About: We stayed in touch. When I later went to New York, I also realized that he had money. Meaning he lived in a big apartment with a terrace, he showed his place to me. All his actors were his friends. So when Jack invited me to visit him, all his "world", all his gay hardcore actors were there. Because sometimes he suddenly wanted to shoot a scene and then they were all around. *(laughs)* It was a family-kind of thing with Jack. I went out with him a couple of times in New York.

Vanisian: Besides the personal aspects, how was it to work with Jack Deveau, especially compared to the non-porn filmmakers you worked with before? Before he worked with you, he had been his own DoP, so I imagine he was very precise regarding what kind of shots he wanted and the images?

About: He was very precise and knew everything he was doing. On the other hand, he would let me do as I thought right; he gave me a lot of freedom. Each of us understood perfectly what the other had in mind. In that age, even a hardcore film was shot for at least one week, because you spent time to do it properly. And since the labs at that time were rather slow – unless you were a big budget production and able to pay high fees – you often would receive the rushes of the whole shots only after a week. Therefore, as a director, you had to have full confidence in the work of the DoP.

Vanisian: There were no difficulties with the labs regarding them having to develop hardcore material?

About: No, not at all. Back at that time, there were three major labs in France, LTC (Laboratoire des Tirages Cinematographiques) in Saint-Cloud, there was Éclair in the north of Paris and there was GTC in Joinville, which still exists, though taken over. And I believe they were too big as to worry about what they were developing, unless it was something really illegal. The great thing back than was that, especially with smaller productions such as the hardcore ones – you didn't have money at all for post-production, as it is nowadays. All these changes of color etc., we couldn't do it back then. The film would, apart from minor corrections, look just the way you recorded it on the film stock.

Vanisian: Most of the American adult movies of the time were shot on 16mm, very few on 35mm – was it the same thing in France, or did you shoot also a lot in 35mm?

About: In that case it was also 16mm, but later on, with Norbert Thierry and his production company Les films de la Troïka, I would also shoot quite some films in 35mm before the video cassettes came.

Vanisian: Did you design the look of the film STRICTLY FORBIDDEN together with Jack or did he leave you alone to express your style? Many sequences remind one of the language of horror movies – how do you remember Jack Deveau's ideas, did he want the movie kind of dark and heavy?

About: These horror elements were my own choice. I always did the lighting with Fresnel spotlights. This is the name of the glass with is in front of the lamp, an episcope, which transforms the light into parallels. So I often would light actors with parallel lights. And yes, you are right; this gives an impression which you often find in horror movies. Nowadays, one doesn't tend anymore to work with reflections; you work with soft light because video or low definition digital is less sensible to highly complex contrasts. I had very few means back then, e.g. sometimes with Philippe Vallois I would only have three spotlights, and once when we went to Morocco to shoot a film there, none of the equipment I had listed beforehand as important arrived. Thus for one whole week I lit the scenes with copper and worked, so to say, with the sun.

Vanisian: There was a disagreement between the producers and Hand In Hand, so the movie remained unfinished, and the print was sneaked out of the country by Jack Deveau. How much do you know about the complications?

About: The problem was that Jack began the editing – and I told him that I was at his disposal if he would have had to reshoot scenes or something alike – and the guy who had rented him the editing room, he was the owner of three cinemas on the Grands Boulevards in Paris, René Chateau. And you know who his lover was at that time? Brigitte Lahaie. I was the first to photograph her in a movie shooting, JE SUIS À PRENDRE (I'M YOURS TO TAKE). It was the first film with horses, because she adores them. So I shot scenes where she was fucked directly beneath a horse. The director of this film was Francis Leroi. Leroi was a director who had before made many films which were not hardcore films at all. One day he started making pornographic films, and he later directed some of the later EMMANUELLE-films, from EMMANUELLE IV on. But he fell out with me because once we went together to Moscow to shoot a porn film there. Imagine, in the 1980s! It was already the time of Gorbachev, but still… Once we arrived there, I realized he was scared all the time. He locked himself up in his room and told me: "François, shut up when we are in a cab, because even there they overhear you." He was afraid to go to jail because of shooting porn scenes in Moscow at that time. Thus we made this wonderful film but didn't enjoy ourselves at all. I had wanted that we use locations or situations such as the May Day parade. I wanted to go there and shoot some footage with a shoulder camera. And once we arrived there, we were asked to participate and represent France! *(laughs)* But because he was obstructing even this pleasure, I clinched with Francis Leroi and said to myself that I would never shoot any film with him again. However, returning to Jack Deveau: This guy, René Chateau, had made a distribution agreement with Jack Deveau, and LE MUSÉE was the first film to be screened in his gay cinema. The problem was that Deveau didn't get along at all with Chateau. They had a quarrel, and Deveau took all the rushes from the editing room and took them with him to New York to edit the film there. And thus the film was released in the U.S. with another title, STRICTLY FORBIDDEN. So you see, it's quite dramatic and disgusting: René Chateau made a film, with the rushes Deveau had left – there was some material which hadn't been in the editing room – which he released in his turn in France, which I haven't seen at all. Instead of Jack Deveau, he asked a young assistant director, Alain Roy, who never made his own feature film, to lend his name as a director for the credits of this film. And subsequently I never contacted Chateau again, because I found his behavior so wrong.

Vanisian: The lighting for the film was made by another Hand In Hand veteran Jack Deveau brought in from New York: Gene Kelton, who was a Broadway person and also worked with pioneer gay filmmaker Wakefield Poole. Can you remember him?

About: No, I must admit that I don't recall him. Basically the only crew member which Jack had brought with him to the shooting I do remember very well is Jean-Étienne Siry. Everybody in the gay scene, back at that time, in the gay nightclubs, knew that his specialty was fistfucking. He was the only one doing it at that time in Paris, yet he didn't want it to be known. He participated in the shooting as Jack's assistant and had a good time making puns at the American actors. *(laughs)*

Vanisian: Did you talk with Jack about the

script, which had been written by Siry?
About: Not at all. I had found this idea – a young American guy locked up in a museum with sculptures coming to life – brilliant, but that was about all I discussed with Jack regarding the script. In the final version of the film, I believe this idea had been wasted due to all these production problems. Deveau died at a very young age and didn't do another film in France. We once went to visit a nightclub together in New York and he gave me something to smoke with was not pot at all, so it is not entirely surprising that he died young.
Vanisian: Do you remember anything regarding the reactions of the French public to STRICTLY FORBIDDEN / LE MUSÉE?
About: I remember foremost entering the cinema – not only for this film, for many others, in Paris as well as in Marseille – and seeing all the guys rushing towards the toilets located next to the main cinema hall. I think this interested them more than all the films that were shown there. *(laughs)*
Vanisian: By the way – did you visit the Adonis in New York? Most of the Troïka-Films and Hand In Hand films were projected in this gigantic cinema. If yes, please tell me your impression. If no, did you go to any adult movie theater in NY?
About: Yes, I remember the wonderful Adonis cinema. And all the liberty you had there: I was hanging out in the nightclubs– more than in the cinemas, surely – and one day, in a three-floor-nightclub, I saw a man enter the room, and a few minutes later I had sex with him, in the middle of one of the floors. I could never have done anything alike in Paris!
Vanisian: Let's talk about the Paris-based adult movie production company Les films de la Troïka. Did they make the same thing like American companies like Hand In Hand and others: Did they sell 8mm prints of the films for private buyers?
About: Well, what happened when I shot for the Films de la Troïka? The Troïka, Norbert Thierry, – who also owned his own cinema in the Rue du Dragon, later on also in Marseille – told me: "François, I want to make French films, we need French actors." And he sent me, without giving me any kind of possibility to choose for myself, some French actors, who were really lousy! *(laughs)* So I mingled the French with some American actors and I made three films in one week for Norbert Thierry, which, as I remember, I had credited as Serge de Beauregard. With an Éclair 16mm in New York. The Americans are not efficient at all with 16mm. Even when loaning a camera. You know, when loaning a camera I always first of all made tests with it, for stability. And each second camera magazine I loaned in New York lacked stability. So I had to throw away the majority of my rushes. Norbert Thierry arrived in New York before we started shooting these three films. Shooting these films in New York was wonderful, for instance filming a hardcore scene on a lovely terrace and with construction sites in the background. You know, I liked using these kind of backgrounds. Even despite the problem of the lacking stability of the majority of my rushes, they were able to edit three films from all the material I shot in New York. During this time, I regularly went to Jack Deveau. And he fell in love with one of the actors Thierry had sent me. Deveau took him out, and at that time, in 1975, all the gay people in New York went to Fire Island, an island not far away from Manhattan. It was unbelievable, there were only homosexuals! *(laughs)* An island of encounters, little amusements. And on this island, Deveau introduced me – you know to whom? A well-known director, William Friedkin. Who otherwise lived next to the place I stay at in New York. And so Friedkin has seen the footage I had shot about the gay world of New York – everybody knew immediately I was homosexual, and I never had problems to enter places – he was invited to the premiere by our producer, and one year later I learned by chance that he had made his film CRUISING. And later he confessed to me: "Yes, it was you who made me keen on doing CRUISING." However, he wasn't able to shoot his film in the real locations, as I could do it. He once tried to shoot in a gay nightclub, but the people there would cut the cables of his equipment, so he had to build the sets in a studio.
Vanisian: LE BEAU MEC – another one of the highly praised gay porn movies of this era – is also a little bit of Hand In Hand history because they distributed the film. Please share some thoughts or anecdotes about the movie, its actors, or director Wallace Potts. For example, did you see the short animation gay porn movie that Wallace Potts had directed a few years before? [DEMI-GODS, a cut-out-animation film and a political satire – also distributed by Hand In Hand in the US]
About: Oh yes, I was the DoP on this film. Wallace was the lover of Nestor Almendros, the young guy I had mentioned previously. And before Almendros, he was the lover of Rudolf Nureyev,

the famous dancer. Nestor had refused to work with him as a DoP, saying he didn't want to risk his career. He then asked me if I would help Wallace. At what time was this? 1977. Wallace was a boy I loved a lot, he was very talented, very calm, and he knew what he wanted. He asked me later to come to San Francisco to shoot another feature film with him which eventually didn't work out and I never saw him again. I don't know what became of him. And I have never seen this film you just mentioned, DEMI-GODS, I only know LE BEAU MEC. You know, I have met people of whom I have wonderful memories, and then some... Let me tell you: I always had been a lover of old-timers. Once I bought a Citroen 15CV, the car of all the robbers and gangsters. And the mechanic who mended the car told me: "I have a younger brother who would love to work in cinema." I said I would like to meet him, and he presented me a boy of 14, 15 years who didn't seem to cut his hair at all; I didn't see his eyes because the hair was hanging over it. He doesn't even say "Hello" to me. However, I was willing to teach him a few things, so I had him come to Paris, and I ended up being something like a father for him for seven years! I took him to all the camera equipment stores, showed him how to handle cameras, how to make tests in order to choose a lens etc. I treated this boy as if he were my son. He was not my lover, please mind! I taught him everything. His name is Thierry Arbogast. Now he is very famous.

Vanisian: Foremostly for his cooperation with Luc Besson.

About: One day I saw a short film of Besson, and saw that Thierry had shot it. Besson had already done two films before he started working together with Thierry. How come? Besson wants to have control of everything, so most of the DoPs didn't get along well with him. He wanted to have a young DoP, inexperienced, who would listen to him. So he somehow learned about Thierry, knew that he had learned from me, and took him as his DoP. What did Thierry do then? I learned this from some producers: He went to see producers and told them: "François prefers to shoot hardcore films". This wasn't true at all. Thus my assistant of almost ten years let me down. But when I saw how he does the lightning, I realized that it's almost like I do it. He has learned a lot from me. There was another person which let me down terribly, who even wants my death. Michel Ricaud, a great director, one who always knew what he wanted, was produced by Marc Dorcel. One day, a big Swedish hardcore production contacted Ricaud and told him they wanted to produce a movie that was to be directed by him. Ricaud told me that, though he was uncomfortable about turning away from Dorcel, he would like to direct for this company since it was a big-budget hardcore film. So we went to the Seychelles to shoot this movie. There was a boy who went there one week earlier than us as a representative of the production to do the preparations. I felt that he had aspirations to direct films himself, and so he did later. Nowadays, he works in Hungary and there invites mothers and daughters to his hotel, lets the mother wait in a room while he fucks her daughter in the neighboring room and records it.

Vanisian: I believe you are talking about Pierre Woodman?

About: Exactly. Woodman was a policeman initially before he was fired from police service because he had raped some of his female colleagues at the police or sometimes girls who had been arrested. Subsequently, one day he became representative of this Swedish production company of hardcore films, and it was him waiting for us in the Seychelles. During the whole shooting he would give comments about the way we filmed, "No, you should put there camera here" and so on. Ricaud soon became fed up with him and even forbid him to be present at the screening of the rushes. He couldn't stand Woodman at all. Actually, we even shot another film during almost the same time, back-to-back, as you say, and at both films there was Woodman with these directorial aspirations. One day, we went to shoot scenes on a small Seychelles island and were supposed to go back by plane on the following day. Beautiful sets, lovely scenes. Ricaud had shot what he wanted and was satisfied while there was still time until our plane would take us back. We returned the cassettes to Woodman, and he noticed that one cassette still was in a "virgin state" – it was already the time when hardcore films were shot on video material. We replied: "Well, yes, we didn't need it, so the better." Whereupon Woodman replied: "It's out of question that we leave here unless all the cassettes have been used! You have to shoot also with this one." Ricaud turned to me and whispered how much this guy pissed him off. Nevertheless, I went to fetch the camera which earlier that morning, during the shooting on a small boat, had caught some water and which I had given to the make-up department to dry. I returned half an hour later to shoot something with the still untouched cassette. I didn't see either Woodman nor Ricaud. I asked somebody where they had gone and was told that they had started quarreling and then went down to the top of the island. I waited. What did I see some minutes later? I saw Woodman returning with a T-shirt soaked in blood. I asked him what had happened, and he told me that Ricaud had stepped on some cliffs, had slipped and fallen into the water and that he, Woodman, had tried to save him. I found this answer most strange, with him covered in blood and all that. I asked him where the accident had happened and went there with my camera. I saw that the cliffs were not even wet, completely dry, and in the water, a dark point far away, I saw a man floating. It was Michel Ricaud. He died there. Ricaud had a wife and two children; one of them has also died by now. What I believe is that they had a fight. Ricaud fell into the water and couldn't swim well. Woodman told later that there had been a wave which had fallen upon them. I doubt that it was an accident, as he tells it. There have, however, been no investigations about this case, as far as I know, no scientific examination. I left the island with the next plane because I had to return back to Paris. On the day of this event, the Seychelles had a national holiday, but still the police came because I had asked them to be called. And what did Woodman do? Michel was crazy about cigars; he had bought two beautiful wooden cigar boxes. When the police arrived, I saw Woodman offering cigars from these boxes bought by Ricaud to the policemen. Well... knowing about my doubts as to how this tragedy had occurred, Woodman had stated that if I would repeat them, he would accuse me of pedophilia. How so? In the hotel where we had stayed during the shooting, the owner had a son of around 14, 15 years. Ricaud had also seen him, and told me to do some screen tests with him since he was extremely beautiful and also interested in working in hardcore movies. So I filmed this boy, asked him questions, how came that he, at his young age, was interested in acting in X-films and other probably rather intimate things. And among all the rushes that Woodman had taken with him after Ricaud's death, there were also a few of these shots with this boy which he probably still has and which he would use against me, even though they are completely harmless.

Vanisian: Let's return back to the positive sides of your film career: Many of the adult films with your cinematography are not only done in high technical standards, a good number of them is considered to be more art than porn. Do you agree on that or did it feel different back then? What are your favorites in terms of having your fingerprint?

About: I don't have a particular favorite, but I can say as much that actors I worked with always said that I have brought them out nicely. While other DoPs in the hardcore business didn't care much about the images, I always tried to make the actors look beautiful. Never did they look ridiculous, even when they fucked in positions which can look embarrassing.

Vanisian: What was your technique regarding the shooting of hardcore scenes? First you shot a large shot and then the close-ups?

About: Yes. The difficult thing about close-ups was... for example, the assistant director of Francis Leroi was a specialist for creating false sperm. So, if it didn't work, if an actor couldn't finish – at that time, almost no actors took drugs or other stimulants – one didn't have time to wait, one called Leroi's assistant who would take egg white and mix it with some other stuff – I don't remember what it was – which eventually looked like sperm. He filled it into a syringe which he held next to my camera and when the time was right, he would "fire" it to simulate a cumshot.

Vanisian: Actors like Jean-Michel Sénécal – who directed also one movie on his own – appeared in straight and gay movies. Was there a lot of gay-for-pay in French adult moviemaking at the time?

About: The number of X-actors was limited in general, so almost all the actors would act in straight as well as gay movies. Likewise the directors who made gay movies: Norbert Thierry, Jacques Scandelari (directing under a false name), Jean-Etienne Siry. That's about it.

Vanisian: Many of the French adult movies you directed or shot as a cinematographer are very serious in tone and narration, not very comedic. Can you confirm that the French porn movie of the time was much darker as those from the US or Germany?

About: I don't think so. Maybe this impression is due to the way how certain films were reedited later on, as e.g. Bijou in the US reedits certain films in order to make them more appealing, excluding certain narrative scenes and thus maybe making them lighter.

Vanisian: Your own feature films, TOP MAN and

À LA RECHERCHE DE DOUGLAS, both were produced by the company Les films de la Troïka. Do you remember something regarding the schedule and budget? Did you have the creative freedom to make the films just as you wanted them to be?

About: Yes, my first feature was produced by Norbert Thierry who had simply asked me one day if I wanted to direct a feature film for once instead of "only" photographing. It was pure chance, I hadn't really thought about directing before. As for Thierry: He knew about my skills as a photographer, and he also knew that directors often have no clue at all! *(laughs)* And that DoPs can be more influential to the look of a film than the directors. Thus, yes, I shot these two and also UN ARABE À NEW YORK for which I "used" my lover at that time, a wonderful person called Nasser. In these films there were not only hardcore scenes. It was lovely to being able to shoot something else than sex scenes.

Vanisian: Did you write the sex scenes in detail or do you let them improvise a lot?

About: There also was a script, but we had such little means and really not enough time, thus we had to adapt the script to the real circumstances. Almost never did I have enough time during the shooting of hardcore films, not even with Philippe Vallois, where we sometimes did shootings in the Province. A normal French film takes six weeks to shoot, and films by auteurs can last up to six months. We are talking about completely other dimensions here. And while shooting my own films, I remembered how it was to work with Philippe Garrel or Philippe de Broca, where every crew member had his fixed duty. And if you will – hardcore cinema has nothing at all to do with these production methods. In a normal film you have two, three hours to set up the lighting, whereas in an X-film you more or less must start shooting immediately. I tried to overcome this disadvantage by adapting a documentary style, similar to the way photographers shoot for news coverage. In terms of artistic freedom: yes, I could do whatever I wanted, in the limits of the budget. Thierry didn't care at all what kind of films I did; they were just supposed to be ready at some point. I shot three films in one week, imagine! And I believe all of them were shown in Thierry's cinemas, some even for over two months.

Vanisian: There are a number of American actors in the movies, do you know anything about how they were brought into the movies? Was there a relationship between the company in Paris and partners like Hand In Hand or Mustang in the United States?

About: We made a casting and chose U.S.-actors of which few didn't do X-films at all. We paid them very little, much less than what they would have received in the U.S. It didn't have a particular reason that they were Americans, and we had nothing to do with Hand In Hand or Mustang. However, once we had cast them, I tried to adapt myself, become part of their community.

Vanisian: Marc Aillaud was, next to you, the second regular cinematographer for the company, he served as a camera operator on some of your films. Do you remember him well, was he a friend, can he be called your student in some way?

About: I can't say much about him but yes, Norbert Thierry employed other cinematographers, too. But we didn't work as close as to be really influenced by each other.

Vanisian: In À LA RECHERCHÉ DE DOUGLAS, there is an orgy scene shot in the tight space of an elevator interior and there's a lot of diversity and movement in the sequence. Do you remember that shooting? Was it complicated? Did you enjoy shooting group scenes; was there a special challenge in it because the camera had to pay attention to a lot of details?

About: In general, I find it easier to shoot a penetration when only two people are involved. The more actors there are, the more difficult it gets, once again, even more so when you don't have neither means nor money. And no crew – for these films, I didn't have one single electrician, I had to do everything myself. And Norbert Thierry knew this.

Vanisian: Catherine Ripert was a key creative person for Troïka. How did she get into the circle; do you have any information about her background? What kind of person was she?

About: I loved this woman, Catherine, a highly intelligent person. She used to be an editor. I have very fond memories of her, and she also appreciated what I made for the company. Since she was an editor, she was the first to see what I shot and liked it. And while I shot scenes, I already anticipated the editing, included certain editing ideas into the shootings. This was not at all usual.

Vanisian: What about Les films du Vertbois? Was that a different company, or was it owned by the same people? Can you say something about the number of people the company was run by?

About: It was Jacques Scandelari's company. The name derives from a street where his company was located in Paris, in the 3rd arrondissement.

Vanisian: Jacques Scandelari clearly was one of the most brilliant adult filmmakers in Europe at the time; I assume that he was very ambitious and a lover of art films? Can you share some memories about his character and his directing style?

About: He was brilliant, yes. He had his own editor, with whom he had used to shoot image and commissioned films about fashion, so he had a proper training before venturing into hardcore cinema. He had started this company in order to make films commissioned by Givenchy, Dior and so on. Only later did he begin to make hardcore films, and the fashion companies were not supposed to know it.

Vanisian: À LA RECHERCHE DE DOUGLAS was the last movie produced by Troïka, is this correct? What was the reason for its end in 1982?

About: Yes, this was the last movie Thierry produced for Troïka. The company stopped due to tax problems, and Thierry soon moved to Thailand where he, until now, spends most of his time.

Vanisian: Looking back on your career and your experiences with so many different filmmakers, actors, creatives, and producers: What was special about this age? Do you think the films had a certain genuine quality and feeling?

About: In fact, I was more than just a DoP. Essentially, a guy like Jacques Scandelari, he let me do everything, drag around the young actors and having me shoot scenes according to my ideas. I would give him the reels, and he would take them to make the dailies. We did three or four films like this. For example for NEW YORK CITY INFERNO, a film which is still shown now and then. The first time I went to New York in 1975 – well, I checked out all the gay clubs of New York *(laughs)*, there were about six or seven, freely, while in Paris you always had the police menace around you. One day, a French director called me up, José Bénazéraf, he wanted to have me as his DoP. I went to meet him in his office. His wife was a model, and he himself had quite some means. We talked; he introduced me to his assistant; then, a few moments later, he presented me his script; and eventually I agreed to be the DoP for his film. Bénazéraf then said

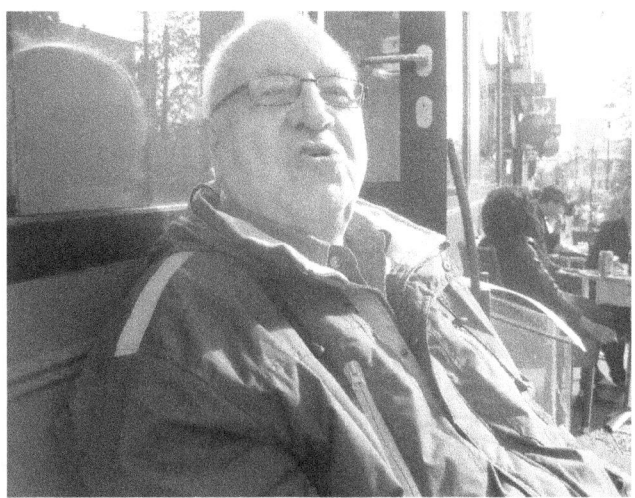

Francois About, Paris 2015
Photo: Gary Vanisian

to his assistant: "We must go and have a look at the films François is doing, one is currently showing in a cinema opposite of the Gare Saint Laraze." It was a film I had done for Francis Leroi. Bénazéraf's assistant declined because he had to go out for dinner with his girlfriend. Suddenly, I saw Bénazéraf and his assistant fighting each other! *(laughs)* Bénazéraf was a violent guy! Eventually, I didn't do the film with him, for different reasons. Later, Bénazéraf called me and asked if I would work with him on another film, which was to be his last. There I saw that he is a real professional. He, in contrast to Jack, told me everything I should do, regarding lighting, colors etc. I had never met anyone who was so fanatic regarding the technical aspect of filmmaking. I often asked myself: Would I prefer a filmmaker who is completely obsessive about the technique and gives me precise orders or one who lets me work freely? I would prefer the one who gives me the most artistic freedom.

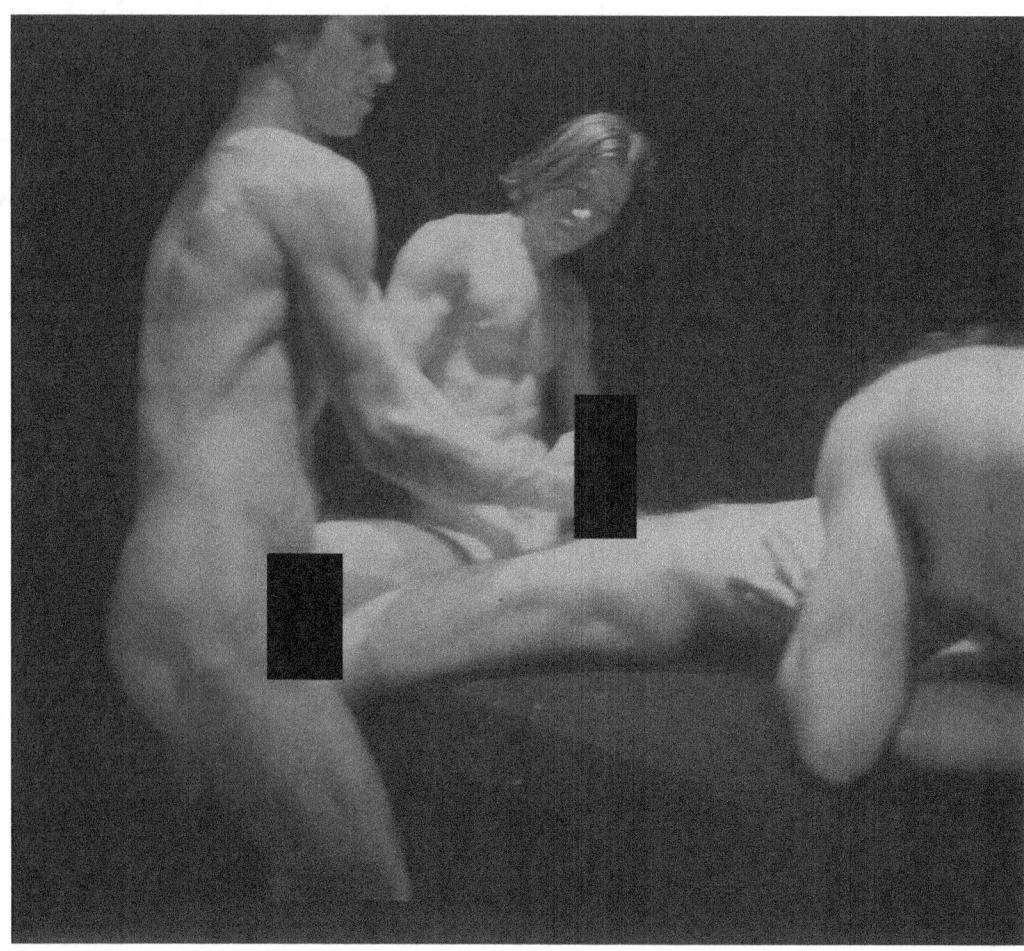

Robert Alvarez (left) in *La Musee*

"Most of the sex was shot in an old, very OLD, bar that somehow or other came out looking like a museum on film. I told you, Mr. Deveau was an artist! We also shot a lot of the exteriors around the Louvre. That whole shooting was a trip - we were working with a French crew that didn't know an on-switch from an off one. Thank God, Bob Alvarez, who edited all of Jack's films, came along after the sixth day and rescued us! If he hadn't arrived, we'd still be there trying to finish the damn thing!" **BILL ELD**

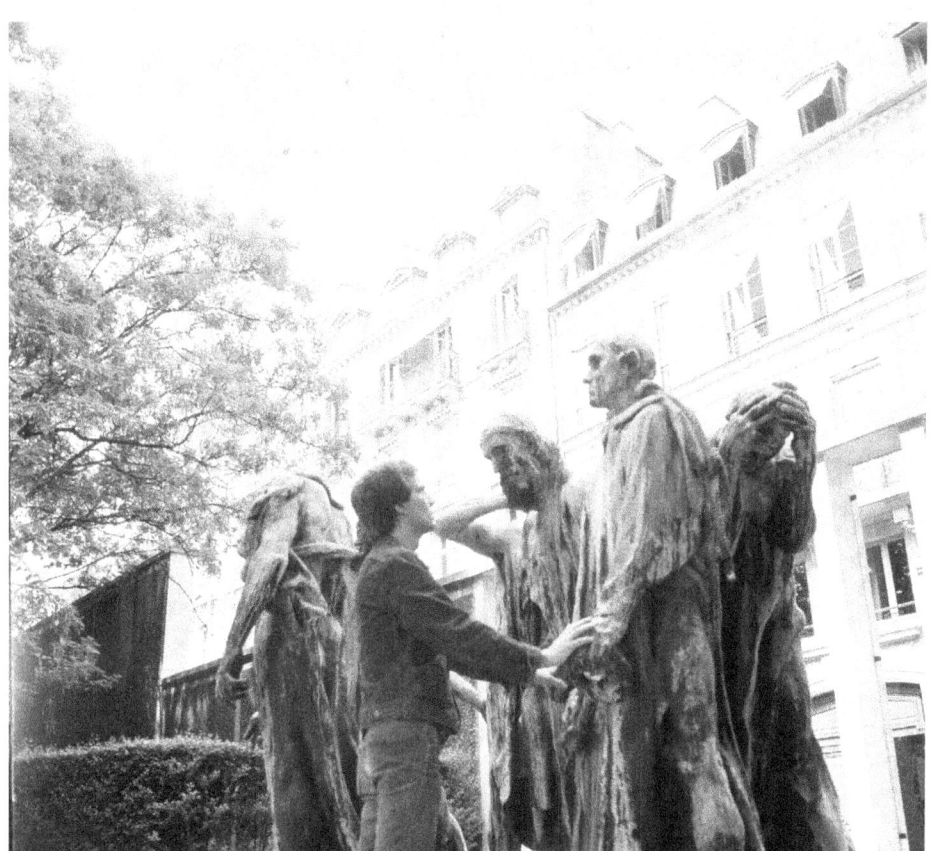

Thomas Jeffries

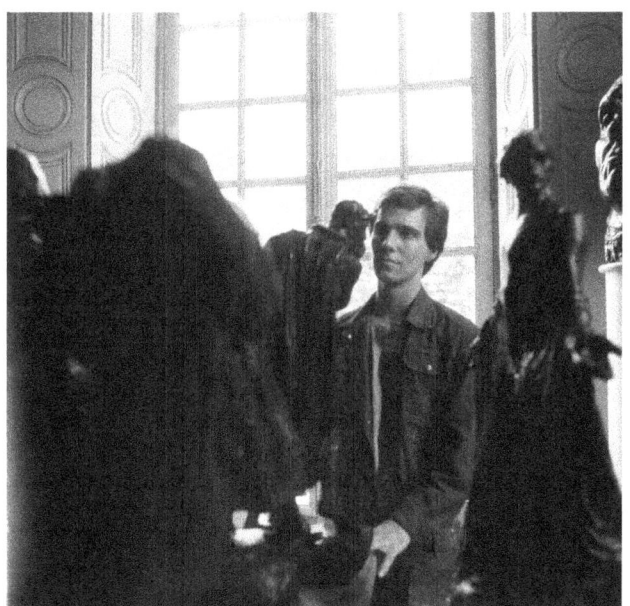
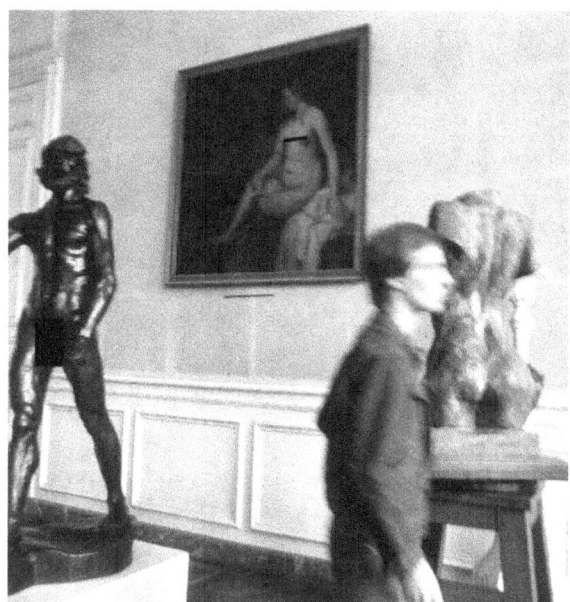

Deveau's description from the *In Touch* interview: "An American student traveling in France finds himself one day in a Paris art museum. Wandering around, he comes upon an unlocked door to a private collection. A guard shoos him away, but his curiosity has gotten the best of him. He returns to the museum, managing to sequester himself there overnight. What he find sin the room is a collection of erotic male statues, which come to life and guide the boy from one sexual act into another. In the end, the boy becomes one of them, a statue. The film is seen from the boy's point of view, and takes on the feeling of one sexual act, an initiation into homosexuality." - Partly filmed in the Musee Rodin and the Musee Gravin (a wax museum) in Paris.

HAND IN HANDS PRIVATE COLLECTION

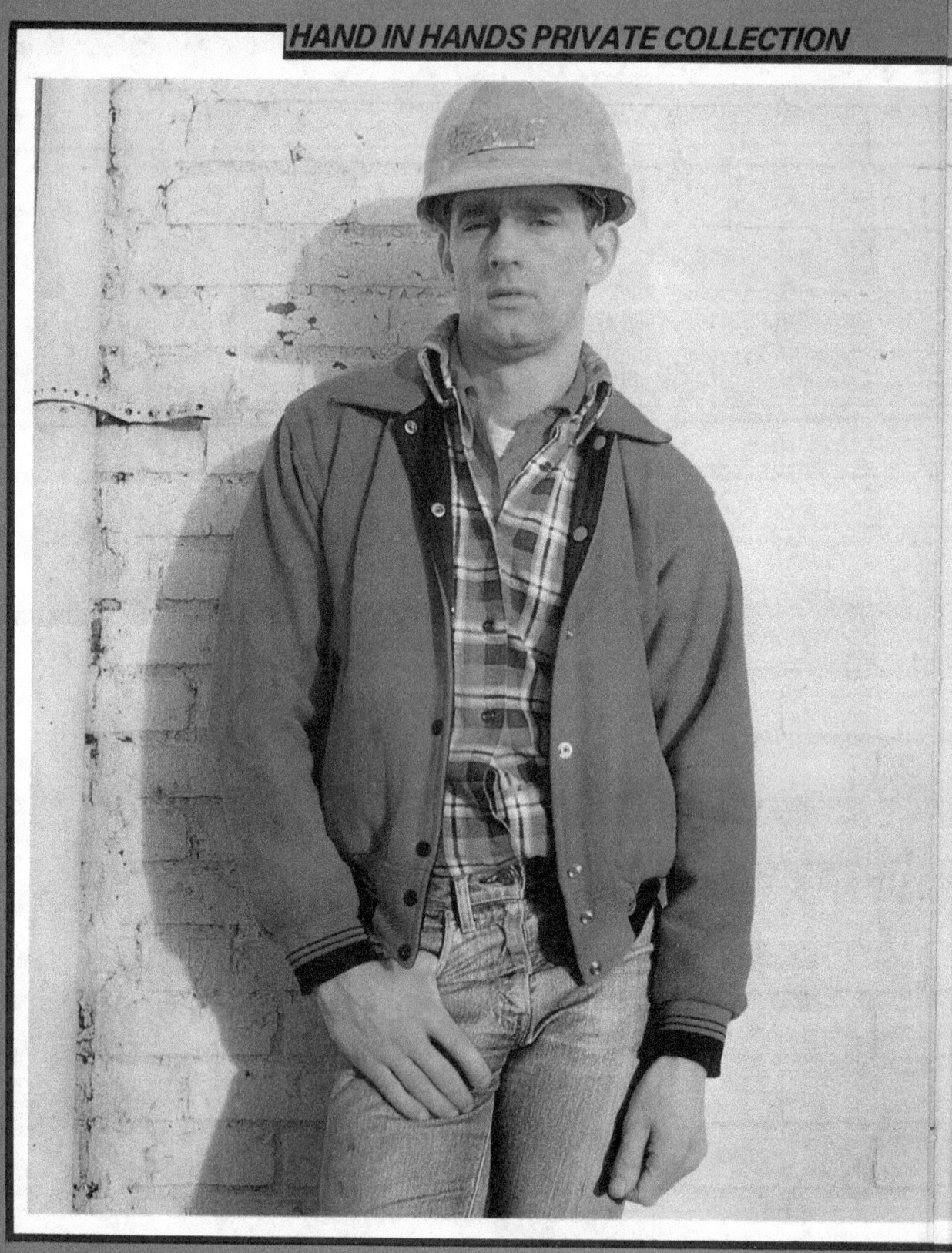

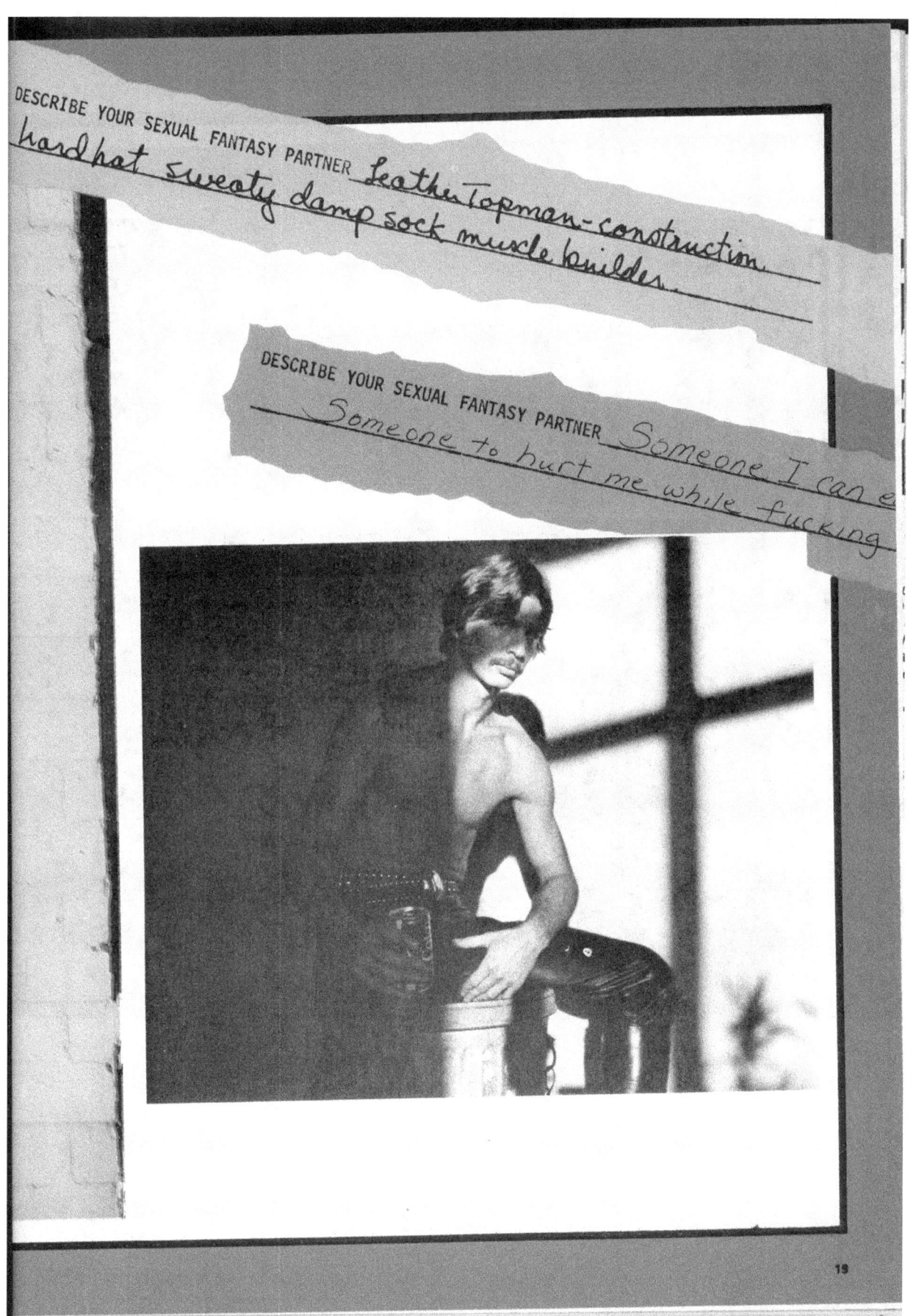

Scorpio in *Double Scorpio* (Segment of *Private Collection*)

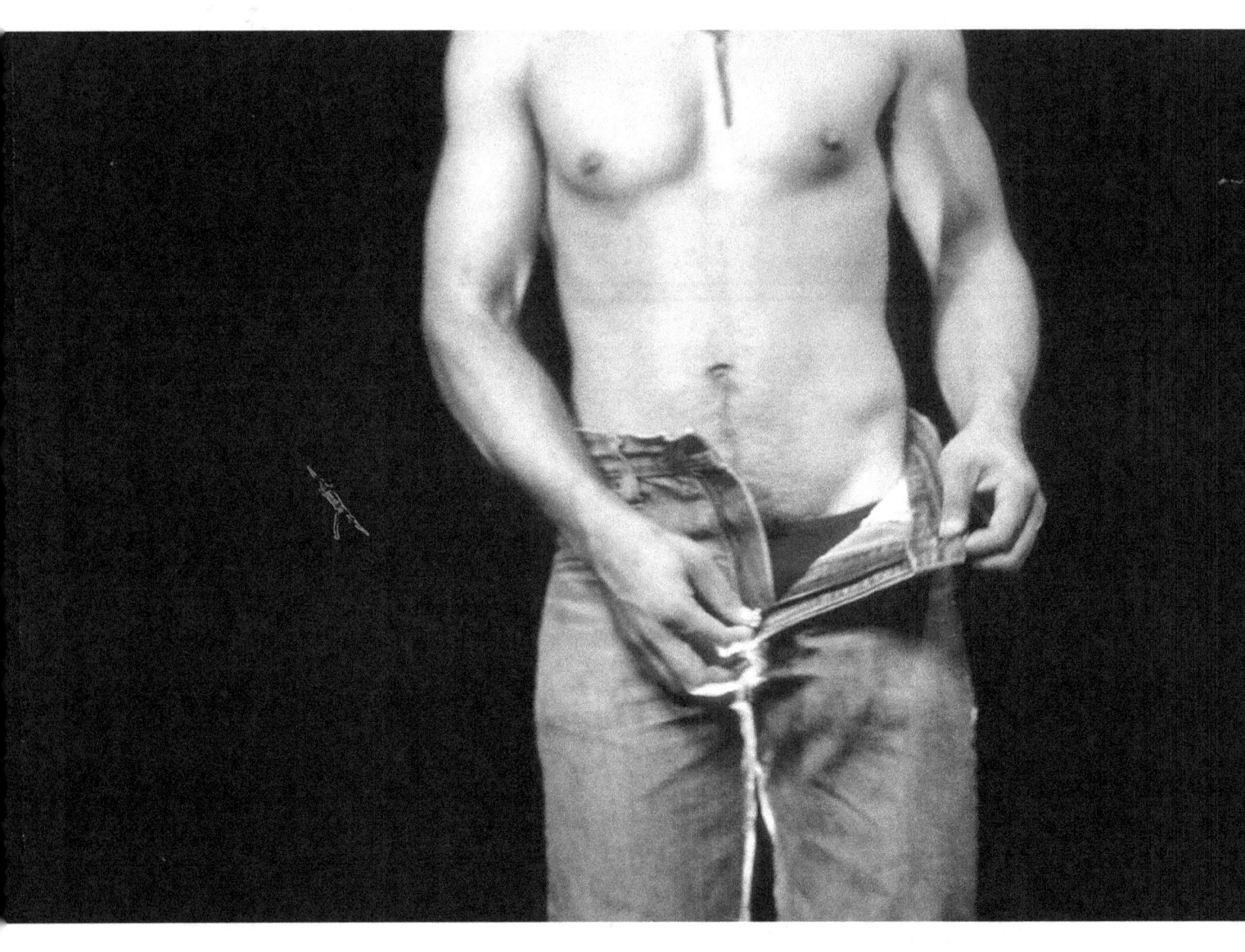

Steve York solo *The Blue Boy* (Segment of *Private Collection*) - He strips out of his leather jacket and blue jeans and jacks off.

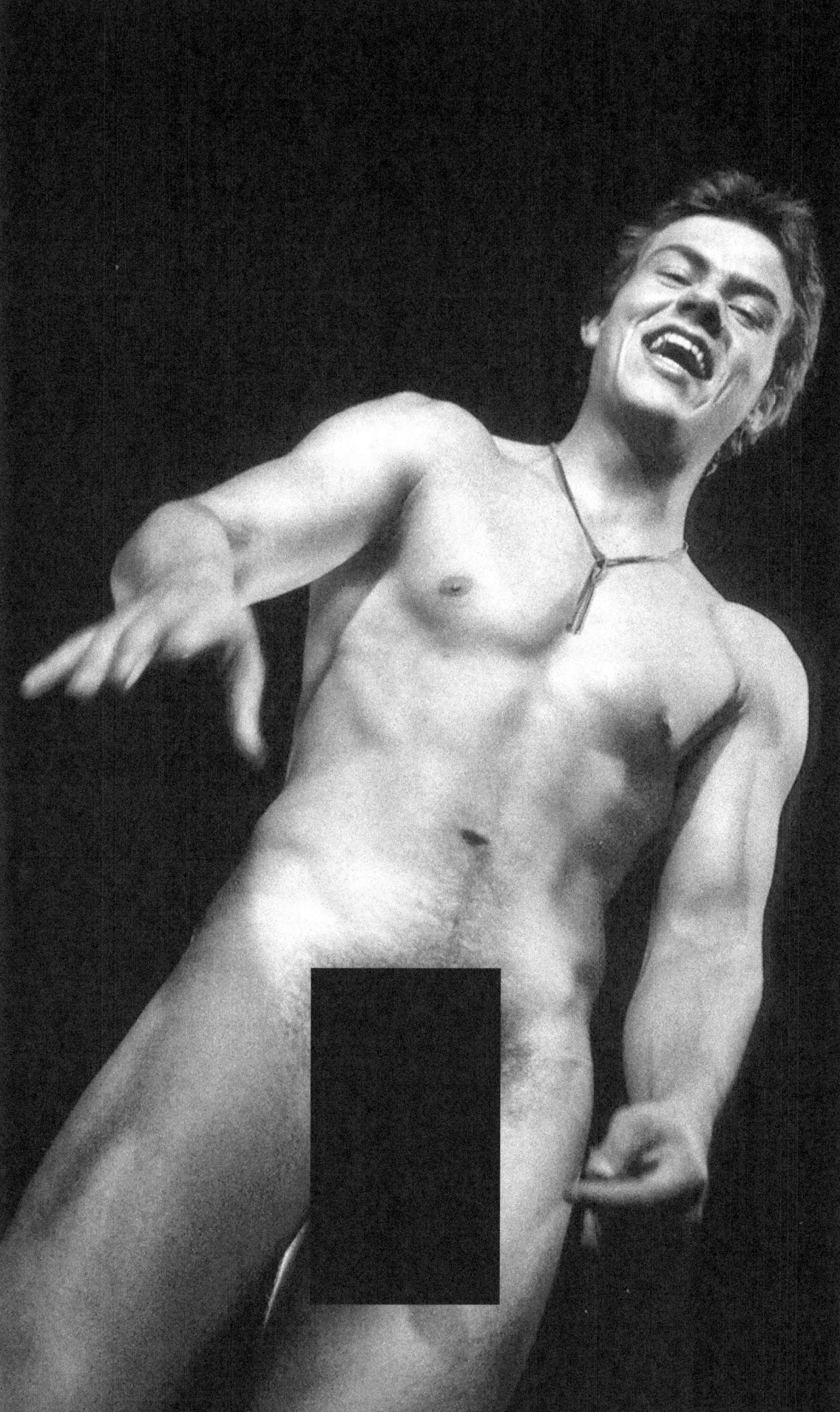

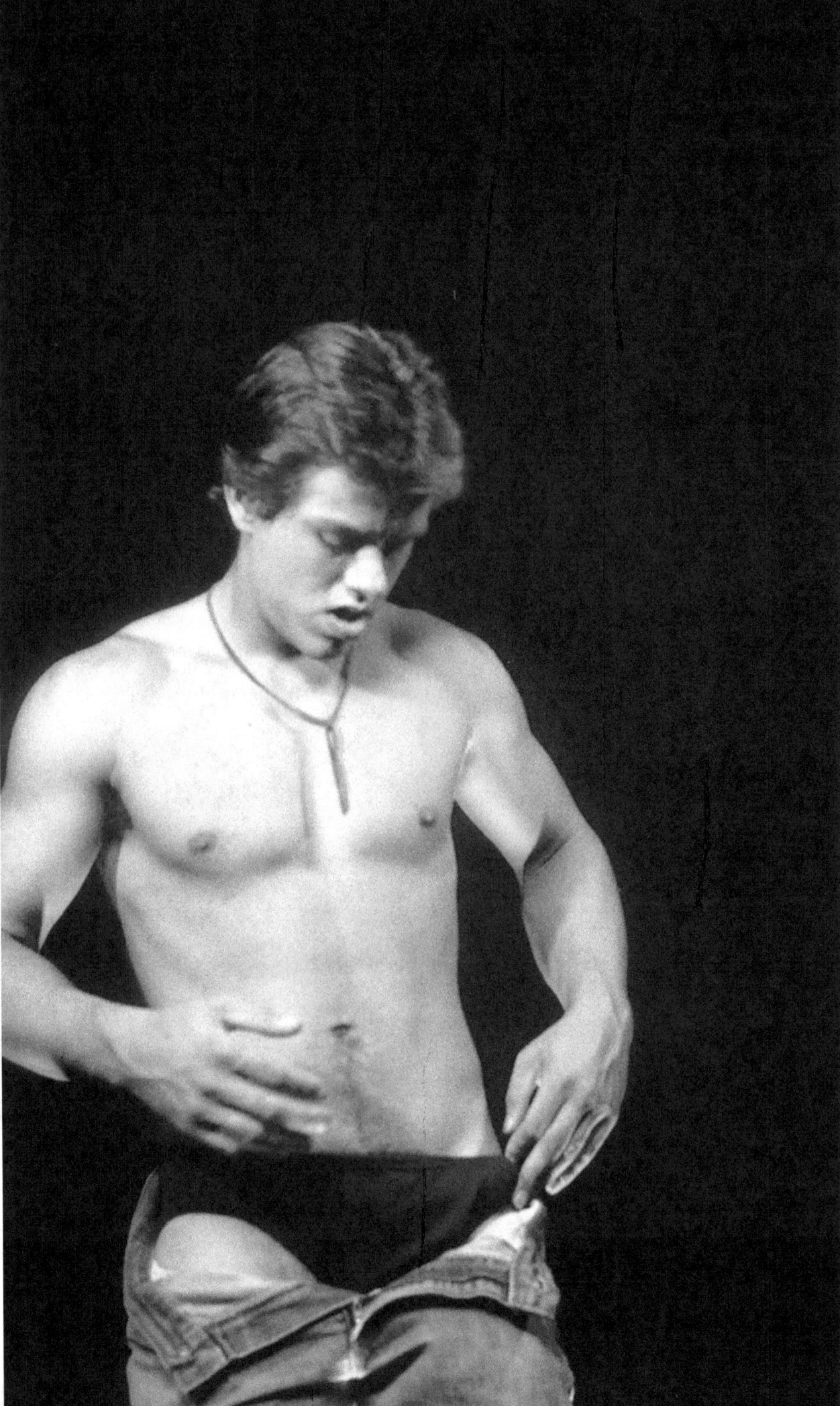

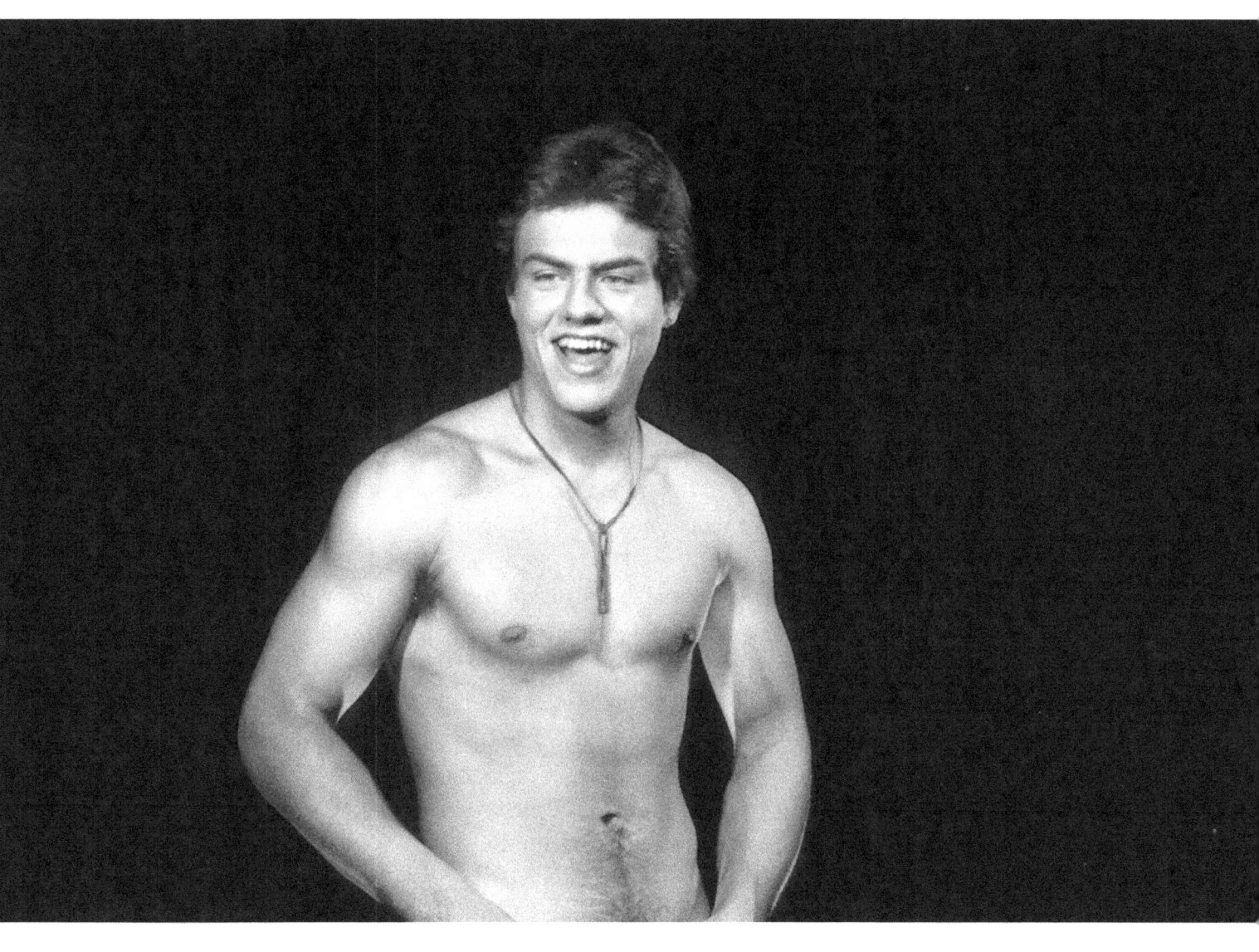

Steve York had already been published in *Blueboy* and Mark Reynolds recognized him on the street in Santa Monica, stopped and asked him to do a movie. He has been spotted in several straight film loops including Diamond Collection's *Long Cowboy* #1 & #2 and *Skin Creme*. (*Gay Erotic Video Index*)

A STAR IS PORN

by Bill Hunter

"I want to be a porn star." About 3,000 men have expressed that desire to Jack Deveau since he began producing and distributing sexually explicit gay films eight years ago. Far and away the East Coast's leading producer of 16-millimeter erotica featuring mostly male casts, Deveau and his Hand In Hand Films production company have made 21 feature-length movies and have had a hand in the distribution of 33 others. As a result, applications for porn stardom pour into the forty-five year old filmmaker's penthouse workshop on the Upper West Side of Manhattan. "I'm always casting," says Deveau, who makes as many as four movies a year. "It's difficult to find the exactly-right people. Single gay men – and by that I mean those who don't have lovers and so forth – are very mobile. Frequently, we find men who would be very good in a porn movie, but they're not available to us when we start assembling a cast. They've taken up residence in Key West for six months or decided to live at a ski resort in Colorado or moved to Hawaii to spend the summer surfing." For that reason, Deveau tries to have five to ten projects ready to go at all times, "just in case the right guy walks in the door." One such project in the "ready to go" file is HANDS IN LEATHER, a gay ROCKY that calls for a Latin lad who gives the appearance of having gone to Yale, where he was an amateur boxer. "That's not an easy type to find among actors, let alone among actors who are willing to put themselves in a porno film," Deveau says, "I have types in mind for pictures, but I can't call up a talent agency and say, 'Send me 100 young, blond men.' But if I run into a lot of blonds, then I do JUST BLONDS." THE IDOL, he recalls, was scripted in 1973, but wasn't produced until 1978 because "we couldn't find actors who could fill all the roles convincingly until then." Deveau got around this problem in his latest offering, HAND IN HAND'S PRIVATE COLLECTION, by striking while the rod was hot, so to speak. "Occasionally, very attractive people come in here and do incredible things, like blow themselves," Deveau says, "Now I don't have a script that calls for someone to blow himself, but I can create little stories around talents like that, and this film has a few things of this nature." PRIVATE COLLECTION is a mélange of stories that were too short to develop into 90-minute features along with a potpourri of unique erotic events, like the guy who sucks himself silly. Hand In Hand Films used to advertise for men who wanted to be porn stars, but "the people who showed up were either overweight, physically unfit or unattractive in a cosmetic way – missing teeth and things like that." Applications that come in "over the transom" prove fruitful in about one in twenty cases, Deveau says. Mostly, porn stars are born (or made, as the case may be) through the "recommendations of actors we've used before, crew members, friends of crew members or writers like yourself." It's sort of a pre-selection process. Someone thinks the guy's hot before he even approaches the casting couch. Who are some of these hot numbers who have been recommended by friends or who have sent Deveau unsolicited Polaroid photos and other "support materials"? On the condition that no last names would be revealed and that certain data would be modified to protect the identities of applicants, Deveau permitted perusal of his confidential files of cast candidates, marked "usable" and "not usable." It was not an unpleasant task, having access to the physical descriptions of

3,000 would-be porn stars. Applicants are required to give not only their cock sizes (hard) but also descriptions of their fantasy sex partners, sexual likes and dislikes and reasons for wanting to appear in a porn movie. Of course, some candidates obviously stretched things. There wasn't a cock in the lot under 6½ inches. John, age 28, had the smallest meat at that precise length. Vic, no age given, listed his shaft at 11½. Eric, 27, noted that his prick was not only 8½ inches long but also 2½ inches wide. Tony, 19, stretched it to the limit with 7½ inches. And J.D. merely remarked in the "size" blank: "no complaints." There are 52 questions on Deveau's application form, among them: "Is there one part of a man's body you prefer?" (The buttocks won out over the penis, and one applicant even sketched a little picture of a man's ass next to his answer.) "What do you prefer to do to others?" ("Fuck them" won hands down.) "What do you prefer other to do to you? ("Fuck me" was the odds-on favorite, but "blow me" was a close second.) "What don't you like in sex?" ("Fisting" and "golden showers" were listed more often than other acts, but most of the applicants were willing to experiment with anything on celluloid.)Applicants, however, frequently "talk backwards" when it comes to dislikes, Deveau says, noting that those who list their objections in great detail usually can't get enough of that particular thing when the action begins. "When an actor goes on and on about a special dislike, that's usually my clue that it's really a fantasy he wants to explore. If not, what made him think about it in such detail?" Other questions range from cruising habits to astrological signs. (In these categories, one applicant listed Fire Island Pines as the best place to find a good fuck, and another noted that he was a triple Scorpio. Scorpios, Leos and Capricorns seemed to dominate the file.) But why? What reasons do applicants give for wanting to put their cocks and balls on the silver screen? Here, verbatim, are some of the answers:

Jerry, 26, 7 inches, Scorpio: "I'd just like to give it a try."

Lee, 19, 9 inches, Leo: "I have acting, dancing and performing ambitions."

Allan, 31, 8 inches, Capricorn: "I am poor at present."

Jose, 28, 8½ inches, Leo: "I'm an aspiring actor. I want experience."

Danny, 27, 9½ inches, Scorpio: "I'd do it for the fun of it and for the experience of acting with others."

J.J., 24, 7 to 8 inches, Pisces: "I'm bizarre and like cash."

J.D., 28, "no complaints," Scorpio: "I'd like to see my cock on a 70-foot screen."

Ray, 32, a perfect "10" (eat your heart out, Bo Derek), Sagittarius: "I enjoy meeting hot men."

Tommy, 20, 9 inches, Libra: "I love to make people happy and would enjoy doing porno."

(This application has a notation by one of Deveau's interviewers: "Has taken some pretty big dildos!")

Manny, 21, 6½ inches, Capricorn: "I'm interested in showing myself off."

Jorge, 32, no size listed, Virgo: "I want proper recognition."

Max, 37, 9 inches, Leo: "Personal glorification."

Louis, 21, 8½ inches, Scorpio: "Basically, I'm sick of seeing the shit that's being shown and feel I could perform better."

Chuck, 33, 8 inches, Taurus: "I need money for my apartment."

Money, says Deveau, is the poorest of motivations. "They're saying they would do anything for a buck," he adds. "We've had them come to us in the worst financial crunches. They thought porno was the way to solve their problems. Those who perform only for financial gain would do better to solve their problems in a hustler bar. I need a conscious participation on the part of the actor. I want him to help me in creating the fantasies that we're trying to project. Unless he's a professional actor, that usually doesn't come out if the motivation is only money." And speaking of money, Deveau's men earn Screen Actors Guild minimum – about $200 a day. Some of them have made up to $2,500 for a feature. The pay, some have told Deveau, is better than they get for appearing in heterosexual films. The best motivation? "Narcissism, vanity," Deveau answers. "The best porn stars are those who can – either because they're skilled at it through acting training or have a natural talent – project some sort of vanity or ego to the camera." Hand In Hand Films sometimes will accept an applicant that it feels might be useful to the company in a large part and give him a small role just to let them gain a little experience before the lenses. "I do this when I'm not sure whether the experience of being in a porno film will blow him away, or when I'm not sure if he has sufficient commitment," Deveau says. "I don't want to start a picture with a brand new actor and find out he doesn't have the stick-to-it-iveness to stay with the project to the end. That can be a disaster for me. I either have to write the character out of the script or abandon the project altogether." Deveau has had some hot numbers apply to become porn stars and then back down when given the opportunity, but that's rare. Those with second thoughts about exhibiting their body while the cameras are whirling usually drop out before the filming begins "because there are enough preliminary meetings about the script and what they're going to do and, in some cases, coaching." If Deveau is the least bit uncertain, he gives the porn star opportunities to drop out. But unearthing a man's motivation usually heads off the drop-out problem, as does finding out if there is anyone close to the actor who might object to seeing him sucking cock or taking it in the ass for theater audiences. "My mother would object," said one candid candidate on his application form. "But she's in Idaho and not even near a theater that shows X-rated films." "My father would object," said another applicant. "But I went to school at a strict religious college in Texas, so he would never suspect." (Note made by the interviewer of this strictly educated applicant: "He would like to be fucked with three or four people holding him down.") Jose said his theatrical booking agent probably would balk, but he also said he didn't give a damn. "I like fucking and being fucked. You name it, I like it. The only thing I don't like is someone who fakes having a good time." One candidate said his lover would object to seeing him in a fuck flick, "but then he won't know about it." On the other hand, Jack Wrangler, whose early application is in Deveau's "usable" file, notes that there not only is no one to object to his doing porn but also that his mother suggested it. Deveau doesn't discard applications that come to him, no matter how "unusable" they may seem at the time. One lad, for example, sent the filmmaker a photo of himself arm-in-arm with his "sweetheart" (yes, female) at the senior prom. "I'm on the left," the applicant wrote on the snapshot. For the time being, Hand In Hand isn't planning any skin flicks about arm-in-arm couples at the senior prom, but then again, who knows when the right script and the right co-star might come along? Deveau doesn't expect to discover the next Jack Wrangler, Peter Berlin or Roger in tomorrow's mail, but would-be showboys who have dreamed or baring body and hole before the cameras can write to Hand In Hand Films, Inc. Get it up, give it up, and get it on!

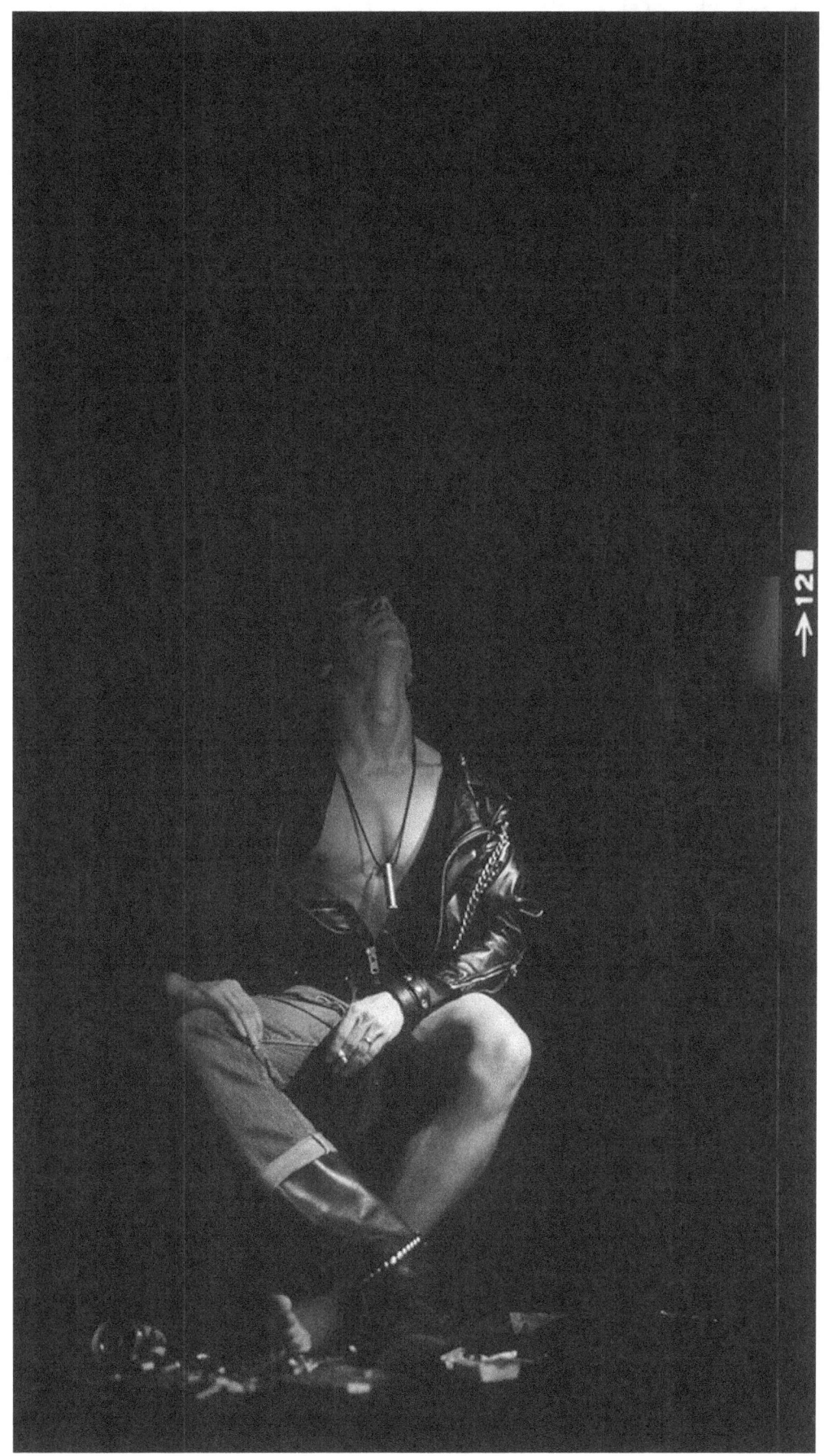

Interview

The answers to the following questions are held in the strictest confide[nce] and are used for casting information only. Please feel free to be as ca[ndid] as you wish, since the information you give us will help in selecting co[-] partners for action scenes.

NAME George Edward Bontot
ADDRESS 428 Winston
CITY Cranston STATE PA.

PHONE: HOME _____
FRIEND _____
BUSINESS _____
ANSWERING SERVICE _____

HOW DID YOU HEAR ABOUT HAND IN HAND from movies
HEIGHT 5'9" WEIGHT 161 EYES Brown HAIR Brown
CHEST 38 WAIST 33 SUIT ? COCK (HARD) _____
DO YOU DRIVE A CAR? yes MOTORCYCLE no RIDE HORSES _____
OTHER ABILITIES singing + sex
WHAT SPORTS DO YOU PLAY WELL? can dress up
HOBBIES toys for sex
DO YOU HAVE ACTING EXPERIENCE? yes IF SO, WHERE? at hom[e]
HAVE YOU HAD PREVIOUS HARD CORE OR NUDE PHOTO EXPERIENCE? _____
WHAT ARE YOUR REASONS FOR BEING IN A FILM? I like people a[nd]
HOW MANY ORGASMS DO YOU HAVE A DAY? MOST 6-10 AVERAGE _____
DESCRIBE YOUR SEXUAL FANTASY PARTNER a short 5'4"-5'[_] be my mother and spanks hard
IS THERE ONE PART OF A MAN'S BODY WHICH YOU PREFER? back
ARE THERE ANY ETHNIC GROUPS YOU PREFER? No
ARE THERE ANY ETHNIC GROUPS YOU DO NOT PREFER? groups of [_]
WHAT DO YOU PREFER TO DO TO OTHERS, SEXUALLY? If male [_] being fucked if female the oppos[ite]
WHAT DO YOU PREFER OTHERS TO DO TO YOU, SEXUALLY? I like [_] diapers on me wet me and fuck [_]
WHAT DON'T YOU LIKE IN SEX? Scars
IS THERE ANYONE (I.E. A LOVER) WHO WOULD OBJECT TO YOUR B[EING IN A] FILM? no

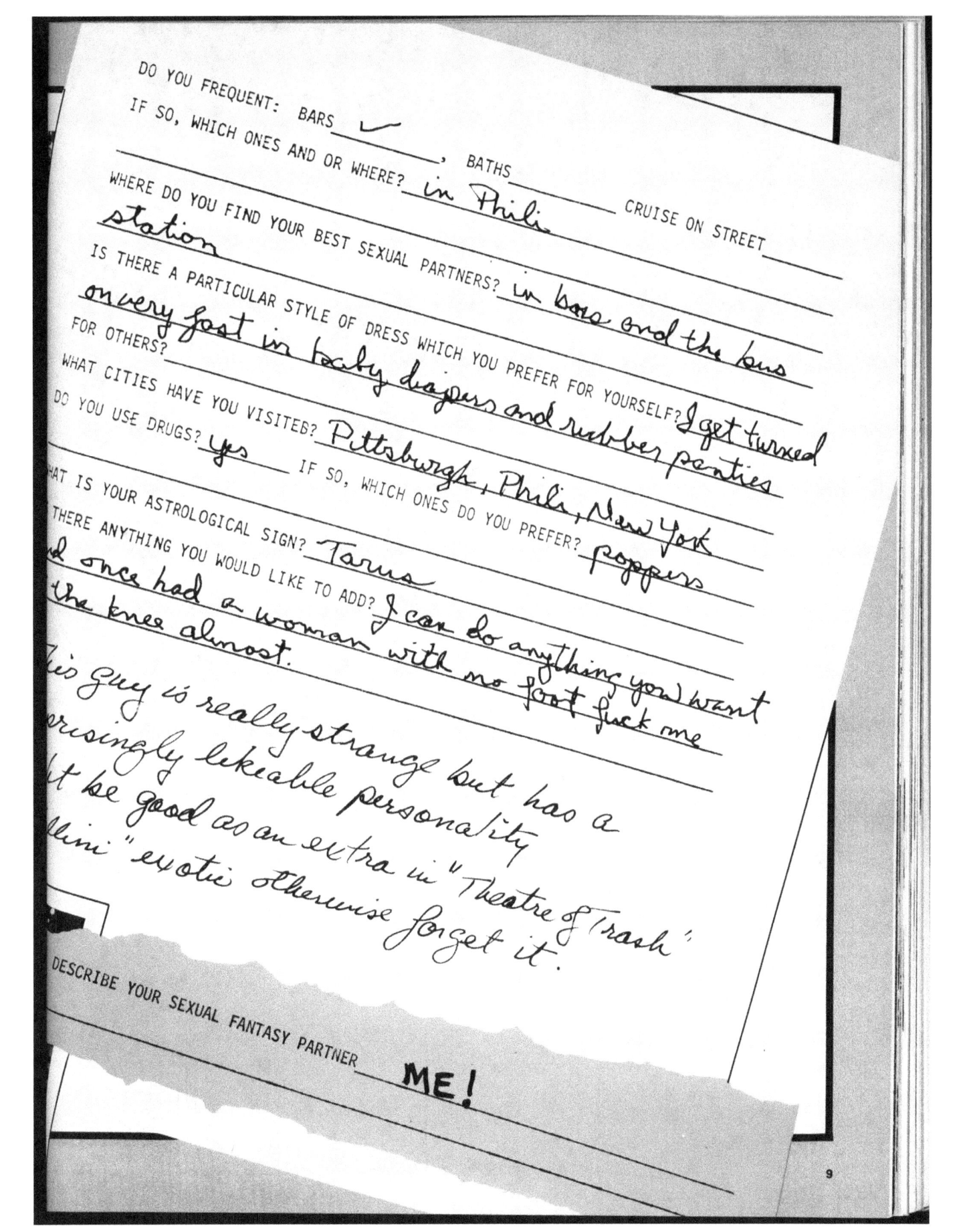

WHAT DO YOU PREFER TO DO TO OTHERS, SEXUALLY? __URINATE, LICK ARMPIT SWEAT__

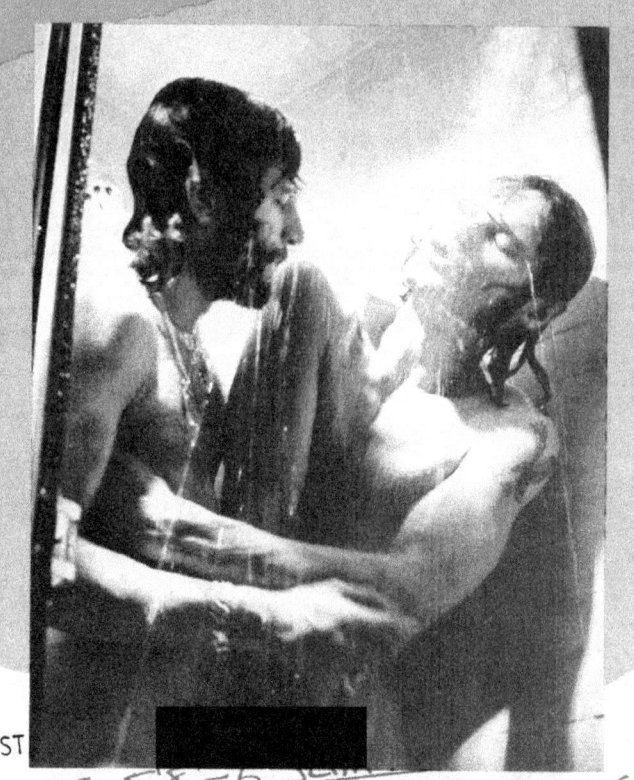

HOW MANY ORGASMS DO YOU HAVE A DAY? MOST
DESCRIBE YOUR SEXUAL FANTASY PARTNER __18-25 5'8-6 SLIM, CLEAN SHAVEN, SMOOTH CHEST, GOOD DEF., BOYISHLY HANDSOME__
IS THERE ONE PART OF A MAN'S BODY WHICH YOU PREFER? __BUTT__
ARE THERE ANY ETHNIC GROUPS YOU PREFER? __CAUCASIAN, LATIN__
ARE THERE ANY ETHNIC GROUPS YOU DO NOT PREFER? __NOT REALLY__
WHAT DO YOU PREFER TO DO TO OTHERS, SEXUALLY? __PLEASE THEM AS BEST I CAN I LIKE TO FUCK__
WHAT DO YOU PREFER OTHERS TO DO TO YOU, SEXUALLY? __DEPENDS ON PARTNER BUT I AM VERSITILE__
WHAT DON'T YOU LIKE IN SEX? __BONDAGE, WATER SPORTS, F.F.__

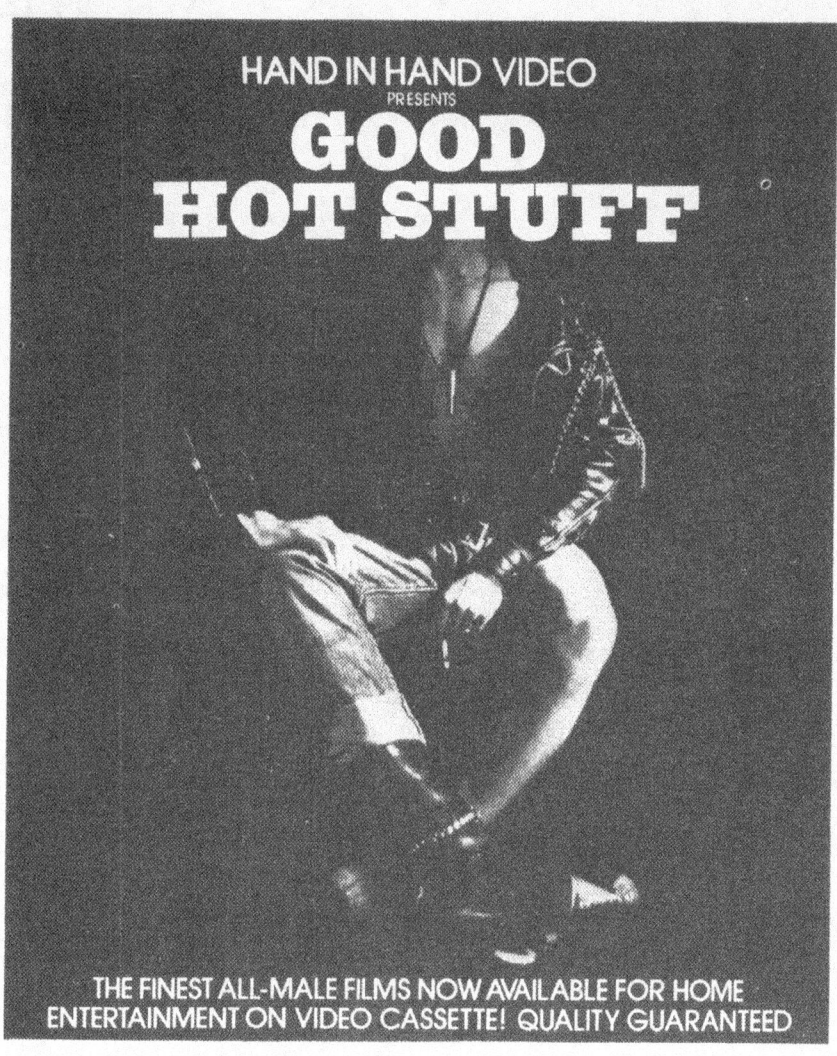

PRESS REVIEWS 5

Another recent Jack Wrangler entry, HOT HOUSE, a product of Jack Deveau's Hand In Hand company, is highlighted by the uncredited appearance, in a smoothly interpolated 8mm black and white sequence, of a genuine curiosity in the male-to-male performer category. The sensuous, sulky teenager who's right in there doing active b.j. and rim work, then appearing to enjoy getting it Greek-style, is Andy Warhol's super-stud, Joe Dallasandro. Deveau works this crude but recognizable underground loop into the action by using it as the featured attraction of a casual afternoon masturbation party involving some of the guys who gather in Wrangler's New York living room to while away the time while their host is in the bedroom, getting it on with Roger, whose screen debut occurred in this otherwise undistinguished feature. Wrangler goes along, amiably but without conviction, in routine suck-me-suck-you situations. Tension – the interaction and conflict of different but mutually attracted personalities – is the stuff of drama. HOT HOUSE has none of it. It's several characters get together as if by routine, falling naturally into each other's arms (and crotches and asses) so swiftly and unemotionally as to suggest that all they wanted to do was get the assignment over with. Jack Deveau has done better than that; so has Wrangler. Let's hope that Roger can, too. So far, he has not had the chance.

*Donald Warman, *In Heat*

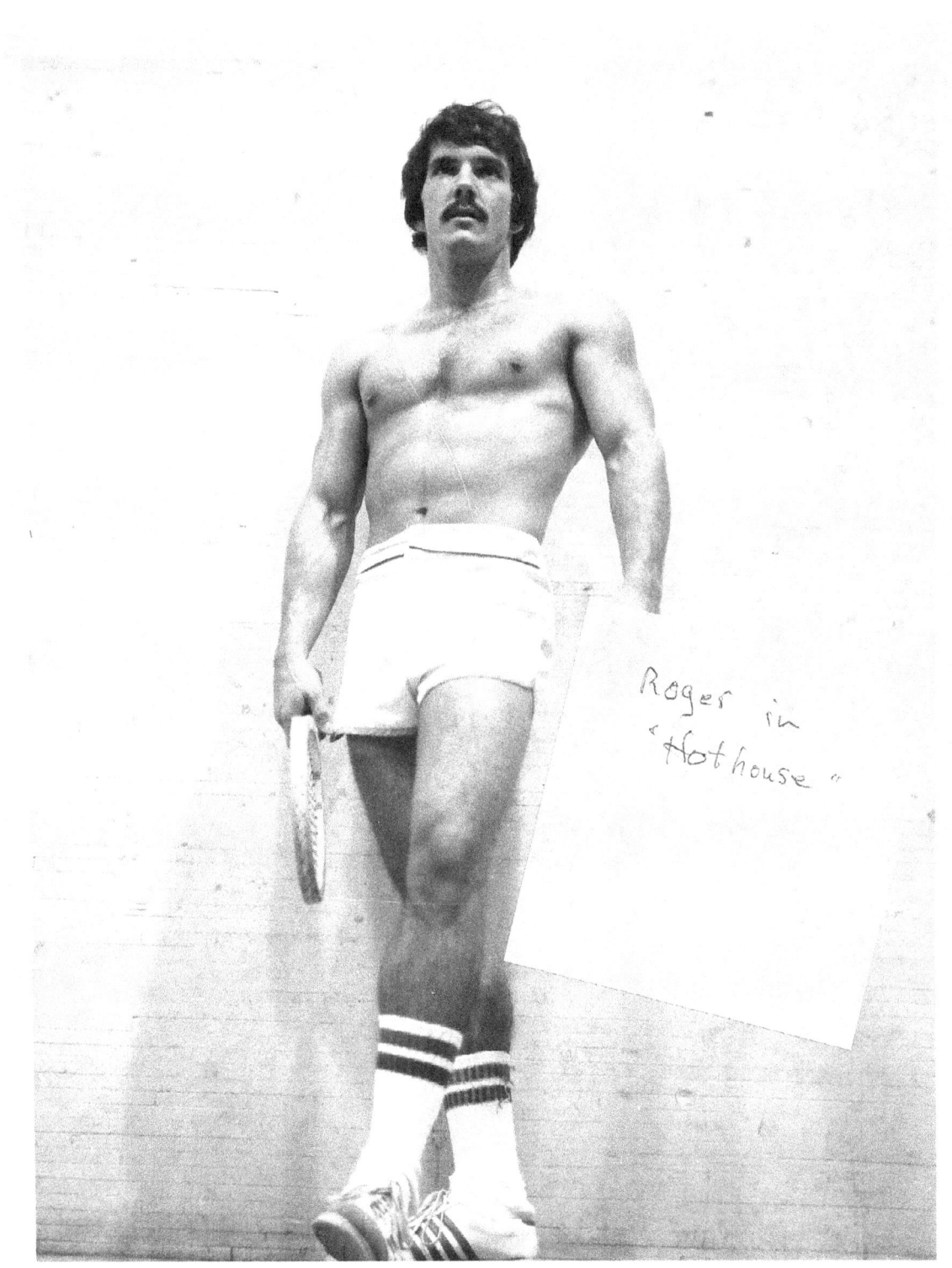

"I used to be a greaser, gettin' into fights, cursing all the time. 'The Fonz' is my favorite TV character, but I'm not a greaser now. I was in the service for two years, and I'm still a distance runner. I could go anywhere. In two years I want to win a bodybuilding title. Maybe even hit Hollywood. Wherever, I'm gonna make it!"

ROGER

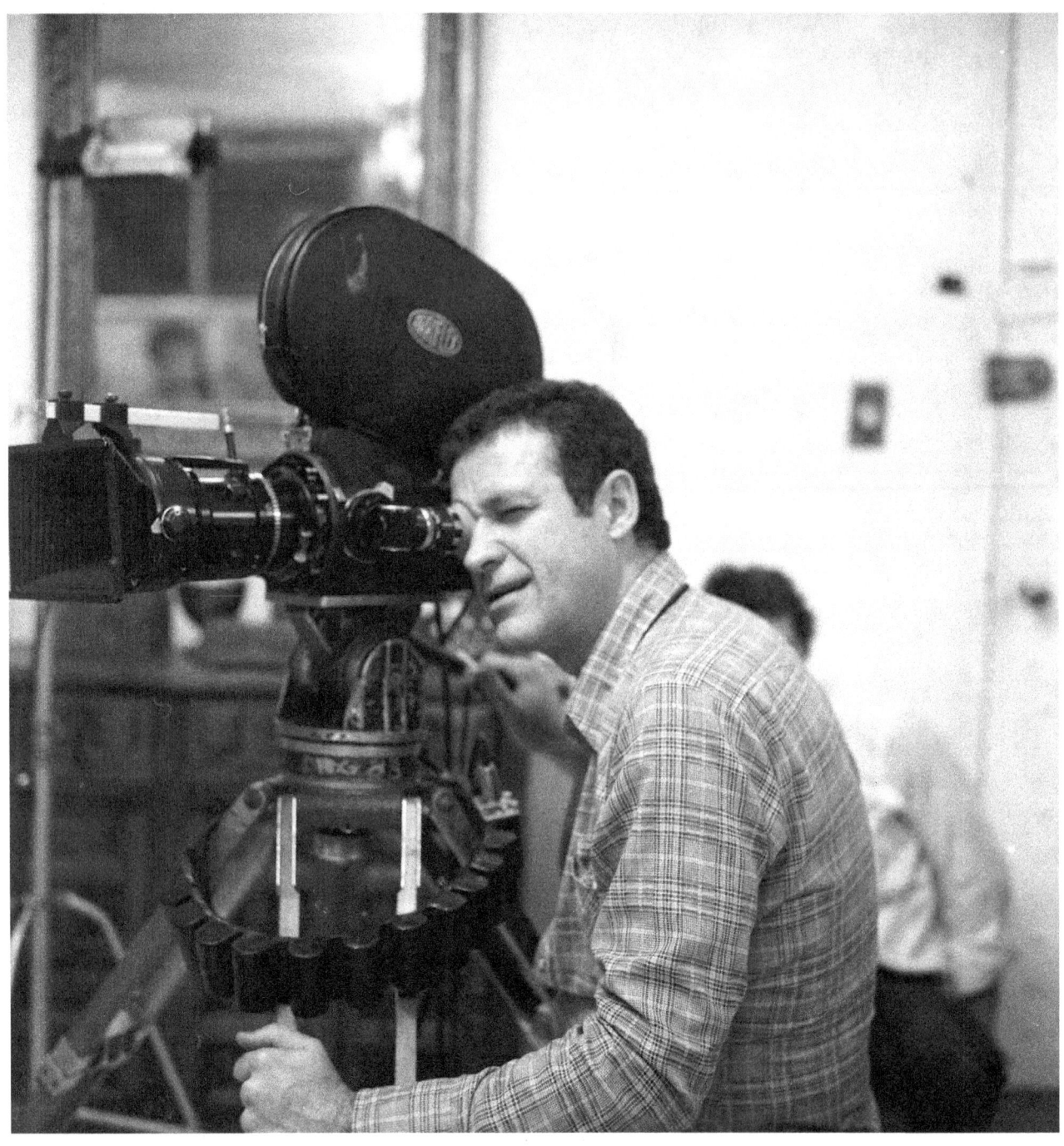

"I usually go over for the Cannes Film Festival, but last year, whe the French censorship system was temporarily relaxed, we opened the first gay hardcore film ever to play in a Paris movie house - Good Hot Stuff, our Hand In Hand anthology film. It was retitled Histoire D'Homme ("Stories of Men"), and it was a great success for us. Not only did we get lots of interesting press and critical attention, most of it quite favorable, but the film outgrossed Nashville our opening week. The most satisfying part of the whlole experience, though, was to be treated as a serious film maker."

JACK DEVEAU

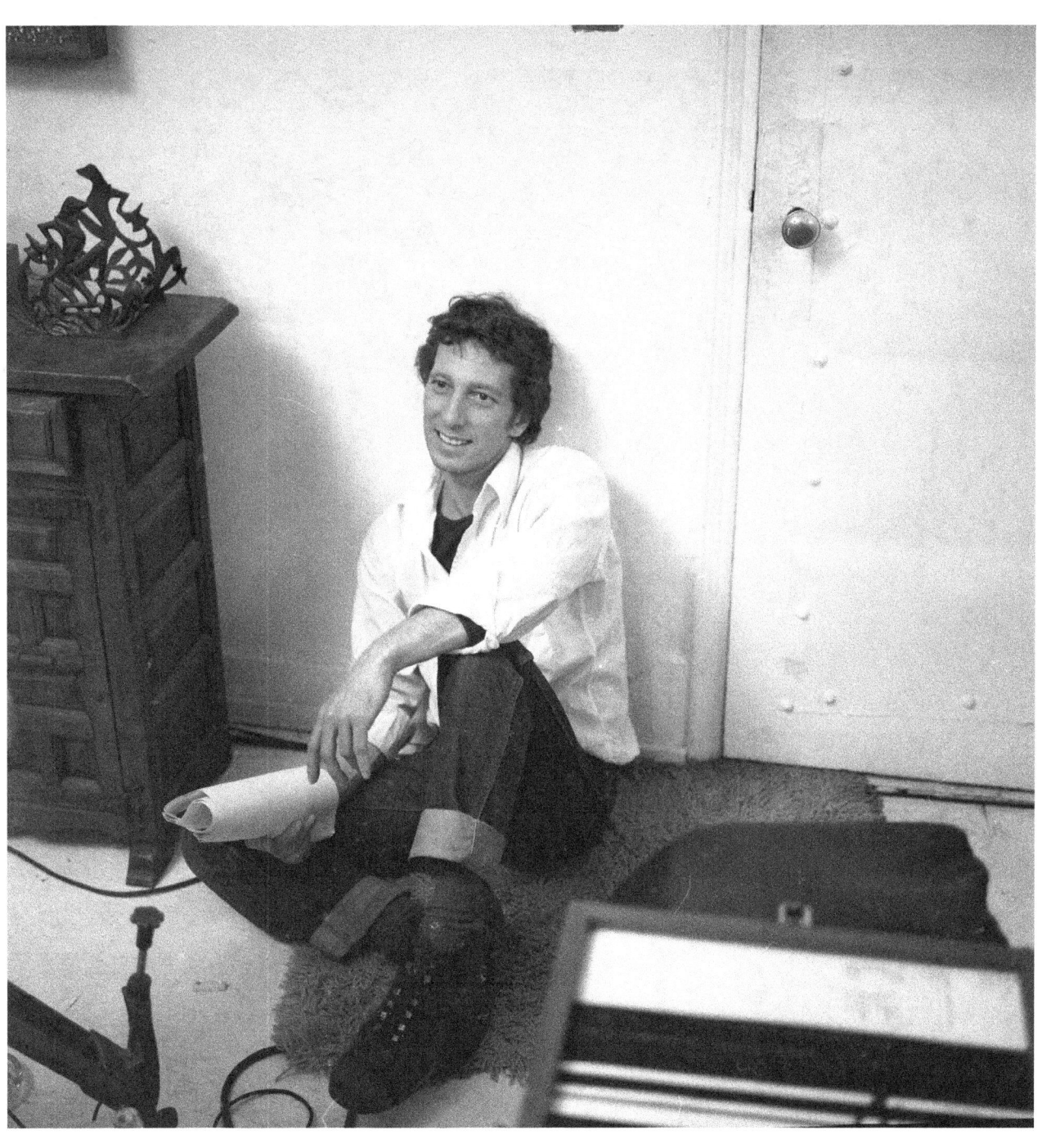

Robert Alvarez on the set of *Hot House*

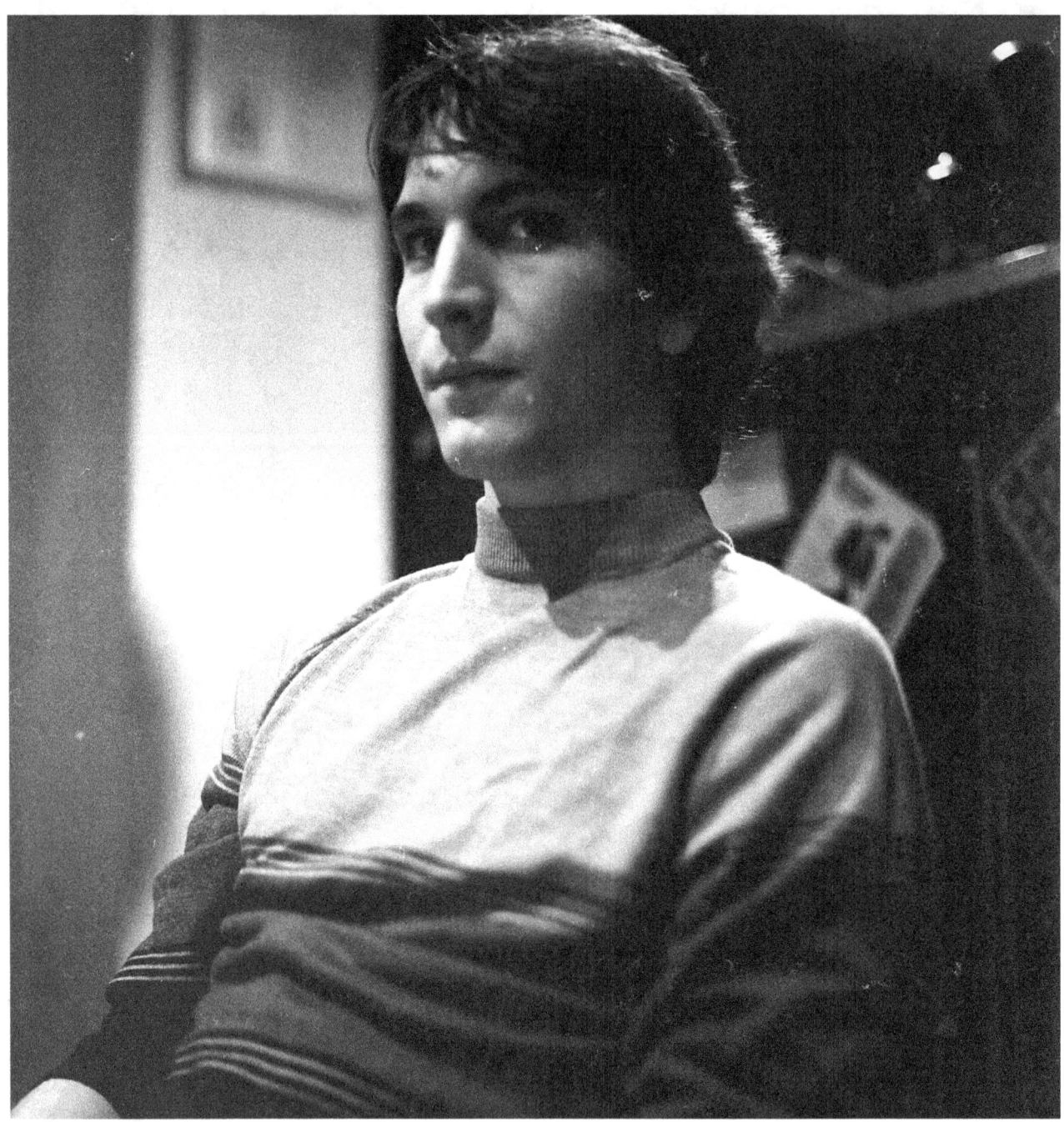
Chris Michaels

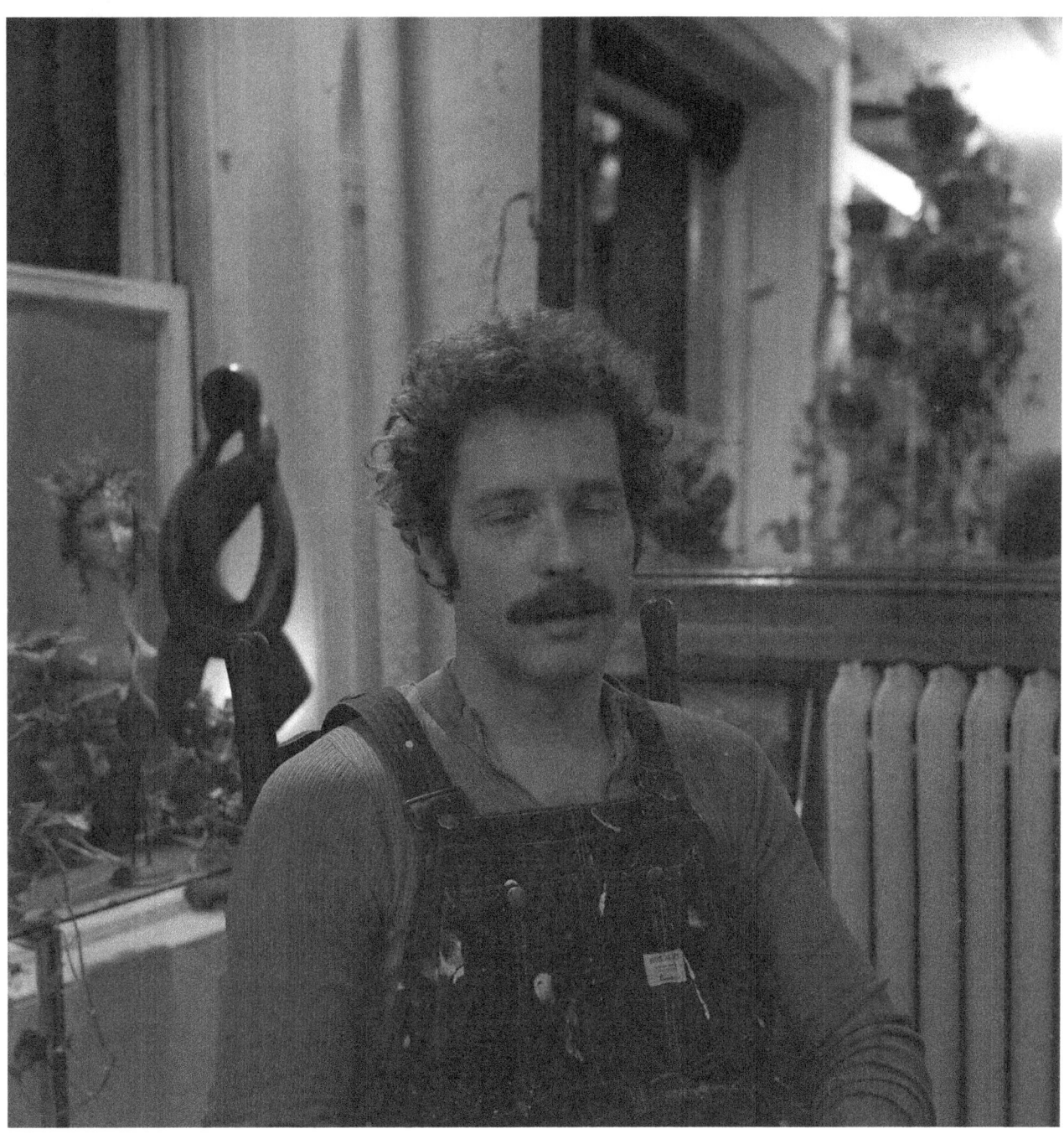

Garry Hunt in another blue-collar part

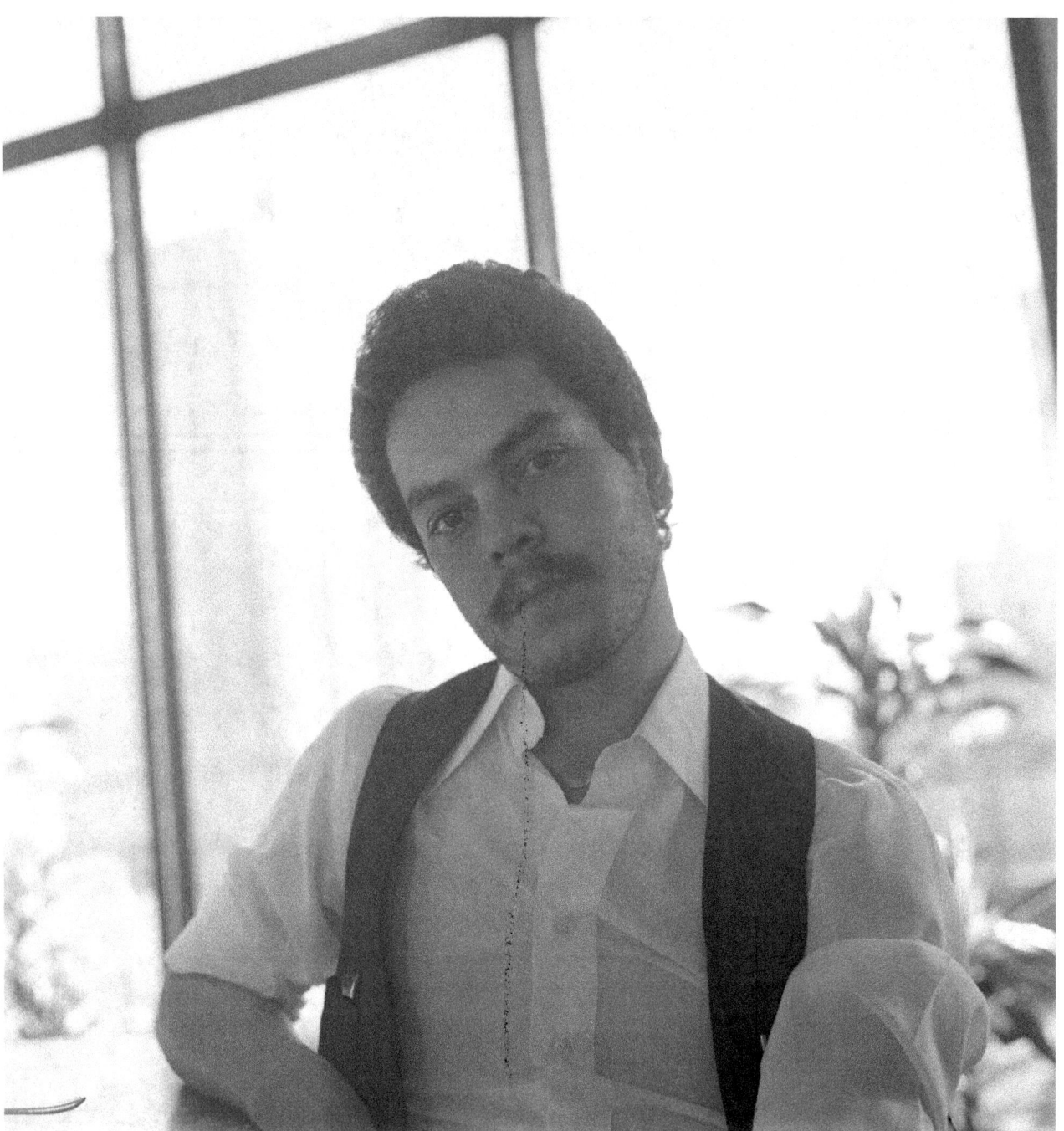

unidentified person behind the scenes of *Hot House*

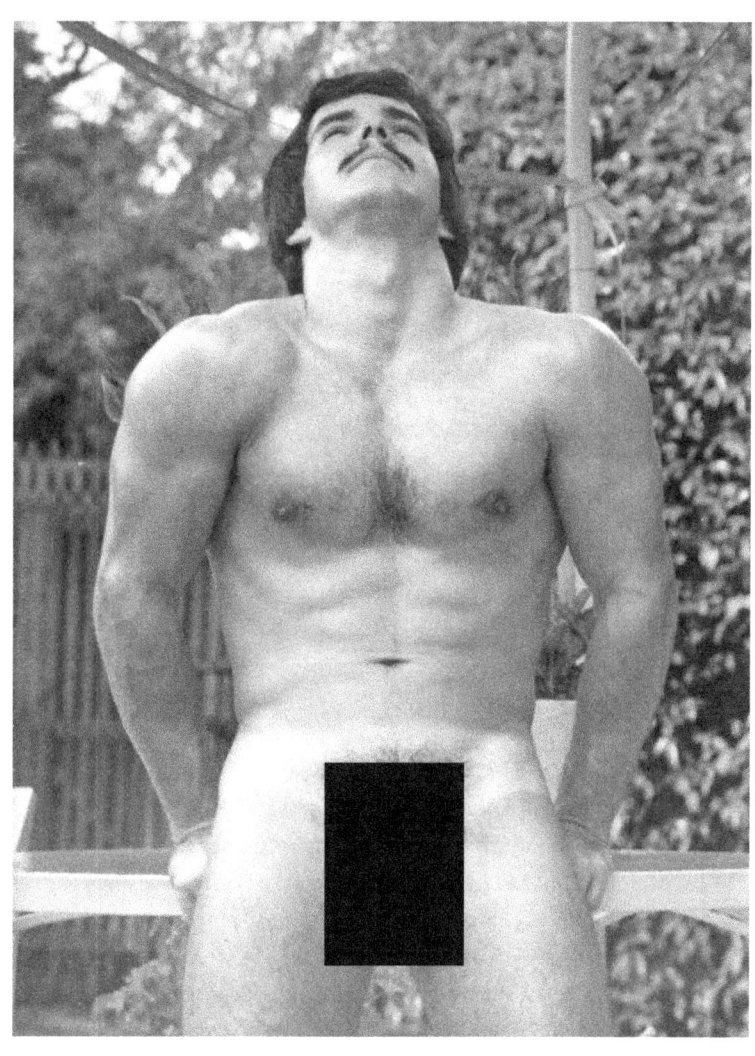

Named Tom Garrett in some of the earlier Target literature for film loops but called Roger in the same scenes in Bullet collection videos. Roger was a straight gay-for-pay performer. He died in a car accident in 1982.
(*Gay Erotic Video Index*)

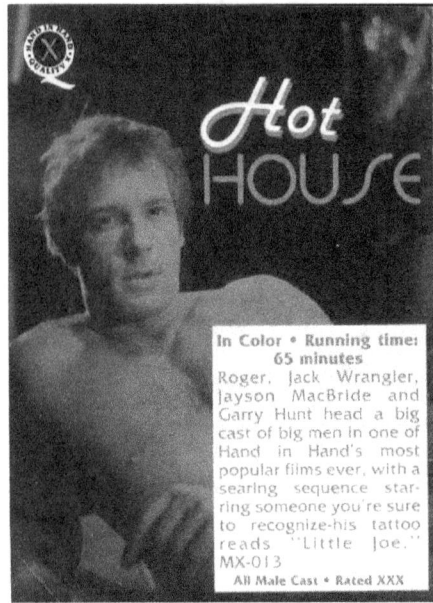

In what is probably the best performance of his career, the ever-popular Jack Wrangler is teamed here with superstud Roger and BALLET DOWN THE HIGHWAY star Garry Hunt in this latest release from Hand In Hand Films. Director Jack Deveau drew from the talents of cameraman Kees Chapman and editor Robert Alvarez, and between them they have created a sizzling piece of celluloid that's now available on video. The exceptionally erotic talents of Jayson MacBride (you'll remember him for his superb performance in CATCHING UP) are featured in an exciting encounter with Jack Wrangler that will rivet your attention to the screen. Roger delivers an overwhelming performance here in HOT HOUSE, one of the few films he's done. Of special interest is a black and white film clip of Joe Dalassandro that was expertly worked into the plot. This short clip is worth the price of the tape, and then some. Why? Quite simply, it is the hottest thing you are ever likely to see on film or video. Anywhere.

*John Mensior, *Torso*

HOTHOUSE

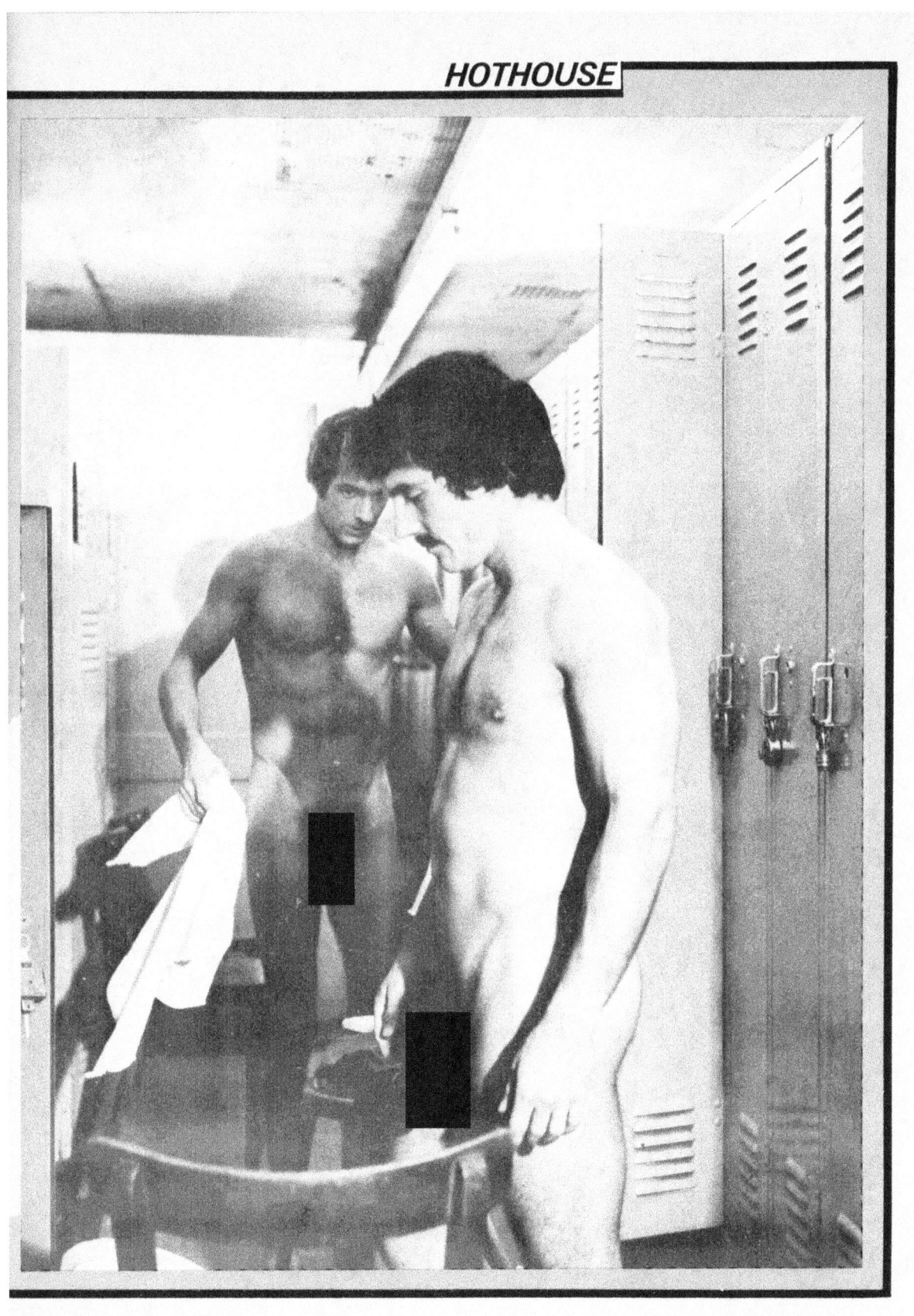

13

"They will be stretched across the screen of the Adonis for the world premiere of Jack Deveau's 'All-American All-Star Movie' *Hot House*. In addition to Roger the X-rated feature boasts blond and bountiful Jack Wrangler. Now that should be hot and heavy."

CHARLES HERSCHBERG, *Michael's Thing*

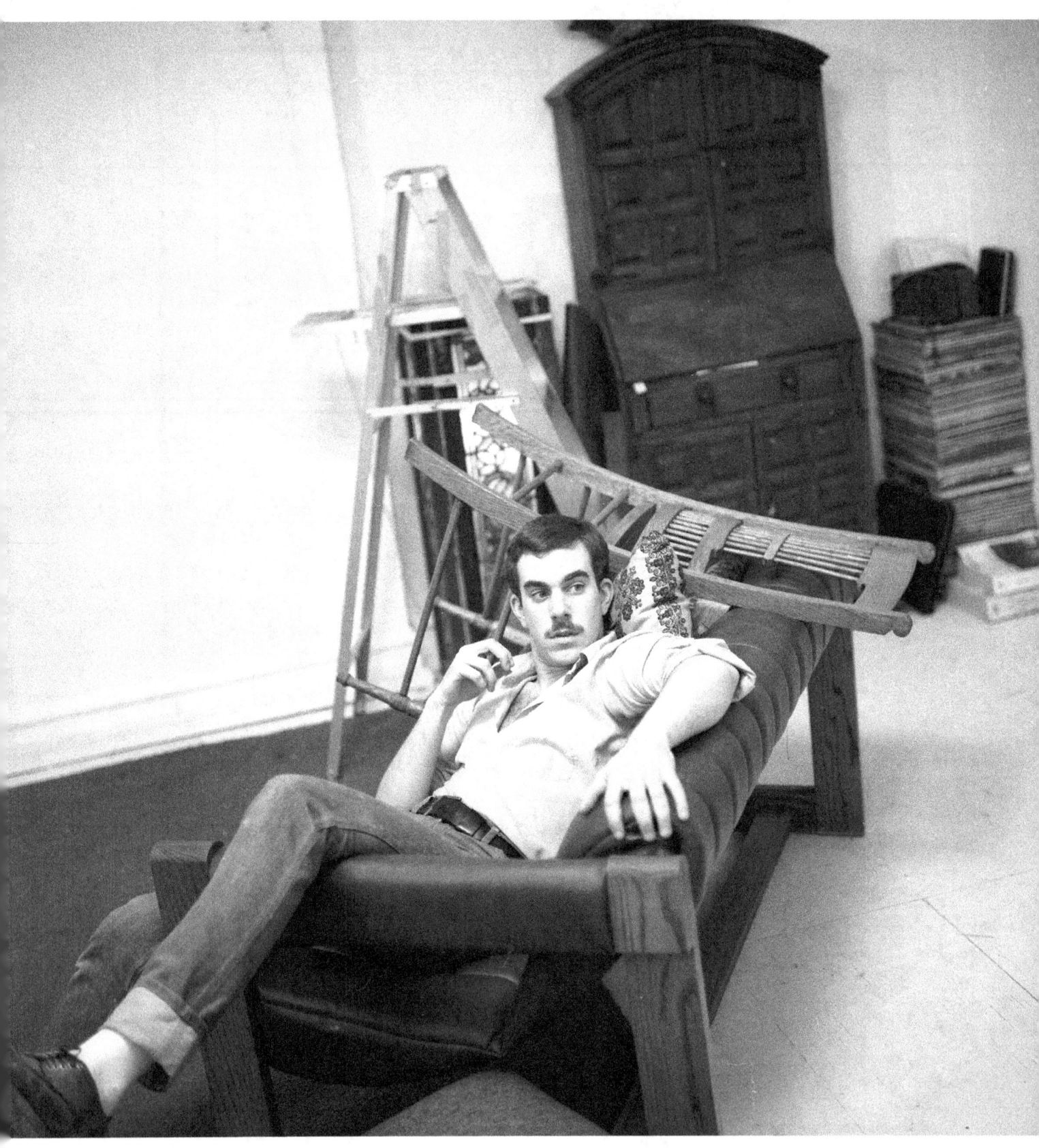

David Hunter in *Hot House*

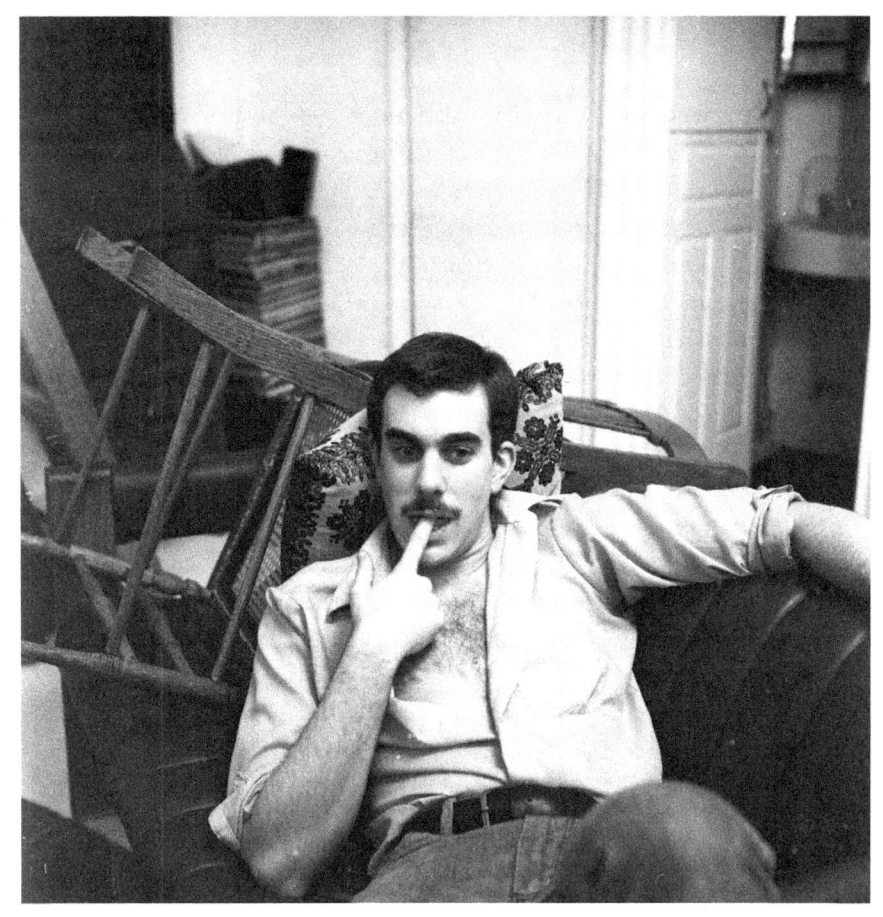
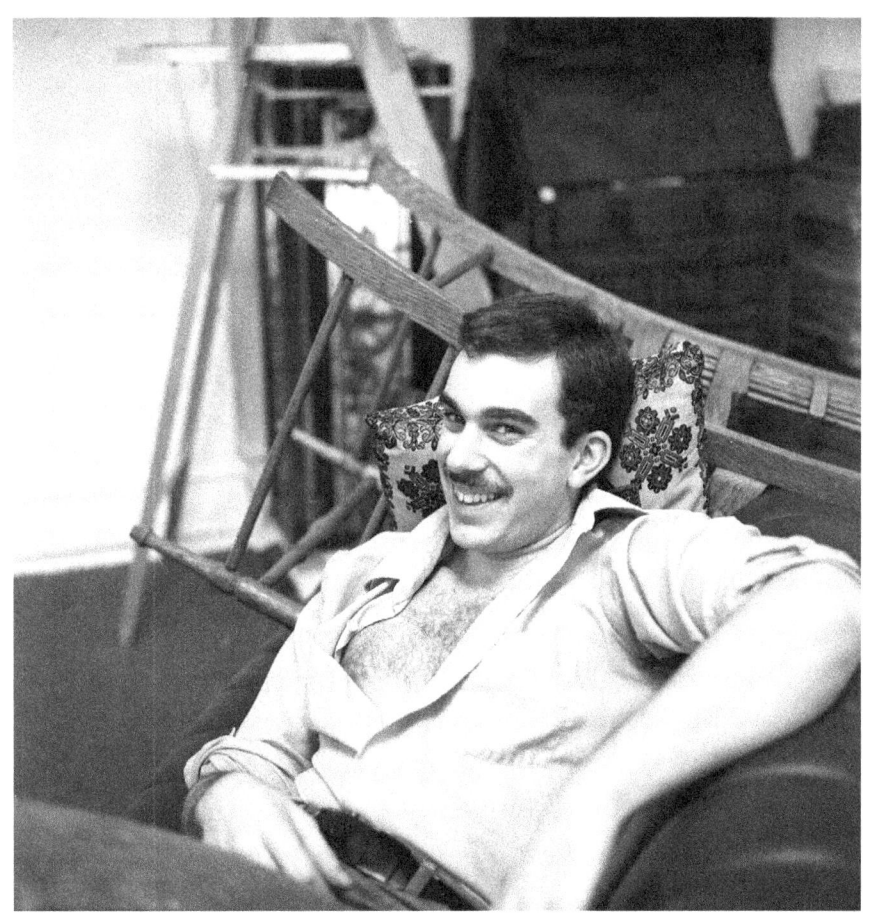

The most ambitious and elaborate of Jack Deveau's films, A NIGHT AT THE ADONIS is a carnalcross between GRAND HOTEL and BOYS IN THE BAND. Set in New York City's legendary porn palace – the Adonis Theatre is still open for business today, but not in the same quarters that were used as the location for this film – this production brings together a shameless crew of assorted studs, all into public sex scenes, and turns them loose on the premises of the original old cavernous playhouse that today awaits demolition. As their lives (and bodies) become intertwined, the building itself functions as a character just as much as any of the hot men who run riot within its confines.

Much like the opening of the film version of *Boys in the Band*, the main characters are introduced under the credits: the opportunistic theatre manager (Chris Michaels); the innocent new assistant manager trainee (Tommy Ruscica); a free-wheeling clothing boutique clerk (Jack Wrangler); a restless lover (Malo) looking for some extra-marital action; a leather-jacketed libertine (Big Al Little); a hedonistic hair stylist (Jayson McBride); an insatiable little bottom (Robert A. Glory); a handsomely endowed, light-skinned black (Geraldo); and a tank-topped hunk (Keith Strickland) at odds with the older man who is keeping him.

As a day in the life of the theatre is traced from opening line-up at the box office to the closing straggle out, nearly everybody connects in one way or another (and almost always, orgasmically) with everyone else. Among the memorable moments: Strickland's angry phone calls to his keeper; McBride and Malo fucking in an old-fashioned barber chair; Wrangler bragging, "There isn't a room in this building I haven't fucked in!" as he leads McBride off to the boiler room; a cum-dripping suck session in the "disco john" by Little and Michaelson; a popper-enhanced plowing of Malo by Geraldo; and a pig-out orgy where virtually everyone gets into action, even (finally) the innocent new trainee.

The fluid camera work with its mysteriously muted shadows; the film-within-the-film excerpts featuring Bill Eld, Roger, and most especially, Myles Longue; the kaleidoscopic editing that paces the whirlwind production; the constantly involving storylines which serve to heighten the sexual heat; and the infernally ruttish performance by Malo – all contribute to this big, extravagant film.

From its opening moments (the marquee lighting up against the strains of an angel choir) to its final fadeout (of the empty house at rest for a few hours), A NIGHT AT THE ADONIS is a voluptuous valentine to the uninhibited joys of an era that is, as they say, gone with the wind.

*Jerry Douglas, *Manshots*

"Sex at the Adonis is all hard celluloid."—The Advocate

ALL MALE CAST

Jack Deveau's
a night at the Adonis

From the balcony to the boiler room, the world famous Male Theater, The Adonis in New York City, is where the hottest, humpiest, horniest men meet to get it on. Prodigiously proportioned patrons thread their way through the nooks and crannies of the movie palace getting and giving the royal treatment to one another. There is more variety in customers and patrons than in a box of bijou jujubes!

Running Time: 85 minutes © MCMLXXXII Evart Enterprises, Inc. All Rights Reserved.

Starring
Jack Wrangler, Malo,
Chris Michaels and Jason Macbride

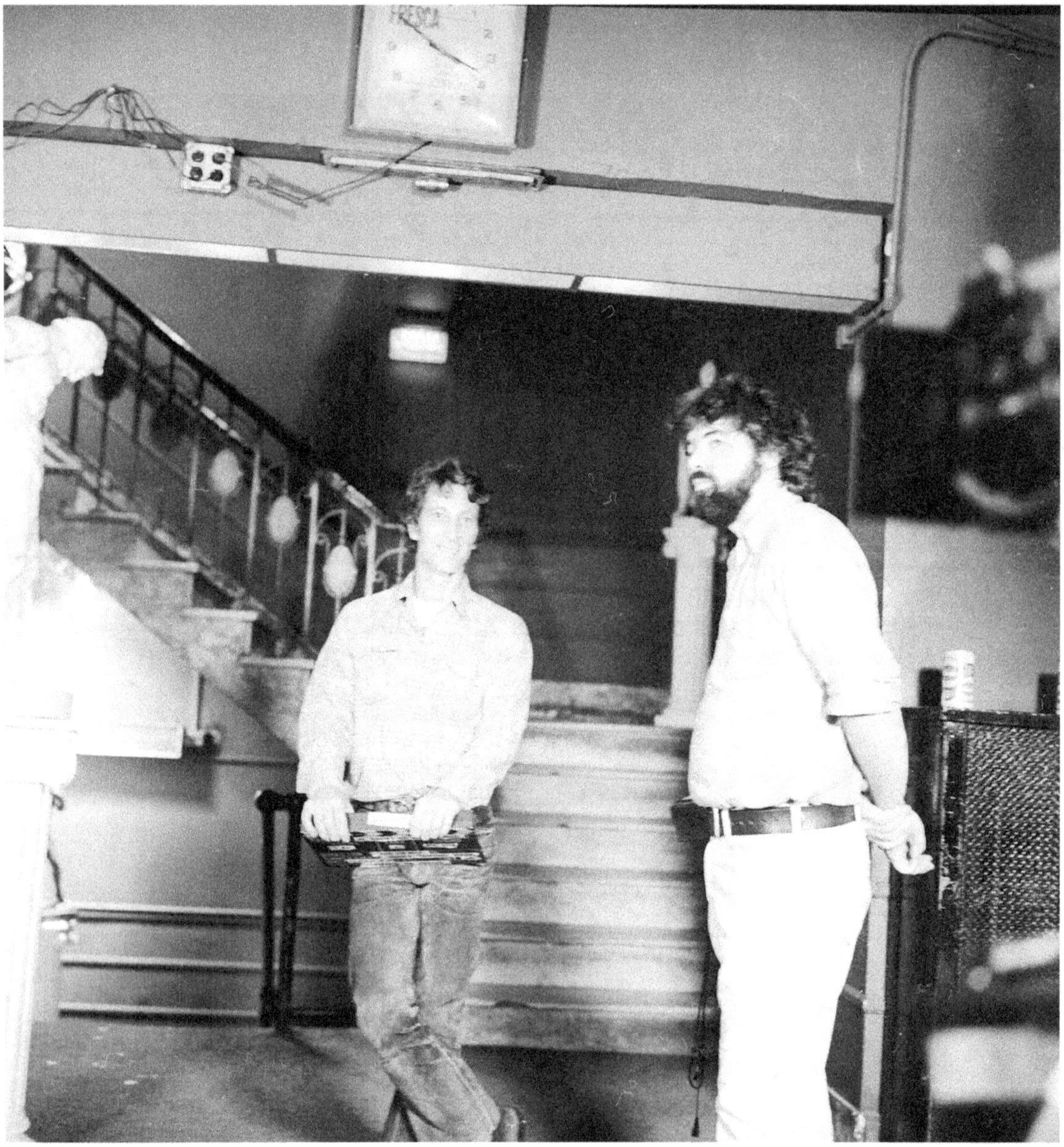

Robert Alvarez (left) and S. Howe

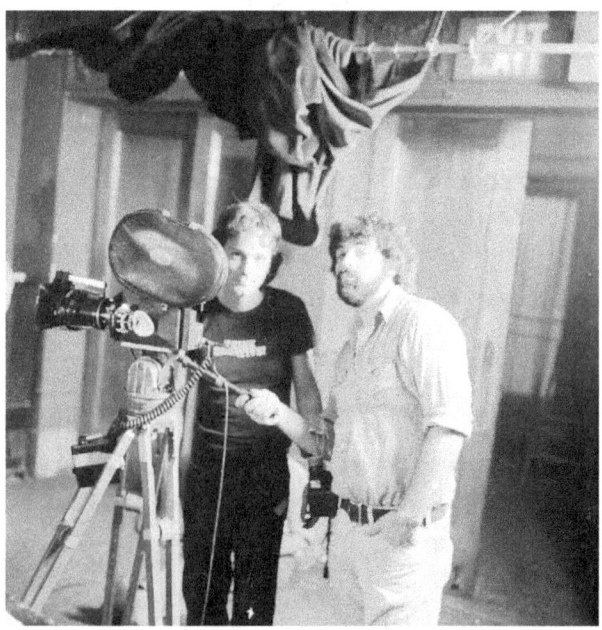
Kees Chapman and S. Howe

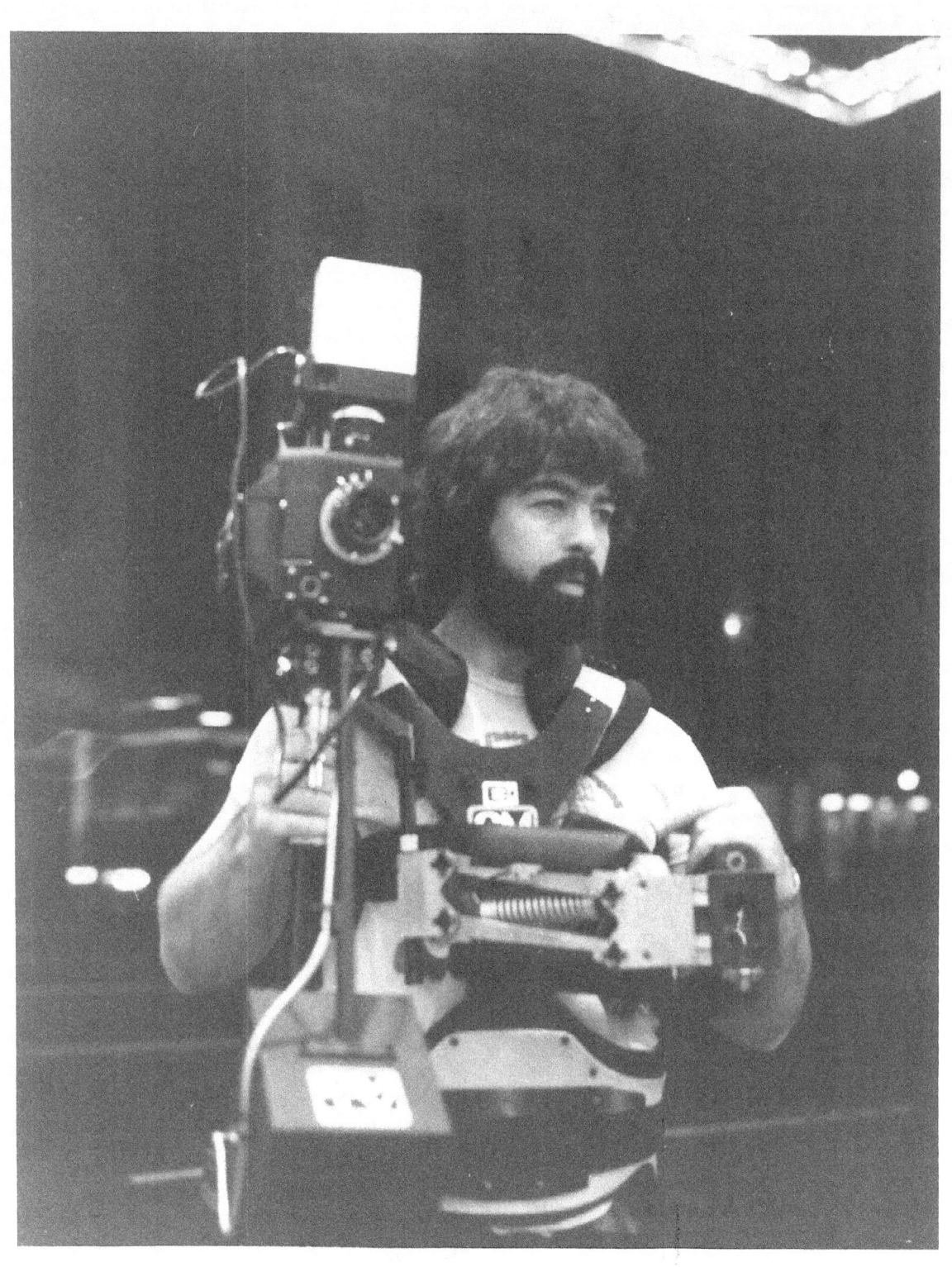

A Night At The Adonis - Special Cameraman S. Howe

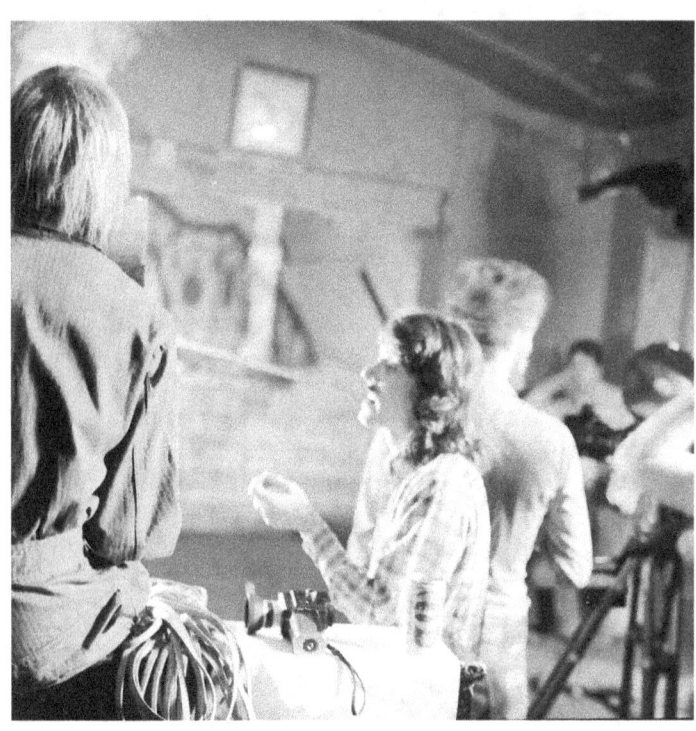

Jim Delegatti

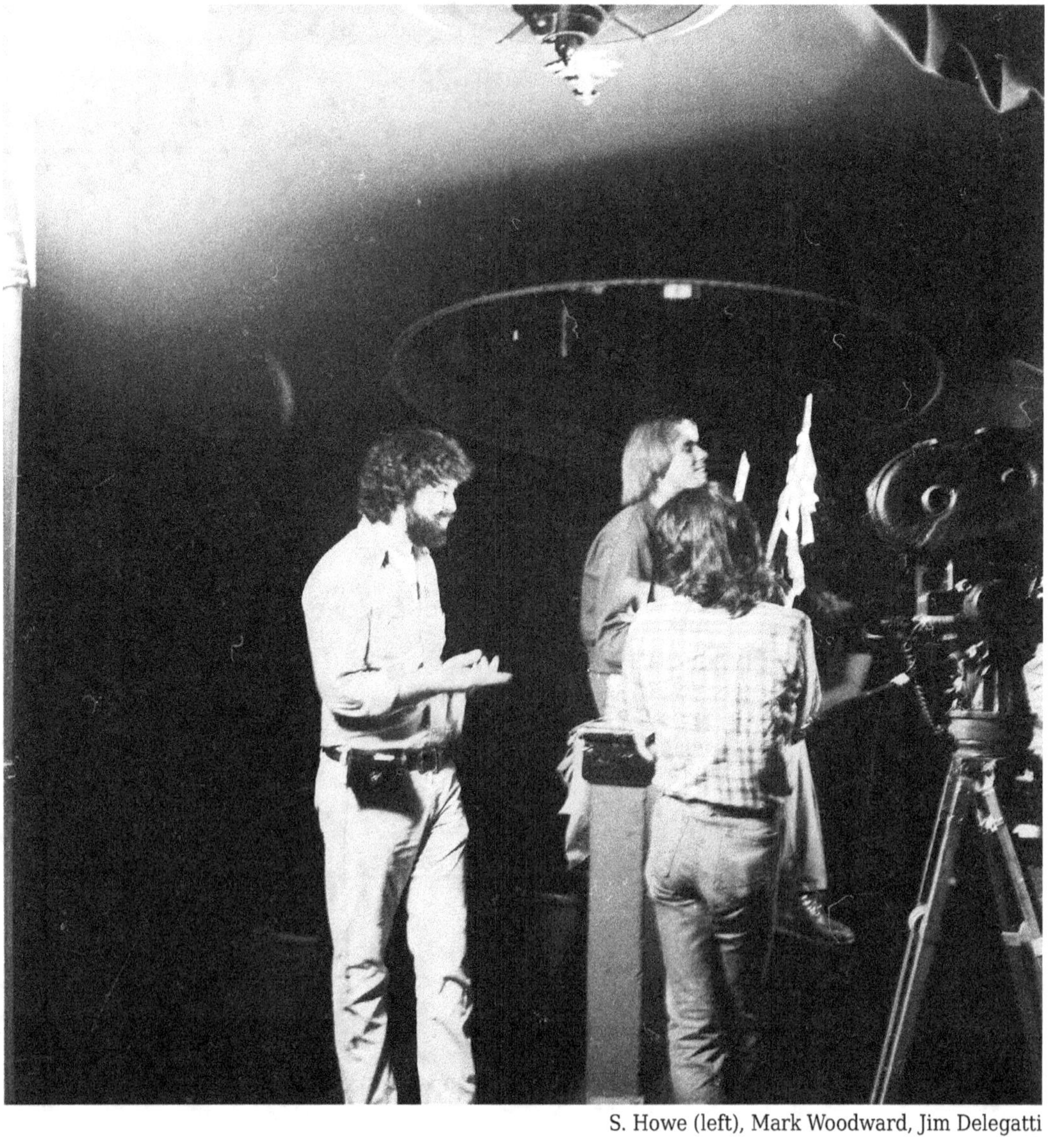

S. Howe (left), Mark Woodward, Jim Delegatti

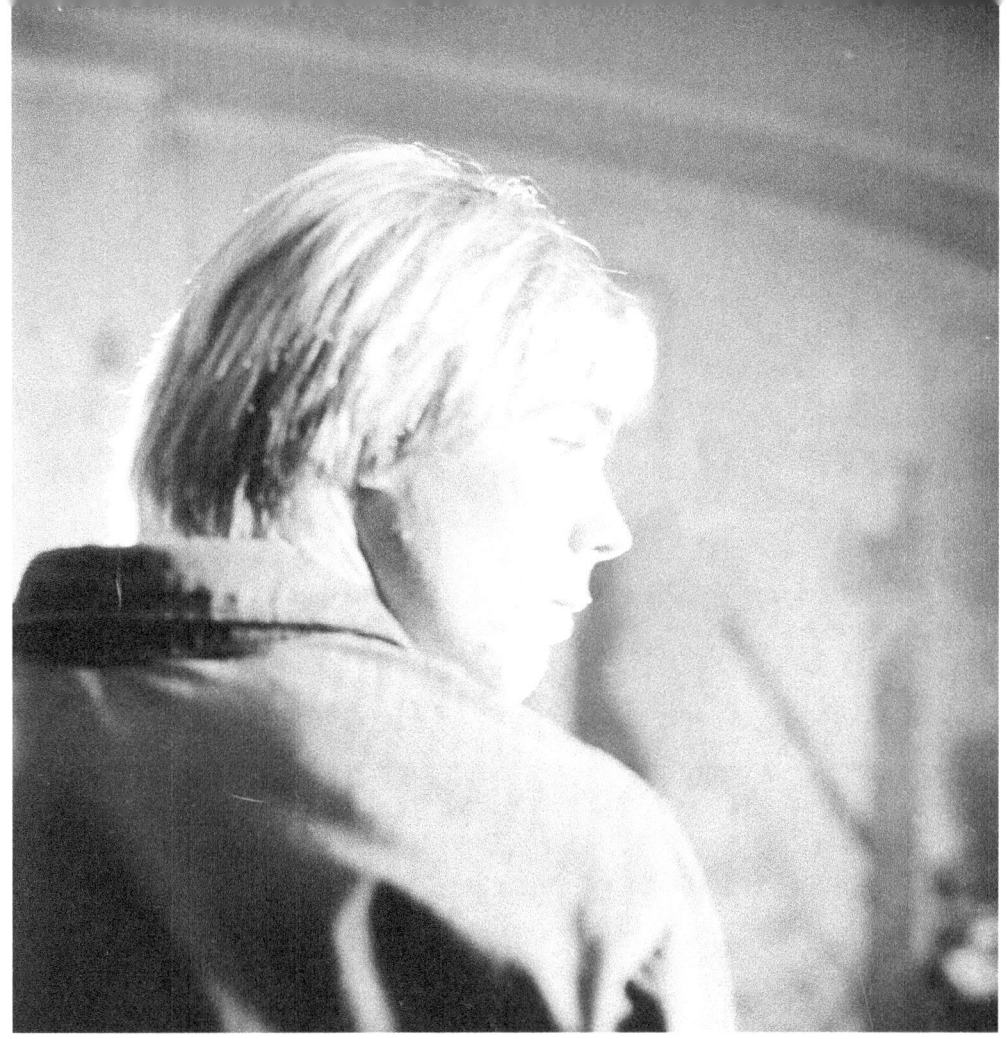

Mark Woodward

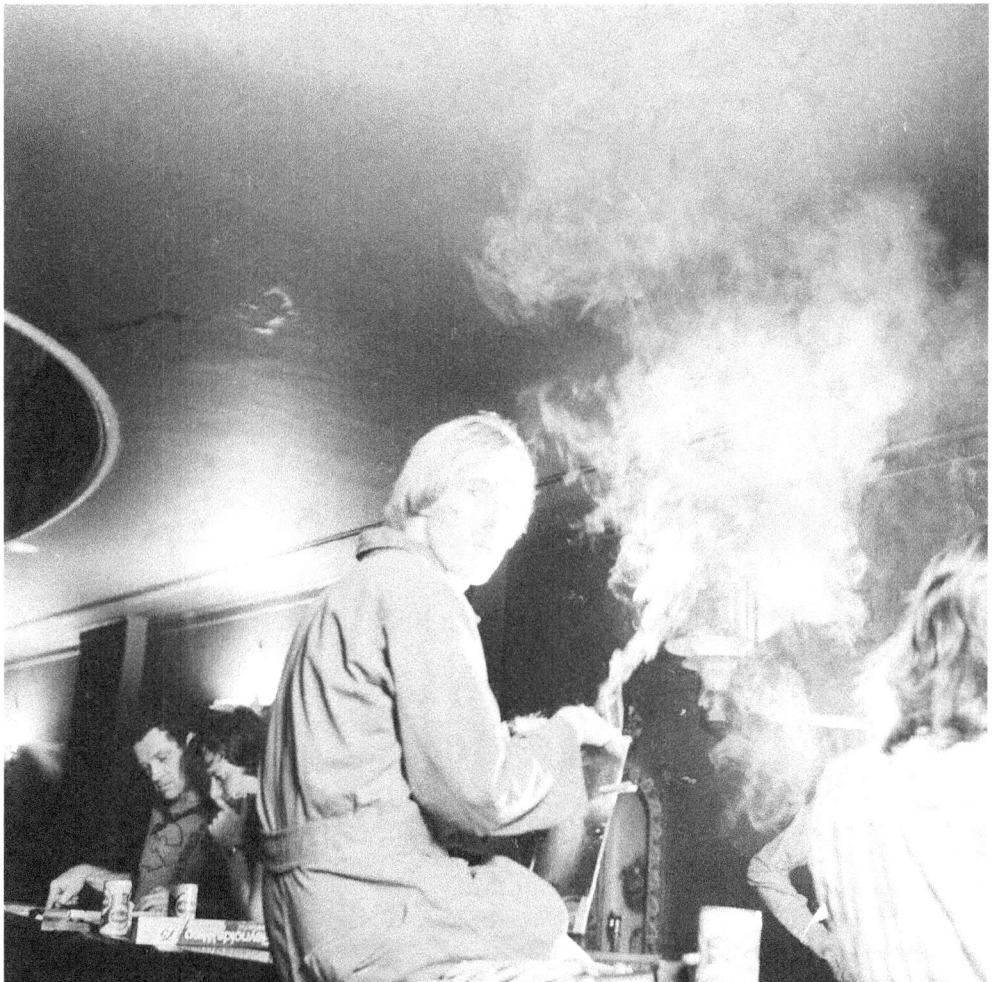

Mark Woodward,
background: Jack Deveau,
Kees Chapman

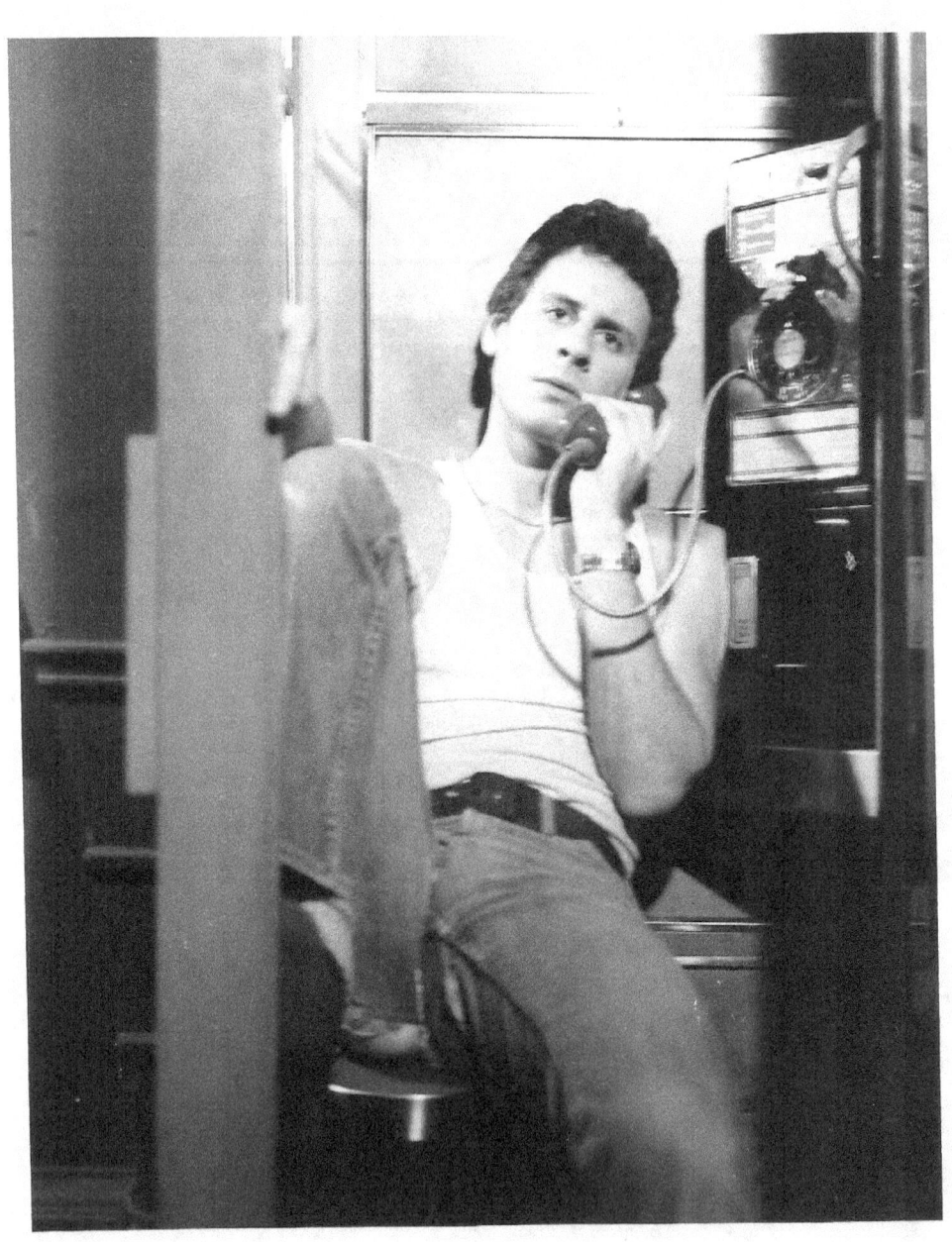

Todd Travers as the theater patron in *A Night At The Adonis*.

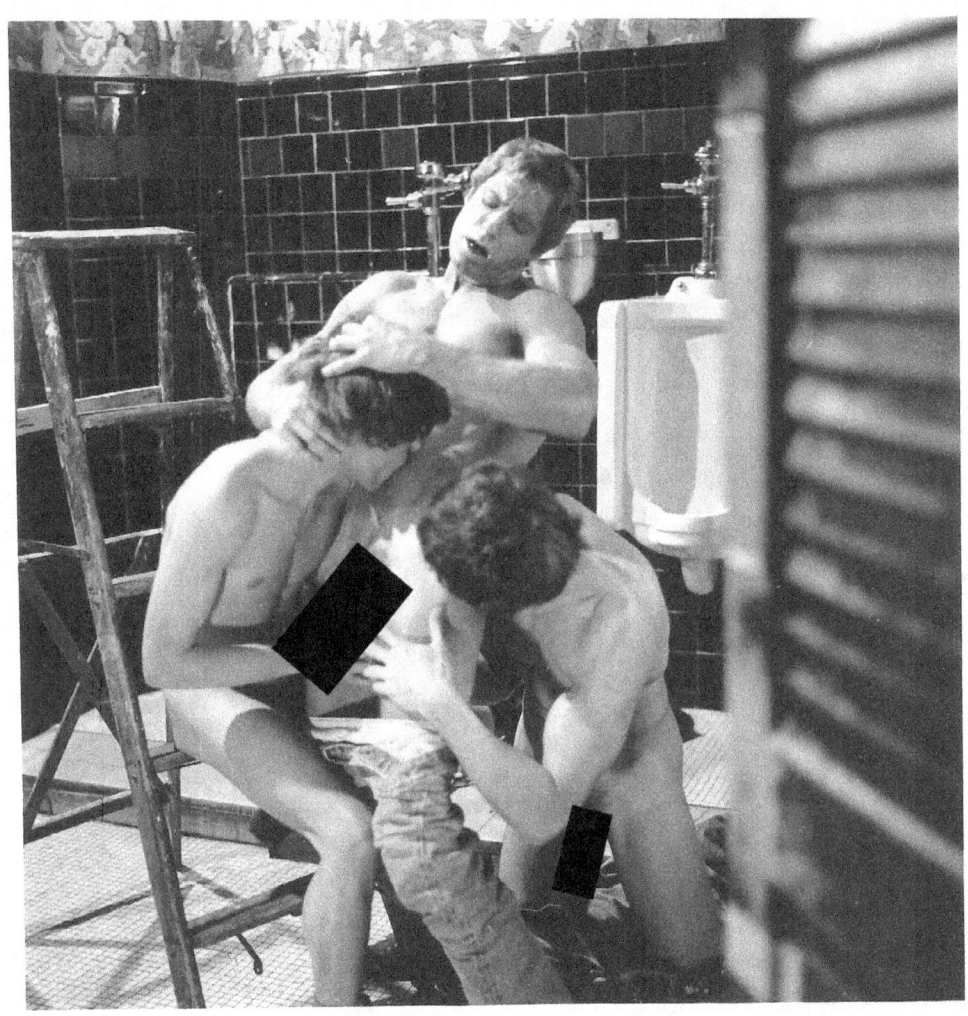

Jack Wrangler, Big Al Little, Robert A. Glory making out at the toilet of the legendary Adonis theatre.

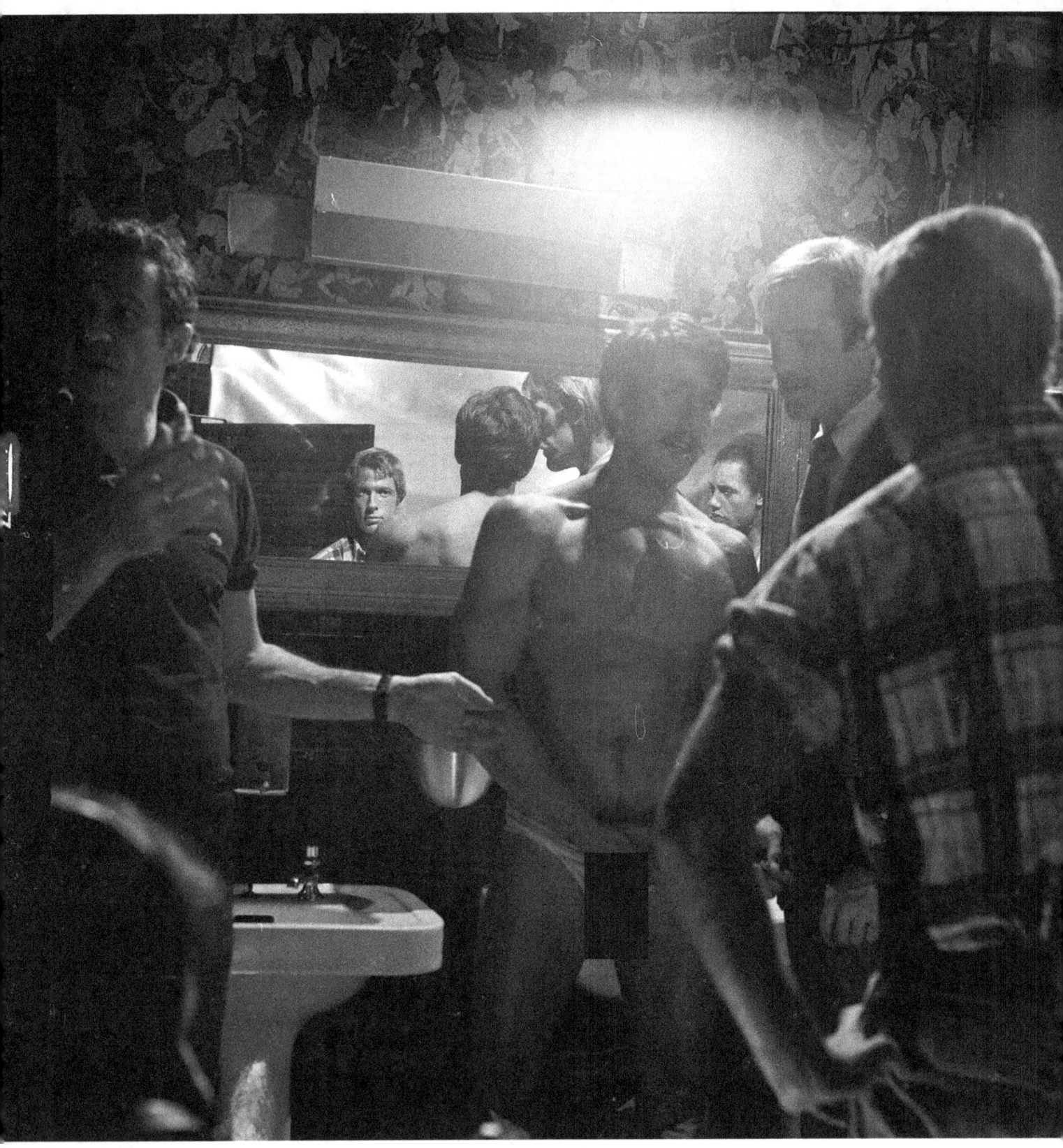

Jack Wrangler stars as a store owner who has designs on his hunky employee Malo. From the balcony to a dark boiler room, director Jack Deveau does a fantastic job of showing us costumers from young to older, from leather types to clean-cut at the Adonis engaging in all sorts of sexual fantasies.

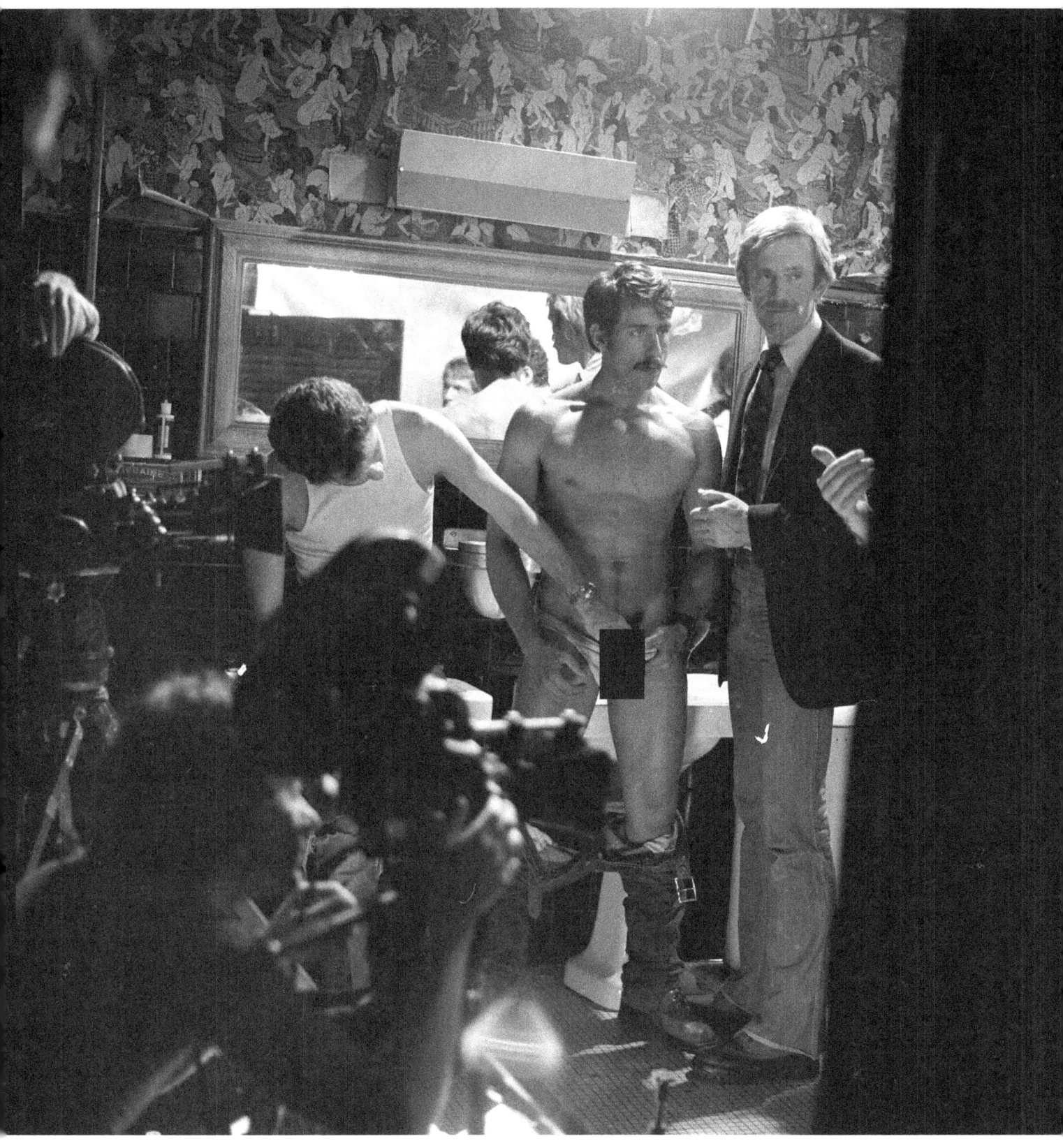

"Truly a fitting tribute and realistic document about this dubious gay porn landmark at the height of its notoriety." *Male Review*

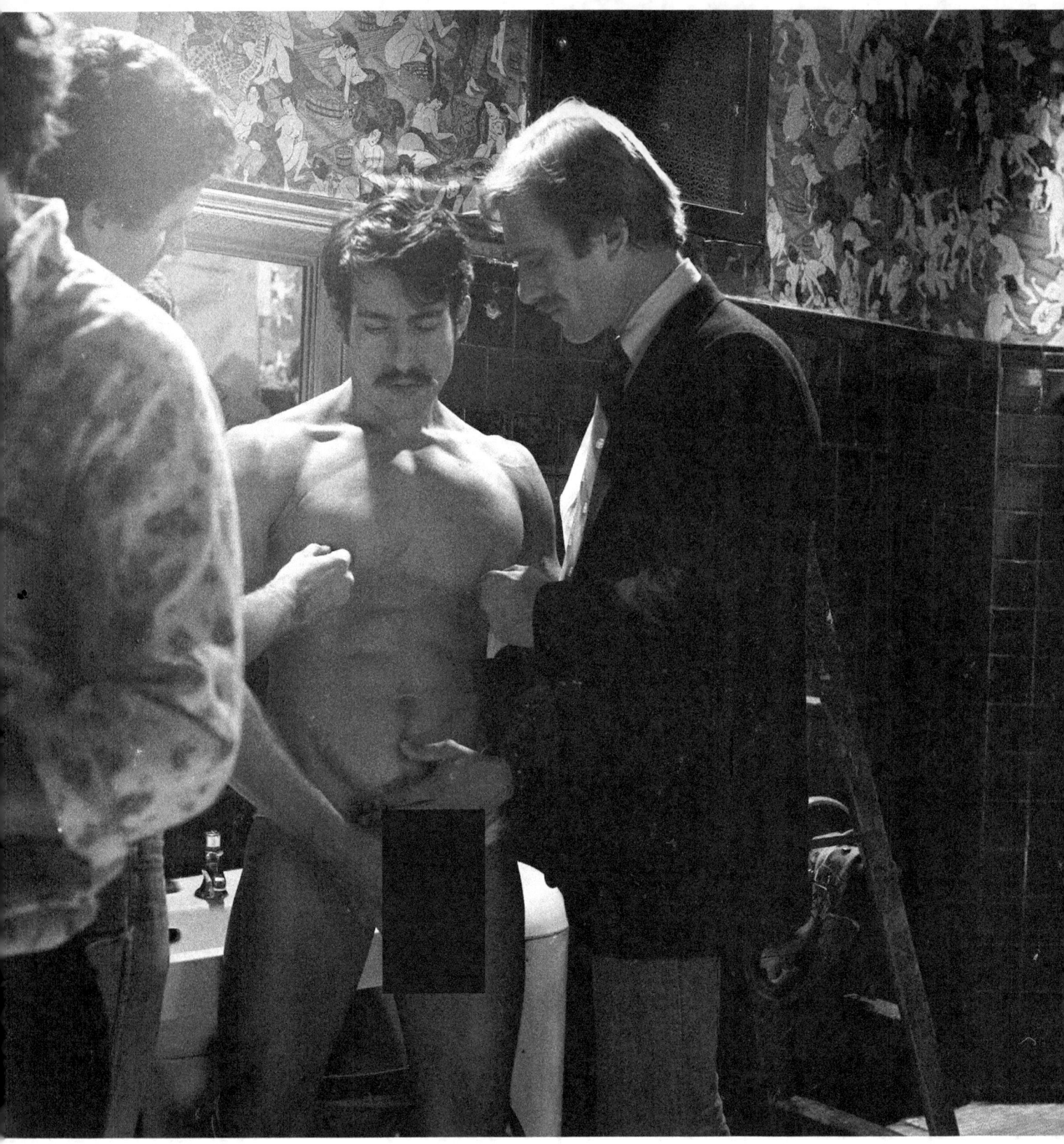

"*A Night at the Adonis* is one of the best, and most interesting, of the 1970s gay porno features shot on film and shown in theatres. It is a remarkably self-reflexive work, not only designed to be shown in adult cinemas but also set by and large in one, a real one - the Adonis in Manhatten. The film follows, in an Altmanesque kind of way, the stories of a number of individual men who end up tonight at the Adonis and sample the hedonistic delights therein." **JAIBO**, *imdb*

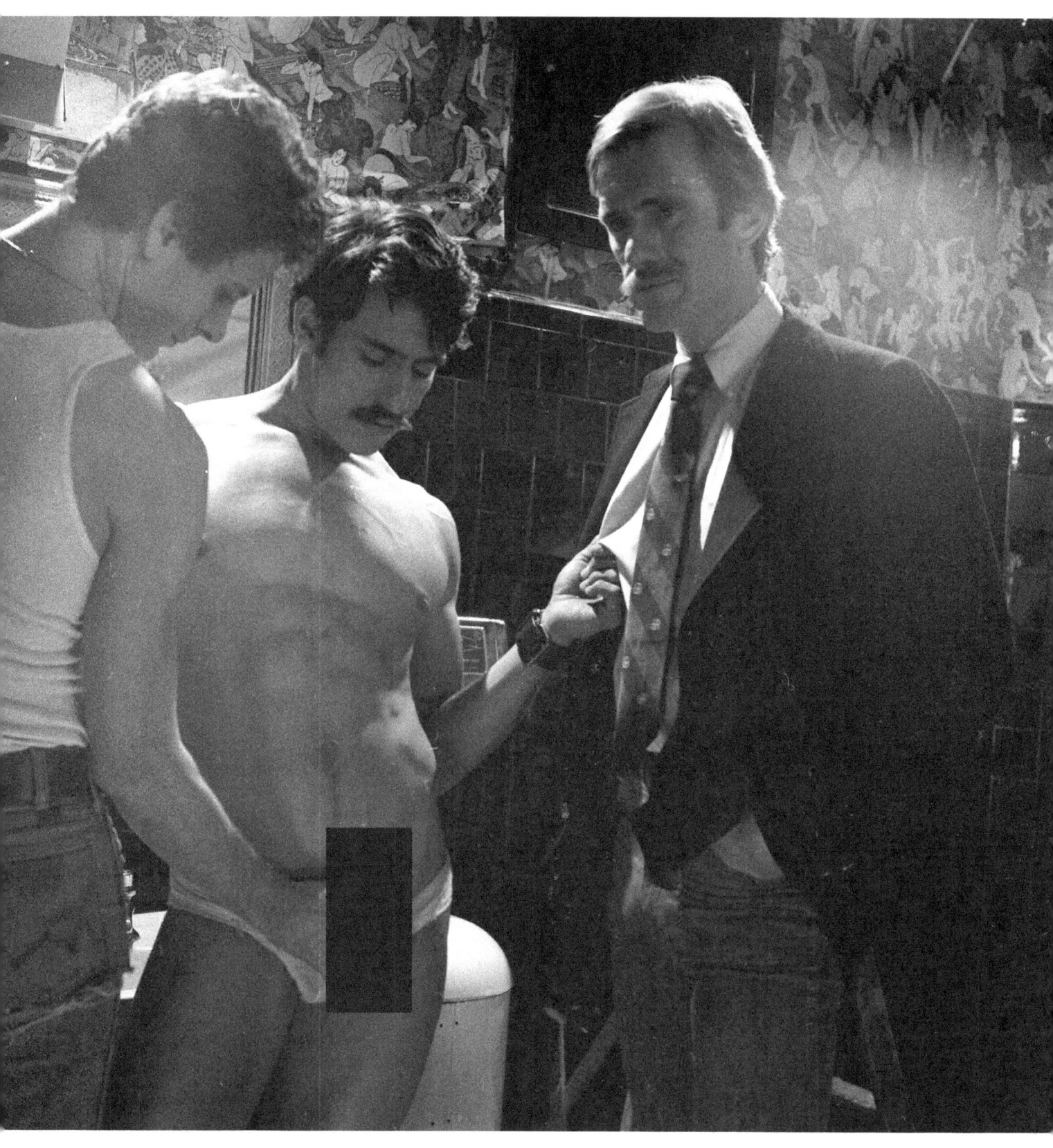

The Jingler Big Al Little (left), Malo (middle), Keith Strickland

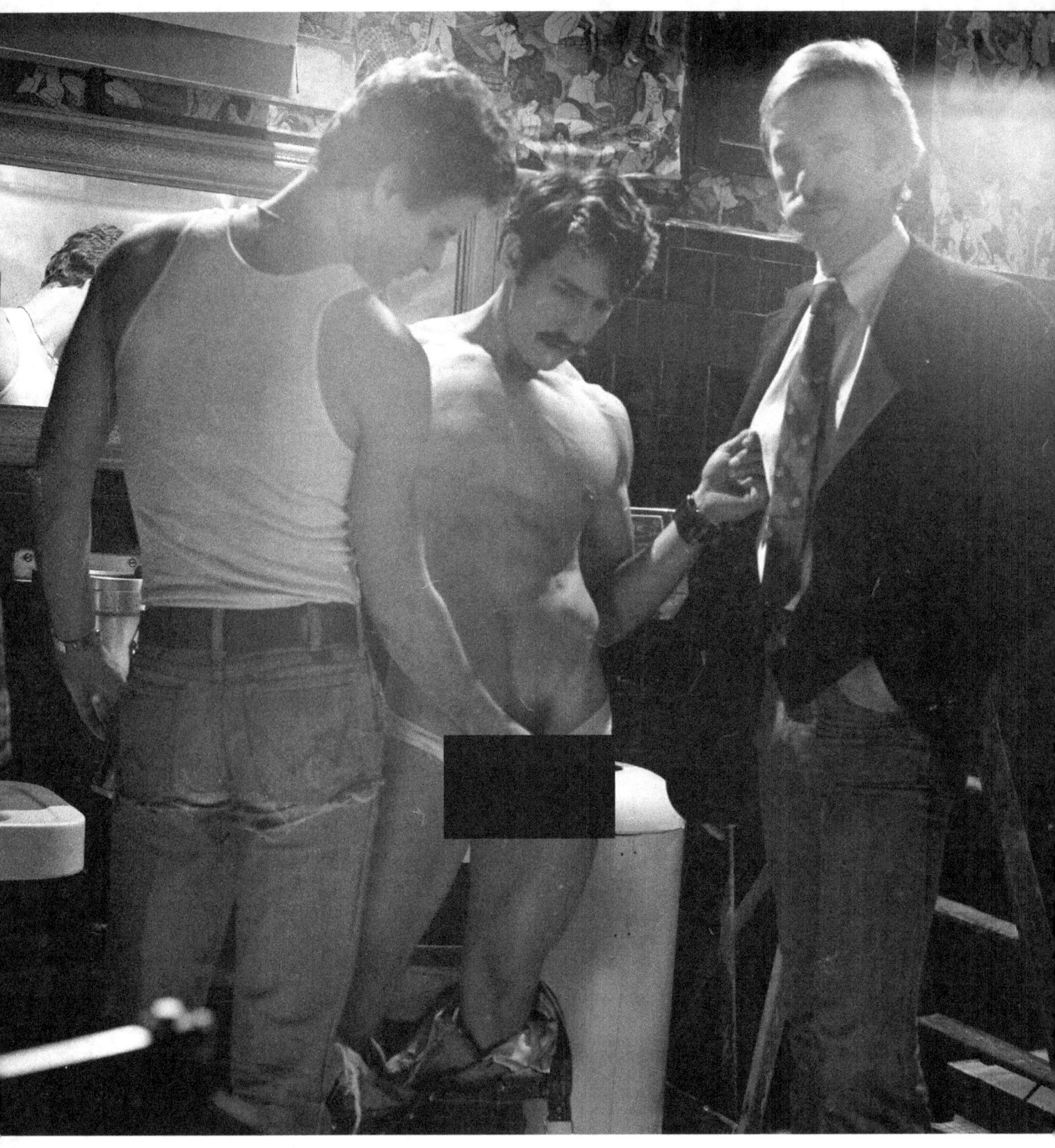

"The main idea Jack and I had about *A Night at the Adonis* was to do our Robert-Altman-movie; many characters that had equal importance. There was not one lead. Doing something like that was our experiment."

MOOSE 100

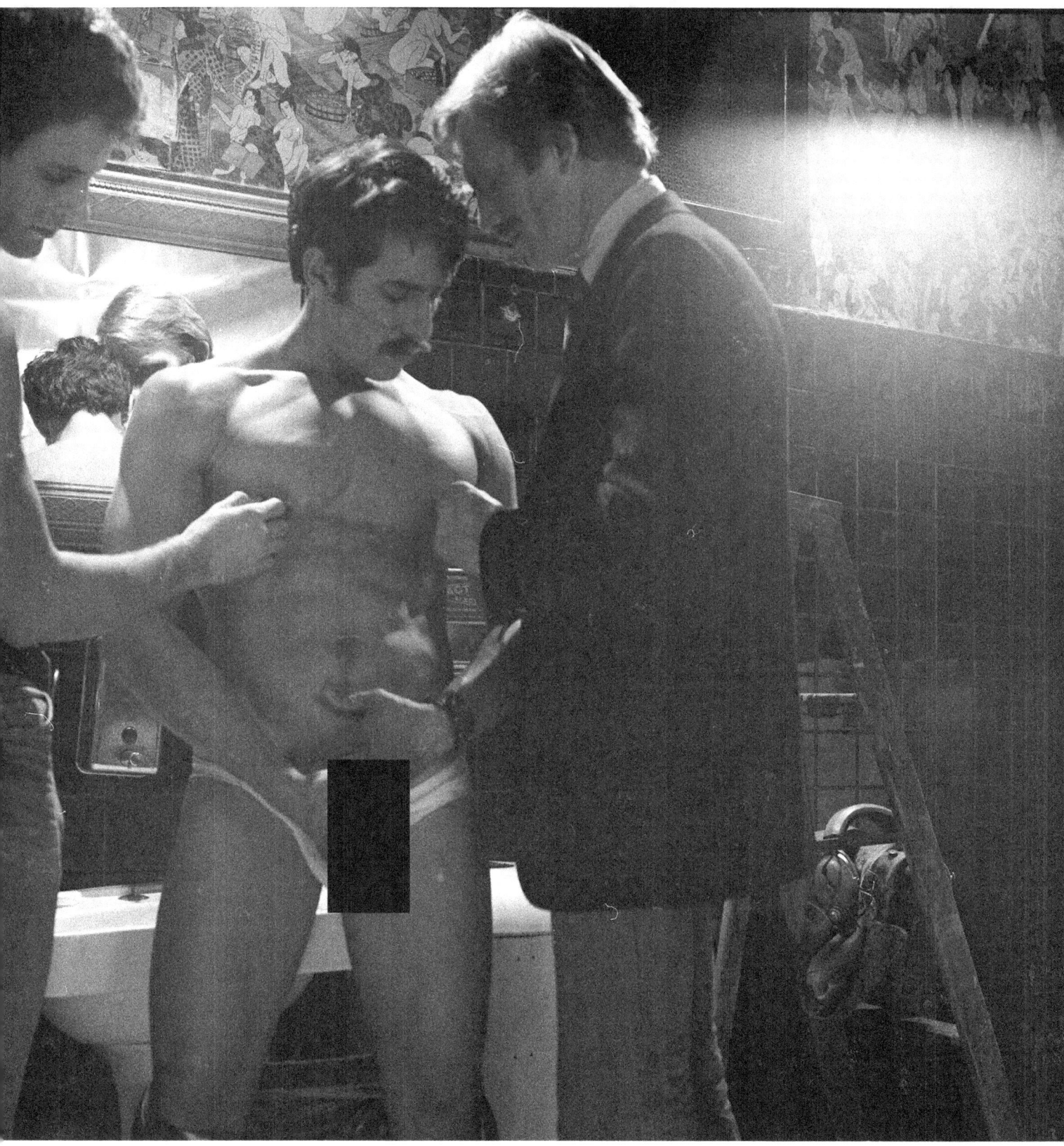

"By carefully building the story around a real-life location, this vintage Gay Adult Film succeeds both as a narrative film and a piece of history. Just as the many soft-core porn films of the 1960s preserve the look and feel of New York City in that era, this provides a mini-time capsule snapshot of the Gay subculture a decade later."

LOR_ ,imdb

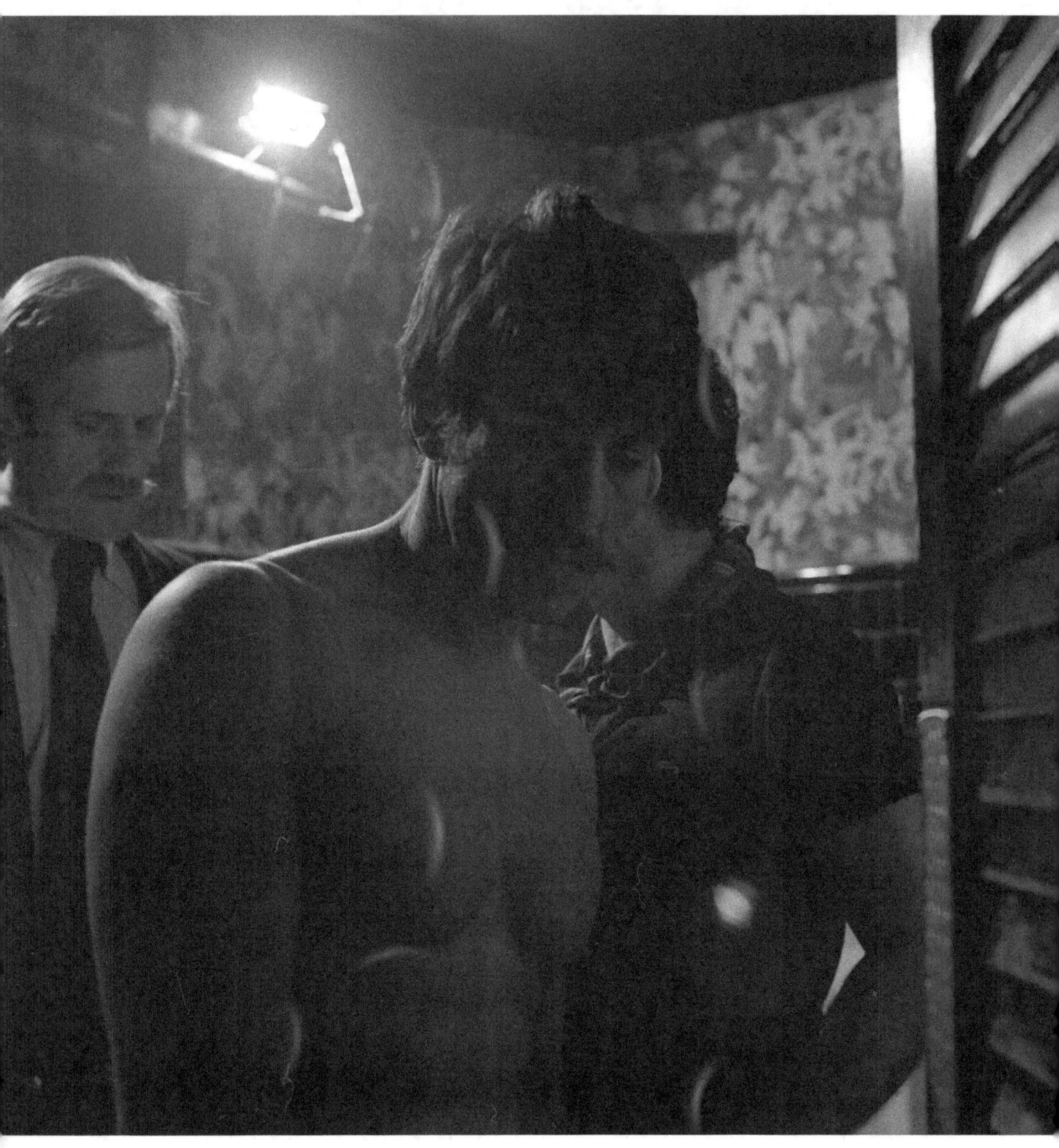

You will meet a tall dark stranger - Malo in *A Night at the Adonis*

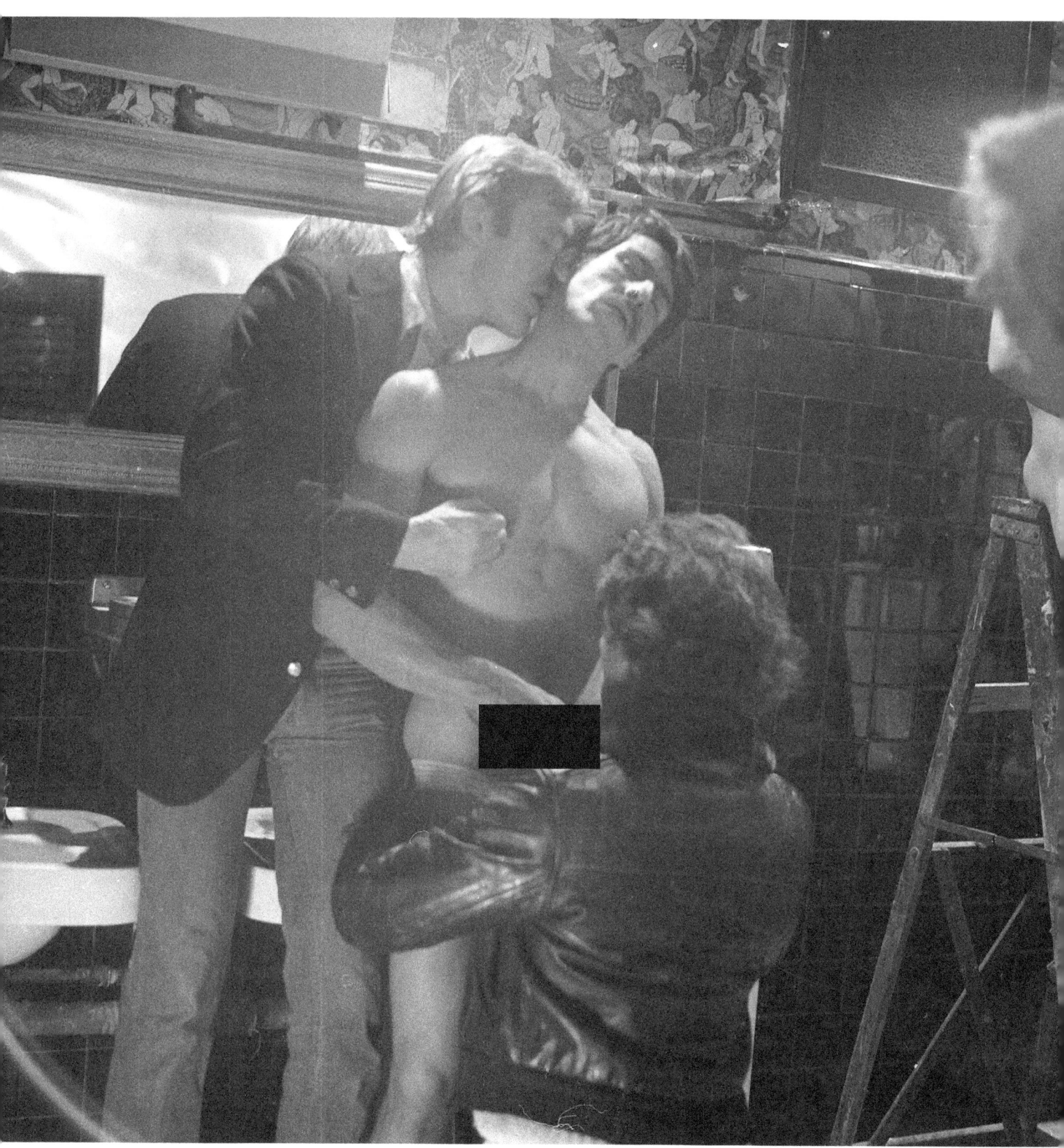

Keith Strickland, Malo, Geraldo

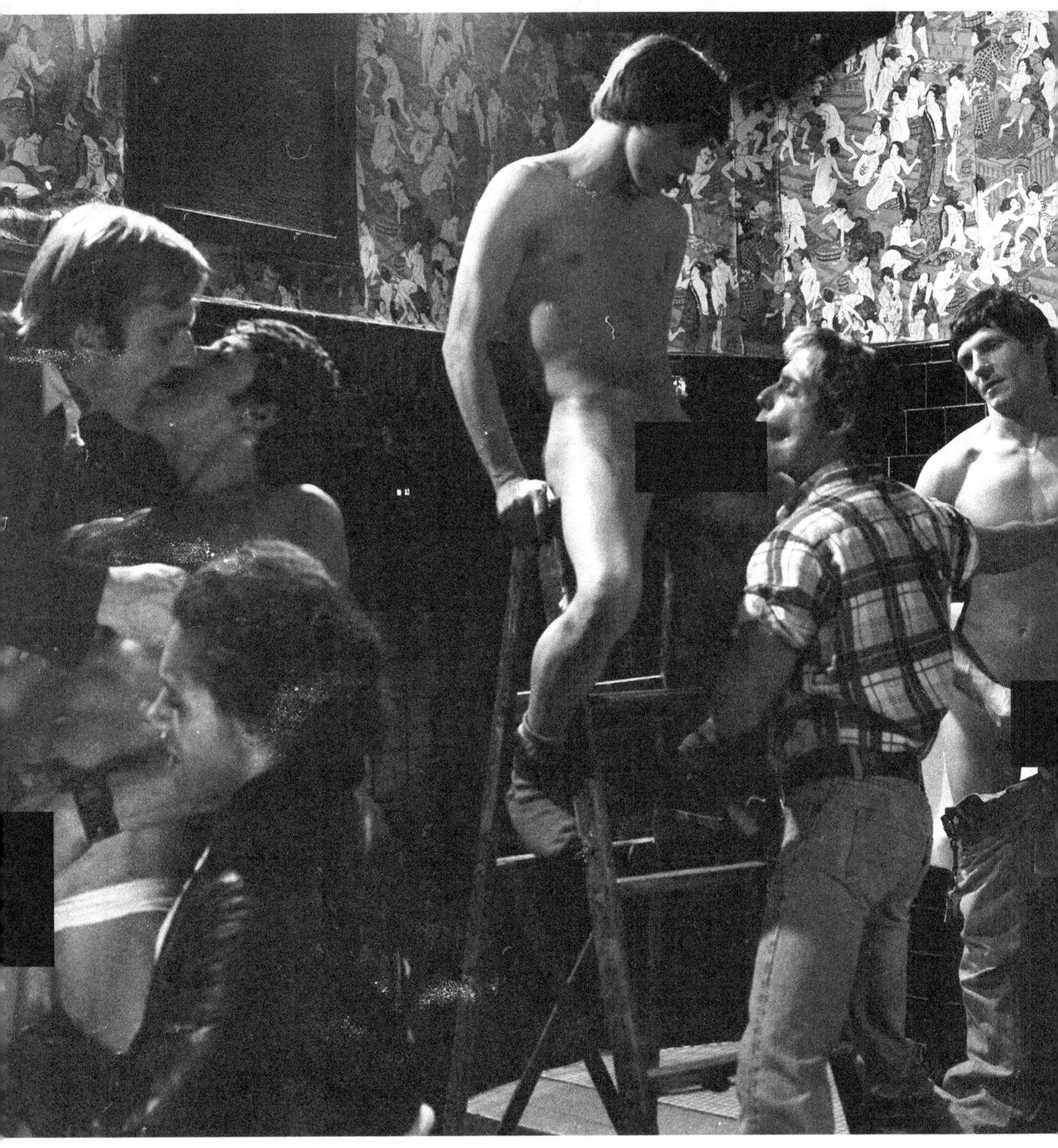

Strickland, Malo, Geraldo (left), Robert Glory gets a blowjob by Jack Wrangler, Big Al Little (right)

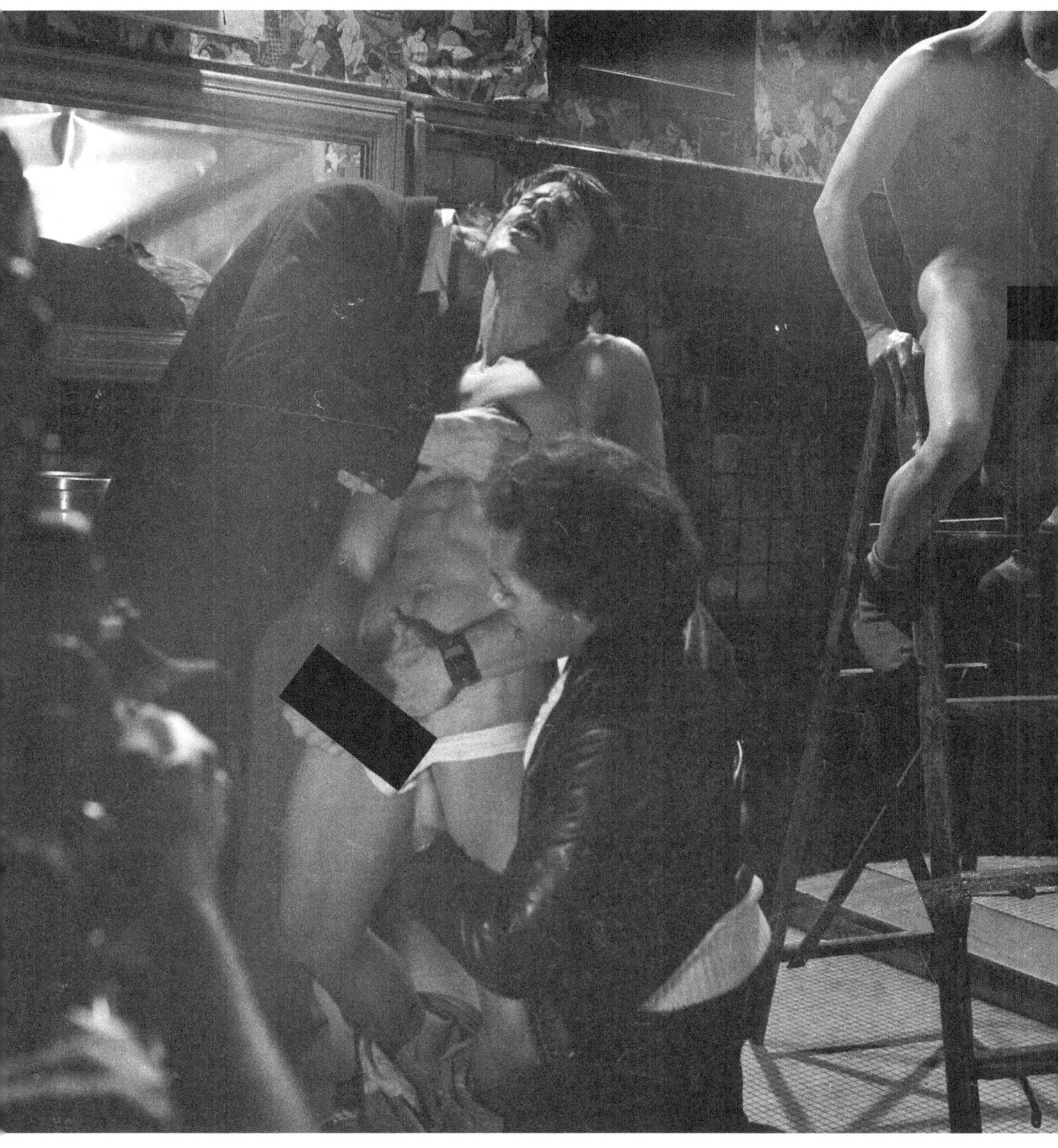

"A cross-section of sexual stereotypes come together in a porn theatre in New York – the Adonis – for a typical night of movies, short-term romance and instant sexual gratification in all the theatre's nooks and crannies. Excellent control exercised by Deveau on all levels." *Studflix*, 100 Best Videos

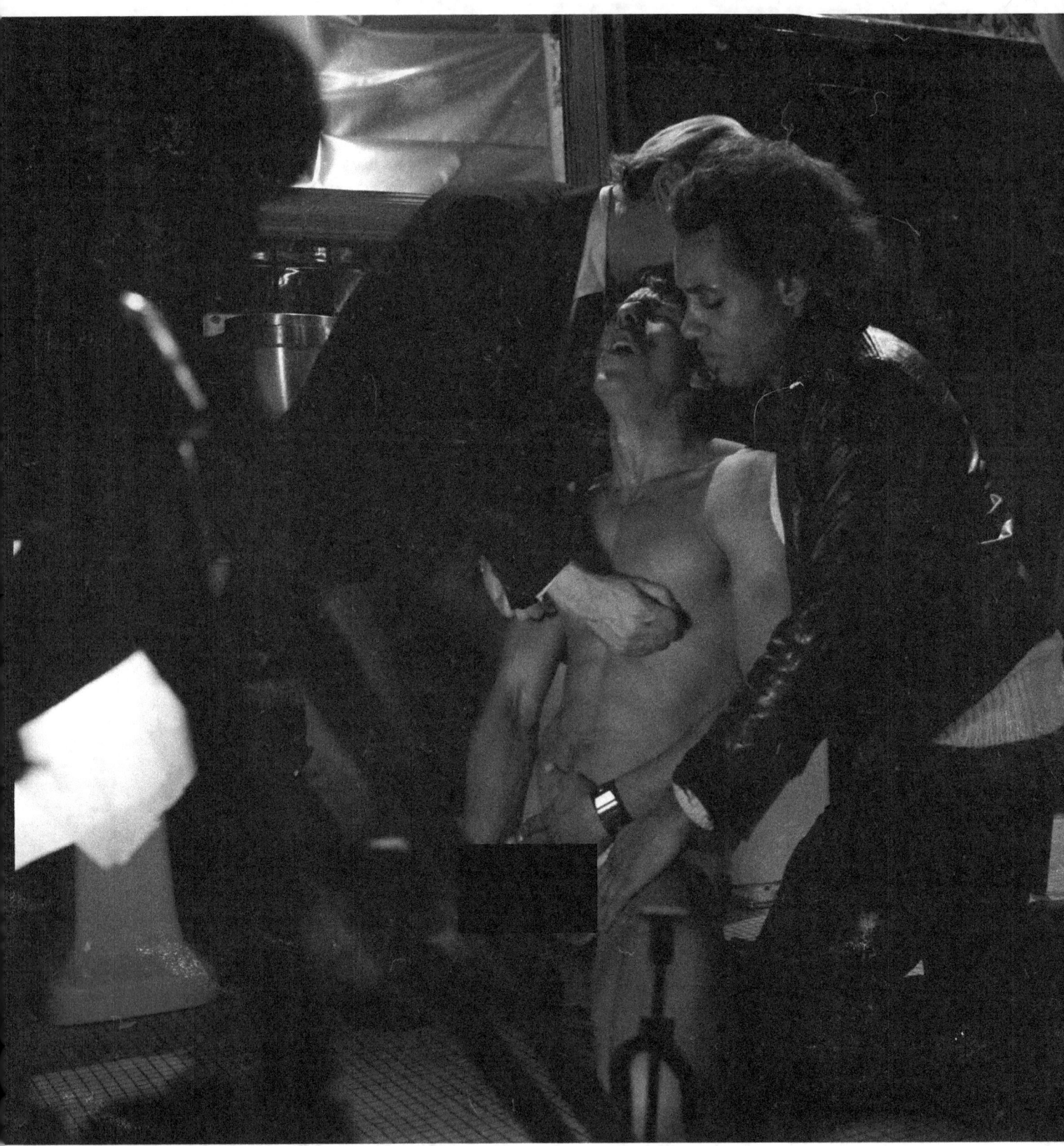

"In sundry ways the film does manage to communicate the ways in which human beings locate themselves in history and space, therein creating themselves through a shared culture. The presence of the prototype Reaganite even makes the film a bit of a prophecy of the future, wherein gay normative self-images in the West will be shaped by business-studies kids out to make bucks from the new gay communities. Yet there's also a sense of timeless continuation going on: the external trappings & attitudes towards and of the homosexuals might chop and change in history, but as one character says - "there's always the Adonis."

JAIBO, *imdb*

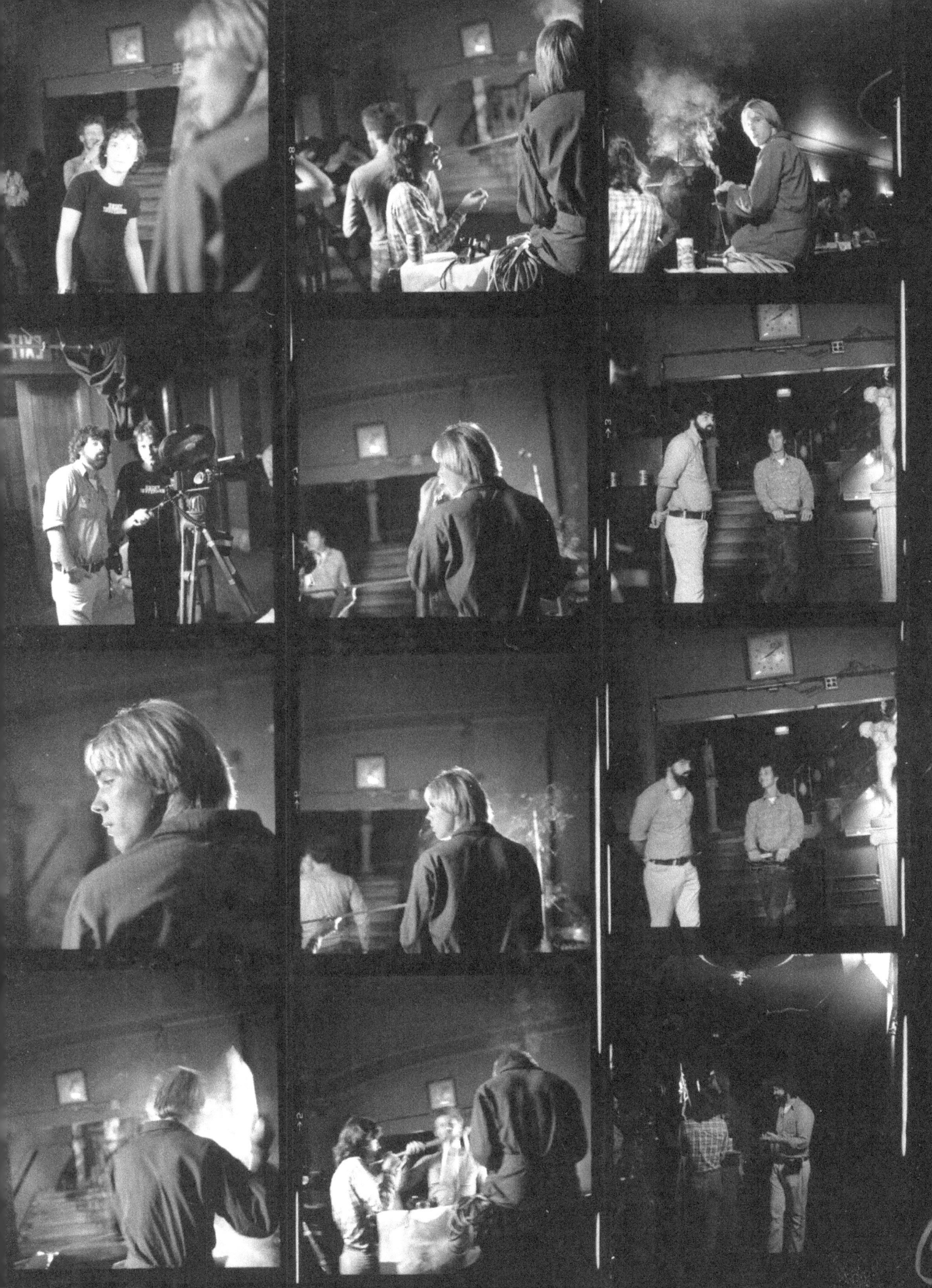

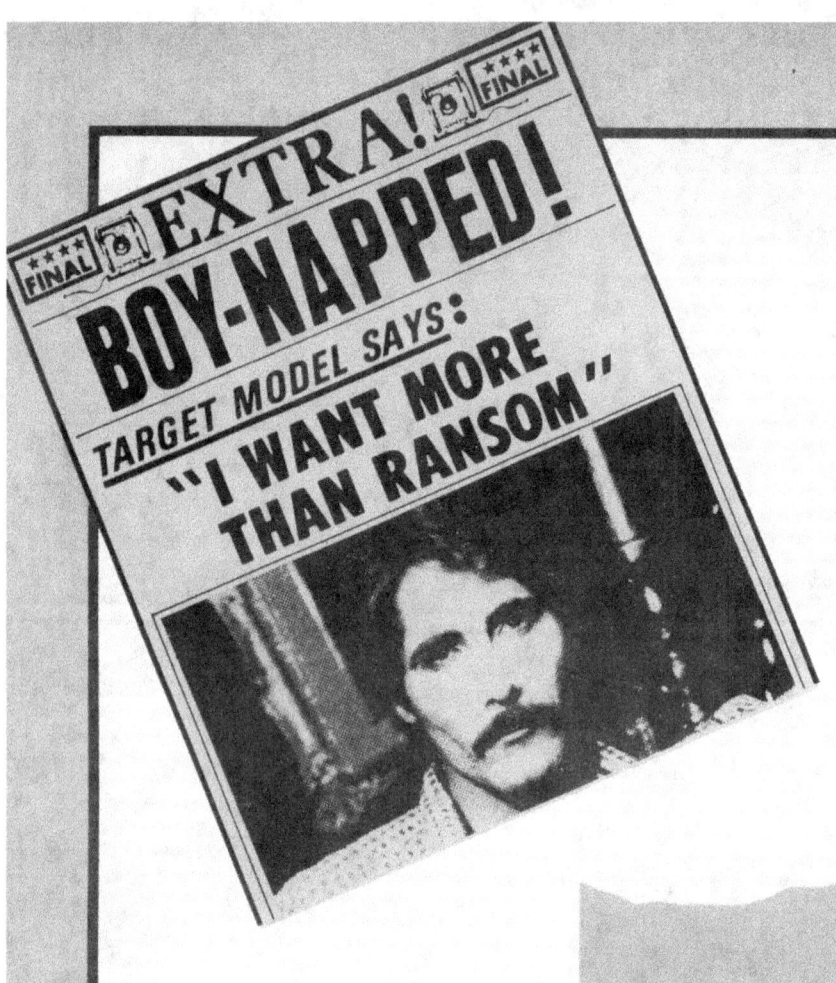

WADE NICHOLS made quite a name for himself as a porno superstar (in both straight and gay films) and he's making a new name for himself these days as a big Disco singer. There's no doubt about his star quality in this feature, as he joins with one of the best-known hungry men in films, MICHAEL HARDWICK (from ADAM & YVES & SPREAD EAGLES.) Add to this combo the talents and good-looks of DWAYNE CARTER and straight porno star JAMEY GILLIS (DEFIANCE), a thick plot that involves kidnap, heavy S & M action, and delicious sex, and you have the kind of film you'll enjoy over and over.

Invite your pals to watch the athlete son of one of the wealthiest men in town as he works out. A freind and he are just getting it on when the two of them are abducted. What follows is a sexual free-for-all that caused New York's **Michael's Thing** to accurately predict BOYNAPPED would become "one of the classic gay films."

There's every kind of combination in this erotic wonder, up to and including heavy action with fists. You'll see men who can dish it out and men who can take it, and all of them love their work.

If you enjoyed watching classic beauties as they join up to get into each other like you've never seen before, get yourself BOYNAPPED. And if you want to find out exactly how versatile these studs that you've seen in the big straight films can be, this is the one you'll want to order. WADE NICHOLS is destined for even bigger things, but one look at this film will show you for sure what it was that those talent scouts spotted. He's got one of the best faces you've ever seen anywhere, and a hot, hot body that's eager to get into every conceivable kind of action.

BOYNAPPED is the one with the excitement, the sex and the action that you'll want to show to your new inductees, and enjoy yourself for years to come.

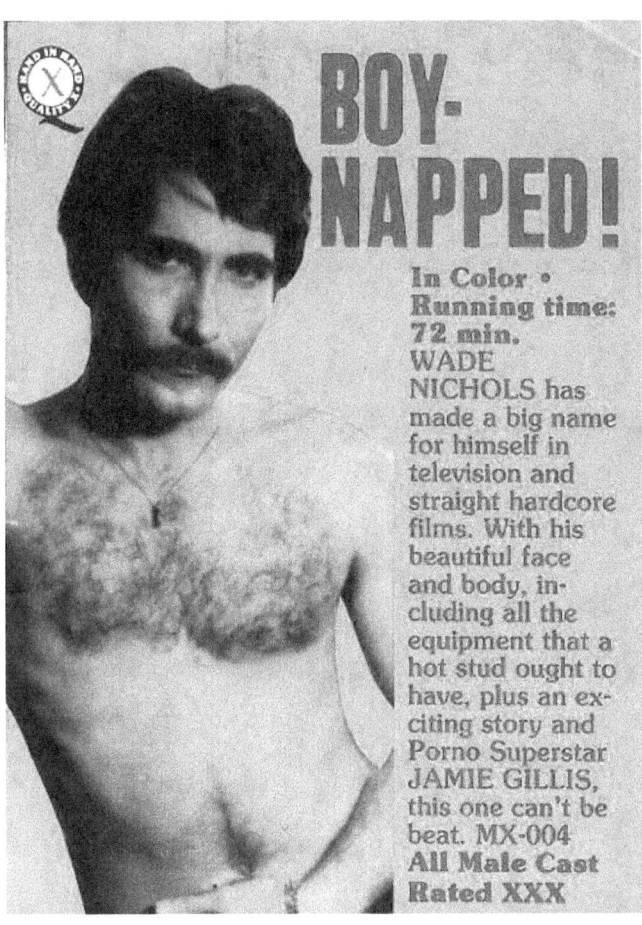

Wade Nichols has made quite a name for himself these past few years prancing around on a daytime soap opera. He also made another name a while back via the disco circuit. You might remember him as Dennis Parker. Under any name, he's got what it takes to turn heads, and you can see exactly what I mean in BOY-NAPPED. There's no doubt about his star quality in this feature. Add to that one of the best known hungry men in films, Michael Hardwick, and the talents and good looks of Dwayne Carter, plus straight porno star Jamie Gillis in a rare all-male appearance, and you have a first-rate cast. A thick plot that involves kidnap, heavy S&M action, and delicious sex is the icing on the cake. The athlete son of a very wealthy man and a friend are just getting it on when the two of them are abducted. What follows is a sexual free-for-all that cannot be missed. There's every kind of combination in this erotic wonder; even some heavy action with fists. You'll see men who can dish it out and men who can take it all; and all of them love it. Though BOY-NAPPED certainly is not the best feature Hand In Hand Films has to offer, it is worth a look. And you'll surely enjoy that look, if not again and again.

*John Mensior, *Torso*

BOY NAPPED

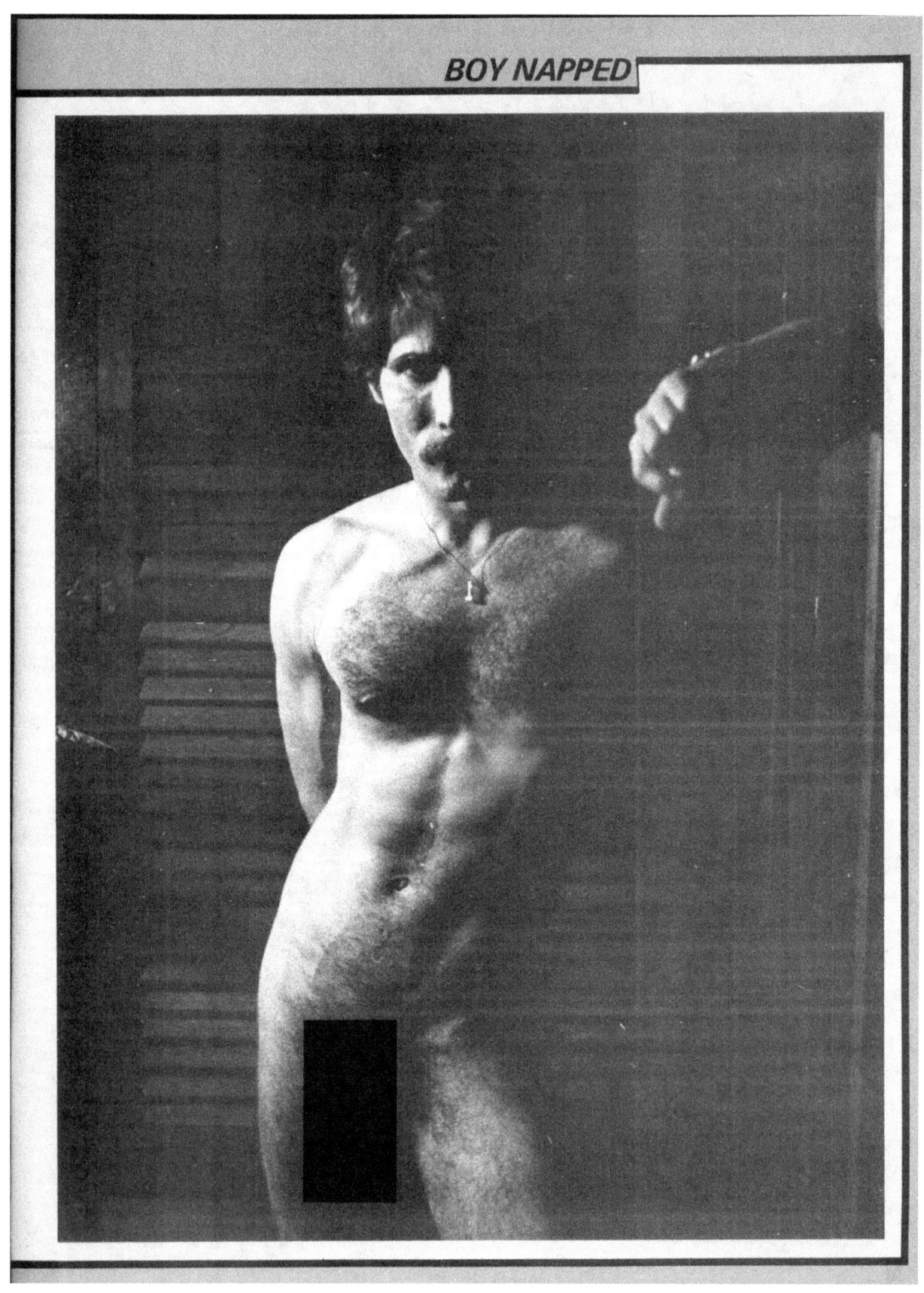

"The creative angles in the porn industry are still there. You just take a different avenue because the media you choose will manifest itself. As an actor in these films, I do my best making them good. I'm serious about my work, but not about myself where I believe I'm going to be a star." **WADE NICHOLS**, *Skin*

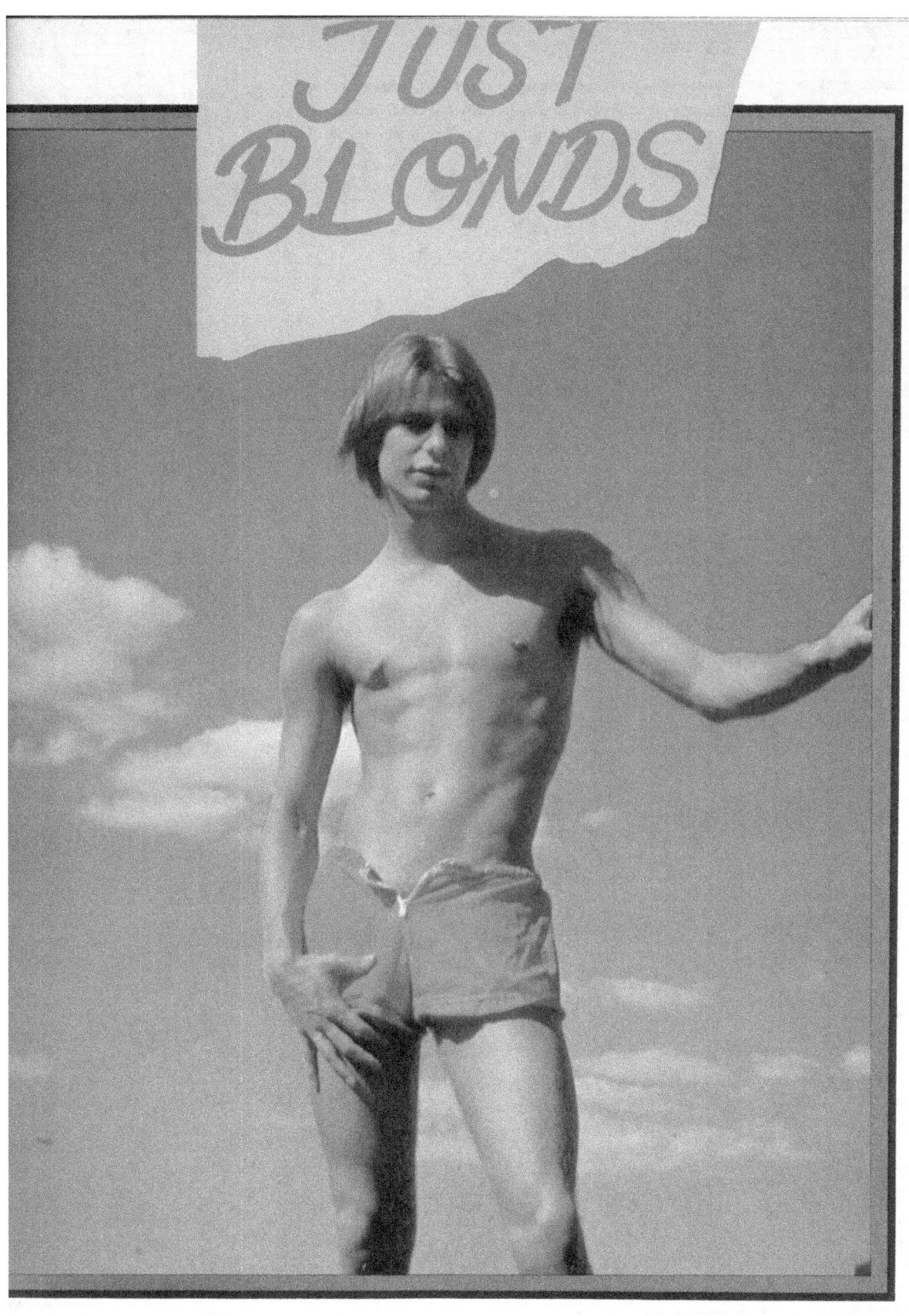

"It was all very fun. He [Jack Deveau] was an extraordinary man and a very good friend - one of the reasons I moved here. And he never condemned anyone, unless they earned it."
LUKE

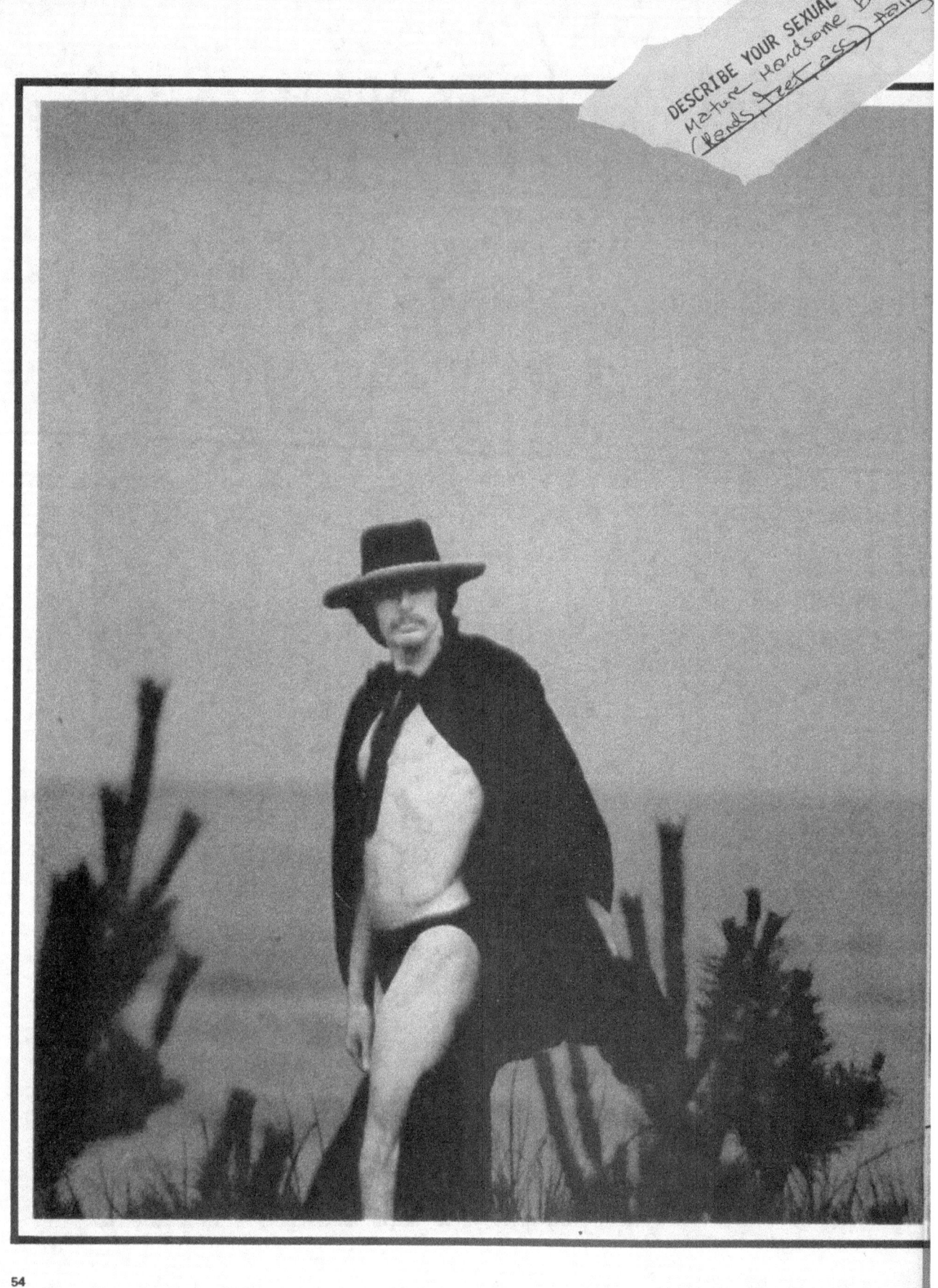

Scorpio in *Just Blondes*

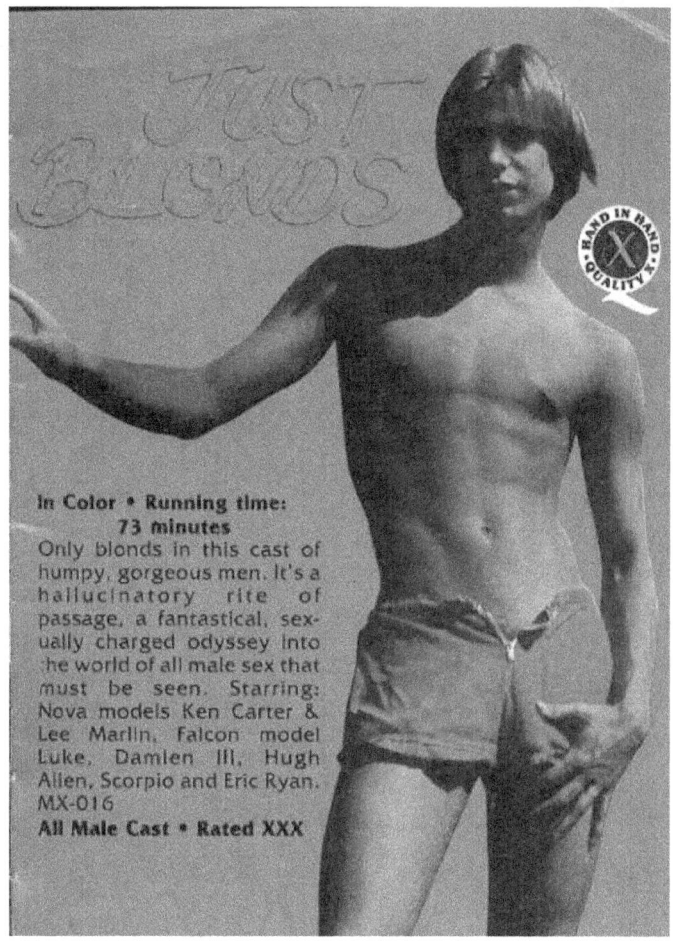

When a smalltown blond boy coming into full sexual awareness runs away from home with a knapsack, a tent, and two hits of windowpane acid, he embarks on a hallucinatory rite of passage – a fantastical, sexually-charged odyssey which takes him from a beautiful, secluded forest to a startling confrontation with his own secret sexual desires. Director Jack Deveau has assembled some of the hottest blonds in the business for this intriguing and sexually super-charged feature. Falcon Studio's Luke, Nova Studio's Lee Marlin and Ken Carter, and BOYS OF VENICE sensation Eric Ryan are joined by Hand In Hand discoveries Hugh Allen, Scorpio, and Damien III. This incredible cast, combined with a dynamite story and exceptional photography, culminate in a visual epic that is first-rate. Jack Deveau has long been known for producing some of the best all-male erotica, and JUST BLONDS is no exception. Deveau combines sensuality with raw sex appeal and the marriage here is perfect. What sets JUST BLONDS apart from most other blue features, however, is Deveau's approach with the camera. He highlights the intensity of the story somehow, bringing you closer to the action. This intimacy is something few filmmakers can achieve and the effect is mind-blowing.

*John Mensior, *Torso*

JUST BLONDES

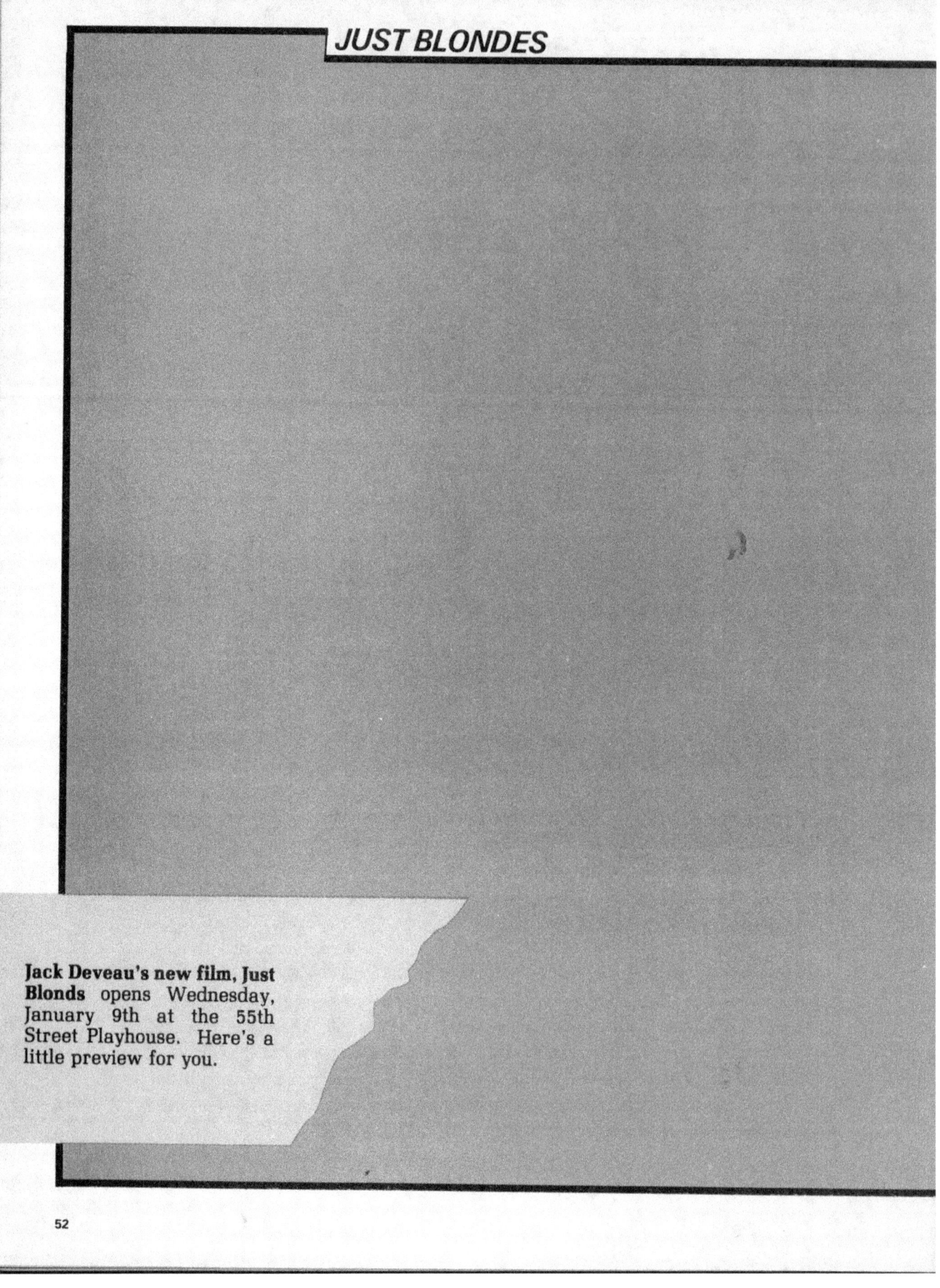

Jack Deveau's new film, Just Blonds opens Wednesday, January 9th at the 55th Street Playhouse. Here's a little preview for you.

An alfresco fantasy trip in which the blond youthful Luke leaves home to find himself, JUST BLONDS begins with a voiceover to his folks: "I'm not doing this to cause you unhappiness or distress, but to seek my own happiness in my own way... Now it's up to me to make my own dreams come true, and that's where I've gone – to the place where dreams come true." That place is a verdant wilderness somewhere between The Garden of Eden and the Meatrack at Fire Island. Along in this paradise, Luke quickly strips to begin the first of his many masturbatory fantasies which constitute the body of the film. Much of JUST BLONDS centers around Luke's voyeuristic observation of others and then his gradual approach/avoidance pursuit of another flaxen-haired free spirit, Lee Marlin, looking much younger and much blonder than he has in his later films. Among the hottest vignettes in the film are a stand-up fuck in which Eric Ryan drills Scorpio against a tree; a heated pairing in which Luke fantasizes Marlin as a leather man screwing Scorpio; Ryan's Tarzan-like rape of Luke in a leafy glade; and the kaleidoscopic finale that culminates in a classic circle jerk. There is a freshly scrubbed, boy-next-door look to each of the cast members, an innocent exuberance to the sex scenes, and a Never-neverland quality to the cinematography. JUST BLONDS is just that – a troop of horny towheads in one outdoor encounter after another – and after it's all over, you'll realize that the film has quietly made some shrewd observations on the fantasy impulse as well as on the various steps toward coming to terms with one's own sexuality.

*Jerry Douglas, *Stallion*

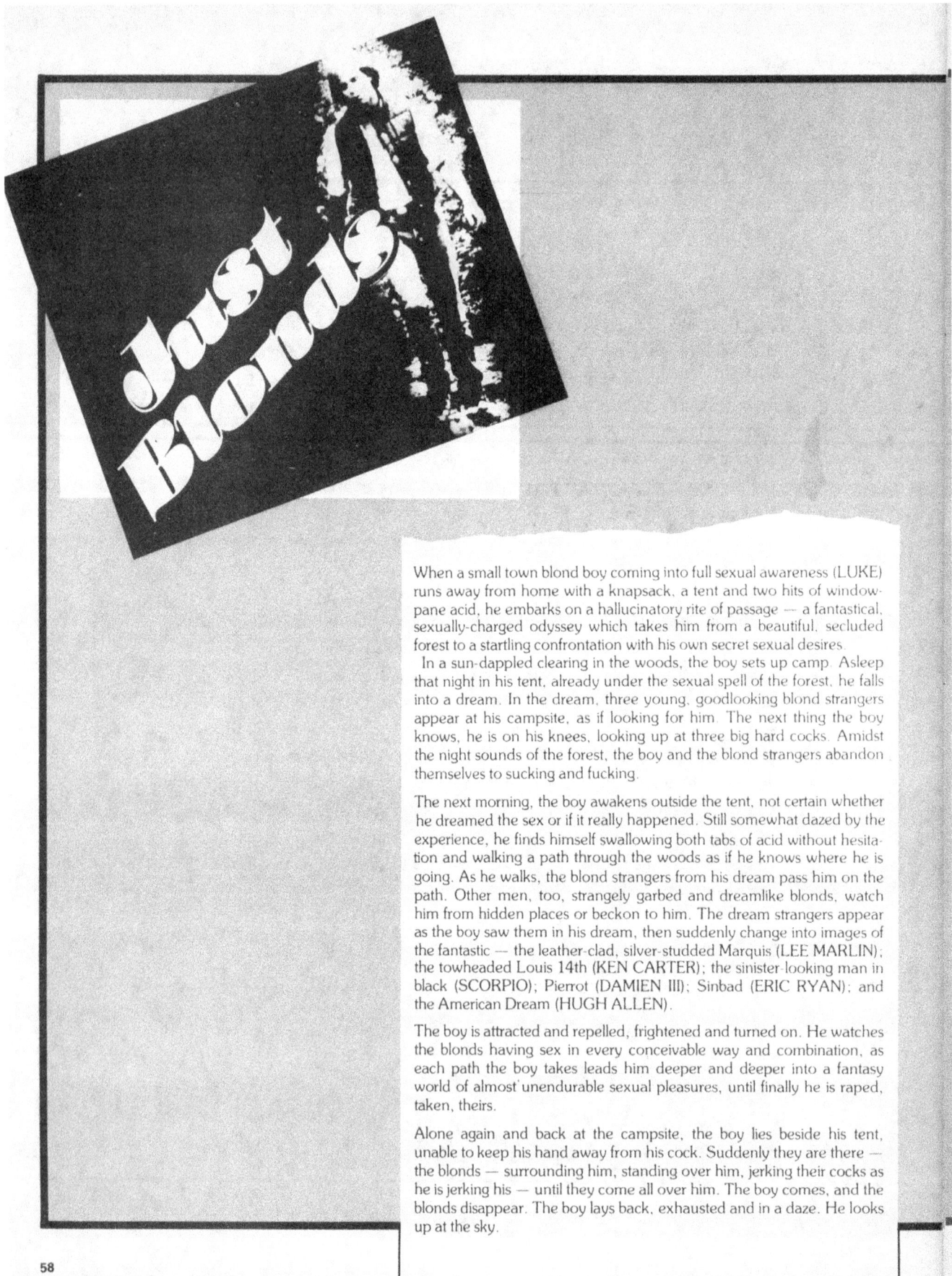

When a small town blond boy coming into full sexual awareness (LUKE) runs away from home with a knapsack, a tent and two hits of windowpane acid, he embarks on a hallucinatory rite of passage — a fantastical, sexually-charged odyssey which takes him from a beautiful, secluded forest to a startling confrontation with his own secret sexual desires.

In a sun-dappled clearing in the woods, the boy sets up camp. Asleep that night in his tent, already under the sexual spell of the forest, he falls into a dream. In the dream, three young, goodlooking blond strangers appear at his campsite, as if looking for him. The next thing the boy knows, he is on his knees, looking up at three big hard cocks. Amidst the night sounds of the forest, the boy and the blond strangers abandon themselves to sucking and fucking.

The next morning, the boy awakens outside the tent, not certain whether he dreamed the sex or if it really happened. Still somewhat dazed by the experience, he finds himself swallowing both tabs of acid without hesitation and walking a path through the woods as if he knows where he is going. As he walks, the blond strangers from his dream pass him on the path. Other men, too, strangely garbed and dreamlike blonds, watch him from hidden places or beckon to him. The dream strangers appear as the boy saw them in his dream, then suddenly change into images of the fantastic — the leather-clad, silver-studded Marquis (LEE MARLIN); the towheaded Louis 14th (KEN CARTER); the sinister-looking man in black (SCORPIO); Pierrot (DAMIEN III); Sinbad (ERIC RYAN); and the American Dream (HUGH ALLEN).

The boy is attracted and repelled, frightened and turned on. He watches the blonds having sex in every conceivable way and combination, as each path the boy takes leads him deeper and deeper into a fantasy world of almost unendurable sexual pleasures, until finally he is raped, taken, theirs.

Alone again and back at the campsite, the boy lies beside his tent, unable to keep his hand away from his cock. Suddenly they are there — the blonds — surrounding him, standing over him, jerking their cocks as he is jerking his — until they come all over him. The boy comes, and the blonds disappear. The boy lays back, exhausted and in a daze. He looks up at the sky.

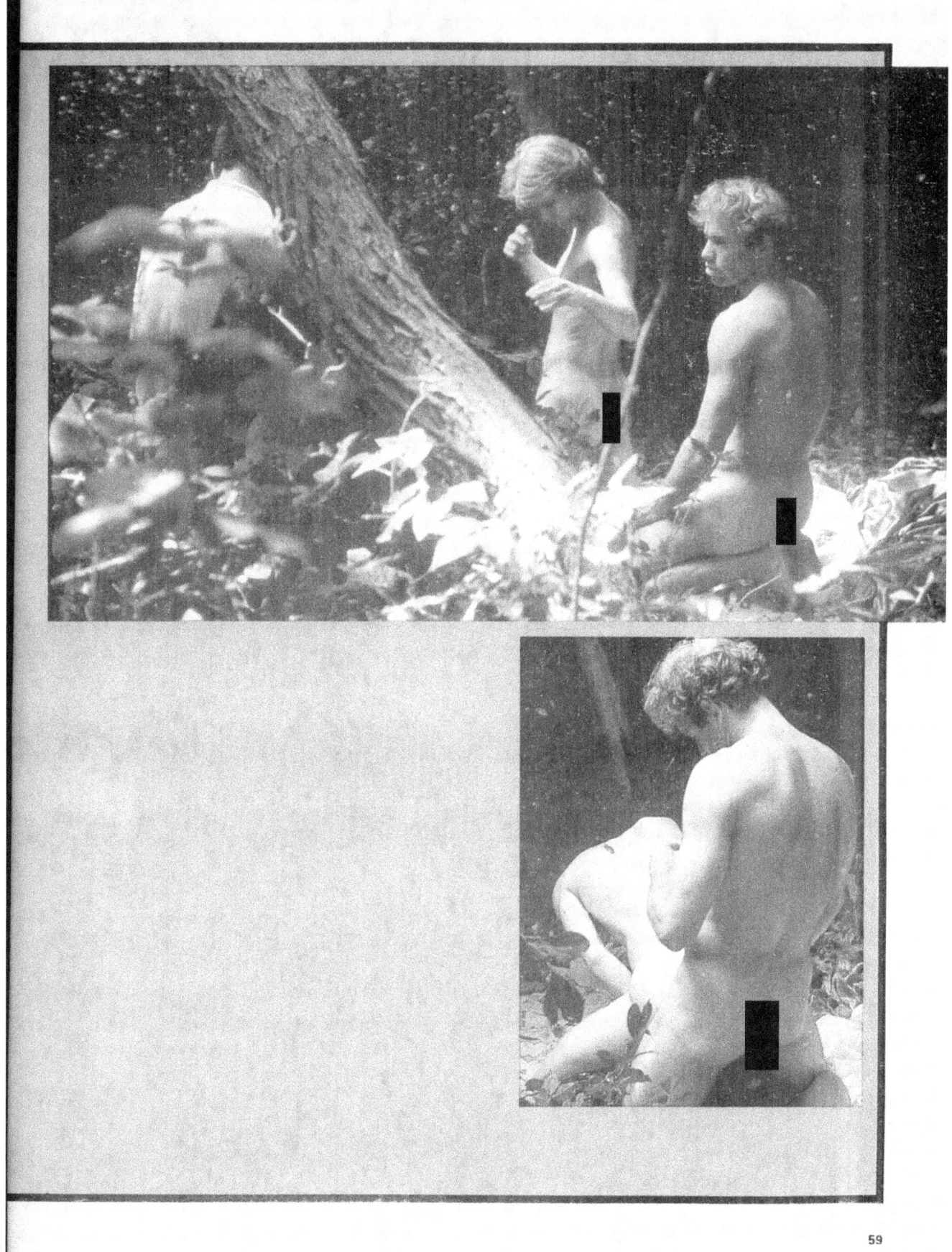

Luke and Eric Ryan

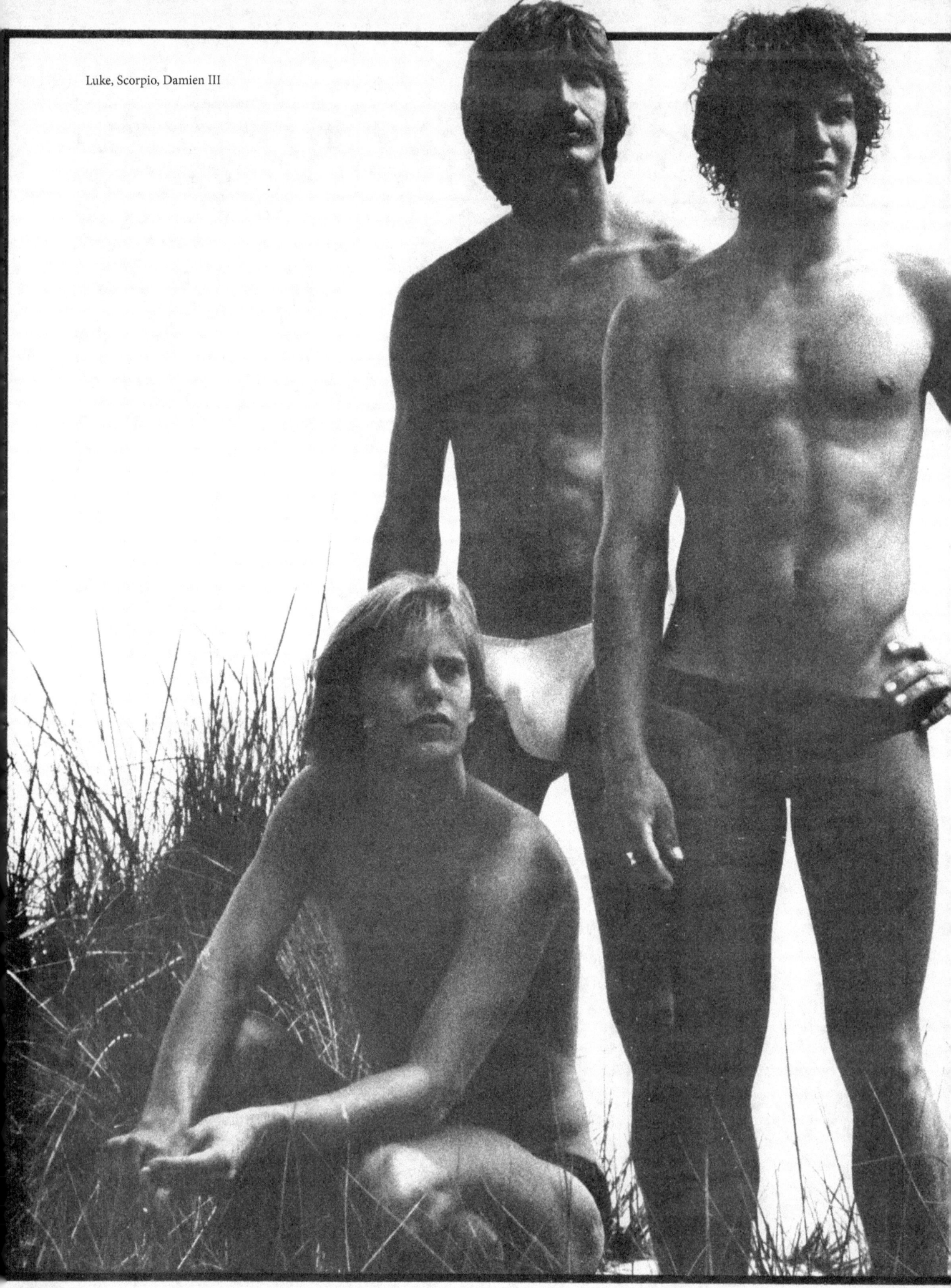
Luke, Scorpio, Damien III

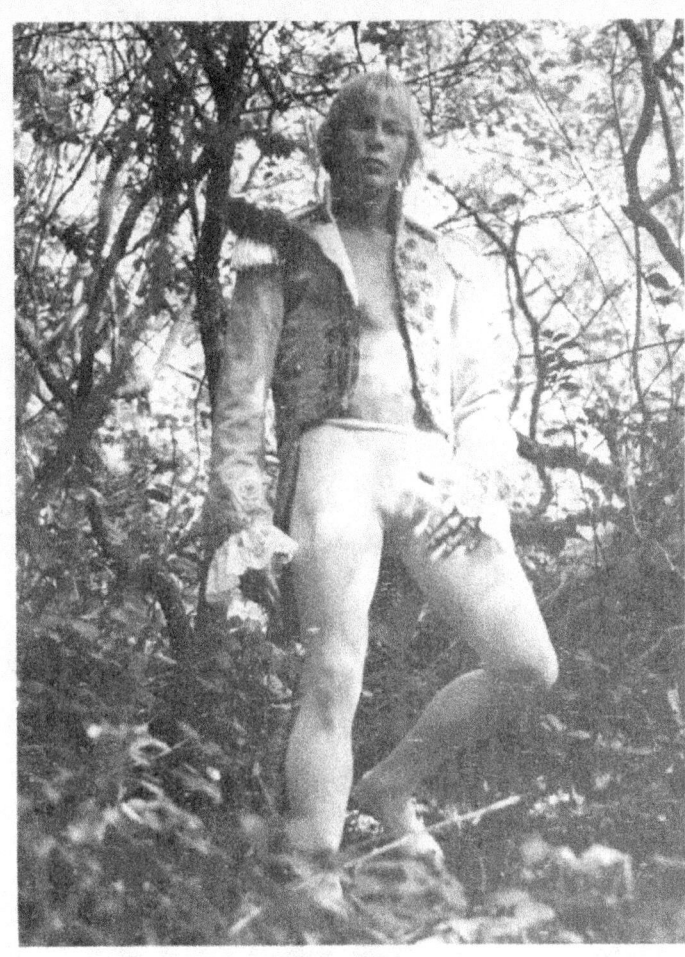

Ken Carter

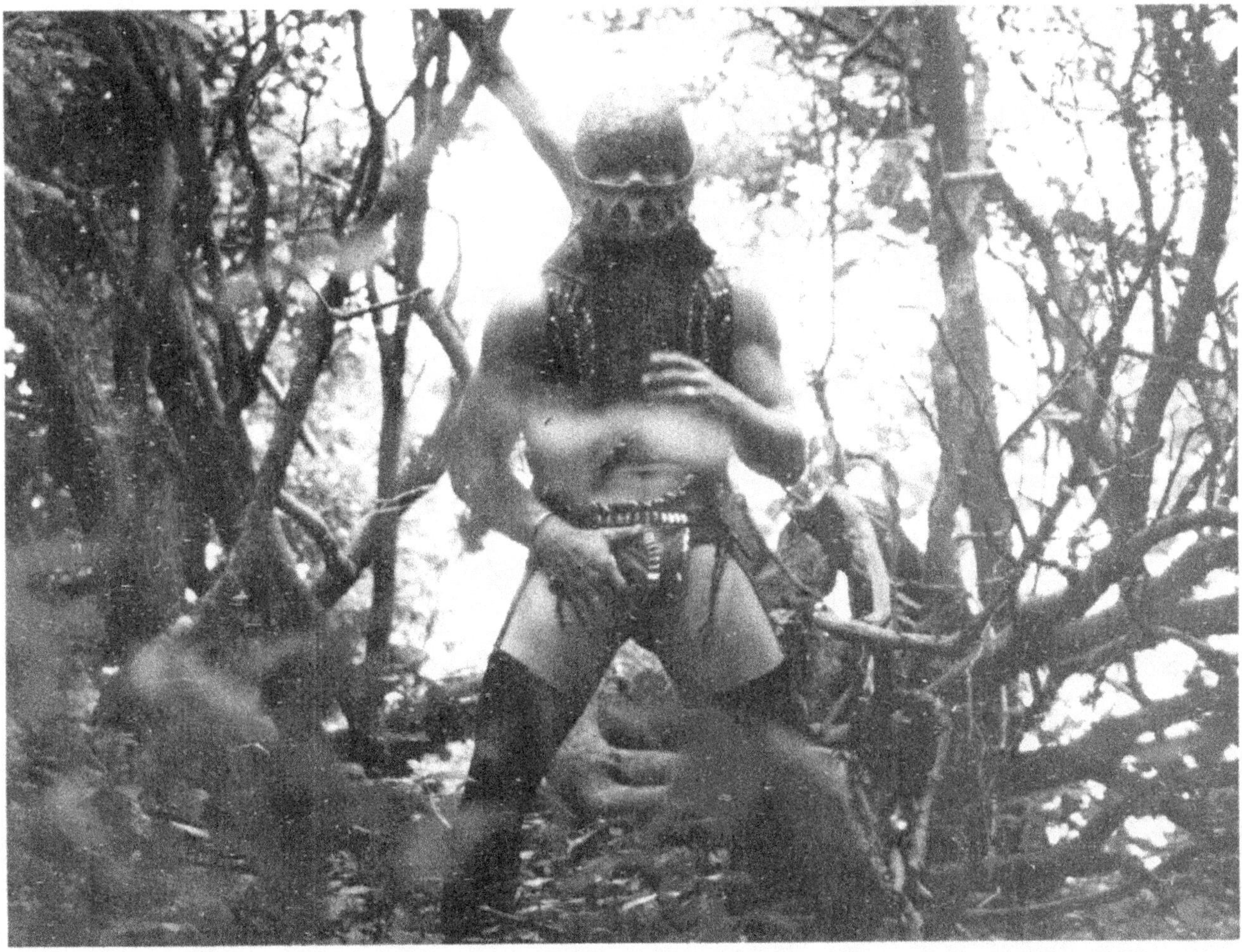

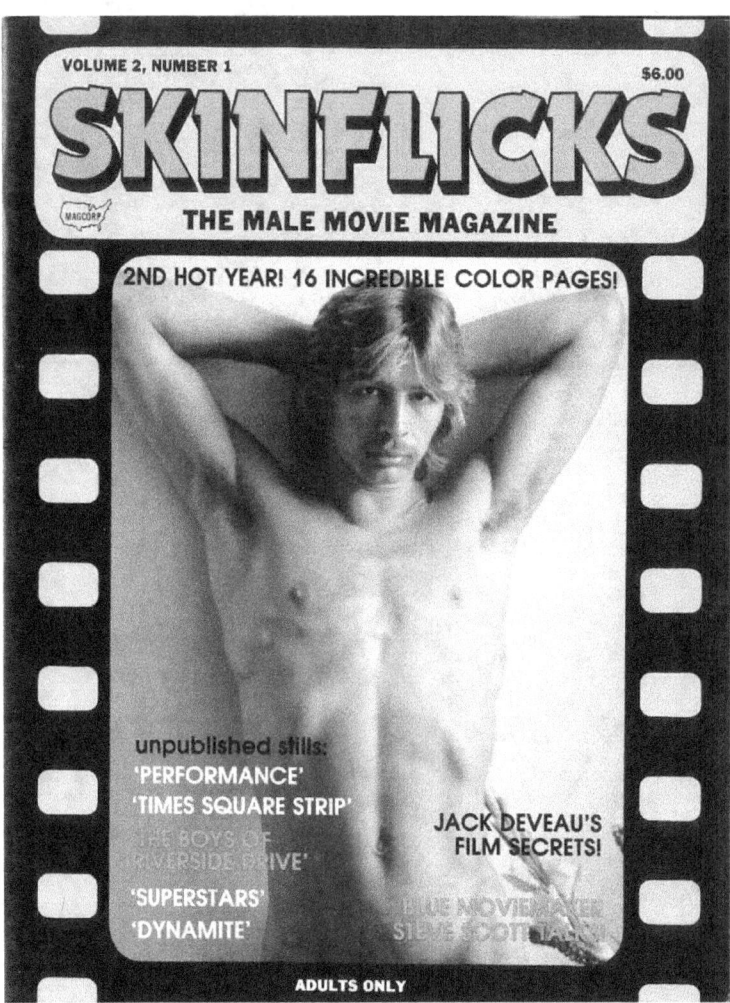

"He'd [Jack Deveau] let you put your input in. It wasn't just, 'I'm going to do it this way.' If you had a thought, then he'd try it out and see what it looked like. It wasn't strictly, 'Okay, now you're going to do this and this and this, and this is the way I want it done.' He'd say, 'Well, if you think something else would be better as you're going along, try it. And if I don't like it, then we won't put it in. But if I like it, then we'll do it.' He was very easy to work for. He wasn't strict. It was casual. [...] That was basically it. 'Lift your leg. I can't see your dick.' That type of thing. There was no choreographin'. That was the enjoyment of working for him, because he didn't have to choreograph. He let you alone. You didn't have to give him the shot. He had to find the shot."

SCORPIO

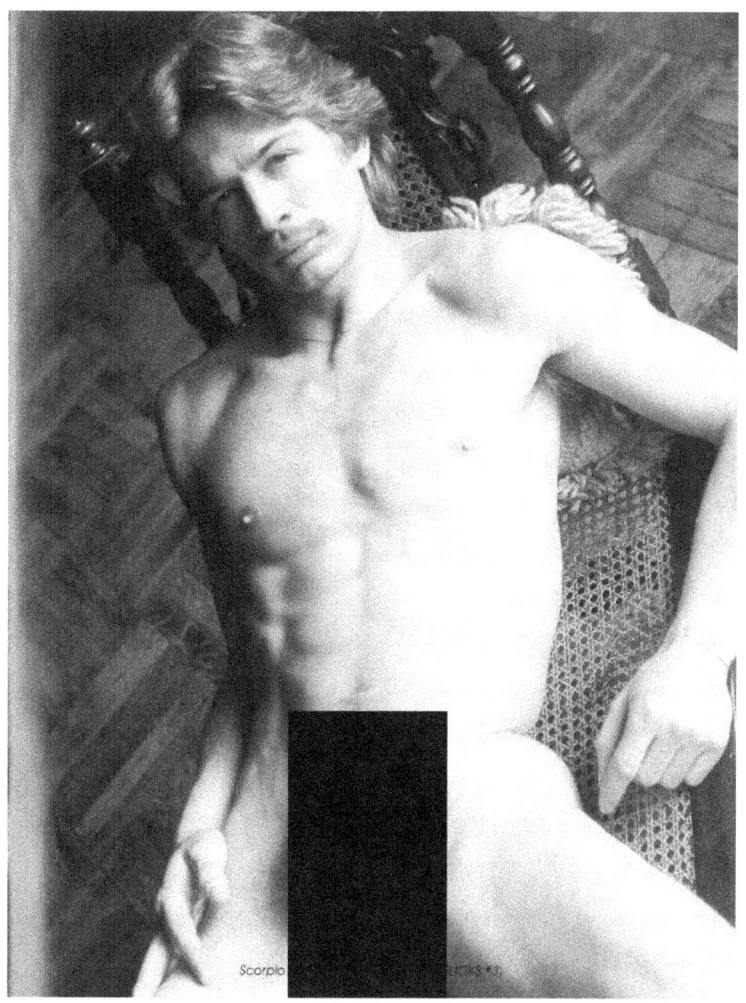

"I think it was Topman that I picked up, and I saw an ad in there saying, 'Models Wanted.' When I answered the ad, they set up a date for me to come in and see 'em - Jack Deveau and Bobby Alvarez and Kees Chapman. They were all there, and they asked their questions. They did their 'Now, take off your clothes and let's see what you look like.' Then they said, ' Well, we don't have anything for you to be in, but how would you like to do a film on your own?' And I said, 'Okay. It's a start.' So then, that's when we did - it's called Double Scorpio.' They knew I could dance, because I had done some dancing up in their little studio. And Jack said, 'We're gonna do this film and it's gonna be you having yourself. And we're going to be in a theatre, and you're gonna find yourself sitting in a theatre watching yourself up onstage. You're gonna pull yourself up onstage and you're gonna do yourself. You're gonna suck yourself, fuck yourself.' [...] It took three days because the only time that we could do it was from midnight until the morning hours, because the theatre was being used." **SCORPIO**

JIM DELEGATTI

Some Moments in Time

Marco Siedelmann: Let's start from the beginning. Do you want to share some information about your origins? What happened before you joined Hand In Hand?
Jim Delegatti: I was born in Pittsburgh, and I left it in my early 20s. I spent some time in Cleveland, Ohio, with another friend. Then I moved to New York. I was designing wigs, and I got involved with a company in Pennsylvania. I worked with them for many years, travelling around the country. I was doing promotional work with wigs and department stores. They would buy the merchandise, and I would go in there. So I used to demonstrate wigs a lot.
Siedelmann: And were you in the closet or could you lead an open life as a gay man?
Delegatti: I wasn't really in the closet before, but it naturally wasn't that open at the time. I went to all the gay bars when I travelled to different cities. It was a great learning experience for me. *(Laughs)*
Siedelmann: Which years are we talking about?
Delegatti: Oh gosh. It was somewhere in the sixties. A couple of promotions I did in the 70s. I've seen a lot of the country, and I had a lot of fun doing that, actually. But then I got out of that, and wanted to become a porno star.
Siedelmann: On camera?
Delegatti: Yes, on camera. So I heard about Jack Deveau, and Hand In Hand Films. I went to meet him, but at the point we weren't really looking for a star. He needed people to help him with his work behind the camera. So that's when I started meeting all these people. Then I got a job working for Gene Kelton. He was the Make-Up artist at Hand In Hand. I was his assistant.
Siedelmann: Had you seen LEFT-HANDED before you went there?
Delegatti: I think there were only one or two films made at the point. So I might have seen it.
Siedelmann: It was the first feature.
Delegatti: Well than that's the one. I saw that one. That's how I got to know him. Then I started meeting some of the actors. We became friends. It was really nice; a good time in my life. And that's when I met Kenny, who is my partner until today.
Siedelmann: You met at Hand In Hand?
Delegatti: No, I meet Kenny in a New Yorker bar in the Village. But I was at Hand In Hand already. Eventually when I went up there, I was doing all kinds of things. I helped Jack with his apartment work. You know, cleaning - all kind of assistant's work. Plus I did this thing with Gene with the make-up. Then I got involved with the camera. I started taking stills. I did that for a while, and Jack used them.
Siedelmann: You did that on set at the actual shootings?
Delegatti: Yes, on several films he did. I also kept all the actors together. We really were like a family in many ways.
Siedelmann: So everybody helped about everything at that time, correct?
Delegatti: Yeah, it was like that. It wasn't a real big company.
Siedelmann: When you met Kenny at the bar - Did you become a couple, and you brought him to Hand In Hand?
Delegatti: Yes, I introduced him to Jack. At that point Kenny had a partner, Nick Justin - a great fella. He owned a lot of porno theaters around Manhattan. At the time I introduced him to the Hand In Hand circle. Justin needed someone to run of the theaters. It was sort of a big one, and they showed a lot of Jack's films. They had two managers. He was one of them. It was a great job, and he really liked it.
Siedelmann: Did it screen gay porn only or straight films as well?
Delegatti: No, this was a strictly gay theater. He managed it for several years. It was called the Adonis.
Siedelmann: Do you remember the ticket lady, Eartha Hugee?
Delegatti: Oh, yeah. We were pretty close. Kenny was there for around eleven years. At the time I thought it was very successful. He saw all the films that went in there during eleven years of work. *(laughing)*
Siedelmann: Let's go back to Gene Kelton; any particular memories about your time as his assistant?
Delegatti: Gene was pretty easy to work with. I tried to learn as much as possible about the make-up stuff. I did make up, but I never did it professionally. It's a whole other thing doing your own make up from the

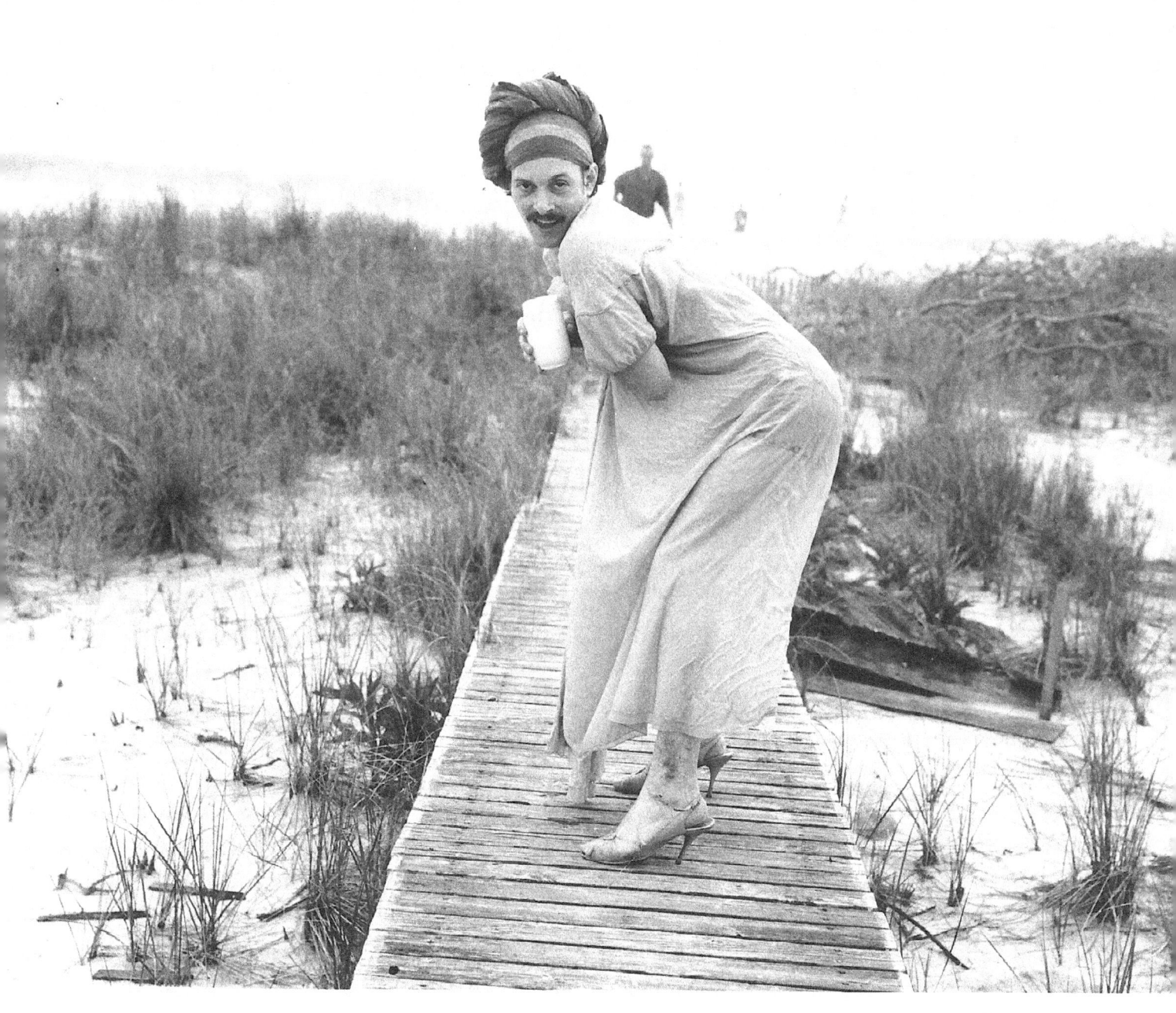

department store, or doing it for motion pictures. It was a whole different thing. I tried to learn. He was a pretty good teacher.
Siedelmann: So that's because you became the major make-up artist for some of the later productions?
Delegatti: Yes I was the make-up artist on three or four feature films.
Siedelmann: Did Gene Kelton go away from Hand In Hand?
Delegatti: I don't know exactly. I think he was doing some kind of other stuff. Also still Broadway. I'm not sure.
Siedelmann: And did you still want to act in front of the camera?
Delegatti: I worked in a few small roles, and I enjoyed it very much. I just got into other things instead of becoming a porn star.
Siedelmann: Did you stay till the end?
Delegatti: Jack became sick, and after he passed I was... he was just a big influence in my life. He meant a lot to me. At the time, I needed someone like him to be around. He was there, and so this was a big family loss. I did a lot of things for him. I went shopping for him, sometimes took care of his apartment; all that kind of stuff. But between the films, you know.
Siedelmann: There was a lot of social and party life in the apartment.
Delegatti: Definitely!
Siedelmann: Later, at Hand In Hand, you participated even more in the films, for example as a decorator on SEX MAGIC, or HOT HOUSE.
Delegatti: Yes, I was still doing this and that. I was learning a lot during the films. Also I went to a school, and learned how to use the camera in a professional way. Then I bought myself a camera. I asked Jack if I could do some stills. He said, sure! He encouraged me to do that. And some of them turned out really great. So that was fun. Sadly, I don't believe I still have any of them. I used to hand them over to Jack right away after the shooting of a film. They are probably lost.
Siedelmann: So do you look back sometimes nowadays?
Delegatti: Well, it was a wonderful time of my life, but it was just a part of it. Not some kind of obsession. I always wanted to do it, and I did it. And it was good. I helped a lot to create these films, because in these kind of films you need a certain atmosphere on set; a special mood. And I helped a lot on that, too. The actors got their buffet. *(laughing)*
Siedelmann: So you help to create the mood on set.
Delegatti: Yeah, the mood. Exactly.

Siedelmann: So how was Jack on set? Did he often ask the crew members about their opinion?
Delegatti: Yeah, he was good at that. I could always say what I was thinking in particular things. Sometimes I mentioned a detail that might be missed. Some of this was going into the movie, other things not. Eventually, a film was changed a bit in such cases. He listened to me, and that was nice. He never rejected the thoughts of others. He was very good with people.
Siedelmann: What about the sex scenes? Did he shoot them based on a strict choreography, or was it more improvised?
Delegatti: He had it set up that it should go a certain way, but if it didn't - he looked at it, and said: "Well, let it go!!" *(laughing)* As long as it looked good, he was doing fine. I thought he handled that great. I guess I would need to fresh up some memories. It's been a long time. *(laughing)*
Siedelmann: Well, I think the films by Hand In Hand are some of the finest examples for a hybrid of adult movies and regular cinema.
Delegatti: Yes it is. Before Jack, it was always like almost amateurish. He did a lot to improve pornography and gay cinema. There was a story behind all of his films, and there is much knowledge about the gay community.
Siedelmann: How long did you spend on an actor before he went on camera?
Delegatti: Hard to say; I guess possibly about one hour.
Siedelmann: And that's how you got in touch with them personally?
Delegatti: Oh yes. I was friends with them all. All the models I worked were really nice boys. *(laughing)*
Siedelmann: There wasn't such a thing like a big porn star ego, correct?
Delegatti: That's true. One of the actors I got very close with was Dennis Walsh. I don't know if he's still with us or not. He worked as a dancer in Chicago in one of the clubs there. I didn't know he was working there, and when I was on one of my trips, I went to a bar. There he was on stage.
Siedelmann: This was after Hand In Hand?
Delegatti: In between. He did a couple of films for Jack. He was one of my very favorites. He did BALLET DOWN THE HIGHWAY. And he was in WANTED: BILLY THE KID.
Siedelmann: So most of the actors went on with their lives and did not stay in the business?

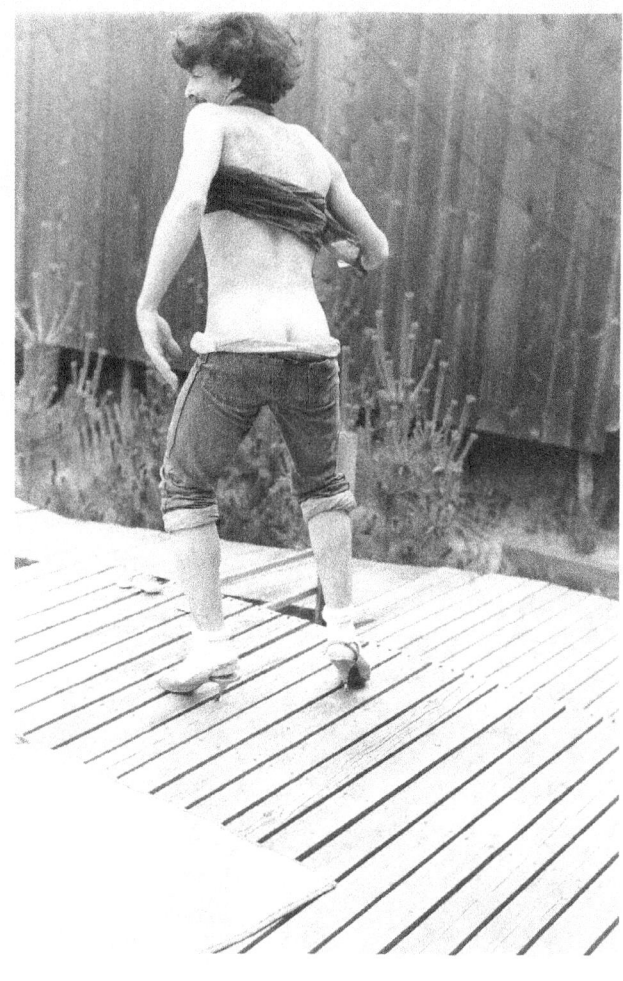

Jim Delegatti on Fire Island

Delegatti: Well, there might have been a couple who stayed in New York. Jack often hired boys from California and other places. Others came by for an interview, and he used them in a film.
Siedelmann: After Hand In Hand went down, you were not interested to stay in the business I guess?
Delegatti: No; not at all. But I thought it was a great experience for me, and I enjoyed the time very much. I really don't think there was such a thing after Hand In Hand. Jack tried to make something out of it, something different than just a porno film. He was a great cinematographer, and he learned to do all this different things by himself.
Siedelmann: You worked with Jack Wrangler, and he actually was a big star at the time. Was it something special to work with him?
Delegatti: Well, he was a California star. That was Hollywood. *(laughing)* The way he acted, and presented himself - He was really into it. The boys we worked with, not that much. They did it mainly for the money or whatever; lots of them.
Siedelmann: Did he bring his very own stylist which was Sigi from Beverly Hills?
Delegatti: Not at the films I worked with him, no.
Siedelmann: So he did not want special treatment? He wasn't a diva?
Delegatti: He was a diva; but a really nice person too. *(laughing)*
Siedelmann: Did he have comedic talent?
Delegatti: Yeah, I think he was funny but didn't know it. You know there are people who are very funny, but they are not intending to be. I think that's the way he was. He was a character. *(laughing)* He was something else.
Siedelmann: So most of the people in the Hand In Hand films were gay men enjoying themselves; very few gay-for-pay actors?
Delegatti: I think so. I mean, you can really see that they enjoy what they are doing. But I don't think many of them were exhibitionists. Jack Wrangler certainly was way more of that kind then the boys Jack Deveau mostly used.

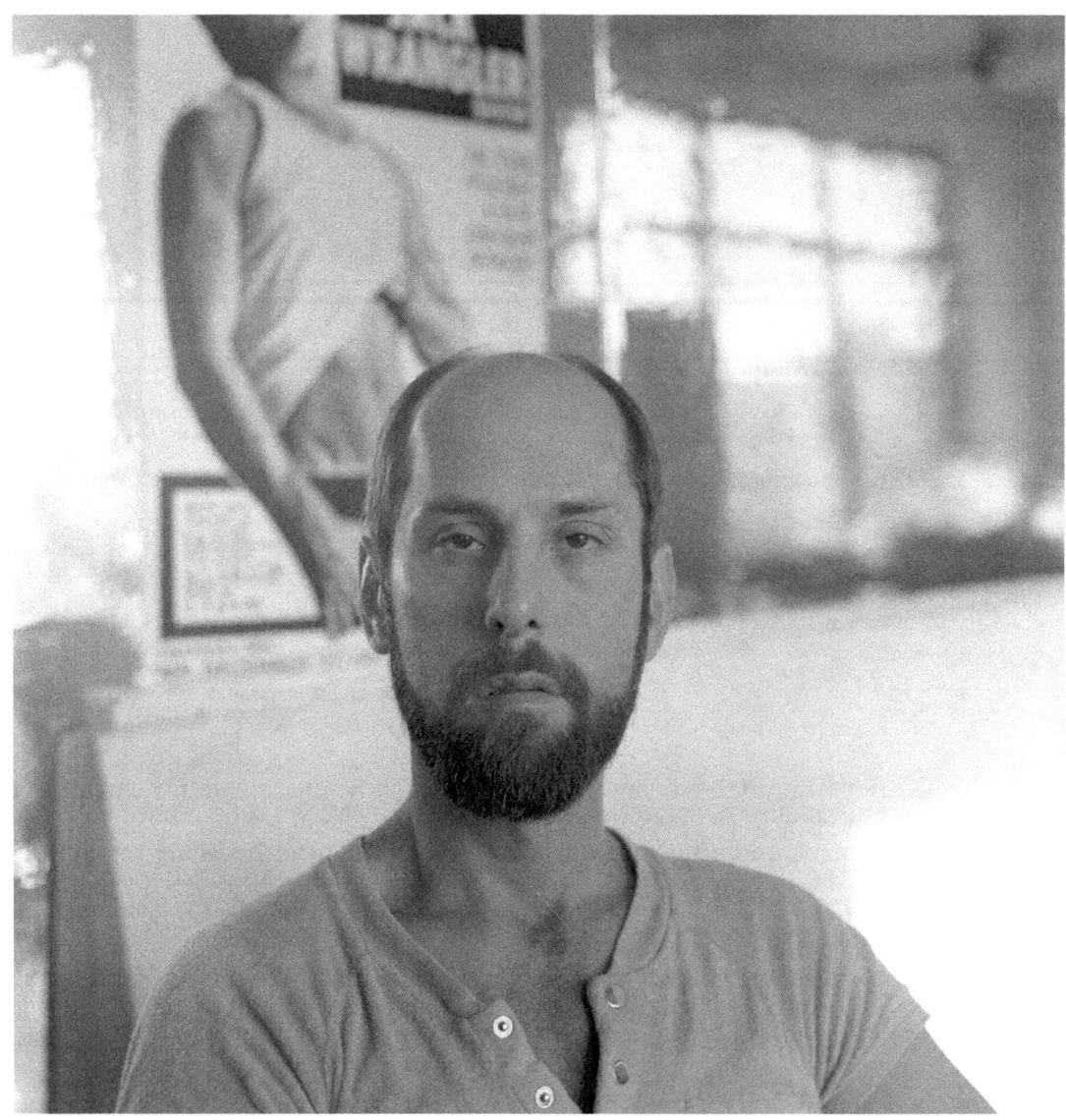

Gene Kelton

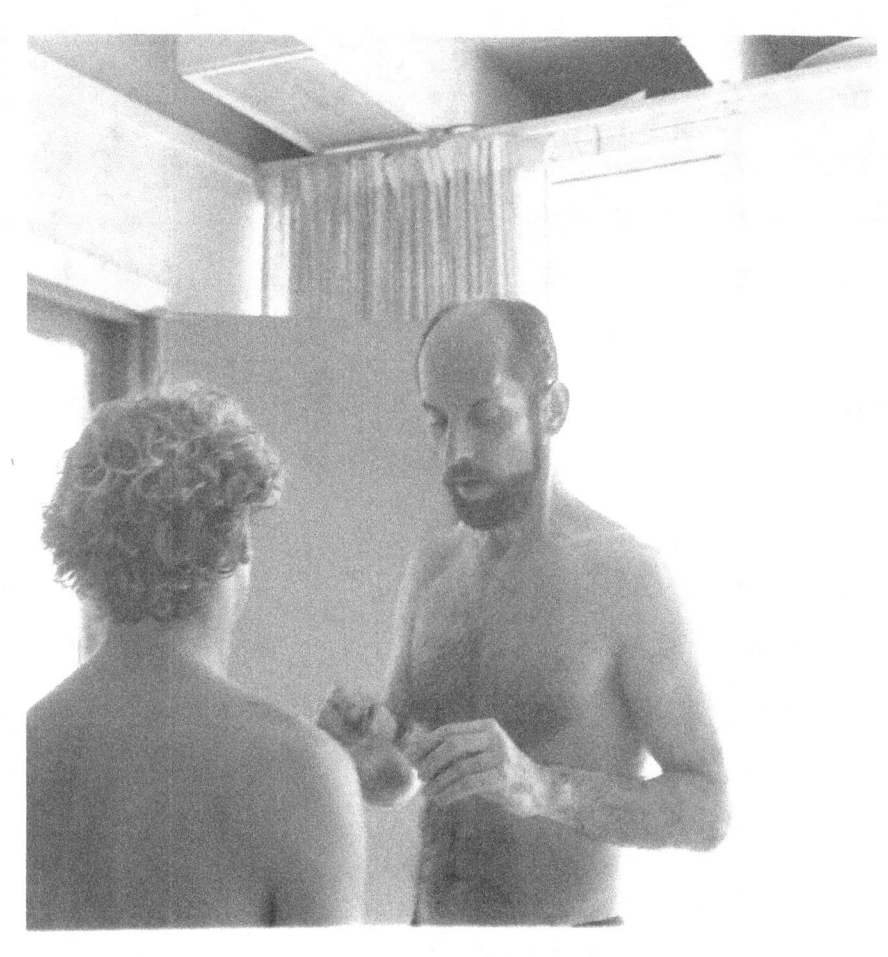

Garry Hunt and Gene Kelton behind the scenes of *Ballet Down the Highway*

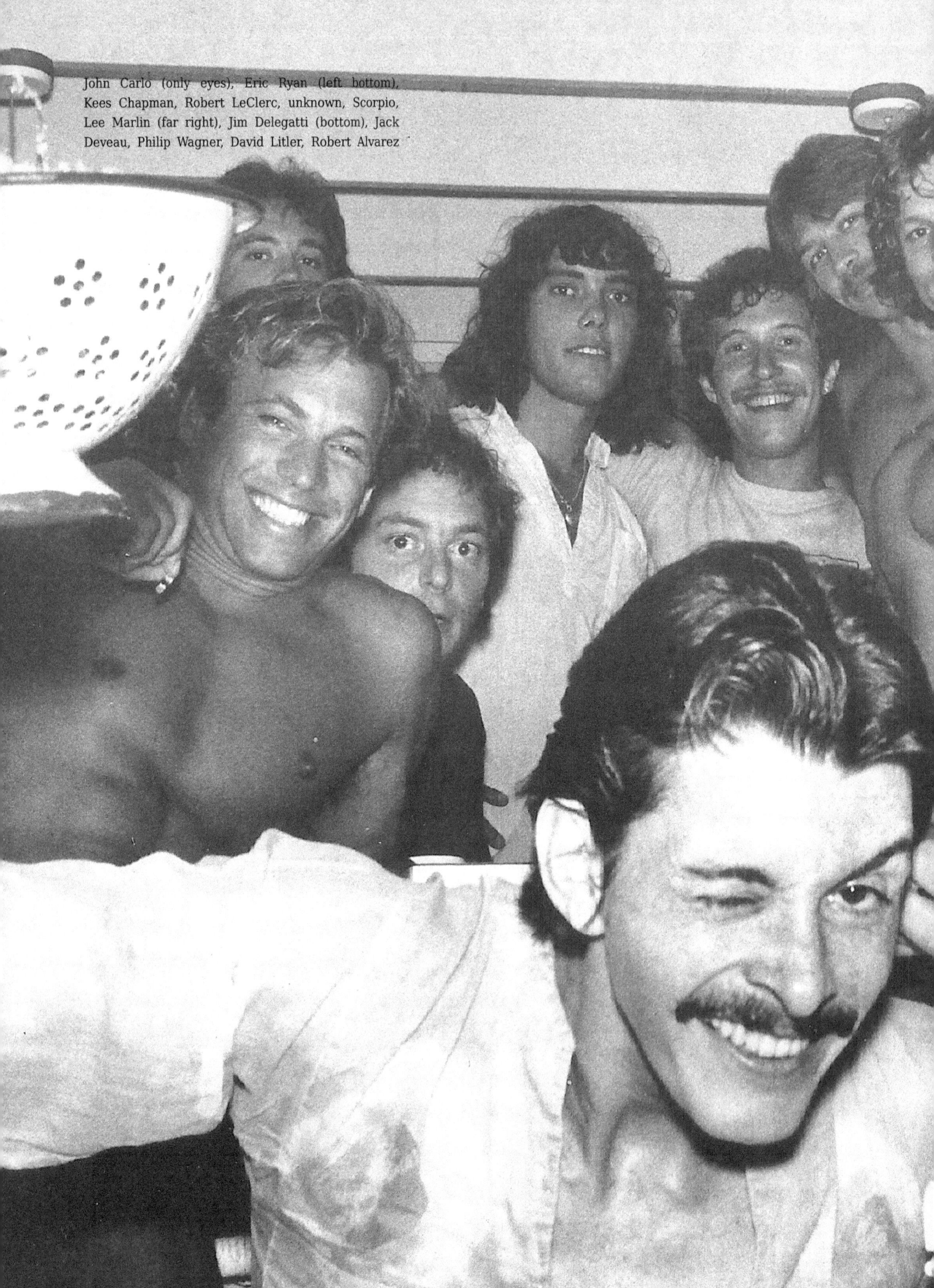

John Carlo (only eyes), Eric Ryan (left bottom), Kees Chapman, Robert LeClerc, unknown, Scorpio, Lee Marlin (far right), Jim Delegatti (bottom), Jack Deveau, Philip Wagner, David Litler, Robert Alvarez

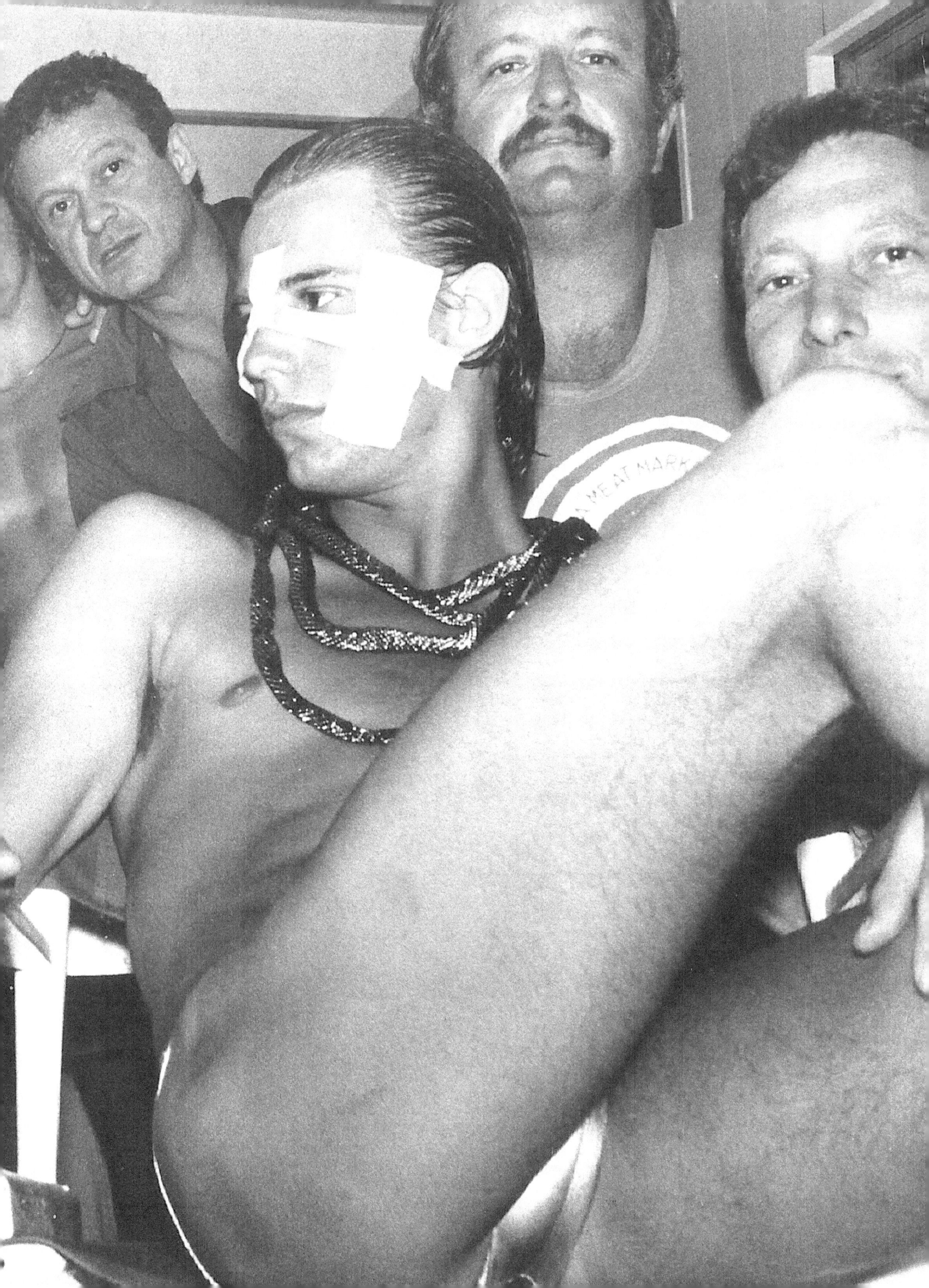

KEN SCHNETZER

A Decade at the Adonis

Marco Siedelmann: You were right there when the golden age was happening. Right in the middle of the New Yorker gay scene you were managing the legendary Adonis.
Ken Schnetzer: I had a lot of fun when I worked at the theatre. *(laughing)*
Siedelmann: How did it come about that you got to manage the Adonis? What did you do before that?
Schnetzer: Oh, I was working as a bartender in one of the gay bars downtown. The name of the bar was Keller's.
Siedelmann: You already had lived an open gay life?
Schnetzer: Yes, I certainly knew what direction I had to go at that point. *(laughing)*
Siedelmann: So you were an insider in the gay scene already?
Schnetzer: Well, I was very familiar with the people, and the things that were going on in the gay scene, yeah.
Siedelmann: And when you met Jim Delegatti you were at work?
Schnetzer: Yes. Man, that was some place too; very wild and crazy. Dancing on the bar, and stuff. Everybody had a good time!
Siedelmann: No trouble with the cops?
Schnetzer: No, we never did. I know some of the places did have issues, but while I was there I never had any legal problems. I went up every morning, and it was business as usual. I mean we were right across the street from the federal detention center that time. So... *(laughing)* The gay community in New York - it was all very liberal. We'll never see those days again, those are long, long gone. It was the beginning of everything. The Gay Pride Movement started about that time. Stonewall was early on. I was very young back then. And life was really good.
Siedelmann: When Stonewall happened, did you feel connected very much in a political way? Did you join the gay pride demonstrations?
Schnetzer: Jim and I were among the ones who helped start them. I mean we were not involved in the paper work, and the organization. We helped things keep going. The demonstrations in front of the mayor's house. We started the march at 5th Avenue. Two years later all the gay pride things started. Later on, I had met Jimmy Kellers, and I had continued to see him on and off at Danny's. That was on Christopher Street. Of course, I had been well known because of my bartender job. In the gay circle they all knew me, you know? *(laughing)*
Siedelmann: So you went on from being a bartender straight to be the manager of a movie theater, or was there something in between?
Schnetzer: There were a few gaps, I'd done some other work in between. I worked for a moving company at a time, and moved people's furniture. All that kind of stuff. Jimmy invited me to a job at one of his cinemas, there was a new one about to open.
Siedelmann: So this was the opening of the Adonis? You were there from the beginning?
Schnetzer: Yeah. They needed a manager. And the next thing I knew, I was hired.
Siedelmann: He had numerous cinemas?
Schnetzer: Justin had a lot; some in Queens, in Brooklyn, New York City. The Adonis was the biggest of them all. It was a great job. I worked there for eleven years.
Siedelmann: So you stayed to the end, or did you move away from New York?
Schnetzer: At the time, Jim and I had moved to New Jersey. The problem was that the driving was getting too much. I came home 1 or 2 o'clock in the morning. I had to get up early the next day, and open up the theater. I just wanted to work in Jersey, so I went to retail. *(laughing)* Bloomingdales!
Siedelmann: Much more quiet!
Schnetzer: Yeah. *(laughing)*
Siedelmann: So Justin was more of a businessman, or was he political, into gay culture?
Schnetzer: I met the guy several times. But I only knew him as a boss, not as a person.
Siedelmann: And as a boss he was comfortable?
Schnetzer: Yes. He was a decent guy. Whenever I had something to do about the theater I got it done, so we really have not been in contact at all.
Siedelmann: Did you choose the films? Did you have to organize the copies from the distributors?
Schnetzer: No; not at all. There was a hell

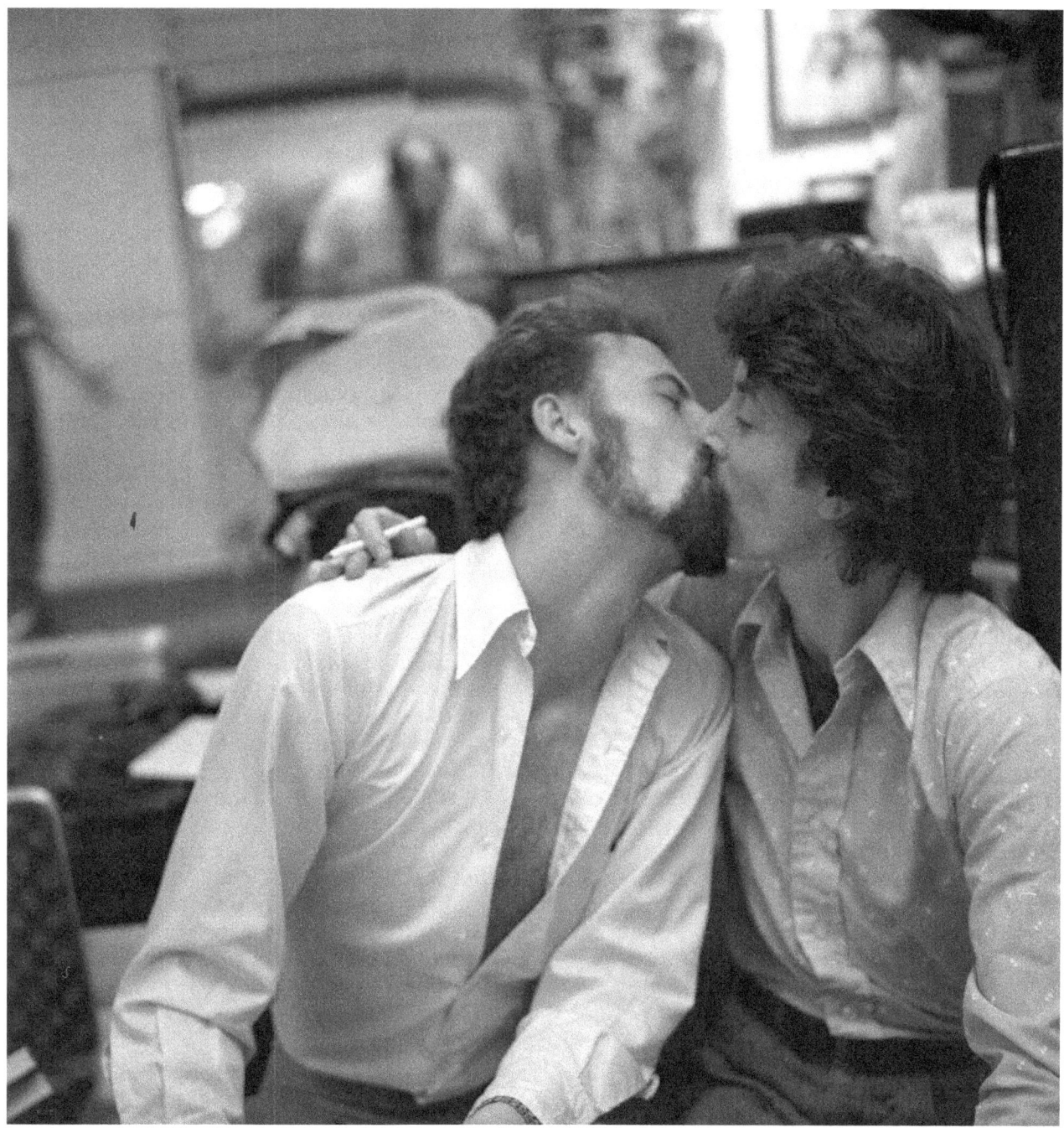
Ken Schnetzer and Jim Delegatti

of organizing, but Justin did all of the arranging. Most of the films we showed were pretty much Jack's films. Hand In Hand. Sometimes from other production companies, of course.
Siedelmann: The Adonis was gigantic, right?
Schnetzer: There were around 2000 seats. So yeah - it was a pretty big theater.
Siedelmann: And how many of these seats were filled with viewers?
Schnetzer: When it was a very well-known film, there were many. In the early days - and with some of the films by Jack Deveau - we could easily pack the house. Sometimes people had to stand in the room, because everything was full. Later on we got around 50 or 60 percent occupancy. At the weekends, 70 or 75 occupancy if it was a real good one; something like that. But when the weather was miserable and everybody had nothing better to do - then we had around 90 percent occupancy.
Siedelmann: That sounds like the theater was doing financially very well.
Schnetzer: Yeah. Think about that: You're filling about 1500 or 1800 seats, and you got

five bucks per ticket; pretty good when you're doing 10-15 performances a day. I don't know what exactly the percentages were that were paid to the producers, and what the theater got. But I'm sure there was a pretty good arrangement though. None of that I really got involved with.
Siedelmann: So what did you do most times?
Schnetzer: My job was basically keeping the theater clean, organize the cleaning people. I had to make sure about the bank, the money of course, the payroll, all that kind of stuff.
Siedelmann: Do you remember the ticket lady Eartha Hugee very well?
Schnetzer: Oh yeah. Her and I - we were very close. We worked together lots of times. I knew her very well.
Siedelmann: Did you hire her right at the beginning?
Schnetzer: She was already there when I came in!
Siedelmann: Amazing! And what kind of woman was she; funny and chatty with the people?
Schnetzer: She was very good - with everybody! She really was quite a character! *(laughing)*
Siedelmann: So she was a part of all this and had to be in A NIGHT AT THE ADONIS?
Schnetzer: People coming into the door, the characters were coming to see the show that was going on. So we needed somebody there, and Eartha did what she always did. Jack Deveau wanted a representation of the people working there, and she was willing to do it. She had a ball! *(laughing)*
Siedelmann: Was she there all eleven years long you managed the Adonis?
Schnetzer: Yes, and she even stayed there when I left. How long, I really don't know. I lost contact with her many years ago.
Siedelmann: So you had more than ten screenings a day. Was this always the same film over and over, on a particular day?
Schnetzer: Yes, mostly. Sometimes they put up a backup, and there was another film we would go with it. That was a "main feature plus". The "plus" could be some excerpts, or trailers for an upcoming film; something like this. We did a lot. Almost exclusively Hand In Hand productions.
Siedelmann: And most of the premiers were done there. So how do you remember the opening night of A NIGHT AT THE ADONIS?
Schnetzer: I was there with Jimmy. *(laughing)* It was quite a night. We actually had a cocktail party on the inside of the lobby. Everybody from the New Yorker porn industry was there as far as I know. Naturally Jack Deveau - because it was his film - and Nick Justin - because he was the owner - were the stars of the show.
Siedelmann: There even was a camera team, is this true?
Schnetzer: There was a camera team, but I don't know exactly who had sent it. So maybe Kees Chapman was there. They definitely were doing lots of still shots. The footage might still be out there. I never got into photography, or something.
Siedelmann: Do you know in which year the Adonis was shut down?
Schnetzer: Gosh, I really can't say, it must have been some year in the 80's. Justin was looking to sell the place, but I don't even know if the building is still there.
Siedelmann: I've heard that it's a high rise now.
Schnetzer: *(laughing hard)* This was the longest time. I don't even know when I was there the last time. It was still there back then, but it was empty. Nothing was going on in there.
Siedelmann: It must have been one of the biggest cinemas in New York?
Schnetzer: Yeah, back in the 20s & 30s, and in the days of Vaudeville they had the theater on the roof. It was one of those which were known for that. And, of course, the next block was where the old Madison Square Garden used to be. The original MSG... It was on 49th/50th. Anyway, I always forget how the Adonis was called in its early days, but it was one of the kind with 900, or 1000 seats at the roof top up there.
Siedelmann: One of those beloved gigantic theaters just like in France in the early silent movie years with all the big serials, and stuff like this.
Schnetzer: Exactly, yeah. It had an elevator - of course that didn't work anymore when I was there. But it would have taken you upstairs to all these offices. It had four floors, and it had a parking building attached to it. It was some place.
Siedelmann: Did you work there on percentage, or on regular salary?
Schnetzer: Everybody was paid by the hour, and so was I.
Siedelmann: You were involved in the film-making of Jack Deveau at some point.
Schnetzer: No, not really. I was always behind the scenes, but not really a crew member. I mean, I had known Jack Deveau, and a lot of the crew members up there. And I also knew a lot of the guys around, Jim introduced me to many of them. But when a new film was going on he tried to keep me

away from that. He didn't want me to see what was going on. *(laughing hard)* He had his very good reasons! He didn't want me to get jealous, or upset about something. I probably would have been, so... *(laughing)*

Siedelmann: But you had earned some credits on the films...

Schnetzer: Yeah, at A NIGHT AT THE ADONIS I really was more of a consultant. I participated on some of them, very few; mostly some kind of help behind the scenes. When they shot A NIGHT AT THE ADONIS I helped out a lot with anything around there. I cared about the projection; I made sure that the air condition kept going. Trying to keep noise at a limitation, stuff like that. The audio what they did was very sensitive. You could pick a pin drop among what they were doing. These things someone had to work out, there was a lot of consulting.

Siedelmann: And that's the credit for the grip?

Schnetzer: Exactly. Mostly for the electrician stuff, I helped with the lighting on location.

Siedelmann: Were you present at the shootings of JUST BLONDS as well?

Schnetzer: Sort of. I have been out there in Fire Island, but I really did not get involved in any of the shooting. I met all the actors, but I really didn't participate. I mean, Jack gave me credit for that. That was because of the good nature of his heart. At least I was there with Jim. *(laughing)* It made a perfect getaway for me!

Siedelmann: When you did FIRE ISLAND FEVER it was shown there, not at the Adonis.

Schnetzer: Actually we did the opening of the film out there. It had its premier in Cherry Grove. I did all the projection work on that. Trust me: It was a packed house! The people were waiting outside in lines to go see this. I remember they came with packed boats to see the film! You had three ways to get to Fire Island: You had to take the ferry, by sea plane, or on your own boat. You couldn't drive, there were no bridges out there. They built bridges later on. I don't know how it looks like today. There was a storm a few years ago that took both of them out. I guess they replaced them. Yeah. Those were the days! *(laughing)* But as far as I know only FIRE ISLAND FEVER was shown up there.

Siedelmann: So you learned about being a projectionist at the Adonis I guess?

Schnetzer: Yeah, we showed the film in 16mm at the event at Fire Island. I mean these were high quality projectors with the audio in 16mm. The ones we showed in New York at the Adonis were all 35mm.

Siedelmann: So the films had to be blown up?

Schnetzer: Yes, it was 35mm there. It was all shot on 16mm, but when it got to the Adonis it was blown up to 35mm. I think there were only one or two films we did in 70mm.

Siedelmann: 70mm?!?

Schnetzer: Yes. So we had to change the projectors temporarily. I had to learn about how to operate these different projectors. That took some time. I mean when do you see this today? It's all IMAX now. You even have to expand the screen. It was huge! We had to modify the screen. I remember that well.

Siedelmann: There were a few gay porn feature films in 3D. Were they screened at the Adonis as well? HEAVY EQUIPMENT starring Jack Wrangler, for example?

Schnetzer: No I don't think we ever did 3D. But I knew Jack Wrangler. Nice guy. *(laughing)* I remember he ended up being married to a woman, and he disappeared from the gay community. Because of AIDS everybody thought he was gone, but he was just about changing his lifestyle.

Siedelmann: So you also have been together with Jim Delegatti as a couple for a very long time, I guess?

Schnetzer: Yeah, we have been together for almost 44 years. We wanted to settle down here before we decided to get married or not. Jim's now 71, going to 72, and I'm going to 65. So we want to do something positive, and we probably will take that step. We're all positive with our lives. It's something we really want to do since we've almost spent the whole time of our lives together. We live a really quiet life now, retired from work.

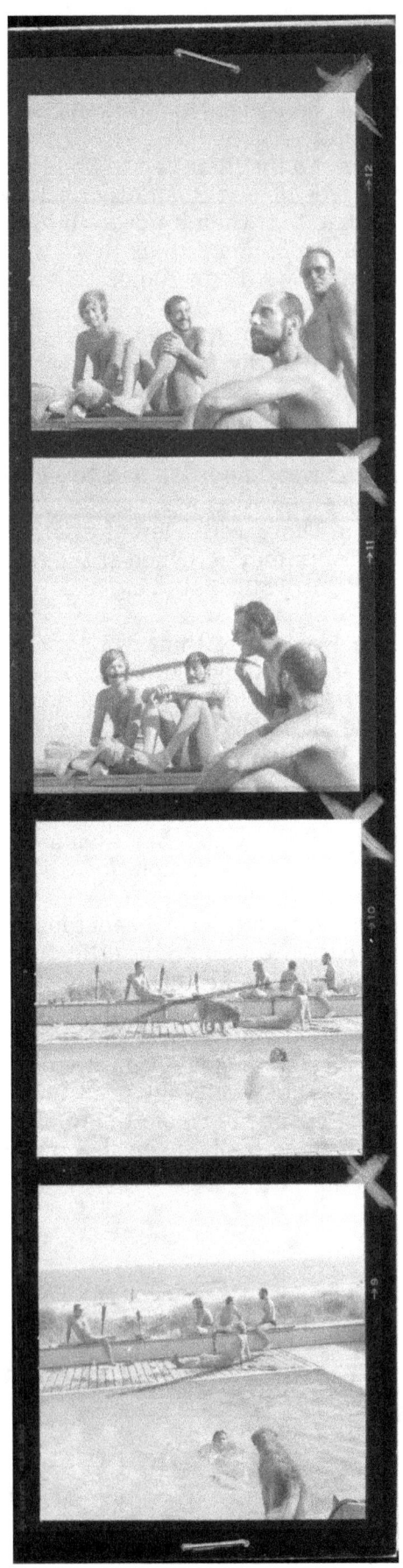

Fire Island Fever

Behind the scenes of *A Night at the Adonis*

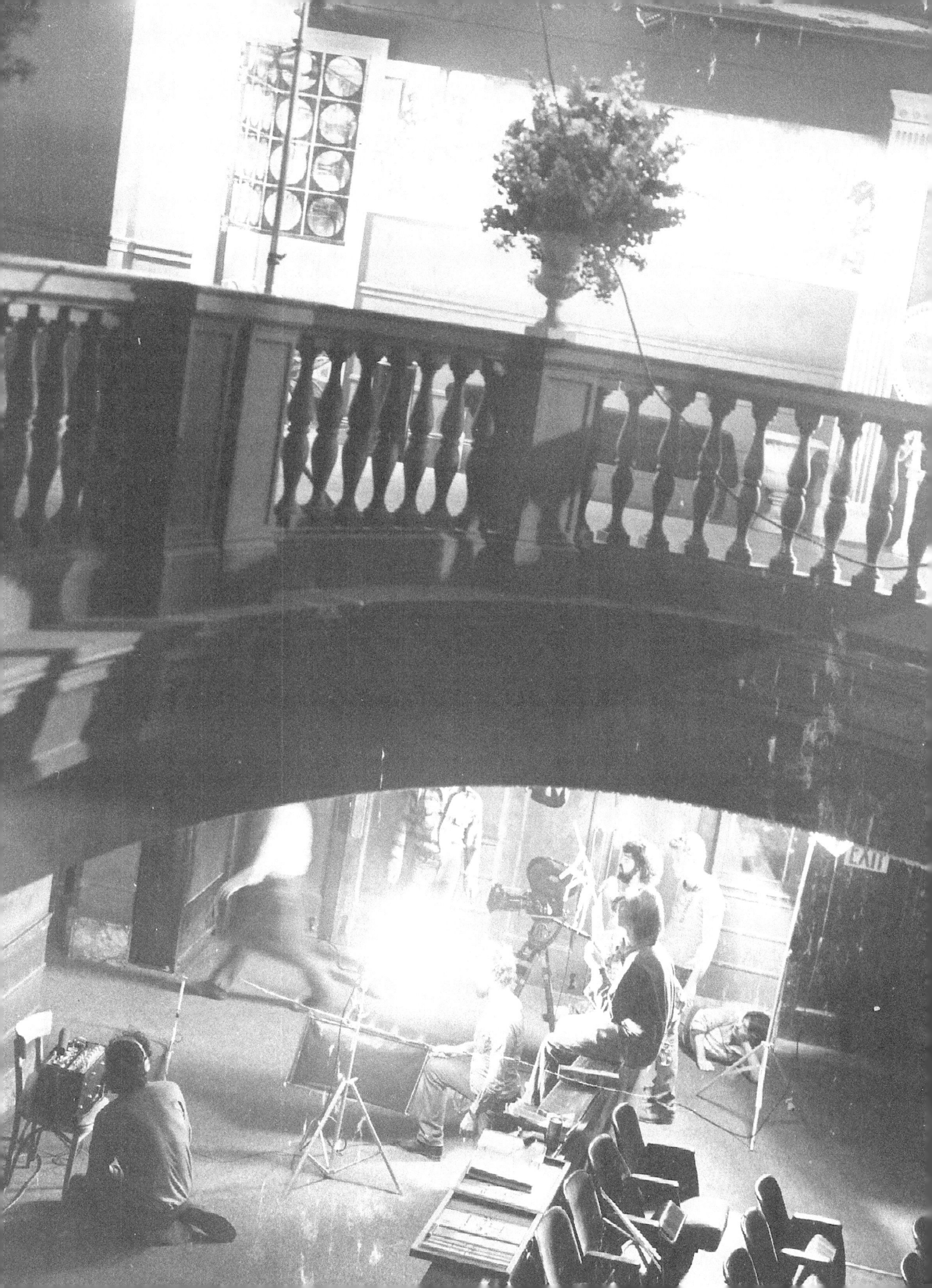

ROLF PARDULA
Coming out with Hand In Hand

Marco Siedelmann: Mr. Pardula, I'm honored to speak with a veteran of American independent filmmaking. In the early years of your very successful career, you worked with legendary adult film director Jack Deveau.
Rolf Pardula: Yes. I was the production sound mixer at Hand In Hand.
Siedelmann: You were one of the straight man in gay porn industry, correct? Have you ever been in a relationship with a man?
Pardula: Well, first I was one of the straight persons in the business. Actually I came out as a gay individual in those days. When I started working with Bob and Jack - that was back in the 70s - this was my first introduction into another world; the homosexual world. I had never been exposed to that. I was having relations with women at the time. Bob and Jack, they liked me. And they allowed me that. I already was in the industry, I had done sound recording for adult films with men and woman; heterosexual films. Sometimes there were sort of art films as well. I was working in that rental company, and they heard that I recorded sound for several X-rated films. So they got in touch with me, and they wanted me to work for them.
Siedelmann: And you were interested right away?
Pardula: I said, sure! They told me that they were making all-male adult films. That was fine for me. I was like, "maybe I can learn something." So they hired me. Their films were made pretty short sometimes, could be within a week. With two days of my work. They realized that I was straight, and they treated me very good. They gave me enough space, and a corner for myself to work in. They were very polite. I was never intimidated, or threatened by them. They treated me as a part of the family, which was very kind. They had love and care, and they didn't want anything to happen to me. In fact, they protected me, and at the same time they allowed me to be on the set, and see these beautiful men having sex with other men.
Siedelmann: Yeah, ok.
Pardula: After a few years, I realized I've been hiding my sexual feelings, and that I really wanted the company of other men. So thanks to Jack and Bob, I was allowed to formulate my personality, who I really was. I wasn't thrown into it. It was a thing over the years. Being with them meant they had always great parties, and they had fabulous men coming there. I was very shy, and introverted. I probably still am, but not so much, of course. Slowly, I came out of my shelf so to speak. So I'm very grateful for them helping me to come out. It wasn't forced by anyone, but it was a natural thing.
Siedelmann: So you literally came out with Hand In Hand!
Pardula: I realized this is the person I really am. I didn't have to suppress my feelings, or to hide them. Why should I hide my homosexuality when Jack and Bob didn't do that? They felt comfortable with themselves, and they had a high self-esteem. They were very well-known all around the country, and in the motion picture circle. They were really well respected, and they were together as lovers. I literally said to myself: "So this must be possible for you as well!" I could become the person I should be.
Siedelmann: They gave you the confidence for all this? Great!
Pardula: And then I worked with them many years. And I always made friends with others from the technicians, or crew members. For example, hair and make-up stylist Jim Delegatti, I'm close friends with him until today. Also with his lover Kenny (Ken Schnetzer) - both worked on several Hand In Hand productions. They brought me out, and told me about the gay world in New York City: the clubs, the bars, the bath houses, and all that. They were always with me, and protected me. They didn't let me go alone; until finally I could do it by myself, and didn't need someone around for that any longer. *(laughing)*
Siedelmann: How did these early experiences feel like?
Pardula: You go to these clubs, and at first you just observe, and learn. You're like a wallflower, you know? You see what goes on between those men, because you have to know some things. How you have to be to be

with another man? How to hold him? How do you kiss? And all this; without feeling shame, or guilt; without feeling like a faggot or a sissy. You want to feel normal, and healthy, and respectable. Feel good about yourself.

Siedelmann: How old were you when they contacted you first?

Pardula: It was sort of my mid-20s. And I got to work with them ... I guess until the time Jack died. I've forgotten when Jack died. I don't even know that.

Siedelmann: It was in '82.

Pardula: Oh, ok. So I must have started there in the mid-70s until something around '82, but actually before that, because the last two years in his life Jack kinda stopped directing; because of his illness. So I guess mid-70s until probably 1980. That's what it is.

Siedelmann: And how did you earn your skills of being a sound engineer?

Pardula: I was involved in a motion picture rental company. I was managing it. That's where they rented out all kinds of cameras, Bolex, 16mm, 35mm, and more related technique. I handed out lighting equipment, and then also sound equipment. The Nagra Kudelski 3 I rented out, which was required for the sound in the film industry back then. I was able to play with the equipment for hours at work, and on the weekends. I fell in love with the sound equipment. I liked the fact of working with sound, and I could be sitting in a corner working with a boom operator. Or a microphone operator - that was the guy who holds it. I could be in my own little world, because nobody understood what a sound mixer does anyway, and still no one knows! *(laughing)* Until you're another sound mixer.

Siedelmann: Very true!

Pardula: They always let you alone in the corner, and all they want to hear from the sound guy is: "Speed"! Which meant something like "ready", or "it's running". Now of course, it's all digital. It's on memory cards, and stuff like this. I was working with quarter-inch-tape, and Sennheiser mics, and a shotgun mic, and so on. I play with microphones as a cameraman plays with filters. Some give a harsher quality, some more sparkle, and some others have more warmth; depending upon the directionality, and the manufacture of the microphone. That was my challenge. After that, I became a production sound mixer; for feature films.

Siedelmann: Do you remember the first film with Hand In Hand? Was it BALLET DOWN THE HIGHWAY?

Pardula: I believe so; sounds familiar. I recall we also did one in a movie house, I've forgotten what it's called.

Siedelmann: The Adonis?

Pardula: Yeah. That's the one. The title was A NIGHT AT THE ADONIS. So that was very great. It was on 50th Street, and 8th Avenue. It's been torn down more than 20 years ago. Now there's a high rise there. It was a huge motion picture theatre, it almost took out the entire block. It was a gay pick-up place. It played gay movies, but it was the place where you could also meet men. It was like going to the bath house. You know: quick sex.

Siedelmann: In the cinema itself?

Pardula: Yes, but it wasn't something I was interested in. But we filmed there - at the Adonis. It was an incredible huge place, and it was never really full. *(laughing)* You know, maybe ten percent of it on any given time. But it showed the films by Hand In Hand, and that's the reason we actually got to film there. I think the shootings took about two weeks.

Siedelmann: Do you remember when A NIGHT AT THE ADONIS had its premier screening, right there where it was shot?

Pardula: Oh yes, that was a very nice evening. The cinema was even full at this event. *(laughing)*

Siedelmann: So that was kinda glamorous?

Pardula: They even had a camera crew there filming that, as I recall! So there should be footage somewhere about the opening night.

Siedelmann: The owner supported Hand In Hand?

Pardula: I think it belonged to a woman, but she had her son manage it. And I think he was also gay. So yeah - he supported Jack and Bob, and I think they knew him. And it all worked out nicely. It was always a great time going to Jack and Bob's. They had great parties in their penthouse apartment. I always expected Andy Warhol to come through the door. But they never connected. They should have! I spoke to Bob about it. Andy was gay, and he shot films. But they never ran in the same circle - it never materialized unfortunately; too bad. I think there would have been great vibrations between the two of them, or the three of them.

Siedelmann: But there were lots of other artists in the Hand In Hand circle, correct?

Pardula: Yes. Sal Mineo and his lover came by. I happened to be there at the time. They were just themselves; totally comfortable. Holding hands and being with each other as a loving couple. It was nice to see that. I thought, oh you can have such a relationship; also with Jack and Bob. They proved you can have a nice relationship being gay. You can have everything that heterosexual people have. You know, you have the right. And the possibilities are there. You can have all this besides producing and having babies. But you can always adopt of course. But you may not want babies. A lot of heterosexual people in New York now don't want them, because they're too expensive.

Siedelmann: And many people want to develop their own careers.

Pardula: Oh yeah, New York is a great career city. You can make it here. I mean I'm here, and I have my own apartment, and I'm single. I had a mate, but he died from complications. Not from AIDS, but from something else.

Siedelmann: I'm very sorry to hear that.

Pardula: We were together for almost 30 years; now I'm living alone the last ten years, or so. I'm a photographer now here in NYC; mostly into black and white journalistic photography.

Siedelmann: So you made a profession out of this?

Pardula: I'm trying to. It took me years to learn how to work with the computer. When I was working, it was an analogue world. Just before I left the film industry, I was working in digital already: digital recorders with tapes. I've done a lot of movies with Spike Lee.

Siedelmann: Yes, I noticed that, of course; very impressive.

Pardula: I did at least six features, among them CROOKLYN, MALCOLM X, SUMMER OF SAM....

Siedelmann: ...also his early feature SCHOOL DAZE?

Pardula: Yes, thanks! That was my first film with Spike. He hired me, because he loves German people. I was born in Hamburg.

Siedelmann: Oh, I didn't know that.

Pardula: Yeah, but my German is horrible these days. I never speak the language. Only with my brother who's living in Florida. If I ever go back to Germany ... I'll pick it up again. *(laughing)*

Siedelmann: How long were you in Germany before you moved to the United States?

Pardula: I left Germany in '56. And I haven't been back since then.

Siedelmann: So you left the country with your family?

Pardula: Yes, with my parents, and my brother, and my grandmother.

Siedelmann: Did they leave Germany because of work?

Pardula: My father always wanted to leave, because he was sick and tired of the political situation in Europe back then. He felt like, you never know what the Russians, or other countries are going to do. There was the fear for the atomic bomb. It was a *Pulverfass* as you say in German. I remember my father saying that. "Pulverfass" - do you see how bad my German is? I was 11, or 12 years old when I left. I remember I was born in the Jadestrasse, and I was playing in the bombed out buildings. I didn't know they were bombed out, but they all have collapsed. They had hidden rooms in the basement, and so it was a playground for us. When I came to America, I learned later that the bombs of the allies caused that damage. And I remember the Stadtpark in Hamburg. There was a huge lake where you could swim. I asked my brother, and that's still there. Everything is still there. *(laughing)*

Siedelmann: So your brother visited Germany?

Pardula: Yes. Because of his business, he went back several times. Four or five times; if not more. I'm the only one who has never gone back.

Siedelmann: So you never had the time?

Pardula: Actually I thought I would work sometimes on a film in Germany. I worked everywhere else but not in Germany. *(laughing)* Italy, Spain, Greece, Egypt, South Africa. Also I went to Brazil, and South America; all on different productions. I thought I was working in Germany at some point, but it never happened.

Siedelmann: In the 80s the German film industry kinda declined for a while, and most things happened in television.

Pardula: Oh, yes. - Anyway, after Hand In Hand ended with Jack's being sick and dying, I went to the union here as a sound mixer, and then graduated to larger films. I met Spike Lee. His MALCOLM X was a huge major production. Almost like a Hollywood film.

Siedelmann: So you met the notorious Spike Lee in his early years.

Pardula: Yes, he was in his thirty-somethings. He liked German products. He always used a German camera, and he was driving German cars. He knew I was in the union, and that I was German by birth. He probably thought: He's from Germany - he has to be good. *(laughing)*

Siedelmann: He's known for being very difficult.

Pardula: Oh, no. Once you get to know him, and if he likes you, he will take very good

care of you. He will treat you very nicely; as Spike did to me, and my assistant.
Siedelmann: Let's go back to Hand In Hand. So when you joined them, you participated on some other adult films as well. Correct?
Pardula: Yes, before I did heterosexual films.
Siedelmann: But parallel you are credited also on straight porn films, just like FIONA ON FIRE.
Pardula: Yes. I did that. It was a very nice film.
Siedelmann: Also another one I like very much: THROUGH THE LOOKING GLASS.
Pardula: Oh yeah, I was thinking about the title. This was a work of art! It was very well received. Actually that really was my first major film. That was a period I worked with Hand In Hand, and also with some other producers who did straight X-rated films.
Siedelmann: So it was obvious for you that THROUGH THE LOOKING GLASS was much more like a common porn feature?
Pardula: Yes. We were shooting it in a Woolworth store. It was a huge estate In Glen Cove, Long Island. It had around 50 or 60 rooms. At that time it had been a private school for girls, and then it was starting to run down. It was collapsing. And that's when we were able to rent it, when no one was in the estate anymore. The building was neglected. Somebody owned it, and the production team rented it. I guess for a month, or so. We spend the time there. Each one had their own bedroom, because there were so many rooms. *(laughing)* Well, the movie was considered as more of an art film than something like an average porno.
Siedelmann: Do you remember Jamie Gillis? He was playing the demon-father in THROUGH THE LOOKING GLASS. He was a heterosexual star, but he worked in a couple of gay films as well.
Pardula: I don't know. I remember the guy very vaguely.
Siedelmann: The Hand In Hand films were not that successful, correct?
Pardula: No, although they were considered to be the best in gay film at that time.
Siedelmann: How important was it for you in what kind of location you filmed?
Pardula: We had rented a gay health club for one movie, and we were filming in there. A lot of the other locations were apartments that Hand In Hand rented. The production designers did great jobs. We did a lot of films in Jack's penthouse, of course.

Siedelmann: So Jack and Hand In Hand were doing very well at the time?
Pardula: Yes. He was very well known, and financially the company did well. It was a respectable company, and everything was going well, until he got sick.
Siedelmann: Did they pay well?
Pardula: Yes, it was always a very nice salary; very comfortable.
Siedelmann: So you were able to make a living out of the sound mixing jobs? Or did you something like commercials also?
Pardula: At the time, I worked as a rental manager - that's how I got to know Jack and Bob - and also on straight films. I worked on weekends in the rental house, but after some time I could totally devote myself to sound. Eventually I left the X-rated industry, and went into regular films.
Siedelmann: He had a very partying lifestyle. How do you remember Jack working on set? Was he very casual, or disciplined?
Pardula: He managed it in a very casual style; never something like the set of a Hollywood film. It was always like having a party. *(laughing)* He was always comfortable. He never screamed, and he was always a gentleman on the set. He said he wants this and that done, but it was always graciously, and with great respect. So that's one of the things Jack Deveau was very well known for.
Siedelmann: Have you experienced different behavior while working on adult films?
Pardula: Oh yeah. I was always very fortunate to work with nice people, and good producers. At least I was always treated nicely. Once or twice I wasn't paid, but that was very rare. I always had good relations with producers, and directors. Honestly that was because I avoided many of them, because in some way I have a sense for persons I feel comfortable with. It was always based on that intuition, simply how I felt about a person.
Siedelmann: Do you recognize Tom De Simone?
Pardula: I remember him, but he wasn't around often.
Siedelmann: Yes - mostly he worked on his own in California, but Hand In Hand financed some of his best films. So there were some intersections between east, and west coast. Have you ever worked on adult films in Los Angeles, or San Francisco?
Pardula: No, I worked strictly in New York at that time; until I was involved in bigger feature films later.
Siedelmann: So as a sound engineer you had to be on set the whole time of production?
Pardula: Yes, I was always there; right behind

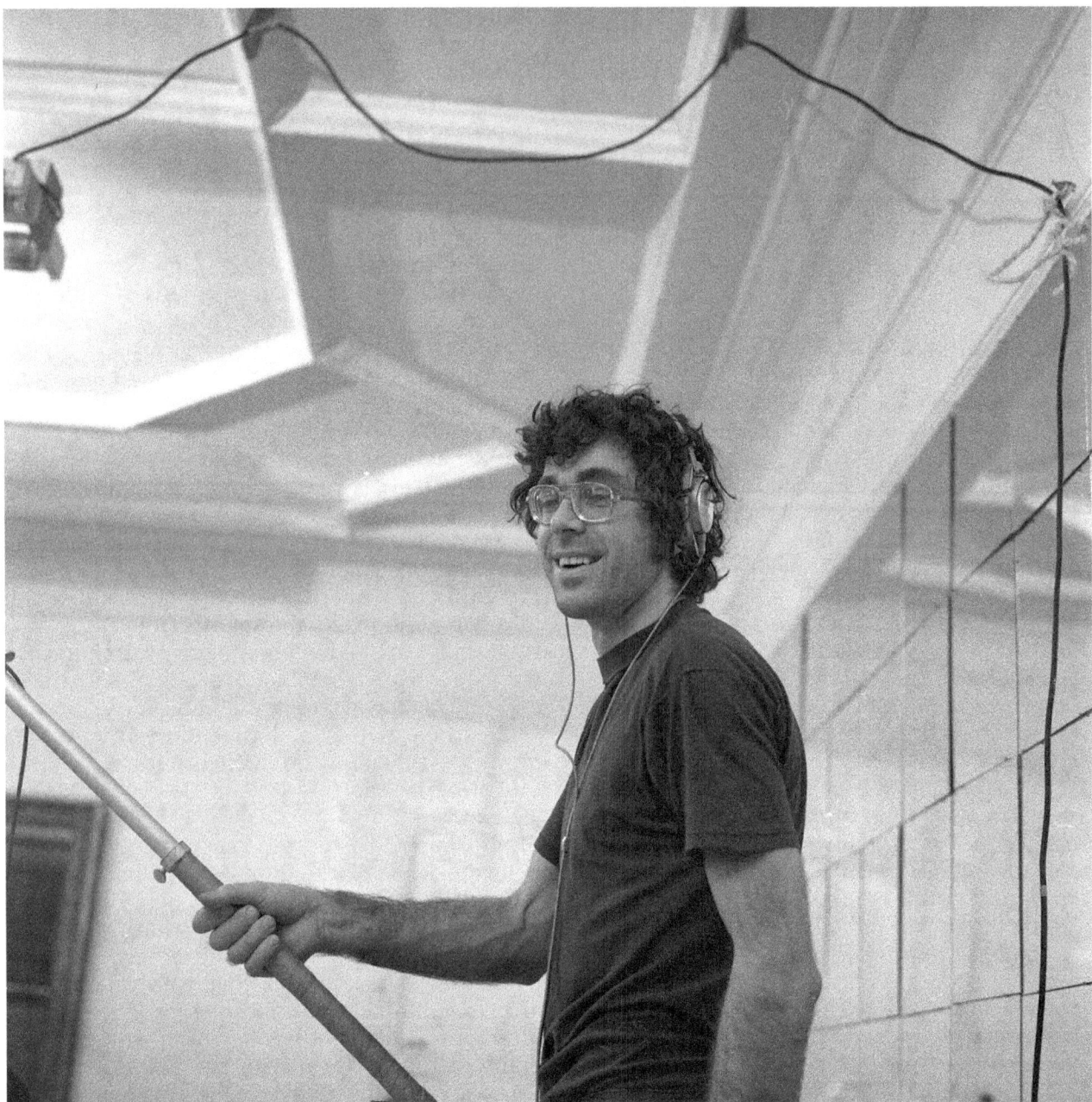
Rolf Pardula during the shooting of *Hot House*

the camera.
Siedelmann: Did you have problems, because of your adult film work?
Pardula: As a sound mixer no one ever minded that I was doing X-rated movies before. At that time it was a way to learn your trade. Editors, or cinematographers, or sound technicians learned to work good and efficient that way. It allowed people such as me to break into the industry. To join the union you had to be working, but how did you learn? By that time: In X-rated films - gay and straight. Nobody ever got upset with me, because of that. They wanted to know how good my sound was, and that was all they cared about.
Siedelmann: That's good. Do you remember David Earnest, the composer of the early Hand In Hand films?
Pardula: Well, not really. He wasn't on set, and I assume he was more present in the editing process. I surely have seen him a couple of times in Jack's apartment, but there were so many great parties, and there were so many men... *(laughing)* They had a small apartment next to the penthouse so they had a place to put you up when you came as a guest. There were always gorgeous men around. I remember that well.

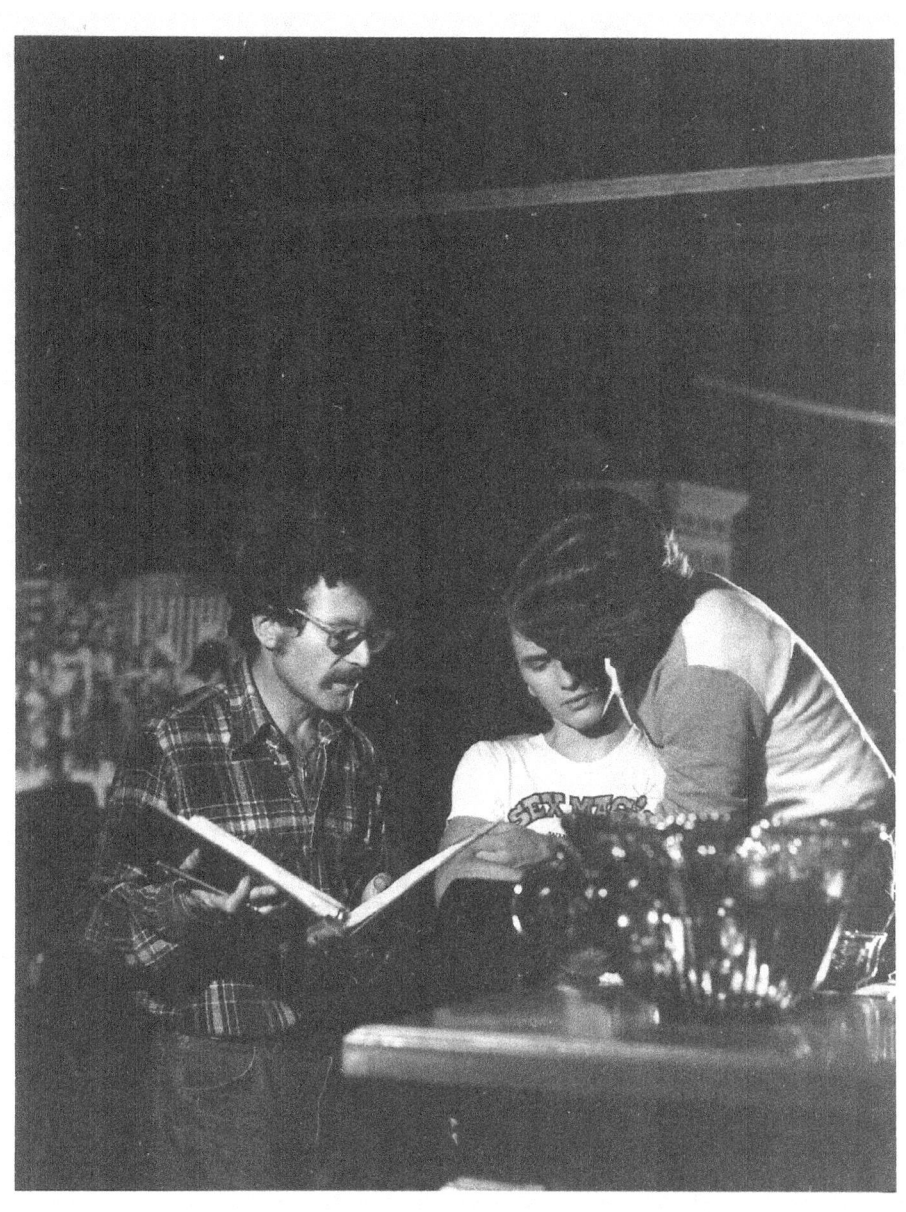

Moose 100 discusses the script behind the scenes of *Sex Magic*

MOOSE 100

Imitation of Life:
The Screenwriter of Hand In Hand

Marco Siedelmann: It wasn't easy to find you, so thanks very much for being available for this conversation.
Moose 100: I'm happy to be able to participate in this. It was a very important period of my life. I like to know that it's remembered, and that I had access to it. So I'm happy to cooperate as best I can. The biggest thing I got out of doing this work was that after the Hand In Hand days ended, that I was able to write the script and lyrics for a new musical. When I was trained as a playwright, I have written the lyrics, but I have never written the script as well. I just sat down and did it. It went just so smoothly that I didn't understand why I haven't had a lot of problems. Then it hit me like a bolt of lightning: A porno movie and a musical - structurally they are the same thing. It's from one number to the next. It could be dancing or fucking.
Siedelmann: Did you meet David Earnest at Yale?
Moose: No, actually we met in the gay world of New York. We were part of the same circle of friends. David and I were friends, and he was composing for them. He thought I might be an interesting person to work with Hand In Hand, so he introduced me.
Siedelmann: Before you joined Hand In Hand, what was the plan? Did you want to write for stage or film?
Moose: I wanted to write musicals for the stage, and I did want to go out for movies as well. But I didn't have a great desire to write movies. I eventually became a film editor on a gay newspaper called *The New York Native*. I worked there until the 90s. I interviewed directors, and reviewed movies all the time.
Siedelmann: Regular movies, not adult movies I guess.
Moose: Well, also adult movies. Some of the advertisers were adult movie companies. Usually the deal was they would advertise if you review the films. So I did that as well.

Siedelmann: You mentioned before that you were very much into the auteur theory. So you were influenced by the French New Wave?
Moose: Not so much. I was more into Hitchcock, Billy Wilder, Fritz Lang. People like this. The only director from the New Wave who really spoke to me was Claude Chabrol whose work I liked a lot, but I was much less influenced by the New Wave then I was influenced by Hollywood movies from the studio era.
Siedelmann: Was this the origin for your adoration of musicals as well? The classic film adaptations by Minnelli and others? Or were you in the Broadway audience even earlier?
Moose: My parents started taking me to Broadway musicals when I was about seven years old. So I saw a lot on stage, and it was also the height of the Gene Kelly and Fred Astaire movies. Those were very powerful for me. I loved the way they made me feel.
Siedelmann: Do you remember when you realized you were attracted to men?
Moose: I was about thirteen.
Siedelmann: Had the numerous queer implications in Broadway plays and musicals been helpful?
Moose: I don't think I recognized it intellectually, but I think I responded to it in a very positive way. I did not understand all of the elements of a musical; it took me a while to figure that out.
Siedelmann: You are born and raised in New York?
Moose: Yes!
Siedelmann: And did you come from a liberal family?
Moose: Yes; a middle class Jewish family. My father owned a Lunchenette.
Siedelmann: What's that?
Moose: That must be an odd word because it's pretty much gone. It's basically a place where you go to have a sandwich. It has a counter, and booths. It's sort of what you call a diner nowadays. But it also had paperback books, cigarettes, magazines, newspapers, candy; all kind of things. My parents both worked there and owned it. We moved from Brooklyn to Queens. So that's where I started out.
Siedelmann: Did you make it official at the time?
Moose: For anybody except my parents; at least as long as I could, because I knew it was going to be a disaster. Finally I was 35

and I lived with the love of my life. He made me do it. I told my dad, and he did the usual response. You know, I am not terribly happy to hear this but I love you, I will not kick you out of my life, and all that stuff. But he insisted to take as long as he needed to tell my mother. It took two years!

Siedelmann: It's interesting that you told your father first.

Moose: I knew he would be more reasonable with it.

Siedelmann: Because of the grandkids that were no longer expected by you?

Moose: Yes. I was an only child so there would definitely be no grandkids. Also both came from very big families, and all of their social life was with family members. When I came out to them and kinda waited for them getting more comfortable with it, they were filled with guilt and shame. The rest of the family was just wonderful! Actually I and Dick - who was my partner for 24 years until he died - had been invited to all family functions. We were treated like every other couple. He was completely accepted. Only my parents couldn't handle to make the transition.

Siedelmann: So that was the love of your life you spoke about.

Moose: Yes. He died of lung cancer 13 years ago. He co-wrote the last two movies that we did for Jack. Our collaboration was a series of horrible arguments. We decided we would never work together again.

Siedelmann: So you joined Hand In Hand in 1974 or '75, and you went on to work with the company until its very end in 1982?

Moose: Yes.

Siedelmann: Were you already in a relationship with Dick when you came to Hand In Hand?

Moose: I met Dick in 1978.

Siedelmann: So right in the middle of your personal history with Hand In Hand?

Moose: Yes. Looking back that feels like a very long period in my life.

Siedelmann: You knew David Earnest socially back then.

Moose: David's boyfriend at the time was a very good friend of mine. We got to know each other, and at one point David told me about his work with Hand In Hand. He knew that I was a writer, and he thought I could really match with them. He made me an appointment, and I just should go out to meet Jack and Bob. Then look what happens. I came back with two treatments I had to write, and I was starting a research mission. I was going to see straight porn films, because I think it was more advanced at the time. I was really interested in trying to do stories. I did the two treatments and went back to Jack's apartment. They bought one of them, and that was WANTED: BILLY THE KID.

Siedelmann: That was your first script.

Moose: Yes. One of things both Jack and I loved very much was to structure a gay adult movie on a Hollywood movie. Of course, adding all kinds of changes, but sort of doing it based on some favorite film. WANTED: BILLY THE KID was loosely based on the Jane Fonda movie KLUTE. Ever heard of that movie?

Siedelmann: Yeah, of course; I like it very much, but frankly I wouldn't have recognized the parallels.

Moose: It's only an idea based on, it's not obvious. It tells another story; we used the plot of several Hollywood movies always as sort of a jumping off point, rather than an adaptation. It's certainly not an adaptation. It's unrecognizable; it's just the center idea.

Siedelmann: Thanks very much by the way for not wasting your time on spoofs!

Moose: Oh gosh, they are mostly not funny at all! Jack, Bob, and I - we were much more ambitious in trying to write and produce real movies! It was our operating philosophy.

Siedelmann: What about JUST BLONDS? I was wondering that you have been credited as a narrator on that one, because it's maybe the most non-narrative feature of Hand In Hand.

Moose: I remember the title, and I guess I've wrote the narration. But I certainly did not narrate it myself. I have absolutely not a voice for that.

Siedelmann: It's obvious that the films are scripted in a very professional way. So what's your educational background?

Moose: I was a Yale playwright. I have a master of fine arts degree from the Yale Drama School. That's what I wanted to bring to gay porn.

Siedelmann: When did you graduate?

Moose: Oh gosh. It was 1967. Five years before Meryl Streep.

Siedelmann: She also graduated from Yale? I did not know about that.

Moose: Oh yes; and several others who became stars. That was the theater school where you could launch a career. When you graduated from Yale any agent would talk to you, any producer. It was a connection that was so valuable. That was my background when I started working for Jack and Bob.

Siedelmann: I think Jerry Douglas also went to

Yale, but he graduated a few years earlier, if I'm not wrong. Do you know about Jerry?
Moose: Oh yeah, sure!
Siedelmann: So, besides the straight porn films I assume you also watched the Hand In Hand films that were already made at that point?
Moose: I did watch the Hand in Hand films. What excited me about them: It was basically a new genre of movie, and it was being created. The idea of working in the field was to be one of those who creating it. There's something very challenging about that. That's what interested me the most. I used to say I'll write movies that people will write college pieces about. *(laughing)* In porn! There were so many possibilities, because it doesn't exist before as a storytelling form. And it was very New York, which was such a rich place back then.
Siedelmann: I assume you had seen the movies by Wakefield Poole before?
Moose: Oh, sure. I remember going to see BOYS IN THE SAND.
Siedelmann: But that was not the kind of film you were going for?
Moose: No. I was much more into dialogue. His films are very handsome to look at, and very effective. But I was coming from a totally different place. I was interested in sort of documenting - in a fictional way - what gay life was like in the city. That's what got me hooked, because you were not able to see it in commercial films at the time. You may have some grotesque gay bar scene that didn't tell you anything about gay culture. Hand-In-Hand offered a chance to do that.
Siedelmann: Speaking of the representation of gay life in mainstream films: Had you seen William Friedkin's THE BOYS IN THE BAND at the time?
Moose: Oh, yeah. I saw the play as well.
Siedelmann: Was the film kind of authentic, or did you feel insulted by it?
Moose: Well, I remember at the time when I saw it - just the fact that there were plausibly gay characters seen on the stage was crazy exciting. I loved it. A couple of years ago I re-watched the movie on DVD, and I was shocked at how ugly it was. How unhappy all the characters were. I think just because gay people in movies were invisible; other than some stereotypes, but any kind of real characters. People were so hungry to see representations of them and their way of living that they didn't notice just how miserable the characters were. *(laughing a little)* It's clear.
Siedelmann: Many gay people have criticized the film.

Moose: It's because, here's a group of people laughing on the outside and crying on the inside. The kind of life I was leading: I was laughing on the outside, and I was laughing on the inside. I wasn't miserable! I had a fabulous life. Being gay was the most wonderful thing in the world. So I had a very different attitude. Maybe I didn't suffer as much as other gay people did. That's why I thought that way. I always lived in New York. A place where gay people had been more accepted than anywhere. I think I felt less isolated then a lot of men all over the world who lived in really oppressive places. I was very lucky to be in an environment where it was easy to be gay. So I was much more interested in sort of the lightness, and the flavor of gay life.
Siedelmann: That's a good keyword. I think the Hand In Hand films can be separated - more or less - in two sections. On one hand we have the kind of darker, melancholic, or even tragic films; LEFT-HANDED for example.
Moose: Yes!
Siedelmann: The lighter, entertaining, and funny ones, on the other hand, are mostly scripted by Moose 100. So you brought much of the sophisticated humor in the films?
Moose: I think that was my strong point as a writer; to be able to do exactly that. There's a scene in A NIGHT AT THE ADONIS where Jack Wrangler has met this other guy at the theater. They are making small talk, and the guy is asking Jack Wrangler, "What do you do?" - And he said, "I'm in mens' pants." Jack Deveau appreciated jokes like that. They put some certain entertainment value into the films.
Siedelmann: Indeed, there are many dialogue lines of that kind in the films. Just like in THE BOYS FROM RIVERSIDE DRIVE when main character Steve (Buddy Preston) calls his best friend Robert (Luke aka Philip Wagner) on the phone. Robert says "I'm tied up at the moment," and when he hangs up the phone we can see what he means.
Moose: *(both laughing)* Yes, exactly!
Siedelmann: Humor is always about timing.
Moose: That's true. The thing is, the way these movies are shown. Most of the films I've written opened at the Adonis Theater. People went there to cruise. The most unusual thing was that somebody would sit down, and watch the movie from the beginning to the end. So the audience saw the films in fragments. Jack and I felt that it

was giving us the opportunity to write the movies just like we wanted to. *(laughing)* Because no one paid that much attention. They were just looking at the sex scenes. They were fantasizing, they were picking up men. That freed us. We felt we were able to experiment. In fact, I used to borrow a print of a new movie, throw a big party, and asked the audience consisting of my straight female friends. They loved them! And they had plenty of hot men to look at. Anyway, that was part of the reality of the time - how the movie theaters functioned. This was before - or at the very beginning maybe- of VCR technology. So, sometimes the movie at the screen you maybe half paid attention to. That was a big factor.

Siedelmann: Can you recall your first introduction to Jack Deveau? What kind of man was he?

Moose: You know, there are so many clichés about people in porno that you expect some horrible creature. *(laughing)* But Jack was a man who inspired confidence. The minute you see him he seemed smart and organized. He seemed to know what he was doing. Plus I've been very impressed; because of Bob Alvarez was one of the editors on WOODSTOCK. David Earnest gave me a very good and personal introduction to them. He said I would like them. And I did right away. They were reliable. When we were shooting a movie Jack would take anybody out to lunch. He gave parties! It was socially very fun to be around them. They were very professional the way they worked. I was invited to the sound mix from the first movie on. I was learning lots of details about filmmaking from the first moving on. They were very generous about sharing what they knew. It was a very positive experience. And also, when you are working in this world - there was something exotic about it. During the years I worked for Jack, another friend of mine said that I had the most exciting life of anybody he knew. Part of it is the legend you get about yourself. For me it was really interesting, and very absorbing. I liked it, and I liked them. Jack knew more about music than almost anybody that I knew. He had an extensive collection. He was a very sophisticated man. It was very easy to be there. He appreciated what I could do, and I appreciated what he could do. So we just worked together over and over.

Siedelmann: Even before WANTED: BILLY THE KID was made, you were credited as a writer for the compilation piece GOOD HOT STUFF.

Moose: Yes. For that one, my job was basically to structure the scenes and write a narration. That's what I did: I put the scenes in an order. It worked pretty well. There was already THAT'S ENTERTAINMENT come out, and that was sort of the model to structure this on.

Siedelmann: But GOOD HOT STUFF was released before WANTED, correct?

Moose: I think what happened was that I wrote WANTED: BILLY THE KID before it was shot, and worked practically on GOOD HOT STUFF. Jack always made two movies at the time, and shared the cast. It was a very smart and economical thing to do. TIMES SQUARE STRIP was the closest thing to a musical we ever did, in a theatrical sense. It was filmed on the Gayety Burlesque. That was really fun. I think that was the last movie Jack ever directed. It was definitely shot back-to-back with THE BOYS FROM RIVERSIDE DRIVE. FIRE ISLAND EVER was shot back-to-back with DUNE BUDDIES. That was how Jack liked to work. I was basically writing two movies at a time.

Siedelmann: But Jack Deveau was not working on a stressful time schedule, right? I've heard he just took the time he needed.

Moose: Yeah. What was interesting is that instead of running out of schedule for the shooting of one movie, he made out a schedule for two movies. He would hire actors who took part in both films. And they would structure it that way. In other words: All their scenes for both films were to be completed in three or four days. So that became an economical way to make two movies for the price of one, in a way.

Siedelmann: But still it was important for Jack Deveau to make two very different films, despite the fact that they were shot back-to-back. Do you agree?

Moose: Oh, yes. The two films made on Fire Island in fact. One of them was shot in the Pines. The other one was shot at Cherry Grove. The whole feeling of the movies was totally different from each other. It's juxtaposition.

Siedelmann: Do you remember Sydney Soons and Kees Chapman very well?

Moose: Oh yeah. They were just a beautiful couple. They were young and good looking - just being present they put something magical in the room. Also both have been nice and intelligent. They were already a very big part of Hand In Hand when I joined the scenery. Both were always good to be around, but I got to know Kees better than Sydney.

Siedelmann: Kees Chapman later was also

391

involved in the cinematography. So he was around a lot on set?

Moose: Yes. But also he did another very important job for Hand In Hand: He was responsible for the schedules. Because he would hire an actor for about four days, the scenes for both movies in which the actor was needed to be in had to be planned very carefully, so Jack would not pay for some actors just waiting one day or even more. Kees Chapman was very helpful in the process and made it happen in a very economic responsible way. He was a well-organized man.

Siedelmann: I don't think it's necessarily the best film produced by Hand In Hand, but for some reason I'm very much into DUNE BUDDIES.

Moose: I like it too. It has some kind of low-key ease about it that's very nice. I think Arnaldo Santana [aka Malo] was quite good. He later was in SCARFACE, and he did Broadway.

Siedelmann: Is he still around?

Moose: I have no idea. He seemed to be somebody at the time that was burning his candle at both ends.

Siedelmann: I see. So you are also not in contact to any of the actors?

Moose: No, not at all; I ran into Robert Alvarez once in a while over the years, but he's the only person of those years that I ever see. You know, so many years had gone by; so many have died of AIDS. Now it's sort of, who is still around at all? I know a couple of the Hand In Hand actors who I got friendly with at the time had died during those years. For example Garry Hunt, who was one of the lead actors in BALLET DOWN THE HIGHWAY. Actually he was a salesman, and because of his work at Hand In Hand, he became a professional actor. He was a very intelligent and nice guy. He died of AIDS. I know that. Garry starred in DUNE BUDDIES, FIRE ISLAND FEVER, and...

Siedelmann: He also was in HOT HOUSE.

Moose: Right! Do you know about the original title of that movie?

Siedelmann: No, actually I don't.

Moose: STOP - IN THE NAME OF LOVE.

Siedelmann: *(both laughing)* That would have been the better title!

Moose: Unfortunately we would have been sued by Motown, and The Supremes. We knew not to do things like that, and we didn't. It was just the working title. Jack used to shoot the movies under such a working title. When a particular film came out, it got a definitive title.

Siedelmann: Did you keep your notifications, treatments and scripts that you made over the years for Hand In Hand?

Moose: No. I had a basement flood, and I lost all kinds of my writing. On the other hand, I tend not to go back and look at it either. I had very little of what you call artifacts from those days. Practically nothing, I don't even have all the movies! I had some of them as VHS copies. A commercial editor I knew borrowed them. He swore he would bring them back to me - and I haven't seen him since. So...

Siedelmann: Does the name Eartha Hugee ring a bell?

Moose: Oh yeah. She was the ticket lady at the Adonis. I remember her! The main idea Jack and I had about A NIGHT AT THE ADONIS was to do our Robert-Altman-Movie; many characters that had equal importance. There was not one lead. Doing something like that was our experiment at A NIGHT AT THE ADONIS. In all of Altman's films there is an amazing way to tell a story about an event, rather than about an individual person. So there were many different characters that contributed to the event. There was not one overwhelming hero, or star. We thought that would be perfect for a film about the Adonis - and we certainly loved to have the real box office lady on camera! She was willing to do it, and we were very happy. It was a treat for sure! That's sort of made it distinctive. She was a familiar base for the audience at the Adonis, and she made the movie really authentic. You walked in to see the movie, and she was sitting there in the box office. When the movie started, there she was on screen! So it really added a great deal to the experience of the film.

Siedelmann: I think so. In fact, you can really feel that she really is the ticket lady, not an actress. Without any information - you just know it immediately. She must have been a character.

Moose: Yeah!

Siedelmann: So, let's go a little bit back in time. You had to deliver a treatment for WANTED: BILLY THE KID, for Jack Deveau. Tell me about your collaboration. How did the creative process work?

Moose: Well, we had a style of working where I would present a first draft. Then we would meet and talk about it, discussing some changes. I used to go home and write them. That was a process. It went on for a while. Once we got a shooting script - and this is what I really liked about the process - I was on set all the time in case I was needed. The minute a sex scene starts, you're shooting a documentary. It's what happens in reality, and sometimes people who act in porn movies got problems, because suddenly there are all these people around, those big hot lights, and they're expected to get erections. Sometimes it doesn't work that way, and things have to change. So having the writer right there can be a helpful thing, or - depending on the people at the cast - sometimes you see one of the actors and you want to sort of customize the role for them.

Siedelmann: Do you have any particular anecdotes about that?

Moose: Well, there was one incident during HOT HOUSE. They were shooting a sex scene, and right when they'd come to the cumshot the film suddenly went out of the camera. And they lost it. Immediately Jack fixed the camera and put in a new film, and by that time they were ready to re-shoot the scene - Jack Wrangler also was sexually ready again. I think he was amazingly good in what he was doing. I used to call him The Sexual Professional. You could tell him: "Jump out of an airplane, jerk off, and come as you land!" *(both laughing)* And he could have done it, because he was totally a pro. In a way that nobody I ever worked with was. He could control his sexuality in a way most people couldn't.

Siedelmann: But Jack Deveau cast also inexperienced faces.

Moose: Yes. Most were not experienced. There was always somebody there to spread the actor's legs, or put his genitals in the frame. That's how the cumshot happened sometimes. But usually part of it was Jack making the actors feel comfortable with each other. So they could function well during the sex scenes. One of the very smart things he used to do was when two people would have the scene together, he would neither introduce them - nor even let them see each other. Right when they were coming to set there was that sort of excitement. Having sex with someone you literally met a few seconds ago.

Siedelmann: So he kept it fresh that way.

Moose: Yes! That was very effective!

Siedelmann: What about the casting? Were you involved in this process, too?

Moose: No. For me it was most interesting when Jack called me up, and told me about an actor he found. He looks like this and his cock is like that. I always told him: "I don't care about any of that. I want to know about his speaking voice." For me, that has as much to do for a character being sexy as what he looks like. It's the quality of voice.

Siedelmann: Do you think that's connected to the acting skills of a person as well?

Moose: Well, the acting was always gonna be a little sketchy. I mean - there were people who were experienced and very good. People like Garry Hunt, Jack Wrangler, Arnaldo Santana - They were smooth on camera. There were other people who were new to it. Not professionals at all. It's something you just have to go with. I had nothing to do with the casting. I would urge him to get people who vocally sounded hot. That would have been it, if I would have been involved in the casting at all. The importance of that! Because if a guy comes along, and he's really butch and good looking, but would have a squeaky little voice - No!! It would not work out. They couldn't afford to dub the movies. This was low budget filmmaking.

Siedelmann: Were you always glad about Jack's casting?

Moose: It's not that I was glad or unhappy about it. It was more like: That's the one who has the role, and so he's the one I'm going to work with. On WANTED: BILLY THE KID, I learned a really big lesson. It was giving too much to any single actor. The pressure on that lead actor - especially sexually - was too much. So after WANTED, the movies had at least two main characters. You could back and forth between them, but it didn't put all the responsibility to the sex on one person.

Siedelmann: Talking about WANTED: BILLY THE KID: Who was Shadow? He's sharing the writing credit with you.

Moose: Shadow was my roommate. We conceived it together. He was a theatrical costume designer. We had a deal. We shared an apartment together - we weren't boyfriends or anything - and we wanted to teach each other what we knew. He suggested he would teach me how to draw, and I would teach him how to write. The culmination of that was WANTED: BILLY THE KID. We developed the idea together.

Siedelmann: Ok, so that was your one and only collaboration on film?

Moose: Yeah. We're sort of in loose touch now. We don't talk often, but at least a little bit every once in a while.

Siedelmann: David Earnest was about to leave soon when you arrived at Hand In Hand, but on his very last Hand In Hand film - which was WANTED - you worked together. Do you play any instruments yourself?

Moose: No, I don't play anything. But I write lyrics for songs.
Siedelmann: What I really enjoyed in THE BOYS FROM RIVERSIDE DRIVE was the mockumentary style. It's made like an anthropological study.
Moose: Yes, but what I was really going for in that movie: I wanted to do my version of a Doris Day & Rock Hudson comedy. *(laughing)*
Siedelmann: A performance that really stuck in my head was the one by George Brown in RIVERSIDE DRIVE. Remember?
Moose: Yes, he was the guy in the elevator!
Siedelmann: So there never was a casting decision that spoiled your ideas totally?
Moose: Not that I recall. Jack and I had a real good communication. We were able to help each other. He was listening to me. Not all the time, we had disagreements. He was the director and the producer so I would serve my work to him at those times. But I was never frustrated or anything. It always was a very pleasant collaboration.
Siedelmann: Did you and Jack have a similar taste when it came to men?
Moose: Hmm - no. I have a very unusual taste. I would never expect in that industry that kind of people I find super-hot. I would almost say it's not at all about how they look like. It's all about the quality of the voice. That's an interesting point in general. When you work on movies like this you are going to ask yourself, what makes somebody hot. To a very large extent, I believe it's self-confidence. I was never attracted to pretty men. I always liked the character actors. I was much more appealed to the bad guys. So I never expected actors in the films that turned me on a lot.
Siedelmann: So you are clearly more of the Bill Harrison guy and not into the William Higgins surfer boys from California?
Moose: Yes! Also I was always attracted to people in my own age, and I still am. My boyfriend is about to turn 70. So I'm not fixated on young flesh. When I was young I was! *(laughing)* I sort of have grown out of it. For me it's more about what somebody does than what he looks like. How they carry themselves, their opinion of themselves; people who find themselves hot.
Siedelmann: And as you probably know: Humor always gets you laid.
Moose: Yes it does. Always. Absolutely true.
Siedelmann: Dick Bettis.
Moose: He was given credit as my co-author on THE BOYS FROM RIVERSIDE DRIVE and TIMES SQUARE STRIP.
Siedelmann: Do you any information about PP Mans, the writer of BALLET DOWN THE HIGHWAY?
Moose: That was Lorenzo Mans. He had written an independent movie that did very well in the 70s. At the times of BALLET DOWN THE HIGHWAY he was around a lot. We had a friendly relationship, because we were the two writers who got to work with Jack at the time. It was a common thing at Hand In Hand: People get along with each other. Partially that was because of Jack and Bob: They set the style. The atmosphere was very friendly. It was very easy to go about the business, and making the movies. You did not have people's emotions all on edge. One of the reasons I wanted to work for Hand In Hand was that I wanted to know if these people were better laid then I was. That was one of my big questions.
Siedelmann: And what was the answer?
Moose: I didn't think they were. I found out that I was very pleased with what I was in that department. At Hand In Hand you were in a world where people generally were confident. They wouldn't be doing this in the first place; talking about their sexuality and their identity. It was an exciting atmosphere to be in.
Siedelmann: So there wasn't much of human drama around? Jealousy?
Moose: No. The only drama I considered was that people were afraid they messed up when the camera hit. Other than that it was a very supportive kind of mood. Jack and Bob were smart enough to realize when you dealing with people's sexuality in a public way, they are vulnerable. They created a very safe environment. It also allowed people to do their best.
Siedelmann: Fassbinder had a circle very similarly built like Hand In Hand. He and Jack had a lot in common, only difference would be that Fassbinder could be a monster.
Moose: It's like with the legendary Jerome Robbins. He did a lot of work for the New Yorker Ballet. He choreographed WEST SIDE STORY for Broadway, and he was brilliant. He put the make on everybody. He was nasty. You hear the worst stories. But years later he is gone, and he has all this brilliant work left. Whatever drama happened in the making - it's eventually forgotten. The work remains.
Siedelmann: Also: Whatever happened - even it's neither forgotten nor forgiven - between the people. Listening to them you can always feel they're talking about one of the most important people they ever met. I

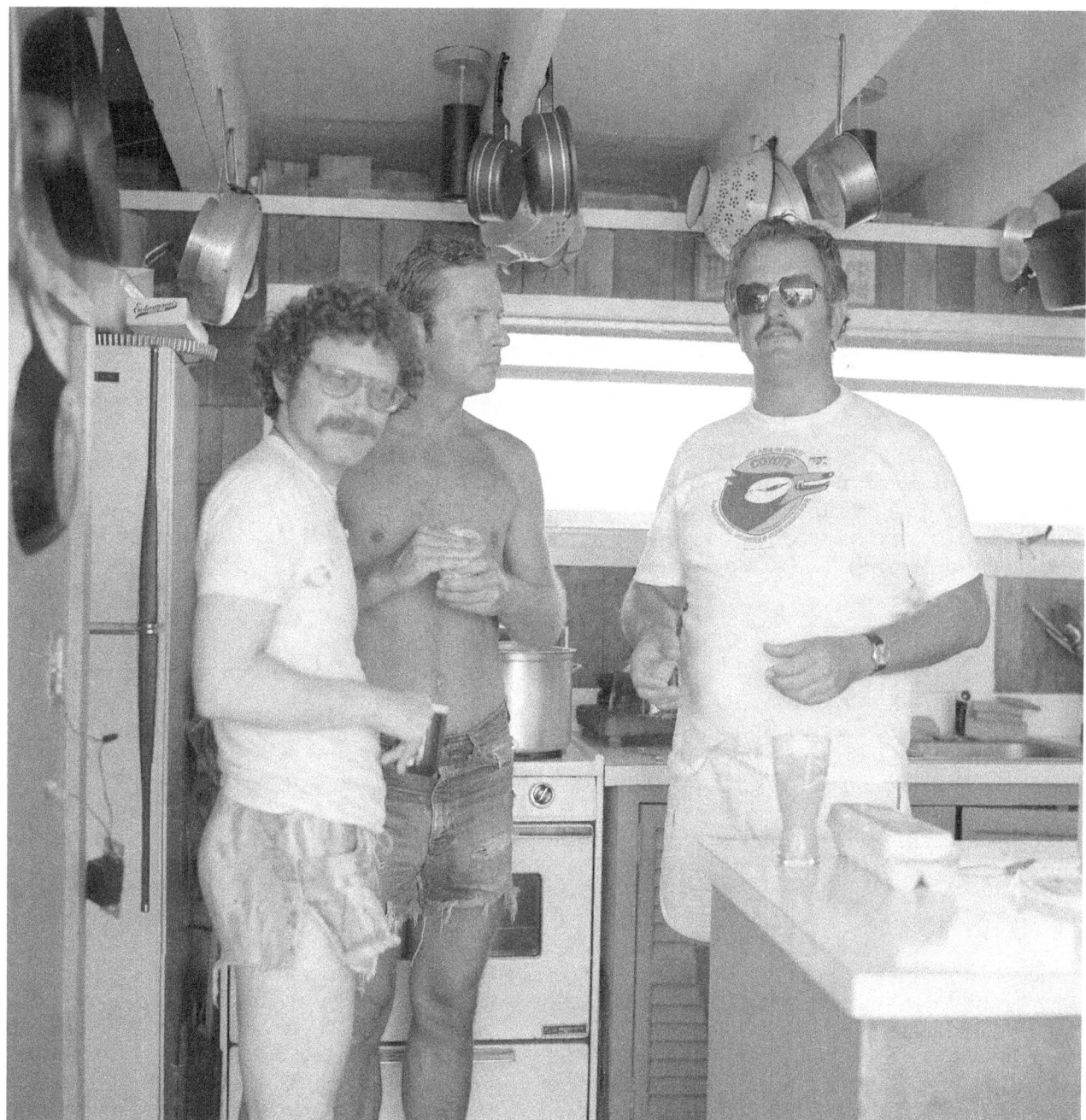

Moose 100, Garry Hunt and David Litler

assume Jack Deveau also was a key person for almost everybody he knew.
Moose: He kind of was, yes. He had sophistication about him. He was like a theater person. His parents worked in the hotel industry, and he had originally been trained for this as well. He was really good with people. He ran around with John Gielgud! Vincent Price! He had the most amazing circle of friends. There was this singer named Bobby Short. At the time he was famous in New Yorker nightclubs. Jack's friends really were all over the place, and his taste was very refined. I think what makes a director great - it's two things: First the ability to create really good work, but also to be with people. To inspire confidence. Jack did. He said: "Let's go." - And people followed him. You never really felt ordered around by him.

SHADOW

A Brief Encounter with Hand In Hand

Marco Siedelmann: We're using your alias Shadow in the book, right?
Shadow: Yes, that's better. It was many years ago, just a different time - when we were young and stupid.
Siedelmann: How old were you when you wrote the script for WANTED: BILLY THE KID with Moose 100?
Shadow: He actually wrote the screenplay. I was more of a visual artist. I'm an artist in New York all my life. I worked as a costume designer in film, television, opera, and theater. I'm not a writer at all.
Siedelmann: But you got that writing credit on the film.
Shadow: Well, I helped Moose out with that. My job at the time was when people got stuck at one point, I would do a storyboard that helped to solve some issues. On WANTED: BILLY THE KID, I didn't deal with words necessarily. I dealt with other levels of reality. I helped Moose and Jack Deveau with the visualization of the words.
Siedelmann: How old were you when you shared an apartment with Moose 100?
Shadow: Um, we were in our thirties. I'm older than Moose, so I was maybe thirty-two when we were working together with Hand In Hand.
Siedelmann: Was it the only film you worked on directed by Jack Deveau?
Shadow: That's correct. I absolutely don't remember how I met Jack, but like I said we did some crazy stupid stuff at the time. We were smoking grass all the time, we were doing cocaine, we had sex with many different people. And somewhere along the line I ran into him, probably because I knew some of the performers that he worked with.
Siedelmann: So you were around in the gay scene in New York, or are you a straight man?
Shadow: Oh, no, gay scene all the way. I had a number of exhibitions with my drawing here in New York at the Leslie Lohman gallery, which is very important for the gay artists here.
Siedelmann: You already were an acclaimed artist at the time?
Shadow: Well, I wouldn't say acclaimed, but it was how I made my living. What my interest was on that particular film is that I wanted to - based on my theater experience here in New York as a designer - paint the wardrobe, so that it showed an indication of the muscle structure that was inside of the pants or the suits, whatever they were wearing. So I was painting those things on the actors, just to help Jack to develop a look for WANTED. And I think it shows on this particular project.
Siedelmann: Was it a more collaborative process with Jack Deveau, or with Moose?
Shadow: I worked much closer to Moose than to Jack. We knew each other very well at the time, so it was very easy and fruitful to deal with.
Siedelmann: Were you satisfied with the finished film?
Shadow: Honestly, it has been so many years ago... *(laughing)* I do not even remember the film, or my thoughts about it. Sorry. I remember a little bit of the events around this film, but actually it's all very vague and shady.
Siedelmann: Ok, that's understandable. But what events related to the film do you remember?
Shadow: I just remember that at least one, if not two of the cast members came over, and I painted their bodies onto the outside of whatever they were going to wear in a particular scene. Then I went to the shoot to make sure that everything was reading on camera in the way it should. And that was it.
Siedelmann: Did you stay in touch with Jack Deveau afterwards?
Shadow: No, not really. From there, I went to a German theater at that point, then I went out to Los Angeles to design a film in Hollywood - so I moved out of that sphere.
Siedelmann: So you never were close to Jack Deveau and the Hand In Hand circle?
Shadow: No, I wasn't.
Siedelmann: What impression did you have about him? Did you like him?
Shadow: I did. I thought he was very personal. He knew what he was doing; he knew what he was going after. Well, this was still very undercover at the time, because of

legal problems. Jack had legal problems, he couldn't work very open. You know, all this changed throughout the years.

Siedelmann: Did you move out at that point as a roommate of Moose?

Shadow: No, I stayed longer. I don't know for sure, but Moose and I lived together in an apartment for about ten years. Then I found a new lover and moved into a loft in Soho.

Siedelmann: But you remained a part of the gay art scene in New York...

Shadow: Well, not really. I never defined myself as a gay artist. I was just an artist. I always considered myself first as a human being. Being gay was never on the top of the list how I considered myself and my personality.

Siedelmann: Did Moose invite you to join the project WANTED: BILLY THE KID?

Shadow: Hmm, I think we both came up with that idea together. Since he was a writer, and I was a visual artist, he kind of presented the idea to Jack Deveau first, and when we had green light for the project we collaborated on the screenplay.

Siedelmann: Do you remember which one of the actors you met or knew?

Shadow: No, I have no idea...

Siedelmann: Did you work more for theater or for movies at the time?

Shadow: Much more for stage, sometimes for movies.

Siedelmann: Are you retired nowadays?

Shadow: I retired this year, 2015. Now I am much more interested in quantum physics. I think I stopped doing all this art work about five years ago.

Siedelmann: What was the reason for that?

Shadow: I wanted to move on. Life is about change, and I've done exhibitions in London, New York, Asia. My art has been published, and all that stuff. So it was time; I just created enough art. This is a new millennium, so I wanted to pursue the massive changes that are about to happen. Last millennium was about reality being structured, it was very externally oriented. This millennium is going to be about the development of internal psychic, it's much more about the relationship with our internal lives. It's going to be a whole other paradigm. And don't forget we're in a global crisis. We're about to find out if we are going to survive as a species, or not. We're all hoping for the best, but this planet can't take much more abuse.

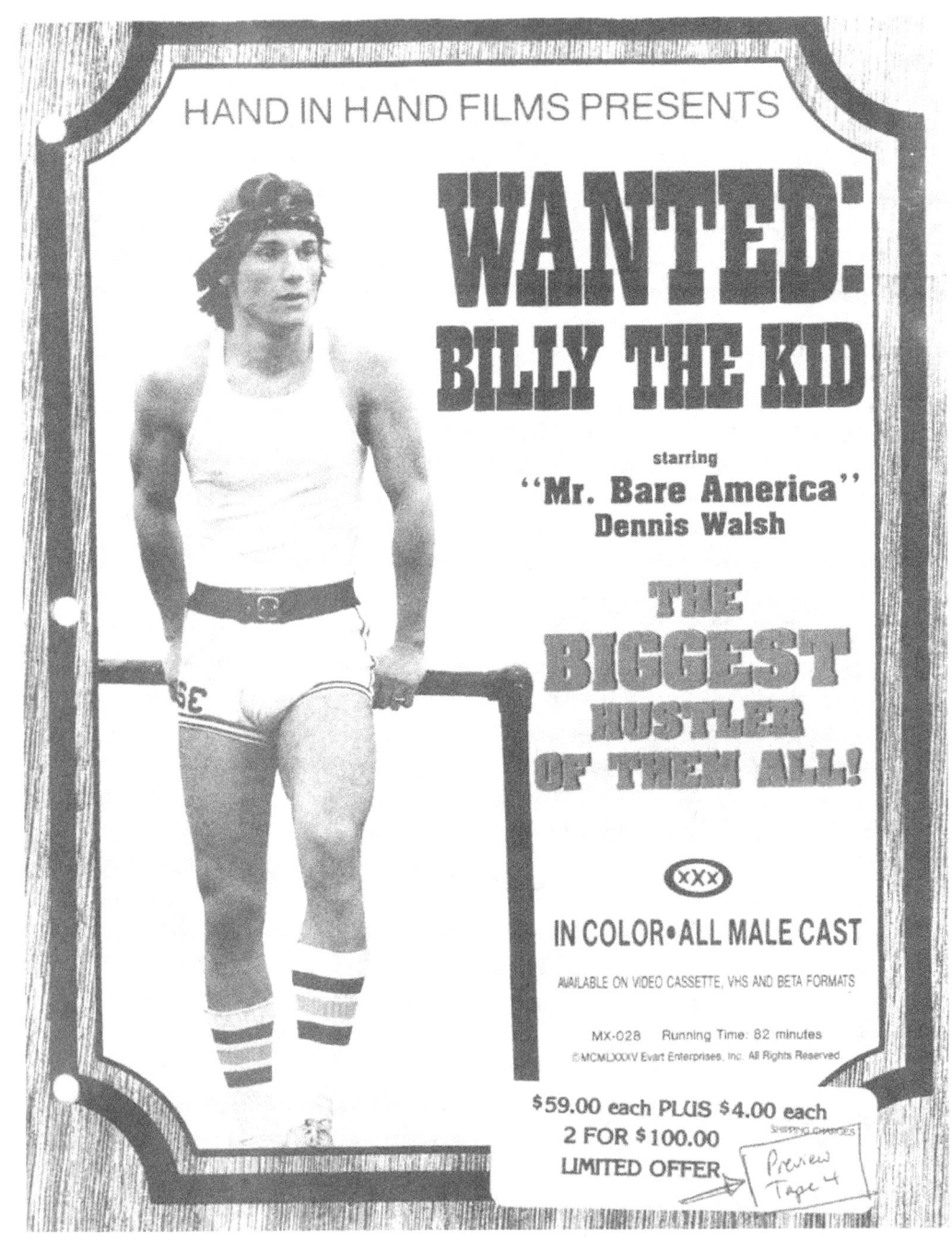

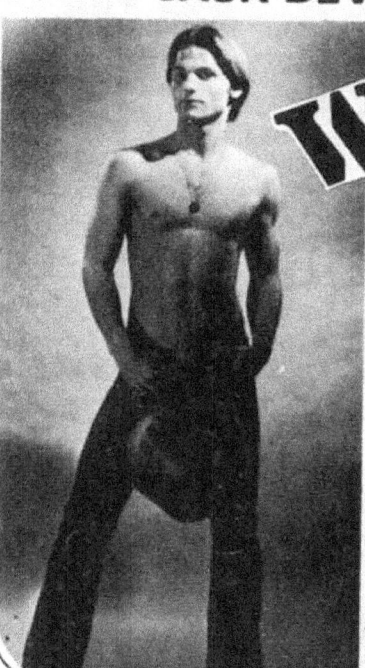

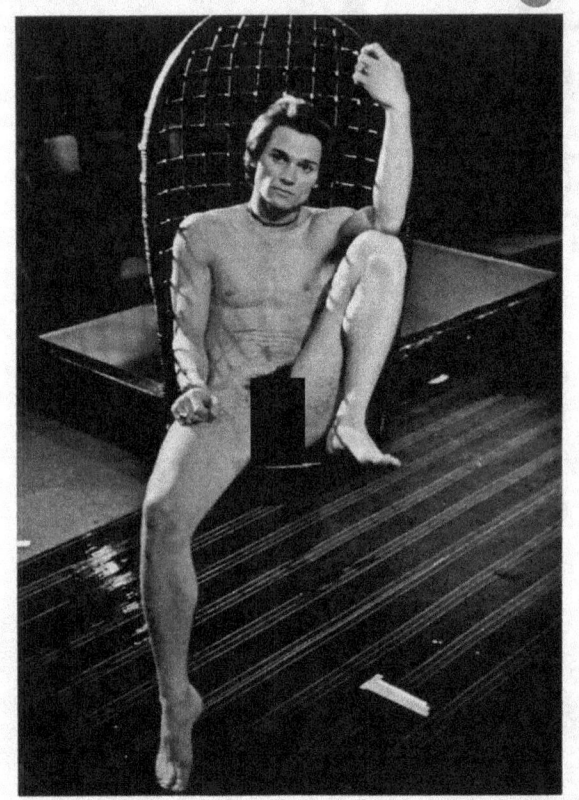
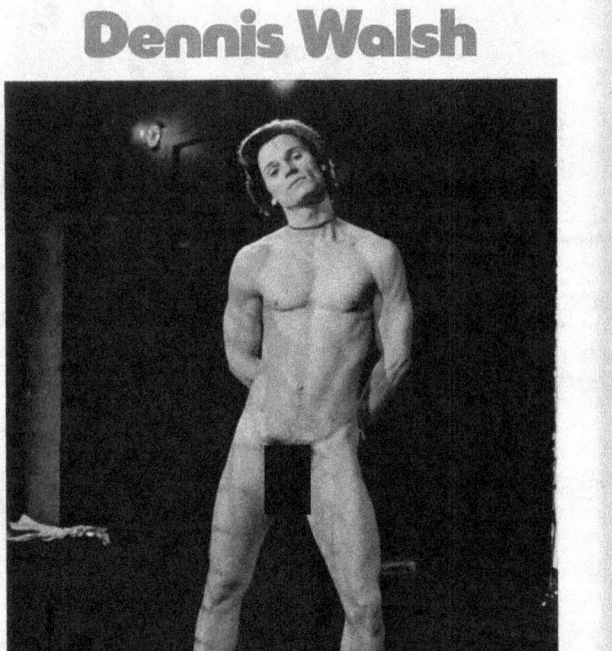

Dennis Walsh aka Bryan Haines

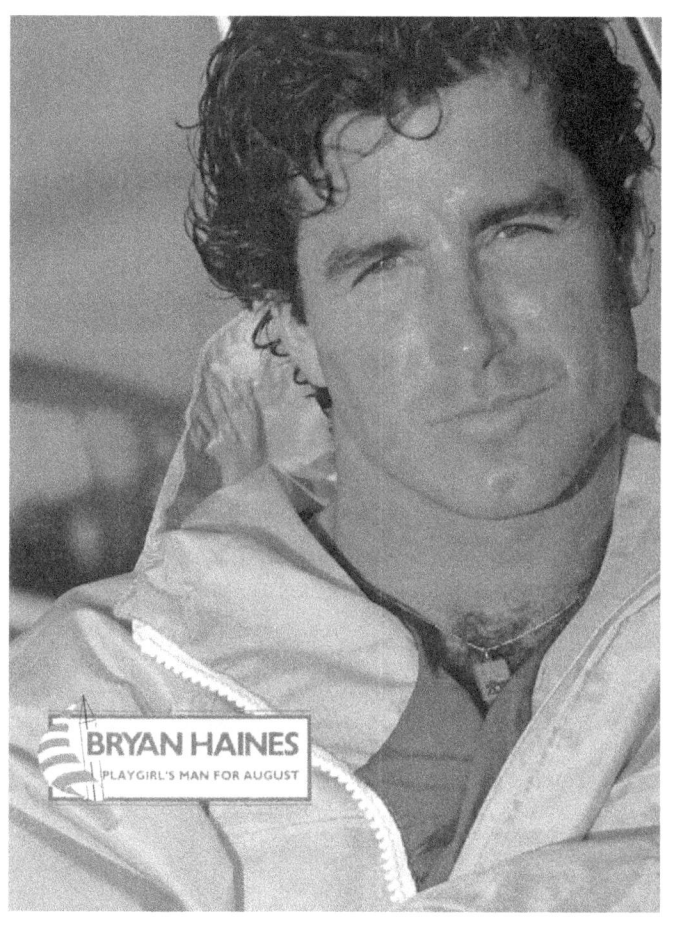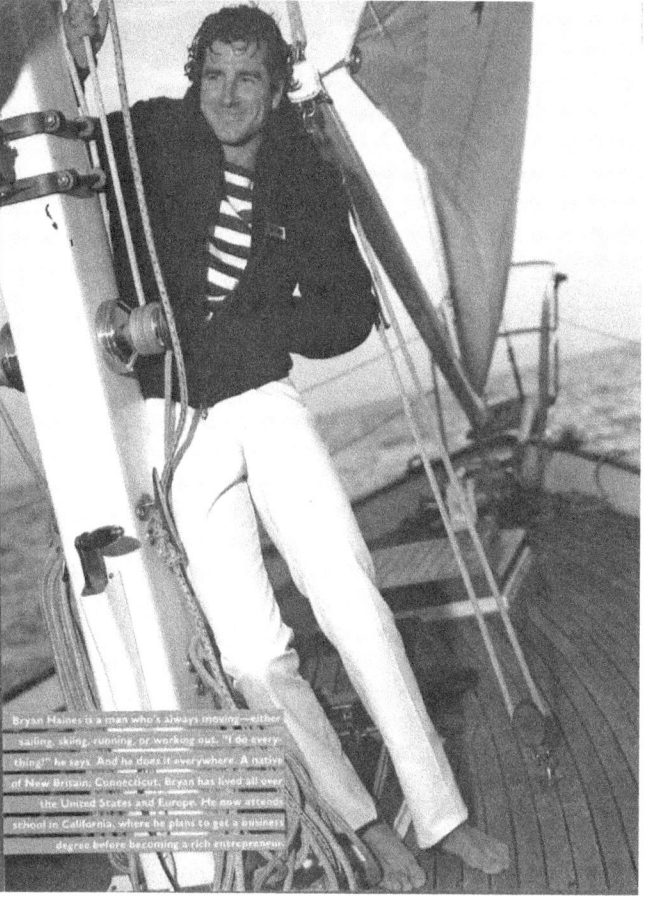

Performed in the New York touring company of Tubstrip. Performed as a stripper and held the title of Mr. Club Baths in 1973. By 1981 when modeling for *Playgirl*, he had lost his definition and sprouted a carpet of curly hair over his torso. (*Gay Erotic Video Index*)

PRESS REVIEWS 6

WANTED: BILLY THE KID, currently playing at the Adonis, focuses on a week in the life of Billy (Dennis Walsh), a young, good-looking and resourceful, but not especially gifted actor who has parlayed his theatrical instincts, his need for money and his sexuality into a successful part-time career as a hustler with a regular, somewhat select clientele. When he is not going to auditions, rehearsing with his actress-friend Karen (Megan Ross) or toning his body in a program of running, gymnastics and Tai Chi, Billy is pursuing his second career with all the devotion and inventiveness he brings to his first.

Among Billy's clients are a British businessman (Crompton Payne); Brian (John Meyers), a photographer with a visceral way of relating to his subjects ("I want to fuck with my camera."); Angelo (Peter Thadliski), a surly apartment building superintendent with a secret identity; Moses (Darc Traid), a client whose interests are athletic ("I like to work up a sweat behind some dude."); Mark (Ron Leigh), a suburban teenager who procures Billy's services for his rites of passage; Beverly (Rene) and Doug (John Tyme), an enlightened married couple in search of the ultimate ménage; Dr. Richard (Larry Marsland), a kinky dentist; and an unidentified nightly telephone caller who fashions elaborately obscene monologues for Billy's benefit and keeps him on a monthly retainer.

From his telephone answering machine to his unusual monthly arrangement with his landlord, Billy has organzed his existence to suit his needs beyond the financial. His sexual encounters have intrigue and imagination, and his actor's ego is satisfied by the variety of roles which he gets to perform. Yet, by the time the week is over, the fabric of Billy's sexual identity begins to unravel, causing him to leave New York and his new-found profession – temporarily?

*Moose 100, *Michael's Thing*

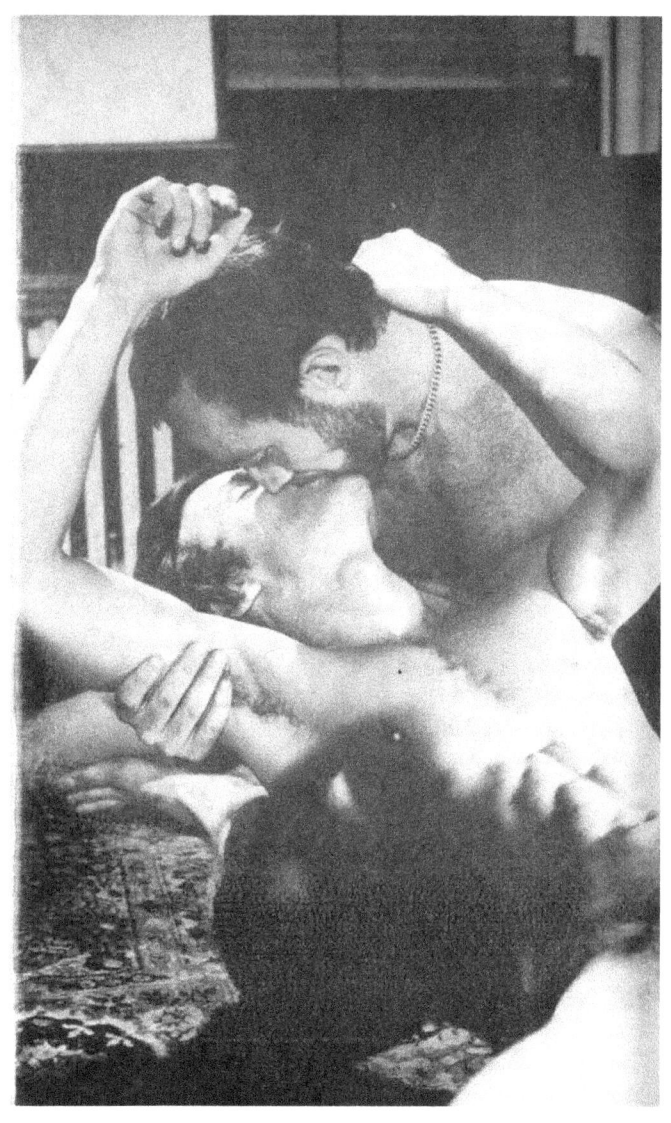

Still from *Wanted - Billy the Kid*
(Photo by Frank Ross)

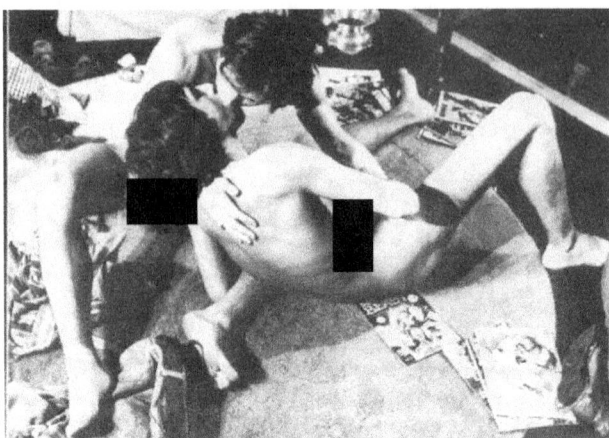

Billy helps Mark come out in Mark's parent's suburban Long Island home while his parents are whooping it up at the Concord.

For Billy it's all in a day's work.

Photos by Frank Loscalzo

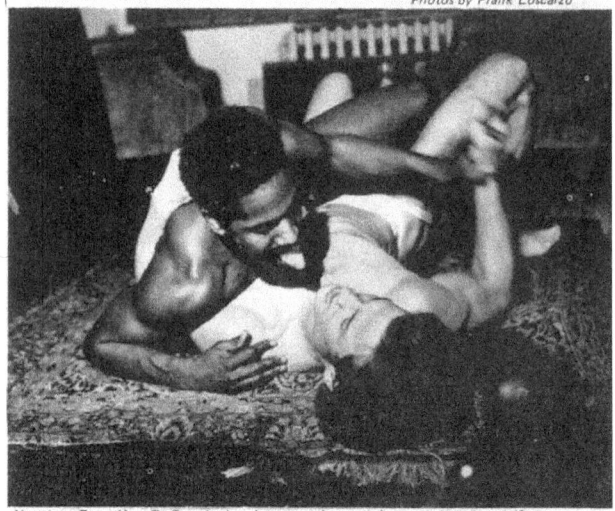

Not since *From Here To Eternity* has the screen shown such stormy love scenes. If you think this shot is hot, wait until you catch the flick and see what they do in the shower.

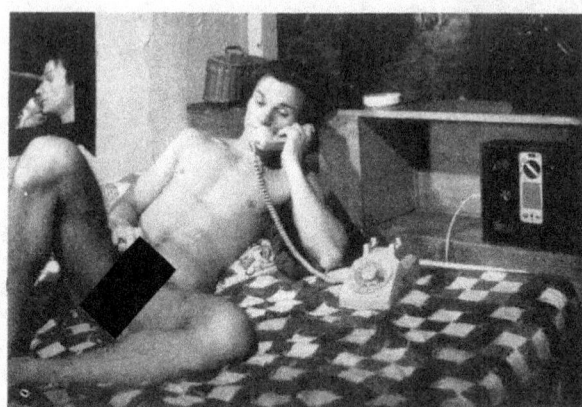

It's an easy way to make money. Billy (Dennis Walsh) gets paid to talk dirty over the phone to an anonymous caller. The Phone Mate on the shelf proves to be a callboy's best friend.

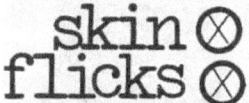

Wanted: Billy The Kid, currently playing at the Adonis, focuses on a week in the life of Billy (Dennis Walsh), a young, good-looking and

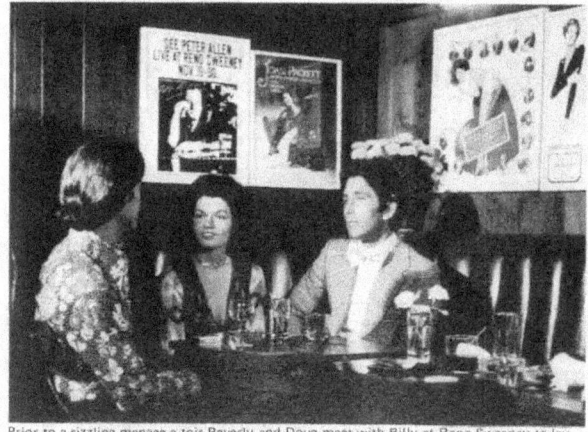

Prior to a sizzling menage a tois Beverly and Doug meet with Billy at Reno Sweeney to lay down the evening's ground rules.

Whenever we take a trip down memory lane with a Jack Deveau film, we are struck over and over again by his genius. Deveau and his New York-based Hand In Hand empire chronicled the birth of freewheeling mansex during the Swinging Seventies in Manhattan. Taking full advantage of all that the sin capital of the world had to offer, Deveau was unique in that he possessed full knowledge of the art of cinema, and at the same time was an expert at capturing unapologetic sex. Sometimes tender and often ferocious, the Deveau style was always in-your-face. Many of his films will forever be ranked as classics, and all are at least worth a look.

The 1976 WANTED: BILLY THE KID tells the tale of a young actor named Billy (Dennis Walsh) who earns his bread and butter by hustling. Toward the end of the film, a trick says to Walsh, "As an object, you are the great American jackoff fantasy." Truer words could not be found to describe the dazzling Walsh. Long and lean, with natural tone, a dark mop of hair, a mushroom-capped cock sprouting from a forest of pubes, and deep pensive eyes that speak louder than any words, he acts and fucks with breathtaking aplomb. Think a young, dreamy Joe Dallesandro with a touch of Ryan Idol and a dash of Tony Ward, and you have the picture. Gentle and gruff, tough and tender, he is (to coin a phrase) flesh made fantasy.

The story opens with Walsh and a trick taking care of business. A quick shower and our star is off to a basement intrigue with Angelo the janitor (Peter Thadiaski). What follows in this dank cellar is an almost mythic power play between the beautiful, leather-jacketed Walsh and the luggish, uncut, horse-hung Thadiaski. Walsh lubes the janitor's butthole with an oil can, and the handy man does him one better by greasing Walsh with all-purpose machine goo and fucking him across a ladder. After multiple climaxes, the real identity of the janitor is revealed, and we become aware of the game that has just been played. Next, we see Walsh on the streets of New York, in the gym working out, and at last, back home for a session of phone sex. As the vice on the line purrs its sexual agenda, Walsh snaps open a popper and floats off to a thunderous jizz-blast.

Subsequently, several more days-in-the-life scenes are played out. From a bathtub suckfest with a black dude, to a druggy adventure with his dentist (replete with nitrous gas and a dildo), to multiple meetings with an obsessed photographer, Walsh has the chameleon-like ability to change, yet remain the same. Hired by a young man to introduce him to the ways of gay sex, Walsh is the understanding teacher. Employed by a kinky, straight couple to provide service, he is the consummate sex machine, totally comfortable fucking the husband while the wife watches. He kisses, he sucks, he fucks and gets fucked – and through it all remains a masculine objet d'art. With an articulate and thought-provoking script by Moose 100 and Shadow, and with sharp production values and crisp editing by Robert Alvarez, this film still impresses after twenty years. Timeless, trippy, transcendental, profane, profound, and passionate, WANTED: BILLY THE KID, starring the staggering Dennis Walsh, is a must see event.

*P.R., *Manshots*

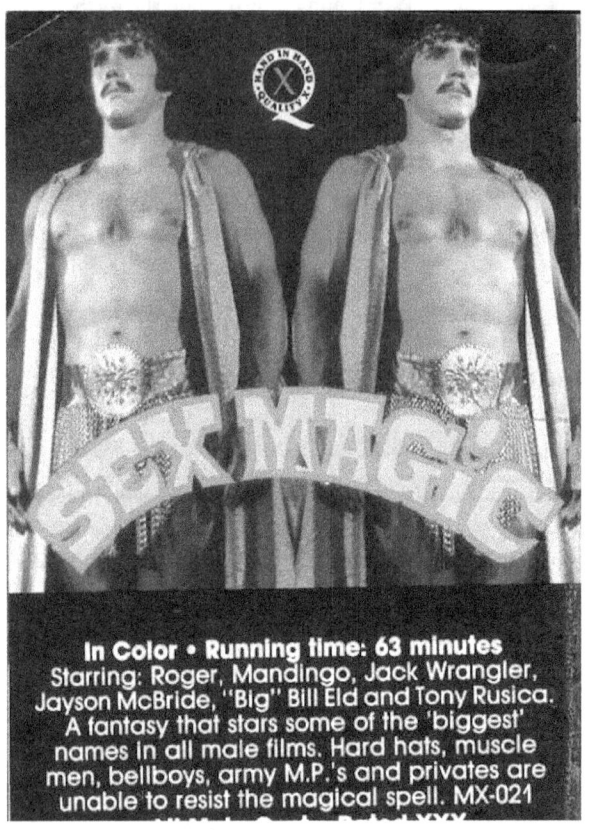

One of the most talked about films Hand In Hand has ever made is SEX MAGIC. And it's no wonder, since two of the "biggest" new names in all-male films, Jack Wrangler and Roger, lead the cast along with Mandingo, "Big" Bill Eld, and Jayson MacBride. That makes sixty inches of cock alone! But there's more, the sensuous boyish looks of Tony Rusica and Lee Foster; plus the only movie appearance of the demanding Tom Trooper. Yes, SEX MAGIC is one of those rare films where the cast is everything. Everything you ever dreamed you wanted. This is the good hot stuff you expect and get from Hand In Hand Productions. SEX MAGIC is a modern day version of Aladdin and his magic lamp. An enchanted ring, discovered by Bo (Roger) on his construction job, is the beginning of an adventure into fantasies with "straight men," turned gay by the ring's "spell" and it's possessors wishful thinking. From then on all sexual hell breaks loose as successively a bellboy and an a.w.o.l. army private become the ring's master. Mr. L.A. ("Big" Bill Eld) is seduced by the wanton Bellhop (Lee Foster); army private Cliff (Tony Rusica) gets his secret fantasies fulfilled by two MP's (Jayson MacBride and Tom Trooper) and Bo gets the best of it, balling with his straight co-worker Valdez (Mandingo) and his fantasy Window Washer (Jack Wrangler). SEX MAGIC leaves no holds barred! Everyone gets it and gives it. Construction workers, muscle men, army MP's, bellboys and army privates are unable to resist the spell cast by SEX MAGIC. It will certainly cast its spell on you and any hot "number" you want to cast your spell on!

*Hand in Hand Promo

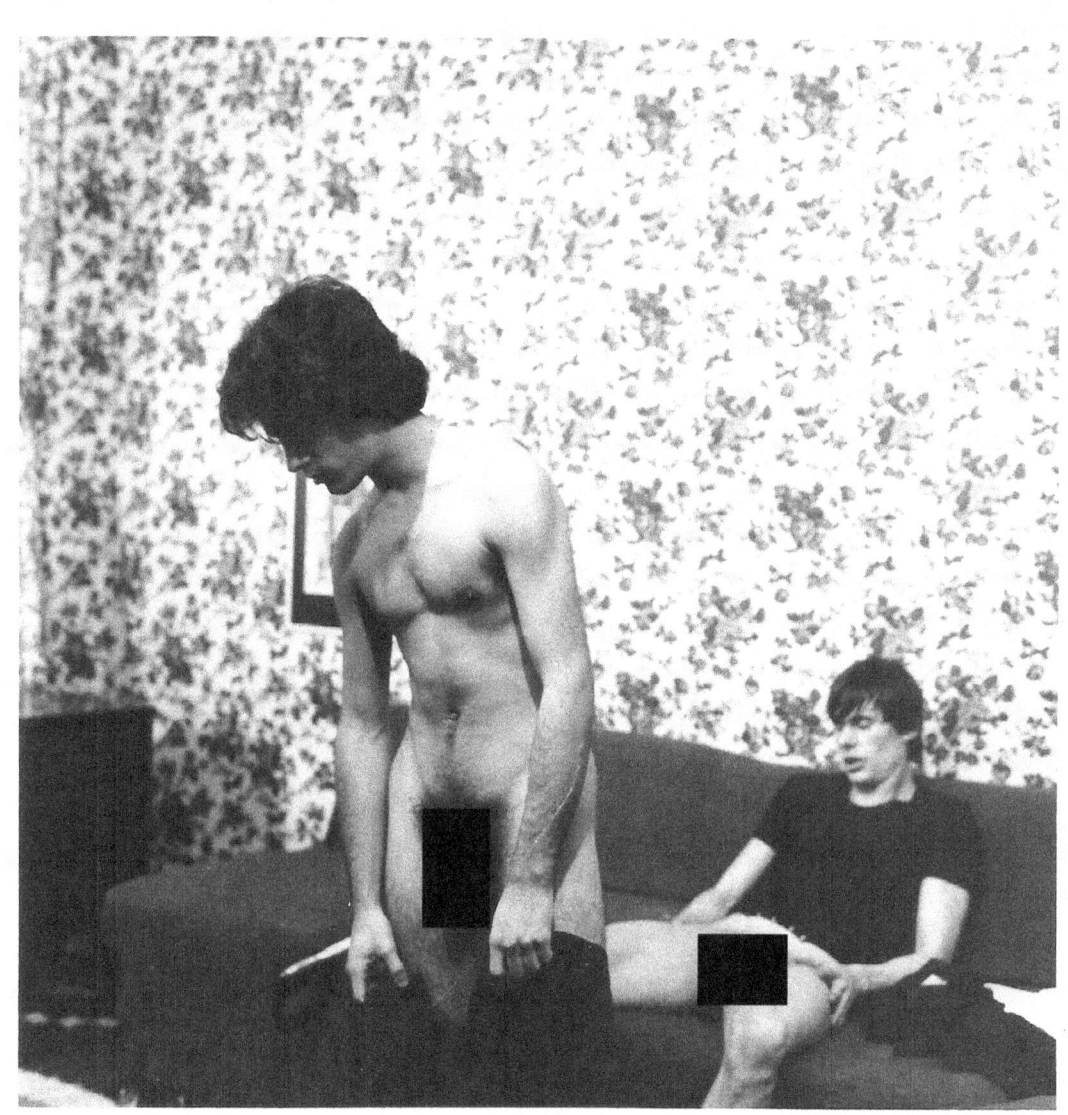

Bellhop (Lee Foster) gets ready for "bottoms up" in the Bellhop Meets the Body Builder scene in *Sex Magic*

JACK WRANGLER and ROGER in

SEX MAGIC

WHO COULD ASK FOR ANYTHING MORE?

with MANDINGO • BIG BILL ELD • JASON MacBRIDE
and introducing new star
TOM TROOPER
X-RATED • COLOR • ALL MALE CAST
A HAND IN HAND FILM

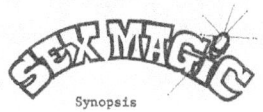

Synopsis

At the height of the ancient Egyptian Empire, the young and spectacularly endowed KING ORSOKON II (Roger) honors Bastet, the goddess of fertility. Deep within a private chamber of the temple, KING ORSOKON II uses his royal hand and cock to honor Bastet. Well pleased with the young King's tribute, Bastet rewards him by transmuting his flowing cum into a silver ring, a ring endowed with a special magic. Whoever puts the ring on his finger immediately realizes the height of sexual pleasure with his chosen one.

New York, in the present, BO, a young Con Edison worker, [Roger (again)] discovers the ring in the excavation in which he is working with VALDEZ (Mandingo). BO has just about given up on ever getting next to the straight VALDEZ, but when he puts on the ring, VALDEZ suddenly "comes on" to him fulfilling the magic prophecy.

Returning from work and a heavy sex scene with VALDEZ, BO finds the sex cassette he ordered from The Advocate has arrived. BO makes himself comfortable in the living room and puts on the cassette. He plays with the ring, which is a bit big, as the cassette ("THE WINDOW WASHER") begins to play. BO can't explain why, (he has sniffed a popper), but when he turns to the window,

Jack Wrangler, in full gear, is strapped to his window, washing it and playing with his cock in the pail of soapy water, rubbing it on the window. BO and the WINDOW WASHER get down on BO's big easychair. During the ensuing duo, the ring slips off BO's finger and falls out of the window, landing on the street.

On the street, CLIFF (Tony Rusica) sees the ring fall, picks it up, tries it on, and walks off. In his room in the Howard Johnson Motor Hotel, CLIFF makes himself a drink and telephones his mother, a child psychologist in Grosse Point, Michigan, to tell her that he's A.W.O.L. from the Army. Then he tells her why. Two M.P.s had been hanging around him, buying him beers, insinuating things. He knew that if he didn't get out of there, he would have "come out" with the M.P.s. His mother accepts this bombshell with utter srenity, thinks he should "come out" if he wants to, and is glad that he won't be marrying his bland sub-deb fiancee. The telephone call is interupted by pounding on the hotel room door. The ring, which CLIFF has been toying with throughout the scene, has come through again. The two uniformed M.P.s come in and show CLIFF where it's at.

Later, as he is leaving the hotel, CLIFF has second thoughts and leaves the ring on the hotel night table.

The BELLHOP (Lee Foster) comes in with the luggage of the room's new occupant and spots the ring. He quickly pockets it. The new hotel guest turns out to be MR.L.A. (Big Bill Eld), a bodybuilder who's come to town for the Ironpumper's Ball. The BELLHOP would obviously like to jump immediately on MR. L.A., but there seems to be no way.

Alone in the hotel pantry, the BELLHOP takes out the ring he has "lifted" from MR. L.A.'s room, examines it, and slips it on his finger. Immediately the room service phone rings. The BELLHOP is surprised to hear the voice of MR. L.A. requesting him to return to MR. L.A.'s room.

When the BELLHOP enters the room, he is even more surprised to find MR. L.A. glistening with sweat, lifting weights in a rubber tanksuit. MR. L.A. is suddenly very approachable, and the BELLHOP approaches him, with obvious consequences; the ring has worked its magic again.

Later, back in the pantry, the BELLHOP is preparing a dinner tray for a guest when the ring falls into a bowl of soup, unnoticed by the BELLHOP. He covers the tray and goes off to deliver it to a hotel guest named Mr. Deveau.

THE END

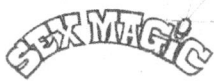

SIXTEEN MILLIMETER   COLOR / SOUND
RUNNING TIME: SIXTY - THREE MINUTES
X — RATING   ALL MALE CAST

CAST
(in order of appearance)

Narration	KEES CHAPMAN
King Orsokom II	ROGER
Bo	ROGER
Valdez	MANDINGO
Window Washer	JACK WRANGLER
Cliff	TONY RUSICA
Mrs. Lucille Sharmat	B. LACKEY
Sergeant No. 1	JASON MacBRIDE
Sergeant No. 2	TOM TROOPER
Bellhop	LEE FOSTER
Mister L.A.	BILL ELD

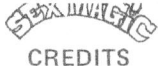

CREDITS

Director of Cinematography	JACK DEVEAU
Cameraman	KEES CHAPMAN
Makeup	GENE KELTON
Assistant to Mr. Kelton	JIM DELEGATTI
Key Grip	KEN SCHNETZER
Set Decoration	JIM DELEGATTI
Production Coordinator	SYDNEY SOONS
Sound Recordist	ROLF PARDULA
Mixer	KEES CHAPMAN
Written by	MOOSE 100
Editor	ROBERT ALVAREZ
Produced and Directed by	JACK DEVEAU

A Hand in Hand Films Production   ©MCMLXXVII

There are very few gay films that withstand the test of time and deserve to be called classics. SEX MAGIC, delivered to us by that superb filmman Jack Deveau, is one of those rare features that truly deserves the title. Roger, with his dominating masculinity and incredible endowment, overpowers you from the very beginning. This man has a sex magic all his own, and his sensual presence captures your attention and holds it until the very last dot of color disappears from your video screen. If you're looking for plot, look no further. The storyline has been weaved in with all the fast-paced sex scenes very smoothly and the result is a roaring turn-on. The music has been perfectly chosen, making everything on screen "come alive." SEX MAGIC is a fantasy film that works.

*John Mensior, *Torso*

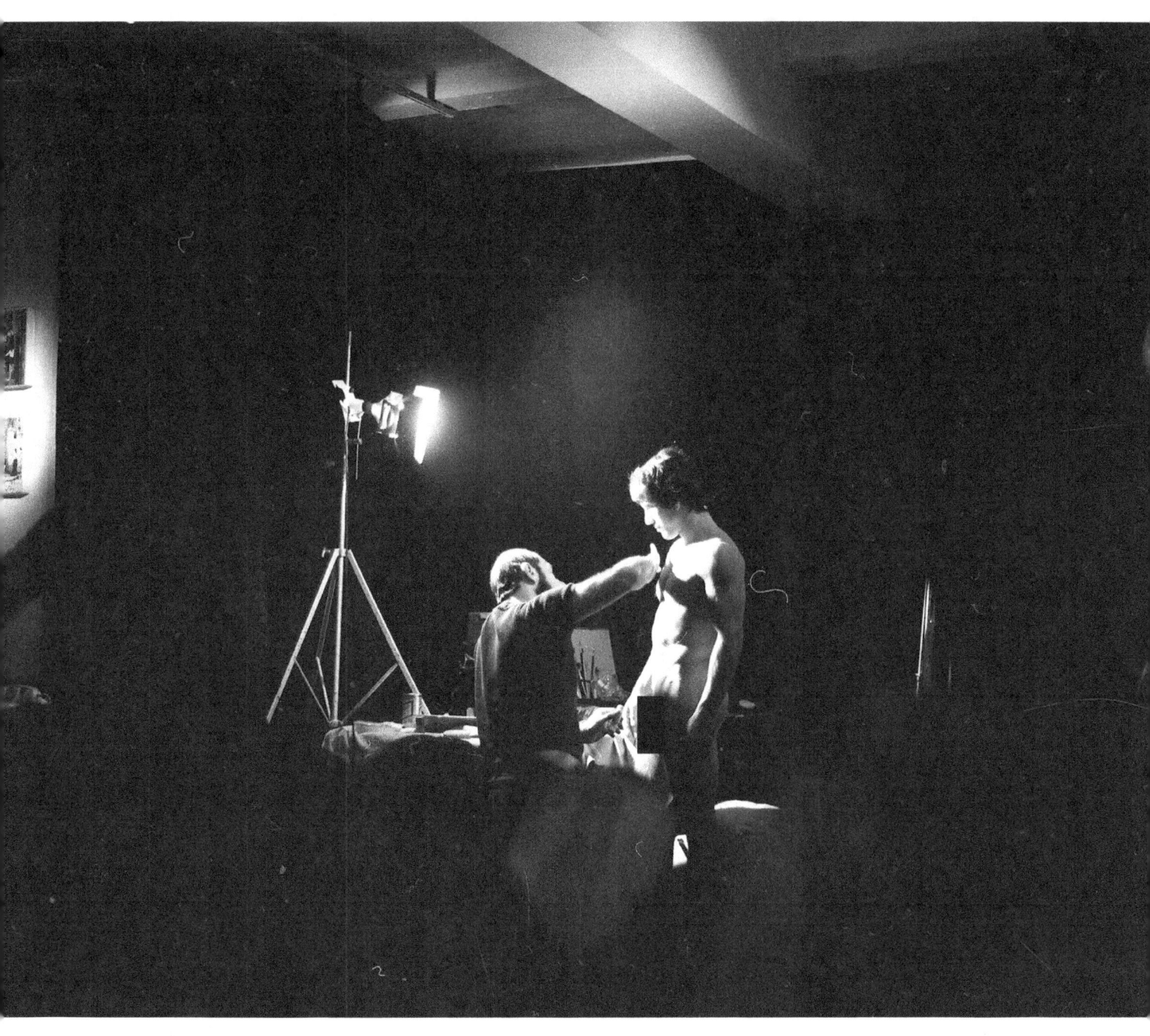

Gene Kelton (left) and Roger behind the scenes of *Sex Magic*

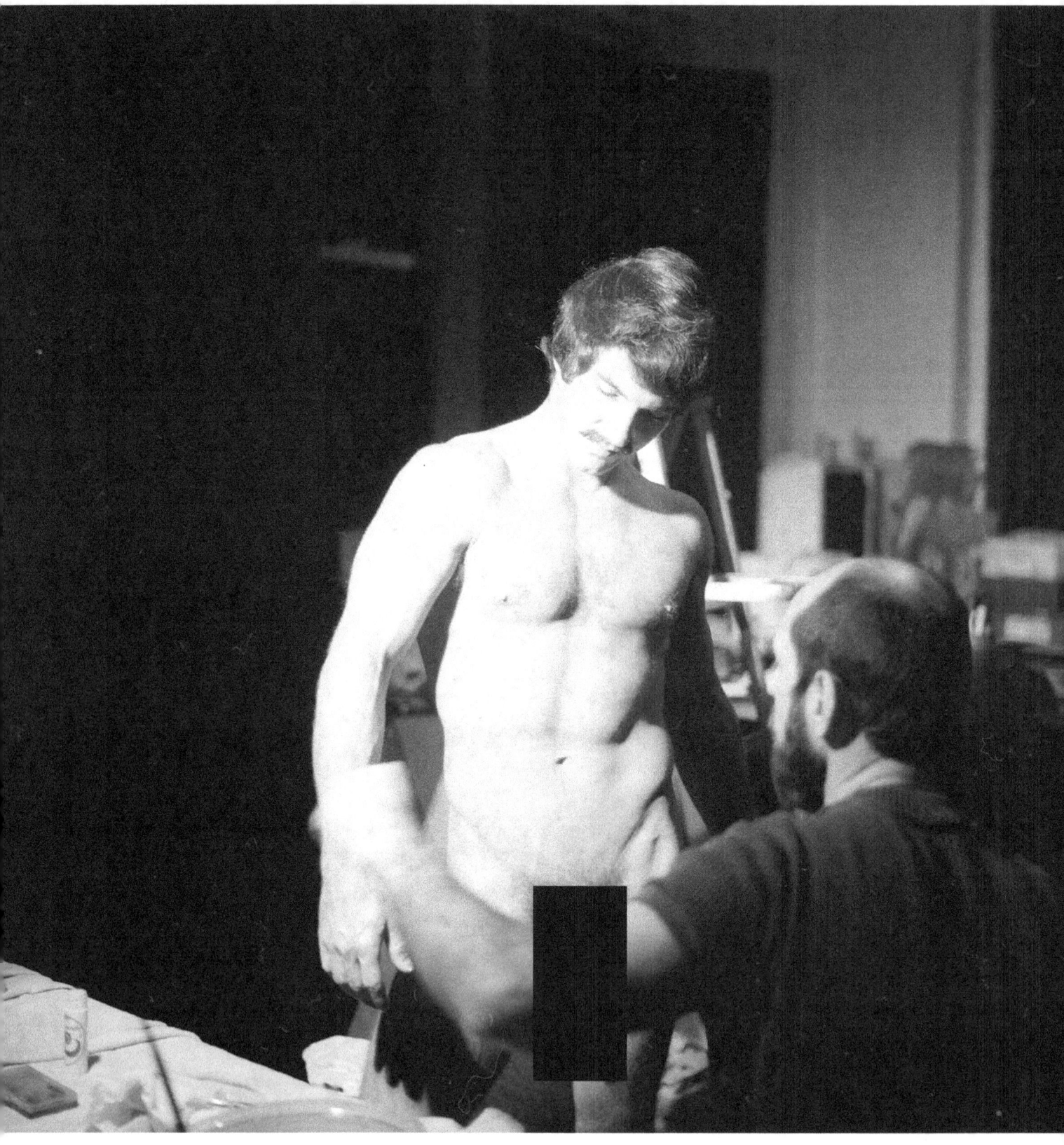

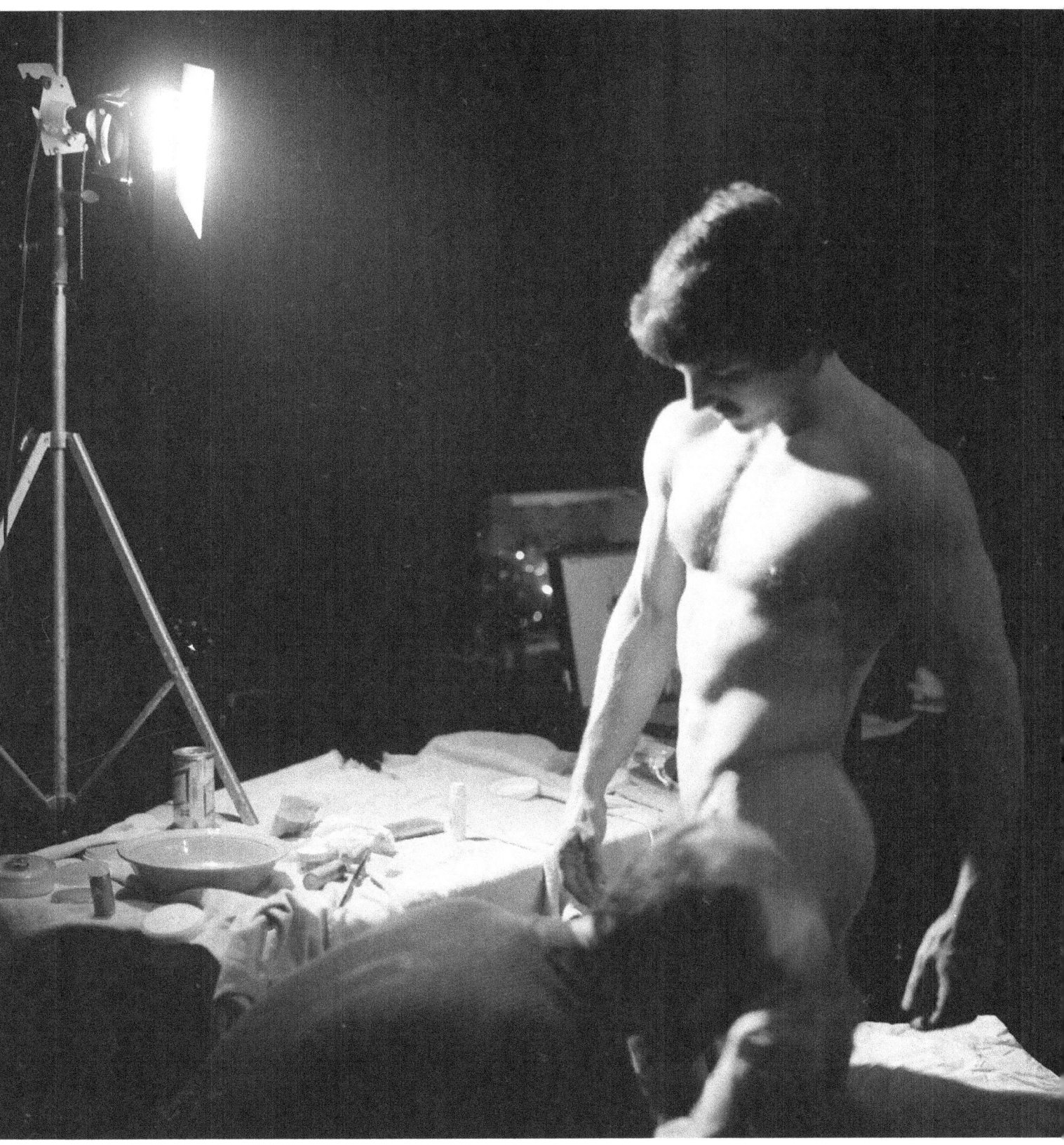

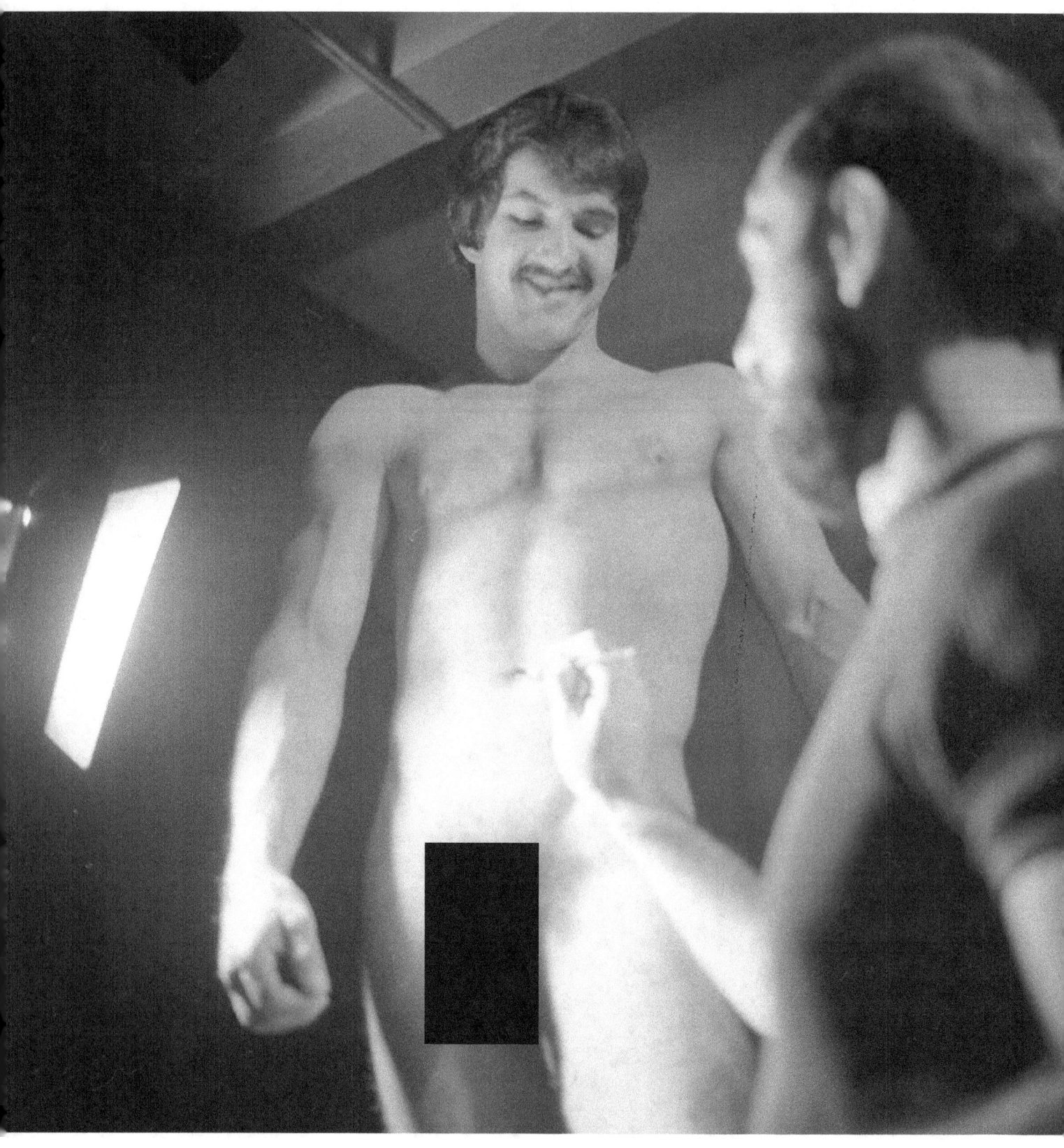

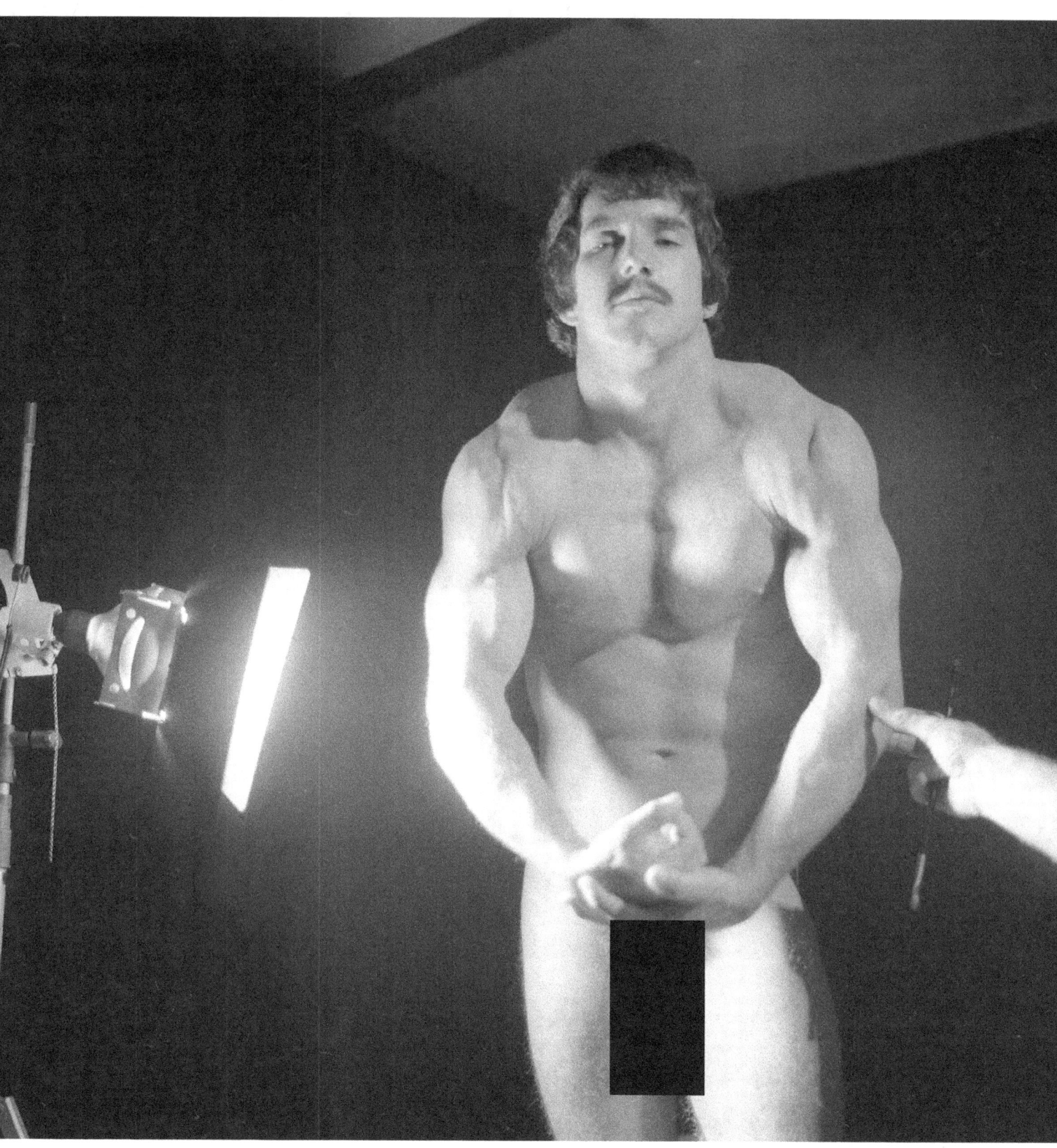

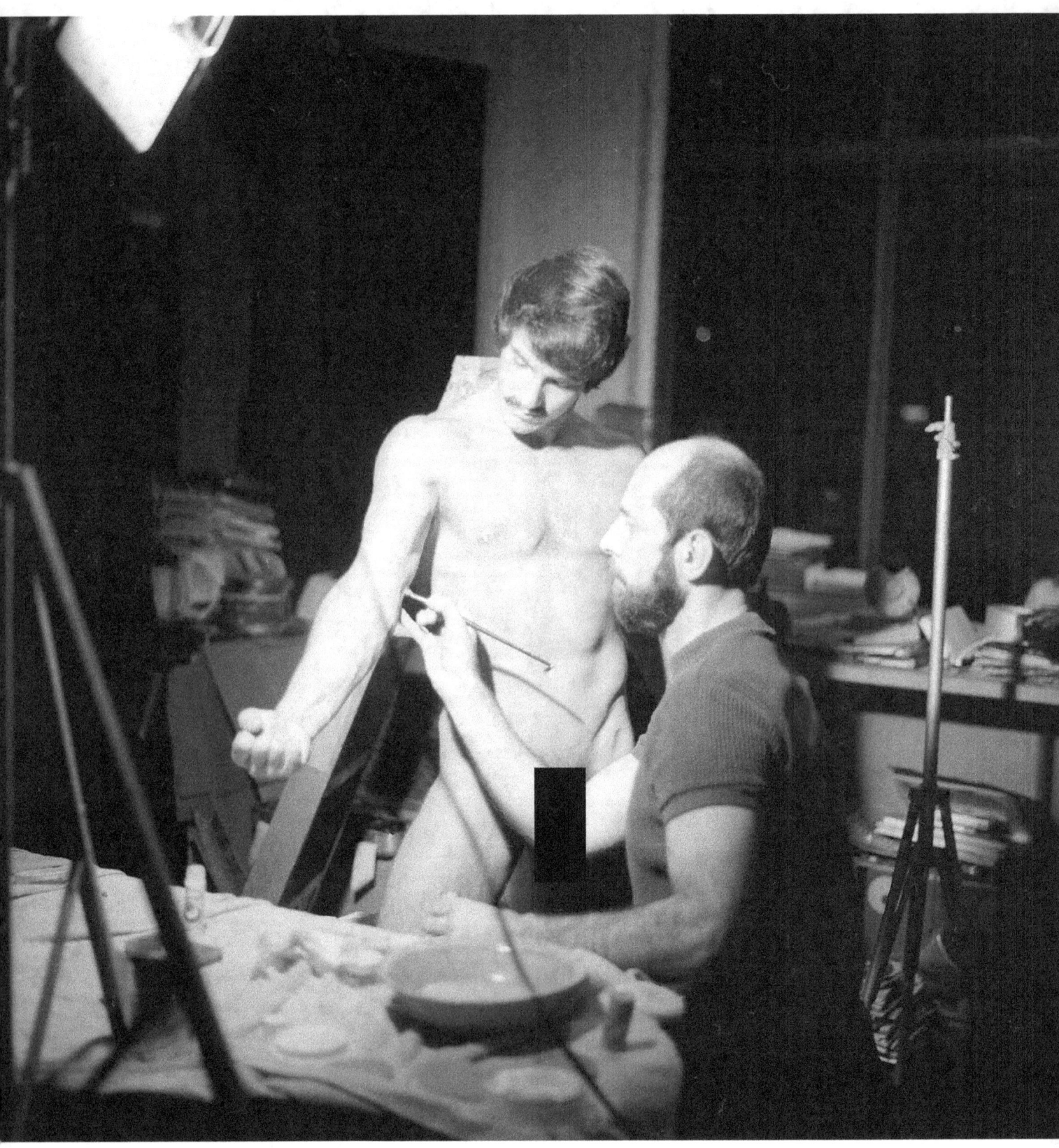

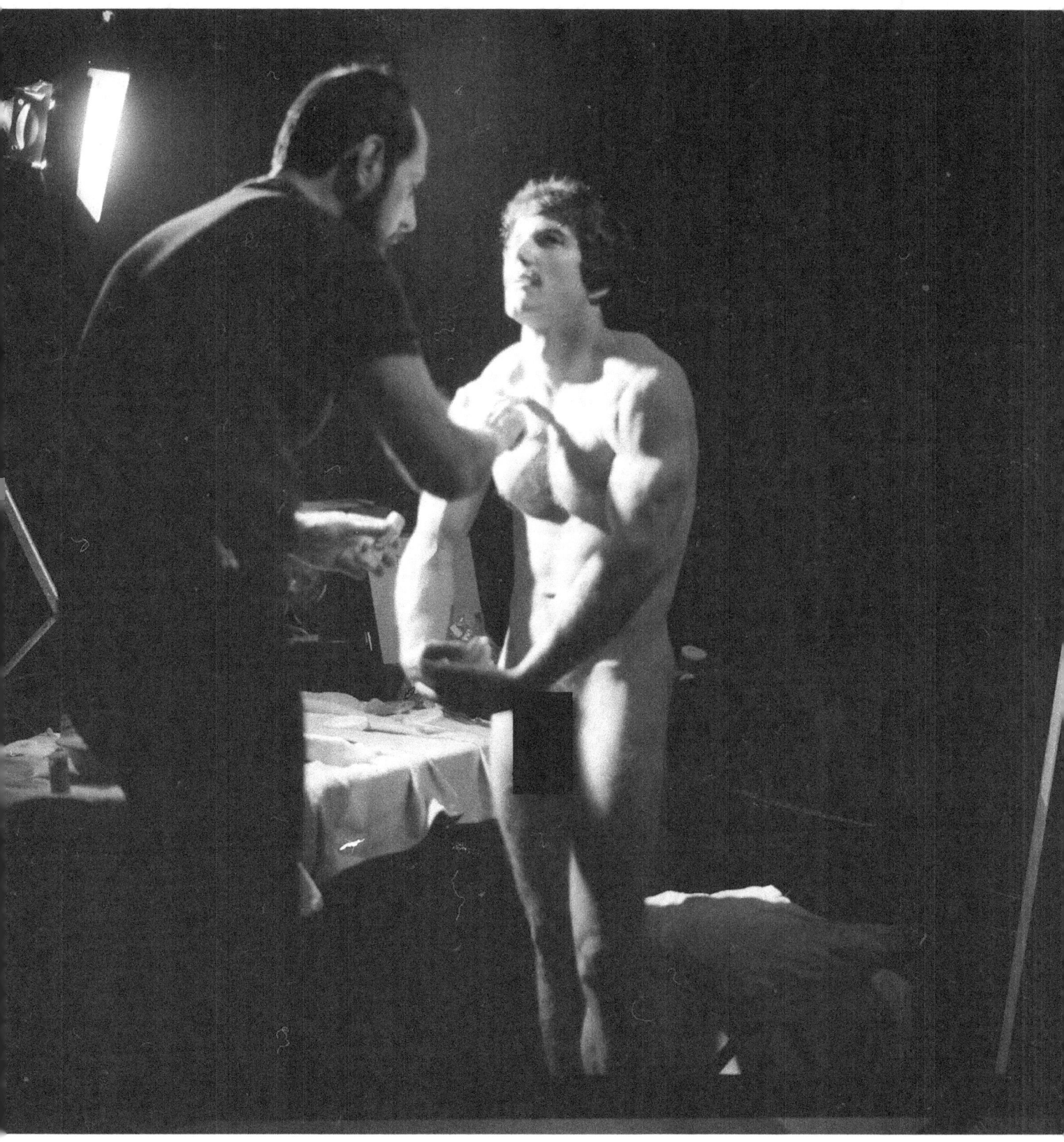

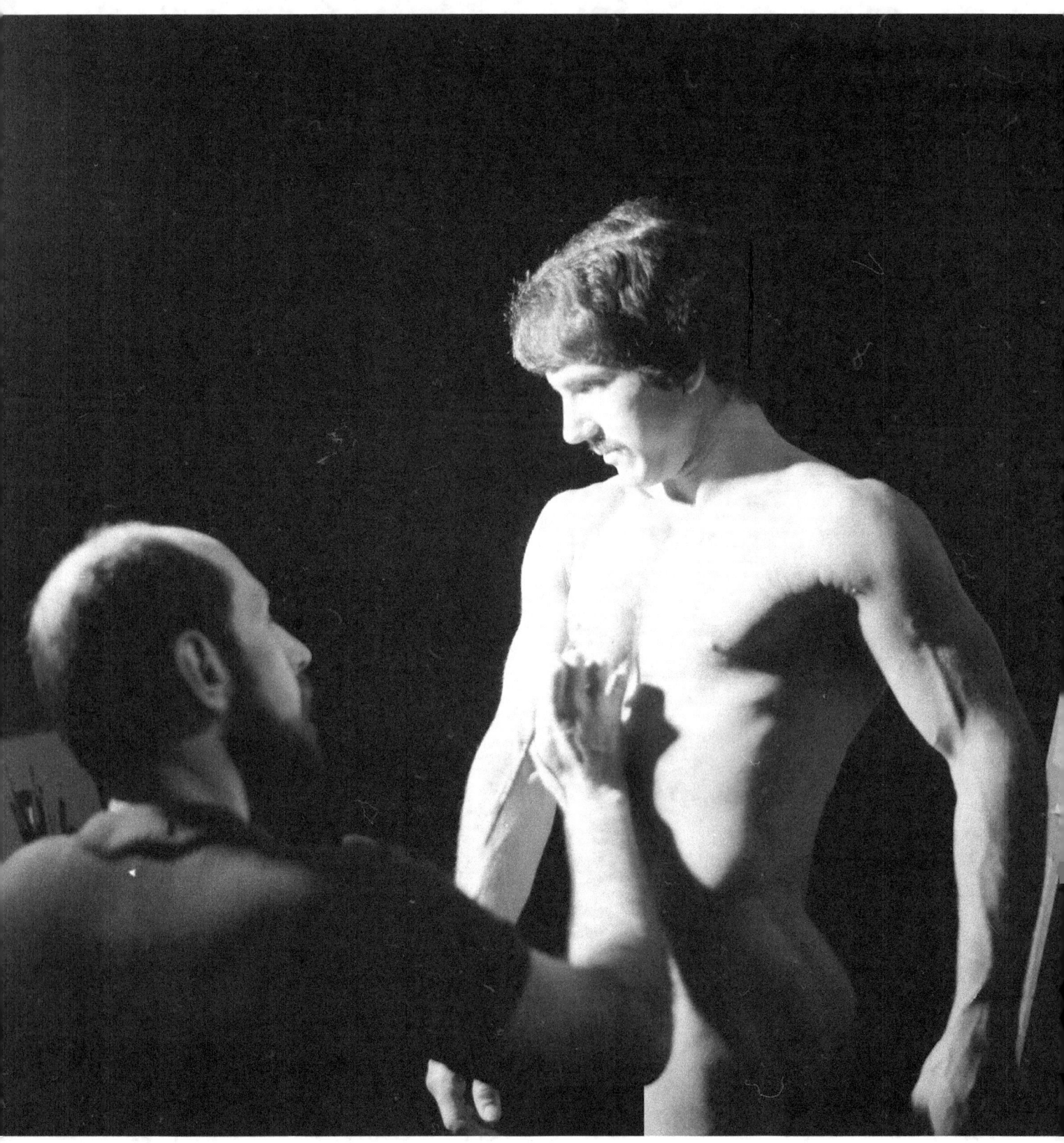

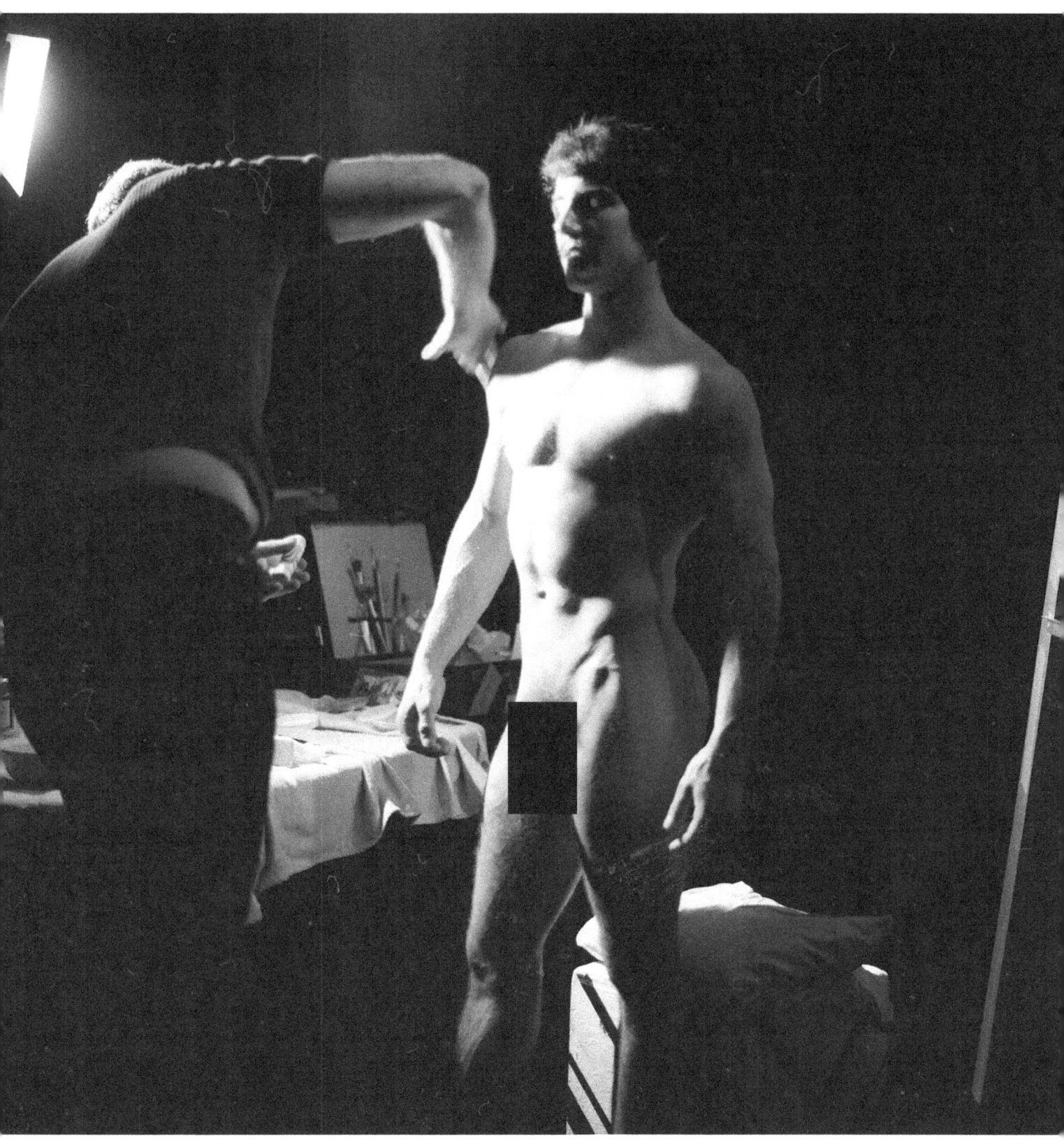

"I need a lot of love." **Roger**

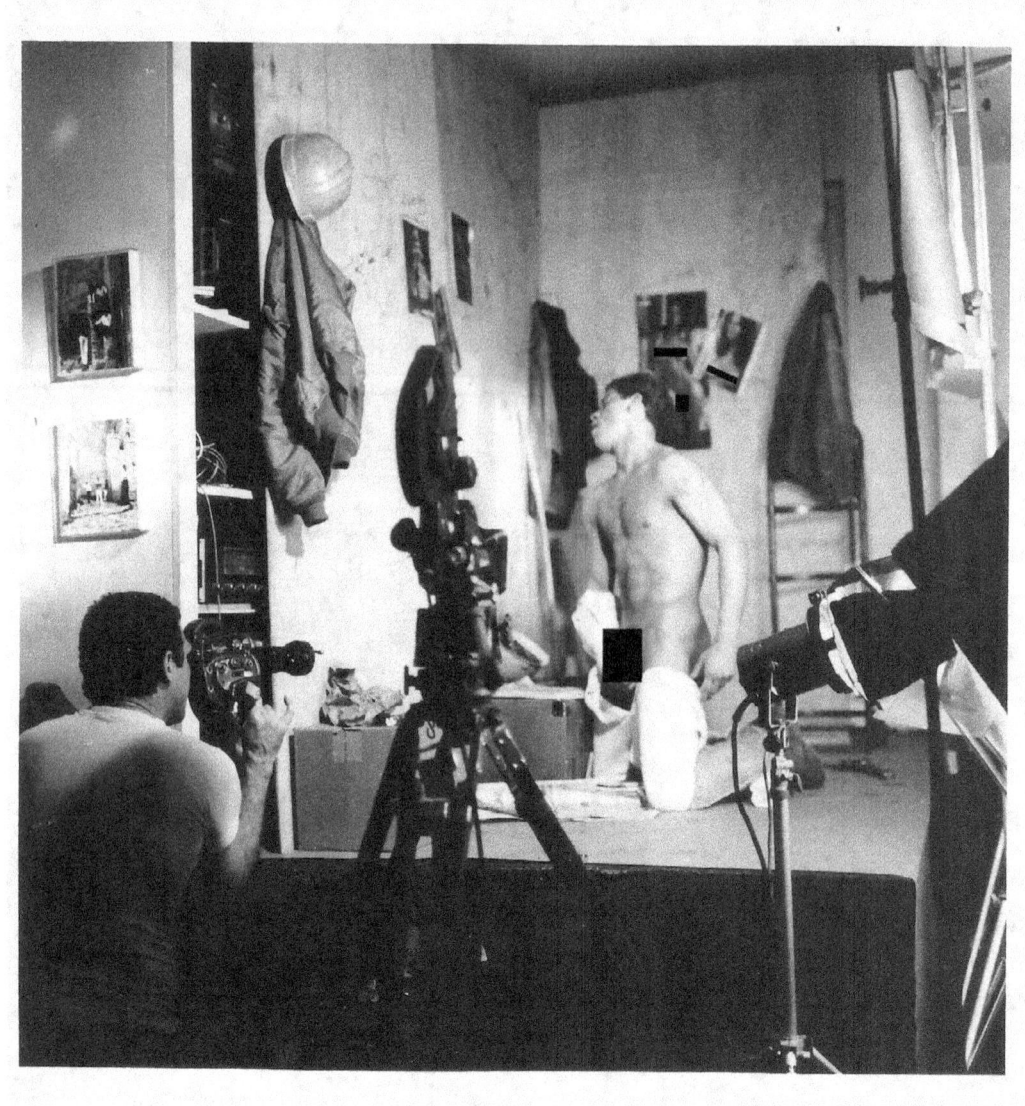

The climax of the construction worker scene seems to be no problem for the director, Jack Deveau (left) and Mandingo on the set of *Sex Magic*.

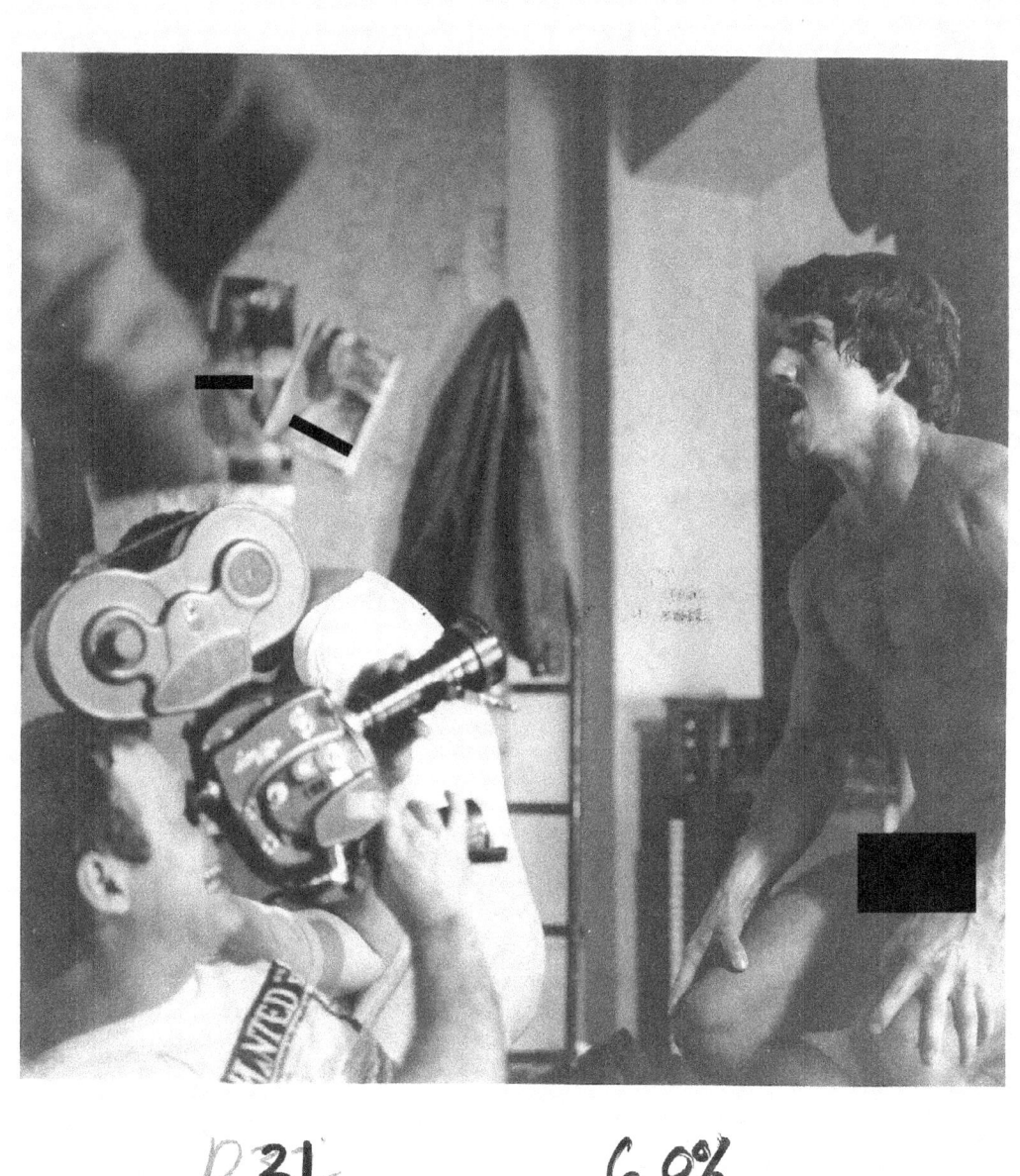

Jack Deveau and Roger shooting *Sex Magic*.

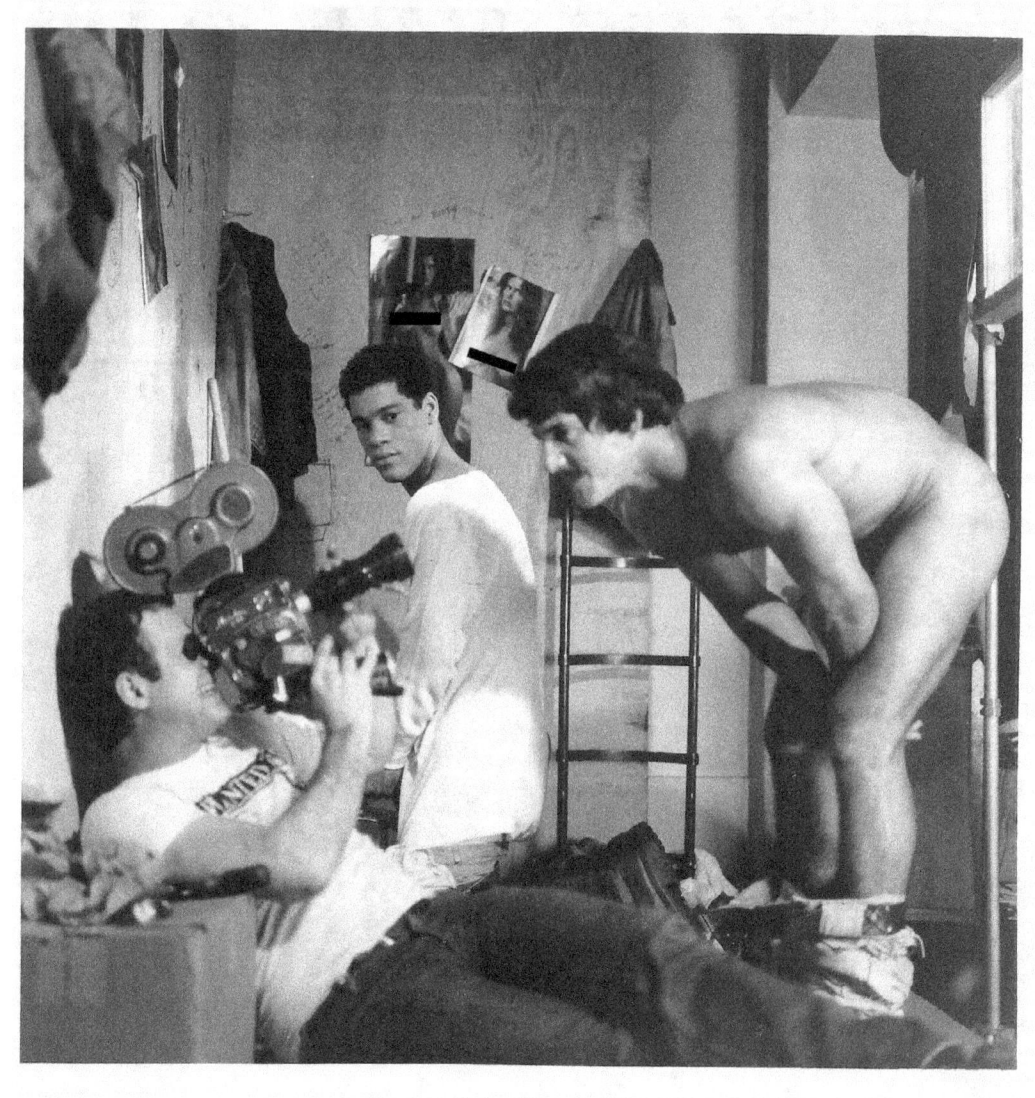

"I´m ready for my close up Mr. de Mille."
Jack Deveau, Mandingo and Roger

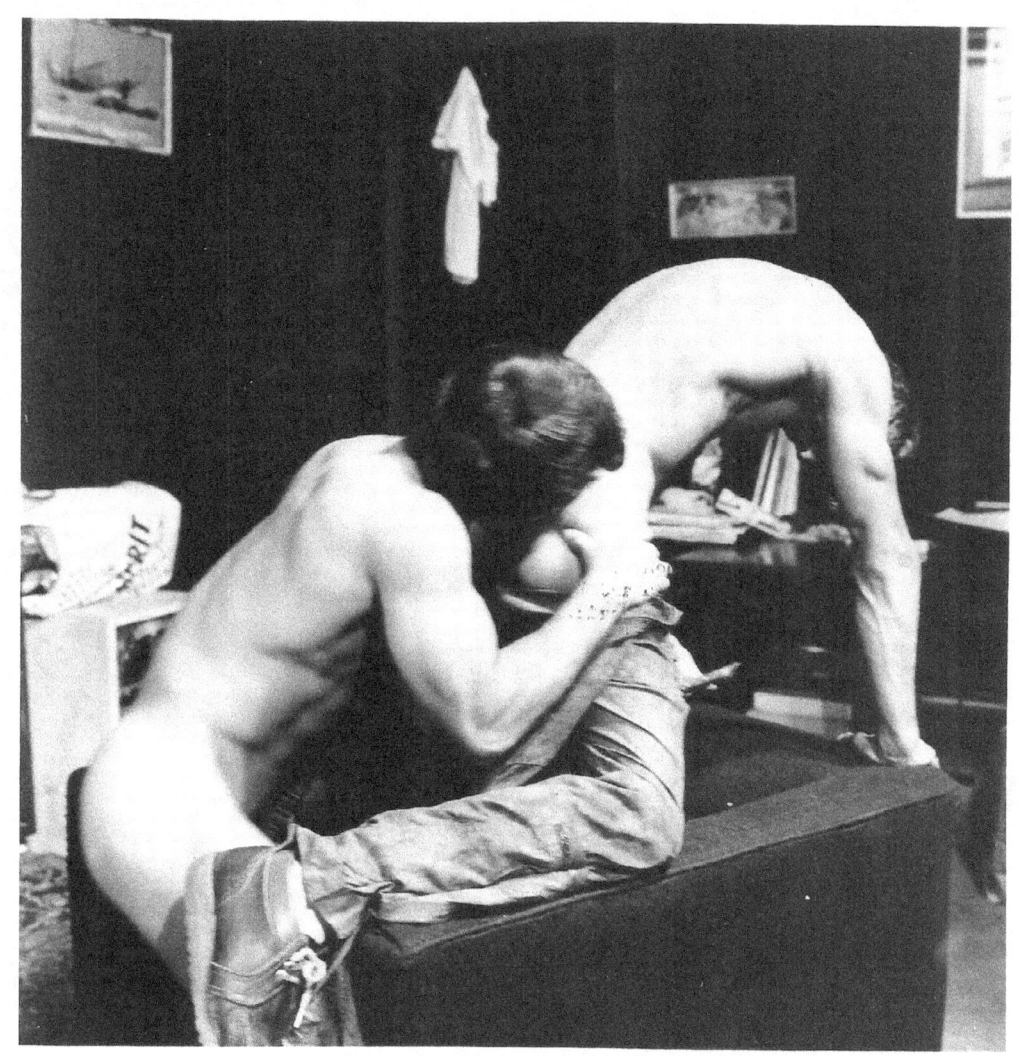

Roger (left) and Jack Wrangler performing in *Sex Magic*.

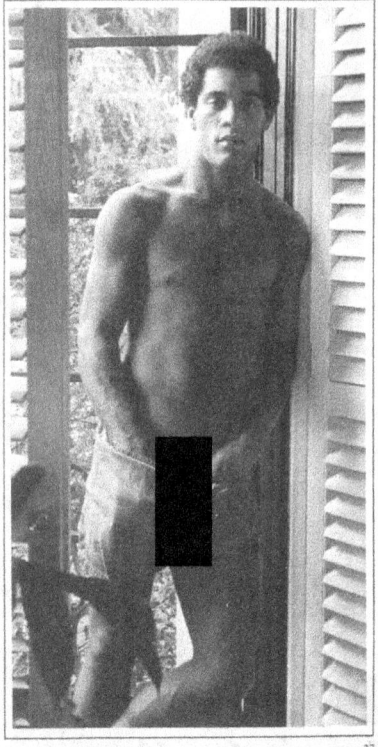
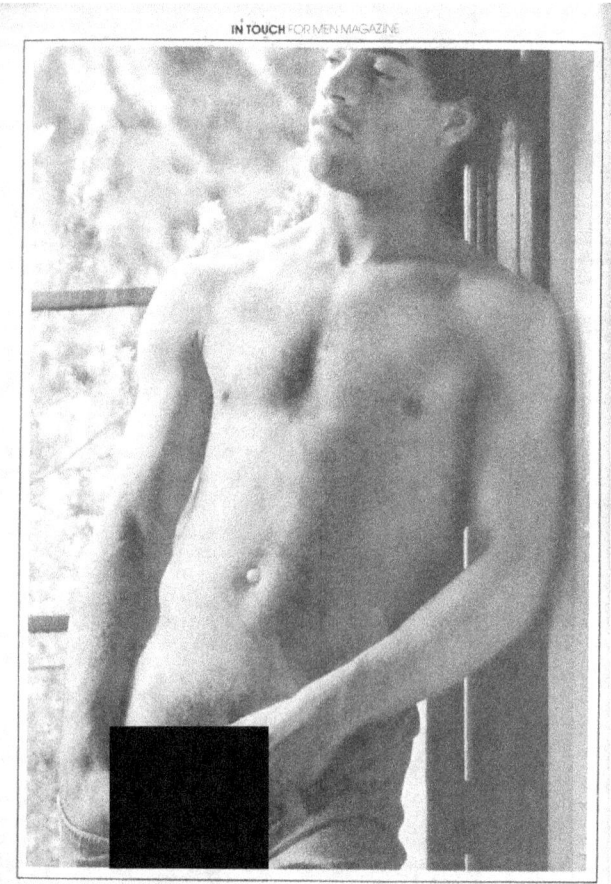

Mandingo aka Mark White

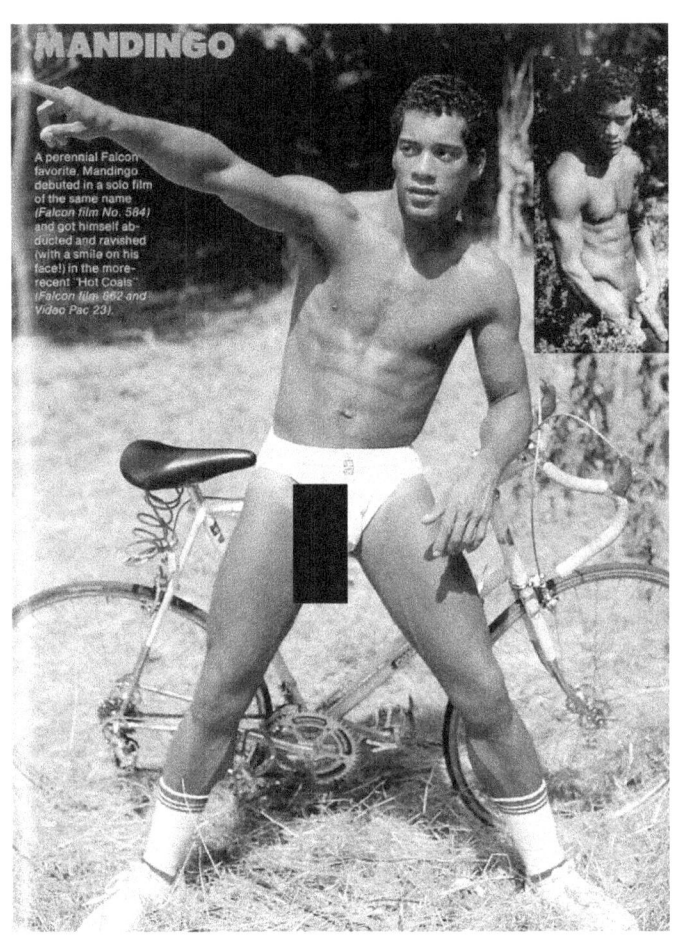

MANDINGO

A perennial Falcon favorite, Mandingo debuted in a solo film of the same name *(Falcon film No. 584)* and got himself abducted and ravished (with a smile on his face!) in the more-recent "Hot Coals" *(Falcon film 662 and Video Pac 23).*

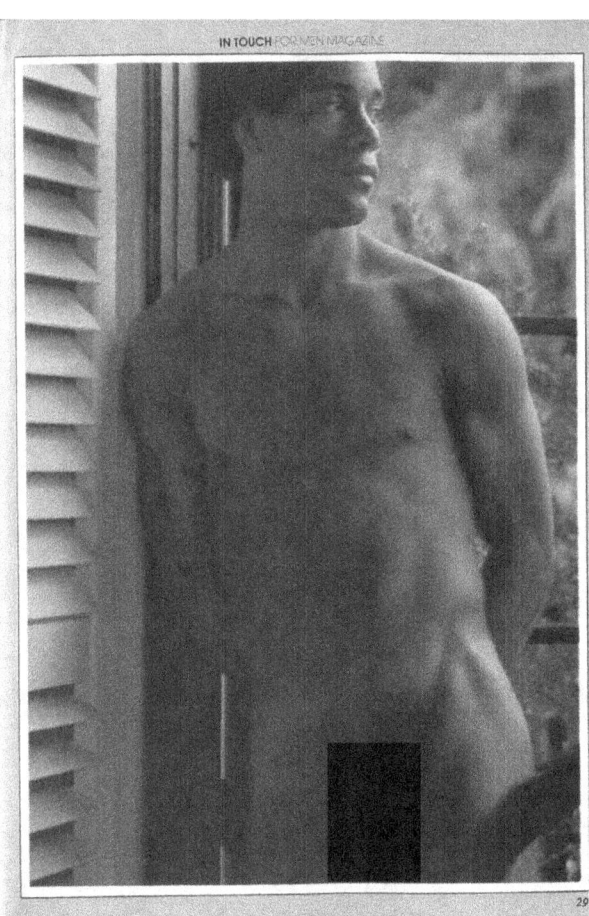

IN TOUCH FOR MEN MAGAZINE

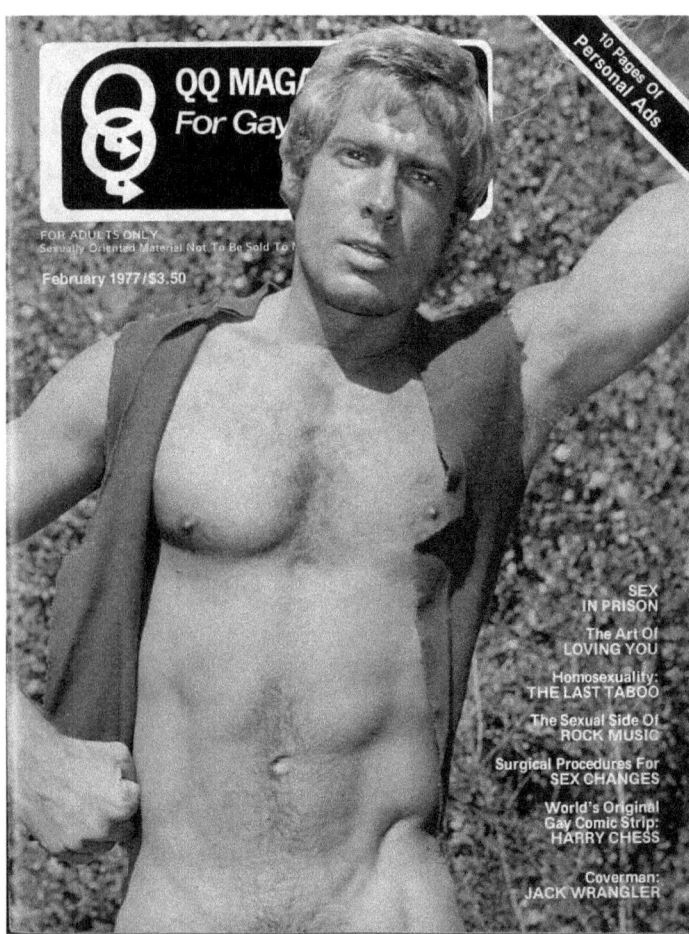 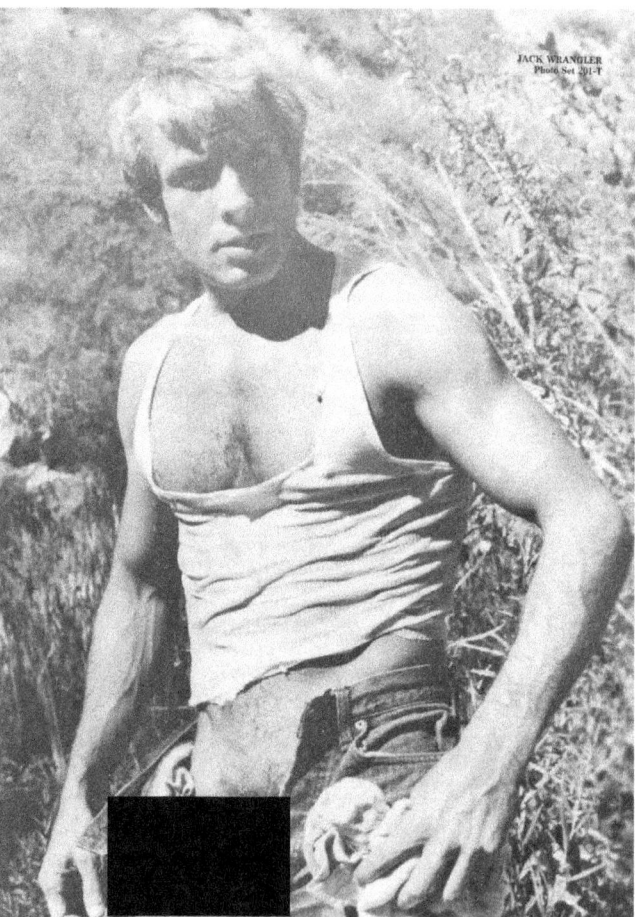

"It seems like forever and then some, but it's only been five years; however, in that short time, I've made eighty-eight features – not loops, features – posed for countless photo layouts, done over 900 performances of my Jack Wrangler – Exclamation Point live show, and done an Off-Broadway play. You might say I've been very high profile! Before I got into this, I was a star-system theatre director. I worked for seven years for the Windmill and County Dinner Theatres with people like Betty Hutton, Jane Russell, Yvonne de Carlo, Gale Storm, and Sal Mineo. Anything they did in theatre, I directed."

JACK WRANGLER

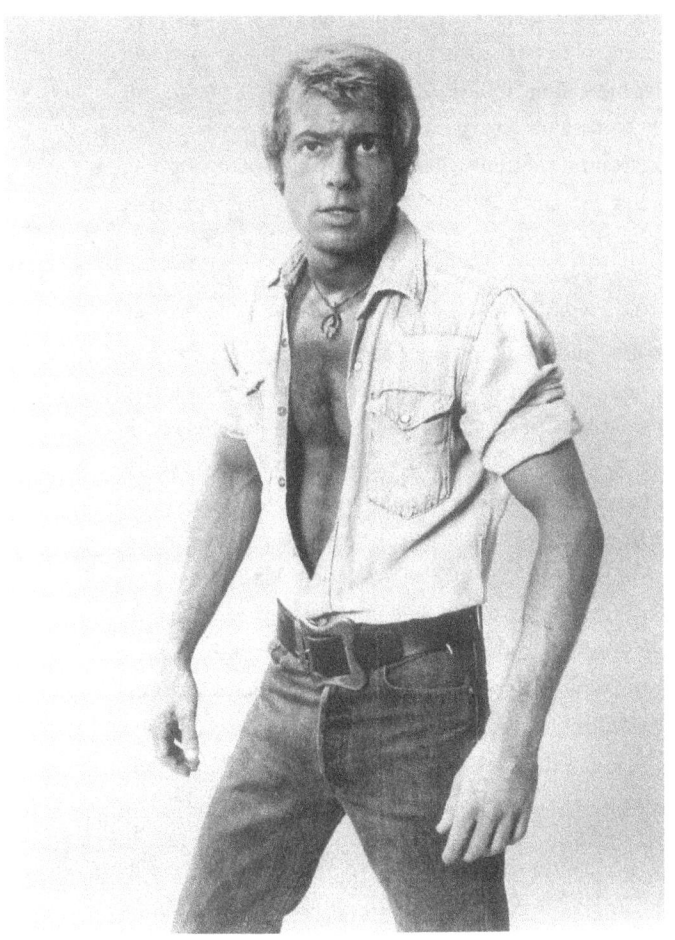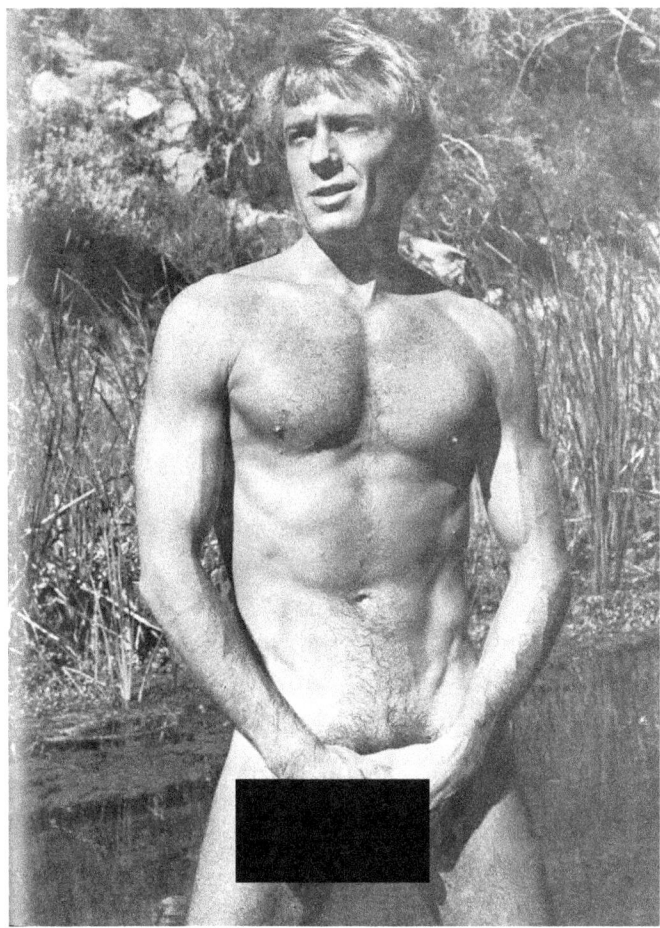

"Deveau is a brilliant man with a great sense of humor, but I just can't understand this! A long time ago when I was working for him, we were sitting on the set relaxing after a scene, and he said to me, 'Jack, I know you've got a plan, but I'll be damned if I can figure out what it is, but someday I'll find out what you're up to and why you did this.' I was never a hustler and never in the mold, and he couldn't see where I was going... I guess he still can't. I'm mystified about why people tear me down all the time now... maybe I've finally arrived." **JACK WRANGLER**

Not only do I enjoy old Hollywood films, I enjoy old porn films as well. What is particularly interesting is that these oldies try to camouflage the fact that they were designed to get the viewers to jack off by investing them with a plot. In DUNE BUDDIES for example we have a Paul, a teacher, renting a house on FiresIsland for the summer in hopes to get away from men and one of his students in particular who has nearly caused him to violate his rule about having sex with students. However when he arrives at his cabin he finds this very same student wearing only a tee shirt that says "I can't live on Love alone" asleep on a bed. The student, Dennis, reminds his teacher that they are no longer in class. The student's exposed penis is the clincher to the argument and Teach soon has it in his mouth sucking away. (Dennis is quite irresistible.) Their fellatio is interrupted by a phone call from Gordon who tells the teacher that one night at a drunken party he was invited to come to Fire Island. Paul heads off to meet his friend at the dock. Dennis says he will get dinner. (I thought Dennis was dinner.) Alone, Dennis—still wearing nothing but his shirt—juggles a few balls. (I'm resisting making a comment here.) He then takes an outdoor shower. Dennis has very nice feet. (I've got a foot fetish.) Dennis starts pounding his dick. (I didn't know anyone had to pound their own dick on Fire Island.) Finally the shirt (now wet) comes off. So does Dennis's dick. Meanwhile Gordon (another good looking young surfer type) is tired of waiting to be picked up by our teacher and hitches a ride with a cute guy in a power boat. (The young boatman and the teacher both have those seventies' moustaches.) The ride pauses for Gordon and the boatman to get it on and we have our first fuck scene as Gordon is banged in several positions. Having missed Gordon Paul is waylaid by a friend who plies him with liquor and dope, a cute young Latino, and a hunky young bear. A four-man orgy is soon underway. Gordon arrives at the cabin and encounters Dennis. We return to the orgy for the climax (literally). Stumbling back to camp Paul sees a light on in a tent where some kind of activity is taking place. The inhabitant is jacking off. (This really begins to disillusion me about Fire Island. Guess I should cash in my ticket.) Paul trips over a rock and sprains his ankle. The masturbator comes to his rescue. Dennis and Gordon have just finished the dinner Dennis made and Gordon says it's only a matter of time before he makes Dennis. Back at the tent, his rescuer having taken care of Paul's ankle is now taking care of Paul's cock. Paul shows his appreciation by going down on the tent dweller. He fucks him too. This night scene is so poorly lit (I don't think it was lit at all) that it's sort of like watching shadow puppets. (And why do we hear a female in orgiastic frenzy on the soundtrack???) Meanwhile back at the cabin Gordon is indeed making Dennis. Though at the moment Dennis is swallowing down Gordon's cock. A ravenous sixty-nine follows. Even though it doesn't include fucking it is the film's best sex scene with Dennis showing some real passion. Both boys fire off nice loads. The next morning however Gordon goes off with the vulgar boatman. Kevin heads into the surf. Paul struggles home. The film ends with Paul giving Dennis the keys to the house and leaving him there. What a silly ninny as a summer with Larry Paige who played Dennis would be unforgettable!

Of course the film can't compare with the technical expertise of our top-grade films today. And although it no doubt was a pud-pounder thirty some years ago, one would have to be very horny to respond that way today. Nevertheless it did put some lead in my pencil and was rather enjoyable. Larry Paige as Dennis and Hugh Allen as Gordon were quite attractive. It is certainly not worth the price of a new DVD so I would suggest renting it if you are interested. That's what I did.

* Joe Shaver, *Adult DVD News*

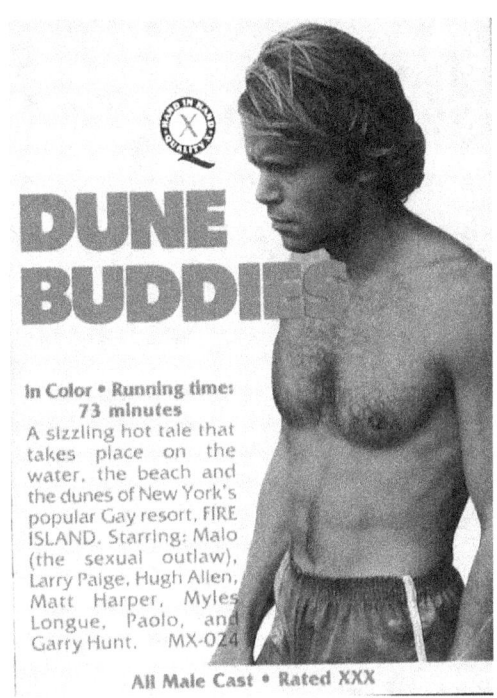

This narrated gay sex film, from the 1970's when Hand In Hand and Jack Deveau were making the best in gay porn, stars Paul Hazzard (body-sculpted Malo) as a teacher from Manhattan who tries to escape a lifestyle of "too much sex" by foolishly renting a house on Fire Island for a month.

Shot on location, the humor, plot and feasible dialogue that are trademarks of Deveau never seem to come completely together, making this a silly, pleasant film that has some very good moments.

Much realism, though, is created in the actor's performances and true lust for one another! A sex-starved student, Dennis (played by Larry Paige), tracks him down to satisfy his crush while Paul's voice-over says, "We stared holes through each other all semester."

Malo proceeds to fuck his ass and work his foreskinned cock to orgasm as we watch in large, excellent close-ups. Larry later joins hunky Matt Harper on a boat for 69ing, rimming and an ass-filling, capturing natural lighting and intense, hard cocks reaching hot orgasms. Fun-loving friends soon arrive by ferry.

His randy real estate agent (played by Garry Hunt) involves him in an orgy and the four-way includes jockstraps, harnesses, face-fucking, face-sitting, a redhead, beard, rimming, a Latin character, and more! Malo later tricks in a tent with a humpy beach bum with a huge cock, Myles Longue.

Myles ends up fucking the man while sucking on his cock! This scene is a bit dark as it is filmed at night, but silhouettes and interesting angles allow for intimate voyeuring and fantasy to work. Some escape! Malo is a wonderfully handsome leading man with a beautiful physique and oodles of charm. Adonis-type bodies, hard and large dicks, and unusually good acting and dialogue make this a good Hand In Hand release.

*Bijou Promo

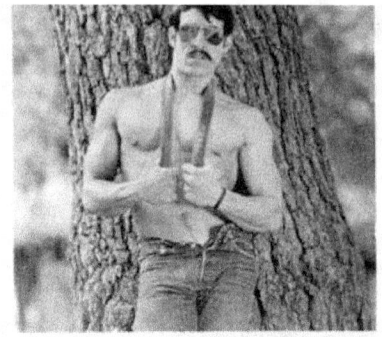

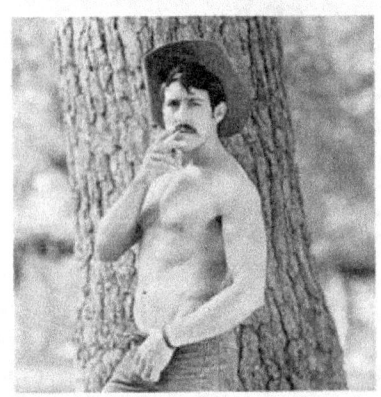

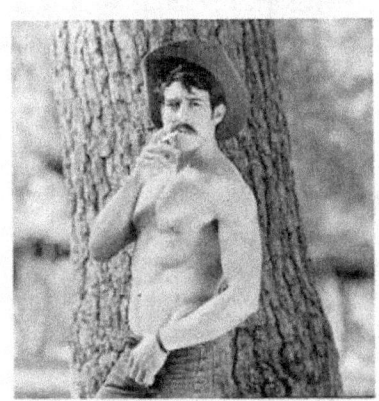

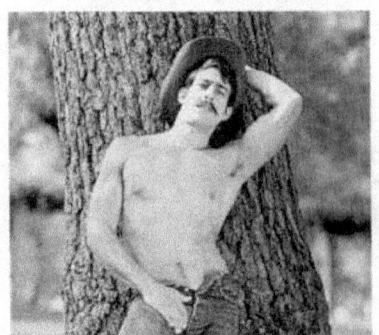

Just when you thought it was safe to go back into the bushes, Hand In Hand Films releases its latest hot pic, DUNE BUDDIES. Filmed entirely on location on Fire Island, DUNE BUDDIES captures the fun, excitement and heartbreak we all go through every summer. The world may change but the Pines and the Grove remain enchanted enclaves where dreams really do come true. Where else, we ask, can you fuck on the bottom of a boat with nobody paying any attention? Where else would a casual flirt be considered a meaningful experience? It takes eight studs performing heavy duty action to give a true picture to what really happens in the dunes, the bushes, on the Burma Road, behind closed bedroom doors. Let's face it, a fast fuck can be a thrilling encounter if you leave your mind at home. (Just ask Erica Jong.) Directed by Jack Deveau, the cast is forceful, handsome and hot to trot. DUNE BUDDIES is the story of chance encounters and shifting identities. It opens next Monday (Oct. 2) at the Adonis on 8th Ave. at 50th St.

*Preview, *Michael's Thing*

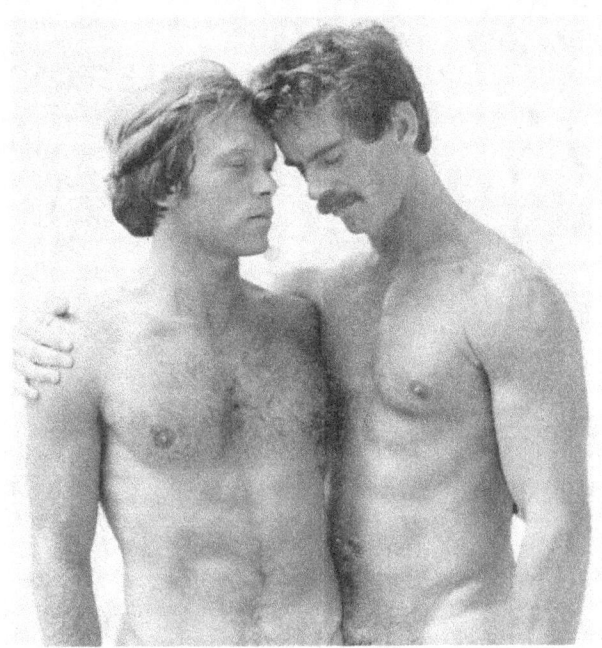

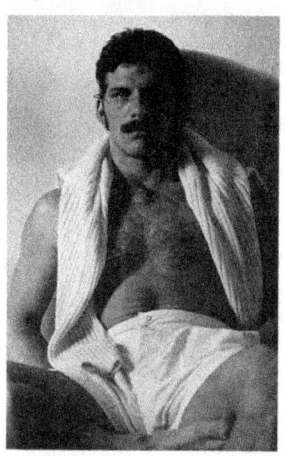

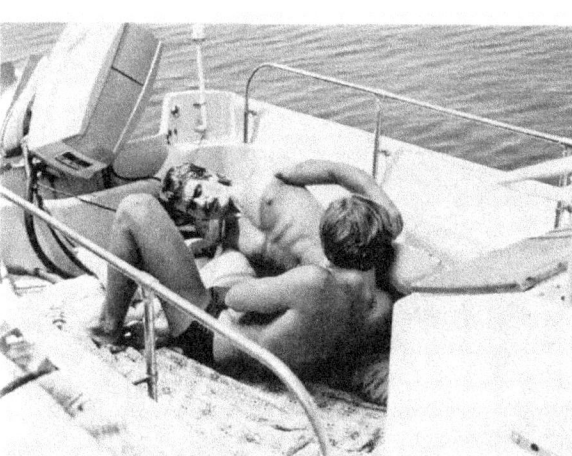

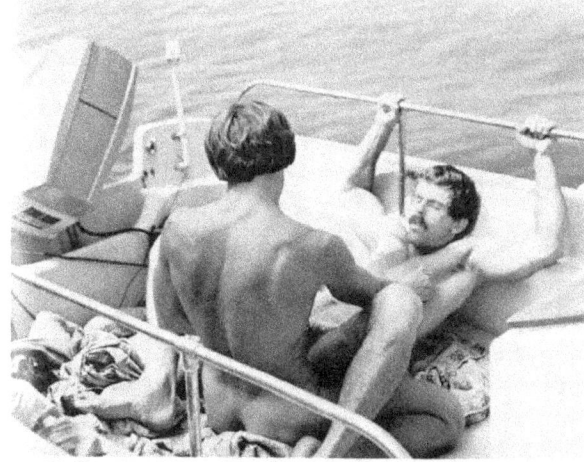

Matt (Target model) Harper and Hugh ("Rough Trades") Allen make the best use of the bottom of a boat since Tallulah and John Hodiak gave the waves a toss for their money in "Lifeboat." This particular sequence may leave you dizzy if you're susceptible to marine motion.

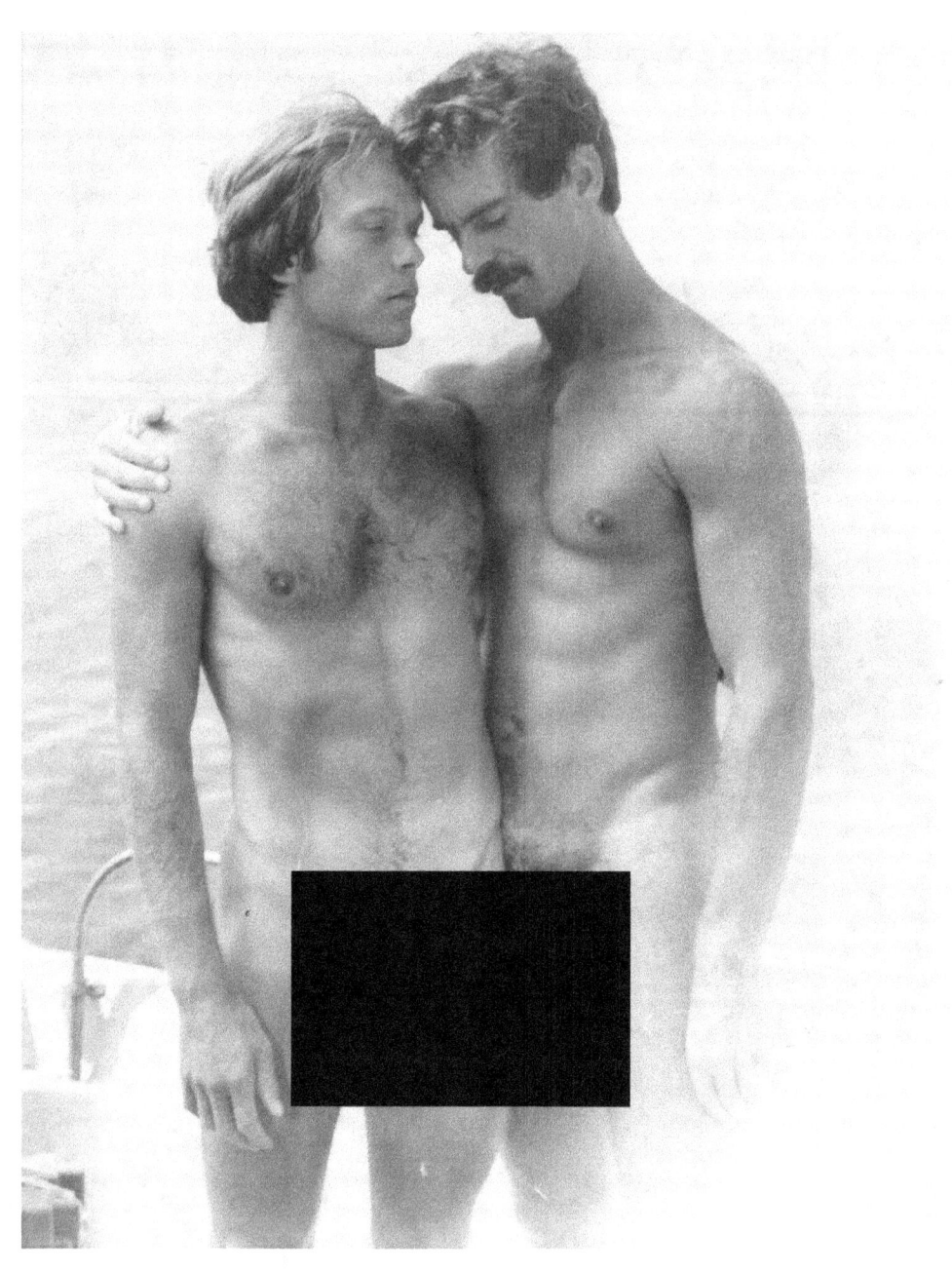

Hugh Allen and Matt Harper in *Dune Buddies*

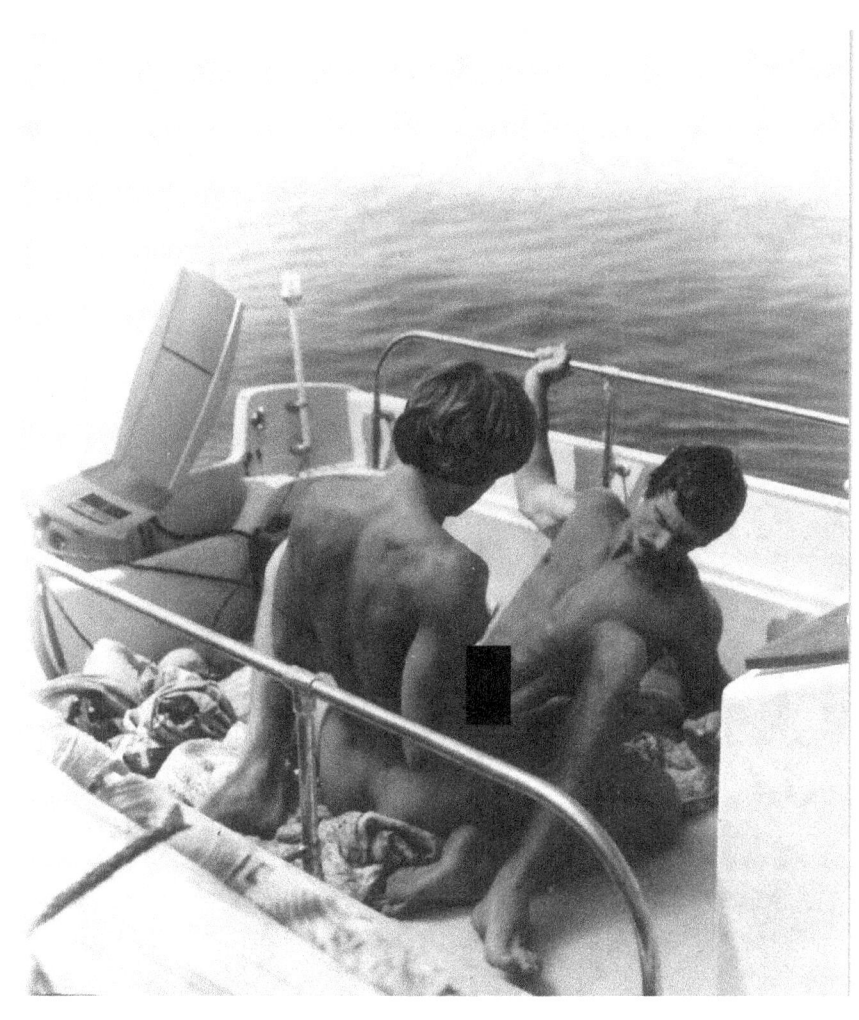

„How pleasing it is to hear laughter during sex."
Bob's Bazaar about *Dune Buddies*

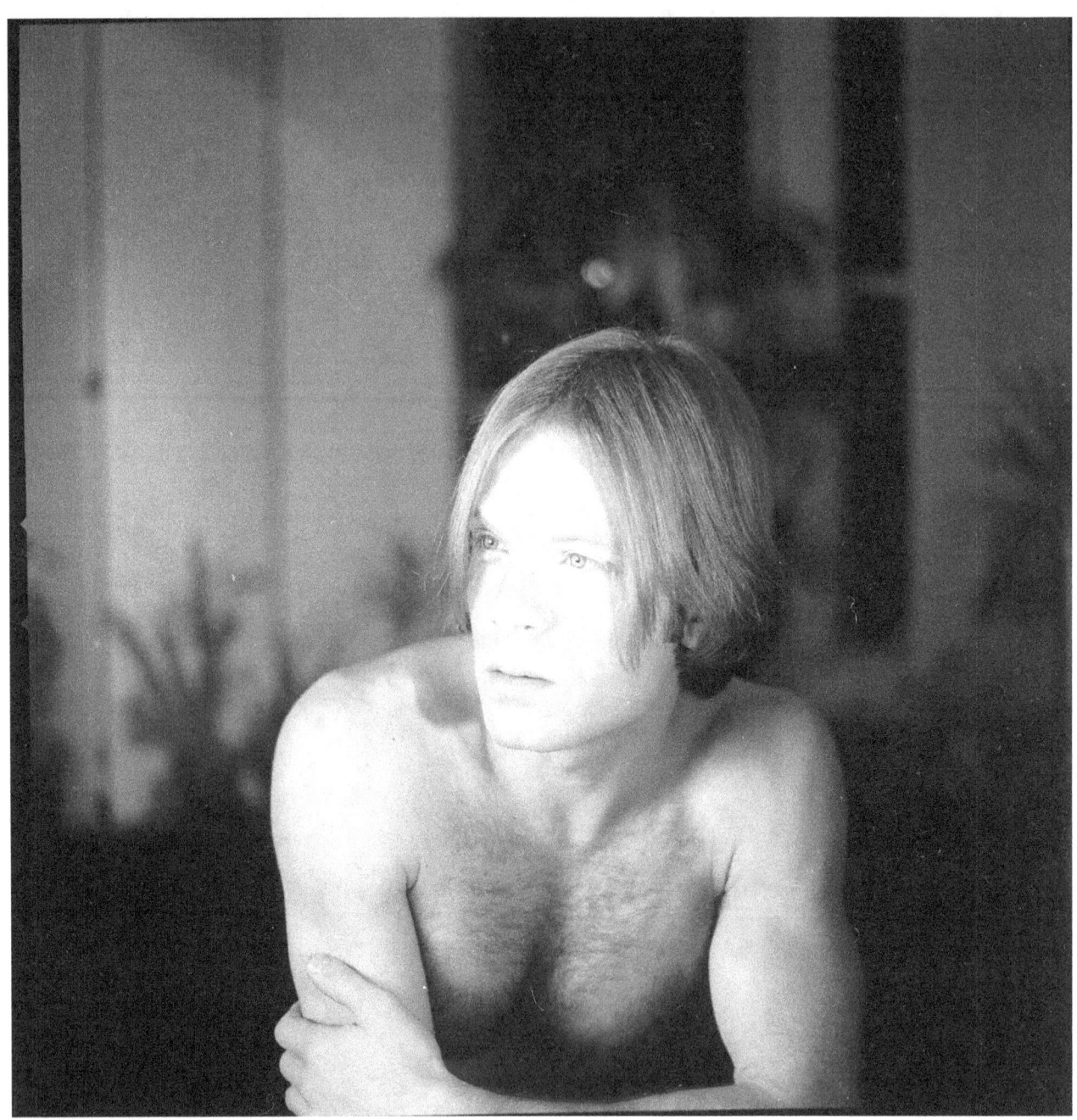

Hugh Allen

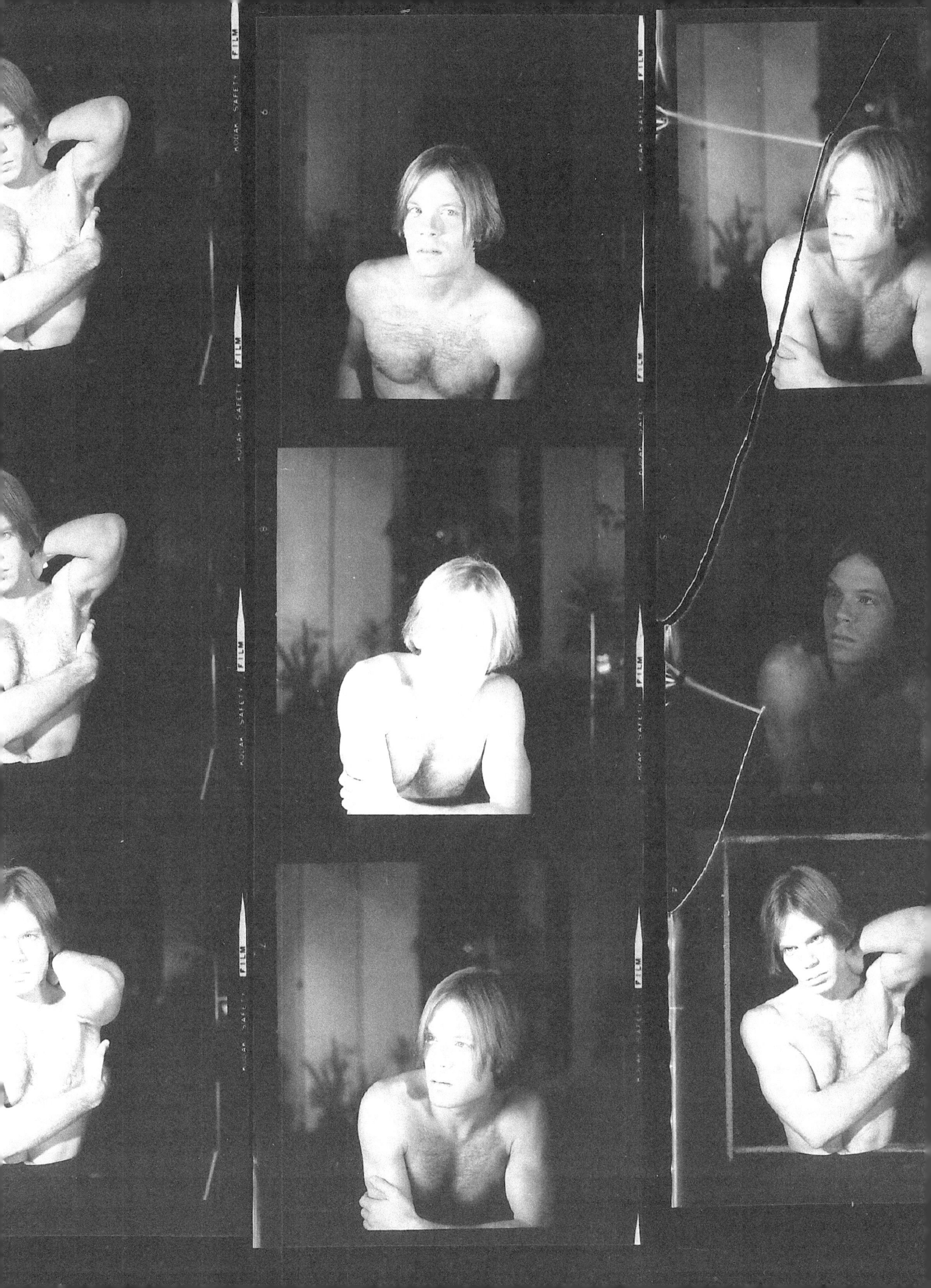

Jack Deveau's Hand In Hand Films was one of the earliest (and most successful) pioneers in creating explicit story films, and almost always they succeeded in maintaining the delicate balance between erotic and narrative components. Unfortunately, their much-ballyhooed 1979 release, FIRE ISLAND FEVER, while built on one of their very best screenplays, is woefully short on hot sex sequences. In a nice touch, the film opens during the Christmas holidays in New York City, where a group of Fire Island regulars hold their midwinter get-together to see "what everyone looks like without a tan." In RASHOMON flashback technique, there unfold three versions of a crisis that occurred the preceding summer at a house in the Pines shared by three roommates: two lovers, Ron and Rich (Larry Paige and John Carlo) and a loner, Jeff (Garry Hunt). Early on, we learn how easy it is to contract a virulent case of "Fire Island Fever," a disease characterized by "constant horniness and a total lack of scruples." Even Ron and Rich's open relationship is soon threatened by each of them moving his own new trick into their summer home. Ron opts for a waiter, Terry (Chris Michaels) and Rich, a trick from the bushes, Greg (Hugh Allen). Through all the lovers' travails, Jeff distances himself, sketching, meditating, and fantasizing over a handsome figure he never meets. This mythic hunk is played by Will Seagers, here working under the name Matt Harper. What actually happened during that summer of sexual excess depends on whose version the viewer believes, and the final resolution is not complete until the Christmas party. But FIRE ISLAND FEVER ends on an upbeat note to rousing strains of a disco version of the "Hallelujah Chorus." The screenplay by Moose 100 is intelligently structured, nicely textured, insightfully probing, and to boot, always clever and often witty in its view of the sex-crazed seventies. The production is well cast and well acted, its level of professionalism way above the norm of much adult films. Fortunately, the best performances in the film are given by the three leads, Paige, Carlo, and Hunt. The problem is the sexual content of the film: Although there are frequent sexual couplings, there is really only one complete sex scene in the film. All the others feel like truncated snippets, many of which do not include money shots. Among these: a brief one-sided oral scene in their bed (Paige/Carlo); two versions of Terry's first encounter with Ron poolside (Michaels/Paige); the encounter in the bushes (Carlo/Allen); the two new tricks cheating on their perspective hosts with each other (Michaels/Allen); and a pair of interestingly cross-cut solos during an acid trip (Hunt/Seagers).

The final scene, a reconciliation between the two lovers is the first and only scene to have a beginning, middle, and an end, including oral and anal action and a pair of money shots. It is also made notable by striking shots of Carlo's extraordinarily hairy ass and Paige's purple, plum-headed, ever-hard erection.

Ultimately, this sixty-eight-minute Bijou version of FIRE ISLAND FEVER (as opposed to the seventy-three-minute version of its original release) is more an art film with all too brief explicit moments than hard-driving, wall-to-wall, get-your-rocks-off erotica.

Jerry Douglas, *Manshots*

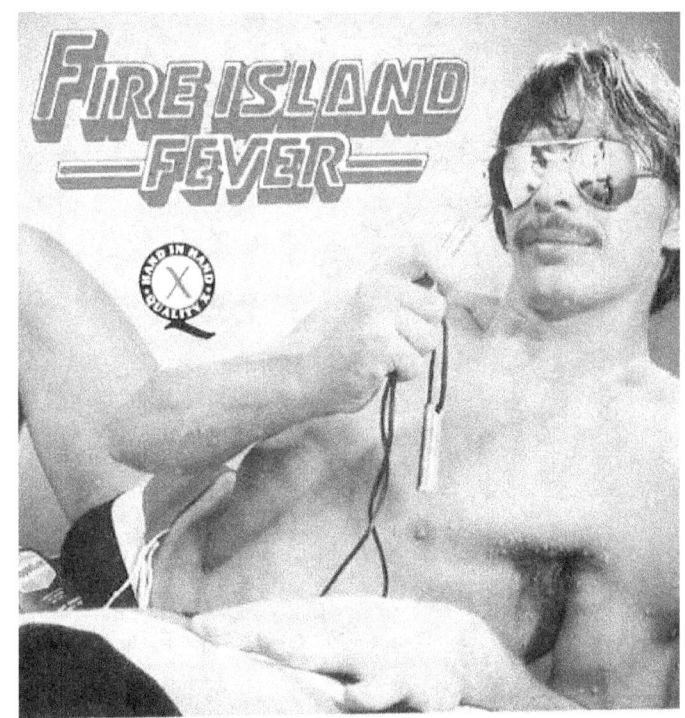

FIRE ISLAND FEVER

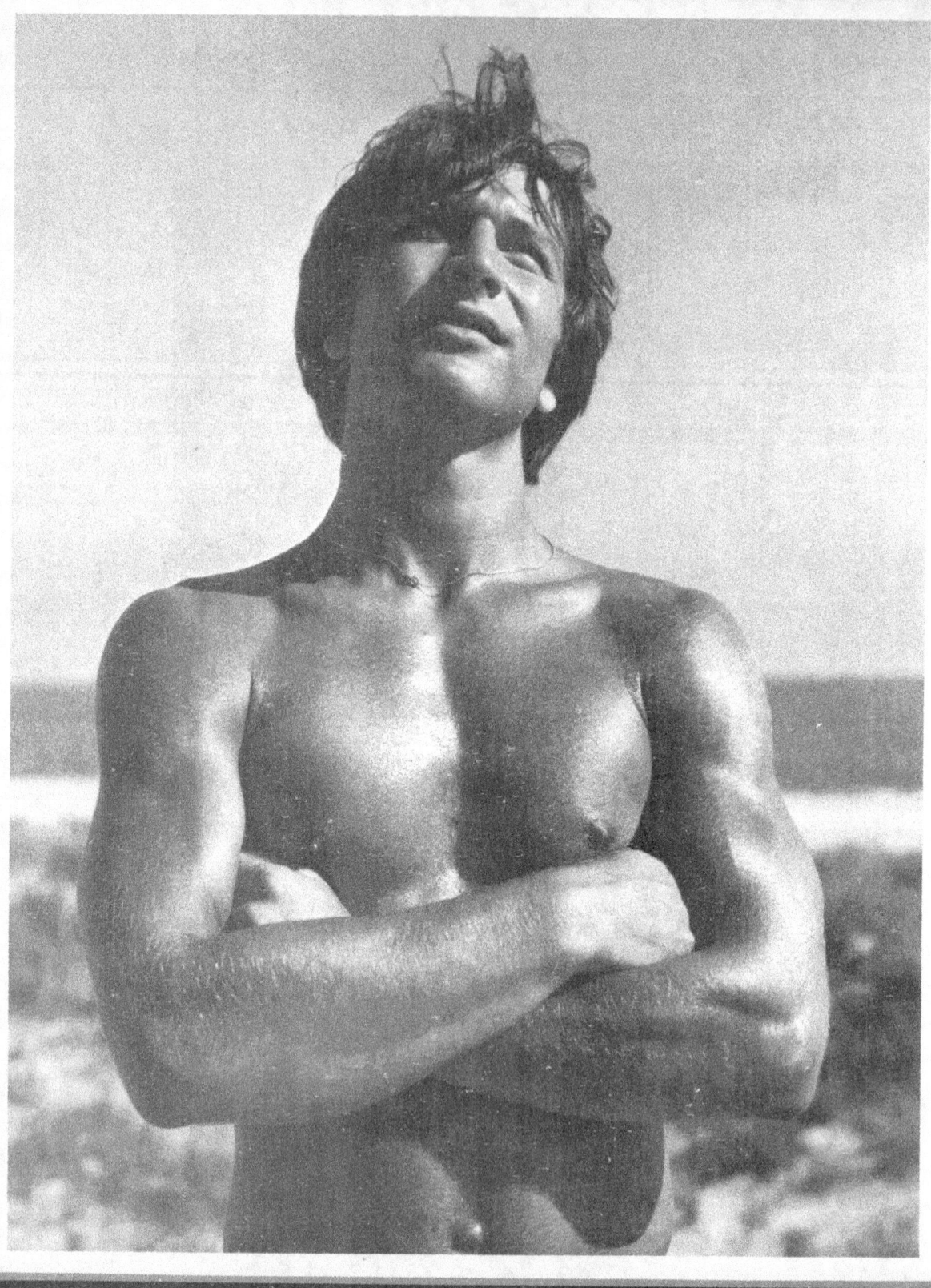

Chris Michaels

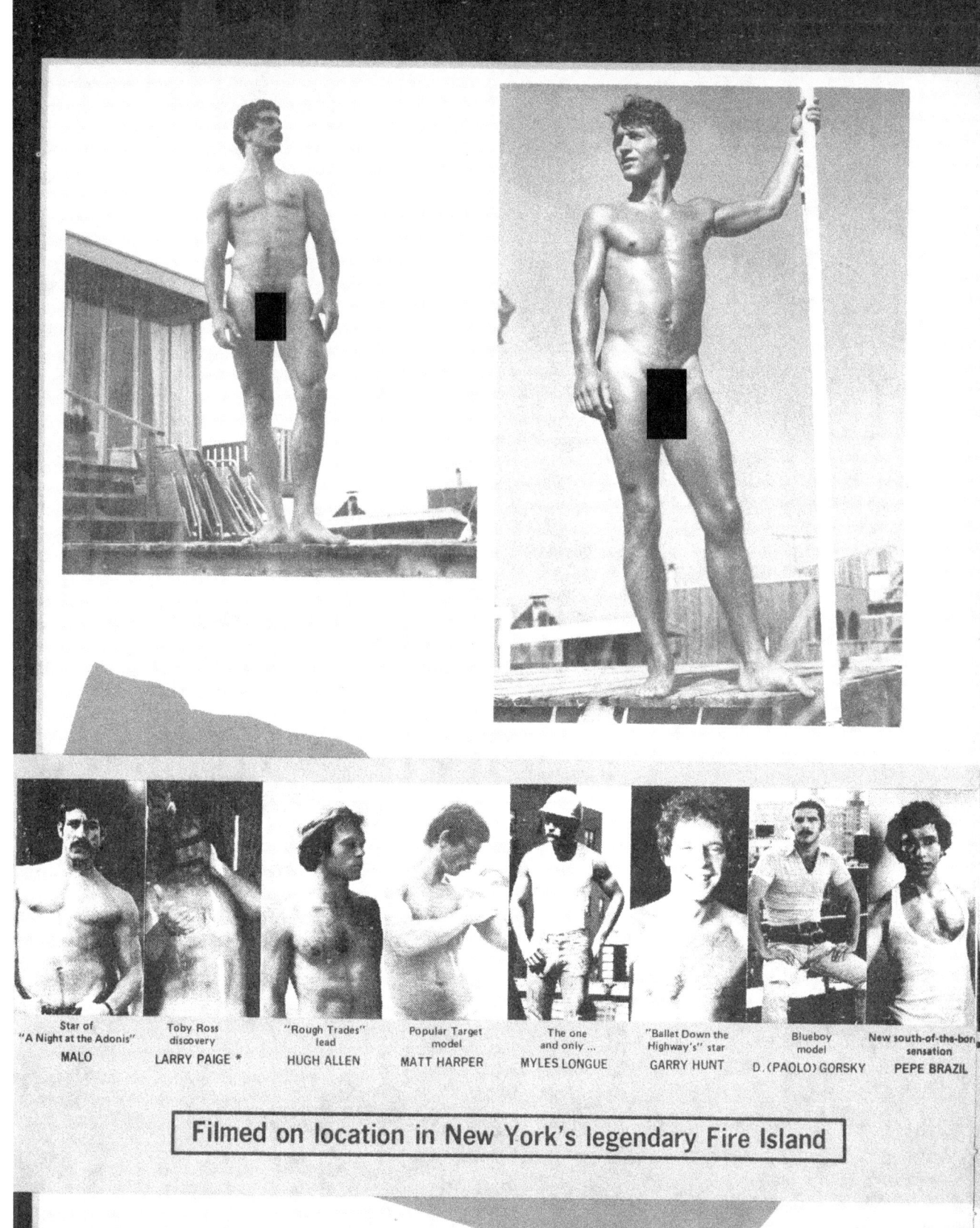

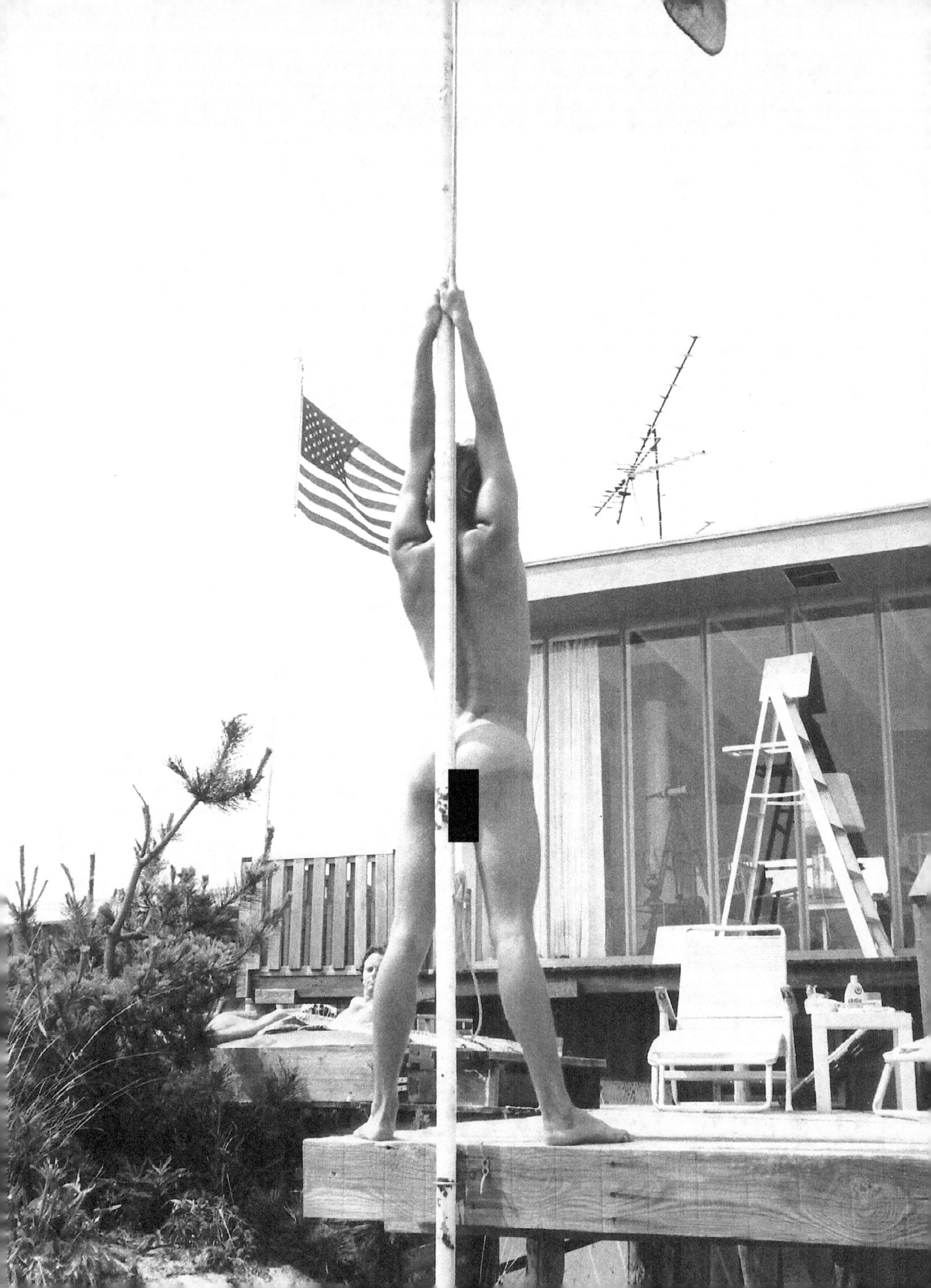

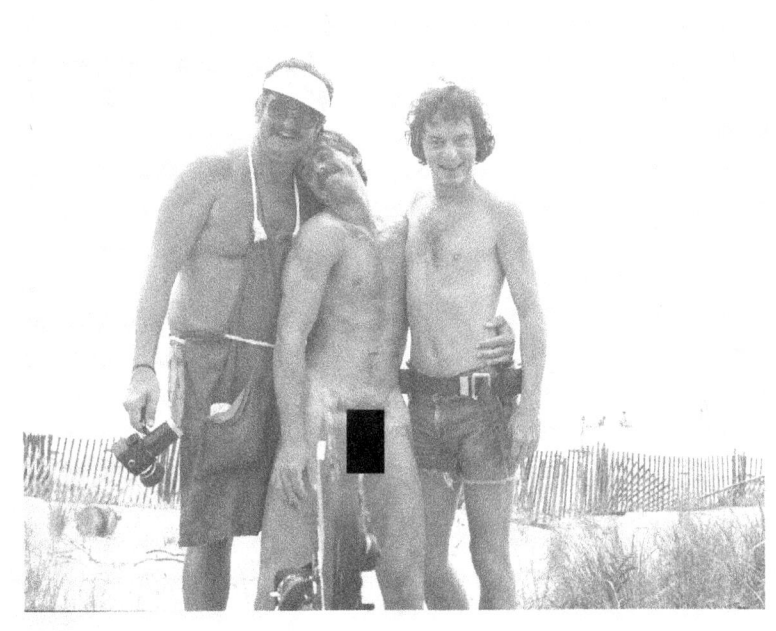

above: David Litler, Matt Harper, Kees Chapman
left: Luke aka Philip Wagner

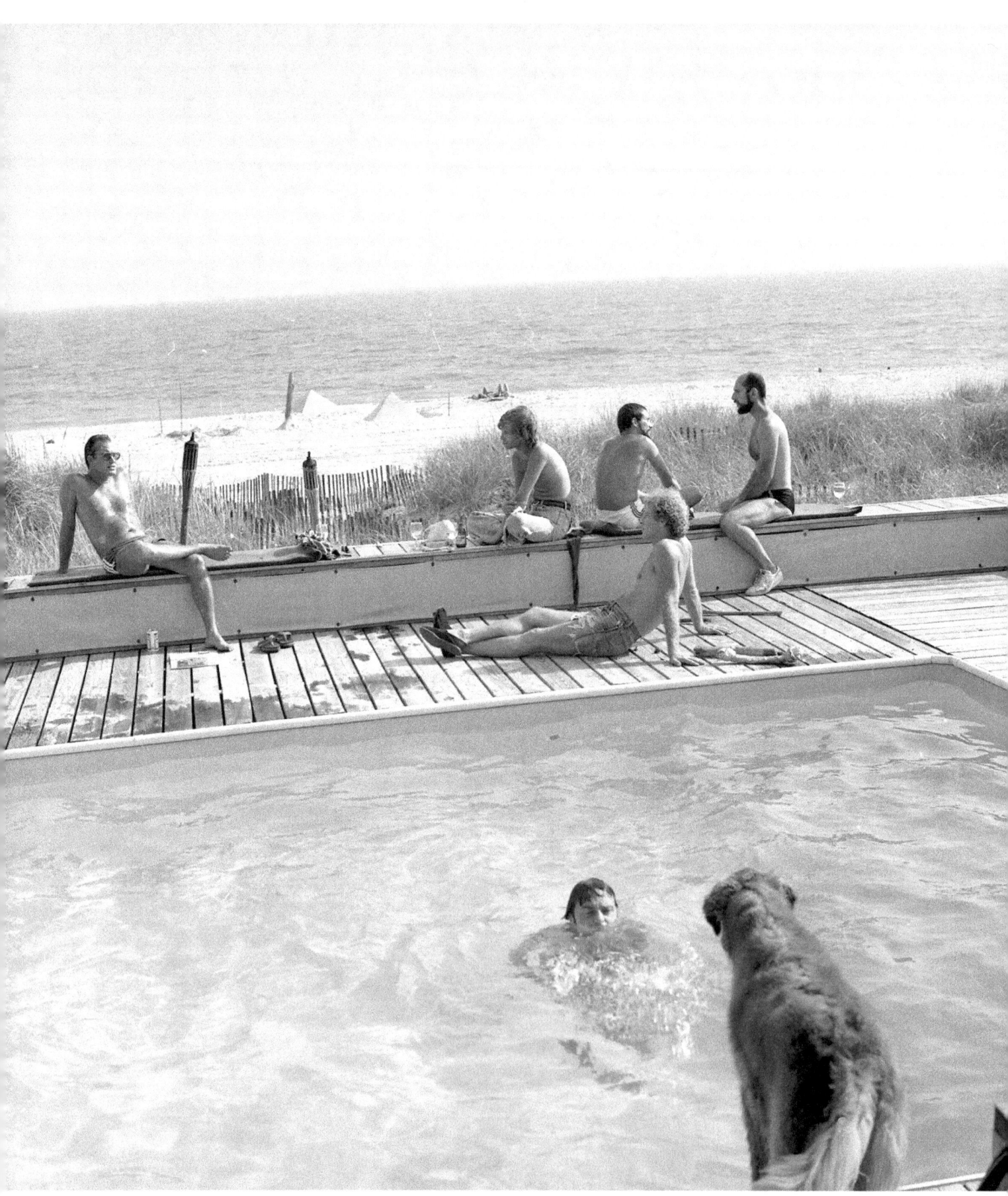

Behind the scenes of *Fire Island Fever*

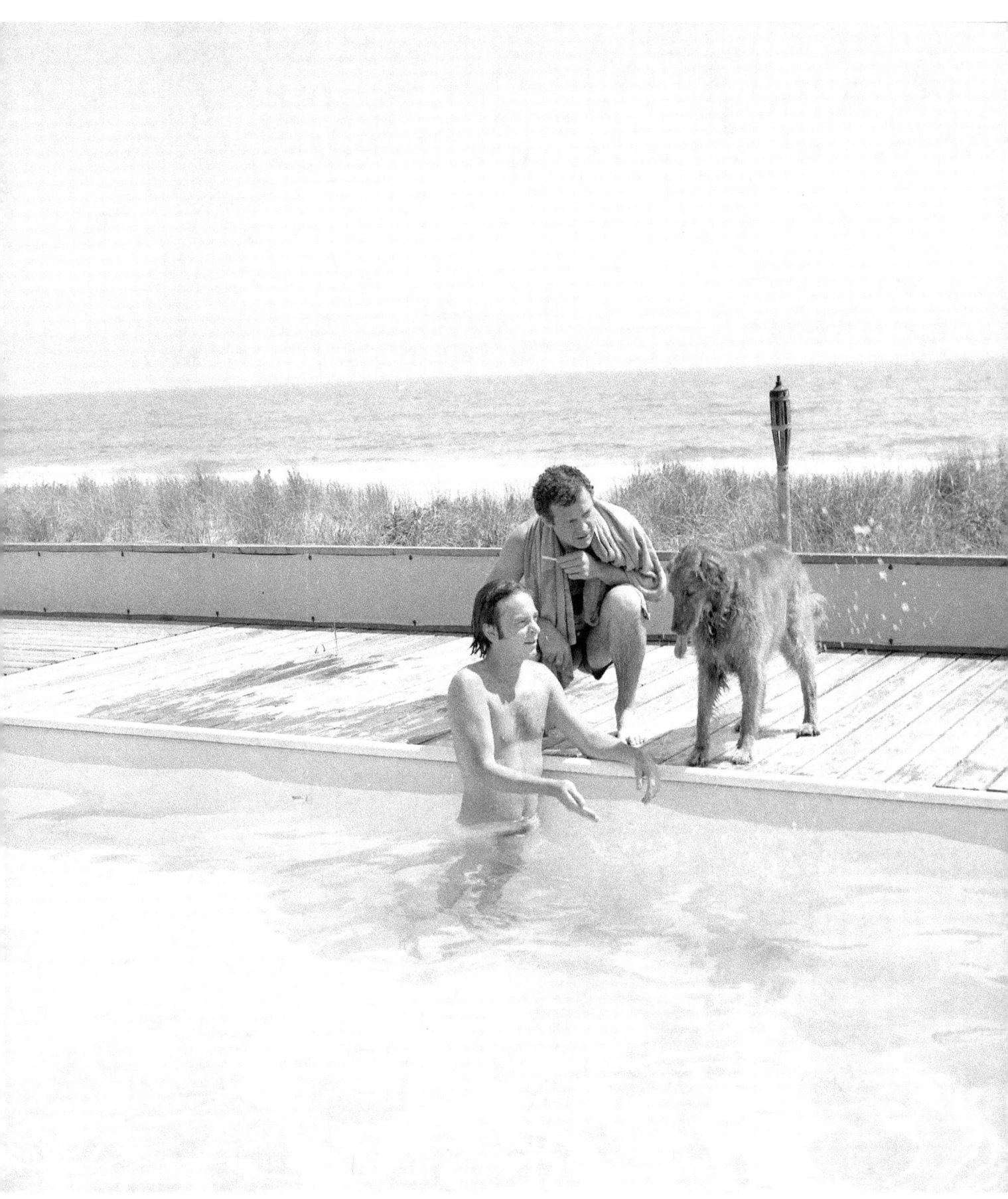

Kees Chapman and Jack Deveau

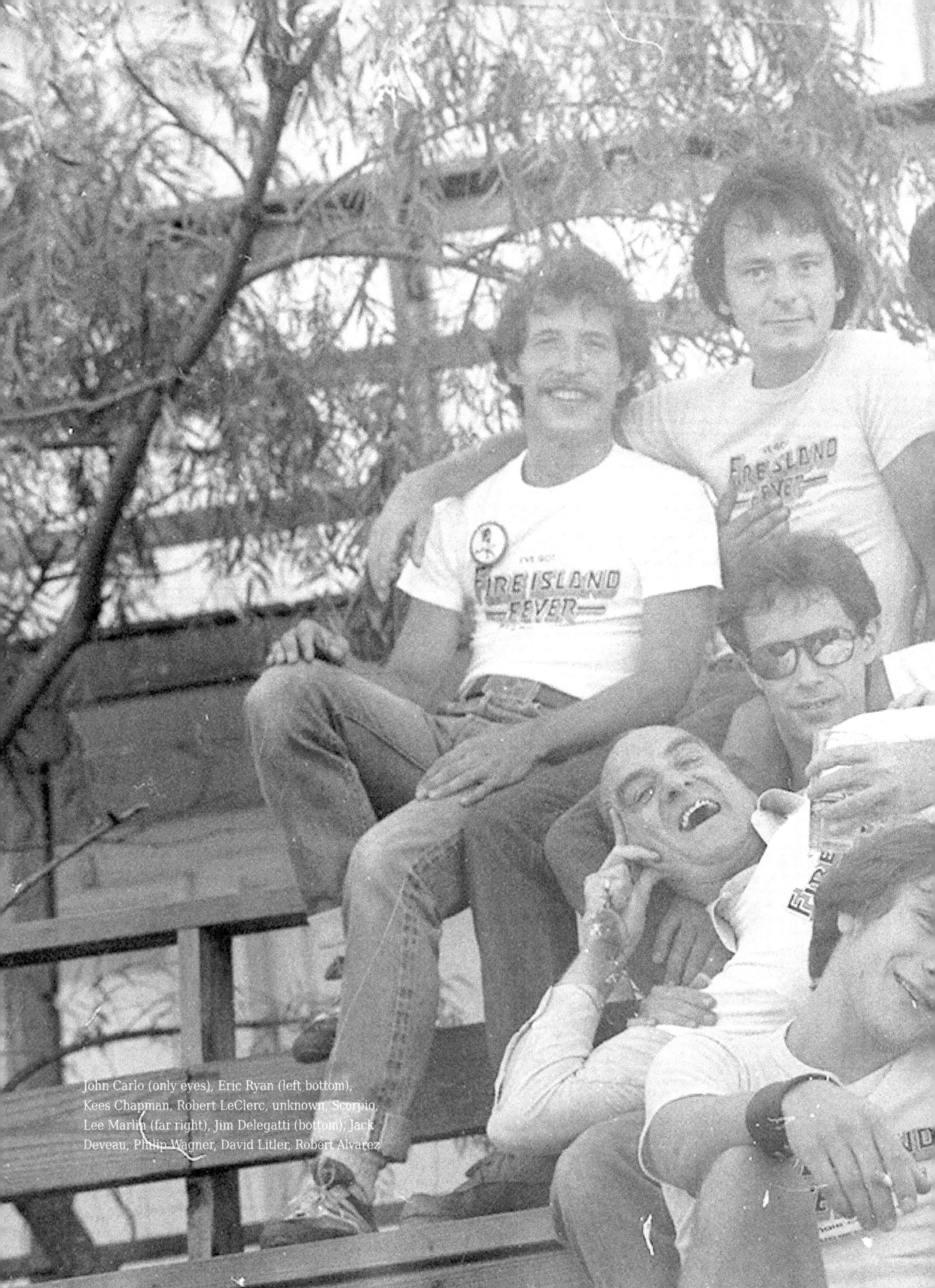

John Carlo (only eyes), Eric Ryan (left bottom), Kees Chapman, Robert LeClerc, unknown, Scorpio, Lee Marlin (far right), Jim Delegatti (bottom); Jack Deveau, Philip Wagner, David Litler, Robert Alvarez

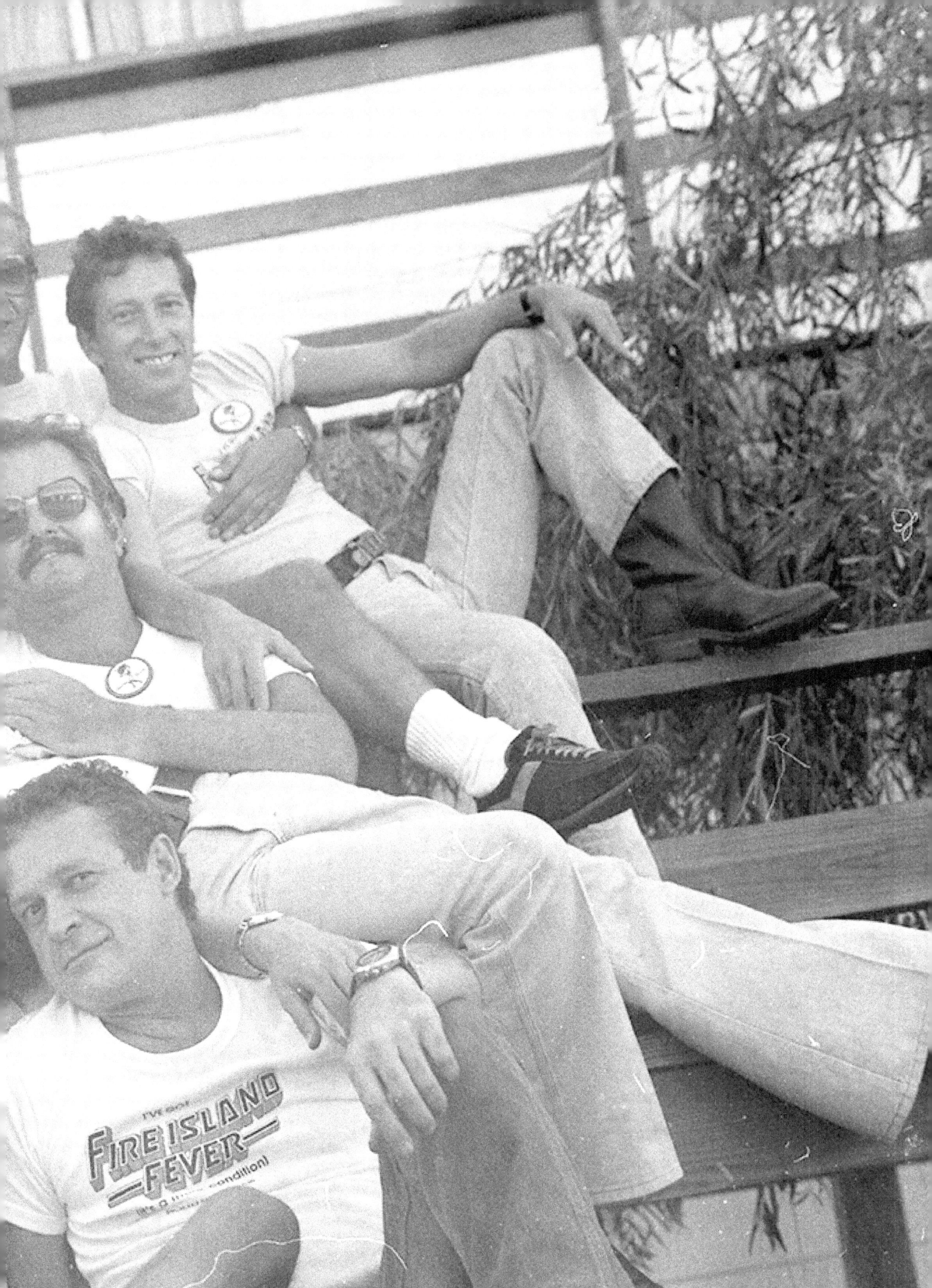

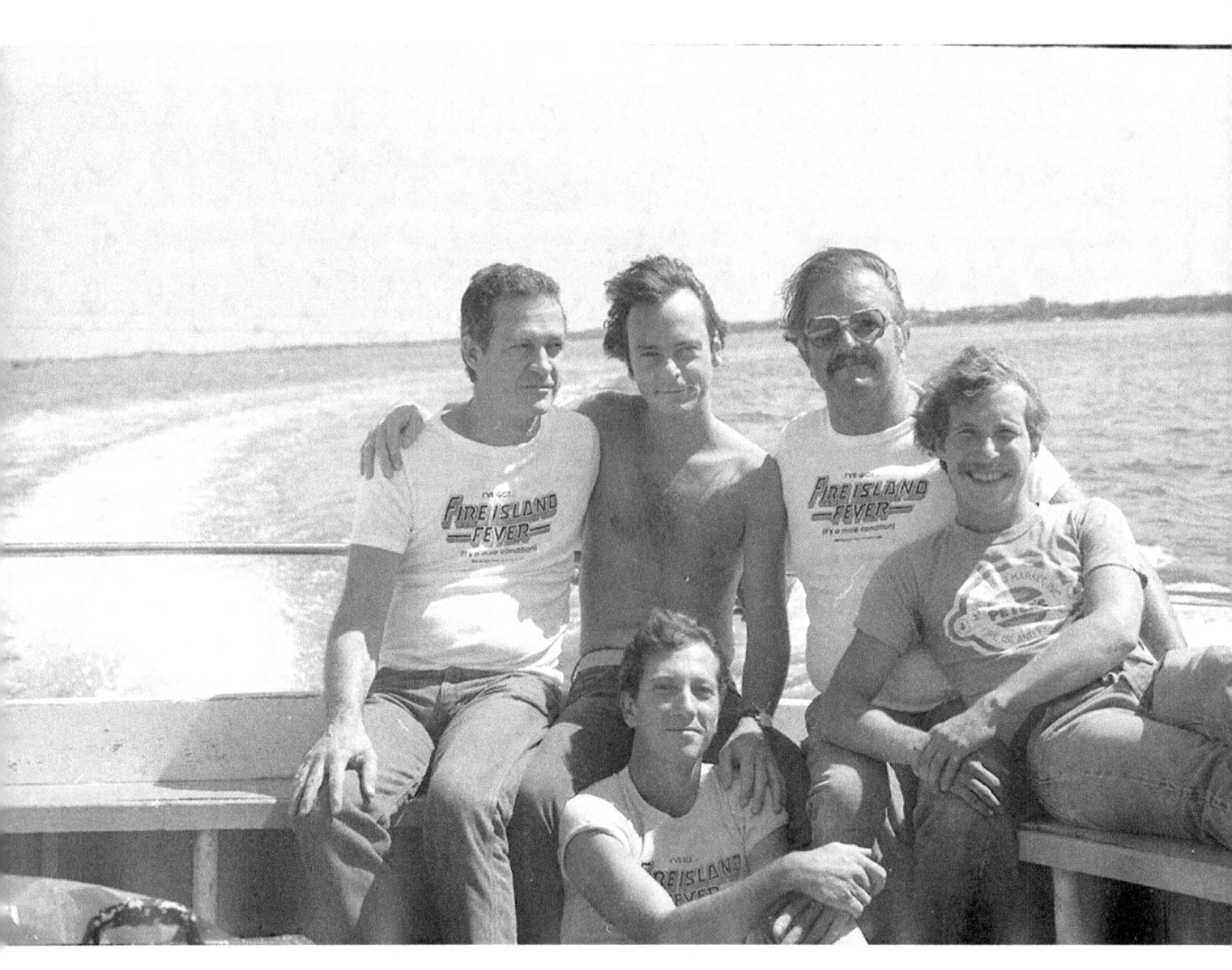

Jack Deveau, Kees Chapman, David Litler, unidentified person and Robert Alvarez

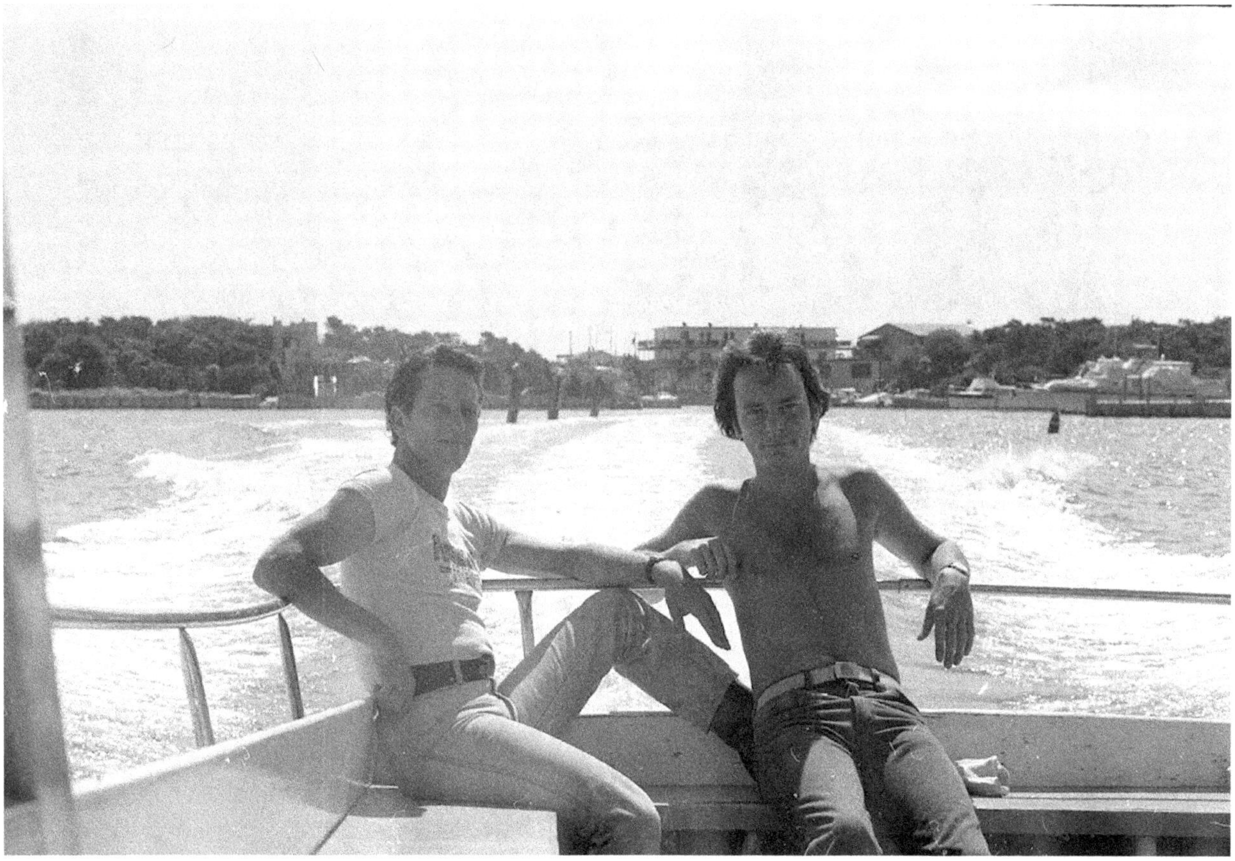

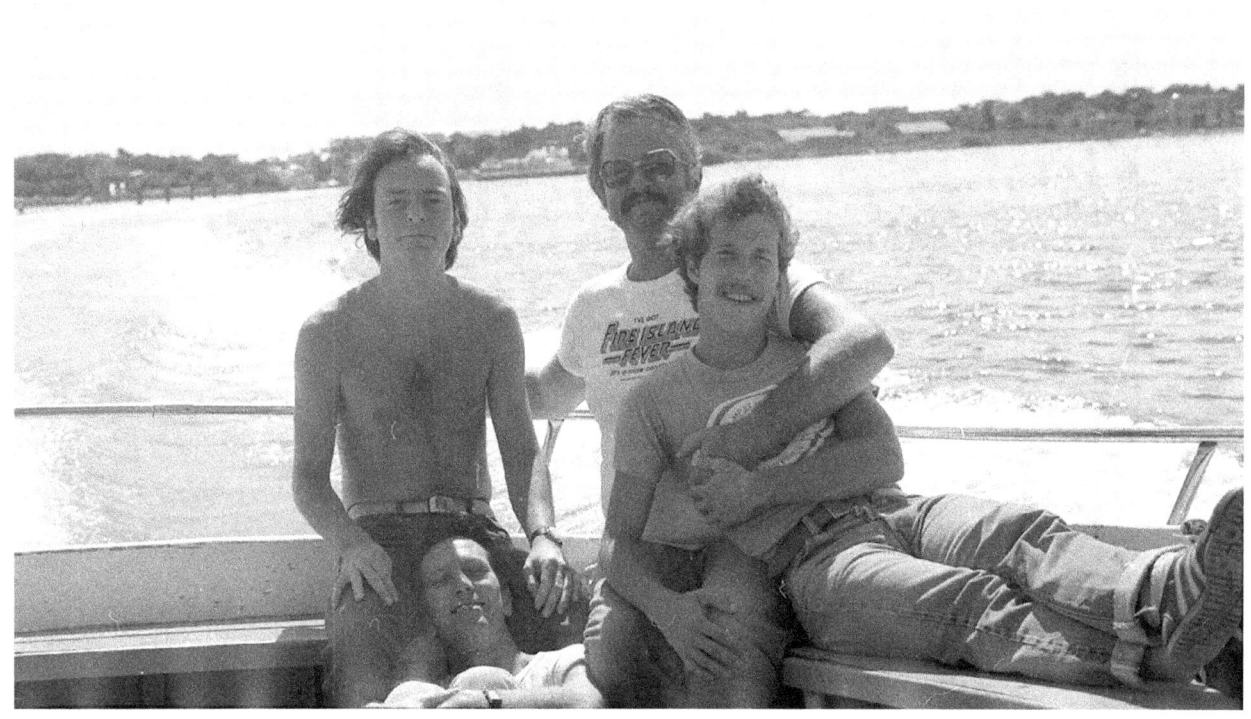

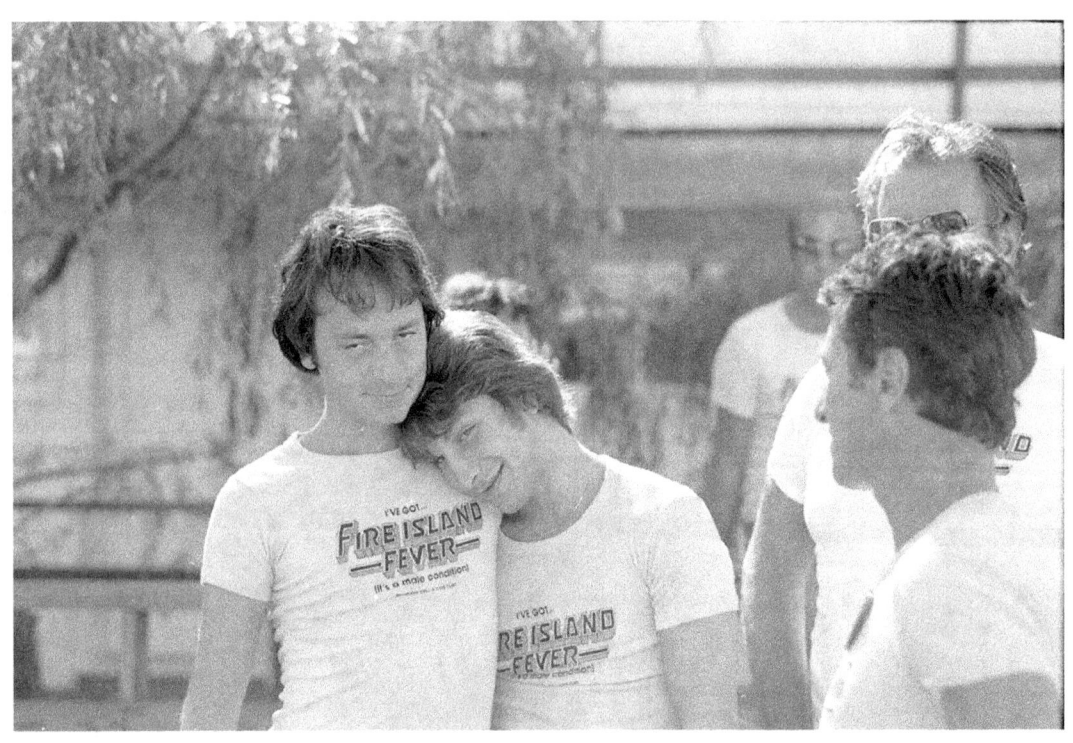

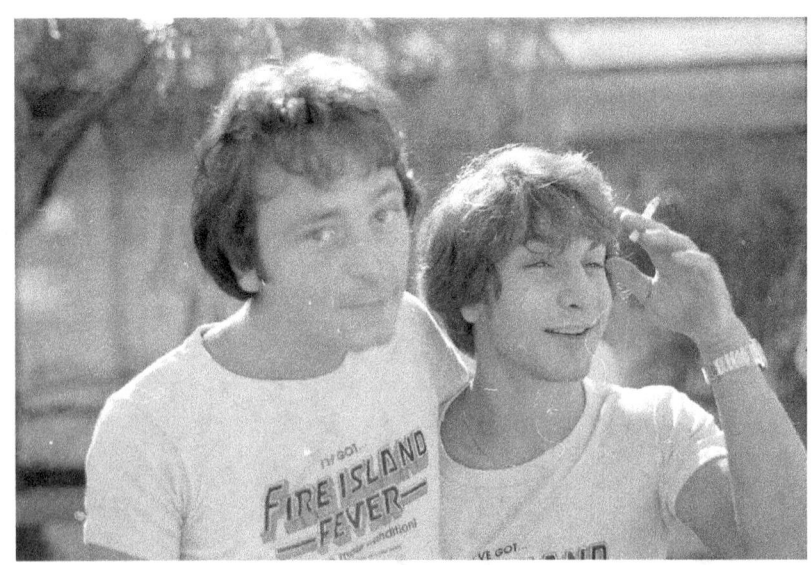

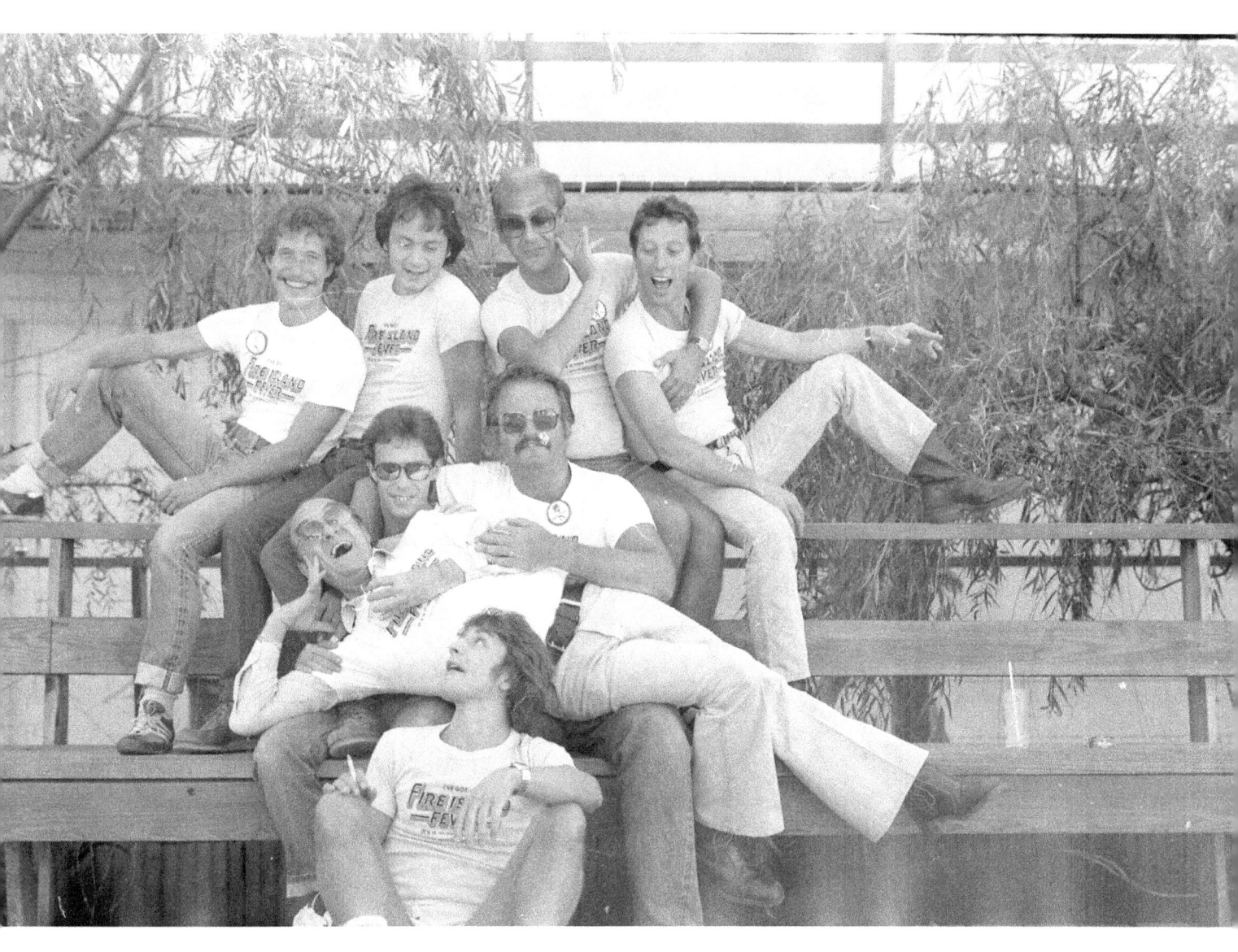

The *Fire Island Fever* crew

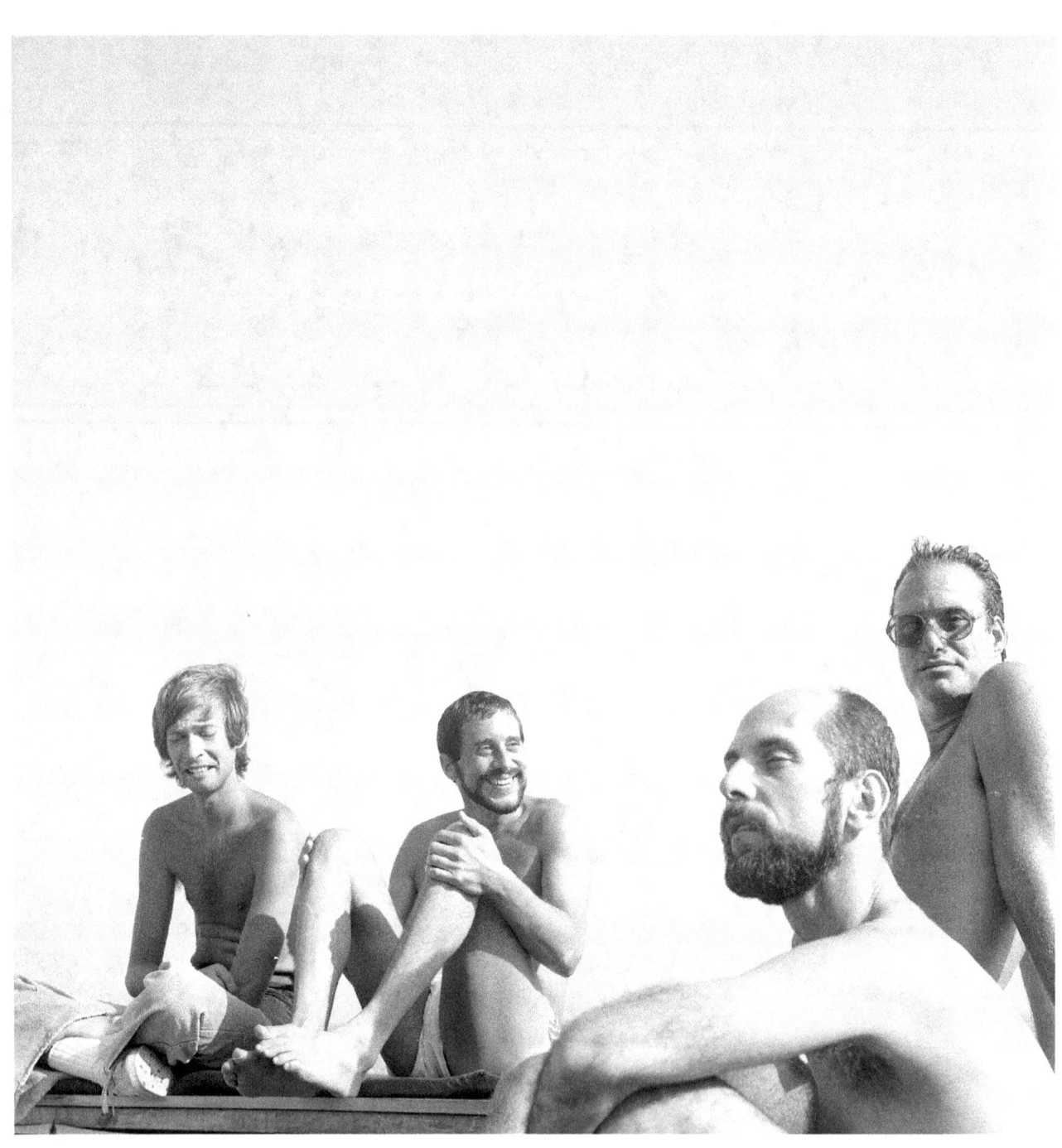

Gene Kelton with other visitors on Fire Island who wanted to hang out and watch the porno stars.

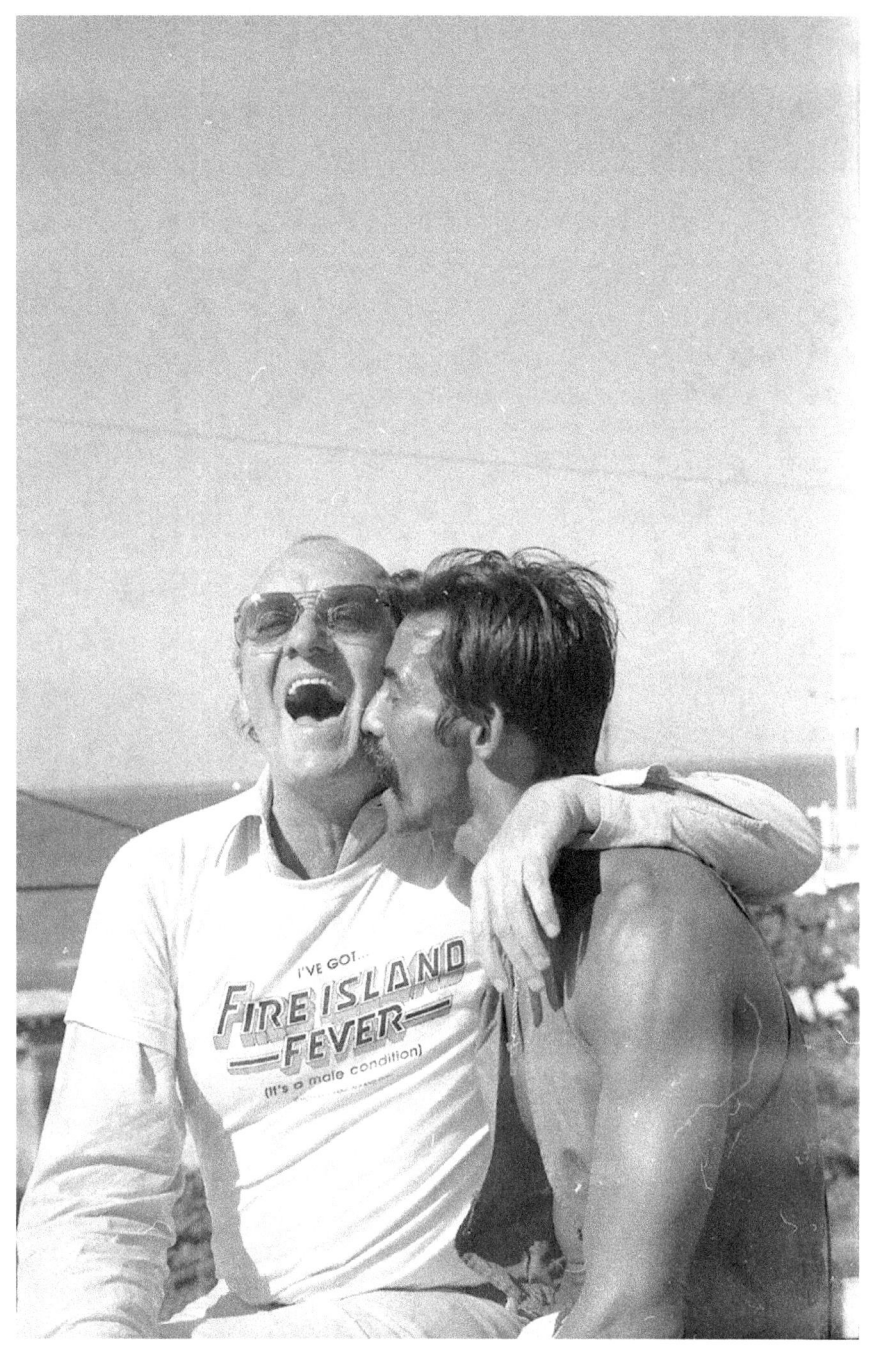

George Sardi. He worked on *Gay Morning America* as columnist and host. He sings a song in *Fire Island Fever: I am just one of those Things,* a parody of a Cole Porter song. He was friends with Jack Deveau and Robert Alvarez.

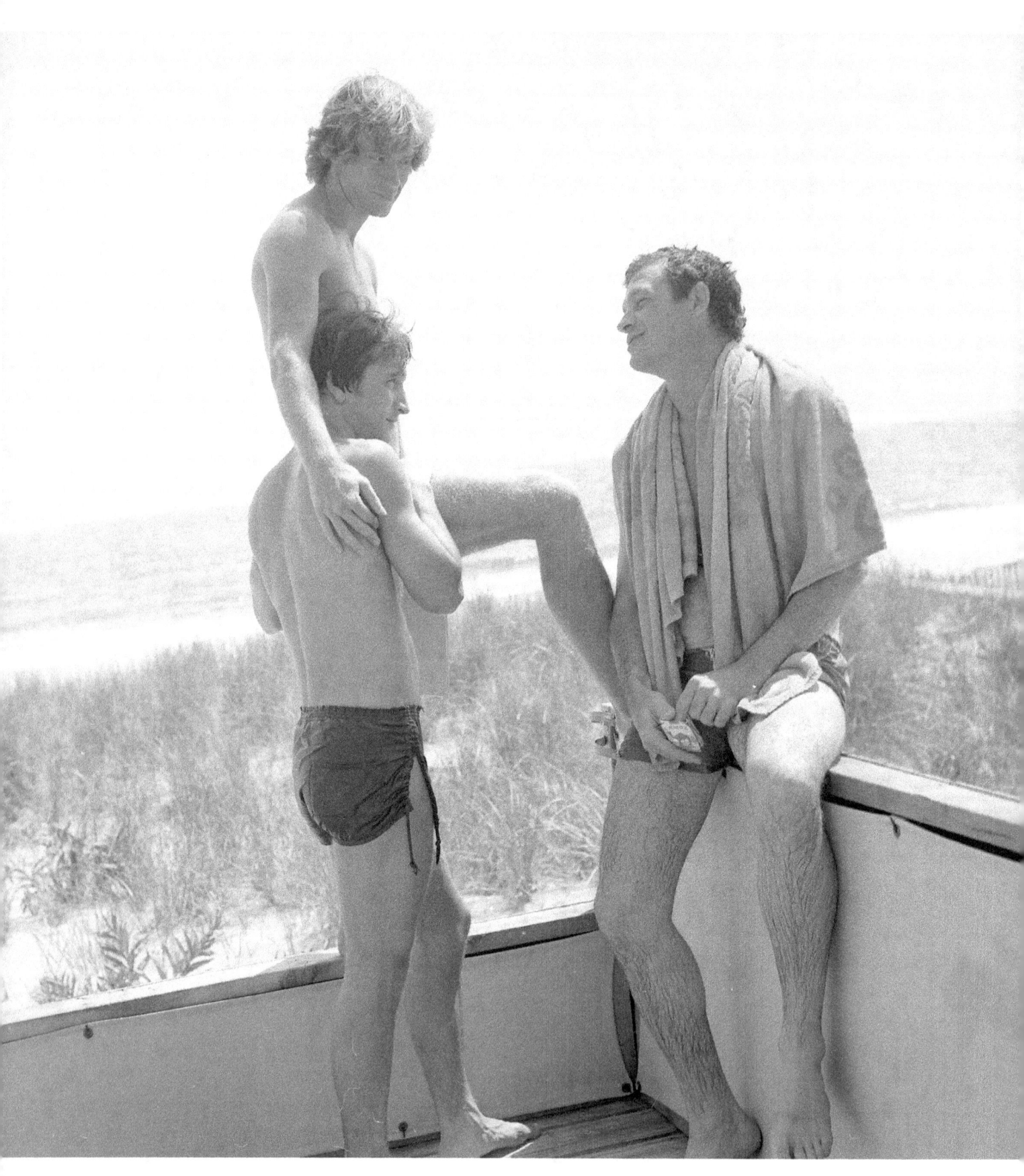

Chris Michaels (standing), Michael Young, Jack Deveau (right)

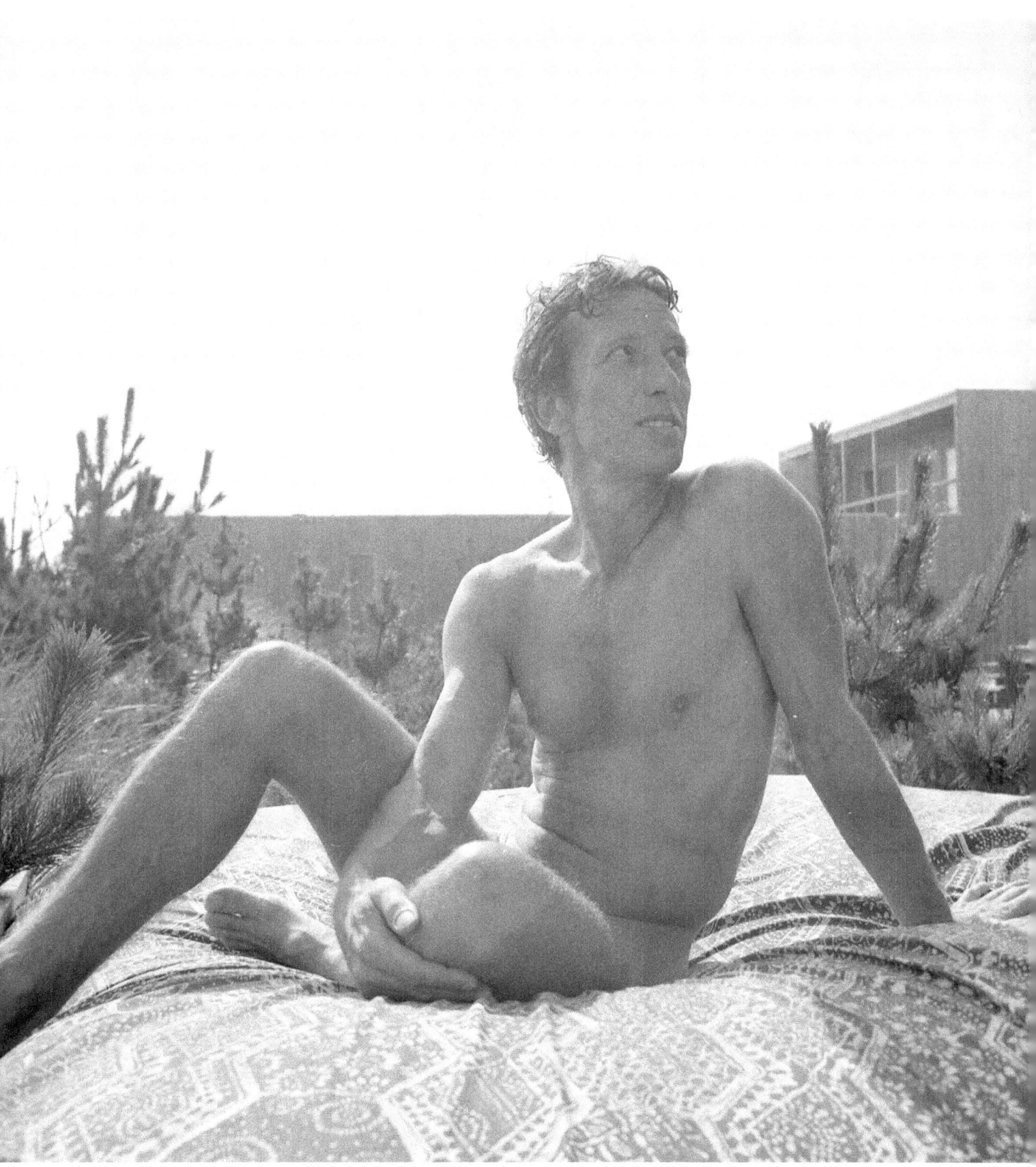

Robert Alvarez

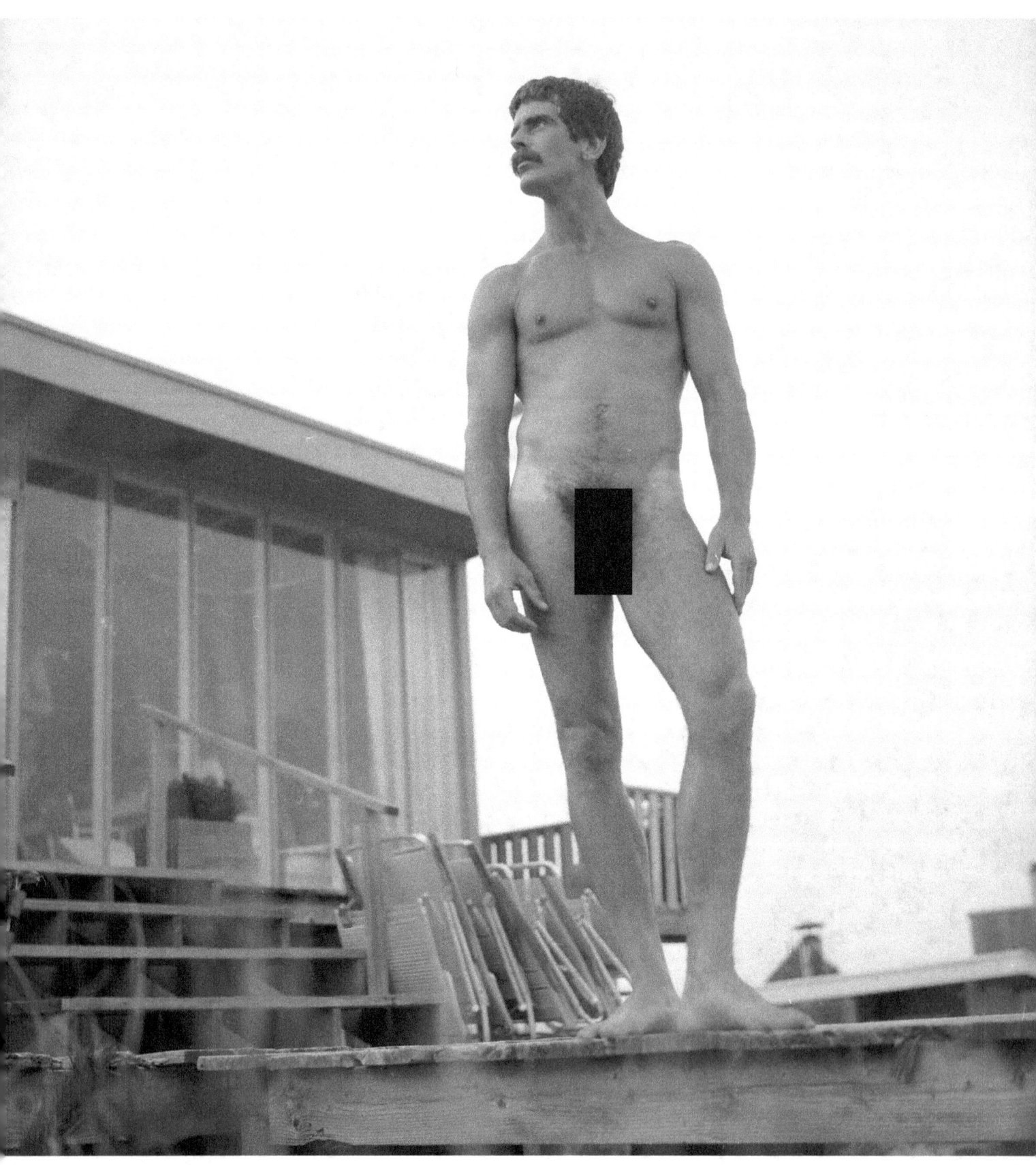

Matt Harper

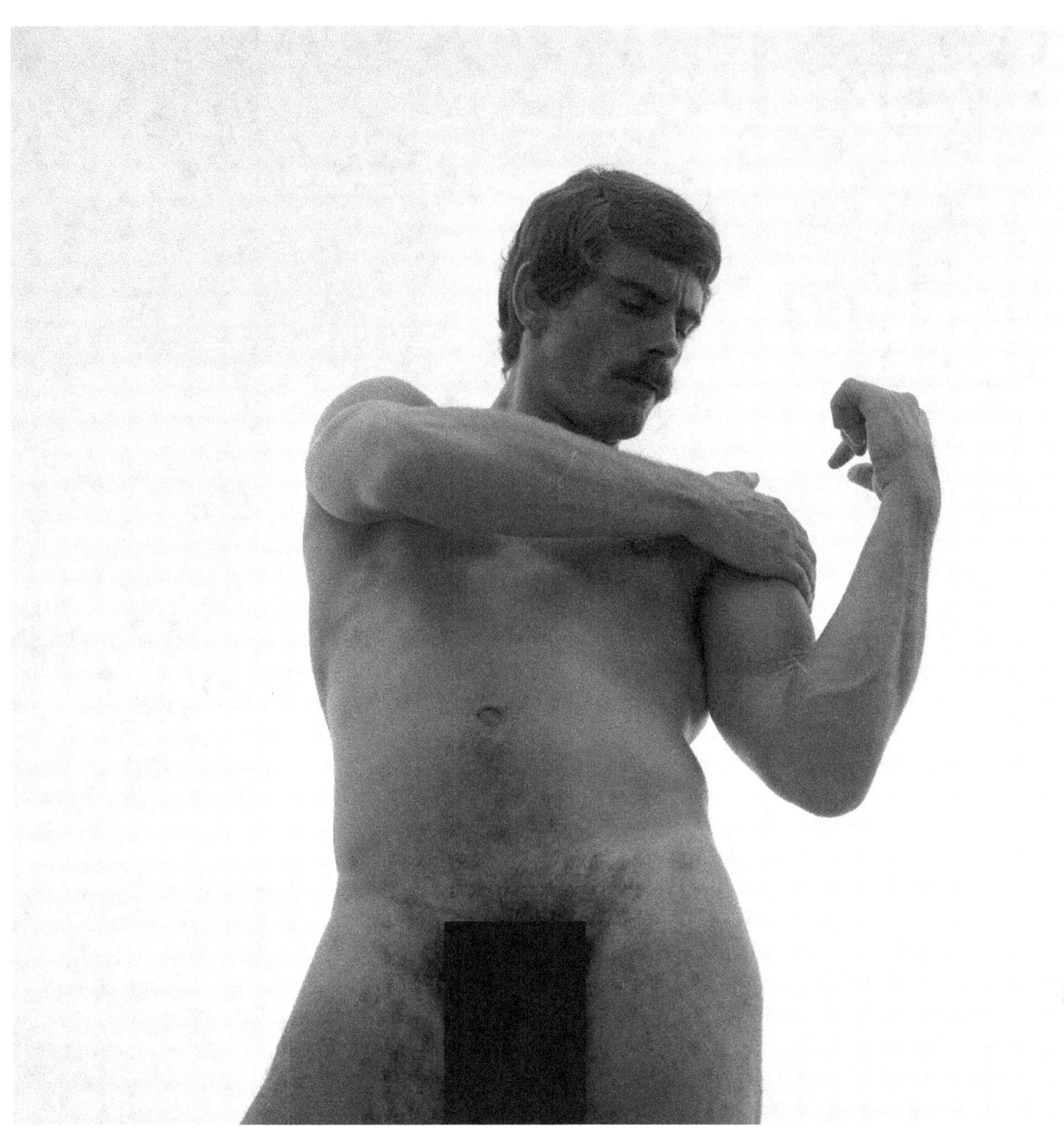

"In this vintage gay porn movie, two lovers decide to try for an open relationship during their vacation in Cherry Grove; jealousies, LSD laced tea going to the wrong guy (Garry Hunt, involving a great trippy sequence featuring Matt Harper), and plenty of sex, of course. Released theatrically in 1979, this movie is one of more ambitious ventures by Hand-In-Hand Films and gathers a gorgeously physical and ample cast of men. In this intelligent and probing story, two lovers, Ron (Larry Paige) and Rick (John Carlo), who think they want an "open relationship" decide to allow each other freedom during their vacation at the swinging gay Fire Island resort, Cherry Grove, in this film by Jack Deveau." *bijouworld.com*

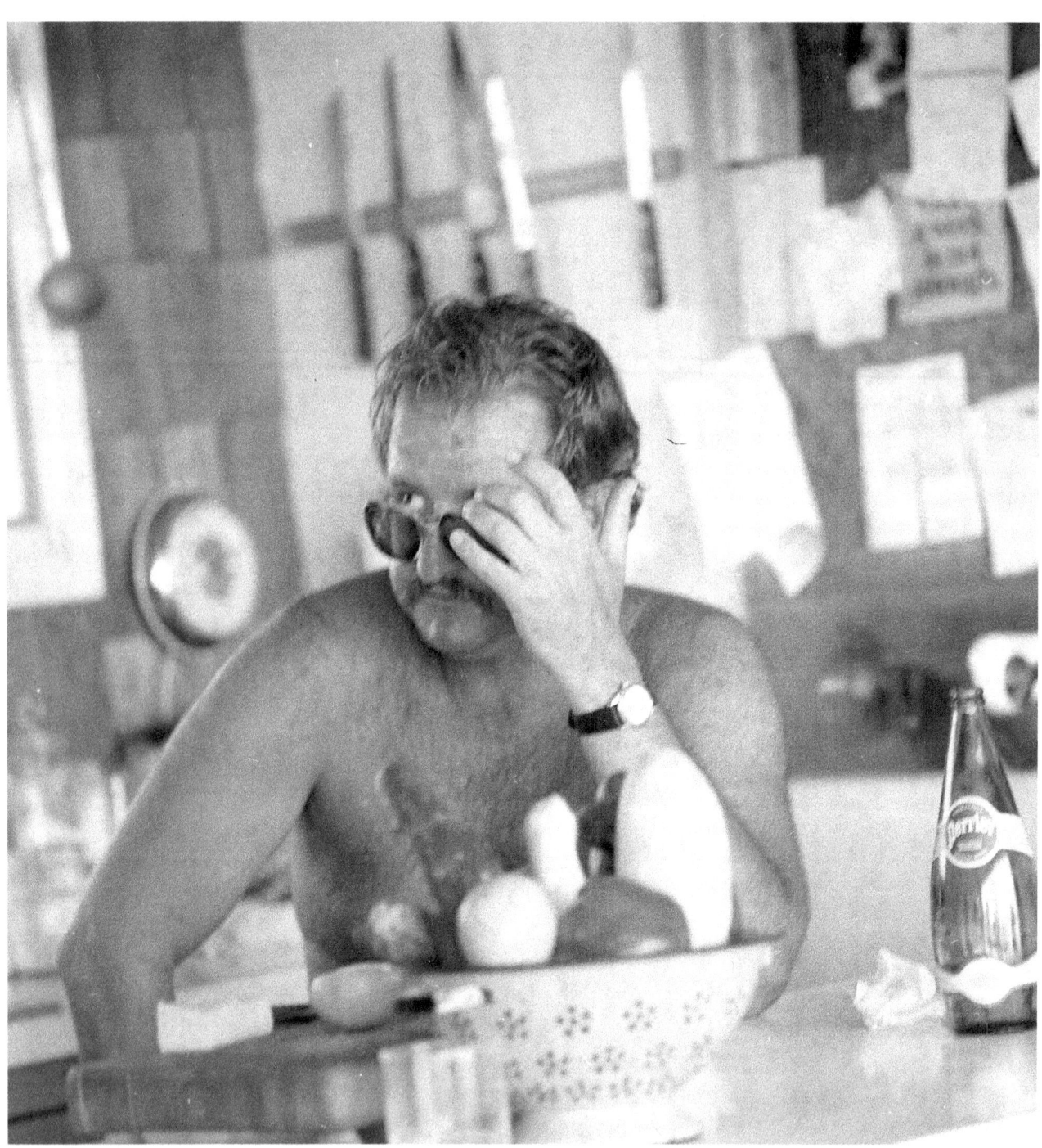

David Litler, Production Coordinator

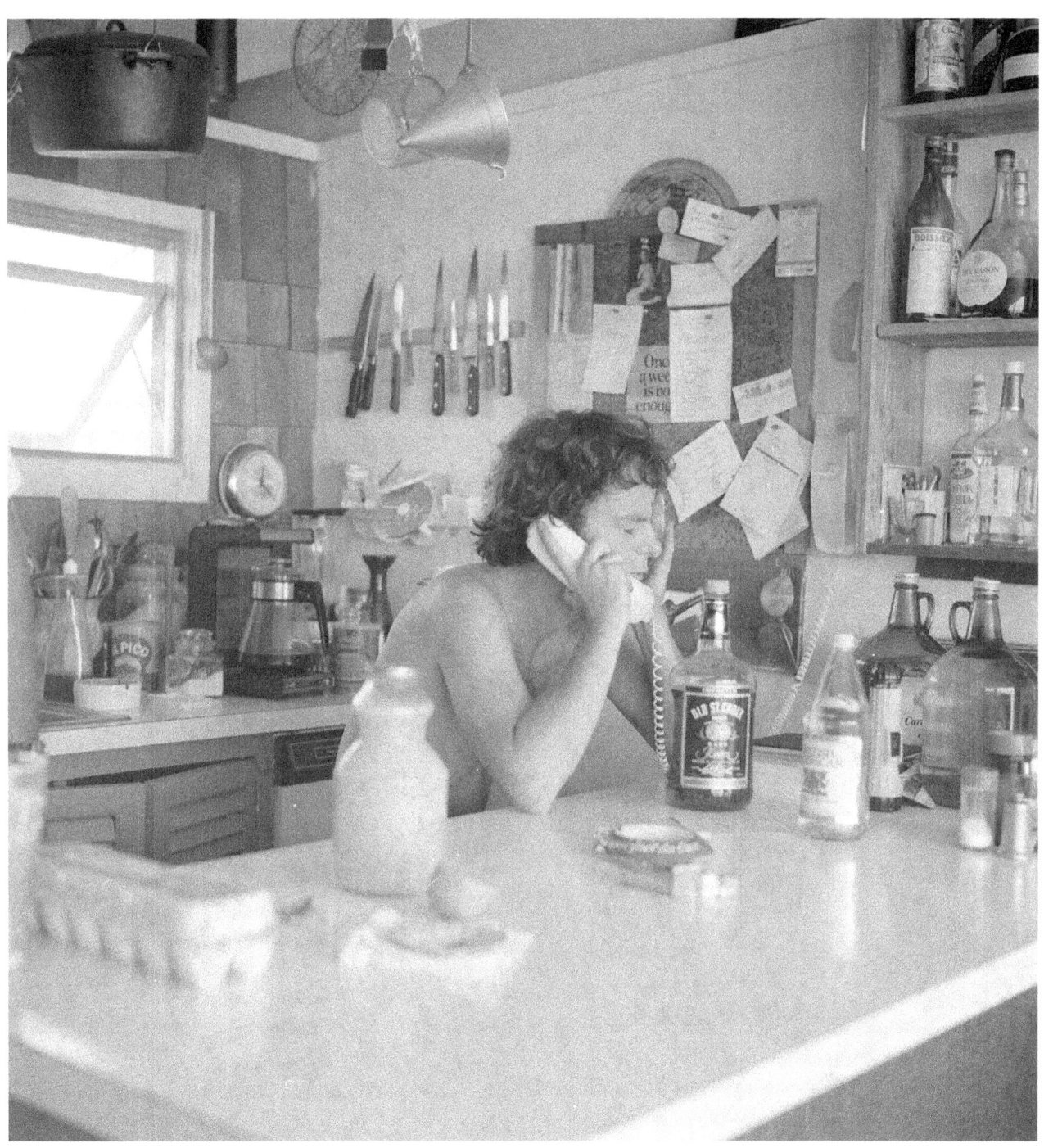

Kees Chapman, Production Assistant

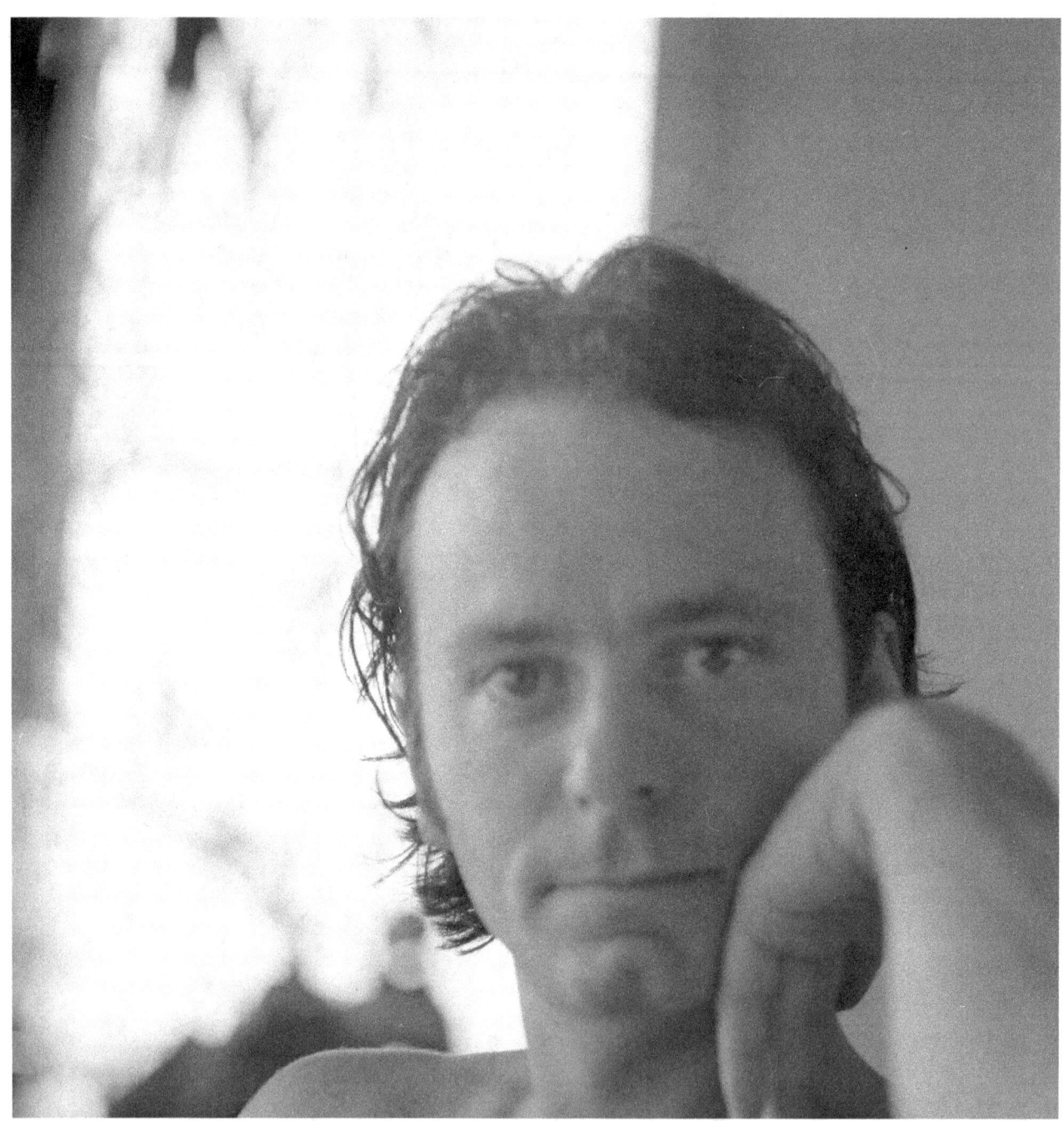

Kees Chapman

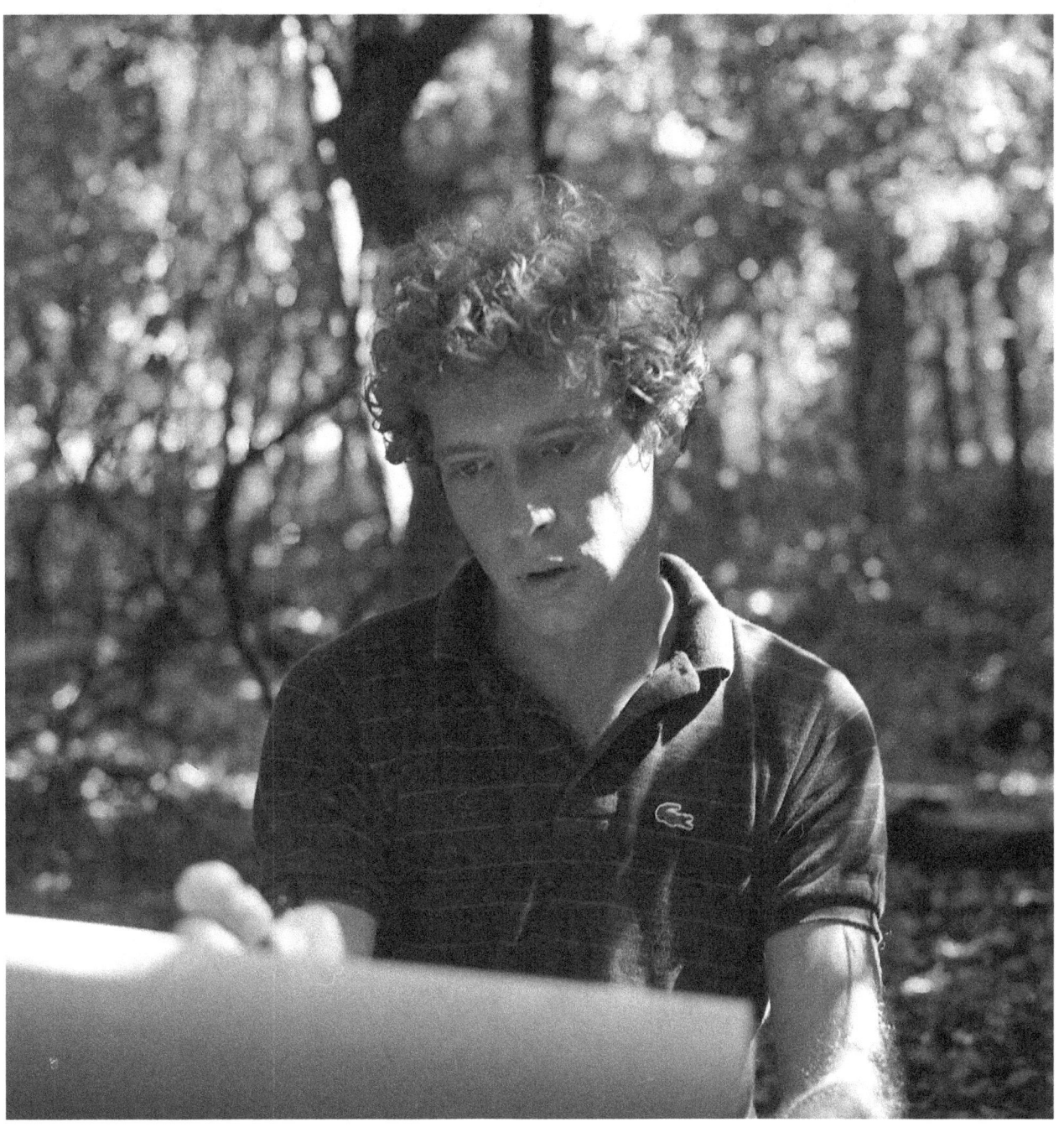

Garry Hunt

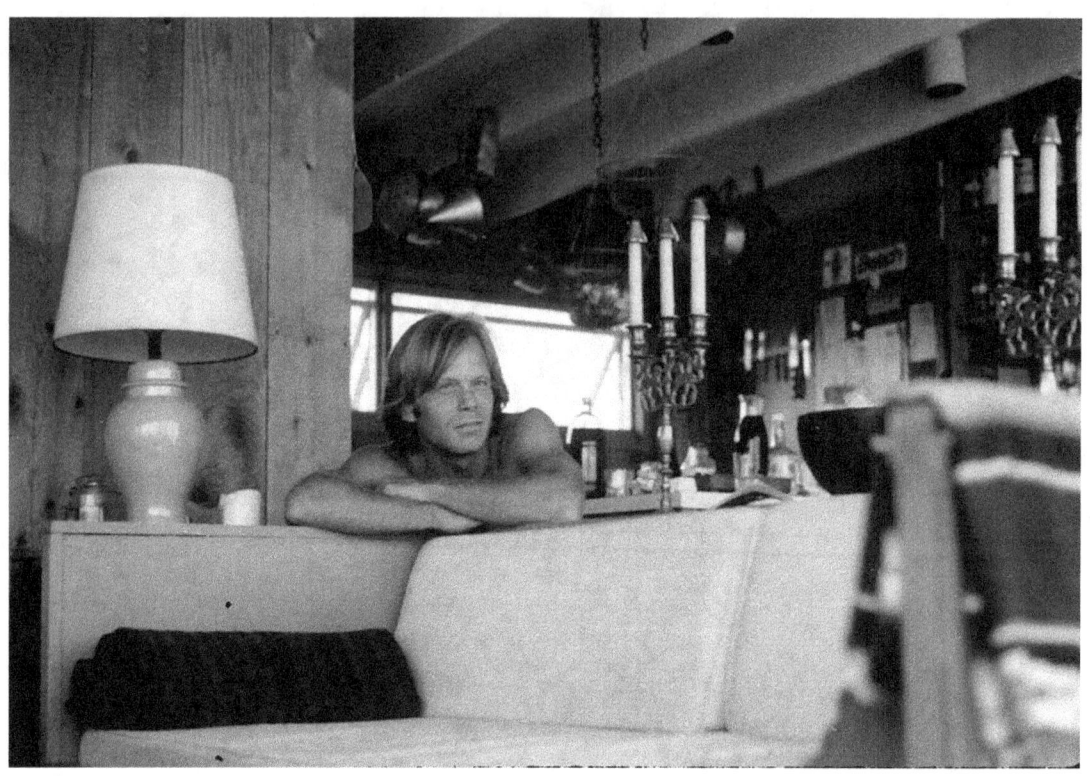

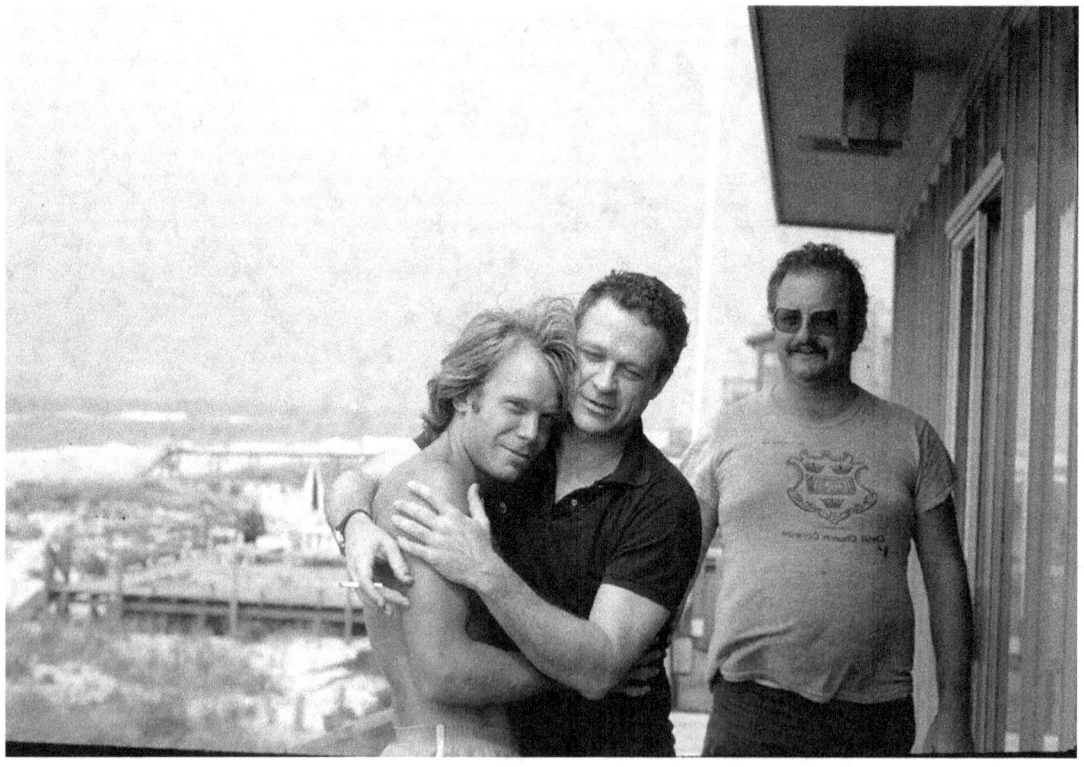

Hugh Allen, Jack Deveau and David Litler

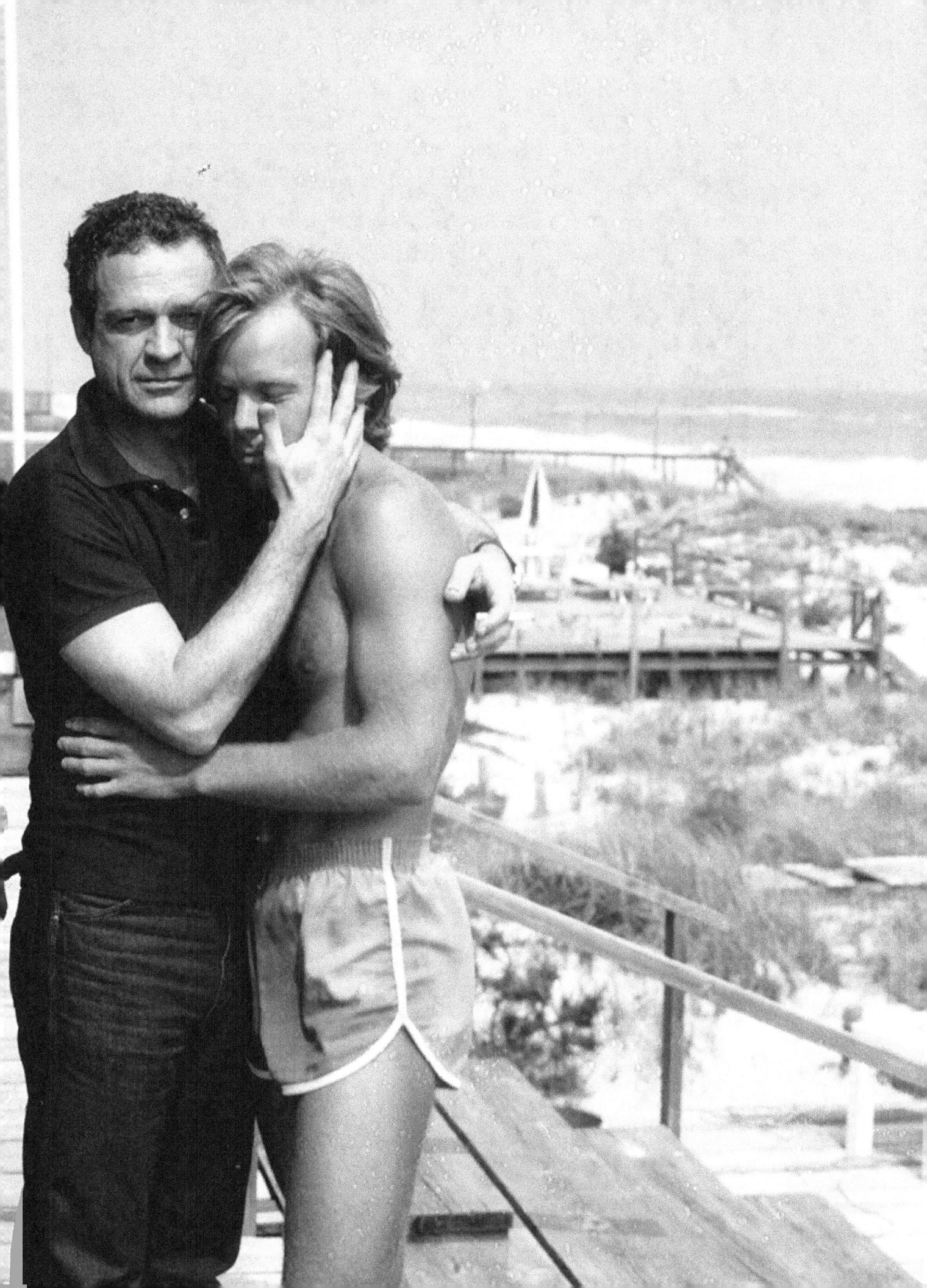

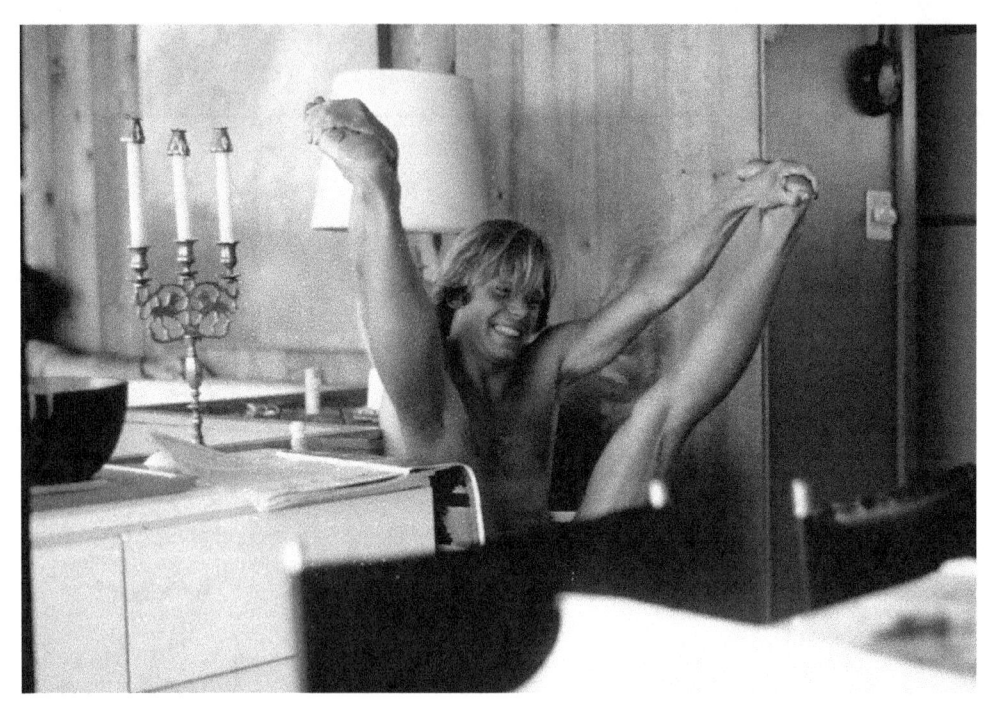

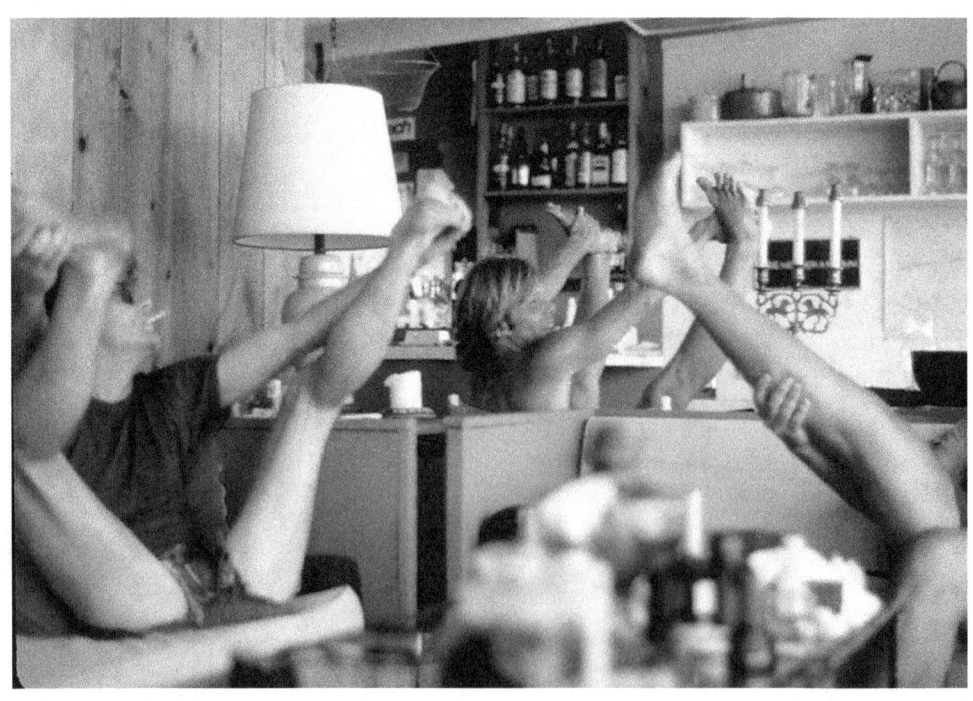

Hugh Allen, Yoga Instructor

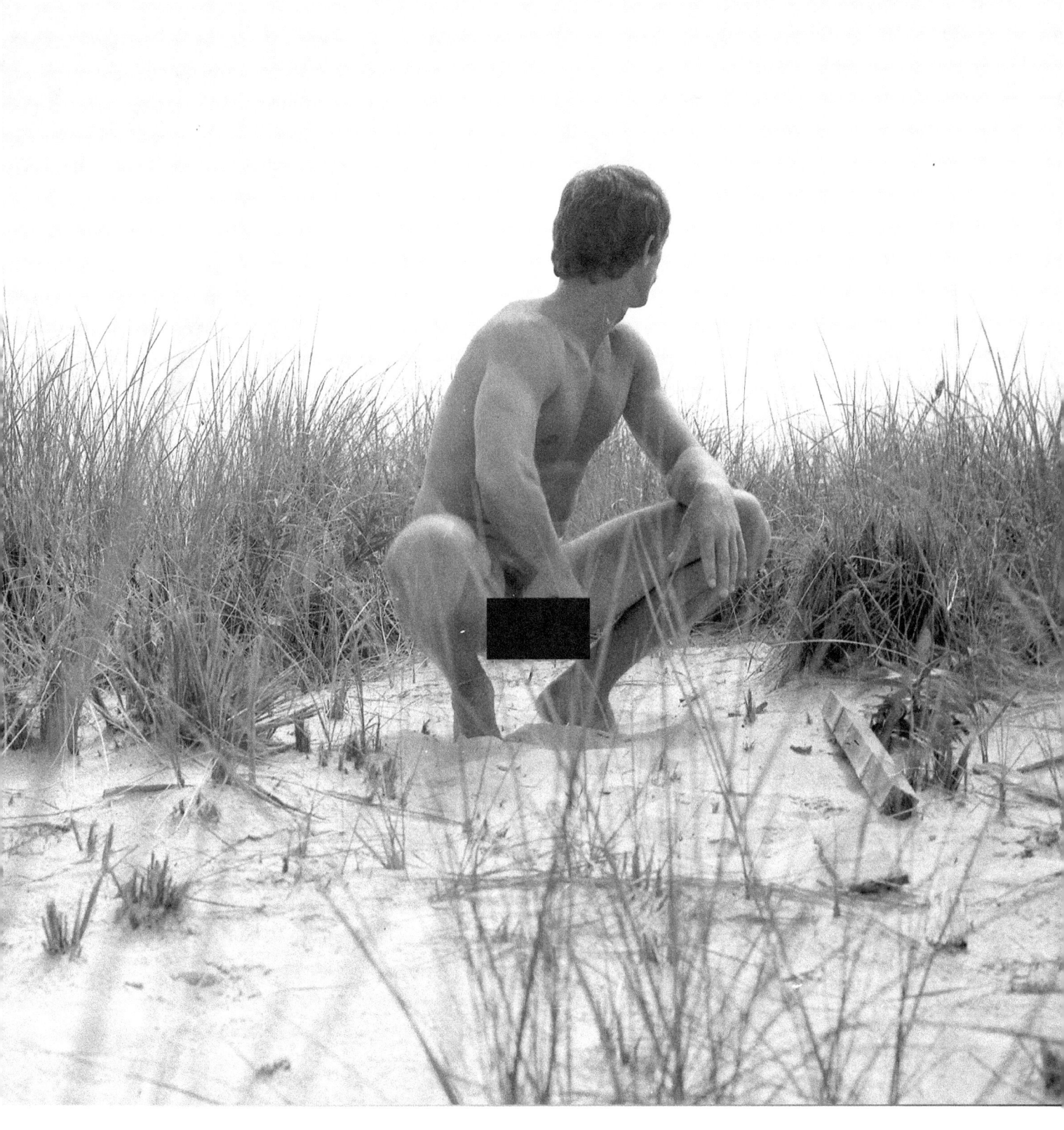

A man in the sand: Matt Harper

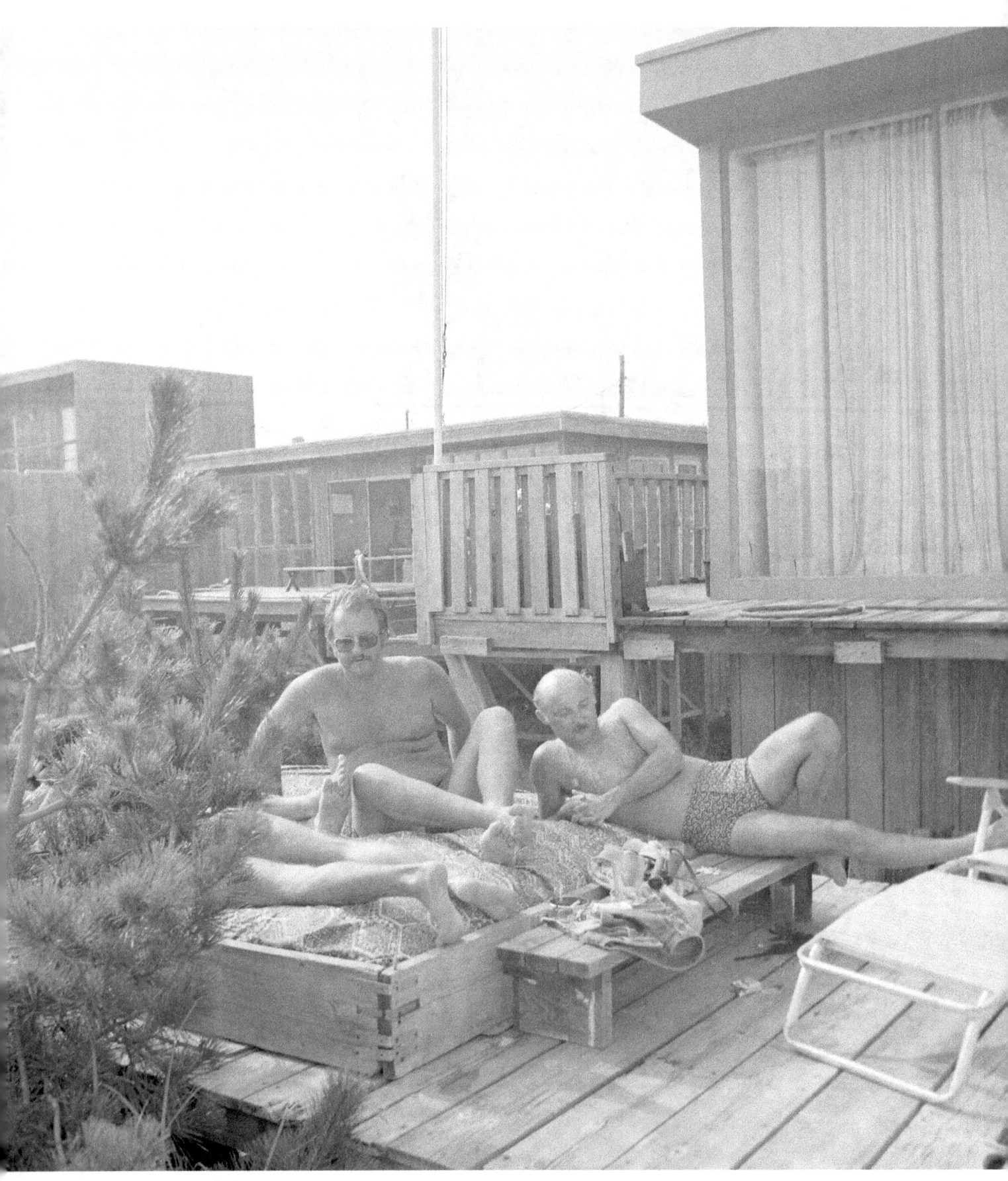

David Litler and unidentified visitor

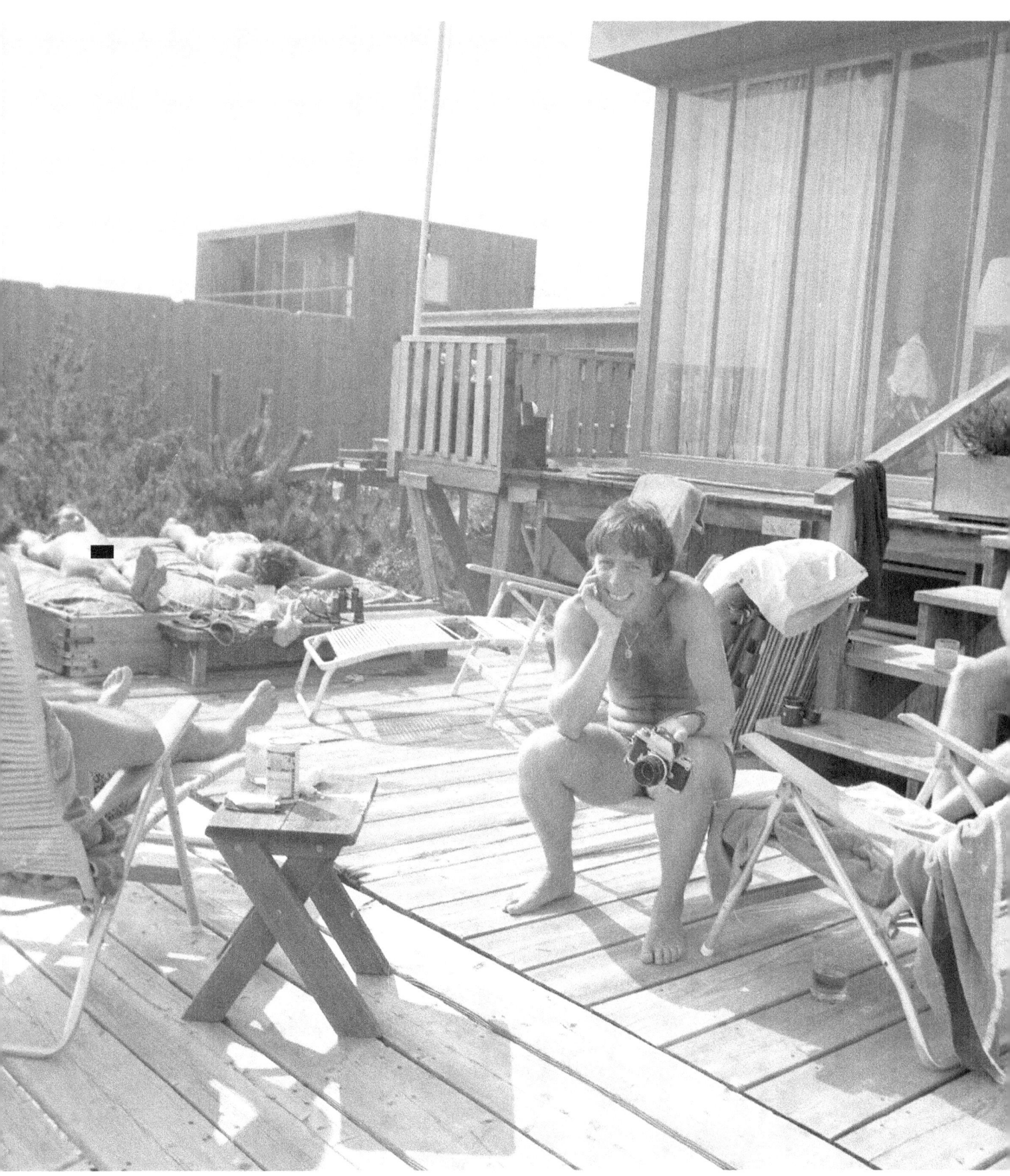

Chris Michaels

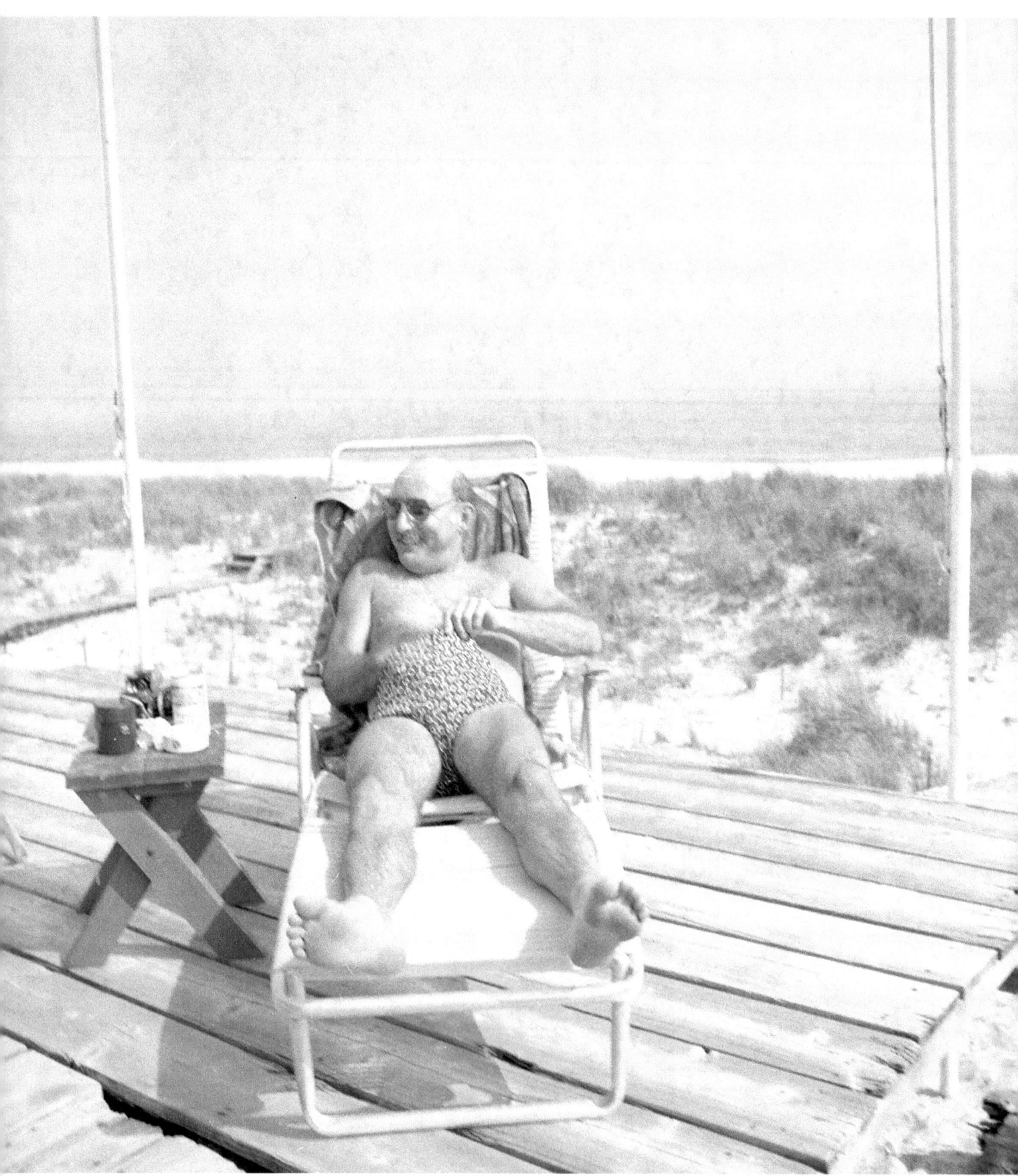
Horny visitor

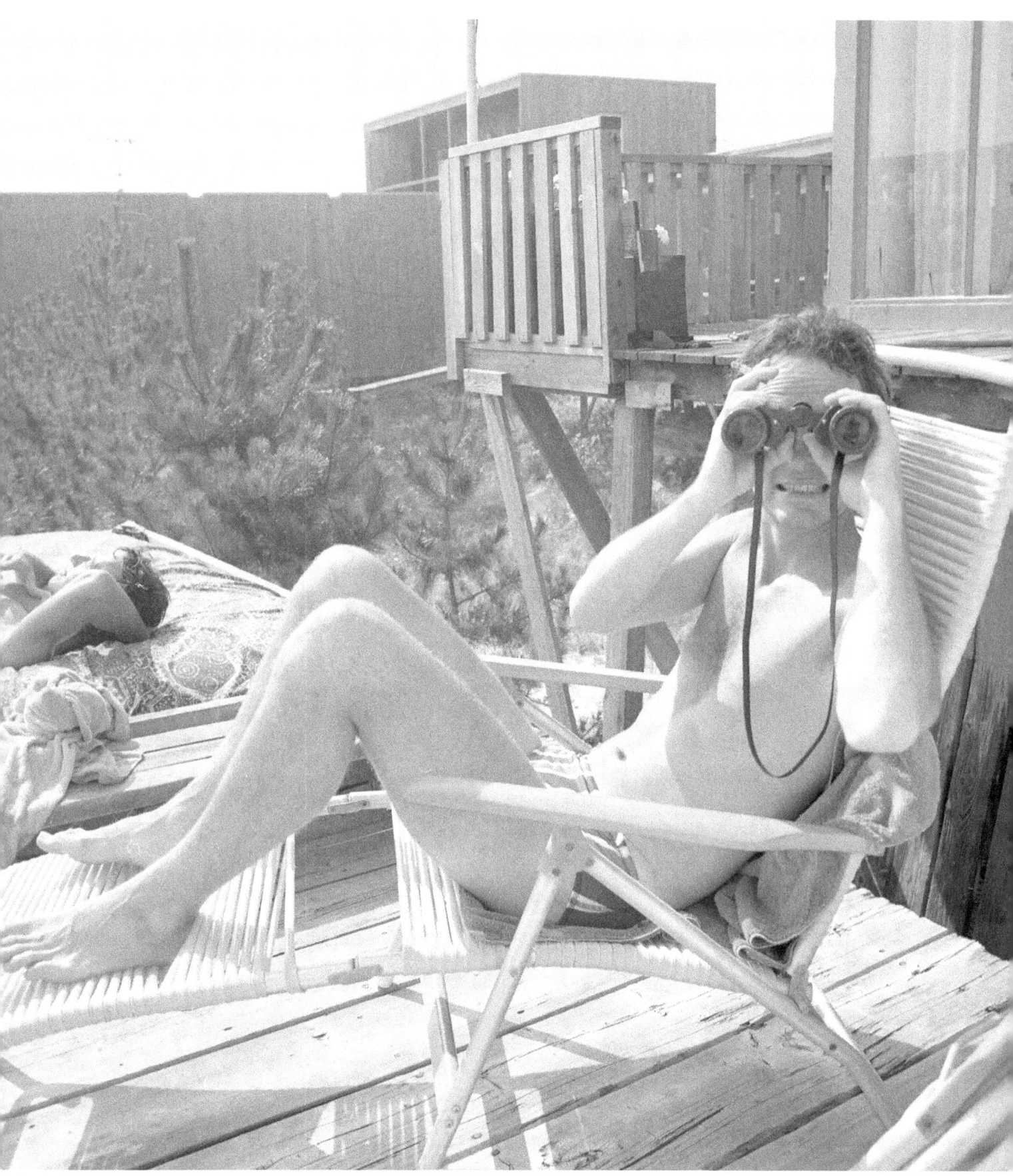

Kees Chapman

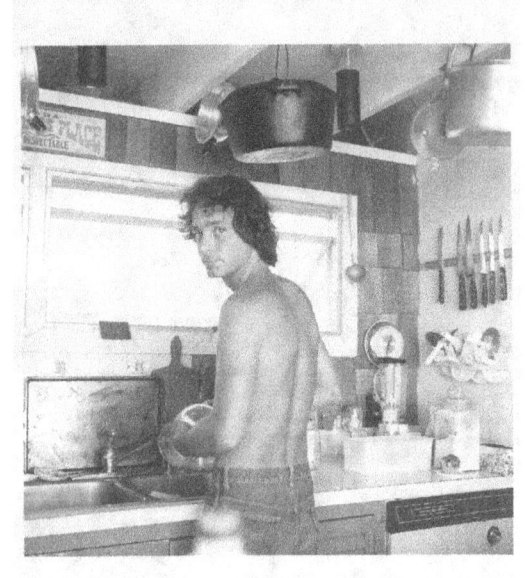
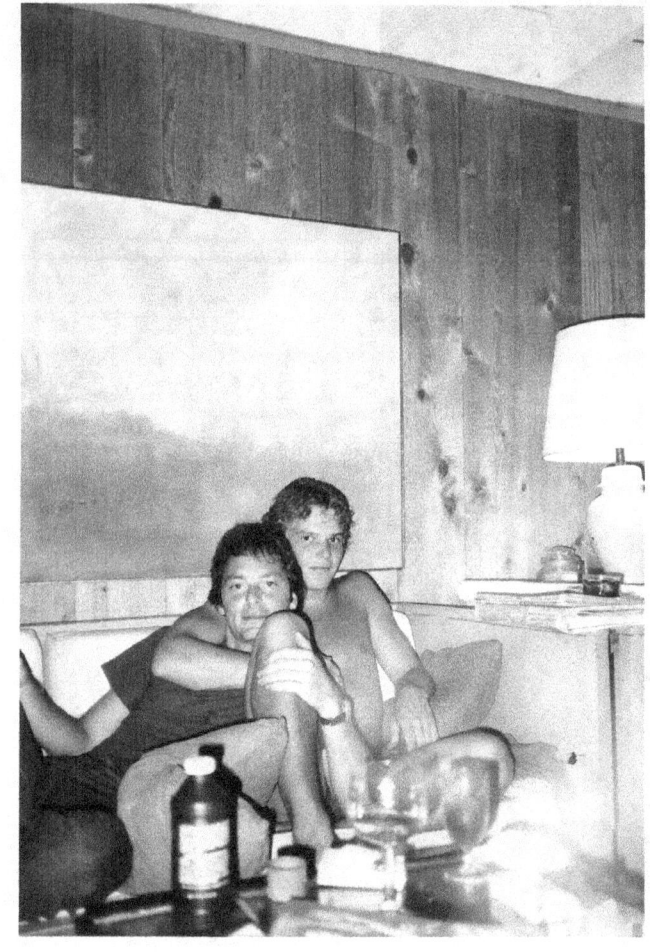
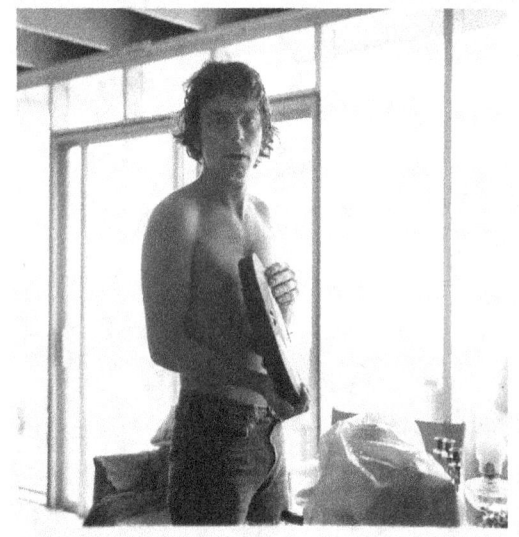

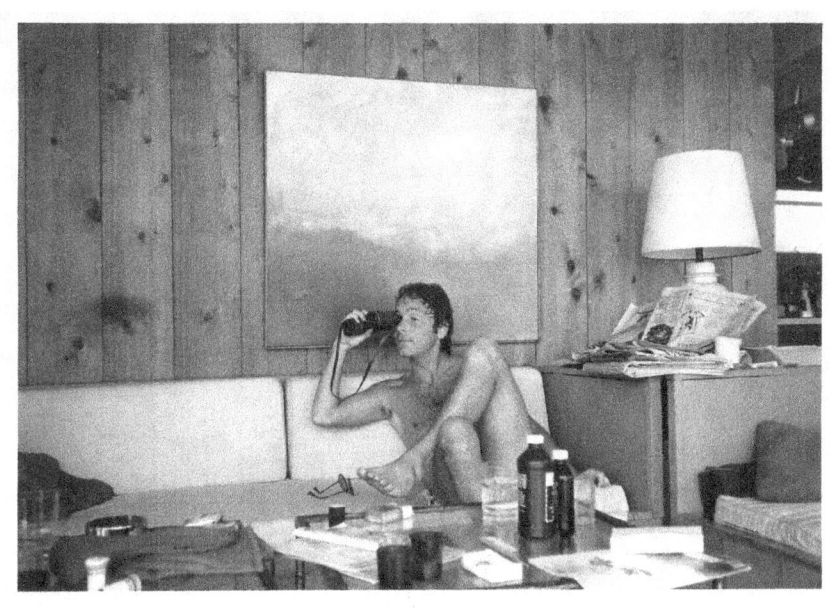
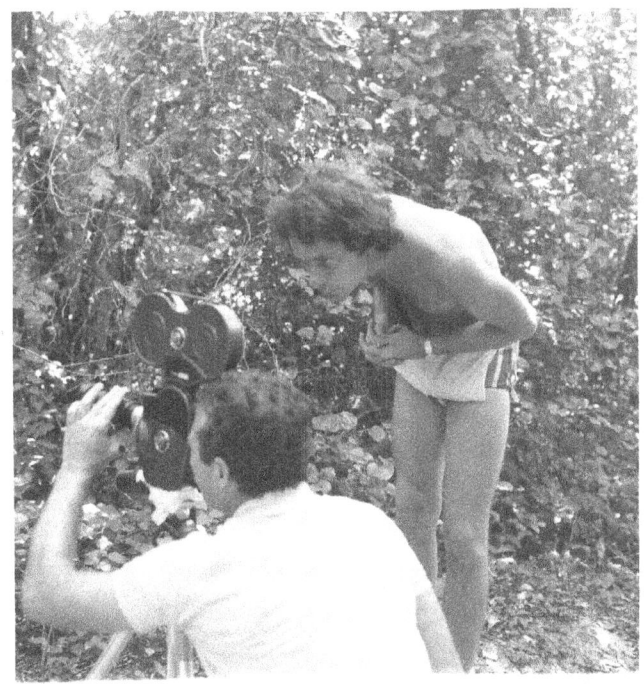

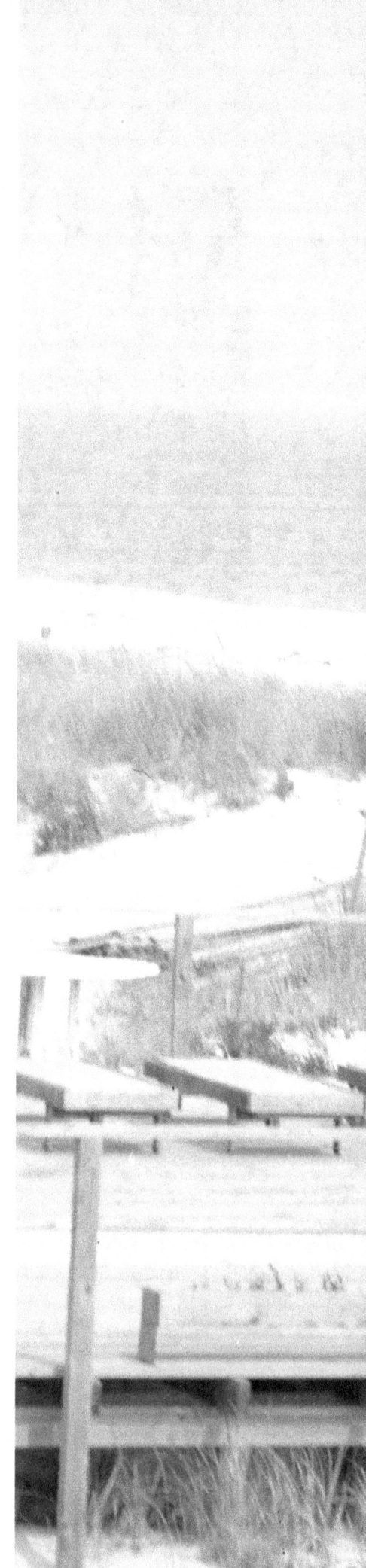

"Fire Island was a fantasy"
WAKEFIELD POOLE

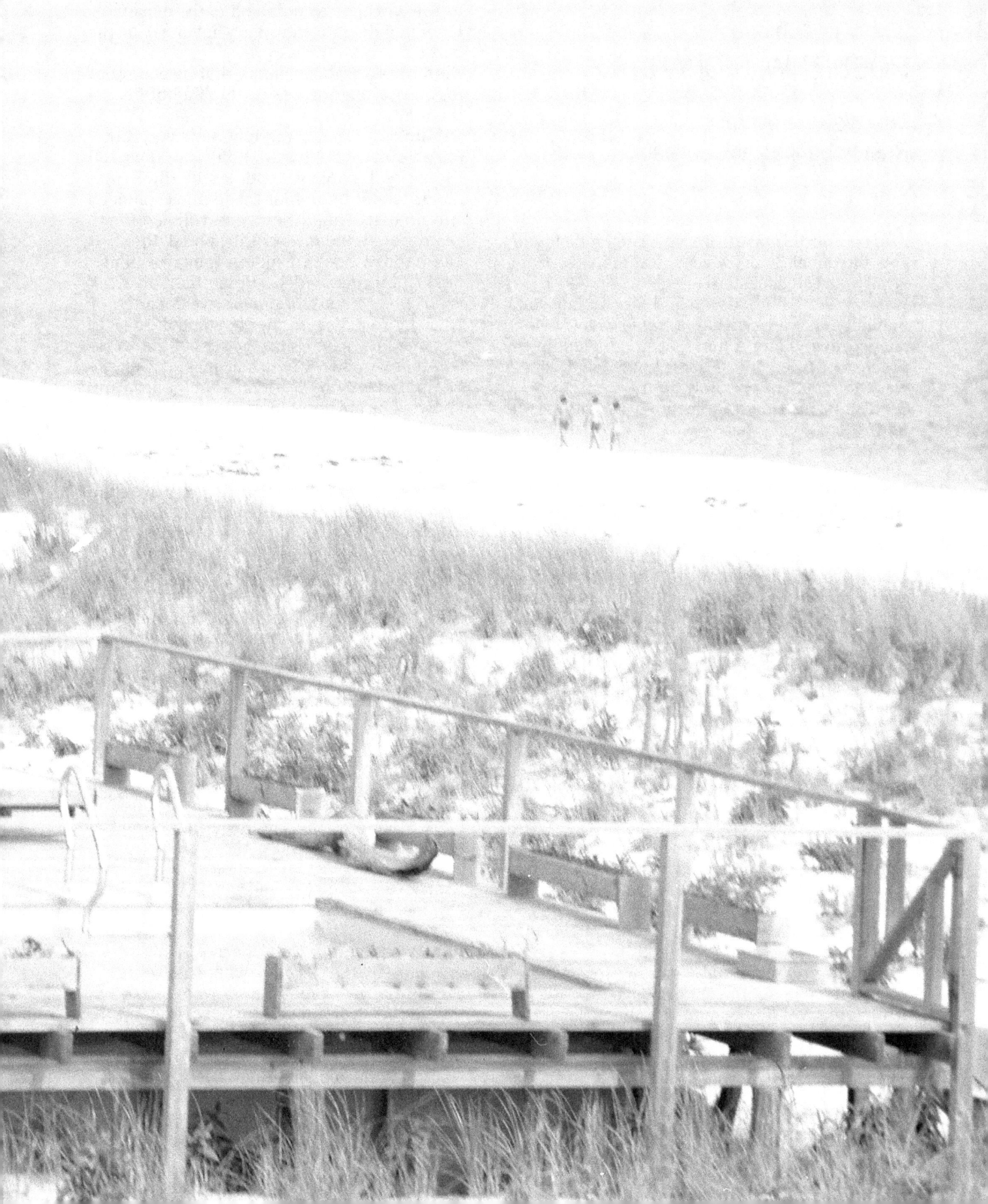

ROBERT W. RICHARDS

The Way We Were: Remembering Jack Deveau

Marco Siedelmann: Do you remember when you did meet Jack Deveau for the first time? What was the occasion?
Robert W. Richards: Yes, I was doing some publicity. I was writing a review, and doing some drawings for a film that he was just in the process of releasing. I don't know what year it was, but you can probably figure it out.
Siedelmann: Do you remember the title of the film?
Richards: Yes, it was BALLET DOWN THE HIGHWAY.
Siedelmann: Did you like it?
Richards: Indeed. I liked Jack's movies because they were complicated. They were more than just sex. I think that Joe Gage and Jack Deveau really are the people who defined that era in which they both were working. They gave some background to the films. I don't mean that Jack used to have a huge storyline; I just mean it was good to know that they were real people, in a place, and they're actually doing something. On a regular porn movie the camera would just open with two guys in bed, and no dialogue of any kind. Just, you know that was it. I never thought that was hot. I like context.
Siedelmann: So do you like the experimental, darker films of Hand In Hand, or do you prefer the lighter, humorous ones?
Richards: I prefer the serious ones, where they really are going to get into it. I want to know how they got to that point. You know, where did the desire start? In other words: I like desire. I think the chase is always more fun than the actual thing. *(laughing)*
Siedelmann: When did you start to develop a personal friendship with Jack Deveau?
Richards: We immediately became friends. He was a very sophisticated man; very, very New York. He lived in a fabulous apartment on 73rd Street. There was a hotel in the building, Jack and Bob Alvarez had the whole roof and the top floor. So it was really a fabulous situation, and of course I was very impressed by that. But he was just a very worldly man; he knew about film, he knew about theatre, he knew what was going on in the museums. He simply was a man very involved in the culture of New York.
Siedelmann: It's a shame that he's more or less forgotten nowadays, thinking of his popularity at the time.
Richards: That's terribly sad, yes. But I am an optimist; I always think that the good things will happen. And I still think that about Jack. I think that those films someday will be discovered. Someone will see them, write about them, and talk about them. It will happen again, I mean, they are films - not just ordinary videos. Sometimes an artist is forgotten about for one or two decades, or even more. Then suddenly someone would become interested, and the rest of the world will follow. When I first met Jack, it was the beginning of my work in that genre. You know what I mean, I knew about porn, and I certainly watched it and all that. But it was the first time that I had myself involved in it. I was very worried about it, because I had a career as an illustrator. I didn't want to sign a phony name to my work, because it's recognizable for being mine. Besides that I don't like that kind of hypocrisy I told Jack that I was a little bit worried. And this is a good quote from him: He said, "Don't worry Robert, 'cause by the year 2000 porn will just be the Disney of its time." *(laughing)* - And that's true. That did happen! It became very much above ground. When Jack was doing it, it was still underground. Also there were theatres, his movies played in theaters. Once the theaters left, that was it. Of course they transferred some on VCR, CD, and DVD.
Siedelmann: What was your impression back then? Did the audience pay attention to the films, or were they mostly been consumed as porn movies?
Richards: I think some people took them seriously as film. You know, they were really good plotted, they had a great cast. I mean, they were more than porno. They were erotic films; that's really what they were.
Siedelmann: You interviewed some of the actors who had starred in Hand In Hand films – for example Jayson McBride, Jack Wrangler, or Luke. Were you ever on location during a shooting of Jack?

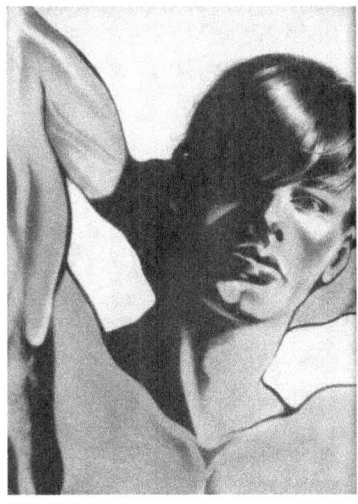
Bill Eld

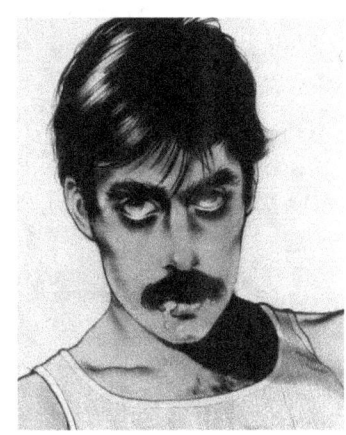
Keith Anthoni

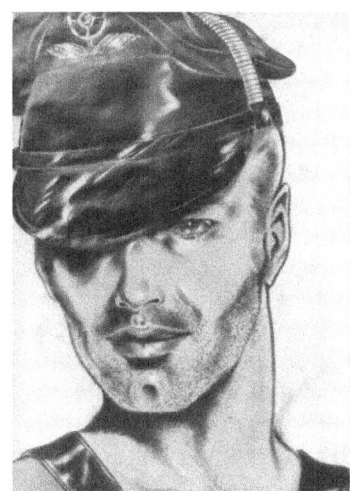
Christopher Rage

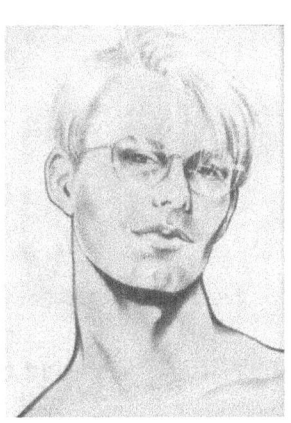
Luke

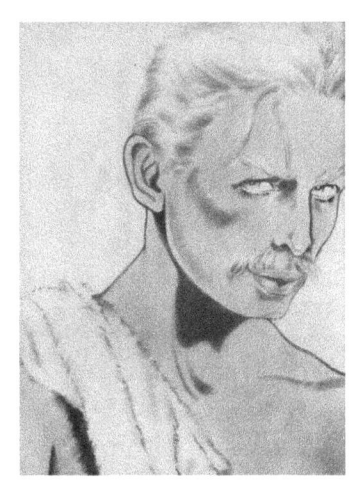
Scorpio

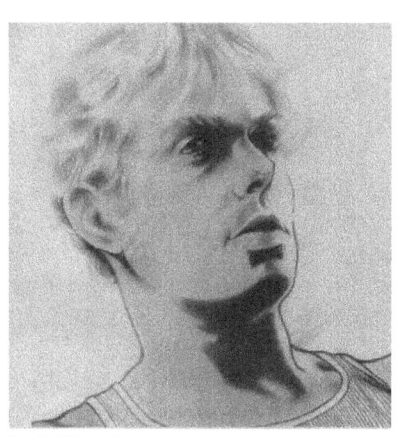
Jack Wrangler

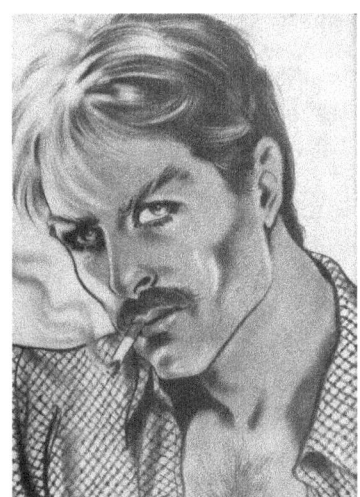
Jayson MacBride

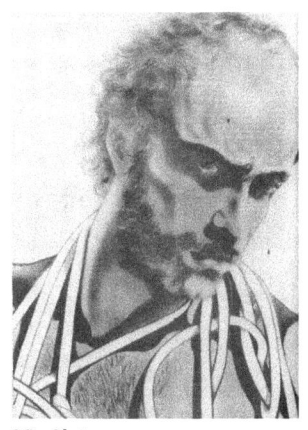
J.D. Slater

ILLUSTRATIONS BY ROBERT W. RICHARDS

Richards: Actually not. I was on set a lot of times with Joe Gage, but never with Jack.
Siedelmann: All of the actors spoke very nicely and kindly about him.
Richards: I have the same opinion, yes. Just everybody spoke about what a gentleman he was, and how smart. He was just first class.
Siedelmann: And that's reflecting in his movies as well. So were you around a lot in the circle of Hand In Hand. Were you close to the other people as well?
Richards: I knew Tray Christopher before I knew Jack, and I became sort of an acquaintance of Jack Wrangler. He wasn't my favorite person. He was like, very... he believed that he was Jack Wrangler. He forgot who he really was.
Siedelmann: Yes, I remember your interview with him, published in *Stallion* or *Manshots*. *(laughing)*
Richards: I did a lot of interviews with the actors, and I once did one with Jack Deveau, but I don't have it anymore.
Siedelmann: That's a shame, would love to read that. Talking about the men of Hand In Hand. Do you have a favorite actor among them?
Richards: Oh, one always does, doesn't one? *(both laughing)* – You got to have to. I like the guy called Malo. He's a big muscle guy, not the type I usually like, but there was something about him. You just knew that he had something more than that. And I liked Christopher Rage. Jayson McBride. And Roger! They were all good, fine men. Not a lot of them worked for other people, most starred only in Jack's films. Not Wrangler, of course - I used to see him socially, because I was also a friend of his wife, the singer Margaret Whiting. So I used to see them often, for music projects and private occasions.
Siedelmann: Did you have a chance to say goodbye to Jack Deveau?
Richards: At some point it was obvious that there was something wrong with Jack. He was suddenly an old man. He was walking with difficulty, he wasn't standing up straight. He became just a completely different character. I don't remember the specific last time, but I remember the last few times that I saw him. I thought, oh, Jack is dying. He just knew it. He had changed so much. He looked like an 80 year old man; even 90. Jack never changed before that. None of us knew that he was as sick as he was. So it all came as a big surprise.
Siedelmann: Did you go to his funeral?
Richards: No, I went to a memorial, but I don't remember much about it. You know, at that particular period you had to go to so many memorials, because of the AIDS crisis and all that. So I don't really remember one from the other anymore. This is very emotional, you know. You cannot imagine, because it was very big here. In New York it was totally intense. Almost every day you heard about another person. Totally terrifying.
Siedelmann: Jack Deveau passed away very early when the AIDS crisis had just arrived. One of my interview partners told me that in a way it was good for Jack to go before he had to see all of the others go.

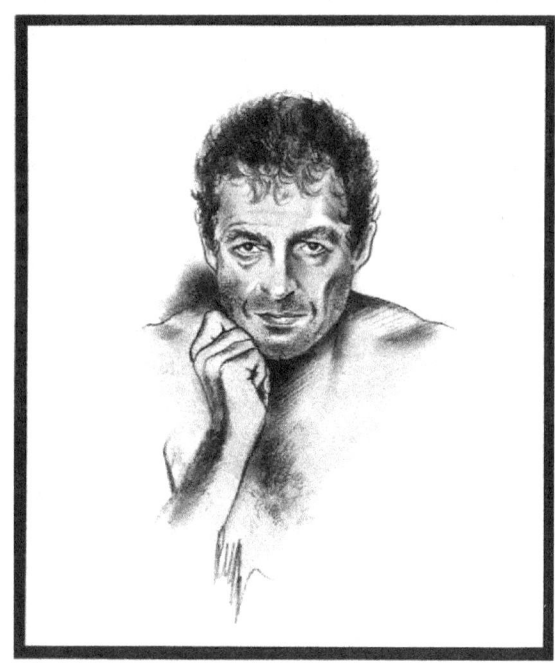

Jack Deveau by Robert W. Richards

Richards: Well, that's true; if he had to go. But yes, that would have been very difficult for Jack. He was a very sensitive and a very loyal man. He liked all those people who worked for him. He would have taken care of them as good as possible, but unfortunately he wasn't there anymore. Sad.
Siedelmann: Can you say something about the theaters in New York? Were you a regular in the 55th Playhouse and the Adonis?
Richards: I wouldn't say regular, but I was there often. Believe it or not, mostly I went there to see the movies. *(laughing)*
Siedelmann: So not for cruising?
Richards: Well, I did some of that, I assure you! But the reason that brought me there was not the cruising, it was more the movies themselves. If I was interested in seeing something, I would go out and see it right away. And of course if you got lucky it was lovely too.
Siedelmann: When did your desire start to be a part of that scene, what made you

start your interviews, and your work as a chronicler of the era?

Richards: Actually there were a couple of people that encouraged me, one being Joe Gage. And then, after I started, Jack became very important for me. He liked my work, because he thought I brought something unusual to it. I didn't ask the same questions that everybody asked all the time. I was more of an individual. So that's how it started and you know once you start, pretty soon people from California are calling, telling you that this boy is coming to town, or that man. They asked if I would want to work with them. I usually said yes, and usually I was happy that I said yes, because mostly they were people that I liked.

Siedelmann: The Hand In Hand movies brought together art, cinema, and porn. Do you think the video technique destroyed that culture and separated the regular film world again from the adult film world?

Richards: I guess that's true, because the theaters were limited when most people began to watch video. Most people watch porn in private as opposed to go into a theater. But of course there weren't many theaters in most cities of the United States, or the world. I think video was a big, radical change for sexual behavior, people suddenly could watch porn at home. They didn't have to depend on going out to a public place to see it. They could watch at home, and alone, or with a friend or friends. I think that made a very big difference, the same difference that it had for actual movies, or Hollywood movies. It certainly affected the attention to the theaters.

Siedelmann: And of course in times of celluloid you needed a real film crew, so they were actual filmmakers.

Richards: Yes, the crew members were very professional. They were all guys who had a couple of days off, and they took these jobs. They knew what they were doing when it came to sound and light, and all the other elements you need for a good film. They knew how to do it, and they were willing to do it. A lot of them were gay anyway, so a lot of them were willing to work in porn to see what it's all about. Because god knows, it was fun.

Siedelmann: The films directed by Peter De Rome are among the darkest produced by Hand In Hand. Do you have an opinion about him and his films?

Richards: I was a big admirer of Peter De Rome, both as a filmmaker and before that as a writer.

Siedelmann: He wrote a great memoir book, *The Erotic World of Peter De Rome*...

Richards: ... which I loved. And don't forget, in ADAM & YVES he had that incredible moment with Greta Garbo. He caught her walking down the street, he filmed her, and of course this was always one of my favorite things. I always loved Greta Garbo, and I still do. It was such a great thing that they caught it, and nobody ever did anything about it. The film was released without the scene having to be taken out. I actually have a feeling that she might have enjoyed it if she would have seen it in private. *(laughing)*

Siedelmann: Well, it's a very tasteful and sensitive movie.

Richards: Yeah, exactly. And she is treated as what she was: legendary. I liked Peter De Rome personally as well. He was a very nice man. His memoir is indeed very memorable; so a big YES! to Peter De Rome.

Siedelmann: Did you ever have an impression about how Jack Deveau and Bob Alvarez worked together?

Richards: I only knew them professionally. At the time they were starting out as filmmakers, I didn't know them at all personally. By the time I met Jack he already was in a relationship with Bob Alvarez for many years.

Siedelmann: After Jack Deveau passed away, did you stay in contact with Bob Alvarez or others from the Hand In Hand circle?

Richards: Yes, kind of. We're in contact, which means we know how to reach each other, but sometimes we don't speak for years or so. But I like Bob a lot, he's a fine gentleman. And I think he's doing a very good job with keeping Jack's work alive. I mean, Jack's films have been transferred from one medium to another, and Bob has a great love for both – the films, and of course for Jack being remembered. Bob is a fine and kind person – and still very good looking. He always was in great shape and very handsome. They had a lot of parties back in the day, and I have to say they had a great space. In the summer the parties happened on the roof and in the winter in their very big apartment. It wasn't divided into little rooms; it was more like a very huge loft. They used to entertain a lot. All the people related to the films were invited: The actors, the crew people, and several other famous people, writers like Michael Musto or Sal Mineo. It was always a very exciting group of people. Jack was a true artist, and he attracted artists. Everybody respected him for that. It was just a big community, you know? I think most

artists regarded "porn" when it was on the level of Jack Deveau, Peter De Rome, Joe Gage, or Wakefield Poole. I think there wasn't a difference; they were considered artists, not porno filmmakers. There wasn't a difference of people who drew fashion, they all used to mix.
Siedelmann: When you think back of Jack Deveau, do you have a certain anecdote which reflects your friendship, or his personality?
Richards: Well, what I liked best about Jack is that he never was a judgmental person. He treated everyone individually, not like putting people in groups, and then not liking that group. In a time where everybody had that strict moral code, Jack had none of that. Jack just wanted for everybody to live their lives and have fun with it. That's what he did, and every time I went there I had a great time. So I don't remember many specific things, but I certainly do remember the overall atmosphere that he created around himself. It was an atmosphere of great freedom and tolerance. People could be whoever they were in front of Jack. There were no limits, because he wasn't going to be judgmental about them, only about himself. That's how I feel about Jack.
Siedelmann: Probably that was the reason because he was able to create that special mood on set.
Richards: Exactly. He was the same as a filmmaker as he was at home. He always was gentle and strong.
Siedelmann: So do you think he was a happy person?
Richards: In the years that I knew him certainly he enjoyed life. He was very, very happy with Bob, and he was happy with the films he was making, and I think he was happy with his place in the artistic community. So yes, I would say he was a very happy man, until disaster struck, until he became ill. That changed everything, as it would change anybody. That's pretty much all I can tell you. All in all, I think he had a good life. His dream was to make films, and he fulfilled that dream. Bob was the love of his life, and he fulfilled that dream as well. He had a great place to live, and more or less enough money to do whatever they wanted. He travelled a lot. He was more happy than most of the people. And I think his happiness made other people happy.
Siedelmann: Yes, lots of people told me that Jack Deveau encouraged them to live their lives open and free.
Richards: Right, and Jack was a living example of that. Jack knew that you have to be free to be happy, that you can't keep secrets and hiding behind things, or thinking that you were something that you were not. He was a very honest man, and he totally believed in having a good life this way. If you need to come out to enhance your life, than you should do it! Do what's going to make you happy. He was an amazing person.
Siedelmann: Did you fall in love with him at some point?
Richards: No, for the simple reason that I knew he wasn't an available man. I didn't want to waste my time and feelings falling in love with him. *(laughing)* – He belonged to somebody else. Don't get me wrong, I don't think there are many men out there who are like Jack Deveau, but there are other wonderful men. Fortunately I had a few of them in my life. So I didn't have to go and fish somebody else's man. Also, I wouldn't compete with Bob Alvarez. Anybody who wanted to compete with Bob was out of their mind. Bob is a very special person as well. I loved them and respected them as a couple always as a couple.
Siedelmann: What would be your favorite film by Hand In Hand?
Richards: I like ADAM & YVES a lot, because it's a very sensitive film, and very sweet. I still like the two boys starring as the leading couple. And I liked DUNE BUDDIES, DRIVE, and I loved A NIGHT AT THE ADONIS. I remember when I went to the Adonis; it was fun to see it on the big screen in the film. I also remember Eartha Hugee, the ticket lady – she was a very great and warm person. She knew all the secrets. *(laughing)* We chatted a lot. I didn't know her well, but she was one of these persons you don't forget. She was the person who sold you the tickets, so she was the face of the Adonis. She made you feel very comfortable. The Adonis always was a quiet place where you could find a companion, where you can jerk off together, or whatever.

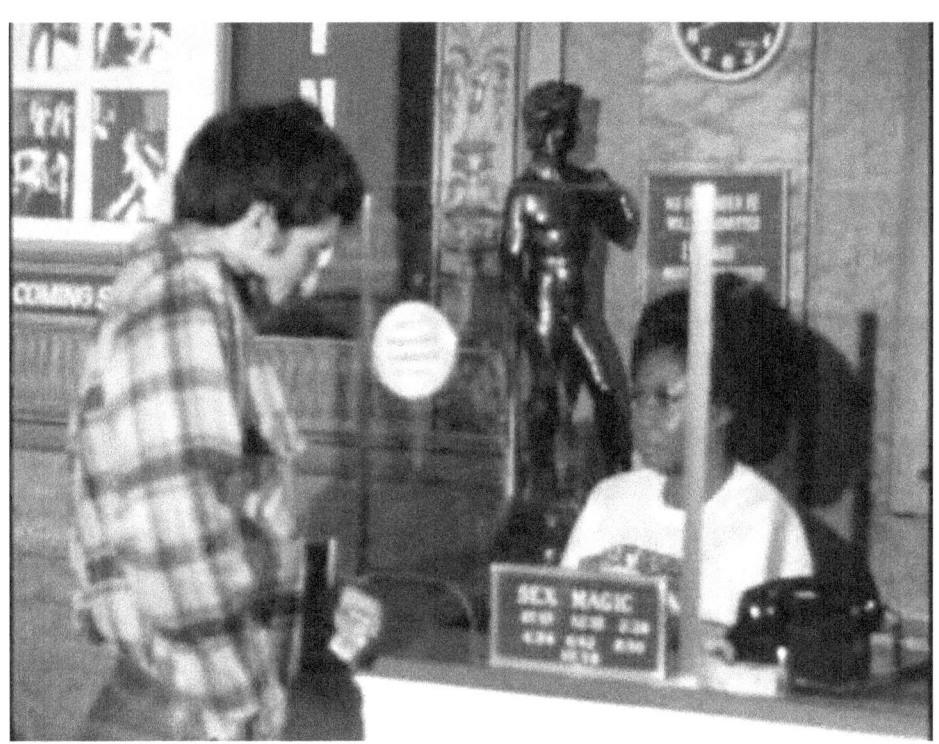

Eartha Hugee in *A Night at the Adonis*

Jack Deveau - A Bluemovie

by Robert W. Richards

Editor's note: Deveau was interviewed prior to the completion of his Hand In Hand pictures TIMES SQUARE STRIP and BOYS OF RIVERSIDE DRIVE, but exclusive, never-published stills became available before press time.

"PRIVATE COLLECTION is a cross between TWILIGHT ZONE and MONDO CANE," says Jack Deveau sitting in his studio on 73rd Street as a Movieola whirls on in the next room, emitting wet, sexual sounds. "It's the first in a series of forthcoming Hand In Hand films using collections of either short, very bizarre items or pieces that were good basic ideas that didn't flesh out into full-length features but worked perfectly as little O'Henry-type vignettes. It's a long film, over 90 minutes, and what put it all into place for me were memories of those little dirty comic books that were around years ago. They were cartoon and very direct – someone would walk through a door and say, 'Boy, I think you're hot, hones, let's fuck!' But there was some plot continuity, one situation led to another, one character to the other, and if anyone misbehaved there was always a little morality – he got his comeuppance. All in 10 or 20 pages! Really tight storytelling." Deveau's Porno Pioneer – his LEFT-HANDED is probably the first gay film with a substantial plot and an attempt at presenting well-developed characters with something more than outright lust on their minds. He got into the movie business at the suggestion of his close friend Sal Mineo, who took him to a meeting on a multi-million-dollar project he was about to become involved in. "At that time I was working with my lover and partner Bobby Alvarez, who still edits all our films, and we were making film strips for schools and government programs – I went to the meeting at Sal's insistence and just sat in the background – stunned! I couldn't believe how incredibly stupid these people were. They were discussing ads and fighting over credits, and the film wasn't even in production yet. After listening to all their bullshit, it seemed like an easy project to tackle, and I made my first film in 1973. Twenty films later I'm still grateful to Sal. One thing I've learned is that gays are very mobile – the most gorgeous man with the biggest dick can walk in here at any time, but I may not have anything for him at the moment – two weeks later the perfect thing comes up, but by now he's living in Switzerland with a john, or he's skiing in Denver or surfing in Hawaii. Another thing that happens is people stick a snake up their ass, ride a unicycle and fuck at the same time – things we simply have no place for. If I'm in the story stage of a film, I'll construct something around their peculiar talent, but as a result of losing lots of these people – at the rate of two or three a month – we decided to shoot them anyway, do a piece of film right on the spot. Now the PRIVATE COLLECTION series has become a way to use all these wild bits in theatrical features. For instance, a beautiful man came in, he can sit in the locus position, concentrate, his dick rises straight up into the air, and he can take an implement like a lobster pick or a toothbrush, stick it into his cock and have an orgasm by just touching himself three or four times. Where on earth could we use it? Luckily, we shot it, saved it, and now it's in the movie." Hand In Hand's doors are always open to newcomers and hopefuls. "We ask everyone who comes

MAKER'S PRIVATE THOUGHTS

up here to fill out a form that's been designed as an ice-breaker. There are some very bold questions and some very benign ones, from 'How many orgasms do you have a day?' to 'What's your astrological sign?' Most of the kids who come up are straight out of *Les Miserables*, but sexual mores are changing and slowly we're getting a better class of people. Porno doesn't have the same onus it once did – there are even a couple of leads in soap operas. Dennis Parker for one, who have done hard-core both gay and straight; the to-do was made among producers, directors, even advertisers is a lot less than it was. I wouldn't be surprised if these boys had to sign pieces of paper denying they've ever done anything even remotely connected to this sort of thing – but they lie. So? Some lawyer has a statement in his files that's totally contrary to the truth – what do they care? They're still working? A few years ago hustlers were totally rejected in homosexual society – now it's become a practical way to make ends meet. If a one bedroom apartment costs $600 a month – how does anyone swing that on a Joffrey scholarship? We don't see the waifs we might have seen a short time ago – and with all this costly equipment, we can't afford to have gutter snipes around. This new wave of people makes life practical for us. These films are almost totally dependent on *who* is in them. Forget the stories, the plots, the clever erotic ideas – they're secondary to the physically beautiful people with the big dicks. I truly believe stars can be manufactured through promotion but that even the most beautiful man will go unnoticed if not presented properly. If, however, you put them in theatrical films, in magazines, in 8 millimeter loops, in video cassettes, you can make someone very big within this genre – though I would imagine they'd be poison anywhere else. Kip Noll is a perfect example of a manufactured star. It's very interesting: I've spoken to him for about three minutes, and I've seen him in pictures and undeniably he has a certain quality; but if you wanted to know what makes a porno star, this guy defies all the preconceptions. He has a long trunk and rather short legs, his skin isn't particularly great, he doesn't have the best grooming, but the mere fact that he's been merchandised in loops, books, a few movies and still, plus the idea that there was Kip Noll and George Noll and Paul Noll creates a mystique that he's able to live up to through chutzpah and charm. Yet, if he were to walk in here off the street, I'd never seen him before, my reaction would be, 'He's O.K. – nothing special!' But he's been sold right, and he's a big item – people are really talking about Kip Noll! Within the milieu of porno, Jack Wrangler has box-office clout – people want to put his name on marquees, in ads and on products – Jack's deliberately cultivated that market. You can gain acting experience, experience of the technical aspect of filmmaking in miniature here which can be very useful in a legitimate career, but Jack's overdone it. His name's on poppers and dildos, and he's become a very specialized product – a freak. I imagine he could get a part in a Broadway show if they wanted a homosexual character very similar to what he portrays in movies – he's just so identified with this kind of product. Still, I do believe it's possible for someone to come in, use his experience and not merchandise himself to every homosexual in the country. There's a big difference between being an *actor* and being just a *sex actor* in these films. There's no thread that ties the boys together – each has his own tale to tell – they either have it or they don't. There's star quality, no doubt, some little magical thing they have, some in terms of being utterly winning, but whatever, when they step in front of the camera – it's there. You can't compare Malo to Roger or Nick Rodgers – you just see it when you turn the first frame of film on the guy – forget the fucking and sucking – that's the easy part on these films. I'm always amazed at how dumb some actors are and yet how effective they are on screen. I'm appalled that people who haven't a wit in their heads can come across with such finesse, poise, carriage and character. It proves acting isn't related to education or I.Q., it's an ability. I prefer having intelligent people around me, but that isn't always the best choice. Sometimes you'll get a great performance out of someone you can't stand – they're temperamental, unpleasant, rude, even their table manners are a disaster – to have lunch with them you have to close your eyes – and yet on film they're marvelous. Like Bill Eld – he's just a mess; he's time-consuming and moribund, but you couldn't ask for more on celluloid – a man in the full bloom of muscular beauty. I'm always delighted with the results of his work, even though I hate working with him. There's a possibility of developing character through sex scenes – Joe Gage does it wonderfully well, and I'm certain I was the first to experiment with building tension and furthering a plot through hardcore scenes. If your people just fuck and suck and come and remain faceless and the viewer isn't intrigued into the next sequence, the movie's over for him, he's already got an erect dick, so why wait for the next sexual episode? He might as well hit the street right away or send his head back to scene one. Plotted porno is like musical comedy, the sex representing the song and dance numbers – it's so tiring if you don't have good human values and plot development to sustain interest between spectaculars. I've changed whole films, because I didn't like a sexual performance – if a guy fucks like a beast and looks like he's beating up his partner when I've written him as a nice guy, I change the script – for the sake of character." In addition to his directorial role Deveau also produces films directed by others for Hand In Hand which gives him a unique overview of the realistic, bottom-line side of the industry as well as the more glamorous creative aspects. "These films are seen in only 12 cities and as silly as this sounds, a film's success depends on how many people see it. Understand the poignancy of that remark – you can't make films for 12 cities and expect 5 million people to see them. Some gay movies have grossed 4, 5, 6, million dollars when they cost $20,000 to make, but the money splits so many ways! Even the cashier in each and every theater can become your partner if he decides to keep two out of every twenty admissions; then there's the distributor, the exhibitor, the ad agency – who knows where the dollars go? We're not in the video cassette business, we only license our films for that purpose. It's too distracting and entirely different from what we do; it means secretaries and typewriters and invoices and all those things we don't want to deal with. When we start a film, we're a big business but only for a couple of weeks – suddenly there are 40 or 50 people on the payroll, but as soon as shooting's finished, it's right back to our family of 4 or 5. The video thing is incomparable with that. And, if I were to make cassettes I'd do them so they'd have a lot more impact scaled to the size and shape of a television

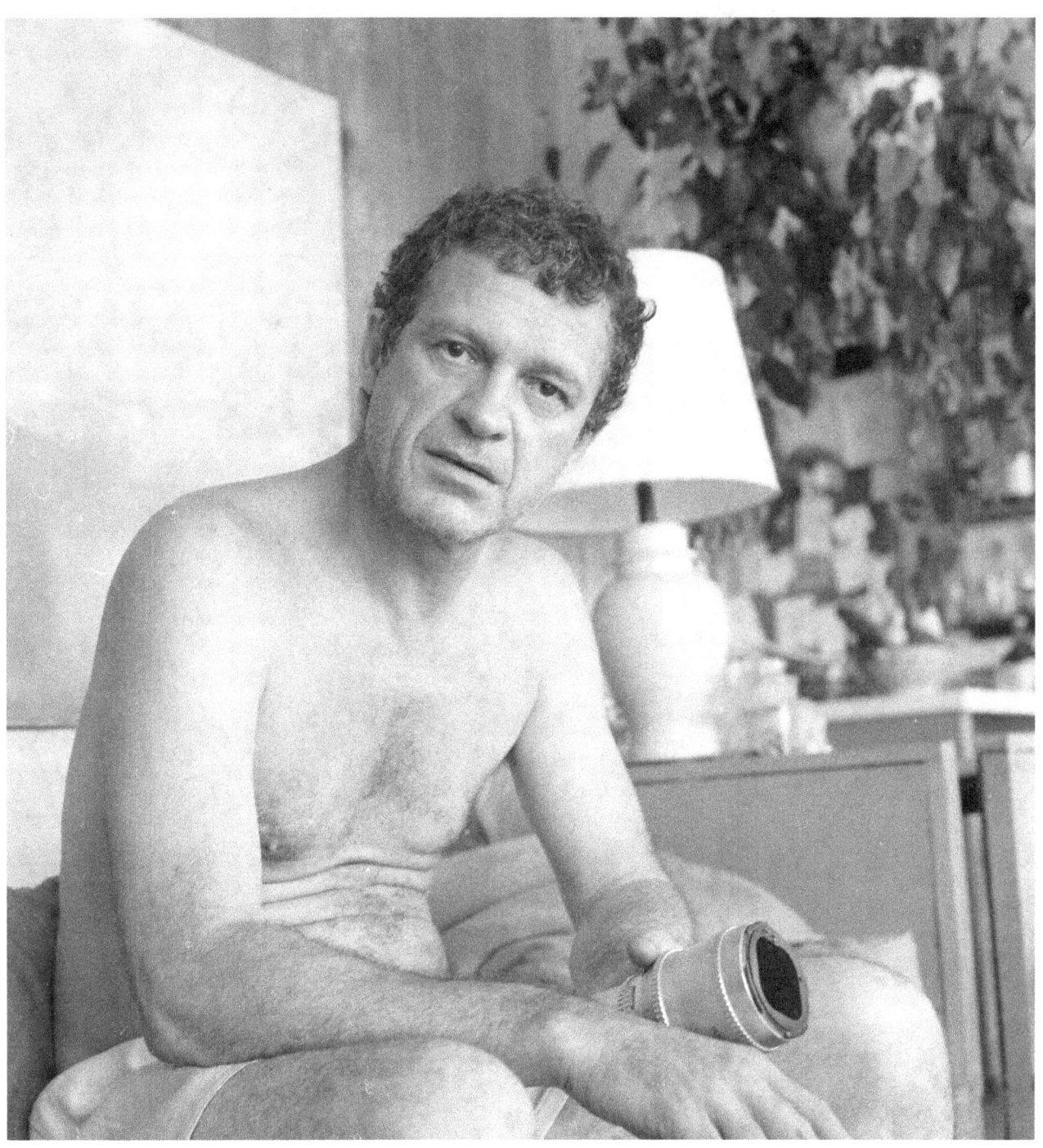

set. Pornography has no date; people's interest in it is a seasonal thing in their lives – I don't know of anyone who's been interested in it from the day they came out until the day they dropped dead, but we deal only with the people who are interested in it at any given moment. Our films are live Disney movies, if we hold them out of circulation for 5 to 6 years, they're PINOCCHIO all over again – playing to a brand-new audience. The number of people interested in porno is probably fixed in relation to the population. This is literature of a kind – I don't know how it's recognized today, but we've created a large body of it – maybe it's the Mickey Mouse of the year 2000!"

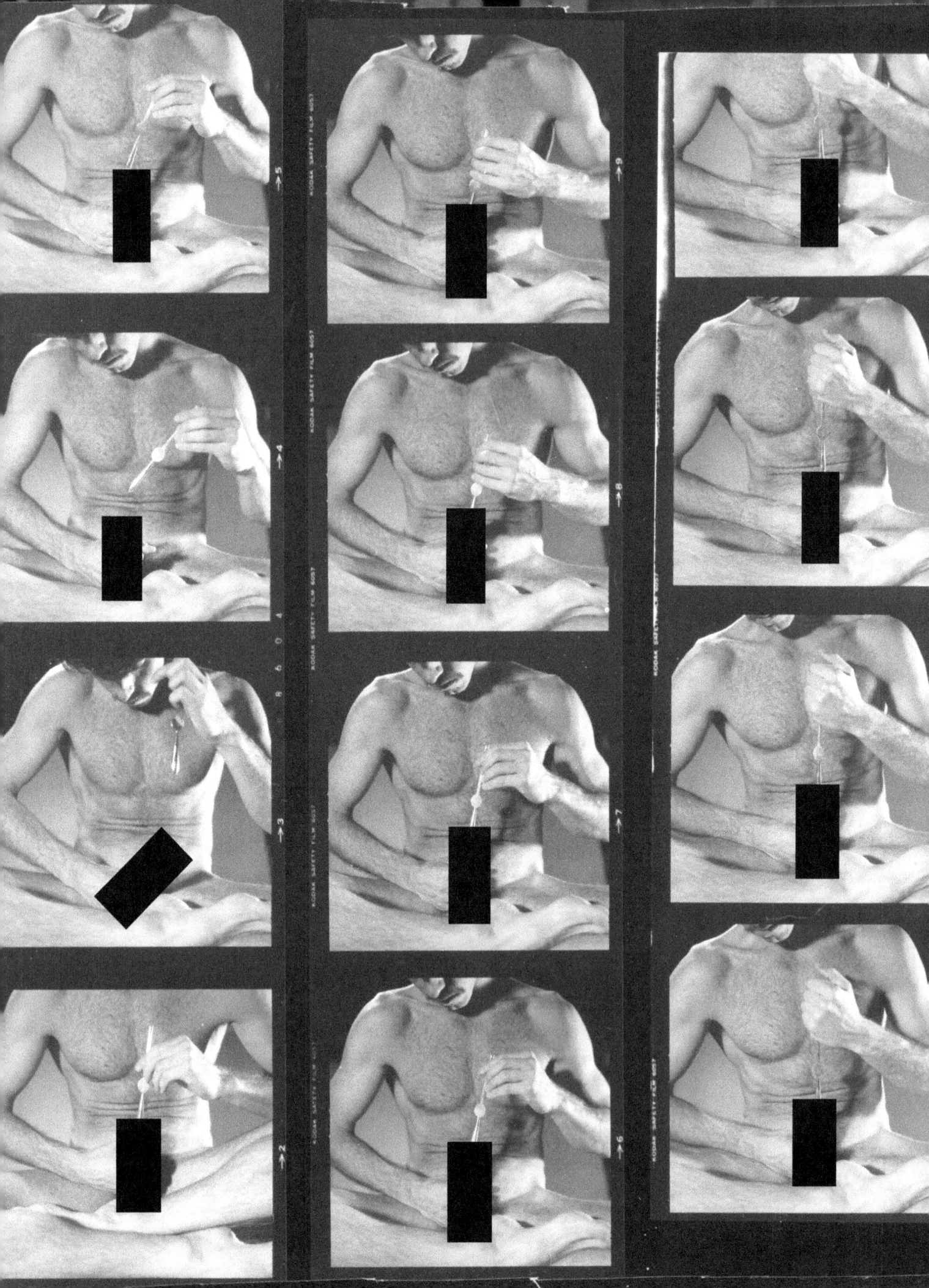

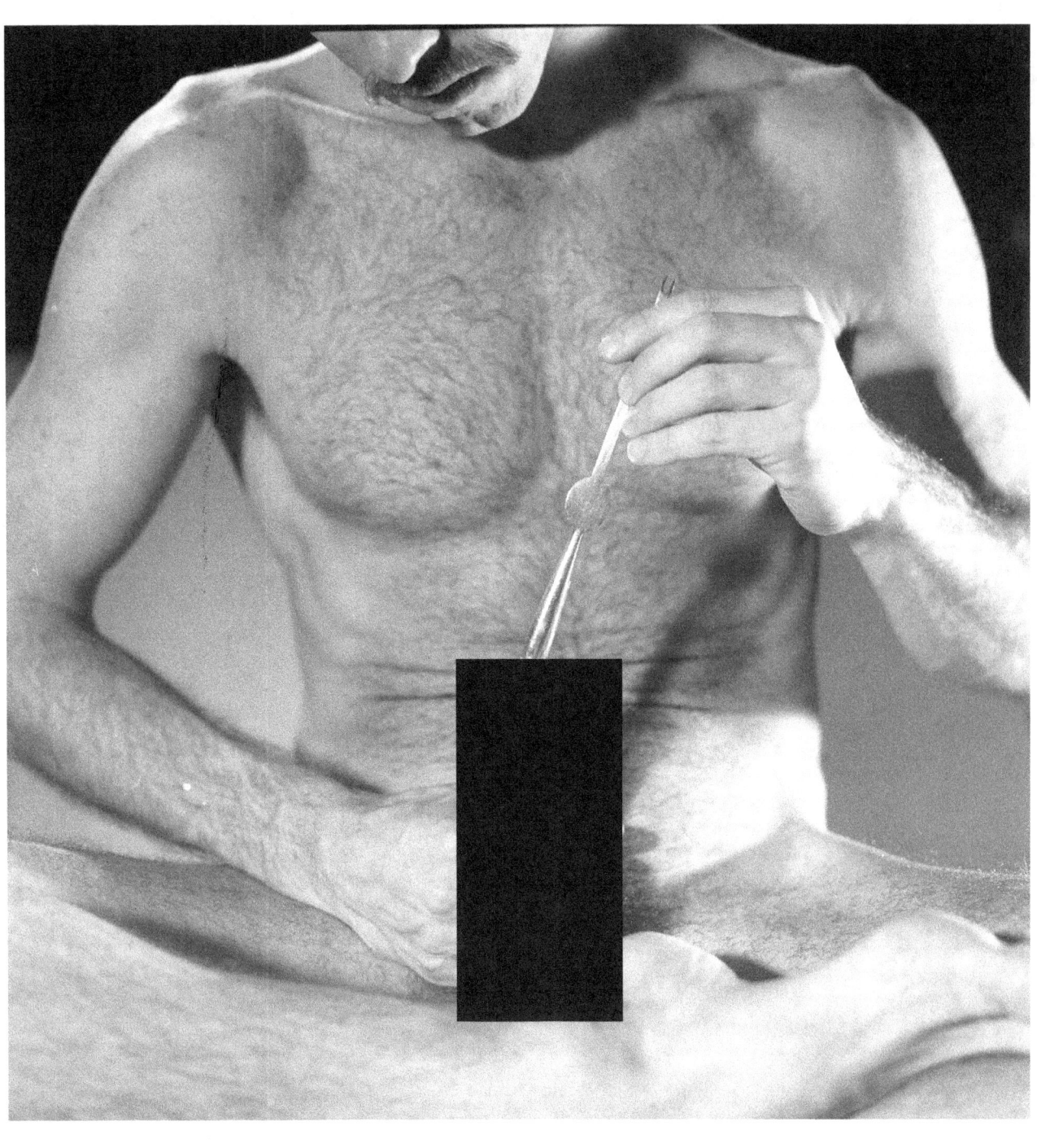

Penetration (Jack Deveau short film, segment of *Private Collection*)
Yogi Rama, a hairy-chested and muscular brunet whose face is never seen, sticks a tuning fork into his piss slit and masturbates.

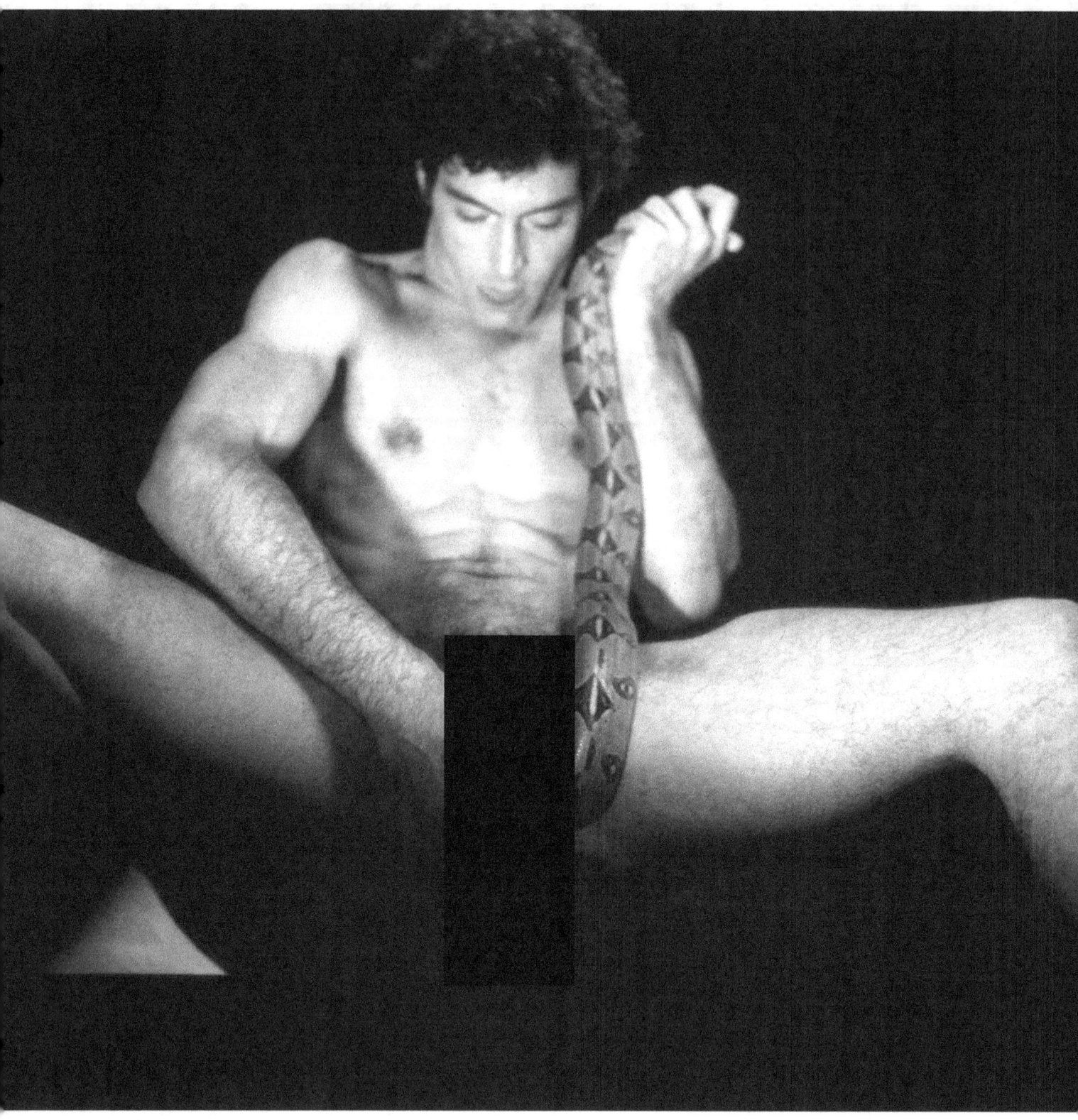

"Another thing that happens is people stick a snake up their ass, ride a unicycle and fuck at the same time - things we simply have no place for. If I'm in the story stage of a film, I'll construct something around their peculiar talent, but as a result of losing lots of these people - at the rate of two or three a month - we decided to shoot them anyway, do a piece of film right on the spot. Now the *Private Collection* series has become a way to use all these wild bits in theatrical features." **JACK DEVEAU**

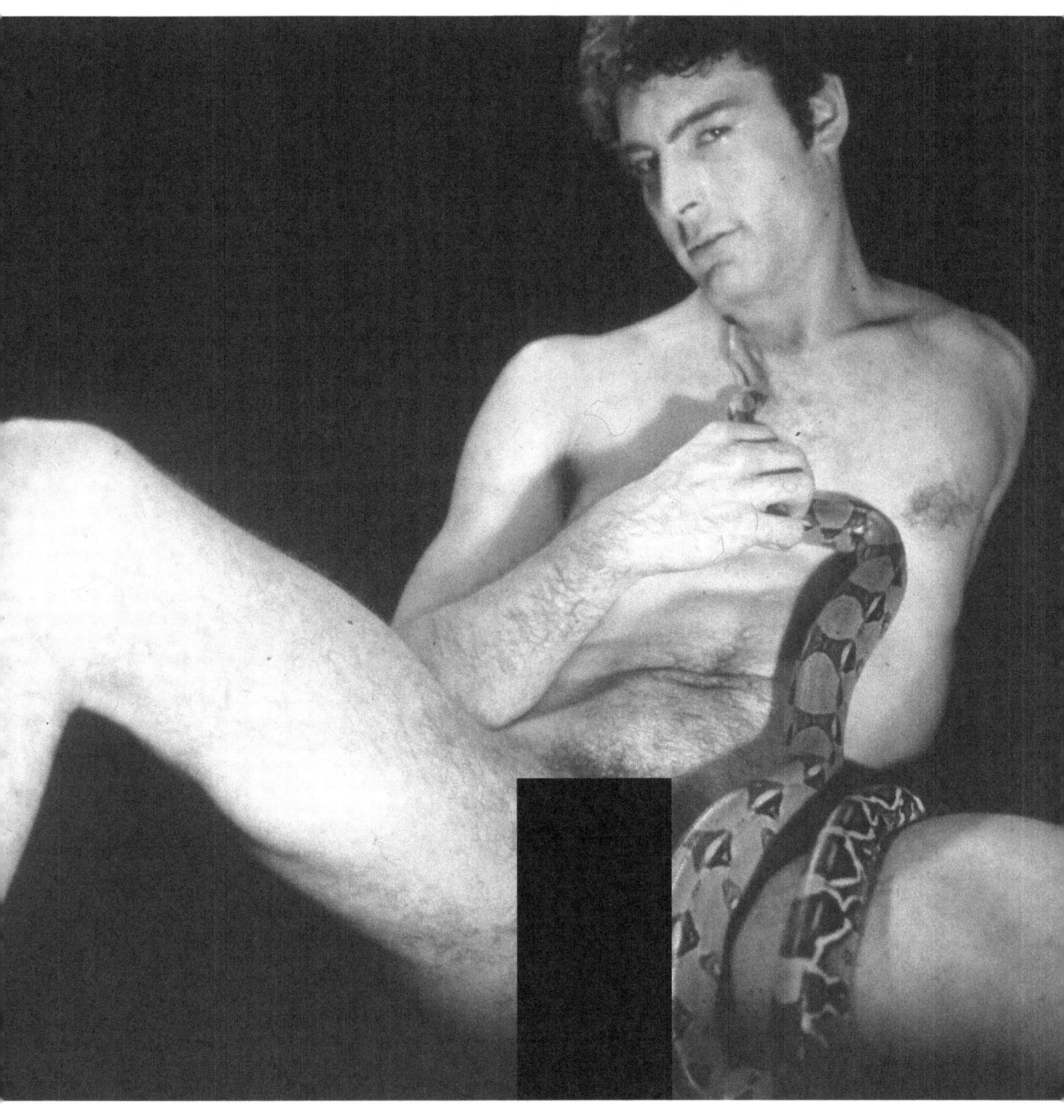

Doug DeMarco in *Before Time* (segment of *Private Collection* and *In Heat*)

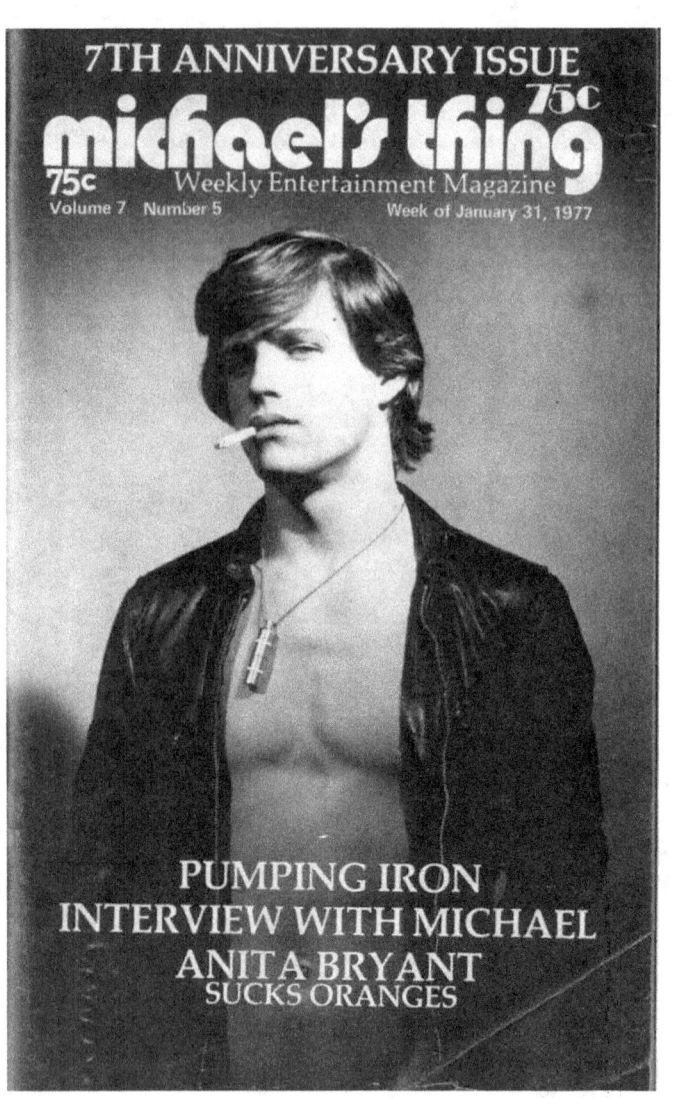

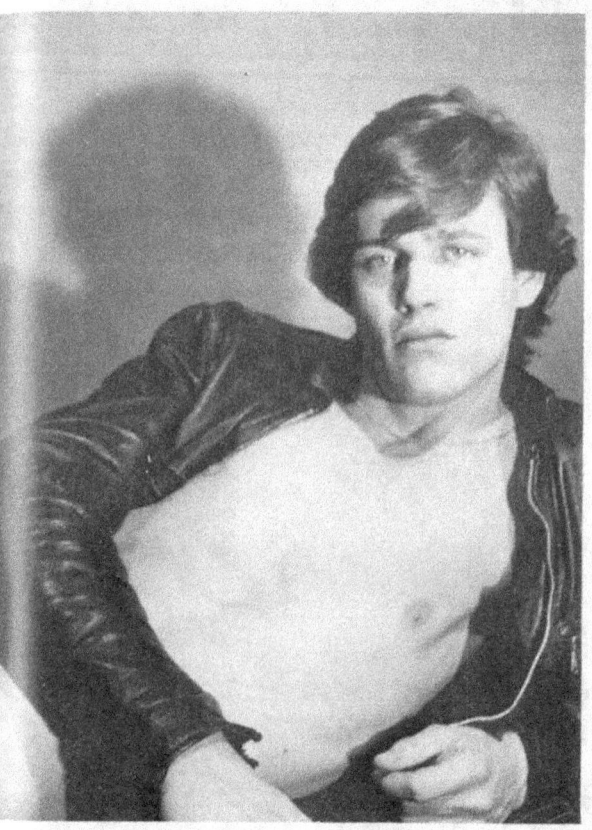

— SWANN SONG —

PHOTOS BY JACK DEVEAU

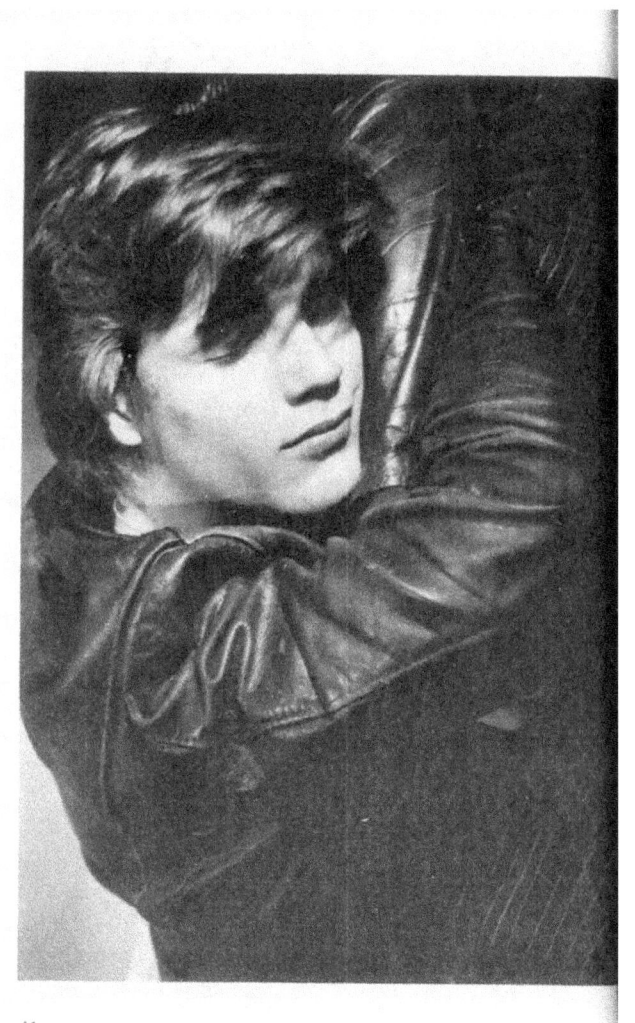

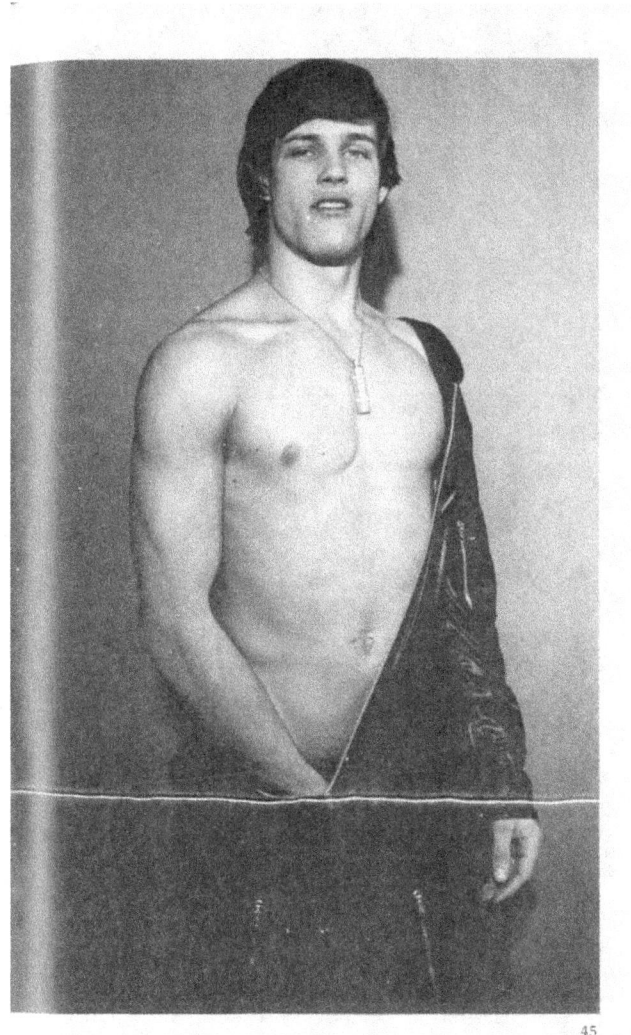

Michael Swana, Photos by Jack Deveau

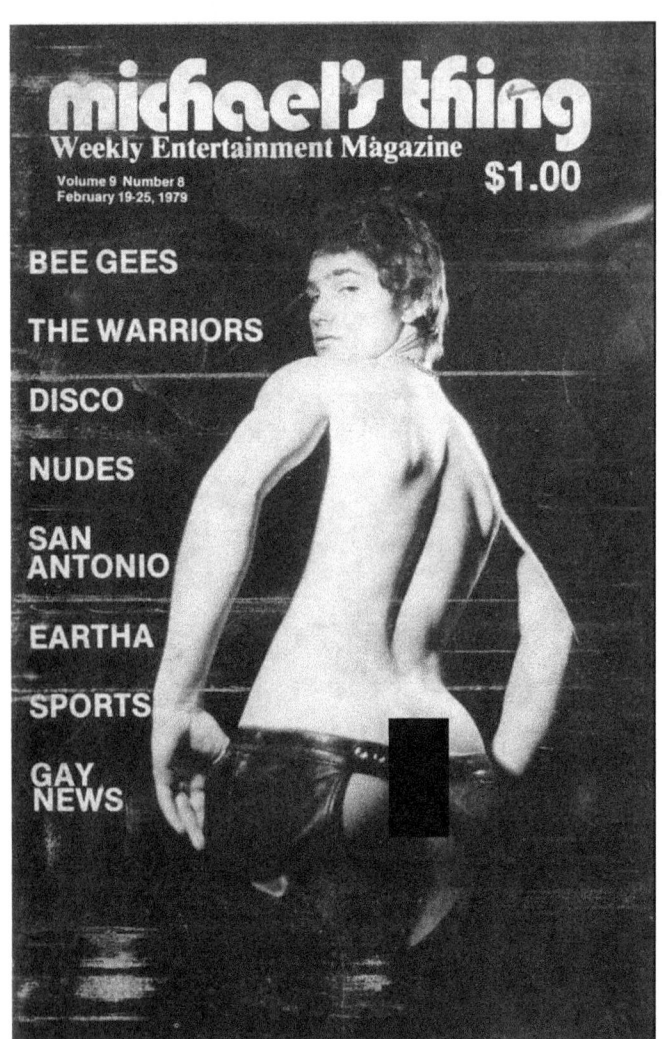
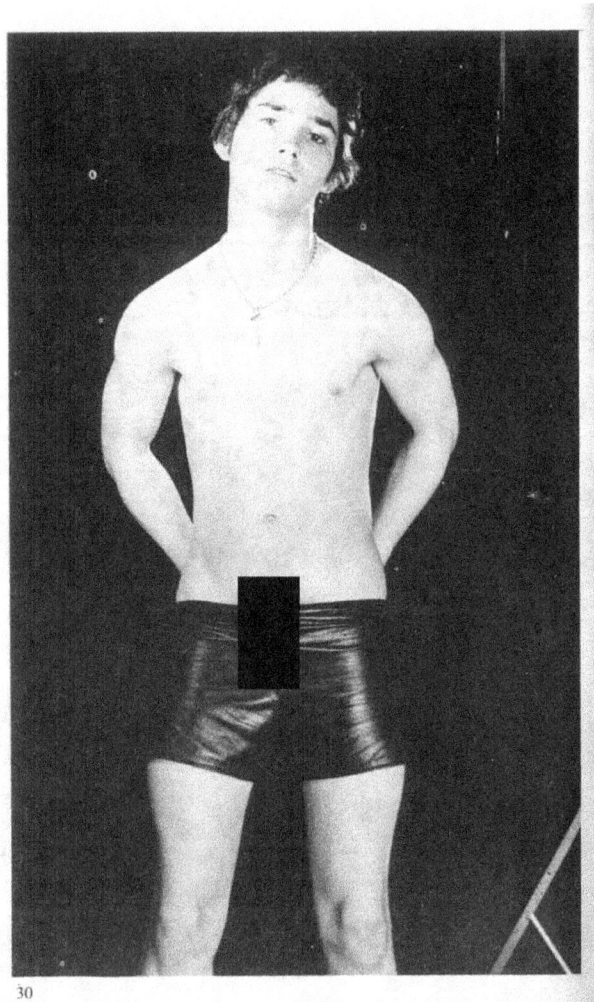

Joshua

JOSHUA

Photos by Jack Deveau

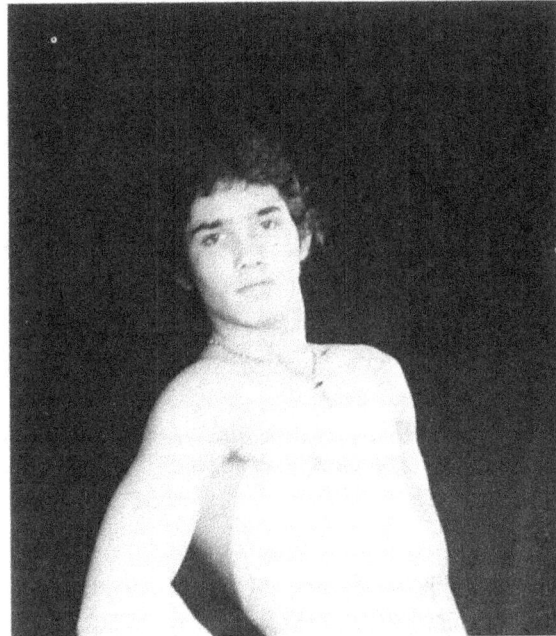

The Gaiety Male Burlesque, 201 W. 46th Street (at B'way), is the home of new faces on the scene. Joshua is a recent addition to the all-star lineup. He takes to the runway like an angel does to flight. He's one of those babes who was born to dance. In addition to Josh, the Gaiety is featuring the N.Y. premiere of "Rough Cut" on the screen.

31

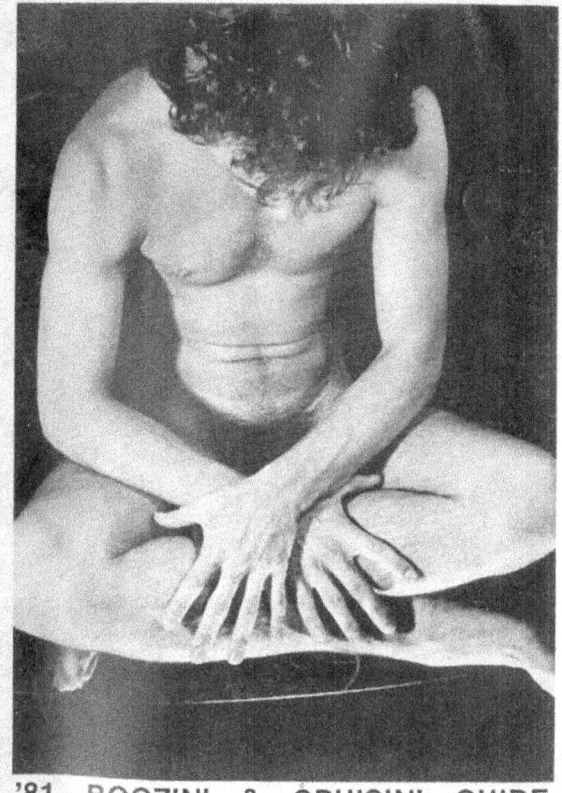

VOLUME 10 NUMBER 47 NOVEMBER 24-30, 1980 ONE DOLLAR

michael's thing
NYC's #1 WEEKLY ENTERTAINMENT MAGAZINE

'81 BOOZIN' & CRUISIN' GUIDE

Yogi Rama

PRESS REVIEWS 7

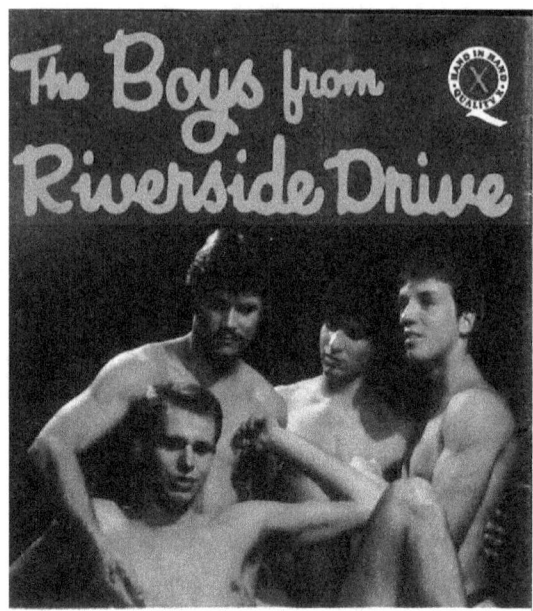

In Color • Running time: 72 minutes
This is an arousing tale that takes place on New York's upper west side. It features that man of muscles, Malo, and the all American favorite Jack Wrangler. The long awaited sequel to the Hand in Hand classic, HOT HOUSE! Also starring: Nova and Higgins' Lee Marlin and Buddy Preston, Falcon Studio's Luke and Tom Stillwater.
MX-005

An excellent vintage porn movie by Jack Deveau from Hand In Hand Studios. Two lovers (David Dion and Buddy Preston), living in a Manhattan high-rise quarrel during their first anniversary dinner. Buddy proceeds to get drunk, David gets locked out. What follows is a series of farce-like situations involving ex-lovers and poking good-natured fun at gay stereotypes. A first, unrelated scene has macho Malo joining Jack Wrangler on a mirrored stage. Good close-up photography captures Malo sucking Jack's big hard-on for a long time before they both jack off. Malo strokes his uncut rod into Jack's face and shoots into his mouth. After the lovers quarrel, David joins doorman George Brown (mustached and hung) in a basement to suck his cock. George fucks his face and cums all over it. Ex-lover Luke (of Falcon fame) swallows the dick of gorgeous and long-haired Tom Stillwater, Tom fucks Like spoon-style. Marcel, the latino-looking janitor, jacks off to a straight porn film. Buddy joins the janitor and gets his face pumped with cock, as well as his asshole. The lovers later make up and fuck ass. Here the film switches between them and Lee Marlin pounding Luke's asshole in the bedroom. A well-photographed gay porn film with humor, a little bit of rope bondage, and much more.

*Bijou Video Promo

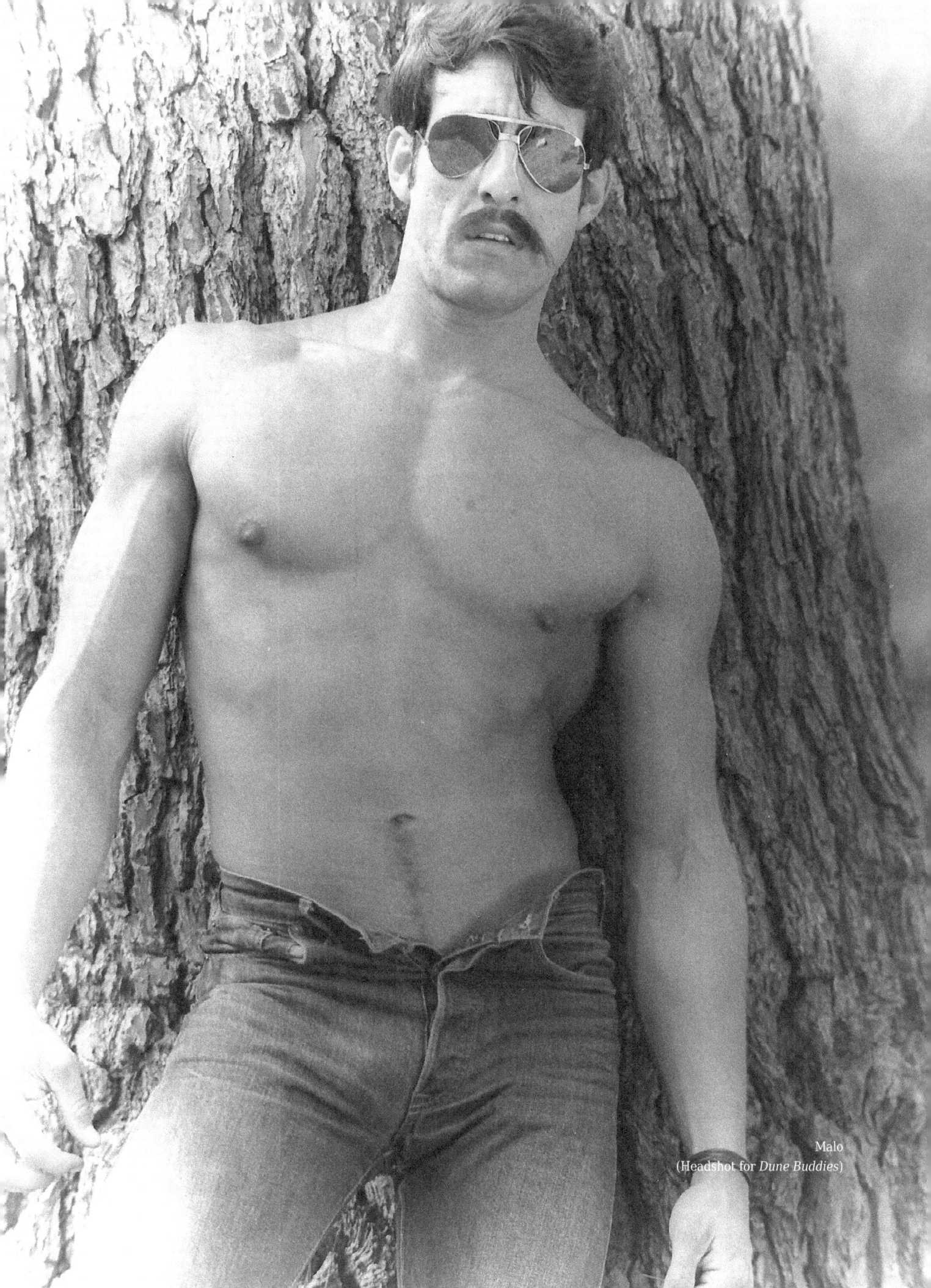

Malo
(Headshot for *Dune Buddies*)

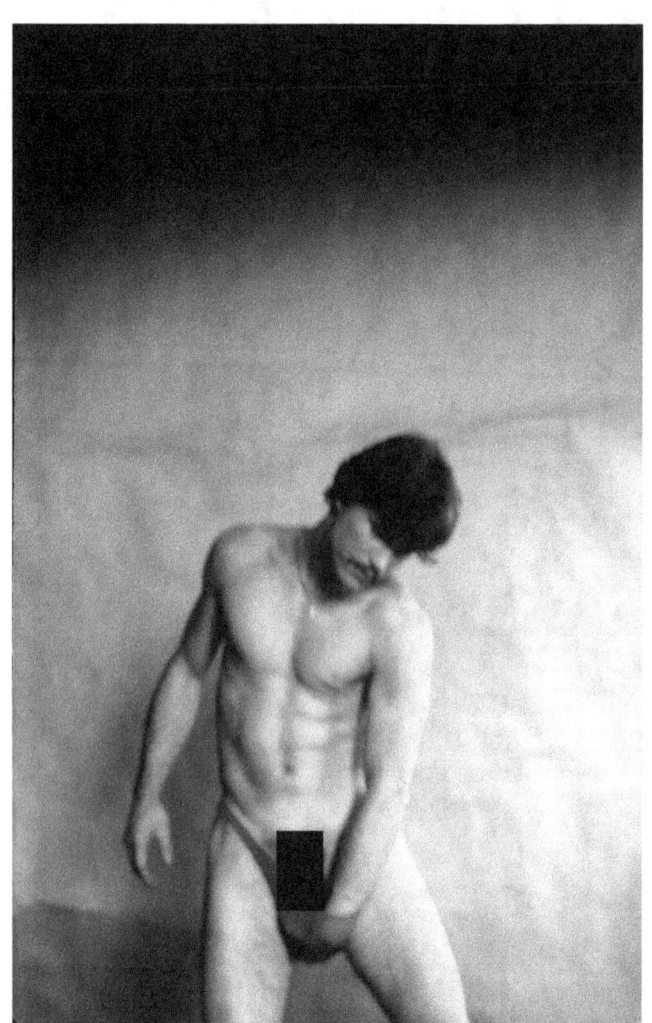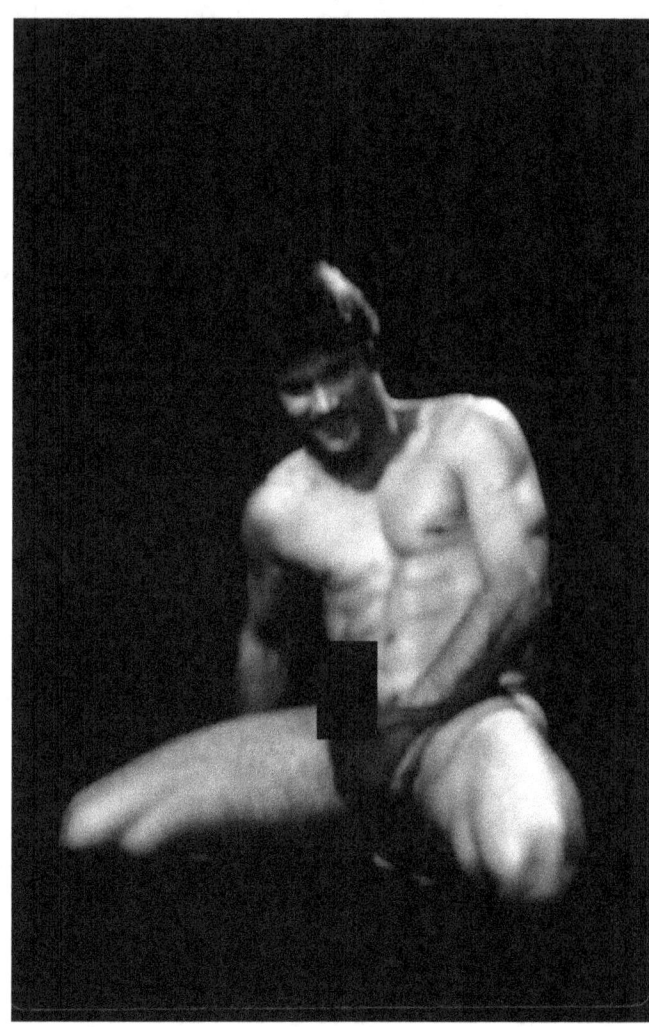

Lee Marlin

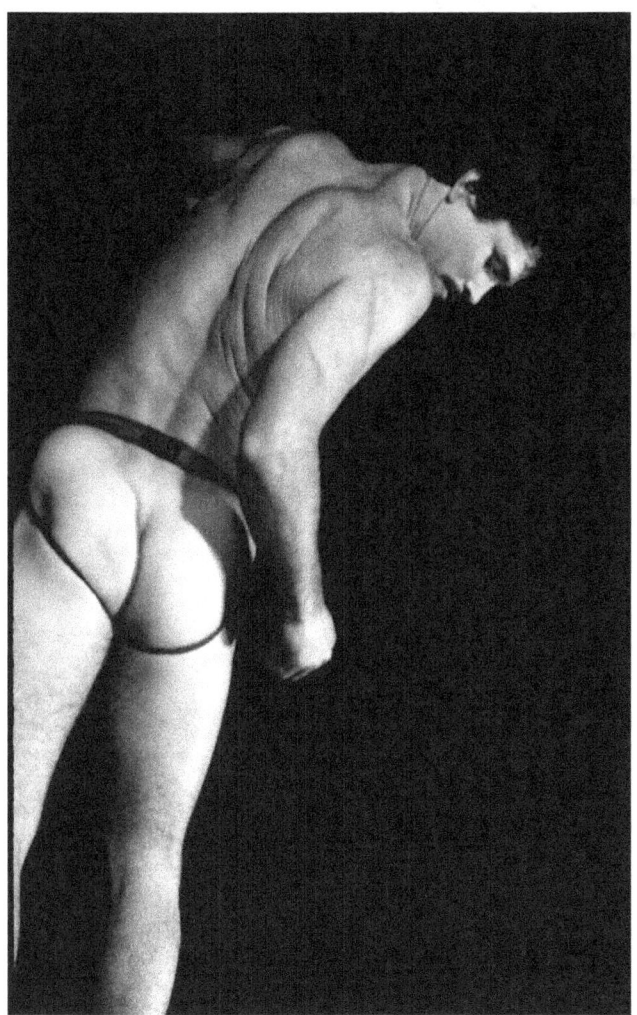 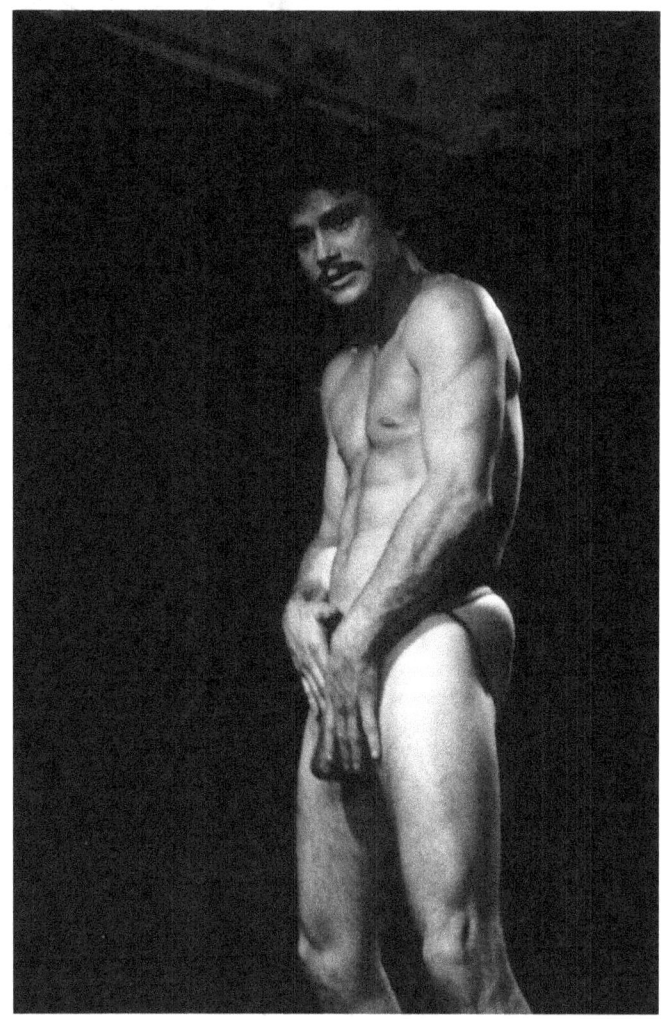

"I have to say, I adore this little bumpkin. He's one of my favorite, vintage hotties. For the life of me, I don't get why Kip Noll was more popular. I love Marlin's attitude in his films. He always seemed so cheerfully insatiable, greedy, and hedonistic. His eyes were always filled with mischief. He also looked pretty adorable wearing an assortment of hats. In my mind, he's the Huck Finn of gay porn. I wonder why Falcon never used him. He was probably too scrappy for them. I also appreciate that he did a moving pictorial, with both of those rugged Italians, Dan Pace and Paul Barresi. He looked great in stills. He obviously was named after Lee Marvin. It was probably during Marvin's famous palimony suit, when the idea was first hatched. One last thing, I noticed you're now concentrating on the younger guys of porn, as opposed to posting about the usual hunks." user comment on Lee Marlin, *bjland.ws*

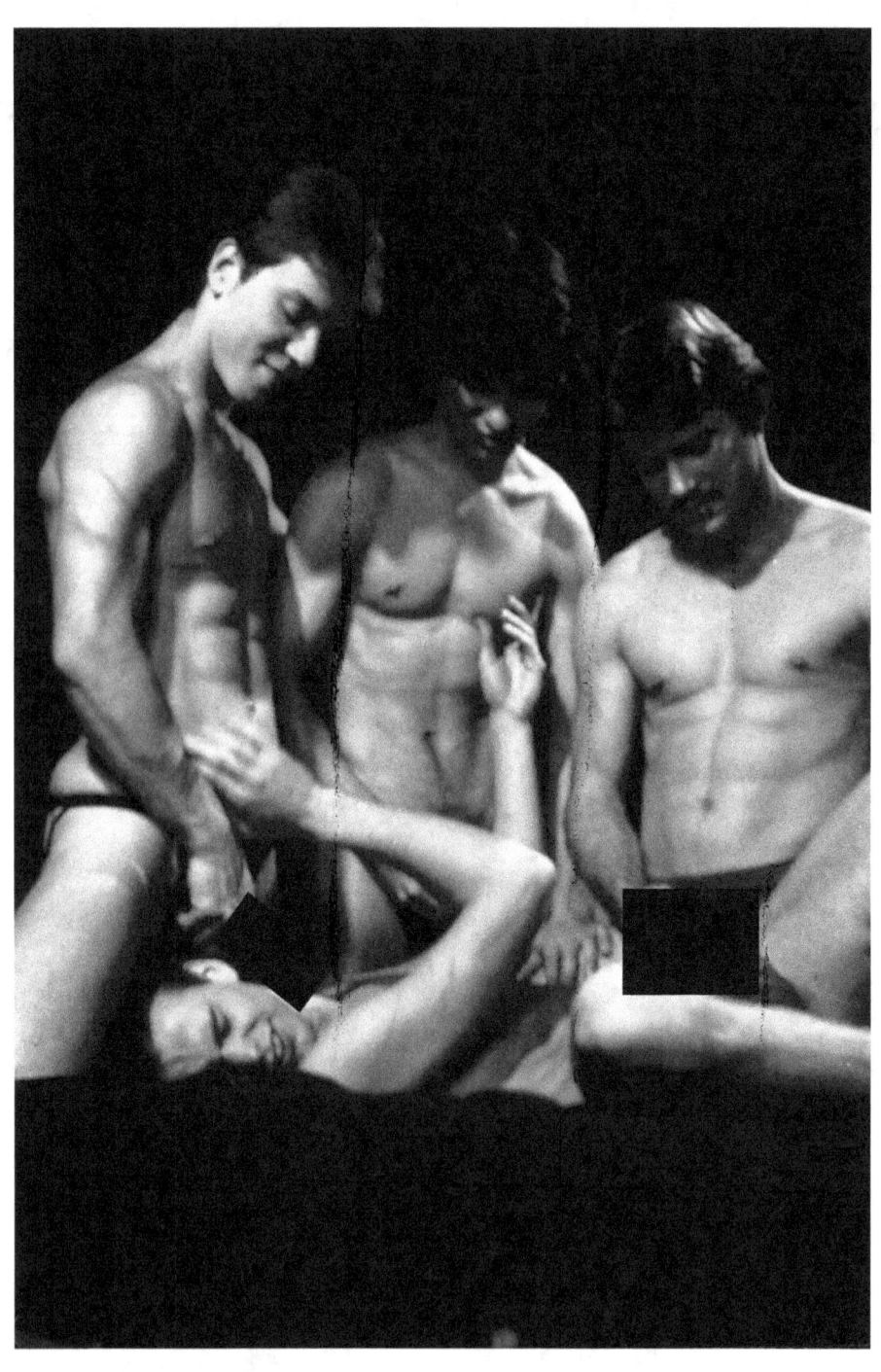

The Boys from Riverside Drive

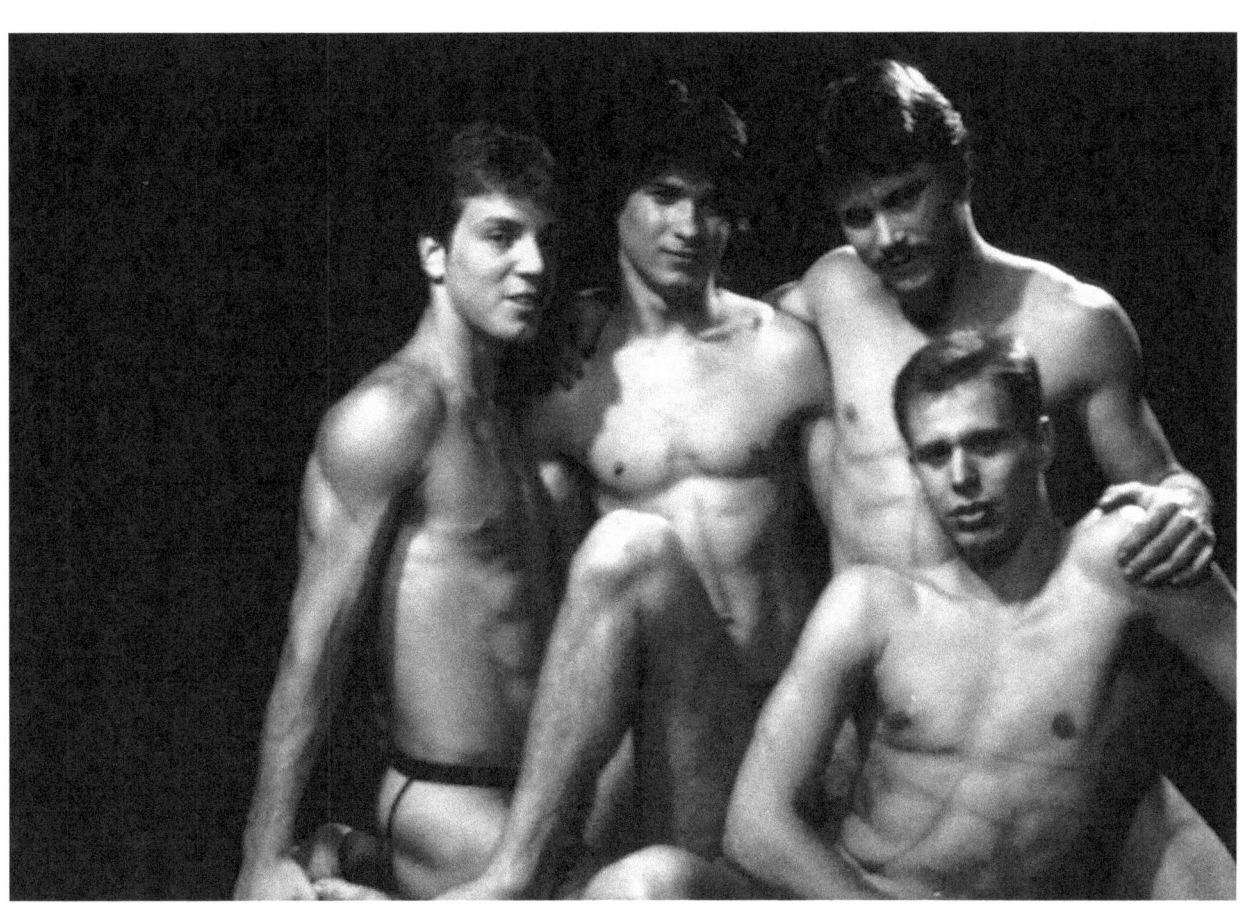

Buddy Preston, Tom Stillwater, Lee Marlin, Luke

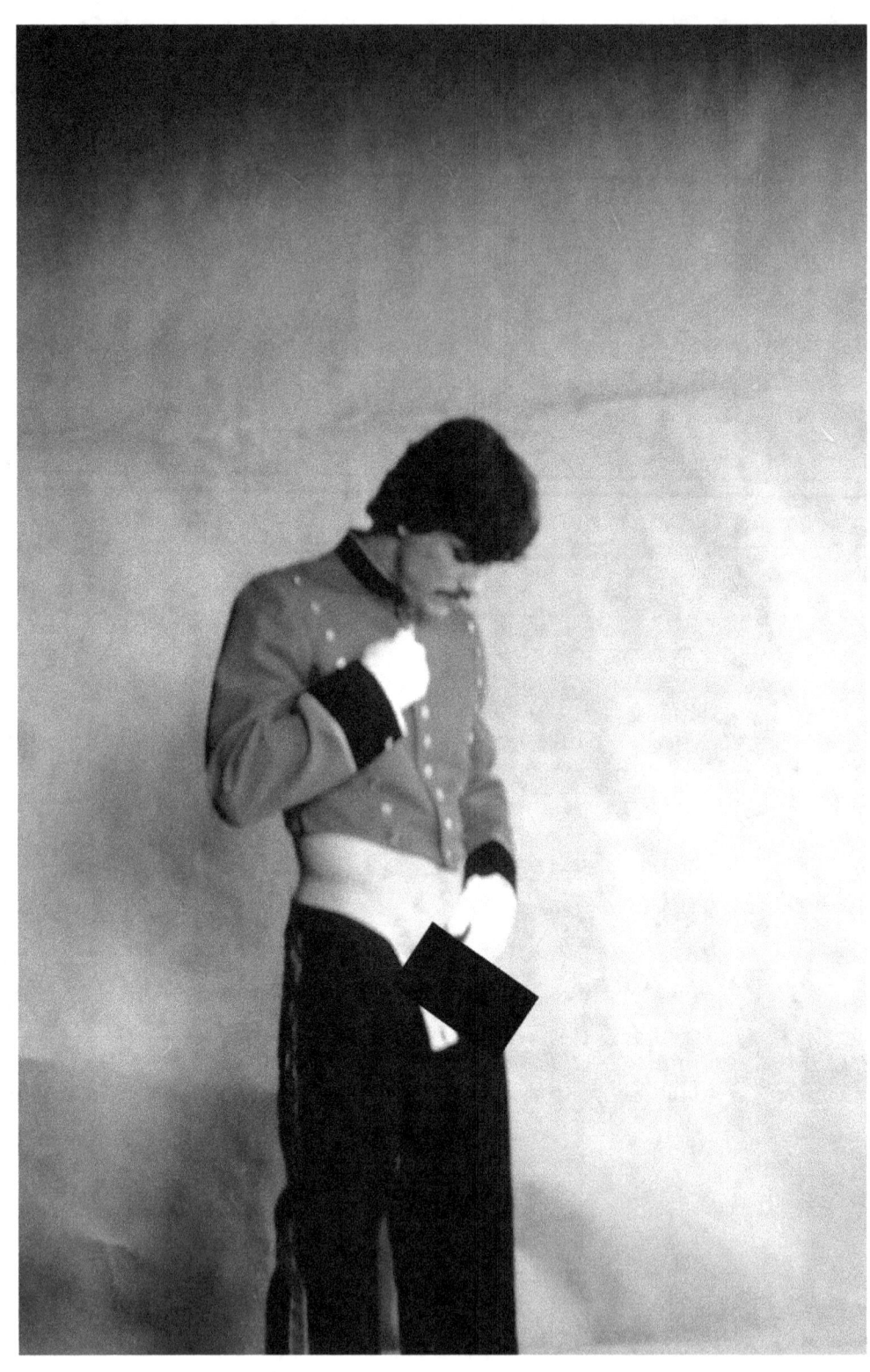

Lee Marlin as the singing telegram

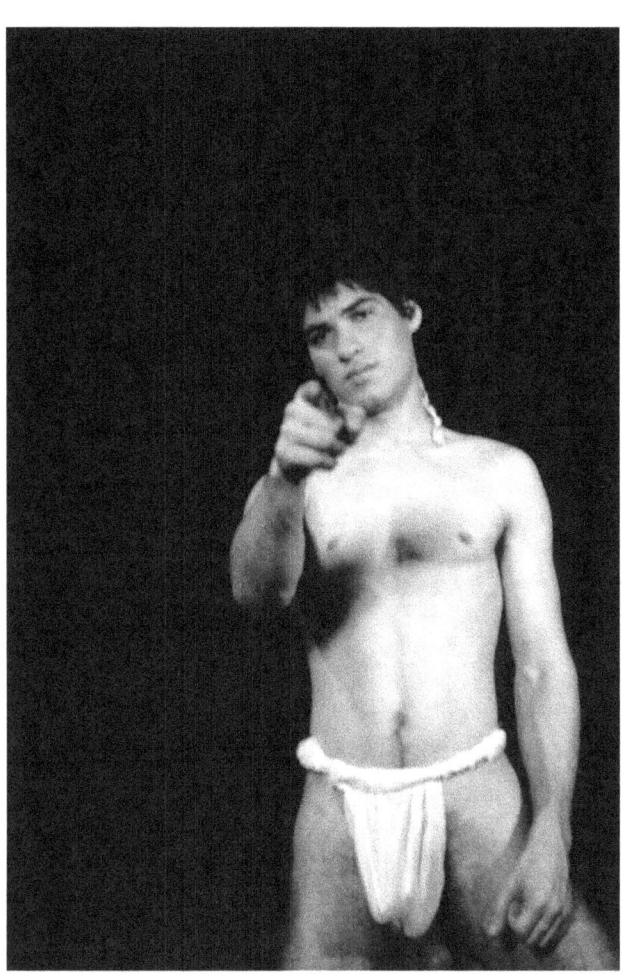 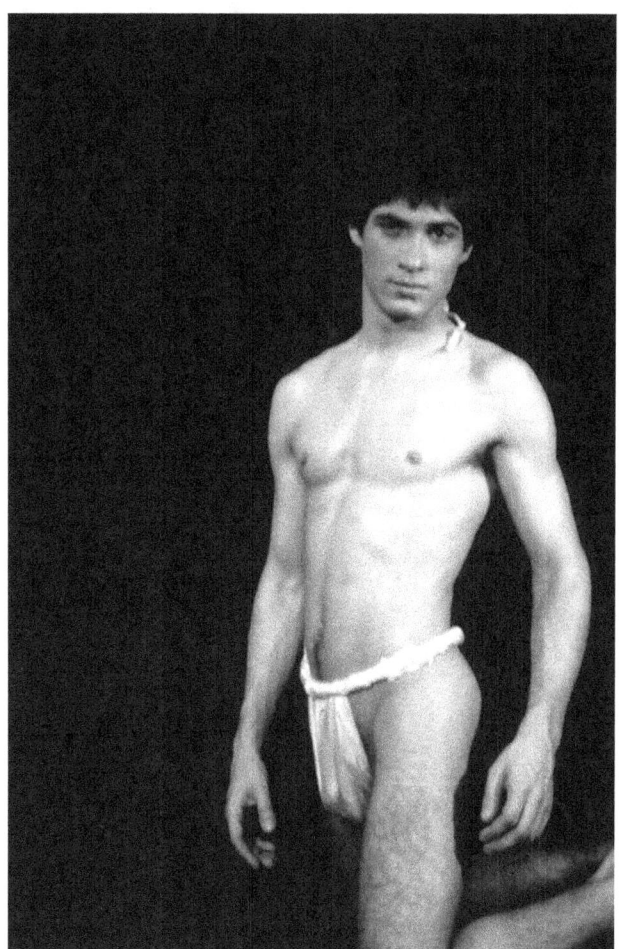

Tom Littlewolf aka Tom Stillwater as the bondage trick

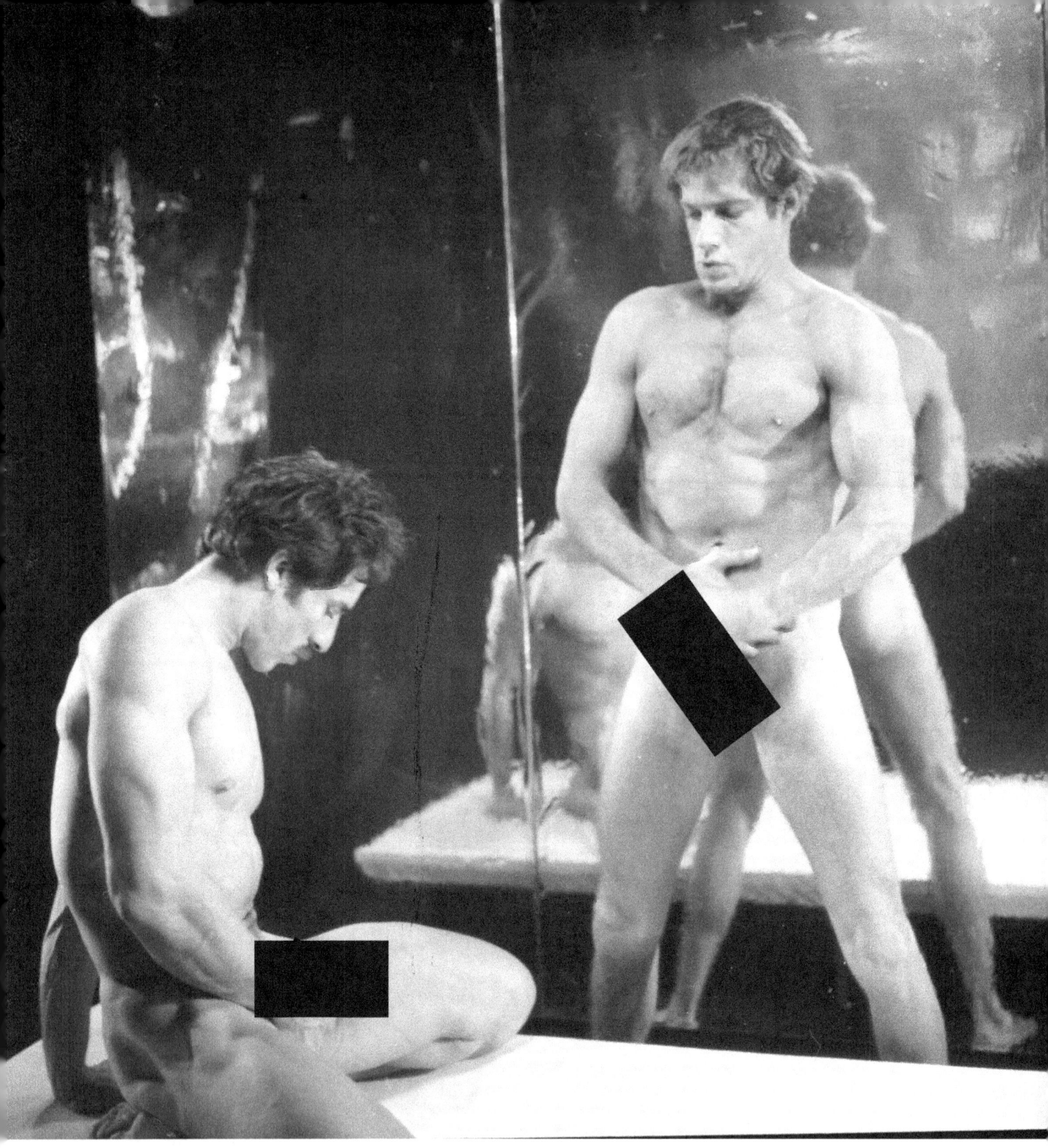

Malo (left) and Jack Wrangler as the ideal couple in *The Boys From Riverside Drive*

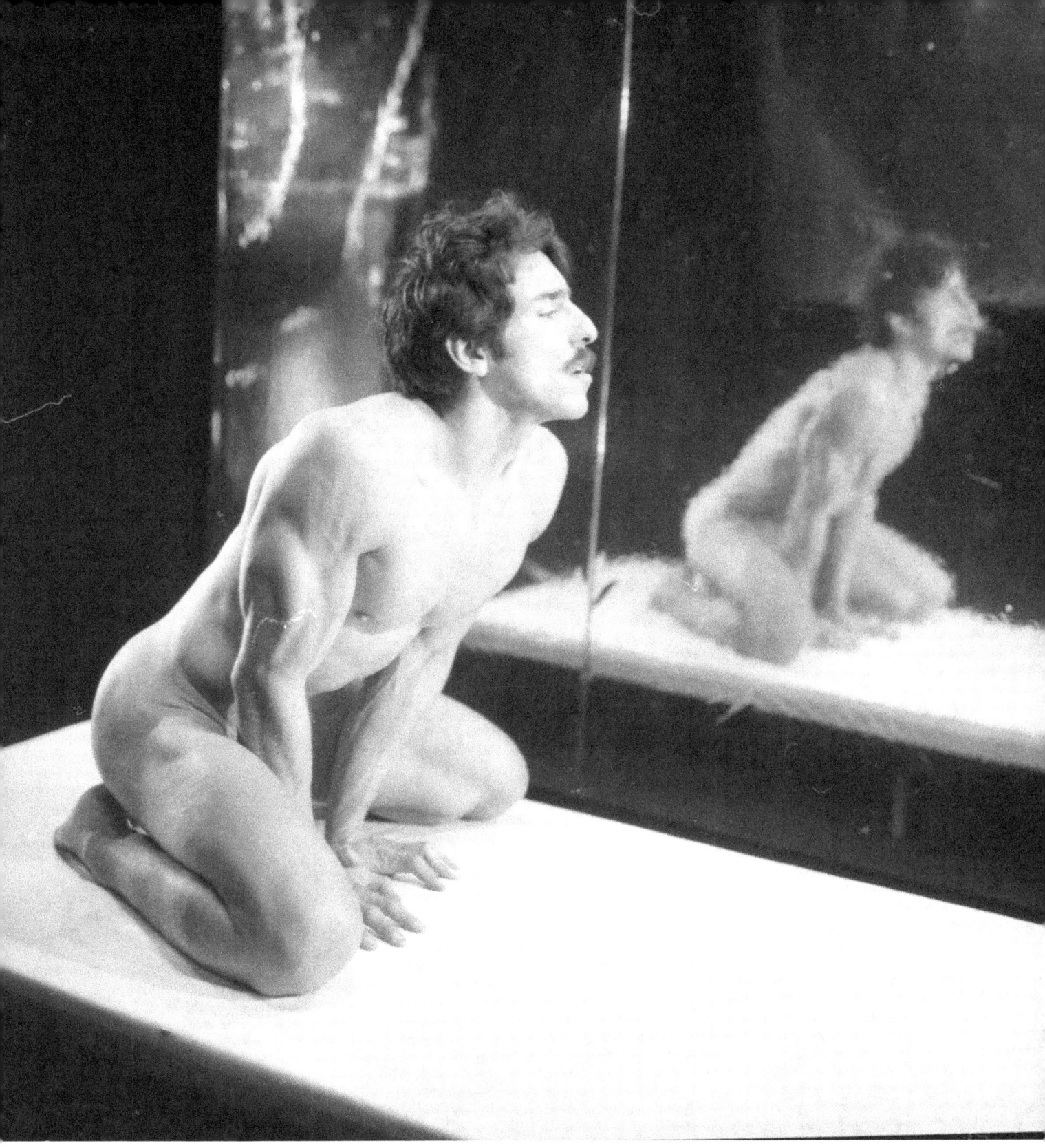

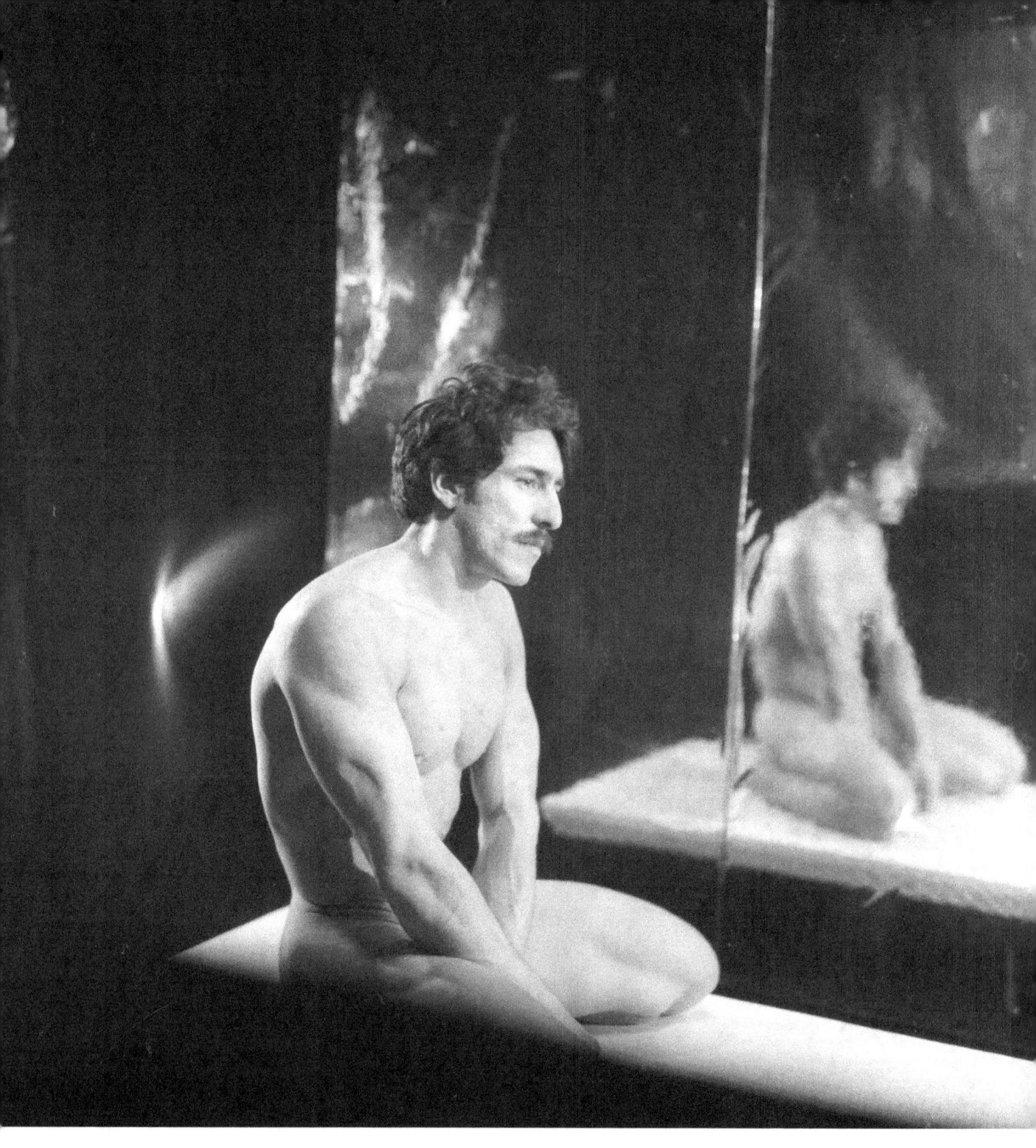

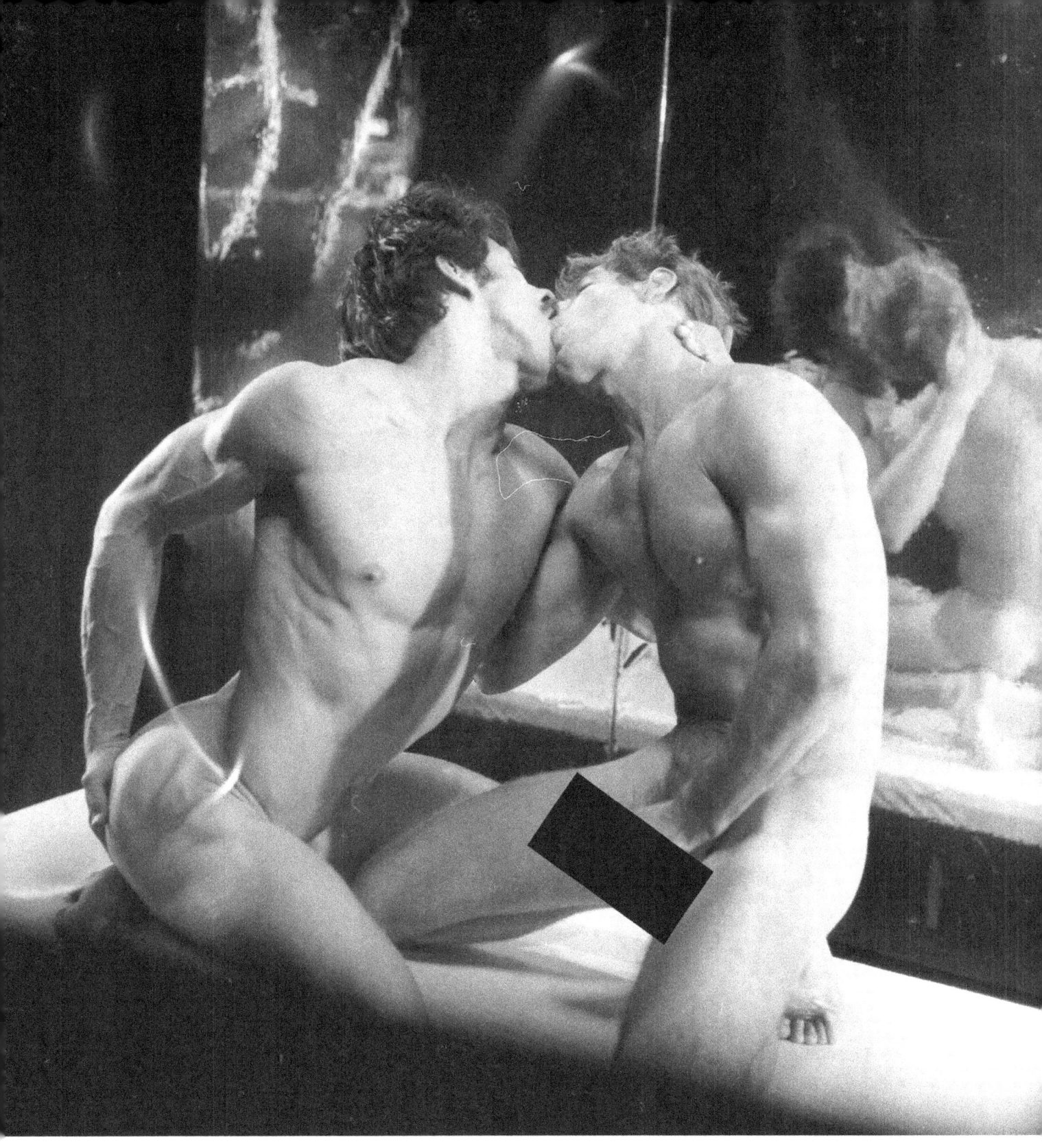

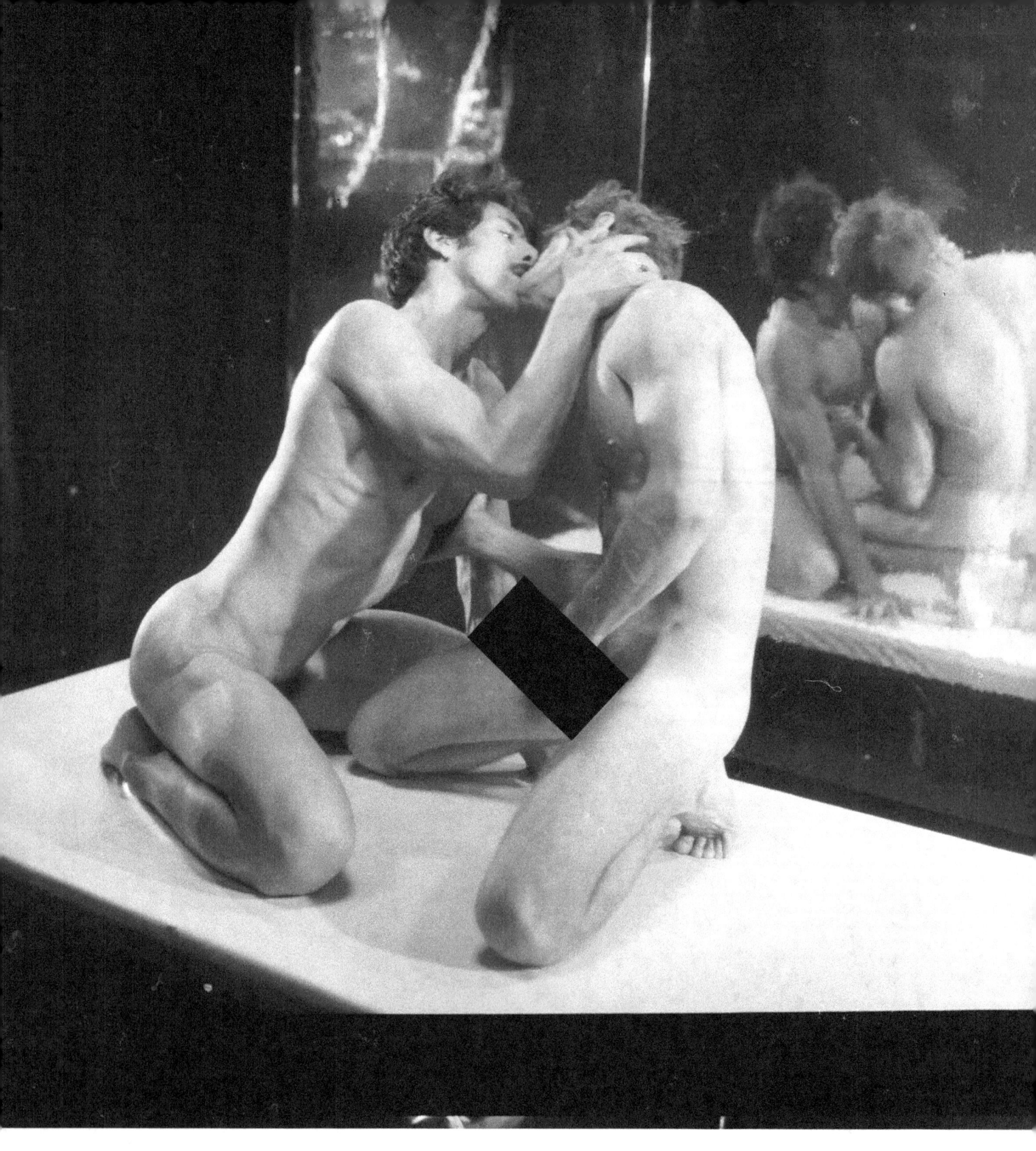

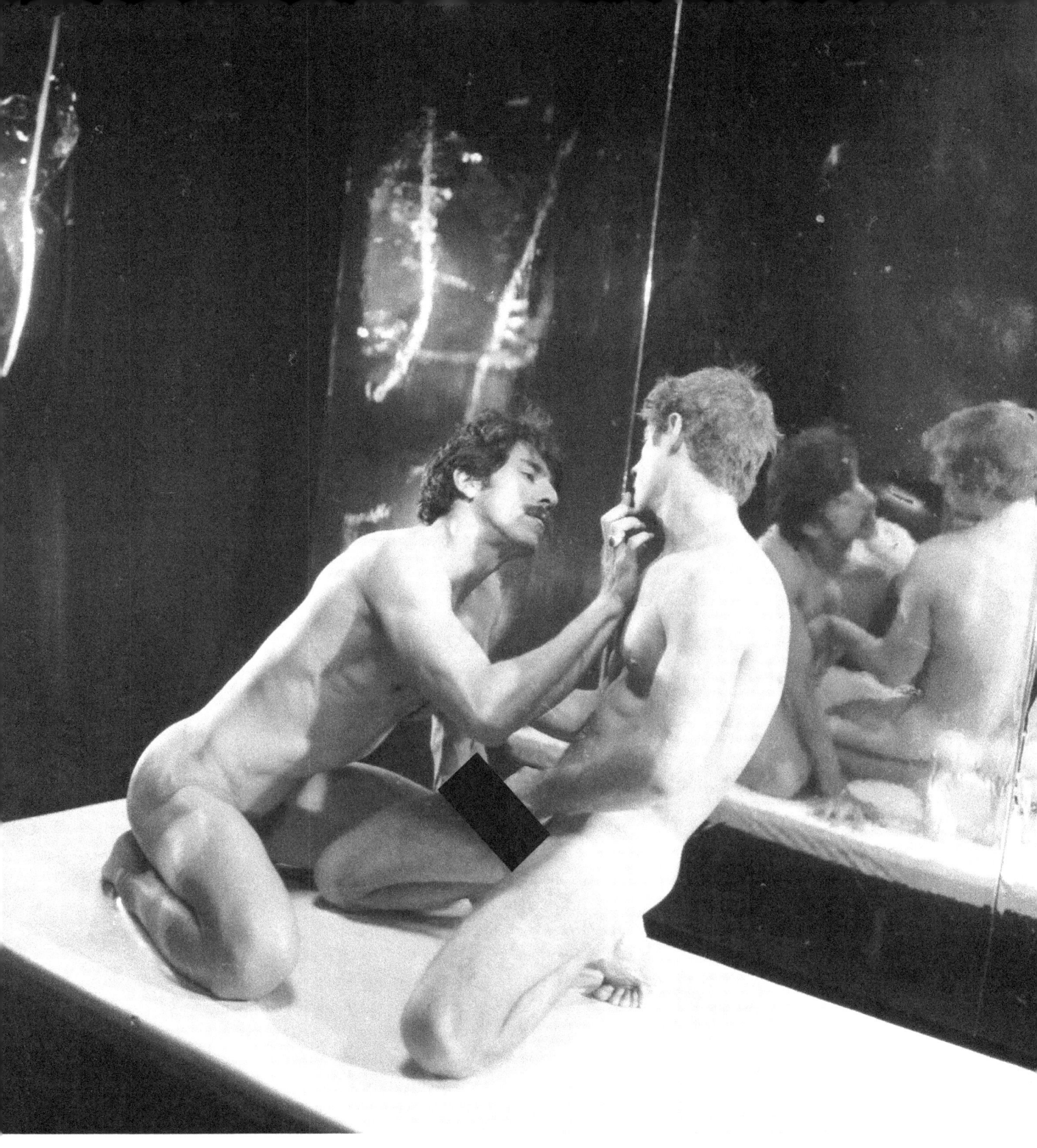

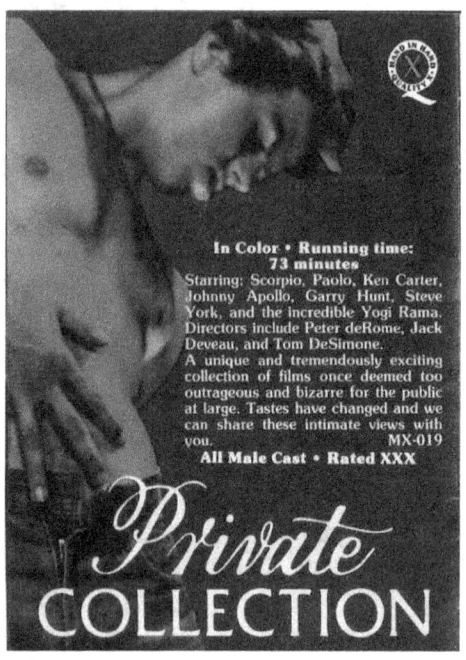

Whether you read about it in *Blueboy* or some other national publication, or perhaps just heard the rumors, you most certainly must be aware Hand In Hand Films has finally released its PRIVATE COLLECTION. But are you aware of just how special this very "private" collection of films is? For the past decade Jack Deveau, producer and director of some of the best known and most extraordinary gay films, has been assembling short films which document some of the outrageously erotic and controversial people and scenes he has encountered. These films were not intended to be shown to the public at large – they were far too exotic at the time they were made – but rather were produced soley for the sake of preserving rare moments of eroticism. By the late Seventies, however, it became clear that public tastes were changing and that it might be possible to show the assembled collection of these remarkable films, at least in a few major cities. Deveau then joined forces with two other well-known and talented filmmakers Peter De Rome and Tom DeSimone, selecting footage from their private files, too. The result of their efforts may well be the most amazing, controversial and erotic film ever released: Hand In Hand Films' PRIVATE COLLECTION. This unique film contains the personal obsessions and private fantasies of the most celebrated names in all-male films. The cast of twenty includes JUST BLONDS stars Scorpio and Ken Carter, *Blueboy*'s Steve York and Paolo, FIRE ISLAND FEVER stars Garry Hunt and John Carlo, Scorpio's identical twin Scorpio II, Bob Damon and new stars Ivan, Johnny Apollo and the incredible Yogi Rama. If you want to treat yourself to the most amazing, explicit sexual experience of the decade, then you owe it to yourself to order Hand In Hand Films' PRIVATE COLLECTION, an erotic masterpiece and an absolutely unforgettable experience.

*Hand In Hand original Promo

HAND IN HAND VIDEO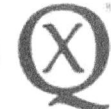

A DIVISION OF
Quality X Video Cassette Company
356 WEST 44TH STREET
NEW YORK, NEW YORK 10036
(212) 541-7880 Outside N.Y. (800) 223-7981

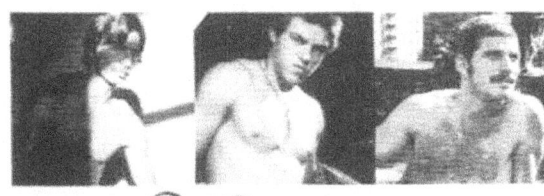

HAND IN HAND FILM'S *Private* COLLECTION

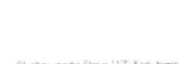

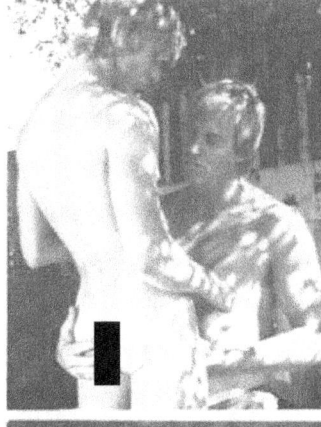

Ken Carter (left), JUST BLONDS star and Falcon model, is ready for hot tub action in Hand in Hand Films' PRIVATE COLLECTION

Blueboy model Steve "12" York bares all in one of the many hot action sequences in Hand in Hand Films' PRIVATE COLLECTION

Whether you read about it in **Blueboy** or some other national publication, or perhaps just heard the rumors, you most certainly must be aware HAND IN HAND FILMS has finally released its *PRIVATE COLLECTION*. But are you aware of just how special this very "private" collection of films is? For the past decade Jack Deveau, producer and director of some of the best known and most extraordinary gay films, has been assembling short films which document some of the outrageously erotic and controversial people and scenes he has encountered. These films were not intended to be shown to the public at large — they were far too exotic at the time they were made — but rather were produced soley for the sake of preserving rare moments of eroticism. By the late Seventies, however, it became clear that public tastes were changing and that it might be possible to show the assembled collection of these remarkable films, at least in a few major cities. Deveau then joined forces with two other well-known and talented filmmakers Peter de Rome and Tom Desimone, selecting footage from their private files too. The result of their efforts may well be the most amazing, controversial and erotic film ever released: *HAND IN HAND FILMS' PRIVATE COLLECTION*.

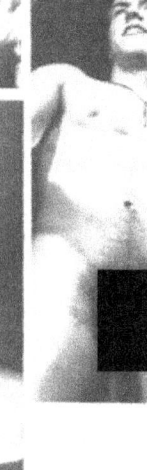
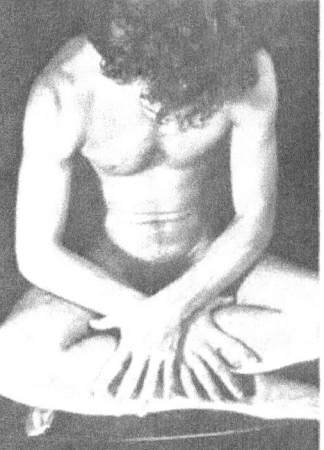

Hand in Hand Films' PRIVATE COLLECTION features a stupifying erotic scene with the magnificent Yogi Rama.

This unique film contains the personal obsessions and private fantasies of the most celebrated names in all-male films. The cast of 20 includes *JUST BLONDS* stars SCORPIO and KEN CARTER. **Blueboy**'s STEVE YORK and PAOLO, *FIRE ISLAND FEVER* stars GARRY HUNT and JOHN CARLO, SCORPIO's identical twin SCORPIO II, BOB DAMON and new stars IVAN, JOHNNY APOLLO and the incredible YOGI RAMA.

If you want to treat yourself to the most amazing, explicit sexual experience of the decade, then you owe it to yourself to order *HAND IN HAND FILMS' PRIVATE COLLECTION*, an erotic masterpiece and an absolutely unforgettable experience.

Cast: Steven York, Garry Hunt, Ivan, Johnny Apollo, John Carlo, Charles Jackson, John Devoe, Kevin Gregory, Ken Carter, Dan Gentry, Beckey Logan, Paolo, Scorpio, Scorpio II, Yogi Rama, Bob Damon, Bart Sommers, John Charles.

Directed by Jack Deveau, Peter deRome and Tom Desimone
Cinematography Jack Deveau, Editors Bob Alvarez, Tom Desimone
Created under the personal supervision of
Jack Deveau   Bob Alvarez   Kees Chapman
Original musical compositions-Slick • Didier Vaffeur

STUDIOSOUND is a special process that guarantees a high fidelity like you've never heard. Instead of the usual optical transfer of sound from film to tape, which limits the reproduction of sound to a narrow range of frequencies, StudioSound is a magnetic transfer of the ORIGINAL MAGNETIC STUDIO sound tracks for the feature, transferred directly to the magnetic tape in your video cassette. This process actually gives you BETTER QUALITY than can be achieved in a cinema. For further enhancement, you can patch your video system into your stereo system and surround yourself with the excitement of these sensual sounds.

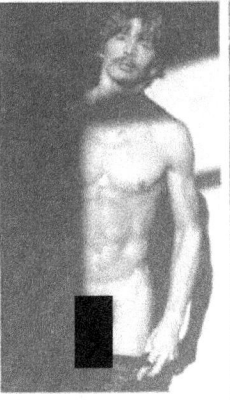
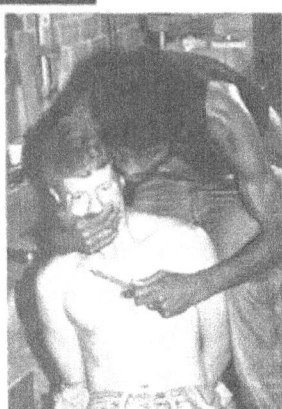

Scorpio's twin, Scorpio II, is every bit the man that his brother is and we see it all in one very special encounter in Hand in Hand Films' PRIVATE COLLECTION

Bob Damon is put through his paces by John Charles, the horny hung burglar, who has more than robbery on his mind!

| PRIVATE COLLECTION | 73 MINUTES | COLOR | ALL-MALE CAST | STUDIOSOUND |

© Quality X Video Cassette Company, 1982

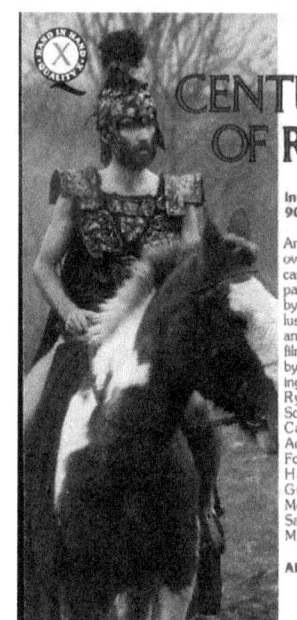

"A long, long time ago..."
"Somewhere outside of Rome..."
"In a village not so far away..."

As you see the opening credits, and then those lines not-so-discreetly adapted from George Lucas STAR WARS epic of a few years ago, you realize CENTURIANS OF ROME is all it's said to be, and more. Not since Joe Gage gave us L.A. TOOL & DIE has there been an all-male erotic release with such quality, action, down-right hot sex, and, yes, even (can you handle all this in one film?) *plot*. Finally the cruelty of the obsessive emperor Caligula and his Generals is unmasked, in a feature that rivals the ancient grandeur of Rome itself. A shocking version of the depravity that slaves endured under the rule of history's most vicious tyrant. The story of two men, in the prime of life, snatched from the countryside and forced to become concubines trained to please every whim of the Roman aristocracy.

CENTURIANS OF ROME is an epic feature capturing all the pomp and pageantry of a society ruled by passion and destroyed by lust. CENTURIANS OF ROME will make you flush as love overcomes lust, and the two valiant slaves bewitch their masters and escape to freedom. Directed by the celebrated John Christopher, CENTURIANS OF ROME showcases the talents of Eric Ryan and Scorpio in several explosive scenes that simply will make you beg for release. George Payne is especially responsible for helping you reach that sought ejaculation. His enticing, lean, perfectly-muscled physique is an instant turn-on in itself, leaving you hard with anticipation, but he tantalizes you even more with a pounding performance of sheer sexuality. Hand In Hand Films brings this exceptional achievement to the screen, and it sets new standards for erotic male entertainment. With its incredible photography, and 31 luscious men sprawled before the camera, it will be a long time before anyone will be able to challenge John Christopher's new stature as master of the all-male epic.

*John Mensior, *Torso*

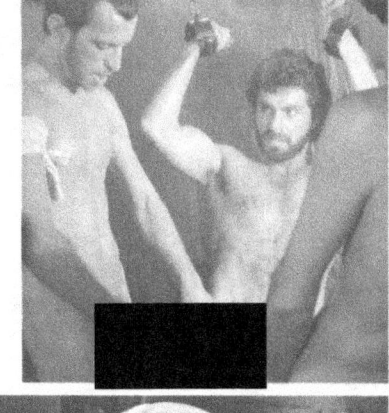
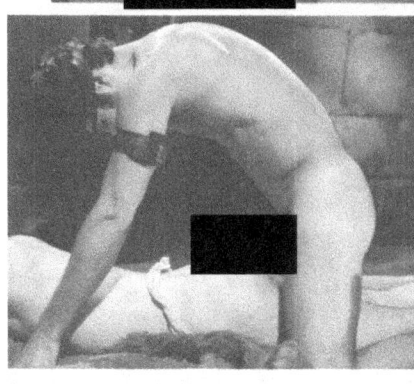
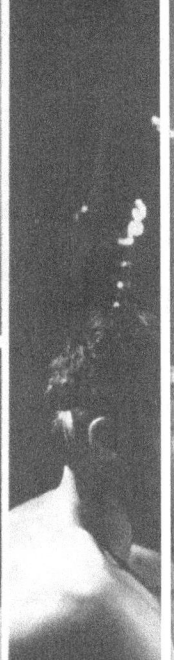
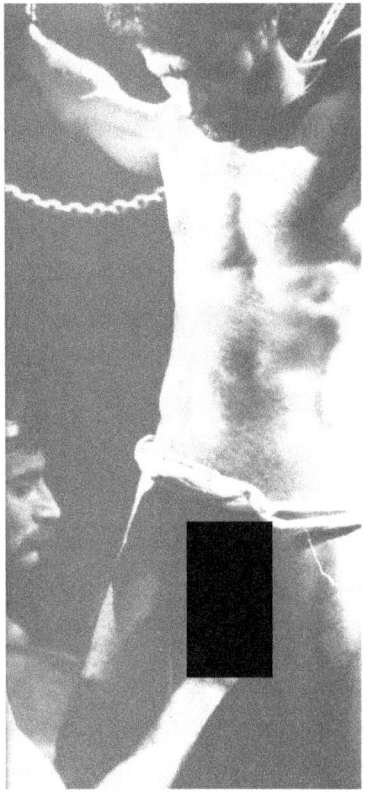
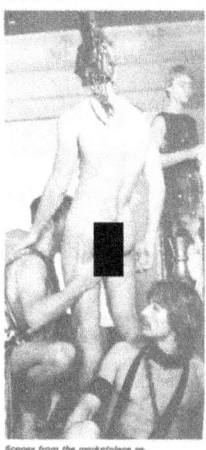

end up with the flick instead of the cash.
Abandoned unfinished for more than a year, the film was finally resurrected by Hand in Hand Films, who put up the completion moneys and are distributing the film.

The plot of the movie itself is far less complicated. Centurions of Rome lives it (their way) recounts the tale of two young Romans, Demetrius and Octavius (George Payne and Scorpio), who live in the time of the depraved Emperor Caligula. Snatched from the fields of their native countryside a few moments

Scenes from the marketplace sequence, in which the two slaves are introduced to Roman decadence.

after their first sexual encounter with each other, they are ravished by their captors and then taken to Rome as slaves.

Sold in the marketplace (where the phrase "Roman orgy" was never more appropriate; they are seen being used sexually by aristocrats and soldiers alike). A Commander (Eric Ryan) takes a fancy

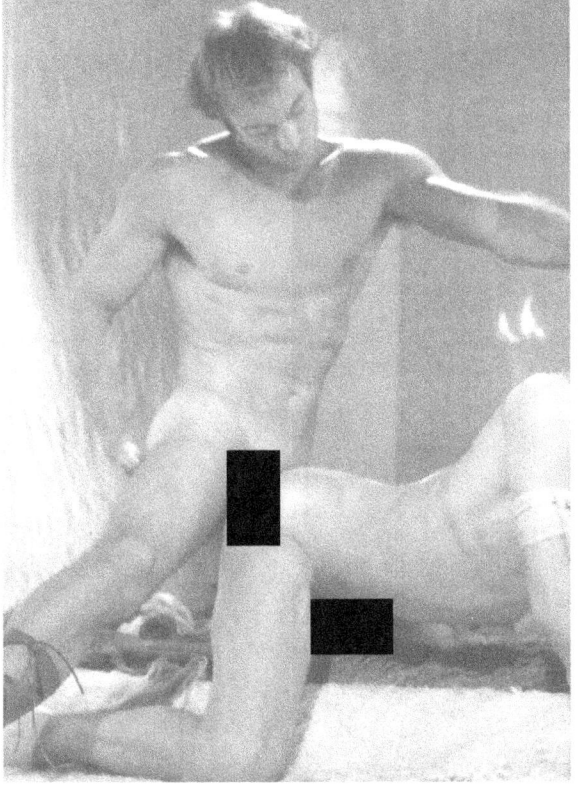
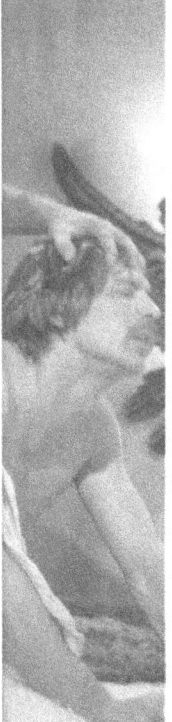
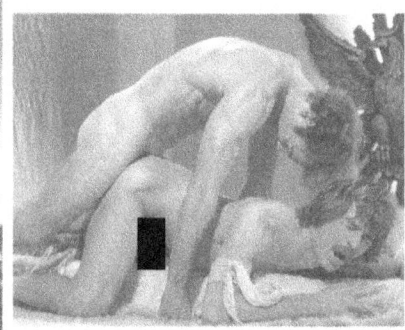
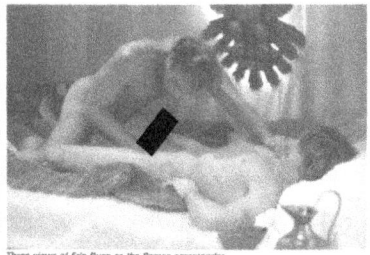

Three views of Eric Ryan as the Roman commander and Scorpio as the less-than-willing object of his passion.

Centurions of Rome, touted as the most expensive film in the history of gay erotica, is an opulent and heated epic in the Cecil B. DeMille tradition. Every care has been lavished on it, save one — somebody along the way misspelled the word "centurion" in its title.

That, however, is the least of the film's problems at the moment. Newspapers from coast to coast have revealed that the world renowned insurance company Lloyd's of London may well own a major piece of the picture. How that happened is a long and complicated story involving a one-time Brink's security guard, who is reported to have, in vested varying amounts of money in the production — estimates reach as high as $200,000. The man currently stands accused of stealing the money from Brink's, who is insured by Lloyd's, which is in turn suing him, but they may

to Octavius, while Demetrius is presented to the Emperor himself and ordered to service him. Between sexual bouts, the two young lovers attempt to get back together and win their freedom.

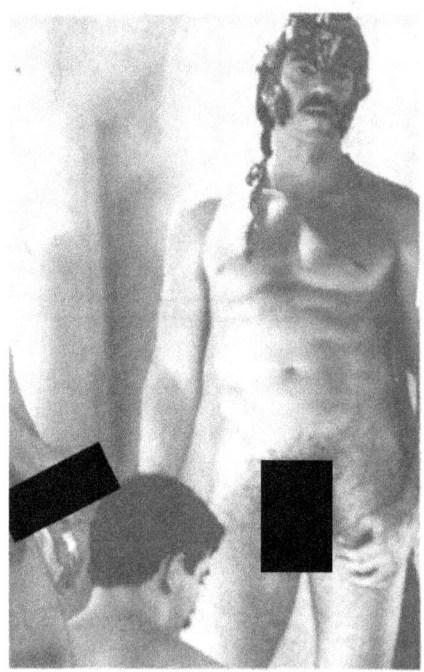

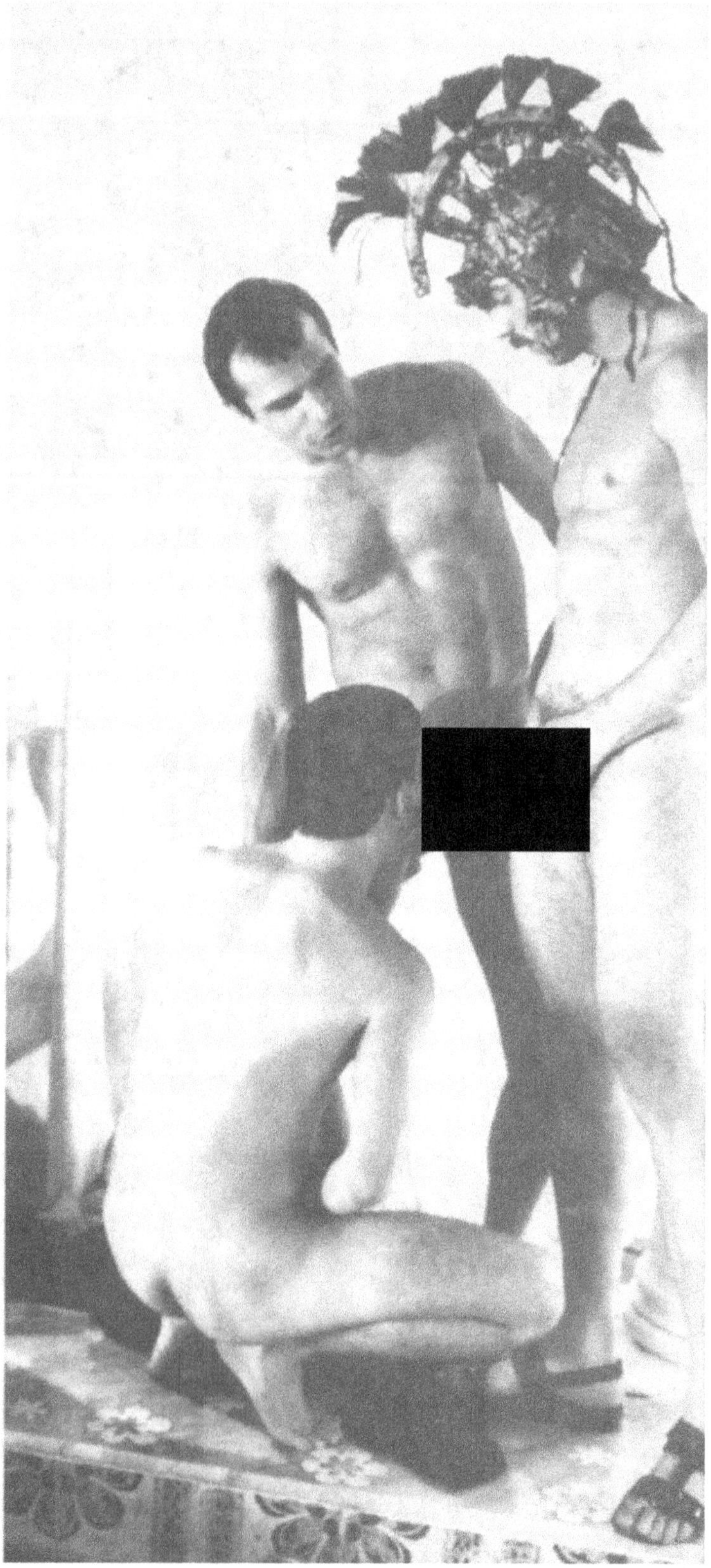

Roman senators, soldiers and slaves.

Hand in Hand Films presents CENTURIANS OF ROME. Directed by John Christopher; Cinematography by Larry Revene; Screenplay by Timothy Michaels; Set Designer, Randal James; Wardrobe, Theodore Aldridge; Sound by Per Sjostedt; Editor, John Christopher; Titles and Optical Effects, Pegasus Graphics Lab. Cast:

Demetrius	GEORGE PAYNE
Commander	ERIC RYAN
Octavius	SCORPIO
Commander's soldiers	JONNY CANNUIC
	JEFFERY SCOTT
Claudius	ADAM DE HAVEN
Auctioneer	JEROME C. FOX
Emperor	MICHAEL FLENT
Argos	MYLES LONGUE
Old Slave	DAVID HADLEY
Bath Slaves	RYDER JONES
	GUISEPPE WELCH
Soldiers	DAVID O'CHELA
	JOHN CANNON
	GREG MONROE
	TOM TRENT
Senators	JOHN KOVACS
	MITCHELL FLYNN
	TIMOTHY MICHAELS
	ROY GARRETT
Slaves	RICHARD COX
	KEN RAMSAVER
	DAVID MORRIS
	ROBERT JONES
Maiden	CHARLOTTE O'HARA
Peasants	TOMMY HAWKE
	BOBBIE BURNS
	KENNETH CARSEIN
	JERRY PURPURA
	JUSTIN SAVAGE
	CHUCK ROEBUCK
	PHIL PHILLIPS

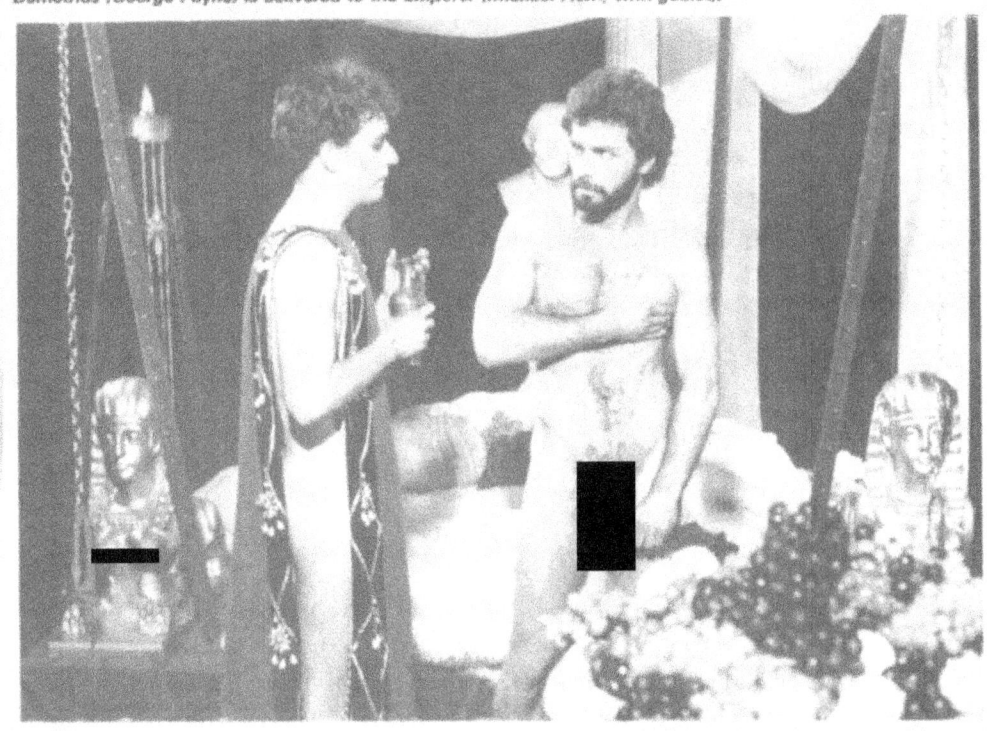

Demetrius (George Payne) is delivered to the Emporer (Michael Flent, with goblet).

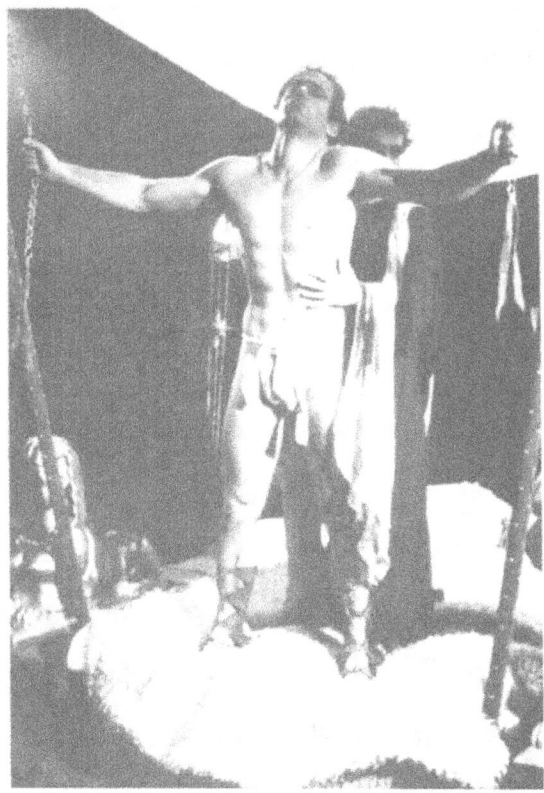

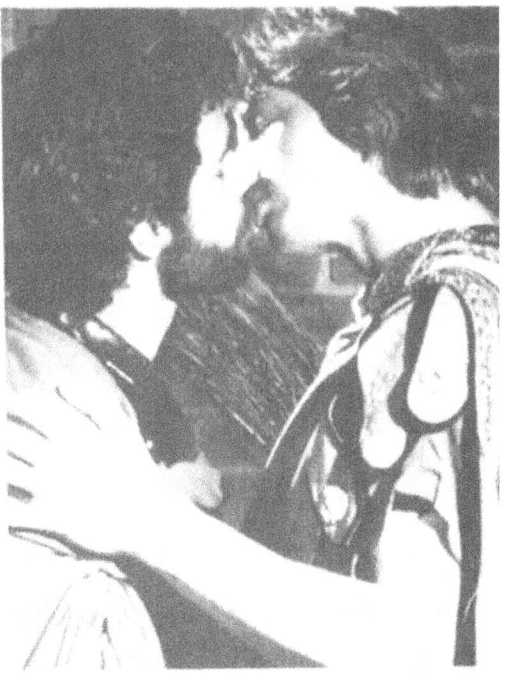

George Payne and Scorpio at the final fadeout.

79 STALLION

Touted as the most expensive gay film of its time, the 1981 CENTURIANS OF ROME purportedly cost $90,000, and if the figure is accurate, it may well be the most costly disaster in the entire history of gay erotica. Every care was lavished on it, save one – somebody along the way misspelled the word "centurion" in its title. Aspiring to the extravagance and decadence of Fellini's SATYRICON, it is instead a mishmash that combines the reverential revisionism so adored by Cecil B. DeMille and the exploitiational pandering of the cloak-and-sandal epics made popular by Steve Reeves. In short, it is an X-rated cross between SAMSON AND DELILAH and HERCULES UNCHAINED. Starring George Payne, Eric Ryan (in the most embarrassing role of his long career), and Scorpio, CENTURIANS OF ROME is handsomely lensed, intelligently directed, and surprisingly well mounted, but the production suffers in two major areas. The script is pretentious and self-conscious – it ain't easy to speak in Biblicalese while fucking – and the sex scenes (though energetically performed and beautifully photographed) seem to be consistently brief, often truncated, and invariably overwhelmed by the heavy-handed script. At the time of its release, newspaper stories chronicled that the world renowned insurance company, Lloyds of London, might well have owned a piece of the film. How that happened is a long and complicated story involving a one-time Brink's security guard who was reported to have invested varying amounts of money in the production – estimates climbed as high as $200,000. The man was accused of stealing the money from Brink's, who was insured by Lloyds, who in turn sued him. He ended up in a California prison, and the film was in limbo for more than a year, until Hand In Hand Films finally resurrected it by putting up the completion monies and initially distributing it.

The plot of the movie is far less complicated. It recounts the tale of two young Romans (Payne and Scorpio), who live in the time of the depraved emperor, Caligula. Snatched from the fields of sunny Italy (by way of New Jersey, where it was filmed), only moments after their first sexual encounter with each other, they are taken to Rome as slaves. Sold in the marketplace, they are soon being used and abused by patricians and plebians alike. A commander (Ryan) takes a fancy to Scorpio, while Payne is given head by almost everyone he encounters – usually while shackled in a standing position, his arms stretched wide in a position not unlike that of Christ on the cross – until at last he ends up in Caligula's chambers. When the Commander has a change of heart and helps to reunite the young lovers, he is seized by the Emperor's guards and forced to become the next royal plaything, a fate worse than death as suggested by the grotesque final freeze frame. Like those colossal mainstream failures, HEAVEN'S GATE, ISHTAR, and BONFIRE OF THE VANITIES, CENTURIANS OF ROME is a monument of profligacy that must be seen to be believed.

*Jerry Douglas, *Manshots*

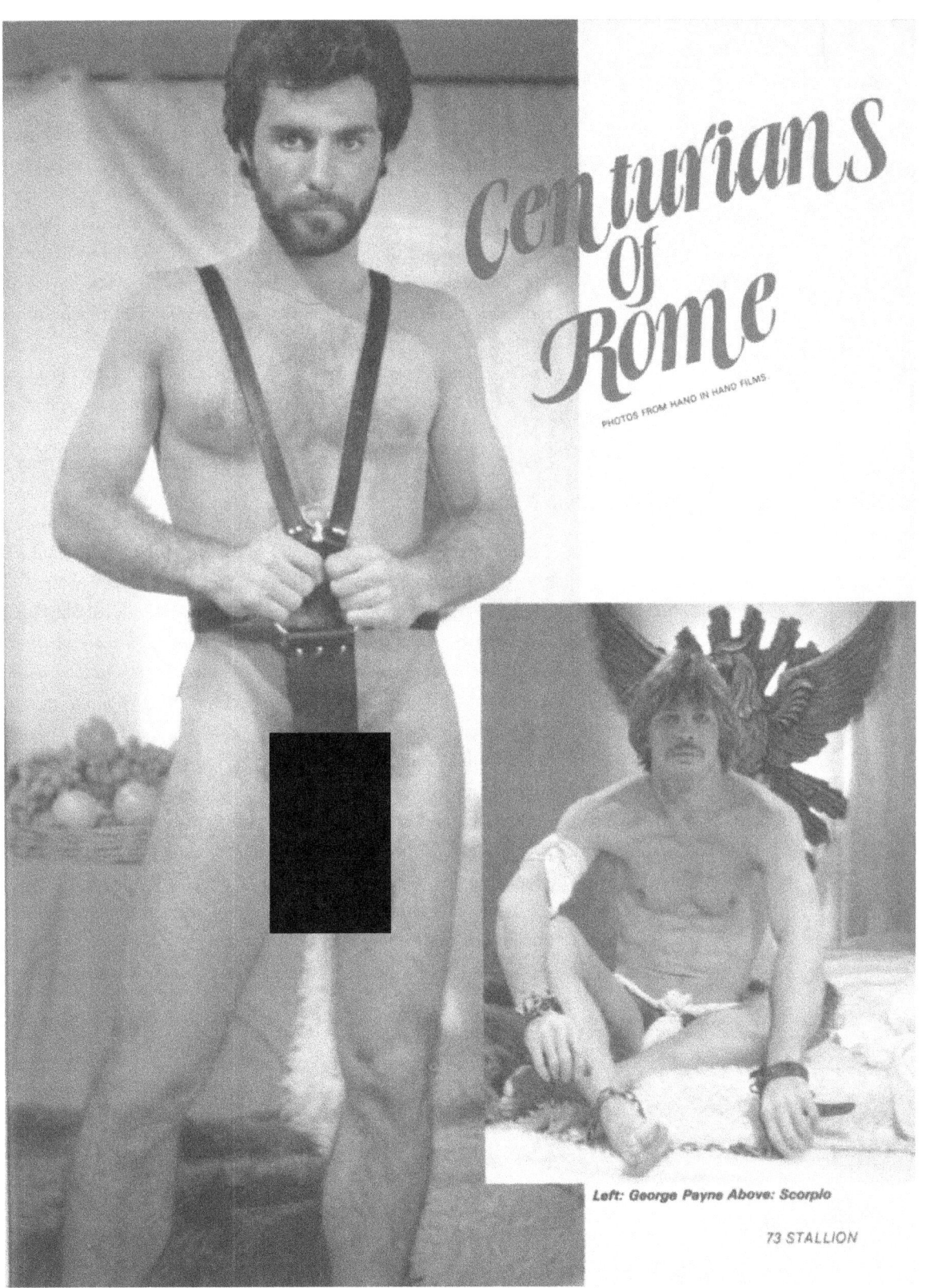

Centurians of Rome

PHOTOS FROM HAND IN HAND FILMS

Left: George Payne Above: Scorpio

73 STALLION

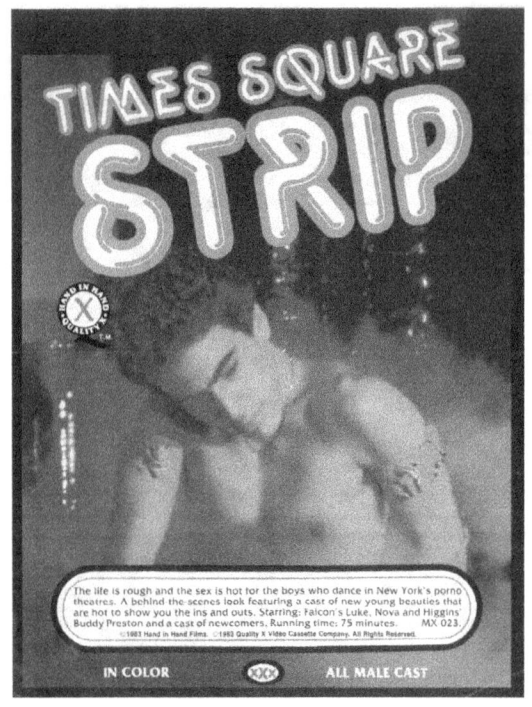

Unless you've spent a wild evening or two trashing through the sleazy porno theatres that fringe New York's Times Square area, the chances are you've never seen any of the live sex shows that draw people from all walks of life to the neon jungle. There, you can see damned near anything you've ever fantasized about – for a price. Now, Hand In Hand Films has created a hot new explicit motion picture that takes you behind the scenes of this demi-world in their wild new work, TIMES SQUARE STRIP. Hand In Hand Films, under aegis of producer-director Jack Deveau, is the production company that has, for more than a decade, produced one gay cinema classic after another, among them LEFT-HANDED, GOOD HOT STUFF, THE IDOL, JUST BLONDS, BALLET DOWN THE HIGHWAY, DRIVE, and FIRE ISLAND FEVER. TIMES SQUARE STRIP stars Buddy Preston (who had appeared in several William Higgins films) and Falcon Studios' Luke, as well as a handful of lean, young new faces. The plot of the piece centers around a new boy in town, Darryl (Preston), right off the bus, and his debut as a stripper at the Gaiety Male Burlesque show. His first performance there especially interests a regular wealthy patron (George Sardi), but most of the other strippers don't feel he has the stuff to make the grade in the business. Much of the film is devoted to the sexual escapades of the other boys in the show: Paco (Jack Moore) who makes it with a cigar-chomping Texan in a ten-gallon hat in an elegant room at the Plaza; Andre (Luke) who gets it on with a wild street hustler in the stairwell of a Hell's Kitchen tenement; Joe (Peter Lopez) who is into scenes of military discipline, and who carries a cassette on which is recorded a lusty drill sergeant's commands; and Kirk (Jerry Overton) and Tony (Tony West), whose specialty is a roller-skating strip. Although Darryl proves again and again that he is a hot man offstage, it takes him a while to learn the knack of getting over his hands-ups to be erotic onstage. By the end of the film, however, he has developed a show-stopping act (thanks to Joe) as a marine who strips out of his full uniform against an American flag. And that, as they say, is how a star is born.

*Jerry Douglas, *Stallion*

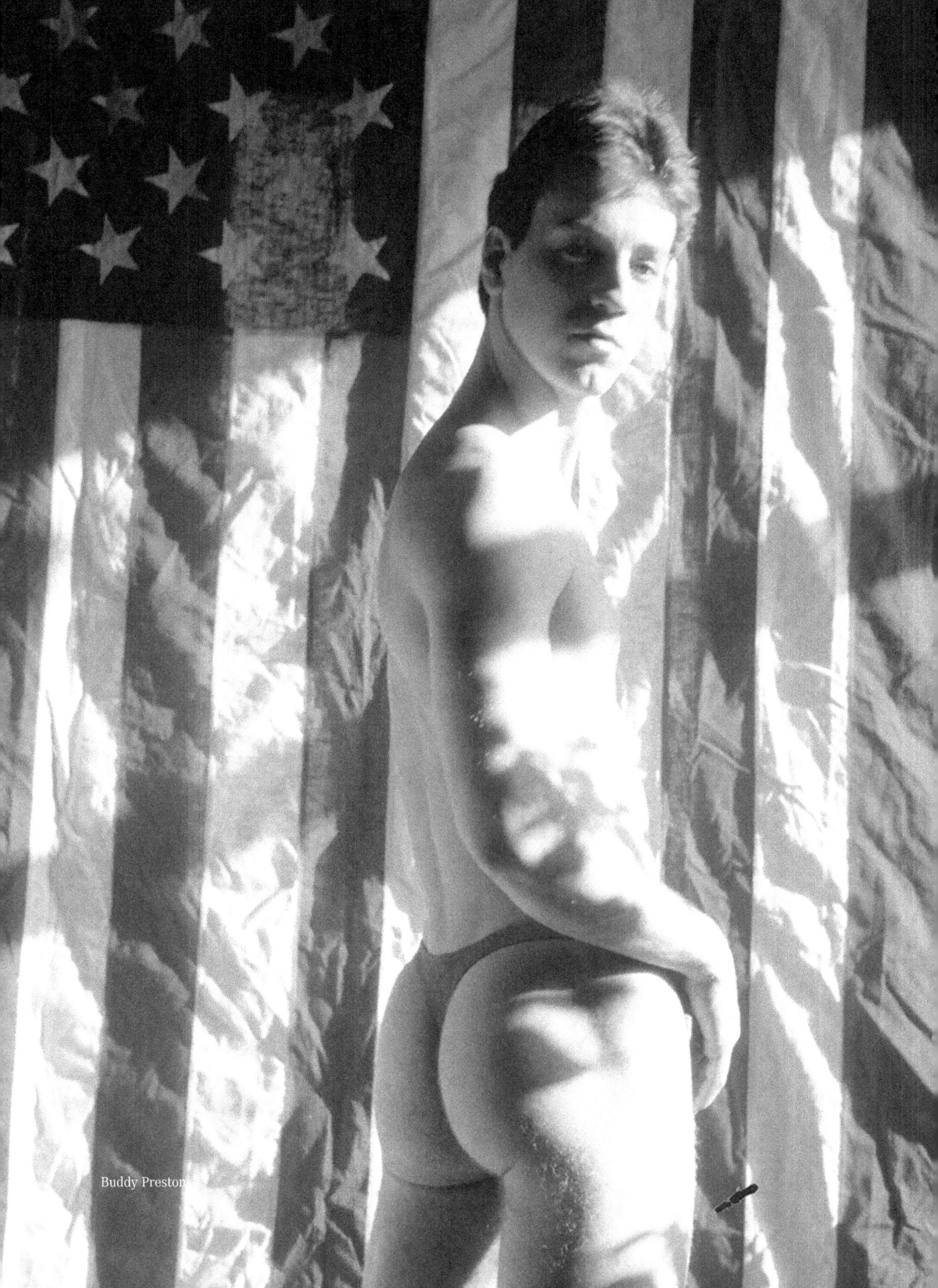

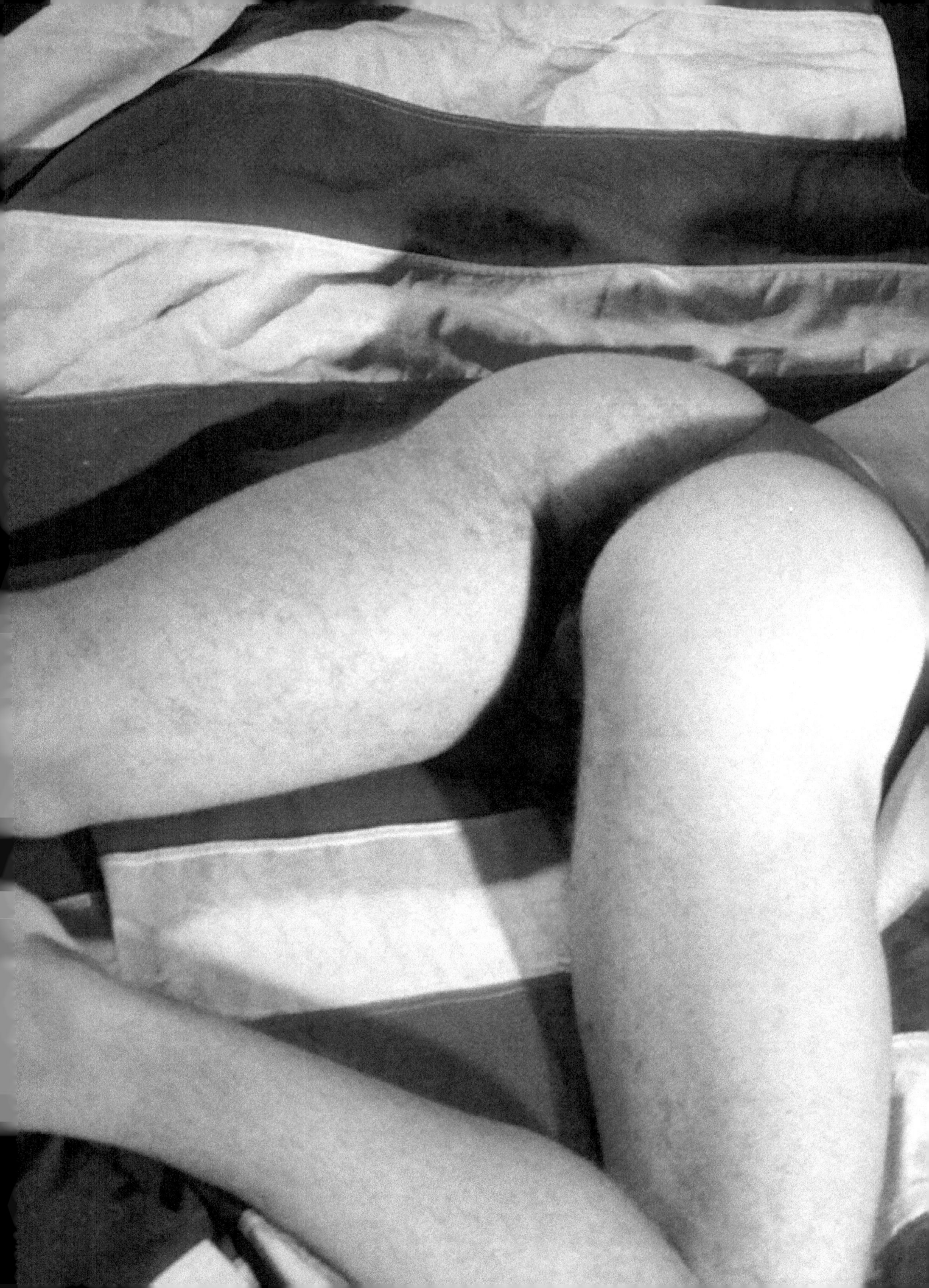

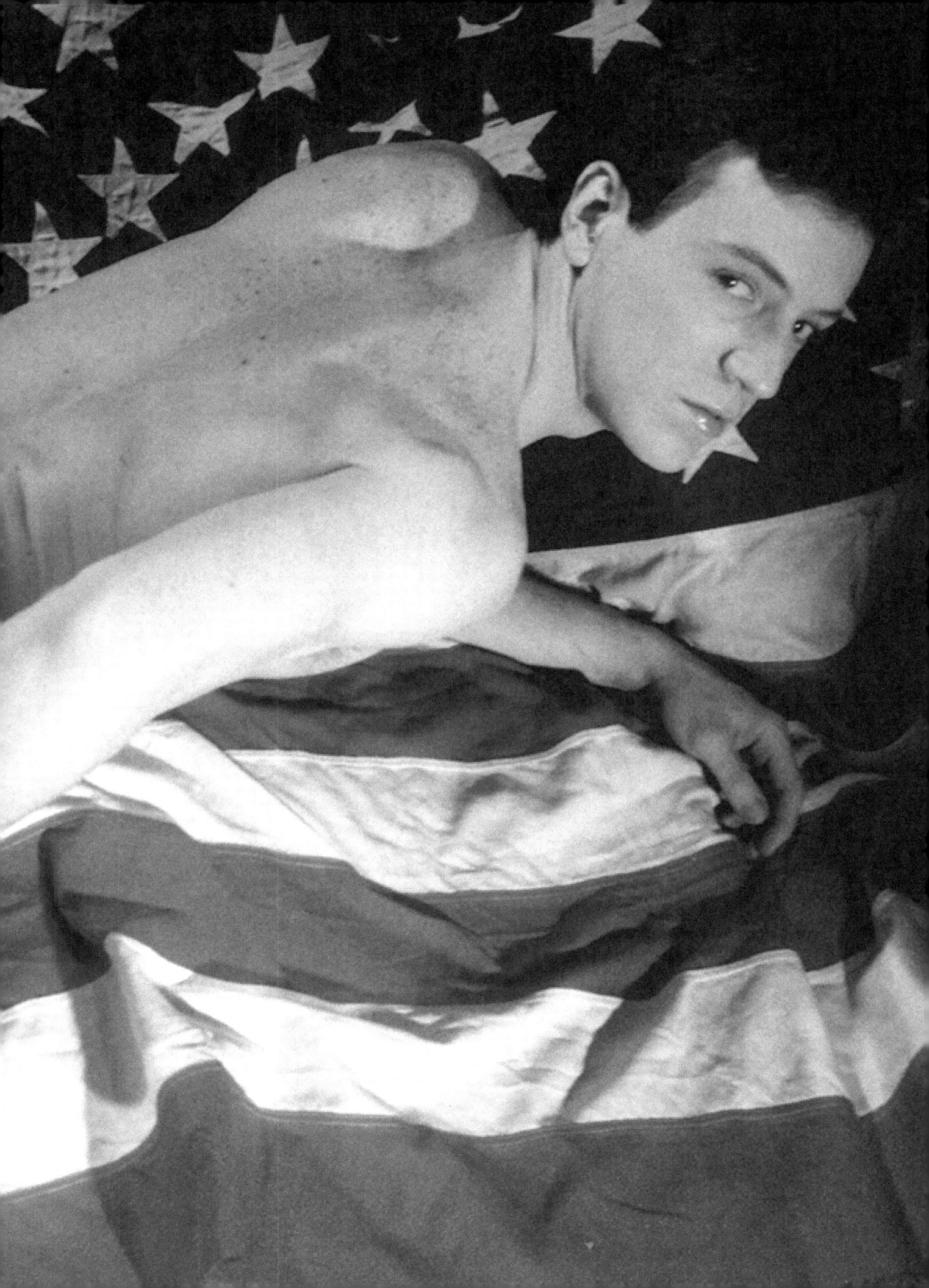

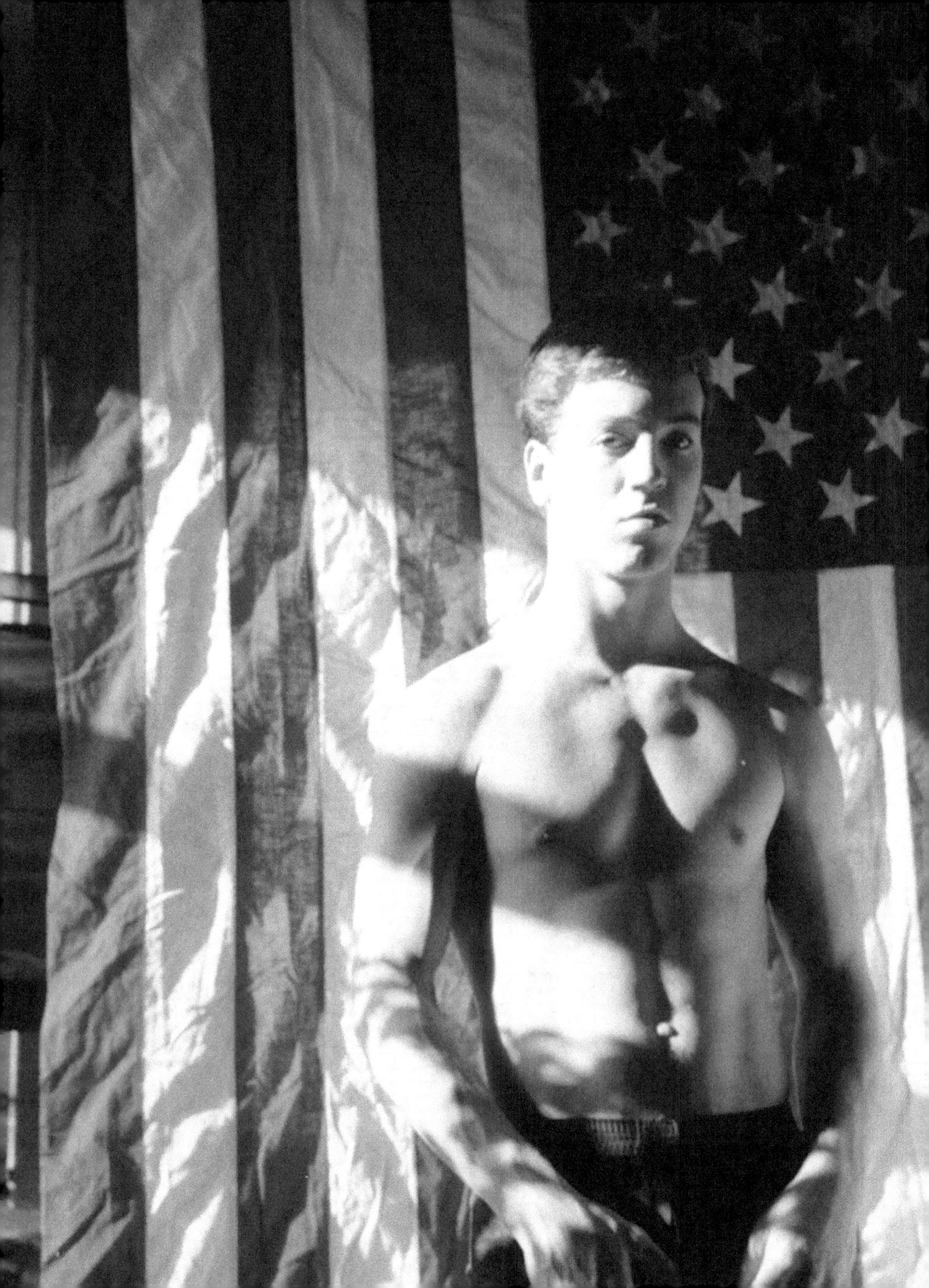

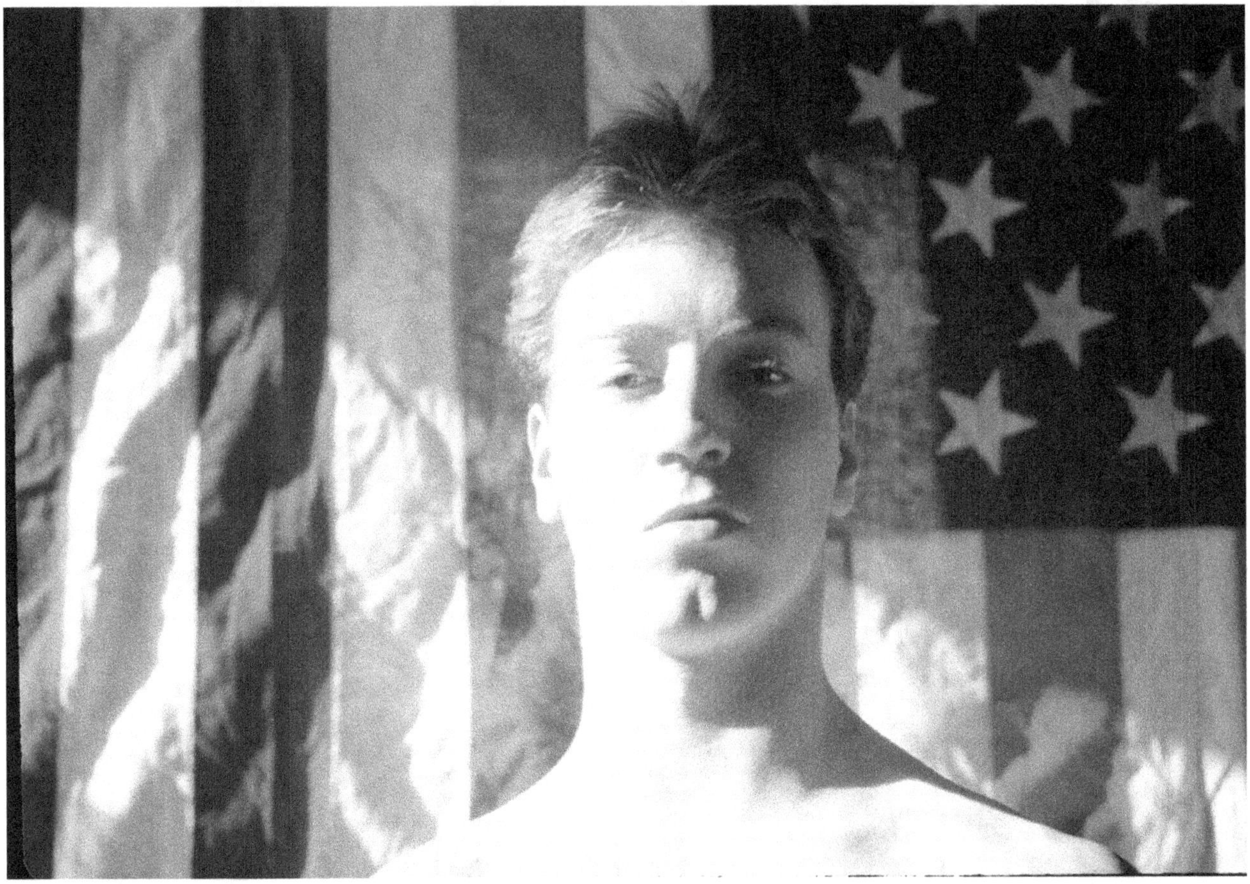

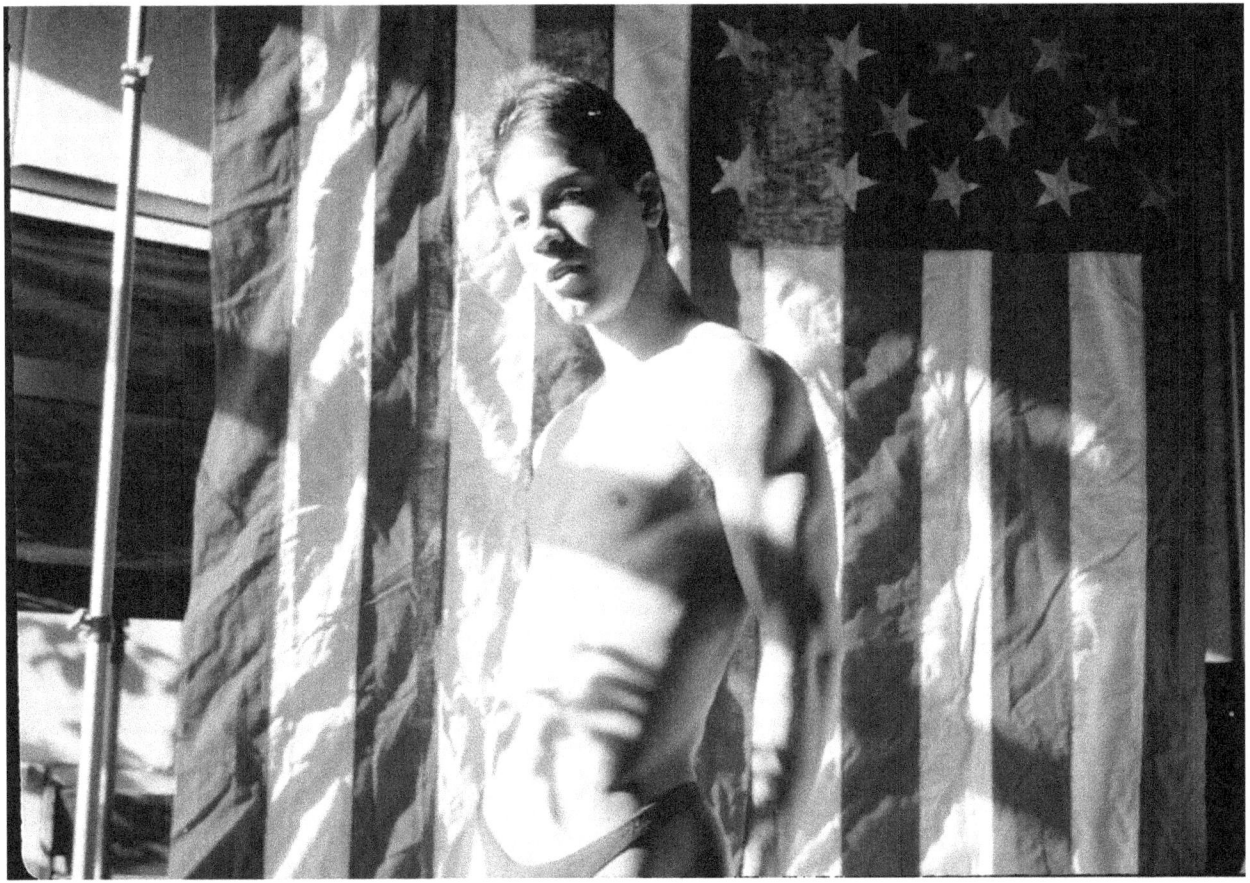

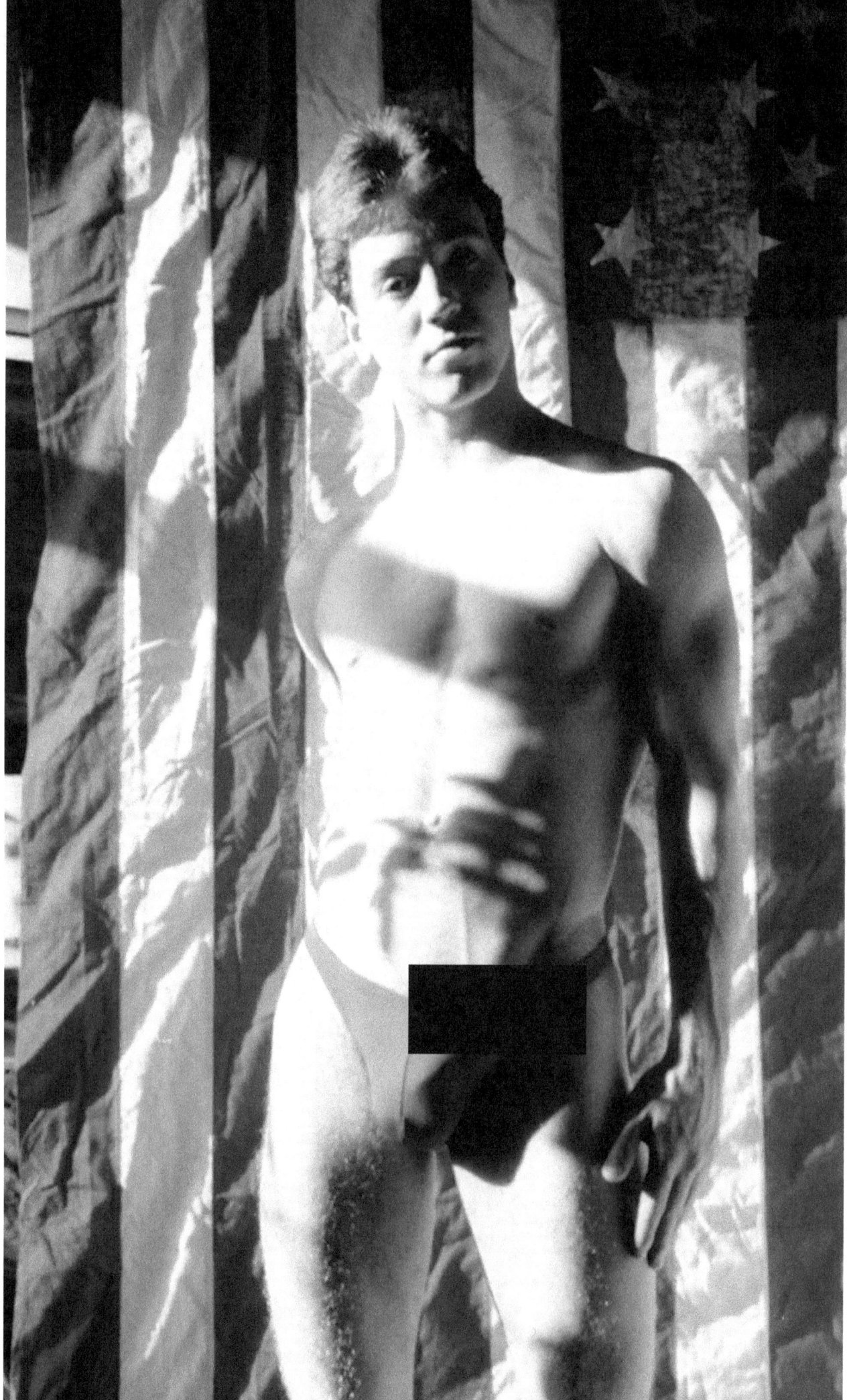

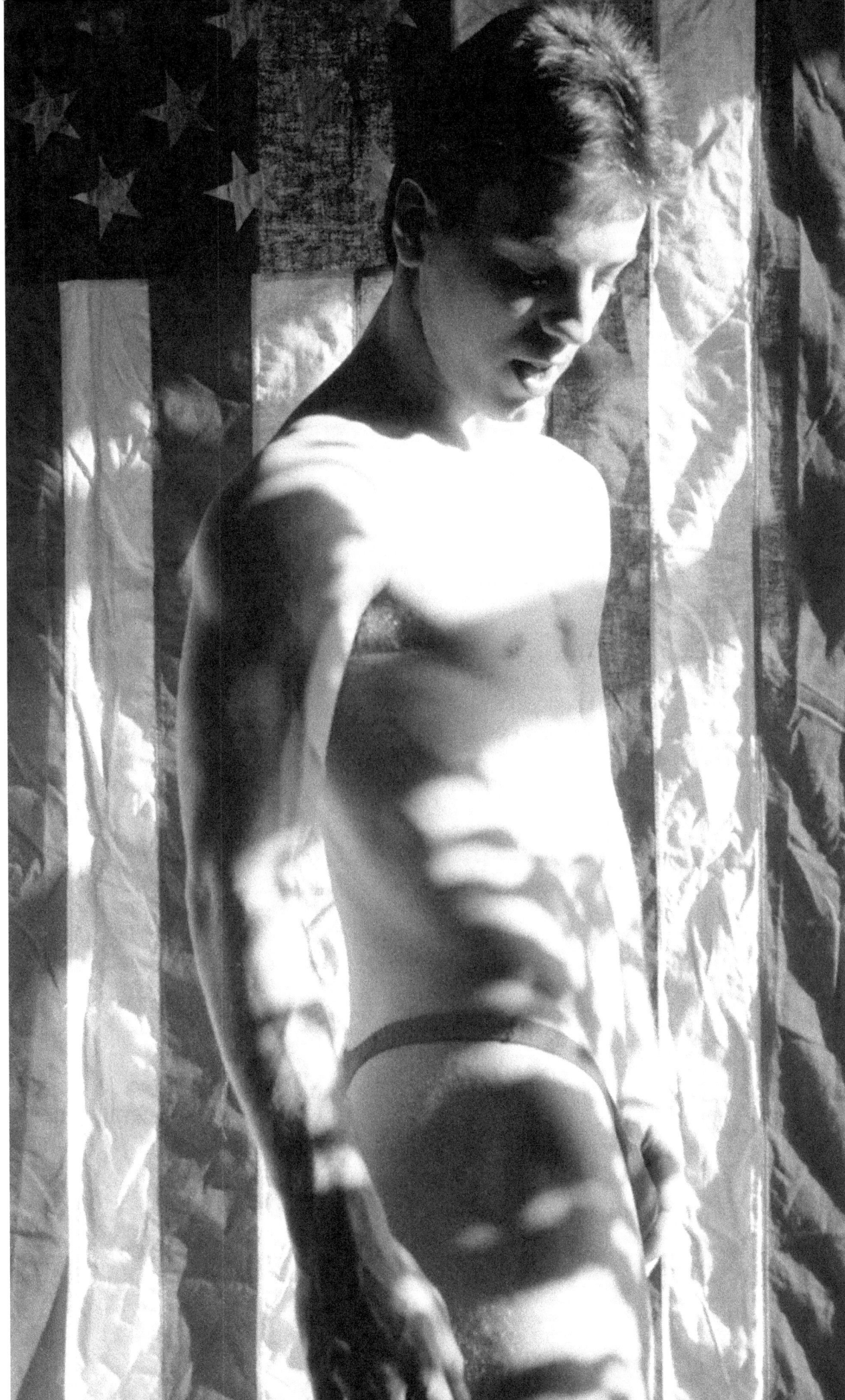

TIMES SQUARE STRIP follows a day in the lives of several go-go boys who work at the Gaiety Theatre in New York. It accurately captures the sleaziness of Times Square, and the kinds of people who are drawn to it. Less of a porn feature than a character study of gays along the Great White Way, the film has plenty of sex, but what makes it so exciting is the overall framework and its honesty in portraying the interaction among the boys and their johns. Heading the cast is Buddy Preston as a new dancer who is not doing well in his first day on the job. The other boys take bets as to whether he will get fired by the end of the day. Therein lies the conflict, because the Preston character *wants* to succeed, and he knows he is failing. Luke and Jack Moore play two dancers who are friends. Between shows they go out – Moore to meet a john from Texas (Jason Jacobi) at the Plaza Hotel, and Luke to find some action. He meets a hustler (David Dion) and they go to a tenement stair landing to do it. The Plaza Hotel and stairwell scenes are juxtaposed. At the Plaza, a cowboy movie is on the television. While Moore and Jacobi get it on, the t.v. posse chases the rustlers. Likewise in the stairwell, Luke and Dion quietly have sex while a dog barks in an apartment and an off-camera argument erupts into a full-scale flight, including breaking dishes and neighbors pounding on the door. At both locations the sound plays a pivotal role in setting the proper atmosphere. A most unusual role is played by Robert Glory, as a backstage hanger-on. Nude throughout the film and horny for any takers, he is ignored by everyone, but he never stops trying. It is a comedy role edged in pathos. Jack Deveau has put together a tight, well produced film (his last before his death in 1982). Kudos go to Rolph Deutch *[Editor's note: Rolf Pardula]* for the cleanest soundtrack we've heard in porn films; to Deveau himself for clear cinematography; to Gene Kelton for always providing enough light, no matter how dark the scene, and for using it creatively, particularly during show numbers. Moose 100 and Dick Bettis have written a good story filled with believable people. Some "witty repartee" is a little forced, but it doesn't stand in the way of the overall mood they have created. Mood is perhaps the best asset of this film, which captures, in a non-sugarcoated way, a segment of the population that gravitates to the busiest few blocks in the world – Times Square.

*Christopher Parrish, *Stallion*

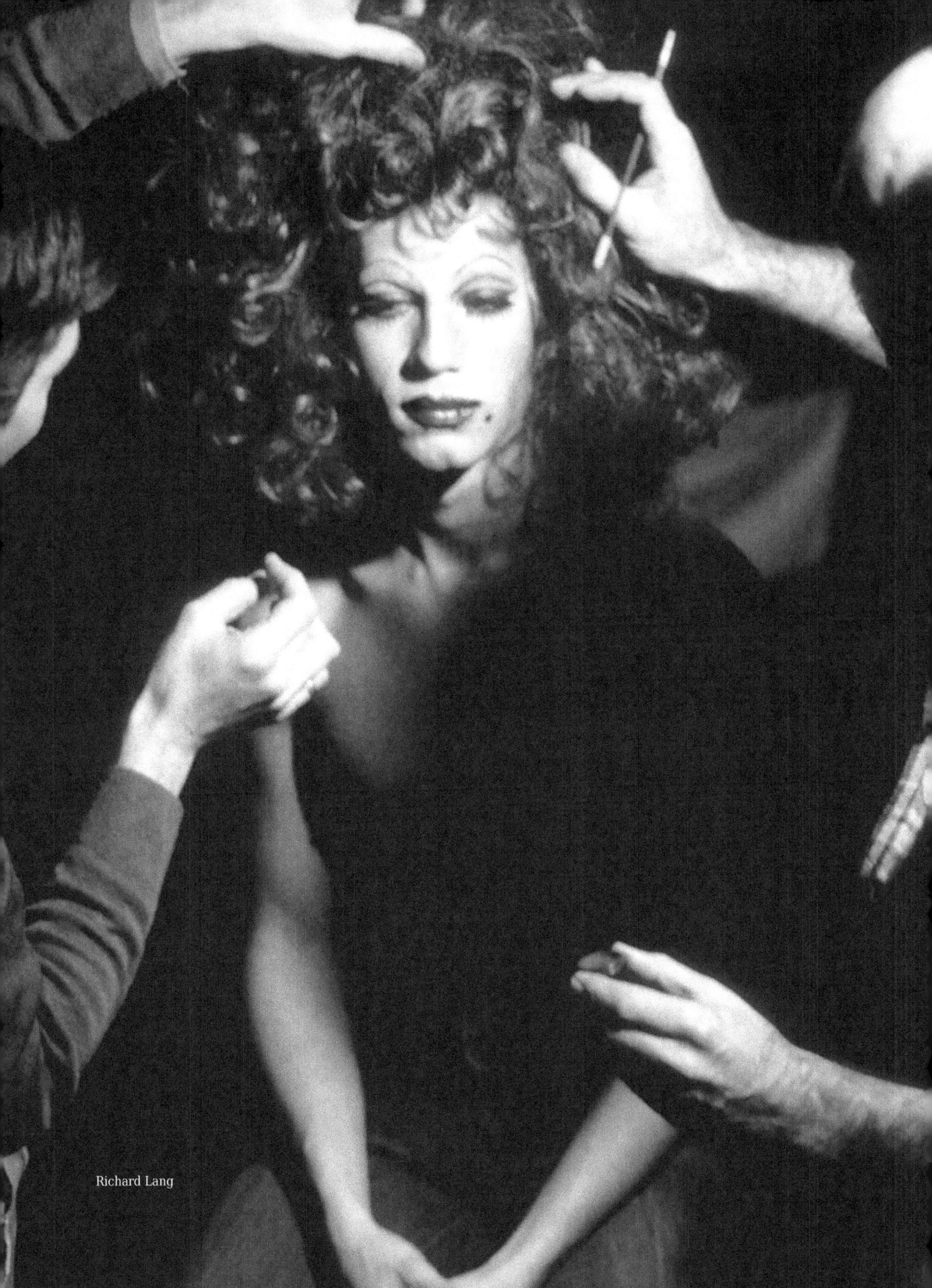

Richard Lang

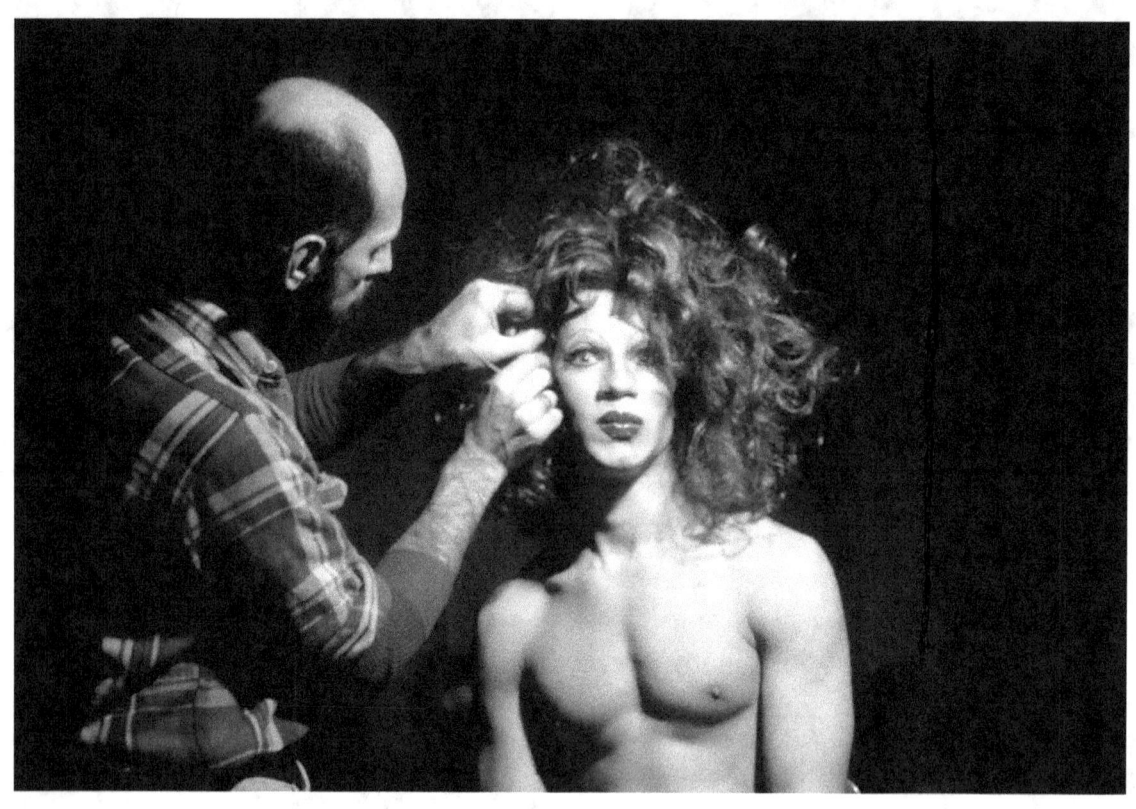
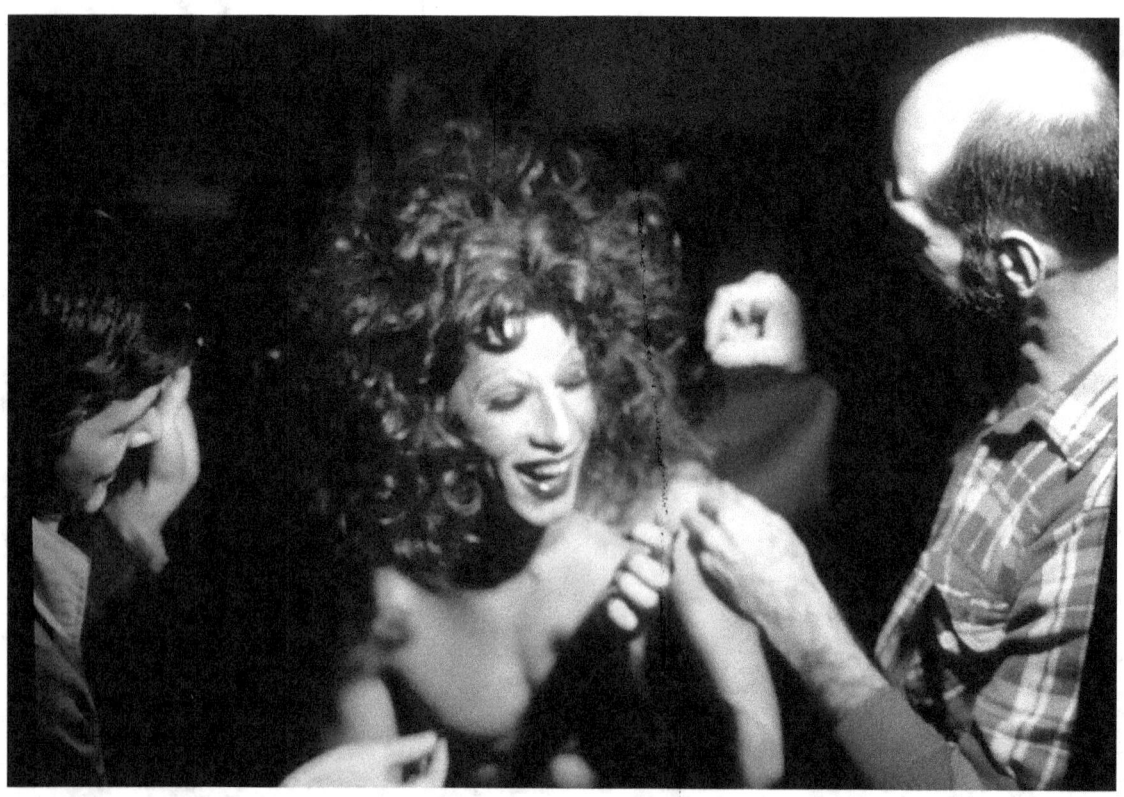

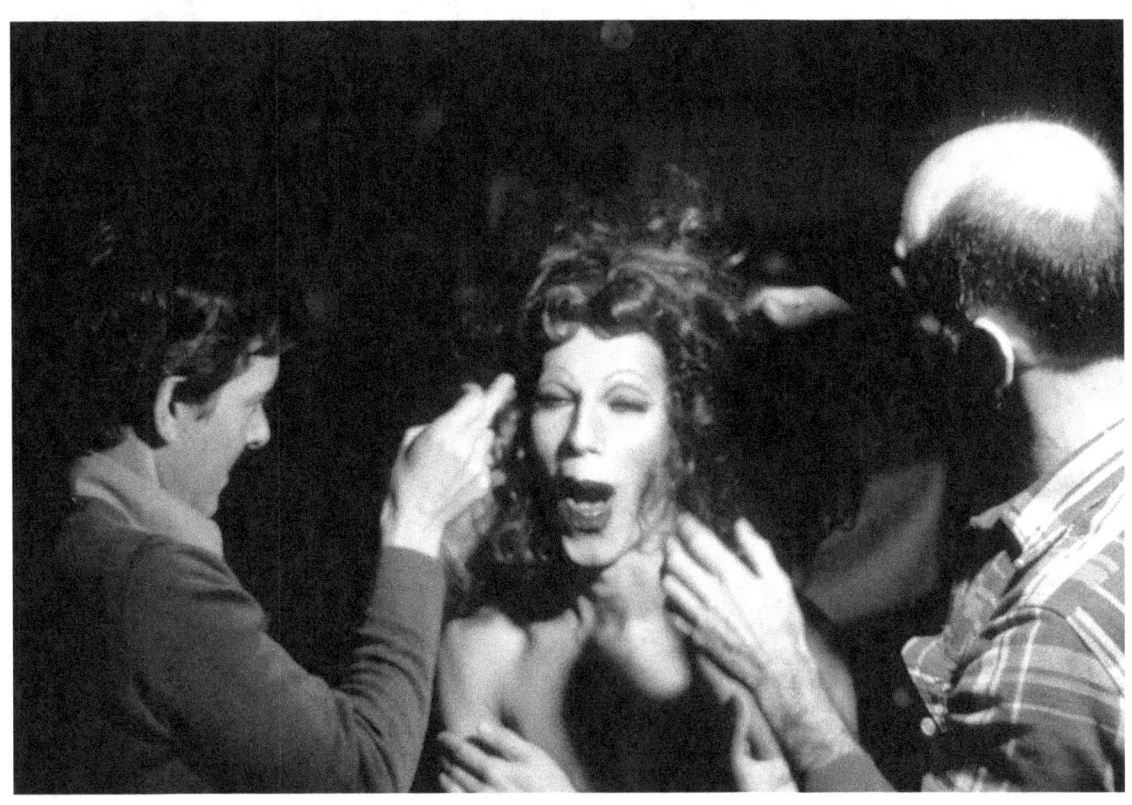

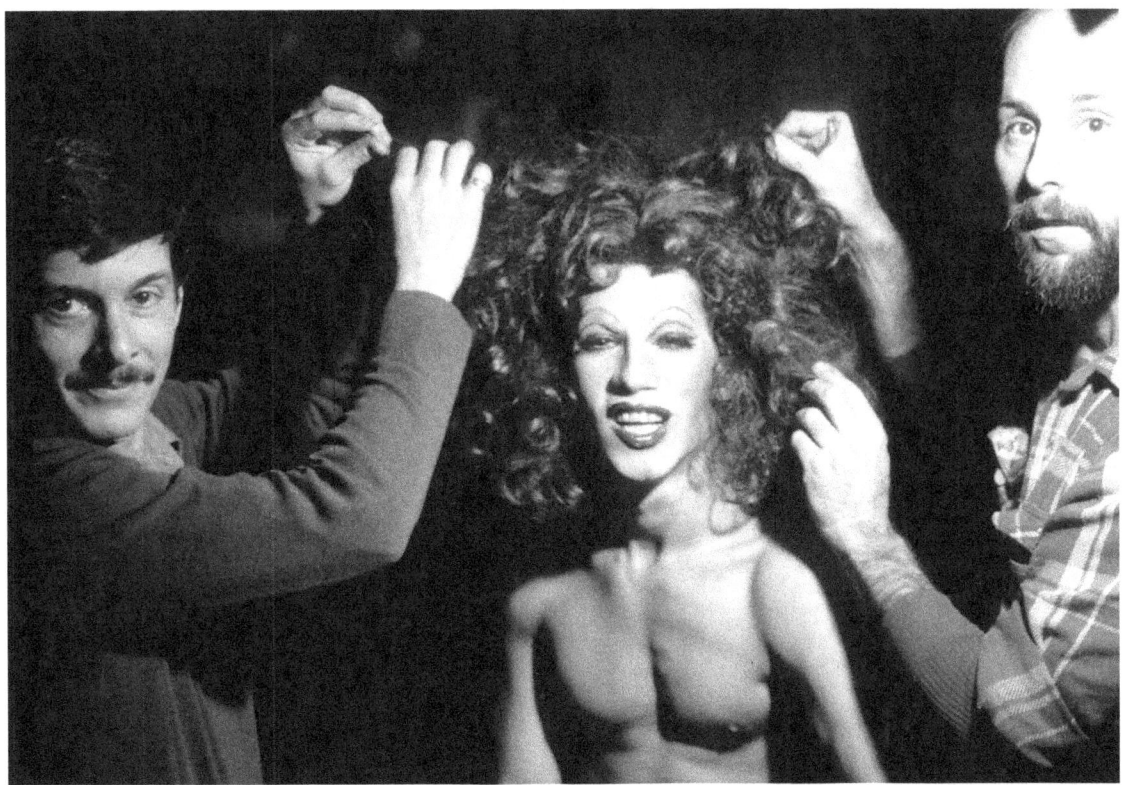

Jim Delegatti, Richard Lang and Gene Kelton

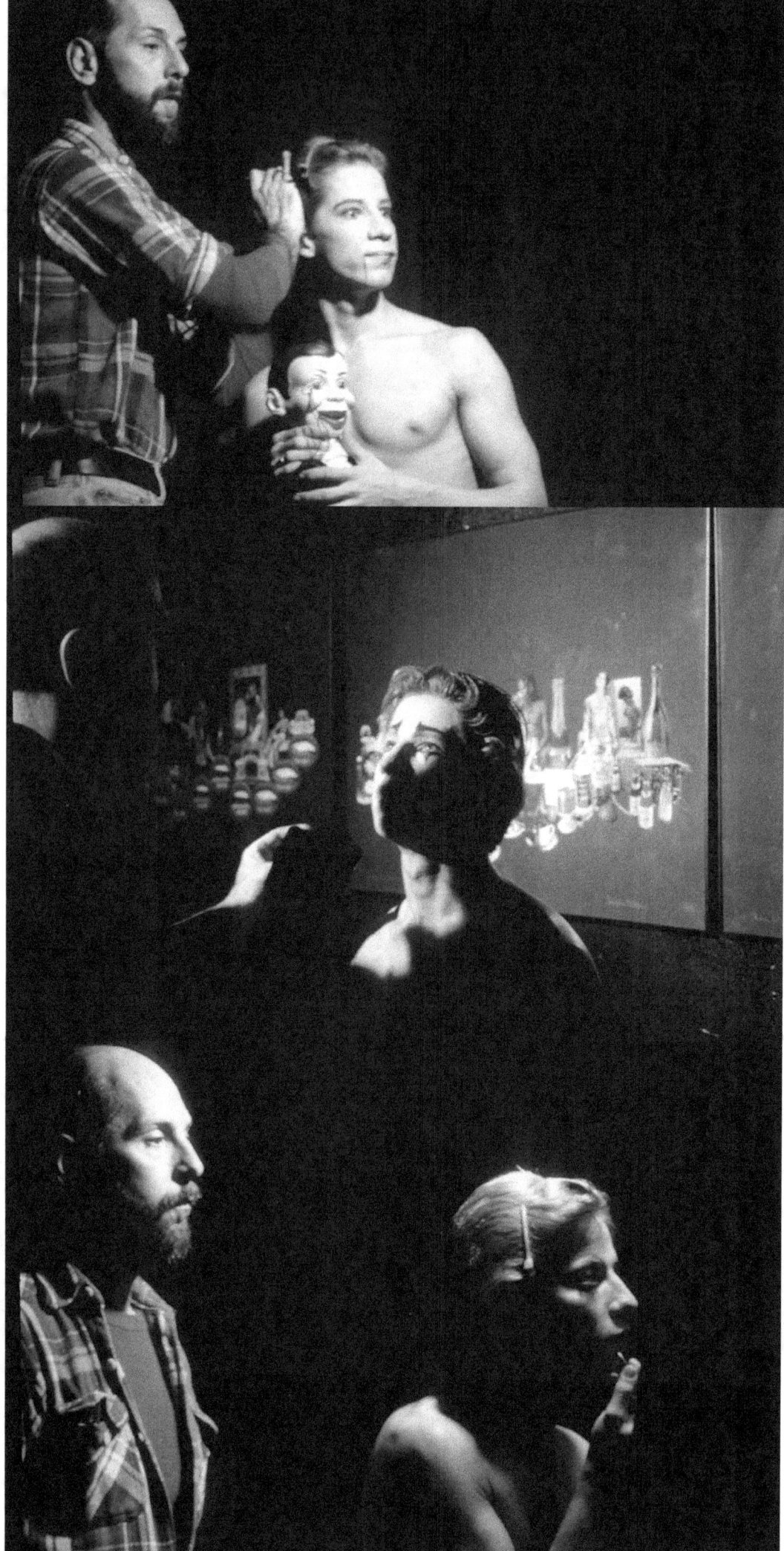

"There is a lot of dialogue, mostly backstage gossip about dates and clothes, the same kinds of conversations you would probably hear in the Rockette's dressing room at Radio City Music Hall. The actors handle this pretty well. Several of the guys in Strip are Hispanic, which is a nice change from the usual all-WASP lineup in gay porn movies, and at least one is hung well enough to satisfy you size queens out there." *GayLife Erotica*

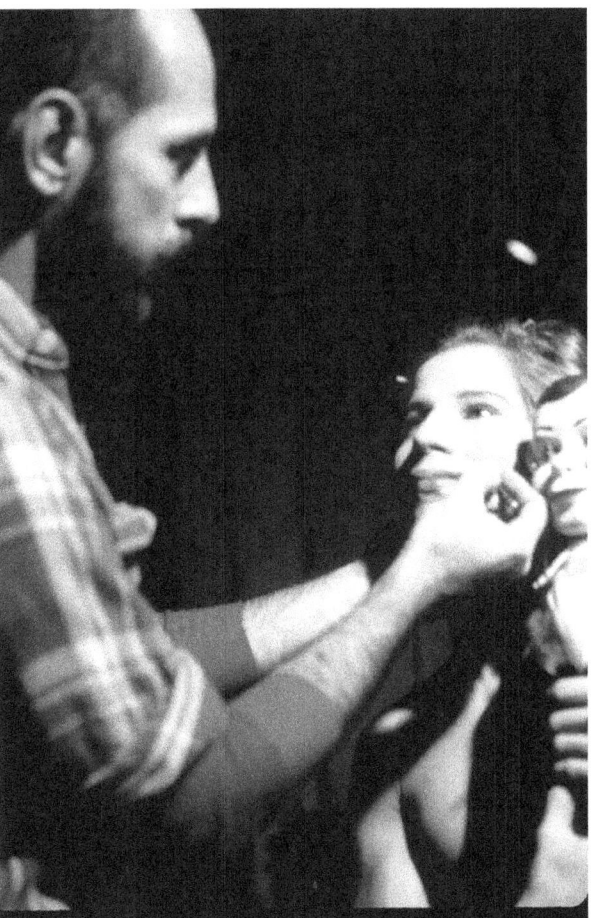

"This film, Jack Deveau's last, features an attractive and diverse cast, and an exciting musical score. "... his passion for preserving sexuality and sensuality on screen goes unsurpassed with this near-perfect production."
John Mensior, *Torso*

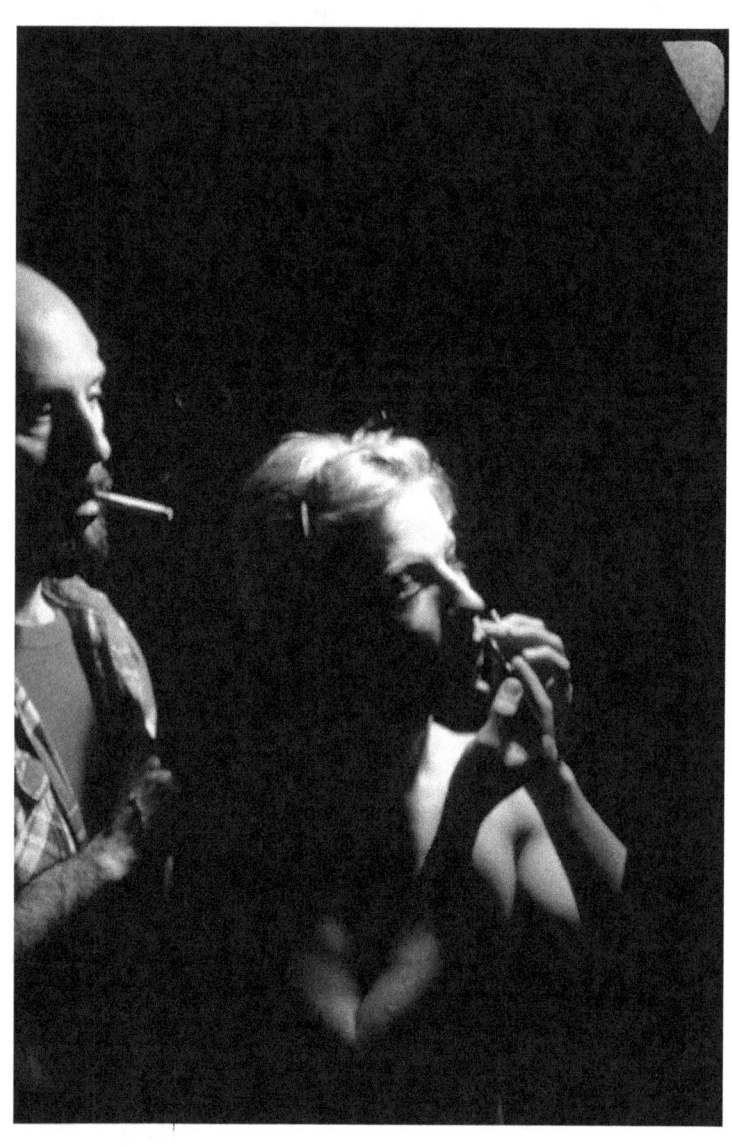

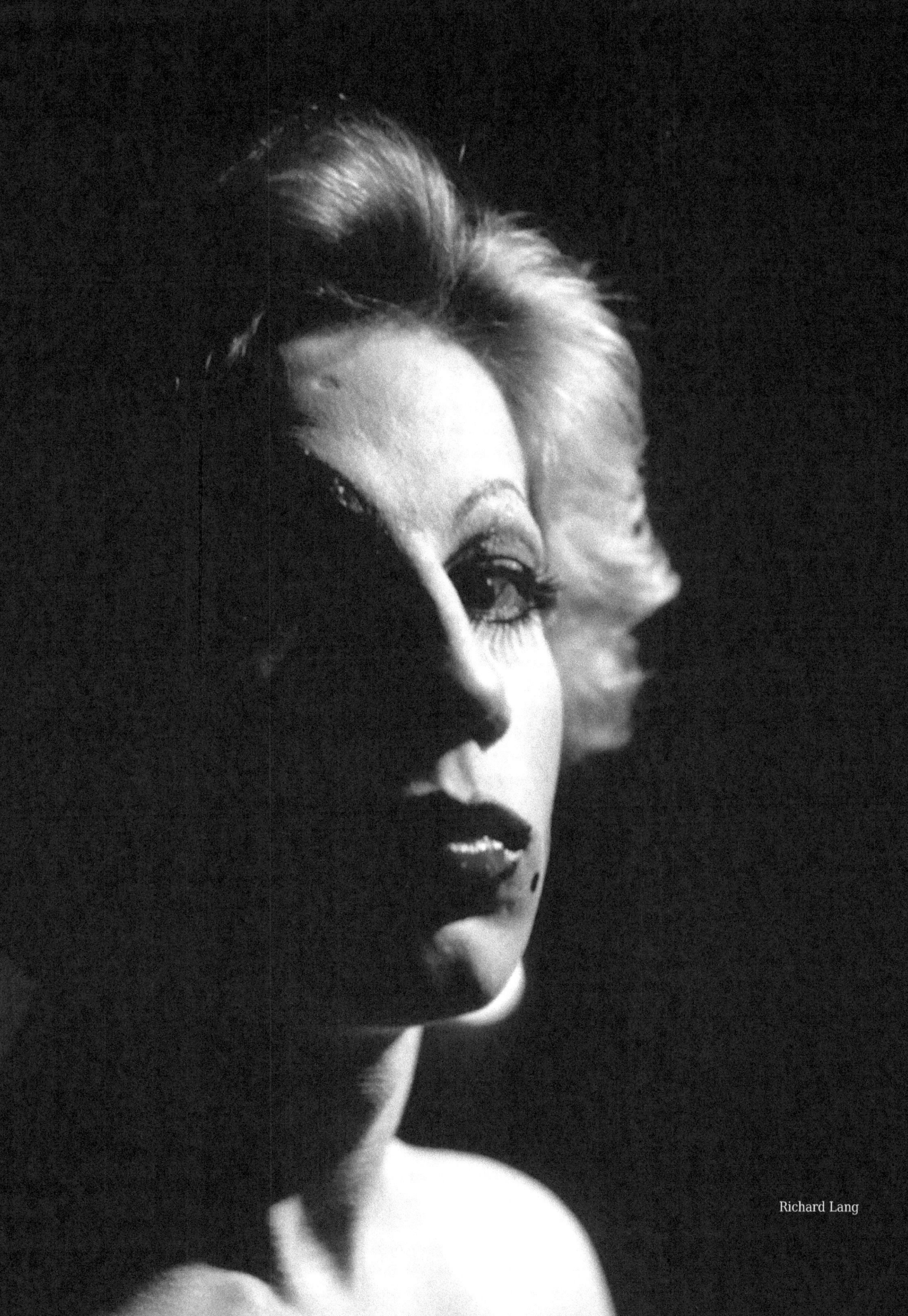

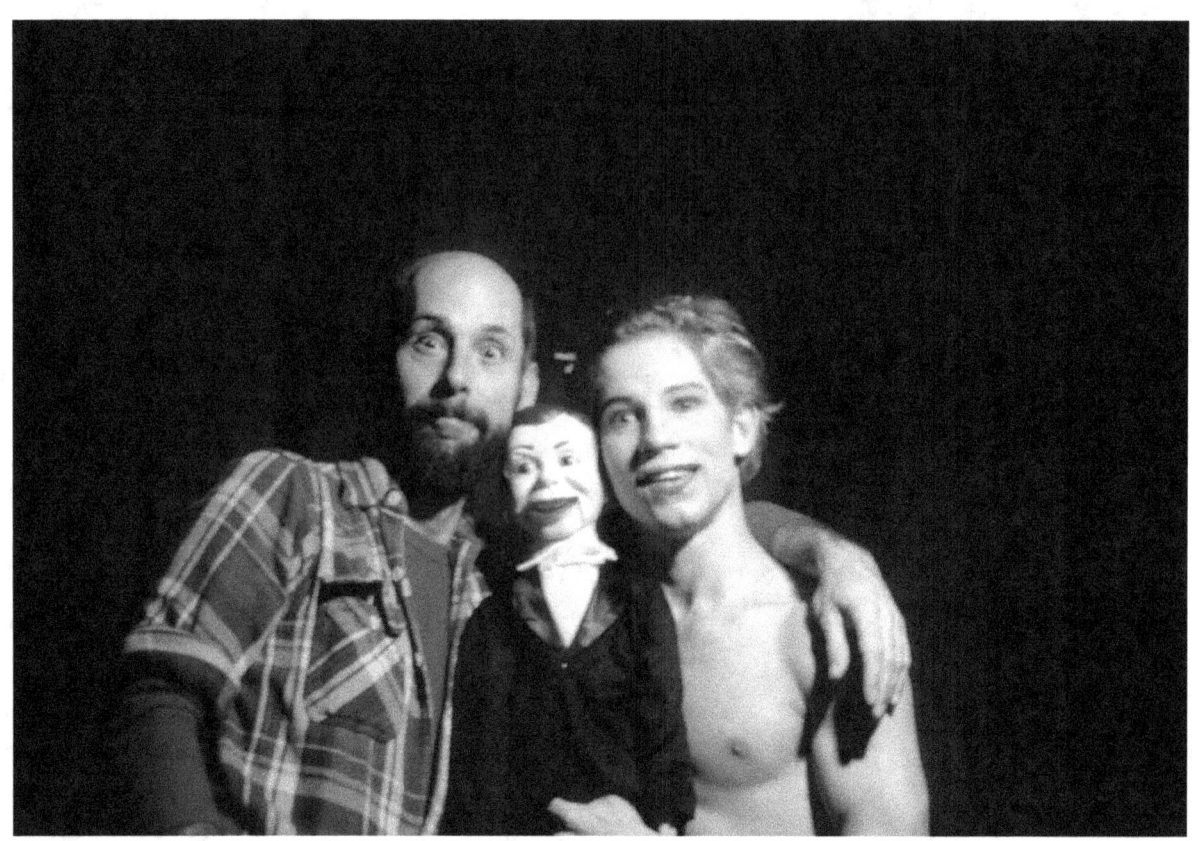

Jack Deveau's last film brings an authentic story with the its real characters to the screen. Life is rough and the sex is steamy, from glitter to the gutter, the Times Square's Gaiety Theater displays the real world of male burlesque. Cock and ball dance numbers are introduced by the costumed M.C; shots of butch men and drag queens intertwine with sex scenes. Like the Adonis Theater and the infamous Mineshaft, the world of Times Square is gone forever.

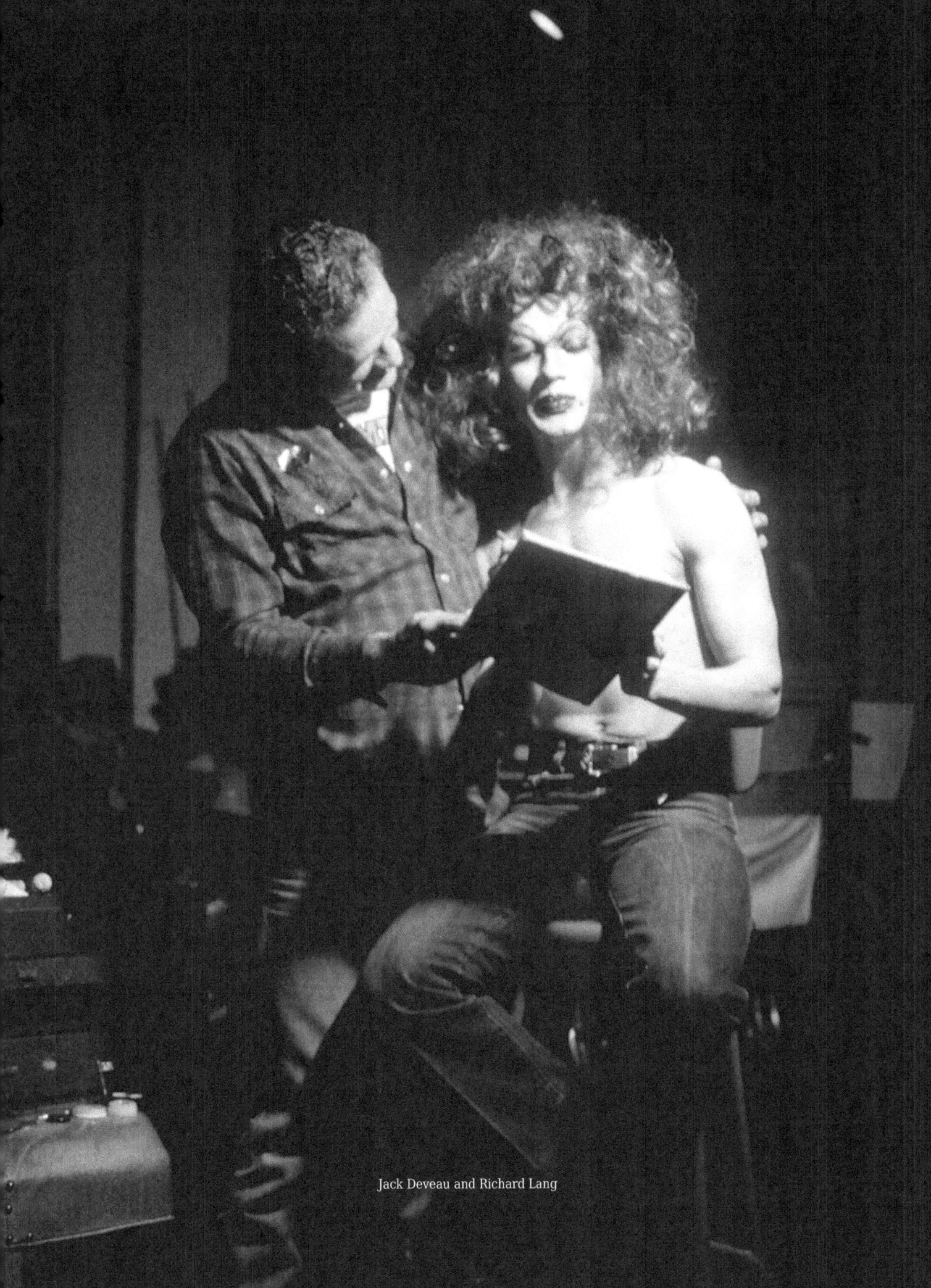

Jack Deveau and Richard Lang

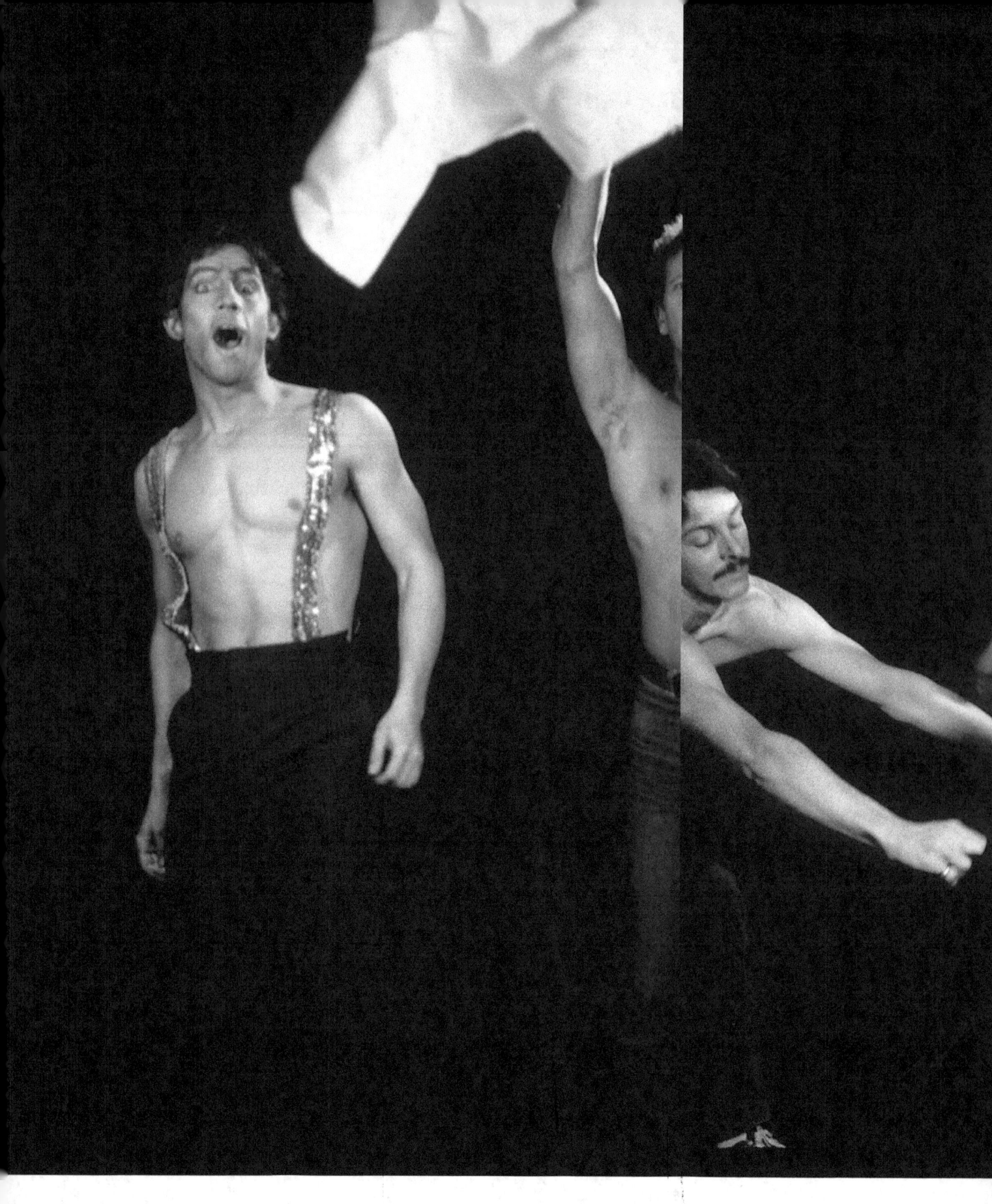

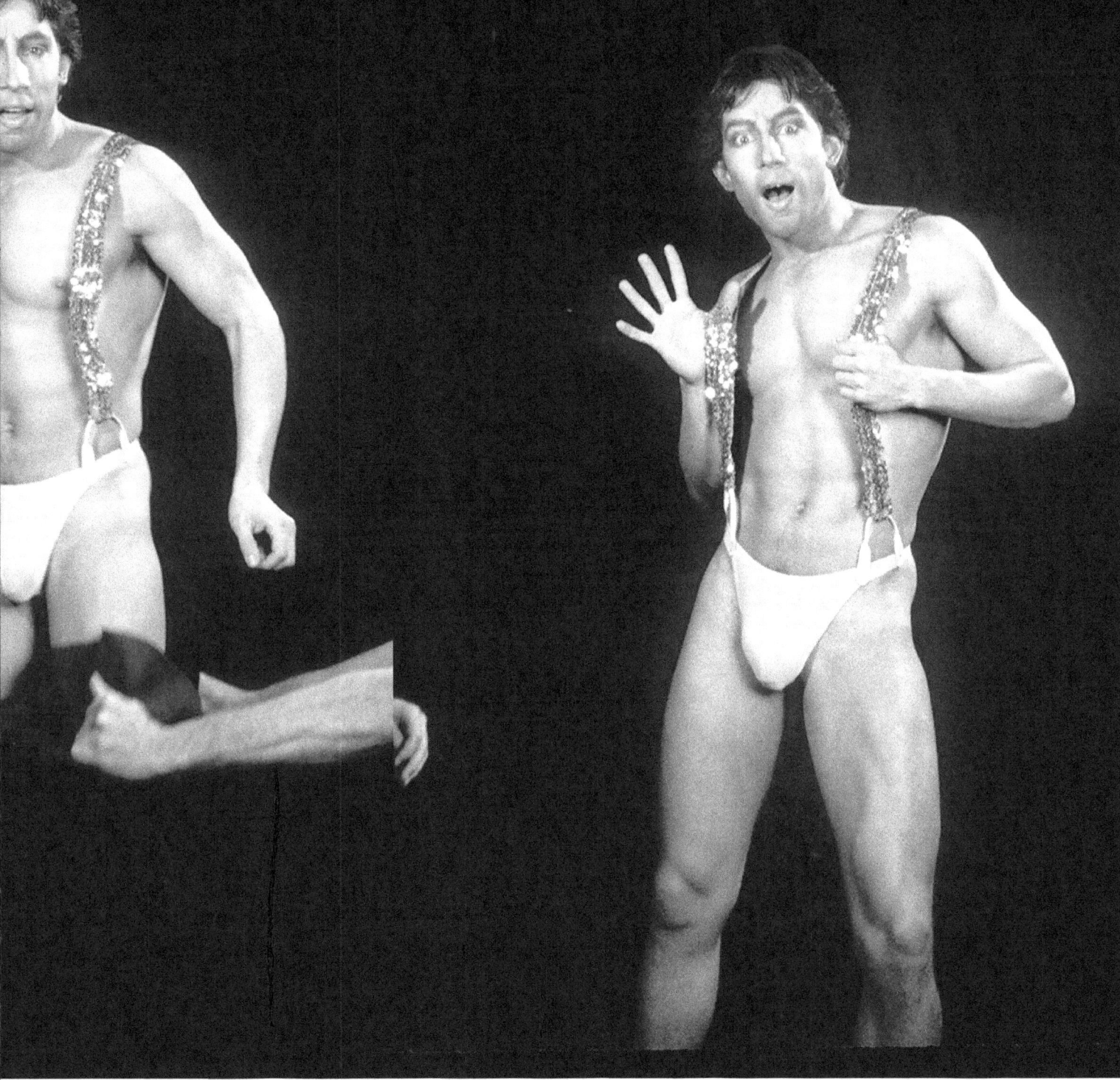

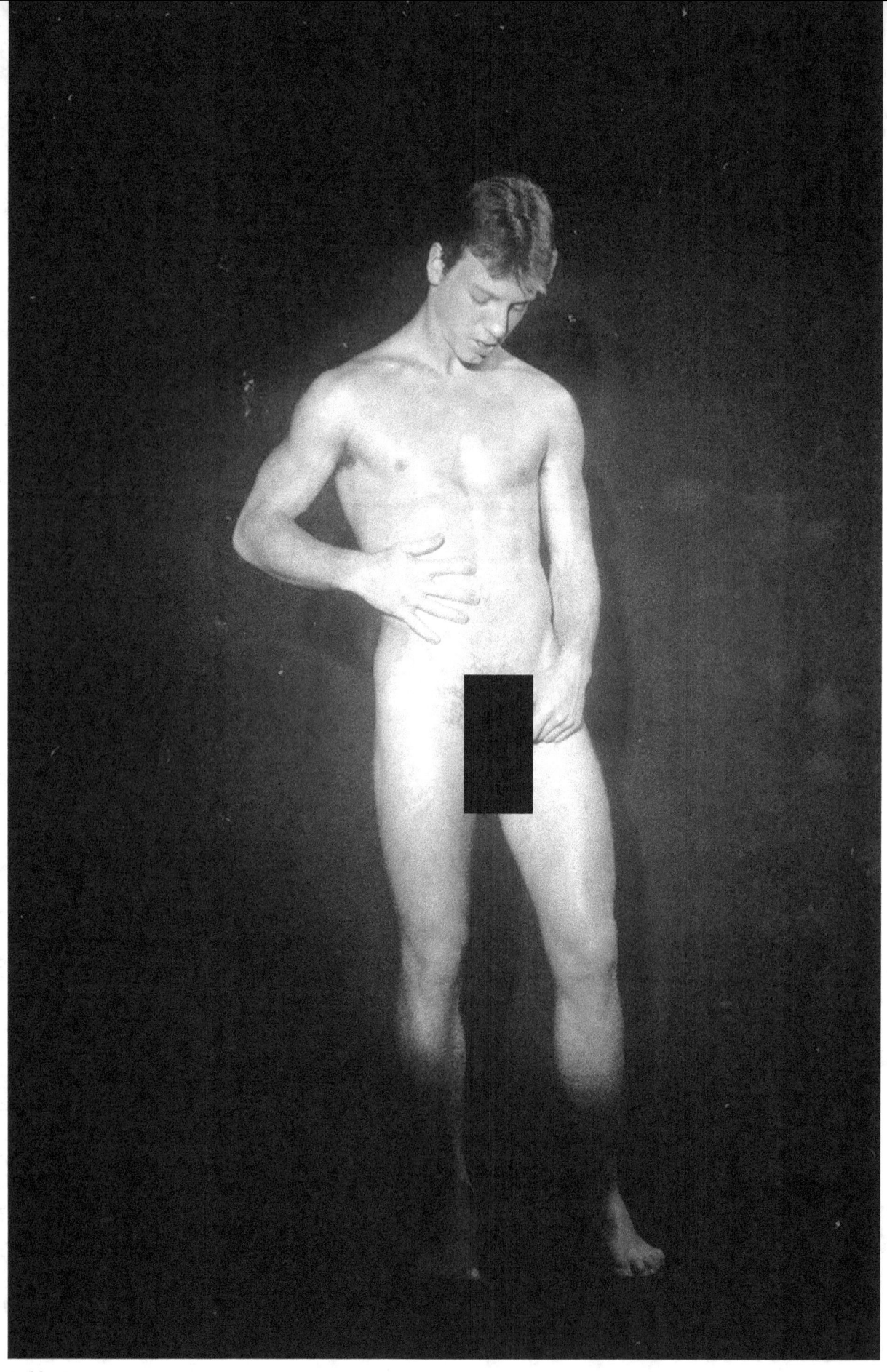

Buddy Preston

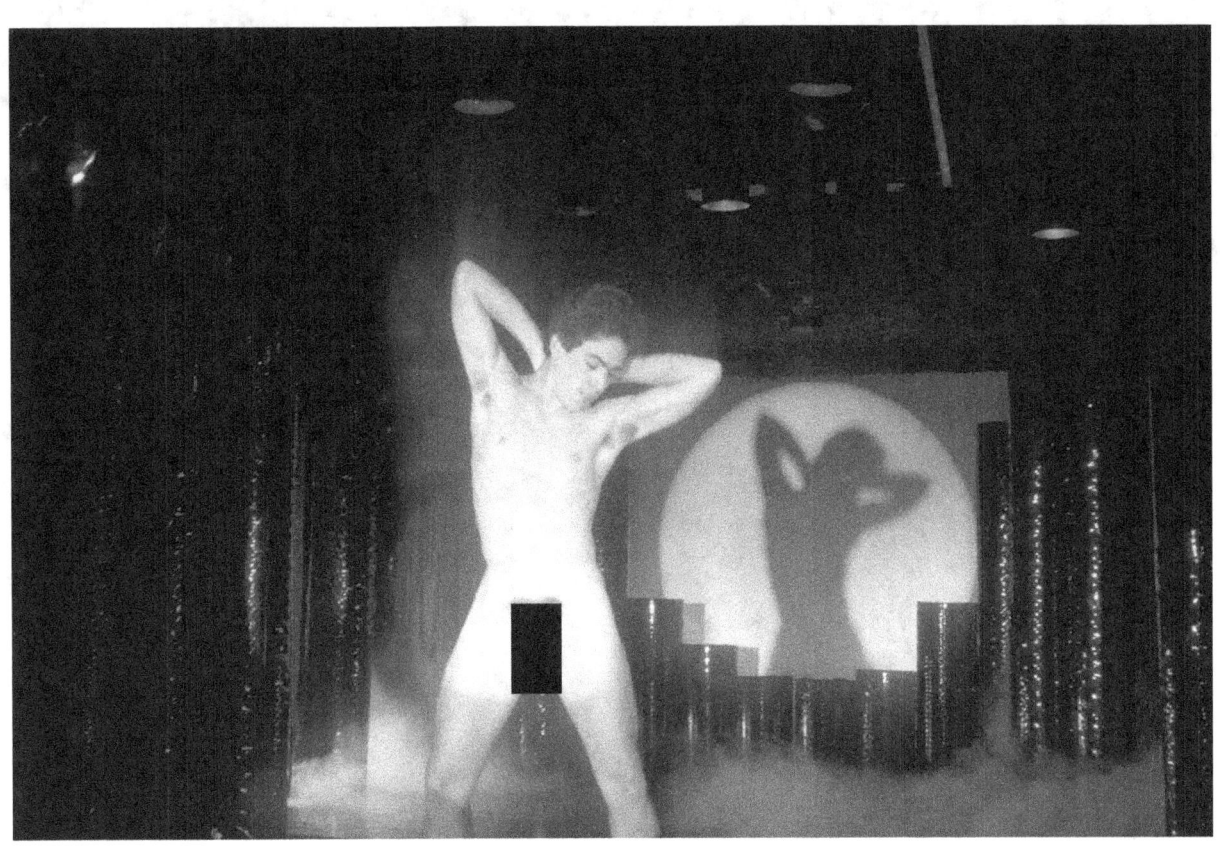

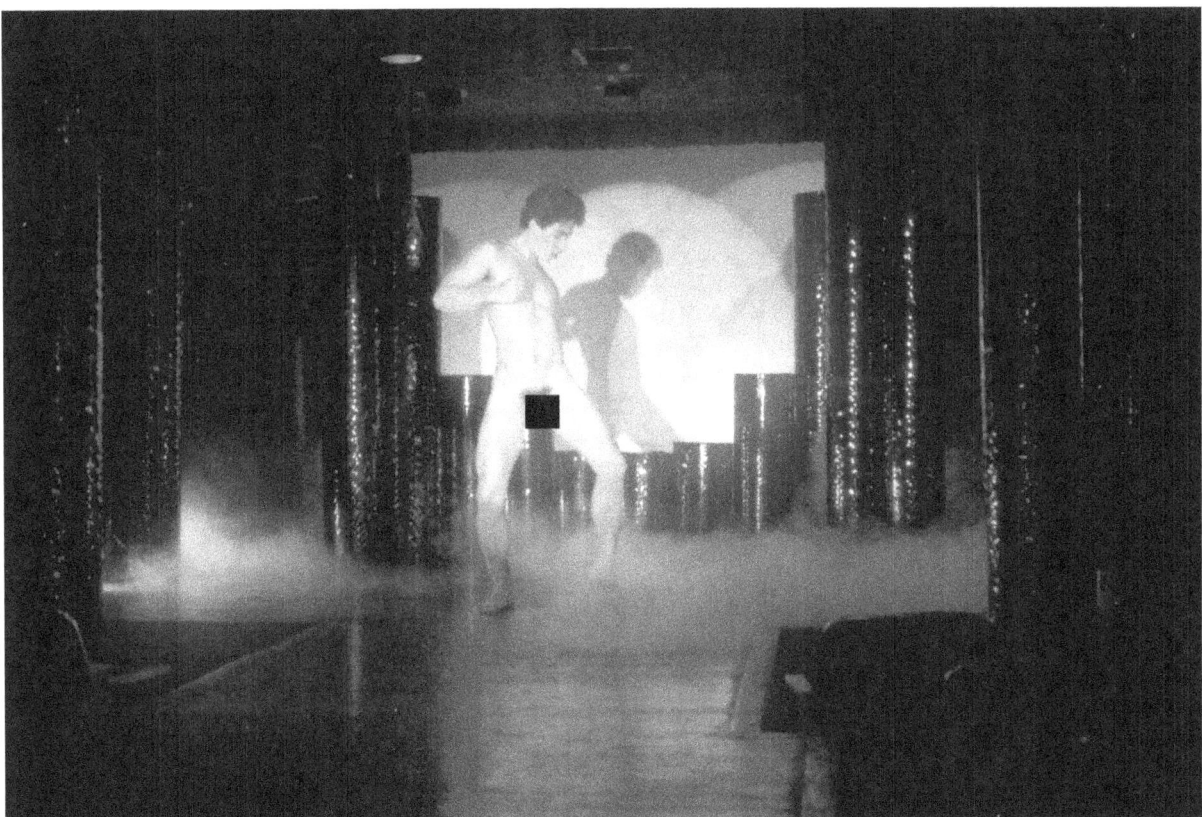

Peter Lopez

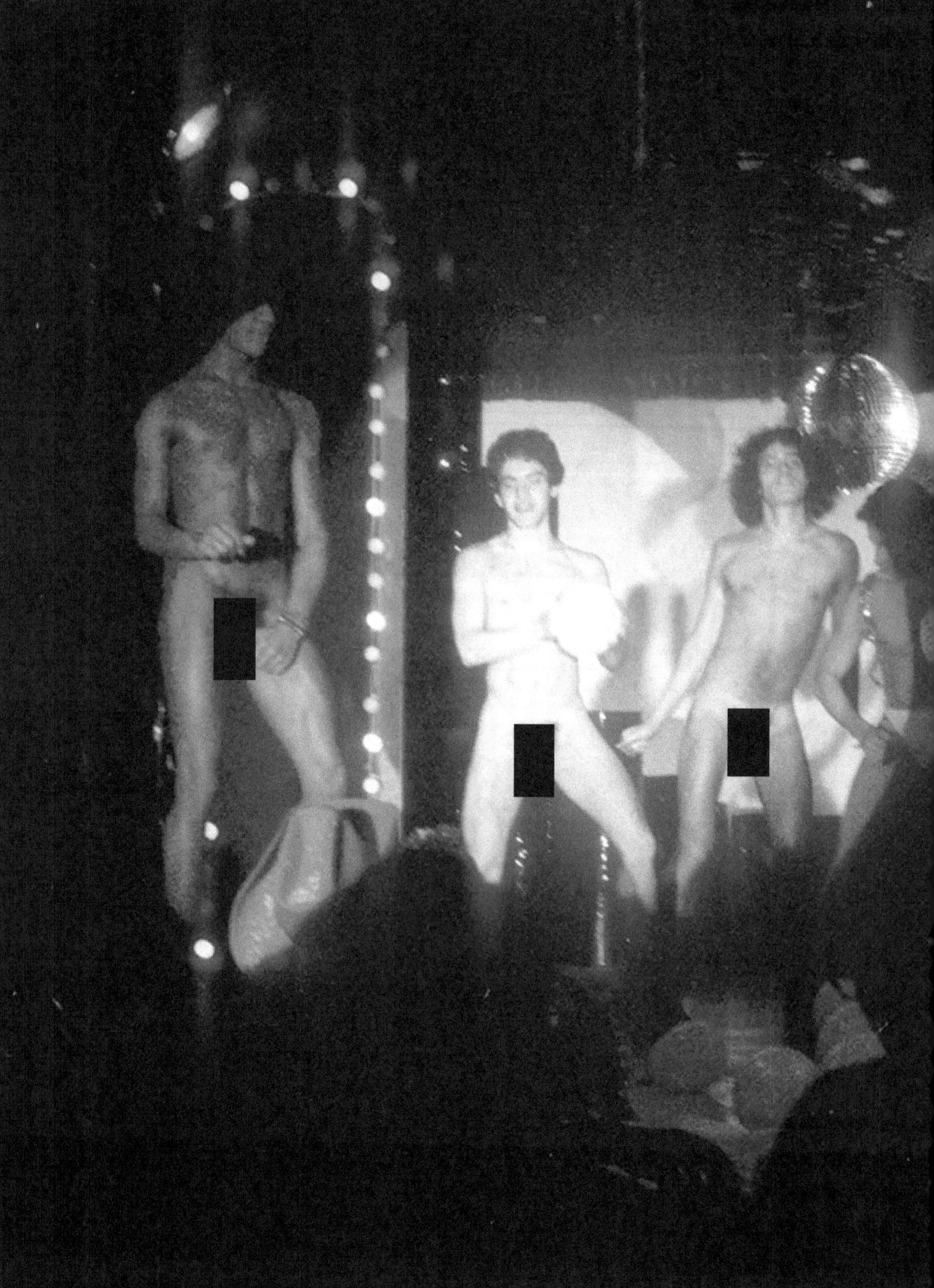

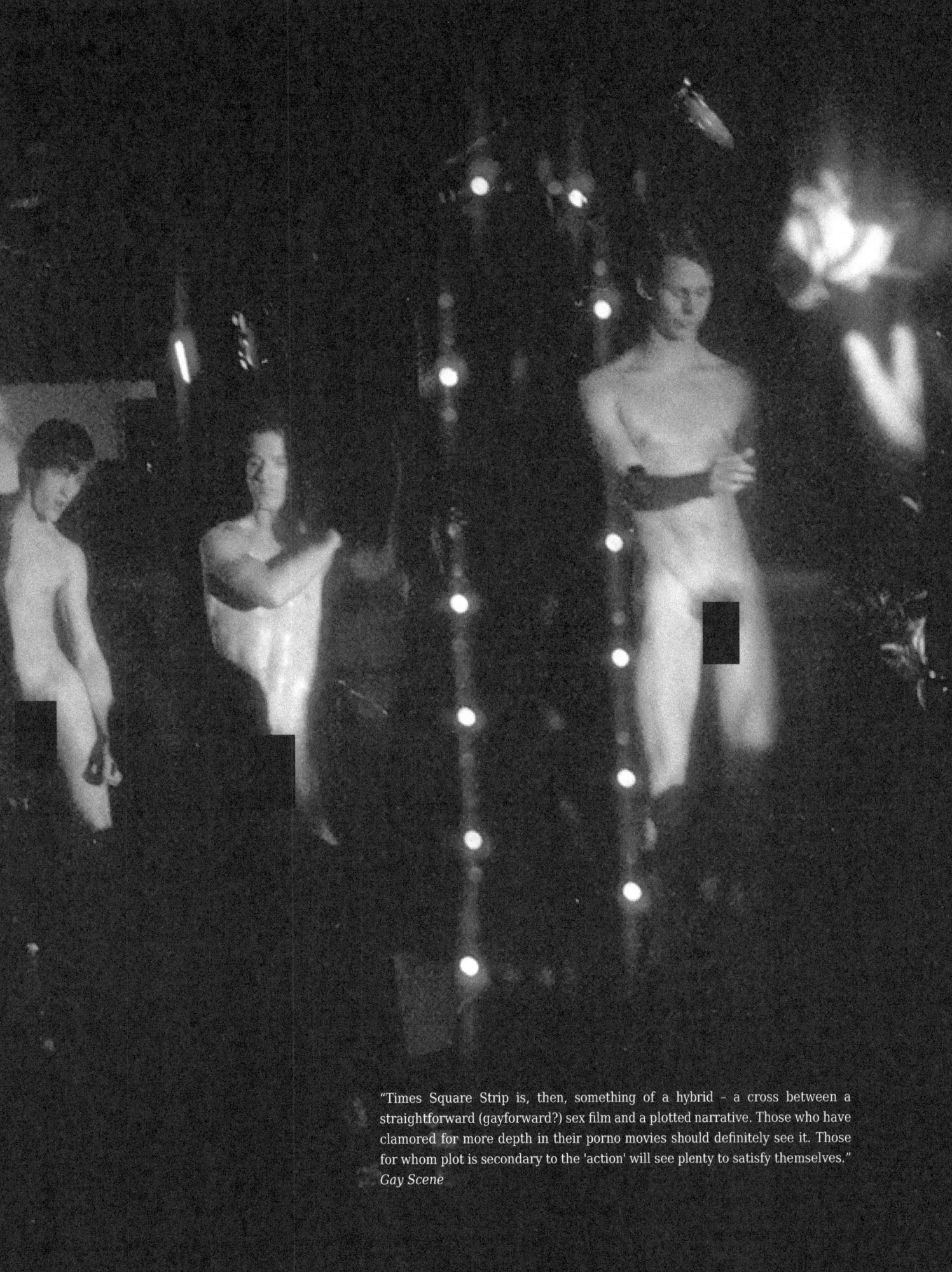

"Times Square Strip is, then, something of a hybrid – a cross between a straightforward (gayforward?) sex film and a plotted narrative. Those who have clamored for more depth in their porno movies should definitely see it. Those for whom plot is secondary to the 'action' will see plenty to satisfy themselves."
Gay Scene

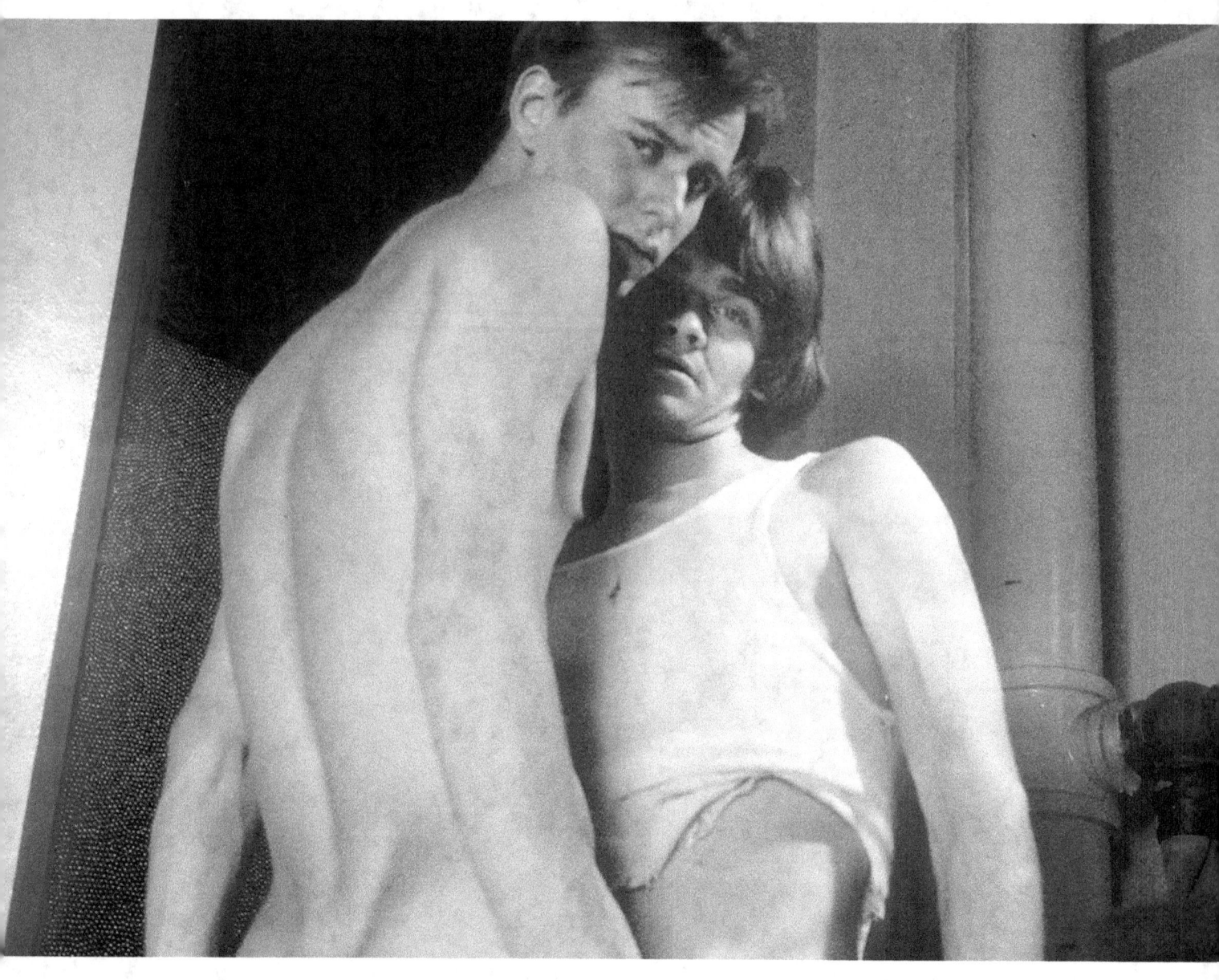

Luke and David Dion

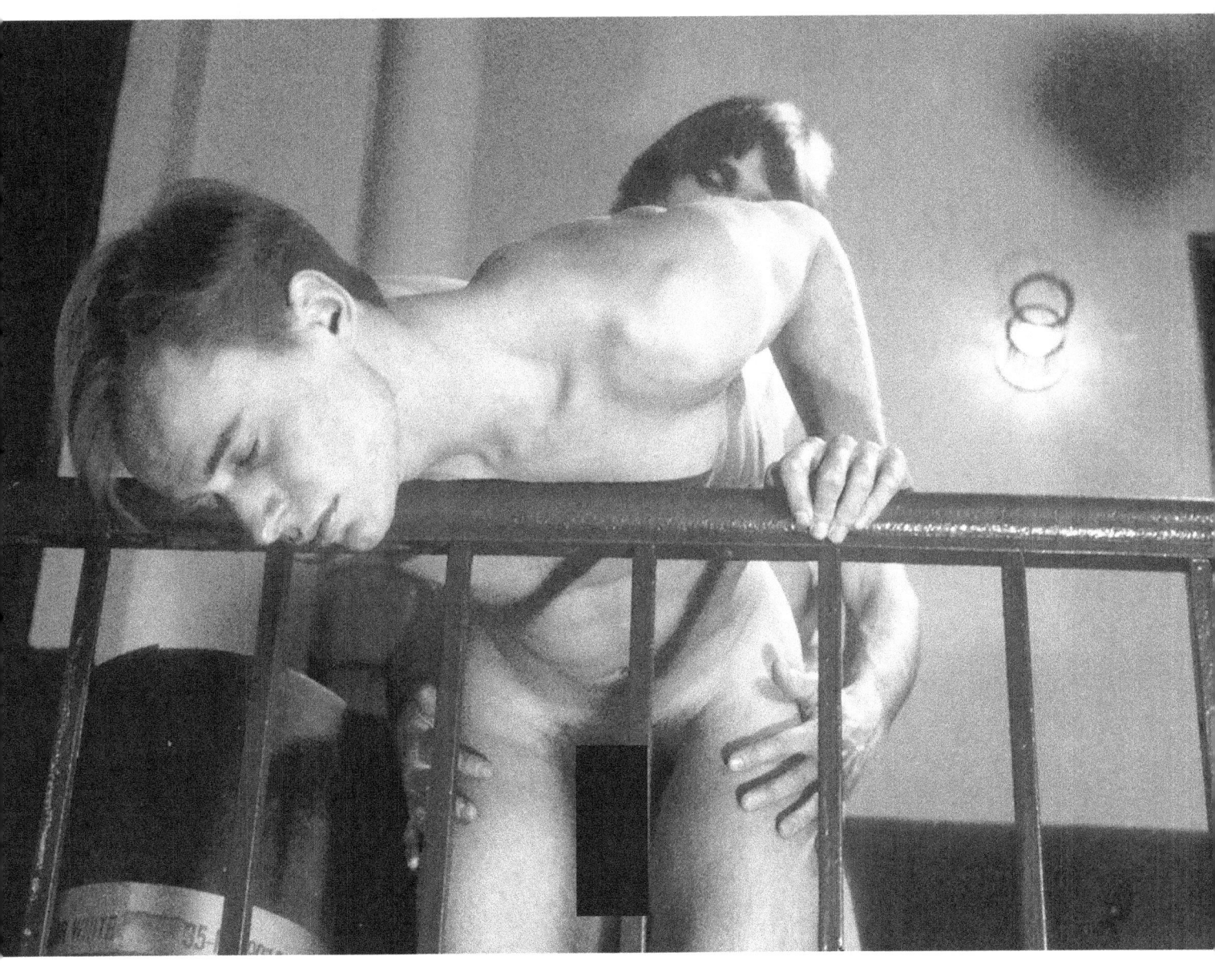

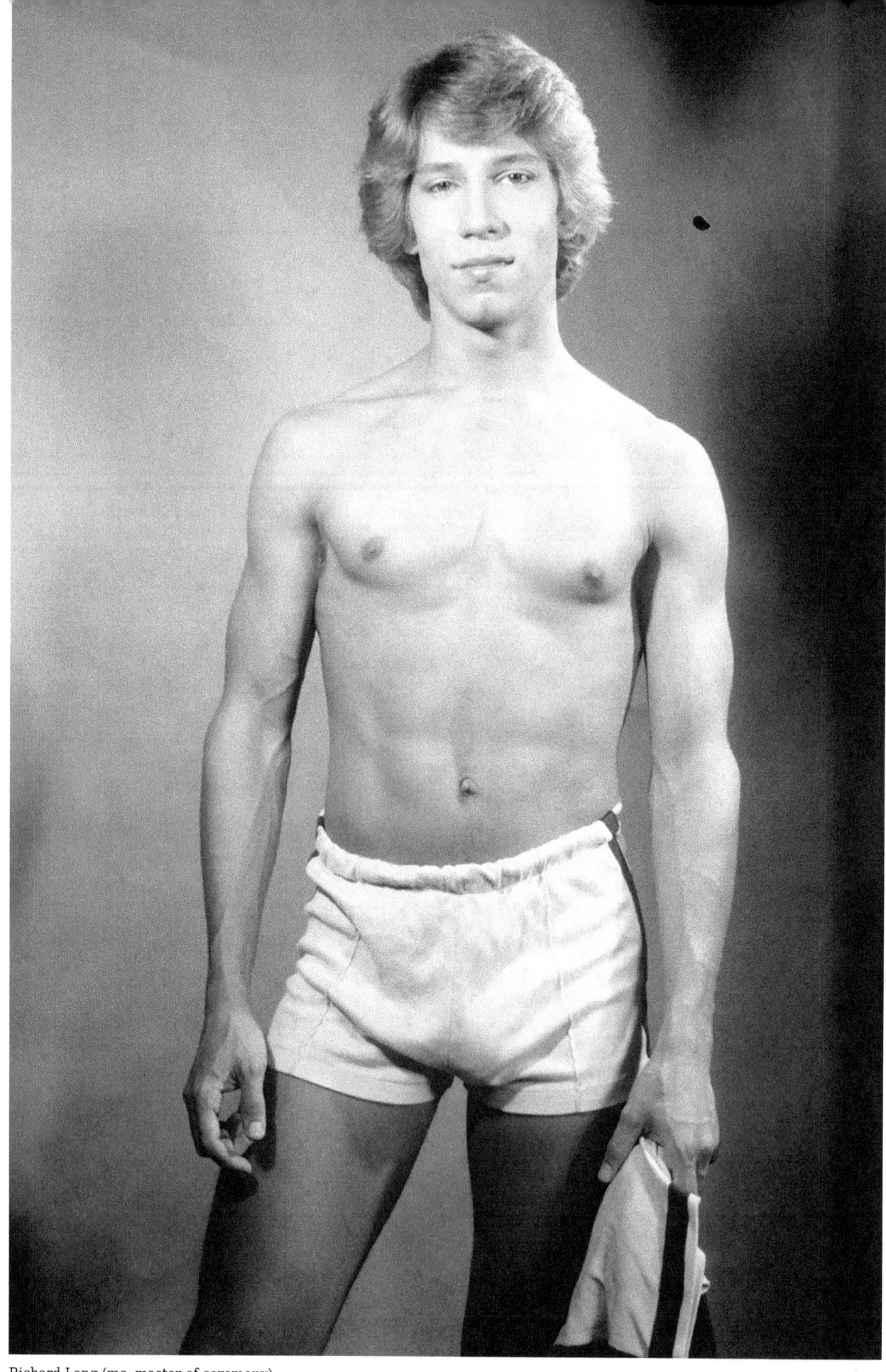

Richard Lang (mc, master of ceremony)

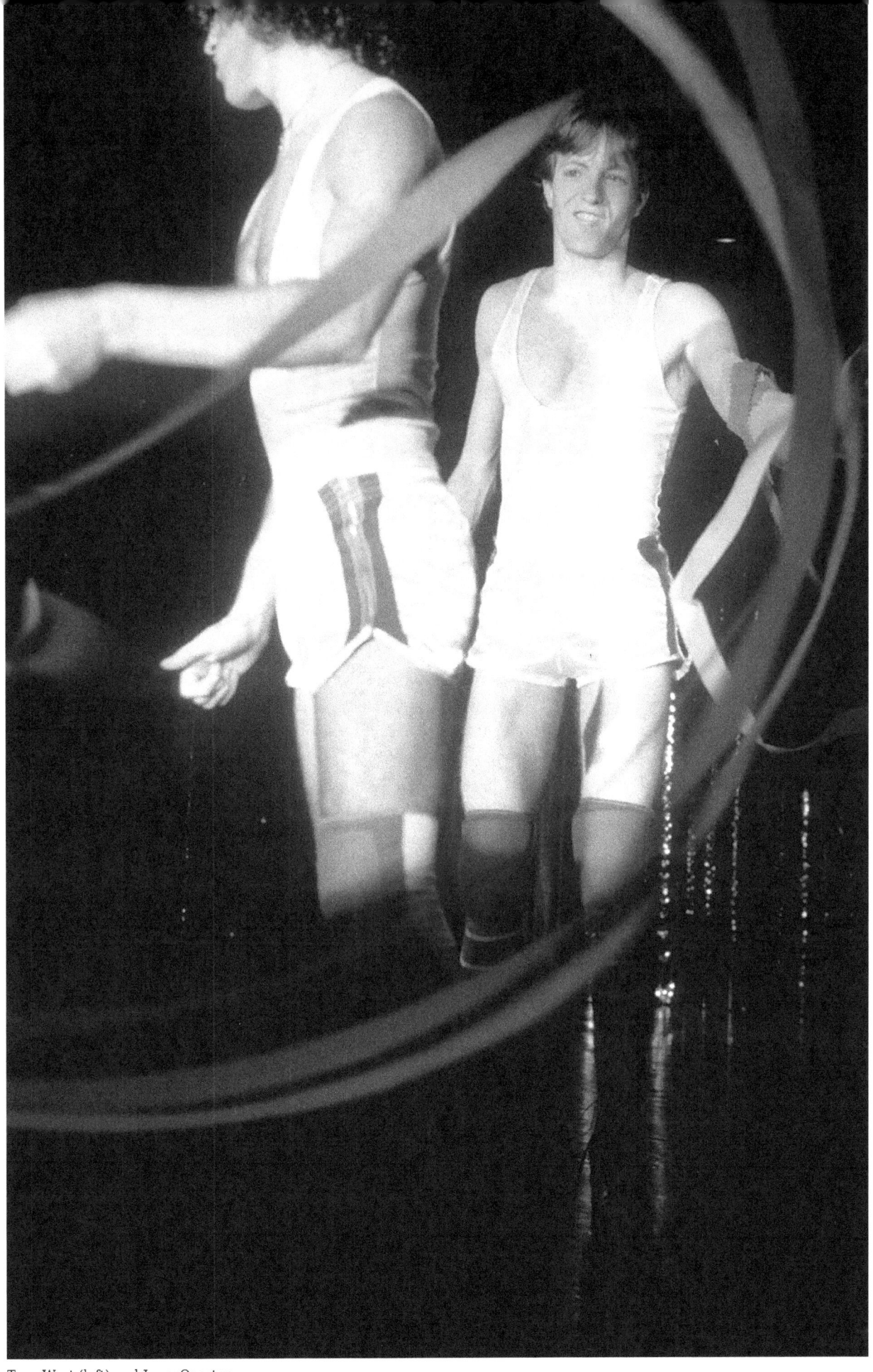

Tony West (left) and Jerry Overton

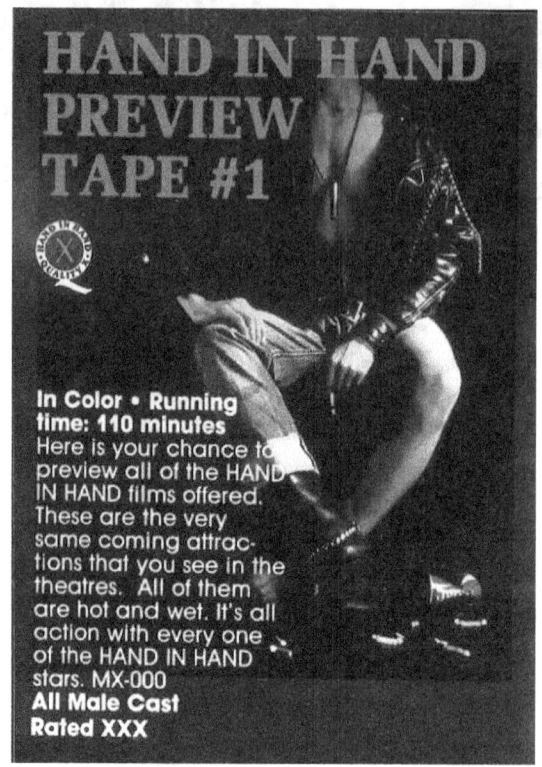

It's nearly two solid hours of rigid cock and solid sex that Hand In Hand Films has become so famous for. You'll get to savor select scenes from all the Hand In Hand greats. Not only will you get to enjoy the choicest cuts, you'll be able to get an idea of what each video is like before you buy. The list of titles is seemingly endless, and includes some of the hottest features available on video. CENTURIANS OF ROME, BOYS FROM RIVERSIDE DRIVE, ROUGH TRADES, HOT HOUSE, THE IDOL, PRIVATE COLLECTION, SEX MAGIC, TIMES SQUARE STRIP, A NIGHT AT THE ADONIS, JUST BLONDS, DESTROYING ANGEL, BALLET DOWN THE HIGHWAY, STATION TO STATION, and DRIVE are just some of the selections you'll see. There is no plot; in fact, the material is a combination of advertisement-type selections. But what's there is *hot* and there is a *lot* of it. You'll certainly be satisfied with this slice of video if only for the price. $39.95 gets you two hours of the best from Hand In Hand Films – and if you pay any more than that, you are paying too much. But don't be weary; it will be a well-invested forty dollars. There is not another video available at that price with so many priceless bodies and scorching sex scenes.

*John Mensior, *Torso*

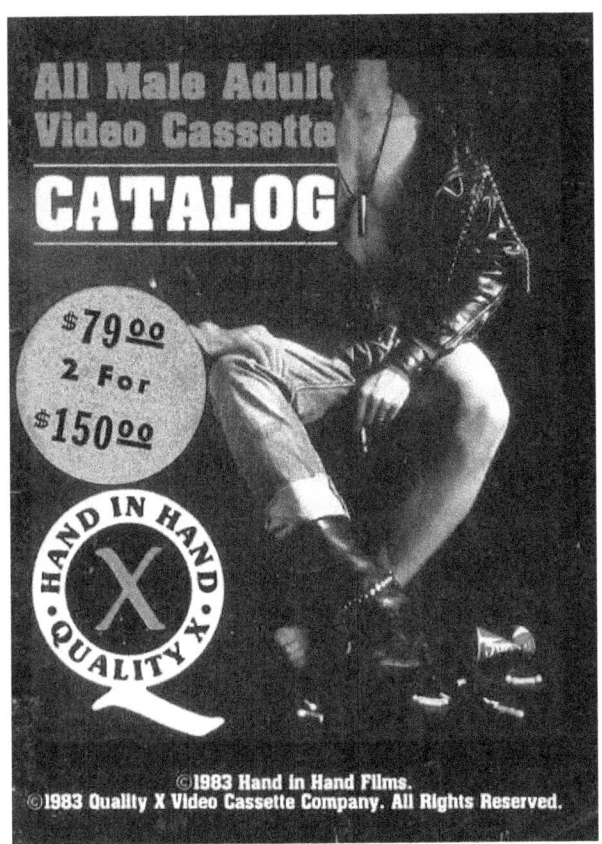
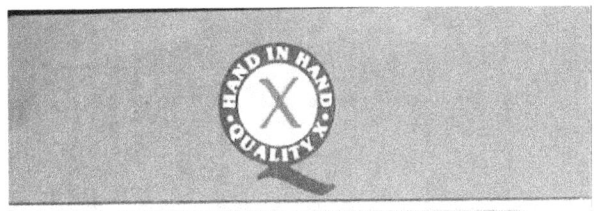
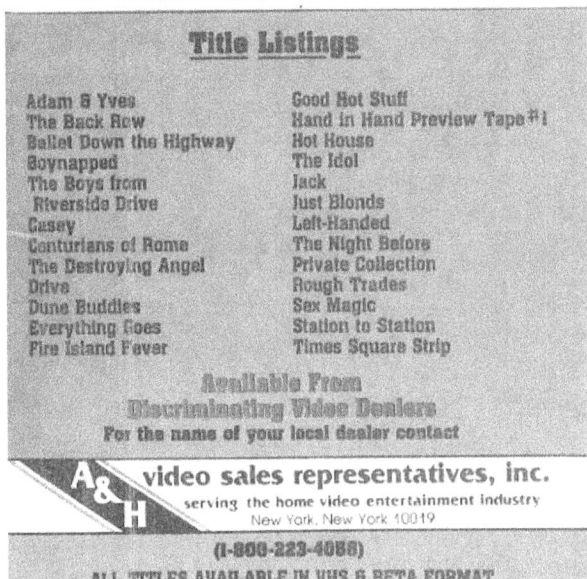

QxQxQxQxQxQxQxQxQxQxQxQxQ xQxQxQxQxQxQxQxQxQxQxQxQxQxQxQxQx

In addition to the foregoing, Quality X Video Cassette Company is pleased to announce that HAND IN HAND Films has granted us the exclusive video cassette distribution of their full-length motion picture titles, described on the following pages.

These feature-length films have never before been released to the video cassette market, and in some instances have not yet been released to theatres in the U.S.

Each casssette is manufactured from the original producer's negative and, as such, we warrant and guarantee the quality of each cassette.

QxQxQxQxQxQxQxQxQxQxQxQxQ xQxQxQxQxQxQxQxQxQxQxQxQxQxQxQxQx

ORDER FORM
HAND IN HAND FILMS
P.O. Box 933 New York NY 10023 212-799-7873

ALL FILMS IN FULL COLOR

No.	Title	VHS	BETA
26.	A NIGHT AT THE ADONIS		
01.	ADAM AND YVES		
02.	THE BACK ROW		
03.	BALLET DOWN THE HIGHWAY		
04.	BOYNAPPED		
05.	BOYS FROM RIVERSIDE DRIVE		
06.	CASEY		
27.	CATCHING UP		
07.	CENTURIANS OF ROME		
08.	THE DESTROYING ANGEL		
09.	DRIVE		
24.	DUNE BUDDIES		
10.	EVERYTHING GOES		
11.	FIRE ISLAND FEVER		
12.	GOOD HOT STUFF		
13.	HOT HOUSE		
14.	THE IDOL		
30.	IN HEAT		
15.	JACK		
16.	JUST BLONDS		
17.	LEFT HANDED		
18.	THE NIGHT BEFORE		
19.	PRIVATE COLLECTION		
20.	ROUGH TRADES		
21.	SEX MAGIC		
22.	STATION TO STATION		
28.	STRICTLY FORBIDDEN		
23.	TIMES SQUARE STRIP		
29.	WANTED: BILLY THE KID		
00.	HAND IN HAND PREVIEW TAPE		

TOTAL TAPES _____
NY Sales Tax _____
Shipping $3.00 per tape _____
GRAND TOTAL _____

Name _____
Address _____
City _____ Apt. _____
State _____ Zip _____

All Tapes: ~~$69.00~~

49.95 ~~$59.00~~

SUPER SPECIAL!
110 Minutes
PREVIEW TAPE
$39.00

Payment:
☐ Check   ☐ Money Order   ☐ MC/Visa

Account Name _____
Account No. _____
Expiration Date _____
Signature _____

NOTE: Signature required to fill order!
I (We) understand that I (We) are acquiring these video programs for home and non-theatrical use only. All other rights, including broadcasting are reserved. Duplication is prohibited. I (We) confirm by my (Our) signature(s) that I (We) am of legal age.

Authorized
Signature _____ Date _____

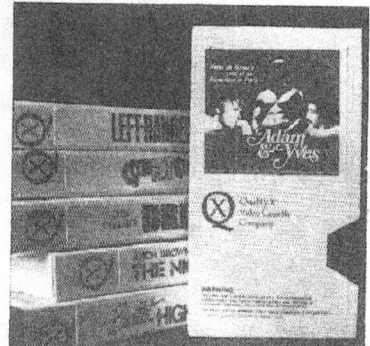

— Order Form —

HAND IN HAND VIDEO

A DIVISION OF
Quality X Video Cassette Company
356 WEST 44TH STREET
NEW YORK, NEW YORK 10036
(212) 541-7860 Outside N.Y. (800) 223-7981

Name ....
Address .... Apt. # ....
City .... State .... Zip ....

Payment: ___ Check   ___ Money Order

Please send: (Check video format required)

Title	2/H Beta $99.50	1/H Beta $99.50	2/H VHS $99.50	3/4"UM $150.00	Price
LEFT-HANDED					
GOOD HOT STUFF					
ADAM & YVES					
THE NIGHT BEFORE					
BALLET DOWN THE HIGHWAY					
DRIVE					

NOTE: SIGNATURE REQUIRED TO FILL ORDER
I/We understand that I/We are acquiring these video programs for home and non-theatrical use only. All other rights including broadcasting are reserved and duplication is prohibited. I confirm by my signature that I am of legal age.

(Signature) _____

Postage: _____
Sales Tax: _____
(New York)
Total Amount: _____

Quality X Video Cassette Company, 1979

Each Quality X Video Cassette Tape is sold seperately, with no obligation towards future purchase.

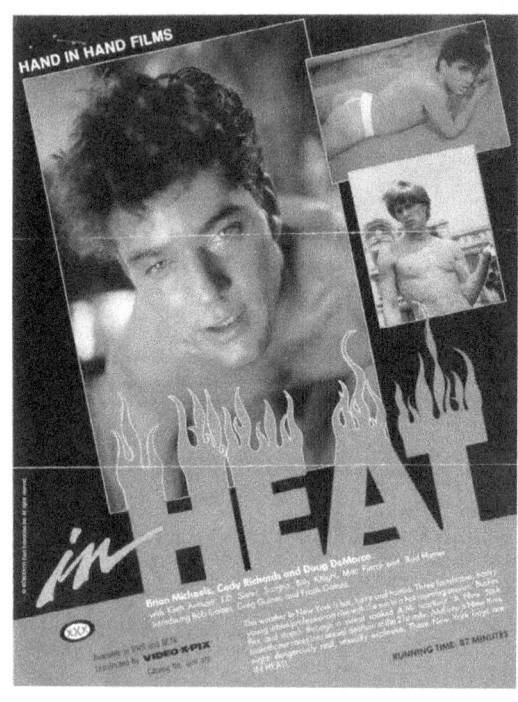

The serious student of gayporn history is going to be delighted with this collection of short films that includes some heretofore unseen pieces by Jack Deveau and Peter De Rome; the general porn fan might find some things to like here as well. A short solo JO sequence by Doug DeMarco with a boa constrictor titled BEFORE TIME opens the package; if snakes frighten you – this act is going to scare the pants off you. A curious tale called 8 AM has a set of three brothers playing peeping tom. A tale set against the New York Marathon has Keith Anthoni lusting after Scorpio. An aerobics class is the setting for a three-way led by J.D. Slater. The final piece is a pseudo SM tableau about a man who finds a leather-clad intruder in his designer apartment. Five very different pieces by three very different directors. Photography is fine, especially for the older pieces, which have been well-transferred to video. Robert Alvarez, who was Deveau's main editor for many years, proves that he is capable of controlling the camera – and the short pieces by him in this anthology just might signal the announcement of a new director in gayporn.

*JWR, *Studflix*

One of the qualities that distinguishes IN HEAT, the final release from Hand In Hand Films, is that each of its segments views the sexual experience from an oblique, often unique, angle. The result is a first-class compendium, filled with fresh and different visions that in no way ignore the traditions of the genre. Included in it are two unreleased, at the time) works created by Jack Deveau prior to his death in 1982, a vintage contribution by Peter De Rome, and two pieces made especially for the film by Bob Alvarez, the editor of Deveau's films, in this, his most impressive directorial debut. Within seconds of the initial fade-in, the viewer knows he is in for something different: under the main titles, a dark-haired hedonist (Doug DeMarco) brings himself off while playing with his pet boa constrictor. There is an eerie fascination to the proceedings, in which DeMarco fondles the snake and his cock with equal ardor, then allows the pet to slither into his mouth. The music and editing are fluid and haunting, and the climactic image of the reptile as a living cockring around the exploding erection is a primal image not to be soon forgotten. Deveau's other posthumous contribution is a sly little tale of a surprise birthday present. The recipient is a blond hunk (Greg Gaines), and the unsigned gift is a pair of binoculars. He goes immediately to the window to discover another blond hunk (Bob Gaines), who except for his curly hair could be a twin. He, too, has a pair of binoculars. In time, a third clone (Frank Gaines) is added to this rear window ménage. He wears glasses, and also has a pair of binoculars. The cross-cutting of the ensuing exhibitionistic jerkoff is as inventive and playful as it is arousing, and we must assume the joke (or the trick photography) is on us – the Gaines boys are all surely played by the same single actor. NOON, the next one-act, is directed by Alvarez, and stars J.D. Slater and Brian Michaels (a/k/a Bobby Madison). Amid mats and mirrors, an all-male aerobics class takes a fuck break as the limbering up exercises almost imperceptibly turn to foreplay. Michaels, apparently as insatiable as ever, plugs into Billy Knight, then shifts roles to let instructor Slater have him. The scene is ingeniously heightened by an infinity of images in the mirrors. Next up is Peter De Rome's lighthearted fantasy about a marathon runner (Scorpio) and a fan (Keith Anthoni) who fantasizes an encounter with the athlete. Enhanced by actual footage of the New York Marathon, the scene clearly equates the eroticism of jogging with explicit carnality. Fans of Scorpio and Anthoni will be particularly delighted by the footage. The final episode, MIDNIGHT, also directed by Alvarez, stars Cody Richards and Matt Pierce as a lonely apartment dweller and the intruder who breaks in and ravishes him – or is the incident merely a fantasy that never happened at all? Pierce, a gritty street type sporting a sweat band and five o'clock shadow, is one hot man, but the real star is Richards, a willing bottom, who writhing ass and explosive money shots make the sequence special. A grand potpourri, IN HEAT brought to a close an era of high standards and popular format set by Jack Deveau and his pioneering Hand In Hand Films.

*Jerry Douglas, *Manshots*

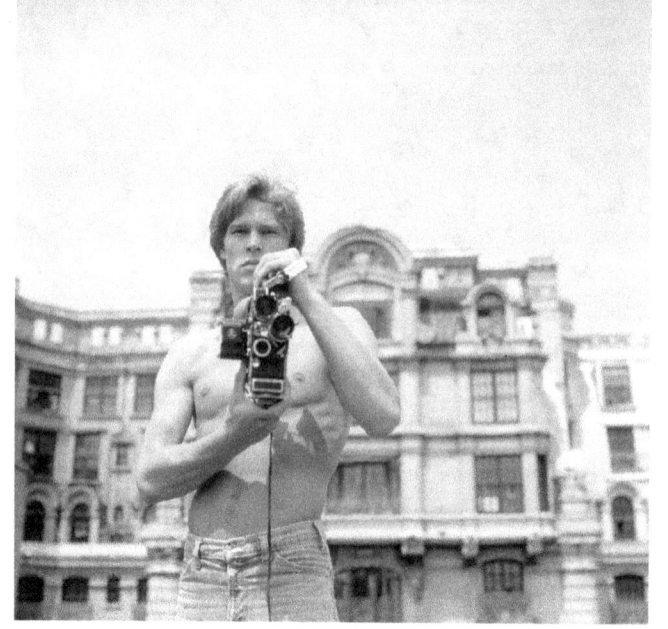

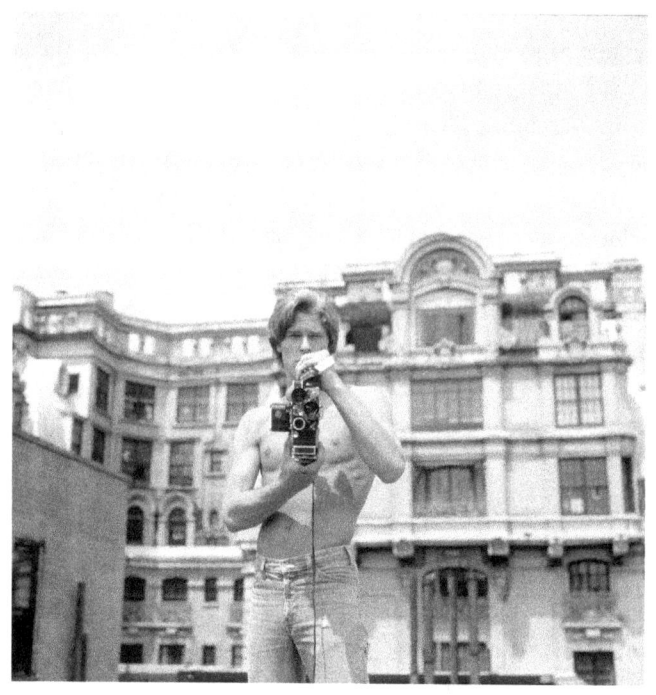

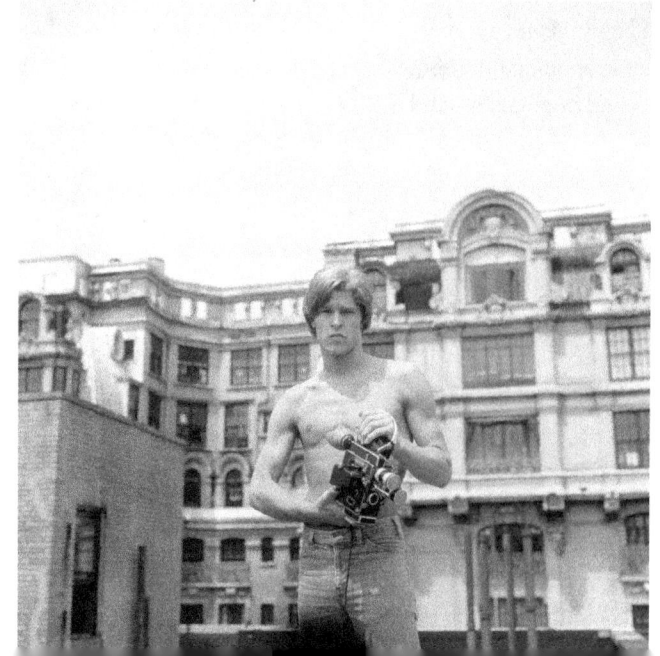

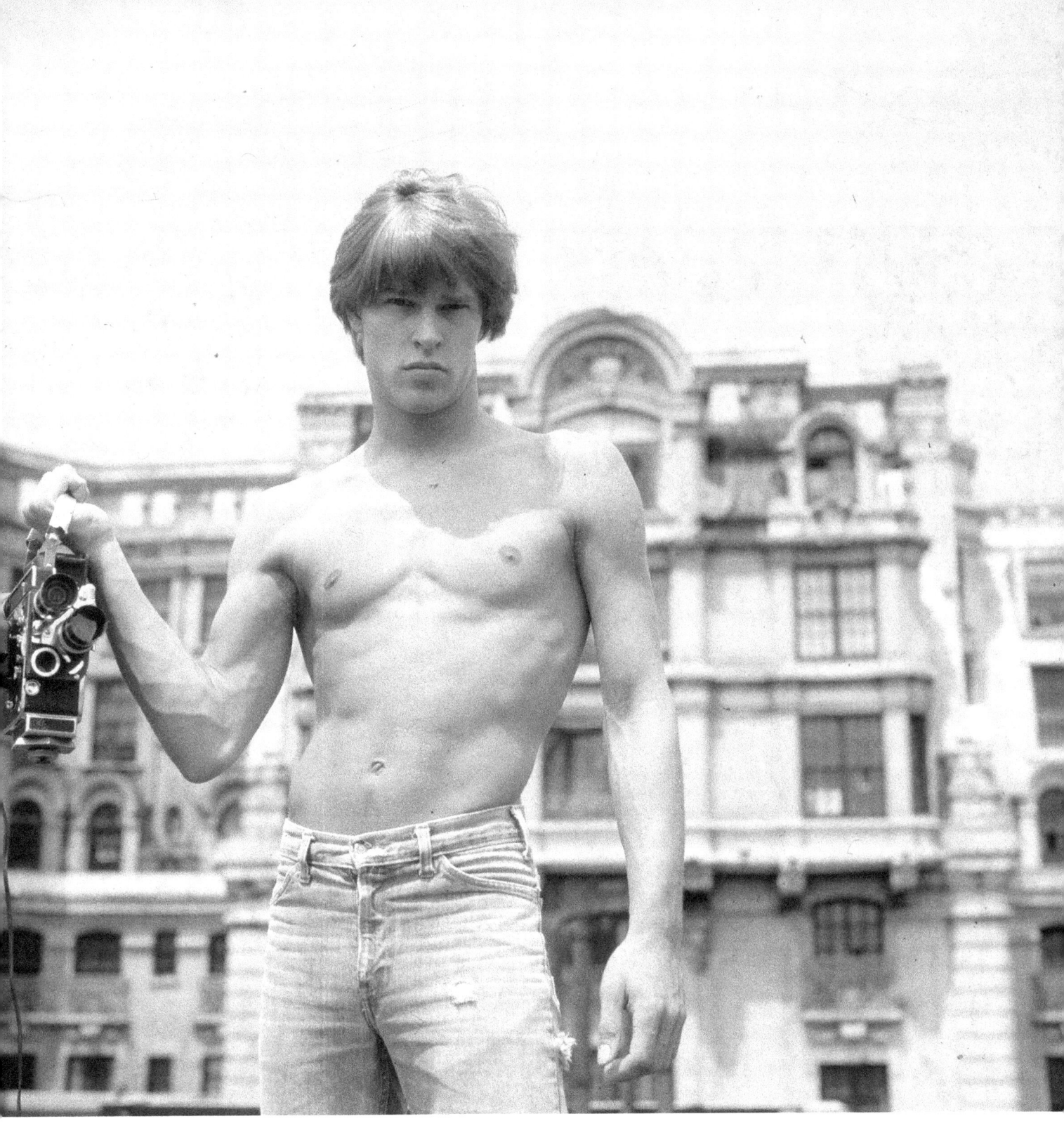

Greg Gaines, *In Heat*

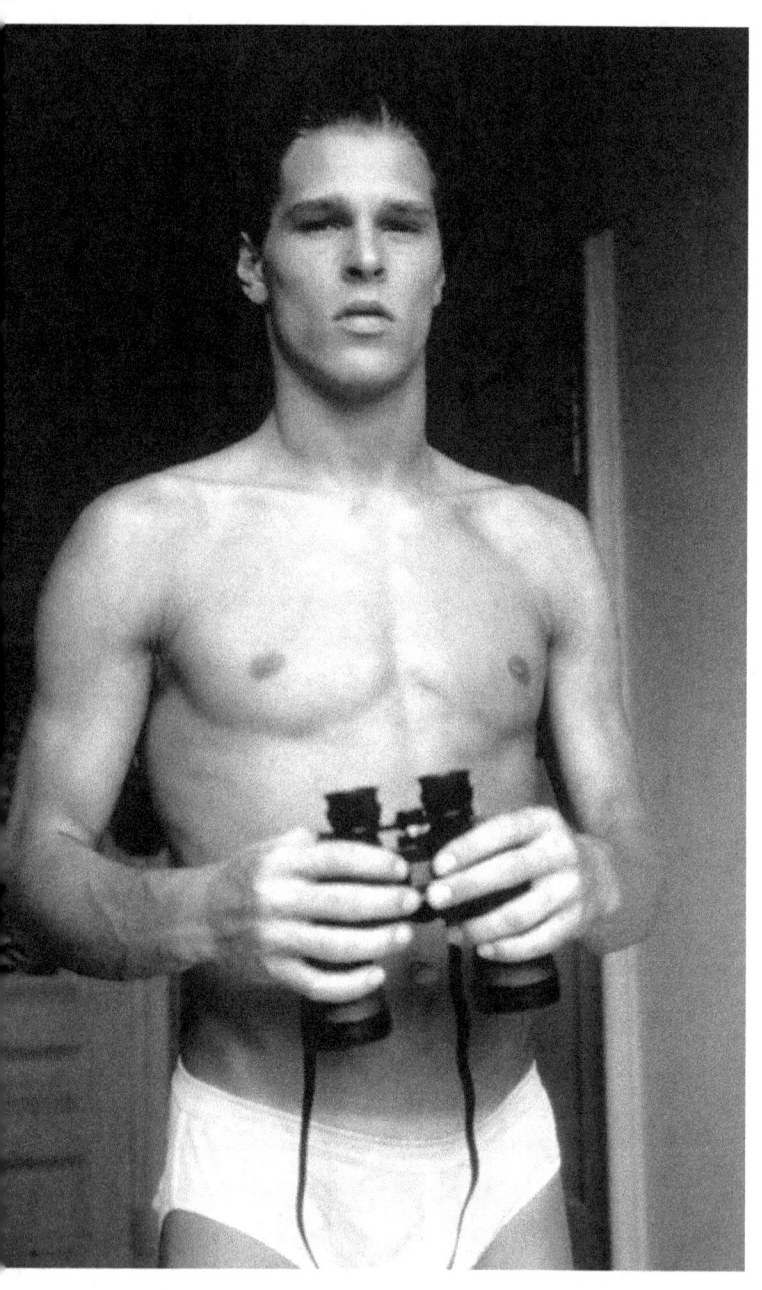 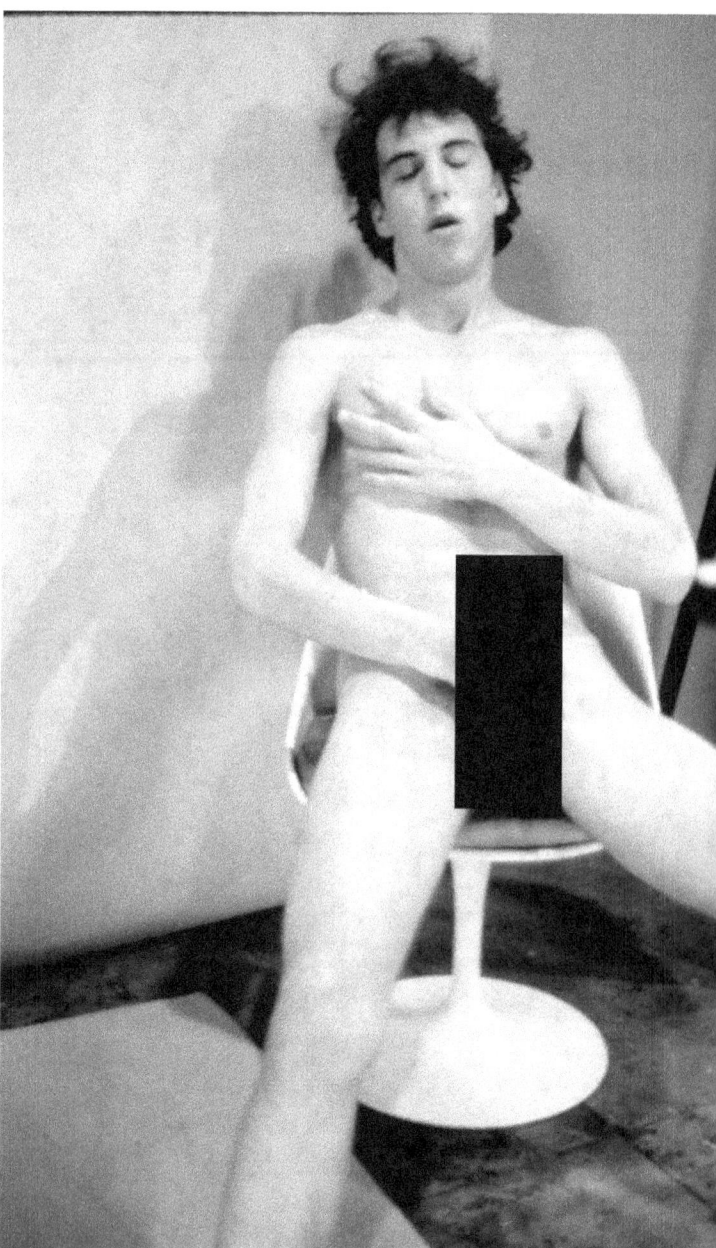

Greg Gaines						Rod Hunter

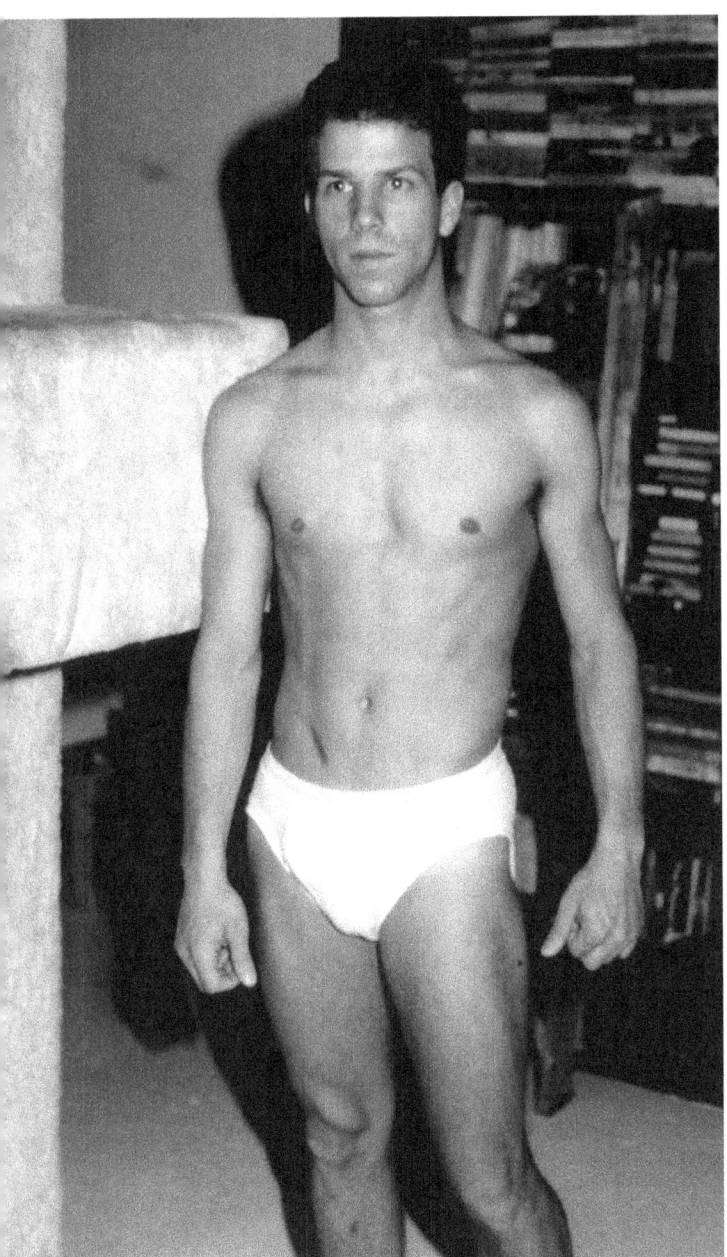

Bobby Medison

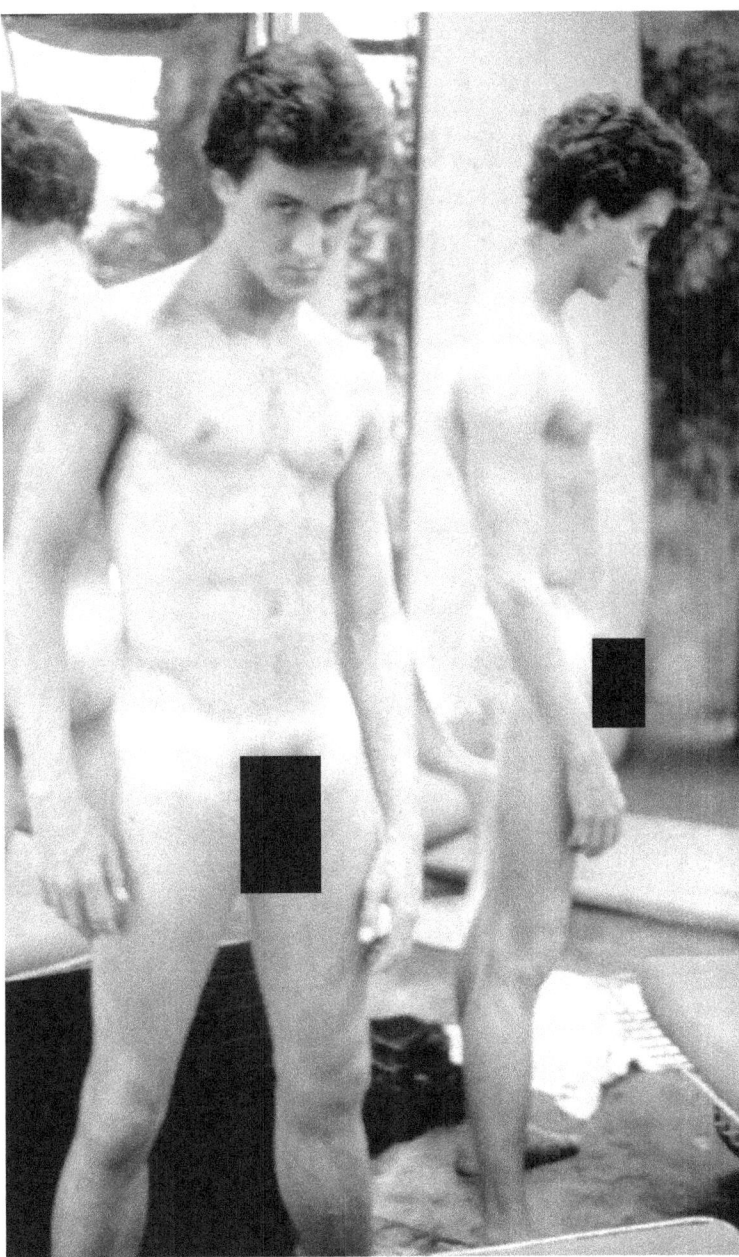

Billy Knight

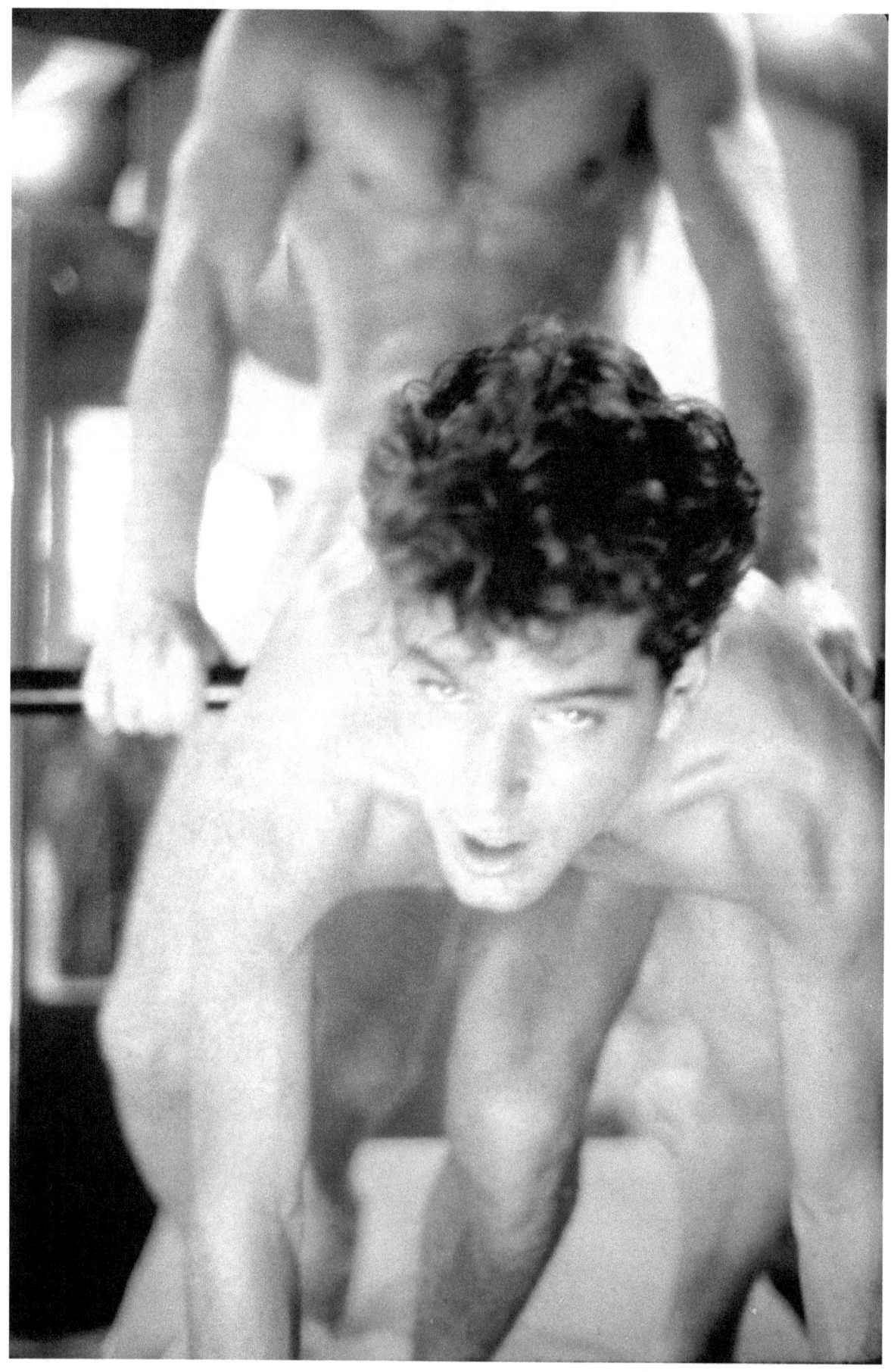

Bob Gaines

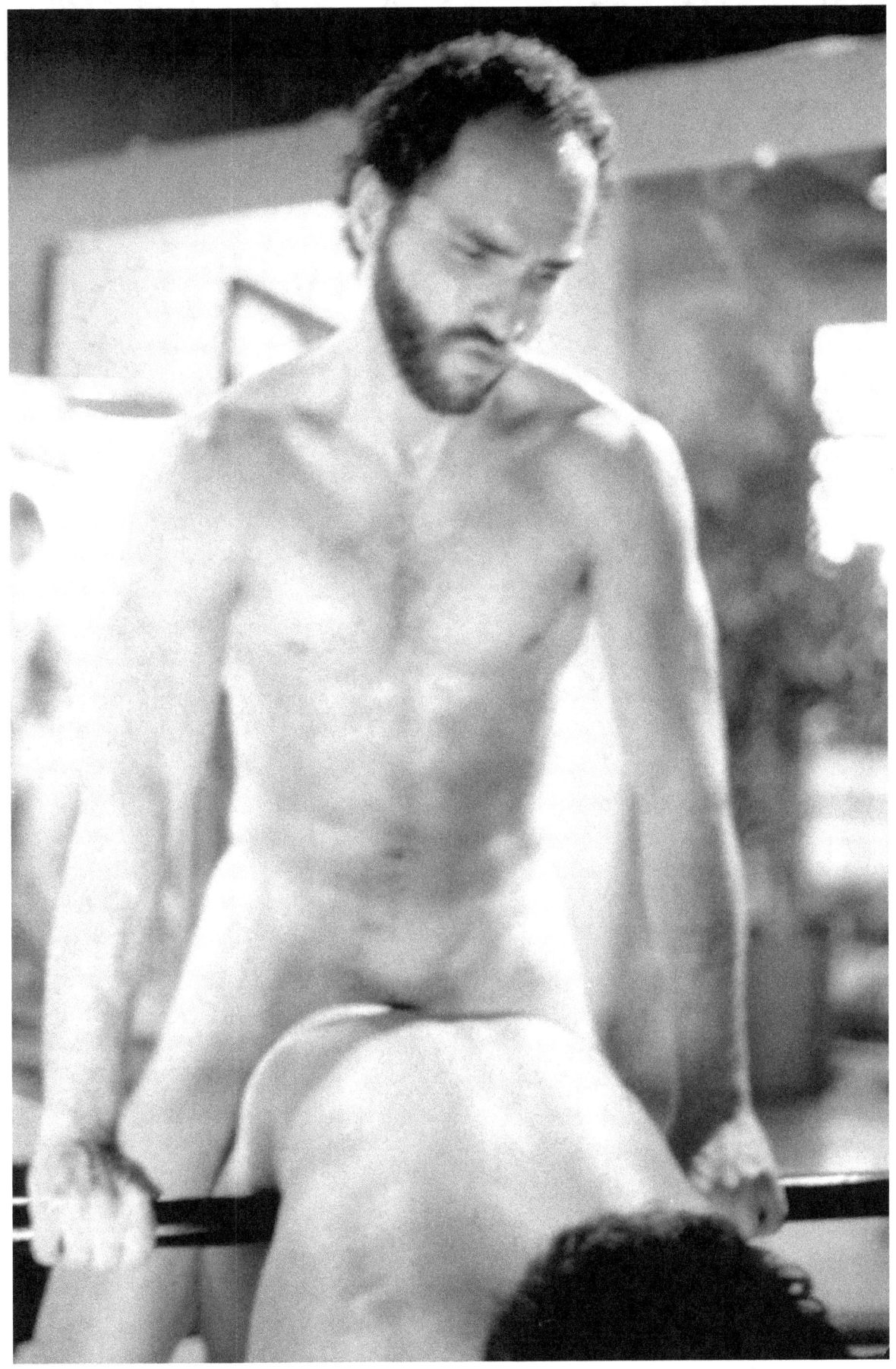

J.D. Slater

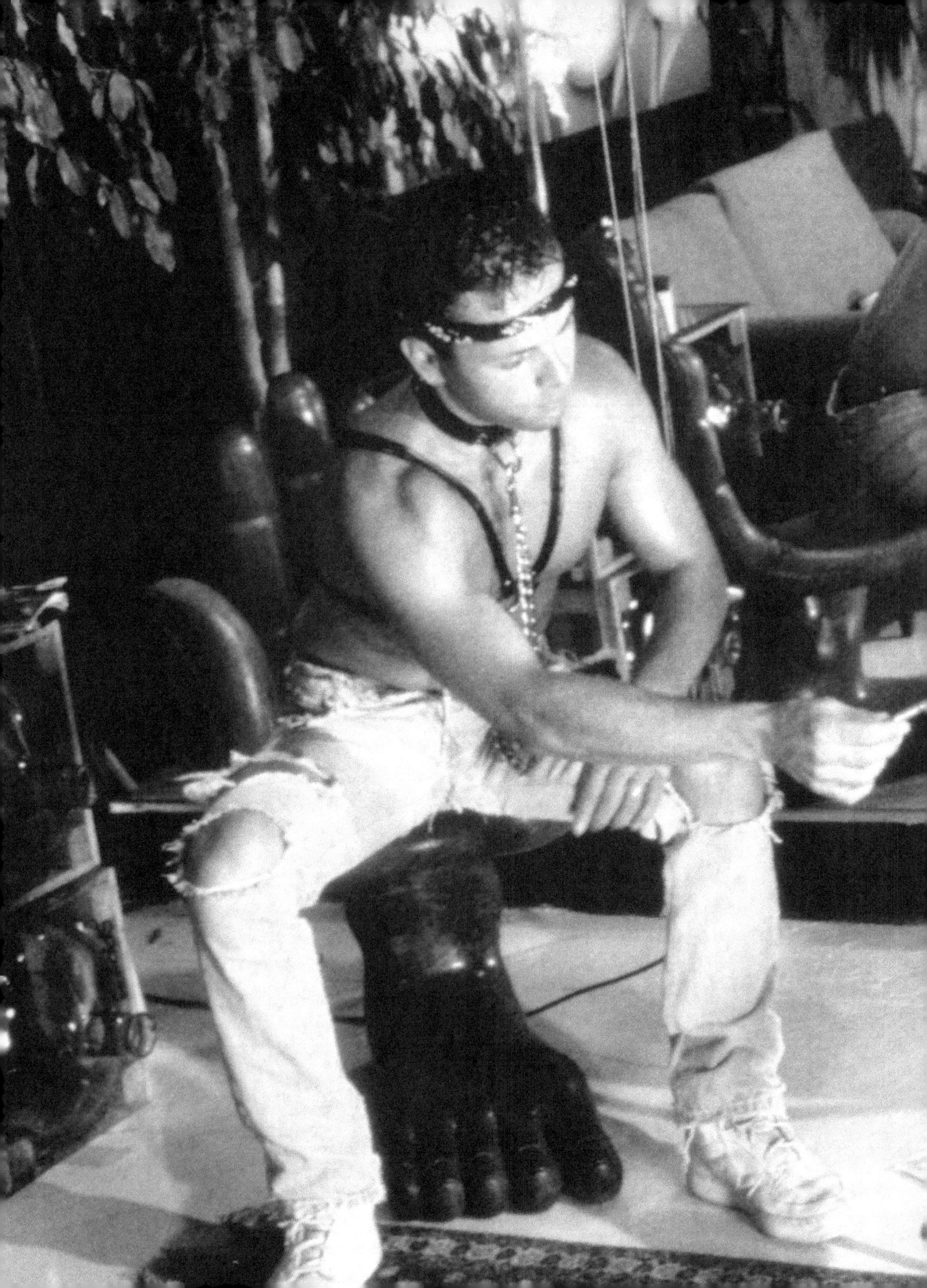

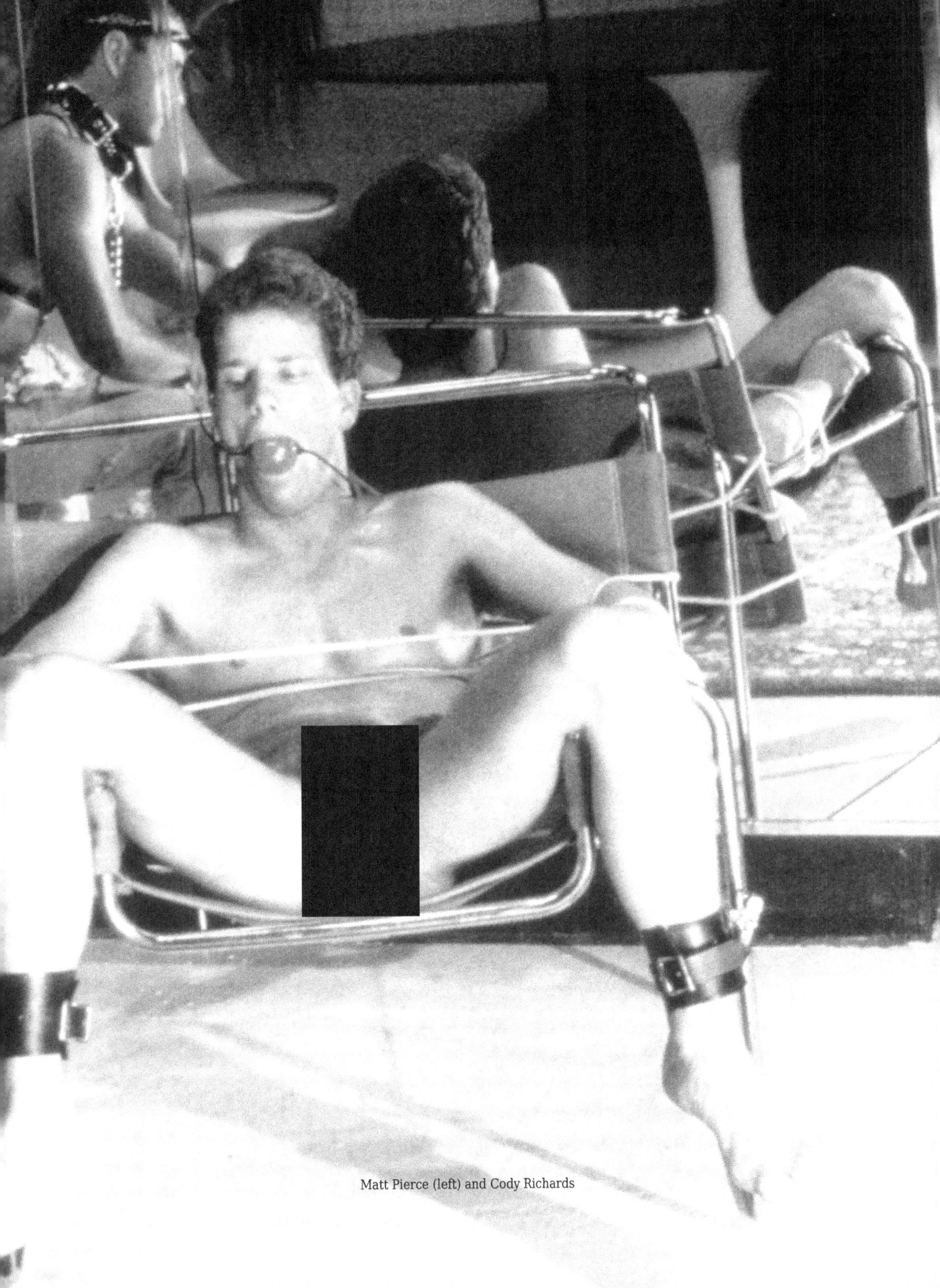

Matt Pierce (left) and Cody Richards

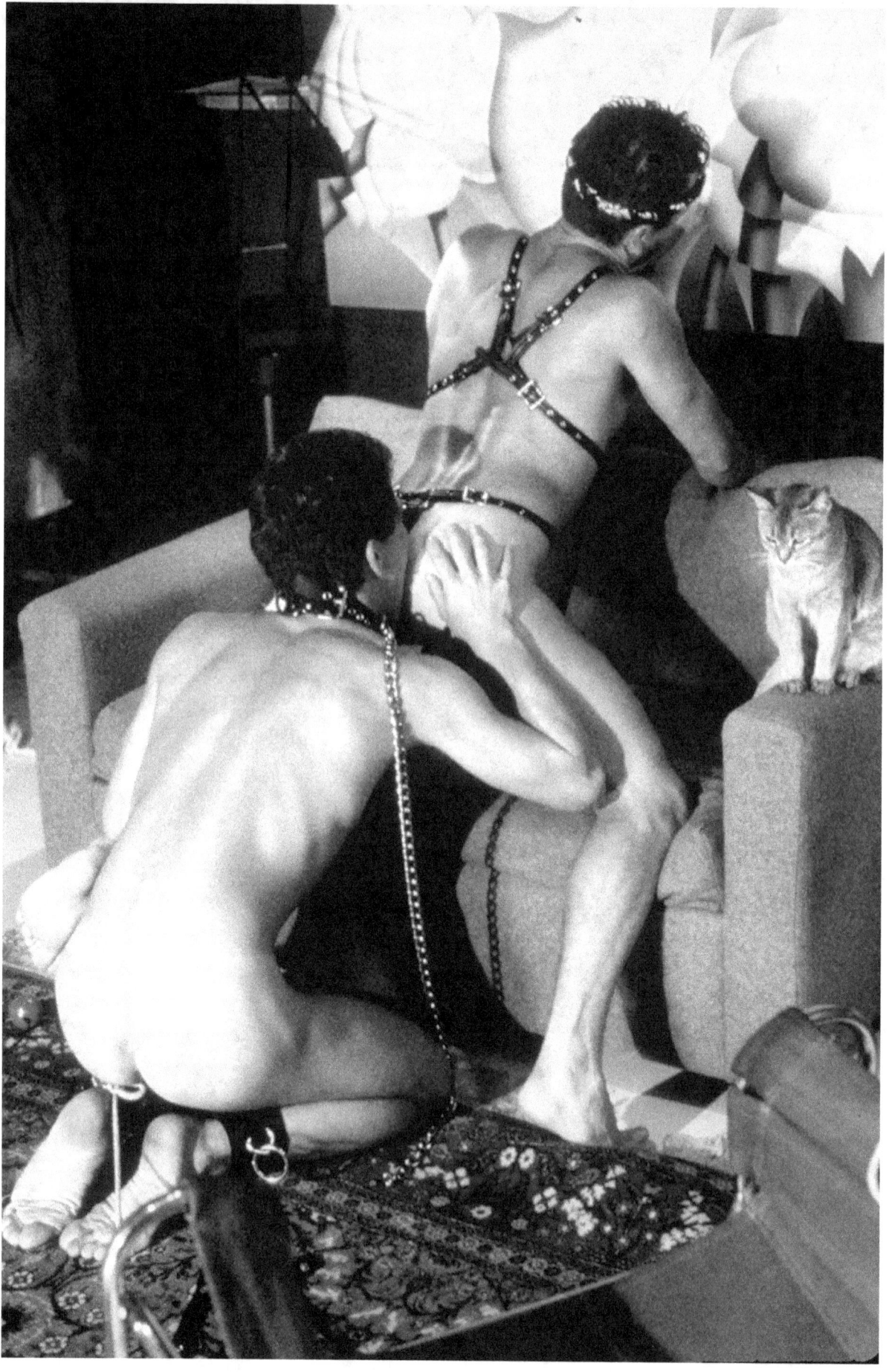

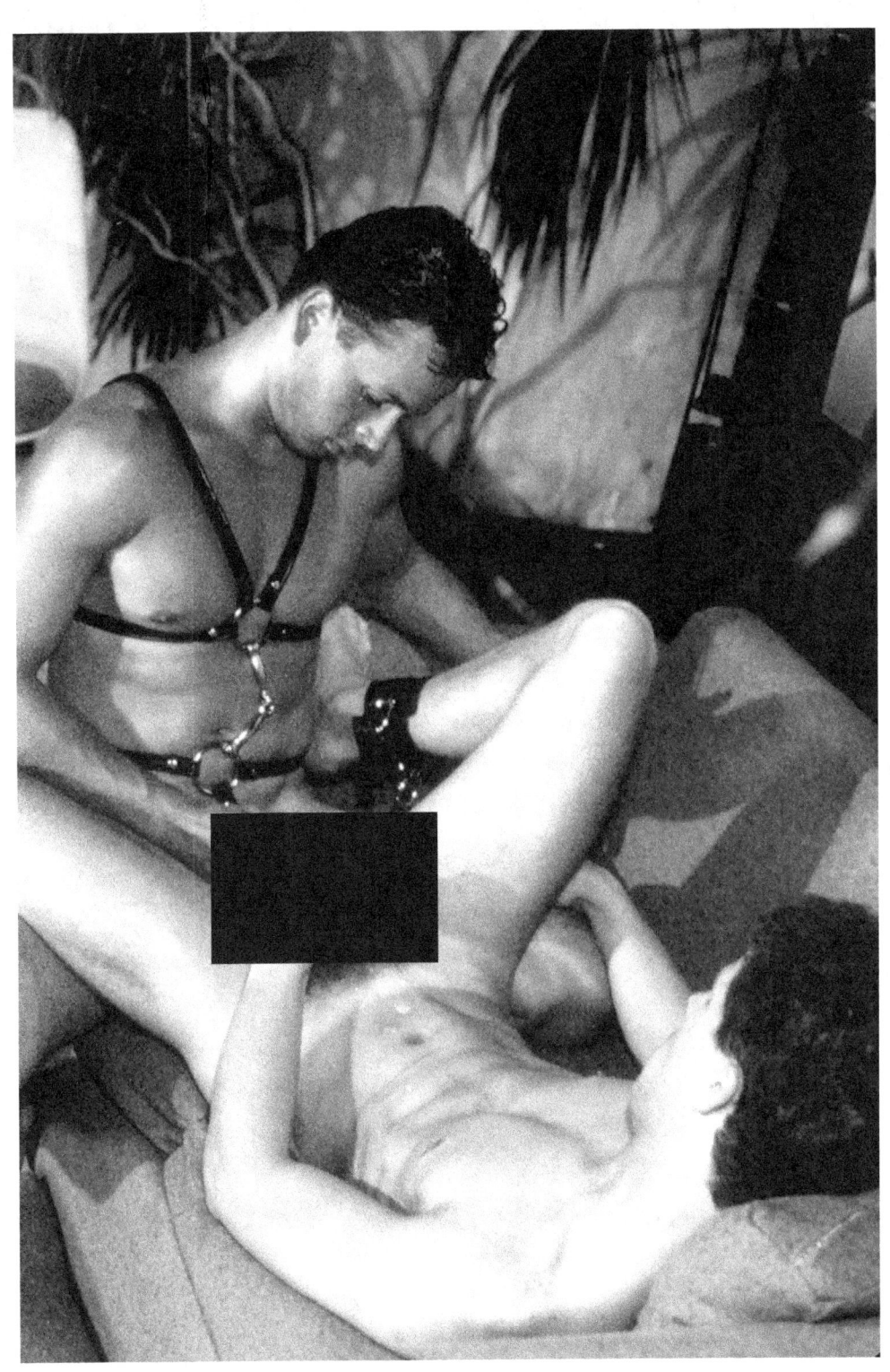

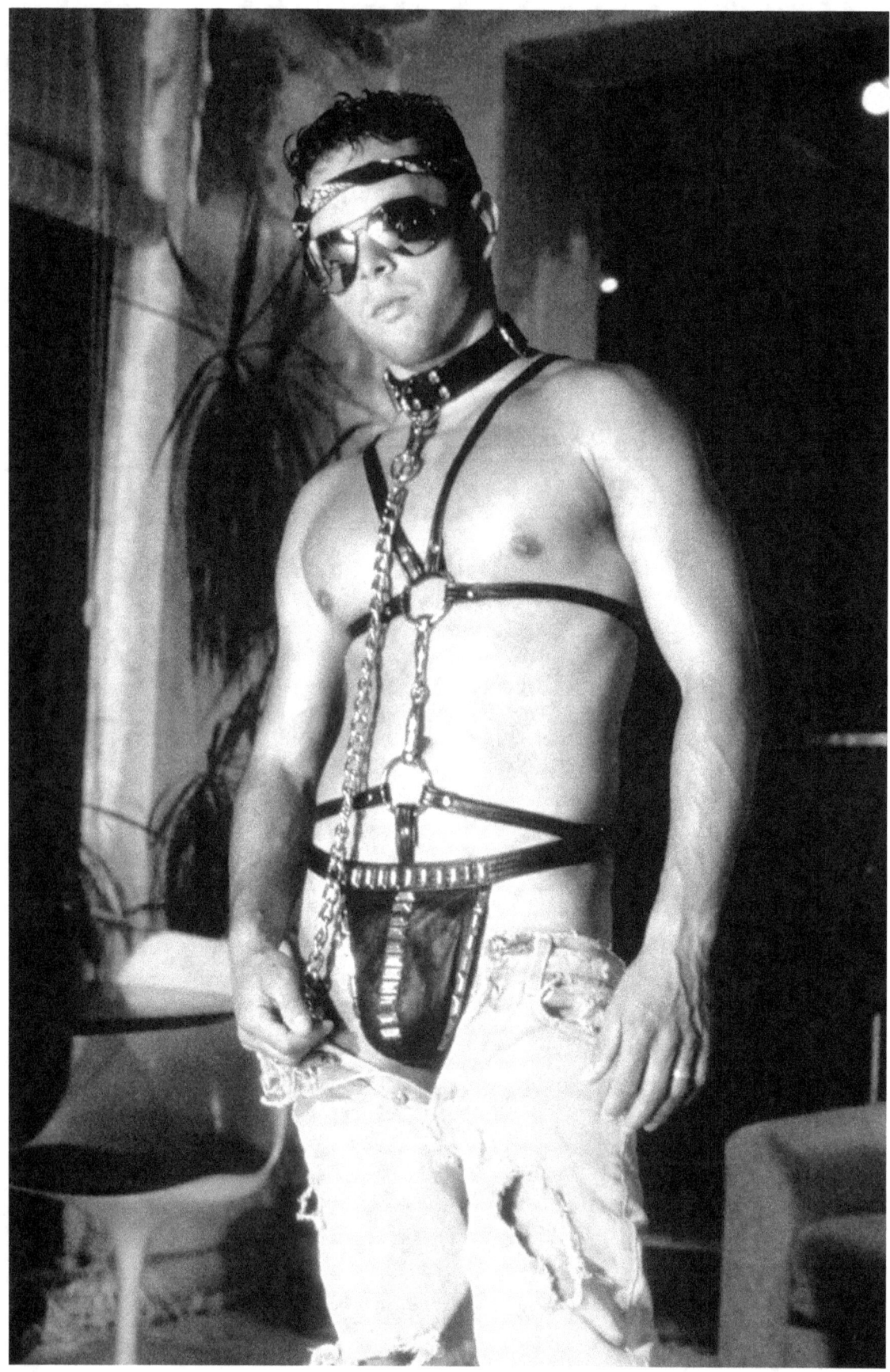

Matt Pierce

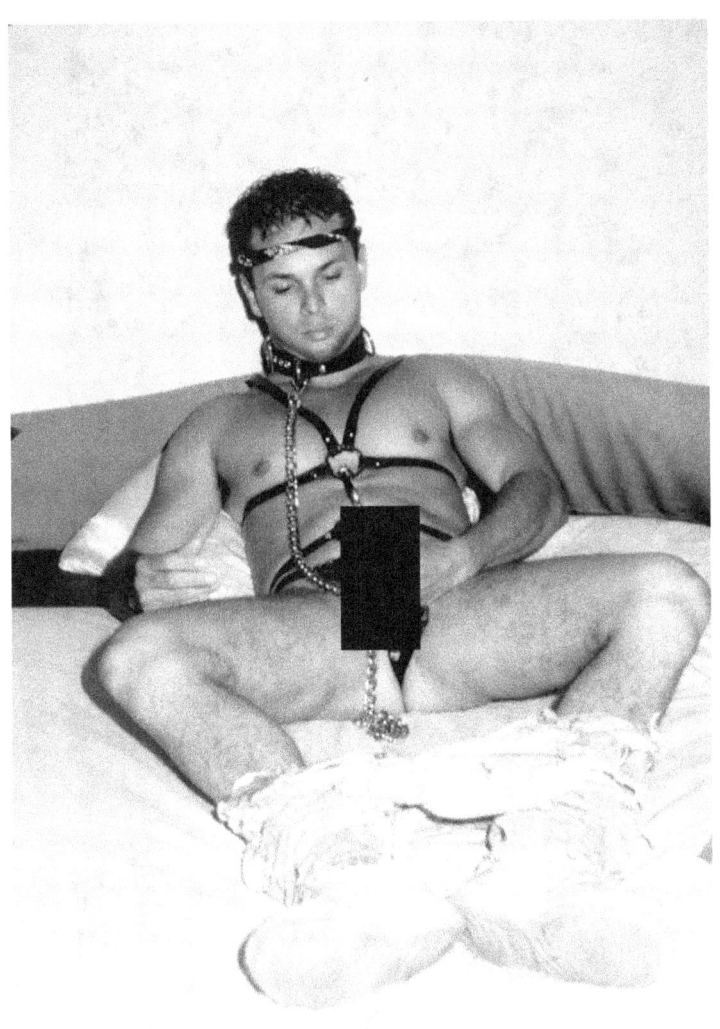

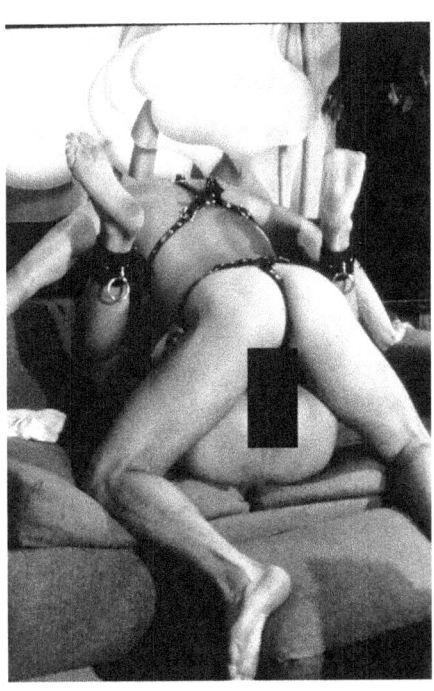

"The final segment, *Midnight*, is a dream-rape sequence featuring Cody Richards as the victim and Matt Pierce as the leather-clad intruder. Fluid camerawork and the intensity of the scene itself show the abilities of director Bob Alvarez at his best."
ROBERT LEIGHTON

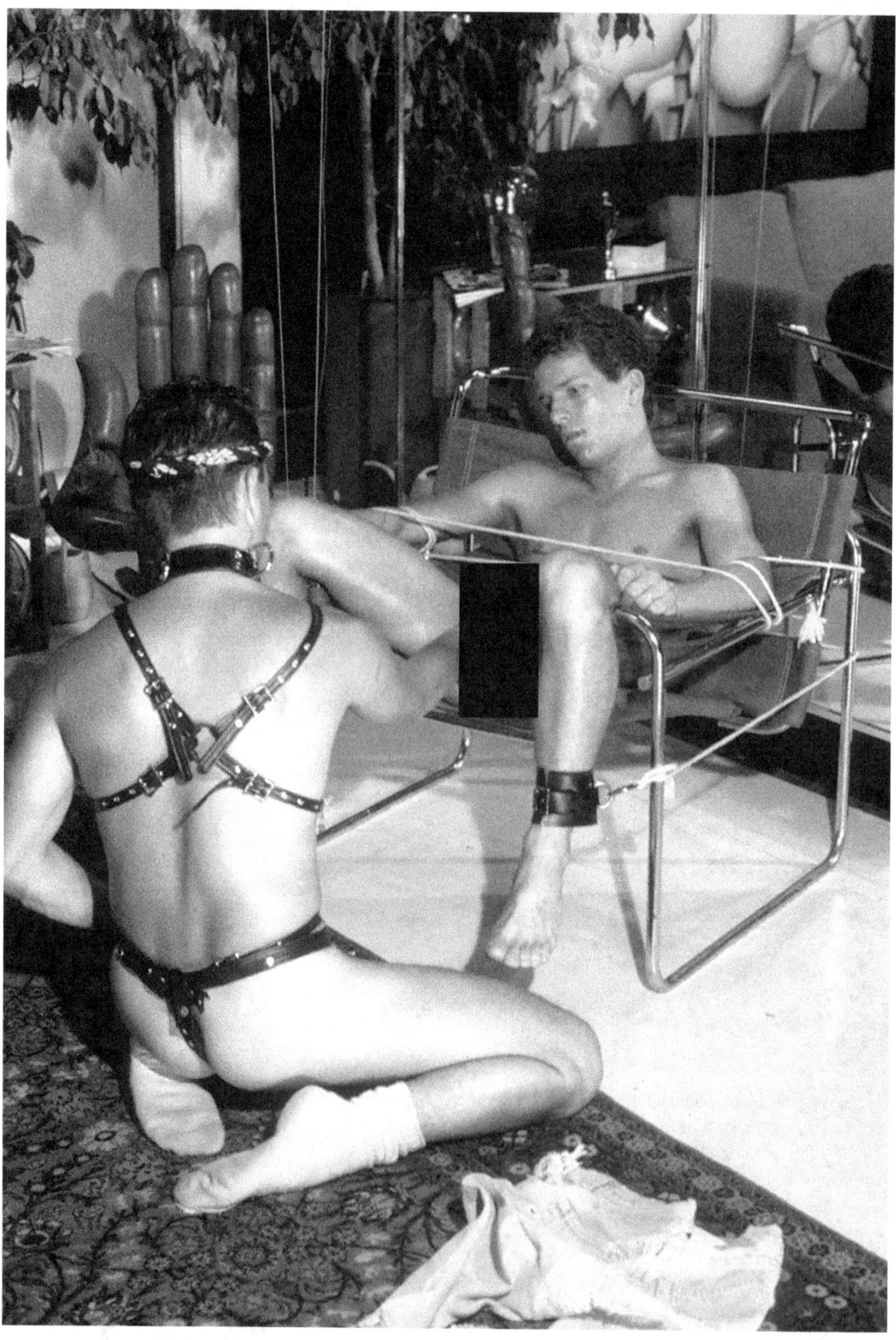

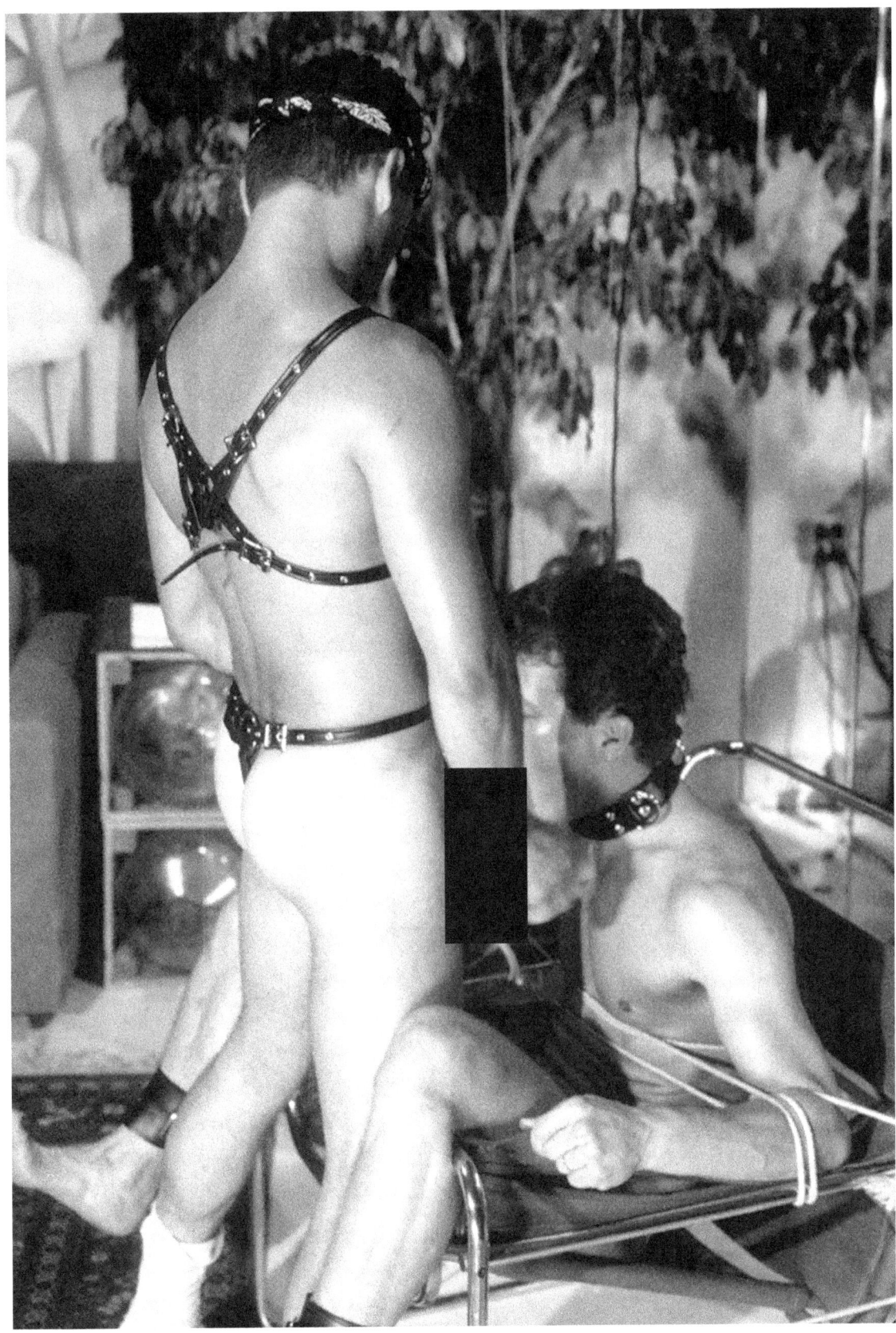

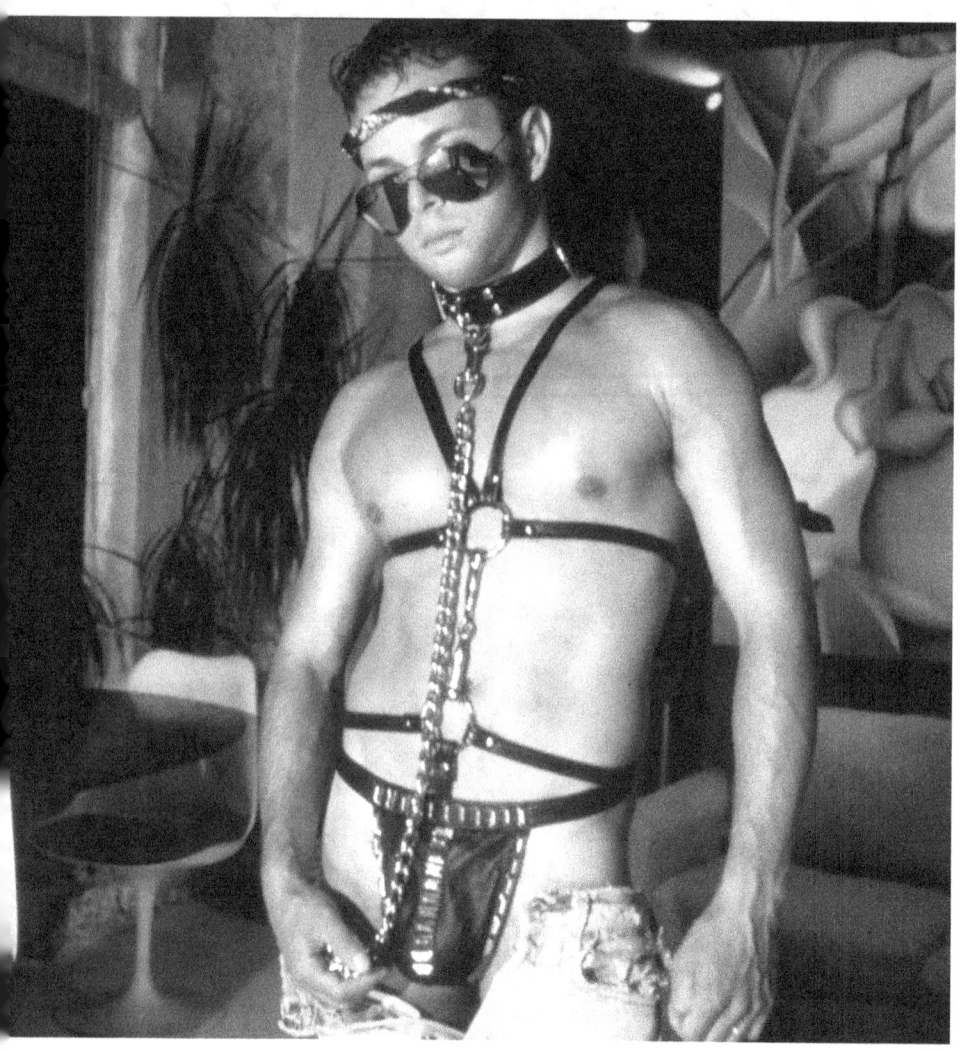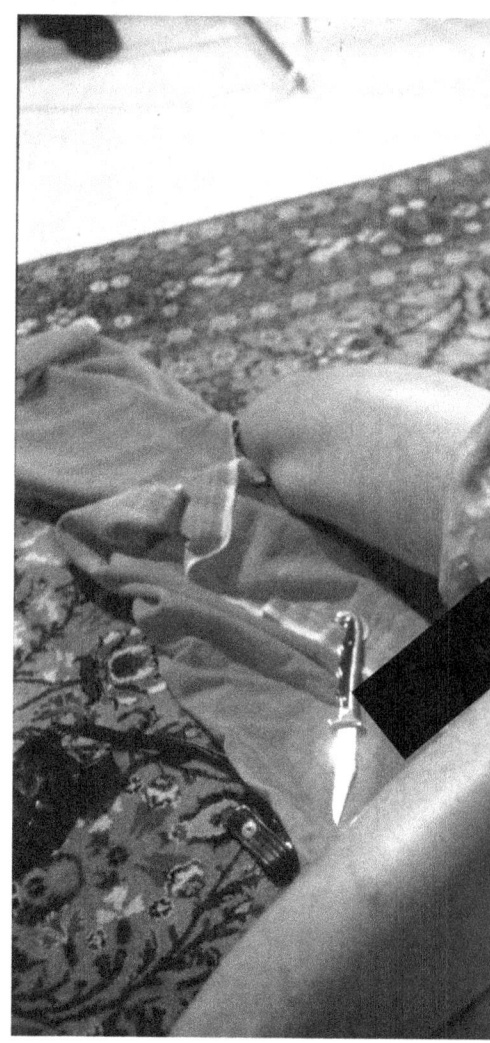

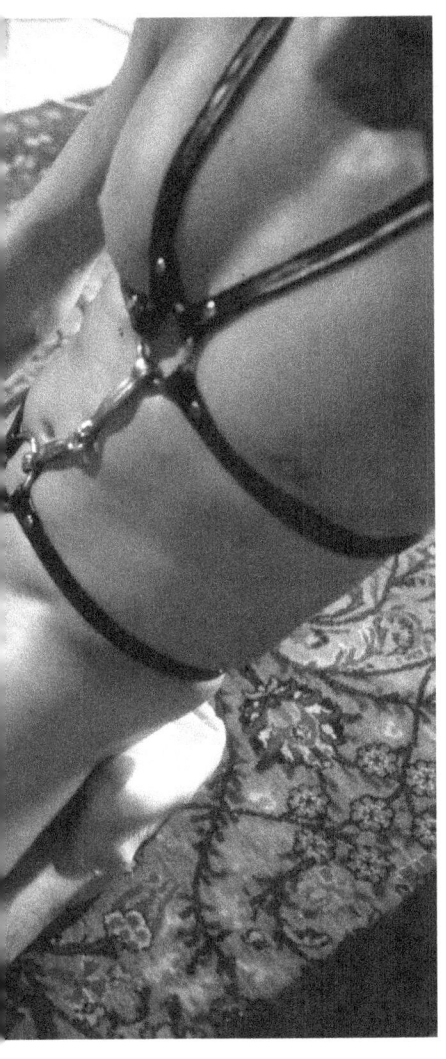
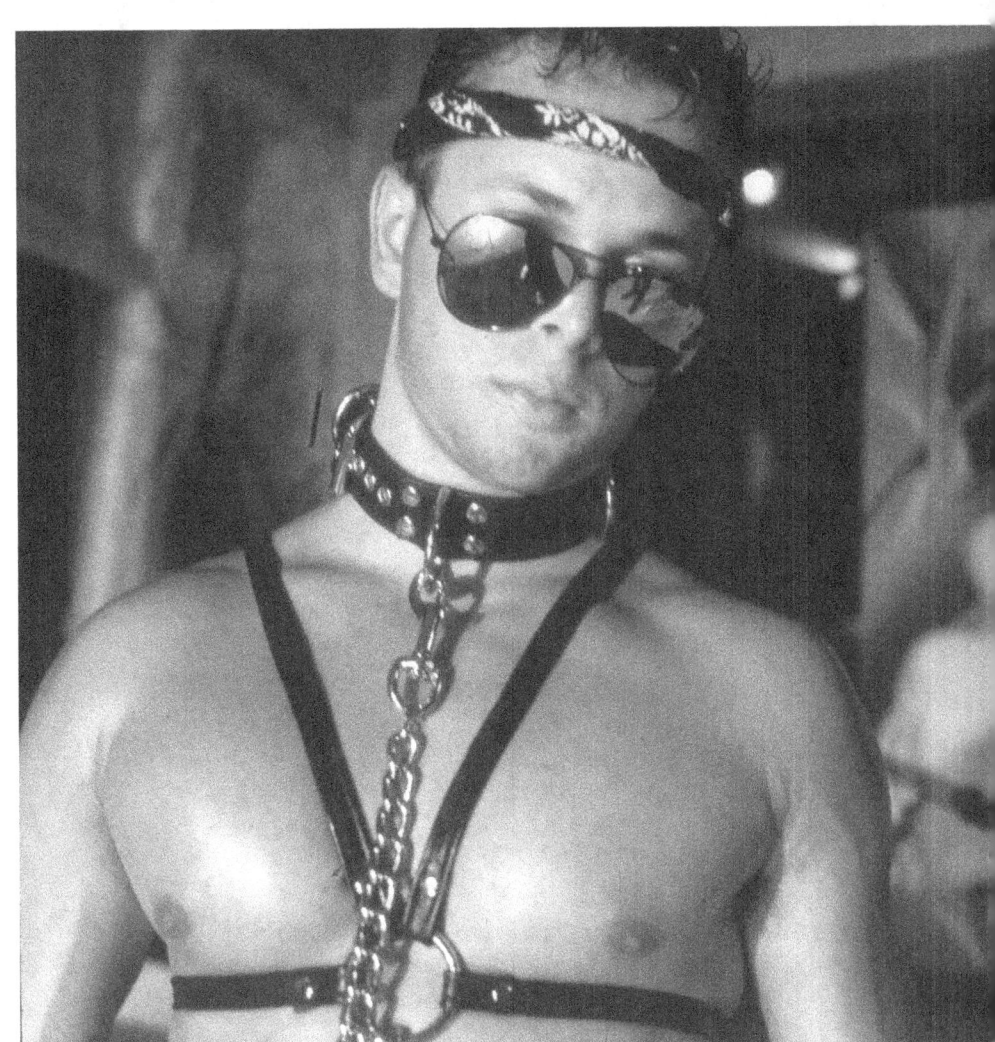

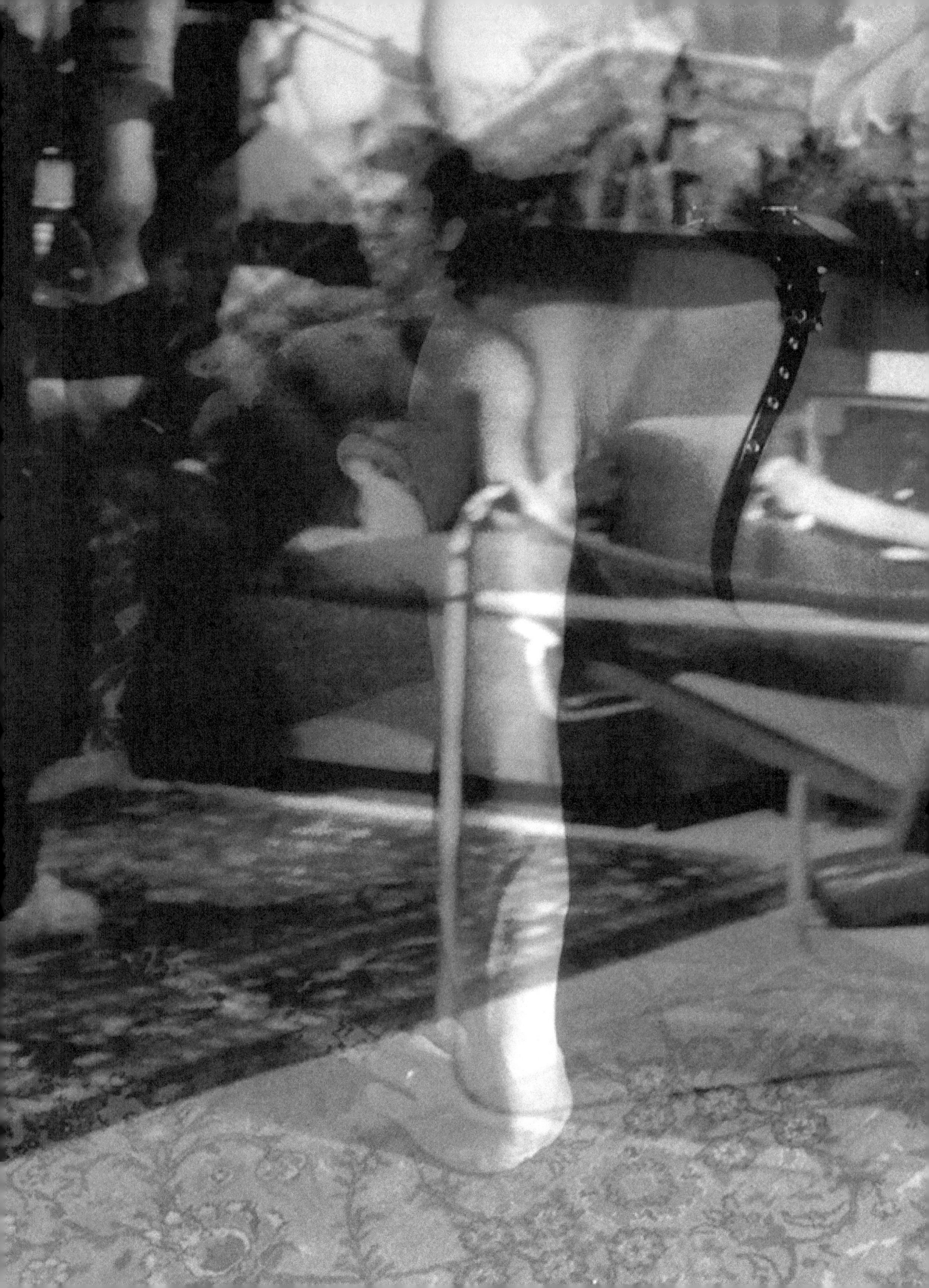

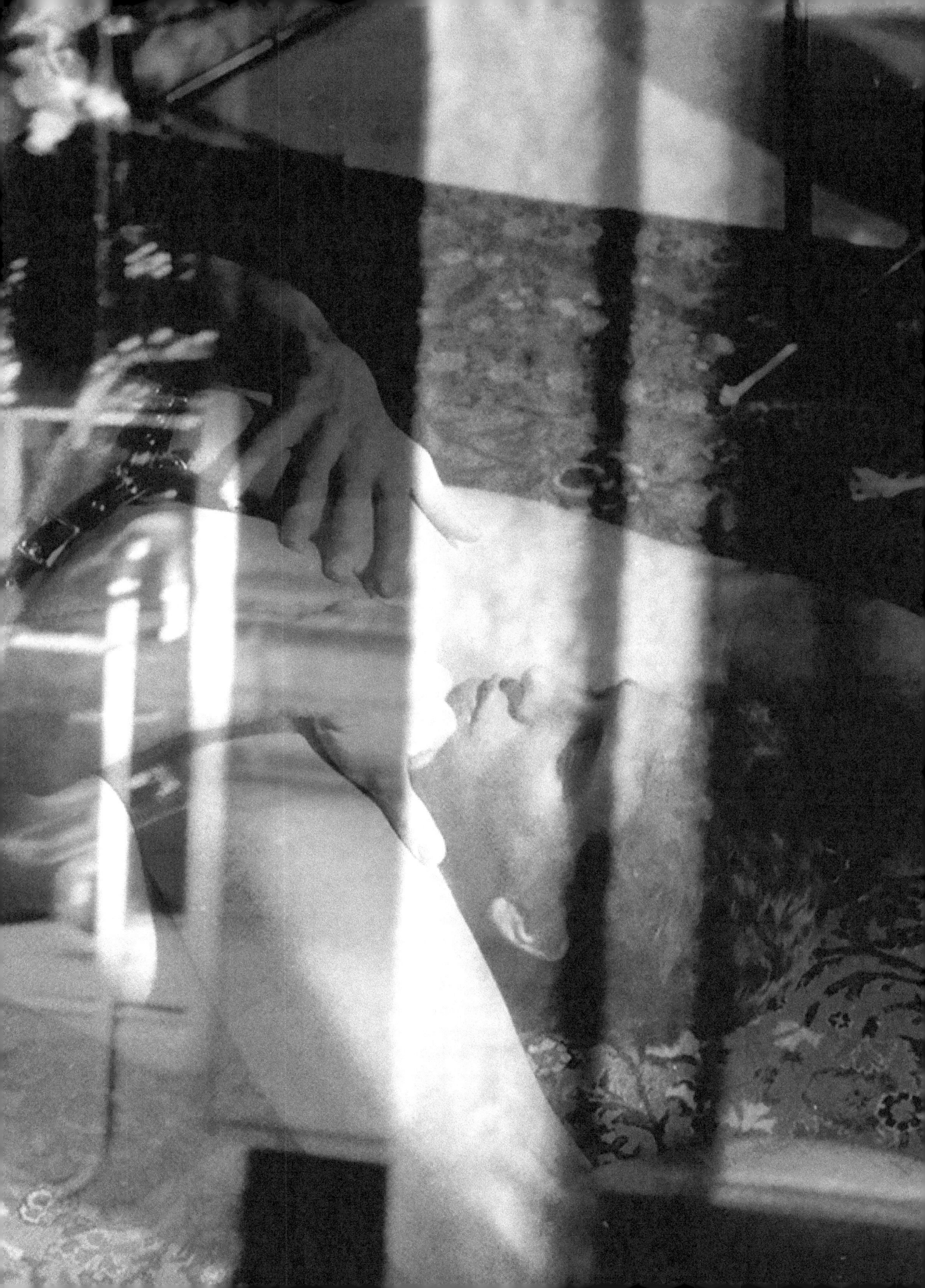

This film consists of five segments, all of which were shot in New York City. Altogether, the action takes 24 hours, which gives still more unity to the video. Jack Deveau directed the first two sequences shortly before his death. I assume this represents his last work, and for that reason alone the film is worth viewing. One of gay porn's pioneers, Deveau was an acknowledged master of the genre, and his mastery shines through in his two sections of IN HEAT. Apparently, Hand In Hand Films assigned the direction of the remaining segments to Bob Alvarez and Peter De Rome so the film could be finished and released, for the opening credits carry a 1984 copyright but a 1985 copyright is displayed at the end. Although I would have liked to be able to compare the finished results with what Deveau might have done had he guided the entire production, the film as a whole does not suffer from too many cooks. In part, this is because each segment is a story that can stand on its own – and each does that very well. The opening segment, BEFORE TIME, which features Doug De Marco with a boa constrictor, is little more than an erotic device for the film's credits, but even here one can see Deveau's vision at work. De Marco and friend's performance is highly erotic (even to someone like myself, who has never been particularly fond of snakes). Watching the boa writhe and slither over De Marco's body, slide his head into De Marco's mouth, glide up his back and between his asscheeks, was both fascinating and arousing. The next sequence, 8 AM, also directed by Deveau, may be even more inventive than the astonishing opening. We discover a young man, Greg Gaines, in the shower. Afterwards he goes to his living room and opens his mail. One package contains a pair of binoculars. Clad in his Jockey briefs, Greg goes to the window and discovers another man, also with binoculars in hand, peering back at him from an adjoining building.

The other man, Bob Gaines, flashes his phone number at Greg. When Greg calls, Bob tells him, in effect, that the binoculars are a birthday present from him, and that if Greg will call another number and ask whoever answers to come to the window, they can have a three-way to help celebrate the event. The call is made, Frank Gaines comes to his window in another nearby building, and an erotic, voyeuristic, three-way masturbation scene ensues. Hot, different, imaginative. It is now NOON, and we are in a studio where an aerobics class is in session. A break is called, and the three students soon turn stretching exercises into sexercises. The performance of Brian Michaels, a Matt Sterling star with classic good looks, illustrates why Michaels has been such a popular performer in Sterling's productions (and, under the name of Bobby Madison, in William Higgins' films). His interaction with Billy Knight, while Rod Hunter looks on, is probably the hottest sex scene in the entire production. J.D. Slater, the trainer, comes back to the studio and turns Michaels into a bottom; he handles this role with the same skill he earlier displayed as a top. Though the sex in this segment is hot, it is the weakest in terms of imagination. There is almost no dialogue, and the scene could be dropped into any other video almost intact. The time shifts to 3 P.M. The New York Marathon is under way. Director Peter De Rome has skillfully intercut footage of an actual marathon with scenes of Scorpio running along a similar route. These shots dissolve to an erotic performance with Keith Anthoni. The sex is satisfying, the editing superb.

The final segment, MIDNIGHT, is a dream-rape sequence featuring Cody Richards as the victim and Matt Pierce as the leather-clad intruder. Fluid camerawork and the intensity of the scene itself show the abilities of director Bob Alvarez at his best. We look forward to seeing more of his work in the future, and the work of Peter De Rome as well.

*Robert Leighton, *Torso*

ROBERT ALVAREZ & KEES CHAPMAN

The Legacy of Jack Deveau

Jack Deveau, the veteran filmmaker who pioneered gay erotica in a series of productions for his Hand in Hand Films, died in New York City on the evening of December 2, 1982, after a long bout with cancer. With him at the time were his lover of twenty-one years, Robert Alvarez, and his close friend and business associate, Kenneth "Kees" Chapman. Two weeks later, in the sprawling penthouse office complex that served as Deveau's home as well as headquarters for Hand in Hand Films, the two survivors sat to discuss the remarkable legacy left by the man who had been a major force in the vanguard of the sexual revolution and a trailblazer in upgrading the art of erotic cinema. Deveau initially gained national prominence with his first film, LEFT-HANDED, in 1972, and went on to write, direct, and/or produce such classics as DRIVE, ADAM AND YVES, GOOD HOT STUFF, BALLET DOWN THE HIGHWAY, WANTED: BILLY THE KID, A NIGHT AT THE ADONIS, FIRE ISLAND FEVER, PRIVATE COLLECTION and his last film, TIMES SQUARE STRIP. Deveau, who was born in Manhattan on January 25, 1935, attended Cornell University for one semester, and was working as a partner in an industrial and architectural design outfit in the early seventies, when, at the prodding of Alvarez (who subsequently edited all his films) he turned to motion picture production.

Jerry Douglas: Why did you prod him?
Bob Alvarez: Because I thought he was a natural. I thought he had a kind of charisma, the ability to make people listen, to make people enjoy what they were doing. Actually, I had become a film editor, maybe four years prior to this time, and that was directly through Jack. I had originally started out to be a dancer, but I wasn't getting anyplace. After one final summer of doing Irma La Duce, Jack said, "I don't think you have the temperament for it," and advised that I look into something else. I did a few underground films —
Douglas: Underground, as opposed to pornographic?
Alvarez: Exactly. There was definitely a connection between what underground films were and what a lot of pornographic films became. They picked up on a lot of the same techniques being experimented with. People like Andy Warhol, Kenneth Anger, and Gregory Markopoulos. The next thing I knew I was hooked. I got my first job as a can carrier for an optical house, worked up to apprentice, assistant film editor, film editor. I did some work on documentaries for NET. Sal Mineo was a good friend of ours, and he also encouraged Jack into this business.
Douglas: What was there about Jack that made you think he would be good at filmmaking?
Alvarez: The way that he handled people. The way that be could meet a stranger at a party or a hustler in a bar. Whoever he set his sights on, he could somehow charm into doing or saying what he wanted. He was the kind of person who, literally, had a lot of tricks up his sleeve — because he'd studied magic when he was just so high — and he was used to dealing with people.
Douglas: So you told him you thought he ought to make a film?
Alvarez: Yes, I did. I told him we should make a film. Because from the beginning I wanted us to work together. That's pan of what the relationship meant to me. I just wanted him around all the time.
Douglas: How did LEFT-HANDED come about?
Alvarez: The money actually came from Jack. He hocked some stocks that he had. I wish I knew what the budget was. By today's standards, it was absurd. Do you have any idea how much we spent, Kees?
Kees Chapman: It was a lot more than was being spent on those kinds of films in those days.
Alvarez: I remember the loans and things.
Douglas: Where did the idea for the story come from?
Alvarez: I don't really know. It was about a guy who was a hustler, and how he gets obsessed with a supposedly straight guy, and manages to seduce him — all to the straight guy's undoing, because at the end

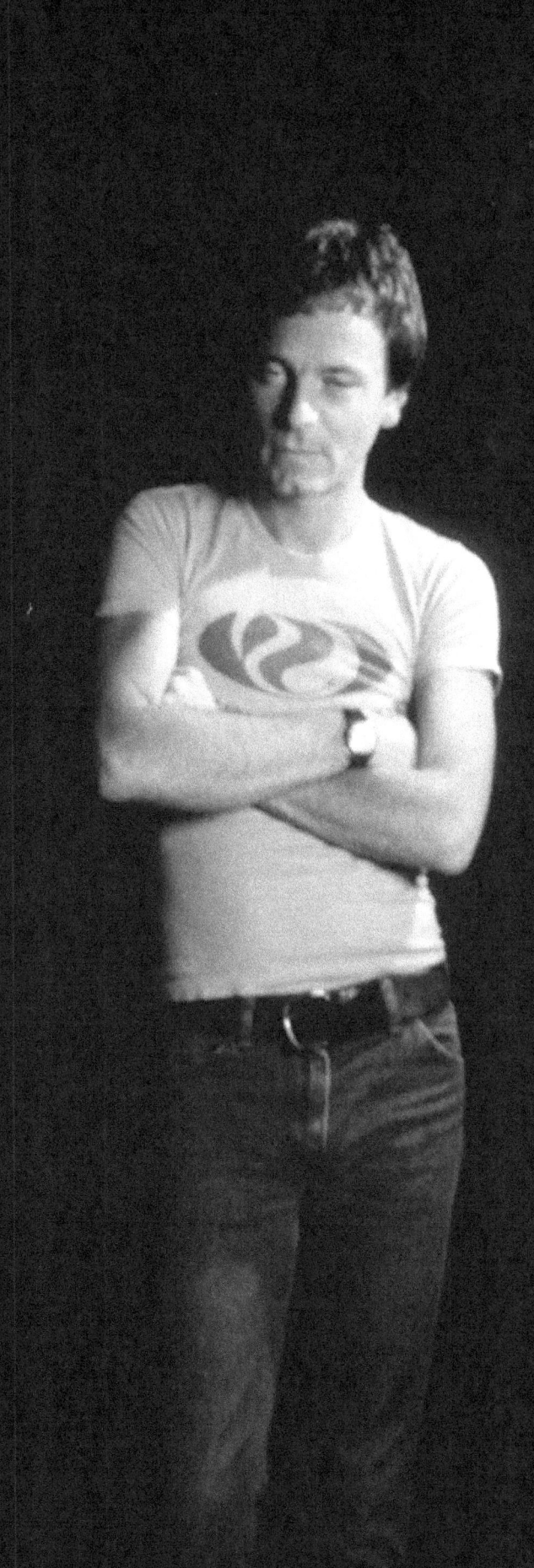

Kees Chapman

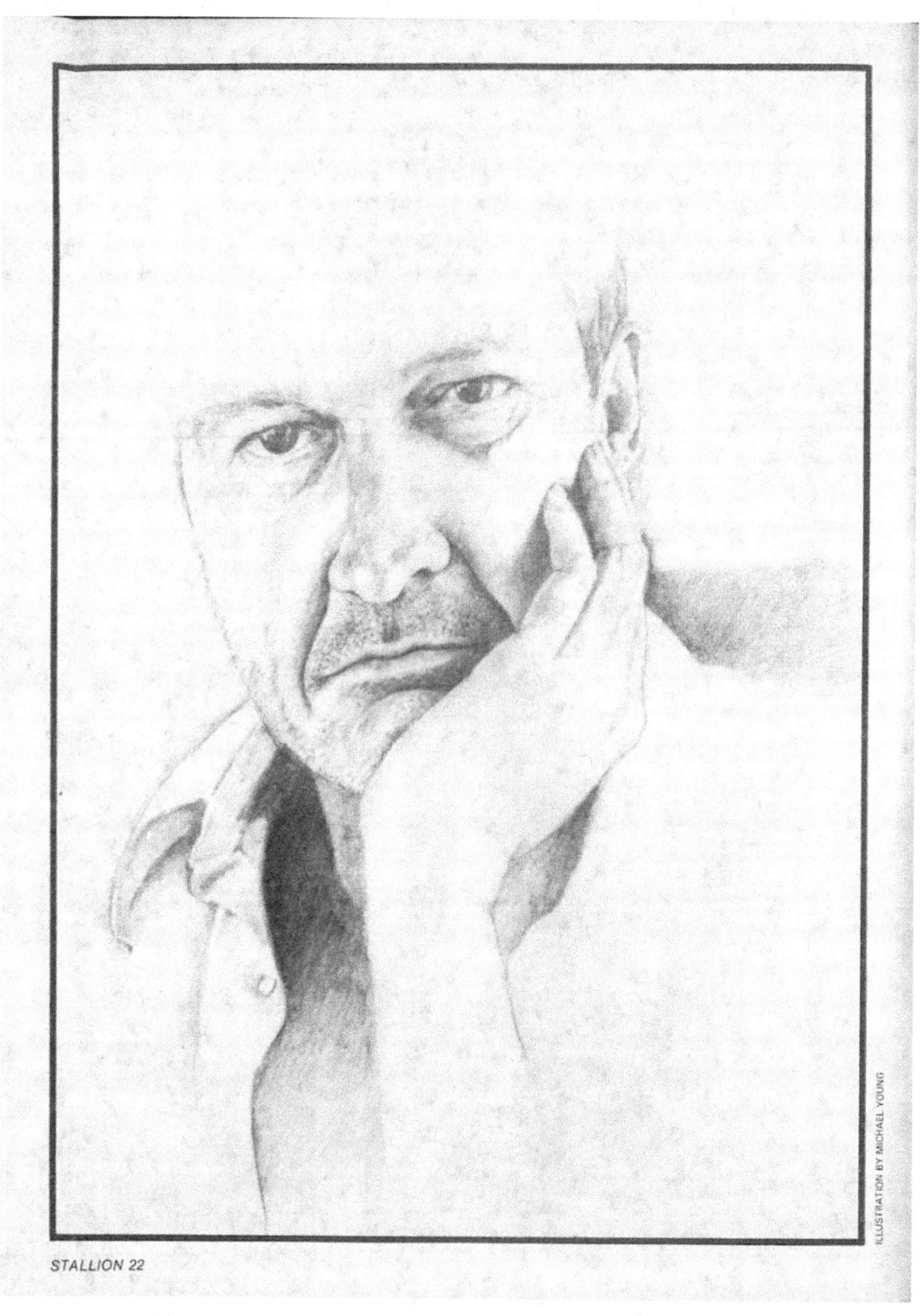

Jack Deveau by Michael Young

the hustler has no real interest in him. It's all about how a straight person's latent gay instinct can be brought out by the right person. It's cynical in a way, because Jack was cynical in a way about a lot of gay relationships and things that happen in gay society.

Douglas: What was it like plunging into the first production?

Alvarez: The feeling, once we got underway, was exciting, because I was at that time very interested in expanding, getting into cinematography, being directly involved with the production rather than sitting behind the editing machine. Since we were just starting out, everybody had a chance to do everything. I even had a sequence in LEFT-HANDED that I shot myself - the overhead sequence.

Douglas: Had either you or Jack had much to do with movie cameras before this time?

Alvarez: I hadn't, no. Jack had had considerable experience with still cameras. He knew about exposures and focus and all that business. He was a tinkerer too. He knew how to take a camera a pan and put it back together. He knew exactly what made it work.

Douglas: How long did it take to make LEFT-HANDED?

Alvarez: Shooting it took about three weeks. We shot on weekends, and about eight weeks to put it together.

Douglas: When it opened, what was the reaction?

Alvarez: Very good. Hardcore was just beginning at this point. BOYS IN THE SAND preceded it, and so had LA. PLAYS ITSELF, which was of course a real shocker. A breakthrough film.

Douglas: In its own way, so was LEFT-HANDED.

Alvarez: I like to think so.

Douglas: What was there about it that was so special?

Alvarez: I think it was the most heavily plotted film of the time. It had a real story to tell. It had characters you could identify with, whether you liked them or not. Like, the lead character is sort of a shit. It was a breakthrough in that sense because it had an anti-hero. It also had all the required elements to make it a hardcore film.

Douglas: Which came first, LEFT-HANDED or Hand in Hand Films?

Alvarez: They were simultaneous.

Douglas: Hand in Hand Films was an organization without precedence. Jack was the first person to make and distribute gay erotica, to provide a sort of national clearing house for gay films.

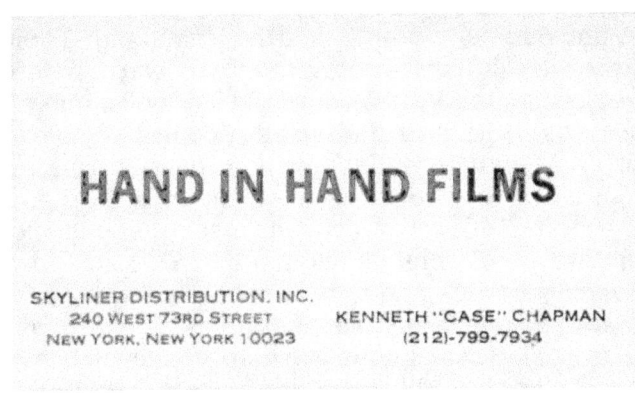

Alvarez: A lot of it bad to do with getting to know the kingpins in the gay film market — by that, I mean the exhibitors. We decided we were not going to do what most people were doing at that time, which was selling prints of their films and calling it a day. Once that happened, the films would just go on forever, and the people who bought them began to pirate them. They would have fourth generation prints playing in the theatres. We decided we would try and keep some sort of control over what we had.

Douglas: In effect, what you were doing was aping the producers of general release films.

Alvarez: Yes. Of course, here we were — we started out with one film, but we weren't under any circumstances going to sell it. Then Jack and I did something I think was really valuable. we took a trip across country. We hit every big city and met the owners of the theatres, saying, "Hello, this is us. We're in the movie business and we're going to be making a lot of movies and we'd like you to rent from us."

Douglas: Was there much resistance to renting instead of buying?

Alvarez: I don ,t know. You'll have to talk to Kees about that.

Chapman: The concept that Jack stressed over and over again was the idea that there would always be something new coming from us. We will have product. You'll get better prints. Prints will be taken care of. Boom! The exhibitors said fine. They weren't really interested in being librarians themselves.

Alvarez: Product was always a problem for them. Getting enough product. Once we got a library of our own films going, plus films from other people that we were distributing, the theatre owners were delighted. It was great for them.

Douglas: Well, let's back up a little. What was Jack's second film?

Alvarez: DRIVE. But then we were involved with THE EROTIC FILMS OF PETER DE ROME. We'd met Peter and we knew be had these eight millimeter films he'd been making. They were really little gems, and we were being experimental in those days. So we took some of Peter's little films and made a collection, blew it up to sixteen millimeter. And gave it a more contemporary look. One of the things Peter wanted to do very much was a sex scene in the subway. I told him he had to do it. See, his films were very nice and very sensual, but we really needed something that had some punch to it. Next thing you know, a whole bunch of of us where on the subway with cameras.

Douglas: What time of day did you shoot?

Alvarez: We started at eight on a weekday morning. It took us all day. It was so exciting — it was just like doing it. For a while Peter was shooting, I was shooting, Jack was shooting. They finally shot the sex scene very late at night. They finally finished on a long express run from Manhattan to Coney Island or somewhere out there. The film has that look about it — starts very crowded, and the car slowly empties out till you reach this empty chamber and these people are united.

Douglas: Now let's talk about DRIVE.

Alvarez: That's when Kees arrived on the scene.

Chapman: I came to audition for a role in Drive. I'd heard that there was this part of a drag queen, and that interested me because I had trained as an actor, and I wasn't interested in doing a real heavyduty sex scene.

Douglas: Tell us about your audition. How did Jack conduct an audition?

Chapman: It was just him sitting here at this marvelous green marble table, quizzing me. The last question was, "Will you take off your clothes and let's have a look at it?" I thought, "This is it. My God, rape! There's no one around to take care of me." And of course he was the gentleman he always is— and was. "Take a turn, put your clothes on, and you'll hear from me." Later, Bob needed an assistant. I was lured away from it. With a ticket to France.

Alvarez: There was a period there where there was a lot of magic going on. It's not ever going to be the same again. There was a period in porn filmmaking when there was hope that you could do something.

Douglas: Much the same as the early days of silent films, I suspect. Everybody was having a good time "making movies."

Alvarez: Yeah. You could do whatever the hell you wanted. You could be as I audacious as you wanted. You were working on a very low budget. You knew there was a limit on how much you could spend. You had that much money to do something. Therefore you could do whatever you wanted as long as you had the required amount of sex scenes. About DRIVE — - don't know exactly how the idea evolved, but we had seen Lynne Carter in Provincetown, and decided it would be great to do a movie with a transvestite/transsexual. We created the movie with Christopher Rage, who ended up playing the role of Arachne. Things just got crazier and crazier. Well, we were turned down by Miss Carter, who had a previous engagement — and really Christopher was the only one who could play Arachne. I see him in that part and I think it's one of the best things I've ever seen.

Douglas: DRIVE is a remarkable film. What do you think is so unique about it?

Alvarez: It's so screwy, and at the same time it's a little bit prophetic. As hedonistic as we were — and we were, very — there's something about the wages of sin, and the movie has a kind of moralistic tone to it. Arachne is not all that far off base. Arachne is an aspect of Jack — maybe, the Catholic side.

Douglas: How did DRIVE do at the box office, compared to LEFT-HANDED?

Alvarez: Not nearly as well. By that time we had acquired the Lincoln Art Theatre on Fifty-Seventh Street.

Douglas: First you made movies, then you started distribution them, then you began to acquire films from other filmmaker for your distribution company and then you acquired a theatre?

Alvarez: It's always better to have your own theatre.

Douglas: So you won't have to share with someone who might be crooked, and you're also assured of a place to open your own film?

Alvarez: Exactly. Well, after DRIVE opened, we planned to turn the place into a gay house. Then THE DEVIL IN MISS JONES came along. It was something we all liked and knew it would be a landmark film. The best pornographic film I've ever seen. We had a chance to book it.

Douglas: It ran forever, and the idea of a gay theatre was victim of your own success with straight porn.

Alvarez: It killed the image of a gay theatre, and by the time it closed, we were on to other things.
Douglas: Such as?
Alvarez: THE EROTIC FILMS OF PETER DE ROME had done fairly well, and we had established ourselves as a national organization. Peter wanted to do something more ambitious — a full-length film, and we came up with the idea of ADAM & YVES.
Douglas: What was the original idea?
Alvarez: An American in Paris who meets a Frenchman and has a brief affair. Very much a take-off on LAST TANGO IN PARIS. Jack loved the idea — and Paris — very much. So he and Peter went off to Paris. Now we weren't at the point where people were coming to us in droves for interviews, so Peter picked a couple of guys who were lovers for the two leads. Perfect, right? Well, they broke up right in the middle of the shooting — we had to chuck the footage and reshoot. We recast the film with one of the guys and someone else. It worked just long enough, because by the end of the film, these two weren't hitting it off. We did manage to get the sex scenes in — and of course a lovely trip to Paris.
Douglas: How did the final film do?
Alvarez: Very well. It has a classy look. It had a European feel.
Douglas: To me, it is Jack's most romantic film.
Alvarez: I think so. Personally, I feel it starts out really well, but somewhere in the middle it just doesn't hold up. The actors weren't getting off on each other. They didn't supply the heat the film needed, and there's no way of getting around that.
Douglas: What happened next?
Alvarez: We assembled GOOD HOT STUFF, made BALLET DOWN THE HIGHWAY, and WANTED: BILLY THE KID in quick succession, then back to Paris, where GOOD HOT STUFF (HISTOIRE D' HOMME) made us a lot of money. It was the first gay film to be shown in Paris.
Douglas: Let's talk a little bit about BALLET DOWN THE HIGHWAY. I think it's one of Jack's best films, if not his best.
Alvarez: Well, it was kind of strange the way it came about. We had decided we were going to become the moguls of gay porn and we began to take other people in. There was a certain man who I thought was very talented, and we started to plan a film called BEYOND THESE DOORS. This guy had this incredible script about all these fantasies we have and love and would just love to see on film. The script was about an innocent boy who has an uncle who runs a whorehouse. Very much like Genet's The Balcony each room had a fantasy. We thought, "Oh, sure, we can make this movie — but only one of them ever got filmed, the Arabian Nights fantasy that showed up in GOOD HOT STUFF. Anyway, we held a lot of interviews for this film. Gary Hunt was one of the people we interviewed. Gary was an original —you look at him and at that incredible cock and balls. It's absolutely obscene. And he has a wonderful manner about him. So we cast him in the film that became BALLET DOWN THE HIGHWAY. All of a sudden, we had this person who had a personality. As a director, once in a while you see someone that is really special and you know that no one else has that quality except that person.
Douglas: Did you reshape BALLET DOWN THE HIGHWAY to fit him?
Alvarez: No, that was the nice thing. It was one of those rare occasions where we didn't have to, because we were constantly reshaping for conditions with actors who couldn't do certain things.
Douglas: Would you say that one of Jack's great talents was his gift for improvisation?
Alvarez: Oh, yeah. He was really good and really quick. He could pick up on something that wasn't going and readjust the scene or half the movie if he had to.
Douglas: It was about the time, 1975, that explicit filmmaking hit its peak, and from then on the market began to drop off.
Chapman: Around '75 there was a general downward trend in theatrical distribution. Jack began to realize that you just couldn't spend the kind of money that we had spent on, say, a picture like DRIVE.
Douglas: How did you change the way you worked?
Alvarez: There really wasn't much difference. The only thing is we tightened our belts and became less profitable.
Douglas: To my way of thinking, A NIGHT AT THE ADONIS was Jack's next major film. What do you remember about it?
Chapman: The shooting of it was the experience that I remember most, because we had to go into that theatre, that cavern of a place, every morning about one AM — go in and light the whole place up, shoot our scenes, and pack it all up by noon, so they could continue operating the business as normal. It was a real bitch.
Alvarez: If you've ever been in a porno house and felt any kind of romance, this would kill it.

Douglas: Where did the idea come from?
Alvarez: Oh, Jack felt it was time to make another film. He was in thick with the guy who owned the Adonis. They thought it was a great idea to make a movie of this pleasure palace where most of our films were being shown at the time.
Chapman: That was '77.
Alvarez: It's very much like his last film, TIMES SQUARE STRIP. The fantasy of what happens in one of these places. h again goes back to Jack's Parisian link. Both films are very much concerned with his French roots.
Chapman: By '77, we started to get people coming to us. We had a great influx of people.
Alvarez: We had all these great-looking people. We just had to do a movie. Jack loved the idea of doing a movie in this space with the high ceilings.
Chapman: He got to use a steady cam, which he was just dying to use, and this was just the place to use it.
Alvarez: Talk about trying to cut back on spending a lot of money — no way.
Chapman: He'd go out and rent the most expensive equipment. I miss Jack's influence that way. Because — as much as I was always trying to pull him back and say "You can't rent another light because we can't afford it" — he'd go rent ten more — and he'd always be right.
Douglas: I want to ask you — what film do you think is Jack's best — and which is your favorite?
Chapman: In watching them over and over again, the best one is DRIVE, but not necessarily my favorite.
Douglas: Why do you think it's the best?
Chapman: It's so weird. It's so off the wall. I have a special feeling, though, for a picture called DUNE BUDDIES. I don't know why — maybe because it's simple nice, and sweet, and it makes a point.
Douglas: Bob, what do you think? Which is the best?
Alvarez: BALLET DOWN THE HIGHWAY.
Douglas: Why?
Alvarez: It best realizes what Jack set out to do.
Douglas: And what's your favorite?
Alvarez: I think LEFT-HANDED, because it was the first.
Douglas: What were his strengths that made his films so special?
Alvarez: I think he touched on subjects that were . . . well, Jack said what he wanted to.
Douglas: The fact that he made erotic films that said anything at all is a rarity.
Alvarez: Yes. I feel it's an unfinished story. I feel that there's more there than even I can comment on. One of the things that Jack always said was that "no matter what — this is recorded literature, or a piece of literature. You can be sure when you're dead that that piece of literature will be around." As long as the film negative doesn't deteriorate or the lab doesn't burn down, it's true. Whatever is there that he made is going to be there for a long time. Who knows what people will make of it — but it will be there.

In the years following the taping of this interview, the number of theatres showing gay adult films in this country shrank to virtually none — just as the video cassette burst into popularity.
Two releases where complete after Deveau's death: STRICTLY FORBIDDEN, with Bill Eld, which had originally been released only in Europe in 1976, and IN HEAT, which was a collection of short films, some of which had been earlier directed by Deveau, some of which represented all new footage directed by Alvarez. A third production, UP FOR IT, starring Bobby Madison, was half-completed before it was abandoned.
Hand In Hand continued through the eighties as a mail order house until Chapman died of AIDS complications on July 8, 1988.
"We managed till Kees died," said Alvarez recently as he talked of the future of Hand in Hand Films. "Like the girl in Green Mansions, the spirit of Jack's films goes on — but not the company." As of this writing, Alvarez has sold the entire film library to the Chicago-based Bijou Video which will soon release new editions of these classic films.

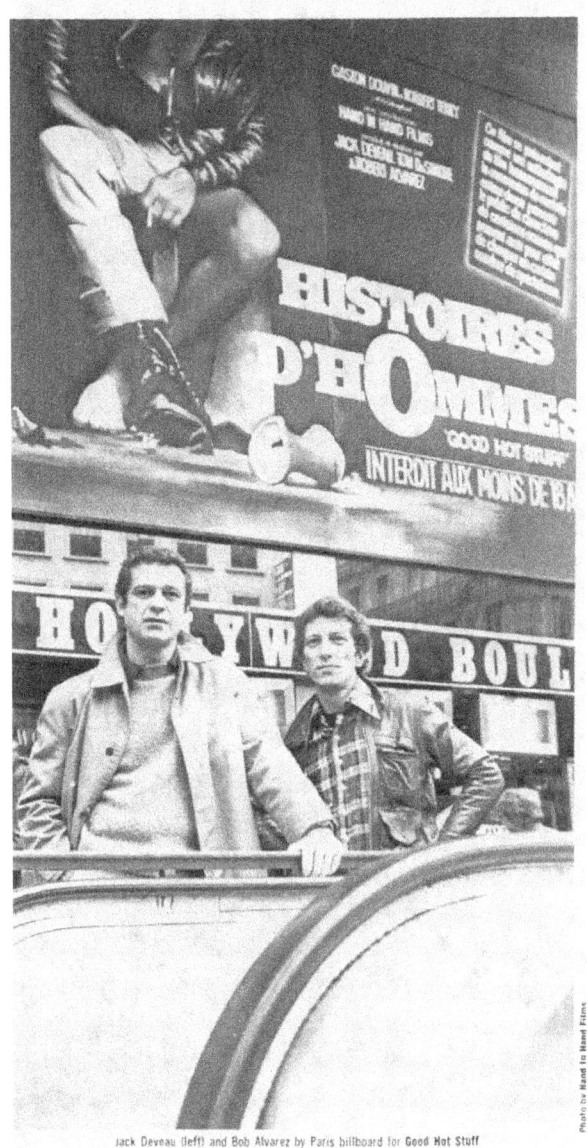

Jack Deveau (left) and Bob Alvarez by Paris billboard for Good Hot Stuff

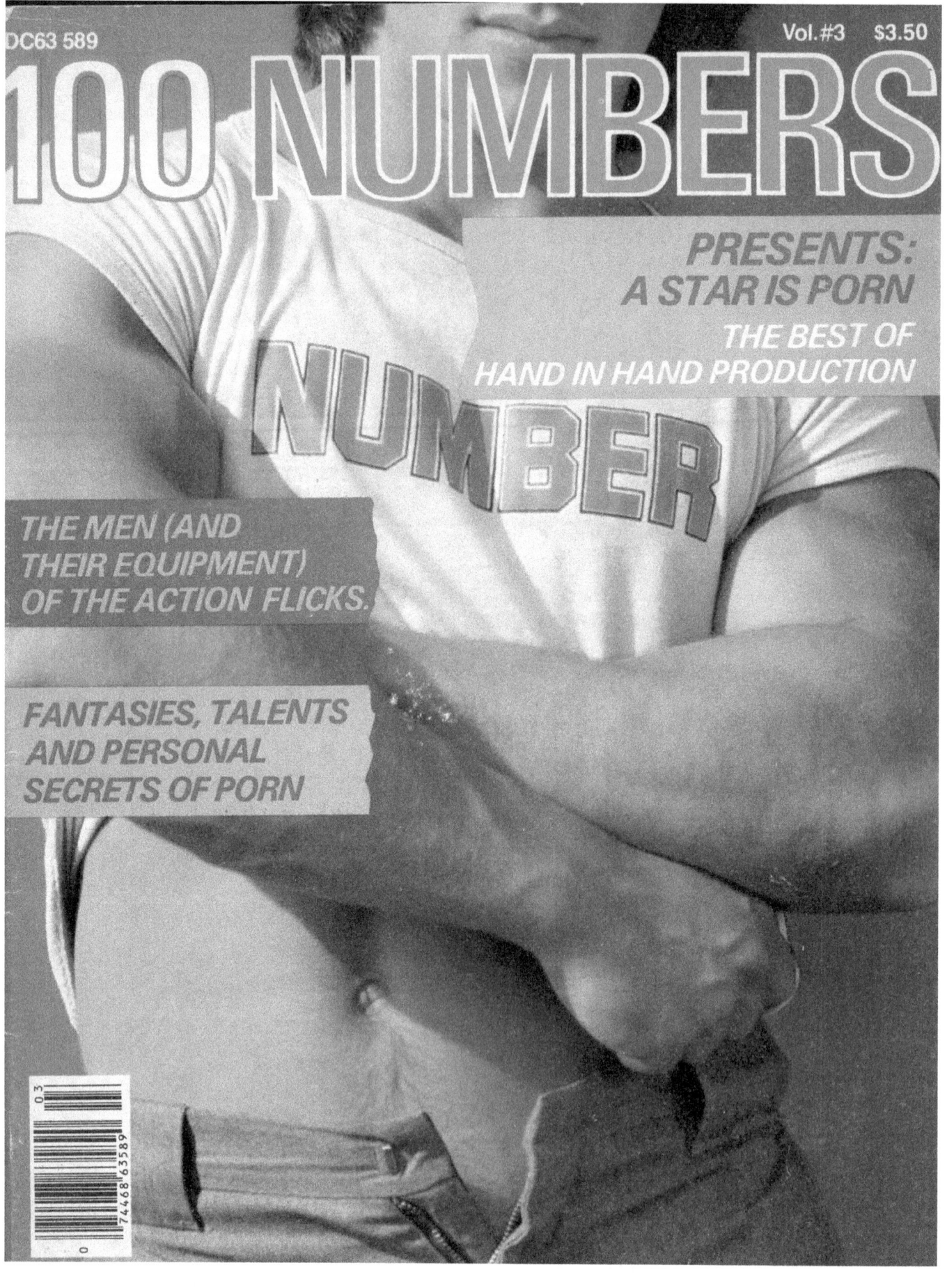

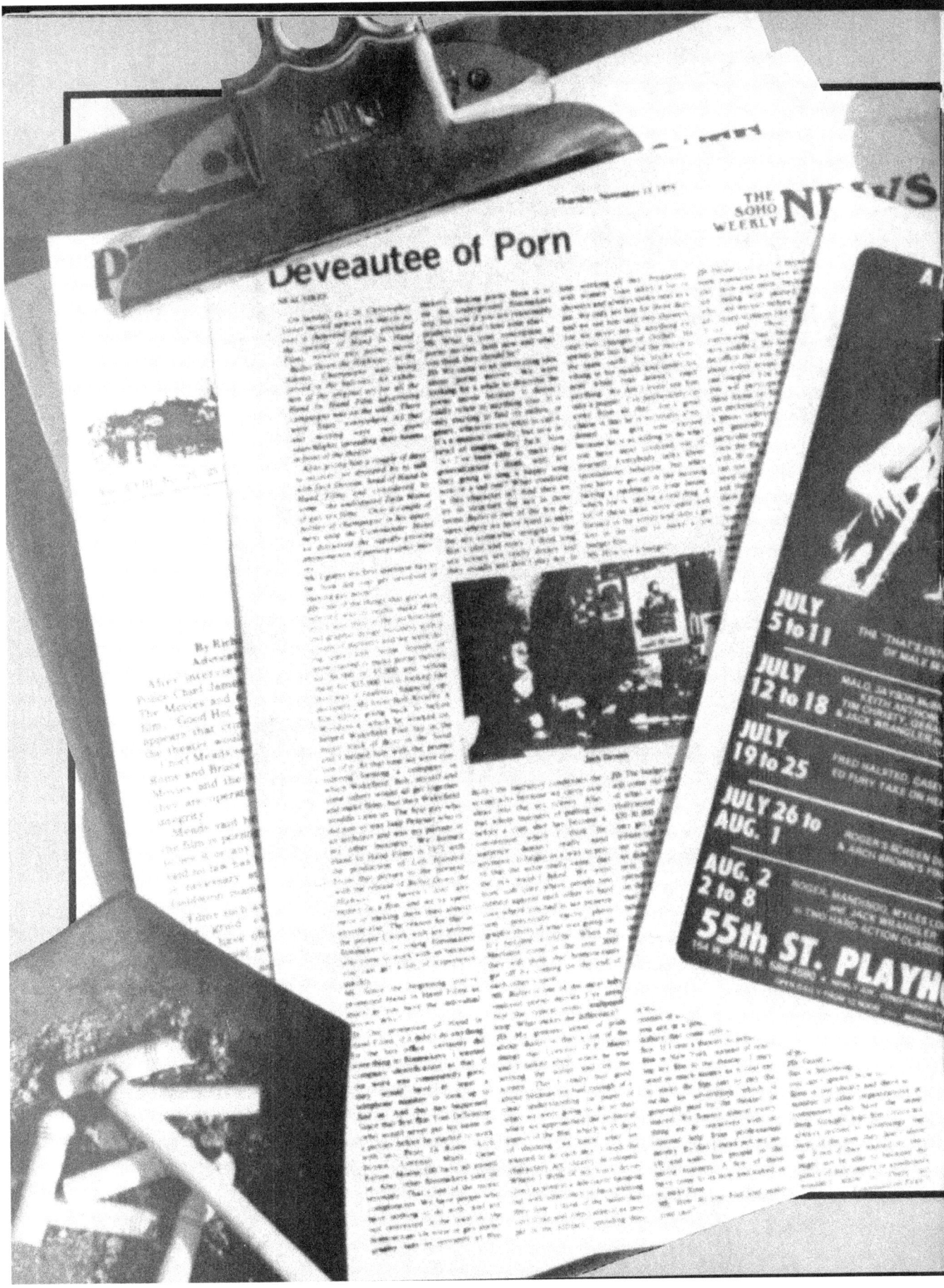

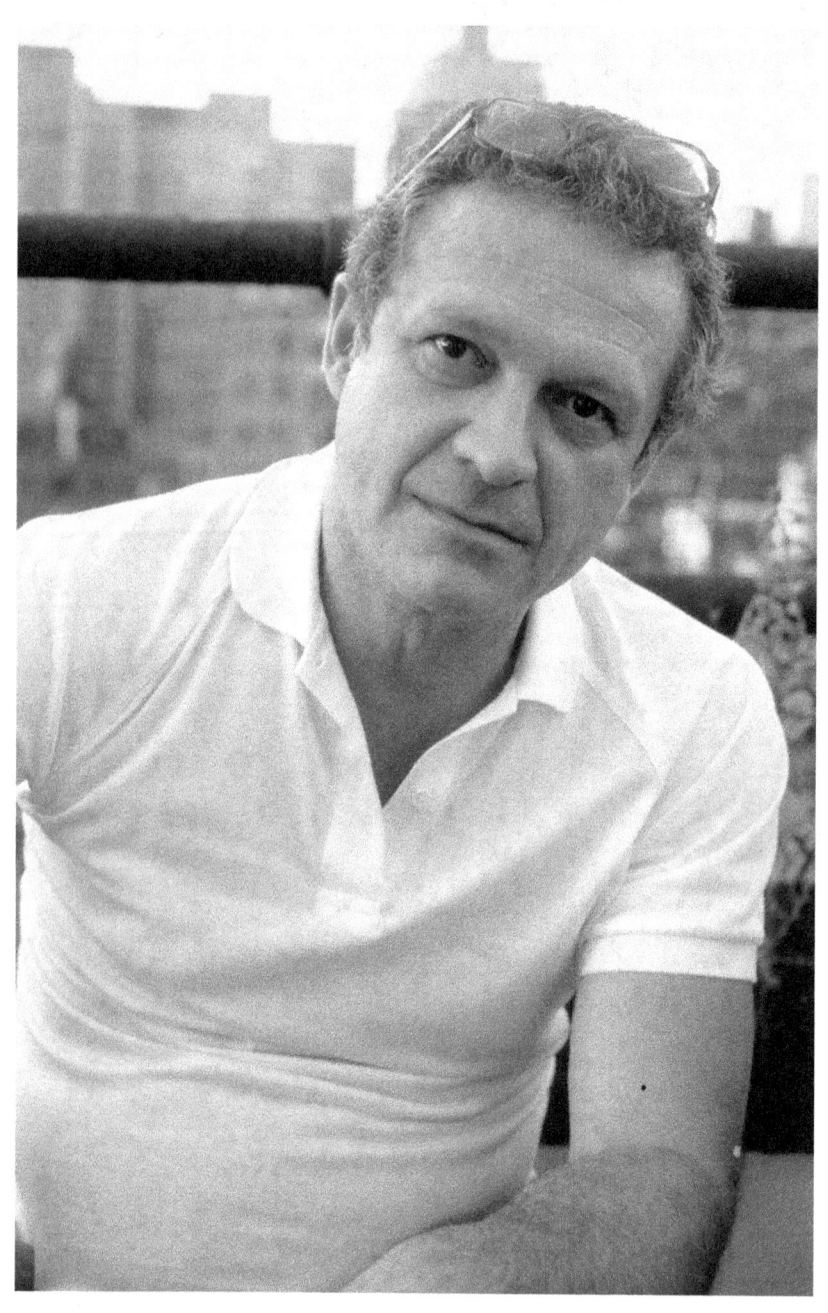

"Our films are live Disney movies, if we hold them out of circulation for five to six years, they're Pinocchio all over again - playing to a brand-new audience. The number of people interested in porno is probably fixed in relation to the population. This is literature of a kind - I don't know how it's recognized today, but we've created a large body of it - maybe it's the Mickey Mouse of the year 2000!" **JACK DEVEAU**

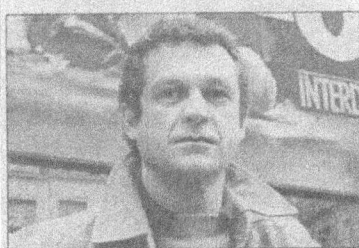

JACK DEVEAU OBITUARY

On Pearl Harbor day, the afternoon sun blazed through the penthouse apartment windows. The rays were so strong that mourners shielded their eyes with black glasses and many of them had their backs to the windows. They were celebrating Jack Deveau's life: the maker of gay erotic films had died of lung cancer the Thursday before. There was plenty to eat and drink. To coin a cliché, "It's the way Jack would have wanted it." Among the mourners were his mother and father, who had flown in from St. Louis (the Deveaus have been married 53 years – Jack was 47 when he died); niece Amy; nephew Terry from San Mateo; Holly Woodlawn, who got tipsy and kissed everybody many, many times; Bobby Short; Frank Schmitt (publisher of *Top Man*); and stars of Jack's films, most notably Jack Wrangler, Peter Berlin, Scorpio, Tray Christopher, Garry Hunt, Arch Brown, and Hugh Allen. Jack's films include BALLET DOWN THE HIGHWAY, WANTED: BILLY THE KID, DRIVE, JUST BLONDS, ROUGH TRADES, LEFT-HANDED, and FIRE ISLAND FEVER, which may be the best porno flick ever made, in that it contained the required fuck scenes, plus a witty commentary on the roundelays that take place each season at the Pines. Jack avoided the clichés of porn filmmaking both in his movies and in his attitude toward his profession. He was a generous spirit, a gentleman, articulate, and he had fun with his work. People of all social and sexual persuasions fought for invites to preview screenings in his living room, which were followed by lavish buffet dinners. Those evenings were great mind-and-muscle soirées. Last July, Jack went for a checkup at the Strang Clinic. They discovered a tumor the size of a softball in his chest. For further tests, he went to Sloan Kettering, where he was diagnosed as having oat cell cancer, a type that's inoperable. He underwent chemotherapy treatment, returning to Sloan Kettering three times for short stays. He died at home. At his bedside were his best friend, Case Chapman, and Bob Alvarez, his lover of many years. Goodbye, Jack. It was a wonderful party and a wonderful life.

*Arthur Bell, *Village Voice*

Hand In Hand Library

The Hand In Hand Production Company

THE EROTIC FILMS OF PETER DEROME 1972
Written & Directed by Peter De Rome // **Produced by** Jack Deveau, Peter De Rome // **Cinematography by** Peter De Rome // **Editing by** Peter De Rome, Robert Alvarez
Cast: Robert Rikas, Barry Lowe, Bill Abney, Bob Powell, David Lejeune, Derek Turner, Ivan Alderman, Joe Leone, Larry Ward, Lee L'Ecuyer, Peter De Rome, Richard Perez, Robin Elphick, Tom Yourk, Tony Williams

LEFT - HANDED 1972
Directed & Produced by Jack Deveau, Jaap Penraat // **Written by** Jack Deveau // **Edited by** Robert Alvarez // **Cinematography by** Jack Deveau, Jaap Penraat, Robert Alvarez // **Music by** Stan Finkelstein, Richard London // **Production Assistance by** Christopher Case, Charles Welz
Cast: Robert Rikas, Larry Burns, Al Mineo, Ray Frank, Teri Reardon, Warren Mans, Alex Marks, Bob Williams, Jack Deveau (narrator, voice only)

THE NIGHT BEFORE 1974
Directed by Arch Brown // **Written by** Arch Brown, Bruce Brown // **Produced by** Jack Deveau // **Edited by** Robert Alvarez // **Cinematography by** Arch Brown // **Music by** David Earnest // **Music Recording by** James P. Shelton // **Production Assistance by** Tom Hinckley // **Title Deisgn by** Tony Falcone // **Choreography by** Christopher Rage (as Tray Christopher) // **Make-Up by** Wayne Webb // **Art Direction by** Bobby Greco // **Assistant Director** Jay Julian
Cast: Coke Hennessy, Alexis Knight, Bill Yort, Bob Plummer, Jamal Jones, Jay Julian, Jeffrey Etting, Jerome Smith, Michael Kade, Mimmi Garth, Nick Kastroff, Tim Clarke, Topaz Worthy

ADAM & YVES 1974
Written & Directed by Peter De Rome // **Produced by** Jack Deveau // **Edited by** Peter De Rome // **Sound Editing by** Robert Alvarez // **Cinematography by** Jack Deveau, Peter De Rome, Tom Hinckley (Director of Photography: Jack Deveau) // **Music by** David Earnest, Peter De Rome // **Music Recording by** Richie Leavy // **Production Manager:** Archie L. Gresham // **Sculptures by** Richard Etts // **Sound Mixing by** Richard Dior, Trans Audio, Inc // **Sound Recording:** Ross-Gaffney, Inc
Cast: Michael Hardwick, Marcus Giovanni. "Big" Bill Young, Kirk Luna, Bob Jones, Daniel Montfort, David Page, Denise Royal, Earl Wilson, Eric Crawford, Gary Keys, Glenn Wilson, John Davis, Luther LeVale, Mark Connors, Tony Skinner, Charles Pooney, Jaap Penraat, Jack Deveau, Geraldo

DRIVE 1974
Directed by Jack Deveau // **Written by** Christopher Rage // **Produced by** Todd Richards // **Edited by** Robert Alvarez // **Cinematography by** Jack Deveau Robert Alvarez, Jaap Penraat, Tom Hinckley, Peter De Rome (Director of Cinematography: Jack Deveau); // **Music by** Stan Freeman, David Earnest // **Production Assistance by** Richard Abel, Paul Berryessa // **Set by** Tom Williams, Jaap Penraat // **Art Direction by** Jaap Penraat // **Make-Up & Hair by** Carlisle Wilson // **Lighting by** Gene Kelton // **Sound by** Jimmy Shelton, Richard Leavy, Walter Sear, Motion Picture // **Recording by** Richard Dior, Trans Audio, Inc // **Casting by** John Jourdan
Cast: Christopher Rage (as Mary Jim Sstunning), Kirk Luna, Shawn Roberts, Mark Woodward, Al Kemis, Arch Fairbanks, Arch Hilborn, Avery Addision, Bill Gillers, Bill Ritter, Brian DeStazio, Carl Manour, Carlyle Taylor, Chris Mosley, Chris Ritter, Clif Dover, Curtis Brown, Denny Mans, Frank Ventgen, Frederick C. Mongue II, Freemann Freeman, George Culver, Harold Reardon, Harvey Shamber, Jaap Penraat, Jack Brusca, Jack Deveau, Jim Case, Joaquin Mineo, Joe Quin, John Fromke, John Willard, Kenric Brown, Kenric Hawley, Lorenzo Lasalle, Mark Sayles, Marty Marks, Marvin DeSimone, Michael Corrigan, Nick Shulman, Paul Conaway, Paul Turley, Peter Fersen, Ray Frank, Renfroe Meyer, Richard Abel, Richard Morrissey, Robert Alvarez, Rusty Lewis, S.V. Newman, Seth Poole, Stan Glinter, Steven Sampson, Ted Yalkus, W. Grippo, Peter De Rome

LE MUSEE (STRICTLY FORBIDDEN) 1974
Directed by Jack Deveau // **Written by** Jean-Etienne Siry (as C. Sebur) // **Produced by** Henri Chateaux, Jack Deveau // **Editing by** Robert Alvarez // **Editing Assistance by** Kees Chapman // **Cinematography by** François About // **Music by** Didier Vasseur // **Make-Up by** Gene Kelton // **Sound by** Adriene Latafere // **Production Coordination by** Mark Woodward (as Sydney Soons)
Cast: Thomas Jeffries, "Big" Bill Eld, Daniel Novan, Alain Queret, Hugh Allen, Jean-Pierre Vierle, Paul McFleet, Robert LeClerc, Daniel Mesplet, Gene Kelton, Jack Deveau

BALLET DOWN THE HIGHWAY 1975
Directed & Produced by Jack Deveau // **Written by** Lorenzo Mans (as P.P. Mans) // **Edited by** Robert Alvarez // **Assistance by** Jim Delegatti // **Assistant Directors** - Tom DeSimone, Robert Alvarez, Jaap Penraat, **Cinematography by** Jack Deveau, Tom DeSimone // **Choreography by** Haynes Owens, Gene Kelton // **Make-Up & Lighting by** Gene Kelton // **Original Music by** David Earnest // **Music performed by** Stan Freeman, Ian Herman // **Music Recording by** Basement Recording Studio, Dick Charles // **Negative Matching by** Noelle Penraat // **Production Assistance by** Kees Chapman, Frank Ross (as Frank LoScalzo) // **Production Coordination by** Mark Woodward (as Sydney Soons), // **Sound by** Rolf Pardula // **Sound Mixing by** Richard Dior, Trans Audio, Inc
Cast: Henk Van Dijk, Garry Hunt, Jeff Sullivan Charles Drucker, Dick Backass, Doug Fay, Frank LoScalzo, Gene Kelton, Grey Rodgers, Haynes Owens, Helen Morganstory, Jaap Penraat, Jack Deveau, Jim Delegatti, Joan Bell, Joe Mayor, Johnny Ventura, Larry Merritt, Lorenzo Mans, Lucille Lucas, Michale Purri, Peter Stephans, Rich Atwell, Robert Alvarez, Robert Anthony, Robin Lane, Roneta Magee, Steven Brown, Susan Tardugno, Tom DeMastri, Tony Duva, Wayne Richards, Zuzane Lynch

CATCHING UP 1975
Written, Edited & Directed by Tom DeSimone // **Produced by** Jack Deveau // **Cinematography by** Robert Shaw, Sound by Tim Christy
Cast: Keith Anthoni, Jayson McBride, Tim Christy, Bob Perry, Dave Daniels, John Farrel, Paul Strand, Scott Heith

GOOD HOT STUFF 1975
Directed by Jack Deveau, Tom DeSimone, Arch Brown, Peter DeRome, Jaap Penraat, James Bidgood //**Written by** Moose 100 // **Produced by** Jack Deveau // **Editing by** Robert Alvarez, Tom DeSimone // **Music by** David Earnest // **Sound by** Rolf Pardula // **Mix by** Rick Dior // **Make-Up & Lighting by** Gene Kelton
Cast: Mark Woodward (narrator), Jack Deveau, Peter De Rome, David Earnest, Alexis Knight, "Big" Bill Eld, Bob Plummer, Coke Hennessy, David Lejeune, Dennis Walsh, Frank Ventgen, Frederick C. Mongue II, Garry Hunt, Henk Van Dijk, Jamal Jones, Jay Julian, Jerome Smith, John Tyme, Kenric Brown, Kirk Luna, Larry Burns, Lee L'Ecuyer, Lionel Jerk, Christopher Rage, Michael Corrigan, Michael Kade, Michael Neill, Nick Kastroff, Ray Frank, Rene, Richard Marks, Robert Rikas, Ron Brooks, Shawn Roberts, Topaz Worthy, Warren Mans, Bill Yort, David Savage, Jaap Penraat, Mimmi Garth, Brian DeStazio, Helen Morganstory, Jack Brusca, Jeffrey Etting, Peter Fersen, Richard Abel, Tim Clarke, Al Mineo, Alex Marks, Bob Williams, George Culver, John Willard, Marvin DeSimone, Paul Conaway, W. Grippo, Arnie Krueger

THE DESTROYING ANGEL 1976
Written & Directed by Peter De Rome // **Produced by** Jack Deveau // **Edited by** Robert Alvarez // **Music by** Joe Mann // **Production Coordination by** Mark Woodward (as Sydney Soons)
Cast: "Big" Bill Eld (as Bill Young), Alain Monceau, Timothy Kent, Thom Aaron, Billy White, Evan DeBraye
Gian-Paolo Cotto, Glenn Middleton, Paul Eden, Philip Darden, Rick Scott, Rufus Michaels

WANTED: BILLY THE KID 1976
Directed & Produced by Jack Deveau // **Written by** Moose 100, Shadow // **Assistant Directors** - Robert Alvarez, Tom DeSimone // **Edited by** Robert Alvarez // **Assistant Editor** - Kees Chapman // **Cinematography by** Jack Deveau, Tom DeSimone // **Make-Up & Lighting by** Gene Kelton // **Make-Up Assistance by** Jim Delegatti // **Music by** David Earnest (Lyrics: Moose 100) // **Music Mix by** Ross-Gaffney // **Production Assistance by** Frank Ross (as Frank LoScalzo), Kees Chapman // **Production Coordination by** Mark Woodward (as Sydney Soons) // **Sound by** Rolf Pardula
Cast: Dennis Walsh, Larry Marsland, Crompton Payne, Darc Traid, John Tyme, Megan Ross, Peter Thadliski, Rene, Ron Leigh, Steve Eberhart, Robert Alvarez, Bob Mularz, Gamin Mantis, Geoffrey Welch, John Meyers, Mark Ekawall, Tony Meyers (voice only)

HOT HOUSE 1977
Directed & Produced by Jack Deveau // **Written by** Moose 100 // **Editing by** Robert Alvarez // **Cinematography by** Jack Deveau, Kees Chapman // **Key Grip** - Ken Schnetzer // **Make-Up & Lighting by** Gene Kelton // **Make-Up Assistance by** Jim Delegatti // **Music Consultant** - Bobby // **Mixer** - Kees Chapman // **Production Coordination by** Mark Woodward (as Sydney Soons) // **Set Decoration by** Jim Delegatti // **Sound by** Rolf Pardula
Cast: Jack Wrangler, Roger, Garry Hunt, Jayson MacBride, Erik Streiff, David Hunter, Joe Dallesandro (uncredited, archive footage), Christopher Rage (voice only, as Tray Christopher)

SEX MAGIC 1977
Directed & Produced by Jack Deveau // **Written by** Moose 100 // **Editing by** Robert Alvarez // **Cinematography by** Jack Deveau, Kees Chapman // **Key Grip** - Ken Schnetzer, Jim Delegatti // **Make-up & Lighting by** Gene Kelton // **Make-Up Assistance by** Jim Delegatti // **Mix** - Kees Chapman // **Production Coordination by** Mark Woodward (as Sydney Soons) // **Set Decoration by** Jim Delegatti // **Sound by** Rolf Pardula
Cast: Roger, Jack Wrangler, "Big" Bill Eld, Jayson MacBride, Lee Foster, Mandingo, Tom Trooper, Tony Rusca, Jim Delegatti, Kees Chapman (narrator, voice only), B. Lackey

ROUGH TRADES 1977
Directed & Produced by Jack Deveau // **Written by** Lorenzo Mans (as P.P. Mans), Jack Deveau // **Editing by** Robert Alvarez // **Cinematography by** Jack Deveau // **Make-Up & Lighting by** Gene Kelton // **Sound by** Rolf Pardula // **Mixer** - Kees Chapman // **Production Coordination by** Mark Woodward (Sydney Soons)
Cast: Myles Longue, Hugh Allen, Bobby Cruz, David Gorsky, Rit Young, Steve Dory

DUNE BUDDIES 1978
Directed & Produced by Jack Deveau // **Written by** Moose 100 // **Editing by** Robert Alvarez // **Cinematography by** Jack Deveau // **Assistant Camera** - Kees Chapman, David Littler // **Direct Sound by** Robert Alvarez // **Make-Up by** Jim Delegatti // **Production Coordination by** Mark Woodward (as Sydney Soons), David Littler
Cast: David Gorsky, Hugh Allen, Garry Hunt, Malo, Matt Harper, Myles Longue, Pepe Brazil, Larry Paige

A NIGHT AT THE ADONIS 1978
Directed & Produced by Jack Deveau // **Written by** Moose 100 // **Edited by** Robert Alvarez // **Cinematography by** Jack Deveau // **Assistant Camera** - Kees Chapman, S. Howe // **Gaffer & Grips** - Jim Delegatti, Ken Schnetzer, Al Legasse // **Make-Up & Lighting by** Gene Kelton // **Make-up Assistance by** Jay // **Sound by** Rolf Pardula // **Production Coordination by** Mark Woodward (as Sydney Soons), Kees Chapman
Cast: Jack Wrangler, Big Al Little, Todd Travers, Keith Strickland, Lee Foster, Malo, Mandingo, Robert A. Glory, "Big" Bill Eld, Robert Alvarez, Chris Michaels, Eartha Hugee, Geraldo, Jayson MacBride, Jim Delegatti, Kees Chapman, Ken Schnetzer, Mark Woodward, Muffie Meyer, Paul Maul,
Myles Longue, Roger, Rolf Pardula, Tommy Ruscica, Victor Williams

FIRE ISLAND FEVER 1979
Directed & Produced by Jack Deveau // **Written by** Moose 100, Jack Deveau // **Edited by** Robert Alvarez // **Cinematography by** Jack Deveau, Kees Chapman // **Make-Up by** Gene Kelton, Jim Delegatti // **Sketches by** Frank Ventgen // **Direct Sound by** Robert Alvarez // **Production Coordination by** Mark Woodward (aka Sydney Soons), David Littler
Cast: Chris Michaels, Matt Harper, Garry Hunt, Hugh Allen, Larry Paige, John Carlo, Pepe Brazil, David Littler, Frank Schmitt, George Sardi, Johnny Savoy, Juanita

THE IDOL 1979
Written & Directed by Tom DeSimone // **Produced by** Jack Deveau, Tom DeSimone // **Cinematography by** Nick Elliot // **Music by** Stan Freeman, David Morgan, Archie Gresham, **Assistant Director** - Rick Jason // **Production Assistance by** Jerry Oliver // **Sound by** Jason Sato
Cast: Kevin Redding, Derek Stanton, Greg Dale, Jerry Foxe, Jim Bartolotta, Mark Bitler, Nick Rodgers, Darla-Lee Barnett, Peter Borchard

JUST BLONDS 1979
Directed & Produced by Jack Deveau // **Written by** Moose 100 // **Editing by** Robert Alvarez // **Cinematography by** Jack Deveau, Kees Chapman; // **Assistant Director** - Kees Chapman // **Costumes by** Warren and Dean // **Make-Up by** Jim Delegatti // **Music by** Didier Vasseur // **Production Assistance by** Les Ribaudo, Ken Schnetzer, Rob Tunnicliff // **Production Coordination by** David Littler
Cast: Philip Wagner (as Luke), Damien III, Eric Ryan, Lee Marlin, Scorpio, Hugh Allen, Ken Carter, David Morgan (narration, voice only)

PRIVATE COLLECTION 1978-1980
Directed by Jack Deveau, Peter De Rome, Tom DeSimone // **Editing by** Robert Alvarez, Tom DeSimone // **Cinematography by** Jack Deveau, Kees Chapman, Nick Elliot, Peter De Rome // **Make-Up by** Jim Delegatti // **Lighting by** Gene Kelton, Steve Uflander // **Sound by** Robert Alvarez, Rolf Pardula, Mike Davis // **Production Assistance by** Rob Tunnicliff, Ricky Rocket
Cast: Bart Damon, Bart Sommers, Becky Logan, Charles Jackson, Dan Gentry, Garry Hunt, Ivan, Jeff Starkey, John Carlo, John Charles, John Devoe, Johnny Apollo, Ken Carter, Kevin Gregory, David Gorsky (as Paolo), Scorpio, Steve York, Yogi Rama

THE BOYS FROM RIVERSIDE DRIVE 1981
Directed & Produced by Jack Deveau // **Written by** Moose 100, Dick Bettis // **Edited by** Robert Alvarez // **Cinematography by** Jack Deveau, Kees Chapman // **Gaffer** - Boyde Masten // **Make-Up by** Jim Delegatti // **Music by** Michael Kester, Dick Slick // **Sound by** Klaus Tinker // **Production Coordination by** Michael Kester
Cast: Buddy Preston, David Dion, George Brown, Jack Wrangler, Malo, Philip Wagner (as Luke), John Holmes (archive footage), Lee Marlin, Marcel, Tom Stillwater, John Elliot

TIMES SQUARE STRIP 1982
Directed & Produced by Jack Deveau // **Written by** Moose 100 // **Edited by** Robert Alvarez // **Cinematography by** Jack Deveau // **Sound by** Rolf Pardula // **Make-Up & Lighting by** Gene Kelton, Jim Delegatti // **Production Coordination by** Kees Chapman
Cast: Philip Wagner (as Luke), Buddy Preston, Robert A. Glory, Jason Jacobi, David Dion, George Sardi, Jack Moore, Jerry Overton, Nick Fordham, Peter Lopez, Richard Lang, Tony West, Dale Caesar, Plato Pastel

IN HEAT 1986
Directed by Jack Deveau, Robert Alvarez, Peter De Rome // **Produced by** Jack Deveau, Robert Alvarez, Kees Chapman // **Edited by** Robert Alvarez, Peter De Rome // **Production Coordination by** Kees Chapman
Cast: Doug DeMarco, Cody Richards, Brian Michaels, Bob/Frank/Greg Gaines, J.D. Slater, Matt Pierce, Scorpio, Keith Anthoni

Hand In Hand Library Distribution Company

THE COLLECTION 1969
Directed by Tom DeSimone // **Produced by** Nick Grippo
Cast: Ash Grover, David Michaels, Nick Grippo (as Max Blue), Poco Alan

THE AMERICAN ADVENTURES OF SURELICK HOLMES 1971
Directed by Ralph Ell // **Written by** Ralph Ell, Charles Lamont, Bear Wilson // **Produced by** Leonard Kirtman // **Editing by** Charles Lamont // **Cinematography by** Billy Hawk // **Assistant Camera by** Conrad Ebish
Cast: David L. Chandler, Frank Massey, Barry Warfel, Chris von Brenner, Rick Valentine, Zebedy Colt

CASEY 1971
Directed by Donald Crane // **Written by** Glenn Jones // **Produced by** Neol Anthony // **Editing by** Fred Chan // **Cinematography by** Ron Almero // **Music by** Cyril Mumford
Cast: Casey Donovan (as Ken Donovan), Angelo Waine, Nat Grey, Sparrow Guano

AMERICAN CREAM 1972
Written, Produced & Directed by Rob Simple // **Cinematography by** Mark Uber // **Costumes by** Eddie Heath // **Art Direction by** Barton Lidicé Benes // **Production Assistance by** Howard, Hank Russo, Georg Whipple
Cast: Robert Rikas, Buddy, Black Barbarella, Doug Roamin, Howard, Joel Stone, Paul D-Fone, Philip St. Albin

BOB & DARYL & TED & ALEX 1972
Directed & Produced by Stan Preston
Cast: Anton Lewis, Danny DiCiccio, Don Sean, Ernie Likens

THE BACK ROW 1973
Written, Produced & Directed by Jerry Douglas (as Doug Richards) // **Music by** William R. Cox
Cast: Casey Donovan, George Payne, Arthur Graham, Chris Villette, David Knox, Robert Tristan, Robin Anderson, Warren Carlton

JACK 1973
Written & Directed by John Stephens // **Produced by** John Stephens, Geoffrey Knower // **Cinematography by** Dom Mori, Chris Larkin // **Editing by** Terry Charles // **Music by** The Beautiful People
Cast: Dano Martin, Phil D'Angelo, Bob Benelli, Bob Jones, Leo Link, Robert Lamb

ANYTHING GOES 1974
Directed by Tom DeSimone (as Lancer Brooks) // **Produced by** Nick Grippo (as Max Blue) // **Cinematography by** Noel Kent // **Sound by** Ned Burke
Cast: Tim Christy, Bob Burke, Bill Travis, Chris Christy, Johnny Johnston, Marc Taylor, Shannon Paul

STATION TO STATION 1974
Directed by Tom DeSimone (as Lancer Brooks) // **Produced by** Nick Grippo (as Max Blue) // **Cinematography by** Noel Kent // **Sound by** Mark Holt
Cast: Tim Christy, Tom Payne, Carl Ford, Ron Fischer, Steve Fox, Linda Hartley, Liz Wolfe, Chris Travis

BOY-NAPPED 1975
Written & Directed by Spencer Logan // **Produced by** David Ransom // **Edited by** Spencer Logan, David Ransom // **Cinematography by** Cecil Signoret // **Assistant Camera by** John Kraus // **Lighting by** George Metesky // **Sound by** Sen Heiser // **Stills by** Jack Logan
Cast: Wade Nichols, Jamie Gillis (as James Rugman), Michael Hardwick, Dwane Carter, Bobby Niles

STAR TRICK 1976
Written & Directed by Tim Knight
Cast: Tim Christy, Carl Simpson, Clay Grant, Jay Salazar, Mary Lou Hopkins, Rick Reyes, Taylor Benson, Tom Manna, Verne Micthel

HOT TRUCKIN' 1977
Directed by Tom DeSimone (as Lancer Brooks) // **Produced by** Todd Richards // **Cinematography by** Robert Shaw, Chris Christy // **Sound by** Tim Christy // **Assistant Director** - Rick Jason
Cast: Gordon Grant, Bob Damon, Bob Snowdan, Claton Cooper, Johnny Dillon, Larry LeBlanc, Tom Marze

BAD, BAD BOYS 1979
Directed by Tom DeSimone // **Written by** Taylor Benson // **Produced by** Taylor Brooks, Editing by Les Kutz // **Cinematography by** Brandon Ryan // **Sound by** Russell Moore
Cast: Bill Leonard, Derrick Stanton, Dick Miller, Guy DeSilva, Guy Lance, Johnny Dawes, Johnny Ryan, Lenny Koto, Rufus, Steve Event

GETTING' DOWN 1979
Directed & Produced by Tom DeSimone (as Lancer Brooks) // **Written by** Jason Sato // **Editing by** Jason Sato // **Cinematography by** Nick Elliot // **Production Assistance by** Hank Charles // **Production Manager** - Jerry Oliver
Cast: Greg Dale, Guy Silva, Chip, Craig Shaw; Jerry Foxe, Rex Wolfe, Cody Houston

CENTURIANS OF ROME 1981
Directed by John Christopher // **Written by** Timothy Michaels // **Produced by** Uranus Films, Marge McGuire // **Edited by** John Christopher // **Cinematography by** Larry Revene // **Assistant Camera by** Scott Jones // **Assistant Director:** Mark Hansen // **Boom** - Dennis Day // **Gaffer** - Phil Hart // **Grip** - Jack Rye // **Make-Up Supervisor** - Jim Bridges // **Production Assistance by** Ken McCord, Justin Tyme, Chuck Roebutt // **Properties by** Navos Oasis // **Publicity by** Flent Associates // **Script Supervisor** - Billy Solobodian // **Set Design by** Randal James // **Sound by** Per Siostadt // **Stills by** Marco Nero // **Titles by** Pegasus // **Transportation by** James Findlay // **Wardrobe by** Theodore Aldridge
Cast: Myles Longue (as Ed Wiley), George Payne, Scorpio, Michael Flent, Adam DeHaven, Adam Kellogg, Bobbie Burns, Chuck Roebuck, David Hadley, David Morris, David O'Chela, Eric Ryan, Greg Monroe, Guiseppe Welch, Gus Monte, Jeffrey Scott, Jerome C. Fox, Jerry Cassode, Jerry Purpura, John Cannon, John Kovacs, John Rowan, Johnny Cannuic, Justin Savage, Ken Ramsaver, Kenneth Purpura, Mitchell Flynn, Phil Phillips, Richard Cox, Robert Jones, Roy Garrett, Ryder Jones, Timothy Michaels, Tom Trent, Charlotte O'Hara, Tommy Hawke

Hand In Hand Pickups Short Films

DEMIGODS [ANIMATED SHORT FILM] 1975
Directed by Wallace Potts

CECK AND CHECKMATE 1975
Directed by J. Davian
Cast: Robert Rikas

THE ILLUSION 1975
Directed by J. Davian
Cast: Robert Rikas

PRISON FOR LIFE 1976
Directed by J. Davian
Cast: Robert Rikas

All the Hand In Hand films are available on DVD and VOD:

www.bijouworld.com

www.bijougayporn.com

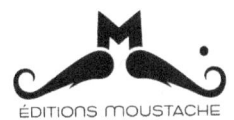

Team Moustache
Ewald Schulz, Michael Gerhardt, Mirjam Pajakowski, Nadia Bruce-Rawlings, Tobias Gossen, Rene Spitzer, Marco Siedelmann

Special Thanks
Robert Alvarez, Jeffrey Escoffier, Dietmar Siedelmann, Gary Vanisian, Jerry Douglas, Tim Wilbur, Jack Fritscher, Bernd Althans, Robert W. Richards, Henk Van Dijk, Robert Satuloff, Marc Ewert, Jerry Jackson Rajaratnam, Christoph Göbbels, Markus Rentmeister, Thomas Krichel, Jochen Werner, Jürgen Brüning, Paul Verstraten, Christoph Draxtra, Nicole Gärtner, Casey Scott, Bruce Harrow, Frank LoSzalo, Tom Hinckley, Gene Kelton, Tom DeSimone, Eartha Hugee, David McGillivray, James Bidgood, Michael Young, Jeffrey Schwartz, Todd Verow, Bruce LaBruce, Rick Castro, Philip Clark, Gavin Geoffrey Dillard, Wakefield Poole, Rolf Pardula, Jim Delegatti, Ken Schnetzer, Lorenzo Mans, Francois About, Jean-Etienne Siry, David Earnest, Christopher Rage, Michael Kienzl, Ute Heyer, Silvia Szymanski, Peter Berlin, Frank Schmitt, John Mensior, Paul Siebenand, John R. Burger, Christopher Parrish, Steve Toushin, Peter De Rome, Tom Udo, Harold Fairbanks, Arch Brown, Clarke Taylor, Freeman Gunter, Barnaby Shackleford, Bruce Benderson, Peter Argus, Dries Vermeulen, David Minton, Ashley West, Grigoris Daskalogrigorakis, Peter Adams, Arthur Bell, Bill Hunter, Joe Rubin, Donald Warman, George Sardi, JWR, Robert Leighton, Jeroen Van Lievenoogen, Ethan Reid, Hervé Joseph Lebrun, Joe Shaver

IMPRINT

Released by Publishing House
Éditions Moustache
Eintrachtstr. 41
52134 Herzogenrath
Germany

Copyright © 2018 Éditions Moustache
ISBN: 978-3-96034-300-4

Cover Artwork // Marc Ewert
Book Jacket // Mirjam Pajakowski
Layout // Michael Gerhardt
Mirjam Pajakowski
Proof Read // Nadia Bruce-Rawlings

Printed by Kindle Direct Publishing, Amazon.com Company
February 2019

The right of contributors to be identified as the Authors of the Work has been asserted by them. All rights reserved. Except for brief passages, quoted in newspaper, magazine, radio, television, internet review, or academic paper, no part of this book may be reproduced, stored in or introduced into a retrieval system, or transmitted in any form with the prior written permission of both the copyright owner and the publisher of this book; nor be otherwise circulated in any form of binding or cover other than that in which it is published and without a similar condition being imposed on the subsequent purchaser.

Éditions Moustache, Entire Collection © 2018 Interviews, articles, and photographs © 2018 Robert J. Alvarez

Inquiries concerning performance, adaptation, or publication rights should be addressed to Publisher,

Éditions Moustache
Marco Siedelmann 1986

place of jurisdiction: Germany

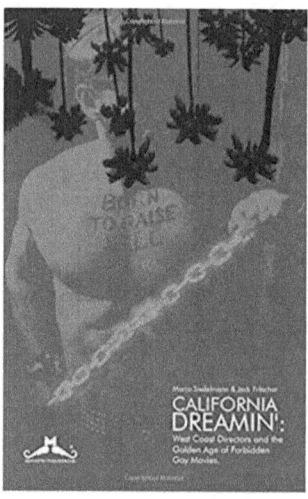

CALIFORNIA DREAMIN': WEST COAST DIRECTORS AND THE GOLDEN AGE OF FORBIDDEN GAY MOVIES

Paperback: 276 pages
Publisher: Editions Moustache // December 14, 2016
Language: English
ISBN-10: 3960341016
ISBN-13: 978-3960341017
Product Dimensions: 5,5 x 8,5 inch

In American pop art, gangster rap, punk rock, and gay filmmaking, there is a Continental Divide between East Coast and West Coast culture typified by New York and California. This esthetic regionalism may be a moot point to today's international viewers of twenty-first-century gay porn which is more "corporate meat loops" than it is the "personal" kind of visionary film narrative made by the pioneer directors. They created gay cinema. They built their box-office fame with their stories and style, and with their superb casting back in the day when the porn stars they discovered were hot guys with real personalities they knew would make audiences hard no matter what coast or country or continent: Jack Wrangler, Casey Donovan, Peter Berlin, and a host of others. No matter the coast or country, Hot is hot. Some things are universal. Essential. Everywhere. Including interviews with J. Brian, Gavin Geoffrey Dillard, Roger Earl, David "Old Reliable" Hurles, Jim West, a guest article by cult filmmaker Toby Ross and numerous pages of pictures and photo art by Mark Hemry, Tom Bianchi, David Pearce, John J. Krause, Tom of Finland, Tom Kellie, and other iconic gay artists.

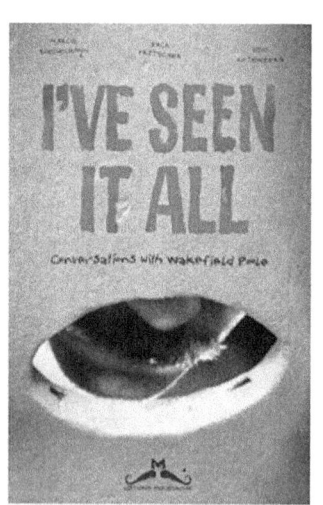

I'VE SEEN IT ALL: CONVERSATIONS WITH WAKEFIELD POOLE

Paperback: 220 pages
Publisher: Editions Moustache // October 20, 2016
Language: English
ISBN-10: 3960341024
ISBN-13: 978-3960341024
Product Dimensions: 5,5 x 8,5 inch

He literally has seen it all. Wakefield Poole experienced a glowing era of American film history and the "golden age" of several glorious things such as Broadway, Porno Chic, Rock Music, Gay Liberation, and the Sexual Revolution itself. After being almost forgotten, the films by adult movie pioneer Wakefield Poole are being re-discovered by a younger generation of cinematics. In a very personal and career-spanning interview, Mr. Poole shares never-heard stories and talks about every single film he made. He discusses several other stations of his life; for example: cooking in the Trump Tower and for Jackie Kennedy. Not only his well-known celluloid-masterpieces like *Boys in the Sand*, or *Bijou* are discussed, but also the often overlooked movies shot on video by the former dancer & choreographer, and his life after retirement. Includes a foreword by documentary filmmaker Jim Tushinski, the historical interview "Dirty Poole" by Jack Fritscher from the legendary *Drummer* magazine which was originally published in 1977, and a conversation with German film critic Udo Rotenberg. On top the interviews are represented visually by many stills, snapshots from private archives, artworks and ephemera pieces.

www.ingramcontent.com/pod-product-compliance
Lightning Source LLC
Chambersburg PA
CBHW081117240526

45470CB00019B/2349